HANDBOOK
of
STRATEGY AND MANAGEMENT

HANDBOOK
of
STRATEGY AND MANAGEMENT

Edited by
ANDREW PETTIGREW,
HOWARD THOMAS
AND RICHARD WHITTINGTON

SAGE Publications
London • Thousand Oaks • New Delhi

First published 2002
Paperback edition published 2006

SAGE Publications Ltd
1 Oliver's Yard
55 City Road
London EC1Y 1SP

SAGE Publications Inc
2455 Teller Road
Thousand Oaks, California 91320

SAGE Publications India Pvt Ltd
B-42 Panchsheel Enclave
Post Box 4109
New Delhi 110 017

British Library Cataloguing in Publication data

A catalogue record for this book is available from
the British Library

ISBN-10 1-4129-2121-X (pbk)
ISBN-13 978-1-4129-2121-3 (pbk)

Library of Congress Control Number: 2005936293

Typeset by C&M Digitals (P) Ltd., Chennai, India
Printed in Great Britain by The Cromwell Press Ltd, Trowbridge, Wiltshire
Printed on paper from sustainable resources

Contents

Part Four   LOOKING FORWARD

Contributors

Edward H. Bowman died in 1998 and Chapter 2 in this Handbook is dedicated to his memory. Edward Bowman was an accomplished and influential scholar of management who made many seminal contributions to the strategy field. He was also an effective institution builder. He held degrees from MIT, The Wharton School, University of Pennsylvania and Ohio State University and served all three institutions. For a time he was Dean of the College of Business at Ohio State and Deputy Dean at the Wharton School. He was also the Founding Director of the Reginald H. Jones Center for Management Policy, Strategy, and Organization at the Wharton School. In recognition of his contributions, the Wharton School has named a Chair after him and established an annual distinguished speaker series.

Balaji S. Chakravarthy is Professor of Strategy and International Management and holds the Shell Chair in Sustainable Business Growth at IMD, Lausanne. His research and teaching interests cover three related areas: strategy processes for sustainable business growth, corporate renewal, and the management and sharing of competencies. He has published four books, several case studies and numerous articles on these topics in top journals. Dr. Chakravarthy has a doctorate from Harvard and has taught at the Wharton School, INSEAD, and the University of Minnesota. He serves on the editorial boards of the *Strategic Management Journal, Long Range Planning Journal and Strategy & Leadership.* He was a member of the Board of Directors of the International Strategic Management Society from 1999 to 2004.

Karel Cool is BP Professor of European Competitiveness and Professor of Strategic Management at INSEAD. Karel Cool's research, teaching and consulting focus is on problems of industry and competitive analysis (e.g. industry over-capacity, profit dynamics, product standards, critical mass races, value creation, building unique resources). He has published in *Management Science*, the *Strategic Management Journal, Organization Studies, Marketing Letters, Advances in Strategic Management,* has edited a book, *European Industrial Restructuring in the 1990s* (London: Macmillan), 1992 with D. Neven and I. Walter, and has contributed to several books on competitive strategy. He is Associate Editor of the *Strategic Management Journal.* During the academic year 1995/6 he was Visiting Professor at the Graduate School of Business at the University of Chicago. He is also Visiting Professor at Northwestern University.

Luís Almeida Costa is Associate Professor of Strategic Management at Faculdade de Economia da Universidade Nova de Lisboa, Portugal, and Visiting Professor at INSEAD, Fontainebleau, France. He received the 'Licenciatura' in Economics degree from Universidade Católica Portuguesa, Lisbon, in 1988, and the MSc. and Ph.D. in Management degrees from INSEAD in 1992 and 1994, respectively. Luís Almeida Costa's research and teaching interests are in the area of industry and competitive analysis as well as in the application of game theory to negotiation analysis. He has worked as a consultant and has conducted executive programmes for companies in several industries, such as retailing, pulp and paper, FMCG, and financial services.

Gerald F. Davis is Wilbur K. Pierpont Professor of Management and Organizations at the Ross School of Business at the University of Michigan. Davis's research examines the influence of politics and social networks on corporate governance. His work appears in *Administrative Science Quarterly*, *Academy of Management Review*, *American Journal of Sociology*, *American Sociological Review*, *Annual Review of Sociology*, *Journal of Financial Economics*, *Journal of Management Inquiry*, *Journal of Personality and Social Psychology*, *Organization Science*, *Research in Organization Behavior*, *Strategic Organization*, and elsewhere.

Ingemar Dierickx is the Director of the INSEAD executive programme on Negotiation Dynamics. As a negotiator, Professor Dierickx has represented the interests of both individuals and major corporate clients. Professor Dierickx has worked as a consultant and has conducted numerous executive programmes throughout Europe, in the US, Israel, China, Singapore, Indonesia, Australia and New Zealand. In particular, he has worked extensively with leading financial services organisations. Before joining INSEAD, he worked at the Division of Research, Harvard Business School and in the Department of Economics, Harvard University. Ingemar Dierickx holds a Ph.D. in Business Economics from Harvard University and an MBA from the Harvard Business School, where he was a Baker Scholar. He also holds law degrees from the Harvard Law School (LLM) and the Rijksuniversiteit Ghent (Lic. Jur).

Kathleen M. Eisenhardt, Stanford Warren Ascherman MD Professor of Strategy and Organization at Stanford University. Professor Eisenhardt's interests centre on high-velocity industries and technology-based companies. She is currently studying corporate strategy, including acquisition of entrepreneurial firms, synergies in multi-business corporations, and the concept of boundaries. She is a co-author of *Competing on the Edge: Strategy as Structured Chaos*, winner of the George R. Terry award for outstanding contribution to management thinking. She has recently published 'Organizational Boundaries and Theories of Organization' (with F.M. Santos) in *Organization Science* and 'The Seller's Side of the Story: Acquisition as Courtship and Governance as Syndicate in Entrepreneurial Firms' (with M.E. Graebner) in *Administrative Science Quarterly*. Professor Eisenhardt is a Fellow of the Academy of Management and the World Economic Forum.

Ewan Ferlie is Professor of Public Services Management and Head of the School of Management at Royal Holloway, University of London. He was previously at

Imperial College Management School, University of London and before that was Deputy Director of the Centre for Corporate Strategy and Change, Warwick Business School. His interests lie in the organization and management of public service organizations, particularly in the health care and higher education sectors. He has written widely on public sector restructuring, the rise of the New Public Management and strategic change processes within the public services. He is also interested in changing professional and managerial roles. He is co-author of two research monographs investigating these issues: *Shaping Strategic Change* and *The New Public Management in Action*.

Raghu Garud's interests lie in exploring the nexus between technology, strategy and organizations. His publications explore path creation, metamorphic change, new organizational forms, economies of substitution, researcher persistence and technology embeddedness. He has co-authored or edited several books on technology: *Technological Innovation: Oversights and Foresights* (co-edited with Zur Shapira and Praveen Nayyar) (Cambridge University Press); *Cognition, Knowledge and Organizations* (co-edited with Joseph Porac) (JAI Press) (Oxford University Press); *The Innovation Journey* (with Andrew H. Van de Ven, Douglas Polley and Suresh Venkatraman, and *Path Dependence and Creation* (co-edited with Peter Karnoe) (Lawrence Earlbaum Associates) and *Managing in the Modular Age: Architectures, Networks and Organizations* (co-edited with Arun Kumaraswamy and Richard Langlois) (Blackwell Publishers). Raghu is Program Chair of the *Technology and Innovation Management* division for the 2001 Academy of Management meetings, Washington DC.

Paul Godfrey is Associate Professor of Strategy at the Marriott School at Brigham Young University. Paul received a bachelor of science degree in political science from the University of Utah, and an MBA and Ph.D. from the University of Washington. He has taught strategy and ethics courses at the Marriott School for the past seven years.

Paul's research interests lie in the intersection of values and strategy, especially the issues of corporate social responsibility, service-learning, values, mission, and organizational culture and identity, and the moral characteristics of leaders. Paul's work has appeared in the *Strategic Management Journal*, the *Journal of Management Inquiry* and the *Journal of High Technology Management*. He has co-edited two books.

Rob M. Grant is Professor of Management at Georgetown University. He has also held positions at City University, California Polytechnic, University of British Columbia, London Business School, and University of St Andrews, and was staff economist at the UK Monopolies Commission. His research focuses upon the nature and management of organisational capability, diversification strategy, the knowledge-based view of the firm, and firm strategy within the oil and gas sector. He was born in Bristol, England and studied economics at the London School of Economics. Although initially a specialist in industrial economics, he moved into strategic management during the early 1980s to escape the game theory revolution. He is married with four children and divides his time between London and Washington DC.

David J. Jeremy is Professor of Business History in the Business School, the Manchester Metropolitan University. His *Transatlantic Industrial Revolution: The Diffusion of Textile Technologies between Britain and America, 1790–1830s* (1981) received the Dexter Prize for the Society for the History of Technology and the John H. Dunning Prize of the American Historical Association. At the London School of Economics he edited the *Dictionary of Business Biography* (6 vols. 1984–6). He is the author of *Capitalists and Christians: Business Leaders and the Churches in Britain, 1900–1960* (1990); *Artisans, Entrepreneurs, and Machines* (1998), and *A Business History of Britain, 1800–1990s* (1998). Currently he is working on an historical study of boardroom culture and governance with special reference to the North West of England. His work has been funded by the Leverhulme Trust and the Economic and Social Research Council.

Bruce Kogut is the Eli Lilly Professor of Innovation, Business and Society at INSEAD and was formerly the Dr. Felix Zandman Chair at the Wharton School, University of Pennsylvania. Over the years, he has been a visitor at the École Polytechnique, the Stockholm School of Economics, Humboldt University, the Wissenschaftszentrum and the Santa Fe Institute. He recently published *The Global Internet* (MIT Press, 2003) and co-edited with Peter Cornelius, *Corporate Governance and Capital Flows in a Global Economy* (Oxford University Press, 2003). He is currently the Scientific Director of the European Institute of Advanced Studies in Management. Bruce works in the areas of direct investment, dynamic networks, corporate governance, and comparative sociology. Most recently, he has focused on privatization and globalization, with papers published by the World Bank, International Monetary Fund, and academic journals.

Christian Knudsen is a professor of economics of the firm at the Copenhagen Business School. He has published extensively on the methodology of economics, theories of the firm and strategy. Among his more recent books are *Rationality, Institutions and Economic Methodology* (with Maki and Gustafsson) (London: Routledge) and *Towards a Competence Theory of the Firm* (with N. Foss) (London: Routledge) His research interests include economic methodology, theories of the firm, sociology of organization and knowledge-based views on strategy. He is currently editing a book (with Haridimos Tsoukas) entitled *The Oxford Handbook of Organization Theory: Meta-theoretical Perspectives*, to be published by Oxford University Press in 2002. (e-mail: knudsen@rocketmail.com)

Rita Gunther McGrath is an associate professor in the Management Division at the Columbia Business School in New York City. Her research concerns entre-preneurship, new technologies and new ventures within established organizations. She is currently using real options reasoning to shed new light on traditional theory in these areas. McGrath has won the *Academy of Management Review* and *Research-Technology Management* 'best paper' awards, and is on the editorial boards of the *Strategic Management Journal*, the *Academy of Management Journal* and the *Journal of Business Venturing*. Her co-authored book, *The Entrepreneurial Mindset: Strategies for Continuously Creating Opportunity in an Age of Uncertainty* was published in 2000 by the Harvard Business School Press.

Prior to joining academia, she was a senior technology manager for the City of New York. Her work experience includes the political election arena as well as two entrepreneurial startups. Her Ph.D. is from the Wharton School.

Constantinos Markides is Professor of Strategic and International Management and holds the Robert P. Bauman Chair of Strategic Leadership at the London Business School. He received his BA (Distinction) and MA in Economics from Boston University, and his MBA and DBA from the Harvard Business School. His research and publications focus on strategic innovation, corporate restructuring, refocusing and international acquisitions. His recent work includes *Diversification, Refocusing and Economic Performance* (MIT Press, 1995) and *All the Right Moves: A Guide to Crafting Breakthrough Strategy* (Harvard Business School Press, 1999). His new book (with Paul Geroski), entitled *Fast Second: How Smart Companies Bypass Radical Innovation to Enter and Dominate New Markets* was published in January 2005 and was shortlisted by the *Financial Times* for the Management Book of the Year award. His publications have also appeared in journals such as the *Harvard Business Review*, *Sloan Management Review*, *Leader to Leader*, *Strategic Management Journal* and the *Academy of Management Journal*.

Keith Pavitt (died 20 December 2002) was R.M. Phillips Professor of Science and Technology Policy at Sussex University in England. He studied engineering, industrial management, and economics at Cambridge (UK) and Harvard (USA), and then worked at the Organisation for Economic Co-operation and Development (OECD) in Paris. During his 28 years at the Science Policy Research Unit, he published widely on the management of technology, and science and technology policy. His central research interests were: corporate and public strategies for technical innovation; the nature and measurement of technology; the reasons why countries, companies and sectors differ in their rates and directions of technical change; the usefulness of basic research; the links between public science and private technology in a period of globalisation and the co-evolution of technology and organisation.

Professor Pavitt advised numerous bodies on policies for technical change. He was a Visiting Lecturer at Princeton University, Visiting Professor at the Universities of Reading, Strasbourg (Louis Pasteur), Padua, Nice, Åalborg, Lyon-Lumière, Paris 13 and Paris-Dauphine, and Visiting Scholar at Stanford University. He was also a main editor of *Research Policy*.

Andrew Pettigrew is Professor of Strategy and Organization at Warwick Business School where between 1985 and 1995 he founded and directed the Centre for Corporate Strategy and Change. He has taught and researched at Yale University, London Business School and Harvard Business School where in the academic year 2001–2002 he will be a Visiting Professor. His most recent research includes studies of the boards and directors of the UK's top 500 companies and new forms of organizing and company performance in major corporations in Europe, Japan and the USA.

He was President of the British Academy of Management (1987–1990) and is a Fellow of both the Academy of Management in the USA and the UK. In 1995 he was the Distinguished Scholar of the Organization and Management Theory Division of the Academy of Management. In 1999 he was elected a Founding Academician of the Academy of Social Sciences.

Joseph F. Porac is the George Daly Professor in Business Leadership at the Leonard Stern School of Business, New York University. His research interests focus on the cognitive bases of markets and organizations, and he is currently pursuing research on knowledge transfer in organizations, the social construction of CEO reputations, and sensemaking between organizations. His research has appeared in a variety of management journals, and his most recent papers include 'Are More Resources Always Better for Growth: Resource Stickiness in Market and Product Expansion' (with Yuri Mishina and Tim Pollock) in *Strategic Management Journal* (25, 1179–97); and 'The Burden of Celebrity: The Impact of CEO Certification Contests on CEO Pay and Company Performance' (with James Wade, Tim Pollock and Scott Graffin) in *Academy of Management Journal* (forthcoming).

Gordon Rands is an associate professor of management at Western Illinois University (WIU). He has also taught at the Pennsylvania State University and at the University of Minnesota, from which he received his Ph.D. in Business Administration. Dr. Rands also has degrees from the University of Michigan (BS in Natural Resources) and Brigham Young University (Masters of Organizational Behavior). His areas of interest and expertise are business and the natural environment, corporate social responsibility and performance, business ethics, environmental sustainability of colleges and universities, service learning and microenterprise. His research has appeared in the *Academy of Management Review, Research in Strategic Management*, and other outlets. He is a member of the International Association for Business and Society and of the Academy of Management, and has served as chairperson of the Academy's Organizations and the Natural Environment Interest Group.

Winfried Ruigrok is a Professor of International Management, Director of the Research Institute for International Management and Academic Director of the MBS programme at the University of St Gallen, Switzerland. He studied political science (BA) and international economic relations (MA) and completed his Ph.D. in international political economy at the University of Amsterdam. He previously worked at the Netherlands Organisation for International Development Cooperation, the European Commission, the Erasmus University Rotterdam and the University of Warwick. He received the 1996 European Association of Evolutionary Political Economy (EAEPE) Mydral Prize. His research interests include multinational restructuring strategies, multicultural top management teams and boards, corporate governance, and the interaction between multinational firms and (international) institutions.

Filipe M. Santos is Assistant Professor of Entrepreneurship at INSEAD. A native of Portugal, Professor Santos holds a Ph.D. in Management Science and Engineering from Stanford University. He also holds a degree in Economics from NOVA University of Lisbon and a Masters in Management and Strategy from

ISEG, Lisbon. His research is at the intersection of strategy, organization theory, and entrepreneurship with a focus on nascent markets. His recent work has appeared in journals such as *Organization Science* ('Organizational Boundaries and Theories of Organization', 2005) and *Technological Forecasting and Social Change*. His current research examines the processes of market emergence, the determinants of organizational boundaries, and the founding and growth of new ventures.

Harbir Singh is Professor and Chair of the Management Department at the Wharton School of the University of Pennsylvania. Dr. Singh joined the Wharton faculty in 1984 after completing his doctorate from the University of Michigan. His research encompasses several areas, including firm scope and performance, effective ways to manage acquisitions and alliances, corporate governance, and processes by which firms cope with the challenges of emerging technologies. He has taught courses in competitive strategy, global strategic management, and corporate development via acquisitions and alliances.

Dr. Singh is Co-Director of Wharton's Mack Center for Technological Innovation, which sponsors inter-disciplinary research on strategies and processes by which firms create and profit from technological innovations.

W. Edward Steinmueller, Professor of Information and Communication Policy at SPRU (Science and Technology Policy Research), University of Sussex received his Ph.D. from Stanford University where he was Senior Research Associate and Deputy Director at Stanford Institute of Economic Policy Research. His areas of research include the economics of the information and information technology industries, the economics of science and technology policy, and the relationships among social, organisational, and technological factors in the production and adoption of new technologies. He is internationally known for his work on the integrated circuit, computer, telecommunication, and software industries and is a policy consultant in areas of industrial policy and high technology competition such as intellectual property rights, competition policy and standardisation.

Mohan Subramaniam is an Associate Professor of strategy at Boston College's Carroll School of Management and specializes in the areas of global strategy, managing multinational companies and the strategic management of knowledge and innovation. He received his DBA from Boston University and an MBA from the Indian Institute of Management at Bangalore. Professor Subramaniam teaches courses focusing on strategy, innovation and managing in a global environment. His research appears in leading management journals including the *Academy of Management Journal, Strategic Management Journal, Journal of Management Studies, Management International Review*, and the *Journal of Product Innovation Management*. His research has also received several grants including those from the National Science Foundation and the Carnegie Bosch Institute, and awards from the Academy of Management, Strategic Management Society, McKinsey & Company and the Decision Sciences Institute. Mohan serves on the editorial board of the *Journal of Management*.

Howard Thomas is Professor of Management and Dean of Warwick Business School. Previously Dean of the College of Commerce and Business Administration at the University of Illinois at Urbana-Champaign, USA since 1991. Prior to this he held posts as Foundation Professor of Management at the Australian Graduate School of Management in Sydney, as Director of the Doctoral Programme at London Business School, and visiting and permanent posts at institutions such as the European Institute of Management in Brussels, the University of Southern California, the University of British Columbia, the Sloan School of Management, MIT and Kellogg School Northwestern University. Former President of the US Strategic Management Society, past Chair of the Board of the Graduate Management Admissions Council, and Fellow of both the Academy of Management in the US and the UK.

His current research interests include: competitive strategy, risk analysis, strategic change, international management and decision theory.

Haridimos Tsoukas is a professor of Organization Theory and Behaviour at the Graduate School of Business, University of Strathclyde and the Athens Laboratory of Business Administration (ALBA). He obtained his Ph.D. at The Manchester Business School and has worked at MBS, Warwick Business School and the University of Essex. He is an associate editor of *Organizations Studies*, a co-editor of *Organization*, and a member of the editorial board of *Organization Science, Human Relations, and Emergence*. He has published widely in several leading journals including the *Academy of Management Review, Strategic Management Journal, Organization Studies, Journal of Management Studies*, and many more. His research interests include: knowledge-based perspectives on organizations, policy sciences and practical reason, the management of change, and epistemological issues in management studies. He is currently editing a book (with Christian Knudsen) entitled *The Oxford Handbook of Organization Theory: Meta-theoretical Perspectives*, to be published by Oxford University Press in 2002.

Michael Useem is William and Jacalyn Egan Professor of Management and Director of the Center for Leadership and Change Management at the Wharton School, University of Pennsylvania. He is the author of *Leading Up: How to Lead Your Boss So You Both Win* (Random House, 2001), *The Leadership Moment: Nine True Stories of Triumph and Disaster and Their Lessons for Us All* (Random House, 1998), *Investor Capitalism: How Money Managers Are Changing the Face of Corporate America* (HarperCollins, 1996), *Executive Defense: Shareholder Power and Corporate Reorganization* (Harvard University Press, 1993), and *The Inner Circle: Large Corporations and the Rise of Business Political Activity in the US and UK* (Oxford University Press, 1984).

Andrew H. Van de Ven is Vernon H. Heath Professor of Organizational Innovation and Change in the Carlson School of Management of the University of Minnesota. He received his Ph.D. from the University of Wisconsin at Madison in 1972, and taught at Kent State University and the Wharton School of the University of Pennsylvania before his present appointment. His current research focuses on processes of organizational innovation and change. He is co-author of *The Innovation Journey* (1999), *Organizational Change and Innovation Processes: Theory and Methods for Research* (2000), and *Handbook of Organizational Change and Innovation* (2004) all published by Oxford University Press. Van de Ven was 2000–2001 President of the Academy of Management.

N. (Venkat) Venkatraman holds the David J. McGrath Jr. Professorship of Management at Boston University School of Management. His research and teaching interests lie at the interface between strategic management and information technology. His current research is on eBusiness strategies for established companies as they embark on competing through the Internet. He is also working on a book on the theme of sustainable business models for the networked economy to be published in early 2002.

His doctoral thesis was awarded the 1986 AT Kearney Award for Outstanding Research in General Management by the Academy of Management and his doctoral students have won prestigious international awards for their doctoral work. His research papers have appeared in several leading academic journals such as *Management Science, Information Systems Research, Academy of Management Review, Academy of Management Journal, Strategic Management Journal*, and others. He has won several awards and recognition for his academic work. He was featured as a top-class faculty in *Business Week Guide to the MBA Programs* (2000). During 1999–2000, he was a Visiting Professor of Management at London Business School.

David A. Whetten is the Jack Wheatley Professor of Organizational Behavior and Director of the Faculty Center at Brigham Young University. He has served as editor of the *Foundations for Organizational Science*, and the *Academy of Management Review*. His pioneering and award-winning management text, *Developing Management Skills*, co-authored with Kim Cameron, is in its sixth edition. He has been very active in the Academy of Management. In 1994 he received the Academy's Distinguished Service Award, and in 1996 he was elected to a five-year term as a national officer in the Academy, which culminated in the position of President in 2000. In 2004 he received the OMT division's Distinguished Scholar Award.

Roderick E. White is an associate professor in the general management area at the Richard Ivey School of Business, The University of Western Ontario where, since 1979, he has taught Business Policy, and Strategic Analysis and Action. Rod received his DBA and MBA (with high distinction) from Harvard University and his Honors Bachelors of Arts in Business from The University of Western Ontario (gold medallist).

His research interests and consulting activities include: the process of strategic renewal, the functioning of top management teams, questions of business strategy – organization relationships within large, complex companies and the strategic management of foreign-owned subsidiaries. Currently, Rod is exploring the origins of social structure, and how this social structure contributes to organizational excellence and strategic renewal. He has an ongoing interest in the financial services industry. Rod has authored or co-authored articles on these and other topics appearing in *Academy of Management Review, Harvard Business Review, Business Quarterly, Policy Options, International Studies of Management and Organization, Planning Review, Organization Dynamics* and *The Strategic Management Journal.* He co-authored *Business Policy: A Canadian Casebook* (2nd, 3rd and 4th editions) and co-edited *Building the Strategically Responsive Organization.*

Richard Whittington is the Millman Fellow in Management at New College and Professor in Strategic Management at the Saïd Business School, University of Oxford. He has previously been Reader in Marketing and Strategic Management at Warwick Business School and Visiting Professor at Groupe HEC, Paris. He has published several single or co-authored books, including *Corporate Strategies in Recession and Recovery* (1989), *What Is Strategy – and Does It Matter?* (1993/2000), *Rethinking Marketing* (1999) and *The European Corporation* (2000). He is Associate Editor of the *British Journal of Management* and on the editorial boards of *Organization Studies* and *Long Range Planning.* His current research is on strategy as social practice, the learning of strategy skills and organizational restructuring.

Acknowledgements

For all three editors this Handbook represents the most ambitious publishing project we have so far attempted. As ever, the easy part was the conception, the hard bit was the delivery.

The idea for the Handbook came from Sue Jones then management editor for Sage Publications in London. She approached Andrew Pettigrew to develop the intellectual concept and structure of the Handbook. We received early advice from Ed Zajac and John McGee. Shortly thereafter Howard Thomas (then Dean at the College of Commerce, University of Illinois) and Richard Whittington agreed to share the editorial responsibilities. When Howard returned to the UK in the summer of 2000, all the editorial team were then located within 50 miles of one another at Warwick and Oxford Universities. This proximity made the team work in drafting the introduction and conclusion that much easier.

When Sue Jones moved on from Sage she was replaced by Rosemary Nixon who was an equally enthusiastic and experienced editor. Latterly, Kiren Shoman as management editor in London and Gladys Calix-Ferguson in her marketing role at Sage Publications have been enormously helpful and patient in guiding the book through to publication.

We thank the entire editorial board for their personal support for the Handbook. The authors are, of course, the Handbook, and we thank them wholeheartedly for their creativity and commitment.

We also wish to acknowledge the special reviewers we called on to help us with this volume. We express our grateful thanks to Andrew Campbell, Stephen Cummings, Charles Galunic, John Gray, Michael Mayer and Joe Tidd.

Shortly before we commenced the Handbook the very successful Sage *Handbook of Organization Studies* was published. We took the opportunity to ask Cynthia Hardy and Stewart Clegg for their advice. Most of the mishaps which occurred on their journey to publication were repeated on our journey. Being fore-warned did not lessen the pain, but nevertheless thanks for the warnings Cynthia and Stewart.

At various times and in various ways secretarial and administrative support has been offered by staff at Warwick Business School. We would like to thank Gill Drakeley, Sheila Frost, Gill Robson and Janet Biddle for all their practical help and support.

We embarked on this Handbook because of a genuine belief that the field of strategic management was at a crossroads, certainly not the last crossroads, but at an important cusp in its development. The authors of the Handbook have confirmed this sense of a turning point and we hope this volume will not just be seen as the mapping of an intellectual terrain, but also as a positive spur for greater critical reflection, more experimentation, and more creativity in strategy and management.

Andrew Pettigrew, Howard Thomas and Richard Whittington
February 2001

Part One

MAPPING A TERRAIN

1

Strategic Management: The Strengths and Limitations of a Field

ANDREW PETTIGREW, HOWARD THOMAS
and RICHARD WHITTINGTON

The purpose of this handbook is to present a major retrospective and prospective overview of research and writing on strategy and management. We make the distinction between the established field of strategic management with its notably successful scholarly journal (*Strategic Management Journal*) and society (Strategic Management Society) and the broader interests in the theory and practice of strategy and management. The classic questions of the strategist have been about the purposes, direction, choices, changes, governance, organization and performance of organizations in their industry, market and social, economic and political contexts. No doubt mindful of the old adage that if you try and see everything, you see nothing, many strategy scholars have chosen to limit their observations by specializing through level of analysis, disciplinary frame of reference and research theme. The field of strategic management has developed in a particular way and this has produced notable strengths and weaknesses, preoccupations and blind spots.

Beyond strategic management, other scholars in the management and social sciences and humanities have also engaged with questions about the direction, organization and performance of institutions most notably in the fields of history, philosophy, political science,

sociology, psychology and economics. Our emphasis on strategy and management in the book title (as distinct from strategic management) is not just a play on words. We take the view that the intellectual development of all fields of management is dependent upon an open and reciprocal relationship with the social sciences and humanities. Progress in developing the theory and practice of strategy and management we believe is more likely to happen though inclusiveness than exclusivity. This means various forms of intellectual bridging and transfer should be encouraged. Bridging across the fields of management has, of course, already occurred most visibly in links between organization theory and strategic management. Industrial economics is well embedded in the field of strategic management and more recently cognitive psychology has also had an impact on theorizing about the nature of competitive strategy within and between organizations. The title is our first invitation for other scholars from the management and social sciences to join us in learning more about strategy and management.

Strategy and management is at the moment an aspiration not an accomplishment. In framing, addressing and synthesizing work in the field of strategy we must start with the existing boundary of strategic management. However, in addressing issues about the future shape and development of the field of strategy we shall be more adventurous. In organizing the chapters into four parts we have set four main challenges for the future. Part 1, Mapping a Terrain, seeks to provide a characterization of the historical, practical and interdisciplinary roots of the field of strategic management and is aspirational about the need to broaden the terrain of strategy. Part 2, Thinking and Acting Strategically, gathers together a group of nine chapters which assess research in some of the core fields of strategic management. The emphasis on thinking and acting offers a dual challenge. Firstly, the need to counterbalance the bias in the strategy field towards analytical thought with a greater concern with action, and in using the verb forms thinking and acting, to give emphasis to the dynamic aspects of both. Part 3, Changing Contexts, provides a range of challenges to the field of strategy from the rapidly transforming settings within which thinking and acting strategically now occurs. Part 4, Looking Forward, consolidates many of the book's strands with a range of epistemological, theoretical, historicist and empirical arguments about the future development of the field.

The design principle as a whole is to encourage intellectual development through seeking focus on the one hand – for example, eschewing an objective of comprehensiveness to seek to map the most significant core terrain for the field – while also acknowledging diversity, of contexts, applications and alternative disciplinary and other paradigms and perspectives threading through this terrain, on the other. Thus the critical analysis and synthesis of diverse disciplinary and other inputs and dynamics around a core set of issues and themes is an important feature and contribution. Contributors have been asked to provide historical overviews of the key strands delineating the topography of their particular themes, addressing the central problem and approaches which have characterized these, to undertake rigorous critical assessments of the state and quality of current theory and knowledge – what is known and not known in the area – and to set out agendas for future theoretical and empirical development. Each author has been asked to consider any salient issues of research methodologies and practice in their topics, as well as addressing the range of literatures and traditions within the social sciences relevant to informed and contextually sophisticated research and

theorizing about strategy and management in a rapidly changing world.

In its contemporary form the field of strategic management is a United States invention and export. However, in an increasingly interdependent and multicultural world it is crucial to recognize differences in institutional and cultural context and diversity in intellectual traditions in different societies. We are sure as editors that we have not gone far enough in recognizing available intellectual diversity. However, the reader will notice that the geographical base of the contributors is 50–50 North American and Europe. Many of the contributors have sought to include published work from the worlds of academia and practice and where possible beyond the intellectual traditions of North America and Europe.

Beyond these opening scene-setting remarks, this introductory chapter has five parts. First, we characterize the history and development of the field of strategic management. We identify major points of development, key authors and schools of thought, notable research themes, strengths and weaknesses, and epistemological and methodological biases. Of necessity this characterization is broad-brush. The more detailed assessment of strengths and weaknesses, gaps and forward looking research agendas are offered in the thematic chapters which follow.

Part 2 of this introduction assesses periodic attempts in the field of strategic management to provide integration and synthesis. It concludes that paradigmatic unity is neither present or desirable in a field opening up yet more to new ideas, and being constantly challenged by rapidly changing contexts. Part 3 provides a brief critical assessment of the field of strategic management from authors inside and outside the traditional boundaries of the field. Part 4 catalogues some of the many contextual challenges to the theory and practice of strategy and in Part 5 we offer brief summaries of each of the 20 chapters which make up the core of this volume.

CHARACTERIZING THE FIELD OF STRATEGIC MANAGEMENT

There are many simplifying statements that can be made to capture aspects of the evolution and development of strategic management. In its contemporary form, but not deeper intellectual history, its roots are in US academia and practice. Most commentators would agree the field began to take shape in the 1960s with the impact of writing by Chandler (1962), Ansoff (1965) and Andrews (1971). Chandler and Andrews were key professors at Harvard Business School. Andrews was part of the powerful general management teaching group at Harvard and Chandler was a Harvard-trained social scientist who virtually single-handedly created a corpus of work using the comparative historical method which had an influence right across the social sciences. Ansoff had a different intellectual and institutional history. He came out of the intellectually dominant Carnegie School, then led by Cyert, March and Simon, but quickly launched himself off into creating a new more interdisciplinary management school at Vanderbilt University before in turn wandering restlessly into Europe and beyond. In *Corporate Strategy*, Ansoff (1965) outlined a more rationalistic and planning orientated view of strategy than the general management focused view of business policy emanating from Harvard.

These early academic roots were complemented by a strong practice element focused around a group of initially US-based strategy consultancy practices. Three of these, McKinsey, BCG and Bain, eventually became world leaders in developing and diffusing the language and techniques of strategy throughout the world. McKinsey quickly picked upon Chandler's path-breaking work on the multidivisional organizational form and his dictum that structure follows strategy. The opening of the London office of McKinsey in 1959 was a key factor in exporting the virtues of the M Form into the boardrooms of Europe. Around the same time, planning functions were building up in many large US and European firms and Shell International became one of the very few European points of influence in developing the technologies of corporate planning (Wack, 1985).

Meanwhile away from the prestige of the Harvard Business School and the consultancy salons of McKinsey, BCG and Bain, an alternative spring of innovation in strategy was taking shape at the Krannert School of Management, Purdue University, Indiana. In 1969 Dan Schendel set up the first doctoral speciality in strategic management. By 1972 he and a junior colleague, Hatten, were using the Academy of Management proceedings to challenge the Harvard intellectual control of the subject. Their 1972 paper 'Business Policy or Strategic Management: a broader view for an emerging discipline' began to push not just a new name and rallying cry, but a more analytical and economics-based view of the field of strategy than had hitherto existed (Schendel and Hatten, 1972). This early claim for influence was allowed to fester until Schendel and Hofer took the much more visible and politically effective step of gathering like-minded professors together at a conference at Pittsburgh University in 1977. If Harvard was to be challenged, a new paradigm for strategic management needed not just an intellectual rallying cry but also a new institutional form which could compete in a way that Purdue alone could not. By 1979 Schendel and Hofer (1979) had published a book-length manifesto for the new field of strategic management. This was quickly followed in 1980 by the publication of Volume 1 of the *Strategic Management Journal* (*SMJ*) and the creation of the Strategic Management Society (SMS) whose annual conferences became a forum for the 'a' (academic) 'b' (business) and 'c' (consultancy) fraternities interested in the strategic management of the firm.

Dan Schendel became the first President of the SMS and remains Editor-in-Chief of the *SMJ* to this day. The *SMJ* has become the pre-eminent journal publishing scholarly work in the field of scientific management and is often rated in the top five of academic journals in the broader field of management. The *SMJ* has been crucial in setting the academic tone for the field. Part of the Schendel manifesto was to create a more scholarly, analytical, positivistic and quantitative treatment of the subject than had existed in the 1960s and 1970s Harvard Business School approach to the subject. This has encouraged the rise in importance of economic theories and econometric methods in strategic management paradoxically at the time in the 1980s when another Harvard Business Professor, Michael Porter, brought his Harvard economics training into the field. A combination of Porter's 1980 and 1985 books, plus the export of Harvard MBAs into the major US consultancy firms and executive corridors, maintained Harvard's influence, but Schendel's energy and presence, together with the new institutions he helped to create, completely altered the intellectual and political landscape of the field of strategic management. The summer and winter special issues of the *SMJ* have been crucial mechanisms to signal major changes and consolidating points in the field. Schendel until very recently used the opening essays in these special issues to put his own gloss on these intellectual developments, and through his selection of the editors of these special issues, reaffirmed and consolidated academic reputations.

Looking back, Schendel has been an enormously skilful surfer of the main waves, never allowing himself or the *SMJ* quite to get left behind. However, this intellectual and institutional trajectory has had its weaknesses as well as its strengths. Both the *SMJ* and SMS have had their critics and there have been periodic questions about the lack of critical reflection and narrowness of the epistemological, methodological and theoretical base of writing in the field of strategic management.

It is now commonplace to talk of the post-Porter era in strategy, perhaps as we shall see the more general changes in epistemological and theoretical discourse in the social sciences at the beginning of the 21st century, together with the empirical challenges from the changing world-wide business, economic and social context, will collectively push the field of strategy and management in some fruitful new directions?

March (1996: 278) has recently reminded us that 'the writing of history is a conceit of survivors'. Certainly it is the case that history is shaped by those with the motivation to grasp opportunities to craft narratives. Truth is socially shaped and so are fields of inquiry. Cannella and Paetzold (1994) – commenting on the paradigm wars in organization theory prompted by Pfeffer (1993) and energized by Van Maanem (1994) – have rightly summarized that 'science is not a magnificent march toward absolute truth, but a social struggle amongst the scholars of the profession to construct truth' (1994: 332). Equally well, there is the important issue of how we characterize the trajectory of development in a field of knowledge. Tsoukas and Cummings (1997) suggest that we can look at a field as a process of progress and progression, upwards and onwards to a set of unifying theories, or we can use

Foucault's (1966) metaphor of a kaleidoscope with its implication of discrete fragments falling into patterns as the kaleidoscope is twisted at key cusps in a field's development. This kaleidoscopic view implies that any new pattern is not necessarily any more true or false, but is merely there. When we explore in a moment some of the key content areas of knowledge in strategic management, we will see clearly that strategic management as a field shares many of the characteristics of its fellow travellers in the social and management sciences. Unlike earlier characterizations of the natural sciences, where the stereotype is of knowledge accumulating progressively and linearly like some clear edged and tidy ribbon, in the social sciences knowledge seems to accumulate more as a mosaic, the patterning on an untidy quilt. This quilt-like form is certainly evident in the management sciences and especially so in the field of strategic management, where the fads and fashions of a field living with the duality of theory and practice periodically emblazon a patch with sharp vibrant colours which pushes the other patterns out of sight and mind.

So what patterns are evident in the patchwork quilt of theory, empirical findings and practice we call strategic management? Is there a clearly defined family tree of knowledge, a clear genealogical structure with notable classics, distinct frames of reference and roots into the social sciences and practice? In Chapter 18 Tsoukas and Knudsen argue that since 1980 the bulk of published research in strategic management has been in the normal science tradition. This, they argue, has been a necessary part of legitimating a new field of study which from the outset faced the combined scepticism of other parts of the social and management sciences and the world of practice. The history of strategic management is a story of promiscuous borrowing from other disciplines and sub-fields of management. Many have implied this borrowing has been one way with little reciprocity between strategic management and other disciplines. This is an accusation, however, that could be made against all the disciplines and fields of management. They have liberally taken but so far have given little back to the core preoccupations of the social science disciplines.

But in amongst the at times casual acquisitions from several disciplines there has been a consistent reaching out to the theoretical apparatus of economics. This approach was part of the manifesto of the new strategic management to give a sharper form of theorizing than that available in the heroic posturing of the Harvard general management tradition laid down in the 1960s and 1970s. Porter's (1980, 1985) enduring contribution has been to bring the language of industrial organization (IO) economics into the field of strategic management. This switched the gaze of the strategist from the firm to the industry structure. The main determinant of firm performance was now to be described and prescribed in terms of industry sector and not the goals, structures, dynamics and leadership of the firm so beloved of the business policy scholars. But this move from an 'inside out' to an 'outside in' paradigm (McKiernan, 1996; Hoskisson et al., 1999) was not deep enough or far enough for some. Camerer (1985) made a sharp plea to economize the field still further and this was followed up by an important paper by Rumelt et al. in 1991 which reaffirmed and blessed the importance of economic thinking in strategy. IO economics had the greatest impact, but the new economics held the greatest promise. This message was softened slightly in the 1994 volume by Rumelt et al. The title of this volume, *Fundamental Issues in Strategy*, switched the focus from the primacy of the discipline as the driver and enabler of intellectual development to the issues and themes in the field, but the tone of the book remained firmly wedded to economics as the core discipline and the section of the 1994 book designed to signal more process-oriented thinking and research was abandoned.

Various other sub-fields of economics other than the original IO approach have continued to have a strong impact on the field. Notable examples include game theory (Camerer, 1991; Saloner, 1991; Nalebuff and Brandenburger, 1997), agency theory (Fama and Jensen, 1983; Hoskisson and Hitt, 1990), transaction costs economics (Williamson, 1975, 1985; Hoskisson, 1987) and evolutionary theories of economics (Nelson and Winter, 1982). These developments have been welcomed by many (for example, Hesterly and Zenger, 1993) but have also led to sharp criticisms about the a priori theorizing of economics, the model of man paraded in both maximizing and satisfying views of economics and the love economists

have of databases rather than seeking direct engagement with phenomena at firm, sector or market levels of analysis (Perrow, 1986; Hirsch et al., 1987; Foss, 1996). Whipp (1996) caught the mood of the sceptics well in arguing that strategy was too important an area of theory and practice to be annexed by a single discipline. Whipp concluded his 1996 review of the field of strategy and organization by noting that a disciplinary takeover of the strategy field was unlikely and there were many encouraging signs of synthetic and boundary spanning work in the field. We will return to issues of integration and cross-fertilization in part 3 of this chapter.

Probably the most comprehensive reviews in article form of theory, research and methods in strategic management have recently been supplied by Hitt et al. (1998) and Hoskisson et al. (1999). The Hoskisson et al. paper on theory and research uses the metaphor of 'swings of a pendulum' to characterize the field's development. The period from the mid 1960s to the late 1990s is portrayed as four eras of development. Throughout what they describe as a period of significant growth in diversity of topics and research methods, Hoskisson et al. see the constant focus being the examination of business concepts that effect firm performance. However, they also see periodic swings from an internal firm focus to external firm focus and then back again. Thus thinking moved from the 1960s and 1970s work in the business policy tradition to an externally focussed era in the 1980s dominated by IO economics, then in the mid 1980s, with the rise of organizational economics, an attempt to mix inside and outside perspectives, and finally with the rise in the 1990s of the resource and knowledge based theories of the firm, a swing back to an internal firm focus in explaining firm performance.

The resource based view of the firm is traceable to the Cambridge based economist Edith Penrose and her classic 1959 book, *The Theory of the Growth of the Firm*. However, the conceptual transfer of this approach into the strategic management literature is generally credited to Wernefelt (1984). Important theoretical developments have also come from Barney (1992) and Grant (1991) but the mass-market popularization of the core competences of the firm had to wait for Prahalad and Hamel (1990) and Hamel and Prahalad (1994). The resource based theory maintained the long-term preoccupation with the determinants of competitive advantage but switched the focus from industry structure, strategy groups and external competitive dynamics to the particular constellation of tangible and intangible resources developed by the firm. The so-called knowledge based theory of the firm perpetuated this internal resource focus but in elaborating a more process orientated view of the acquisition, maintenance and utilization of knowledge resources gave a further twist to the particularities of firm behaviour and deepened the pendulum swing to internal firm dynamics (Kogut and Zander, 1992; Nonaka and Takeuchi, 1995).

With the pendulum swings in theory and research, Hitt et al. (1998) also argue, have come switches in levels of analysis, theoretical orientation and then research method. They note that the early business policy work tended to use single case studies or comparative case studies. The IO work and its derivatives moved to incorporate the econometric analysis of surveys and databases, and with the switch of interest to the particularities of resource acquisitions and knowledge development processes there has been a return to smaller sample studies sometimes accompanied by surveys of limited samples of firms. Schwenk and Dalton's (1991) paper on the changing shape of strategic management research gives a useful overview of the central tendencies of strategy research up to 1987 and just before the resource based theory of the firm began to take hold. They noted the standard criticisms of strategic management research up to the mid 1980s had been the absence of studies of strategy implementation, and of the determinants of firm performance, the overuse of nominal and single-item scales and the lack of attention to construct validity of scales. Longitudinal studies were very rare, comparative and cross sectional research using surveys and databases was the great preoccupation.

In their survey of published strategic management research in six top US academic journals in the years 1986 and 1987 Schwenk and Dalton (1991) found more continuity than change in the content and methods of strategy research. One-third of the articles used the static metaphor of 'fit' from contingency theory to address issues to do with the content of strategy. Some 72% of strategic management research relied on data derived from surveys and archival material. There was a continuing strong emphasis on

performance as a dependent variable, using hard and soft measures of performance. Seventy-five per cent of studies were cross-sectional. Of the 25% of studies which had longitudinal data, only 12% of these analysed the data in time series terms. In spite of conclusions about the increasing maturity of the field, the picture before the rise of the resource and knowledge based theories of the firm was of little experimentation in theory and method. If strategic management in the mid 1980s was adapting at all it was through low risk exploitation and not through higher risk exploration (March, 1991).

There are at least two important conditioning statements to be made about the otherwise very useful synthetic reviews of the field supplied by Schwenk and Dalton (1991), Hitt et al. (1998) and Hoskisson et al. (1999). The first is the overwhelming geographical bias of all three reviews. Schwenk and Dalton (1991) report only on strategic management research published in top US journals. Scholarship in Europe and beyond is totally ignored. The more recent assessments of work in strategic management by Hoskisson et al. and Hitt et al. is equally partial. Both of these review papers cite around 250 items of published research. The Hitt et al. paper is solely dependent on US-based work and Hoskisson et al. can only manage to incorporate six or seven references to non-US work in their assessment of theory and research. As McKiernan (1996: xiv) in Volume 1 of his *Historical Evolution of Strategic Management* curtly puts it, there is a constant 'need to counter-balance any easy assumption that any single geographical source has monopolized the history of thought in the subject'.

The other major limitation of the Schwenk and Dalton, Hitt et al. and Hoskisson et al. reviews is their lack of critical reflection on the field, including their reluctance to cite authors who have pointed to the limitations of theory and research in strategic management. Thus Hoskisson et al. ignore the gentle epistemological critique of Bourgeois (1984), the more radical reflections of Shrivastava (1986) and the European critical management theorists such as Knights and Morgan (1991) and Alvesson and Willmott (1995). Even harder to understand is the complete disregard of Mintzberg's alternative process view of strategy (1978, 1990, 1994) and the entire field of strategy process and change research (Pettigrew, 1985, 1992; Chakravarthy and

Doz, 1992; Johnson, 1987). But if the field of strategic management more generally has been short on reflexity (Whipp, 1996), it has not been devoid of thematic and theoretical eclecticism. In the 1990s there has been a clear trend to tidy up the resultant fragmentation by seeking out cross-fertilization, integration and complementary scholarly development.

INTEGRATION AND CROSS-FERTILIZATION IN STRATEGIC MANAGEMENT

In a range of carefully argued papers, Abrahamson (1991, 1996) uses the language of fads and fashions and band wagons to characterize management techniques as fashion commodities. Unlike many aesthetic and cultural forms, Abrahamson argues management techniques emerge and are justified through a combination of rational efficiency (sound means to achieve important ends) and progressive (new as well as improved relative to older management techniques). He cites the rise and eclipse of quality circles in the United States in the 1980s as a contemporary example, but also draws on historical data to show that management fashions about, for example, employee stock ownership schemes have gained and lost popularity since the turn of the twentieth century. Crucially, Abrahamson also argues that management fashions are not cosmetic and trivial. They have done and continue to shape the behaviour of managers all over the world and can have massive – sometimes helpful, but also questionable – impacts on organizations and their people.

All of the fields of management theory and research have been exposed to fads and fashions. The crucial interest and role of senior executives and external consultants in the strategy domain alongside their academic collaborators has made the field of strategic management more susceptible than most to the rise and fall of bandwagons. Academic reputations and consultancy practices in the social and management sciences are often built upon this rise and fall of analytical language and their associated programmatic management techniques. The fact that the field of strategic management has constantly pivoted between concerns for theory and practice has in some sense kept the field

honest and alive. Detached a priori theorizing at some point will be challenged by the practical agenda of the senior executive or consultant – or indeed by the sceptical gaze of the empirical researcher. Nevertheless, in an over-published world the constant drive for recognition and a place in the scholarly and consultancy marketplace has meant that novelty is prized over the careful accumulation of evidence-based knowledge. So apparent innovation may be spurious and ephemeral, a language game just as easily won as lost.

But the resultant fragmentation in strategic management research is not just a product of drives for linguistic novelty. The core of strategy's interest in the direction, purpose, strategic leadership, organization and competitive performance of organizations has created a multidisciplinary melting pot crowded by aspirants claiming 'twas from my loins it came!'. Claims for originality are often expressed initially in didactic terms – this innovation is at the expense of that now fading framework or technique. The past is pushed off-stage by the hard edge of exclusivity of a new paradigm or frame of reference. In time, however, extreme positions get watered down and some scholars look for the supremacy of unifying paradigms (Camerer, 1985; Sanchez and Heene, 1997), or more integration and cross-fertilization between complementary approaches (Barney, 1992; Zajac, 1992; Seth and Thomas, 1994). All these patterns in the social production of knowledge are apparent in the history of development of strategic management.

As we have already argued, the strongest history of the search for a unifying paradigm in strategic management research is associated with the drive for unity through the theoretical and methodological approaches of various strands of economics – from IO economics, through transaction costs economics, agency theory, game theory and latterly organizational economics (Camerer, 1985; Rumelt et al., 1991; Mahoney, 1992). These aspirations remain unfulfilled, indeed the rise of the resource based theory of the firm and its consolidation and development in the knowledge based theory have provided for some an alternative unifying paradigm. One of the strongest statements of this is the recent paper by Sanchez and Heene (1997) which is critical of the 'split personality' in the field with the bi-polar focus on inside-out and outside-in approaches to strategy. The way forward, argue Sanchez and Heene (1997: 304), lies in unifying the field around the language of competence-based competition which 'requires the effective integration of internal organizational and external competitive dynamics'. This the authors argue is not just because of evident fragmentation and polarization in the field but because the understanding of the ever changing global context of business requires a dynamic, systemic, cognitive and holistic treatment of competence-based competition within and between firms.

In their search for cross-fertilization and complementarity, others have been more circumspect, arguing the jigsaw should be put together piece by piece rather than attempting a Herculean synthesis. Thus Barney (1992) has argued that the rise of the resource-based theory of the firm offers new opportunities to bring more organization theory into the strategy domain but this time not just to deepen appreciation of strategy processes but also to help disentangle the origins and development of socially complex competitive resources such as trust, change and choice capability and creativity. Zajac (1992) has argued for greater cross-fertilization of economic and behavioural science approaches to strategy. He shows how questions reliant on economic thinking alone (from IO economics, agency and transaction costs theories) can be enriched by posing complementary behavioural questions.

Later empirical work in the corporate governance area by Zajac and Westphal (1996, 1998) shows that Zajac has practised what he preached. Seth and Thomas (1994) are also preoccupied with the links between strategy research and economics and, like Zajac, they are wise enough to see that this is only possible where surface posturing is shed to examine incommensurable theoretical assumptions from any perspectives attempting a rapprochement. Zajac (1992) makes the point that any cross-fertilization work is only as strong as its weakest link and that the integrative scholar needs to pass the tough test of being able to speak both languages with equal depth and fluency. Seth and Thomas (1994: 186) have an equally hard-headed message for those still searching for a unifying paradigm. More reflexivity they argue is necessary to create a field where researchers 'are particularly sensitive to the various assumptions underlying

their frames of reference, the utility of those assumptions in framing theory and to communicating these'.

The rise of organizational economics and institutional theory in the 1990s have also benefited theory development and empirical research in strategic management. In a kaleidoscopic treatment of the literature on organization economics and strategy, Mahoney (1992) rests his case on a heightened conversation between the two fields and on the rejection of Kuhn's (1970) incommensurability of paradigms thesis. Mahoney (1992) sharply dismisses incommensurability as an approach designed to legitimate intellectual vested interests, and not much else. However, Mahoney's over-inclusive definition of organizational economics (particularly the inclusion of the behavioural theory of the firm and the resource-based theory of the firm) mispleased Eisenhardt and Brown (1992).

Sociological insights into the strategic analysis of firms have come from a variety of directions. Pettigrew (1985, 1992, 1997) has brought Giddens' (1979) theory of structuration and Sztompka's (1991) theory of social becoming to deepen theorizing about strategy processes. These theoretical developments have been enriched and illustrated by a whole series of empirical studies at the Centre for Corporate Strategy and Change, Warwick University (Pettigrew, 1985; Pettigrew and Whipp, 1991; Pettigrew et al., 1992; Ferlie et al., 1996; McNulty and Pettigrew, 1998; Pettigrew and Fenton, 2000). Oliver (1997) has sought to link developments in institutional theory with the resource-based theory of the firm. Her argument is a complementary one, that a firm surely needs resource capital and institutional capital for longer-run competitive advantages. The dynamic perspective now available in institutional theory brings a welcome temporal perspective to earlier variants of the resource-based theory which were curiously uncurious about how resources were created, modified and utilized over time.

A third and most recent dialogue between sociological theory and strategic management is now occurring between economic sociologists and strategists (Dobbin and Baum, 2000). Again, the way forward is to eschew vague notions of unity of perspective and to start by disentangling common research themes and questions; identifying similarities and differences in core assumptions and then search for complementarity rather than integration.

In spite of periodic cries for a unifying paradigm in strategic management, one has not appeared, it is unlikely to do so and it would be creatively destructive if it did arrive. As Schendel (1994) and many others have pointed out, the sheer complexity of the subject matter of the strategy field, the historical pathway of eclecticism of theory and method, and the field's roots in multiple disciplines and in practice, have all created a rich body of theory and practice. Recent attempts to look for bridges across complementary traditions, combined with an increasing visibility of sociological and psychological approaches, have counter-balanced earlier dependence on economic theorizing about firms, markets and industries.

Further maturity is likely to come from the cross-fertilization of theories in big empirical studies using multiple methods, and from an increasing willingness to critically reflect on old assumptions and novel developments. It is to this historical predisposition not to critically reflect that we now turn.

STRATEGIC MANAGEMENT: SOME CRITICAL REFLECTIONS

As Whipp (1996) and others have commented, one of the most serious and intellectually debilitating aspects of strategic management as a field is its lack of reflexivity. There are a few notable iconoclasts (Camerer, 1985; Shrivastava, 1986; Mintzberg, 1990, 1994) but by and large it is a field unendowed with a developed critical tradition. We can speculate why this might be so. One reason is certainly the theory and practice duality and the need to meet the often conflicting expectations of the various stakeholders interested in the subject. Few senior executives and consultants we have met have much tolerance for academic deconstruction, which is often seen as a form of irritating self-abuse. Practitioners of strategy are much more likely to be impressed by creative problem-solving ability – 'if it works for me, it works' is the emblem for that form of pragmatism. The stage of development of the field in a constantly changing context is also a factor.

In its contemporary form the field is only 40 years old and that has been an era of laying down foundations, building a reasonably consistent intellectual language and trying to establish some basic patterns in what is known and not known. In this pioneering era it may not be surprising that few scholars have been prepared to challenge the core beliefs and assumptions of the field whether they are about the concept of knowledge, rules of evidence, levels of analysis or mode of human action grounded in the field. Until recently it has been very difficult to identify any epistemological writing on strategic management, but the critical reflections from this source are now beginning to flow, most especially from European-based scholars such as Pettigrew (1992), Calori (1998), Tsoukas and Knudsen (see Chapter 18) and Cummings and Wilson (in press).

One form of meta level critical reflection which is evident is the preparedness of some authors to organize writing in the field into classificatory schemes in order to clarify central tendencies in the field and thereby identify areas of focus and relative inattention. Whittington's (1993) book *What is Strategy And Does it Matter?* is one such contemplative assessment of the field and the more recent book by Mintzberg et al. (1998) is another. The forthcoming book by Cummings and Wilson (in press) is a further attempt to offer critical reflection through juxtaposing alternative frames of reference and illustrations of strategy making in action.

Bourgeois (1984) was a very early questioner of the determinism of IO economics in the field of strategic management and at a time when the Porter era was beginning to take hold. He noted the reductionist and determinist character of IO economics, the failure to examine mutual causal links between industry structure and firm behaviour, the need to study the content and process of strategy reciprocally and simultaneously and the obvious value of combining qualitative and quantitative data in a field which constantly needed to move between the particular and the general. This was dangerous stuff in 1984.

However, Shrivastava outmatched Bourgeois in his direct attack on the uncritical ideological bias of the field of strategic management. His stated aim was to encourage researchers to 'examine their unstated managerial values and assumptions, and to encourage them to generate less ideologically value-laden and more universal knowledge about the strategic management of organizations' (Shrivastava, 1986: 364). This criticism by Shrivastava, which ended by concluding that the ideological character of strategic management research was a crucial legitimator of existing power structures, has since been used as a totem and point of entry for critical management theorists such as Alvesson and Willmott (1995), but Shrivastava has been virtually ignored in most other subsequent reviews of the field.

Mintzberg has been a much more sustained, effective and creative critique of the field of strategic management. After some early high-impact empirical work on the nature of managerial work (Mintzberg, 1973) and the character of strategic decision processes (Mintzberg et al., 1976), Mintzberg has found his place in a series of iconoclastic challenges of the nature of strategy and of strategy processes (Mintzberg, 1978, 1990, 1994; Mintzberg and Walters, 1985; Mintzberg et al., 1998). At a time when IO economics was dominating the field, with the black box of the firm bobbing helplessly around the economic bath tub, it could be said that Mintzberg's writing began to humanize the field of strategic management. He used his energy and Herculean reading, combined this with great skills in conceptual pattern recognition and evocative writing, to attack one cherished belief after another.

Strategy was no longer to be seen just as rationally intended purposeful thought. The strategists were no longer to be portrayed as heroic general managers, but might involve actors in and outside the boardroom. Even the unthinkable was articulated, action might precede thought. Strategizing could now be thought of as reconstructions after the fact, rather than rationally intended plans. Strategies could be intended, emergent and unrealized. The linear view of process explicit in the old cartesian dichotomy of strategy formulation and strategy implementation was questioned. With increasing interest in the enduring characteristics of structural and strategy context, Chandler's dictum that structure followed strategy was modified to include the possibility that strategy may indeed follow structure. These criticisms carried on unabated and had a tremendous influence on establishing the field

of strategy process research and strategy change research. Mintzberg's 1994 book further dissected the notion of the purposeful organization and provided an extended obituary for planning as a technology to aid processes of strategy development.

Meanwhile a similar challenge to some of the core rationalist and contingent thinking in organizational analysis and strategic management was developing in Europe. Pettigrew (1973, 1977) drew attention first of all to the significance of the distribution and use of power as a shaper of decision and strategy outcomes, a perspective at that time virtually ignored in the literature on strategic management. Later work (Pettigrew, 1979) then brought in the language of culture in organizational analysis, and then a combined political and cultural view of process was fashioned around a large-scale empirical study of strategic change processes in ICI (Pettigrew, 1985). The latter study and subsequent theoretical writing (Pettigrew, 1992) attempted to break the two absurd dichotomies then so accepted by strategy scholars (strategy formulation and implementation and strategy content and process). The series of large-scale empirical studies at Warwick Business School (Pettigrew, 1985; Pettigrew and Whipp, 1991; Pettigrew et al., 1992; Ferlie et al., 1996; Pettigrew and Fenton, 2000) articulated and developed a new approach to strategy process research which combined the content, process and context of change with longitudinal data collected at firm, sector and economic levels of analysis. Parallel empirical research by Johnson (1987) and Smith et al. (1990) helped to establish a European tradition of research on strategy process, but the key to the door of strategy process research had been provided by Mintzberg.

The field of strategy process research has helped to open up the black box of the firm and humanize the field of strategic management. The old dichotomies of strategy process and content and formulation and implementation have withered away and a new impetus has been given to time, agency and dynamics in addressing important issues to do with the strategic development of the firm alongside processes of choice and change. Strategy process has also brought a new epistemological and methodological tradition into the field of strategic management. The examination of processes over time has demanded longitudinal data often collected through retrospective and real time analyses (Pettigrew, 1990, 1997). The exploration of processes in their contexts has required skill in collecting time series data over multiple levels of analysis. Power, politics, culture, learning, evolution and development are now appropriately at the centre stage of the discourse of the field. However, there is still much to do in developing this dynamic tradition in the study of strategy processes and we will suggest some important lines of development in the concluding chapter.

Before we leave time and process it is important to discuss the potential of history and the historical method for the development of strategic management. Many of the strategy process researchers already mentioned have shown a strong interest in the relationship between the past, the present and the future. They have been interested in the heavy hand of the past, the tensions between free will and determinism in historical explanation and many have tried to collect retrospective data sometimes over 30 years to underpin their analyses of changing (for example, Pettigrew and Whipp, 1991; Miles and Cameron, 1982). Notwithstanding this tradition of process research, as Hendry (1992: 207) has rightly argued, 'despite the early influence of Aldred D. Chandler's *Strategy and Structure* on the field of business strategy, the interaction between business history and business strategy research has been minimal'. This is surprising since the two fields, with their interest in change and the responses of organizations to changing environments, appear to have much in common. Given the interest in the discipline of history in European scholarship and the tremendous impact across the social sciences of Chandler's earlier work, it is also surprising that aside from Chandler's home base at the Harvard Business School, no other US or European business school has strongly invested in the field of business history or of historical investigation.

Of course, some of the shine has been taken off Chandler's reputation by the much more critical stance taken to some of his later work. As Chandler moved from the within country analyses of the rise of the 'M' form in the USA to the cross country analyses of business history in the United States, Britain and Germany (see *Scale and Scope*, 1990) so his evident qualities as a grand theorist were taxed more and more by the twin perils of universal theorizing and the disentangling of very long chronologies set in quite different social, cultural and institutional contexts. Some examples of this respectful criticism of Chandler's later cross-country comparative work include Supple (1991), Church (1993), Hannah (1999) and Whittington and Mayer (2000). As Hannah (1995) has succinctly put it 'only the exceptionally gifted and brave (or the criminally foolhardy) venture into both grand theory and comparative empirical work!'. Hannah (1999) later did try this comparative historical research himself, and rightly so, for with the sociological tradition of similar comparative historical research, history is well placed to ask big questions over a long time series and thus act as another counterpoint to the largely ahistorical field of strategic management.

Hannah's (1999) analysis of the survival and size mobility of the world's largest 100 industrial corporations, 1912–1995, is, of course, the link with the other two fields of work – economic sociology (Baum and Dobbin, 2000) and evolutionary perspectives of strategy (Barnett and Burgleman, 1996) – where there has been a serious treatment of history and the historical method. The evolutionary perspective as summarized by Barnett and Burgleman is a humanized variant of population ecology theory now itself facing revisionist critiques (Aldrich, 1999). Barnett and Burgleman (1996) return to the old strategy management theme of what determines the success and failure of organizations, but do this in an altogether more dynamic and historical fashion. They explore how variation in firm strategy impacts on variation in the rate and pace of innovation and thereby affects firm performance. They also offer the much needed connection to another long held bias in the strategy field, the preference for studying apparent high performers in isolation from a comparable set of lesser performers in similar product market and economic conditions. This kind of analytical approach is helping to keep history in the field of strategic management but we concur with Hendry (1992) that the field will continue to be found wanting without more comparative and historical studies. Jeremy (see Chapter 19) develops the theme and importance of business history and strategy.

In the 1980s probably the two dominating figures in strategic management research and writing were Mintzberg and Porter. Given the quality, visibility and impact of their work it is surprising how few critical assessments have appeared in writing. Aside from the well known acerbic dialogue between Mintzberg (1990) and Ansoff (1991), we can find no comprehensive review and evaluation of Mintzberg's work. Tsoukas (1994) offers a partial assessment of Mintzberg's writing. Aside from an excellent published assessment by Foss (1996) and an unpublished conference paper in the critical management tradition by Harfield (1999), we can find no other penetrating review of Michael Porter's work. Foss's (1996) paper is valuable because it assesses the Porter contribution alongside the wider debate about the contribution of economists to strategy research.

Foss portrays the strategy field as a fragmented adhocracy, a field which has become too pluralistic, idiosyncratic and uncoordinated. He also sees Porter's work becoming more eclectic over time with practice issues in the 1985 and 1990 Porter books driving the increased variety of sources away from the more pure exposition of IO economics evident in the 1980 book. However, the distinctive and additive teaching and consultancy message was evident in each book. The 1980 Porter book provided the five forces framework, the value chain analysis came in 1985, and Porter's 1990 book provided the diamond framework. Between them these three frameworks for a time dominated the classrooms and consultancy salons where strategy was on the agenda, but their impact on the research agenda for strategy were not as deep or enduring. As Foss (1996: 16) concludes 'Porter turned IO economics into a normative framework for strategy' and this is where his enduring reputation will be counted.

Thus far we have discussed some of the critical reflections of authors largely from within the mainstream of the strategy literature. However, we would be partial if we did not recognize the critical management community and their more radical critique of the field of strategic management. Mainstream strategy research and writing is a particular target for the critical management theorist. Why? One factor has been its rapid growth and pervasiveness as a language system within

management studies. As Whipp (1996) cogently argues and illustrates, the strategy word has become not just a keyword but an all-embracing buzzword signifying not just generalship and competitive behaviour, but also significance. The fact that the strategy literature is embedded in many literatures, but also emphatically looks to theory and practice and the thoughts and actions of the very top organizations, incites accusations of non-reflective managerialism. The association with the worldwide consultancy industry and a cadre of often senior and presumably well-paid academic consultant professors attracts envy and cries of intellectual superficiality. We can all think of examples which warrant these sort of barbs.

The critical management research community is, of course, still developing (there is now even a group within the US Academy of Management). However, it is as broad a church and just as ideologically conscious and fragmented as the field of strategic management itself. Looking for central tendencies in this critical treatment of strategy management is not easy. The fact that only a limited amount of the output of critical theorists is published in established journals and monographs is understandable but regrettable. Much of the writing from critical theorists still circulates around as working papers and conference papers or in unofficial issues of unofficial journals. Thus far the net effect is an extremely uneven quality of debate and little empirical work to substantiate critical assessments of mainstream work, or any new empirical possibilities raised by this developing tradition of censorious writing.

Much of the critical theory now available originates in Europe. The most developed is associated with scholars much influenced by Foucault and other discourse analysts (Knights and Morgan, 1991; Knights, 1992). Another tradition also evident in Europe is based on philosophical and epistemological critiques of management studies as a whole as well as that most visible of targets – strategic management (Alvesson and Willmott, 1995; Tsoukas and Cummings, 1997; Calori, 1998). However, Shrivastava's (1986) contribution in the US pre-dates much of this publishing and has been developed further a decade later in Shrivastava and Stubbart (1995). Knights and Morgan (1991) articulate views about the all-embracing power of strategy discourse, an influence attached to language alone, which is hard to empirically justify but nevertheless offers a well-developed and novel critique of the field of strategy.

Shrivastava (1986) had also picked up the domination possibilities of strategy ideas, techniques and language but wanted to extend this to strategy praxis. In an unpublished paper, Thomas (1999) carries this tradition forward and begins to pin down a developing research agenda which would incorporate three levels of analysis. These are the discourse analysis of discursive texts in strategy, the behavioural analysis of discursive practices and also the social contexts in which strategic management occurs in organizational settings. A similar agenda is being developed by Whittington (2001) who argues that studying strategy as a social practice (taking strategists and their work seriously) is a long overdue research theme in strategy which fits well the qualitative research traditions in European management research and the bigger theme of strategy process research.

However, in amongst these more considered developments in the critical management theory tradition is a host of polemical, accusatory and loosely written discourse about mainstream strategic management. We are variously informed that strategy discourse is systematically distorted by power and leads to false ideologies and needs myth makers (Ehrensel, 1999); that strategic management is a medium and outcome of domination (Alvesson and Willmott, 1995); and that 'strategy is there to serve the narrow sectional interests of those who can make the claim that they are strategists' (Alvesson and Willmott, 1995: 600). And most messianic of all, 'critical theory values sociological analysis for its capacity to yield insights into the dynamics of domination and oppression, and thereby to provide a stimulus for emancipating change' (Alvesson and Willmott, 1995: 103). Even Alvesson and Willmott admit this is value laden posturing of the most utopian sort, arguing that 'this may appear utopian and unrealistic given the present corporate context' (1995: 605).

But what of the present corporate context and the challenges it may present to the development of a more reflexive, critical and empirically attuned field of strategic management?

SOME CONTEXTUAL CHALLENGES TO THE FIELD OF STRATEGIC MANAGEMENT

The history of the social production of knowledge in the natural and social sciences shows clearly that ideas appear and are blessed or sidelined in particular social, political and economic contexts (Gibbons et al., 1994; Ziman, 1994). Scientists are also citizens of particular settings and cannot readily disengage from the settings that have helped to create them. This view of the social construction of knowledge applies to all forms of knowledge creation but it is a particularly powerful way of interpreting the rise and fall of ideas in the social and management sciences. In a recent assessment of the characteristics of the European Corporation, Whittington and Mayer (2000) debate the veracity of Chandler's (1962) universal propositions about the character and evolution of the modern corporation. They place Chandler's important work on the M Form as an archetype of assumed American managerial superiority and as a form of practice other nations would do well to appreciate and then practise. Indeed, Whittington and Mayer (2000: 23) make the additional and all-embracing point that 'the social sciences made America the universal pattern'.

Not any more, argue Whittington and Mayer. Time and place are a constant reminder of the rise and fall of managerial practices and the patterns of organizational behaviour associated with those practices. Temporal oscillations are clear enough. Think of the anxiety in America with the rise in the power and performance of Japanese corporations in the 1980s. Consider also the revisionist onslaught on this view in the late 1990s as the Far East economic bubble was deflated. Recent research on the variation in governance arrangements across different societies (Scott, 1991; Davis and Useem, see Chapter 11), divergent forms of capitalism throughout the world (Whitley, 1999) and new forms of organizing in Europe and Japan (Pettigrew et al., 2000) indicate how and why national cultures and institutions can shape the strategy and behaviour of corporations. So the management sciences in the past may have been 'not culture free but culture blind' (Whittington and Mayer, 2000: 31). But this contextualist challenge to managerial and corporate universalism does not mean a retreat to cultural or institutional relativism. Patterns may still be observable within and between corporations in and between different societies, but in an age of globalization and multiculturism it is a wise scholar who thinks hard about why and how various levels of context shape the strategies and behaviour of firms and the people who work in them.

The present and future development of the field of strategic management is likely to be driven by two compulsions. Firstly, contemporary developments in social and economic theory, some of which have been mentioned in this chapter and to which we will return in the concluding chapter. And, secondly, recent changes in the nature of the business and economic context which we address here. In recognizing the significance of business context as a shaper of research agendas in strategic management we are, of course, acknowledging the inevitable. By and large the social and management sciences follow events rather than create them. This means that one crucial input into deliberations about what are the key researchable questions should be the big themes and issues around us.

The view that strategic management research should be theme-driven rather than theory or technique driven does not, of course, mean that strategy research can make real progress without adequate techniques of data collection and analysis. Neither is it conceivable that knowledge development will flow in the absence of accessible theoretical languages and insights. The question is the balance and reciprocal relation between themes, theories and techniques. Themes are very important in a field like strategic management, which pivots between theory and practice. The themes are the initial problem framer, the necessary condition which exposes the problem, opens up the possibility for interdisciplinary engagement and draws in partners, co-funders and co-producers from the worlds of policy and practice. Crucially, the themes have to meet the double hurdle of embeddedness in the social sciences and the worlds of policy and practice. The aim is also to meet the complementary double hurdle of scholarly quality and relevance (Pettigrew, 1997). In a field such as strategic management it should be possible to meet the challenge and opportunity of these double hurdles to make sure that practical

and academic knowledge work together and mutually raise rather than lower the standards.

The writing on the new competitive environment of business at the end of the 20th century is at times apocryphal and dramatic. The new context for strategic management has been variously described as a 'silent industrial revolution' (Prahalad and Hamel, 1994) or as hyper-competitive (D'Aveni, 1994), brought about by a linked set of market, technological, global competitive, deregulatory and environmental changes. Thus instead of long, stable periods in which firms can achieve sustainable competition advantages, the hyper-competitive context allows only short periods of advantage, punctuated by frequent interruption. In these circumstances, stable end-states are illusory and the re-thinking of strategy and form of organization becomes more or less continuous (Fenton and Pettigrew, 2000). In these conditions Teece et al. (1997) argue the resource based theory of the firm needs to move from a static view of existing stocks of resources, towards an appreciation of innovation and renewal implied by 'dynamic capabilities'. Under contexts of fast-paced change, particular resources and strategies are soon redundant. These changes in form and strategy of organizations have encouraged Whittington et al. (1999) to drop the nouns of organization and strategy and to revert to the more active language of organizing and strategizing to capture the new dynamism in the field of strategic management. We will return to develop this theme of the dynamic character of strategy in the concluding chapter.

Prahalad and Hamel (1994) give a comprehensive overview of the forces impacting on the nature of the competitive environment within industry in Europe, the US and Japan. They cite deregulation, structural changes due to technological and customer expectations, excess capacity, increasing merger and acquisition activity, environmental concerns, less protectionism, technological discontinuities, the emergence of trading blocks and global competition. These, or a subset of these, have impacted upon almost all industries during the 1990s.

The importance of technology as a driver for strategy and organization change is another dominant theme in the management literature. The evolution of technology towards an 'information age' and 'the knowledge age' are having multiple effects on organizing and strategizing. I.T. is having a widespread impact on information flows within and between firms, on the structural configuration of the firm and management's ability to integrate changes in strategy and organizational form (Pettigrew and Fenton, 2000). Organizing of knowledge resources is now also seen as a key component of market-place competition with the continuous generation and synthesizing of knowledge regarded as key sources of organizational advantage. Knowledge cannot be controlled centrally and is continually changing. The exploitation of knowledge within the firm requires a continuous chase after shifting properties, a process better captured by the dynamics of organizing than the finality of organization (Whittington et al., 1999). All these considerations and more mean that the interface between strategizing and organizing represents one of the key themes in the future research agenda for strategy and management.

Lowendahl and Revang (1998) present a complementary analysis of the challenges to strategic management from what they describe as a post-industrial society. However, they crystallize their analysis around the need for scholars to study the ever more demanding customer with highly individualized needs and the powerful and knowledgeable employee ever more prepared to challenge traditional hierarchical arrangements in older, mechanistic forms of organization. The core strategic issue in the new world they characterize as 'the ability to build and maintain relationships to the best people for maximum value creation both internally to firm representatives and externally to customers' (1998: 757).

Lowendahl and Revang (1998) see the professional service firm as the archetype of the resultant high external and internal complexity. Such firms have dispersed critical competences, loosely coupled internal units with tight coupling to external actors through long-term relationships and increasing complexity in terms of both types and numbers of interaction. With the growth of such firms heavily dependent on recruitment of high calibre people, often with multiple career options, professional service firms are also located at the centre of the war for talent in the new economy. These considerations have many implications for the analytical approach of strategic management. One is, of course, a

new concern for people and relationships in the context of the information and knowledge age. More generally, the trend for strategy frameworks to look simultaneously outside and inside the firm will be reinforced by the rise of the duality of internal and external complexity.

The strategy consultancy industry is normally faster to see and to exploit contextual changes than academic observers. Recently McKinsey have published an anthology 'On Strategy' as a special issue of the *McKinsey Quarterly* – June 2000. The anthology is organized into three parts, corresponding to the main phases in the development of their work over the period 1978–2000. 'Foundations' covers the period 1978–1989, the early years of McKinsey strategy practice. 'The Changing Landscape' contains articles from the mid 1990s and 'Strategy in the New Economy' represents work in progress. This anthology is an extremely valuable archive and source of linguistic analysis for the discourse analysts of the practice of strategy. It is also a useful compendium of consultant views of the changing analytical challenges faced by strategy analysts in the front line of practice.

The first three articles in the changing landscape section discuss the increasing complexity and uncertainty of the strategy task, deficiencies in the five forces model of Porter in the new competitive structures of many industries and the new challenges of conceptualizing the strategy task in 'webs' – clusters of companies that collaborate in and around particular technologies (Coyne and Subramanian, 2000; Courtney et al., 2000; Hagel, 2000).

Coyne and Subramanian (2000) convincingly show how the rise of co-dependent systems cross industry structures such as alliances, networks and economic webs in both the new and old economies are undermining three of the core assumptions of the now dated five forces model of Porter (1980). Prescriptively Coyne and Subramanian (2000) argue that higher levels of uncertainty than those envisaged by Porter in the early 1980s requires not just static notions of posture or position but the active management of an evolving strategy. This they argue can be facilitated by the highly situational use of quantitative and qualitative game theory and an enhanced sensitivity to skills in the execution of strategy.

The Hagel paper in the changing landscape section and the Hagel and Singer paper on 'unbundling the corporation' in the new economy section provide pointers to the strategic impact of webs and networks on the modern corporation. These papers characterize the big strategic issues in webs as which webs to participate in and which role to play in the chosen web. Again there is a close overlap between the strategic issue and organizational choices of the firm. A combination of highly porous firm boundaries, denser information links, pervasive issues of trust and reciprocity and the constant imperative to find, retain and motivate talent make the interface between strategizing and organizing a constant challenge.

The theme of continuous adaptation is picked up in the paper by Beinhocker originally published in 1997 and titled 'Strategy at the Edge of Chaos'. This paper builds on theoretical developments in chaos and complexity theory. The practice focus is the need for robust strategies capable of performing well in a variety of possible future environments. Again flexibility and agility of strategy is explicitly linked to dualities in organizing, this time the need for firms to be simultaneously conservative and radical.

These perspectives from the McKinsey knowledge bank resonate with our own experience of the innovating organization in Europe, the USA and Japan (Pettigrew et al., 2000; Pettigrew and Fenton, 2000; Whittington et al., 1999). They have also been acknowledged by other scholars interested in competitive processes in strategic networks. Bettis (1998) has noted that the units of analysis in the strategy field have not kept up with either available analytical or methodological tools or the nature of competition and strategy in the late 20th century. He argues that the usual units of analysis, the business unit, firm and industry, surely now need to be complemented by work on dynamically changing network or webs of firms. (For a development of this theme see Venkatraman and Subramaniam, Chapter 20.)

Again never quite allowing itself to get left behind, the *Strategic Management Journal* in March 2000 published a special issue on Strategic Networks. In their editorial introduction to this special issue Gulati et al. (2000) push the argument for a new relational approach to strategy. Location in, access to

and skill in operating in networks are now seen to be key additional factors in explaining the old strategy questions of 'why do firms differ in their conduct and profitability?'. The traditional way into network analysis has, of course, been to measure the structural characteristics of these forms (Burt, 1992). Increasingly scholars are now interested in the role of networks as depositories of resources. This approach is now much more processual and relational with skill in entering, bargaining, reciprocating and utilizing the network seen to be fateful for the future development of the firm and the network.

This brief view of some of the contextual challenges to the theoretical, empirical and practical developments in strategic management has emphasized a number of key prompts for future work. We have emphasized the power of context as a shaper of research themes and the analytical languages and methods used to study them. With the growth of management research communities throughout the developed world, there is a greater variety of scholarship and a new awareness of variation in the form and conduct of business throughout the world. This is producing within the USA and other academic communities an increasing challenge to the implied universalism and hegemony of the US social and management sciences. The rise of internationalism and multiculturism is also heightening awareness of diversity in the strategies, structures, cultures and systems of organizations. However, progress in developing knowledge in any field of the social sciences is dependent upon a balancing act between universalism and contextualism and the retreat into relativism will be self-defeating. In the field of strategic management, which historically has tried to live with theory and practice, there is a further special challenge in meeting the double hurdles of scholarly quality and relevance, and embedding this research agenda in the social and management sciences and the world of policy and practice.

Our contextual review has also mentioned a variety of new and complementary research themes which arise naturally from the emerging context around us. We have dwelt on the new forms of competition arising in both the old and new economies. These provoke challenges to the units of analysis in our studies, the concept we have of strategy and organization, or as we would prefer strategizing and organizing. They also require an approach to strategic analysis which is more dynamic, processual and contextual than hitherto. But this is a sketch, a taster of what is to come. In what follows we now go on to describe the main menu of this Handbook. From Chapter 2 onwards, detailed analyses are then provided, theme by theme, of the past, present and future of strategy and management.

STRUCTURE AND INTELLECTUAL LOGIC OF THE HANDBOOK

The field of research and practice we call strategy is too important to be annexed by a single discipline. One way forward intellectually lies in nourishing and exploiting its pluri-disciplinary roots across the social and management sciences. Openness about epistemology and the social production of knowledge is surely also essential. Strategy may at last be on the point of breaking free from the constraints of its origins in the modernist social sciences of the mid 20th century. As we argue in the concluding chapter, strategy research is now reaching for new directions that are, if not 'post modernist', most certainly 'after modernism' (Clark, 2000). Throughout this introductory chapter, we have also emphasized the crucial significance of spatial and temporal contexts as shapers of the past and future direction of the field of strategy. The importance of strategy in a contextually dynamic and plural world makes the US bias in the literature not only internationally myopic, but theoretically and empirically restrictive. The double hurdle of scholarly quality and relevance so emblematic of the field of strategy also requires a heightened sensitivity to variations across national cultures, company cultures and within the inner contexts of firms.

The main purpose of a scholarly handbook should be to literally attempt to map the terrain of a field. However, the map should not just be a historical synthesis, but should offer a sharp critical reflection on past and present work. We have encouraged all the authors to criticize, entice and provoke. Handbooks also need to address the question 'what of the future?'.

All the authors, to varying degrees, have articulated a future research agenda for the sub-field of strategy research they have synthesized and reviewed.

Many of the authors take the view that strategy research is at a 'cross-roads'. There is ample praise and critical reflection of past and present contributors, but also an impatience for innovation and creativity in the field of strategy. As editors, our own view about the justification for a strategy handbook at this time is also based upon a sense that the field needed reconsideration and renewal. But how might this intellectual development be encouraged? We took the view that in a disparate field progress was more likely to be encouraged through a combination of focusing on the one hand, and acknowledging diversity of contexts, themes, paradigms and perspectives on the other. We have not sought comprehensiveness of coverage for its own sake. The reader will notice, for example, there is no chapter assessing the important strategy research using game theoric approaches. The four parts do assess many of the key themes in strategy, and do this sensitive to the past, present and the future, and always aware of spatial and temporal context. We have also encouraged intellectual diversity by choosing authors on a 50–50 basis from North American and European intellectual traditions. As ever, the book is limited by its restricted awareness and use of strategy writing emanating from beyond North America and Europe. A challenge for authors in Asia, Central and South America and Africa is to educate us all.

Chapter 2 is written as a testament to the intellectual contribution of Edward H. Bowman who has written many seminal pieces on strategy (Bowman, 1974, 1990) and who died in 1999. Ed Bowman, Harbir Singh and Howard Thomas provide a complementary personal view of the history and evolution of strategic management to stand alongside this introductory chapter. They emphasize and value the field's essential theoretical pluralism and outline the varying contributions of institutionalists, economists and behaviourists. Throughout their overview they note the reciprocal relationship between the development of theoretical ideas and empirical themes in strategy, and the changing economic, political and social context of organizations between 1960 and 2000.

Bowman, Singh and Thomas locate practical and intellectual contributions in a review of the major tools of strategic analysis and some of the classic books in the field published over the 40-year development of strategic management. In sketching some future directions for strategy research they highlight the need for more longitudinal, processual analysis and the value of taxonomic schemes to simplify, order and give emphasis to the proliferating and sometimes confusing analytical languages in strategy. They share their concerns about the endless march of novel but imprecise conceptual terminology by asking us to be more exact in the operational definition of terms, and by being more open to using a wider range of methodologies, and to combine them more imaginatively in any particular study.

In Part 2, Thinking and Acting Strategically, we move on to consider some of the core themes evident in strategy research. Here we juxtapose the words thinking and acting to emphasize their essential duality and dynamic character, whilst recognizing that historically many fields of strategy have divided these terms in simple dichotomies such as formulation and implementation, or content and process. Karel Cool, Luis Almeida Costa and Ingemar Dierickx review research and writing in one of the central questions of strategy research – what are the sources of a firm's competitive advantage? In discussing this core question they juxtapose and interrogate the complementary approaches of the currently fashionable resource based view of the firm and the market-position view of competitive advantage long established in industrial economics. Crucially, Cool, Costa and Dierickx pose their question not just across two levels of analysis – the firm and the market – but also over time. How can firm specific resources and/or privileged market positions be accumulated and sustained over the medium and long term?

Cool, Costa and Dierickx provide many useful analytical categories and mechanisms to discuss the sustainability of unique resources and privileged market positions. For the protection and development of internal firm resources issues of 'perfectly immobile' and 'imperfectly mobile resources' stand alongside more familiar discussions in the literature about the imitability of scarce resources. Privileged market positions as a source of competitive advantage are discussed through the making of 'strategic commitments' in products, processes and production capacity as well as through the proliferation of product varieties and absolute cost advantages. They note that in the resource-based view, conceptual language development has far outstretched the careful empirical analysis that might have underpinned the proliferating vocabulary. Future research on competitive advantage, Cool, Costa and Dierickx suggest, requires a blending of the complementary strengths of the industrial organization research on market interaction and competition with the strategic management research on firm specific resources. At this time such integrative research endeavours are limited only by the tendency of scholars to specialize in levels of analysis and the evident failure to develop theories and research methodologies which comfortably cross different perspectives and levels of analysis.

One of the longest and deepest traditions in strategy research is concerned with the scope and content of strategy. With admirable clarity, Robert Grant's Chapter 4 first defines the central questions of corporate strategy, then draws a map of the key literature, reviews the quality of empirical work and subsequent theoretical developments, and then points to the content and direction of future research. Grant helps to focus reader attention by identifying the three main questions pursued by scholars interested in corporate strategy. These are:

1   What determines the scope of a firm's business, how diversified or specialized should it be?
2   What is the linkage between scope and firm performance? and
3   What do we know about the management of multi-business firms in terms of structure, management systems and leadership?

In Chapter 4, Grant pursues the first two of these questions. Constantinos Markides addresses the third question in Chapter 5.

Grant critically addresses the well-established work in strategy on growth and diversification. Importantly, he does this against the backcloth of the changing economic and political context in the period 1960–1980, and recognizing the varying experiences of large firms in North America and Europe compared with those in emerging-market economies.

Strangely, research on growth and diversification persisted long after firms had had to adjust their broad goals and incorporate pressures towards risk reduction, survival and profitability (see also Webb and Pettigrew, 1999). Grant saves his sharpest scalpel for research seeking to link diversification to firm performance by arguing that more than 100 academic studies have failed to determine if diversification enhances profitability or whether related diversification outperforms unrelated diversification. Interestingly, Grant contends that a tradition of empirical inconsistencies may be a spur for theoretical innovations. He notes that research on corporate strategy has been greatly assisted by parallel theoretical developments in transaction costs economics, the resource based theory, agency theory and financial theory. Like Cool, Costa and Dierickx, Grant sees the way forward in posing the more sophisticated (and in this case) practically relevant questions which arise from work at the boundaries of strategy and organization. Grant is particularly encouraging of future research on corporate strategy which looks both to the characteristics of the resources and capabilities that underlie corporate strategy and to the organizational structures and mechanisms that implement it.

Constantinos Markides addresses the related and narrower question in corporate strategy: What is the role of the centre in a multi-business firm? He then breaks this broad question into its descriptive form. What does the centre do? And its prescriptive form: What should the centre do? Both questions, he argues, have generated theoretically uninformed laundry lists of various sizes and perceptivity. Markides then contends that theoretical guidance may be offered by re-stating the descriptive and prescriptive questions as: What is the economic rationale for the multi-business firm? He answers this question by drawing on literature on the exploitation of economies of scope and the creation of efficient internal capital markets. These two economics-based answers are then complemented by an answer from management and organization theory. The multi-business firm has the potential to create the efficient sharing and transfer of core competences across divisions so that the divisions can accommodate new strategic assets more quickly and cheaply than competitors. Markides' guidance for future research is built

around four themes which bear upon the strategy, structure, processes and leadership of the multi-business firm. He is particularly interested in the degree of freedom claimed and negotiated by different divisions within the same firm and the implications of such a differentiated approach for the leadership and performance of such firms.

After two chapters on corporate strategy which productivity bridged into the field of corporate stucture, Richard Whittington takes us firmly into the deep tradition of research and writing on corporate structure. Whittington argues that over the last 40 years structure has maintained its interest and significance to practitioners and consultants as a key area of managerial choice, but as a field of research it declined in importance after the heyday of the 1960s and 1970s. More recently, a new research agenda has emerged amongst scholars which is altogether more contextual, dynamic, holistic and practical than 'the general and lifeless reifications' that previously had dominated debates on structure.

Whittington organizes his statement of the evolving theoretical and empirical perspectives on structure using the categories of policy, proxy, periphery and practice. The foundational work which examined appropriate structures for diversification and internationalization he labels as policy work. Whittington defines proxy studies where the structure becomes a proxy variable in other debates, for example, in the literature on strategic choice. The periphery option is when structure was effectively marginalized in studies of organizational culture, change and control. Whittington argues that it is in structure as practice that a more holistic treatment of the subject, drawing on elements of the policy, proxy and periphery traditions, may yet emerge. The practical perspective would start from the apparently mundane but largely unstudied territory of the choices and changes made by practitioners of structure: what makes structure work? But this general question could be located within any of the other emerging streams of structural investigation which treated organization and organizing as the interdependencies between strategy, structure, processes, systems and people. Thus holistic work in the policy tradition is now attempting to define and discover innovative forms of organizing in the post-industrial knowledge economy. Some of this work is using large scale international surveys to compare and contrast the differential pace of change across different dimensions of organizing in different countries and regions whilst also incorporating contextually sensitive case study work to discover the practititioners of structure in action (Pettigrew and Fenton, 2000; Pettigrew et al., 2002).

In Chapter 7, we move from corporate structure, one of the oldest areas of inquiry in strategy, to knowledge and knowing, one of the newest. Kathleen Eisenhardt and Filipe Santos pose some tough questions about the so-called knowledge based view (KBV) of strategy and organization. Is the KBV a passing fad? Is it a new theory of strategy or a new theory of organization, or neither? What is the evidence, if any, for the oft-repeated assertion that knowledge is a source of competitive advantage?

Eisenhardt and Santos draw on North American, European and Japanese scholarship, and the diverse epistemological and theoretical assumptions they entail, to underpin an appropriately balanced yet sceptical treatment of the theme of knowledge, knowing and strategy. In their review of the limited empirical work on knowledge and strategy they examine research findings on knowledge processes of sourcing, internal transfer, external transfer and integration. In conclusion, Eisenhardt and Santos assume that the knowledge-based theory is neither a new theory of strategy or a new theory of organization, and that the evidence to link knowledge resources to competitive advantage is questionable. They suggest three important areas for further research. Firstly, there is an important need for conceptual ground-clearing to produce a more consistent and coherent language to guide research. Secondly, they call for more bridging between static and reified treatments of knowledge and the more processual and contextually sensitive exploration of knowing now evident in European scholarship. Finally, they contend that the KBV would usefully develop alongside insights now available in various branches of social psychology, sociology and evolutionary biology. The knowledge area is one of many instances in the book where a reciprocal relationship between developments in the social sciences and management can underpin real intellectual progress in the broad field of strategy and management.

Historically, economics has been the dominating perspective in the development of strategic management. Latterly, through their influence in organization theory, sociological and political concepts have also become influential. Only recently have psychological ideas risen in significance. The chapter by Joseph Porac and Howard Thomas on cognition and strategy brings those psychological ideas to the fore. Porac and Thomas discuss the literature on cognition and strategy around three central questions: What are cognitive structures? How do such structures develop and with what measurable consequences? Their focus is on the upper echelons of the firm where the assumption is that the beliefs and mental maps of key players are likely to have the biggest impact on processes of strategic choice and change. Their review appropriately crosses levels of analysis considering in turn the existence, causes and consequences of strategic cognitive structures at the individual, top management team, organization and population of top management teams in industries. Their chapter concludes by providing an agenda for future research on managing cognition and strategy.

Chapters 9 and 10 comprehensively document and assess research on the linked areas of strategy process and strategic change processes. Bala Chakravarthy and Roderick White focus on one of the central questions in the theory and practice of strategy: how are strategies formed, implemented and changed? They frame their review by making a number of strong assertions which they then return to in their concluding comments about the future direction of research on strategy process. They insist that strategy process cannot be studied in isolation from the content of strategy and the outcomes of strategy making. Theorizing about strategy process, they argue, has been partial in particular studies, with authors favouring one or other of the various theoretical lenses (boundedly rational, emergent, political, or incremental). They call for future approaches to attempt more holistic theorizing and to embed their conceptual approach in studies which combine a long time series, multiple levels of analysis and expose process variation in comparative analysis. Such empirical studies are likely to demand high levels of resourcing with teams of researchers being kept together for long enough to build a truly cumulative set of findings. They note the existence and impact of such teams in North America and Europe and suggest that further scale commitments of that sort may be the more appropriate stepping stone to building research of scholarly quality and practical relevance on how strategies are made and executed.

Research on strategic change processes has perhaps been misguidedly equated with the broader category of work on strategy process. Change processes are now regarded as at the centre of the strategy field, but are only one of the key elements in strategy process research. Raghu Garud and Andrew Van de Ven review existing studies of strategic change process against the backcloth of four broad social science theories of changing: teleological, life cycle, dialectical and evolutionary. They then point to the strengths and limitations of each theoretical lens and suggest that the character of change in contemporary organizations now demands the increased explanatory power evident in non-linear dynamics. Like Chakravarthy and White, they focus their observations about future research on strategic change processes more on the character and style of future research than its content. They recommend, however, that the central question of strategic change process research should switch from a concern with the antecedents or consequences of strategic changes to the analysis of how strategic change processes emerge, develop, grow or terminate over time.

Scholarly and policy attention to issues of comparative governance has flowered in the 1990s, and no handbook of strategy could be complete without acknowledging the important developments which have taken place. Gerald Davis and Michael Useem introduce us to the pluri-disciplinary work on top management, company directors and corporate control. This research is theoretically eclectic, drawing on theories from financial economics, agency theory, sociology, political sciences and a variety of traditions in management studies. Davis and Useem note how work in the governance area has crossed multiple levels of analysis. Over time the central questions have broadened from narrow issues of board composition and control – Is it better for shareholders for a corporation's board to have more 'outside' directors? – to the characteristic question of the early 21st century: What ensemble of institutions best situates a nation

for economic growth in a post-industrial information-based economy? Thus research on corporate governance has come to span levels of analysis from within the organization to the nation-state and beyond.

Respecting the breadth of work in the field in the US and beyond, Davis and Useem organize their extended review around a number of core questions: One capitalism or many? Who are top managers and company directors? How do shareholders and other stakeholders influence the corporation? Do top managers really make a difference? How do corporations shape society? Is a worldwide model for top management and corporate governance emerging?

They conclude that research in the corporate governance area will be energized by work which clarifies what governance arrangements and leadership styles work well both within national settings and across cultural divides. They recommend further research in five areas: boards and directors, corporative governance, financial globalization, inequality in a globalized world and business and political leadership.

Bruce Kogut introduces us to the field of international strategy with its interests in the international activities of firms and their interaction with foreign governments, competitors and employers. Kogut also uses the device of posing and answering key researchable questions to structure his presentation of the highlights in past and present research and what is known and not known about international management and strategy. Historically, the major question in this field has been 'why do firms go overseas and how and when do they do it?'. This broad question has opened up a plethora of sub-fields of research concerned with foreign entry modes, the strategies, structures and systems of multinationals, the factors which shape location decisions, and the increasing importance of new forms of organizing and new technologies in shaping the possibilities and processes of international firm behaviour.

For future research Kogut identifies a range of possibilities, many of them influenced by a heightened interest in the way societal and institutional factors are creating differential responses of international firms to regional and national conditions. As research capabilities in management are being developed throughout the world, and North American and European scholars are investing more in international comparative investigations, so variations in business practices, levels of technological investment and pace of change in implementing innovative forms of organizing are all being recognized. There are rich possibilities to examine how and why the internet economy may be bringing about fundamental changes in strategic thinking and action about location and place.

The major purpose of a handbook is to review, assess and develop existing themes in an intellectual terrain. However, it should have the licence to add to a map and not just reinforce what is there. We take two opportunities to re-configure the conventional map of strategic management. In Chapter 13 Ewan Ferlie signals the enormous potential of studying strategy in the changed conditions of the contemporary public sector. In Chapter 15 Winfried Ruigrok begins the process of articulating the scholarly and policy agenda for strategy research on the myriad of international institutions which now shape the political, economic and industrial landscape around us.

By and large business and management schools throughout the world are private sector ghettos. This is surprising because as late as 1997 32% of GDP in the USA, 35% in Japan, 39% in the UK and 62% of GDP in Sweden was accounted for by government revenues. Irrespective of the intrinsic interest in strategic change in the contemporary public sector throughout the world, it seems somewhat perverse of business schools to virtually ignore 35% or more of their potential market. Ewan Ferlie argues the case for why the analysis of public sector organizations should be taken more seriously within the strategic management literature. Drawing on research in Europe, North America, Australia and New Zealand, Ferlie documents the widespread and profound re-structuring now underway in public services throughout the world. The rise of this new public management, he contends, is drawing the public sector context closer to management practices in the private sector (whilst also retaining important differences), thereby opening up the public sector to its own brand of strategic analysis. The rise of quasi markets in the public sector, increased pressure for performance, the managerialization of the public sector and the move from

maintenance management to the management of strategic change have all re-shaped the conduct and process of strategic management.

Ferlie proposes a research agenda to explore the extent of convergence between the public and private sectors. He asked penetrating questions about the extent to which politicians have ceded policy making to senior managers in the public sector and raises an important research theme about the evolving role of public sector professionals in the changing context for the delivery of public services. This is an area wide open for intellectual leadership for a new generation of scholars leaving doctoral programmes in strategic management.

Rita Gunther McGrath raises the flag of entrepreneurial research and signals its importance and overlap with research on strategic management. McGrath's chapter is premised on the assumption that the fields of strategy and entrepreneurship may be merging. She argues that the changing competitive context of large enterprises towards greater uncertainty, complexity and volatility mirrors well the conditions faced by those engaged in entrepreneurial action. Throughout Chapter 14, McGrath uses the metaphor of real options reasoning to explore some of the core entrepreneurial processes of option identification, formulation of a new business, growth development and profit, and business termination. These processes she explores across five levels of analysis: the individual entrepreneur, the network, the organization, the region, and the institutional context of entrepreneurial action. In each cell in her 4 by 5 matrix she identifies novel and interesting researchable questions which could frame a new research agenda at the boundary of strategy and entrepreneurship.

Since the Second World War, international institutions such as the European Union (EU), the International Monetary Fund (IMF) and the World Trade Organisation (WTO) have acquired a crucial role in the international, political and economic arena. With the increased interdependency of the world and the recognition and exploitation of nation state, regional and international interests, so such international institutions have acquired greater material and symbolic significance. But with this rise in visibility has come ever-rising expectations for policy delivery from such institutions. Many of these expectations lie unfulfilled. International institutions are regularly criticized for their lack of transparency, accountability and for the gaps between their policy statements and their capacity to deliver on them.

Winfried Ruigrok's chapter on the strategy and management of international institutions raises the prospect of a new area of inquiry for strategy scholars and for stronger links to be made between strategic management researchers and colleagues in political science and international relations. Ruigrok notes that international institutions are notoriously difficult to manage. They rarely have strong and omnipotent chief executive officers or coherent executive teams who can define strategic direction. It is rare for any length of time for one nation state in such international bodies to impose their will. Diverse, conflicting and sometimes irreconcilable demands are often the order of the day. The challenges of strategy and management in international institutions are pervasive, real and under researched.

Ruigrok's chapter begins to prepare the ground for strategy research in this important area. In turn, he traces the evolution of international institutions and reviews the literature on domestic and international institutions developed by sociologists, political scientists, economists and management scholars. His research agenda for the future targets the effectiveness of international institutions. This will require a pluri-disciplinary approach combining the skills of strategy scholars with those of political scientists, sociologists and economists. Here, as in many other areas of this Handbook, our future lies not just in the concepts and methods of strategic management but in the even more pluri-disciplinary field of strategy and management.

At the beginning of the 21st century we cannot ignore the relationship between technology and strategy. Keith Pavitt and W. Edward Steinmueller draw on their extensive knowledge of technology in corporate strategy and in so doing place it at the heart of the future research agenda on strategy and management. They argue that the effective mobilization of technology for competitive advantage depends on the orchestration, integration and application of increasingly specialized knowledge from both inside and outside the firm. In spite of rapid improvements in underlying scientific understanding, they contend that corporate

innovation activities remain complex and uncertain in their outcomes. Rapid improvements in information and communication technologies (ICTs) will generate potentially revolutionary and disruptive changes in a number of corporate functions, including transactions, distribution, technological development and strategy. Yet the revolution will be incrementalist in nature, since experimentation based on past experiences (including past failures) will remain the norm. Key subjects requiring further research include the changing nature of professional networks, co-evolution of technology (including ICTs) and organizational practices and the management of change in increasingly complex systems.

Our final chapter in Part 3 bounded by the theme of 'changing contexts' embraces the relationship between business and society. David Whetten, Gordon Rands and Paul Godfrey argue that in spite of its long history and now contemporary visibility, the research and policy theme of business and society has developed somewhat in isolation from the more mainstream approaches to the study of strategy and management. Their chapter suggests that now is the time to bring business and society relationship into centre stage in the strategy field. Whetton, Rands and Godfrey offer an historical overview of business and society scholarship and then discuss future directions for research and study. Important areas of inquiry for the future include: the study of effective and/or moral practices of firms; issues of organizational reputation, image and identity; the links, if any, between firm ethical behaviour and competitive advantage; collaborative strategies between firms and other societal stakeholders; and the important role played by human resource strategies in firms on the choices and changes made in business and society relationships.

Part 4 looks forward through four lenses. In Chapter 18 Haridimos Tsoukas and Christian Knudsen look to the future through the twin lenses of philosophy and epistemology. David Jeremy consolidates the temporal and contextual agenda of the book by signalling the importance of history to the development of strategy. N. Venkatraman and Mohan Subramaniam suggest how and why the changing shape of the knowledge economy may require new forms of theorizing in strategy. The fourth lens is offered by the editors who draw together many of the scholarly and policy threads and then articulate their own view about some of the future directions for the conduct of strategy research.

Earlier in this chapter the editors noted that one sign and symptom of a lack of maturity in the strategy field was the absence of critical reflection. Haridimos Tsoukas and Christian Knudsen provide some of this missing reflexivity by their critical examination of the ontological, epistemological and praxeological foundations of strategic management. Following their epistemological exploration of the theoretical foundations of strategy research, Tsoukas and Knudsen outline a meta-theoretical framework which allows them to interrogate the field's answer to two core questions: how is thinking related to action, and who sets strategy? Their thesis is that strategic management has been dominated by one particular mode of explanation (the covering law model) and one particular view of how thinking is related to action (representationalism) both of which have their problems. They argue that strategy research will become more relevant, encompassing, and subtle if it moves closer toward a process-oriented view of the firm and opens itself to a constructivist view of strategy making.

For many, Alfred Chandler and Douglas North represent the peak of recent scholarship in business and economic history. Although both have been much quoted and admired, and Chandler is widely regarded as one of the founders of strategy research, their success so far has not brought the investigative capabilities of the historian and the subtlety and power of historical explanation to the forefront of strategy research. Indeed, beyond the Harvard Business School it is difficult to identify a business school throughout the world which has sustained any form of teaching and research in the history of business in its economic, social and political context.

David Jeremy carries the flag of history most explicitly into this volume, although it is note-worthy that many other authors acknowledge the importance of history, and the historical perspective to the further development of strategy research (see especially Chapters 1, 6, 9, 13, 15, 16, 17 and 18). Recognizing that business history draws upon several disciplines, including history, economics and management, Jeremy articulates many of the key requirements and stepping-stones to bring business history and strategy closer together. In turn, he marshals the evidence to reveal a history of business history, to explore the existing relationship between business history and strategy; to identify what business history has already contributed to thinking about strategy, and the value of historical methods for investigating strategy. He concludes by offering a wide agenda for future research in strategy demanding historical investigation.

The penultimate chapter encourages strategy research to look forward through the challenges of the knowledge-based economy. N. Venkatraman and Mohan Subramaniam place the changing context of the knowledge-based economy in historical perspective by arguing that thinking about strategy may be considered over three eras. First, when strategy was viewed as a portfolio of businesses, second, as a portfolio of capabilities, and third, as it is now surfacing, as a portfolio of relationships. They emphasize that throughout these three eras cumulative development has occurred with each era supplementing rather than supplanting earlier periods of thinking.

Venkatraman and Subramaniam argue that each of the three eras has had a distinct paradigmatic focus. The portfolio era was associated with economies of scale, the capabilities era with economies of scope, and the relationship era, economies of expertise. Theorizing about strategy in the current expertise era they see bounded and enabled by four key questions: How do we conceptualize economies of expertise? Do we need a new unit of analysis for theorizing about strategy? Does economies of expertise lead to differential performance and do we need new organizing principles in this latest era of relationships and expertise?

Finally, we conclude with a thematic overview. This is not a search for uniformity, which is neither available or desirable. However, the editors pick up some important threads and overlay them with a number of personal observations about the future direction of research on strategy and management. We take the view that strategy research may be at the point of breaking free from the constraints of its origins in the modernist social sciences of the mid 20th century. After modernism, research in strategy will search less for universal laws, give more due to temporal and spatial context; it will admit the possibility of holistic analysis; and where once it fixed on the static and detached, now it will seek change and action. In all these ways the new strategy research will move beyond simple reliance on scientific abstraction and at last meet the double hurdles implied in seeking scholarly quality and relevance.

REFERENCES

Abrahamson, E. (1991) 'Managerial fads and fashions', *Academy of Management Review*, 16: 586–612.

Abrahamson, E. (1996) 'Management fashion', *Academy of Management Review*, 21(1): 254–85.

Aldrich, H. E. (1999) *Organizations Evolving*. London: Sage.

Alvesson, M. and Willmott, H. (1995) 'Strategic management and domination and emancipation: from planning and process to communication and praxis', in P. Shrivastava and C. Stubbart (eds), *Advances in Strategic Management: Challenges from Outside the Mainstream*. Greenwich, Conn: JAI Press. pp. 85–112.

Andrews, K. R. (1971) *The Concept of Corporate Strategy*. New York: Dow Jones-Irwin Inc.

Ansoff, H. I. (1965) *Corporate Strategy*. Homewood, Illinois: Dow Jones-Irwin.

Ansoff, H. I. (1991) 'Critique of Henry Mintzberg's The Design School: reconsidering the basic premises of strategic management', *Strategic Management Journal*, 12: 449–61.

Barnett, W. P. and Burgleman, R. A. (1996) 'Evolutionary perspectives on strategy', *Strategic Management Journal*, 17 (Special Issue): 5–19.

Barney, J. B. (1991) 'Firm resources and sustained competitive advantage', *Journal of Management*, 17: 99–120.

Barney, J. B. (1992) 'Integrating organizational behaviour and strategy formulation research: a resource based analysis', in P. Shrivastava, A. Huff and J. Dutton (eds), *Advances in Strategic Management*. Greenwich, Conn. JAI Press, Vol. 8: pp. 39–61.

Baum, J. A. C. and Dobbin, F. (eds) (2000) 'Economics meets sociology in strategic management', *Advances in Strategic Management*, volume 17. Greenwich, Conn: JAI Press.

Beinhocker, E. D. (2000) 'Strategy at the edge of chaos', *The McKinsey Quarterly*, Anthology on Strategy, June: 109–18.

Bettis, R. A. (1998) 'Commentary on Redefining Industry Structure for the Information "Age" by J. L. S. Sampler', *Strategic Management Journal*, 19 (Special Issue): 357–61.

Bourgeois, L. J. (1984) 'Strategic management and determinism', *Academy of Management Review*, 9(4): 586–96.

Bowman, G. H. (1974) 'Epistemology, corporate strategy and academe', *Sloan Management Review*, 23(4): 33–42.

Bowman, G. H. (1990) 'Strategy changes: possible worlds and actual minds', in J. W. Fredrickson (ed.), *Perspectives on Strategic Management*. New York: Harper Business. pp. 9–37.

Burt, R. S. (1992) *Structural Holes: The Social Structures of Competition*. Cambridge, MA: Harvard University Press.

Calori, R. (1998) 'Essai: philosophizing in strategic management', *Organization Studies*, 19(2): 281–306.

Camerer, C. F. (1985) 'Redirecting research in business policy and strategy', *Strategic Management Journal*, 6: 1–15.

Camerer, C. F. (1991) 'Does strategy research need game theory? *Strategic Management Journal*, Special Issue, 12: 137–52.

Cannella, A. A. and Paetzold, R. L. (1994) 'Pfeffer's barriers to the advance of organizational science, a rejoinder', *Academy of Management Review*, 19(2): 331–41.

Chakravarthy, B. S. and Doz, Y. (1992) 'Strategy process research: focussing on corporate self-renewal', *Strategic Management Journal*, 13, Special Issue: 5–14.

Chandler, A. R. (1962) *Strategy and Structure: Chapters in the History of the Industrial Enterprise*. Cambridge, Mass: MIT Press.

Chandler, A. D. (1990) *Scale and Scope: The Dynamics of Industrial Capitalism*. Cambridge, Mass: Harvard University Press.

Church, R. (1993) 'The family firm in industrial capitalism', *Business History*, 35: 17–43.

Clark, P. (2000) *Organisations in Action: Competition between Contexts*. London: Routledge.

Courtney, H. G., Kirkland, J. and Viguerie, S. P. (2000) 'Strategy under uncertainty', *The McKinsey Quarterly*, Anthology on Strategy, June: 81–90.

Coyne, K. P. and Subramaniam, S. (2000) 'Bringing discipline to strategy', *The McKinsey Quarterly*, Anthology on Strategy, June: 61–70.

Cummings, S. and Wilson, D. C. (eds) (In Press) *Images of Strategy*. Oxford: Blackwell.

D'Aveni, R. (1994) *Hypercompetition*. New York: Free Press.

Dobbin, F. and Baum, J. A. C. (2000) 'Introduction: economics meets sociology in strategic management' in J. A. C. Baum and F. Dobbin (eds), *Advances in Strategic Management*, Greenwich, Conn: JAI Press.

Ehrensel, P. A. L. (1999) 'Calling the Shots: How Elite Discourses Constrain Local Strategic Actors', *Critical Management Studies Conference (Strategy Stream)*, Manchester, UK, July 14–16.

Eisenhardt, K. and Brown, S. L. (1992) 'Commentary on Mahoney, J. T. "Organizational Economics Within the Conversation of Strategic Management"', *Advances in Strategic Management*, 8: 157–62 Greenwich, Conn: JAI Press.

Fama, G. F. and Jensen M. C. (1983) 'Separation of ownership and control', *Journal of Law and Economics*, 26: 327–49.

Fenton, E. M. and Pettigrew, A. M. (2000) 'Theoretical perspectives on new forms of organizing', in

A. M. Pettigrew and E. Fenton (eds), *The Innovating Organization*. London: Sage. pp. 1–46.

Ferlie, E., Ashburner, L., FitzGerald, L. and Pettigrew, A. M. (1996) *The New Public Management in Action*. Oxford: Oxford University Press.

Foss, N. J. (1996) 'Research in strategy, economics and Michael Porter', *Journal of Management Studies*, 33(1): 1–24.

Foucault, M. (1966) *The Order of Things: An Archeology of the Humanities*. London: Tavistock/Routledge.

Gibbons, M., Limoges, C., Notwotny, H., Schartman, S., Scott, P. and Trow, M. (1994) *The New Production of Knowledge*. London: Sage.

Giddens, A. (1979) *Central Problems in Social Theory*. London: Macmillan.

Grant, R. M. (1991) 'The resource-based theory of competition advantage', *California Management Review*, 33(3): 114–35.

Gulati, R., Nohria, N. and Zaheer, A. (2000) 'Strategic networks', *Strategic Management Journal*, 21, Special Issue: 203–16.

Hagel, J. (2000) 'Spider versus spider', *The McKinsey Quarterly*, Anthology on Strategy, June: 71–80.

Hagel, J. and Singer, M. (2000) 'Unbundling the corporation', *The McKinsey Quarterly*, Anthology on Strategy, June: 147–56.

Hamel, G. and Prahalad, C. K. (1994) *Competing for the Future*. Boston, Mass: Harvard Business School Press.

Hannah, L. (1995) 'The American miracle, 1875–1950, and after: a view in the European mirror', *Business and Economic History*, 24(2).

Hannah, L. (1999) 'Marshall's "trees" and the global "forest": were "giant redwoods" different?', in R. Naomi, D. Lamoreaux, M. G. Raff and P. Temin (eds), *Learning by Doing in Markets, Firms, and Countries*. Chicago: University of Chicago Press.

Harfield, T. (1999) 'Strategic management and Michael Porter: a postmodern reading', *Critical Management Studies Conference (Strategy Stream)*, Manchester, UK, July 14–16.

Hendry, J. (1992) 'Business strategy and business history: a framework for development', *Advances in Strategic Management*, 8: 207–25 Greenwich, Conn: JAI Press.

Hesterly, W. S. and Zenger, T. R. (1993) 'The myth of monolithic economics: fundamental assumptions and the use of economic models in policy and strategy research', *Organization Science*, 4(3): 496–510.

Hirsch, P., Michaels, S. and Friedman, R. (1987) 'Is sociology in danger of being seduced by economics?', *Theory and Society*, 16: 317–38.

Hitt, M. A., Gimeno, J. and Hoskisson, R. E. (1998) 'Current and future research methods in strategic management', *Organizational Research Methods*, 1(1): 6–44.

Hoskisson, R. E. (1987) 'Multidivisional structure and performance: the contingency of diversification strategy', *Academy of Management Journal*, 30: 625–44.

Hoskisson, R. E. and Hitt, M. A. (1990) 'Antecedents and performance outcomes of diversification: a review and

critique of theoretical perspectives', *Journal of Management*, 16: 461–509.

Hoskisson, R. E., Hitt, M. A., Wan, W. P. and Yin, D. (1999) 'Theory and research in strategic management: swings of a pendulum', *Journal of Management*, 25(3): 417–56.

Johnson, G. (1987) *Strategic Change and the Management Process*. Oxford: Basil Blackwell.

Knights, D. (1992) 'Changing spaces: the disruptive impact of a new epistemological location for the study of management', *Academy of Management Review*, 17(3): 514–36.

Knights, D. and Morgan, G. (1991) 'Strategic discourse and subjectivity: towards a critical analysis of corporate strategy in organizations', *Organization Studies*, 12(2): 251–73.

Kogut, B. and Zander, H. (1992) 'Knowledge of the firm, combinative capabilities and the replication of technology', *Organization Science*, 3: 383–97.

Kuhn, T. (1970) *The Structure of Scientific Revolutions*. Chicago: University of Chicago Press.

Lowendahl, B. and Revang, D. (1998) 'Challenges to existing strategy theory in a post industrial society', *Strategic Management Journal*, 19(8): 755–74.

McKiernan, P. (ed.) (1996) *Historical Evolution of Strategic Management*, Volume I. Aldershot: Dartmouth.

McKiernan, P. (ed.) (1996) *Historical Evolution of Strategic Management*, Volume II. Aldershot: Dartmouth.

McNulty, T. and Pettigrew, A. M. (1998) 'Strategists on the board', *Organization Studies*, 20(1): 47–74.

Mahoney, J. T. (1992) 'Organizational economics within the conversation of strategic management', *Advances in Strategic Management*, 8: 103–55.

March, J. G. (1991) 'Exploration and exploitation in organizational learning', *Organization Science*, 2: 71–87.

March, J. G. (1996) 'Continuity and change in theories of organizational action', *Administrative Science Quarterly*, 41: 278–87.

Miles, R. M. and Cameron, K. S. (1982) *Coffin Nails and Corporate Strategies*. Englewood Cliffs: Prentice Hall.

Mintzberg, H. (1973) *The Nature of Managerial Work*. New York: Harper & Row.

Mintzberg, H. (1978) 'Patterns in strategy formation', *Management Science*, 24: 934–48.

Mintzberg, H. (1990) 'The design school: reconsidering the basic premise of strategic management', *Strategic Management Journal*, 11: 171–96.

Mintzberg, H. (1994) *The Rise and Fall of Strategic Planning*. New York: Free Press.

Mintzberg, H. and Walters, J. A. (1985) 'Of strategies, deliberate and emergent', *Strategic Management Journal*, 6(3): 257–72.

Mintzberg, H., Raisinghani, D. and Theoret, A. (1976) 'The structure of unstructured decision processes', *Administrative Science Quarterly*, 21: 246–75.

Mintzberg, H., Ahlstrand, B. and Lampel, J. (1998) *Strategic Safari: A Guided Tour Through the Wilds of Strategic Management*. New York: The Free Press.

Nalebuff, B. and Brandenburger, A. M. (1997) *Co-opetition*. London: Harper Collins Business.

Nelson, R. and Winter, S. (1982) *An Evolutionary Theory of Economic Change*. Cambridge, MA: Belknap.

Nonaka, I. and Takeuchi, K. (1995) *The Knowledge-Creating Company: How Japanese Companies Create the Dynamics of Innovation*. Oxford: Oxford University Press.

Oliver, C. (1997) 'Sustainable competitive advantage: combining institutional and resource-based views', *Strategic Management Journal*, 18(9): 697–713.

Penrose, E. T. (1959) *The Theory of the Growth of the Firm*. New York: John Wiley.

Perrow, C. (1986) 'Economic theories of organization', *Theory and Society*, 15: 11–45.

Pettigrew, A. M. (1973) *The Politics of Organizational Decision Making*. London: Tavistock Publications.

Pettigrew, A. M. (1977) 'Strategy formulation as a political process', *International Studies of Management and Organization*, 7(2), Summer 1977: 78–87.

Pettigrew, A. M. (1979) 'On studying organizational cultures', *Administrative Science Quarterly*, 24(4): 570–81.

Pettigrew, A. M. (1985) *The Awakening Giant: Continuity and Change in ICI*. Oxford: Basil Blackwell.

Pettigrew, A. M. (1987) 'Context and action in the transformation of the firm', *Journal of Management Studies*, 24(6): 649–69.

Pettigrew, A. M. (1990) 'Longitudinal field research on change: theory and practice', *Organization Science*, 1(3): 267–92.

Pettigrew, A. M. (1992) 'The character and significance of strategy process research', *Strategic Management Journal*, 13, Special Issue: 5–16.

Pettigrew, A. M. (1997) 'What is processual analysis?', *Scandinavian Journal of Management*, 13(4): 337–48.

Pettigrew, A. M. and Whipp, R. (1991) *Managing Change for Competitive Success*. Oxford: Blackwell.

Pettigrew, A. M., Ferlie, E. and McKee, L. (1992) *Shaping Strategic Change*. London: Sage.

Pettigrew, A. M. and Fenton, E. M. (eds) (2000) *The Innovating Organization*. London: Sage.

Pettigrew, A. M., Massini, S. and Numagami, T. (2000) 'Innovative forms of organizing in Europe and Japan', *European Management Journal*, 18(3): 259–73.

Pettigrew, A. M., Whittington, R., Melin, L., Ruigrok, W., Sanchez-Runde, C. and Van den Bosch, F. (eds) (2002) *Innovative Forms of Organizing: Complementarities and Dualities*. London: Sage.

Pfeffer, J. (1993) 'Barriers to the advance of organization science: paradigm development as a dependent variable', *Academy of Management Review*, 18: 599–620.

Porter, M. E. (1980) *Competitive Strategy*. New York: Free Press.

Porter, M. E. (1985) *Competitive Advantage*. New York: Free Press.

Porter, M. E. (1990) *Competitive Advantage of Nations*. New York: Free Press.

Prahalad, C. K. and Hamel, G. (1990) 'The core competence of the corporation', *Harvard Business Review*, 68(3): 79–91.

Prahalad, C. K. and Hamel, G. (1994) 'Strategy as a field of study: why search for a new paradigm?', *Strategic Management Journal*, Special Issue, 15: 5–16.

Rumelt, R. P., Schendel, D. and Teece, D. J. (1991) 'Strategic management and economics', *Strategic Management Journal*, 12: Special Issue: 5–29.

Rumelt, R. P., Schendel, D. and Tecce, D. J. (eds) (1994) *Fundamental Issues in Strategy: A Research Agenda*. Boston, MA: Harvard Business School Press.

Saloner, G. (1991) 'Modeling, game theory and strategic management', *Strategic Management Journal*, Special Issue, 12: 119–36.

Sanchez, R. and Heene, A. (1997) 'Reinventing strategic management: new theory and practice for competence-based competition', *European Management Journal*, 15(3): 303–17.

Schendel, D. (1994) 'Introduction to the Summer 1994 Special Issue – strategy: search for new paradigms', *Strategic Management Journal*, Special Issue, 15: 1–5.

Schendel, D. and Hatten, K. J. (1972) 'Business policy or strategic management: a broader view for an emerging discipline', *Academy of Management Proceedings*, 99–102.

Schendel, D. and Hofer, C. W. (1979) *Strategic Management: A New View of Business Policy and Planning*. Boston: Little Brown & Co.

Schwenk, R. R. and Dalton, D. R. (1991) 'The changing shape of strategic management research', *Advances in Strategic Management*, 7: 277–300.

Scott, J. (1991) 'Networks of corporate power: a comparative assessment', *Annual Review of Sociology*, 17: 181–203.

Seth, A. and Thomas, H. (1994) 'Theories of the firm: implications for strategy research', *Journal of Management Studies*, 31(2): 165–91.

Shrivastava, P. (1986) 'Is strategic management ideological?', *Journal of Management Studies*, 12(3): 363–77.

Shrivastava, P. and Stubbart, C. (eds) (1995) *Advances in Strategic Management: Challenge from Outside the Mainstream*. Greenwich, Conn: JAI Press.

Smith, C., Child, J. and Rowlinson, M. (1990) *Reshaping Work: The Cadbury Experience*. Cambridge: Cambridge University Press.

Supple, B. (1991) 'Scale and scope: Alfred Chandler and the dynamics of industrial capitalism!', *Economic History Review*, 44: 500–14.

Sztompka, P. (1991) *Society in Action: The Theory of Social Becoming*. Chicago: University of Chicago Press.

Teece, D. J., Pisano, G. and Shullen, A. (1997) 'Dynamic capabilities and strategic management', *Strategic Management Journal*, 18(7): 509–33.

Thomas, P. (1999) 'Ideology and the discourse of strategic management: a critical research framework', *Critical Management Studies Conference (Strategy Stream)*, Manchester, UK: July 14–16.

Tsoukas, H. (1994) 'Refining common-sense: types of knowledge in management', *Journal of Management Studies*, 31(6): 761–80.

Tsoukas, H. and Cummings, S. (1997) 'Marginalization and recovery: the emergence of Aristotelian themes in organization studies', *Organization Studies*, 18(4): 655–83.

Van Maanem, J. (1994) 'Style and theory', *Organization Science*, 6: 2–12.

Von Tunzelman, G. N. (1999) 'Big business, growth and decline: review article', *The Journal of Economic History*, 59(3): 787–94.

Wack, P. (1985) 'Scenarios, uncharted waters ahead', *Harvard Business Review*, Sept–Oct: 73–90.

Webb, D. and Pettigrew, A. M. (1999) 'The temporal development of strategy: patterns in the UK insurance industry', *Organization Science*, 10, 5, 601–21.

Wernefelt, B. (1984) 'A resource based theory of the firm', *Strategic Management Journal*, 5: 171–80.

Whipp, R. (1996) 'Creative deconstruction: strategy and organization', in S. R. Clegg, C. Hardy and W. R. Nord (eds), *Handbook of Organization Studies*. London: Sage. pp. 261–75.

Whitley, R. (1999) *Divergent Capitalisms*. Oxford: Oxford University Press.

Whittington, R. (1993) *What is Strategy, and Does it Matter?* London: Routledge.

Whittington, R. (2001) 'The practice of strategy: a European agenda', paper presented to the *European Academy of Management Conference*, IESE Barcelona, April 20–21.

Whittington, R., Pettigrew, A. M. and Melin, L. (1999) 'Organizing/strategizing', paper presented to *Academy of Management Conference*, Chicago, August 1999.

Whittington, R., Pettigrew, A. M., Peck, S., Fenton, E. M. and Conyon, M. (1999) 'Change and complementarities in the new competitive landscape: a European panel study 1992–1996', *Organization Science*, 10(5): 583–600.

Whittington, R. and Mayer, M. (2000) *The European Corporation: Strategy, Structure and Social Science*. Oxford: Oxford University Press.

Williamson, O. E. (1975) *Markets and Hierarchies: Analysis and Antitrust Implications*. New York: Collier Macmillan.

Williamson, O. E. (1985) *The Economic Institutions of Capitalism*. New York: Free Press.

Zajac, E. (1992) 'Relating economic and behavioural perspectives in strategy research', *Advances in Strategic Management*, 8: 69–96, Greenwich, Conn: JAI Press.

Zajac, E. and Westphal, J. D. (1996) 'Who should succeed? How CEO/board preferences and power affect the choice of new CEOs', *Academy of Management Journal*, 39: 64–90.

Zajac, E. and Westphal, J. D. (1998) 'Toward a behavioural theory of the CEO–board relationship', in D. C. Hambrick, D. A. Nadler and M. C. Tushman (eds), *Navigating Change: How CEO's, Top Teams, and Boards Steer Transformation*. Boston: Harvard Business School Press. pp. 256–77.

Ziman, J. (1994) *Prometheus Bound: Science in a Dynamic Study State*. Cambridge: Cambridge University Press.

2

The Domain of Strategic Management: History and Evolution

EDWARD H. BOWMAN, HARBIR SINGH
and HOWARD THOMAS

The field of strategic management has advanced substantially in the past 40 years. The field has progressed significantly from its beginnings as a capstone course in the business school curriculum and an applied area providing practical insights to strategic executives and assessing the key strategic choices faced by top managers. In its present more rigorous state it has developed a strong disciplinary focus and a substantial academic base on particular strategic decision processes and their performance consequences. Consequently, this chapter takes a historical perspective on the evolution of the field. We trace the development of key ideas in the field, and attempt to make linkages between ideas developing in strategic management and the challenges facing managers.

Strategic management (Bowman, 1974) has three elements: its roots in practice, its methodology, and its theoretical underpinnings. For academics working in this field, practice is typically captured in cases and business histories. The methodology, or applications, of strategic management is elaborated in the implementation of planning systems, and associated tools for strategic analysis, in the process of strategic decision-making. Theoretical roots come primarily from economics and/or the social and behavioral sciences. A review of academic writing and the challenges faced by executives in various time periods indicates that practice and theory are not always well connected. Bettis (1991) notes that our research in strategic management has not yet produced the volume of useful results expected by managers. Thus, although the field has advanced, there continue to be some gaps between what is known from an academic perspective (more often in the positive, descriptive mode), and what is, or can be, prescribed to managers (in the normative mode).

It is important, therefore, to review the progress in the strategy field and thoroughly

This chapter is dedicated to the memory of
Professor Edward H. Bowman, Reginald H. Jones Professor at the Wharton School,
Founding Director of the Reginald H. Jones Center for Management Strategy, Policy,
and Organization.

examine its evolution and future potential. Such a critical review of the field should take stock of both its progress and theoretical orientation. We believe, following Bowman (1990) that theoretical pluralism is necessary for the development of the field. This viewpoint is convincingly demonstrated by Allison (1971), when he argues that there is much to be gained in understanding the Cuban Missile Crisis by framing the problem using alternative conceptual lenses.

In this pluralistic, multi-lectic spirit (Huff, 1982) it is relevant to take note of Bowman's (1990) suggestion that processes of dialogue, intellectual exchange and argument should be used to advance the field. Indeed, the many articles examining and reflecting the elements and content of strategy research (Bourgeois, 1984; Bowen and Wiersema, 1999; Camerer, 1985; Chakravarthy and Doz, 1992; Hirsch et al., 1990; Langley, 1999; Montgomery et al., 1989; Pettigrew, 1987b, 1992; Rumelt et al., 1994; Spender, 1992; Zaheer et al., 1999) have each advanced a set of propositions and criticism about the field and its development.

We do not seek to replicate the views of others here, nor attempt a totally comprehensive review. Rather, we present a personalistic and, perhaps, biased view about the field's domain and evolution. We address academic styles and patterns in the field's development and link these patterns to environmental challenges and changes. We not only review key elements in the literature but also monitor changes in management practice. We attempt to assess those critical ideas and issues that shape and frame the strategic management problem. We provide a set of insights about future research directions and also a set of conjectures about the boundaries of the field.

ACADEMIC STYLES IN STRATEGY

The field of strategy, as viewed from a historical perspective in the academic world, has nurtured at least three types of academics in the past few decades. While all three co-exist and thrive today, their relative significance and importance has changed. The first set of strategy scholars can be described as field researchers, the institutionalists, whose influence

was paramount in the middle 1960s and early 1970s. Though they varied in their approaches, they focused on a rich description of the elements of strategy and the strategy process from a top manager's perspective, both from within the firm and looking out at the environment. They could supply rich descriptions of strategy-related issues. They offered cases, histories, and planning systems. These contributions were exemplified by authors like Alfred Chandler (1962), who provided a disciplinary base for studying the modern corporation and inspired others at Harvard (for example, Rumelt, 1974) to build upon and further research his theoretical base. Because of their approach, they were able to investigate a broad range of problems and issues. Their method allowed them to be broad in scope as they delved into concepts related to strategy and planning. Because of the detailed descriptions they provided of strategic decisions, they were able to engage in field studies and prescription, part of which later scholars would re-examine. However, the textured descriptions of managerial challenges in corporate settings provided a good backdrop for future research and thinking.

Indeed, Chandler (1972) and others (Quinn, 1980; Pettigrew, 1987; Mintzberg, 1978) have developed a research tradition – the so-called processual approach to strategy – which still persists and provides an enduring stream of insights about the strategy process for other researchers to pursue in a variety of ways, including empirical hypothesis testing.

A later influence came from economists in the late 1970s and 1980s, most exemplified by Porter (1980). Industrial organization economics was the background on which they drew to analyze the problems of the firm, but especially the industries in which they existed. They posed the fundamental question of whether industry structural characteristics constrain the strategies of competing firms. Issues of industry concentration, barriers to entry, cost and price structures, economies of scale and scope, investment choices, vertical integration, profitability rates, and growth patterns were explored. A later generation of economists, whose interest in strategy has increased, are game theorists, who have examined issues that surface in the competitive environment associated with industry competition and competitive rivalry. These individuals

(Saloner, 1991; Dixit and Nalebuff, 1991; Camerer, 1985, 1991, etc.) have brought insights derived from the new industrial organization economics using disciplined ways of thinking about competitive interactions.

The third set of influences came from behavioral scientists, and gained increased momentum in the 1980s and the 1990s, following the earlier path-breaking work of March and Simon (1958), Simon (1958, 1991), Pettigrew (1987) and Argyris (1985). These include the organization psychologists, political scientists, sociologists (Burt, 1997; Granovetter, 1985; Scott, 1995), population ecologists (Hannan and Freeman, 1977, 1989) and cognitive scientists (Tversky and Kahneman, 1986; Porac and Thomas, 1990). Their work has dealt with a broader spectrum – from the individual to firm, to the industry, to the population of industries. They focus not on the optimization and equilibrium of the economist, but the functioning and survival of the organization, and the behavior of its people and the intra- and inter-organizational networks they adopt. Cooperative networks as distinct from competitive markets start to inform this analysis.

It is clear that the relative impact of these three groups, institutionalists, economists, and behavioralists, has followed a historical progression yet, over time, the views of these different groups have become much more integrated. They are all present today in the academic world, working on issues of strategy, and they all cope, though imperfectly, with the two central questions of strategy: first, why are some firms more successful than others? (a question of the type 'what is'), and secondly, how can we make a given firm more successful? (a question of the type 'how to'). Herbert Simon (*The Sciences of the Artificial,* 1969) has taken the academic community to task for being more interested in and more comfortable with the 'what is' question, and less so with the professional questions, 'how to' (Bowman, 1990). They both feel that the education of professionals in our universities suffers from this bias.

As we examine the way strategic thinking has evolved over time, it is useful to take a parallel look at how environmental challenges have changed over the past few decades. We will argue that many of the changes in thinking in strategic management have been catalyzed and influenced by some of the challenges faced by executives during these periods.

In the 1960s, for example, there was the continuation of the period of post World War II recovery and prosperity, and the parallel evolution of the form of the modern business enterprise. Industry in the US and in many developed countries was burgeoning. It was a growth decade for many organizations and, in order to enhance this growth, many businesses moved toward diversification. This led to the development of the conglomerate form and rationale for the corporation as a mini-capital market (Williamson, 1975; Armour and Teece, 1978). Thus, in the late 1960s, there was also the perception that larger firms had a lower cost of capital and more talented managers than smaller firms. As a result, much academic research in this period focused on growth, expansion, acquisition, diversification, and corporate control of the conglomerate enterprise (Amit and Livnat, 1988; Chatterjee, 1986; Christensen and Montgomery, 1981; Dess and Robinson, 1984; Lubatkin, 1987; Palepu, 1985; Rumelt, 1982; Singh and Montgomery, 1987). ITT under Harold Geneen, which diversified via acquisition into a vast number of unrelated businesses, was one such corporation (Prahalad and Bettis, 1986; Ramanujam and Varadarajan, 1989).

The 1970s were characterized by a combination of stagnation and inflation. The business community returned to conservative styles of management, moving away from diversification and towards the discipline of financial control systems. At the same time, there was the perception that the firm needed to increase its market share in its core businesses, and use the cash flow from such businesses to fund new ventures. This became the era of portfolio management and the invention of approaches such as the strategic business unit (SBU) form of organization and portfolio matrices (Henderson, 1979). The petroleum industry had major upheavals in this decade, particularly with the OPEC oil-price shock, with consequences for other large industries, such as the automobile industry in terms of fuel efficient vehicles and new product niches.

In the 1980s, there was strongly increased foreign competition, which led to the phenomenon of 'globalization' of industries and companies (Porter, 1988). There was an increase in emphasis on financially-driven strategies. Budget deficits and foreign trade imbalances, mainly with respect to Japan, caused a rethinking – particularly in American industry. It became apparent that American and European firms were not as efficient as Japanese corporations. The impact of perceived quality differences between American and Japanese manufacturers (Powell, 1995) was the realization that industrial markets had rapidly globalized, competitive strategies had shifted along with significant movements in market share among various manufacturers. This was also a time when financial strategy became important – many companies were under pressure from corporate raiders who determined that they could take over the companies and redeploy financial resources to more productive uses. Corporate restructuring and denominator management toward the end of the decade became the dominant mode, with detractors decrying 'the hollowing of the American Corporation' (Hamel and Prahalad, 1994). Sometimes this restructuring was abetted by the US Government, with American Telephone & Telegraph being a salient example – business portfolios changed, organizations and people were rearranged, and often the capital structure changed, as with RJR Nabisco. Much academic research in this period focused on aspects of restructuring or derivative issues, such as leveraged buyouts, divestments of divisions, organization downsizing, and top management teams (Bantel and Jackson, 1989; Singh, 1990).

During the 1990s, there was rapid and discontinuous economic and political change in the international environment. The cold war ended, Eastern Europe opened up, Japan began to have its own share of problems, and the European Union grew in stature. In view of these changes, corporate networks began to form. IBM, originally the leader in the computing industry, reinvented itself in the face of its problems by creating networks and alliances around the world, and selling solutions, rather than products, to corporations. Academic research in this period dealt with multinational alliances, corporate ventures, technology change, and continuing restructuring.

The new century comes in with further evolution towards networks – the rise of the knowledge worker and the knowledge-based organization, and the creation of flatter organizations. It is also the time of the internet-based corporation, with small staff sizes, and the use of the internet to sell products globally.

The rapid rise and fall of internet firms has underscored the broader volatility experienced by investors in the stock market. At the same time, analysts in the stock market continue to be strong figures, and CEOs have increasingly been concerned about meeting or exceeding ever-rising quarterly earnings targets. This tension between creating slack resources and investing in employees (to train and develop stronger knowledge workers) and providing investors with continued streams of cash flow has added new complexity to the lives of senior executives.

All these changes over the past decades have changed the face of the issues considered central to the field of strategy. With these changes in issues, we have had changes in practice and the literature of strategic management.

Changes in the Practice of Management

Changes in practice, in the form of changes in the methods of planning, have been documented by Gluck et al. (1980), McKinsey Quarterly Anthologies (2000) and by Chakravarthy and Lorange (1991). First came financial planning (1950s and earlier), then long range planning (1960s), then strategic planning (1970s), and then strategic management (1980s onward).

Financial planning largely focused on budgets for one and two years. The data and variables were all largely financial measures. These were projections from the past into the future as computed by the financial executives of the firm. This is what Chakravarthy and Lorange (1991) call budgeting. Their argument is that early planning in corporations was almost entirely budgeting and did not effectively take into account the strategic priorities of the firm.

Long range planning in the 1960s used a functional view of the firm, and focused essentially on the arrangement of each of the functions – marketing, production, finance, human resources – to achieve long-term goals. Frequently, staffs were employed and trained to develop these long range plans at both the corporate level and for each function. However, in the relatively placid environment of the 1960s, this planning process with a functional orientation was appropriate.

Strategic planning, often in the 1970s called forecast-based planning, began focusing both on external factors, such as the market and competitors, and internal functional factors. Here customers and competitors were the major focus, and the organization of the firm was rearranged in SBUs to map these customers and competitors.

Strategic management (1980s) was the last stage, and included both strategic planning and implementation. In some ways, the practice of strategic planning in GE, under CEO Jack Welch (see, for example, *Business Week*, June 8, 1998), epitomized this approach. Line managers were responsible for the strategies, both in planning and implementation, and the measure was the development of competitive advantage in each major line of business. The appropriate line executives had to be involved, incentives established, information systems designed, and programs articulated. Strategic management can connote other changes such as well away from a calendar driven system and toward an analysis that can be continuous and line-executive centered.

Changes in the Literature of Strategy: Patterns and Disciplinary Frameworks

It is quite clear that the strategy field's growth has reflected a tradition of theoretical pluralism (Bowman, 1990) in its borrowing of concepts and theories from other disciplines (economics, psychology, political and behavioral sciences) and in the evolution of its concepts and frameworks with changes in the styles and practice of management.

Writers in the strategy field have offered a wide range of alternative models of strategy (Bowman, 1974, 1990; Chaffee, 1985; Gluck et al., 1980; MacCrimmon, 1988, 1993; McKinsey Quarterly Anthologies, 2000; Porter, 1996). Yet, serious communication among strategy scholars has continued and allowed progress to be made in empirical, theoretical and methodological issues in strategic management research (Thomas and Pruett, 1993). And each of these different views of strategy has influenced the development of alternative research streams in the field. We try to identify these research streams as we discuss these different views of strategy and their evolution.

Earlier concepts of strategy were somewhat mechanistic in orientation and could be described in terms of the notion of 'organizational fit' – 'strategy as integrating organisational functions' (Barnard, 1938; Chandler, 1972) or 'strategy as fit between the organisation and the environment' (Andrews, 1971) or 'strategy as a planning perspective in terms of ends-means' (for example, matching policies to organizational goals – MacCrimmon, 1993).

The 'strategy as integration or organizational fit' theme developed from a substantial tradition of writing in scientific management (Barnard, 1938; Fayol, 1949; Taylor, 1911). Chandler (1962, 1972) built on this tradition in a fine-grained study of the historical evolution of a small number of firms. His model of corporate development examined diversification and growth patterns and identified a generalized set of relationships between strategy and structure of exceptional richness and depth. It was a major study grounded in the tradition of economic and business history research – as Nelson and Winter (1982) pointed out much later in their important book, 'history matters'. This one study motivated a stream of research involving researchers at Harvard Business School (Wrigley, 1970; Rumelt, 1974; Channon, 1973; Thanheiser, 1972; Pooley-Dyas, 1972), which teased out more thoroughly the character of Chandler's organizational forms and examined diversification strategies in the US and other Western European countries. It also generated a typology of diversification strategies based on the concept of 'relatedness' (Rumelt, 1982). Chandler's pioneering efforts, therefore, created a path-breaking direction for strategy research involving both in-depth, historical, longitudinal research and empirical testing of alternative diversification strategies. This stream was a dominant one in the strategy literature in the 1970s and 1980s.

Almost simultaneously, a stream of research emanated from the 'strategy as planning, strategy as ends-means' viewpoints. Writers such as Ansoff (1965), Ackoff (1970) and Steiner (1979) pioneered this deductive modeling stream and incorporated concepts drawn from operational research, decision theory, game theory and economics to model strategic situations. It focussed on firm-level planning using the OR tradition of modeling the web of economic relationships characterizing the firm and then devising frameworks to address firm level policy and strategy questions (Thomas, 1984). An outgrowth of this modeling tradition was the use of the so-called SWOT analysis (Andrews, 1971) – the analysis at the firm-level of *strengths, weaknesses, opportunities* and *threats*. This SWOT framework in its earliest applications led firms to search for their distinctive competences (a term first coined by Newman and Logan, 1971) and, thus, assess their competitive positioning.

SWOT was also an early example of the 'organization–environment' notion of 'fit' and linkage – matching a firm's strengths and weaknesses to its opportunities and threats. In turn, this led to an analytical literature attempting to analyze and forecast environmental opportunities and threats (Fahey and Naranayan, 1989). Indeed, Porter's analytical 'five-forces' model (Porter, 1980) was a classic example of such an 'organization–environment' model and framework. Using the industry as the unit of analysis, it analyzes how a firm's strategy can match, or be constrained by, its industry environment. The 'five-forces' model is anchored theoretically in Joe S. Bain's (Bain, 1956, 1968) industrial organization economics model, known colloquially as the structure–conduct–performance (SCP) paradigm. As a consequence, the analysis focuses on such industry characteristics as entry/exit barriers, competitive rivalry, supply, demand and substitution to assess the structure of the industry competitive landscape from the perspective of the firm. It has spawned a huge stream of literature on competitive strategy (Thomas and Pollock, 1999) in order to understand the puzzles of competitive strategy (who competes with whom?, how do they compete and why?).

Some of this analytic research and planning stream – particularly that grounded in the logical positivist tradition of OR – drew criticism from students of organization and strategic decision processes. They observed that strategizing is a political process (Pettigrew, 1987b) and involves a thorough understanding of organizational and political processes. As a consequence, a range of more 'organic' perspectives of strategy were presented, based on the premise that strategy is, in part, a work of art, not science, and is not intendedly rational. Rather, it emerges as a pattern in a stream of conscious, managerial decisions (Mintzberg, 1978; Miles and Snow, 1978), aimed at

ensuring organizational adaptation. In this sense, it is often associated with a 'learning by doing' mode and processes or organizational learning (Lyles and Thomas, 1988).

Quinn's (1980) set of rich, fine-grained case studies of strategic decision processes also built upon March and Simon's (1958) notion of bounded rationality. In this research, he identifies a strategy process which is step-wise and evolutionary, and characterized by organizational processes of logical incrementalism and well-developed organizational routines.

A number of key writers have contributed to this view of strategy as an emergent, evolutionary process. Perhaps the most noteworthy is Henry Mintzberg, whose paper 'Structure of unstructured decision processes' (Mintzberg et al., 1976) is a modern classic. It identifies the uncertainty inherent in the process and the iterative, feedback nature of organizational decision processes. Another cohort of strategy process researchers led by Andrew Pettigrew (1987) and Joseph Bower's (1970) descriptive model of the capital budgeting process followed the Chandlerian tradition of processual research and tried to identify patterns of strategy development and organizational learning (e.g. Johnson, 1987). The method here is to opt for rich, detailed descriptions of process which create insight and develop a range of hypotheses for future research.

Nelson and Winter's (1982) evolutionary models of strategy build upon concepts of emergent decision processes and bounded rationality to examine the path dependent and evolutionary nature of strategy processes. They re-framed important perspectives such as the role of organizational routines and recipes (also Quinn, 1980; Spender, 1989; Huff, 1982) in framing organizational strategy.

Cognitive psychologists (Porac and Thomas, 1990; Weick, 1987) expanded on these concepts and incorporated cognitive perspectives into thinking about strategies. They developed notions of organizational sense-making; of collective strategies and of organizational meaning and learning. These notions were a natural outgrowth of a closer examination of individual and organizational roles in the strategy process. The exemplar study of Porac et al. (1989), quoted in Weick (1995), pointed out how the interplay between individual and organizational cognition plays out in the processes of strategy-making in the Scottish knitwear industry.

More recent integrative perspectives have identified the firm as a rent seeking mechanism (Barney, 1991; Bowman, 1974, 1990) and have advanced the resource-based view of the firm (Amit and Schoemaker, 1993; Wernerfelt, 1984; Peteraf, 1993). Following Coase (1937) and Penrose (1958), they have asked what is the role of the firm and what are the critical resources to make it grow. In this sense, strategy is the ability to define and create uniqueness and research should focus on firms (not industries) and their uniqueness and how to predict success based on those unique actions and characteristics (often called 'core competences') (Prahalad and Hamel, 1990).

It is instructive to note that even Porter (1996) has moved to a more balanced view of strategy and the strategy process. He defines 'strategy as fit' as the key construct, and stresses the importance of understanding the roles of the top management team and strategic leadership in the strategy process. Clearly, induction and deduction both matter in studying strategy – in other words, both content and process matter in gaining a rich understanding of strategic management.

Tools of Strategic Analysis

A significant feature of work in strategy has been the development of tools for analysis in the world of practice, with parallel development taking place in the world of academia. Therefore, a discussion of the domain of strategy would not be complete without examining the tools used in strategic analysis, which are often used as frameworks to enhance policy dialogue about appropriate strategies in competition (Thomas, 1984). Thus, frameworks are useful in identifying the relevant variables and the questions which the manager must answer in order to develop conclusions tailored to a particularly industry and company (Furrer and Thomas, 2000). We discuss below some of the more important tools used in strategic analysis over the past several years.

SWOT (1960s)

The SWOT framework, among the earliest tools of strategic management, suggests that firms obtain sustained competitive advantages by implementing strategies that exploit their internal strengths, through responding to environmental opportunities, while neutralizing external threat and avoiding internal weaknesses (Ansoff, 1965; Andrews, 1971; Hofer and Schendel, 1978). Most research on sources of sustained competitive advantage has focused either on isolating a firm's opportunities and threats (Porter, 1980, 1985), describing its strengths and weaknesses (Hofer and Schendel, 1978; Penrose, 1958; Stinchcombe, 1965), or analyzing how these are matched to choose strategies.

BCG Growth-Share Matrix (1970s)

The limitations of the discounted cash flow model were particularly apparent to corporate executives of large, diversified firms in the early 1970s. Many firms had acquired an array of businesses but because of a recession, they also faced financial problems. Corporate strategists were anxious to find approaches that enabled them to evaluate various opportunities and to determine which businesses should receive funds and which should be divested. Portfolio models provided a convenient method to evaluate available investment opportunities as well as factors associated with superior long-term performance (Sudharshan, 1995). Competitive portfolio analysis, which was developed by the Boston Consulting Group (BCG) (Henderson, 1979), is based on the close relationship between market share and cash generation. What distinguished competitive portfolio analysis from the PIMS (profit impact of market share) analysis (Buzzell and Gale, 1987) was its focus on the specific role of each product in the overall strategy of the firm. Based on its cash flow characteristics and relative market share, each product could be positioned in a product portfolio matrix. Two important concepts underlay this matrix – the product life-cycle concept and the experience curve concept. Applications of this concept are available in Hambrick et al. (1982) and McCabe and Narayanan (1991).

GE Matrix: Market Attractiveness– Business Strength (1970s)

The market attractiveness–business strength matrix was developed by General Electric (GE) and McKinsey. GE corporate planners felt it was simplistic to make important investment decisions based on only two factors – market growth and relative market share.

The basis of this matrix is that the long-term profitability of an investment alternative is a function of the attractiveness of the market in which the business operates. This and the business position relative to other competitors' positions were assessed using multiple factors (Sudharshan, 1995). Variations of this model have been developed by Royal Dutch Shell (Directional Policy Matrix) and Arthur D. Little (Industry Maturity–Competitive Matrix) (Hofer and Schendel, 1978; Sudharshan, 1995).

PIMS Analysis (1970s, early 80s)

The profit impact of market strategy (PIMS) project was organized in early 1972 by the Marketing Science Institute at the Harvard Business School. A large data base containing information on more than 600 businesses was established and used to develop different PIMS profit models (Schoeffler et al., 1974). These models were designed to answer the following questions: What factors influence profitability in a business, and how much influence does each one have? How does ROI change in response to changes in strategy and in market conditions? The PIMS project was established to overcome some limitations concerning financial planning models and the market attractiveness–competitive position matrix. Although these models were conceptually appealing, they did not provide insight into factors that make opportunities attractive-factors which result in long-term performance. The PIMS project attempted to identify the factors related to long-term performance (Sudharshan, 1995). Rather than use a theoretical framework to identify key factors related to long-term profitability, variables were included in the PIMS models because they have a potential empirical relationship with the performance of a business. Research applications of these tools can be found in Buzzell and Gale (1987).

Industry Analysis – Five Forces (early 80s)

Industry analysis, as noted earlier, was introduced by Michael Porter to the field in the early 1980s, and was a transformation of the structure–conduct–performance paradigm in industrial organization economics to apply to strategic analysis. It was a way to provide substantially greater sharpness to the analysis of the environment involved in SWOT analyses. Five attributes of industry structure, according to Porter (1979, 1980), could influence the ability of a firm to either maintain or create above-normal returns – barriers to entry, the intensity of rivalry, barriers to substitutes, and the relative power of suppliers, and buyers. Implicitly, this work adopted two simplifying assumptions. First, these environmental models of competitive advantage assumed that firms within an industry are identical in terms of the strategically relevant resources they control and the strategies they pursue. Second, these models assume that should resource heterogeneity develop in an industry, that this heterogeneity will be very short lived because the resources that firms use to implement their strategies are highly mobile (Barney, 1991).

Value Chain Analysis (mid 80s)

Most goods or services were recognized to be produced by a series of vertical business activities – acquiring supplies of raw materials, manufacturing intermediate products, manufacturing of final products, sales and distribution, and service (Porter, 1985). The use of value chain analysis involved an examination of the rent-generating potential of each link in the chain. This analysis served as a guide to action on investment in various links, and possible recommendations on outsourcing or expansion of particular activities. Value chain analysis was proposed initially both by consultants McKinsey and company, and by Porter (1985). Kogut (1985) also extended the value-chain concept to the analysis of global competition.

Scenario Analysis (1970s)

Scenario analysis provided decision-makers with the ability to address uncertainty by representing future states through a limited set of internally consistent 'scenarios'. Scenarios could be applied in testing the viability of alternative strategies or as background information in strategy formulation or contexts to evaluate specific capital investment projects. Scenarios tended to be used when conventional analytical/statistical forecasting techniques proved inadequate for environmental assessment (Furrer and Thomas, 2000). Increases in environmental uncertainty and the growing importance of political and social issues in corporate decision-making tended to foster scenario use (Nair and Sarin, 1979; Linneman and Klein, 1981, 1982, 1983; Lanzenauer and Sprung, 1982; Becker, 1983; Wack, 1985).

Seven-S Framework (1980s)

The 7-S framework, developed by McKinsey and company, stated that it was not enough to think about strategy implementation as a matter only of strategy and structure. In this context, the 7-S framework indicated that effective strategic management is at least a function of seven variables: strategy, structure, systems, style, staff, skill, and shared values. The overall consistency and fit between these seven variables were presumed to result in a successful strategy (Waterman et al., 1980, Waterman, 1982; Peters and Waterman, 1982).

Value Based Planning (1980s)

Value based planning had its roots in financial theory. The decision criterion of this method was the maximization of shareholder wealth. From a financial standpoint, maximizing shareholder wealth was the appropriate objective for a company. This tool allowed managers to examine their strategies in the context of the contributions of each investment decision to shareholder value. Several firms during this period focused on creating value in each of their businesses, computing independent valuations of each line of business and monitoring how these valuations would change based upon strategic decisions made in a given period (value based strategic management) (Rappaport, 1986; Newport et al., 1991).

EVA (Economic Value Added) (1990s)

Given the numerous limitations of accounting measures of divisional performance, several firms began adopting alternative methods of evaluating this performance. These alternatives focus directly on the present value of the cash flow generated by a division. The most popular of these economically-oriented measures of division performance is economic value added (EVA) (Stern et al., 1995; Tully, 1993). By measuring the value added over all costs, including the cost of capital, EVA measures the productivity of all factors of production. It does not, by itself, tell a decision maker why a certain product or a certain service does not add value, or shed light on courses of action to recover value. EVA does show which product, service operation, or activity has unusually high productivity and which activities can add unusually high value.

Capability Analysis (1990s)

Capability-based competition is based on four basic principles: the building blocks of corporate strategy are not products and markets but business processes; competitive success depends on transforming a company's key processes into strategic capabilities that consistently provide superior value to the customer; companies create these capabilities by making strategic investments in a support infrastructure that links together and transcends traditional SBUs and functions; and because capabilities necessarily cross functions, the champion of a capabilities-based strategy is the CEO (Stalk et al., 1992). In addition, the literature on the resource-based view of the firm has uncovered key characteristics of resources and capabilities that have strategic value. It is structured in a series of four questions: the question of value, the question of rareness, the question of inimitability, and the question of organization (Barney, 1996).

Strategic Option Analysis (1990s)

The strategic option approach incorporates both the uncertainty inherent in business and the active decision making required for a strategy to succeed. Business strategy can be conceptualized as a series of options in the face of uncertainty. Executing a strategy almost always involves making a sequence of major decisions. Some actions are taken immediately, while others are deliberately deferred, so managers can optimize as circumstances evolve. The strategy sets the framework within which future decisions will be made but, at the same time, it leaves room for learning from ongoing developments and for discretion to act based on what is learned. This approach considers strategies as portfolios of related real options (Luehrman, 1998a, b). Recent work has shown how the real options approach represents a more theoretically appealing valuation approach to certain kinds of investment projects than the discounted cash flow approach. In particular, it has been shown that under conditions of high uncertainty, the conventional discounted cash flow approach to valuation can understate the value of a project, and thereby has important limitations. In contrast, since the real options approach facilitates quantification of the benefits of flexibility of managerial action, it has a strong advantage for strategic decision making under conditions of uncertainty. The real options approach is frequently applied to value projects with uncertain returns such as oil exploration, manufacturing and production, and R&D projects (Seth and Kim, 1999). It has also been recognized as useful for the valuation of joint ventures (Kogut, 1991; Balakrishnan and Koza, 1993; Hurry, 1993; Seth and Kim, 1999).

From the above discussion, it is clear that the strategy literature provides a range of different tools to frame and analyze strategy, competition and competitive dynamics. It is important, however, to note that they have usually been developed to answer certain specific strategy or competitive questions. Their growth is embedded in, and influenced by, the critical ideas and issues of strategic management.

Evolution of Critical Ideas in Strategic Management

If we examine the path of change in academic influences and managerial challenges, some shifts in the emphases of strategic management research are clearly discernible. We contend that, in the mid-1960s, the *firm* was the primary focus of strategic management research, with its strengths and weaknesses as a key element. Moving on to the late 1970s through the early eighties, the *environment* and its relationship to the firm was the emphasis, with industry analysis at its center. Later in the 1980s, *industries and markets and firm scope* were the dual foci, with the strategy performance relationship as the focus. Throughout the 1990s, *firm capabilities and core competences* (Prahalad and Hamel, 1990) became the development of central concern and led, more recently, to *knowledge* as an emphasis, with its links to the building of capabilities and competitive advantage as the focus (Spender and Grant, 1996; Nonaka, 1994).

All the factors listed above are, of course, given consideration in an analysis of strategy of the firm, but this change in emphasis or focus has been apparent in the literature and in practice. For instance, Robert Hayes (1985) suggested, 'In short, the logic here is: Do not develop plans and then seek capabilities; instead build capabilities and then encourage the development of plans for exploiting them. Do not try to develop optimal strategies on the assumption of a static environment; instead seek continuous improvement in a dynamic environment.' Early in the 1990s, Prahalad and Hamel (1990) argued, 'In the 1990s they (top executives) will be judged on their ability to identify, cultivate, and exploit core competencies that makes growth possible – indeed, they'll have to rethink the concept of the corporation itself.'

The shifts in emphasis can also be examined in the context of practice. One company very visible to students of strategy in its chief executive officers and in its strategy thinking has been General Electric (see the range of Harvard Business School cases). In the 1960s, Fred Borsch made the visible move to SBUs in conjunction with McKinsey, permitting a focus on each unit's strategy and performance. The strategy of the competitive business unit could be presented by its managers and understood by top management. Reginald Jones in the 1970s built a very strong and well documented, strategic planning practice for competitive analysis. The organization shifted into 'sectors' in order to permit the continuing attention to competitive strategy throughout the company. Important resource commitment choices could be made between key strategic units. Jack Welch in the 1980s worked at a simplification of both the strategy ('Be number one or two in your industry') and the strategy process, with a special emphasis on the executive group to be inclusive in strategy consideration through organization 'workouts'. The 'boundaryless' organization could be advocated and sought. If our previous argument for the shifting emphasis in strategic analysis from the 1960s to the 1990s is correct, then our estimate is that the 1990s have brought to GE a renewed interest in the core competence of the firm, with a focus on capabilities reinforcement. Most recently in the year 2000, Jack Welch (see Sherman, 2000) instituted a policy that each line of business of

GE would have to reinvent itself in light of the internet, thus addressing the latest shift in the competitive environment of the firm.

Strategy Research: Classic Books in the Field of Strategy

We discuss here how classic books, rather than research articles reviewed earlier, have impacted theory and practice in the development of the field of strategy. The 1960s were the start of the modern era in strategy and their authors' impact is still felt. Alfred Chandler, Igor Ansoff, and Kenneth Andrews were all institutionalists – in one way or another. They all provided a look at strategy from within the firm, looking out. They offered a richly desciptive view of managers in the firm, coping with issues relating to strategy.

Chandler's *Strategy and Structure* was the classic strategy history book focusing on the developing history of four major American corporations – DuPont, General Motors, Standard Oil of New Jersey, and Sears Roebuck. The book examines the relationships between strategy and structure as these firms evolve. As the firms grew, expanded geographically and diversified, they were virtually forced to change their organization structures (and processes) to cope with these changes. The decentralized, divisionalized operating corporation, with centralized control, as designed by GM's Alfred Sloan came into being.

The book *Corporate Strategy*, by Igor Ansoff, had an analytical focus and laid out a systematic series of analyses that would allow the corporation to determine what its strategy would be and how to take the important next steps. Major considerations examined were product market domains, competitive advantage, synergy, growth direction, and make-or-buy choices. Growth and diversification were virtually assumed in this treatment of strategic planning.

Kenneth Andrews was the co-author of *Business Policy: Text and Cases*, who wrote the text material (later rewritten in a separate book *The Concept of Corporate Strategy*). This book allowed the reader to work through the major questions in strategy formulation and strategy implementation. Cases were amply supplied to facilitate group discussion of these questions. Andrews argued that though he was not interested in theory *per se*, he was providing 'an everyman's theory' for corporate strategy. All three of these books emphasized corporate strategy in all its particulars.

In the early 1980s, the switch in corporate strategy literature was substantial. The leading book in this era, anticipated by earlier articles, was Michael Porter's *Competitive Strategy*. This book relied strongly and explicitly on industrial organization economics. Though of many parts, the book's major emphasis was on the competitive actors in the firm's industrial, competitive environment – 'the five forces'. These forces for consideration and analysis were suppliers, competitors, possible substitutes, potential entrants, and customers. Around these forces were arranged the factors that would be present in various life cycle stages of a corporation's existence and how to think about them.

Another important book was *Organizational Strategy, Structure, and Processes*, by Miles and Snow (1978), which was empirically based, and presented a field research-based view of how organizational processes and strategy were inter-related. It dealt with a number of industry studies, identified strategic taxonomies and showed how generic strategies of the firm came about and how influential such generic strategies seemed to be in all aspects of a coordinated strategy. Their discovered generic strategies were: the prospector, the analyzer (positioned between prospector and defender), the defender, and the reactor. The first three were all viable approaches to positioning within most industries, while the reactor was not an effective strategy, but nevertheless was observed in the field.

A book somewhat earlier than Porter's but fitting into this period was Oliver Williamson's *Markets and Hierarchies* (1975). The treatment here was the efficacy of the divisionalized structure (the M-form) for managerial control and the appropriate boundaries of the firm. The boundaries of the firm are involved with the make-or-buy decisions, and are influenced by the nature of the assets and the markets involved.

The 1980s and beyond have brought a new literature looking at the implementation issues and problems of the corporation's strategies. Hax and Majluf's *Strategic Management: An Integrative Perspective* (1984) offered an extended treatment of the planning steps necessary for strategy. Rappaport's (1986) financial treatment of strategy issues, *Creating Shareholder Value: The New Standard for Business Performance*, offered a value added or value based approach to strategy with a continuing look to the stock market for guidance and calibration. Itami and Roehl's book, *Mobilizing Invisible Assets* (1987), asked the reader to look at the more intangible aspects of the firm's nature, especially its people commitments, in order to capture the advantage of these assets. Teece's book, *The Competitive Challenge: Strategies for Innovation and Renewal* (1987), supplied an intellectual breadth addressed to the issues of strategic management by several leading authors of the day. Nelson and Winter's book, *An Evolutionary Theory of Economic Change* (1982), deals with skills within the firm, and how they are searched for, changed, and selected. Firm capabilities, routines, learning, change, and flexibility are key concepts in this important work.

It is interesting that many of the ideas presented in these books from the past decades are relevant and pertinent to today's problems. Strategic management has had a rich and pluralistic history, and many of the key works are still current in their impact on ideas in the field.

Strategy Research: Influences on Work in Strategy

Strategic management research has been characterized by multiple influences – of industrial economics on the study of positioning in industries, of the economics and sociology of organization on the study of firm resources and capabilities, and of game theory on the study of competitive interactions.

In the area of *positioning*, the earliest work was best exemplified by Porter (1980), and by a large number of studies of strategy and its link to performance. This was also a period in which a lot of researchers explored the relationships between various strategies and financial performance or market share (see, for example, Hambrick et al., 1982). In addition, there was the study of economic uncertainty, and guides to action in such settings. Porter and Spence (1982) offered a scenario study of capacity

expansion in an industry under conditions of uncertainty of demand, prices, and technology. Based on assumptions of rational expectations and equilibrium (standard fare in economic analysis), the several companies in this oligopoly and their choices could be approximated based on their characteristics. Several other industry-specific studies have followed, such as Lieberman (1989) on the factors influencing first mover advantages in the specialty chemical industry, and Thomas (1990) in the study of research productivity in the pharmaceutical industry.

There was also a lively debate on the existence and predictive value of the concept of strategic groups – which argues that firms in an industry form groups according to the similarity of their strategies and, normatively speaking, these strategic groups show persistent performance differences. While researchers such as Hatten and Hatten (1987) and Barney and Hoskisson (1990) have questioned the existence and stability of the construct, Tang and Thomas (1992) link theories of strategic choice (Child, 1972), spatial competition (Hotelling, 1929) and cognitive taxonomy (Weick, 1991; Porac and Thomas, 1990) to demonstrate that the concept of strategic groups is not an analytical convenience but a valid theoretical construct.

On a more behavioral front, Frederickson and Mitchell (1984) investigated the efficacy of comprehensiveness in strategic planning under different conditions of industry turbulence. Their use of scenarios for executive questionnaires was instructive for other researchers. Hirsch's (1975) comparative study of institutional strategy in the phonographic records and pharmaceutical industries showed how important the government and critical gatekeepers can be in the implementation of strategy throughout a whole industry. He argues average profits differ by a factor of three largely due to these factors.

In the area of *capabilities and resources*, the early work in strategic management very clearly had an institutionalist flavor, focusing on strategy and choices of firms. The work of Penrose (1958) was seminal in its treatment of the drivers of corporate growth through the generation and utilization of firm-level resources. Rumelt's book on the efficacy of diversification used the *Fortune* 500 companies to show how some kinds of diversification (related) were more effective than others, and how the organization structures of these companies were influenced by these moves. In many ways, Rumelt's (1974) arguments about the benefits of particular types of diversification (related linked and related constrained) pointed to the development and exploitation of firm-level critical resources that could be used effectively only in a defined range of markets. Later work by Montgomery (1982) showed that industry effects also influenced returns, and not just the resource profile of the firm.

A large amount of research was spawned on resources and the scope of the firm, including studies of risk and return (Montgomery and Singh, 1984; Amit and Livnat, 1988). At about this time, Wernerfelt (1984) wrote the first paper on the resource-based view of the firm based on the seminal work of Penrose (1958). This paper received substantial interest because it was a crisp articulation of the conditions under which a firm's resources could be used to generate rents. Rumelt's (1984) *Strategic Theory of the Firm* was also framed from a similar resource-based view and advanced concepts such as isolating mechanisms (Lippman and Rumelt, 1982) which created uniqueness at the firm level. Later work by Barney (1986, 1991) provided more of a texture on the conditions under which resources could generate rents. Subsequent applications to areas such as acquisitions (Singh and Montgomery, 1987; Lubatkin, 1987; Barney, 1988; Seth, 1990) explored how firms could generate rents from significant decisions involving changes in firm scope, and found support for the idea that firms generate value only from unique configurations of rent-generating resources. Teece et al. (1997) came up with the idea of dynamic capabilities, and argued that capabilities were dynamic and needed reinvestment over time to stay as significant sources of rents for the firm.

More recently, research on the development of firm-level capabilities has evolved into *knowledge management* within the firm. The early work of Nelson and Winter (1982) and Spender (1989) was already pointing in this direction, through the concept of routines and recipes, which embody systematic, codified knowledge within the firm. Later research, such as Winter (1987), identified the conditions under which knowledge could be a strategic asset. Dierickx and Cool (1989) offered the argument that knowledge can be thought of in terms of stocks and flows. Accumulated stocks of knowledge can be a source of advantage, while flows of knowledge may change the configuration of stocks over time. Kogut and Zander (1993), along with other authors, suggested that knowledge as a source of advantage is path-dependent in nature. A way to continue to generate advantage was to not allow knowledge to be easily replicable, but to recombine knowledge in creative ways to pursue new market opportunities. Other theoretical work by Grant (1996) hypothesizes that tacit knowledge is the source of sustained competitive advantage. Further empirical work (Szulanski, 1996) identified the role of the firm as an entity in managing the transfer of knowledge among divisions, and found support for the notion of 'stickiness', that it was actually very difficult to transfer specialized knowledge within the firm. Later work has further explored the role of knowledge management in developing key firm-level capabilities in many contexts, such as the development of alliance management capability (Kale et al., 2000). Cohen and Levinthal's (1990) study of the absorptive capacity effects of R&D spending offers a new look at learning in the critical fields of technology as supporting the competence of the firm. The work of Henderson and Cockburn (1994) distinguishes between architectural and component competence of the firm, and stresses the importance of coordination mechanisms in positively influencing research productivity in the pharmaceutical industry.

Game theory has played a significant role in deepening our understanding of *competitive interactions* (Furrer and Thomas, 2000). Although competitive interactions have often been at the heart of teaching and practical discussion of strategy, the research on this area is early in developing teachable insights. Arguments about competitive interaction were implicit in Porter and Spence's modeling of strategy decisions under uncertainty. Due to the high level of rationality and information processing capability imputed to decision-makers in game-theoretic models, many researchers in strategy have been somewhat skeptical of the insights obtainable from this set of tools. However, Camerer (1991) addresses this concern by indicating that game theory can be used to formally think about interdependence of competitive moves in an industry. A careful application of game theoretic thinking can be very helpful in this sense. The work by Ghemawat (1991) on large strategic commitments as sources of competitive advantage is illustrative. Saloner (1991) offers the perspective that rather than using game theoretical modeling for global generalizations, researchers would find it productive to use this technique to solve specific, stylized competitive problems. Additionally, Weigelt and Camerer (1988) have found empirical evidence supporting the idea that even though individual players in a game do not solve for the equilibrium, a collection of players arrives at the theoretically calculated equilibrium through their collective moves. Clearly, there is unexploited potential in the broad area of study of competitive interaction, through multiple theoretical lenses.

Conjectures for Further Research

We list below a number of areas that we believe to be important in developing future research for the field.

Longitudinal, Processual Analysis

Mintzberg and his colleagues (Mintzberg, 1978; Mintzberg and Waters, 1982, 1985; Mintzberg et al., 1976) and Pettigrew (1987) have demonstrated the key role and benefits of a historical and longitudinal perspective within strategic management. If we subscribe to the view that strategies do not change on schedule and that, when they do change, the process is complex (Mintzberg and Waters, 1982, 1985), the role of intensive longitudinal research can be better appreciated. Such attempts typically mean small sample sizes and large investments of research time. The rich body of results and tentative propositions developed from such a study can be subsequently tested and refined by other researchers adopting different methodologies. The aim is often to provide insights for such theory building attempts as Rumelt's (1984) interdisciplinary strategic theory of the firm.

Development of Gestalts and Taxonomies

Within the strategic management discipline, many recent studies have adopted a taxonomic or 'gestalt' perspective. A taxonomic approach involves the ordering, classification or grouping of objects (or phenomena) (Blalock, 1971) with a marked focus on the commonality which exists between objects rather than on their uniqueness. The benefit in using a taxonomic approach in strategic management is the opportunity to collapse large amounts of information into convenient and parsimonious categories (Carper and Snizek, 1980), which can be used for testing hypotheses and examining relationships.

A number of taxonomic perspectives are currently evident in the literature. The first main perspective follows traditional research in industrial organization and looks for strategic groups *within an* industry (Cool and Schendel, 1988; Fiegenbaum and Thomas, 1995; McGee and Thomas, 1986). The second main perspective identifies firms employing similar strategies, usually within a homogeneous environment (not necessarily restricted to an industry), and defined using multiple characteristics (Miller, 1987; Miller and Friesen, 1986; Miles and Snow, 1978; Miles and Cameron, 1982).

Clearly, it is necessary to understand both the conditions underlying the formulation of strategic taxonomies and the factors likely to influence the movement or stability of taxonomies (gestalts) over time and across contexts. Whereas existing research has focused upon the formation of taxonomies, relatively little research has been directed towards the movement of firms across taxonomic groups (Oster, 1982, 1999).

Enhancing Precision in the Measurement of Concepts

Measurement still remains a little-researched area within strategic management but, as indicated earlier, greater attention and enhanced precision is evident in certain studies (Frederickson, 1984; Dess and Davis, 1984; Venkatraman and Ramanujam, 1987). Improving measurement approaches is a key requirement for the development of a field, since a 'failure to represent explicitly the degree of correspondence between measurement and

concepts undermines the test of the theory'
(Bagozzi and Phillips, 1982: 459).

Emphasis on Alternative Research Methods

Strategy researchers need to enrich their range
of research approaches. We believe that, for
example, simulation and game theoretic
approaches can provide increasingly valuable
frameworks for strategy research (Furrer and
Thomas, 2000). Simulation methods are being
used in several areas of strategy research. In a
classic study, Hall (1976) examined strategic
decision-making processes and strategy evaluation in the *Saturday Evening Post* magazine,
using a systems dynamics form of simulation.
More recently, Morecroft (1999) and Warren
(1995) at London Business School have
strongly advocated the use of systems dynamics models. From an industrial organization
perspective, Porter and Spence (1982) modeled
decisions to expand capacity in the corn wet
milling industry using simulation to analyze
alternative industry scenarios.

Camerer (1985) suggests that competitive
reaction can be anticipated and explicitly modeled in business strategy settings using game
theoretic concepts and frameworks. Indeed,
Camerer makes a good case for the increased
use of deductive models in strategy but
ignores the role of hybrid inductive/deductive
models and theoretical and methodological triangulation (Boland, 1982; Caldwell, 1982;
Denzin, 1978; Jick, 1979; Smith, 1975: ch. 12)
in strategy. Oster (1999) notes that game
theory has been used by numerous companies
to make decisions about marketing issues,
capacity expansion and reduction, entry and
entry deterrence, acquisitions, bidding and
negotiations.

CONCLUSION

Theories from a number of disciplines (economics, sociology, psychology) have been
used to understand phenomena in strategic
management research. Each perspective provides a unique set of theoretical insights but
there has not been sufficient success in putting
the pieces of the puzzle together. The strategic
management field can be conceptualized
as one centered on problems relating to the

creation and sustainability of competitive
advantage, or the pursuit of rents. This
problem-oriented approach has served the
field well, but bringing in influences from
multiple disciplines to address interesting
research questions related to the creation of
competitive advantage. Of course, many
process-oriented pieces of research, on the
process of strategy formation, and on strategic
decision-making, have added richness to the
literature, as have pieces of research on top
management teams and corporate governance.

While pluralism is a strength of the field, it
has also generated some concerns, mostly
about the lack of existence of a single, unifying
paradigm. The costs can often be a lack of rigor
in research that is an application of theories
and techniques developed in adjacent fields.
Some of this concern is well founded, although
there have been some very thoughtful
approaches recommended to deal with these
concerns – namely that work done in the field
should meet the highest standards of related
disciplines (Saloner, 1991; Camerer, 1991).

Early research in strategic management
moved from field-based institutional research,
with little theory, to research that drew rather
heavily upon economics, with an emphasis on
high levels of rationality of decision-makers.
More recently, with the rise of interest in firm-
level capabilities, and on the knowledge-based
view of the firm, there has been an increase in
the behavioral component of the field, with
decision-making criteria based upon bounded
rationality. Hopefully the next steps in research
will develop insights from the tensions between
these different views of decision-making,
or will combine the best of each of these
traditions.

A set of limitations that have caused concern for several writers is the tendency within
the field to invent new terms to label a construct even in instances where existing terms
may work well. A related concern is with a
lack of attention to prior treatments of a topic,
and a lack of reconciliation between new
terms used by an author with those that
already exist in the literature. A consequence
of this proliferation of terms is a reduction in
the extent to which research is cumulative,
because prior and later work cannot be compared effectively. However, as increasing
numbers of authors are aware of these limitations, there is greater and greater comparability

of research across studies, resulting in a cumulative body of knowledge in the field.

It is unlikely that interdisciplinary theories will be developed in fields which are relatively more narrowly defined. Interdisciplinary research is, and should be, one of the primary distinctive competences of strategic management as a field, and there seems to be sufficient demand for interdisciplinary research within this field to make such ventures possible and fruitful. Further, it is reasonable to assume that neighboring fields would find it useful to import interdisciplinary theories. Efforts to develop, and to disseminate, such theory are a natural role for strategic management research.

The value to be added by strategic management can be put into business terms by conceiving technology as knowledge structures (Spender, 1996; Spender and Grant, 1996; Nonaka, 1991, 1994). The licensing of technology can reduce start-up costs (for example, R&D expenditures) for the receiving organization. Technology can be applied directly or combined with other technologies in novel ways within the receiving organization as they develop their own innovations. In an academic environment, exporting interdisciplinary theories to more sharply-defined fields can allow their researchers to expand the boundaries of knowledge with substantially less effort and greater benefit – the technology (knowledge structures) for linking their known body of theories to a wealth of theories in other disciplines can be provided by strategic management researchers. From an entrepreneurial perspective, this represents a remarkable opportunity for strategic management as a field.

Strategic management has several perspectives that clearly have their home in the field, such as the resource-based view, the relational view, the dynamic capability perspective, and the knowledge based perspective of the firm. These perspectives of the firm have developed mainly through research within strategic management. There also have been several applications in related fields, such as information strategy, information systems design, human resource management, and organization theory. Strategic management continues to be an interesting domain, with several driving questions and a commitment to pluralism in theoretical perspectives that will serve the field well.

REFERENCES

Ackoff, R. L. (1970) *A Concept of Corporate Planning.* New York: John Wiley and Son.

Allison, G. T. (1971) *Essence of Decision: Explaining the Cuban Missile Crisis.* New York: HarperCollins.

Amit, R. and Livnat, J. (1988) 'Diversification and the risk-return trade-off', *Academy of Management Journal*, 31(1): 154–66.

Amit, R. and Schoemaker, P. J. H. (1993) 'Strategic assets and organizational rent', *Strategic Management Journal*, 14(1): 33–46.

Andrews, K. R. (1971) *The Concept of Corporate Strategy.* Homewood, Ill: Dow-Jones Irwin.

Ansoff, H. I. (1965) *Corporate Strategy: An Analytic Approach to Business Policy for Growth and Expansion.* New York: McGraw Hill.

Argyris, C. (1985) *Strategy, Change, and Defensive Routines.* Boston: Pitman Publishing Co.

Armour, H. O. and Teece, D. J. (1978) 'Organization structure and economic performance: a test of the multidivisional hypothesis', *Bell Journal of Economics*, 9: 106–22.

Bagozzi, R. P. and Phillips, L. W. (1982) 'Representing and testing organisational theories: a holistic construal', *Administrative Science Quarterly*, 27(3): 459–90.

Balakrishnan, S. and Koza, M. P. (1993) 'Information asymmetry, adverse selection and joint-ventures', *Journal of Economic Behavior and Organization*, 20(1): 99–117.

Bain, J. S. (1956) *Barriers to New Competition.* Cambridge, MA: Harvard University Press.

Bain, J. S. (1968) *Industrial Organisation*, second edition. New York: John Wiley.

Bantel, K. A. and Jackson, S. E. (1989) 'Top management and innovations in banking: does the composition of the top team make a difference?', *Strategic Management Journal*, 10: 107–24.

Barnard, C. I. (1938) *The Functions of the Executive.* Boston, MA: Harvard University Press.

Barney, J. B. (1986) 'Strategic factor markets: expectations, luck, and business strategy', *Management Science*, 32(10): 1231–41.

Barney, J. B. (1988) 'Returns to bidding firms in mergers and acquisitions: reconsidering the relatedness hypothesis', *Strategic Management Journal*, 9 (Special Issue): 71–8.

Barney, J. B. (1991) 'Firm resources and sustained competitive advantage', *Journal of Management*, 17(1): 99–120.

Barney, J. B. (1996) *Gaining and Sustaining Competitive Advantage.* Reading, MA: Addison-Wesley.

Barney, J. B. and Hoskisson, R. E. (1990) 'Strategic groups: untested assertions and research proposals', *Managerial and Decision Economics*, 11(3): 187–98.

Becker, H. S. (1983) 'Scenarios: a tool of growing importance to policy analysts in government and industry', *Technological Forecasting and Social Change*, 23: 95–120.

Berle, A. A. and Means, G. C. (1932) *The Modern Corporation and Private Property*. New York: Medallion Co.

Bettis, R. A. (1991) 'Strategic management and the straitjacket: an editorial essay', *Organization Science*, 2(3): 315–19.

Bettis, R. A. and Mahajan, V. (1985) 'Risk/return performance of diversified firms', *Management Science*, 31(7): 785–99.

Blalock, H. M. (1971) *Causal Models in the Social Sciences*. Chicago: Aldine Books.

Bourgeois, L. J. (1984) 'Strategic management and determinism', *Academy of Management Review*, 9: 586–96.

Bowen, H. P. and Wiersema, M. F. (1999) 'Matching method to paradigm in strategy research: limitations of cross-sectional analysis and some methodological alternatives', *Strategic Management Journal*, 20(7): 625–36.

Bower, J. (1970) *Managing the Resource Allocation Process*. Boston: Harvard Business School.

Boland, L. (1982) *The Foundations of Economic Method*. London: Allen and Unwin.

Bowman, E. H. (1974) 'Epistemology, corporate strategy, and academe', *Sloan Management Review* 5(2): 35–50.

Bowman, E. H. (1990) 'Strategy changes: possible worlds and actual minds', in J. W. Frederickson (ed.), *Perspectives on Strategic Management*. New York: Harper and Row. pp. 9–37.

Bowman, E. H. and Hurry, D. (1993) 'Strategy through the option lens: an integrated view of resource investments and the incremental-choice process', *Academy of Management Review*, 18(4): 760–82.

Bowman, E. H., Singh, H., Useem, M. and Bhadury, R. (1999) 'When does restructuring improve economic performance?', *California Management Review*, 41(2): 33–54.

Bowman, E. H. and Kunreuther, H. (1988) 'Post-Bhopal behaviour at a chemical company', *Journal of Management Studies*, 25(4): 387–402.

Bruner, J. (1986) *Actual Minds, Possible Worlds*. Cambridge, MA: Harvard University Press.

Burt, R. S. (1997) 'The contingent value of social capital', *Administrative Science Quarterly*, 42(2): 339–65.

Buzzell, R. D. and Gale, B. T. (1987) *The PIMS Principles: Linking Strategy to Performance*. New York: Free Press.

Caldwell, B. (1982) *Beyond Positivism: Economic Methodology in the Twentieth Century*. London: Allen and Unwin.

Camerer, C. (1985) 'Redirecting research in business policy and strategy', *Strategic Management Journal*, 6(1): 1–15.

Camerer, C. (1991) 'Does strategy research need game theory? *Strategic Management Journal*, 12 (winter): 137–52.

Carper, W. B. and Snizek, W. E. (1980) 'The nature of organizational taxonomies', *Academy of Management Review*, 5: 65–75.

Chaffee, E. E. (1985) 'Three models of strategy', *Academy of Management Review*, 10: 89–98.

Chakravarthy, B. S. and Lorange, P. (1991) *Managing the Strategy Process*. Englewood Cliffs, NJ: Prentice-Hall, Inc.

Chakravarthy, B. S. and Doz, Y. (1992) 'Strategy process research: focusing on corporate self-renewal', *Strategic Management Journal*, 13 (Special Issue): 5–14.

Chandler, A. D. (1962) *Strategy and Structure: Chapters in the History of American Enterprise*. Cambridge, MA: MIT Press.

Chandler, A. D. (1972) *Strategy and Structure*. Cambridge: MIT Press.

Chang, S-J. and Singh, H. (2000) 'Corporate and industry effects on business unit competitive position', *Strategic Management Journal*, 21(7): 739–52.

Channon, D. F. (1973) *The Strategy and Structure of British Enterprise*. New York: Macmillan.

Chatterjee, S. (1986) 'Types of synergy and economic value: the impact of acquisitions on merging and rival firms', *Strategic Management Journal*, 7(2): 119–39.

Child, J. (1972) 'Organisation structure, environment and performance: the role of strategic choice', *Sociology*, 6: 1–22.

Christensen, C. R., Andrews, K. R., Bower, J. L., Hamermesh, R. G. and Porter, M. E. (1980) *Business Policy: Text and Cases*. Homewood, IL: Irwin.

Christensen, H. K. and Montgomery, C. A. (1981) 'Corporate economic performance: diversification strategy versus market structure', *Strategic Management Journal*, 2: 327–43.

Coase, R. H. (1937) 'The nature of the firm', *Economica*, 4: 386–405.

Cohen, W. M. and Levinthal, D. (1990) 'Absorptive capacity: a new perspective on learning and innovation', *Administrative Science Quarterly*, 35: 128–52.

Cool, K. and Schendel, D. (1988) 'Performance differences among strategic group members', *Strategic Management Journal*, 9(3): 207–23.

Denzin, N. K. (1978) *The Research Act*, second edition. New York: McGraw-Hill.

Dess, G. G. and Davis, P. S. (1984) 'Porter's (1980) generic strategies as determinants of strategic group membership and organizational performance', *Academy of Management Journal*, 27(3): 467–88.

Dess, G. G. and Robinson, R. (1984) 'Measuring organisational performance in the absence of objective measures: the case of privately-held firm and conglomerate business unit', *Strategic Management Journal*, 5(3): 255–73.

Dierickx, I. and Cool, K. (1989) 'Asset stock accumulation and sustainability of competitive advantage', *Management Science*, 35(12): 1504–14.

DiMaggio, P. J. and Powell, W. W. (1983) 'The iron cage revisited: institutional isomorphism and collective rationality in organization fields', *American Sociological Review*, 48: 147–60.

Dixit, A. K. and Nalebuff, B. J. (1991) *Thinking Strategically: The Competitive Edge in Business, Politics, and Everyday Life*. New York and London: Norton.

Dyer, J. H. and Singh, H. (1998) 'The relational view: cooperative strategy and sources of interorganizational competitive advantage', *Academy of Management Review*, 23(4): 660–79.

Fahey, L. and Naranayan, V. K. (1989) 'Linking changes in revealed causal maps and environmental change: an empirical study', *Journal of Management Studies*, 26(4): 361–78.

Fayol, H. (1949) *General and Industrial Management*. Pitman: London.

Fiegenbaum, A. and Thomas, H. (1995) 'Strategic groups as reference groups: theory, modeling and empirical examination of industry and competitive strategy', *Strategic Management Journal*, 16(6): 461–76.

Frederickson, J. W. (1984) 'The comprehensiveness of strategic process: extension, observations, future directions', *Academy of Management Journal*, 27: 445–66.

Frederickson, J. W. and Mitchell, T. R. (1984) 'Strategic decision processes: comprehensiveness and performance in an industry with an unstable environment', *Academy of Management Journal*, 27(2): 399–423.

Furrer, O. and Thomas, H. (2000) 'The rivalry matrix: understanding rivalry and competitive dynamics', *European Management Journal*, 18(6): 619–38.

Ghemawat, P. (1991) *Commitment: The Dynamics of Strategy*. New York: Free Press.

Gluck, F. W., Kaufman, S. P. and Walleck, A. S. (1980) 'Strategic management for competitive advantage', *Harvard Business Review*, 58(4): 154–60.

Granovetter, M. (1985) 'Economic action and social structure: the problem of embeddedness', *American Journal of Sociology*, 91: 481–510.

Grant, R. M. (1991) *Contemporary Strategy Analysis*. Cambridge, MA: Basil Blackwell.

Grant, R. M. (1996) 'Toward a knowledge-based theory of the firm', *Strategic Management Journal*, 17 (winter): 109–22.

Gulati, R. and Singh, H. (1998) 'The architecture of cooperation: managing coordination costs and appropriation concerns in strategic alliances', *Administrative Science Quarterly*, 43(4): 781–814.

Hall, R. I. (1976) 'A system pathology of an organisation: the rise and fall of the *Saturday Evening Post*', *Administrative Science Quarterly*, 21: 185–211.

Hambrick, D. C., Macmillan, I. C. and Day, D. L. (1982) 'Strategic attributes and performance in the BCG matrix: a PIMS-based analysis of industrial product businesses', *Academy of Management Journal*, 25(3): 510–31.

Hamel, G. and Prahalad, C. K. (1989) 'Strategic intent', *Harvard Business Review*, 67(3): 63–76.

Hamel, G. and Prahalad, C. K. (1994) 'Competing for the future', *Harvard Business Review*, 72(4): 122–8.

Hannan, M. T. and Freeman, J. H. (1977) 'The population ecology of organizations', *American Journal of Sociology*, 82(5): 929–64.

Hannan, M. T. and Freeman, J. H. (1989) *Organisational Ecology*. Boston, MA: Harvard University Press.

Hatten, K. J. and Hatten, M. L. (1987) 'Strategic groups, asymmetrical mobility barriers and contestability', *Strategic Management Journal*, 8(4): 329–42.

Hax, A. C. and Majluf, N. S. (1984) *Strategic Management: An Integrative Perspective*. Englewood Cliffs, NJ: Prentice-Hall.

Hayes, R. H. (1985) 'Strategic planning – forward in reverse?', *Harvard Business Review*, 63(6): 111–19.

Henderson, B. (1979) *Henderson on Strategy*. Boston: ABT Books.

Henderson, R. and Cockburn, I. (1994) 'Measuring competence? Exploring firm effects in pharmaceutical research', *Strategic Management Journal*, 15 (Special Issue): 63–84.

Hirsch, P. M. (1975) 'Organizational effectiveness and the institutional environment', *Administrative Science Quarterly*, 20: 327–44.

Hirsch, P. M., Friedman, R. and Koza, M. P. (1990) 'Collaboration or paradigm shift: caveat emptor and risk of romance with economic models for strategy and policy research', *Organization Science*, 1(1): 87–97.

Hofer, C. W. and Schendel, D. (1978) *Strategy Formulation: Analytical Concepts*. St. Paul, MN: West Publishing.

Hotelling, H. (1929) 'Stability in competition', *Economic Journal*, 39: 41–57.

Huff, A. (1982) 'Industry influences on strategy formulation', *Strategic Management Journal*, 3: 55–75.

Hurry, D. (1993) 'Restructuring in the global economy: the consequences of strategic linkages between Japanese and US firms', *Strategic Management Journal*, 14 (Special Issue): 69–82.

Itami, H. and Roehl, T. W. (1987) *Mobilizing Invisible Assets*. Cambridge, MA: Harvard University Press.

Jick, T. D. (1979) 'Mixing qualitative and quantitative methods: triangulation in action', *Administrative Science Quarterly*, 24: 602–11.

Johnson, G. (1987) *Strategic Change and the Management Process*. Oxford: Blackwell.

Kale, P., Singh, H. and Perlmutter, H. (2000) 'Learning and protection of proprietary assets in strategic alliances: building relational capital', *Strategic Management Journal*, 21(3): 217–37.

Kogut, B. (1985) 'Designing global strategies: profiting from operational flexibility (part 1)', *Sloan Management Review*, 27(1): 27–38.

Kogut, B. (1991) 'Joint venture and the option to expand and acquire', *Management Science*, 37(1): 19–33.

Kogut, B. and Zander, U. (1993) 'Knowledge of the firm and the evolutionary theory of the multinational corporation', *Journal of International Business Studies*, 24(4): 625–45.

Langley, A. (1999) 'Strategies for theorizing from process data', *Academy of Management Review*, 24(4): 691–710.

Lanzenauer, C. H. and Sprung, M. R. (1982) 'Developing inflation scenarios', *Long Range Planning*, 15(4): 37–44.

Learned, E. A., Christensen, C. R., Andrews, K. R. and Guth, W. D. (1965) *Business Policy: Text and Cases*. Homewood, IL: Richard D. Irwin.

Levitt, B. and March, J. (1988) 'Organization learning', *Annual Review of Sociology*, 14: 319–40.

Lieberman, M. B. (1989) 'The learning curve, technology barriers to entry, and competitive survival in the chemical processing industries', *Strategic Management Journal*, 10(5): 431–47.

Linneman, R. E. and Klein, H. E. (1981) 'The use of scenarios in corporate planning – eight case histories', *Long Range Planning*, 14(5): 69–77.

Linneman, R. E. and Klein, H. E. (1982) 'The use of multiple scenarios by US industrial companies', *Long Range Planning*, 15(4): 37–44.

Linneman, R. E. and Klein, H. E. (1983) 'The use of multiple scenarios by US industrial companies: a comparison study, 1977–1981', *Long Range Planning*, 16(6): 94–101.

Lippman, S. A. and Rumelt, R. P. (1982) 'Uncertain imitability: an analysis of interfirm differences in efficiency under competition', *Bell Journal of Economics*, 13: 418–38.

Lubatkin, M. (1987) 'Merger strategies and stockholder value', *Strategic Management Journal*, 8(1): 39–53.

Luehrman, T. (1998a) 'Investment opportunities as real options: getting started on the numbers', *Harvard Business Review*, 76(4): 51–67.

Luehrman, T. (1998b) 'A strategy as a portfolio of real options', *Harvard Business Review*, 76(5): 89–99.

Lyles, M. A. and Thomas, H. (1988) 'Strategic problem formulation: biases and assumptions embedded in alternative decision making models', *Journal of Management Studies*, 25: 131–45.

MacCrimmon, K. R. (1998) 'Essence of strategy: ends, means and conditions.' In J. Grant (ed.), *Strategic Management Frontiers*. Greenwich, CT: JAI Press. pp. 42–72.

MacCrimmon, K. R. (1993) 'Do firm strategies exist?', *Strategic Management Journal*, 14 (Special Issue): 113–30.

March, J. G. (1980) 'How we talk and how we act: administrative theory and administrative life.' In M. D. Cohen and J. G. March (eds), *Leadership and Ambiguity*. Boston, MA: Harvard Business School Press. pp. 273–90.

March, J. G. and Shapira, Z. (1987) 'Managerial perspectives on risk and risk taking', *Management Science*, 33(11): 1404–18.

March, J. G. and Simon, H. A. (1958) *Organizations*. New York: Wiley.

McCabe, D. L. and Narayanan, V. K. (1991) 'The life cycle of the PIMS and BCG models', *Industrial Marketing Management*, 20(4): 347–52.

McGee, J. and Thomas, H. (1986) 'Strategic groups: theory, research and taxonomy', *Strategic Management Journal*, 7(2): 141–60.

McKinsey Quarterly Anthologies (2000) *On Strategy*. June.

Miles, R. E. and Snow, C. C. (1978) *Organization, Strategy, Structure, and Processes*. New York: McGraw-Hill.

Miles, R. H. and Cameron, K. S. (1982) *Coffin Nails and Corporate Strategy*. Englewood Cliffs, NJ: Prentice-Hall.

Miller, D. (1987) 'Strategy making and structure: analysis and implications for performance', *Academy of Management Journal*, 30(1): 7–32.

Miller, D. and Friesen, P. H. (1986) 'Porter's (1980) generic strategies and performance: an empirical examination with American data – Part II: performance implications', *Organization Studies*, 7(3): 255–61.

Mintzberg, H. (1976) 'Planning on the left side and managing on the right', *Harvard Business Review*, 54: 49–58.

Mintzberg, H. (1978) 'Patterns in strategy formation', *Management Science*, 24(9): 934–48.

Mintzberg, H. (1987a) 'Crafting strategy', *Harvard Business Review*, 87(4): 66–77.

Mintzberg, H. (1987b) 'The strategy concept 1: five Ps for strategy', *California Management Review*, 30(1): 11–24.

Mintzberg, H., Raisinghini, D. and Theoret, A. (1976) 'The structure of unstructured decision process', *Administrative Science Quarterly*, 21: 246–75.

Mintzberg, H. and Waters, J. A. (1982) 'Tracking strategy in an entrepreneurial firm', *Academy of Management Journal*, 25(3): 465–99.

Mintzberg, H. and Waters, J. A. (1985) 'Of strategies, deliberate and emergent', *Strategic Management Journal*, 6(3): 257–72.

Montgomery, C. A. and Singh, H. (1984) 'Diversification strategy and systematic risk', *Strategic Management Journal*.

Montgomery, C. A. and Thomas, A. R. (1988) 'Divestment – motives and gains', *Strategic Management Journal*, 9(1): 93–7.

Montgomery, C. A. (1982) 'The measurement of firm diversity: some new empirical evidence', *Academy of Management Journal*, 25: 299–307.

Montgomery, C. A., Wernerfelt, B. and Balakrishnan, S. (1989) 'Strategy content and the research process', *Strategic Management Journal*, 10(2): 189–98.

Morecroft, J. D. W. (1999) 'Visualising and rehearsing strategy', *Business Strategy Review*, 10(3): 17–32.

Morrison, A. and Wensley, R. (1990) *Boxing Up or Boxing In? A Short History of the Boston Consulting Group Share/Growth Matrix*. Coventry, UK: Warwick Business School.

Nair, K. and Sarin, R. K. (1979) 'Generating future scenarios – their use in strategic planning', *Long Range Planning*, 12: 57–61.

Nelson, R. R. and Winter, S. G. (1982) *An Evolutionary Theory of Economic Change*. Cambridge, MA: Prentice-Hall.

Newman, W. H. and Logan, J. P. (1971) *Strategy, Policy and Central Management*. Cincinnati: South-Western.

Newport, S., Dess, G. G. and Rasheed, A. M. A. (1991) 'Nurturing strategic coherency', *Planning Review*, 19(6).

Nonaka, I. (1991) 'The knowledge-creating company', *Harvard Business Review*, 69(6): 96–104.

Nonaka, I. (1994) 'A dynamic theory of organizational knowledge creation', *Organization Science*, 5(1): 14–37.

Oster, S. (1982) *Modern Competitive Analysis*, first edition. New York: Oxford University Press.

Oster, S. (1999) *Modern Competitive Analysis*, second edition. New York: Oxford University Press.

Palepu, K. (1985) 'Diversification strategy, profit performance and the entropy measure', *Strategic Management Journal*, 6(3): 239–55.

Penrose, E. T. (1958) *A Theory of the Growth of the Firm*. New York: Wiley.

Perrow, C. (1986) *Complex Organizations: A Critical Essay*. New York: Random House.

Peteraf, M. A. (1993) 'The cornerstones of competitive advantage: a resource-based view', *Strategic Management Journal*, 14(3): 179–91.

Peters, T. J. and Waterman, R. H. Jr. (1982) *In Search of Excellence: Lessons from America's Best-Run Companies*. New York: Harper & Row.

Pettigrew, A. M. (1987b) 'Researching strategic change', in A. M. Pettigrew (ed.), *The Management of Strategic Change*. Oxford: Basil Blackwell.

Pettigrew, A. M. (1992) 'The character and significance of strategy process research', *Strategic Management Journal*, 13: 5–16.

Pooley-Dyas, G. (1972) 'Strategy and structure of French enterprise', Doctoral Dissertation, Harvard Business School, Boston, MA.

Porac, J. F. and Thomas, H. (1990) 'Taxonomic mental models in competitor definition', *Academy of Management Review*, 15(2): 224–40.

Porac, J. F., Thomas, H. and Baden-Fuller, C. (1989) 'Competitive groups as cognitive communities: the case of Scottish knitwear manufacturers', *Journal of Management Studies*, 26(4): 397–416.

Porter, M. E. (1979) 'How competitive forces shape strategy', *Harvard Business Review*, March–April: 137–56.

Porter, M. E. (1980) *Competitive Strategy*. New York: Free Press.

Porter, M. E. (1985) *Competitive Advantage: Creating and Sustaining Superior Performance*. New York: Free Press.

Porter, M. E. (1988) *The Competitive Advantage of Nations*. New York: Free Press.

Porter, M. E. (1996) 'What is strategy?', *Harvard Business Review*, 74(6): 61–78.

Porter, M. E. and Spence, A. M. (1982) 'The capacity expansion process in a growing oligopoly: the case of corn wet milling', in J. J. McCall (ed.), *The Economics of Information and Uncertainty*. Chicago: University of Chicago Press. pp. 258–309.

Powell, T. C. (1995) 'Total quality management as competitive advantage: a review and empirical study', *Strategic Management Journal*, 16(1): 15–37.

Prahalad, C. K. and Bettis, R. A. (1986) 'The dominant logic: a new linkage between diversity and performance', *Strategic Management Journal*, 7(6): 485–501.

Prahalad, C. K. and Hamel, G. (1990) 'The core competence of the corporation', *Harvard Business Review*, 68(3): 79–91.

Quinn, J. B. (1980) *Strategies for Change: Logical Incrementalism*. Homewood, IL: Irwin.

Ramanujam, V. and Varadarajan, P. (1989) 'Research on corporate diversification: a synthesis', *Strategic Management Journal*, 10(6): 523–51.

Rappaport, A. (1986) *Creating Shareholder Value: The New Standard for Business Performance*. New York: Free Press.

Rorty, R. (1979) *Philosophy and the Mirror of Nature*. Princeton, NJ: Princeton University Press.

Rumelt, R. P. (1974) *Strategy, Structure, and Economic Performance*. Boston: Harvard Business School, Division of Research.

Rumelt, R. P. (1982) 'Diversification strategy and profitability', *Strategic Management Journal*, 3: 359–69.

Rumelt, R. P. (1984) 'Towards a strategic theory of the firm'. In R. B. Lamb (ed.), *Competitive Strategic Management*. Englewood Cliff, NJ: Prentice Hall. pp. 556–570.

Rumelt, R. P. (1987) 'Theory, strategy, and entrepreneurship', in D. Teece (ed.), *The Competitive Challenge: Strategies for Industrial Innovation and Renewal*. Cambridge, MA: Ballinger. pp. 137–58.

Rumelt, R. P., Schendel, D. E. and Teece, D. J. (1991) 'Strategic management and economics', *Strategic Management Journal*, 12 (winter): 5–29.

Rumelt, R. P., Schendel, D. E. and Teece, D. J. (1994) *Fundamental Issues in Strategy*. Boston, MA: Harvard Business School Press.

Saloner, G. (1991) 'Modeling, game theory, and strategic management', *Strategic Management Journal*, 12 (winter): 119–36.

Schoeffler, S., Buzzell, R. D. and Heany, D. F. (1974) 'Impact of strategic planning on profit performance', *Harvard Business Review*, March–April.

Schon, D. A. (1983) *The Reflective Practitioner: How Professionals Think in Action*. New York: Basic Books.

Scott, R. W. (1995) *Institutions and Organisations*. Thousand Oaks, CA: Sage.

Seth, A. (1990) 'Sources of value creation in acquisitions: an empirical investigation', *Strategic Management Journal*, 11(6): 431–46.

Seth, A. and Kim, S-M. (1999) 'Valuation of international joint ventures: a real options approach', presentation at the Valuation of Intangible Assets in Global Operations Conference at Rutgers University, February 5, 1999.

Sherman and Stanford, A. (2000) Article on Jack Welch, *Business Week*, 6 June.

Simon, H. A. (1958) *Administrative Behaviour*, second edition. New York: Macmillan.

Simon, H. A. (1960) *The New Science of Management Decision*. New York: Harper & Row.

Simon, H. A. (1969) *The Sciences of the Artificial*. Cambridge, MA: MIT Press.

Simon, H. A. (1991) 'Organizations and markets', *Journal of Economic Perspectives*, 5: 25–43.

Singh, H. (1990) 'Management buyouts: distinguishing characteristics and operating changes prior to public offering', *Strategic Management Journal*, 11: 111–29.

Singh, H. and Montgomery, C. A. (1987) 'Corporate acquisition strategies and economic performance', *Strategic Management Journal*, 8(4): 377–86.

Smith, H. W. (1975) *Strategies of Social Research: The Methodological Imagination*. Englewood Cliffs, NJ: Prentice-Hall.

Spender, J. C. (1989) *Industry Recipes*. Oxford: Basil Blackwell.

Spender, J. C. (1992) *Advances in Strategic Management*, Volume 8. A Research Annual, 3–32.

Spender, J. C. (1996) 'Making knowledge the basis of a dynamic theory of the firm', *Strategic Management Journal*, 17: 45–62.

Spender, J. C. and Grant, R. M. (1996) 'Knowledge and the firm: overview', *Strategic Management Journal*, 17: 5–9.

Stalk, G., Evans, P. and Shulman, L. (1992) 'Competing on capabilities: the new rules of corporate strategy', *Harvard Business Review*, March–April: 57–69.

Steiner, G. (1979) *Strategic Planning: What Every Manager Must Know*. New York: Free Press.

Stern, J., Stewart, B. and Chew, D. (1995) 'The EVA financial management system', *Journal of Applied Corporate Finance*, 8: 32–46.

Stinchcombe, A. L. (1965) 'Social structure and organizations', in I. G. March (ed.), *Handbook of Organizations*. Chicago: Rand-McNally. pp. 142–93.

Sudharshan, D. (1995) *Market Strategy: Relationships, Offerings, Timing & Resource Allocation*. Englewood Cliffs, NJ: Prentice-Hall.

Szulanski, G. (1996) 'Exploring internal stickiness: impediments to the transfer of best practice within the firm', *Strategic Management Journal*, 17 (winter): 27–43.

Tang, M-J. and Thomas, H. (1992) 'The concept of strategic groups: theoretical construct or analytical convenience', *Managerial and Decision Economics*, 13(4): 323–9.

Taylor, F. W. (1911) *The Principles of Scientific Management*. New York: Norton.

Teece, D. J. (ed.) (1987) *The Competitive Challenge: Strategies for Industrial Innovation and Renewal*. Cambridge, MA: Ballinger.

Teece, D. J., Pisano, G. and Shuen, A. (1997) 'Dynamic capabilities and strategic management', *Strategic Management Journal*, 18(7): 509–33.

Thanheiser, H. T. (1972) 'Strategy and structure in German industrial enterprise', Doctoral Dissertation, Harvard Business School, Boston, MA.

Thomas, H. (1984) 'Strategic decision analysis: applied decision analysis and its role in the strategic management process', *Strategic Management Journal*, 5(2): 139–56.

Thomas, H. and Pollock, T. (1999) 'From I-O economics' S–C–P paradigm through strategic groups to competence-based competition: reflections on the puzzle of competitive strategy', *British Journal of Management*, 10(2): 127–40.

Thomas, H. and Pruett, M. (1993) 'Perspectives on theory building in strategic management', *Journal of Management Studies*, 30(1): 3–11.

Thomas, L. G. (1990) 'Regulation and firm size: FDA impacts on innovation', *Rand Journal of Economics*, 21(4): 497–517.

Tully, S. (1993) 'The real key to create wealth', *Fortune*, September 20: 38–50.

Tversky, A. and Kahneman, D. (1986) 'Rational choice and the framing of decisions', *Journal of Business*, 59(4): S251–78.

Tversky, A., Slovic, P. and Kahneman, D. (1990) 'The causes of preference reversal', *American Economic Review*, 80(1): 204–17.

Venkatraman, N. and Ramanujam, V. (1987) 'Planning system success: a conceptualization and an operational model', *Management Science*, 33(6): 687–705.

Von Hippel, E. (1988) *The Sources of Innovation*. Oxford: Oxford University Press.

Wack, P. (1985) 'Scenarios: uncharted waters ahead', *Harvard Business Review*, September–October: 73–89.

Warren, K. B. (1995) 'Exploring competitive futures using cognitive mapping', *Long Range Planning*, 28(5): 10–22.

Waterman, R. H. Jr. (1982) 'The seven element of strategic fit', *Journal of Business Strategy*, 2(3): 68–72.

Waterman, R. H. Jr., Peters, I. J. and Phillips, J. R. (1980) 'Structure is not organization', *Business Horizons*, 23(3): 14–26.

Weick, K. E. (1987) 'Substitutes for strategy', in D. J. Teece (ed.), *The Competitive Challenge*. Cambridge, MA: Ballinger.

Weick, K. E. (1991) 'The nontraditional quality of organizational learning', *Organizational Science*, 2(1): 116–24.

Weigelt, K. and Camerer, C. (1988) 'Reputation and corporate strategy: a review of recent theory and applications', *Strategic Management Journal*, 9(5): 443–54.

Weick, K. E. (1995) *Sense-making in Organisations*. London: Sage.

Wernerfelt, B. (1984) 'A resource-based view of the firm', *Strategic Management Journal*, 5: 171–80.

Williamson, O. E. (1975) *Markets and Hierarchies: Analysis and Antitrust Implications*. New York: Free Press.

Winter, S. G. (1987) '"Knowledge" and competence as strategic assets'. In D. J. Teece (ed.), *The Competitive Challenge*. Cambridge, MA: Ballinger. pp. 159–184.

Wrigley, L. (1970) 'Divisional autonomy and diversification'. Unpublished Ph.D. dissertation, Harvard Business School.

Zaheer, S., Albert, S. and Zaheer, A. (1999) 'Time scales and organizational theory', *Academy of Management Review*, 24(4): 725–41.

Part Two
THINKING
AND ACTING
STRATEGICALLY

3

Constructing Competitive Advantage

KAREL COOL, LUÍS ALMEIDA COSTA
and INGEMAR DIERICKX

A firm achieves a competitive advantage in a given market whenever it outperforms its competitors. A competitive advantage may result from a lower cost of production, from the ability to provide a group of customers with higher perceived benefits, or from a combination of both (Porter, 1980, 1985). One important stream, often referred to as the 'resource-based' view of strategy, emphasizes firm-specific *resources* as the fundamental determinants of competitive advantage and performance (Rumelt, 1984, 1987; Wernerfelt, 1984; Barney, 1986a; Dierickx and Cool, 1989a; Prahalad and Hamel, 1990; Peteraf, 1993). Following Daft (1983) and Barney (1991), we define firm resources as all assets, capabilities, competencies, information knowledge and reputations that are owned or controlled by the firm and that enable the firm to conceive of and implement strategies that improve its efficiency and effectiveness.[1]

The resource-based view maintains that firms may be heterogeneous with respect to the bundle of resources they control. Furthermore, since some of these resources, such as a firm's reputation or other information-based resources, cannot be traded in factor markets and are difficult to accumulate and imitate, resource heterogeneity may persist over time. This perspective offers important insights about which resources lie at the heart of the firm's competitive position, and, therefore, are

worth protecting and developing (Wernerfelt, 1984; Barney, 1986a, 1991; Dierickx and Cool, 1989a; Peteraf, 1993), and about the major mechanisms that drive the accumulation and imitation of resources (Barney, 1986a; Dierickx and Cool, 1989a).[2]

While the resource-based view focuses on the internal analysis of firms' resources, sustainable competitive advantages may be based, not on unique firm-specific assets or capabilities, but on *privileged market positions* (Caves, 1984; Shapiro, 1989; Peteraf, 1993; Kay, 1993). A strategy may lead to a sustainable competitive advantage either because it results from the deployment of unique (scarce) resources 'or because its adroit implementation by a limited number of firms makes its replication unprofitable for latecomers' (Caves, 1984: 131). Industrial organization economists have identified a number of dimensions in which *commitments* that are irrevocable for nontrivial periods of time may lead to privileged market positions and sustainable competitive advantages.[3] For example, firms may expand production capacity (Spence, 1979; Dixit, 1980; Eaton and Lipsey, 1981), may use product strategies such as brand proliferation (Schmalensee, 1978; Eaton and Lipsey, 1979), or may invest in intangible property (Dasgupta and Stiglitz, 1980; Lee and Wilde, 1980; Reinganum, 1981, 1983). In such cases, the firm's competitive advantage is sustainable, not because competitors cannot accumulate or imitate a similar resource bundle, but because they do not have the incentive to do so. The competitive advantage follows from industry structure, rather than from strategic resources.

In this chapter, we discuss the nature and sources of competitive advantage, paying attention both to firm-specific resources and privileged market positions. The rest of this chapter is organized as follows. Below we elaborate on the distinction between returns to unique resources and returns to privileged market positions and discuss the managerial and analytical problems that may result from not recognizing the real source of a firm's above normal returns. We then analyze the basic criteria resources should meet to yield a sustainable stream of above normal returns and describe the major mechanisms that drive the accumulation and imitation of resources. This is followed by a discussion of the strategic role of commitments and discuss different sources of privileged market positions.

SOURCES OF COMPETITIVE ADVANTAGE

To motivate the importance of the distinction between returns to unique resources and returns to privileged market positions, we introduce a simple example, taken from Dierickx and Cool (1994). Suppose a petroleum refiner has access to low cost crude oil at $10 per barrel, while his competitors must buy crude on the open market at $20 per barrel. Does the refiner have a cost advantage? Will this refinery be more profitable? While at first sight one may be tempted to say 'yes', the answer is negative for both questions. In using a barrel of his $10 crude, the refiner really incurs a cost of $20. Indeed, he is sacrificing that revenue by not selling the crude on the market. Yet, will he not earn more than his competitors? Yes, *but not in refining*; his access to 'low cost' crude oil does not give him a cost advantage in refining. He is simply earning money from his ownership of a valuable asset – a deed to property with easily accessible oil underneath (or possibly a long-term supply contract at some earlier and lower price). The refiner's above-normal returns result from a scarce resource (the deed) which merely happens to be deployed to a particular

use or product market opportunity (refining), rather than from his product market activities *per se*. Indeed, rather than refining his 'low cost' crude, he could also simply sell property, keep the property and sell the oil, or lease the property to other producers at a royalty.

This example illustrates a general class of cases where a firm's above-normal returns result, not from a privileged market position, but from the possession or control of a unique resource. But, is it really important to identify a firm's *source* of above-normal returns? Is it not enough to evaluate its cost and differentiation position relative to competitors?

Failure to correctly identify the real source of a firm's above-normal earnings may lead to several kinds of problems.[4] First, failure to correctly identify the real source of a firm's returns may lead to a bias towards captive use. A firm that owns or controls a unique resource often faces several deployment options. The decision to deploy a unique resource captively, in an attempt to create a competitive advantage in product markets, is only one of the possible alternatives. In our example, rather than refining his 'low cost' crude, the oil refiner could simply sell the property, keep the property and sell the oil, or lease the property to other producers. Yet, unless the specific asset responsible for the firm's superior earning potential has been explicitly identified, competitive strategy is likely to be biased toward captive use. As a result, a broader range of options for the deployment of valuable resources may be left unexplored.

A second problem may result from hidden cross-subsidization of unprofitable activities. Unless the oil refiner understands that the 'low cost' crude is its valuable asset and compares its alternative uses, the 'opportunity cost' of refining the 'low cost' crude is not correctly accounted for. If the opportunity cost of using valuable resources is not correctly accounted for, measured profits from operations will be inflated. This hidden cross-subsidization may distort performance appraisal and investment decisions. Returning to the oil refiner case, high measured profits in refining when the opportunity cost of oil is not correctly accounted may give a misleading signal for further investments in refining facilities. Furthermore, measurement problems caused by hidden cross-subsidization may give the wrong incentives to the subsidized activities since high measured performance is almost guaranteed by the subsidy.

In addition, failure to correctly identify the real source of a firm's returns may lead to inadequate protection of scarce resources. Unless the firm's sources of above-normal returns are correctly identified, one may neglect to carefully examine the forces which threaten to destroy this potential. As we discuss below, to the extent that a similar resource can be easily bought or sold, competitors could quickly deploy a similar resource. Even if the resource cannot be bought or sold, competitors may accumulate a similar stock of their own. This may, however, be a complex and time-consuming process.

In sum, a firm's competitive strategy often tends to be biased toward captive use of resources. Access to low cost or differentiation inputs is frequently believed to be a sufficient reason for pursuing a cost leadership or differentiation strategy. While a strong product market position might be achieved, captive use of resources is not necessarily the optimal deployment option.[5] The identification of the different deployment options obliges firms to move beyond product market positioning and to address the broader issue of how to fully appropriate the rent potential of its valuable assets.

Strategic Resources and Competitive Advantage

The inquiry into the conditions for sustained competitive advantage constitutes the major research theme of the resource-based perspective.[6] Clearly, for resources to yield a competitive advantage, they have to be *unique*. Resource heterogeneity, leading to efficiency differences and, therefore, rents, is a necessary condition for a resource bundle to constitute the basis for competitive advantage. If all firms in a market have the same stock of resources, no strategy is available to one firm that would not also be available to all other firms in the market. However, uniqueness is not a sufficient condition for resources to yield a sustainable competitive advantage and economic profits. We now discuss the basic criteria unique resources should meet to yield a sustainable stream of above normal returns.

Imperfectly Competitive Factor Markets

As Barney (1986a) points out, the attainability and desirability of a competitive advantage can only be assessed by taking into account the cost of obtaining the resources needed to implement it. For resources to yield above normal returns, they have to be acquired at a price below their discounted net present value. Therefore, unless factor markets are imperfectly competitive, buyers will not be able to extract superior economic performance from buying the factor.

This argument can be further elaborated by distinguishing between *tradeable* and *nontradeable* resources. Some resources are tradeable, in the sense that they may be acquired in factor markets. For example, a firm may be able to increase its production capacity by acquiring a new factory, or it may be able to gain access to a new technology through a licensing agreement. Barney defines a 'strategic factor market' as a 'market where the resources necessary to implement a strategy are acquired' (1986a: 1231). *Nontradeable* resources are resources which, due to factor markets' incompleteness, cannot be sold or bought in factor markets (Caves, 1980; Itami, 1987; Dierickx and Cool, 1989a). A firm's reputation or brand loyalty are examples of nontradeable resources. They have to be accumulated inside the firm in a complex and time-consuming process.

The distinction between tradeable and nontradeable resources is not always obvious. Consider the case of organizational capabilities. Capabilities are sets of highly routinized and complex activities, which define a set of things the organization is capable of doing confidently (Nelson and Winter, 1982; Prahalad and Hamel, 1990; Nelson, 1991; Collis, 1994; Lado and Wilson, 1994; Teece et al., 1997). Behind this notion is Nelson and Winter's (1982) idea that firms can be seen as a hierarchy of practiced organizational routines. Routines are intrinsically social and collective phenomena created and developed over time inside the firm. They are patterns of interaction that reside in group behavior, although certain sub-routines, involving individual skills, may reside in individual behavior. Because of their complexity and tacit dimension, the creation and development of organizational capabilities is a difficult and time-consuming process. For the same reason, they cannot be fully captured in codified form. Does this mean that organizational capabilities are nontradeable? Not necessarily. In particular, the imitation of a capability under the guidance of the firm being imitated may still be possible.[7] For example, a firm characterized by high manufacturing flexibility may be able to transfer the skills and organizational routines that make up that capability to another firm by training the workers of the recipient, by helping the recipient in changing the way the work is organized, etc.

Barney's 'imperfect factor markets' argument is straightforward in the case of tradeable resources. When can a firm make above normal returns by buying a tradeable resource and deploying it in product markets? Unless there is some imperfection in the corresponding factor market, buyers will not be able to extract superior economic performance from buying the factor. In the absence of imperfections, the cost of the resource (its market price) will approximately equal the value of the resource once it is used to implement product market strategies. Firms may be able to make above normal returns by buying a tradeable resource only if the corresponding factor market is imperfectly competitive – if firms 'have different expectations about the future value of the resource' (Barney, 1986a: 1231).[8] Thus, as forcefully argued by Rumelt (1984) and Barney (1986a), firms may obtain above normal returns by buying a tradeable resource if they are *lucky* or if they have *exceptional foresight* to buy the resource before its value becomes clear to a large set of firms.

Strategically, it is of little value to know that one has to be either lucky or have foresight. Few businesses are systematically lucky or have exceptional foresight all the time. If a firm does not have superior information about the value of a tradeable resource, does that preclude shareholder value creation? Not necessarily: similar to the use of market power in product markets, a firm with a *privileged market position* may be able to wield power with the owner of the resource, paying a lower price. A firm with a dominant market position based on, for instance, economies of scale or accumulated production capacity may be able to obtain favorable prices.

For firms that do not have such bargaining power, there is yet another alternative: the synergistic use of the tradeable resource with their *unique complementary resources*. For example, a latecomer to a booming ski resort who wants to put up a hotel will probably have to pay a high access fee to get land. However, if this business has some unique resources (a unique booking system, casino rights, etc.), then it may still be able to realize above-average returns by combining the land with its unique resources. Similarly, the makers of PC clones may create shareholder value if, for example, they can draw on unique skills in manufacturing to make the PCs.

As noted by Dierickx and Cool (1989a, b) and Barney (1989), the imperfect factor market argument can be extended to nontradeable resources. To accumulate a given nontradeable resource, like a reputation for quality or firm specific labor, a firm must engage in a consistent pattern of activities for a long period of time. As Barney puts it, '[t]he strategic factor markets model enters the analysis by comparing the total cost of developing these kinds of assets – summed, over time, as "step by step" firms create these assets – with the value they create when used to implement strategies' (1989: 1512). In other words, 'Barney's fundamental argument about competition for resources may be extended from competition in factor markets to competition in resource accumulation' (Dierickx and Cool, 1989b). However, in the case of nontradeable resources, better expectations about the value of the activities the firm undertakes in each period to accumulate the resource may result, not only from superior information about the *use* of the accumulated stock, but also from superior information about its *accumulation* process. Since these resources have to be acquired and accumulated over time, it is less likely that the full value of such resources will be anticipated in the cost of acquiring them. That is to say, the strategic factor markets associated with the accumulation of nontradeable resources are imperfect, and, therefore, investments in such assets may lead to above normal returns (Barney, 1989; Peteraf, 1993).

Imperfect Mobility

Resource uniqueness and factor market imperfections are conditions for resources to yield a competitive advantage and above normal returns. However, the profits earned from resources depend, not only on their ability to establish competitive advantage, but also on how long that advantage can be sustained. The resource-based view offers important insights about which resources can generate a *sustainable* stream of above normal returns.[9] The sustainability of a competitive advantage depends on how easily rival firms are able to build a similar resource position. The simplest way to obtain the resources necessary to implement a given strategy is to acquire them. Under the assumption that all the resources necessary to implement a strategy can be bought and sold in an open market, competitors can replicate any asset bundle simply by purchasing the required components at going market prices. Furthermore, as the oil refiner case presented above illustrates, firms may well realize the value of their asset stocks by selling them in the appropriate markets, instead of deploying them in product markets. Therefore a sustainable competitive advantage must be underpinned *by imperfectly mobile* resources – resources that are not traded in well-functioning markets.

Following Peteraf (1993: 183), we distinguish between 'perfectly immobile' and 'imperfectly mobile' resources. Resources are perfectly immobile if they cannot be traded. Nontradeable resources cannot, by definition, be transferred between companies. They have to be developed and accumulated inside the firm in an often complex and time-consuming process. Imperfectly mobile resources are resources that are tradeable but more valuable within the firm that currently employs them than they would be in other employ. Imperfect mobility may result from firm-specific investments by owners of factors employed by the firm (Montgomery and Wernerfelt, 1988); from the transaction costs associated with the transfer of those resources (Williamson, 1975, 1985; Rumelt, 1987); or from cospecialization of assets (Teece, 1986; Peteraf, 1993).[10]

Since perfectly immobile and imperfectly mobile resources cannot be acquired in factor markets or are less valuable to other users, they cannot be bid away from their current employer. They remain bound to the firm and can, thus, be a source of sustained competitive advantage. Rival firms may, however, either attempt to imitate them, by accumulating similar asset stocks of their own, or they may try to substitute for them with other assets. To the extent that the accumulation process of nontradeable or imperfectly mobile resources is complex and time consuming, and to the extent that rival firms cannot find substitutes for those resources, resource positions based on nontradeable or imperfectly mobile resources are sustainable.

Nonimitability

The limits to *imitation* have received extensive attention in the literature (Rumelt, 1984, 1987; Ghemawat, 1986; Dierickx and Cool, 1989a). Rumelt (1984) coined the term 'isolating mechanisms' to refer to the impediments to immediate imitation of a firm's resource position. Property rights to scarce resources, response lags, and information asymmetries constitute examples of isolating mechanisms. Isolating mechanisms are to a firm what an entry barrier is to an industry and a mobility barrier is to a strategic group or market segment. Bain (1956) defines barriers to entry as anything that allows firms already in the market to earn above normal profits without facing the threat of entry.[11] Caves and Porter (1977) extend the notion of barriers to entry from the industry level to groups or segments within an industry. They define mobility barriers as anything that allows firms in a group to earn above normal profits without facing the threat of entry into that group, both from firms in other groups in the same industry, or from outside the industry. Finally, Rumelt argues that there is no reason to limit mobility barriers to groups of firms, and proposes the concept of isolating mechanisms as an extension of the notion of mobility barriers to the firm level.

Different authors propose different classifications of isolating mechanisms (Ghemawat, 1986; Rumelt, 1987; Dierickx and Cool, 1989a). Dierickx and Cool relate the imitability of a resource position to the characteristics of the process by which the underlying resources may be accumulated. The starting point of their discussion is the distinction between state variables and control variables which has a long history in optimal control theory (Bellman, 1957; Pontryagin et al., 1962). The stock of an asset can be seen as a state variable, while the flow, i.e., the change in the value of the stock at a given point in time, can be seen as a control variable. Although a firm's competitive position depends on its accumulated stock of assets, at any point in time the firm only controls the flows. It takes a consistent pattern of resource flows (advertising, training) to accumulate a given stock of nontradeable resources (brand loyalty, firm specific labor). Elaborating on Dierickx and Cool's discussion of the accumulation process of nontradeable resources, we distinguish two main types of isolating mechanisms: economies of resource accumulation and barriers to imitation.

Economies of Resource Accumulation

Economies of resource accumulation result from isolating mechanisms that, once a firm develops a competitive advantage, set in motion a dynamic that *increases* the magnitude of that advantage relative to other firms. Clearly, when economies of resource accumulation are important, building asset stocks starting from low initial levels may be difficult. Dierickx and Cool (1989a) identify two types of economies of resource accumulation: 'asset mass efficiencies' and 'interconnectedness of asset stocks'.

Asset Mass Efficiencies Sustainability will be enhanced to the extent that firms which develop a high level of an asset stock before competitors achieve an increase in the asset stock at a lower cost than competitors. This is a 'success breeds success' phenomenon: the higher the stock, the higher its growth, leading to a higher stock, etc. Asset mass efficiencies may result from learning curve effects. A firm that has a higher cumulative output than its competitors will move further down the learning curve and achieve lower unit costs. Therefore, a firm with greater cumulative experience can profitably charge lower prices than its competitors, further increasing its cumulative output and its cost advantage. Similar effects may arise in industries where a firm's cumulative sales are an important determinant of its current sales. This happens when 'word of mouth' increases product awareness, in the presence of network externalities, or when buyers incur substantial switching costs.

Interconnectedness of Asset Stocks The pace of an asset's accumulation may be influenced, not only by the existing stock of that asset, but also by the level of *other* asset stocks. For example, to the extent that customer requests or suggestions are a valuable input for the development of new products and processes, firms that have an extensive service network may find it easier to develop technological know-how. Asset stocks are interconnected when the difficulty of building one stock is related, not to the initial level of that stock, but to the low initial level of another stock which is its complement.

Barriers to Imitation

Instead of setting in motion a dynamic that *increases* the magnitude of the advantage relative to other firms, barriers to imitation simply impede competitors from duplicating a firm's valuable resources. We discuss three types of barriers to imitation: time compression diseconomies, causal ambiguity and exclusivity.

Time Compression Diseconomies Latecomers who wish to shorten the time needed to build the resources may have to accept diseconomies of time compression. This happens when maintaining a given rate of investment for a given interval produces a larger increase in the resource level than maintaining twice the investment rate over half the interval. Time compression diseconomies reflect the 'law of diminishing returns' when one output, *viz.* time, is held constant. For example, 'crash' R&D programs are typically less effective than programs where annual outlays are lower but spread over a proportionally longer period of time. Similarly, firms do not achieve the same learning from consultants if these double their efforts in half the period compared to an effort of lower but sustained intensity.

Causal Ambiguity It may be difficult for imitating firms to fully identify which factors play a role in the accumulation process. Even if rival firms are able to identify all relevant variables, they may not be able to control them. In such cases, imitation becomes next to impossible. As Reed and DeFillippi (1990) point out, causal ambiguity may result from three characteristics of resources: tacitness, complexity, and specificity. Tacitness refers to the implicit and noncodifiable accumulation of skills that results from learning by doing. Complexity results from having a large number of interdependent skills and assets. Finally, specificity refers to the transaction-specific skills and assets that are utilized in the production processes and provision of services for particular customers. Individually or in combination, these characteristics can produce ambiguity between resource accumulation actions and outcomes. This, in turn, creates barriers to imitation.[12]

Exclusivity Barriers to imitation may result, not only from time compression diseconomies or causal ambiguity, but also from *exclusive* access to resources or markets. Legal restrictions, such as patents, copyrights, trademarks or licenses to operate in a given market, often constitute a source of exclusivity.[13] In addition, firms often benefit from long-term exclusive contracts with suppliers or customers. To the extent that such exclusive contacts allow the firm to obtain access to inputs or customers on more favorable terms than competitors, they may be a source of sustainable competitive advantage. Notice, however, that the sources of exclusivity are often tradeable. For example, patents, copyrights, trademarks and contracts giving the firm favorable access to suppliers or customers can be bought and sold. Therefore, firms may well realize the rent potential of these assets by selling them in the appropriate factor markets, instead of deploying them in product markets. In such cases, as we discussed above, the sources of exclusivity should not be seen as sources of competitive advantages in *product markets.*

Nonsubstitutability

Even when imitation is not possible, competing firms may develop what Barney (1991: 111) calls 'strategically equivalent resources'. Two resources are strategically equivalent when they allow firms to implement the same strategies. According to Barney, substitutability can take at least two forms. On the one hand, a competing firm may be able to develop a *similar* resource that enables it to conceive for and implement the same strategy. For example, even though it may be difficult for a firm to imitate another firm's high quality top management team, it may still be able to develop its own unique top management team. The two teams may be different, but strategically equivalent. On the other hand, a competing

firm may rely on a very *different* resource to implement the same strategy of another firm. For example, a very clear vision of the future of a given industry may result from the insights of a charismatic leader or from a formal planning process. A firm not having a charismatic leader may, therefore, rely on a strategic planning process to formulate and implement the same strategy.

In sum, for unique resources to yield a sustainable stream of above normal returns they have to meet several criteria. First, they have to be acquired in imperfectly competitive factor markets. Otherwise, their price equals their discounted net present value and buyers will not be able to extract superior economic performance from buying the factor. Second, a sustainable competitive advantage must be underpinned by imperfectly mobile resources. To the extent that similar resources can be easily bought and sold, competitors could quickly deploy a similar resource bundle simply by buying the required components at the corresponding market prices. Furthermore, a firm that owns or controls a resource may well realize the value on its resource by selling it in the appropriate factor markets, instead of deploying it in the product market. Third, for resources to yield a sustainable competitive advantage they have to be difficult to imitate. Unless the accumulation process of resources is complex and time consuming, competitors may accumulate similar asset stocks of their own, eliminating the firm's competitive advantage. Finally, resources must be nonsubstitutable. Even when imitation is not possible, competitors may replicate a firm's competitive position by developing strategic equivalent resources – resources that allow competitors to implement the same strategies.[14]

Empirical Evidence

The resource-based view has been insightful in explaining the conditions under which firm resources can serve as sources of sustainable competitive advantages. However, despite the renewed theoretical interest on the internal analysis of firm resources, relatively few empirical studies on this perspective exist. Most empirical studies on the resource-based view discuss the relationship between resources, competitive advantage and performance (Henderson and Cockburn, 1994;

Maijoor and van Witteloostuijn, 1996; Brush and Artz, 1999; Yeoh and Roth, 1999). These papers support the idea that nonimitable firm-specific assets and capabilities are important sources of competitive advantage and superior performance. Furthermore, they identify the assets and capabilities that are critical in specific industry contexts.

For example, in a study of the role of firm-specific resources on research productivity in the pharmaceutical industry, Henderson and Cockburn (1994) found support for the importance of resources as a source of advantage in research productivity. Firms with the right set of complementary capabilities are able to implement product development strategies that are not available to firms that do not possess those resource bundles. Yeoh and Roth also found that 'sustained competitive advantage in the pharmaceutical industry requires firm strategies that capitalize on resources and capabilities' (1999: 649). More specifically, the authors found 'important resources to be those that depend on scale imperatives (for example, salesforce and R&D expenditures), are difficult to understand (for example, development of therapeutically differentiated drugs), and in which the firm possesses clear ownership and control (for example, knowledge and understanding of drug development in certain therapeutic areas)' (1999: 649–50).

The literature on first-mover advantages provides important insights about the interaction between resource accumulation and timing of market entry.[15] The bulk of this literature focuses on the conditions under which early entrance can enhance the firm's accumulation of superior resources. Several studies provide evidence that early entrants may gain a head start in developing a set of organizational capabilities that are key to the product or service in question.[16] For example, Levin et al. (1987) and Lieberman and Montgomery (1988) showed that learning and experience curve effects in manufacturing or marketing are typically important sources of advantages. However, '[t]here is (…) no guarantee that these potential advantages of pioneers will be sufficient to ensure a strong position as the market evolves, [because] [e]arly entrants are often overtaken by competitors with more potent resources or capabilities' (Lieberman and Montgomery, 1998: 1113). In fact, early entrants often miss the best opportunities,

which are obscured by technological and demand uncertainties. As summarized by Lieberman and Montgomery, '[t]he sustainability of a first-mover advantage depends upon the initial resources captured by the pioneer, plus the resources and capabilities subsequently developed, relative to the quality of resources and capabilities held by later entrants' (1998: 1113).

The first-mover advantages literature also discusses to what extent the initial resources of a firm affect its optimal (and actual) timing of entry. Lieberman and Montgomery (1988) propose that pioneering is likely to be a desirable strategy for firms whose relative skills are in new product development, whereas firms with relative strengths in marketing and manufacturing may prefer to enter later, after the initial technological and demand uncertainties have been resolved. These ideas have been tested by Robinson et al. (1992). They found that early entrants had significantly different skill and resource profiles than later entrants. As expected, firms with greater marketing skills and shared manufacturing tended to be followers, but, surprisingly, R&D skills had no discernible effect on entry timing. Interestingly, the overall quality of resources did not differ much between early movers and latecomers, suggesting that the idea that pioneers are intrinsically stronger or more proficient than later entrants is not necessarily true.

A related issue is to what extent the resource base of incumbents affects the timing and success of their entry in the new product generation. Thomas (1995, 1996) found that in the ready-to-eat cereal industry, where most new product generations are incremental, larger incumbents were typically the first to enter. However, studies on different industries suggest that if the shift to the new generation is radical enough, incumbents' existing capabilities may make it more difficult for them to adapt (Henderson and Clark, 1990; Henderson, 1993; Christensen, 1993).

PRIVILEGED MARKET POSITIONS
AND COMPETITIVE ADVANTAGE

The resource-based view of strategy associates the sustainability of competitive advantage to the ownership or control of unique and hard-to-replicate resources. However, a competitive advantage may be sustainable, not because rival firms cannot replicate the underlying resource position, but because they do not have the incentive to do so. In such cases, the source of the sustainable competitive advantage is a *privileged market position*. The advantage follows from industry structure, rather than from strategic resources.

Strategic Commitments

In their efforts to create a competitive edge relative to competitors, firms often make *strategic commitments*. Strategic commitments are decisions that have long-term impact and are difficult (or costly) to reverse. The decision to investment in production capacity, to adopt a cost-reducing process innovation, to introduce a new product, or to launch a new advertising campaign constitute examples of strategic commitments. All these decisions require significant up-front expenditures and result in the creation of highly specific assets. Once these assets have been created, the firm's ability to use them outside their initial intended use is limited. Therefore, the decision to invest in such assets involves important *sunk costs*.

Because of their irreversibility, these decisions change a firm's competitive incentives. A capacity expansion, for instance, may increase a firm's incentives to cut price. This, in turn, may intensify pricing rivalry in the industry, or reduce other firms' incentives to expand their production capacity. As this example illustrates, to the extent that strategic commitments are visible and understandable, they may have an important impact on the nature and intensity of competition in the industry. Therefore, if firms are farsighted, they will anticipate the effect of strategic commitments on market competition and use them to shape competitors' expectations and behavior. A commitment that induces competitors not to introduce a new product, to abandon a capacity expansion plan, or to cut back on the amount of investment on a cost-reducing process innovation is likely to be beneficial to the firm making the investment.[17] By inducing competitors to behave less aggressively, such strategic commitment

may improve the firm's competitive situation. In particular, a commitment that creates a competitive advantage may simultaneously eliminate competitors' incentives to make a similar investment. The underlying mechanism is *preemption*. By occupying existing and potential market positions, a firm reduces the range of investment opportunities open to rivals, avoiding competitive challenges. In such cases, the sustainable competitive advantage is based, not on unique firm-specific resources, but on the firm's dominance and market position.

To illustrate this argument, consider the market situation represented in Figure 3.1.[18] Two firms, a large firm and a small firm, produce a homogeneous product and face the same long-run average cost curve (LAC). The downward sloping straight line is the market demand curve. Production technology is characterized by economies of scale, with the long-run average cost curve declining until the minimum efficient scale of 4000 units per year is reached. The large firm has an installed capacity of 5000 per year and the small firm has an installed capacity of 1000 per year. The large firm's volume exceeds minimum efficient scale (MES), while the small firm's volume is less than MES. The large firm benefits from economies of scale and, therefore, has a cost advantage relative to the small firm. However, both firms make positive profits. If both firms produce at full capacity, the market price would be equal to $10, higher than the small firm's average cost. The small firm may, however, decide to invest in additional capacity and expand output to MES in an attempt to lower its average cost. If the small firm increases capacity to 4000 units, and both firms produce at full capacity, the market price falls to $4.25. Since the market price falls below the minimum of the long-run average cost ($5), the small firm is unable to earn an adequate rate of return on its investment in the new plant. Thus, imitation is deterred.

As this simple numerical example illustrates, economies of scale (or scope) may discourage a smaller competitor from seeking to grow larger to replicate the cost advantage of a firm that has obtained a high market share.[19] When the minimum efficient scale is a significant proportion of the industry demand and a firm has secured a large share of the market,

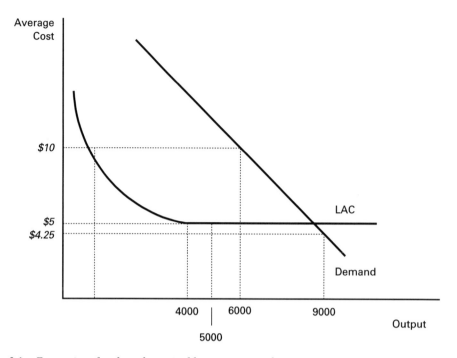

Figure 3.1   *Economies of scale and sustainable competitive advantage*

imitation may be deterred. While it may be possible for a small firm to imitate the source of the large firm's advantage, it may not have the incentive to do so. Imitation would result in increased market competition and in lower economic profits.

Economies of scale and scope constitute a source of privileged market positions because they force small firms to increase their scale of production or to increase product variety in order to achieve unit cost parity with the dominant firms. Notice, however, that the only reason why small firms cannot earn an adequate rate of return on such investments is that the small firm cannot recover its upfront costs if it subsequently decides to reduce its scale (or scope) of production or exit the market. A small firm whose upfront costs were not sunk could expand capacity, undercut the large firm's prices, and sell the capacity and recover its investment if the incumbent firms retaliate. Therefore, as Spulber (1989) points out, it is the existence of *sunk costs*, not scale or scope economies *per se*, that constitutes the source of the privileged market position. Notice, however, that, in most markets, economies of scale and scope can only be achieved by making irreversible commitments. Therefore, the

distinction between whether economies of scale and scope represent the source of privileged market positions or sunk costs represent the source of privileged market positions is not that critical. The same reasoning applies to all the other sources of privileged market positions.

Sources of Privileged Market Positions

In the section above we saw that *economies of scale and scope* may discourage a smaller competitor from seeking to grow larger to replicate the cost advantage of a firm that has obtained a high market share or a larger product variety. Industrial organization economists have identified several other potential sources of privileged market positions. Some of them are briefly discussed below.

A dominant position may result from *absolute cost advantages*, or cost advantages independent of scale, that result from the fact that certain firms have already made investments that reduce their cost of production. For example, firms may have incurred insignificant advertising expenditures (Salop,

1979; Schmalensee, 1983), or they may have accumulated physical capital (Spence, 1977, 1979; Dixit, 1979, 1980; Eaton and Lipsey, 1981). The strategic role of capacity has been extensively studied by industrial organization economists.[20] Large investments in production capacity ahead of growth of market demand may allow a large firm to credibly commit to compete aggressively if entry occurs or if a small competitor expands capacity. Rivals may interpret such investments as bad news about the profitability of the market, refraining from making similar investments.

Many industries are characterized by *network externalities*. Network externalities are present when the benefit a consumer derives from the use of a product increases with the number of other consumers purchasing compatible items – with the installed base of the selected technology. Network externalities arise 'when buyers wish to "communicate" directly with each other, such as when files are transferred from one computer to another or software is shared among users, … [or] when a large installed base allows manufacturers of complementary goods to exploit economies of scale, leading, for example, to a higher density of repair facilities for more popular automobile models or a greater variety of software to run on more popular computer hardware platforms' (Katz and Shapiro, 1992: 55).[21]

In such markets, firms' installed bases are critical objects of strategic rivalry: firms with large installed base of consumers have a differentiation advantage relative to firms with smaller installed base. Clearly, small firms may try to increase their customer base, for example, by launching aggressive advertising campaigns. However, as in the case of economies of scale, to the extent that such decisions involve nonrecoverable costs, the reaction of large firms may render such decisions unprofitable. The dynamics of competition in markets with network externalities has been extensively studied in the economics literature (Farrell and Saloner, 1985, 1986; Katz and Shapiro, 1985, 1986, 1994; Economides and White, 1994; Kristiansen, 1998).

A privileged market position may also result from the *proliferation of product varieties*. In many industries, firms choose to produce several products that are differentiated according to brand, product-specific characteristics or location. Several authors have argued that dominant firms can crowd a product space in order to gain market share at the expense of their rivals (Schmalensee, 1978; Shaked and Sutton, 1990; Eaton and Lipsey, 1979; Gilbert and Matutes, 1993). By cornering the right niches in the product space, a market leader may leave smaller rivals with few opportunities for establishing a significant market presence. Notice, however, that the dominant firm's investment has a preemptive value only if the investment corresponds to an irreversible commitment. A market leader that can withdraw some of its product offerings at zero or low cost may not be able to use the proliferation of product varieties as a source of a sustainable competitive advantage.[22]

In sum, there are several situations where a sustainable competitive advantage results, not from the deployment of unique firm specific assets and capabilities, but from privileged market positions. Replication is feasible, but uneconomical. In such cases, the competitive advantage follows from industry structure rather than from strategic resources.

CONCLUSION

A fundamental question in the strategic management field is how firms achieve and sustain competitive advantage. The resource-based view of strategy has answered this question in terms of what Ghemawat calls *intrinsic inimitability*, 'inimitability stemming from factors such as unique historical circumstances, causal ambiguity, and the social complexity of organizational phenomena that may make it impossible for firms to systematically manage or influence them' (1997: 84). This research stream provides important insights about the preconditions a resource must fulfill in order to be a potential source of sustainable competitive advantages and about the major mechanisms that drive the accumulation and erosion of resources. However, as Ghemawat correctly points out, 'in stressing the strict infeasibility of imitation, … ["resource-based" theorists] exclude consideration of the important possibility that imitation may be feasible but uneconomical' (1997: 84).

In contrast, industrial organization economists have identified a number of dimensions in which commitments that are irrevocable for nontrivial periods of time may lead to privileged market positions and sustainable competitive advantages, not because competitors cannot accumulate and deploy a similar resource bundle, but because they do not have the incentive to do so. While the existing literature is predominantly framed in terms of barriers to entry, it provides nevertheless many important insights about how privileged market positions may lead to sustainable competitive advantages. The emphasis of economists on industry structure, rather than nontradeable and nonimitable resources, as the explanation for competitive advantage and inter-industry profitability differences results, at least in part, from their assumption that relatively few factors of production have inelastic supply (Barney, 1997: 40). By focusing on the complex and time-consuming accumulation process of capabilities and other information-based resources, resource-based research indicates that, contrary to economists' beliefs, intrinsic inimitability is often a fundamental source of competitive advantage and profitability differences.

In this perspective, the strategic management and the industrial organization economics approaches to the problem of how to construct sustainable competitive advantages are largely complementary. Both unique resources and privileged market positions should be seen as important sources of sustainable competitive advantages. However, while we have a rich taxonomy of markets and substantial theoretical and empirical knowledge about market structures, we need a better understanding of the accumulation process and the competitive implications of different types of resources. Although the number of articles that focus on specific resources is rapidly growing (Barney, 1986b; Oliver, 1997; Majumdar, 1998; McEvily and Zaheer, 1999), our understanding about the accumulation process and deployment of specific resources is still limited. As Wernerfelt puts it:

> To make the resource-based view more useful we need to map the space of resources in more detail. At the moment this work is going on in several directions. On the theory side we are developing a better understanding of specific resources (such as culture; Barney, 1986b), the fact that rigidities in acquiring resources may be different from the rigidities in shedding resources (Montgomery, 1995; Rumelt, 1995), and the related fact that some resources at some points may have negative value (Leonard-Barton, 1992). On the empirical side, we are starting to use much better measures of specific resources (Davis and Thomas, 1993; Farjoun, 1994; Helfat, 1994; Henderson and Cockburn, 1994). (Wernerfelt, 1995: 172)

The enrichment of our understanding about which resources lie at the heart of the firm's competitive position, and, therefore, are worth protecting and developing, clearly requires more emphasis on empirical research. Despite the renewed theoretical interest on the internal analysis of firm resources, relatively few empirical studies on this perspective exist. As Henderson and Cockburn pointed out some years ago, while '[s]tudies of the evolution of capability at individual firms have greatly enriched our understanding of the nature of particular competencies, (…) relatively little empirical work has attempted to combine the richness of measures of competence derived from fieldwork with large-scale statistical studies of competition' (1994: 63). In spite of the recent increase in the number of empirical studies available, this statement remains valid.

Another important area for further research is the relationship between unique resources and the competitive environment. As noted by Henderson and Mitchell (1997: 6), this issue has not received sufficient attention in the literature. The understanding of the competitive implications of different resource positions under different competitive situations requires an effective integration of the industrial organization research on market interaction and competition with the strategic management research on firm-specific resources. This raises a methodological issue: which disciplinary approaches are better suited to study the complex interactions between unique resources and market competition? While several approaches may yield valuable insights, some authors (Conner, 1991; Mahoney and Pandian, 1992) argue that the resource-based view can be enriched by incorporating game-theoretic models that study the implications of the interactions among competitors' resource positions and competitive strategies under given environmental constraints. As Conner puts it:

It is apparent that a resource-based approach views a firm's performance as resulting from the simultaneous interaction of at least three forces: the firm's own asset base; the asset bases of competitors; and constraints emanating from the broader industry and public policy environment. Although further development of the resource-based approach will benefit from employment of a variety of research methods, developing the theoretical implications of such complex interactions is an area in which the resource-based theory may gain from application of the new IO's game-theoretic techniques. (1991: 145)[23]

NOTES

1 Some authors make a distinction between resources and capabilities wherein resources are firm-specific assets and capabilities are sets of highly routinized and complex activities that define sets of things an organization is capable of doing confidently (Amit and Schoemaker, 1993; Markides and Williamson, 1996; Teece et al., 1997). In contrast, we use the term resources broadly to refer to both assets and organizational routines.

2 It is noteworthy that although only in the last fifteen years the focus on the strategic role of firms' idiosyncratic resources came to the core of the strategic management field, the roots of the 'resource-based' view can be traced back, among other contributions, to David Ricardo's (1817) discussion of resource deployment and rents, to Selznick's (1957) notion of 'distinctive competencies', to Penrose's (1959) theory about the growth of the firm, or to Nelson and Winter's (1982) evolutionary theory of the firm.

3 As Barney (1997: 140) points out, in contrast with strategic management researchers, economists tend to assume that relatively few factors of production have inelastic supply. This explains their emphasis on privileged market positions as the source of sustainable competitive advantages.

4 See Dierickx and Cool (1994) for a more complete discussion of these problems.

5 This is true, in particular, for *tradeable* resources. Resources are tradeable whenever they may be bought or sold in the corresponding market. In the next section we elaborate on the distinction between tradeable, non-tradeable and imperfectly mobile resources.

6 The perhaps most systematic exposition of the characteristics of the assets that give rise to sustainable competitive advantage is due to Peteraf (1993). See also Barney (1991, 1997, ch. 5).

7 Nelson and Winter (1982, ch. 5) elaborate on the distinction between *replication* – the situation where a firm is trying to apply a routine it already possesses on a larger scale – from *imitation* – the situation where one firm is trying to copy a routine of some other firm. What distinguishes imitation from replication 'is the fact that the target routine is not in any substantial sense available as a template' (1982: 123). Therefore, imitation is more problematic than replication. *Imitation with the active support of the firm being imitated* is seen as an intermediate case between imitation and replication.

8 Barney argues that all the other apparent factor market imperfections (such as the control of unique resources by a given firm, or the access to lower cost capital by a given firm) are special cases of differences in expectations held by firms about the future value of a strategic resource.

9 Important contributions on this topic include Rumelt (1984, 1987), Ghemawat (1986), Dierickx and Cool (1989a), Reed and DeFillippi (1990), Hall (1992, 1993), and Collis (1994).

10 Cospecialized assets are assets which must be used together or which have a higher value when used together (Teece, 1986). If these resources are transaction specific (they have no other equivalent uses), and if at least one of the assets is firm-specific, they are imperfectly mobile (Peteraf, 1993).

11 Bain identified four types of barriers to entry: economies of scale (e.g., fixed costs), absolute cost advantages, product differentiation advantages, and capital requirements.

12 Lippman and Rumelt (1982) use the notion of 'uncertain imitability' to explain why performance differences may persist even when the market is perfectly competitive. Essentially, uncertain imitability also refers to this causal ambiguity about the process of asset stock accumulation (see also Rumelt, 1984: 567).

13 The available evidence on the importance of patent protection indicates that patents are not the exclusive, or even the primary, device for protecting inventions in most industries, and that patent protection is a much more important source of private returns to R&D in some industries, as the pharmaceutical industry, than in others (Mansfield et al., 1981; Levin et al., 1987; Lieberman and Montgomery, 1988; Schankerman, 1998). In general, firms use various methods to protect their innovations, including secrecy, licensing agreements and different forms of first-mover advantage.

14 Since organizational capabilities (and other information-based resources) are accumulated over time in a firm-specific and path-dependent manner and cannot be bought or sold in factor markets, they often meet these criteria. Therefore, such resources tend to be sources of sustainable competitive advantages. Understanding the mechanisms through which organizations develop

capabilities has been a major focus of recent theorizing in the strategic management field (Nonaka, 1994; Levinthal and March, 1993; McGrath et al., 1995; Teece et al., 1997; Zollo and Winter, 1999). The firm is viewed, not simply as a contractual entity, but as a repository of knowledge stocks that are accumulated inside the firm, in a complex and time-consuming process. Several authors push these arguments further to propose a 'knowledge-based' theory of the firm (Kogut and Zander, 1992, 1996; Conner and Prahalad, 1996; Grant, 1996). See also Foss (1996a, b). This literature is reviewed in Chapter 7 and, therefore, we do not discuss it here.

15 Our discussion of this literature closely follows the first part of the survey by Lieberman and Montgomery (1998).

16 The first-mover advantage literature also discusses the conditions under which pioneers are able to create privileged market positions, for example by preempting superior positions in geographic space or customer perceptual space. The sources of privileged market positions are discussed below.

17 The fact that there is a preemptive advantage to moving first when costs are sunk has been shown by Industrial Organization economists in a variety of contexts. Some of them are discussed below.

18 This numerical example is taken from Besanko et al. (2000: 460–1).

19 The predominance of large corporations in many manufacturing and service industries reflects the impact of economies of scale. Economies of scale exist when proportionate increases in the amounts of inputs employed in a production process result in a more than proportionate increase in total output. As a result, firms that produce more of a good or service benefit from lower unit costs.

20 While game-theoretic analysis of preemptive capacity expansions are abundant (see also, among others, Ware, 1984; Allen, 1993; and Bagwell and Ramey, 1996), empirical evidence is not (Lieberman, 1987; Smiley, 1988). One exception is the US titanium dioxide industry in the 1970s (Ghemawat, 1984, 1990).

21 For a discussion of the sources of network externalities see, for example, Katz and Shapiro (1985).

22 See Judd (1985) for a discussion of the importance of commitment in determining whether product proliferation can function as a preemption strategy.

23 For discussions on the importance and the limitations of the use of game-theoretic modeling in the strategic management field see also Shapiro (1989), Camerer (1991), Saloner (1991), Porter (1991), Rumelt et al. (1991), and Ghemawat and McGahan (1998).

References

Allen, B. (1993) 'Capacity precommitment as an entry barrier for price-setting firms', *International Journal of Industrial Organization*, 11: 63–72.

Amit, R. and Schoemaker, P. J. H. (1993) 'Strategic assets and organizational rent', *Strategic Management Journal*, 14(1): 33–45.

Bagwell, K. and Ramey, G. (1996) 'Capacity, entry, and forward induction', *Rand Journal of Economics*, 27(4): 660–80.

Bain, J. (1956) *Barriers to New Competition*. Cambridge, MA: Harvard University Press.

Barney, J. (1986a) 'Strategic factor markets: expectations, luck and business strategy', *Management Science*, 32(10): 1231–41.

Barney, J. (1986b) 'Organizational culture: can it be a source of sustained competitive advantage?', *Academy of Management Review*, 11: 656–65.

Barney, J. (1989) 'Asset stocks and sustained competitive advantage: a comment', *Management Science*, 35: 1511–13.

Barney, J. (1991) 'Firm resources and sustained competitive advantage', *Journal of Management*, 17(1): 99–120.

Barney, J. (1997) *Gaining and Sustaining Competitive Advantage*. Reading, MA: Addison-Wesley.

Bellman, R. (1957) *Dynamic Programming*. Princeton, NJ: Princeton University Press.

Besanko, D., Dranove, D. and Shanley, M. (2000) *The Economics of Strategy*. New York: Wiley.

Brush, T. H. and Artz, K. W. (1999) 'Toward a contingent resource-based theory: the impact of information asymmetry on the value of capabilities in veterinary medicine', *Strategic Management Journal*, 20: 223–50.

Camerer, C. F. (1991) 'Does strategy research need game theory?', *Strategic Management Journal*, 12 (Special Issue): 137–52.

Caves, R. E. (1980) 'Industrial organization, corporate strategy and structure', *Journal of Economic Literature*, 18: 64–92.

Caves, R. E. (1984) 'Economic analysis and the quest for competitive advantage', *American Economic Review*, 74(2): 127–32.

Caves, R. E. and Porter, M. E. (1977) 'From entry barriers to mobility barriers: conjectural decisions and contrived deterrence to new competition', *Quarterly Journal of Economics*, 91: 241–62.

Christensen, C. M. (1993) 'The rigid disk drive industry: a history of commercial and technological turbulence', *Business History Review*, 67: 531–88.

Collis, D. J. (1994) 'How valuable are organizational capabilities?', *Strategic Management Journal*, 15: 143–52.

Conner, K. R. (1991) 'An historical comparison of resource-based theory and five schools of thought within industrial organization economics: do we have a new theory of the firm?', *Journal of Management*, 17(1), 121–54.

Conner, K. R. and Prahalad, C. K. (1996) 'A resource-based theory of the firm: knowledge versus opportunism', *Organization Science*, 7: 477–501.

Daft, R. (1983) *Organization Theory and Design*. New York: West.

Dasgupta, P. and Stiglitz, J. (1980) 'Uncertainty, industrial structure, and the speed of R&D', *Bell Journal of Economics*, 11: 1–28.

Davis, R. and Thomas, L. G. (1993) 'Direct estimation of synergy: a new approach to the diversity–performance debate', *Management Science*, 39: 1334–46.

Dierickx, I. and Cool, K. (1989a) 'Asset stock accumulation and sustainability of competitive advantage', *Management Science*, 35(12): 1504–11.

Dierickx, I. and Cool, K. (1989b) 'Asset stock accumulation and sustainability of competitive advantage: reply', *Management Science*, 35(12): 1514.

Dierickx, I. and Cool, K. (1994) 'Competitive strategy, asset accumulation and firm performance', in H. Daems and H. Thomas (eds), *Strategic Groups, Strategic Moves and Performance*. Oxford: Pergamon Press.

Dixit, A. (1979) 'A model of duopoly suggesting a theory of entry barriers', *Bell Journal of Economics*, 10: 20–32.

Dixit, A. (1980) 'The role of investment in entry deterrence', *Economic Journal*, 90: 95–106.

Eaton, B. C. and Lipsey, R. G. (1979) 'The theory of market preemption: the persistence of excess capacity and monopoly in growing spatial markets', *Econometrica*, 47: 149–58.

Eaton, B. C. and Lipsey, R. G. (1981) 'Capital, commitment, and entry equilibrium', *Bell Journal of Economics*, 12: 593–604.

Economides, N. and White, L. J. (1994) 'Networks and compatibility: implications for antitrust', *European Economic Review*, 38: 651–62.

Farjoun, M. (1994) 'Beyond industry boundaries: human expertise, diversification, and resource-related industry groups', *Organization Science*, 5: 185–99.

Farrell, J. and Saloner, G. (1985) 'Standardization, compatibility, and innovation', *Rand Journal of Economics*, 16: 70–83.

Farrell, J. and Saloner, G. (1986) 'Installed base and compatibility: innovation, product preannouncements, and predation', *American Economic Review*, 76: 940–55.

Foss, N. J. (1996a) 'Knowledge-based approaches to the theory of the firm: some critical comments', *Organization Science*, 7: 470–6.

Foss, N. J. (1996b) 'More critical comments on knowledge-based theories of the firm', *Organization Science*, 7: 519–22.

Ghemawat, P. (1984) 'Capacity expansion in the titanium dioxide industry', *Journal of Industrial Economics*, 32: 145–63.

Ghemawat, P. (1986) 'Sustainable advantage', *Harvard Business Review*, September–October: 53–8.

Ghemawat, P. (1990) 'The snowball effect', *International Journal of Industrial Organization*, 8: 335–51.

Ghemawat, P. (1997) *Games Businesses Play: Cases and Models*. Cambridge, MA: MIT Press.

Ghemawat, P. and McGahan, A. M. (1998) 'Order backlogs and strategic pricing: the case of the US large turbine generator industry', *Strategic Management Journal*, 19(3): 255–68.

Gilbert, R. J. and Matutes, C. (1993) 'Product line rivalry with brand differentiation', *Journal of Industrial Economics*, 41(3): 223–40.

Grant, R. M. (1996) 'Towards a knowledge-based theory of the firm', *Strategic Management Journal*, 17 (Special Issue): 109–22.

Hall, R. (1992) 'The strategic analysis of intangible resources', *Strategic Management Journal*, 13: 135–44.

Hall, R. (1993) 'A framework linking intangible resources and capabilities to sustainable competitive advantage', *Strategic Management Journal*, 14: 607–18.

Helfat, C. (1994) 'Firm specificity in corporate applied R&D', *Organization Science*, 5: 173–84.

Henderson, R. (1993) 'Underinvestment and incompetence as responses to radical innovation: evidence from the photolithographic alignment equipment industry', *Rand Journal of Economics*, 24(2): 248–70.

Henderson, R. and Clark, K. (1990) 'Architectural innovation: the reconfiguration of existing product technologies and the failure of established firms', *Administrative Science Quarterly*, 35: 9–30.

Henderson, R. and Cockburn, I. (1994) 'Measuring competence: exploring firm-effects in pharmaceutical research', *Strategic Management Journal*, 15 (Special Issue): 63–84.

Henderson, R. and Mitchell, W. (1997) 'The interactions of organizational and competitive influences on strategy and performance', *Strategic Management Journal*, 18 (Special Issue): 5–14.

Itami, H. (with Roehl, T. W.) (1987) *Mobilizing Invisible Assets*. Cambridge, MA: Harvard University Press.

Judd, K. (1985) 'Credible spatial preemption', *Rand Journal of Economics*, 16: 153–66.

Katz, M. L. and Shapiro, C. (1985) 'Network externalities, competition, and compatibility', *American Economic Review*, 75: 424–40.

Katz, M. L. and Shapiro, C. (1986) 'Technology adoption in the presence of network externalities', *Journal of Political Economy*, 94: 823–41.

Katz, M. L. and Shapiro, C. (1992) 'Product introduction with network externalities', *Journal of Industrial Economics*, 40(1): 55–83.

Katz, M. L. and Shapiro, C. (1994) 'Systems competition and networks effects', *Journal of Economic Perspectives*, 8: 93–115.

Kay, J. (1993) *Foundations of Corporate Success*. Oxford: Oxford University Press.

Kogut, B. and Zander, U. (1992) 'Knowledge of the firm, combinative capabilities, and the replication of technology', *Organization Science*, 3: 383–97.

Kogut, B. and Zander, U. (1996) 'What do firms do? Coordination, identity, and learning', *Organization Science*, 7: 502–17.

Kristiansen, E. G. (1998) 'R&D in the presence of network externalities: timing and compatibility', *Rand Journal of Economics*, 29(3): 531–47.

Lado, A. and Wilson, M. (1994) 'Human resource systems and sustained competitive advantage: a competency-based perspective', *Academy of Management Review*, 19: 699–727.

Lee, T. and Wilde, L. (1980) 'Market structure and innovation: a reformulation', *Quarterly Journal of Economics*, 194: 429–36.

Leonard-Barton, D. (1992) 'Core capabilities and core rigidities: a paradox in managing new product development', *Strategic Management Journal*, Summer Special Issue, 13: 111–26.

Levin, R., Klevorick, A., Nelson, R. and Winter, S. (1987) 'Appropriating the returns from industrial research and development', *Brookings Papers on Economic Activity: Microeconomics*, 783–820.

Levinthal, D. A. and March, J. G. (1993) 'The myopia of learning', *Strategic Management Journal*, 14: 95–112.

Lieberman, M. (1987) 'Excess capacity as a barrier to entry: an empirical appraisal', *Journal of Industrial Economics*, 35: 607–27.

Lieberman, M. and Montgomery, D. (1988) 'First-mover advantages', *Strategic Management Journal*, 9 (Special Issue): 41–58.

Lieberman, M. and Montgomery, D. (1998) 'First-mover (dis)advantages: retrospective and link with the resource-based view', *Strategic Management Journal*, 19: 1111–25.

Lippman, S. and Rumelt, R. (1982) 'Uncertain imitability: an analysis of interfirm differences in efficiency under competition', *Bell Journal of Economics*, 13: 418–38.

Mahoney, J. T. and Pandian, J. R. (1992) 'The resource-based view within the conversation of strategic management', *Strategic Management Journal*, 13(5): 363–80.

Maijoor, S. and van Witteloostuijn, A. (1996) 'An empirical test of the resource-based theory: strategic regulation in the Dutch audit industry', *Strategic Management Journal*, 17(7): 549–69.

Majumdar, S. K. (1998) 'On the utilization of resources: perspectives from the US telecommunications industry', *Strategic Management Journal*, 19: 809–31.

Mansfield, E., Schwartz, M. and Wagner, S. (1981) 'Imitation costs and patents: an empirical study', *Economic Journal*, 91: 907–18.

Markides, C. C. and Williamson, P. J. (1996) 'Corporate diversification and organization structure: a resource-based view', *Academy of Management Journal*, 39: 340–67.

McEvily, B. and Zaheer, A. (1999) 'Bridging ties: a source of firm heterogeneity in competitive capabilities', *Strategic Management Journal*, 20: 1133–56.

McGrath, R. G., MacMillan, I. and Venkataraman, S. (1995) 'Defining and developing competence: a strategic process paradigm', *Strategic Management Journal*, 16(4): 251–75.

Montgomery, C. A. (1995) 'Of diamonds and rust: a new look at resources', in C. A. Montgomery (ed.), *Resources in an Evolutionary Perspective: A Synthesis of Evolutionary and Resource-Based Approaches to Strategy*. Norwell, MA, and Dordrecht: Kluwer Academic.

Montgomery, C. A. and Wernerfelt, B. (1988) 'Diversification, Ricardian rents, and Tobin's *q*', *Rand Journal of Economics*, 19: 623–32.

Nelson, R. (1991) 'Why do firms differ, and how does it matter?', *Strategic Management Journal*, 12: 61–74.

Nelson, R. and Winter, S. (1982) *An Evolutionary Theory of Economic Change*. Cambridge, MA: Belknap Press.

Nonaka, I. (1994) 'A dynamic theory of organizational knowledge creation', *Organization Science*, 5(1): 14–37.

Oliver, C. (1997) 'Sustainable competitive advantage: combining institutional and resource-based views', *Strategic Management Journal*, 18(9): 697–713.

Penrose, E. T. (1959) *The Theory of the Growth of the Firm*. New York: Wiley.

Peteraf, M. A. (1993) 'The cornerstones of competitive advantage: a resource-based view', *Strategic Management Journal*, 14(3): 179–91.

Pontryagin, L. S., Boltyanskii, V. G., Gamkrelidze, R. V. and Mischenko, E. F. (1962) *The Mathematical Theory of Optimal Processes*. New York: Interscience.

Porter, M. E. (1980) *Competitive Strategy: Techniques for Analyzing Industries and Competitors*. New York: The Free Press.

Porter, M. E. (1985) *Competitive Advantage: Creating and Sustaining Superior Performance*. New York: The Free Press.

Porter, M. E. (1991) 'Towards a dynamic theory of strategy', *Strategic Management Journal*, 12 (Special Issue): 95–117.

Prahalad, C. K. and Hamel, G. (1990) 'The core competence of the corporation', *Harvard Business Review*, 68(3): 79–91.

Reed, R. and DeFillippi, R. J. (1990) 'Causal ambiguity, barriers to imitation, and sustainable competitive advantage', *Academy of Management Review*, 15(1): 88–102.

Reinganum, J. (1981) 'Market structure and the diffusion of new technology', *Bell Journal of Economics*, 12: 618–24.

Reinganum, J. (1983) 'Technology adoption under imperfect information', *Bell Journal of Economics*, 14: 57–69.

Ricardo, D. (1965, Original 1817) *The Principles of Political Economy and Taxation*. Reprinted. London: J. M. Dent and Son.

Robinson, W. T., Fornell, C. and Sullivan, M. (1992) 'Are market pioneers intrinsically stronger than later entrants?', *Strategic Management Journal*, 13(8): 609–24.

Rumelt, R. (1984) 'Toward a strategic theory of the firm', in R. Lamb (ed.), *Competitive Strategic Management*. Englewood Cliffs: Prentice Hall. pp. 556–70.

Rumelt, R. (1987) 'Theory, strategy and entrepreneurship', in D. Teece (ed.), *The Competitive Challenge*. Cambridge, MA: Ballinger. pp. 137–58.

Rumelt, R. P. (1995) 'Inertia and transformation', in C. A. Montgomery (ed.), *Resources in an Evolutionary Perspective: A Synthesis of Evolutionary and Resource-Based Approaches to Strategy*. Norwell, MA, and Dordrecht: Kluwer Academic.

Rumelt, R., Schendel, D. and Teece, D. (1991) 'Strategic management and economics', *Strategic Management Journal*, 12 (Special Issue): 5–29.

Saloner, G. (1991) 'Modeling, game theory, and strategic management', *Strategic Management Journal*, 12 (Special Issue): 119–36.

Salop, S. (1979) 'Strategic entry deterrence', *American Economic Review*, 69: 335–8.

Schankerman, M. (1998) 'How valuable is patent protection? Estimates by technology field', *Rand Journal of Economics*, 29(1): 77–107.

Schmalensee, R. (1978) 'Entry deterrence in the ready-to-eat breakfast cereal industry', *Bell Journal of Economics*, 9: 305–27.

Schmalensee, R. (1983) 'Advertising and entry deterrence: an exploratory model', *Journal of Political Economy*, 91: 636–53.

Selznick, P. (1957) *Leadership in Administration*. New York: Harper & Row.

Shaked, A. and Sutton, J. (1990) 'Multiproduct firms and market structure', *Rand Journal of Economics*, 21: 45–62.

Shapiro, C. (1989) 'The theory of business strategy', *Rand Journal of Economics*, 20: 125–37.

Smiley, R. (1988) 'Empirical evidence on strategic entry deterrence', *International Journal of Industrial Organization*, 6: 167–80.

Spence, A. M. (1977) 'Entry, capacity, investment and oligopolistic pricing', *Bell Journal of Economics*, 8: 534–44.

Spence, A. M. (1979) 'Investment strategy and growth in a new market', *Bell Journal of Economics*, 10: 1–19.

Spulber, D. F. (1989) *Regulation and Markets*. Cambridge, MA: MIT Press.

Teece, D. J. (1986) 'Profiting from technological innovation: implications for integration, collaboration, licensing and public policy', *Research Policy*, 15(6): 285–305.

Teece, D. J., Pisano, G. and Shuen, A. (1997) 'Dynamic capabilities and strategic management', *Strategic Management Journal*, 18(7): 509–33.

Thomas, L. A. (1995) 'Brand capital and incumbent firms' positions in evolving markets', *Review of Economics and Statistics*, 77(3): 522–34.

Thomas, L. A. (1996) 'Brand capital and entry order', *Journal of Economics and Management Strategy*, 5(1): 107–29.

Ware, R. (1984) 'Sunk costs and strategic commitment: a proposed three-stage equilibrium', *Economic Journal*, 94: 370–8.

Wernerfelt, B. (1984) 'A resource-based view of the firm', *Strategic Management Journal*, 5(2): 171–80.

Wernerfelt, B. (1995) 'The resource-based view of the firm: ten years after', *Strategic Management Journal*, 16: 171–4.

Williamson, O. E. (1975) *Markets and Hierarchies*. New York: Free Press.

Williamson, O. E. (1985) *The Economic Institutions of Capitalism*. New York: Free Press.

Yeoh, P-L. and Roth, K. (1999) 'An empirical analysis of sustained advantage in the US pharmaceutical industry: impact of firm resources and capabilities', *Strategic Management Journal*, 20: 637–53.

Zollo, M. and Winter, S. G. (1999) 'From organizational routines to dynamic capabilities', working paper. Fontainebleau, France: INSEAD.

4

Corporate Strategy: Managing Scope and Strategy Content

ROBERT M. GRANT

The strategy of an enterprise is defined by the answers to two questions: *where* does the firm compete and *how* does it compete? The first question concerns the scope of the firm's activities: in which products, markets, and activities should the firm be involved? The second question is concerned with how the firm plans to establish a competitive advantage over its rivals within the markets that it serves. Conventional approaches to strategy have attempted to dichotomize strategic decision-making between issues relating to scope (or 'domain selection') and those relating to competing within a market or sector ('domain navigation'). The former set of decisions defines the firm's corporate strategy; the latter set defines its competitive, or business, strategy.[1]

Research into corporate strategy has emphasized three sets of issues. First, the determinants of firm scope: why is it that some companies are highly specialized in what they do while others embrace a wide range of products, markets and activities? Second, what is the linkage between scope and performance? Clearly, specialized firms will tend to be smaller than diversified firms, but what about profitability and shareholder returns? Third, what can we say about the management of multibusiness firms in terms of structure, management systems and leadership? In this chapter I shall focus on the first two of

these sets of issues; Chapter 5 will address the third.

While the issues of corporate scope draw upon common theoretical principles – most notably the presence of economies of scope in resources and capabilities and the role of transaction costs – each of the three primary dimensions of firm scope have developed distinct streams of research. In relation to product scope, the fundamental question of 'How broad a range of products should the firm supply?' has generated research into the determinants and effects of diversification that has spanned four decades. Why is it that companies such as Coca Cola, Levi Strauss and Nintendo focus upon a narrow range of products, while Hitachi, Vivendi and 3M span many product areas? When a specialized company, such as Rolls Royce in jet engines, competes with highly diversified companies, General Electric and United Technologies, which type of company has the advantage?

In relation to geographical scope, what determines the geographical area that a firm serves? An inner-city convenience store may serve customers within a few blocks; multinational enterprises, such as Unilever and Marriott International, span the globe. Ever since the work of Hymer (1957), Dunning (1958) and others in the late 1950s, scholars have sought to explain the existence of multinational enterprises and the circumstances in which operating across multiple geographical markets can create value.

Research into vertical integration has explored the range of vertically-linked activities that firms encompass. Ever since the acquisition of Fisher Body by General Motors in the early 1920s (Klein et al., 1978) academics have analyzed the potential for vertical integration to create value for firms. Different firms have very different vertical structures. In computers, Dell Computer relies heavily upon third-party suppliers and service providers. By contrast, IBM's mainframe business continues to be relatively vertically integrated: extending from the production of components and software through to sales and customer service.

These dimensions of corporate strategy are interdependent. Breadth of scope along one dimension tends to be associated with narrow scope along the other two. Among British manufacturing companies, highly multinational companies tended to have only moderate levels of product diversification (and vice versa), suggesting that firms face managerial limits to complexity (Jammine, 1984). Similarly, the re-integration of South Africa within the international economy has encouraged domestic conglomerates such as Barlow and Gencor to expand overseas while refocusing upon core businesses (Ferreira, 1999).

However, some companies have successfully combined broad product, vertical and geographical scope. General Electric and Samsung are highly diversified corporations with broad global and vertical scope. Similarly, the oil majors Exxon and Shell are vertically integrated from primary extraction to retailing and supplying products that range from lubricants to plastics to almost all the world.

Accounting for these differences between firms in the scope of their business activities requires that we address the fundamentals of strategy and the theory of the firm. The importance of these issues has meant that corporate strategy has been central to the study of strategic management since the origins of the subject during the late 1950s. Indeed, during its early development, issues of corporate strategy – product diversification in particular – were the primary focus of emerging interest in strategic management. For economics, the growing role of large, diversified, multinational corporations challenged the subject's preoccupation with

markets and encouraged industrial economists to shift their attention from the market towards the firm, asking fundamental questions such as 'Why does the firm exist?' and 'What determines its boundaries?'.

Because these issues of firm scope are complex, the study of corporate strategy has drawn upon a wide range of disciplines and theories. As a result, research in corporate strategy represents the confluence of a number of streams of literature and study. Figure 4.1 identifies the major issues and areas of research that have shaped the development of the field of corporate strategy. In the following sections I shall refer to these issues and research streams in more detail.

The goal of this chapter is to assess the present state of knowledge in the area of corporate strategy. Specifically, what does research reveal about the relative benefits of specialization and diversity, about the characteristics of the firm and its external environment that determine the scope of the firm's activities, and about the potential for creating value from the linkages between the different activities of the firm? My primary focus of attention will be upon the firm's diversification across different product markets, chiefly because this dimension of corporate scope has been central to the analysis of corporate strategy. Furthermore, despite a huge volume of research, the determinants and the performance implications of corporate diversification remain contentious. The fact that so much empirical research has failed to establish consistent answers to any of the most basic questions concerning corporate diversification is humbling for strategic management researchers, and raises awkward questions concerning the most promising avenues for future research.

Let us begin with an historical view of the development of company scope, then go on to consider the underlying theoretical issues.

The Historical Perspective

Origins of the Modern Corporation

Although the firm is long been recognized as the fundamental unit of business, as an institution for organizing productive activity, the company is a recent phenomenon. Of course, human beings have engaged in production and

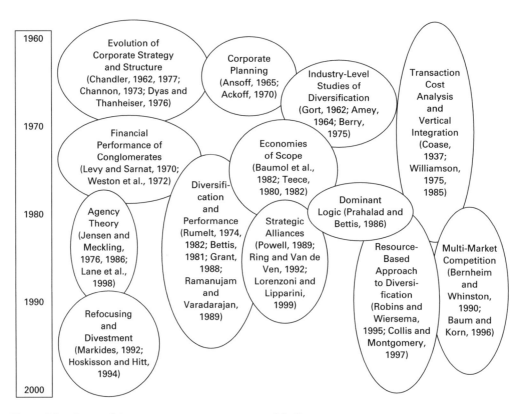

Figure 4.1   *Research into corporate strategy: a map of the literature*

trade since mankind's earliest days, but most of these 'business' activities were undertaken within families and tribes. Even during the early phases of the industrial revolution in Britain, companies were comparatively scarce in most trades: production and trade were carried out mainly by individuals and families, typically with close linkages between them. Those companies that did exist were small, and by the early 19th century, the only sizeable enterprises were colonial trading companies such as the Dutch East India Company and Hudson's Bay Company. As late as the 1840s, the largest enterprises in the US in terms of both capital employed and numbers of workers were agricultural plantations (Chandler, 1977: Chap. 2).

Even where economies of scale encouraged larger production units, the limited size of their local markets constrained the growth of individual establishments, while multiplant firms were not possible without effective means of communication. The advent of railroads and the telegraph changed all that. Very quickly,

regional and national markets could be supplied from a single establishment in a timely manner, and the activities of multiple establishments could be coordinated from a single office. With the increasing size of firms, management developed as a specialized activity. Indeed, it was the railroad companies themselves that were the first to realize the potential of the new transportation and communications technologies to establish the 'first administrative hierarchies in American business' (Chandler, 1977: 87) using 'line and staff' structures with line operations organized around separate geographical divisions and head offices organized in functional staff departments.

These modern corporations utilized administrative hierarchies and standardized systems of decision-making, financial control, and information management. These structures enabled companies to expand the size and scope of their activities. Consolidation through merger and acquisition resulted in the appearance of the first 'holding companies' during the late 19th century. These were created by one company acquiring controlling interests in a number of subsidiaries. Beyond the appointment of the subsidiary boards of directors, the parent exercised little strategic or operational influence over the subsidiary companies. Warren Buffett's Berkshire Hathaway is a present-day example of this structure.

The Multidivisional Corporation

The multidivisional corporation was a response to the problems posed by increasing size and diversification both for traditional industrial enterprises and the new holding companies. As DuPont, a functionally-organized producer of explosives and chemicals, expanded its product line: '...the operations of the enterprise became too complex and the problems of coordination, appraisal and policy formulation too intricate for the small number of top officers to handle both long-run, entrepreneurial and short-run, operational administrative activities' (Chandler, 1962: 382–3).

Pierre DuPont's solution in 1920 was to create separate product divisions, each independently responsible for operations, sales and financial performance, leaving to the corporate head office the tasks of coordination, strategic leadership and control. A few years later, General Motors, a holding company created from mergers and acquisitions among many automobiles and components producers, adopted a similar multidivisional structure. The divisional chief executives of Cadillac, Oldsmobile, Buick, Pontiac, and Chevrolet were responsible for the operation and performance of their divisions, while the corporate president monitored performance, established the terms for inter-divisional transactions, and formulated company-wide product and technology policies (Sloan, 1963: 42–56). During the next 30 years, the multidivisional structure that allowed product and national divisions to pursue their operational strategies while the corporate head office managed corporate strategy and financial planning became increasingly prevalent within the US (Chandler, 1962) and Europe (Daems, 1989; Hannah, 1991).

Postwar Patterns of Diversification

Not only were companies becoming more diversified, but their diversification strategies progressed from closely-related to more loosely-related businesses, and then towards unrelated businesses. An international research project at Harvard Business School extended Chandler's original work on strategy and structure. For the US, Wrigley (1970) and Rumelt (1974) found that the number of single business companies among the *Fortune* 500 fell steadily, whereas the most diversified companies – both related business and unrelated business – increased in number (see Table 4.1). Parallel studies for the UK (Channon, 1973), Germany (Thanheiser, 1973), France (Dyas, 1972), Italy (Pavan, 1972) and Japan (Itami et al., 1982) found similar results. Recent research by Whittington et al. (1999) has updated the European evidence (see Table 4.2). They show European developments in corporate strategy and structure parallel those of the US, albeit with some time lag.

The postwar diversification trend was a consequence of several factors. The multidivisional structure was just one of many organizational and managerial innovations that facilitated the establishment of companies with unprecedented business and geographical scope. The result of the rapidly advancing 'science of management' was the view that the essence of management was not the deployment of industry-specific experiential knowledge, but rather the application of the general tools and principles. The universality of the principles of management implied that professional managers armed with the appropriate tools of financial controls, capital appraisal systems, human resource management techniques, and decision rules could successfully manage any type of business (Katz, 1955; Koontz, 1969).

The development of the concepts and techniques of corporate strategy during the late 1960s and early 1970s (Ansoff, 1965) reinforced the view that professional managers were not constrained by industry boundaries. Tools of strategic analysis developed in the 1970s and 1980s permitted standardized yet sophisticated approaches to diversification and resource allocation decisions (Goold and Luchs, 1993). These tools included business portfolio analysis (Haspeslaugh, 1983), industry analysis (Porter, 1980), and quantitative approaches to the performance implications of market structure and competitive positioning (Buzzell and Gale, 1987).

Table 4.1   *Corporate strategies of the* Fortune *500, 1949–1974*

	1949 %	1954 %	1959 %	1964 %	1969 %	1974 %
Single business companies	42.0	34.1	22.8	21.5	14.8	14.4
of which, vertically integrated companies	12.8	12.2	12.5	14.0	12.3	12.4
Dominant business companies	15.4	17.4	18.4	18.4	12.8	10.2
Related-business companies	25.7	31.0	38.6	37.3	44.4	42.3
Unrelated-business companies	4.1	4.7	7.3	8.7	18.7	20.7
	100.0	100.0	100.0	100.0	100.0	100.0

Note: Single business companies have more than 95% of their sales within their main business. Vertically integrated companies have more than 70% of their sales in vertically related businesses. Dominant business companies have between 70% and 95% of their sales within their main business. Related-business companies have more than 70% of their sales in businesses that are related to one another. Unrelated-business companies have less than 70% of their sales in related businesses.
Source: Rumelt (1982).

Table 4.2   *Corporate strategies of large European companies, 1950–1993*

	1950 %	1960 %	1970 %	1983 %	1993 %
France					
Single business	45	35	20	24	20
Dominant business	18	22	27	11	15
Related business	31	36	41	53	52
Unrelated business	5	5	9	12	14
Germany					
Single business	37	27	27	18	13
Dominant business	22	24	15	17	8
Related business	31	38	38	40	48
Unrelated business	9	11	19	25	32
UK					
Single business	24	18	6	7	5
Dominant business	50	36	32	16	10
Related business	27	48	57	67	62
Unrelated business	–	–	6	11	24

Notes:
1. Some column totals do not equal 100 due to rounding.
2. The categorization of firms by strategies is consistent for each country over time, but is not consistent between countries.

Sources: The table is adapted from Whittington et al. (1999). The data for the period 1950–1970 is from Dyas and Thanheiser (1976) and Channon (1973). The data for 1983 and 1993 is from Whittington et al.

The growing scale and scope of companies was widely seen as a fundamental change in the capitalist system. 'Managerial' or 'corporate' capitalism operated by professional managers using new scientific tools of management was inherently superior to the old market capitalism in allocating resources, organizing production and managing innovation. J. K. Galbraith's *The New Industrial State* (1969) anticipated the dominance of the capitalist economies by a small number of giant corporations. However, the rise of 'professional management' had other implications too. The separation of ownership from control encouraged salaried top managers to pursue diversification as a means of growth, often at the expense of profitability (Marris, 1964).

The Conglomerates

By the early 1970s, the emergence of a new type of company with no 'core business' and no obvious linkages between their many businesses represented the pinnacle of the diversification trend. These 'conglomerates' included ITT, Gulf & Western, Textron, and Allied-Signal in the United States and Slater-Walker, Hanson Trust, and BTR in the UK. All were created by multiple acquisitions. These conglomerates exemplified the belief in the generality of management principles and the irrelevance of industry-specific knowledge to the top management tasks of leadership, control, and strategic direction. At ITT, Harold Geneen perfected his system of 'management by the numbers' (Geneen, 1969), while at Hanson, chairman Lord Hanson made a point of never visiting the companies that he acquired.

The new conglomerates were of particular interest to finance scholars armed with the tools of modern portfolio theory (Sharpe, 1964; Lintner, 1965). If individual investors could spread risk through diversifying their portfolios of securities, what advantages could the conglomerate firm offer? The evidence from a series of finance studies was that, overall, conglomerates did not outperform mutual funds in terms of risks and returns. Studies of conglomerates in the United States have shown that their risk-adjusted returns to shareholders are typically no better than those offered by mutual funds or by matched portfolios of specialized companies (Levy and Sarnat, 1970; Weston et al., 1972; Mason and Goudzwaard, 1976; Melicher and Rush, 1973). Subsequent research has also cast doubt upon the ability of conglomerate diversification to lower risk. Lubatkin and Chatterjee (1994) found that unrelated diversification failed to lower either systematic or unsystematic risk, but moderate, closely related diversification did reduce both.

Downsizing, Outsourcing, and Refocusing

Just when industrial economists and business historians were recognizing the transition to managerial capitalism and proclaiming the giant, diversified, integrated, multinational corporation as the final stage in the evolution of the business enterprise, countervailing trends became evident. The dominant trends of the last two decades of the 20th century were 'downsizing' and 'refocusing' as large industrial companies reduced both their product scope through focusing on their core businesses and their vertical scope through outsourcing. International expansion has continued, however. These changes coincided with a more turbulent business environment: the oil shock of 1973–1974, the floating of exchange rates in 1972, the invention of the integrated circuit, and the upsurge of international competition. The implication seems to be that during periods of market turbulence, the effectiveness of firms' internal administrative mechanisms (strategic planning, internal resource allocation, financial control, and the like) in managing across industries, countries, and within the value chain, is reduced (Cibin and Grant, 1996). External volatility increases the pressure of decision-making on top management and can overwhelm traditional management systems. In these circumstances, smaller, more focused firms operating close to their markets for inputs and outputs can be more efficient and effective than multibusiness firms. Two processes contributed to narrowing the corporate scope of large companies: outsourcing and refocusing.

Outsourcing

Reductions in vertical integration through outsourcing have involved not simply greater vertical specialization, but also the redefinition of vertical relationships. The new supplier–buyer partnerships typically involve long-term 'relational contracts' that avoid much of the bureaucracy and administrative inflexibility associated with vertical integration. They also avoid many of the problems of opportunism associated with market contracts where the parties are 'locked-in' by transaction-specific investments. The integration model for many Western companies has been the collaborative relationships that many Japanese companies have with their suppliers. These relationships have allowed Japanese companies to adopt highly streamlined operations. For example, during the late 1980s, Toyota and Nissan directly produced only about 20 to 23% of the value of their cars, compared to 50% for Ford and about 70% for GM. Nevertheless, Japanese carmakers have collaborated very closely with their suppliers on technology, quality control, design, and scheduling (Dyer, 1996a, b, 1997).

Western companies now need to replace supplier relationships defined by competitive tendering and short-term contracts with longer term 'vertical partnerships' with fewer vendors (Johnston and Lawrence, 1988). IBM and Chrysler are among the once-integrated companies that now outsource components and services and have restructured supplier relationships. Hewlett-Packard, Cisco Systems, Sun Microsystems, and Benetton (Dubini, 1997) are companies whose collaborative supplier networks are central to their strategies.

The extent of outsourcing and vertical de-integration has given rise to a new organizational form: the virtual corporation, where the primary function of the company is coordinating the activities of a network of suppliers (Davidow and Malone, 1992; *Business Week*, 1993). Although the virtual corporation has advantages of flexibility and the ability to select from a wide range of external capabilities, there is a danger that increasing reliance upon other firms' resources and capabilities could cause the loss of innovation and integrative capability (Chesborough and Teece, 1996).

Refocusing upon Core Businesses

Narrowing of corporate scope is also apparent in firms' retreat from product diversification. In Britain, the most highly diversified companies of the late 1960s became less diversified during the late 1970s and early 1980s (Jammine, 1984). In the US, the average index of diversification for the *Fortune* 500 declined from 1.00 to 0.67 between 1980 and 1990 (Davis et al., 1993). The surge of US M&A (mergers and acquisitions) activity in the late 1980s and early 1990s was driven by divestiture of unprofitable diversified businesses. (Hoskisson and Hitt, 1994). Most of the acquisitions were horizontal in direction. Of the $1.3 trillion in assets acquired during the 1980s (which included 113 members of the *Fortune* 500), only 4.5 percent represented unrelated diversification (Shleifer and Vishny, 1990). Among the acquisitions occurring in the 1980s, many were conglomerates that were subsequently broken up. Shleifer and Vishny (1991: 59) concluded that: 'The most plausible interpretation of the evidence is that the takeover wave of the 1980s served largely to reverse unrelated diversification of the '60s. Over a 30-year period, corporate America took

a detour.' Of the surviving conglomerates, most divested unrelated businesses and restructured themselves around fewer, more closely related businesses (Williams et al., 1988). Markides (1992a) found that, within the *Fortune* 500, refocusing firms outnumbered diversifying firms and that the refocusers tended to be highly diversified firms. Although a general trend towards greater specialization is difficult to establish,[2] the 1980s and 1990s were a period of unprecedented divestment and spin-offs.

The overwhelmingly important factor driving the retreat from diversification and vertical integration was the shifting of corporate goals from growth to profitability. The new emphasis on profitability and creation of shareholder value was due both to the economic downturns and interest-rate spikes of 1974–76, 1980–82, and 1989–1991 that exposed the inadequate profitability of many large, diversified corporations, and to increased pressure from shareholders and financial markets. Institutional investors led the rise of shareholder activism; especially pension funds such as California's Public Employees Retirement System. The ousting of a number of CEOs during the early 1990s also indicated an increasing independence of corporate board members. These included Robert Stempel at General Motors, James Robinson at American Express, Ken Olsen at Digital Equipment, and John Akers at IBM (*Fortune*, 1993). An even bigger threat to incumbent management was the surge in leveraged buyouts. The use of debt financing by corporate raiders to acquire then restructure underperforming companies culminated in Kohlberg Kravis Roberts' $25 billion takeover of the tobacco and food giant RJR Nabisco in 1989. The lesson to other sluggishly performing giants was clear: either restructure voluntarily or have it done through hostile acquisition. Nor was the trend restricted to the US. By the late 1990s, leading European companies including BAT, ICI, and BTR had been forced into extensive restructuring, while others such as Daimler-Benz, ENI, Olivetti, and Philips voluntarily divested diversified businesses in order to increase shareholder value. By 1999, the restructuring wave had reached South Korea and Japan.

New ideas about strategic management have also influenced corporate strategies. If the 1970s were dominated by optimism over the universality of management principles, in the 1990s, the development and exploitation of organizational capability was a central theme. There has also been recognition that a strategy of exploiting linkages between different business sectors does not necessarily require diversification: a wide variety of alliances and other synergistic relationships can exploit economies of scope across independent companies. These concepts and theories are discussed further later in this chapter.

Diversification in the Emerging-Market Economies

This refocusing trend is less evident in Asia, Eastern Europe and other emerging market economies than it is in the advanced market economies of North America and Western Europe. A handful of *chaebols* – Samsung, Daewoo, Hyundai, and Goldstar – continue to dominate the South Korean business sector, while in Southeast Asia sprawling conglomerates such as Charoen Pokphand of Thailand, Lippo of Indonesia, and Keppel Group of Singapore have even increased in prominence (*Economist*, 1993). These geographical differences may be partly explained by lack of efficient, well-developed capital markets outside the United States and Western Europe, thus offering internalization advantages to diversified companies (Khanna and Palepu, 1997). The result may be that cross-country differences in the relative costs of organization through market transactions and internal management may create international differences in the boundaries of firms (Hill, 1995). Thus, Lee and Sirh's (1999: 14) research on Korean chaebols concluded that 'the optimal diversification level...is higher in Korea than in advanced countries such as the US'.

More generally, despite the common trends towards diversification and divisionalization across countries identified by the Harvard studies of the early 1970s, substantial international differences remain in corporate strategies of large companies. Not only does 'stakeholder capitalism' associated with continental Europe and Asia tend to promote higher levels of diversification than the 'Anglo-Saxon shareholder capitalism' associated with the English-speaking world (between cross-national differences in corporate strategy between large companies [Choi et al., 1999]), but country-specific organizational forms (Japan's keiretsu, Korea's chaebols, the holding companies of continental Europe) tend to persist. The global diffusion of market capitalism accompanied by privatization and deregulation has created only limited convergence in corporate strategy. Indeed, in Chile and India, deregulation and internationalization during the 1990s did little to undermine the role of diversified business groups, on the contrary, these large conglomerates appear to have thrived and increased their internal linkages over the period (Khanna and Palepu, 1999).

Beyond Historical Trends

The evidence of history has exerted a strong influence on the study of corporate strategy. Studies by business historians, Alfred Chandler in particular, have provided fascinating insights into the evolution of corporate scope and the links between strategy, organizational structure and the entrepreneurial drive of business leaders. This evidence has provided a strong impetus to strategic management scholars to develop theory that can explain the patterns of corporate development that have been observed and test more rigorously some of the relationships. Let us proceed by exploring the primary driving force behind strategic management research: the link with performance. What does empirical research tell us about the relative success of different corporate strategies?

CORPORATE STRATEGY AND PERFORMANCE

Rumelt's *Strategy, Structure and Economic Performance* (1974) represents a landmark in the study of corporate strategy. Prior research into corporate strategy and organizational structure had viewed the trends from specialization to diversification and from closely related to unrelated diversification and concluded that the broadly diversified corporation was a superior strategy to being more focused. Introducing financial performance into his analysis, Rumelt provided an explicit linkage between corporate strategy and profitability. His key finding was the superiority of related over unrelated diversification. In particular, those firms whose diversification was closely linked to their core business ('constrained diversifiers') were the most profitable. The ensuing torrent of empirical studies of the relationship between diversification strategy and performance initially confirmed the superiority of related over unrelated diversification (Bettis, 1981; Christensen and Montgomery, 1981; Rumelt, 1982; Lecraw, 1984). The apparent consistency of the evidence was such that Peters and Waterman (1982: 294) were able to conclude: '…virtually every academic study has concluded that unchannelled diversification is a losing proposition.' One of their 'golden rules of excellence' was 'Stick to the Knitting'.

However, as the volume of empirical work on the relationship between diversification strategy and performance grew, the findings became increasingly inconsistent. Some studies found no significant relationship between relatedness in diversification and profitability (Grant et al., 1988) while other studies found unrelated diversification to be more profitable than related diversification (Michel and Shaked, 1984; Luffman and Reed, 1984; Lubatkin, 1987). On the relationship between profitability and the extent of diversification, several studies have observed a curvilinear relationship – diversification is beneficial up to a point, after which the costs of complexity overwhelm the benefits of diversification (Grant et al., 1988; Lubatkin and Chatterjee, 1994; Palich et al., 2000).

Of course, statistical association does not imply causation. If diversification is associated with higher levels of profitability, which is driving which? Grant et al. (1988) suggested that the positive relationship between profitability and diversity might well be the result of companies investing retained profits in diversification, while Burgelman (1983) found that diversification initiatives were a response to declining performance in core businesses.

Recent investigations of the relationship between corporate strategy and performance have featured more refined methodologies. These investigations have deployed more sophisticated measures of diversification (Hoskisson et al., 1993; Nayyar, 1992; Robins and Wiersema, 1997) and the use of a wider range of control variables. Particular attention has been devoted to the interactions

between corporate strategy and industry characteristics (Montgomery and Wernerfelt, 1991; Stimpert and Duhaime, 1997) in addition to the links between resources and diversification (Chatterjee and Wernerfelt, 1991). Attention has also been given to different performance measures – while most studies have used accounting measures of profitability, some studies have used stock market returns (Amit and Livnat, 1988; Dubofski and Varadarajan, 1987). In addition, increasing attention has been given to the need to adjust for risk (Bettis and Mahajan, 1985).

However, despite these refinements, additional studies have done little to reconcile the inconsistencies of the early research findings or to clarify our understanding of the relationship between diversification and firm performance. A survey of 37 empirical studies of the relationship between diversification and corporate performance was unable to identify any consistent relationships and concluded, despondently, 'the prospect for gaining new empirical insights by explaining cross-sectional relationships between alternative measures of diversity and performance seems to be slim' (Ramanujam and Varadarajan, 1989).

In other areas of corporate strategy, the picture is less confusing. In contrast to the contradictory findings with regard to product diversification, much greater consistency is found in relation to vertical integration and international diversification. In relation to vertical integration, Rumelt's (1974) finding that vertically integrated firms underperform both specialized and diversified firms has been confirmed by subsequent evidence. In relation to international diversification, multinationals have tended to outperform nationally focused firms (Grant, 1987; Grant et al., 1988; Hitt et al., 1997).

Recent evidence concerning the relationship between diversification and performance includes the consequences of refocusing initiatives by a large number of North American and European companies. The results of the divestments of diversified businesses by conglomerates such as ITT and Hanson, as well as the oil majors, tobacco companies, and engineering companies such as Daimler-Benz, suggest that narrowing business scope leads to increased profitability and increased stock market valuation. The stock market's verdict on diversification is unambiguous. The high price-earnings ratios attached to conglomerates during the 1960s have been replaced by a 'conglomerate discount'. The result was that diversified companies came under attack from leveraged-buyout specialists seeking to add value by dismembering these companies. The tendency for acquisition announcements to generate abnormal stock market returns to the acquiring companies during the 1960s and 1970s was reversed in the 1980s (Jarrell et al., 1988), while Markides (1992b) found that refocusing announcements by diversified companies were accompanied by abnormal stock market returns. Whether these findings of superior returns to refocusing are stable over time remains to be seen.

The main conclusion that arises from the empirical literature is that there is no simple and consistent relationship between diversification and firm performance. In answering the question: 'Does diversification enhance firm performance?' the most we can say is: 'It all depends.' To make further progress in unraveling the factors that influence the performance impact of diversification, we need to address the underlying theoretical relationships that link corporate strategy to value creation.

THE DETERMINANTS OF CORPORATE SCOPE

Corporate Strategy, Multimarket Competition and Market Power

The traditional industrial economics approach to firms' operations across multiple products, multiple markets, and multiple activities was to assume that such strategies were driven by a quest for market power. Thus, in the case of vertical integration, a firm with a monopoly at one stage of the value chain could use market foreclosure to extend its monopoly to adjacent stages of the value chain – Rockefeller's Standard Oil being the classic example (Chernow, 1998). To the extent that vertical integration forces competitors to vertically integrate, this raises barriers to entry.

In the case of diversification, it has been claimed that large, diversified companies could exercise market power through three mechanisms:

1 Predatory pricing. The ability of diversified companies to cross-subsidize one division

with their profits from another gives them the power to discipline or even drive out specialized competitors in individual product markets. The key competitive weapon is predatory pricing – the ability to cut prices below the level of rivals' costs and sustain losses over the period needed to cause the competitor to exit or sell out. Hamel and Prahalad (1985) argued that such cross-subsidization is fundamental to the effectiveness of global strategies.

2 Reciprocal buying. A diversified company can leverage its market share across its businesses by reciprocal buying arrangements with customers. This means giving preference in purchasing to firms that become loyal customers for another of the conglomerate's businesses.

3 Mutual forbearance. Corwin Edwards argued that: 'When one large conglomerate enterprise competes with another, the two are likely to encounter each other in a considerable number of markets. The multiplicity of their contacts may blunt the edge of their competition. A prospect of advantage in one market from vigorous competition may be weighed against the danger of retaliatory forays by the competitor in other markets. Each conglomerate may adopt a live-and-let-live policy designed to stabilize the whole structure of the competitive relationship' (US Senate, 1965).

Despite the plausibility of these arguments, evidence of anticompetitive practices of these types is sparse. Although common patterns of diversification among competing firms in the same industry point to firms' awareness of the need to build countervailing strategic positions, examples of firms exercising anticompetitive practices based on diversified market positions are few, judging by the scarcity of antitrust actions of this type. However, on the topic of predatory pricing, the pricing policies of the major airlines and Microsoft in the web browser market have given cause for concern.

Recent studies have explored the phenomenon of 'multimarket competition' among firms with diversified products or diversified geographical markets in greater detail. Where the products produced by different divisions of a diversified company are substitutes, coordinated pricing increases margins – a result referred to as the 'efficiency effect'

(Besanko et al., 1996: 428–9). In repeated games involving players that meet in multiple markets, companies are likely to refrain from aggressive action in any one market for fear of triggering more generalized warfare (Bernheim and Whinston, 1990). Most research into multi-market contact has explored the competitive implications of firms that meet in multiple geographical markets for the same product or service (e.g. airlines, supermarkets, and banks). In the US airline industry Baum and Korn (1996) found that extensive multimarket contact encouraged mutual forbearance in the form of reluctance to compete on routes dominated by one or other of the airlines. However, it seems plausible that the tendency for contact in multiple geographical markets to discourage competition might also exist among diversified companies that meet in multiple product markets (Korn and Baum, 1999).

Economies of Scope in Resources and Capabilities

A central theme in discussions of corporate strategy both at the academic and practitioner level has been the concept of 'synergy' – the advantages from exploiting linkages between different businesses, different markets and different activities. These linkages have directed attention to the resources and capabilities that can be shared across businesses, activities and markets. Research by industrial economists into inter-industry patterns of firm diversification provided some clues as to what these resources and capabilities might be. The work of Gort (1962), Amey (1964), and Berry (1975) pointed to the role of technological resources and brand equity (as indicated by R&D and advertising expenditures) in driving diversification decisions. However, Penrose (1959) provides a more fundamental model of the firm as a collection of firm-specific resources where excess capacity in these resources drives diversification. If resources and capabilities are to be drivers of corporate strategy, the essential characteristics are that they can be applied across product markets and they are subject to some form of indivisibility such that the marginal cost of deploying them in an additional application is less than the marginal cost of their initial use. In other words, they should be subject to 'economies

of scope' which is defined formally in terms of 'sub-additivity' (Baumol et al., 1982). Economies of scope exist in the production of goods x_1, x_2, ... x_n, if:

$$C(X) < \Sigma_i c(x_i)$$

Where $X = \Sigma_i x_i$, $C(X)$ is the cost of producing all n goods within a single firm, and $\Sigma_i c(x_i)$ is the cost of producing the goods in n specialized firms. The nature and extent of economies of scope varies across different resources and capabilities.

During the 1990s, the analysis of corporate strategy was transformed by the so-called 'resource-based view of the firm' (Wernerfelt, 1984; Grant, 1991; Barney, 1991). This approach views the firm as a set of resources and capabilities. The challenge of strategy is to deploy these resources and capabilities in order to maximize the Ricardian rents that they can yield. While resources and capabilities are critical to competitive strategy in terms of establishing positions of sustainable competitive advantage in individual markets, the ability to deploy resources and capabilities across multiple markets means that the resource-based view also provides a foundation for corporate strategy (Chatterjee and Wernerfelt, 1991; Collis and Montgomery, 1997).

The resource-based approach to corporate strategy places emphasis upon the particular resources and capabilities that can be deployed across industry borders. Thus:

First, tangible resources such as distribution networks, communications infrastructure, sales forces, and research laboratories offer economies of scope by eliminating the duplication of facilities between businesses and creating a single shared facility. Similar economies of scope are available from the centralized provision of accounting, finance, legal, and IT services to different businesses within diversified corporations. Similar benefits arise to companies such as Philips, IBM, Matsushita, DuPont, and Xerox from centralizing research within corporate R&D labs.

Second, intangible resources such as brands, corporate reputation, and technology offer economies of scope primarily due to the ability to transfer them from one business area to another at low marginal cost. General Electric advertises a wide range of products and services under the slogan 'GE brings good things to life'.

Third, organizational capabilities offer economies of scope because they can be transferred between the divisions of the diversified company. Canon applies its synthesis of optical and microelectronic technologies to products ranging from cameras to semiconductor manufacturing equipment (Prahalad and Hamel, 1990). Philip Morris's brand management capabilities are applied to Marlboro cigarettes, Miller beer, and Kraft dairy products. General management capabilities play an especially important role in many diversified corporations. For example, General Electric's capabilities in motivating and developing its managers, and 3M's capabilities in developing and marketing new products have been key components of the success they have enjoyed.

This analysis suggests that a key determinant of a firm's business scope is the extent to which its resources and capabilities offer economies of scope. Collis and Montgomery (1998) show that differences in firms' diversification strategies are closely linked to the degree of specialization of their resources and capabilities. Sharp Corporation's core capability is its world-class optoelectronics technology that have caused it to focus around a tightly-linked group of calculators, computers, printers, flat screens, and associated products. At the other end of the scale, Berkshire Partners' core capability is its deal making skill. Berkshire has diversified over a wide range of loosely-related businesses.

Economies from Internalizing Transactions

Economies of scope provide cost savings from sharing resources and transferring capabilities. But why does a firm need to diversify across products and markets in order to exploit economies of scope? Economies of scope can be exploited simply by selling or licensing the use of the resource or capability to another company. In relation to geographical diversification, most western pharmaceutical companies supply Japan by licensing their drugs to local companies to manufacture and distribute. In relation to product diversification, Harley-Davidson extends its brand to clothing, toiletries, cigarettes, cafes, and studded leather underwear by means of licensing its trademarks to the manufacturers of these products. Even

tangible resources can be shared across different businesses through leases and licenses.

As recognized by Teece (1980, 1982), the choice of whether to exploit economies of scope internally through diversification or externally through market contracts with independent companies depends upon relative efficiency – what are the transaction costs of market contracts, as compared to the costs of managing economies of scope within the diversified enterprise? Transaction costs include the costs involved in drafting, negotiating, monitoring, and enforcing a contract. The costs of internalization consist of the management costs of establishing and coordinating the diversified business.

If a company has defined property rights in its trademarks and patents, licenses with third parties offers a low cost means of appropriating the returns to these resources. Also, such licensing arrangements avoid a company from having to enter markets and business sectors where it lacks the capabilities needed to establish competitive advantage. On the other hand, many companies do choose diversification as the most effective means of exploiting economies of scope in resources and capabilities. For example, 3M uses its adhesives and coating technologies to diversify across a broad range of products from Scotch tape and Post-it notes to surgical dressings, road traffic signs and videotapes. It chooses to exploit its technical and product development capabilities internally – first, because 3M cannot establish clear property rights in many of its most important technical capabilities, and second, because 3M has built an organization that is effective and efficient both in transferring and deploying its many capabilities and in continually extending and developing them.

The relative costs of internal versus external exploitation of resources and capabilities depends to a great extent on the characteristics of the resource or capabilities. The more deeply embedded a firm's resource or capability within the management systems and the culture of the organization, the greater the likelihood that its value is best appropriated internally.

Firms and Markets: The Coase/ Williamson Contribution

The concept of transaction costs is central to the existence of the firm and the relative roles of firms and markets within the economy. Faced with evidence of the growing role of large industrial corporations in the US economy during the interwar years, Ronald Coase asked the question, 'Why firms?' His answer, that the firm can organize certain transactions at lower cost than can markets, gave birth to transaction cost economics (Coase, 1937). Although the capitalist economy is frequently referred to as a 'market economy', Simon (1991) reminds us that it comprises two forms of economic organization: the market mechanism, or 'invisible hand' as characterized by Adam Smith, and the administrative mechanisms of firms, the 'visible hand' as characterized by Chandler (1977).

The scope of the firm depends upon the costs of market transactions as compared to administered transactions within the firm. With regard to vertical scope, which is more efficient: three independent companies, one producing raw materials, the next producing components from those raw materials, and the third assembling components into a final product? Or having all three stages of production within a single company? In the case of geographical scope, which is more efficient: three independent companies, each operating an ice cream business in three separate countries? Or a single company operating the three national units? In the case of product scope, should cigarettes, beer, and food products be produced by three separate companies each acquiring resources from external markets, or are there efficiencies to be gained by merging all three into a single company where corporate management allocates resources between the three businesses?

Oliver Williamson's (1975, 1985) contribution to corporate strategy has been to analyze the nature and sources of these transaction costs. Markets tend to be efficient where there are many buyers and sellers for a product and where information is distributed among the market participants. Markets fail where there are few buyers and sellers and where transactions require transaction-specific investments by one or both of the parties to the contract, and where information is asymmetrically distributed between the parties. In these situations, one or both parties become locked into the transaction encouraging opportunistic behavior by the other party ('hold-up').

The growth in the scope of firms' activities during the 100 years up to 1980 that we discussed above can be explained in terms of transaction costs. Technological developments such as the telegraph, telephone and electronic computer, and management developments such as systems of managerial accounting, strategic planning systems, and the multi-divisional structure, reduced the costs of administering transactions within firms relative to the costs of contracting across markets. Similarly, recent narrowing of firm scope through outsourcing and refocusing suggests that the turbulent market conditions of the past two decades have raised the costs of internal transactions as compared with market transactions. This is partly because the reorganized management systems of firms are best suited to standardized transactions under stable environmental conditions, but also because the costs of interfirm transactions have been lowered through strategic alliances, vertical partnerships and the like.

The Diversified Firm as an Internal Market System

Efficiencies in the internal allocation of resources provide a basis for efficiency in the diversified firm even where economies of scope from resource indivisibility are not present. Where significant costs are incurred in using external capital markets (the margin between borrowing and lending rates, and the underwriting costs of issuing securities), diversified companies can benefit from lower costs of capital by building a balanced portfolio of cash generating and cash absorbing businesses. A central role of the corporate head office in such a company is to allocate capital among the different businesses according to the potential returns of each. In this respect, the diversified corporation represents an internal capital market in which the different businesses compete for investment funds (Liebeskind, 2000). The efficiency of external capital markets in North America and Western Europe means that the advantages of internal capital markets do not, on their own, provide an adequate justification for the diversified firm. However, in Russia, Indonesia and Brazil, the transaction costs of capital markets may be sufficient to offer significant advantage to the diversified corporation with an internal capital market.

Efficiencies may also arise from the ability of diversified companies to transfer employees, especially managers and technical specialists, between their divisions. As companies develop and encounter new circumstances, different managerial, professional and technical skills are required. The costs associated with using external labor markets – advertising positions, recruitment, and recruitment agency fees – are high, as are the costs of shedding employees. Diversified corporations such as Matsushita, General Electric, Unilever, and Nestle have pools of managerial and specialist employees that can be moved between businesses to respond to the need for particular skills or expertise.

An important benefit of internal capital and labor markets within the diversified corporation is that the corporate head office of the diversified corporation has better access to information than is available to external capital and labor markets. As a result, the diversified corporation may be more efficient in reallocating labor and capital among its divisions than external capital and labor markets in allotting labor and capital among independent businesses. These information advantages may be especially important in the case of labor. A key problem of hiring from the external labor market is not just cost but limited information. A company has limited information as to the performance potential of a new hire. The diversified firm that is engaged in transferring employees between business units and divisions has access to much more detailed information on the abilities, characteristics, and past performance of each of its employees. This informational advantage exists not only for individual employees but also for groups of individuals working together as teams (Alchian and Demsetz, 1972). As a result, in diversifying into a new activity, the established firm is at an advantage over the new firm, which must assemble a team from scratch with poor information on individual capabilities and almost no information on how effective the group will be at working together.

Organizational Capability and Firm Scope

If thinking about corporate strategy during the 1960s and 1970s was dominated by the beliefs concerning the unbounded potential of modern management, the primary influence on corporate strategy during the 1990s was the idea of 'focusing upon core competences'. The underlying proposition is that the limits to the scope of the firm are in relation to resources and capabilities rather than in relation to activities or products or markets. Faced with increasing competition, firms have been forced to focus upon activities, products and markets where they possess competitive advantage over actual and potential rivals. This 'capability-based' view of firm scope contrasts with the more conventional transaction cost approach. Argyres (1996) finds that relative strengths in capabilities offer a better explanation of vertical integration decisions than transaction costs.

A central issue in capability-based analysis of corporate scope concerns limits to the range of a firm's capabilities. The strategic evolution of some firms suggests that the number of capabilities they sustain outstanding performance in is clearly limited. Intel abandoned DRAMs for microprocessors in the belief that it could not sustain world leadership in both (Grove, 1996). Eastman-Kodak sold off its health sciences and chemicals businesses in order to concentrate upon building leadership in digital imaging. Yet General Electric, 3M, Matsushita, and Samsung seem able to maintain successfully a broad range of organizational capabilities.

Research in this area is underdeveloped. While some research points to the benefits of integrating complementary capabilities (Helfat, 1997; Krishnan et al., 1997), systematic research into capabilities and firm scope has been constrained by the empirical problems of classifying and measuring organizational capability.

It is possible that organizational conditions – structure, systems, and culture – may be the factors that limit firms' ability to achieve high levels of performance across a wide range of capabilities. For example, the lack of vertical integration between manufacturing and retailing companies may reflect the different types of capabilities required in each type of business. Manufacturing requires technological, process, and product development capabilities. Retailing requires rapid response capability, astute buying, and constant attentiveness to managing the customer interface. Designing a company that can accommodate such different capabilities is a difficult organizational challenge.

AT&T's divestment of its manufacturing businesses, NCR and Lucent, can also be attributed to the organizational tensions of developing telecommunication service capabilities and equipment development and manufacturing capabilities within a single corporation. Even Sony and Matsushita, companies that have shown tremendous versatility in integrating multiple technical capabilities across a range of consumer electronics products, have experienced difficulties in extending from hardware into software, as indicated by the difficulties of their acquisitions of Columbia and MCA.

The Role of Alliances and Networks

The challenge of reconciling the economies of scope in certain resources and capabilities with the advantages of specialization in the developing distinctive capabilities has encouraged the development of organizational forms that are neither market-based nor hierarchical but are described as alliances or network forms (Powell, 1989; Ring and Van de Ven, 1992). These collaborate forms have been regarded as hybrid organizational forms that are capable of avoiding both the transaction costs associated with market contracts and the inflexibility costs associated with full internalization. While bilateral alliances take a wide variety of forms, interfirm networks comprising many companies tend to be organized either around a hub company (Lorenzoni and Baden-Fuller, 1995), or within a single geographical area such as California's Silicon Valley (Saxenian, 1990) or the Emilia Romagna region of Italy. Some of the most interesting aspects of strategic alliances and interfirm networks are the mechanisms through which organizational capabilities are integrated across multiple firms and are reconfigured to produce different products. In the Italian packaging machinery industry, Lorenzoni and Lipparini (1999) point to the management of interfirm relationships as a distinct organizational capability.

THE GOALS OF CORPORATE STRATEGY

In describing the recent trend towards a narrowing of corporate scope, the chapter emphasized the reordering of corporate goals during the late 1980s and the 1990s. Similarly, the elusiveness of clear empirical relationships between corporate strategy and performance reflects, in part, the different motives that have driven firms' decisions to extend their scope. Three goals have been paramount: growth, risk reduction, and profitability. To what extent have corporate strategies been directed to goals other than the pursuit of profit, and to what extent are these different goals consistent with shareholder interests?

Growth and Risk Reduction

Much of the diversification trend of the 1960s and 1970s was oriented towards corporate growth where the primary drivers were the interests of managers rather than shareholders. If managers are motivated by financial gain, status, and power, and if their salaries and prestige are correlated with corporate size rather than corporate profitability, they are likely to pursue growth at the expense of profitability. The result is that firms will tend to invest at a greater rate than is consistent with profit maximization, causing valuation ratios to decline to just short of the point where the firm becomes vulnerable to acquisition (Marris, 1964). The tendency for growth objectives to drive diversification is likely to be especially strong for companies located in slow growth or declining industries. Thus, the diversification by tobacco companies and oil companies during the 1970s and 1980s was driven by declining sales in domestic markets, although most of the diversification went into less profitable industries and had the effect of destroying shareholder value – RJR Nabisco was a classic example (Burrough, 1990). Agency theory has contributed substantially to the analysis of management behavior through careful analysis of the incentives determining the relationships of agents (managers) to principals (shareholders) (Jensen and Meckling, 1976).

The goal of risk reduction, too, is associated more with the interests of managers than with shareholders. The capital asset pricing model postulates that the risk that is relevant to determining the price of a security is not the overall risk (variance) of the security's return, but its 'systematic risk' – that part of the variance of the return that is correlated with overall market risk (as measured by the security's beta coefficient). Corporate diversification does not reduce systematic risk: if separate companies are brought under common ownership, in the absence of any other changes, the beta coefficient of the combined company is simply the weighted average of the beta coefficients of the constituent companies. The underlying argument is that, if shareholders can diversify risk through holding portfolios of securities, firms cannot create value by diversifying on their behalf. Firms that diversify in order to reduce risk are likely to be pursuing the security goals of managers. Amihud and Lev (1981) showed that managerially-controlled firms made more conglomerate mergers and became more diversified than owner-controlled firms, however, Lane et al. (1998) challenged these findings.

The only exception to this argument is where some form of inefficiency exists within securities markets, such that diversification by firms is more feasible or efficient than 'home-made' portfolio diversification by investors. For example, if individuals are unable to purchase the securities of companies in Russia or China, multinational diversification by Western companies may offer benefits of global risk spreading that investors cannot access individually. Special issues arise once we consider the risk of bankruptcy. For a marginally profitable firm, diversification can help avoid cyclical fluctuations of profits that can push it into insolvency. It has been shown, however, that diversification that reduces the risk of bankruptcy is beneficial to the holders of corporate debt rather than to equity holders. The reduction in risk that bondholders derive from a diversifying merger is the 'coinsurance effect' (Ross and Westerfield, 1988: 681).

Top management's ability to pursue objectives other than profitability is constrained by at least two factors. First, over the long term a firm must earn a return on capital greater than its cost of capital or it does not survive. Second, if management sacrifices profitability for other objectives, managers run the risk of losing their jobs either from a shareholders' revolt or from acquisition. This explains why companies sell off diversified businesses when their control of the firm is threatened by a takeover bid or by a fall in profitability that attracts potential predators (Ravenscraft and Scherer, 1987). The key to aligning the interests of managers with those of shareholders is

to remove management control over free cash flow (Jensen, 1986). The surge of leveraged buy-outs during the 1980s and 1990s may be viewed as a response to the agency problem.

Are there circumstances where reductions in unsystematic risk can create shareholder value? If there are transaction costs in using external capital markets, then the stability in the firm's cash flow that results from diversification may support a firm's independence from the capital markets. An implicit assumption behind the use of portfolio models for corporate planning was the desirability of balancing cash using and cash generating businesses (Haspeslaugh, 1983). Among the major oil companies (Exxon, Shell, Mobil, BP), one of the benefits of extending across upstream (explorations and production), downstream (refining and marketing), and chemicals is that the negative correlation of the returns from these businesses increases the overall stability of the companies' cash flows. This in turn increases their capacity to undertake huge risky investments such as offshore oil production, transcontinental pipelines, and natural gas liquefaction plants.

Agency theory suggests linkages between a firm's ownership and capital structure and its corporate strategy. Based upon the assumption that diversification is more in the interests of mangers than of shareholders, several studies offer empirical support for the prediction that companies with greater ownership concentration are less diversified (Amihud and Lev, 1999; Denis et al., 1999).

Implications of Shareholder Value Maximization for Corporate Strategy

If firms are to operate in the interests of their shareholders, then maximization of shareholder value implies maximizing the company's net cash flow discounted at its cost of capital. Selecting the corporate strategy that can best achieve this goal involves two basic questions: which products, markets and activities are the most attractive in terms of their inherent attractiveness, and in which products, markets and activities does the firm have the best potential for establishing competitive advantage?

For firms contemplating diversification, Michael Porter (1987) proposes three 'essential tests' to be applied in deciding whether diversification will truly create shareholder value:

1 *The attractiveness test.* The industries chosen for diversification must be structurally attractive or capable of being made attractive.
2 *The cost-of-entry test.* The cost of entry must not capitalize all the future profits.
3 *The better-off test.* Either the new unit must gain competitive advantage from its link with the corporation or vice versa.

The Attractiveness and Cost-of-Entry Tests

An important insight in Porter's 'essential tests' is that industry attractiveness is insufficient on its own. Although diversification is a means by which the firm can access more attractive investment opportunities than are available in its own industry, it faces the task of entering the new industry. The second test, cost of entry, explicitly recognizes that the attractiveness of an industry to a firm already established in an industry may be different from its attractiveness to a firm seeking to enter the industry. Indeed, many industries offer above-average profitability precisely because they are protected by barriers to entry. Firms seeking entry to attractive industries such as pharmaceuticals, management consulting, or investment banking have a choice of entry strategies. They may enter by acquiring an established company, in which case not only does market price of the target firm reflect the superior profit prospects of the industry, but the diversifying firm must also offer an acquisition premium of between 20 and 40% over the market price to gain control. Alternatively, if diversifying firms enter by creating new corporate ventures, then they must directly confront the barriers of that industry. A study of 68 diversifying ventures by established companies found that, on average, break-even was not attained until the seventh and eighth years of operation (Biggadike, 1979).

The 'Better-Off' Test

Porter's third criterion for successful diversification addresses the basic issue of competitive advantage: if two businesses producing different products are brought together under the

ownership and control of a single enterprise, is there any reason why they should become any more profitable? This takes us into the issues of market power, economies of scope, and transaction costs that were discussed earlier.

Porter goes on to distinguish corporate strategies in relation to the extent to which they exploit economies of scope. The loosest strategy is that of *portfolio management*, where the lack of shared resources and capabilities means that the only source of value is the firm's ability to 'beat the market' in trading companies. Warren Buffett's Berkshire Hathaway follows a classic portfolio management strategy.

A *restructuring strategy* is one where the critical source of value added is corporate management's intervention in the acquired company so as to change top management, restructure the asset portfolio, change the financial structure, and reduce costs. Conglomerates Hanson, BTR, Tomkins and Tyco Internationals and leveraged buyout specialists such as Kohberg Kravis and Roberts were classic restructurers. However, the potential for value creation through exploitation of economies of scope are, according to Porter, limited. For a restructuring strategy to keep creating value requires a continuing process of acquisition, restructuring and disposal (divestment or spin-off).

The major opportunities for value creation through diversification arise from fuller utilization of resources and capabilities. Here Porter defines two types of corporate strategy to exploit linkages between businesses. *Transferring skills* involves moving knowledge, particularly that related to technology and markets, from one business to another. Thus, 3M transfers its technological capabilities and knowledge of customers among its many divisions. Similarly, Philip Morris transfers its knowledge of branding, market segmentation, target marketing, and managing within highly regulated markets between its cigarette business, Miller Brewing, and Kraft-General Foods. Alternatively, diversifying companies may use a strategy of *sharing activities*. Procter & Gamble employs common sales and distribution systems for paper towels and disposable diapers. General Electric shares its advertising across all its products. Porter argues that the shared activities model of diversification offers the most substantial opportunities for value creation.

THE QUESTION OF RELATEDNESS

These discussions of economies of scope in shared resources and capabilities and Porter's categorization of corporate strategy types raises important issues for the nature of relatedness between different businesses. The literature on diversification has made a key distinction between 'related' and 'unrelated' diversification. The problem has been that the criteria for distinguishing these forms of diversification are hazy. The industrial economics literature has tended to fall back on standard industrial classification (SIC). Thus, related diversification is directed towards 'adjacent sectors', normally defined as within the same SIC two-digit industry code, while unrelated diversification is between two-digit codes (Berry, 1975). Other studies, notably the Wrigley classification, have defined related diversification in terms of technological linkages (a common core technology) and market linkages (a common customer need and channels of distributions).

Resource-Based Approaches to Relatedness

The resource-based view of the firm offers a broader-based and more rigorous approach to the analysis of business relatedness. If the primary source of value creating in diversification is economies of scope in resources and capabilities, then it is the ability to deploy common resources and capabilities that is the basis for relatedness between businesses. However, such an approach focuses upon a subset of resources and capabilities. Recent analysis of relatedness in diversification has offered a broader based approach that focuses upon the identification and analysis of common resources and capabilities (Robins and Wiersema, 1995). Markides and Williamson (1996) focus upon the deployment in different markets of similar nontradable, nonsubstitutable, hard to accumulate assets. They identify five types of asset: *customer assets* (brand recognition, customer loyalty, installed base), *channel assets* (channel access, distributor loyalty), *input assets* (knowledge of factor markets, supplier loyalty, financial capacity), *process assets* (proprietary technology, functional capabilities), and *market knowledge assets*.

Dominant Logic and Strategic Relatedness

Prahalad and Bettis (1986) propose an alternative approach to the analysis of relatedness in diversification. They propose the term *dominant logic* to refer to 'a mind set or world view or conceptualization of the business and the administrative tools to accomplish goals and make decisions in that business'. This concept of relatedness rests, not on the presence of economies of scope in resources and capabilities, but upon top management's perception of similarity between businesses. While Prahalad and Bettis develop the idea of dominant logic as a common cognitive 'schema' through which corporate and business-level managers can understand the nature of their company and its strategic rationale, operationalization of the concept requires that we specify the common strategic characteristics of the different businesses that permit the firm to apply its management capabilities and common corporate management systems in order to create value (Grant, 1988). Without such a specification, there is a danger that dominant logic may not be underpinned by any true economic synergies. There is a history of failed diversification where the dominant logic of the corporation has not been supported by genuine economic synergies.[3]

The linkage between dominant logic and the performance of diversified firms most likely exists through the implications of dominant logic for the overall configuration between corporate strategy, resources and capabilities, organizational structure, and management systems. Those companies that possess a stable consensus concerning dominant logic are better able to achieve fit between resources, strategy, structure, systems and style. Markides and Williamson (1996) point to the important and complex role played by organizational structure in linking commonality in strategic assets to superior profitability. In particular, the centralized, multidivisional form ('CM-form') appeared to facilitate the sharing of some types of strategic assets, but not others.

A key theme arising from several writings has been emphasis on 'strategic' rather than 'operational' level linkages between the business units of the diversified firm. Much of the traditional analysis of relatedness in diversification has emphasized commonalities in

Table 4.3   *The determinants of strategic relatedness between businesses*

Corporate management tasks	Determinants of strategic similarity
Resource allocation	Similar sizes of capital investment projects. Similar time spans of investment projects. Similar sources of risk. Similar general management skills required for business unit managers.
Strategy formulation	Similar key success factors. Similar stages of the industry life cycle. Similar competitive positions occupied by each business within its industry.
Targeting, monitoring, and control of business unit	Goals defined in terms of similar performance variables. Similar time horizons for performance targets.

Source: Grant (1988).

technology and markets. These relate primarily to relatedness at the *operational* level – in manufacturing, marketing, and distribution activities. Although Porter suggests that these operating-level commonalities involving the sharing activities across businesses require the closest integration between the businesses, this does not necessarily mean they offer the greatest potential for yielding economies of scope. Moreover, such sharing of activities typically imposes substantial coordination costs. These costs involve not simply the management time and effort to coordinate the linkages across businesses, but also the loss of clarity in financial control and performance monitoring that results from the presence of shared costs.

The dominant logic approach to corporate strategy emphasizes on strategic rather than the operational linkages between businesses. If dominant logic rests ultimately upon the resources and capabilities of the top management team, then the domain over which these resources and capabilities can be deployed is dependent upon a set of common strategic characteristics of the various businesses. Thus, Berkshire Hathaway is involved in insurance, candy stores, furniture, kitchen knives, jewelry, and footwear. Despite this diversity, all these businesses have been selected on the basis of their ability to benefit from the unique style of corporate management established by Chairman Warren Buffett and CEO Charles Munger. Berkshire Hathaway's hands-off management style is dependent upon its top management's ability to identify and acquire well-managed medium-sized businesses in industries with strong underlying economics and which are not complicated by either rapid technological change or strong international competition. The same is true with Richard Branson's Virgin group of companies that span airlines, soft drinks, and financial services.

This array of businesses is linked, first, by the Virgin brand and, second, by the group's capabilities in managing start-up businesses with a strong customer orientation, innovative differentiation, and entrepreneurial, risk taking cultures.

Grant (1988) argues that the essence of these strategic linkages is the ability to apply similar strategic planning processes, resource allocation procedures, and control systems across the different businesses. Table 4.3 illustrates some of the features of strategic similarity that facilitate the application of common corporate management systems.

Parenting Advantage

Empirical research shows that there are no generally superior corporate strategies. The critical issue is achieving fit between the resources and capabilities of a company and its corporate strategy, organization structure and management systems. The resources and capabilities that reside at the headquarters level of a company are fundamental determinants of the optimal strategy/structure/systems configuration. To gain insight into these linkages, Goold, Campbell and colleagues invoke the concept of 'parenting' to analyze the relationship between the corporate headquarters and the individual businesses of the diversified company (Goold et al., 1994, 1995). The core principle underlying corporate strategy decisions is that of 'parenting advantage': a corporate parent should be able to 'create more value from its businesses than any alternative owner' (Goold et al., 1994: 14). Corporate parents can add value to their individual businesses through four primary mechanisms:

Stand-alone influence whereby the corporate parent improves business performance by applying its standardized tools of financial control and strategic planning, appointing and motivating business managers, and, possibly, influencing strategic and operational management at the business level. Examples include BTR, Emerson and RTZ.

Linkage influence whereby the corporate parent manages linkages between the businesses including the transfer of best practices, the sharing of technology and information, and the exploitation of other business-level economies of scope. Examples include Bank One, Unilever, ABB, and Canon.

Functional and services influence whereby the corporate parent takes responsibility for developing and providing administrative services such as IT, legal and HR services and key functional such as R&D, marketing, and logistics. Examples include Cooper Industries, Shell, and 3M.

Corporate development influence whereby the primary role of the corporate parent is nurturing the development of the individual businesses. Examples include Hanson and TI plc.

This concept of fit between resources and capabilities, corporate and business-level strategies, organizational structure, and management systems and style is also the central theme of Collis and Montgomery's (1997, 1998) analysis of corporate strategy. They propose a triangle of corporate strategy that links resources, businesses and organization. The key feature of resources is their degree of specialization. The more specialized the firm's resources and the narrower the firm's business scope, the greater the emphasis on sharing resources rather than transferring skills, and the greater the emphasis on operating controls rather than financial controls.

CONCLUSION: CHALLENGES FOR FUTURE RESEARCH

Corporate strategy has been a minefield both for managers and researchers. For senior executives, diversification may be compared to sex: its attractions are obvious, even irresistible, but the actual experience is often disappointing. The diversification histories of large corporations are littered with expensive mistakes: Exxon with Exxon Office Systems, GE with Utah International and Kidder Peabody, Philip Morris with Seven-Up, American Express with Shearson Lehman, Daimler-Benz in aerospace, Coca-Cola in wine, AT&T with NCR. Yet despite so many costly failures, the urge to diversify continues to captivate chief executives. One problem is top management's willingness to sacrifice shareholder value for corporate empire building. Another problem is hubris. A company's success in one line of business tends to result in the top management team becoming overconfident of its ability to achieve similar success in other businesses (Miller, 1990). Collis and Montgomery (1997: 83) point to two key managerial miscalculations: 'First, they tend to overestimate the transferability of specific resources. Sears, for example, misjudged the value of its customer base and reputation would bring to financial services.... Second, companies overestimate the value of very general resources in creating competitive advantage. General Mills, for example, thought its valuable resource was understanding the needs and wants of the homemaker, and so diversified unsuccessfully into fashion retailing, toys, jewelry, and clothing during the seventies.'

Have corporate strategy scholars done much to educate managers? Even after nearly a half-century of research, the advice we academics can offer managers in designing and implementing their corporate strategies is tentative at best. Much of the research into corporate strategy, especially those studies that attempted to link corporate strategy with performance, seems naïve. More than a hundred academic studies have failed to determine if diversification enhances profitability or whether related diversification outperforms unrelated diversification.

As with other areas of management science, progress has been achieved less by empirical testing as through the displacement of prevailing theories by better theories. During the past 20 years, the study of corporate strategy has been transformed by transaction cost economics and the resource-based theory of the firm, with further contributions from agency theory and modern financial theory.

Current research is looking beyond simple relationships between corporate strategy and performance and is coming to terms with the complex relationships between the scope of the firm, corporate performance and the wide range of variables that characterize both the external and the internal environment of the firm. The most promising approaches to the analysis of corporate strategy are those that look both to the characteristics of the resources and capabilities that underlie corporate strategy and to the organizational structures and mechanisms that implement it. Collis and Montgomery's resource-based analysis of corporate advantage and Goold and Campbell's corporate parenting model are initial explorations of the overall configuration of resources, strategy, structure, systems and style. At the empirical level, Markides and Williamson's research has established a bridge between the resource-based approach to strategy formulation and organization-theory approach to strategy implementation.

To make further progress, key gaps in our knowledge need to be filled. These include:

Analysis of organizational capabilities. Despite the surge of interest in a firm's capabilities and competences, the anatomy, development and scope of organizational capability represents *terra incognito* for strategy scholars. The concept and importance of organizational capability is well established, yet we know little about their taxonomy and measurement, let alone their internal structure or processes of creation and replication. Unless we know how organizational capability is created, performed, transferred within the organization, and what limits the number and range of capabilities that an organization can successfully embrace, then progress in unraveling the relationship between firm scope and competitive advantage will be limited. But help is at hand, research into routines and the evolutionary theory of the firm (Nelson and Winter, 1982; Teece et al., 1994; Pentland and Rueter, 1994), the knowledge-based theory of the firm (Kogut and Zander, 1992; Nonaka, 1994), and coordination theory (Malone et al., 1999) has the potential to deepen our understanding of how multibusiness firms create value.

Analysis of organizational structures and processes. The organizational capabilities that form the foundation of corporate strategy are dependent upon organizational structures and processes. If value creation in the multibusiness firm rests upon the deployment of organizational capabilities across multiple businesses, then organizational structures and systems must be adapted to the characteristics of those capabilities and the ways in which they are deployed to enhance the competitive advantage

of the individual businesses. However, our understanding of the role structure in the linkage between corporate strategy and performance remains primitive. Transaction cost economics offers penetrating insights into the relative efficiencies of multibusiness firms compared with specialized firms linked by markets, but our understanding of the costs of market transactions is not matched by our understanding of costs of corporate management. Better understanding of the capacity of diversified corporations to allocate resources, transfer capabilities, and adapt to external change will need to draw upon promising developments in corporate coherence (Teece et al., 1994), the management of convergent expectations (Camerer and Knez, 1996), complexity theory (Anderson, 1999), and corporate management processes (Ghoshal and Bartlett, 1999).

The nature of the firm. As yet we have little understanding of why Matsushita, General Electric, ABB, Canon, Walt Disney Company, Tyco International and Hewlett Packard are able to create value through diversification while other companies (RJR Nabisco, Hanson, AT&T, Eastman Kodak, and BTR) have released shareholder value through breaking up their diversified structures and returning to their core businesses. Further analysis of the role of organizational structures and management systems in linking resources and capabilities to strategies can help, but ultimately we need to consider the fundamentals of why firms exist and what their roles are. Until recently the theory of the firms has been shaped mainly by transaction cost economics. The recent debate is over transaction cost versus resource-based and knowledge-based views of the firm (Foss, 1996; Connor and Prahalad, 1996; Kogut and Zander, 1996). To understand how firms can create value across multiple businesses we need to know what firms are. This requires looking beyond transaction cost theory to consider the role of the firm as a set of routines (Nelson and Winter, 1982), a residue of property rights (Hart and Moore, 1990), collection of 'higher-order organizing principles' (Kogut and Zander, 1992), a reservoir of productive knowledge (Grant, 1996), a unit of social capital (Dasgupta and Serageldin, 1999), and a complementary group of competences (Dosi and Teece, 1998).

In common with many other areas of strategic management research, the quest for consistent, stable relationships between strategic variables and firm performance, even when contextual variables representing the business environment are taken into account, has proved to be fruitless. The challenge is not so much to refine the empirical methodology, but to delve into the underlying theoretical issues. What are the sources of value in the competitive capitalist economy? What is the role of the firm as an institution for organizing production? How does the firm deploy resources and create organizational capability? What does the firm reconcile the benefits of specialization with the gains from complementarities in terms of the range of capabilities that it encompasses? What factors determine the efficiency with which a firm deploys resources and capabilities across multiple markets and activities as compared with alternative economic and social institutions?

The trends we have observed from the conglomerate diversification of the 1970s to the refocusing of the 1990s have been driven by ideology and imitation rather than by analysis. The corporate strategies of the future need to be based not on slavish acceptance of prevailing management philosophy but upon depth of understanding of the relationships between strategy, structure, resources, and environment. The coexistence of successful specialized companies and successful diversified companies underlines the fact that there are no simple relationships that link corporate strategy to performance. Developing better understanding of what determines the scope of the firm and how corporate strategy links with firm performance will require drawing upon better developed theories of the firm and undertaking the fine-grained, exploratory research needed to uncover the specifics of how value is created within multibusiness firms.

NOTES

1 As we shall see, ultimately, this distinction breaks down: corporate strategy decisions are highly dependent upon a firm's ability to establish competitive advantage within specific markets and sectors. However, as a starting point this distinction is useful.

2 Although Lictenberg (1992) points to US firms operating in fewer industries between 1985 and 1989, Hatfield et al. (1996) observe increased industry specialization during 1981–89. Meanwhile, in Europe,

Whittington et al. (1999) point to a continuation of large company diversification in France, Germany and the UK between 1983 and 1993.

3 Examples include Allegis Corporation's attempt to combine United Airlines, Hertz car rental, and Westin hotel in a corporation designed to 'meet the needs of the traveler'; General Mills' diversification into toys, fashion clothing, specialty retailing, and restaurants on the basis of 'understanding the needs and wants of the home-maker'; and Sears Roebuck's merging of Allstate Insurance, Dean Witter, and Coldwell Banker real estate to create the 'Sears Financial Network'.

REFERENCES

Ackoff, R. C. (1970) *The Concept of Corporate Planning.* New York: Wiley.
Alchian, A. A. and Demsetz, H. (1972) 'Production, information costs, and economic organization', *American Economic Review*, 62: 777–95.
Amey, L. (1964) 'Diversified manufacturing businesses', *Journal of the Royal Statistical Society, Series A*, 127: 157–74.
Amihud, Y. and Lev, B. (1981) 'Diversification strategies, economic cycles, and economic performance', *Bell Journal of Economics*, 12: 605–17.
Amihud, Y. and Lev, B. (1999) 'Does corporate ownership structure affect its strategy towards diversification?' *Strategic Management Journal*, 20: 1063–9.
Amit, R. and Livnat, J. (1988) 'Diversification and the risk/return trade off', *Academy of Management Journal*, 31: 154–66.
Anderson, P. (1999) 'Complexity theory and organizational science', *Organization Science*, 10: 321–36.
Ansoff, I. (1965) *Corporate Strategy.* London: Penguin Books.
Argyres, N. (1996) 'Evidence on the role of firm capabilities in vertical integration decisions', *Strategic Management Journal*, 17: 129–50.
Barney, J. B. (1991) 'Firm resources and sustained competitive advantage', *Journal of Management*, 17: 395–410.
Baum, J. A. C. and Korn, H. J. (1996) 'Competitive dynamics of interfirm rivalry', *Academy of Management Review*, 39: 255–91.
Baumol, W. J., Panzar, J. C. and Willig, R. D. (1982) *Contestable Markets and the Theory of Industry Structure.* New York: Harcourt Brace Jovanovich. pp. 71–2.
Bernheim, B. D. and Whinston, M. D. (1990) 'Multimarket contact and collusive behavior', *Rand Journal of Economics*, 2: 1–26.
Berry, C. H. (1975) *Corporate Growth and Diversification.* Princeton, NJ: Princeton University Press.
Besanko, D., Dranove, D. and Shanley, M. (1996) *Economics of Strategy.* New York: Wiley.

Bettis, R. A. (1981) 'Performance differences in related and unrelated diversified firms', *Strategic Management Journal*, 2: 379–94.

Bettis, R. A. and Mahajan, V. (1985) 'Risk-return performance of diversified firms', *Management Science*, 31: 785–99.

Biggadike, R. (1979) 'The risky business of diversification,' *Harvard Business Review*, 57 (May–June).

Burgelman, R. (1983) 'Corporate entrepreneurship and strategic management: insights from a process study', *Management Science*, 29: 1349–64.

Burrough, B. (1990) *Barbarians at the Gate: The Fall of RJR Nabisco*. New York: Harper & Row.

Business Week (1993) 'The virtual corporation', February 8: 98–104.

Buzzell, R. D. and Gale, B. T. (1987) *The PIMS Principles: Linking Strategy to Performance*. New York: Free Press.

Camerer, C. and Knez, M. (1996) 'Coordination, organizational boundaries and fads in business practices', *Industrial and Corporate Change*, 5: 89–112.

Chandler, A. Jr. (1962) *Strategy and Structure*. Cambridge: MIT Press.

Chandler, A. Jr. (1977) *The Visible Hand: The Managerial Revolution in American Business*. Cambridge: MIT Press.

Channon, D. (1973) *The Strategy and Structure of British Enterprise*. Cambridge: Harvard University Press.

Chatterjee, S. and Wernerfelt, B. (1991) 'The link between resources and type of diversification', *Strategic Management Journal*, 12: 33–48.

Chernow, R. (1998) *Titan: The Life of John D. Rockefeller Sr*. New York: Random House.

Chesbrough, H. W. and Teece, D. J. (1996) 'When is virtual virtuous? Organising for innovation.' *Harvard Business School* (January–February), 65–74.

Choi, C. J., Raman, M., Oussoltseva, O. and Lee, S. H. (1999) 'Political embeddedness and institutional analysis in the new global triad', *Management International Review*, 45: 30–48.

Christensen, K. and Montgomery, C. A. (1981) 'Corporate economic performance: diversification strategy versus market structure', *Strategic Management Journal*, 2: 327–43.

Cibin, R. and Grant, R. M. (1996) 'Restructuring among the world's leading oil companies', *British Journal of Management*, 7: 283–308.

Coase, R. H. (1937) 'The nature of the firm', *Economica*, 4: 386–405.

Collis, D. J. and Montgomery, C. A. (1997) *Corporate Strategy: Resources and the Scope of the Firm*. Burr Ridge, IL: Irwin.

Collis, D. J. and Montgomery, C. A. (1998) 'Creating corporate advantage', *Harvard Business Review*, 76: 71–83.

Connor, K. R. and Prahalad, C. K. (1996) 'Resource-based theory of the firm: knowledge versus opportunism', *Organization Science*, 7: 477–501.

Daems, H. (1989) 'The performance of European industrial groups', Discussion paper, Harvard Business School.

Dasgupta, P. and Serageldin, I. (1999) *Social Capital: A Multifaceted Perspective*. Washington, DC: World Bank.

Davidow, W. H. and Malone, M. S. (1992) *The Virtual Corporation*. New York: HarperCollins.

Davis, G. F., Diekman, K. A. and Tinsley, C. F. (1993) 'The decline and fall of the conglomerate firm in the 1980s: a study in the de-institutionalization of an organizational form', Northwestern University.

Denis, D. J., Denis, D. K. and Sarin, A. (1999) 'Agency theory and the influence of equity ownership structure on corporate diversification strategies', *Strategic Management Journal*, 20: 1071–6.

Dosi, G. and Teece, D. (1998) 'Organizational competencies and the boundaries of the firm', in R. Arena and C. Longhi (eds), *Markets and Organizations*. New York: Springer.

Dubini, P. (1997) 'The United Colors of Benetton', in A. Sinatra (ed.), *Corporate Transformation*. Norwell, MA: Kluwer. pp. 415–46.

Dubofski, P. and Varadarajan, P. (1987) 'Diversification and measures of performance: additional empirical evidence', *Academy of Management Journal*, 30: 597–608.

Dunning, J. H. (1958) *American Investment in British Manufacturing Industry*. London: George Allen and Unwin.

Dyas, G. (1972) 'The Strategy and Structure of French Enterprise', DBA dissertation, Harvard Business School.

Dyas, G. and Thanheiser, H. (1976) *The Emerging European Enterprise*. London: Macmillan.

Dyer, J. H. (1996a) 'Specialized supplier networks as a source of competitive advantage: evidence from the auto industry', *Strategic Management Journal*, 17: 271–92.

Dyer, J. H. (1996b) 'How Chrysler created an American keiretsu', *Harvard Business Review*, July–August: 42–56.

Dyer, J. H. (1997) 'Effective interfirm collaboration: how firms minimize transaction costs and maximize transaction value', *Strategic Management Journal*, 18: 535–56.

Economist, 'South-East Asia's Octopuses', July 17, 1993: 61.

Fereira, M. A. (1999) 'The evolution of corporate advantage: Gencor's unbundling, 1986–1999', Ph.D. thesis, IESE, Barcelona.

Fortune (1993) 'The king is dead', January 11: 34–46.

Foss, N. J. (1996) 'Knowledge-based approaches to the theory of the firm: some critical comments', *Organization Science*, 7(5): 473.

Galbraith, J. K. (1969) *The New Industrial State*. Harmondsworth, UK: Penguin.

Geneen, H. (1969) 'The strategy of diversification', Statement to the Antitrust Subcommittee of the Committee on the Judiciary, House of Representatives, November 20.

Ghoshal, S. and Bartlett, C. (1999) *The Individualized Corporation*. New York: Harper Paperback.

Goold, M., Campbell, A. and Alexander, M. (1994) *Corporate-Level Strategy: Creating Value in the Multibusiness Company*. New York: Wiley.

Goold, M., Campbell, A. and Alexander, M. (1995) 'Corporate strategy: the quest for parenting advantage', *Harvard Business Review*, March–April: 120–32.

Goold, M. and Luchs, K. (1993) 'Why diversify? Four decades of management thinking', *Academy of Management Executive* 7, 3: 7–25.

Gort, M. (1962) *Diversification and Integration in American Industry*. Princeton, NJ: Princeton University Press.

Grant, R. M. (1987) 'Multinationality and performance among British manufacturing companies', *Journal of International Business Studies*, 22: 249–63.

Grant, R. M. (1988) 'On dominant logic, relatedness, and the link between diversity and performance', *Strategic Management Journal*, 9: 639–42.

Grant, R. M. (1991) 'The resource-based theory of competitive advantage: implications for competitive advantage', *California Management Review*, 33(3): 114–35.

Grant, R. M. (1996) 'Toward a knowledge-based theory of the firm', *Strategic Management Journal*, 17: 109–22.

Grant, R. M., Jammine, A. P. and Thomas, H. (1988) 'Diversity, diversification and profitability among British manufacturing companies, 1972–84', *Academy of Management Journal*, 31: 771–801.

Grove, A. (1996) *Only the Paranoid Survive*. New York: Doubleday.

Hamel, G. and Prahalad, C. K. (1985) 'Do you really have a global strategy?', *Harvard Business Review*, July–August: 138–48.

Hannah, L. (1991) 'Scale and scope: towards a European visible hand?', *Business History*, 33: 297–309.

Hart, O. and Moore, J. (1990) 'Property rights and the nature of the firm', *Journal of Political Economy*, 98: 1119–58.

Haspeslaugh, P. C. (1983) 'Portfolio planning approaches and the strategic management process in diversified industrial corporations', doctoral dissertation, Harvard Business School.

Hatfield, D. E., Liebeskind, J. P. and Opler, T. C. (1996) 'The effects of corporate restructuring on aggregate industry specialization', *Strategic Management Journal*, 17: 55–72.

Helfat, C. (1997) 'Know-how and asset complementarity and dynamic capability accumulation', *Strategic Management Journal*, 18: 339–60.

Hill, C. (1995) 'National institutional structures, transaction cost economizing and competitive advantage', *Organization Science*, 6: 119–31.

Hitt, M. A., Hoskisson, R. E. and Kim, H. (1997) 'International diversification: effects on innovation and firm performance in product-diversified firms', *Academy of Management Journal*, 40: 767–98.

Hoskisson, R. E. and Hitt, M. A. (1994) *Downscoping: How to Tame the Diversified Firm*. New York: Oxford University Press.

Hoskisson, R. E., Hitt, M. A., Johnson, R. A. and Moesel, D. D. (1993) 'Construct validity of an objective categorical measure of diversification strategy', *Strategic Management Journal*, 14: 215–35.

Hymer, S. (1957) *The International Operations of National Firms: A Study of Direct Investment*, Ph.D. dissertation, MIT.

Itami, H., Kagono, T., Yoshihara, H. and Sakuma, S. (1982) 'Diversification strategies and economic performance', *Japanese Economic Studies*, 11(1): 78–110.

Jammine, A. P. (1984) *Product Diversification, International Expansion and Performance: A Study of Strategic Risk Management in UK Manufacturing*, Ph.D. dissertation, London Business School.

Jarrell, G. A., Brickly, J. A. and Netter, J. M. (1988) 'The market for corporate control: empirical evidence since 1980', *Journal of Economic Perspectives*, 2, 1 (Winter 1988): 49–68.

Jensen, M. C. (1986) 'Agency costs of free cash flow, corporate finance, and takeovers', *American Economic Review*, 76: 323–9.

Jensen, M. C. and Meckling, W. F. (1976) 'Theory of the firm: managerial behavior, agency costs, and ownership structure', *Journal of Financial Economics*, 3: 305–60.

Johnston, R. and Lawrence, P. R. (1988) 'Beyond ver-tical integration: the rise of the value adding partnership', *Harvard Business Review*, 66, July–August: 94–101.

Katz, R. L. (1955) 'Skills of an effective administrator', *Harvard Business Review*, January–February: 33–42.

Khanna, T. and Palepu, K. (1997) 'Why focussed strategies may be wrong for emerging markets', *Harvard Business Review*, 75 (July–August): 41–51.

Khanna, T. and Palepu, K. (1999) 'Policy shocks, market intermediaries, and corporate strategy: the evolution of business groups in Chile and India', *Journal of Economics and Management Strategy*, 8: 271–310.

Klein, B., Crawford, R. and Alchian, A. A. (1978) 'Vertical integration, appropriable rents and the competitive contracting process', *Journal of Law and Economics*, 21: 297–326.

Kogut, B. and Zander, U. (1992) 'Knowledge of the firm, combinative capabilities, and the replication of technology', *Organization Science*, 3: 383–97.

Kogut, B. and Zander, U. (1996) 'What firms do? Coordination, identity, and learning', *Organization Science*, 7: 502–18.

Koontz, H. (1969) 'A model for analyzing the universality and transferability of management', *Academy of Management Journal*, 12: 415–30.

Korn, H. J. and Baum, J. (1999) 'Chance, imitative and strategic antecedents to multimarket contact', *Academy of Management Journal*, 42: 171–93.

Krishnan, H. A., Miller, A. and Judge, W. Q. (1997) 'Diversification and top management team complementarity', *Strategic Management Journal*, 18: 361–74.

Lane, P. J., Cannella, A. A. and Lubatkin, M. H. (1998) 'Agency problems as antecedents to unrelated mergers and diversification: Amihud and Lev reconsidered', *Strategic Management Journal*, 19: 555–78.

Lecraw, D. J. (1984) 'Diversification strategy performance', *Journal of Industrial Economics*, 32: 179–98.

Lee, J-H. and Sirh, J-Y. (1999) 'Institutional context, structural adaptation, and diversification of Korean chaebols', Paper presented at the Academy of International Business, London Business School.

Levy, H. and Sarnat, M. (1970) 'Diversification, portfolio analysis and the uneasy case for conglomerate mergers', *Journal of Finance*, 25: 795–802.

Lictenberg, F. R. (1992) 'Industrial de-diversification and its consequences for productivity', *Journal of Economic Behavior and Organization*, 18: 427–38.

Liebeskind, J. P. (2000) 'Internal capital markets: benefits, costs and organizational arrangements', *Organization Science*, 11: 79–92.

Lintner, J. (1965) 'Security prices, risk, and maximal gains from diversification', *Journal of Finance*, 20: 587–615.

Lorenzoni, G. and Baden-Fuller, C. (1995) 'Creating a strategic center to manage a web of partners', *California Management Review*, 37(3): 146–63.

Lorenzoni, G. and Lipparini, A. (1999) 'The leveraging of interfirm relationships as a distinctive organizational capability: a longitudinal study', *Strategic Management Journal*, 20: 317–38.

Lubatkin, M. (1987) 'Merger strategies and stockholder value', *Strategic Management Journal*, 8: 218–25.

Lubatkin, M. and Chatterjee, S. (1994) 'Extending modern portfolio theory into the domain of corporate strategy: does it apply?', *Academy of Management Journal*, 37: 109–36.

Luffman, G. A. and Reed, R. (1984) *The Strategy and Performance of British Industry, 1970–80*. London: Macmillan.

Malone, T. W., Crowston, K. and others (1999) 'Tools for inventing organizations: toward a handbook of organizational processes', *Management Science*, 45: 425–43.

Markides, C. (1992a) 'The economic characteristics of de-diversifying firms', *British Journal of Management*, 3: 91–100.

Markides, C. (1992b) 'Consequences of corporate refocusing: ex ante evidence', *Academy of Management Journal*, 35: 398–412.

Markides, C. and Williamson, P. J. (1996) 'Corporate diversification and organizational structure', *Academy of Management Journal*, 39: 340–67.

Marris, R. (1964) *The Economic Theory of Managerial Capitalism*. London: Macmillan.

Mason, R. H. and Goudzwaard, M. B. (1976) 'Performance of conglomerate firms: a portfolio approach', *Journal of Finance*, 31: 39–48.

Melicher, F. W. and Rush, D. F. (1973) 'The performance of conglomerate firms: recent risk and return experience', *Journal of Finance*, 28: 381–8.

Michel, A. and Shaked, I. (1984) 'Does business diversification affect performance?', *Financial Management*, 13, 4: 18–24.

Miller, D. (1990) *The Icarus Paradox*. New York: Harper Business.

Montgomery, C. A. and Wernerfelt, B. (1991) 'Sources of superior performance: market share versus industry effects in the US brewing industry', *Management Science*, 37: 954–9.

Nayyar, P. R. (1992) 'On the measurement of corporate diversification strategy', *Strategic Management Journal*, 13: 219–35.

Nelson, R. and Winter, S. (1982). *An Evolutionary Theory of Economic Change*. Cambridge, MA: Belknap Press.

Nonaka, I. (1994) 'A dynamic theory of organizational knowledge creation', *Organization Science*, 5: 14–37.

Palich, L. E., Cardinal, L. B. and Miller, C. C. (2000) 'Curvilinearity in the diversification–performance linkage: an examination over three decades of research', *Strategic Management Journal*, 21: 155–74.

Pavan, R. (1972) 'The strategy and structure of Italian enterprise', DBA dissertation, Harvard Business School, Boston.

Penrose, E. (1959) *Theory of the Growth of the Firm*. New York: Wiley.

Pentland, B. and Rueter, H. (1994) 'Organizational routines as grammars of action', *Administrative Science Quarterly*, 39: 484–500.

Peters, T. and Waterman, R. (1982) *In Search of Excellence*. New York: Harper & Row.

Porter, M. E. (1980) *Competitive Strategy*. New York: Free Press.

Porter, M. E. (1987) 'From competitive advantage to corporate strategy', *Harvard Business Review*, (May–June): 46.

Powell, W. W. (1989) 'Neither market not hierarchy: network forms of organization', in B. M. Staw and L. L. Cummings (eds), *Research in Organizational Behavior*, 12. pp. 295–336.

Prahalad, C. K. and Bettis, R. A. (1986) 'The dominant logic: a new linkage between diversity and performance', *Strategic Management Journal*, 7: 485–502.

Prahalad, C. K. and Hamel, G. (1990) 'The core competences of the corporation', *Harvard Business Review*, (May–June): 79–91.

Ramanujam, V. and Varadarajan, R. P. (1989) 'Research on corporate diversification: a synthesis', *Strategic Management Journal*, 10: 523–51.

Ravenscraft, D. A. and Scherer, F. M. (1987) 'Divisional selloff: a hazard analysis', in *Mergers, Selloffs and Economic Efficiency*. Washington, DC: Brookings Institute.

Ring, P. S. and Van de Ven, A. H. (1992) 'Structuring cooperative relationships between organizations', *Strategic Management Journal*, 13: 483–98.

Robins, J. and Wiersema, M. F. (1995) 'A resource-based approach to the multibusiness firms: empirical analysis of portfolio interrelationships and corporate financial performance', *Strategic Management Journal*, 16: 277–300.

Robins, J. and Wiersema, M. F. (1997) 'Measurement of related diversification: are the measures valid for the concepts?', GSM Working Paper 97010-ST, University of California, Irvine.

Ross, S. A. and Westerfield, R. W. (1988) *Corporate Finance*. St. Louis: Times Mirror/Mosby College. p. 681.

Rumelt, R. P. (1974) *Strategy, Structure and Economic Performance*. Cambridge, MA: Harvard University Press.

Rumelt, R. P. (1982) 'Diversification strategy and profitability', *Strategic Management Journal*, 3: 359–70.

Saxenian, A. (1990) 'Regional networks and the resurgence of Silicon Valley', *California Management Review*, 33, Fall: 39–112.

Sharpe, W. F. (1964) 'Capital asset prices: a theory of market equilibrium under conditions of risk', *Journal of Finance*, 19: 425–42.

Shleifer, A. and Vishny, R. W. (1990) 'The takeover wave of the 1980s', *Science*, 248 (July–September, 1990): 747–9.

Shleifer, A. and Vishny, R. W. (1991) 'Takeovers in the '60s and the '80s: evidence and implications', *Strategic Management Journal*, 12 (Winter special issue): 51–9.

Simon, H. A. (1991) 'Organisations and markets', *Journal of Economic Perspectives*, 5(2): 25–44.

Sloan, A. P. (1963) *My Years at General Motors.* London: Sidgewick & Jackson.

Stimpert, J. L. and Duhaime, I. M. (1997) 'In the eyes of the beholder: conceptualizations of relatedness held by managers of large diversified firms', *Strategic Management Journal*, 18: 111–26.

Teece, D. J. (1980) 'Economies of scope and the scope of the enterprise', *Journal of Economic Behavior and Organization*, 1: 223–47.

Teece, D. J. (1982) 'Towards an economic theory of the multiproduct firm', *Journal of Economic Behavior and Organization*, 3: 39–63.

Teece, D. J., Rumelt, R., Dosi, G. and Winter, S. (1994) 'Understanding corporate coherence: theory and evidence', *Journal of Economic Behavior and Organization*, 23: 1–30.

Thanheiser, H. (1973) 'The strategy and structure of German enterprise', DBA thesis, Harvard Business School.

US Senate, Subcommittee on Antitrust and Monopoly Hearings, *Economic Concentration*, Part 1, Congress, 1st session, 1965: 45.

Wernerfelt, B. (1984) 'The resource-based view of the firm', *Strategic Management Journal*, 5: 171–80.

Weston, J. F., Smith, K. V. and Shrieves, R. E. (1972) 'Conglomerate performance using the capital asset pricing model', *Review of Economics and Statistics*, 54: 357–63.

Whittington, R., Mayer, M. and Curto, F. (1999) 'Chandlerism in post-war Europe: strategic and structural change in France, Germany and the UK, 1950–1993', *Industrial and Corporate Change*, 8: 519–50.

Williams, J. R., Paez, B. L. and Sanders, L. (1988) 'Conglomerates revisited', *Strategic Management Journal*, 9: 403–14.

Williamson, O. E. (1975) *Markets and Hierarchies: Analysis and Antitrust Implications.* New York: Free Press.

Williamson, O. E. (1985) *The Economic Institutions of Capitalism: Firms, Markets and Relational Contracting.* New York: Free Press.

Wrigley, L. (1970) *Divisional Autonomy and Diversification*, doctoral dissertation, Harvard Business School.

5

Corporate Strategy:
The Role of the Centre

CONSTANTINOS MARKIDES

What is the role of the centre in multibusiness firms? This question lies at the heart of what academics call 'corporate strategy' (as opposed to business strategy). As a result, it has received extensive attention in the academic literature and has been the subject of numerous studies since the early 1960s – Chandler's (1962) book being the catalyst for the ensuing research on the subject.

This question has obvious managerial relevance as well and this has not gone unnoticed by consultants. As a result, to the voluminous academic literature on the subject, one could add an equally impressive body of work coming out of consulting houses – the BCG portfolio matrix being the most famous 'contribution' to the issue.

Unfortunately, the majority of this work has not been anchored in theory. By this I mean that in order for anyone to answer the question: 'What is the role of the centre?' in a meaningful way, one must *begin* by answering the question: 'What is the economic rationale for multibusiness firms?' – a point also raised by Hill (1990). Without answering this question first, all answers to the first question would amount to nothing more than laundry lists of things that the 'centre' ought to be doing. Such laundry lists can be short or long, elegant or coarse, sensible or stupid, but at the end of the day will simply reflect the biases

and (limited) mental capacity of the person preparing the laundry list.

One need not dig too deep to see the logic in my assertion. Even a casual survey of the literature produces numerous papers attempting to answer the question. In paper after paper, you get lists after lists of what the centre 'ought' to be doing. For example, Chandler (1994: 327) argues that the centre has to carry out two closely-related functions. 'One [is] entrepreneurial or value-creating, that is, to determine strategies for maintaining and utilizing in the long term the firm's organizational skills, facilities, and capital and to allocate resources... The second [is] more administrative or loss preventive. It [is] to monitor the performance of the operating divisions; to check on the use of the resources allocated; and, when necessary, to redefine the product lines of the divisions so as to continue to use the firm's organizational capabilities effectively.'

This is an impressive list and one could hardly disagree with any of the functions listed – they all sound logical and common sense. But how exhaustive is this list? Does it cover all the functions that the centre ought to be doing or has Chandler missed a few? (In fact, much lengthier lists than this have been produced. For example, Collis and Montgomery [1997] propose that the centre has four major functions – to

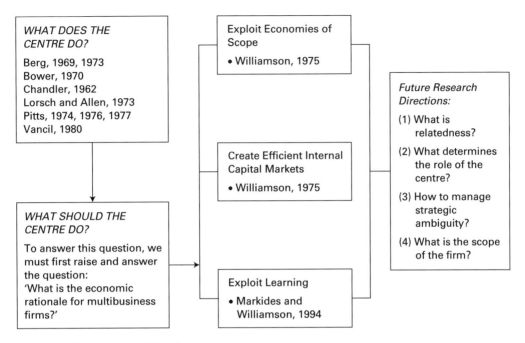

Figure 5.1   *The structure of this chapter*

set strategy, to guard resources, to set the administrative context and to carry out general overhead functions. Campbell et al. [1995], on the other hand, provide a list of ten areas where the centre can add value, for example, exploit linkages between divisions, provide special expertise to the divisions, manage external relations, and so on.) When I asked the same question in an executive class, I assembled a list of 27 functions that the centre is or should be performing in the modern firm – from promoting entrepreneurship at the divisional level to developing the norms and values that guide the corporation forward. With a bigger class, one hopes to generate an even longer list! Add to this the numerous authors that claim to have uncovered the role that the 'new' centre ought to perform in these fast-changing and exciting times and one gets the distinct feeling that the list may be endless.

Even worse, lack of a theoretical underpinning means that we have no basis for judging whether what we propose that the centre ought to be doing is the right thing. In other words, apart from judging these proposed functions on the criterion of 'common sense', how do we know that these are indeed the appropriate functions that the centre *ought* to be doing?

Other than common sense, what other criteria should we be using and on what basis should we be making recommendations to managers? Again, there is nothing wrong with using common sense, but surely this is not enough. We must have some logical theory on which to base our prescriptions.

In this chapter, I will try to avoid providing my own list of things that the centre ought to be doing. Instead, I'd like to argue that to make any meaningful progress in this area, we must first distinguish between two interrelated questions: 'What *does* the centre do?' and 'What *should* the centre do?' The first one requires us to simply describe what we see, something that had been the preoccupation of several studies primarily coming out of Harvard Business School in the 1960s and 1970s (Berg, 1969, 1973; Bower, 1970; Lorsch and Allen, 1973; Pitts, 1974, 1976, 1977; Vancil, 1980). The second question, however, requires that we take a position. And whatever position we take cannot be based on castles in the sand or common sense. It must be based on a theory that explains the economic rationale for the existence of multibusiness firms. The structure of this chapter is visually presented in Figure 5.1.

WHAT SHOULD THE CENTRE DO?
THE ECONOMIC PERSPECTIVE

To begin to understand the appropriate role of the corporate centre in multibusiness firms, we must first understand why multibusiness firms exist. That is, why do we have (say) 10 units organized under one corporate umbrella rather than as 10 autonomous and separate firms? The only acceptable answer must be that it is economically superior to organize these 10 units under one corporate umbrella than do anything else with them. We must, therefore, identify the conditions under which this is the case.

But before we even attempt to identify the conditions under which it is better to organize these units under one corporate umbrella, we must first make clear whose perspective we are taking. In particular, we need to emphasize that when we say 'economically superior' we mean from society's point of view (rather than the firm's). There are many occasions when it may make sense for a particular firm to diversify but this may not be in the interests of society. For example, a newspaper company may decide to diversify into online publishing to exploit opportunities in that market. This may make perfect sense for the newspaper company to do but is it the best option for society? Could a young entrepreneur have done a better job starting an online business to exploit the opportunities in that market?

I don't mean to imply that the latter is a better option for society. It may, in fact, be the case that the newspaper company is in possession of valuable knowledge about publishing which would allow it to exploit the online publishing opportunities better and more efficiently than a new start up. All I am trying to suggest is that we need to identify the conditions under which it is economically superior *for society* when we put 10 units under one corporate umbrella rather than keep them as independent companies.

There has been a lot of work on this issue and the academic literature provides some unambiguous answers to the question: 'what is the economic rationale of the multibusiness firm?' Specifically, theory suggests two rationales.

First, according to transaction cost theory (Williamson, 1975), firms diversify to exploit excess, firm-specific assets which cannot be traded in the open market because of high transaction costs. For example, Teece (1980, 1982) has argued that if a firm possesses excess specialized physical capital, it does not make sense to lease it because such an action exposes the firm to the risk of opportunism. If it wants to utilize this excess asset, it will have to do it itself by diversifying into another business where the excess asset can be applied. Teece (1982) and Hill (1990) have identified other scenarios under which the firm cannot trade its excess assets in the market, which means that the firm can make use of them only through diversification.

The natural implication of this way of thinking is that a multibusiness firm which has diversified for this purpose must develop the strategy and administrative context that would allow it to achieve this objective. In other words, the answer to the question: 'what is the role of the centre in such firms?' is quite simply: 'the centre must do whatever is necessary to achieve optimal exploitation of economies of scope.' Under the title 'whatever is necessary' one can then put a variety of things such as deciding what specific businesses to diversify into; how to allocate the firm's scarce resources among divisions; how to exploit synergies among divisions; how to design the appropriate administrative context (i.e. incentives, culture, measurement and evaluation systems; structure, etc.) to encourage exploitation of synergies; and so on.

Unavoidably, this will produce a laundry list of things that the centre ought to do but notice that at least this laundry list has a common purpose: it is all the things that the centre can do to achieve economies of scope.

The second rationale for the existence of multibusiness firms is again based on Williamson's (1975) transaction cost theory and explains the existence of unrelated diversifiers and conglomerates. The argument here is that the corporate centre can act as an internal capital market – that is, as an alternative to the outside capital market – in allocating resources to the divisions.[1] Under certain circumstances, the internal capital market can be more efficient than the outside capital market. For example, a firm can draw capital from slow-growing divisions to supply high-growing ones without having to disclose sensitive information to the outside world. In addition, corporate managers tend to have information advantages over outside investors in evaluating and disciplining divisions, as well as deciding what division needs cash and what division can supply this cash (Salter and Weinhold, 1979).

In general, the internal capital market is argued to have three kinds of advantages over the external capital market: (1) information asymmetries are lower in internal capital markets than in external ones (Williamson, 1975); (2) agency costs of free cash flow are lower in internal capital markets than external capital markets (Williamson, 1975); (3) capital supply is more reliable in internal capital markets than in external ones (Donaldson, 1994). Even though there is little empirical evidence demonstrating the existence of these benefits and despite arguments that the added costs of internalizing capital market functions far outweigh these benefits (Liebeskind, 1995), this rationale for the existence of multibusiness firms has taken hold in the literature and is now taken for granted.

Again, this way of thinking suggests that the role of the centre in conglomerate firms should be to do whatever is necessary to enable the firm to behave like an efficient internal capital market. This will include functions such as deciding what businesses to acquire and what to dispose; and designing an appropriate organizational context to facilitate the functioning of an internal capital market. Williamson (1975) has provided a very detailed description of what this organizational context must look like.

The recognition that the appropriate role of the centre depends on what the firm is trying to achieve, and that there is a fundamental difference between what the related diversifier is trying to achieve versus what the unrelated diversifier is trying to achieve, is one of the most significant new developments in the diversification field. This contribution can be credited to the work of Hill and Hoskisson (1987), Hill (1988) and Hill et al. (1992).

According to Hill (1990: 50): 'The dominant theme that surfaces from the reviews of both the management literature and the economic literature is that there are two different strategies for becoming a multibusiness enterprise, and that the successful pursuit of these strategies requires fundamentally different organizational arrangements. Both the strategies themselves and the structural context required to implement those strategies suggest very different roles for the headquarters' unit in the multibusiness firm.'

What is Missing from the Economic Perspective?

Although transaction costs theory provides a useful way to explore the question: 'what is the economic rationale for the existence of multibusiness firms?', it has recently come under attack for missing an important benefit of diversification, that of learning. In other words, in response to the question: 'why do we have 10 units organized under one corporate umbrella rather than as 10 autonomous and separate firms?', the answer is that by being under one corporate umbrella, the units can exchange knowledge and learning that would allow them to gain competitive advantage over their non-diversified rivals.

The argument put forth by Markides and Williamson (1994) is that simply exploiting existing strategic assets (simply exploiting economies of scope) will not create long-term competitive advantage. In a dynamic world, only firms that are able to continually build new strategic assets faster and more cheaply than their competitors will earn superior returns over the long term. Core competences have a pivotal role to play in this process. By transferring core competences between its divisions, a corporation can accelerate the rate and lower the cost at which it accumulates new strategic assets.

The full argument goes as follows: strategic assets are the imperfectly imitable, imperfectly substitutable and imperfectly tradeable assets necessary to underpin an SBU's cost or differentiation advantage in a particular market. Core competences, on the other hand, are the pool of experience, knowledge and systems that exists elsewhere in the same corporation which can be deployed to reduce the cost or time required either to create a new strategic asset or expand the stock of an existing one.

A division that has access to valuable, rare, imperfectly tradeable and costly-to-imitate assets will have a competitive advantage. But this advantage will eventually decay as a result of asset erosion and imitation by single-business rivals. In the long-run, therefore, only accumulated competences that enable the firm to build *new* strategic assets more quickly and efficiently than its competitors will allow it to sustain supernormal profits.

How can the firm accumulate new strategic assets? One way is through experience or learning by doing. However, this process is subject to various types of frictions, more fully discussed by Dierickx and Cool (1989). Another way is to utilize the firm's core competences.

Competences are potential catalysts to the process of accumulating strategic assets. If the firm knows from past experience how to efficiently build the type of distribution network which will improve the competitiveness of its product, then it will be able to put the necessary asset in place more quickly and cheaply than a firm which lacks this competence. Competences may also act as a catalyst to the processes of adapting and integrating assets that an SBU has accessed through acquisition, alliances or sharing.

But where can a firm get hold of the competences that would allow it to speed up its rates of asset accumulation, adoption and integration? The first place to look is the open market. But competences themselves often have characteristics which render markets inefficient as a mechanism for exchange. Characteristics such as information impactedness and scope for opportunism make competences, like other intangible assets, difficult to sell at arms-length (Williamson, 1975 and Caves, 1982: chapter 1). This leads to excess capacity in competences which cannot easily be utilized by seeking buyers in the open market. Unique competences developed by an SBU through learning by doing therefore risk becoming 'imprisoned' in that unit, even though they could be potentially valuable catalysts to the process of asset accumulation in other businesses (Prahalad and Hamel, 1990).

Compared with the problems associated with trading competences in the open market, it is often more efficient to transfer competences between businesses using conduits *internal* to a single organization (Williamson, 1975). Such internal mechanisms include posting staff from one business unit to another, bringing together a corporate task force with individuals from a number of businesses to help solve a problem for one of them, passing market intelligence or other information between SBUs which could act as catalysts to asset accumulation and so on. This implies that a crucial role for the centre in any multibusiness firm is to develop the

processes and the structures that would allow for the efficient sharing and transfer of core competences across divisions (Markides and Williamson, 1996).

Markides and Williamson (1994: 150) have broken down the 'learning' benefit of diversification into four sub-categories or types. The argument is that the role of the centre will differ depending on which of these types of learning the firm aims to achieve. The four types are:

1 The potential to reap economies of scope across SBUs that can share the same strategic asset (such as a common distribution system); this is the 'asset amortization' benefit.

2 The potential to use a core competence amassed in the course of building or maintaining an existing strategic asset in one SBU to help improve the quality of an existing strategic asset in another of the corporation's SBUs (for example, what Honda learns as it gains more experience of managing its existing dealer network for small cars may help it improve the management of its largely separate network for motorbikes); this is the 'asset improvement' benefit.

3 The potential to utilize a core competence developed through the experience of building strategic assets in existing businesses, to create a *new* strategic asset in a *new* business faster, or at lower cost (such as using the experience of building motorbike distribution to build a new, parallel distribution system for lawn mowers – which are generally sold through a different type of outlet); this is the 'asset creation' benefit.

4 The potential for the process of related diversification to expand a corporation's existing pool of core competences because, as it builds strategic assets in a new business, it will learn new skills. These, in turn, will allow it to improve the quality of its stocks of strategic assets in its existing businesses (in the course of building a new distribution system for lawn mowers, Honda may learn new skills that allow it to improve its existing distribution system for motorbikes); this is the 'asset fission' benefit.

A different approach to the same issue has recently been proposed by Foss (1997: 313). He has argued that 'an important part of the rationales of the corporate HQ lies in its ability to perform "knowledge-direction" (use, blend and direct the initial knowledge endowments of input owners) and exploit the flexibility of incomplete contracts, particularly with respect to growing capabilities through coordinated organizational learning'. Here again, the contribution is to go beyond the static, economies of scope benefit of diversification to a more dynamic, 'learning' benefit.

So, What is the Role of the Centre?

By starting our thinking with the question: 'what is the economic rationale for multibusiness firms', we have identified three major reasons why diversified firms exist: to exploit excess firm-specific assets which cannot be traded in the open market because of high transaction costs (to exploit economies of scope); to create efficient internal capital markets which have informational (and other) advantages over the external capital market; to promote the efficient sharing and transfer of core competences across divisions so that the divisions can create and accumulate *new* strategic assets more quickly and cheaply than competitors.

Of course, one could probably identify additional benefits associated with diversification. These include market-power advantages emphasized in the industrial organization (IO) literature (Berry, 1971, 1974; Caves, 1981; Gort, 1962; Markham, 1973; Rhoades, 1973); tax benefits and other financial advantages emphasized in the finance literature (Galai and Masulis, 1976; Lewellen, 1971); the benefits associated with growth emphasized in the strategy literature (Guth, 1980); the strategic benefits from competing with the same competitors in multiple markets (Gimeno, 1999); and other miscellaneous benefits associated with reductions in agency problems (Aron, 1988; Marshall et al., 1984).

There is no question that these benefits do exist. The question, of course, is whether these benefits are firm-specific or does the whole society benefit from them? Maybe a firm saves taxes by diversifying – but is that value creation or simply value redistribution for society? Similarly, a firm can diversify and gain market power in the process or become a growing and attractive place to work for but is society better off? Could we not receive the

same benefits by having 10 separate firms do what one diversified firm with 10 divisions is doing?

Even if we can identify additional benefits to diversification which are good for society, my purpose is not to develop a complete and exhaustive list of the benefits to diversification. Rather, I want to suggest that the answer to the question: 'what is the role of the centre?' depends on what the centre is trying to achieve. If it is trying to exploit economies of scope, then the centre ought to be doing things which may be different from what it is supposed to be doing if the objective is to create internal capital markets or transfer core competences across divisions.

More specifically, if the objective is to exploit economies of scope, the centre has to decide what businesses the firm should be in (a decision that might lead to acquisitions, divestitures or strategic alliances, the overall scope of the firm and the strategic allocation of resources across businesses) and then design the appropriate structural context (Bower, 1970) to promote coordination between divisions (Galbraith, 1977). This has implications as to the appropriate balance to be struck between centralization and decentralization (more about this later) as well as the appropriate measurement and evaluation systems that must be put in place to facilitate coordination. A huge academic literature exists detailing the specifics of these corporate functions and interested readers are referred to this literature (Ackerman, 1970; Berg, 1969; Ghoshal and Bartlett, 1995; Govindarajan and Fisher, 1990; Gupta and Govindarajan, 1986; Halal et al., 1993; Hill, 1988; Hill and Hoskisson, 1987; Hill et al., 1992; Kerr, 1985; Lorsch and Allen, 1973; Pitts, 1977; Vancil, 1980).

On the other hand, if the objective is to create efficient internal capital markets, the centre has to decide what businesses the firm should be in and then design the structural context to facilitate the functioning of an internal capital market. The main features of a structural context that might achieve this goal have been sketched out by Williamson (1975): cash flows are reallocated by the centre between competing claims and are *not* returned to source divisions; operating functions are decentralized so that the centre does not get involved in the daily operating decisions of the divisions; the centre is profit-oriented and evaluates divisional performance according to abstract profit criteria; and the centre exercises central strategic and financial controls but limited operational control.

Finally, if the objective is to facilitate the sharing and transfer of core competences across divisions, the centre has to put in place a structural context to facilitate such transfers. For example, Hill (1988) and Hill and Hoskisson (1987) have proposed that the CM-form organizational structure may be such a structure. This is because the CM-form structure allows the corporate centre to get involved in the operating decisions of the SBUs and become active in exploiting interrelationships or transferring skills and competences across SBUs. This is in direct contrast to the M-form structure where the SBUs operate with no interference from the head office. The M-form structure is therefore more appropriate for unrelated diversifiers who are only interested in realizing benefits from an internal capital market.

The literature contains many more specific ideas like the one specified above. Again, interested readers are referred to this literature for the details (Birkinshaw, 2000; Campbell et al., 1995; Collis and Montgomery, 1998; Ghoshal and Bartlett, 1995; Goold and Campbell, 1987; Grant, 1995: chapter 15; Halal et al., 1993; Porter, 1987; Nonaka and Takeuchi, 1995).

UNEXPLORED RESEARCH FRONTIERS

What Exactly is Relatedness?

As described above, the role of the centre depends on whether the corporation is diversifying so as to exploit firm-specific assets that cannot be traded in the open market or whether it is diversifying to create an efficient internal capital market. This distinction boils down to the difference between related and unrelated diversification. It is therefore crucial for the firm to decide whether it is engaged in related or unrelated diversification.

Simple as this might appear, it is one of the most thorny issues in diversification research. Is Virgin, a corporation that competes in the airline, transport, music and retailing businesses, a related or unrelated diversifier? How about General Electric, Canon or Disney? The question that needs further exploration is simple: 'what is the appropriate measurement of relatedness?'

Recent work by Markides and Williamson (1994) and Robins and Wiersema (1995) has suggested that traditional measures of relatedness provide an incomplete and potentially exaggerated picture of the scope for a corporation to exploit interrelationships between divisions. This is because traditional measures look at relatedness only at the industry or market level whereas the relatedness that matters is that between strategic assets.

The full argument goes as follows: even though the advantages of the strategy of related diversification are usually cast in terms of the cost and differentiation benefits that arise from the cross-utilization of the firm's underlying assets, the actual measurement of relatedness between two businesses often does not even consider the underlying assets residing in these businesses. Relatedness has been traditionally measured in two basic ways (Montgomery, 1982; Pitts and Hopkins, 1982): using an objective index like the entropy index or SIC count (Caves et al., 1980; Jacquemin and Berry, 1979; Palepu, 1985) which assumes that if two businesses share the same SIC they must have common input requirements and similar production/technology functions; and/or using a more subjective measure such as Rumelt's diversification categories which consider businesses as related: '...when a common skill, resource, market, or purpose applies to each' (Rumelt, 1974: 29).

The traditional measures could be acceptable proxies for what they are trying to measure. In fact, if these measures did not suffer from any *systematic* bias, one would consider them as a 'good enough' way to substitute for a costly and time consuming ideal measure. However, they do suffer from one systematic bias. Consider a firm using the strategy of related diversification so as to exploit the relatedness of its SBU-level assets. Suppose, however, that the SBU-level assets that the corporate centre is trying to exploit are not 'strategically important' (as defined below). For example, suppose that the SBU-level assets that Firm X is trying to cross-utilize are in fact assets that any other firm can easily obtain in the open market through purchase. In that case, even if Firm X achieves short-term competitive advantage through exploitation of economies of scope, it will not really achieve any sustainable competitive advantage *over time* – other firms will quickly achieve similar positions by purchasing similar assets.

This implies that any measure of relatedness should take into consideration not only whether the underlying SBU-level assets of a firm are related, but also consider whether these assets are important. Even if the traditional measures of relatedness do a good job in capturing the relatedness of the underlying assets, they *consistently* ignore the evaluation of whether these assets are the 'right' assets; and they do so because in measuring relatedness, they do not *explicitly* consider the underlying assets.

This implies that it is not broad market-relatedness that matters. Two markets may be closely related, but if the opportunity to rapidly build assets using competences from elsewhere in the corporation does no more than generate asset stocks which others can buy or contract in at similar cost, then no competitive advantage will ensue from a strategy of diversification between them. 'Strategic relatedness' between two markets – in the sense that they value non-tradeable, non-substitutable assets with similar production functions – is a requirement for diversification to yield super-normal profits in the long-run. By failing to take into account differences in the opportunities to build strategic assets offered by different market environments, the traditional measures suffer from an 'exaggeration' problem – they will wrongly impute a benefit to related diversification across markets where the relatedness is primarily among non-strategic assets.

This is certainly a neat argument but more work needs to take place on the subject of strategic relatedness (Teece et al., 1994). In particular, researchers still need to develop measures of relatedness that take into consideration its cognitive aspects (Prahalad and Bettis, 1986). A more careful definition of what is a strategic asset is also needed (Farjoun, 1994). Finally, future research needs to provide a more precise explanation as to the difference between strategic assets, competences and capabilities.

What Determines the Role of the Centre?

The discussion up to this point has argued that the role of the centre depends primarily on the strategic objectives of the firm, as embodied in the firm's corporate strategy. Thus, if the objective is to exploit economies of scope, then the centre ought to be doing things which may be different from what it is supposed to be doing if the objective is to create internal capital markets or transfer core competences across divisions.

Implicit in this idea is the assumption that the firm's corporate strategy (or strategic objectives) are the only contingency factors that determine what the firm's structure should be. This simplification has recently come under attack by a number of scholars who argue that another variable that influences a diversified firm's choice of structure is the business-level strategy that each division follows (Govindarajan, 1986; Govindarajan and Fisher, 1990; Gupta, 1987; Gupta and Govindarajan, 1984). Their key argument has been that different SBUs within the same multibusiness firm often pursue different business-level strategies and, therefore, the administrative mechanisms that the corporate HQ should use to manage these divisions should differ accordingly.

This argument is based on a central proposition of organizational theory: that the appropriate structure of an organization is determined by the task uncertainty facing that organization. Since the differentiation strategy entails more task uncertainty relative to the cost strategy, Govindarajan (1986) and Gupta (1987) have argued that the two strategies require different structural arrangements. Task uncertainty, in turn, is one element of what other researchers have termed the 'external environment' of an organization. Past research has singled out this variable (external environment) as one of the key determinants of the structure of complex organizations (Lawrence and Lorsch, 1967; Thompson, 1967).

This point has raised concerns on two levels. First, is such a differentiated approach towards divisions even possible, given the administrative complexity it imposes and the administrative flexibility it requires? Second, even if it is possible, is it more efficient than a standardized approach?

Several recent empirical studies have provided evidence which suggests that such a differentiated approach towards divisions is indeed possible (Chu, 1997; Govindarajan and Fisher, 1990; Gupta and Govindarajan, 1986; Lioukas et al., 1993). For example, Gupta and

Govindarajan (1986) report findings which show that the appropriate evaluation and incentive systems for SBUs following a 'low cost' strategy were different from those of SBUs following a 'differentiation' strategy. Similarly, Chu (1997) found that corporate HQs in diversified companies grant varying degrees of autonomy to their divisional managers to take strategic, operational and financial decisions. This, in turn, would imply that different systems of assessment, evaluation and reward will be applied to each division (Pugh et al., 1968).

If such a differentiated approach towards divisions is indeed feasible, the next logical area of inquiry will be to determine what factors influence how each division is managed. The work of Gupta and Govindarajan suggests that the competitive strategy that each division follows should have a significant impact on how the division is managed by HQ. However, other factors may be at work: for example, we would expect that the reputation and prestige of the divisional management team may influence how HQ views and manages that division; similarly, the relative size and profitability of the division (a proxy for how important this division is in the whole group) may also have an important effect on HQ behaviour towards this division.

In summary, therefore, future work on this subject ought to be examining questions such as: Do corporate headquarters (HQs) manage different divisions differently? If so, which factors determine why some divisions receive more autonomy than others? What are the performance implications of a differentiated management approach from headquarters?

Managing Strategic Ambiguity

If the above line of inquiry is pursued, it is likely that a number of factors which influence how much autonomy each division gets will be unearthed. The literature suggests that prominent among these will be the following three variables: the volatility of the external environment that the division is facing; the strategy that the division is following; and whether the division is interdependent or shares resources with other divisions in the group. It is suggested that divisions which face a volatile environment or follow a differentiated strategy or share resources with other divisions should receive decision making autonomy from the centre.

The rationale for the existence of a positive relationship between autonomy and these three contingency factors is well accepted in the literature: divisions that face an uncertain and volatile external environment need a more decentralized organization if they are to deal effectively with the higher information processing requirement they face and react quickly and flexibly to environmental changes (Govindarajan, 1986; Lawrence and Lorsch, 1967). Similarly, divisions that follow a differentiation strategy face higher levels of task uncertainty and therefore require high degrees of autonomy and decentralization (Gupta, 1987). On the other hand, divisions which share critical resources with other divisions in the business group (and are therefore interdependent) cannot be given too much autonomy otherwise opportunities for coordination and integration will be lost (Gupta and Govindarajan, 1986; Porter, 1985; Thompson, 1967).

If we accept these basic propositions from the diversification literature, then an interesting – and as yet unexplored – conundrum emerges. Namely, what happens in situations where a division faces conflicting strategic imperatives? For example, how should we manage a division facing a volatile environment which is also very interdependent with other divisions in the group? Theory suggests that because of the volatility of its environment, this division should be granted autonomy; but because of high interdependence with other divisions, it should be centrally controlled and should be given little autonomy.

This is an example of what Hamel and Prahalad (1983: 341) have called 'situations of strategic ambiguity' – that is, situations where divisions face conflicting demands for integration and responsiveness which makes management of these divisions especially difficult. Several such situations may present themselves. For example, a division in a stable (mature) business which is following a differentiation strategy faces a situation of strategic ambiguity. The same is true for a division in a volatile business which has adopted a cost leadership strategy. In fact, given the three contingency variables identified above, we could come up with eight possible scenarios of strategic ambiguity. While I do not want to pretend that these are the only instances when strategic ambiguity may creep in, I do want to argue that these situations happen often enough in practice to warrant further examination.

Situations such as these have been identified and examined in the *multinational* literature. For example, Bartlett and Ghoshal's (1989) examination of the management of the 'transnational' organization tackled exactly this issue. Similar issues have also been explored by Hamel and Prahalad (1983) and by Prahalad and Doz (1987). By building on the insights that have emerged from this literature on multinationals one could study this phenomenon within a *diversified* firm.

For example, Markides and Chu (1999) have proposed that for divisions facing strategic ambiguity, the corporate centre should grant them operational autonomy but centralize their strategic and financial decisions in order to achieve coordination and integration within the firm. In addition to this structural autonomy solution, they proposed that a cultural solution (conceptualized as shared values among divisions) can be used to manage strategic ambiguity – the existence of strong shared values can allow headquarters to grant autonomy to divisions without losing control over them. Finally, they proposed that communication, rotation of managers and training programmes can all be employed as integrative mechanisms that allow divisions to receive decision-making autonomy and still remain integrated within the firm. All these ideas are a step in the right direction but much more work, especially empirical research, needs to be done for us to get a better understanding on how situations of strategic ambiguity are managed in practice.

The Scope of the Firm

As presented above, one of the key roles of the centre in any multibusiness firms is to decide what businesses the firm should be in – in a sense, to decide what the scope of the firm should be. This is a function that the centre must perform whatever its strategic objective might be.

In the West, it is now taken for granted that there is a limit to how much a firm can diversify and that many firms diversified beyond their limit (for a variety of reasons) in the 1960s and the 1970s. As a result, their performance suffered and many of them fell victims to a virile market for corporate control in the 1980s which led to them being taken over and broken up. Although this thesis has received plenty of support in the US (Markides, 1995), it would certainly come as a surprise to students of Asian conglomerates such as the Korean chaebols or the Taiwanese groups. It appears that while Western conglomerates were engaging in massive refocusing, Asian conglomerates continued to diversify and continued to remain profitable (Lee, 1999). This is certainly a mystery that deserves further exploration. What might explain the continuing prosperity of the Asian conglomerates? Are they not subject to the same limits to size as Western conglomerates or have they discovered a much better way of managing diversity in Asia?

From a theoretical point of view, there is still some debate in the economics literature as to whether there is a limit to how much a firm can diversify (Calvo and Wellisz, 1978; Mueller, 1987: 26–9; Williamson, 1967). In the strategy literature, on the other hand, it is now accepted that a firm cannot diversify indefinitely without running into diseconomies – especially *managerial* diseconomies to scale. For example, in their survey of the existing literature on diversification, Hoskisson and Hitt (1990: 474) argue that: '…research and theory…suggest an overall curvilinear relationship between performance and diversification…' Similarly, in their examination of diversification in Britain, Grant and Thomas (1988: 73) reported that: '…the relationship between product diversity and [profitability] was quadratic in form.'

Intuitively, it would seem that in a world where transaction costs are not assumed away, there must be a limit to how much a firm can grow in size (coordination costs lead to U-shaped average cost curves). Had this not been the case, the world would have been dominated by a single mega-firm. That the world is not ruled by a huge monopolist implies that a firm cannot grow indefinitely without running into some form of diseconomies – especially *managerial* diseconomies to scale (see Keren and Levhari, 1983).

The issue of whether there is a limit to how much a firm can diversify can be formulated in terms of marginal benefits (MB) and marginal costs (MC) to diversification. On the one hand, we know from the literature that there exist certain benefits to diversification. For example, transaction cost economists (Caves, 1971; Gorecki, 1975; Montgomery and Wernerfelt, 1988; Teece, 1982) have emphasized the benefits that arise when a firm diversifies to exploit its excess firm-specific assets (such as brand names, managerial skills, consumer loyalty, technological innovations, etc.), the markets for which are characterized by imperfections. These assets cannot be traded in the market because of a variety of imperfections such as transaction costs in transferring the assets, and externalities in the use of the assets (Gorecki, 1975). The firm, therefore, diversifies so as to exploit these assets in other markets.

The existence of these and other benefits to diversification have been well-emphasized in the literature. In addition, and perhaps more importantly, the literature also tells us that the marginal benefits to diversification tend to decrease as the firm diversifies further and further away from its basic business. For example, Montgomery and Wernerfelt (1988) argue that a firm contemplating diversification will first try to apply its excess assets to the closest market it can enter. If excess capacity remains, the firm will enter markets even further afield. But as these factors are applied in more and more distant fields, they lose their competitive advantage and thus earn lower rents. This implies that the *marginal* benefits to diversification tend to decrease as the firm diversifies more and more.

These benefits to diversification are not achieved without cost. Penrose (1959), for example, has emphasized the long-run constraints associated with recruiting, training, and assimilating new managers as the firm grows. Williamson (1967) looked at the costs to diversification in terms of information processing. He argues that top management must gather information from the operating layers of the firm and send down directions based on the information gathered. Some of this information gets lost or gets distorted as it passes from one layer of the hierarchy to another. The loss of information and the inefficiencies that are created as a result constitute the costs of diversification.

Other types of costs emphasized in the literature include control and effort losses arising from increasing shirking as the firm diversifies (Calvo and Wellisz, 1978); coordination costs and intrinsic diseconomies of scale in the expansion of the firm's hierarchical structure (Keren and Levhari, 1983); X-inefficiencies created when managers continue to apply their existing 'dominant logic' on newly-acquired, strategically-dissimilar businesses (Prahalad and Bettis, 1986); disproportionate increases in the costs of coordination and control relative to real output, as a result of limited managerial spans of control (Sutherland, 1980); and the costs created when a 'detached' corporate staff makes inappropriate *and* untimely interventions in the operations of the units (Ravenscraft and Scherer, 1987).

That such costs exist in today's firms has been demonstrated by many researchers (Finkelstein, 1986; Kitching, 1967; Ravenscraft and Scherer, 1987; Yavitz and Newman, 1982). But again, the literature also tells us what kind of functional relationship we should expect between diversification and the marginal costs of diversification. As the firm diversifies, the costs to diversification increase. For example, Williamson (1967) argues that as the firm diversifies, its hierarchy becomes steeper (more managerial layers are created) and as a result, more information gets lost or distorted. Hence, the costs of diversification increase. Similarly, Prahalad and Bettis (1986) argue that as the firm diversifies into more strategically-dissimilar businesses, the costs of applying an inappropriate dominant logic in a variety of businesses rise disproportionately.

The optimal diversification level is the point where the marginal benefits to diversification equal its marginal costs. A firm that starts from zero diversification level can diversify *profitably* up to point D^*. After point D^*, however, the costs outweigh the benefits of additional diversification, so it doesn't pay for the firm to diversify any more. Even though every firm has a different optimal point D^* (according to its resources), the important issue to note is that every firm has a limit to how much it can diversify.

Even though the above discussion has not explicitly addressed the issue of related versus unrelated diversification, the basic ideas presented above should not be affected by this distinction. For example, consider a firm that is primarily engaged in unrelated diversification. All that this implies is that the marginal benefit and marginal cost curves facing this firm are *steeper* than the curves facing a firm engaged in related diversification. This means that the unrelated diversifier will have a much lower optimal diversification level D^*, and will find itself in an over-diversified position much sooner than the related diversifier. Note, however, that both firms still have a limit to how much they can diversify, and both will suffer if they go past their limit. The same argument applies to firms that learn how to manage diversification as they go along: organizational learning affects the *slope* of their MB and MC curves, but does not prevent them from having a limit, or from running into diseconomies once they pass this limit.

If a firm is *profit-maximizing*, it should diversify up to the optimal point D^* (assuming it knows what this is) and then stop. According to Montgomery and Wernerfelt (1988), this is what all firms do – they stop diversifying when the marginal rents from an additional diversification move become subnormal (i.e., when they reach D^*). In their own words: 'We envision a firm…as having a queue of potential diversification opportunities. We argue that a firm, in electing to diversify, will begin with the most profitable opportunities and move toward the least profitable ones. Our expectation is that this process will end when marginal rents become subnormal' (Montgomery and Wernerfelt, 1988: 631).

The implication is that firms that go beyond their optimal point (for whatever reason) will have inferior performance. Several studies have demonstrated that this is indeed the case – at least in the USA and Europe. However, Lee (1999) has shown that Korean chaebols with similar high levels of diversity do not display inferior performance. He has hypothesized that Korean chaebols may have a higher optimal level of diversification compared to western firms. He has offered two possible reasons for this.

First, he has argued that the existence of inefficient capital and labour markets in Asia means that the internal markets which diversification creates allow the chaebol to substitute for the inefficient external markets. This is a benefit of diversification which is not available (or is available to a lesser extent) in the West. This basically means that the marginal benefit curves that chaebols face do not

decline as sharply as the ones that western firms face.

Second, he has argued that Korean chaebols also face a less steep marginal cost curve compared to western firms. The reason for this is that Korean firms are more keen to use their strong cultures as well as strong shared values to manage their divisions without too much interference from the centre. Thus, whereas western firms tend to emphasize structural or incentive mechanisms for controlling their divisions, Korean chaebols use these same mechanisms along with additional cultural ones. This is believed to lead to more efficient management of diversity.

The combination of marginal benefit and marginal cost curves which are not as steep as the curves that western firms face leads to a much higher optimal level of diversification for Korean chaebols. This explanation will provide an acceptable answer to the mystery of Asian firms having high levels of diversification without suffering any performance deterioration, but of course this explanation needs empirical support. In addition, if the 'cultural' way of managing diversity is indeed found to lead to efficiencies, what are the implications for western diversified firms? These are all issues that need additional research to be resolved.

CONCLUSION

In this chapter, I have argued that it is a mistake to pose the question: 'What is the role of the centre in multibusiness firms?' without first answering the question: 'What is the economic rationale for the existence of multibusiness firms?' It is only after we develop an acceptable theory of the diversified firm that we will be able to offer meaningful prescriptions as to what the centre ought to be doing and how. And it is only after we develop this theory that we would be able to judge whether what the centre is doing is the right thing to be doing after all.

The search for a theory of diversification has led us to uncover three possible reasons for the existence of diversified firms: to exploit excess firm-specific assets which cannot be traded in the open market because of high transaction costs (to exploit economies of scope); to create efficient internal capital markets which have informational (and other) advantages over the external capital market; to promote the efficient sharing and transfer of core competencies across divisions so that the divisions can create and accumulate *new* strategic assets more quickly and cheaply than competitors.

Pursuit of these different strategic objectives requires different competencies at the centre. It also requires different structural contexts to be put in place. Prescriptions as to what the centre ought to do must be contingent on the strategic rationale for why the firm diversified in the first place. One size does not fit all.

I believe that of the three rationales given above, the first two have received the bulk of attention and research from academics. Future research must explore the dynamic aspects of diversification embedded in the third rationale. By transferring core competencies across divisions, a corporation will be able to accelerate the rate and lower the cost at which it accumulates new strategic assets. Future research must explore how the centre can carry out this important role in an efficient and productive way.

NOTES

1 This argument can be extended beyond the capital market to propose that the diversified firm can act as an alternative to inefficient labour, legislative and educational markets and institutions. Thus, the more inefficient the outside institutions, the higher the benefits that diversification confers. This is the argument that I used (Markides, 1990, 1995) to explain why firms are currently refocusing. Basically, I argued that because outside institutions like the capital and labour markets have improved in efficiency in the period 1960–1985, diversification has lost some of its beneficial effects. This leads firms to reduce their diversification (to refocus). For a more recent treatment of this same issue, see Khanna and Palepu, 1997.

REFERENCES

Ackerman, R. W. (1970) 'Influences of integration and diversity on the investment process', *Administrative Science Quarterly*, 15: 341–51.

Aron, J. D. (1988) 'Ability, moral hazard, firm size, and diversification', *Rand Journal of Economics*, 19(1): 72–87.

Bartlett, C. A. and Ghoshal, S. (1989) *Managing Across Borders*. Boston, Mass: Harvard Business School Press.

Berg, N. A. (1969) 'Strategic planning in conglomerate companies', *Harvard Business Review*, 43, May–June: 79–92.

Berg, N. A. (1973) 'Corporate role in diversified companies', in B. Taylor and K. MacMillan (eds), *Business Policy: Teaching and Research*. New York: Halsted Press.

Berry, C. H. (1971) 'Corporate growth and diversification', *The Journal of Law and Economics*, XIV: 371–83.

Berry, C. H. (1974) 'Corporate diversification and market structure', *The Bell Journal of Economics and Management Science*, 5: 196–204.

Birkinshaw, J. (2000) *Entrepreneurship in the Global Firm*. London: Sage Publications.

Bower, J. L. (1970) *Managing the Resource Allocation Process*. Boston, Mass: HBS Press.

Calvo, G. A. and Wellisz, S. (1978) 'Supervision, loss of control, and the optimum size of the firm', *Journal of Political Economy*, 86: 943–52.

Campbell, A., Goold, M. and Alexander, M. (1995) 'Corporate strategy: the quest for parenting advantage', *Harvard Business Review*, March–April, 120–32.

Caves, R. E. (1971) 'International corporations: the industrial economics of foreign investment', *Economica*, 38, February: 1–28.

Caves, R. E. (1981) 'Diversification and seller concentration: evidence from changes, 1963–72', *The Review of Economics and Statistics*, LXIII: 289–93.

Caves, R. E. (1982) *Multinational Enterprise and Economic Analysis*. Cambridge: Cambridge University Press.

Caves, R. E., Porter, M. E., Spence, M. A. and Scott, J. T. (1980) *Competition in the Open Economy: A Model Applied to Canada*. Cambridge, Mass: Harvard University Press.

Chandler, A. D. Jr. (1962) *Strategy and Structure*. Cambridge, Mass: MIT Press.

Chandler, A. D. Jr. (1994) 'The functions of the HQ unit in the multibusiness firm', in R. Rumelt, D. Schendel and D. Teece (eds), *Fundamental Issues in Strategy*. Boston: HBS Press. pp. 323–60.

Chu, W. (1997) 'Managing diversification: an empirical study of Taiwanese business groups', Unpublished doctoral dissertation, London Business School, University of London.

Collis, D. J. and Montgomery, C. A. (1997) *Corporate Strategy: Resources and the Scope of the Firm*. Chicago, IL: Irwin.

Collis, D. J. and Montgomery, C. A. (1998) 'Creating corporate advantage', *Harvard Business Review*, May–June: 71–83.

Dierickx, I. and Cool, K. (1989) 'Asset stock accumulation and sustainability of competitive advantage', *Management Science*, December: 1504–14.

Donaldson, G. (1994) *Corporate Restructuring: Managing the Change Process from Within*. Boston: Harvard Business School Press.

Farjoun, M. (1994) 'Beyond industry boundaries: human expertise, diversification and resource-related industry groups', *Organization Science*, 5(2): 185–99.

Finkelstein, S. (1986) 'The acquisition integration process', in J. A. Pearce II and R. B. Robinson Jr. (eds), *Best Papers Proceedings 1986*. New York: Academy of Management. pp. 12–16.

Foss, N. J. (1997) 'On the rationales of corporate head-quarters', *Industrial and Corporate Change*, 6(2), March: 313–38.

Galai, D. and Masulis, R. (1976) 'The option pricing model and the risk factor of stock', *Journal of Financial Economics*, 3(1–2): 53–82.

Galbraith, J. (1977) *Organization Design*. Lexington, Mass: Addison Wesley.

Ghoshal, S. and Bartlett, C. (1995) 'Building the entre-preneurial corporation', *European Management Journal*, 13(2): 139–55.

Gimeno, J. (1999) 'Reciprocal threats in multimarket rivalry: staking out spheres of influence in the US airline industry', *Strategic Management Journal*, 20(2): 101–28.

Goold, M. and Campbell, A. (1987) *Strategies and Styles*. Oxford: Basil Blackwell.

Gorecki, P. K. (1975) 'An inter-industry analysis of diver-sification in the UK manufacturing sector', *Journal of Industrial Economics*, 24, December: 131–46.

Gort, M. (1962) *Diversification and Integration in American Industry*. Princeton: National Bureau of Economic Research.

Govindarajan, V. (1986) 'Decentralization, strategy and effectiveness of strategic business units in multibusi-ness organization', *Academy of Management Review*, 11: 844–56.

Govindarajan, V. and Fisher, J. (1990) 'Strategy, control system, and resource sharing: effects on business-unit performance', *Academy of Management Journal*, 33: 259–85.

Grant, R. (1995) *Contemporary Strategy Analysis*, 2nd edition. Cambridge, Mass: Blackwell.

Grant, R. M. and Thomas, H. (1988) 'Diversity and profit-ability: evidence and future research directions', in A. M. Pettigrew (ed.), *Competitiveness and the Manage-ment Process*. Oxford: Basil Blackwell. pp. 68–85.

Gupta, A. K. (1987) 'SBU strategies, corporate-SBU rela-tions, and SBU effectiveness in strategy implementa-tion', *Academy of Management Journal*, 30: 477–500.

Gupta, A. K. and Govindarajan, V. (1984) 'Business unit strategy, managerial characteristics, and business unit effectiveness at strategy implementation', *Academy of Management Journal*, 27: 25–41.

Gupta, A. K. and Govindarajan, V. (1986) 'Resource shar-ing among SBUs: strategic antecedents and administra-tive implications', *Academy of Management Journal*, 29: 695–714.

Guth, W. D. (1980) 'Corporate growth strategies', *The Journal of Business Strategy*, 1(2).

Halal, W. E., Geranmayeh, A. and Pourdehnad, J. (1993) *Internal Markets: Bringing the Power of Free Enterprise Inside Your Organization*. New York: Wiley.

Hamel, G. and Prahalad, C. K. (1983) 'Managing strategic responsibility in the MNC', *Strategic Management Journal*, 4: 341–51.

Hill, C. W. L. (1988) 'Internal capital market controls and financial performance in multidivisional firms', *The Journal of Industrial Economics*, XXXVII: 67–83.

Hill, C. W. L. (1990) 'The functions of the head quarters unit in multibusiness firms', unpublished manuscript, University of Washington, Seattle.

Hill, C. W. L., Hitt, M. A. and Hoskisson, R. E. (1992) 'Cooperative versus competitive structures in related and unrelated diversified firms', *Organization Science*, 3: 501–21.

Hill, C. W. L. and Hoskisson, R. E. (1987) 'Strategy and structure in the multiproduct firm', *Academy of Management Review*, 12: 331–41.

Hoskisson, R. E. and Hitt, M. A. (1990) 'Antecedents and performance outcomes of diversification: review and critique of theoretical perspectives', *Journal of Management*, 16: 461–509.

Jacquemin, A. P. and Berry, C. H. (1979) 'Entropy mea-sure of diversification and corporate growth', *The Journal of Industrial Economics*, XXVII: 359–69.

Keren, M. and Levhari, D. (1983) 'The internal organiza-tion of the firm and the shape of average costs', *The Bell Journal of Economics*, 14(2).

Kerr, J. L. (1985) 'Diversification strategies and manage-rial rewards: an empirical study', *Academy of Management Journal*, 28: 155–79.

Khanna, T. and Palepu, K. (1997) 'Corporate scope and institutional context: an empirical analysis of diversi-fied Indian business groups', HBS working paper 96-051, Rev. 5–29–97.

Kitching, J. (1967) 'Why do mergers miscarry?' *Harvard Business Review*, November–December: 22–33.

Lawrence, P. R. and Lorsch, J. W. (1967) *Organization and Environment*. Boston: Division of Research, Harvard Business School.

Lee, J-H. (1999) 'Organizational context, institutional context and the management of diversification', unpub-lished manuscript, London Business School.

Lewellen, W. (1971) 'A pure financial rationale for the conglomerate merger', *Journal of Finance*, 26: 521–37.

Liebeskind, J. P. (1995) 'Internal capital markets in diver-sified firms: benefits versus costs', unpublished manu-script, University of Southern California.

Lioukas, S., Bourantas, D. and Papadakis, V. (1993) 'Decision making autonomy in state-owned enter-prises', *Organization Science*, 4: 135–53.

Lorsch, J. W. and Allen, S. A. (1973) *Managing Diversity and Interdependence*. Boston: Harvard Business School.

Markham, J. W. (1973) *Conglomerate Enterprise and Public Policy*. Boston: Harvard Business School.

Markides, C. C. (1990) 'Diversification, refocusing and economic performance', unpublished doctoral disserta-tion, Harvard Business School.

Markides, C. C. (1995) *Diversification, Refocusing and Economic Performance*. Cambridge, Mass: MIT Press.

Markides, C. C. and Chu, W. (1999) 'Autonomy versus strategic control in diversified companies: the management of conflicting strategic imperatives', unpublished manuscript, London Business School.

Markides, C. C. and Williamson, P. J. (1994) 'Related diversification, core competences and corporate performance', *Strategic Management Journal*, 15, Special Issue: 149–65.

Markides, C. C. and Williamson, P. J. (1996) 'Corporate diversification and organizational structure: a resource-based view', *Academy of Management Journal*, 39: 340–67.

Marshall, W. J., Yawitz, J. B. and Greenberg, E. (1984) 'Incentives for diversification and the structure of the conglomerate firm', *Southern Economic Journal*, 51: 1–23.

Montgomery, C. A. (1982) 'The measurement of firm diversification: some new empirical evidence', *Academy of Management Journal*, 25: 299–307.

Montgomery, C. A. and Wernerfelt, B. (1988) 'Diversification, Ricardian rents, and Tobin's Q', *Rand Journal of Economics*, 19: 623–32.

Mueller, D. C. (1987) *The Corporation: Growth, Diversification and Mergers*. London: Harwood Academic Publishers.

Nonaka, I. and Takeuchi, H. (1995) *The Knowledge-Creating Company*. Oxford: Oxford University Press.

Palepu, K. (1985) 'Diversification strategy, profit performance, and the entropy measure', *Strategic Management Journal*, 6: 239–55.

Penrose, E. (1959) *The Theory of the Growth of the Firm*. Oxford: Blackwell.

Pitts, R. A. (1974) 'Incentive compensation and organizational design', *Personnel Journal*, 53: 338–44.

Pitts, R. A. (1976) 'Diversification strategies and organizational policies of large diversified firms', *Journal of Economics and Business*, Spring–Summer: 181–8.

Pitts, R. A. (1977) 'Strategies and structures for diversification', *Academy of Management Journal*, 6: 239–55.

Pitts, R. A. and Hopkins, H. D. (1982) 'Firm diversity: conceptualization and measurement', *Academy of Management Review*, 7: 620–9.

Porter, M. E. (1985) *Competitive Advantage: Creating and Sustaining Superior Performance*. New York: Free Press.

Porter, M. E. (1987) 'From competitive advantage to corporate strategy', *Harvard Business Review*, May–June: 43–60.

Prahalad, C. K. and Bettis, R. A. (1986) 'The dominant logic: a new linkage between diversity and performance', *Strategic Management Journal*, 7: 485–501.

Prahalad, C. K. and Doz, V. (1987) *The Multinational Mission: Balancing Local Demands and Global Vision*. New York: Free Press.

Prahalad, C. K. and Hamel, G. (1990) 'The core competence of the corporation', *Harvard Business Review*, May–June: 71–91.

Pugh et al. (1968) 'Dimensions of organization control', *Administrative Science Quarterly*, 13 (June): 65–105.

Ravenscraft, D. J. and Scherer, F. M. (1987) *Mergers, Sell-Offs and Economic Efficiency*. Washington, DC: The Brookings Institution.

Rhoades, S. A. (1973) 'The effect of diversification on industry profit performance in 241 manufacturing industries: 1963', *The Review of Economics and Statistics*, LV: 146–55.

Robins, J. and Wiersema, M. F. (1995) 'A resource-based approach to the multibusiness firm: empirical analysis of portfolio interrelationships and corporate financial performance', *Strategic Management Journal*, 16: 277–99.

Rumelt, R. (1974) *Strategy, Structure, and Economic Performance*. Cambridge, Mass: Harvard Business School.

Salter, M. S. and Weinhold, W. A. (1979) *Diversification Through Acquisition: Strategies for Creating Economic Value*. New York: Free Press.

Sutherland, J. W. (1980) 'A quasi-empirical mapping of optimal scale of enterprise', *Management Science*, 26: 963–81.

Teece, D. J. (1980) 'Economies of scope and the scope of the enterprise', *Journal of Economic Behavior and Organization*, 1: 223–47.

Teece, D. J. (1982) 'Towards an economic theory of the multiproduct firm', *Journal of Economic Behavior and Organization*, 3: 39–63.

Teece, D. J., Rumelt, R., Dosi, G. and Winter, S. (1994) 'Understanding corporate coherence: theory and evidence', *Journal of Economic Behavior and Organization*, 23: 1–30.

Thompson, J. D. (1967) *Organizations in Action*. New York: McGraw-Hill.

Vancil, R. (1980) *Decentralization: Managerial Ambiguity by Design*. Homewood, Ill: Dow-Jones Irwin.

Williamson, O. E. (1967) 'Hierarchical control and optimum firm size', *The Journal of Political Economy*, 75: 123–38.

Williamson, O. E. (1975) *Markets and Hierarchies: Analysis and Antitrust Implications*. New York: Free Press.

Yavitz, B. and Newman, W. H. (1982) 'What the corporation should provide its business units', *The Journal of Business Strategy*, 3(1): 14–19.

6

Corporate Structure: From Policy to Practice

RICHARD WHITTINGTON

For a long time, the study of corporate structure has seemed rather old-fashioned. Certainly, the energy created by Alfred Chandler (1962) has gone. Back in the 1960s, structure was seen as a crucial variable. Since then, structural research has gone down a wide range of by-ways. Many of these have been productive, but none has reclaimed the intellectual high-ground. Research energy has largely by-passed explicit concern for structure, preferring new avenues. This chapter, however, will contend that these new avenues have not so much left structure behind as opened up new opportunities for investigation that can take structure back towards a lively and central place in strategy and management research. Where research has put structure on the margins, it has discovered new issues and methods that can now be fruitfully redirected to the study of structure. Where economic change has superseded old preoccupations, new urgency and relevance have been given to the structural agenda. Next generation research on corporate structure will not look like that of the hey-day of the 1960s. But it will have at least as great a claim for centrality in strategy and management research.

The argument of this chapter is that the future of research on structure will lie in a move beyond the general and lifeless reifications that came to dominate by the late 1960s and early 1970s. The agenda will be informed by new issues emergent from the very different environment of the twenty-first century, particularly the demands of continuous change, a more knowledge-based economy and an increasingly international and multicultural environment. The agenda will be invigorated by the infusion of wider perspectives brought about by the developments of management and organization theory during the 1980s and 1990s, when structure seemed to get left behind. The result will be an approach to corporate structure that will be more contextual, less aseptic and, above all, of more practical value for the managers who form our ultimate audience.

The argument will be developed as follows. The next section affirms the continuing importance both of corporate structure and of the large corporations for whom structure is such a central concern. It also outlines a framework for considering evolving theoretical perspectives on structure, distinguishing between policy, proxy, periphery and practice. The following section introduces the foundational work on structure as *policy choice*, particularly that concerned with appropriate structures for various kinds of diversification or internationalization strategies. While there continues to be a lively agenda in this field of structure as policy – particularly in the areas of appropriate structures for international and knowledge-intensive organizations – it is argued that this stream of research became marginalized during the last two decades by research with different purposes and, often, different methods.

The next section, therefore, examines how in this recent period, structure often became either a *proxy variable* in other debates, such as the role of rational strategy formulation and the extent of strategic choice, or a *peripheral variable* relegated to the background of studies of organizational culture, change or control. This marginalization of structure has not, however, been all bad. Typically drawing upon the sociological imagination, the new work on structure as proxy and periphery has amplified structural understandings that had become unduly formulaic. The following section, therefore, draws from proxy and periphery studies to outline the emerging agenda for research on structure as *practice*. Here the appreciation of organizational politics and pluralism achieved by the work on proxy, and new concerns for both change and continuity developed on the periphery, can fuse with some of the enduring and more novel themes of the policy stream to constitute a renewed practical agenda for structural research in the coming decades.

The shift in perspective implied in moving from policy to practice can be summed up in Michel de Certeau's (1984: 73) analogy of the knowledge involved in tight-rope walking. Traditional science can measure the height of the tight-rope; it can measure the span. Policy does the same for the heights of organizational hierarchies and the spans of managerial control. But, however precise the measurements, this kind of knowledge is only a small part of what an acrobat needs to cross a rope, or a manager to structure an organization. What matters is the practical wisdom of the performer. To do what they do, the acrobat and the manager rely on skills and knowledge that are barely accessible to traditional approaches. It is this practical wisdom that the practice perspective seeks to capture.

AN ENDURING ISSUE

The field of corporate structure became established with the great work of Alfred Chandler (1962), *Strategy and Structure: Chapters in the History of the American Industrial Enterprise*. Its case studies were marked by a sense of choice and complexity, practice and politics that is still unusual in structural studies 40 years later. It was not these characteristics, however, that were initially to be most influential. In defining two variables – strategy in terms of diversification, structure in terms of corporate organization – Chandler (1962) offered the emerging discipline of strategic management a handy means to rapid progress. Rumelt et al. (1994) trace the foundation of strategic management as a modern and independent research field back to the publication of *Strategy and Structure*, and commend the manner in which its clear constructs and propositions provided a template as the discipline began to advance in the direction of a 'positive' science in the late 1960s. Jason Spender (1992: 43) indeed suggests that the first generation of doctoral students engaged on the Harvard strategy and structure research programme in the 1960s and 1970s effectively built what was to become the strategy field. It was great that structure should become so central, but in some ways Chandler would be too successful. The strategies and structures of large corporations would be done to death in the following years.

By the early 1980s, according to Jeffrey Pfeffer (1997: 162, 190), careful empirical work on organizational structure had virtually come to an end. This obituary was somewhat unfair on continuing work on structural issues. However, Pfeffer's (1997) essential point is taken: the heyday of structural research was over. The problem was both impracticality and boredom. Too much of the literature on organizational structure was impractical, being concerned with opaque and formalistic variables. A great deal had become routinized, affording academics little scope for career-enhancing innovation. From another point on the organizational theory spectrum, Mary Jo Hatch (1999: 75) reports a collapse in traditional interests in organizational structure, the contemporary 'black hole' in organization theory. Traditional theories of organization structure appear inadequate to the global, networked and knowledge-intensive organizations of the turn-of-the-century. Pfeffer (1997) and Hatch (1999) do not despair, however. Each advances their own new agenda, Pfeffer

Table 6.1 *The world's largest firms by revenues*

Rank		Revenues $bn.	Employees	Foundation Date
1.	General Motors	161.3	594,000	1908
2.	Daimler-Chrysler	154.6	441,502	1883
3.	Ford	144.4	345,175	1903
4.	Wal-Mart	139.2	910,000	1962
5.	Mitsui[1]	109.4	32,961	1673
6.	Itochu[1]	108.7	5,775	1858
7.	Mitsubishi[1]	107.2	36,000	1870
8.	Exxon	100.7	79,000	1882
9.	General Electric	100.4	293,000	1892
10.	Toyota	99.7	183,879	1926

[1] Trading companies.
Source: The Global 500, *Fortune*, 2 August, 1999; Derdack, 1988.

concerned with physical design, Hatch with the active improvisation of structure. As Hatch (1999: 75) continues, 'like a collapsing star that forms a black hole, the collapsing notion of organizational structure does not disappear. Its absence is felt as an empty space that attracts.' New issues and approaches to organization structure are pulled in, and Pfeffer's concern for practicality and Hatch's for the activity in structure will be two of the themes that will be argued here.

First, though, we need to affirm the continued need for good knowledge about corporate structures. The Chandlerian concern was with the large corporations arising from the technological and managerial revolutions of the late 19th and early 20th centuries. Teece (1993) accuses Chandler (1990) of being obsessed with an antiquated form of economic organization, producers of chemicals, steel and automobiles. He points to the new forms of fragmented and flexible forms of economic organization created in the latest industrial revolution of information, biotechnology and materials. Companies such as Dell and Sun are the models now. For theorists of a new 'disorganized capitalism' (Offe, 1985; Lash and Urry, 1987; Castells, 1996), the era of the large corporation, with its carefully articulated structures of control and coordination, is over.

We should not be so hasty. Empirically, the traditional large corporation is alive and well. Table 6.1 lists the world's 10 largest corporations by 1998 revenues. Six are more than a century old. Chandler's (1962) own model company, General Motors, is still top of the tree. Dell ranks 210 and Sun 455. Apart from the three Japanese trading companies, these old economy giants are all massive employers, with

Wal-Mart approaching a million employees. These are not companies for which traditional concerns for structure have been abolished. Large firms still matter and seem to do so over the long-run. As veteran structural researcher Elliott Jacques (1990) contends, structure is an issue that is not going to go away.

Indeed, new structural challenges are emerging with economic change. The companies with which Chandler and the first generation of structural researchers dealt with were largely domestic, American and industrial. Today, the old jibe that so-called multinational companies are really 'national companies with international subsidiaries' (Hu, 1992) is giving way to a more global and complex reality. Before the set-back of the Asian crisis, the average proportion of overseas turnover amongst the *Fortune* Global 500 companies had moved steadily during the early to late 1990s from 38% to 42% (Gestrin et al., 2000). To take one highly admired example from Table 6.1: between 1987 and 1998, General Electric's share of turnover from overseas doubled, from a fifth to just over 40% (Slater, 1999: 251). As traditional Western companies have expanded into new regions, they have had to confront more directly alternative business models, particularly the *keiretsu* of Japan, the *chaebol* of Korea and the networks of Chinese business (Whitley, 1999). At the same time, advanced nations have been transforming themselves into service economies, and old manufacturing companies have turned into new service companies. Between 1980 and 1998, General Electric's share of turnover from services rather then products increased from 15% to two-thirds (Slater, 1999: 244). In short, it is not just that Chandlerian corporations still

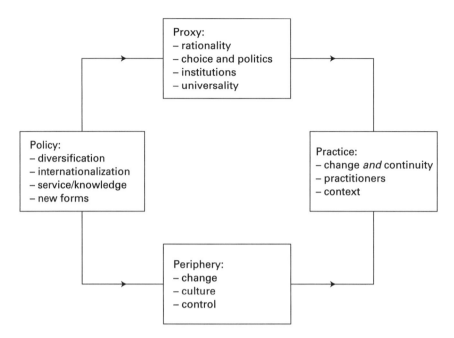

Figure 6.1   *Evolving concerns in research on corporate structure*

dominate the landscape; it is that structural research is actually becoming more interesting as these venerable institutions engage with an increasingly international, diverse and service-oriented economy.

Amidst these economic changes, we are now also recognizing new levers in structure. For early theorists such as Chandler (1962) and Williamson (1975), the achievement of structure lay simply in controlling the vast bulk and complexity of the modern corporation. This is a somewhat negative achievement. But the staying power of large organizations in general, and some in particular, argues for structure's more positive role in the creation of value. With the rise of the contemporary knowledge economy, this positive role is becoming more relevant, not less. Ghoshal and Moran (1996) have spoken of the 'organizational advantage' of the firm over markets in today's conditions. Firms seem capable over time of building up collective senses of 'identity' (Kogut and Zander, 1996) or 'social capital' (Nahapiet and Ghoshal, 1998) that facilitate the exchange and novel combination of knowledge. In many circumstances, markets and networks fail to assemble the appropriate conditions for knowledge

accumulation and advance. By comparison with firms, moreover, markets and networks are limited in the means of protecting and embedding the valuable types of knowledge that increasingly form the basis of competitive advantage (Liebeskind, 1996). In the new economy, therefore, structure will not only continue to be important to the control of large and increasingly international organizations, but will need to be recognized as deeply implicated in value-creating and preserving processes of knowledge co-ordination, combination and learning (Kogut and Zander, 1996). Corporate structures are not so much iron cages as knowledge reservoirs.

Research on structure must move on, therefore. Figure 6.1 offers a map of how the field has been developing. We start with the policy tradition, stemming from Chandler's (1962) classic work on strategy and structure. Here the key question is one of policy choice: *what* structure is most appropriate to particular strategies and contexts, whether of diversification, internationalization or knowledge-intensity. This is the tradition of structural contingency theory, which had its heyday in the 1960s and which Pfeffer (1997) proclaimed effectively dead by the early 1980s.

Approaches to structure have since developed in two principal directions. On the one hand, some researchers took advantage of the success of traditional structural research in defining clear and measurable variables to use structure as a proxy in various key debates in strategy and organization theory. The most prominent debates were those over the sequence of rational strategy formulation, the politics of strategic choice, the influence of institutional context and the universality of the management sciences. As these proxy debates introduced other rationales for structural adoption than simple economics, so they effectively asked *why* particular types of structures tended to be adopted. The second concern, however, placed structure firmly in the background. During the 1980s and early 1990s, a good deal of strategy and management research relegated structure to the periphery, a contextual issue in studies of organizational change, organizational culture and organizational control. Structure became just one of many organizational aspects for change; one of many means of control. To push the alliterative theme a bit further, the question raised by the peripheral work was *whether* formal structure in itself mattered very much. Instead of an abstracted single variable fitted alongside strategy, the peripheral work promoted a more holistic vision of organization.

As Figure 6.1 indicates, the proxy and periphery approaches do not necessarily represent irretrievable deviations. Nor, contrary to Donaldson's (1995) *cri* in favour of traditional structural research, do they commit irredeemably to an 'anti-managerial' impracticality. The more sophisticated appreciation of organizational logics derived from the work on structure as proxy, combined with the richer understanding of organizational complexity and dynamics obtained from the peripheral work, together flow into a concern for structure as practice. Here the concern is with *how* structures are created, adjusted and actually made to work. This requires a practical wisdom that extends beyond the abstract fits of policy theory, drawing more upon the internal pluralism discovered in the proxy tradition and the appreciation of idiosyncracy and intractability so readily accepted on the periphery. This kind of practical wisdom, of course, is at least as managerially-relevant as the traditional approach of policy.

The next section examines structure through the lens of policy. The purpose here will be not so much to offer a comprehensive review of past research as to identify opportunities for the future. While some policy avenues are now nearly exhausted, others are opening up. The policy experience has, moreover, lessons to be carried over to practice.

STRUCTURE AS POLICY

Alfred Chandler's (1962) *Strategy and Structure* was foundational in at least two senses. It provided crucial and influential definitions of key concepts. It also set an agenda for strategy and management research that would last for a good two decades or more. The main concern of this policy agenda was with establishing which structures were most effective in terms of performance, both generally and in terms of 'fit' with different strategies. These issues were pursued in a detached, quantitative mode that has, to date, largely failed to deliver on its original promise.

Structure was defined by Chandler as:

> ... the design of organization through which the enterprise is administered. This design, whether formally or informally, has two aspects. It includes, first, the lines of authority and communication between the different administrative offices and officers, and, second, the information and data that flow through these lines of communication and authority. Such lines and such data are essential to assure the effective coordination, appraisal, and planning so necessary in carrying out the basic goals and policies and in knitting together the total resources of the enterprise. These resources include financial capital; physical equipment such as plants, machinery, offices, warehouses, and other marketing and purchasing facilities; sources of raw materials, research and engineering laboratories; and, most important of all, the technical, marketing and administrative skills of its personnel. (Chandler, 1962: 14)

What is striking in this early definition of structure is the comprehensiveness of the concept. It is concerned with more than the organization chart. It includes both the formal and the informal; not just what is connected, but the content of what flows through the connections; financial and physical assets, but also the knowledge assets incorporated in the skills of its people. It is true that much of what followed in the Chandlerian tradition was highly attenuated, but Chandler's (1962) own original definition of structure did allow for a richer conceptualization that is still useful today. This section traces the evolution of the policy tradition from preoccupation with Chandler's own ideal, the multidivisional, through to the alternative conceptions of structure that have emerged in response to more recent economic challenges.

The Multidivisional Structure

The summit of structural design for Chandler (1962) was, of course, the multidivisional structure, developed by Irenée Du Pont at DuPont and Alfred Sloan at General Motors in the 1920s. Oliver Williamson (1970) gave the multidivisional theoretical flesh, prescribing its combination of operational decentralization and strategic centralization as essential for all large corporations. For this generation of scholars, the adoption of the multidivisional form became of urgent importance around the world (Williamson, 1970; Scott, 1973). Chandler (1962) had been more nuanced, rendering the multidivisional structure contingent upon adoption of strategies of diversification. In his classic formula: 'Unless structure follows strategy, inefficiency results' (Chandler, 1962: 314). Whatever these small differences, by the early 1970s, Chandler and Williamson had set a powerful research agenda around three kinds of question: first, regarding the diffusion of the multidivisional; then regarding the performance advantages of the multidivisional for large firms in general; and finally regarding the contingency of performance on fit between strategy and structure. Common denominators for all this research were a preoccupation with a largely undifferentiated notion of the multidivisional and a preference for quantitative research at a distance from particular organizations.

The first major effort of the policy tradition, therefore, was simply to track the spread of the multidivisional form amongst big business worldwide. In the United States, there is little doubt: Rumelt (1974) and Fligstein (1990)

show overwhelming adoption by large industrial firms of the multidivisional structure, reaching 84% by 1979. Europe got off to a slower start (Dyas and Thanheiser, 1976), but by the early 1990s, the multidivisional accounted for between 70% and 90% of large, domestically-owned industrial firms in France, Germany and the United Kingdom (Mayer and Whittington, 1999). Outside the United States and Western Europe, there is some debate, as we shall return to: even so, in Japan the proportion of large manufacturing firms with divisional structures had reached about 45% by 1980 (Kono, 1984). Interesting questions about diffusion remain in the emergent and new capitalist economies, but, at least in the advanced Western nations, the multidivisional seems broadly to have achieved saturation.

If there has been success in tracking the diffusion of the multidivisional, the second effort of the policy tradition has been less conclusive. Williamson's (1975) original sweeping M-form hypothesis had proposed that the multidivisional would outperform all other structures (explicitly the functional or U-form; implicitly the holding or H-form). Large-scale statistical tests are still unsatisfactory. Amongst the classic American studies, Rumelt (1974) found more positive impact of divisionalization on growth measures than on financial performance ratios, while Harris (1983) could find little significant evidence for a positive impact of divisionalization on performance. The picture has been even patchier elsewhere round the world. In the United Kingdom, Steer and Cable's (1978) early finding of positive returns to divisionalization has been countered by Hill and Pickering's (1986) and Hill's (1988a) conclusions in favour of holding company structures. In a later United Kingdom study, Ezzamel and Watson (1993) were unable to distinguish significant structural effects at all. Elsewhere research is scanty, but findings so far are equivocal. Germany and Japan do not seem to yield significant advantages for the multidivisional (Cable and Dirrheimer, 1983; Cable and Yasuki, 1984). From Korea, Chang and Choi (1988) do claim a positive multidivisional effect, but their structural definition appears to include quite loose chaebol relationships rather foreign to the original American conceptualizations. At this stage, Cable's (1988) conclusion for strong culture dependency regarding the multidivisional is still hard to reject. This may be disappointing for seekers of universal relationships, but at least it may point up the issue of context.

Of course, it may be that Williamson's (1975) M-form hypothesis was too broad, simply claiming a general superiority for multidivisional organization in large firms. Chandler's (1962) argument was in terms of fit between strategy and structure. Findings are again inconclusive. In an early United Kingdom study, Grinyer et al. (1980) did not find any effect of strategy–structure fit on performance. However, re-analysis of Rumelt's (1974) American data suggests some small positive fit effects (Donaldson, 1987), while Hamilton and Shergill (1992) found the same, with larger co-efficients, for a New Zealand group of firms. More complexity has been added, however, by Hoskisson's (1987) finding in an American sample that the positive effects of fit depended upon the type of diversification strategy: divisionalization had a positive effect on performance for unrelated diversifiers, but not for related diversifiers.

This kind of differentiated finding has prompted a second more discriminating stream of work that distinguishes usefully not only between types of diversification strategy but also types of divisional structure. Here dominant approaches have taken their cue from Williamson and Bhargava's (1972) sub-categories of 'corrupt' and 'transitional' multidivisionals. Distinguishing between the corrupted multidivisional, where the centre compromises its detachment by intervening in operations, and the pure, where the centre remains austerely aloof, allows for two types of multidivisional in place of one. Reserving firms in the process of moving towards the multidivisional structure to a 'transitional' category makes possible, by comparing with stable categories, some account for costs of change.

Researchers pursuing this more discriminating analysis of structure find previously unsuspected virtues in the 'corrupt' multidivisional. This kind of multidivisional has been reappraised as the 'centralized' multidivisional (CM) (Hill, 1988a, b) or the 'co-operative' multidivisional (Hill et al., 1992) and attributed advantages in managing scope economies in related diversified firms (the simple multidivisional, with detached centre and discrete divisions, is favoured for unrelated diversifiers). Although some support has been found for co-operative or centralized structures for related diversifiers in particular (Hill, 1988a; Hill et al., 1992), others have been less positive (Markides and Williamson, 1996). On traditional measures of relatedness, Markides and Williamson (1996) arrive at the surprising result that it is unrelated diversifiers that do best with CM-form structures. Markides and Williamson's (1996) more innovative measures of relatedness provide contradictory results according to particular kinds of business relationships, but again tend not to favour CM-form fit with related strategies of diversification.

Treating firms currently involved in changing structures separately as transitional forms has not helped much either, even where this has been combined with the more discriminating CM-form of multidivisional. Markides and Williamson (1996) found some advantage for completed multidivisionals over transitional multidivisionals, but Hill (1988b) found the reverse, while Ezzamel and Watson (1993) uncover no robust differences. The transitional form may be too limited to picking up structural changes between the major types, rather than potentially costly changes within types. Alternative approaches to structural change, looking at the impact of adoption of the multidivisional structure on subsequent performance, have also had mixed results – Hoskisson and Galbraith (1985) finding quite positive effects for early transitions, while Armour and Teece (1978) find rather insignificant effects as the innovation diffused amongst their later sample. Armour and Teece (1978) suggest that the benefits of divisionalization are likely to diminish over time as populations reach equilibrium. Given the near exhaustion of the pool of organizations still available for divisionalization, and likely equilibrium of those retaining alternative structures, the need now is to examine the performance impact of finer changes within broad structural types. As Bowman et al. (1999) indicate, this remains an area with little research and, again, ambiguous performance results.

So far, then, it seems that neither the differentiation between just two types of multidivisional or allowance for major structural change has been enough to deliver stable results.

Markides and Williamson (1996) conclude that the ambivalent findings of their study and previous ones suggest that the issues of strategic and structural fit are still too complex for large scale statistical analysis. They urge small-sample study of limited numbers of diversified firms in detail. For many policy researchers, this is nearly the counsel of despair.

But frustrations over the multidivisional have not been entirely unproductive. They have raised awareness of context, particularly of possible cultural and institutional effects; they have helped develop a more differentiated perspective on the multidivisional; they have prompted a greater sensitivity to the implications of change; and finally, though with an air of last resort perhaps, they have increased the readiness to contemplate small number studies. Many of the methods developed in the policy tradition have also been carried over into other debates, particularly those of proxy. But within the broad policy tradition itself, these methods have also provided a starting point for exploration of different types of organization that have become more important since the original Chandlerian formulations, particularly international business and service and knowledge-intensive firms.

Alternative Structures

An obvious alternative basis for structure has been geographical diversification. Research here has started in the same organizational demographic mode as that on the original diffusion of the multidivisional structure, and sought out equivalent kinds of strategic fit. Scholars such as Stopford and Wells (1972), Daniels et al. (1984), Egelhoff (1988) and Leong and Tan (1993) have established different kinds of multinational structures (international, product or area divisions, with or without matrix co-ordination) and then associated them with different types of international strategy (degree of foreign product diversity, extent of foreign sales and extent of foreign manufacturing). Again, there are cross-national differences, but these are interpreted principally in terms of the very different sizes of domestic markets, especially between European and United States multinationals (Egelhoff, 1988). Generally there has been a tendency to underplay or relegate to

history distinctive national forms of international organization, as for instance in Bartlett and Ghoshal's (1989) discussion of European firms' shift from 'multi-domestic' structures to the more universal 'transnational' structure. There are very few performance studies in this tradition, but those that do exist are equivocal. Thus Habib and Victor (1991) conclude that fit between international strategy and international structure does not predict profitability very well, particularly for service multinationals.

By adding an additional geographic dimension, and by recognizing the variable relationships national subsidiaries are likely to have both between themselves and with their multinational centres, the international business literature is well-placed to develop a much more differentiated and internally-complex picture of organizational structure. For example, Nohria and Ghoshal (1994) found that the degrees of centralization and decentralization are highly differentiated according to subsidiary resources and shared values. Other studies of multinationals have shown how subsidiaries' roles may vary in terms of initiative and scope, ranging from highly dependent local implementers of strategy to relatively autonomous holders of world mandates (Birkinshaw and Morrison, 1995). Another study of multinationals' subsidiaries in the United Kingdom distinguishes between confederate subsidiaries, strategic auxiliaries and autarchic subsidiaries, again implying a good deal of differentiation in how divisional structures operate with regard to particular businesses (Taggart, 1998). By focusing on subsidiaries, students of international business have succeeded in getting *inside* their structures, understanding the different ways they work and the perspectives of those who operate within them (Birkinshaw, 2000). This is a good start, and there is plenty of mileage left in developing these more differentiated notions of structure, tracking their demographics and, especially, in testing their performance consequences.

Another area of catch-up is the service sector. A disproportionate part of the work in the policy tradition has been undertaken in industrial firms, reflecting its origins in the 1960s and early 1970s. The growth of the service sector, and particularly of knowledge-intensive firms within it (Starbuck, 1992), poses new questions for the policy tradition:

these are questions not just about structure but about the nature of strategy.

Again, the service and knowledge-intensive sectors have the potential to add richness to the rather sparse structural typology that the policy tradition started out with. From early on Channon (1973) recognized some fundamental differences in large service firms, in particular the likelihood of centralization of critical functions. Mintzberg's (1979) Professional Bureaucracy, common in the public and quasi-public sectors, is a type apart from the traditional multidivisional form, with greater levels of decentralization. Likewise, Greenwood et al.'s (1990) P^2-form professional partnerships – typically accounting or legal firms – are distinguished clearly from the multidivisional by their weaker emphasis on strategic controls but strong centralized control of standards and quality at the operating level. These different structures have prompted also a more complex notion of strategy than in the original stark dependency of Chandler's (1962) *Strategy and Structure*. In Mintzberg's (1979: 363–4) Professional Bureaucracy it is as fruitful to think of each professional's personal strategy at least as much as 'the strategy' of the organization as a whole. Strategy in the P^2 professional partnership organization is not the apparently clean-cut decision-making process but a consensual, non-analytical process (Greenwood et al., 1990; cf. Cooper et al., 1996; Hinings et al., 1999). Structure emerges not so much as a discrete and dependent variable as potentially a deeply embedded part of the organizational whole – a view developed in both the periphery and the practice approaches.

Many of the insights arising from work on the structures of multinationals and professional service firms have converged in the recent work on new forms of organizing (Daft and Lewin, 1993; Volberda, 1998). This work claims to go 'beyond the M-form': the focus shifts 'from allocating capital to managing knowledge and learning as the key strategic task' (Bartlett and Ghoshal, 1993: 41). This shift produced its own neologism, the N-form (Hedlund, 1994; Nohria, 1996). The N-form corporation is characterized by combination rather than division, temporary constellations rather than permanent structures, lateral communication rather than vertical, focus rather than diversification, heterarchy rather than hierarchy. Top management's role becomes one of catalyst, architect and protector of knowledge, rather than monitor and resource allocator (Hedlund, 1994: 82–3). Indeed, the implications of the knowledge-based view of the firm tend to turn notions of hierarchy on their head. The firm becomes 'decentred' as critical knowledge is distributed amongst dispersed organizational participants beyond the control of any single corporate mind (Tsoukas, 1996). The result is to render strategic planning increasingly diffuse, as critical knowledge and decision-making become necessarily 'co-located' (Grant, 1996). Rather than hierarchies, internal and external networks become critical to accessing and mobilizing knowledge (Grant, 1996; Gulati et al., 2000).

These new forms of organization pose several critical issues. Again, they challenge the instinct to sharp distinctions typical of orthodoxy. Networks blur traditional boundaries between and within firms; knowledge-intensity undermines top-down and sequential notions of strategy and structure. The convenient reduction of organizational characteristics into distinct variables for counting and correlating becomes harder and harder to do. In any case, the novelty of these new forms of organization implies a methodological turn. Attention is focused on those pioneering firms that claim to represent the future, rather than the mass of firms that reflect the past. To this extent, the new forms of organization promote research methods based on case studies of innovators rather than the pursuit of averages (Starbuck, 1993; Daft and Lewin, 1993; Pettigrew and Fenton, 2000). Nevertheless, quantitative issues remain. The new forms raise new issues of organizational demographics, as their diffusion within the wider population becomes moot: the few extant studies tend to be conservative (Nohria, 1996; Ruigrok et al., 1999; Pettigrew et al., 2000). As they add new dimensions to organizational structure, they open up further opportunities for a richer typology of organizations. Now that the pool of possible multidivisional adoptions is nearly exhausted, transitions from old to new forms of organization offer the chance for more studies of structural change and its performance consequences (Whittington et al., 1999a).

The policy tradition clearly has a full agenda still, but it should be frank about its mixed success so far. It has defined a paradigm of research, facilitating the development of rigorous research methods. But this research may have done more for the skills and careers of academics than for practising managers. Decades of careful empirical research have provided few convincing results, especially across countries. A great deal of the research effort remains focused on counting what practising managers have already discovered for themselves: it is small news to tell corporations that the multidivisional is a good thing when it is what they and their competitors have been doing for a long time. It is not just that the categories are too broad to be useful: the multidivisional is so comprehensive that it masks the continuous changes *within* form that are endemic to organizational life. The multidivisional has become reified as a static monolith that obscures as much as it reveals. There is a need both to get deeper inside these structures and to make more distinctions, as particularly the international business research has begun to do. As these become theoretically better defined, then again there will be opportunities for tracking the demographics of these finer structural types and searching out performance consequences.

The policy tradition has too long been trapped between two poles. The broad and discrete categories that it has developed, while readily researchable, are now both too commonplace to gain the attention of practising managers and too crude to distinguish either outstanding performance or significant changes. Although Donaldson (1995) has claimed for this kind of work a practical bent, it has not yet delivered as much as it has promised. As Gresov and Drazin (1997: 424) suggest, this tradition still fails '... to speak to the complexity of design and the experience of managers engaged in designing'. The pursuit of averages for broad categories is unlikely to yield practical value (Starbuck, 1993). Even if the Holy Grail of a high performing strategy–structure fit, robust across time and countries, is discovered, managers would still need to have a route-map to achieve the fit, and an estimate of the costs of getting there.

A substantial research agenda for the policy tradition remains, however. There is an important opportunity in defining new types of structure more appropriate to the post-industrial, knowledge-based economy. There will be no need here to surrender to the nihilist notions

of 'dis-organized' capitalism. What will be critical, however, is to continue the task of refining structural types in ways that are able to capture the complexity of organization and pick up the implications of normal change: we should not let the N-form follow too simply on the M. It is likely that these new types will challenge, as professional service organizations already have, the instinct towards neat dependencies between structure and strategy, pressing researchers towards a more holistic approach. Another challenge is posed by the increased economic pluralism of world capitalism since the early theorists of the multidivisional. It will be necessary to be more cautious than the early theorists of the multidivisional about the cultural and institutional contexts in which performance advantages hold (Khanna and Palepu, 1999). Researchers will have to make greater efforts to theorize the fit of new types, such as the network, with older types, such as the Chinese family network, already well-established around the world (Li, 1998).

However, it is hardly surprising that, as Donaldson (1995) admits, the policy tradition has lost its old centrality to so many alternative approaches. The next section will point to how structural issues have been relegated either to a background peripheral variable or to a proxy in other debates. But rather than accepting Donaldson's (1995) dismissal of these diversions as 'anti-management', I shall argue that they offer many insights capable of being turned to practical managerial advantage.

STRUCTURE AS PROXY AND PERIPHERY

Part of the success of the policy tradition has been to develop measures of structure that lend themselves to the efforts of other scholars to prove quite different points. Part of the failure has been to banalize the study of structure so that many have simply left it behind in order to advance their careers through innovation in other areas (Pfeffer, 1997). Structure has either been reduced to a proxy variable, or sunk into the peripheral vision of many contemporary scholars. There are, however, useful new directions emerging from both proxy fights and these alternative approaches. We shall consider first structure's involvement in arguments over managerial rationality, strategic choice, institutional pressures and the question of universality. The treatment of structure in this proxy stream has generally borrowed unproblematically from the policy tradition, with few advances in research methods or structural definitions. The contribution from the proxy stream, rather, has been to develop a more sophisticated understanding of the workings of structure and its different rationales. On the other hand, innovative methods and concepts have emerged where structure has been relegated to the periphery. The potential contribution of the peripheral work is a more holistic, fine-grained and active appreciation of structure in context. In other words, the literatures on structure as both proxy and periphery are not so much sterile deviations as exploratory ventures from which we can return with new insights capable of significantly reinvigorating the old agendas of structural research.

Proxy Fights

The first proxy fight is over the role of rationality in strategic management, represented by the logical sequence of structure following strategy. Here, strategy formulation is distinguished from strategy implementation and given a priority that reduces organization to an infinitely adaptable and plastic tool. Mintzberg (1990) has incorporated the formulation-implementation sequence as one of his seven 'premises' of the Design School of strategy, to which he attributes dominance in the field. The contrary view is that structures can work backwards on strategy, through the options they facilitate and the opportunities they filter (Hall and Saias, 1980). Mintzberg (1990: 183) rejects the simple sequence of the Design School, therefore, by asserting that '... structure follows strategy as the left leg follows the right'. Organizational structure is too important to be relegated to the status of dependent variable on strategy. As Robins (1993) suggests of the American film industry, and Lorenzoni and Baden-Fuller (1995) write for Benetton, distinctive modes of organizing are intrinsic to competitive advantage. Structure *is* the strategy.

Empirical work investigating the sequence in practice still tends to favour the priority of strategy over structure, while accepting some

influence in the opposite direction (Donaldson, 1987; Amburgey and Dacin, 1994; cf. Harris and Ruefli, 2000). Reanalysis of Rumelt's (1974) original data leads, for example, to the conclusion that '... strategy and structure do follow one another as the left foot follows the right – but they do not have equal strides' (Amburgey and Dacin, 1994: 1449). It seems that the Design School's sequence holds largely good, but that nevertheless organization must be allowed a greater role than admitted in simpler formulations of the strategy–structure relationship. No doubt this debate will rumble on, but in this proxy fight so far, the structural variable has helped us to be less dogmatically linear in our thinking, while nevertheless retaining sound respect for the rationality of the original Chandlerian sequence.

The imperfect subordination of structure to strategy provides the grounds for a second proxy fight, over the role of internal politics in the strategic choices of large corporations (Child, 1972, 1997). Donaldson (1987) admits that the lags between strategic and structural change can be very long, two decades or more. Such extended periods of structural 'misfit', perhaps including several generations of top management team, suggest that structural choice (or refusal) may well be driven by political interests within the firm (Whittington, 1989: 40–1). Hence structure becomes a proxy for measuring the extent to which managers are able to exercise discretion according to internal politics, regardless of economic rationality.

This political perspective has associated particular structural alternatives with different professional or ownership interests within the firm. The multidivisonal, with its capacity to rely on detached, quantitative measures of control, is often deemed particularly suitable to a financial control approach to management (Hayes and Abernathy, 1980; Fligstein, 1990). Engineering and production managers will distrust and resist the multidivisional for its abstraction; sales and marketing managers will support it as favouring sales expansion and diversification; managers with financial backgrounds will promote it as pushing the enterprise as a whole into their own hands (Fligstein, 1987). Similarly, family owners and managers are said to be suspicious of the transparency and decentralization inherent in the multidivisional, constraining the power and discretion they might otherwise enjoy (Palmer et al., 1987, 1993). Banking shareholders too may be reluctant to support the multidivisional, as its role in allocating capital between different businesses competes with banks' own traditional functions (Cable and Dirrheimer, 1983; Palmer et al., 1987). For these political theorists, therefore, decisions to adopt or resist the multidivisional form provide good opportunities to reveal the internal balance of power within firms.

Tests have focused on adoption of the multidivisional in the United States. Fligstein (1987), Palmer et al. (1987) and Mahoney (1992) do find significant ownership effects on multidivisional adoption, with families and banking interests generally opposing. However, Palmer et al.'s (1993) more recent re-analysis, using a different methodology, has found no significant family effects and even a positive effect of bank ownership on divisionalization. As to the political interests of various managerial groups, Fligstein (1987) did uncover positive influence of corporate presidents with sales or finance backgrounds on the likelihood of divisionalization, while Palmer et al. (1993) only found this effect for presidents with sales backgrounds. Whittington and Mayer (2000) could find little effect amongst their European firms. The empirical findings so far are not, therefore, entirely consistent. Nevertheless, it does seem worth holding on to the notion that structural choices are not neutral vis-à-vis the various internal and external interests of the firm. There is room for more work here, particularly perhaps with more differentiated forms than the simple multidivisional.

The third proxy fight into which the multidivisional has been drawn is that around the force of institutional pressures in determining firm policy. Here sociology confronts economic reasoning head-on. Meyer and Rowan (1977) draw attention to the role of 'formal structure as myth and ceremony'. Rather than by rational economic choice, as policy theorists might have it, organization structures are often selected in ceremonial conformity to the prevailing 'myths' of the local context (DiMaggio and Powell, 1983: 156). Structures follow legitimacy rather than strategy. Institutional fit is important, not just economic efficiency.

The multidivisional has again been seized upon as a convenient measure for the extent to which firms simply imitate legitimate managerial models. In the post-war period, the multidivisional rapidly became a highly visible symbol of modern management, an attractive signal to the outside world of appropriate managerial policy. In fact the evidence that imitative search for legitimacy drives divisionalization is equivocal. For the population of American divisionalizers as a whole, Mahajan et al. (1988) and Venkatraman et al. (1994) did not find significant evidence that the adoption curves for the multidivisional fitted typical innovation diffusion models emphasizing imitation. However, looking more at the industrial level, Fligstein (1987), Palmer et al. (1993) and Kogut and Parkinson (1998) do find that the proportion of firms that had already adopted the multidivisional can be a significant predictor of divisionalization by remaining non-divisional firms, suggesting imitation of leaders. Again, therefore, the relationship between strategy and structure emerges as potentially more complex than the simple rational economic sequence of structure following strategy.

Fligstein (1990) also suggests that the spread of the multidivisional reflected a more general rise to domination in American business of a 'finance conception of the corporation'. This was a national historical phenomenon, going beyond the interests of particular groups within firms, and linked to the changing nature of American capitalism as a whole. In other words, the multidivisional has a nationally specific character that may not generalize more widely. Fligstein (1990) in particular doubts that the finance conception of the corporation would transfer to France, Japan or the United States, where the state and banks play different roles than in the United States: '...unique interactions between the state and the largest firms in the economies of various advanced countries has resulted in different organizational forms driven by different conceptions of control. There exists no abstract market that disciplines firms to one and only one efficient standard' (Fligstein, 1990: 312). Here sociology and economics are not offering competing logics of organization. It is sociological context that defines economic efficiency.

The multidivisional has thus got sucked into its fourth proxy fight, the debate concerning universals in organization theory. For Chandler (1992 [1984]: 156), evidence of the early spread of divisional form in Europe, the United States and Japan was enough for him to claim '… convergence in the type of enterprise and system of capitalism used in all advanced industrial economies for the production and distribution of goods'. Donaldson (1996: 146) includes the Chandlerian work on strategy and structure within the broader framework of structural contingency theory: 'Structural contingency theory yields generalizations that are valid globally. They are general relationships on which the sun never sets.' This is provocative. Hofstede (1991: 22) confronts Chandler head-on when he declares 'structure follows culture'. 'Business Systems' theorists (Hollingsworth and Boyer, 1997; Whitley, 1994, 1999) suggest now that the performance of organizations depends upon the distinct institutional arrangements of particular countries. Whitley (1994) argues that the financial markets and professional management of Anglo-Saxon countries particularly favours multidivisionalization; traditional German banking relationships and French statism militate against.

Again the evidence is contradictory, but enough to cast some suspicion on a universally-transferrable approach to organizational structures. Despite continued institutional differences in terms of ownership and control, large organizations in France, Germany and the United Kingdom do now seem all equally likely to adopt the multidivisional structure as American organizations (Mayer and Whittington, 1999). However, institutional analyses of the diffusion of these structures in Europe suggest that it was more than bare economics that drove the process. Using the Boolean method suited to the comparative analysis of small numbers of cases (Ragin, 1987), Guillén (1994) and Djelic (1998) have shown that the adoption of structures across the major European economies could be strongly influenced by country-specific institutional factors, such as the power of the state or national systems of politics and industrial relations. On this analysis, some countries – Italy and to a lesser extent Spain – were slower to adopt the multidivisional than their economic development would otherwise merit; other countries, such as Germany and France, began divisionalization before the economic

conditions were strictly in place. Such national institutional factors, precipitating or inhibiting particular kinds of organization, might help explain the instability of the relationship between structure and performance so often found outside the United States. As we go further afield, particularly towards emerging and Asian economies, it becomes more necessary to take account of such persistent alternatives to Western orthodoxies as the traditional conglomerate holding company (Granovetter, 1995; Khanna and Palepu, 1999) and the extensive family networks of Chinese business (Hamilton and Biggart, 1988; Li, 1998). Bearing in mind the need for external legitimacy, here we should beware surface conformity to dominant norms of professional organization. In struggling or emergent economies, there are strong incentives for companies to present themselves externally as multidivisionals, while inside operating very differently. There is certainly a case for getting deeper inside apparently similar structures to discover what is really going on.

It is a paradoxical achievement of the policy tradition that in fashioning such a clearly-defined variable as the divisional structure it has also furnished the sceptics of universality and economic efficiency with the means for arguing quite different rationales for organizations. By and large, the sceptics have been no more successful in finding robust statistical relationships than the policy scholars. Nevertheless, the various proxy battles into which the multidivisional has been drawn have helped to articulate a more complex understanding of the forces surrounding structure and structure's relationship to strategy. It is clear that for the policy tradition to go forward, it needs to recognize more readily national propensities in organizing. Structure's reciprocal influence back on strategy warns against simply treating it as a discrete and subordinate variable, rather than as a property intimately and potentially equally involved in strategy. The staying power of structures, and the ways in which they favour some managerial groups more than others, sharpen our sensitivities to the difficulties of structural change. Recognizing the importance of legitimacy should highlight the scope for surface conformity. All this can be helpful to practice too. Practice can take from the proxy studies an appreciation of both internal and external context: the mediating influences of societal conditions and the plural forces engaged in structural change and structural inertia. Over all, the proxy approach to structure makes us less glib, more far-seeing.

On the Periphery

The readiness to accept complexity introduced by the proxy tradition is reinforced also by the work on culture, change and control. Much of this work is in self-conscious reaction to the earlier dominance of structural contingency theory (Martin and Frost, 1996). In Barley and Kunda's (1992) account, the managerial literature during the 1980s and early 1990s turned away from old preoccupations with formal, rational forms of control towards an interest in normative and cultural controls. Structure *per se* typically became a peripheral issue. The quantitative techniques developed in the policy tradition were largely discarded.

As Rowlinson (1995: 122) observes: 'corporate culture writers pay little attention to structure'. Whereas once structure was the key variable, in the corporate culture writing of the last two decades it is norms, symbols and values that have the deeper importance. In a particularly influential polemic, Richard Pascale (1984: 65) was dismissive: 'Structural remedies, by their unambiguous two-dimensional nature, impose a falsehood – organizational charts.' Informal structure no longer bids for attention besides formal structure; it is now the behaviours that represent the informal structures that typically have predominance. The formal structure may only be a symbolic representation of the underlying culture determining actual behaviour. For Schein (1985), indeed, structure is merely an artefact of culture.

Unlike the policy tradition, cultural studies from the start recognized organizational issues as intimately and problematically related to strategy. Culture and strategy meshed together (Barney, 1986). Another marked departure from the structural tradition of policy was a resistance to typology and insistence on uniqueness (Schein, 1985; cf. Martin, 1992). Indeed, the strategic value of corporate cultures lay in their ability to differentiate particular firms in sustainable, non-inimitable fashion (Barney, 1986). A third distinctive

tenet of the culture camp was that change initiatives, especially the deliberate engineering of corporate cultures, are prone to failure and unintended consequences (Martin and Frost, 1996; Legge, 1994; Ogbonna and Harris, 1998). Much more so than in the policy tradition, change and transition had to be taken seriously. More than this: sheer continuity began to be recognized as an achievement. As researchers probed into their complex constructions, they more and more appreciated how cultures required of practitioners skilled and continuous performances for their instantiation (Rosen, 1985; Munro, 1999). It is not just a matter of what the culture is but 'how culture happens' (Munro, 1999: 621). This recognition of practitioners has even brought back into the picture that missing presence, concrete individuals. Whether as founders, heroes or manipulative charlatans, the culture studies are full of people (Rosen, 1985; Schein, 1985; Martin, 1992).

This cultural research offers several important insights worth taking forward into an emergent practice perspective. The objective need no longer be confined to boxing organizations into general categories; rather it may be developing managers as sensitive, skilled interpreters of organizational specificity. Cultural research suggests too that skilful interpretation is likely to rely upon the holistic appreciation of organizational phenomena, rather than the reduction to discrete dependent and independent variables. This kind of appreciation is to be advanced more by detailed, rich ethnography than by research at a distance. Finally, the cultural work has not only accentuated the perils of change, but also revealed something of the precarious, effortful performance involved in continuity. The notion of performance reminds us too that structures, no less than cultures, need performers.

One further by-product of the cultural research has been a more complex understanding of control. The cultural notion both suggests that organizations are less amenable to rational control than might have been thought and that culture can substitute for the formal hierarchical controls of structure (Martin, 1992). Indeed, Jermier (1998) suggests that it is a characteristic of contemporary life that the mechanisms of control are shifting from overt bureaucracy to more unobtrusive and insidious means. Advanced technologies enable surveillance by the 'electronic eye'; the behavioural sciences develop unseen disciplines through culture and teams (Willmott, 1993). Indeed, the new Foucauldian appreciation of micro-technologies of discipline subverts the old duality of strategy and structure from yet another angle. Knights and Morgan (1991) argue that the discourse of strategy as it is diffused and internalized within organizations achieves a transformation of potentially recalcitrant employees into disciplined subjects for whom the formulation and conduct of strategy comes to secure their sense of purpose and reality. For example, Oakes et al. (1998) demonstrate how the introduction of business planning processes into the Canadian public service allowed a certain language and set of commercial assumptions to transform behaviour in an entirely taken-for-granted manner. In this sense, strategy *is* the structure. I have argued that structure itself will not go away. But it is clear that the practicalities of structure are inseparable from broader issues of culture and control.

The work on organizational change likewise has tended to put the issues of structure on the sidelines. Since Pettigrew's (1985) pioneering research on ICI, the many case studies of strategic change have typically dealt with a broad gamut of cultural, business, management and process issues (Johnson, 1987; Child and Smith, 1987; Pettigrew and Whipp, 1991; Leavy and Wilson, 1994). Structural change, however, is rarely treated as an issue in itself. In Pettigrew's (1985) study, ICI's different divisions principally provide a means by which to order the overall narrative of transformation on many dimensions. Only quite recently have there emerged studies in which structure is explicitly treated as the central subject in the management of change (Rowlinson, 1995; Chakravarthy and Gargiulo, 1998; Pettigrew and Fenton, 2000; Bate et al., 2000). As yet, these are all quite short accounts. Chandler's (1962) detailed accounts of the internal debates over divisionalization at DuPont and General Motors are still unmatched.

In good part, this is the fault of the policy tradition. Policy scholars have been too successful in attuning researchers of change only to gross movements between broad forms – typically, from functional structure or holding structure to multidivisional. However, such

changes are epochal and infrequent (Donaldson, 1987; Amburgey and Dacin, 1994). What has emerged from the change literature is that large organizations are more typically characterized by continuities rather than clean breaks, the accumulation of incremental changes rather than dramatic transformations (Pettigrew, 1990). 'Sedimentation' of new ways on top of old is often the appropriate metaphor (Cooper et al., 1996). The policy tradition, with its need for unambiguous variables visible from outside, is poorly equipped to deal with this kind of complexity. It promotes a view of abrupt shifts from one discrete structural category to another that accords ill with practical reality. Even if the change literature has been slow to tackle restructuring specifically, its broader endeavour does underline the need for a more differentiated conceptual apparatus adequate to grasping the nuanced shifts *within* broader structural forms that are the everyday reality of large organizations (Brickley and van Drunen, 1990).

The proxy and periphery streams could easily be accused of trivializing the structural issue in recent years – either by relegating it to a routine variable in the service of different debates, or by putting it on the margins of other issues such as culture, change and control. A less defensive response is to recognize how their insights can actually be taken forward within a renewed structural agenda. As we shall see, the practice perspective in particular relies on the more holistic conception of structure as not simply a subordinate variable to strategy, but as jointly-embedded in the complex web of relationships and elements that make up the firm and define control. The proxy and periphery streams have also underlined the importance of context, internal and external. The practice perspective will require sensitivity both to the diversity of business models around the world and to the plurality of rationales that must be negotiated within the firm. The recognition of competing political interests in the proxy view, and of cultural intractability in the peripheral work, have together problematized the processes of structural change. The change literature in particularly has taught a more subtle language of incrementalism and sedimentation, supplanting the simple policy notions of one form replacing another in neat succession. At the same time, the cultural tradition enjoins a greater appreciation of the skilled performance involved in structural maintenance. Structures are not reified and static, but created and elaborated by real people. The peripheral stream has, moreover, demonstrated that the subtle operations of organizational production and reproduction are best appreciated through case study and close ethnography. These methods have brought rich insight into the working of organizations in ways that the broad abstractions of policy, frankly, have not.

STRUCTURE AS PRACTICE

While Figure 6.1 positions the practice perspective as drawing on earlier traditions of strategic and organizational theorizing, it nevertheless places it apart. The practice perspective has a distinct agenda, concerned with organization as a skilled performance, achieved in routine as well as in change, and with its success dependent upon holistic, contextual and particular understandings, rather than the detached manipulation of discrete and universal variables. The practice perspective also claims for itself a different label (Whittington, 1996). In a crowded field, where its agenda shares concerns with others and there are already many voices shouting for attention, this new label needs a moment's justification.

Introducing the terminology of practice is not conceptual innovation for own sake. Like so many, Lewin and Stephens (1993) have noticed the gap between management practice and the theory of organization design and structure. They also have a proposal: '... much is in a name, and organization theory by some other name might be more acceptable and accessible to non-academics' (Lewin and Stephens, 1993: 397). The shift to a terminology of practice adopted here, while not their own, responds to the failure of access that they identify. A focus on the practice of structure makes an obvious and direct appeal to managerial practitioners. But, as well as casting many traditional problems of organization structure in more appealingly practical terms, it also opens up new theoretical resources from within contemporary theories of social practice (Bourdieu, 1990; de Certeau, 1984; Ortner, 1984; Turner, 1994). While originating in the wider social sciences, such theories of

practice are developing fast within management too (Schön, 1983; Brown and Duguid, 1991; Cook and Seeley-Brown, 1999; Orlikowski, 2000). With regard specifically to structure, these theoretical resources imply an anthropological regard for the situated, often routine but typically skilful activities of structure's practitioners – especially the managers and consultants who make structures and keep them going.

Framing the problem of structure as practice evokes many similar themes to that of process, an increasingly powerful perspective in strategy and management theory (Van de Ven, 1992; Pettigrew, 1992). But, while practice embraces many of the themes of process, there are at least two important differences of emphasis. First, the language of process pushes us in a particular direction: 'The idea of process implies impermanence' (Weick, 1979: 42). Process is closely identified with change (Pettigrew, 1992). Organizations proceed from one state to another. Whether in analyses of strategic change processes, or of strategic decision-making processes, what is at stake typically is some kind of initiative or break from the past. This applies particularly to those arguing for an explicit language of process in understanding organization structure. Thus Kimberly (1984) calls for an analysis of design processes in understanding organizations' 'developmental trajectories'; Galunic and Eisenhardt (1994: 249) propose a process approach in exploring whether and how the traditional policy variables of strategy–structure-performance align in the context of change; while Orton (2000) suggests that the important questions of organizational theory have shifted from description (how are organizations structured?) to process (how do organizations change from one form to another?). The shift from policy's usual static perspective to a concern for dynamic processes is a useful one, something that should be held onto. The language of practice incorporates this, but also gives weight to continuity. Practice's roots in anthropology endow it with a respect for the simple accomplishments of continuity and routine (Ortner, 1984).

The second difference from process is again a fine one, but concerns the level of analysis. Processes tend to be properties of organizations; practice connects more directly to the practitioners. For Schön (1983: viii) a practice approach is concerned with 'what practitioners ... actually do'. Brown and Duguid (2000: 95) talk of practice as being 'the internal life of process'. The focus of practice is typically micro-level, interested in the skills and performance of people before those of the organization. It is first of all their practices that make up processes. Here the modesty of this micro-level perspective resonates closely with the mundane achievements of continuity. The practice perspective seeks out the unglamorous.

This section continues by introducing in quite general theoretical terms three key elements in the practice perspective: the notion of everyday practice; actors as practitioners; and the importance of local contexts. It then turns attention to specific questions concerning corporate structure: making structures work; the practitioners of structure and restructuring; and contextual understanding.

The Theory of Practice

In de Certeau's (1984: ix) definition, practices are about 'ways of operating or doing things'. These are established procedures that actors carry with them from the previous experience of their communities and apply to the exigencies of particular situations. Following practices involves more than the effortless running of pre-set programmes. In shifting, always microscopically unique circumstances, even just doing the same as before requires artful adjustments. Something of this continuous labour of adjustment is implied by the ordinary use of practice in music: repetition, but also gradual and laborious refinement (Schön, 1983). De Certeau (1984) makes a distinction between the strategic – involving autonomous transformation – and the tactical – the use, manipulation and diversion of what is in place. As well as the grand crashes of transformation, the practice notion is concerned with the tactical 'murmerings of the everyday' (de Certeau, 1984: 70). Everyday continuity is not merely passive, but involves effortful achievement. Celebrated are the practical accomplishments of the mundane. Girard's (1998) focuses on the everyday routines and improvisations of 'doing cooking'. In their study of 'laboratory life', Latour and Woolgar (1979) show how scientific work relies upon the repetitious, relentless chores of simple documentation.

Orr (1996) studies photocopier maintenance, Wenger (1998) insurance clerks. In short, the practice perspective uncovers the ordinary strategems and skills upon which human achievements – family life, scientific progress and business organization – depend.

In this recognition of everyday activity, the practice notion also highlights the role of practitioners – people. It is their tactical manoeuvres and manipulations that oil the wheels of everyday life. It is their skilful exploitation of everyday knowledge that contributes to success. In Bourdieu's (1990) account of marriage strategies in Algerian tribes, it is not just position in kinship structures that matters, but how a tribesman plays the particular cards dealt by tradition and inheritance to maximize his personal advantage. Students of kinship need to be connoisseurs of how good players play the game as well as just experts in the rules. This calls for a shift of attention towards the actual activities of practitioners, their routines and their creativity (Schön, 1983; Orlikowski, 2000: 421). Here there need be no exclusive concern with the powerful. We are all practitioners. De Certeau (1984) in particular is concerned with the users of our cultural products, as well as their makers. Important is understanding how ordinary people interpret and use, through creative tactical manipulations, the cultural and material artefacts furnished to them by their environments. In urban design, this entails a shift of perspective from that of technocratic urban planners, to one that is sensitive to the actual practice of local people making daily use of their townscapes. We can chart pedestrian traffic intensity, but what we really need to understand is whether the pavements are being used for travelling to work or leisure, shopping or window-shopping (de Certeau, 1984). The gain in urban design is a more sympathetic environment, intimate and responsive rather than grandiose and alienating. Organizational design has available similar gains from an equivalent shift to understanding 'structures-in-use'.

De Certeau's (1984) sense of situational context is important too in the practice perspective. As Chaiklin (1996) insists, practices are always 'situated'. Thus to understand the practices involved in and surrounding 'doing cooking' within a French household, Girard (1998) insists on detailing the local shops, familial relationships, and even the physical layout of the apartment. Appreciation of context implies as well a heightened awareness of actors' skilful interaction with material and symbolic artefacts. These are the tools of practice. Latour and Woolgar (1979) photograph not only the people but the computers, the desks, the paper, the pens and the pencils involved in the production of scientific knowledge. As we see the scatter of print-outs, notes, pens and cups on the crowded desk of a scientist working at 'cleaning the data', we recognize that scientific knowledge is a precarious product of human activity, not the objective, reified 'facts' of the textbooks. Uncovering the messy, effortful achievements behind the stark and static lines of an organizational chart should be at the heart of a practice approach to structure too.

The Practice of Structure

The practice perspective's emphases on the active achievement of continuity, on the role of practitioners in maintaining and refining the routine, and the implications of context contribute to our understanding of structure in at least three ways. First, there is the practical business of making structures work, involving everyday maintenance but also manipulation and adjustment. Then there is a new awareness of the role of practitioners in structure – both the top managers, advisers and consultants that produce structures, but also the middle managers and others who use and interpret these structures. Finally, the practice perspective implies a holistic and nuanced appreciation of context, of structures as embedded within both organizations and environments, each with very particular characteristics.

Making Structures Work

To start with, the practice perspective points to the relative paucity of research on how different structures can be made to work. Research has been more easily done from a distance – by counting structures and regressing them on performance – than by understanding structures from the inside. In fact, Chandler's colleagues at Harvard made a good start to understanding the practicalities of decision-making and planning within the multidivisional structure, in studies that combined

quantitative and qualitative insights (Bower, 1970; Lawrence and Lorsch, 1967; Vancil, 1978). As the nature of business has changed since these pioneering studies, so there is room for extending this tradition to more contemporary conditions. Another opportunity lies in understanding the role of particular functional areas and skills to the working of structure. Here useful prototypes include Roberts' (1991) study of accounting functions within a conglomerate structure; Purcell and Ahlstrand's (1994) work on human resource functions within different kinds of multidivisional structure; and the Ashridge programme on the role of the centre (Goold and Campbell, 1987; Goold et al., 1994). All of these get inside the actual workings of different kinds of organization, furnishing practical insight into how particular functions fit within and contribute to corporate structures. There remains, however, a good deal to be done, especially in systematically exploring functional contributions to the more differentiated kinds of structure that are now emerging from the policy tradition. The work on the role of information systems within the transnational corporation (Earl and Feeney, 1996) provides one model for this kind of research.

In a world of rapid change, the achievement of any sort of order depends in part upon the capacity for constant micro-adjustments and flexibility. Here already there is a promising stream of research that matches the practice perspective's attention to the constant manipulations and adjustments required for the maintenance of continuity. Rather than seeing structural change as an episodic and transformatory phenomenon, change here is seen as a chronic condition of successful organization (Schoonhoven and Jelinek, 1990; Galunic and Eisenhardt, 1994; Brown and Eisenhardt, 1997; Eisenhardt and Brown, 1999). The achievement of structural continuity requires that structures should never quite be the same from one period to another. The rise of knowledge-intensive firms and the importance of innovation make this appreciation of continuous change still more important. Innovative strength lies not just in the laboratories but in organizational capabilities for continuous structural combination and recombination of the firm's resources (Galunic and Rodan, 1998). We need to know more about the characteristics of organizations adept at frequent structural change and the demands and trade-offs involved (Eisenhardt and Brown, 1999).

The Practitioners of Structure

Schoonhoven and Jelinek (1990) point particularly to the skills and expectations required of practising managers in organizations operating under chronic structural change. Such managers have to be self-critical, outwards-looking and confident handlers of tension and uncertainty. The practice perspective of de Certeau (1984) in particular would encourage further exploration of how these 'consumers' of structure and structural change respond to and manipulate their organizational environments. If, as Schoonhoven and Jelinek (1990) suggest, different structural conditions require particular skills, we need to develop our understanding of what these skills are and how practitioners acquire them. If, moreover, we are moving from a paradigm of structure based on control to one embracing knowledge creation (Ghoshal and Moran, 1996), then we should search for a bottom-up, user-centred understanding of structure and its effects. We should design structures for consumer comfort as well as technocratic convenience.

At the same time, however, we know very little about the 'producers' of structure, the consulting firms, management gurus and top managers who together articulate and introduce new structural designs. Useful pioneering work here has been done on the role of consulting firms like McKinsey & Co. in the evolution and dissemination of the multidivisional structure (McKenna, 1997; Kipping, 1999), but even looking back we still lack in-depth understanding of how consultants and clients actually work together in the tailoring of standard structural solutions to the specific demands of particular firms. We are sorely in need of careful studies of the producers of new structures: who the practitioners are; the skills they bring; the standard tools they employ; their means of structural representation; and the techniques of implementation. If, following Bourdieu (1990), we are interested not just in the rules of the game, but in how successful players take particular tricks, we would want to understand both the contents of consultants' structural repertoires and the manner in which they use them. Practice needs to capture the street-wisdom of the consultant, not just the abstractions of the academic.

The Context of Structure

The understanding of practice should necessarily be situated. The study of structure is marked by its origins in an era pre-dating the internationalization of business and recent challenges to American economic hegemony. The early Harvard policy researchers in Europe perceived it a problem that the same basic multidivisional structure operated differently across France, Germany and the United Kingdom (Channon, 1973; Dyas and Thanheiser, 1976). This kind of local interpretation of structure might be better recognized as discovery than felt as frustration. As the multidivisional structure continues to spread around the world, we need to confront more willingly the varying interpretations that may be laid upon it in different national contexts. An interesting example of this is Clark and Soulsby's (1999) study of structural changes in the Czech Republic: here divisionalization could be adopted totemistically as marker of Westernization on the one hand, while on the other being readily compromised by value-commitments to employment. The skilled practitioners of structure – whether as consumers or as producers – will be more effective as they become more sensitive to the variety of local interpretations of structural types. Here the policy tradition's preference for neat and limited categories amenable to demographic enumeration works to suppress sensitivity rather than enhance it.

Truly more practical would be to accept structural complexity and individuality in the tradition of the corporate cultural studies. Entailed would be a more subtle appreciation of all the elements of internal context, of which structure and strategy make barely separable parts. A holistic recognition of the roles of culture, information and accounting systems, human resource policies and so on *alongside* strategy and structure would likely forearm structural practitioners against simple recipes and enhance their skills in negotiating both change and continuity. The model for this kind of holistic recognition, of course, is the tradition of rich case studies of organizational cultures (e.g. Kunda, 1992; Martin, 1992): the difference would be to put structure centre stage, not culture (cf. Bate et al., 2000).

Clearly, this research agenda has methodological implications. The practice perspective would not rule out quantitative methods – Bourdieu (1988) uses large-scale statistical data to ground his analysis of the practices of academic elite production, while the Boolean method used by Guillén (1994) for the comparative analysis of countries could equally be applied to the intensive study of contrasting cases of structure. Nevertheless, there is a predisposition towards the close study of practice and practitioners in particular contexts, very much in the mode developed by scholars of organizational culture. The ambition is not to establish general laws for others to apply, but to develop the skills of performance through appreciation of the complexities and artfulness of practice. Important here is ethnographic or semi-ethnographic understanding. Orr (1996) conducts his research by driving out with the photocopying engineers on their visits and listening to their stories over coffee-breaks. Girard (1998) chats over the kitchen table. Latour and Woolgar (1979) use the camera. The ethnographic eye should not be merely reflective, however. The practice perspective recognizes that practitioners are rarely fully able to articulate what they do and why. Unselfconsciousness may even be a condition for skilled performance – if the Pacific Islanders had theoretical knowledge of the gift-exchange relationship, they would no longer be able to carry it out (Bourdieu, 1990). Orr (1996) had to overcome his own previous experience as photocopying engineer in order to spot what was really remarkable. While the policy tradition tends to keep its distance, the practice perspective favours first immersion, then detachment.

Many of the concerns that arise from the practice perspective will not be unrecognizable to other traditions within strategic management and organization theory. The improvisation metaphor (Weick, 1993; Hatch, 1999) is close in its evocation of the arts of performance. Practice's concern for continual structural adjustment is shared by scholars from an avowedly process perspective (Schoonhoven and Jelinek, 1990; Galunic and

Eisenhardt, 1994). Structuration theory too is similar in its understanding of the continuous production and reproduction of structures (Barley and Tolbert, 1997; Ranson et al., 1980; and Orlikowski and Yates, 1994). The recent post-modern turn in organization theory has counterposed a language of being and becoming against the reified and static concepts of the policy view (Chia, 1997), while Lyotard's (1984) post-modern celebration of local *savoir faire* over generalized *savoir* promotes practical contextualized skills. Theories of configurations (Miller, 1986), complementarity (Milgrom and Roberts, 1995; Whittington et al., 1999b) and co-evolution (Koza and Lewin, 1998; Lewin and Volberda, 1999) all accept the intimate and dynamic relationship between structure and organizational contexts. A very practical turn allied to the process tradition is the recent interest in assembling and documenting the tools of organization (Malone et al., 1999).

None of these various streams is foreign to the practice perspective and all provide their own special insights. What practice can do, however, is link these to a common resource in social theory, particularly the work of Bourdieu and de Certeau. Practice offers additional theoretical grounding to the metaphors of jazz; it balances the dynamic language of process with an anthropological regard for continuity; it foregrounds the practitioner rather than the organization. Finally – and not negligibly – the very title of the practice perspective makes a direct and positive appeal to those who are actually out there 'doing structure'.

CONCLUSIONS

Corporate structure needs to reclaim its central position on the strategy and management agenda. Companies like General Motors are not going away. With internationalization and the move to a knowledge economy, their structural challenges are becoming more interesting, not less. But we should admit that traditional academic research has not served these companies' structural needs particularly well. It was a practitioner, General Motor's own Alfred Sloan, who in large part invented the multidivisional. Sloan played a leading role in keeping this structure going at General

Motors over three decades. It was even Sloan (1963) himself who was amongst the very first to articulate and publicize the multi-divisional's advantages. For too long, the principal contribution of academia has been to try to prove performance advantages in the multidivisional that managers world-wide had grasped intuitively already. Even in this endeavour, the policy tradition has largely failed. Researchers and their audiences are hardly to be blamed for switching their attention.

Never the less, we can be more positive about the policy tradition than Pfeffer (1997). Policy has exciting prospects in defining, mapping and testing the organizations of the new, knowledge-based and international economy. However, policy is more likely to be successful in pursuing its agenda as it addresses the origins of its earlier frustrations. It will need to develop more discriminating organizational types, take more account of the costs and nature of change, and understand organizations more holistically and from the inside. Some of this renewed policy agenda will be informed by the shift in perspective that is also proposed in this chapter, namely taking more seriously structural practice and structure's practitioners. But the practice perspective proposed here has a distinct agenda, with intellectual debts of its own. The practice perspective learns from the proxy and periphery approaches even as it asserts the urgent relevance of the issues that they left behind. Practice takes from them a complexity and a specificity that have been too absent from the distant approach of the policy tradition. Instead of abstract measurement, it is intimately concerned with the practical wisdom involved in the hard work of making structures and keeping them going.

This practical wisdom is most effectively to be advanced by observing closely how practitioners actually manage structure. After all, managers and their advisers should be pretty good at structure – they do it for their living. We researchers should not be ashamed to ask. Then we can do what we are good at – codifying and conditioning, refining and testing, packaging and disseminating. The kind of knowledge that will emerge is likely to be very different from the contingency theory of first generation structural research. A practical wisdom of structure will entail a holistic recognition of the reciprocity between strategy and structure, an awareness of structure's political repercussions, acceptance of institutional as well as economic logics and a suspicion of universal rules and broadly-defined categories. We can expect that this practical wisdom will be unflinching in its commitment to continued structural adjustment, yet modest in its expectations of major structural transformation. It will respect the creativity of actors at every level of the structural hierarchy, allow them to ease structures to workable shapes and be concerned for their capacities to manage repeated structural change. There will be people – designers and leaders, implementers and interpreters, saboteurs and resisters. Alongside this wisdom of practice, structural contingency theory will seem something of a blunt instrument.

In a sense, this takes us full circle, back to the richness of Alfred Chandler's (1962) original studies of DuPont and General Motors. Certainly, we should avoid this time the temptation to premature abstraction of simple variables. We should regard more carefully aspects of organization, such as culture and change, whose importance has only been revealed by subsequent research. We should incorporate new influences on structure, such as business schools, consulting firms and systems houses, insignificant in an earlier age. We should look more internationally for our models and be more cautious about their universality. Fundamentally, however, the practice approach will have a similar starting point. We need to find the new Alfred Sloans, the new McKinsey consulting companies, watch them closely and learn not only from what they design but – this time especially – from how they do it.

ACKNOWLEDGEMENTS

This chapter has benefited from the comments of Charles Galunic, Michael Mayer and Howard Thomas.

REFERENCES

Amburgey, T. L. and Dacin, T. (1994) 'As the left foot follows the right? The dynamics of strategic and structural change', *Academy of Management Journal*, 37: 1427–52.

Armour, H. O. and Teece, D. J. (1978) 'Organizational structures and economic performance: a test of the multidivisional programme', *Bell Journal of Economics*, 9: 106–22.

Barley, S. and Tolbert, P. S. (1997) 'Institutionalization and structuration: studying the links between action and institution', *Organization Studies*, 18: 93–118.

Barley, S. R. and Kunda, G. (1992) 'Design and devotion: surges of rational and normative ideologies of control in managerial discourse', *Administrative Science Quarterly*, 37: 363–99.

Barney, J. B. (1986) 'Organizational culture: can it be a source of sustainable competitive advantage?', *Academy of Management Review*, 11: 656–66.

Bartlett, C. A. and Ghoshal, S. (1989) *Managing Beyond Borders*. Boston: Harvard Business School.

Bartlett, C. A. and Ghoshal, S. (1993) 'Beyond the M-form, towards a managerial theory of the firm', *Strategic Management Journal*, 14, Special Issue: 23–46.

Bate, P., Khan, R. and Pye, A. (2000) 'Toward a culturally sensitive approach to organization structuring: where organization design meets organization development', *Organization Science*, 11: 197–211.

Birkinshaw, J. (2000) *Entrepreneurship in the Global Firm*. London: Sage.

Birkinshaw, J. and Morrison, A. (1995) 'Configurations of strategy and structure in subsidiaries of multinational corporations', *Journal of International Business Studies*, 26(4): 729–53.

Bourdieu, P. (1988) *Homo Academicus*. Cambridge: Polity.

Bourdieu, P. (1990) *The Logic of Practice*. Cambridge: Polity.

Bower, J. L. (1970) *Managing the Resource Allocation Process*. Boston: Harvard Business School Division of Research.

Bowman, E. H. and Singh, H. (1993) 'Corporate restructuring: reconfiguring the firm', *Strategic Management Journal*, 14, Special Issue: 5–14.

Bowman, E. H., Singh, H., Useem, M. and Bhadura, R. (1999) 'When does restructuring improve economic performances?', *California Management Review*, 41: 33–54.

Brickley, J. A. and van Drunen, L. (1990) 'Internal corporate restructuring: an empirical analysis', *Journal of Accounting and Economics*, 12: 251–80.

Brown, S. J. and Duguid, P. (1991) 'Organizational learning and communities-of-practice', *Organization Science*, 2: 40–57.

Brown, J. S. and Duguid, P. (2000) *The Social Life of Information*. Boston, Mass: Harvard Business School.

Brown, S. L. and Eisenhardt, K. M. (1997) 'The art of continuous change: linking complexity theory and time-paced evolution in relentlessly shifting environments', *Administrative Science Quarterly*, 42: 1–34.

Cable, J. (1988) 'Organizational form and economic performance', in S. Thompson and M. Wright (eds), *Internal Organization, Efficiency and Profits*. Oxford: Philip Allan.

Cable, J. and Dirrheimer, M. J. (1983) 'Hierarchies and markets: an empirical test of the multidivisional hypotheses in West Germany', *International Journal of Industrial Organization*, 1: 43–62.

Cable, J. and Yasuki, H. (1985) 'Internal organisation, business groups and corporate performance: an empirical test of the multidivisional hypothesis in Japan', *International Journal of Industrial Organisation*, 3(4), 401–21.

Castells, M. (1996) *The Rise of the Network Society*. Oxford: Blackwell.

Chaiklin, S. (1996) 'Understanding the social scientific practice of "understanding practice"', in S. Chaiklin and J. Lave (eds), *Understanding Practice*. Cambridge: Cambridge University Press. pp. 377–401.

Chakravarthy, B. and Gargiulo, M. (1998) 'Maintaining leadership legitimacy in the transition to new organizational forms', *Journal of Management Studies*, 35: 435–56.

Chandler, A. D. (1962) *Strategy and Structure: Chapters in the History of the American Industrial Enterprise*. Cambridge, Mass: The MIT Press.

Chandler, A. D. (1984) 'The emergence of managerial capitalism', *Business History Review*, 58: 473–503.

Chandler, A. D. (1990) *Scale and Scope: The Dynamics of Industrial Capitalism*. Cambridge, Mass: Harvard University Press.

Chang, S. J. and Choi, U. (1988) 'Strategy, structure and performance of Korean business groups: a transactions cost approach', *Journal of Industrial Economics*, 37: 141–58.

Channon, D. (1973) *The Strategy and Structure of British Enterprise*. Cambridge, Mass: Harvard University Press.

Chia, R. (1997) 'Thirty years on: from organization structure to the organization of thought', *Organization Studies*, 18: 685–707.

Child, J. (1972) 'Organisational structure, environment and performance: the role of strategic choice', *Sociology*, 6: 1–22.

Child, J. (1997) 'Strategic choice in the analysis of action, structure, organizations and environment: retrospect and prospect', *Organization Studies*, 18: 43–76.

Child, J. and Smith, C. (1987) 'The context and process of organizational transformation: Cadbury limited in its sector', *Journal of Management Studies*, 24: 563–93.

Clark, E. and Soulsby, A. (1999) 'The adoption of the multi-divisional form in large Czech enterprises: the role of economic, institutional and strategic choice factors', *Journal of Management Studies*, 36: 335–59.

Cook, S. D. N. and Seeley-Brown, J. (1999) 'Bridging epistemologies: the generative dance between organizational knowledge and organizational knowing', *Organization Science*, 10: 381–400.

Cooper, D. J., Hinings, R., Greenwood, R. and Brown, J. L. (1996) 'Sedimentation and transformation in organizational change: the case of Canadian law firms', *Organization Studies*, 17: 623–49.

Daft, R. and Lewin, A. (1993) 'Where are the theories of the new organizational forms?', *Organization Science*, 4(4): 1–16.

Daniels, J. D., Pitts, R. A. and Tretter, M. J. (1984) 'Strategy and structure of US multinationals: an exploratory study', *Academy of Management Review*, 27: 292–307.

de Certeau, M. (1984) *The Practice of Everyday Life*. Berkeley: University of California Press.

Derdack, T. (1988) *International Directory of Company Histories*. Chicago: St. James Press.

Di Maggio, P. and Powell, W. W. (1983) 'The iron cage revisited: institutional isomorphism and collective rationality in organisational fields', *American Sociological Review*, 48: 147–80.

Djelic, M-L. (1998) *Exporting the American Model: The Postwar Tranformation of European Business*. Oxford: Oxford University Press.

Donaldson, L. (1987) 'Strategy and structural adjustment', *Journal of Management Studies*, 24: 1–24.

Donaldson, L. (1995) *American Anti-Management Theories of Organization*. Cambridge: Cambridge University Press.

Donaldson, L. (1996) *For Positivist Organization Theory: Proving the Hard Core*. London: Sage.

Dyas, G. P. and Thanheiser, H. T. (1976) *The Emerging European Enterprise*. London: Macmillan.

Earl, M. J. and Feeney, D. (1996) 'Information systems in global business: evidence from European multinationals', in M. J. Earl (ed.), *Information Management: The Organizational Dimension*. Oxford: Oxford University Press.

Egelhoff, W. G. (1988) 'Strategy and structure in multinational corporations: a revision of the Stopford and Wells model', *Strategic Management Journal*, 9: 1–14.

Eisenhardt, K. and Brown, S. (1999) 'Patching: restitching business portfolios in dynamic markets', *Harvard Business Review*, May–June, 72–80.

Ezzamel, M. and Watson, R. (1993) 'Organisational form, ownership structure, and corporate performance: a contextual analysis of UK companies', *British Journal of Management*, 4: 161–76.

Fligstein, N. (1987) 'Intraorganizational power struggle: the rise of finance personnel to top leadership in large corporations 1919–1979', *American Sociological Review*, 52: 44–58.

Fligstein, N. (1990) *The Transformation of Corporate Control*. Cambridge, Mass: Harvard University Press.

Galunic, D. C. and Eisenhardt, K. M. (1994) 'Renewing the strategy–structure–performance paradigm', *Research in Organizational Behavior*, 16: 215–55.

Galunic, D. C. and Rodan, S. (1998) 'Resource recombinations in the firm: knowledge structures and the potential for Schumpeterian innovation', *Strategic Management Journal*, 19: 1193–201.

Gestrin, M., Knight, R. and Rugman, A. (2000) *Templeton Global Performance Index 2000*. Oxford: Templeton College.

Ghoshal, S. and Moran, P. (1996) 'Bad for practice: a critique of transaction cost theory', *Academy of Management Review*, 21: 13–47.

Girard, L. (1998) 'The nourishing arts', in L. Girard, P. Mayol and M. de Certeau (eds), *The Practice of Everyday Life*. Minneapolis: University of Minnesota Press.

Goold, M. and Campbell, A. (1987) *Strategies and Styles*. Oxford: Blackwell.

Goold, M., Campbell, A. and Alexander, M. (1994) *Corporate Level Strategy: Creating Value in the Multibusiness Company*. London: Wiley.

Granovetter, M. (1995) 'Coase revisited: business groups in the modern economy', *Industrial and Corporate Change*, 4: 93–130.

Grant, R. (1996) 'Towards a knowledge-based theory of the firm', *Strategic Management Journal*, 17, Winter Special Issue: 109–22.

Greenwood, R., Hinings, C. R. and Brown, J. (1990) 'P²-form strategic management: corporate practices in professional partnerships', *Academy of Management Journal*, 33: 725–55.

Gresov, C. and Drazin, R. (1997) 'Equifinality: functional equivalence in organizational design', *Academy of Management Review*, 22: 403–28.

Grinyer, P., Yasai-Ardekani, M. and Al-Bazzaz, S. (1980) 'Strategy, structure, the environment and financial performance in 48 United Kingdom companies', *Academy of Mangement Journal*, 23: 193–220.

Guillén, M. F. (1994) *Models of Management: Work, Authority and Organization in Comparative Perspective*. Chicago: University of Chicago Press.

Gulati, R., Nohria, N. and Zaheer, A. (2000) 'Strategic networks', *Strategic Management Journal*, 21: 203–16.

Habib, M. M. and Victor, B. (1991) 'Strategy, structure and performance of US manufacturing and service MNCs: a corporate analysis', *Strategic Management Journal*, 12: 589–606.

Hall, D. J. and Saias, M. A. (1980) 'Strategy follows structure!', *Strategic Management Journal*, 1: 149–63.

Hamilton, G. C. and Biggart, N. W. (1988) 'Market, cultures and authority: a comparative analysis of management and organisation in the Far East', *American Journal of Sociology*, 94, Supplement: 52–94.

Hamilton, R. T. and Shergill, G. S. (1992) 'The relationship between strategy–structure fit and financial performance in New Zealand: evidence of generality and validity with enhanced controls', *Journal of Management Studies*, 29: 95–113.

Harris, B. C. (1983) *Organization: The Effect on Large Corporations*. Ann Arbor, Michigan: UMI Research Press.

Harris, I. C. and Ruefli, T. W. (2000) 'The strategy/structure debate: an examination of the performance implications', *Journal of Management Studies*, 37: 557–603.

Hatch, M. J. (1999) 'Exploring the empty spaces of organizing: how improvisational jazz helps redescribe organizational structure', *Organization Studies*, 20: 75–100.

Hayes, R. H. and Abernathy, W. (1980) 'Managing our way to economic decline', *Harvard Business Review*, July–August: 67–85.

Hedlund, G. (1994) 'A model of knowledge management and the N-form corporation', *Strategic Management Journal*, 15: 73–90.

Hill, C. W. L. (1988a) 'Corporate control type, strategy, size and financial performance', *Journal of Management Studies*, 25: 403–17.

Hill, C. W. L. (1988b) 'Internal capital market controls and financial performance in multidivisional firms', *Journal of Industrial Economics*, 37: 67–83.

Hill, C. W. L. and Pickering, J. F. (1986) 'Divisionalisation, decentralisation and performance of large United Kingdom companies', *Journal of Management Studies*, 23: 26–50.

Hill, C. W. L., Hitt, M. A. and Hoskisson, R. E. (1992) 'Cooperative versus competitive structures in related and unrelated diversified firms', *Organization Science*, 3: 501–21.

Hinings, C. R., Greenwood, R. and Cooper, D. (1999) 'The dynamics of change in large accounting firms', in M. Powell, C. R. Hinings and D. Brock (eds), *Restructuring the Professional Organization*. London: Routledge.

Hofstede, G. (1991) *Cultures and Organizations*. London: McGraw-Hill.

Hollingsworth, J. R. and Boyer, R. (1997) 'The coordination of economic actors and social systems of production', in J. R. Hollingsworth and R. Boyer (eds), *Contemporary Capitalism: The Embeddedness of Institutions*. Cambridge: Cambridge University Press.

Hoskisson, R. E. (1987) 'Multidivisional structure and performance: the contingency of diversification strategy', *Academy of Management Journal*, 30: 625–44.

Hoskisson, R. E. and Galbraith, C. S. (1985) 'The effect of quantum versus incremental M-form reorganization on performance – a time-series exploration of intervention dynamics', *Journal of Management*, 11(3): 55–70.

Hu, Y-S. (1992) 'Global or stateless corporations are national firms with international operations', *California Management Review*, Winter: 115–26.

Jacques, E. (1990) 'In praise of hierarchy', *Harvard Business Review*, January–February: 127–32.

Jermier, J. M. (1998) 'Introduction: critical perspectives on organizational control', *Administrative Science Quarterly*, 43: 235–56.

Johnson, G. (1987) *Strategic Change and the Management Process*. Oxford: Blackwell.

Khanna, T. and Palepu, K. (1999) 'Policy shocks, market intermediaries and corporate strategy: the evolution of business groups in Chile and India', *Journal of Economics and Management Strategy*, 8: 271–310.

Kimberly, J. R. (1984) 'The anatomy of organizational design', *Journal of Management*, 10: 109–26.

Kipping, M. (1999) 'American management consulting companies in Western Europe, 1920 to 1990: products, reputation and relationships', *Business History Review*, 73: 190–220.

Knights, D. and Morgan, G. (1991) 'Corporate strategy, organisations and subjectivity', *Organization Studies*, 12: 251–73.

Kogut, B. and Parkinson, D. (1998) 'Adoption of the multidivisional structure: analysing history from the start', *Industrial and Corporate Change*, 7: 249–74.

Kogut, B. and Zander, U. (1996) 'What do firms do? Coordination, identity and learning', *Organization Science*, 7: 502–18.

Kono, T. (1984) *Strategy and Structure of Japanese Enterprises*. London: Macmillan.

Koza, M. P. and Lewin, A. Y. (1998) 'The co-evolution of strategic alliances', *Organization Science*, 9: 255–64.

Kunda, G. (1992) *Engineering Culture*. Philadelphia: Temple University Press.

Lash, S. and Urry, J. (1987) *The End of Organised Capitalism*. Oxford: Polity.

Latour, B. and Woolgar, S. (1979) *Laboratory Life: The Social Construction of Scientific Facts*. London: Sage.

Lawrence, P. and Lorsch, J. W. (1967) *Organization and Environment: Managing Differentiation and Integration*. Boston, MA: Harvard Business School Press.

Leavy, B. and Wilson, D. C. (1994) *Strategy and Leadership*. London: Routledge.

Legge, K. (1994) 'Managing culture: fact or fiction?', in K. Sisson (ed.), *Personnel Management: A Comprehensive Guide to Theory and Practice in Britain*. Oxford: Blackwell.

Leong, S. W. and Tan, C. T. (1993) 'Managing across borders: an empirical test of the Bartlett and Ghoshal (1989) typology', *Journal of International Business Studies*, 24: 494–564.

Lewin, A. Y. and Stephens, C. U. (1993) 'Designing postindustrial organizations: combining theory and practice', in G. P. Huber and W. H. Glick (eds), *Organizational Change and Redesign*. New York: Oxford University Press.

Lewin, A. Y. and Volberda, H. W. (1999) 'Prolegomena on coevolution: a framework for research on strategy and new organization forms', *Organization Science*, 20: 519–34.

Li, P. P. (1998) 'Towards a geocentric framework of organizational form: a holistic, dynamic and paradoxical account', *Organization Studies*, 19: 829–62.

Liebeskind, J. P. (1996) 'Knowledge, strategy and the theory of the firm', *Strategic Management Journal*, 17, Winter Special Issue: 93–108.

Lorenzoni, G. and Baden-Fuller, C. (1995) 'Creating a strategic centre to manage a web of partners', *California Management Review*, 37: 146–63.

Lyotard, J-F. (1984) *The Postmodern Condition: A Report on Knowledge*. Manchester: Manchester University Press.

Mahajan, V., Sharma, S. and Bettis, R. A. (1988) 'The adoption of the M-form organizational structure: a test of the imitation hypothesis', *Management Science*, 34: 1188–200.

Mahoney, J. T. (1992) 'The adoption of the multidivisional form of organisation: a contingency model', *Journal of Management Studies*, 29: 49–72.

Malone, T. W., Crowston, K., Lee, J. and Pentland, B. (1999) 'Tools for inventing organizations: toward a handbook for inventing organizations', *Management Science*, 45: 425–43.

Markides, C. and Williamson, P. (1996) 'Corporate diversification and organizational structure: a resource based view', *Academy of Management Journal*, 39: 340–67.

Martin, J. (1992) *Cultures in Organizations: Three Perspectives*. New York: Oxford University Press.

Martin, J. and Frost, P. (1996) 'The organizational culture war games: a struggle for intellectual dominance', in C. Hardy, W. Nord and S. Clegg (eds), *Handbook of Organization Studies*. London: Sage. pp. 599–620.

Mayer, M. C. J. and Whittington, R. (1999) 'Strategy, structure and "systemness": national institutions and corporate change in France, Germany and the UK, 1950–1993', *Organization Studies*, 20: 933–59.

McKenna, C. D. (1997) 'The American challenge: McKinsey & Company's role in the transfer of decentralization to Europe, 1957–1975', *Academy of Management Best Paper Proceedings*, 226–31.

Meyer, J. W. and Rowan, B. (1977) 'Institutionalised organisations: formal structure as myth and ceremony', *American Journal of Sociology*, 83: 340–63.

Milgrom, P. and Roberts, J. (1995) 'Complementarities and fit: strategy, structure and organizational change in manufacturing', *Journal of Accounting and Economics*, 19: 179–208.

Miller, D. (1986) 'Configurations of strategy and structure: towards a synthesis', *Strategic Management Journal*, 7: 233–49.

Mintzberg, H. (1979) *The Structuring of Organizations*. Englewood Cliffs, NJ: Prentice-Hall.

Mintzberg, H. (1990) 'The design school: reconsidering the basic premises of strategic management', *Strategic Management Journal*, 11: 171–95.

Munro, R. (1999) 'The cultural performance of control', *Organization Studies*, 20: 619–40.

Nahapiet, J. and Ghoshal, S. (1998) 'Social capital, intellectual capital, and the organizational advantage', *Academy of Management Review*, 23: 242–66.

Nohria, N. (1996) 'From the M-form to the N-form: taking stock of changes in the large industrial corporation', Harvard Business School Working Paper, Division of Research.

Nohria, N. and Ghoshal, S. (1994) 'Differentiated fit and shared values: alternatives for managing headquarters–subsidiary relations', *Strategic Management Journal*, 15: 491–502.

Oakes, L. S., Townley, B. and Cooper, D. J. (1998) 'Business planning as pedagogy: language and institutions in a changing institutional field', *Administrative Science Quarterly*, 43: 257–92.

Offe, C. (1985) *Disorganized Capitalism*. Cambridge: Polity.

Ogbonna, E. and Harris, L. C. (1998) 'Managing organizational culture: compliance or genuine change?', *British Journal of Management*, 9: 273–88.

Orlikowski, W. J. (2000) 'Using technology and constituting structures: a practice lens for studying technology in organizations', *Organization Science*, 11: 404–28.

Orlikowski, W. J. and Yates, J. (1994) 'Genre repertoire: examining the structuring of communicative practices in organizations', *Administrative Science Quarterly*, 39: 541–74.

Orr, J. E. (1996) *Talking about Machines: An Ethnography of a Modern Job*. New York: Cornell University Press.

Ortner, S. B. (1984) 'Theory in anthropology since the sixties', *Comparative Studies of Society and History*, 26: 126–66.

Orton, D. (2000) 'Enactment, sense-making and decision-making: redesign processes in the 1976 reorganization of US intelligence', *Journal of Management Studies*, 37(2): 213–34.

Palmer, D. A., Devereux Jennings, P. and Zhou, X. (1993) 'Late adoption of the multidivisional form by large US corporations: institutional, political and economic accounts', *Administrative Science Quarterly*, 38: 100–31.

Palmer, D., Friedland, R., Devereux Jennings, P. and Powers, M. (1987) 'The economics and politics of structure: the multidivisional form and the large US corporation', *Administrative Science Quarterly*, 32: 25–48.

Pascale, R. T. (1984) 'Perspectives on strategy: the real story behind Honda's success', *California Management Review*, 24: 47–72.

Pettigrew, A. (1985) *The Awakening Grant: Continuity and Change in ICI*. Oxford: Basil Blackwell.

Pettigrew, A. M. (1990) 'Longitudinal field research on change: theory and practice', *Organization Science*, 1, 3.

Pettigrew, A. M. (1992) 'The character and significance of strategy process research', *Strategic Management Journal*, 13: 5–16.

Pettigrew, A. and Fenton, E. (2000) *The Innovating Organization*. London: Sage.

Pettigrew, A. M. and Whipp, R. (1991) *Managing Change for Competitive Success*. Oxford: Blackwell.

Pettigrew, A. M., Massini, S. and Numagami, T. (2000) 'Innovative forms of organizing in Europe and Japan', *European Management Journal*, 18: 259–73.

Pfeffer, J. (1997) *New Directions for Organization Theory*. New York: Oxford University Press.

Purcell, J. and Ahlstrand, B. (1994) *Human Resource Management in the Multi-Divisional Company*. Oxford: Oxford University Press.

Ragin, C. C. (1987) *The Comparative Method*. California: California Press.

Ranson, S., Hinings, R. and Greenwood, R. (1980) 'The structuring of organizations', *Administrative Science Quarterly*, 25: 1–17.

Roberts, J. (1991) 'The possibilities of accountability', *Accounting, Organizations and Society*, 16: 355–68.

Robins, J. (1993) 'Organization as strategy: restructuring production in the film industry', *Strategic Management Journal*, 14, Summer Special Issue: 103–18.

Rosen, M. (1985) 'Breakfast at Spiros: dramaturgy and dominance', *Journal of Management*, 11(2): 31–48.

Rowlinson, M. (1995) 'Strategy, structure and culture: Cadbury, divisionalization and merger in the 1960s', *Journal of Management Studies*, 32: 121–40.

Ruigrok, W., Pettigrew, A. M., Peck, S. and Whittington, R. (1999) 'Corporate restructuring and new forms of organizing: evidence from Europe', *Management International Review*, 39(2): 41–64.

Rumelt, R. (1974) *Strategy Structure and Economic Performance*. Boston: Harvard Business School Press.

Rumelt, R., Schendel, D. and Teece, D. (1994) 'Fundamental issues in strategy', in R. Rumelt, D. Schendel and D. Teece (eds), *Fundmental Issues in Strategy*. Boston: Harvard Business School Press.

Schein, E. H. (1985) *Organizational Culture and Leadership*. San Francisco: Jossey-Bass.

Schön, D. A. (1983) *The Reflective Practitioner: How Professionals Think in Action*. New York: Basic Books.

Schoonhoven, C. B. and Jelinek, M. (1990) 'Dynamic tension in innovative high technology firms: managing rapid technological change through organizational structure', in M. von Glinow and S. Mohrman (eds), *Managing Complexity in High Technology Firms*. Oxford: Oxford University Press. pp. 90–115.

Scott, B. R. (1973) 'The industrial state: old myths and new realities', *Harvard Business Review*, March–April, 135–48.

Slater, R. (1999) *The GE Way Fieldbook*. New York: McGraw Hill.

Sloan, A. P. (1963) *My Years with General Motors*. London: Sedgewick and Jackson.

Spender, J. C. (1992) 'Business policy and strategy: an occasion for despair, a retreat from disciplinary specialisation, or for new excitement?', *Academy of Management Best Papers Proceedings*: 42–6.

Starbuck, W. (1992) 'Learning in knowledge-intensive-firms', *Journal of Management Studies*, 29: 713–40.

Starbuck, W. (1993) 'Keeping a butterfly and an elephant in a house of cards: the elements of exceptional success', *Journal of Management Studies*, 30: 885–912.

Steer, P. and Cable, J. (1978) 'Internal organization and profit: an empirical analysis of large UK companies', *Journal of Industrial Economics*, 27: 13–30.

Stopford, J. and Wells, L. T. (1972) *Managing the Multinational Enterprise*. New York: Basic Books.

Taggart, J. H. (1998) 'Configuration and coordination at subsidiary level: foreign manufacturing affiliates in the UK', *British Journal of Management*, 9: 327–40.

Teece, D. J. (1993) 'The dynamics of industrial capitalism: perspectives on Alfred Chandler's scale and scope', *Journal of Economic Literature*, 31: 199–225.

Tsoukas, H. (1996) 'The firm as a distributed knowledge system: a constructionist approach', *Strategic Management Journal*, 17, Winter Special Issue: 11–26.

Turner, S. (1994) *The Social Theory of Practices: Tradition, Tacit Knowledge and Presuppositions*. Cambridge: Polity.

Van de Ven, A. (1992) 'Suggestions for studying strategy process: a research note', *Strategic Management Journal*, 13, Summer Special Issue: 169–88.

Vancil, R. E. (1978) *Decentralization: Managerial Ambiguity by Design*. Homewood, Illinois: Dow Jones-Irwin.

Venkatraman, N., Loh, L. and Koh, J. (1994) 'The adoption of corporate governance mechanisms – a test of competing diffusion models', *Management Science*, 40(4): 496–507.

Volberda, H. W. (1998) *Building the Flexible Firm: How to Remain Competitive*. Oxford: Oxford University Press.

Weick, K. E. (1979) *The Social Psychology of Organising*. Massachussetts: Addison-Wesley.

Weick, K. E. (1993) 'Organizational design as improvisation', in G. P. Huber and W. H. Glick (eds), *Organizational Change and Redesign*. New York: Oxford University Press.

Wenger, E. (1998) *Communities of Practice: Learning, Meaning and Identity*. Cambridge: Cambridge University Press.

Whitley, R. (1994) 'Dominant forms of economic organization in market economies', *Organization Studies*, 15: 153–82.

Whitley, R. (1999) *Divergent Capitalisms*. Oxford: Oxford University Press.

Whittington, R. (1989) *Corporate Strategies in Recession and Recovery: Social Structure and Strategic Choice*. London: Unwin Hyman.

Whittington, R. (1996) 'Strategy as practice', *Long Range Planning*, October: 731–5.

Whittington, R. and Mayer, M. (2000) *The European Corporation: Strategy, Structure and Social Science*. Oxford: Oxford University Press.

Whittington, R., Mayer, M. and Curto, F. (1999a) 'Chandlerism in post-war Europe: strategic and structural change in France, Germany and the UK, 1950–1993', *Industrial and Corporate Change*, 8: 519–50.

Whittington, R., Pettigrew, A., Peck, S., Fenton, E. and Conyon, M. (1999b) 'Change and complementarities in the new competitive landscape: a European panel study, 1992–1996', *Organization Science*, 10: 583–600.

Williamson, O. E. (1970) *Corporate Control and Business Behaviour*. Englewood Cliffs, New Jersey: Prentice-Hall.

Williamson, O. E. (1975) *Markets and Hierarchies: Analysis and Antitrust Implications*. New York: The Free Press.

Williamson, O. E. and Bhargava, N. (1972) 'Assessing and classifying the internal structure and control apparatus of the modern corporation', in K. Cowling (ed.), *Market Structure and Corporate Behaviour*. London: Gray Mills.

Willmott, H. (1993) 'Strength is ignorance; slavery is freedom: managing culture in modern organizations', *Journal of Management Studies*, 30: 515–52.

7

Knowledge-Based View: A New Theory of Strategy?

KATHLEEN M. EISENHARDT
and FILIPE M. SANTOS

The knowledge movement is sweeping through the field of strategy. The last several years have witnessed the widespread use of a knowledge perspective for research on a variety of topics within strategy, including alliances (Mowery et al., 1996; Simonin, 1999), capabilities transfer (Zander and Kogut, 1995; Szulanski, 1996), acquisitions (Ranft and Lord, 1998; Zollo and Singh, 1999) and product development (Hargadon and Sutton, 1997; Hansen, 1999). An emerging knowledge-based view (KBV) of strategy underlies this research. This perspective considers knowledge as the most strategically significant resource of the firm (Grant, 1996a), and its proponents argue that heterogeneous knowledge bases and capabilities among firms are the main determinants of sustained competitive advantage and superior corporate performance (Decarolis and Deeds, 1999; Winter and Szulanski, 1999).

What is the impact of this focus on knowledge for the field of strategy? The answer is unclear because agreement on the nature of organizational knowledge, the specifics of the KBV, and whether such a view constitutes a theory of strategy, a theory of the firm, or both, has yet to emerge. Additionally, empirical research based on the knowledge perspective is extensive, but there is no consensus

understanding on whether that research supports the existing theory (Patriotta and Pettigrew, 1999) or adds predictive power to other theories of strategy.

Some researchers argue that KBV is an outgrowth of resource-based thinking where the concept of resources is extended to include intangible assets and, specifically, knowledge-based resources (Grant, 1996a; Decarolis and Deeds, 1999). But then, is KBV really just a relabeling of resource-based thinking that adds little to our current understanding of the sources of superior performance? Other researchers see KBV as a useful extension of organizational learning to strategy and organization theory, an extension that is capable of informing research and providing new insights into organizational functioning (Kogut and Zander, 1992, 1996). Still others argue that knowledge should be treated as a process of ongoing social construction and not as a resource (Spender, 1996). Finally, some believe that a theory of strategy must be a theory of the firm if it is to be a theory of strategy at all (Conner and Prahalad, 1996). Given this variety of perspectives, is the knowledge movement just a fad? Or does it represent the emergence of a new theory of strategy, contributing to our ability to understand the sources of superior firm performance? Or is it more accurately a new theory of organization? The purpose of this chapter is to address these questions.

The chapter is organized into four sections. We begin with a theoretical discussion of KBV that covers varying views on the nature of knowledge, several streams of thinking that underlie KBV, and a variety of theoretical statements about what a knowledge-based theory of strategy might be. We then examine the empirical literature on KBV, within strategy and closely related fields, by focusing on four major streams of research on knowledge: sourcing, internal transfer, external transfer, and integration. We end by addressing the questions that we posed at the beginning of this chapter and offering some directions for future research.

There are several major conclusions. First, KBV offers a number of useful and empirically-grounded insights into the multi-level social processes through which knowledge is sourced, transferred, and integrated, within and across organizations. Second, since the empirical research indicates that these knowledge processes are largely similar within and across organizations, KBV is not as yet a theory of organization. There is, however, some exciting new theoretical work emphasizing organizational identity and 'knowledge as knowing' that may become such a theory. Finally, when KBV is used as a theory of strategy, knowledge is conceptualized as a resource that can be acquired, transferred, or integrated to achieve sustained competitive advantage. In our view, KBV then reduces to simply a special case of resource-based thinking, rather than a unique theory of strategy. Further, it rests on the tenuous assumption that knowledge is the firm's most important resource. Therefore, knowledge-based thinking is enormously important for understanding a number of central topics in strategy, including acquisitions, alliances, and strategic choice, but it is not as yet a unique theory about how firm managers create competitive advantage. It is not as yet a new theory of strategy.

ORIGINS AND DEVELOPMENT OF
THE KNOWLEDGE-BASED VIEW

Researchers in the strategy field have traditionally used a concept of knowledge that is grounded in Western epistemology.[1] Knowledge is considered as 'justified true belief' and the focus of theories is on the explicit nature of knowledge (Nonaka and Takeuchi, 1995). In other words, knowledge is modeled as an unambiguous, reducible and easily transferable construct, while knowing is associated with processing information. This approach to knowledge has given rise to several theories that suggest a machine-like functioning of organizations. For example, scientific management theories posit that the organization of work should be entirely determined by codified knowledge, and that the knowledge of the firm is held by a select number of individuals. Similarly, the information-processing perspective treats organizations as machines that use rules and routines to address the individual information processing requirements caused by interdependent work and environmental uncertainty (Santos, 1999).

In contrast with this traditional conception, a newer view of knowledge, based on the distinction between explicit and tacit knowledge (Polanyi, 1962), has emerged. Tacit knowledge is linked to the individual and is very difficult, or even impossible, to articulate. Only through observation and doing is it possible to learn this type of knowledge. As knowledge is explored, put into action and socially justified, some part of it may be codified (made more explicit), by being converted into messages that can then be processed as information and transmitted. Nonetheless, information and explicit knowledge are considered distinct constructs, since there is always a certain degree of interpretive ambiguity due to specific contexts and individual perspectives (Tell, 1997). The process of knowledge codification requires the development of mental models and the existence of a language in which knowledge can be articulated. In addition, since codification entails a transformation in the organization of knowledge, it is always a process of creation (Cowan and Foray, 1997) and does not replace entirely the more tacit knowledge on which it is based. This distinction between tacit and explicit knowledge has proven to be particularly important in the dominant knowledge-based approach to strategy (Kogut and Zander, 1992; Grant, 1996a). That approach identifies tacit knowledge as the most strategic resource of firms. The argument is that, since tacit knowledge is difficult to imitate and relatively immobile, it can constitute the basis of sustained competitive advantage (Grant, 1996a; Decarolis and Deeds, 1999; Gupta and Govindarajan, 2000).

Yet, even as mainstream strategy scholars began emphasizing the implications of tacit vs explicit knowledge, a more recent epistemology has emerged in the strategy and learning literatures, particularly in Europe (Blackler, 1993; Weick and Roberts, 1993; Blackler, 1995; Spender, 1996; Von_Krogh et al., 1998; Cook and Brown, 1999; Patriotta and Pettigrew, 1999). The foundations of this approach are deeply rooted in cognitive psychology and sociology. As such, this approach focuses more on the process of knowing than on knowledge as an objective and transferable resource. Knowledge is considered socially constructed and the creation of meaning occurs in ongoing social interactions grounded in working practices (Weick and Roberts, 1993; Cook and Brown, 1999) and the specifics of the social and cultural setting (Blackler, 1995; Galunic and Rodan, 1998). Instead of a cognitive representation of reality, knowledge is a creative activity of constructing reality (Von_Krogh et al., 1994). Thus, truth should be considered more as a goal of the knowledge creation process than an absolute characteristic of knowledge (Tell, 1997).

Overall, this approach goes beyond the dominant conception of knowledge as a resource that can assume tacit or explicit forms. In this newer epistemology, knowledge is associated with a process phenomenon of knowing that is clearly influenced by the social and cultural settings in which it occurs. With these varying views of knowledge in mind, we turn now to the streams of thinking that underlie KBV.

Organizational Learning as a Foundation for the Knowledge-Based View

Organizational learning is part of the foundation that underlies knowledge-based thinking. Learning can be defined as the process by which new information is incorporated into the behavior of agents, changing their patterns of behavior and possibly, but not always, leading to better outcomes. The initial focus of learning theory was on individuals, using the mechanism of stimulus–response (Weick, 1991). More recently, it has been conceptualized at the organizational level as well, where it is viewed as a key process in the adaptation of organizations to the environment (Argote, 1999).

Penrose's seminal work on the growth of the firm (1959) is an important starting point for understanding organizational learning. Penrose describes how learning processes create new knowledge and form the basis of the growth of organizations through the recombination of existing resources. Shortly thereafter, Cyert and March (1963) developed significant thinking around the concept of organizational routines. Organizational routines form the basis of collective learning in organizations. They are seen as executable capabilities for repeated performance that have been learned by an organization in response to selective pressures (Cohen et al., 1996). These routines represent a manifestation of organizational memory in that they encode inferences from history, and guide individual and group behavior in organizations. Organizational learning is thus perceived as an adaptive change process that is influenced by past experience, focused on developing and modifying routines, and supported by organizational memory (Nonaka and Takeuchi, 1995).

Nelson and Winter (1982) were among the first to integrate organizational knowledge and routines with the notion of dynamic competitive environments. In their approach to evolutionary economics, the firm is understood to be a repository of knowledge, which is represented by routines that guide organizational action. The authors see individuals as responding to information complexity and uncertainty through their own skills and routine organizational activity, in line with the behavioral tradition (Simon, 1965; Cyert and March, 1963).

Cohen and Levinthal (1990) related organizational learning and innovation to the evolving knowledge base of the firm. The authors define absorptive capacity as the ability to recognize the value of external information, assimilate it and apply it to commercial ends. According to the authors, absorptive capacity is largely a function of the level of the firms' prior knowledge (which emphasizes them cumulative nature of knowledge) and is history or path dependent (which emphasizes the importance of earlier decisions). Important determinants of absorptive capacity are the internal channels of communication, the distribution of knowledge in the environment and in the firm, and the pattern of R&D investment decisions. Specifically, in an environment where knowledge development is widely dispersed and learning requires a strong knowledge base, internal R&D efforts will more significantly contribute to absorptive capacity.

Brown and Duguid (1991) proposed a unified view of working, learning and innovation, which links individual and organizational levels of knowledge. The authors start by pointing out that codification of work procedures can be quite different from actual working practices, and sometimes it is even contradictory. They argue that learning theory should be distanced from codified, transferable and objective notions of knowledge, and focus instead on knowledge in context. In their view, meaningful knowledge is deeply related to daily work, and the acquisition of new knowledge (learning) is socially constructed from working practices. This social construction of knowledge occurs within informal communities-of-practice, where knowledge is freely shared through collaborative mechanisms such as narration and joint work. The authors also argue that these communities-of-practice are likely to engage in innovative activities because their view of the world is constantly challenged by the demands of daily work. The informal character of these communities and their fluid membership facilitates innovation and mitigates the ossifying tendencies of large organizations. The dysfunction of this ossification has been clearly demonstrated by Leonard-Barton (1992). She found that when the level of congruence between capabilities and an innovation project is low, the core capabilities of a firm could become core rigidities and hinder innovation. An organization composed of communities with a certain degree of autonomy and legitimacy to enact new experiments might be able to overcome these rigidities and engage in innovation (Brown and Duguid, 1991).

This perspective on organizational learning and innovation implies a view of organizations as multiple communities-of-practice. Each community-of-practice is engaging in experimental and interpretative activities with the environment from which sensemaking emerges, leading to adaptive behavior. Organizations thus evolve based on the competing perspectives of different communities-of-practice (Martin and Carlile, 1999). A number of authors (Lave and Wenger, 1991; Blackler, 1995; Whitaker, 1996; Nahapiet and Goshal, 1998; Galunic and Rodan, 1998) have extended this emphasis on communities-of-practice, recognizing knowledge as contextual and situated in a broader range of settings.

Dynamic Capabilities as a Foundation for the Knowledge-Based View

The dynamic capabilities approach is a second foundation that underlies knowledge-based thinking. In the traditional economic vision of the firm, managers' decisions are based on a set of productive and environmental conditions. Since this is an equilibrium-based perspective, theory does not need to explain how knowledge in organizations is created or how it changes over time (Nonaka and Takeuchi, 1995). Managers need not change their firms routinely because the basic characteristics that define the environment and the structure of competition are stable, or at least predictable. Given these assumptions, a strategic theory that addresses the cross-sectional problem of explaining superior performance at a given point in time is helpful in addressing the more important longitudinal problem of explaining how firms achieve superior performance over time (Porter, 1991). In other words, competitive advantage is sustainable in static or slow-moving environments.

Until the past decade, this equilibrium-based thinking dominated the major paradigms of strategy. For example, according to the industrial organization approach, sustainable competitive advantage can be achieved by developing and defending profitable positions in attractive industries (Porter, 1985). According to the resource-based view, valuable, rare, inimitable and non-substitutable (VRIN) resources (Wernerfelt, 1984; Barney, 1991) and related sets of operational routines and technological skills (Pralahad and Hamel, 1990; Stalk et al., 1992) are sources of sustainable advantage for firms. Even strategic conflict approaches – using game-theory concepts to explore the dynamics of competition – argue that superior performance can be sustained by competing through a clever sequence of strategic moves and counter-moves in a well-defined strategic game (Shapiro, 1989). This last approach can thus be described as 'exploring the dynamics of a largely static world' (Porter, 1991: 106).

The increasing dynamism of the environment, with its frequent and rapid changes in technology, customer preferences, and competition, has led a number of researchers (Eisenhardt, 1989; D'Aveni, 1994) to question the sustainability of superior performance of any given strategic position, bundle of resources or set of moves. This means that understanding superior performance at a point in time explains very little of how superior performance is consistently achieved over time (Grant, 1996a) or indeed, if it can be achieved at all (D'Aveni, 1994; Eisenhardt and Martin, 2000). In high-velocity environments – an extreme form of dynamic markets where even basic industry characteristics such as boundaries, competitors and customers are in flux – no specific advantages are sustainable. Rather, superior performance occurs by continuously creating temporary advantages. In these situations, the ability to learn quickly in order to alter the resource configuration in adaptation to market change becomes crucial to performance.

Given these observations, strategy theorists began a quest for a dynamic theory of strategy, a theory that could reveal the sources of superior performance in dynamic environments (Porter, 1991; Spender, 1996; Teece et al., 1997; Brown and Eisenhardt, 1998). This quest was approached both by developing new strategic paradigms like complexity approaches to strategy (Brown and Eisenhardt, 1998), as well as by extending existing ones, like the dynamic capabilities extension to the resource-based view (Teece et al., 1997). The dynamic capabilities approach argues that competitive advantage is dependent on particular organizational and managerial processes, termed 'dynamic capabilities', that are defined as the firm's ability to integrate, build and reconfigure internal and external competencies to address rapidly changing environments (Teece et al., 1997). The main challenges for strategy researchers have been to define the construct of dynamic capabilities, test their contribution to performance, and understand the evolution of capabilities over time (Eisenhardt and Martin, 2000).

Knowledge-Based View of Strategy

A number of researchers have attempted to integrate the above insights into a theory of strategy and, in some cases, a theory of the firm based on a knowledge perspective. One of the earliest attempts was by Dierickx and Cool (1989). They conceptualized the knowledge of firms in terms of stocks and flows. Stocks of knowledge are accumulated knowledge assets, while flows are knowledge streams within and across organizations that contribute to the accumulation of knowledge. Superior stocks and flows are seen as sources of sustained competitive advantage and superior performance.

Kogut and Zander (1992) also emphasized the strategic importance of knowledge as a source of advantage and established the foundation for a theory of the firm. They posited that what firms do better than markets is the creation and transfer of knowledge within the organization. In their view, knowledge is held by individuals (know-what and know-how), and yet it is also embedded in the organizing principles by which people voluntarily cooperate in an organizational context. Because the creation of new knowledge depends on existing capabilities and organizing principles, the knowledge of the firm evolves in a path-dependent way, through the replication and recombination of existing knowledge. In what could form the basis for a theory of strategy, the authors also argue that the ability to replicate knowledge determines the firm's rate of growth, but that such replication also facilitates imitation by competitors. Therefore, firms are able to grow and deter competitive imitation only by continuously recombining their knowledge and applying it to new market opportunities. That is, in a competitive environment, superior performance can only be sustained through continuous innovation.

Nonaka and Takeuchi (1995) complement the work of Kogut and Zander by providing a framework for understanding the integration of individual and organizational knowledge. Consistent with their observations of Japanese companies, the authors argue that organizational knowledge should be understood as the processes that amplify the knowledge created by individuals and crystallize it as a part of the knowledge network of the organization. These processes constitute a knowledge spiral, which is highly iterative and occurs mainly through informal networks of relations in the organization. This spiral involves continuous interplay between tacit and explicit knowledge at individual and organizational levels. The proposed model identifies some enabling conditions for the knowledge creating process, namely the existence of redundancy, requisite variety and a creative chaos.

Grant further articulated the theoretical foundations for a knowledge-based view, both as a theory of organization (1996a) and as a theory of strategy (1996b), in what has become probably the most widely used perspective on knowledge within the strategy field. In this view, tacit knowledge is the source of sustained competitive advantage. However, since production activities usually require the combination of a wide array of specialized knowledge that resides in individuals, organizational capabilities are essential to the achievement of that advantage. In particular, the essence of organizations is their ability to integrate individual specialized knowledge and apply it to new products and services. These capabilities are structured hierarchically according to the scope of knowledge that they integrate. The key integration mechanisms are direction and routines, and the central organizational problem is one of coordination (Grant, 1996a).

Based on this understanding of organizations, Grant (1996b) proposed a knowledge-based theory of strategy. He argues that the source of competitive advantage in dynamic environments is not knowledge that is proprietary to the organization, because the value of such knowledge erodes quickly due to obsolescence and imitation. Rather, sustained competitive advantage is determined by non-proprietary knowledge in the form of tacit individual knowledge. Tacit knowledge can form the basis of competitive advantage because it is both unique and relatively immobile. Yet, because that knowledge is possessed by individuals and not the organization, a critical element of sustained competitive advantage is the ability to integrate the specialized and tacit knowledge of individuals. Grant identifies three characteristics of knowledge integration that increase its strategic value. The first is the efficiency of integration, which is a function of common knowledge, frequency and variability

of tasks, and a structure that economizes on communication. The second is the scope of that integration, with a broader scope facilitating the creation and preservation of competitive advantage. The third is the flexibility of integration to include new knowledge and the reconfiguration of existing knowledge.

In addition, Grant makes the point, also emphasized by other scholars (Kogut and Zander, 1996; Kogut, 2000), that knowledge can also be integrated externally through relational networks that span organizational boundaries. These networks provide efficient mechanisms for accessing and integrating new knowledge, especially in high-velocity environments, where the speed and scope of knowledge integration are paramount for sustaining competitive advantage. Overall, Grant's approach extends the dynamic capabilities view of strategy (Teece et al., 1997) and can be considered an outgrowth of resource-based thinking.

Challenges to the Dominant Knowledge-Based View of Strategy

Although the approach of 'knowledge as resource' has become the dominant perspective of KBV in strategy (Grant, 1996b), it is not without challenge. For example, Spender (1996) argues that a dynamic theory of the firm based on knowledge should be conceptually different from a resource-based approach. Knowledge is not an observable and transferable commodity. Organizations are not collections of rational agents. Rather, Spender argues that organizations learn and have knowledge to the extent that their members are malleable beings whose sense of self is influenced by the organization's evolving identity, a theme argued by Kogut and Zander (1996) as well. Collective knowledge thus becomes the basis of human meaning and communication. The firm is seen as a system of knowing activity, rather than as a system of applied knowledge bundles that can be shuffled about the organization. Specifically, the firm is seen as an evolving, quasi-autonomous system of knowledge production and application, with emergent and self-organizing properties that derive from the interactions of its semi-autonomous elements with one another and the external environment (Spender, 1996).

Spender's approach to KBV is very similar to Brown and Duguid's view of organizations as systems of communities-of-practice (Brown and Duguid, 1991). Further, both these perspectives have much in common with conceptualizing organizations as complex adaptive systems, in which innovative behavior emerges from loosely connected structures among modular actors (Anderson, 1999; Eisenhardt and Bhatia, 2001). This approach to organizations has several normative implications. For the system to be active, managers should preserve and enhance the interpretive flexibility, manage the boundaries of the firm, and identify the institutional influences in the environment (Spender, 1996). In addition, it is important to distinguish between the systemic and component parts of the system. For example (and in contrast to Grant's approach), a core competence is not a collection of knowledge components, but a systemic property emerging from the organization's ongoing activity. Finally, Spender argues that identification of the internal knowledge processes and their organizational meaning is essential for an effective management of organizations. Kogut and Zander (1996) echo similar themes in their discussion of social identity as a basis for a knowledge-based theory of the firm.

Dissatisfaction with the dominant perspective on KBV as a theory of strategy is also clear in the work of other researchers. Similar to Spender (1996), some scholars (Cook and Brown, 1999; Patriotta and Pettigrew, 1999) suggest that the treatment of knowledge that is inherent in the 'knowledge as resource' view is clearly incomplete. These and other authors (Blackler, 1995; Kogut and Zander, 1996) argue for a more contextual, processual, and situated view of knowledge, with closer ties with learning theory and social identity. Others attack KBV from the perspective of transaction-cost economics, arguing that the knowledge-based view of the firm can be subsumed by this earlier perspective (Foss, 1996). Still others question the strategic logic of KBV. Can knowledge be the most important resource without considering either its strategic value (Lane and Lubatkin, 1998; Eisenhardt and Galunic, 2000; Gupta and Govindarajan, 2000) or whether that value will actually be appropriated by the firm rather than retained by individual knowledge-holders (Chacar and Coff, 2000)? More

fundamentally, other authors (Eisenhardt, 1989; D'Aveni, 1994; Eisenhardt and Martin, 2000) question whether sustained competitive advantage is even possible in dynamic environments, especially high-velocity ones. As such, they focus on the ability to change, rather than the possession and use of knowledge, as the central driver of a flow of temporary advantages that leads to superior performance in such environments.

REVIEW OF EMPIRICAL RESEARCH

In the previous section, we discussed KBV from a theoretical perspective. In this section, we switch our focus to the empirical research on KBV in strategy and related fields. Our thinking is that theoretical discourse goes hand-in-hand with empirical exploration and theory testing.

We have organized this review according to specific knowledge processes: sourcing, internal transfer, external transfer, and integration. Although many categorizations are possible, we chose this one because it is closely linked with the dominant theoretical conception of 'knowledge as resource' and with the dominant conception of KBV as theory of strategy in which these knowledge processes are the source of sustained competitive advantage and superior performance (Grant, 1996b). As such, this categorization reveals significant insights into the empirical validity of current theory, the shape of a potentially more valid theory, and an agenda for future research. In each of the following sub-sections we describe the specific knowledge process, relevant empirical literature and main findings, and draw implications for KBV as both a theory of strategy and a theory of organization.

Knowledge Sourcing

To keep pace with dynamic environments, managers frequently need to adapt their firm's knowledge base (Grant, 1996a). Given the dispersion of knowledge (both within and outside the firm) and the uncertainty in the environment, knowledge sourcing is an important knowledge process by which managers identify and gain access to relevant knowledge that is being created in the environment.

Recent empirical literature reveals some of the mechanisms for effective knowledge sourcing.

In a pharmaceutical industry study, Henderson and Cockburn (1994) used knowledge sourcing arguments to explain research productivity, as measured by patents. The authors collected both qualitative and quantitative data, at the level of research programs, to construct detailed measures of both component and architectural competences. Component competence was associated with specific areas of knowledge such as expertise in hypertension, whereas architectural competence (like dynamic capability) refers to the ability to integrate component competencies in new and flexible ways. The authors found that the allocation of key resources through collaborative rather than dictatorial processes, and the existence of pro-publication incentives that promoted links to the wider external scientific community were strongly correlated with research productivity. These variables accounted for 40–50% increases in productivity. Pro-publication incentives were also strongly correlated with other measures of external knowledge sourcing, namely the proximity of headquarters to a research university and the involvement in collaborative R&D projects with major research universities.

In more recent work, Henderson and Cockburn (1996) used the same data to test the effect of economies of size and knowledge spillovers in pharmaceutical research productivity, as measured by important patents. They found that research programs located within larger firms are significantly more productive than rival programs located within smaller firms. In particular, research programs in large firms benefited primarily from economies of scope in the form of a larger and more diversified knowledge pool, rather than from scale economies due to sharing fixed costs and greater specialization.

These findings are consistent with other studies that link external knowledge sourcing with innovation and performance. For example, Powell et al. (1996) used a knowledge sourcing argument to explain the patterns of alliances in biotechnology firms. Traditional explanations of inter-firm collaborations focus on risk sharing, access to new markets and technologies, speeding products to market and pooling complementary skills. Nevertheless, the authors argue that when the knowledge base of an industry is complex, expanding, and widely dispersed, the locus of innovation will be found in networks of learning, rather than in individual firms. In these situations, building external collaborations is central to updating the knowledge base of the firm. R&D collaborations become admission tickets to the knowledge network, and vehicles for the rapid communication of new knowledge.

To test these arguments, Powell and his colleagues used a longitudinal social network analysis, with five years of data that included measures of the number of R&D ties, the diversity of ties and the network centrality of each company. They found support for their hypotheses, indicating that a firm's portfolio of alliances and resultant network position were dependent on previous network experience, and that the size of a firm was positively related with previous network centrality. Thus, the establishment of a network of collaborations in biotechnology firms seems to be a cumulative process, and the development of a central position in the network enables future growth.

In a similar vein, Liebeskind et al. (1996) also use knowledge sourcing arguments to explain research collaboration behavior in the biotechnology industry. But, in contrast to the focus on formal R&D alliances by Powell and colleagues (1996), these authors studied informal research collaborations. They argued that, in a knowledge environment characterized by complexity and rapid change, boundary-spanning networks based on informal relations represent opportunities for sourcing scientific knowledge from external experts.

Their analysis of the publication and patent records of two highly successful biotechnology firms revealed a myriad of research collaborations with external parties (mainly research laboratories and universities), which were not covered by either contractual or market arrangements. These collaborations did not decrease over time and did not lead to problems in appropriating knowledge, since the biotechnology firms had mainly exclusive (not shared) patents. In addition, the findings of the study also pointed to the importance of long-term employment of scientists that enabled a stable organizational context, creating conditions that were helpful for sharing knowledge.

The importance of external ties in the previous studies is consistent with the probing process identified by Brown and Eisenhardt (1997). In their multiple case study of major computing firms, the authors observed that the managers of the most successful businesses gathered information about the future in an active and externally oriented way, through the use of a wide variety of low-cost probes, including experimental products, futurists and strategic alliances. Relying on explanations from learning theory, the authors describe how these probes helped managers to gain insight into future industry trends and so effectively position their firms for the future, especially in terms of new products. They also noted the importance of integrating the knowledge from probes with current activities.

Bierly and Chakrabarti (1996) used a longitudinal analysis of 21 pharmaceutical firms across a 15-year period to synthesize knowledge sourcing tradeoffs. The authors developed a taxonomy of knowledge strategies, based upon the four key strategic decisions concerning the knowledge development of a firm: internal vs external sources of knowledge, radical vs incremental knowledge evolution, depth vs breadth of knowledge base, and speed of knowledge acquisition and application. The collective responses to these four choices form the knowledge sourcing strategies of firms. Using measures of these four factors (based on R&D spending, patent analysis and approval of new products) and cluster analysis techniques, the authors identified four consistent strategy patterns, which they named *explorers*, *exploiters*, *loners* and *innovators*. Innovators were aggressive knowledge developers, achieving high levels of internal and external knowledge acquisition, focusing on both radical and incremental innovation, and applying knowledge very quickly. Loners were slow and inward oriented. They had a focused knowledge base and few external linkages. Exploiters had little internal knowledge sourcing and were essentially incremental learners, showing a high level of external linkages and a broad knowledge base. Explorers were characterized by very radical knowledge evolution and average values on the other dimensions. The authors found sustained profit differentials favoring innovators and explorers.

Tripsas (1997) found evidence of a positive impact on long-term performance of establishing external research links. In an historical analysis of the evolution of three major firms in the typesetter industry, the author found that only one company was able to survive the three stages of competence-destroying technological change that swept the industry in the second half of the 20th century. Her analysis indicated that the successful adaptation of the firm's knowledge base depended upon the capability to source and then integrate external knowledge. This capability was developed through early investments in R&D that led to the accumulation of absorptive capacity in a variety of technologies, and through the development of an external communication infrastructure to source the relevant knowledge. Moreover, the investments in absorptive capacity were cumulative and self-reinforcing, because initial investments did not immediately lead to better performance in integrating new knowledge. Rather, they led to more successful developments over time. The external communication infrastructure was developed through regular collaborations with experts and through knowledge scanning activities. These activities allowed firm managers to identify new technologies, unrelated to their knowledge base, which were important for the future path of technological development in the industry. Another important factor for the successful adaptation was the existence of multiple locations for R&D activities, as opposed to having a central research laboratory. These multiple locations were a source of variety and enabled managers to cope with the overlap between different generations of technological knowledge.

In a related study, Rosenkopf and Nerkar (1999) found that firms in the optical disk industry with few external contacts became locked into fixed paths of technological evolution. The authors analyzed the impact of a firm's technological developments on the subsequent technological evolution of the industry, using knowledge exploration strategy as the predictor variable. The authors defined four main strategies to source new knowledge: local search (building upon similar technology within the organizational boundaries), radical search (spanning both technology and firm boundaries), organizational boundary spanning, and technological boundary spanning. Rosenkopf and Nerkar examined technological impact, as measured by patent citations, of the 22 firms with most patenting activity in the industry between 1971 and 1995. They found that local search (measured by extensive self-citation) was negatively correlated with impact. In contrast, the highest impact approach was organizational boundary-spanning exploration, in which managers extensively used the findings of other firms in the industry to inform their own knowledge development. The second most effective approach was radical search, whereby managers crossed both organizational and technological boundaries. Therefore, an inward learning focus was not effective for achieving technological impact.

Two recent studies provide complementary insights on knowledge sourcing. Hansen (1998) adopts an internal focus for the study of knowledge sourcing. The complex and evolving nature of knowledge and the sheer size of some firms create the need for sourcing knowledge across organizational sub-units. This situation occurs in product development activities, where relevant knowledge can be identified and shared among project teams throughout a corporation. Hansen used the speed of completion of projects as the dependent variable in a sample of 120 development projects of a large electronics firm. Using measures of network centrality and knowledge relatedness as independent variables, the author concludes that effective knowledge sourcing requires both a central position in the network of relations and the possession of related knowledge that builds absorptive capacity. Further, this central position is most effectively achieved by indirect relations, because too many direct relationships are so costly to maintain that the costs may override the potential benefits.

Recent research by Jett (1999) focuses on the relationship between external connections for knowledge sourcing and organizational action. Using a sample of 47 SBUs in the computer, networking and telecommunications industries, the author explored the impact of different probing mechanisms on managers' ability to adapt their product portfolios to changing competitive conditions. He found that strategic alliances for the exploration of new markets enabled knowledge acquisition and fostered introduction of new products. Further, and consistent with Brown and Eisenhardt (1997), these results suggest that probes, such as futurists and exploratory products, should be well-linked to the present competitive position of firms. If the probes are too far into the future, with few links to present markets and technologies, then managers will not be able to effectively use the newly sourced knowledge to improve their firms.

Summary

Taken together, these studies and others (Allen, 1977; Katz and Tushman, 1981; Brown and Eisenhardt, 1998; McEvily and Zaheer, 1999) on knowledge sourcing suggest that external linkages are important for a variety of innovation-related outcomes such as patents, patent citations, speed of product development, quality of the product pipeline, and introduction of new products. External linkages appear to help managers become aware of the content and location of new technical knowledge, and gain insight into the trajectory of their industry. Thus, in dynamic environments, searching for, identifying, accessing, and sharing new knowledge are important activities for innovative performance. These external linkages include incentives that motivate scientists to stay connected with the larger scientific community (Henderson, 1994), formal network relationships (Powell et al., 1996; Brown and Eisenhardt, 1997; McEvily and Zaheer, 1999), exploratory products (Brown and Eisenhardt, 1997; Jett, 1999), gatekeepers (Allen, 1977; Katz and Tushman, 1981), and informal networks (Henderson and Cockburn, 1994; Liebeskind et al., 1996; Tripsas, 1997; Rosenkopf and Nerkar, 1999). These external linkages emerge as clearly valuable in industries such as biotechnology, pharmaceuticals, and optics where knowledge is at the cutting-edge of science. More surprisingly, they are also valuable in less knowledge-intensive industries such as computing (Brown and Eisenhardt, 1997; Jett, 1999) and even in machine shops (McEvily and Zaheer, 1999) where they provide insights into market and technical trends. Finally, the concept of a portfolio of external knowledge sourcing activities emerges. A diverse portfolio of such activities increases opportunities for experimentation and learning (Brown and Eisenhardt, 1997), especially when the knowledge probes are low-cost and so create occasions for small failures. Such portfolios are particularly relevant when the knowledge objective is to have a broad insight into the trajectory of future product and market arenas, rather than some specific piece of cutting-edge (often technical) knowledge.

In addition, a few studies suggest that similar knowledge sourcing processes occur within corporations and can also lead to more innovation (Henderson and Cockburn, 1996; Hansen, 1998). Moreover, these processes occur in loosely-coupled organizations in which business units (Hansen, 1998), R&D facilities (Tripsas, 1997), and research programs (Henderson and Cockburn, 1994) are only partially connected. Hansen (1998), for example, argues that greater connection would be too time-consuming to be advantageous, while Tripsas (1997) notes the value of retaining some randomness in research in order to enhance adaptability.

Overall, these studies are useful for understanding the linkage of internal and external knowledge sourcing with innovation-related outcomes. Yet, this research stream leaves unexamined several fundamental issues related to KBV as a theory of strategy. One such issue is the relationship between knowledge sourcing and firm performance. Only a few studies examine firm performance, and those that do rely on a variety of performance outcomes, including survival (Tripsas, 1997), growth (Powell et al., 1996), market segment dominance (Brown and Eisenhardt, 1998), and profit (Bierly and Chakrabarti, 1996). As a result, there is no cumulative demonstration of the power of KBV as a theory of strategy for any specific conception of performance. Further, the studies do not examine whether sustainable competitive advantage exists as predicted by KBV. Indeed, Roberts (1999) recently showed that competitive advantage in the pharmaceutical industry is not sustained, but rather is a series of temporary advantages. Even if sustained advantage were demonstrated, the research does not distinguish between whether that advantage stems from the knowledge sourcing process *per se*, as argued by Grant (1996b), from the knowledge gathered during the process, or from some other unexamined factors.

Finally, the research suggests time is a relevant addition to KBV thinking. For example, Tripsas (1997) found that the timing of different technological innovations forced managers to adopt complex learning strategies

involving different sectors of the corporation, while Jett (1999), as well as Brown and Eisenhardt (1997, 1998), noted that future-oriented knowledge sourcing needs to be linked with current activities in order to be effective.

Internal Knowledge Transfer

A second stream of KBV research addresses internal knowledge transfer. This research explores how knowledge transfer within an organization depends upon the characteristics of that knowledge, the sender, the recipient, and their mutual relationship. This is an important stream of research because the efficacy of knowledge transfer within organizations is a primary rationale for KBV as both a theory of organization (Kogut and Zander, 1992; Grant, 1996a; Kogut and Zander, 1996) and a theory of strategy (Grant, 1996b).

Zander and Kogut (1995) analyzed the speed at which manufacturing capabilities related to product innovations were transferred across borders by Swedish firms. The transfer of capabilities involved knowledge codification, in which the tacit knowledge embedded in the innovations was made more explicit in order to be more easily communicated and understood by the recipients. One possible drawback of such codification is that it might also speed imitation by competitors. The authors thus analyzed the impact of knowledge characteristics and competitive environment on the speeds of both internal transfer and external imitation. They used a detailed multidimensional construct for knowledge, including codifiability, teachability, complexity, systems dependence, and product observability by competitors, based on previously suggested knowledge taxonomies (Rogers, 1980; Winter, 1987). The authors found that greater codifiability and teachability were associated with faster transfer, but not with faster imitation. The speed of imitation was positively related only to the knowledge spillovers among firms (mainly caused by employee turnover), and to the levels of common knowledge and competence across the industry. Other findings suggested that the pressure of competition made firms more efficient in transferring capabilities and that continuous innovation impeded imitation by competitors.

Szulanski (1996) also analyzed the transfer of knowledge within the firm. His objective was to understand the causes of stickiness in the transfer of complex best practices. Based on prior research, the author focused on four main causes of stickiness: the characteristics of the knowledge transferred, the source of knowledge, the recipient, and the context of the transfer. Using a sample of 38 technical and administrative complex best practices, encompassing a total of 122 transfers, the author found that the three most important barriers to knowledge transfer were lack of absorptive capacity of the recipient, causal ambiguity of the knowledge transferred, and difficulty in establishing personal interactions between the source and the recipient. The author also found that higher knowledge retention impeded transfer because recipients were less able to unlearn old knowledge and replace it with new. Szulanski concluded that knowledge variables, not lack of motivation or cooperation, were the primary barriers to knowledge transfer.

In contrast to Szulanski's emphasis on knowledge characteristics, Lord and Ranft (1998) found that organizational structure and incentives were significant factors affecting the effectiveness of knowledge transfer. Based on a survey of 104 market entries of multinational companies, the authors analyzed the impact of knowledge characteristics and organizational variables on the internal transfer of knowledge about local markets. They concluded that, alongside tacitness of knowledge, the organizational structure, communication mechanisms, and incentives were also significant. Specifically, they found that formal vertical reporting channels and incentive systems linked to performance were positively related to knowledge sharing and transfer. Moreover, knowledge sharing and transfer were positively related to divisional performance.

Athanassiou and Nigh (1999) used a social network perspective to study knowledge sharing among top management teams in 37 multinational companies based in the US. The authors showed that the top management of these companies developed advice networks for sharing tacit knowledge about international business issues. These advice networks were important mechanisms for internal coordination. Furthermore, the density of these networks, defined as the ratio of advice-seeking

relationships to the total possible relationships, was shaped by the international strategy of the firm. A more extensive international strategy and a higher inter-dependence of subsidiaries' activities increased the density of the network. The formal governance mechanism of the subsidiaries (wholly owned and majority-owned vs minority participation) surprisingly had no significant relationship with the density of advice networks. This latter result suggests that the governance mechanism of subsidiaries does not change the need for tacit knowledge exchange through advice networks.

Gupta and Govindarajan (2000) also analyzed inter-firm knowledge flows across 374 subsidiaries within 75 multinational corporations in a very comprehensive study of internal knowledge transfer. Their independent variables included the strategic value of the knowledge, motivation of the source, motivation and absorptive capacity of the recipient, and communication channels, as measured in the transfer of seven types of procedural knowledge (know how). The authors separately analyzed knowledge transfer horizontally among peer subsidiaries and hierarchically with the parent. They found that knowledge flow from the parent to subsidiaries was the most pervasive type of internal knowledge transfer. Further, the communication channel (as measured by formal integrative mechanisms and socialization), absorptive capacity, and strategic value of the knowledge facilitated knowledge transfer, while incentives to share knowledge had no effect.

Hargadon (1998) provides interesting insights into how organizational structure and culture can facilitate knowledge transfer within the firm. The author developed case studies of firms that act as knowledge brokers (product design firms, management consultants and consulting sub-units within large corporations). Knowledge brokers place themselves in a network of clients that cuts across different industries and technology areas, and are thus able to link problems in one area with their knowledge of solutions from other areas. These firms thus rely extensively on internal transfers of knowledge to operate successfully. Hargadon found that knowledge brokers used fluid project teams. Further, their organizational structure mimicked the diverse and relatively disconnected domains in which they operated. Within knowledge broker firms, individuals adhered to norms that required sharing knowledge freely with other organizational members. Hargadon found that the most important barriers to knowledge transfer were employee turnover, organizational size, and increasing demands on individual time and individual efficiency.

Similarly, Brown and Eisenhardt (1998) examined inter-firm cooperation (including knowledge transfer) in their study of 12 major computing firms. They found that more effective firms limited knowledge transfer to the most strategically valuable information, rather than all possible information. The managers of these firms accomplished this by having regular meetings among business unit heads to share opportunities to collaborate, and then letting these business leaders choose whether or not to collaborate. The former created the social bonds and information necessary for collaboration to occur, while the latter helped to ensure that the best opportunities were chosen. Thus, in the best performing firms, senior executives set the context for collaboration among businesses. In less effective firms, senior executives either ignored cross-business collaboration or forced collaboration from the top. Finally, in related work, Eisenhardt and Galunic (2000) indicated that, when knowledge was transferred effectively, business unit heads were rewarded for their own business' success, not for collaboration *per se*.

In a study of 120 development projects in a large electronics firm, Hansen (1999) addressed the different relationship requirements for the transfer of simple vs complex knowledge. Speed of project completion was the dependent variable while the complexity of knowledge to be transferred (measured in terms of tacitness and systems dependence) and strength of the relationships of the project team (measured by tie weakness) were the independent variables. The author found that weak ties favor knowledge search but impede the transfer of complex knowledge, as compared with strong ties. Based on these findings, Hansen asserted that effective organizational design should consider the type of knowledge likely to flow within the organization. When knowledge is simple and easily transmitted, weak ties are likely to solve the problem of obtaining knowledge. When knowledge is more complex, effective internal

transfer is more challenging, and requires strong ties in the form of formal mechanisms and frequent interaction.

Summary

Taken together, many of these studies indicate that knowledge characteristics affect the efficacy of internal knowledge transfer. These characteristics include tacitness (Zander and Kogut, 1995; Lord and Ranft, 1998), causal ambiguity (Szulanski, 1996), and complexity (Hansen, 1998), which impede knowledge transfer, and strategic value (Brown and Eisenhardt, 1998; Gupta and Govindarajan, 2000), which enhances knowledge transfer.

These studies also indicate that the relationship between the sender and recipient is crucial for knowledge transfer. When the sender and recipient have difficulty in establishing interpersonal interactions (Szulanski, 1996), such as when they are distant, knowledge transfer is impaired. In contrast, when integrative mechanisms such as teams, liaisons, informal social networks, norms for collaboration, and formal meetings exist (Hargadon, 1998; Gupta and Govindarajan, 2000; Eisenhardt and Galunic, 2000), knowledge transfer is facilitated. Overall, appropriate organizational structure and culture can ease knowledge transfer.

Moreover, several studies indicate an interaction between knowledge characteristics and the relationship between sender and recipient. If the transfer is more difficult because of complex knowledge (Hansen, 1999) or knowledge that requires significant local adaptation (Hargadon, 1998), then the relationship between sender and recipient must be stronger with frequent and personal face-to-face interactions in order for effective knowledge transfer to occur. In addition, the greater the absorptive capacity of the recipient, the more easily knowledge is transferred (Szulanski, 1996; Gupta and Govindarajan, 2000).

The most controversial aspect of the empirical studies surrounds the role of incentives for the sender and the related top-down enforcement of knowledge transfer. Lord and Ranft (1998) found that incentives and vertical reporting relationships enhanced transfer of knowledge about international market entry and improved performance. Gupta and Govindarajan (2000) found that vertical reporting did enhance knowledge transfer, but incentives did not. Finally, Eisenhardt and colleagues (Brown and Eisenhardt, 1998; Eisenhardt and Galunic, 2000) indicate that senior executives in the most effective firms create a collaborative context through culture and organizational structure, but they do not force or even reward collaboration *per se*.

These diverse findings suggest that when knowledge is relatively simple and static, top-down enforcement and incentives improve knowledge transfer by dealing with motivation issues. When that knowledge is also strategically valuable, transfer will enhance performance (Lord and Ranft, 1998). In contrast, when knowledge is complex, knowledge and relationship characteristics dominate the motivational issues in knowledge transfer (Szulanski, 1996). Further, when knowledge is varied and changing, context setting activities based on organizational structures and cultural norms that make managers aware of knowledge transfer opportunities are effective, but incentives to collaborate are not. Such incentives may not only be ineffective in knowledge transfer (Gupta and Govindarajan, 2000), but they may also negatively impact performance by encouraging managers to waste time and resources transferring non-strategic knowledge (Eisenhardt and Galunic, 2000).

In summary, these studies are very useful for understanding internal knowledge transfer. But they are less helpful in dealing with the performance issues that are at the heart of strategy. Many of these studies implicitly link knowledge transfer and performance. Nevertheless, both Gupta and Govindarajan (2000) and Brown and Eisenhardt (1998) argue that the strategic value of the knowledge is crucial to whether improved performance is actually achieved. These authors suggest that the managers of effective firms should concentrate their efforts on transferring only the most strategically valuable knowledge. In fact, less knowledge transfer can be more effective than more transfer, especially in high-velocity environments where the time of managers is so limited (Eisenhardt and Galunic, 2000). Further, only two studies (Brown and Eisenhardt, 1998; Lord and Ranft, 1998) actually measured performance.

More broadly, these studies, like those on knowledge sourcing, do not deal with important aspects of KBV theory. They do not indicate

whether knowledge transfer results in sustained or even temporary competitive advantage. Similarly, they do not address whether advantage derives from the knowledge transfer process, the knowledge itself, or both. Finally, the theoretical rhetoric of KBV asserts that knowledge is the most strategically important resource. Yet it is unclear from these studies what constitutes valuable knowledge, when to transfer it, or whether extensive internal knowledge transfer is strategically wise.

External Knowledge Transfer

A third stream of research addresses knowledge transfer across firm boundaries through alliances and acquisitions. This stream is significant because it sheds light on several fundamental theoretical assertions of KBV as a theory of strategy and of organization, namely that effective knowledge transfer is a source of sustained competitive advantage and that it is more effectively accomplished within organizations rather than markets.

Several studies address specifically how organizations transfer knowledge through their participation in alliances. Lane and Lubatkin (1998) explored the impact of partner characteristics on the acquisition of new knowledge in the form of new skills and capabilities. Their study examined 31 R&D alliances between pharmaceutical and biotechnology companies, where the pharmaceutical firm is the learning entity and the biotechnology firm is the teacher. In their view, learning tacit and embedded knowledge requires absorptive capacity in the recipient firm, which is relative in that it depends on the teacher firm. In an unusual conception, the authors measured relative absorptive capacity by a three-dimensional construct, using indicators of knowledge overlap, similarity in knowledge processing systems, and similarity of commercial logic. The dependent variable of knowledge acquisition was measured by a panel of industry experts who assessed how much the recipient firms had learned in terms of new capabilities and knowledge spillover. The authors found that the similarity of basic knowledge was positively related to learning, while the similarity of specialized knowledge was negatively correlated. Presumably in the latter case, the knowledge of the sender was too similar to be of value to the recipient. The results for similarities of knowledge processing systems (measured by the degree of formalization and centralization of the organizational structure) were mixed. Similarity in lower level management and research structures was positively related to learning, while similarity in top management and business decision structures was negatively related. Finally, the authors found that the sharing of research communities was positively related to knowledge transfer. Overall, the results validate that knowledge transfer is dependent on measures of distance or dissimilarity to the partner firm.

In a similar vein, Inkpen and Dinur (1998) found that effective transfer of knowledge exhibited an inverse relationship between tacitness of knowledge and the organizational level at which the transfer took place. Based on a longitudinal analysis of five case studies of North-American-based automotive joint ventures between US and Japanese companies, the authors analyzed the processes by which parent companies accessed and transferred the knowledge created in the context of the joint venture. The research results suggest that individuals are the best agents for the transfer of highly tacit knowledge, when compared to groups or higher organization levels. It also suggests that the transfer of tacit knowledge demands a high level of individual interaction, through regular meetings, temporary sharing of human resources and frequent visits to manufacturing facilities. Moreover, there were indications that managers who focus their attention on acquiring only explicit knowledge undervalued the relationship potential by neglecting tacit knowledge-based opportunities. Finally, there was a positive relation between the transfer of tacit strategic knowledge and the development of strategic relationships between the firms.

Similarly, Simonin (1999) studied the effects of the characteristics of knowledge, sender, and recipient–sender relationship on knowledge transfer. His sample included 147 alliances executed by US multinationals, with data provided by single informants. The results indicate that tacitness and complexity of knowledge lowered knowledge transfer, as did cultural and organizational distance between the two firms. These factors, however, were all mediated by knowledge ambiguity, which

emerged as the principal factor affecting knowledge transfer. The author also replicated his previous finding (Simonin, 1997) that collaborative know-how from past alliances improved knowledge transfer.

The next two studies offer compelling insights into how the knowledge base of alliance partners changes over time. In one of the studies, Mowery et al. (1996) used data on patent citations to trace the changes in technological portfolio of partner firms as a consequence of alliances. Using a sample of 792 alliances including at least one US firm, the authors had several findings that were consistent with those of others. That is, strong ties (equity joint ventures) were more likely to be used to transfer complex capabilities than weak ties (contract-based alliances). Further, strong ties (bilateral contracts) were more effective than weaker ties (unilateral contracts) for knowledge transfer. In addition, alliances between two US partners and between partners with experience in related technological areas (greater sender–recipient similarity) resulted in greater knowledge transfer.

The most intriguing result of the study, however, was that the partners in a substantial subset of the alliances exhibited technological divergence. This sharply contrasts with the technological convergence that would be expected in alliances geared toward knowledge acquisition and capabilities transfer. So, while knowledge transfer was one outcome of alliances, so too was the coevolution of the partners into increasingly unique roles. In this latter situation, knowledge transfer evolved into knowledge integration, while the overall system of relationships came to resemble a complex adaptive system based on partially connected and specialized partners (Anderson, 1999; Eisenhardt and Bhatia, 2000).

A similar coevolution among alliance partners into increasingly specialized knowledge positions also appeared in a longitudinal analysis of three inter-firm alliance networks in the Italian packaging machine industry (Lorenzoni and Lipparini, 1999). The firms developed networks of inter-firm relationships around the specialized knowledge necessary to assemble and supply packaging machines. These machines had many interdependent groups and parts, which required extensive mutual adjustment and inter-firm coordination.

Comparing firm strategies in 1988 and 1995, the authors found evidence that managers had narrowed their firm's scope of technological competence and increased their reliance on a network of long-term relationships with other suppliers as the best way to pursue product quality and flexibility. Using co-design and co-manufacturing processes, managers developed relational capabilities with one another across their firms. They further exchanged goods and knowledge on a daily basis, which allowed their firms to increasingly develop specific competencies. Trust developed between partners, which further eased problems of coordination and control of the exchanges, while decisions began to transcend considerations of short-term economic efficiency. Similar to the firms in Mowery et al. (1996), these firms coevolved into networks of more specialized organizations that came to resemble complex adaptive systems. Not surprisingly then, the emergent networks created increased capacity to adapt to environmental change and so enabled managers to more effectively keep pace with technological developments within the industry.

Using a different lens on knowledge transfer, Almeida (1996) examined whether and how managers could overcome impediments in alliance relationships. Specifically, he studied foreign semiconductor multinationals whose managers established plants in the US in order to take advantage of the regional knowledge-sharing networks. Using patent citations to analyze inter-firm knowledge flows, the author found that these firms learned more than similar domestic firms. The explanation for this success in external knowledge transfer was that firm managers were very motivated to learn and did so by joining local knowledge networks, mainly through hiring local employees and using local suppliers. That is, the 'liability of foreignness' that creates dissimilarity can be overcome by the motivation to learn locally using mechanisms that reduce the 'distance' between partners in a knowledge transfer. In addition, these foreign firms also contributed more to local knowledge, suggesting that knowledge transfer is rarely one-way.

A different line of research focuses on acquisitions as a means for external knowledge transfer. Ranft and Zeithaml (1997) argued that the recent wave of acquisitions in high-technology industries has the goal of expanding the knowledge base of the acquiring companies. Thus, long-term value creation from this kind of acquisition depends on knowledge transfer between firms. Yet, this knowledge can be difficult to extract from acquired firms because it is often tacit and embedded within the organization and within key individuals who may leave due to the acquisition. The authors analyzed the process of post-acquisition knowledge transfer in 75 high-tech acquisitions during 1994–95. Overall, they found that a greater tacitness of knowledge had a negative impact on the transfer of knowledge. Additionally, higher levels of communication increased the transfer of all types of knowledge, while higher autonomy of the acquired firm's personnel and longer acquisition integration periods reduced knowledge transfer.

Using the same sample of acquisitions, Ranft and Lord (1998) explored the impact of employee retention (middle managers, R&D people, engineers, and salespeople) on knowledge transfer. These employees often possess the tacit knowledge of the firm that is being acquired. The authors found that the retention of key employees is positively correlated with knowledge transfer. They also established that post-acquisition autonomy, corporate commitment from the acquiring firm, and a high relative standing position for the acquired personnel were important factors in the retention of key employees. Surprisingly, the effect of financial incentives was not significant, which suggests that, when dealing with highly skilled or experienced people, material incentives are not important when compared to other factors related to work definition or working environment.

Summary

Taken together, these and other studies of external knowledge transfer (Simonin, 1997; Capron, 1999; Dyer, 1999; Kale et al., 1999) indicate that knowledge transfer is affected by knowledge characteristics and by the relationship between the sender and the recipient. As such, these studies replicate the studies of internal knowledge transfer. In particular, the tacitness (Inkpen and Dinur, 1998; Ranft and Lord, 1998; Simonin, 1999), complexity, and ambiguity of knowledge (Simonin, 1999) reduced knowledge transfer. Knowledge that was too similar and so lacked strategic value also led to less knowledge transfer (Lane and Lubatkin, 1998).

The relationship between the sender and recipient also affected knowledge transfer as it did in the internal knowledge transfer literature. Similarities in general knowledge base (Mowery et al., 1996; Lane and Lubatkin, 1998), organizational structures (Simonin, 1999) including similar lower level management and research structures (Lane and Lubatkin, 1998), organizational culture (Mowery et al., 1996; Simonin, 1999), and strategy (Inkpen and Dinur, 1998) improved knowledge transfer. Further, integrative mechanisms such as meetings, personnel exchange, bilateral contracts, and personal interaction were effective in overcoming the challenges of transferring tacit and/or complex knowledge (Mowery et al., 1996; Inkpen and Dinur, 1998) and the organizational differences (Almeida, 1996; Ranft and Lord, 1998). Conversely, structural and procedural barriers (Dyer, 1999) can inhibit knowledge transfer in both alliances and acquisitions (Capron, 1999). Firms that have translated their experience into know-how (Simonin, 1997, 1999) that is embedded in organizational structures (Kale et al., 1999) have more successful knowledge transfers. Finally, as in the case of internal knowledge transfer, stronger ties are needed to transfer more complex knowledge (Mowery et al., 1996).

But, the research on external knowledge also suggests some twists when compared with the internal knowledge transfer literature. One such twist is the emergence of specialization among alliance partners (Mowery et al., 1996; Lorenzoni and Lipparini, 1999) such that relationships that may have begun as knowledge transfers become ones of knowledge access and integration. This divergence and specialization suggests that alliances can be a way to gain access to knowledge (Powell et al., 1996), without transfer of that knowledge into the organization. Further, it suggests that networks of alliance relationships can become complex adaptive systems in which different firms coevolve into specialized roles to form highly adaptive networks. Since limited evidence (Brown and Eisenhardt, 1998; Eisenhardt and Galunic, 2000) indicates that the emergence of specialized, coevolving

actors can also occur inside corporations, comparison of this phenomenon inside and outside organizations is an intriguing research opportunity.

A second twist from the internal transfer literature is that knowledge extrication poses difficult challenges in external knowledge transfer situations. For example, a dilemma of knowledge transfer via alliances and acquisitions is that very often the desired knowledge is highly tacit, deeply embedded in individual experiences and organizational context, and co-mingled with other knowledge and resources that are not of interest. Successful knowledge transfer, therefore, requires a focus on the interactions of individuals and the preservation of organizational context (Inkpen and Dinur, 1998; Ranft and Lord, 1998). And, especially in the case of acquisitions, there is a further dilemma. Retention of key employees improves knowledge transfer (Ranft and Lord, 1998), but the high degree of autonomy for the acquired firm that leads to this retention of key employees (Ranft and Lord, 1998) lowers knowledge transfer (Ranft and Zeithaml, 1997). The implication of this research is that extrication of externally located knowledge can be complex and difficult to accomplish, especially in the case of acquisitions (see also Capron, 1999; Graebner, 1999).

Finally, this research stream does not sharply answer the critical questions of whether external knowledge transfer is either easier or qualitatively different from internal knowledge transfer. Yet, a primary of assumption of KBV as a theory of organization (Kogut and Zander, 1992; Grant, 1996a) is that knowledge transfer is facilitated within organizations as compared with markets. Certainly, the two knowledge transfer research streams indicate that similarities in organizational structure and culture, which seem more probable within organizations, should ease transfer. The external knowledge transfer stream also suggests that acquisitions pose particular challenges. But we found no studies that compared intra- and inter-organizational knowledge transfer *per se*. Further, integrative mechanisms such as meetings and personal interaction may overcome the advantages of organizations for knowledge transfer, where such advantages exist (Almeida, 1996). In terms of KBV as a theory of strategy, the current research does not address whether the source of advantage is a more effective external knowledge transfer process *per se*, or if the knowledge itself creates advantage, or whether that advantage is sustained or temporary.

Knowledge Integration

A fourth stream of research focuses on how specialized knowledge is integrated from different sources to generate new knowledge or to apply that knowledge to the creation of new products and services. In particular, much of this research centers on how individuals from different communities-of-practice integrate their specialized knowledge. As such, it emphasizes the micro-processes of interaction, mostly within organizations, that enable the integration of knowledge. This stream of research is especially relevant to KBV because of the assertion that knowledge integration (especially integration of the tacit knowledge that is held by individuals) is a primary source of superiority of firms over markets and a major way in which competitive advantage is achieved (Grant, 1996a).

Eisenhardt (1989) conducted an inductive study on the strategic decision-making processes of top management teams in the computer industry. These teams integrated their different functional and personal perspectives to achieve group decisions regarding crucial strategic issues such as major alliance formation and financing. The author studied the process by which speed and quality were achieved in strategic decisions. She found that the extensive use of concrete and real-time information, as opposed to abstract and accounting-based information, and the simultaneous consideration of multiple alternatives, accelerated decision speed and linked to higher firm performance. She also found that a specific procedure for conflict resolution – consensus with qualification – was very effective for achieving rapid and high-quality decisions.

Dougherty (1992) also focused on knowledge integration. This work was motivated by the observation that product innovators often fail to link technological and market issues, and to collaborate across departments. The author attempted to explain these knowledge integration problems through an analysis of 18 case studies of product innovation in large computer/communications and chemical firms.

Based on extensive interviews, the author found that different departmental 'thought worlds' (the knowledge that people from each functional area have about product innovation) systematically varied. Moreover, the systems of meaning on issues like the perspective on the future, or the identification of the critical aspects of the innovation process, also varied across thought worlds. This meant that people 'not only know different things, but also know things differently', thus creating difficulties in knowledge integration.

These difficulties were exacerbated by many established routines (job descriptions, criteria for market-technology research and standards definition) that encouraged the separation of thought worlds. Successful innovators broke away from these established routines and created new social orders based on mutually adaptive interactions in which knowledge developed as the work unfolded. In particular, the successful innovators overcame the barriers of different thought worlds by creating a customer focus, made tangible and realistic through concrete experiences such as joint participation in focus groups, customer visits, and technology audits. Structural solutions like liaison people or boundary-spanning roles were not enough to ensure the bridging of thought worlds.

In an ethnographic study at the largest product design firm in the US, Hargadon and Sutton (1997) described how the firm routinely innovated by integrating and recombining knowledge across several industries. The designers of the firm were coached to learn about technological and design solutions in different areas and industries, and to keep available artifacts and archives exemplifying those solutions. Some of these artifacts were kept at the organizational level and translated into a collection of concrete solutions to possible design problems, representing a very tangible form of organizational knowledge. The culture of the firm also fostered knowledge integration among the designers through the use of informal discussions and e-mail requests to share knowledge and link solutions to problems. Knowledge sharing and integration were also institutionalized by frequent brainstorming sessions where a particular problem would be addressed and possible solutions freely discussed by designers, with the aid of drawings and tangible representations. Drawing analogies between past solutions and the present problem was also an important element of these sessions, and a key mechanism of knowledge integration as well.

In a recent ethnographic study of a production floor, Bechky (1999) also addressed knowledge integration across thought worlds. The author studied three different communities-of-practice (engineers, technicians and assemblers) whose members collaborated on the development and production of new machines. The different understandings of these communities were based on distinct work practices, ranging from the schematic understanding of the engineers to the spatio-temporal understanding of the assemblers. Their language reflected the different work practices and created communication problems between the communities. Status differences made communication more difficult, especially the upstream feedback from the production floor to the drawing board. Language problems arose in the course of interactions, mainly by attributing different meanings to the same word or using different words to represent the same objects. Interruptions of the production floor activities, due to failures, created occasions for interaction across occupations. During these interruptions, shared understanding and related knowledge integration was developed by translation (through the brokering of technicians) and by tangible examples and physical objects. These concrete problems were thus effective mechanisms for individuals in different communities to learn from each other.

The above account has striking similarities with a recent description of knowledge integration among firms in the US automobile industry (Helper et al., 1999). Based on a survey of suppliers, the authors found evidence of an extraordinary increase in interaction between customers and key suppliers (named 'super suppliers' or first-tier suppliers), through different means of communication, on a daily or weekly basis. The greatest increase occurred in contacts geared to 'joint efforts to improve the product or processes', which indicates an effort to integrate knowledge across firms in the context of concrete issues and tangible processes.

Summary

Overall, these studies highlight the importance of concrete and tangible expressions of knowledge, especially in the context of actually solving real problems, for knowledge integration within and across firms. Such expression of knowledge in realistic contexts appears to be an important way to overcome the challenges of knowledge integration created by the existence of different knowledge, different modes of knowing, and different ways of expressing knowledge. The extensive use of artifacts (Hargadon and Sutton, 1997), real-time operating information (as opposed to abstract accounting data) (Eisenhardt, 1989), joint customer visits (Dougherty, 1992), specific alternatives (Eisenhardt, 1989; Hargadon and Sutton, 1997), and tangible representations of problems (Hargadon and Sutton, 1997; Bechky, 1999) helped in breaking down communication barriers while increasing analogic thinking and related understanding, so that knowledge integration became more effective.

In addition, the work by Dougherty (1992) suggests that established routines and rules, such as formal and complicated standards, job descriptions, and criteria for market research, can create barriers to knowledge integration across communities. Yet, several of the other studies include examples of routines and rules that promote knowledge integration, like consensus with qualification, consideration of multiple alternatives (Eisenhardt, 1989), and brainstorming sessions (Hargadon and Sutton, 1997). Obviously then, rules and routines have enormous power both to improve and impede knowledge integration. The more effective rules and routines appear to encourage and legitimate airing different points of view, while leaving leeway for individual interpretation and creative implementation. In contrast, the less effective rules locked behavior into defined procedures, many of which quickly become obsolete and created further barriers among disparate individuals.

Finally, with a few exceptions (Eisenhardt, 1989), the research on knowledge integration lies outside the traditional strategy literature despite the theoretical importance of knowledge integration to KBV arguments (Grant, 1996a). Not surprisingly then, this research stream does not address key issues of strategy such as the nature of competitive advantage and implications for firm performance.

DISCUSSION

We began this chapter by asking if the knowledge-based view (KBV) provides distinctive insights about the sources of superior performance, and could thus be considered a new theory of strategy and perhaps of organization as well. In addressing these and related questions, we discussed varying views of knowledge, several streams of thinking that underlie KBV, and the variety of theoretical statements regarding what KBV might be. We then reviewed four streams of empirical research that relate to major knowledge processes. Based on this analysis, we have several observations.

First, our review indicates divergence on the meaning of knowledge between the theoretical and the empirical literatures. On the one hand, the theoretical literature contains several rich conceptions of knowledge. These include articulating knowledge-based thinking in terms of different kinds of knowing (Cook and Brown, 1999), spiral theories linking individual and organizational knowledge (Nonaka and Takeuchi, 1995), and understanding knowledge in terms of emergence and identity (Kogut and Zander, 1996; Spender, 1996). On the other hand, the empirical literature, particularly within the strategy field, has largely focused on one, relatively simplistic conception of 'knowledge as resource'. Although there are other conceptions of knowledge within the empirical literature (for an exception see Lam, 1997), they exist mostly outside of the strategy field (Hargadon, 1998; Bechky, 1999).

Second, our review reveals that knowledge sourcing leads to more innovative outcomes when managers engage in a portfolio of activities, both inside and outside the corporation, to gain knowledge. These activities include rewarding scientists for publication (Henderson and Cockburn, 1994), formal network relationships (Powell et al., 1996), and exploratory products (Brown and Eisenhardt, 1997). In other words, a portfolio of externally oriented connections leads to more innovation.

Third, our review suggests significant similarity between internal and external knowledge transfer processes. Characteristics of knowledge like tacitness (Zander and Kogut, 1995; Lord and Ranft, 1998), complexity (Hansen, 1999; Simonin, 1999), and ambiguity (Szulanski, 1996) affect knowledge transfer both within and across organizations. Similarly, the recipient's absorptive capacity (Gupta and Govindarajan, 2000), the sender's motivation, and the distance between sender and recipient (Szulanski, 1996) also influence the efficacy of knowledge transfer, both inside and outside the firm. These results imply that organizations may not be unique in their ability to efficiently transfer knowledge.

Fourth, the literature suggests a subtle interplay between knowledge per se and the structures that are the conduits through which knowledge flows. In some situations, structures can clearly impede knowledge flow (Dougherty, 1992; Dyer, 1999). Yet, structures such as teams, liaisons, and meetings can also improve knowledge flow within and across organizations (Almeida, 1996; Brown and Eisenhardt, 1998; Hargadon, 1998; Inkpen and Dinur, 1998). At a more basic level, loosely-linked organizational structure is related to innovative knowledge flows and adaptive organizational outcomes (Henderson and Cockburn, 1994; Tripsas, 1997; Brown and Eisenhardt, 1998; Hansen, 1999). Over time, organizations may coevolve into more distinctly specialist roles within systems of knowledge integration among organizations (Mowery et al., 1996; Lorenzoni and Lipparini, 1999). Overall, this suggests that organizations and groups of organizations become complex adaptive systems (organized into loosely linked systems of unique knowledge specialists), and when they do so, they become collectively more innovative, adaptive, and ultimately successful in dynamic markets.

Finally, our review sheds light on the question of whether KBV is a new theory of strategy, a new theory of organization, or both. In our view, it is none of these. The basic tenets of KBV have not received much empirical examination. As we noted earlier, the theory has not been tested with regard to the nature of competitive advantage (temporary vs sustained) or the source of that advantage (knowledge vs knowledge processes). Even the normative implications of the theory have received little empirical examination. Rather, the typical approach is to measure performance indirectly by using a mediating dependent variable such as speed of knowledge transfer (Zander and Kogut, 1995; Szulanski, 1996), learning (Lane and Lubatkin, 1998), or number of patents (Henderson and Cockburn, 1994). While such measures are suggestive of performance, they are not actually measures of performance that can yield insights into the nature of competitive advantage, the source of that advantage, or whether that advantage exists at all.

More significant, KBV as a theory of strategy rests on the assumption that knowledge is the most important resource. While this assumption has surface appeal, there appears to be little, if any, empirical evidence that this assumption is true. Indeed, several authors (Eisenhardt and Galunic, 2000; Gupta and Govindarajan, 2000) suggest that it is crucial to consider the strategic value of knowledge. In other words, not all knowledge is equally valuable. More knowledge sourcing, transfer, and even integration is not necessarily advantageous unless the knowledge is strategically valuable. Others (Chacar and Coff, 2000) find that the returns to knowledge may go to the individuals who possess that knowledge, not to the firm.

Perhaps most problematic is that the strategic logic of KBV is a special case of the resource-based view. That is, when knowledge is conceptualized as a resource that can be acquired, transferred, and integrated, the strategic logic is simply an extension of the resource-based view of strategy in general, and the dynamic capabilities approach in particular. Therefore, KBV is simply not a new view of strategy.

Finally, KBV is also not as yet a new theory of organization. From a theoretical standpoint, it is unclear exactly what the organization is, or why organizations are likely to be more effective than markets in the execution of various knowledge processes. As we noted in the empirical review, internal and external knowledge transfer seem quite similar, suggesting that knowledge processes may not uniquely distinguish organizations. More significant, a growing number of authors (Blackler, 1993; Kogut and Zander, 1996; Spender, 1996; Von_Krogh et al., 1998; Patriotta and Pettigrew, 1999) – especially from the fields of sociology, cognitive psychology and critical European perspectives – take exception to the assumption of knowledge as a

resource, and the view of organizations that follows from that assumption. They regard such thinking as mechanical and reductionist. These authors prefer to frame knowledge as a process of knowing, and see organizations as complex activity systems of knowledge emergence and application. Thus, KBV lacks a sharply defined and consensus set of assumptions about organizations and knowledge.

So what is KBV? The extensive empirical literature within the strategy field reveals important insights about fundamental knowledge processes that are related to strategic phenomena, ranging from alliances and acquisitions to strategic decision-making and innovation. In other words, KBV offers a wide-range of important insights that are relevant for improved understanding of many strategic processes. But, it is not as yet a new theory of strategy or of organization.

A RESEARCH AGENDA
FOR THE KNOWLEDGE-BASED VIEW

Knowledge-based thinking is still in its early stages, and may yet become a theory of strategy and of organization. In order to accelerate the development of KBV, we offer three broad suggestions for future research.

Develop Consistent Knowledge Taxonomies

Research on KBV rests on fundamental inconsistencies in how knowledge is conceptualized and measured, beyond the commonly accepted distinction between tacit and explicit knowledge. Even this distinction is troublesome since some researchers believe that tacit knowledge can be made more explicit through a process of codification (Kogut and Zander, 1992) while others see tacit and explicit knowledge as essentially distinct and complementary forms of knowledge (Cook and Brown, 1999).

The studies reviewed in this chapter illustrate these inconsistencies. The most cited framework for knowledge was proposed by Winter (1987) and was based on earlier work on the diffusion of innovations (Rogers, 1980). In this taxonomy, knowledge is classified along four dimensions: tacitness, complexity, systems dependence and observability. Tacitness is further divided into teachability and codifiability. Some authors used this detailed taxonomy (Zander and Kogut, 1995) while others just focused on an aggregate construct like ambiguity (Szulanski, 1996). Still others defined tacitness using codifiability, teachability and complexity constructs (Lord and Ranft, 1998). Others relied on a very aggregate construct of complexity, based on measures of codifiability and systems dependence (Hansen, 1999).

This inconsistent conceptualization and measurement of knowledge creates confusion, especially when trying to compare findings across different studies, and so retards the accretion of understanding about KBV. Therefore, a useful future direction for research would center on developing a consistent classification for knowledge. From our review of the empirical literature, we suggest that such knowledge taxonomy should at least include measures of codifiability (the extent to which the knowledge can be articulated) and complexity (number of interrelated elements that compose the knowledge). Additional dimensions of knowledge could be used in specific studies. Simonin (1999), for example, develops and applies a comprehensive taxonomy of knowledge in the context of knowledge transfer in strategic alliances.

Bridge Knowledge and Knowing Perspectives

A second direction for future research is to pull together the varied views of knowledge to create a more complete understanding. As we noted earlier, an emphasis on the process of knowing, as opposed to knowledge as a resource, has been the focus of the critical perspective towards the dominant KBV approach (Blackler, 1995; Spender, 1996; Tsoukas, 1996). If KBV is to develop beyond being just an extension of RBV, then its proponents need to incorporate the insights from this critical approach, and so bridge the two theoretical frameworks to create a more complete and accurate picture of the role of knowledge and knowing in organizations.

Cook and Brown (1999) proposed an epistemological template on which such an integrated knowledge-based view can be developed. The authors argue that tacit and explicit knowledge are distinct forms of knowledge. While tacit knowledge might be useful to generate explicit knowledge and vice-versa, one type of knowledge cannot be converted into another. The authors also argue that individual and group knowledge are distinct forms of knowledge. An example of explicit group knowledge is reflected in the 'war stories of communities of practice' (Orr, 1996), while an example of tacit group knowledge might be the different knowledge structures identified by Lam (1997) in an engineering setting. Combining these two dimensions of knowledge gives a 2*2 matrix that defines four distinct types of knowledge. These types of knowledge are linked to the processes of knowing, which are deeply related to the interaction of individuals with the world. The authors argue that it is through the interplay of knowledge and knowing that innovation takes place in organizations (Cook and Brown, 1999).

The bridging of knowledge and knowing implies that less focus should be given to the idea of knowledge transfer (moving a piece of knowledge from one place to another) while more focus should go to knowledge integration processes, in which the development of meaning and the creation of new knowledge occurs through individual interactions and is affected by social contexts (Galunic and Rodan, 1998). In a similar vein, another useful research direction is to continue to develop the perspective of social identity within the organization, and study its relation to the effectiveness of knowledge processes (Kogut and Zander, 1996; Spender, 1996; Kogut, 2000). Such theoretical development may prove to be essential to frame KBV as a theory of organization.

Enrich KBV with Ideas from Other Fields of Research

A third research direction centers on expanding the intellectual base of KBV. In our view, KBV researchers have neglected the potential insights related to knowledge that are being developed in other fields such as social psychology, sociology, and evolutionary biology. Relating these insights to KBV might help in further developing the organizational and strategic logic of KBV.

In social psychology, for example, Weick and Roberts (1993) focused on the concept of collective mind. This concept raises cognition to a higher level of analysis and helps to explain why some organizations are extremely reliable in face of great complexity. Another example is the concept of transactive memory (Moreland et al., 1996) that suggests the importance of distinguishing transactive knowledge (who knows what) from declarative (what is known). Such a distinction might prove valuable in understanding knowledge integration and transfer processes. Transactive memory is often more crucial to effective knowledge transfer than the actual transfer itself (Hargadon, 1998). A third example is the social psychology surrounding interruptions and breakdowns in daily working routines as an instance for knowledge creation (Bechky, 1999; Patriotta and Pettigrew, 1999).

Drawing from sociology, the concepts of social identity and shared understanding could be further developed in order to explain why the organizational context makes a difference in knowledge flows (Kogut and Zander, 1996; Kogut, 2000) as argued by KBV proponents. In this regard, a deeper understanding of the institutions where organizational knowledge is created, and of the social and cognitive mechanisms within which individuals work, is of crucial importance for the development of the knowledge-based view of the firm (Kogut, 2000).

Finally, drawing from evolutionary biology and more specifically from complexity theory, analysis of loosely-coupled systems as structural arrangements that enable the flexible flow of knowledge is an interesting area for further research (Anderson, 1999).

CONCLUSION

Given the current theoretical perspectives on knowledge, KBV is not yet a theory of strategy (a theory that links independent variables to a specific conception of firm performance) that goes beyond the insights provided by the resource-based view and the related dynamic capabilities approach. That is, once knowledge is conceptualized as a resource, the thinking simply becomes a special case of the resource-based view of the firm. Similarly, the empirical literature suggests that it is unlikely that we have a new theory of organization, given that internal and external knowledge transfer processes are not appreciably different.

So, what is the knowledge-based view? Our view is that KBV offers enormously useful theoretical insights, well grounded in empirical findings that address the multi-level social processes through which knowledge is sourced, transferred and integrated within and across organizations. Although KBV is not fully developed, there is already a surprisingly consistent body of empirical results that is capable of informing theory-building and managerial practice. These findings point to a knowledge-based theory that is consistent with a pluralistic understanding of knowledge, and a view of organizations as complex adaptive systems, where meaning is socially constructed through ongoing activities of semi-autonomous groups. The implications for strategy remain more distant.

ACKNOWLEDGEMENTS

The authors gratefully acknowledge the helpful comments from Andrew Pettigrew, Gerardo Patriotta, Steffen Bohm, Jeff Martin and Mahesh Bhatia. They acknowledge the financial support from the Stanford Technology Ventures Program and Program PRAXIS XXI (BD 16210/98).

NOTES

1 This discussion represents a simplification of a highly complex theme. For a deeper overview of individual knowledge, drawn mostly from cognitive psychology, see Sparrow (1998). For an in-depth discussion of organizational knowledge, see Tell (1997). For an interesting discussion on the contrast between Western and Eastern epistemology see Nonaka (1994).

REFERENCES

Allen, T. J. (1977) *Managing the Flow of Technology.* Cambridge, MA: The MIT Press.
Almeida, P. (1996) 'Knowledge sourcing by foreign multinationals: patent citation analysis in the US semiconductor industry', *Strategic Management Journal*, 17 (Winter Special Issue): 155–65.

Anderson, P. (1999) 'Complexity theory and organization science', *Organization Science*, 10(3): 216–32.

Argote, L. (1999) *Organizational Learning: Creating, Retaining and Transferring Knowledge.* Norwell, MA: Kluwer Academic Publishers.

Athanassiou, N. and Nigh, D. (1999) 'The impact of US company internationalization on top management team advice networks: a tacit knowledge perspective', *Strategic Management Journal*, 20: 83–92.

Barney, J. (1991) 'Firm resources and sustained competitive advantage', *Journal of Management*, 17(1): 99–120.

Bechky, B. A. (1999) 'Creating shared meaning across occupational communities: an ethnographic study of a production floor', Working Paper.

Bierly, P. and Chakrabarti, A. (1996) 'Generic knowledge strategies in the US pharmaceutical industry', *Strategic Management Journal*, 17 (Winter Special Issue): 123–35.

Blackler, F. (1993) 'Knowledge and the theory of organizations: organizations as activity systems and the reframing of management', *Journal of Management Studies*, 30(6): 863–84.

Blackler, F. (1995) 'Knowledge, knowledge work and organizations: an overview and interpretation', *Organization Studies*, 16(6): 1021–46.

Brown, J. S. and Duguid, P. (1991) 'Organizational learning and communities of practice: toward a unified view of working, learning and innovation', *Organization Science*, 2(1): 40–57.

Brown, S. L. and Eisenhardt, K. (1998) *Competing on the Edge – Strategy as Structured Chaos.* Boston, MA: Harvard Business School.

Brown, S. L. and Eisenhardt, K. M. (1997) 'The art of continuous change: linking complexity theory and time-paced evolution in relentlessly shifting organizations', *Administrative Science Quarterly*, 42: 1–34.

Capron, L. (1999) 'The long-term performance of horizontal acquisitions', *Strategic Management Journal*, 20: 987–1018.

Chacar, A. S. and Coff, R. W. (2000) 'Deconstructing a knowledge-based advantage: rent generation, rent appropriation and performance in investment banking', Working Paper.

Cohen, M. D., Burkhart, R. et al. (1996) 'Routines and other recurring action patterns of organizations: contemporary research issues', *Industrial and Corporate Change*, 5: 653–98.

Cohen, W. M. and Levinthal, D. A. (1990) 'Absorptive capacity: a new perspective on learning and innovation', *Administrative Science Quarterly*, 35(1): 128–52.

Conner, K. R. and Pralahad, C. K. (1996) 'A resource-based theory of the firm: knowledge vs. opportunism', *Organization Science*, 7(5): 477–501.

Cook, S. D. N. and Brown, J. S. (1999) 'Bridging epistemologies: the generative dance between organizational knowledge and organizational knowing', *Organization Science*, 10(4): 381–400.

Cowan, R. and Foray, D. (1997) 'The economics of codification and the diffusion of knowledge', *Industrial and Corporate Change*, 6(3): 595–622.

Cyert, R. M. and March, J. G. (1963) *A Behavioral Theory of the Firm.* Englewood Cliffs, NJ: Prentice-Hall.

D'Aveni, R. A. (1994) *Hypercompetition: Managing the Dynamics of Strategic Maneuvering.* New York: Free Press.

Decarolis, D. M. and Deeds, D. L. (1999) 'The impact of stocks and flows of organizational knowledge on firm performance: an empirical investigation of the biotechnology industry', *Strategic Management Journal*, 20: 953–68.

Dierickx, I. and Cool, K. (1989) 'Asset accumulation and sustainability of competitive advantage', *Management Science*, 35: 554–71.

Dougherty, D. (1992) 'Interpretive barriers to successful product innovation in large firms', *Organization Science*, 3(2): 179–202.

Dyer, J. H. (1999) 'Interorganizational learning, barriers to knowledge transfers and competitive advantage', Working Paper.

Eisenhardt, K. (1989) 'Making fast strategic decisions in high-velocity environments', *Academy of Management Journal*, 32(3): 543–76.

Eisenhardt, K. M. and Bhatia, M. M. (2001) 'Organizational computation and complexity', in J. Baum (ed.), *Companion to Organizations.* Oxford: Blackwell.

Eisenhardt, K. M. and Galunic, D. C. (2000) 'Coevolving: at last, a way to make synergies work', *Harvard Business Review* (January–February): 91–101.

Eisenhardt, K. M. and Martin, J. A. (2000) 'Dynamic capabilities: the evolution of resources in dynamic markets', *Strategic Management Journal*, 21: 1105–21.

Foss, N. J. (1996) 'Knowledge-based approaches to the theory of the firm: some critical comments', *Organization Science*, 7(5): 470–6.

Galunic, D. C. and Rodan, S. (1998) 'Resources recombinations in the firm: knowledge structures and the potential for Schumpeterian innovation', *Strategic Management Journal*, 19: 1193–201.

Graebner, M. (1999) *A Review of Recent Research on Mergers and Acquisitions.* Chicago, IL: Academy of Management.

Grant, R. M. (1996a) 'Toward a knowledge-based theory of the firm', *Strategic Management Journal*, 17 (Winter Special Issue): 109–22.

Grant, R. M. (1996b) 'Prospering in dynamically-competitive environments: organizational capability as knowledge integration', *Organization Science*, 7(4): 375–87.

Gupta, A. K. and Govindarajan, V. (2000) 'Knowledge flow within multinational corporations', *Strategic Management Journal*, 21: 473–96.

Hansen, M. T. (1998) 'Combining network centrality and related knowledge: explaining effective knowledge sharing in multiunit firms', Harvard Business School, Working Paper.

Hansen, M. T. (1999) 'The search-transfer problem: the role of weak ties in sharing knowledge across organizational subunits', *Administrative Science Quarterly*, 44(1): 82–111.

Hargadon, A. (1998) *Knowledge Brokers: A Field Study of Organizational Learning and Innovation*. Chicago, IL: Academy of Management.

Hargadon, A. and Sutton, R. I. (1997) 'Technology brokering and innovation in a product development firm', *Administrative Science Quarterly*, 42: 716–49.

Helper, S., MacDuffie, J. P. and Sabel, C. (1999) 'Pragmatic collaborations: advancing knowledge while controlling opportunism', *Industrial and Corporate Change*, 9(3): 443–88.

Henderson, R. (1994) 'The evolution of integrative capability: innovation in cardiovascular drug discovery', *Industrial and Corporate Change*, 3(3): 607–29.

Henderson, R. and Cockburn, I. (1994) 'Measuring competence? Exploring firm effects in pharmaceutical research', *Strategic Management Journal*, 15: 63–84.

Henderson, R. and Cockburn, I. (1996) 'Scale, scope, and spillovers: the determinants of research productivity in drug discovery', *RAND Journal of Economics*, 27(1): 32–59.

Inkpen, A. C. and Dinur, A. (1998) 'Knowledge management processes and international joint-ventures', *Organization Science*, 9(4): 454–68.

Jett, Q. R. (1999) 'All the right moves: linking organizational capabilities with competitive product moves in dynamic markets', Working Paper.

Kale, P., Dyer, J. H. and Singh, H. (1999) 'Alliance capability, stock market response, and long term alliance success', Working Paper.

Katz, R. and Tushman, M. L. (1981) 'An investigation into the managerial role and career paths of gatekeepers and project supervisors in a major R&D facility', *R&D Management*, 11: 103–10.

Kogut, B. (2000) 'The network as knowledge: generative rules and the emergence of structure', *Strategic Management Journal*, 21: 405–25.

Kogut, B. and Zander, U. (1992) 'Knowledge of the firm, combinative capabilities, and the replication of technology', *Organization Science*, 3(3): 383–97.

Kogut, B. and Zander, U. (1996) 'What firms do? Coordination, identity, and learning', *Organization Science*, 7(5): 502–23.

Lam, A. (1997) 'Embedded firms, embedded knowledge: problems of collaboration and knowledge transfer in global cooperative ventures', *Organization Studies*, 18(6): 973–96.

Lane, P. J. and Lubatkin, M. (1998) 'Relative absorptive capacity and interorganizational learning', *Strategic Management Journal*, 19: 461–77.

Lave, J. and Wenger, E. (1991) *Situated Learning: Legitimate Peripheral Participation*. Cambridge, UK: Cambridge University Press.

Leonard-Barton, D. (1992) 'Core capabilities and core rigidities: a paradox in managing new product development', *Strategic Management Journal*, 13: 111–25.

Liebeskind, J. P., Oliver, A. L., Zucker, L. and Brewer, M. (1996) 'Social networks, learning and flexibility: sourcing scientific knowledge in new biotechnology firms', *Organization Science*, 7(4): 428–43.

Lord, M. D. and Ranft, A. L. (1998) 'Transfer and sharing of local knowledge within the firm & entry into new international markets', *Academy of Management Best Papers* Proceedings '98.

Lorenzoni, G. and Lipparini, A. (1999) 'The leveraging of interfirm relationships as a distinctive organizational capability: a longitudinal study', *Strategic Management Journal*, 20: 317–38.

Martin, J. A. and Carlile, P. R. (1999) 'Designing agile organizations: organizational learning at the boundaries', in R. E. Quinn, R. M. O'Neill and L. S. Clair (eds), *Pressing Problems in Modern Organizations*. New York: Amacom.

McEvily, B. and Zaheer, A. (1999) 'Bridging ties: a source of firm heterogeneity in competitive capabilities', *Strategic Management Journal*, 20: 1133–56.

Moreland, R. L., Argote, L. and Ranjani, K. (1996) 'Socially shared cognition at work: transactive memory and group performance', *What's Social about Social Cognition*, 57–84.

Mowery, D. C., Oxley, J. and Silverman, B. (1996) 'Strategic alliances and interfirm knowledge transfer', *Strategic Management Journal*, 17 (Winter Special Issue): 77–91.

Mowery, D. C. and Rosenberg, N. (1998) *Paths of Innovation*. Cambridge, MA: Cambridge University Press.

Nahapiet, J. and Goshal, S. (1998) 'Social capital, intellectual capital and organizational advantage', *Academy of Management Review*, 23(2): 242–66.

Nelson, R. R. and Winter, S. G. (1982) *An Evolutionary Theory of Economic Change*. Cambridge, MA: Belknap – Harvard University Press.

Nonaka, I. (1994) 'Dynamic theory of organizational knowledge creation', *Organization Science*, 5(1): 14–37.

Nonaka, I. and Takeuchi, H. (1995) *The Knowledge-Creating Company*. New York: Oxford University Press.

Orr, J. E. (1996) *Talking about Machines: An Ethnography of a Modern Job*. Ithaca, NY: Cornell University Press.

Patriotta, G. and Pettigrew, A. (1999) 'Studying knowing and organization', Working Paper.

Penrose, E. (1959) *The Theory of the Growth of the Firm*. Oxford: Basil Blackwell.

Polanyi, M. (1962) *Personal Knowledge – Towards a Post-Critical Philosophy*. London: Routledge and Kegan Paul.

Porter, M. E. (1985) *Competitive Advantage: Creating and Sustaining Superior Performance*. New York: Free Press.

Porter, M. E. (1991) 'Towards a dynamic theory of strategy', *Strategic Management Journal*, 12: 95–117.

Powell, W. W., Koput, K. W. and Smith-Doerr, L. (1996) 'Interorganizational collaboration and the locus of innovation: networks of learning in biotechnology', *Administrative Science Quarterly*, 41: 116–45.

Prahalad, C. K. and Hamel, G. (1990) 'The core competence of the organization', *Harvard Business Review*, (May–June): 79–90.

Ranft, A. L. and Lord, M. D. (1998) 'The challenges of acquiring knowledge-based resources: evidence from high-tech acquisitions', Working Paper.

Ranft, A. L. and Zeithaml, C. P. (1997) 'Preserving and transferring knowledge-based resources during post-acquisition implementation: a study of high-tech acquisitions', Working Paper.

Roberts, P. W. (1999) 'Product innovation, product-market competition and persistent profitability in the US pharmaceutical industry', *Strategic Management Journal*, 20: 655–70.

Rogers, E. (1980) *Diffusion of Innovations*. New York: Free Press.

Rosenkopf, L. and Nerkar, A. (1999) 'Beyond local search: boundary-spanning, exploration and impact in the optical disc industry', Working Paper.

Santos, F. M. (1999) 'The cognocratic organization: towards a knowledge theory view of the firm', Presented at The Academy of Management '99, Chicago, IL.

Shapiro, C. (1989) 'The theory of business strategy', *RAND Journal of Economics*, 20(1): 125–37.

Simon, H. (1965) *Administrative Behavior*. New York: Free Press.

Simonin, B. L. (1997) 'The importance of collaborative know-how: an empirical test of the learning organization', *Academy of Management Journal*, 40(5): 1150–74.

Simonin, B. L. (1999) 'Ambiguity and the process of knowledge transfer in strategic alliances', *Strategic Management Journal*, 20: 595–623.

Sparrow, J. (1998) *Knowledge in Organizations*. London: Sage Publications.

Spender, J-C. (1996) 'Making knowledge the basis of a dynamic theory of the firm', *Strategic Management Journal*, 17 (Winter Special Issue): 45–62.

Stalk, G., Evans, P. and Shulman, L. E. (1992) 'Competing on capabilities: the new rules of corporate strategy', *Harvard Business Review*, (March–April): 57–69.

Szulanski, G. (1996) 'Exploring internal stickiness: impediments to the transfer of best practice within the firm', *Strategic Management Journal*, 17 (Winter Special Issue): 27–43.

Teece, D. J., Pisano, G. and Shuen, A. (1997) 'Dynamic capabilities and strategic management', *Strategic Management Journal*, 18(7): 509–33.

Tell, F. (1997) *Knowledge and Justification – Exploring the Knowledge Based Firm*. Linkoping: Linkoping University.

Tripsas, M. (1997) 'Surviving radical technological change through dynamic capability: evidence from the typesetter industry', *Industrial and Corporate Change*, 6: 341–77.

Tsoukas, H. (1996) 'The firm as a distributed knowledge system: a constructionist approach', *Strategic Management Journal*, 17 (Winter Special Issue): 11–25.

Von_Krogh, G., Roos, J. and Kleine, D. (eds) (1998) *Knowing in Firms: Understanding, Managing and Measuring Knowledge*. London: Sage.

Von_Krogh, G., Roos, J. and Slocum, K. (1994) 'An essay on corporate epistemology', *Strategic Management Journal*, 15: 53–71.

Weick, K. E. (1991) 'The nontraditional quality of organizational theory', *Organization Science*, 2(1): 116–24.

Weick, K. E. and Roberts, K. H. (1993) 'Collective minds in organizations: heedful interrelating on flight decks', *Administrative Science Quarterly*, 38: 357–81.

Wernerfelt, B. (1984) 'A resource-based view of the firm', *Strategic Management Journal*, 5: 171–80.

Whitaker, R. (1996) 'Managing context in enterprise knowledge process', *European Management Journal*, 14(4): 399–406.

Winter, S. (1987) 'Knowledge and competence as strategic assets', in D. Teece (ed.), *The Competitive Challenge – Strategies for Industrial Innovation and Renewal*. Cambridge, MA: Ballinger.

Winter, S. G. and Szulanski, G. (1999) 'Replication as strategy', Working Paper – Presented at the 1999 Academy of Management Conference.

Zander, U. and Kogut, B. (1995) 'Knowledge and the speed of the transfer and imitation of organizational capabilities: an empirical test', *Organization Science*, 6(1): 76–92.

Zollo, M. and Singh, H. (1999) 'Post-acquisition strategies, integration, capability, and the economic performance of corporate acquisitions', Working Paper – INSEAD 99/42/SM.

8

Managing Cognition and Strategy: Issues, Trends and Future Directions

JOSEPH F. PORAC and HOWARD THOMAS

The study of cognition and cognitive science is not new in the field of psychology (Hunt, 1982; Reed, 1982; Kahneman et al., 1982), but its popularity and relevance has grown in the field of strategic management over the last 20 years or so. Extensive reviews by Stubbart (1989) and Walsh (1995) have examined the potential linkages between managerial and organizational cognition and the theory and practice of strategic management. Clearly, the cognitive approach and its linkage with the process of strategy has received increasing attention from strategy researchers with the development of a division on Managerial and Organisational Cognition in the Academy of Management and several dedicated journal issues on the subject (for example, *Journal of Management Studies, Organisational Science*).

At least three distinct research streams are evident from the literature: first, the cognitive literature in behavioural decision theory, which focuses upon the cognitive biases, heuristics and limitations inherent in the process of judgement and choice (Hogarth, 1980); second, an extensive methodological literature, specifying techniques for eliciting cognitive maps and structures from individuals (Huff, 1990); third, an ever-widening literature examining the linkages between 'cognitive structures' and decision processes in strategic management with regard to strategy

formulation and implementation (Stubbart, 1989; Walsh, 1995).

While this paper lists and briefly reviews the literature in the first two areas, we will emphasize the linkages between cognition, strategy and strategic decision making, and examine the contents of the managerial 'black box' – the cognitive models used by senior/top managers (strategic) in a strategy process. We will focus upon the cognitive structures of top management – beliefs about the environment, about strategy and about the business portfolio and state of the organization. Our organizing framework is summarized in Figure 8.1, through which we will examine the causes and origins of strategic cognitive structures, their empirical descriptions, and their consequences for the conduct of the process of strategic decision-making. We will focus on strategic cognition at various levels of analysis: the individual (top manager), the top management team (TMT), the organization, and populations of TMTs – so-called cognitive communities.

We first briefly review the breadth of the cognitive science paradigm in strategy. We follow with a discussion of the key findings and concepts from a range of selected studies using each of the levels of analysis to illustrate the discussions. We will conclude by providing conjectures about an agenda for, and interesting directions in, future research.

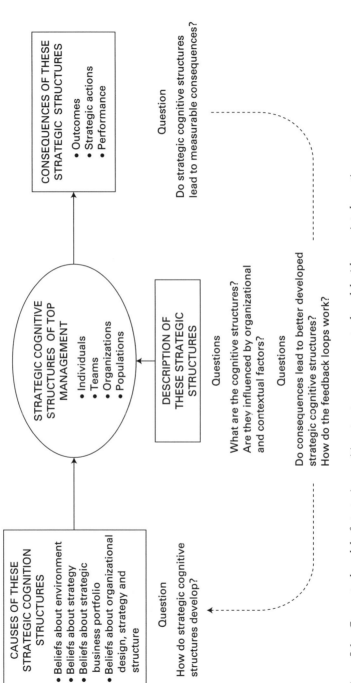

Figure 8.1   *Conceptual model of strategic cognitive structures: a conceptual model with associated questions*

THE LANDSCAPE OF MANAGERIAL AND ORGANIZATIONAL COGNITION (MOC)

The landscape of the field of managerial and organizational cognition is driven by the need to understand the role of the individual decision-maker in the process of problem formulation and strategic decision-making. Indeed, this has been a central theme in developing cognitive perspectives in organizational and management theory at least since the Carnegie School's work in the 1950s. March and Simon (1958) proposed that organizations can be understood as cognitive phenomena that derive from and, in turn, influence the mental models, frames-of-reference and routinized knowledge structures of their participants. Indeed, in their stress on the centrality of individual knowledge representations as the basis of organizing, March and Simon and their colleagues pioneered a cognitive stance in both organization theory and the social sciences as a whole. Their emphasis on processes of 'bounded rationality' (Simon, 1955, 1957; March and Simon, 1958) countered the view that decision processes were intendedly rational – rather, individual decision-makers are more likely to simplify reality and be resistant to change.

Taking a cognitive perspective, researchers in behavioural decision theory emphasize that individuals exhibit biases and use cognitive simplification mechanisms (often called heuristics or 'rules of thumb') in processes of strategic decision and choice. Hogarth (1980) and Kahneman et al. (1982) catalogue this literature in depth and draw attention to such factors as cognitive limitations on information processing (Miller, 1956), hindsight biases in assessing predictions of past events, and heuristics (for example, adjustment and anchoring) in assessing probability judgements (Moore and Thomas, 1975) and simplifying reality. Barnes (1984), Schwenk (1984) and Schwenk and Thomas (1983) also extended this literature to the strategy field by pointing out the influence of cognitive biases, simplification mechanisms and heuristics in framing strategic problems, identifying and diagnosing strategic issues, and in making strategic decisions.

However, simply noting that individuals are imperfect and exhibit a range of cognitive heuristics and biases is not sufficient for advancing cognitive organizational and management theory. In order to move theory forward, we must return to a central assumption of cognitive organizational theory, namely that an individual's behaviour toward external stimuli is mediated by his or her cognitive representations of those stimuli (Dill, 1958, 1962). Consequently, an alternative approach to cognitive modelling suggests that an understanding of how organizations respond to their environments (whether internal, competitive or external) must rely on understanding the 'mental models' of key decision-makers, who must interpret and understand these environments and eventually make critical strategic choices. Extant research indicates that mental models of key decision-makers shape their environmental sensing capabilities (Daft and Weick, 1984; Fahey and Naranayan, 1989), influence their selective perception of key issues in the environment (Starbuck and Milliken, 1988), and affect their diagnoses of such strategic issues as environmental opportunities and threats (Dutton and Jackson, 1987). Mental models also influence diversification strategies (Ginsberg, 1989) and determine how an organization's 'dominant logic' (Prahalad and Bettis, 1986) may shape its growth, diversification, and business portfolio strategy. Barr et al. (1992) also track from a cognitive perspective how organizations' views of the strategy–environment linkages change over time. And a range of researchers (Porac et al., 1989; Porac and Thomas, 1990; Reger and Huff, 1993; Hodgkinson and Johnson, 1994) examine how individual managers' mental models enable the costs and benefits of various competitive strategies to be assessed. Weick (1979, 1995) and Porac et al. (1989) go even further and argue that, since competitive environments are enacted, the mental models of organizational-decision makers actively shape the nature and character of their competitive environments. Indeed, Porac et al. (1995) show how cognitive communities – networks of firms – form in the interplay of competitive rivalry in the Scottish knitwear industry.

However, in order to capture cognitive phenomena, researchers must be able to adequately map the mental models of key organizational participants. Huff (1990) catalogues several approaches, which range from 'causal mapping' (Axelrod, 1976), cognitive mapping (Eden et al., 1992), the use of

Kelly's (1956) repertory grid (Reger and Huff, 1993) to multi-dimensional scaling and a range of taxonomic mapping procedures (Porac and Thomas, 1990). Unfortunately, it is clear that these approaches currently make different cognitive demands on individual decision-makers and, consequently, yield quite significant differences in the structure and content of decision-makers' representations of key strategic problems (Hodgkinson and Johnson, 1994).

As mentioned earlier, we try to frame processes of individual group and organizational cognition in terms of the model shown in Figure 8.1. The central element in Figure 8.1 is the strategic cognitive structures of top managers, described individually or collectively. We focus on the informational content of these structures as it forms the foundation for beliefs about the environment, strategy, the business portfolio and organizational structure. We are not only interested in describing managerial knowledge structures but also in explaining how they arise. In turn, we need to link the mental models to key strategic outcomes and choices about resource deployment and performance. Obviously, the model in Figure 8.1 is dynamic and involves feedback loops. Information and knowledge about outcomes influences, develops insight about, and re-shapes the maps and frames of individual managers.

In subsequent sections, we apply this model to different units of analysis in the cognitive domain: the key individual manager (CEO), the top management team (TMT), the organization itself, and the industry community encompassing the firm.

INDIVIDUAL MANAGERIAL COGNITION AND THE STRATEGY PROCESS

Table 8.1 summarizes the application of Figure 8.1 to the cognitive structures of the individual manager. As with the concept of strategy itself, strategy researchers use many definitions and descriptions for an individual's knowledge structures (March and Simon, 1958) or mental model (Hodgkinson and Johnson, 1994; Porac and Thomas, 1990). The term 'cognitive map' (Weick and Bougon, 1986; Axelrod, 1976) is used almost interchangeably

alongside 'cause map' (Eden et al., 1992), 'schemata' (Schwenk, 1984, 1985), 'world view' (Mason and Mitroff, 1984) and 'strategic frame' (Huff, 1982). Since the words are used interchangeably, it is perhaps valuable to quote Fombrun's view (Fombrun, 1994: 71) of how cognitive maps help managers in practice: 'Much as generals use cartographers' maps to deploy armies, so do managers rely on cognitive mappings of the competitive landscape to deploy their products, resources and personnel ... But maps are only representations of the world. They, too, are incomplete. A road map does not advise a driver about road conditions, nor does it indicate traffic congestion.'

This leads us quite naturally to ask how good the map of an individual manager may be. Individuals' maps can reflect both processing of current information and a myriad of factors associated with the demographic and job characteristics of the individual. Finkelstein and Hambrick (1996: 57) discuss three main elements and underlying causes of a top manager's cognitive map. These elements are cognitive content, cognitive structure and cognitive style. Cognitive content 'consists of the things he or she knows, assumes and believes' (1996: 57). Cognitive structure is 'how the content is arranged, connected or studied in the executive's mind' (1996: 57) and cognitive style 'refers to how a person's mind works – how he or she gathers and processes information' (1996: 57).

Cognitive content can be learned through a manager's job and educational background, and the set of professional and educational experiences that have patterned his or her career. Hodgkinson and Johnson (1994) show clearly that managers' mental models (in the case of a competitive situation) vary widely in detail and depth. Experiences, job training, educational background and career patterns are strongly linked to differences in mental models. Finkelstein and Hambrick suggest that cognitive content, structure and style affect not only managers' perceptions, interpretation and processing of information but also their ability to frame strategic problems and devise key strategic choices. However, it is equally clear that these three elements of cognition are inter-related and strongly interactive. For example, cognitive style may limit an individual's ability to perceive new content, while

Table 8.1   *Individual level of analysis (top manager) cognitive models*

	Causes	Description	Consequences
Papers	Axelrod (1976) Bougon et al. (1997) Eden (1988) Huff (1982) March and Simon (1958) Porac and Thomas (1990) Stubbart (1989) Walsh (1995)	Isenberg (1987) Mintzberg (1976) Calori et al. (1994a, b) Schneider (1989) Hodgkinson and Johnson (1994)	Fiol (1989) Ginsberg and Venkatraman (1992) Dutton et al. (1989)

Key concepts/
findings
	Cognitive maps
	Cause maps
	Frames of references
	Taxonomic mental
	   models
	Knowledge structures
		Cognitive maps and thinking
		   frameworks of managers
		   in practice
			Prediction from cognitive
			   maps of outcome
			   consequences, e.g. joint
			   ventures, adoption of
			   technology, strategic
			   issues diagnosis

new cognitive content may have a significant effect on cognitive structure.

A simple conclusion can be drawn from existing evidence. Managers' maps (mental models) are highly individualized and personal (Porac et al.'s knitwear study, 1989) and may not change in accordance with new data or information. (However, Barr et al. [1992] note that their managers' maps changed significantly as environmental discontinuities occurred.) Indeed, as Weick (1983) points out: they can become self-fulfilling and self-reinforcing. This tendency can be exacerbated by the impact of neuroses, emotion and other psychoanalytic factors (Kets de Vries and Miller, 1984) and by such personality factors as charisma (Agle and Sonnenfeld, 1994) and risk-taking and intolerance for ambiguity (Gupta and Govindarajan, 1984). Hill and Levenhagen (1995) also note that managers must make sense of highly ambiguous environments and tend to use metaphors in framing their cognitive models of business development and competition. Since such maps are highly individual, it is very clear that we need to identify mapping methods with a less qualitative researcher-driven orientation and with a design which can prove to be applicable and reliable across a range of cognitive studies.

It is clear that the mapping process can lead to a range of unacceptable outcomes – 'bad maps' (Kiesler and Sproull, 1982). For example, Zahra and Chapple (1993) identify the presence of competitive 'blind spots' in cognitive modelling of competition, often involving

managers' inability to recognize the actions of competitors. Reger (1988) and Gripsrud and Gronhaug (1985) also indicate that managers in banks and retail contexts respectively both have a narrow field of vision in strategic decision-making. Lorsch (1989) has also described this tendency as 'strategic myopia'. In Reger's case, bank managers tended to rely on a limited set of factors, including geographical scope, target market identification and size, in mapping their perceptions of competition. Individuals may also be guilty of distorting reality (Fombrun, 1994) and biasing their perception of outcomes through relying on their past experience of certain events (Tversky and Kahneman, 1974) and their educational and cultural background (Meyer, 1982; Bantel and Jackson, 1989) in framing their cognitive maps.

Finally, in examining the role of the individual CEO in the strategy process, it is important to remember the findings of Mintzberg (1983) and Pettigrew (1973, 1985). They emphasize that the framing of strategy takes place in an organizational, social and political context and that the art of devising strategy is inherently a political process. Indeed, an individual actor such as a CEO may, in fact, dominate the strategy framing process and, therefore, may use a power position to create a highly personalized map which may turn out to be an inappropriate cognitive map (Dearborn and Simon, 1958).

We now turn to another element of the socio-political arena, namely how the cognitive structures may change as the CEO interacts with his top management team.

Table 8.2   *TMT (top management team) level of analysis cognitive models*

	Causes	Description	Consequences
Papers	Hambrick (1989) Hambrick and Mason (1984) Finkelstein and Hambrick (1996) Prahalad and Bettis (1986) Sims and Gioia (1979) Ginsberg (1989)	Barr et al. (1992) Dutton and Dukerich (1991)	Barr et al. (1992) Fiol (1993) Dutton and Dukerich (1991)
Key concepts/ findings	Dominant (general management) logic Socio-cognitive models	Chief executives' (TMTs') framing of strategic issues, business strategy and environmental issues	TMT cognitive models predict actions on strategic issues and joint ventures

TMT Cognitive Structure and the Strategy Process

The term 'top management team' (TMT) refers to the top management group responsible for setting the overall direction of the organization (Table 8.2) (Mintzberg, 1979). Hambrick and Mason (1984) and Finkelstein and Hambrick (1996) have defined and catalogued much of the work on the upper echelons of organizations, TMTs, and strategic leadership. They suggest that there are three main conceptual elements of a TMT – composition, structure and process. Composition of the TMT includes personality factors and aspects of executive experience (age, education, etc.). Structure of a TMT relates to the roles of the members and the size of the team, whereas process refers to the inter-action mechanisms among TMT members in terms of the degree of social integration and consensus in the team and the relative power relationships among members of the team.

From a cognitive perspective, the team is made up of individuals with a series of different mental models and beliefs. The key question is whether it is possible to aggregate the individual belief structures of TMT members to achieve a TMT group mental model. Or, framing the question in terms of Prahalad and Bettis' (1986) concept of the 'dominant logic', defined as 'the way in which managers conceptualize the business and make critical resources allocation decisions', is it possible to identify and measure the dominant logic of a TMT? Current research suggests that consensus in a TMT is positively related to TMT homogeneity and high levels of social integration (Dess and Keats, 1987; Dutton and

Duncan, 1987; Wiersema and Bantel, 1992). TMT consensus is also likely to be positively related to a small team size (Hambrick and d'Aveni, 1992), and to occur in environments which are relatively stable (Mintzberg, 1979) and uncomplicated (Keats and Hitt, 1988). Consensus is also affected by the power distribution among members of the TMT (Finkelstein, 1992). Westphal and Zajac (1994) point out that the presence of a dominant CEO can create a homogenous TMT with a dominant consensual mental model.

Dissensus and cognitive heterogeneity in a TMT is probably a much more likely outcome than consensus and cognitive homogeneity. Indeed, the quality of strategic decisions measured in terms of the generation of a range of feasible alternatives and a full evaluation of those alternatives is positively correlated with TMT heterogeneity and size (Finkelstein and Hambrick, 1996: 147). And, cognitively heterogeneous TMTs will tend to have greater levels of problem-solving skills and innovativeness (Bantel and Jackson, 1989; Jackson, 1992).

Fombrun (1992), Ginsberg (1989), Prahalad and Bettis (1986) and others stress some of the advantages of consensus. Corporations and the TMT can implicitly adhere to a strong dominant logic and pursue consistent corporate-level strategies with respect to growth and diversification. Adverse consequences, however, can occur from such a consensual map of the world. These include a pattern of strategic inertia in the TMT involving resistance to change and the inability to adapt to environmental trends. Also, in facing adversity, the TMT may act to 'batten down the hatches', restrict information flows, and reinforce the consensus. Strong CEOs and networks may also influence and drive TMT consensus to the extent that it may lead, in some cases, to the misinterpretation of strategic trends and an inability to undertake strategic re-orientation and change.

However, in the translation from the consensual mental model to the entire organizational level, the next relevant question is to ask whether, and under what conditions, TMT consensus and learning may influence the construction of an organizational-level consensus about strategic options. In turn, we may also ask how organizational learning, belief systems and cultures develop to create both short-term and long-term organizational strategies.

ORGANIZATIONAL COGNITION AND THE STRATEGY PROCESS

Daft and Weick (1984) set out a basic framework for understanding cognition at the organizational level by arguing that organizations are 'interpretation systems' that collect information from the environment, interpret such information by incorporating it into organizational level shared beliefs, and then act upon those beliefs in the course of adapting to the environment (Table 8.3). Such action then provides environmental input for additional information, interpretation, and learning. Daft and Weick suggest that although this information collection–interpretation–action cycle is most associated with top level decision makers in an organization, given their environmental scanning and decision-making responsibilities, all levels of the organization are involved in enacting its environment and incorporating external information into its collective cognitive structures. Differences across organizations can be observed in how they collect information and form beliefs about the environment.

For Daft and Weick's view of organizations as collective cognitive units to be theoretically and practically useful, the basic processes of storing and retaining information in organizations must be explicated and understood. Walsh and Ungson (1991) take on this challenge by fleshing out the basic components of what they label an organization's 'memory' system. In their view, organizational memory 'refers to stored information from an organization's history that can be brought to bear on present decisions' (1991: 61). It

consists of a variety of information retention mechanisms, the information retained by these mechanisms, and routines for the acquisition, storage, and retrieval of such information over time. At the heart of Walsh and Ungson's model is a set of five 'retention facilities' that store acquired information in organizations and make it available for use by organizational members. Individuals store information through their own recollections of past organizational events and procedures. Organizational culture is a retention mechanism because it consists of a shared nomenclature and set of symbols, stories, and assumptions about an organization's functioning and characteristics. Transformations within the core technology of an organization retain information through standard operating procedures and formalized systems for handling and acting upon organizational inputs. Organizational structures, as embodied in constellations of formal and informal roles, store information by stabilizing activities, decision rights, and individual responsibilities. Finally, the physical ecology of an organization encodes organizational characteristics such as status relationships (the relative size of offices, etc.), assumptions about worker motivation (color of office or factory walls), and organizational culture (informal or formal office buildings and décor, etc.).

Walsh and Ungson's retention mechanisms lay the foundation for theorizing about the collective cognitive structures that bind organizational members together in coordinated action. Cognitive constructs such as organizational culture, ideology, routines, tacit and explicit knowledge, and frames have all been imputed to organizations by researchers studying organizational cognition. All of these constructs must have some basis in the fundamental memory systems of organizations to be meaningful. At the same time, however, not all information retained in organizational memory is directly connected to the strategic processes of a firm – that is, to those processes that are involved in defining the business and setting the general direction of the organization. In this regard, Lyles and Schwenk (1992) provide a useful discussion about core and peripheral cognitive structures in organizations and how these are involved in strategy formulation. According to Lyles and Schwenk, 'firms are characterized by core elements of a generalized knowledge framework about

Table 8.3   *Organizational level of analysis cognitive models*

	Causes	Description	Consequences
Papers	Lyles and Schwenk (1992) Walsh and Ungson (1991) Daft and Weick (1984)	Lyles and Schwenk (1992) Fiegenbaum et al. (1996) Dutton et al. (1989) Albert and Whetten (1985)	Lyles and Schwenk (1992) Dutton et al. (1989) Dutton and Dukerich (1991)
Key concepts/ findings	Organizational knowledge structures Organizational memory Organizations as interpretive structures	Strategic reference points Organizational identity	Images and identity lead to organizational adaptation Cognitive dimensions lead to action

which there is widespread agreement. The core facilitates understanding about the firm's general purpose, mission and competitors' (1992: 160). In contrast to the core, more peripheral elements of organizational knowledge structures are characterized by less agreement and concern an organization's subgoals and the operational means for achieving them.

Lyles and Schwenk suggest that core cognitive structures involve basic strategic beliefs about an organization's position in its industry or field, various recipes for dealing with clients or customers, and a consensual understanding of the identity and attributes of competitors. In their case analysis of a consulting firm, for example, Lyles and Schwenk observed that the firm's core beliefs held that the firm was moving away from manufacturing consulting to a broader base of activities that was split evenly among international and domestic markets. The firm's consultants believed that their role was to provide sophisticated and increasingly non-manufacturing clients with a set of best 'experts' that would sell the client on the firm. In Lyles and Schwenk's model, core beliefs such as these are deeply embedded within the strategy formulation process and influence a firm's strategy by shaping perceptions of opportunities and threats and by serving as background assumptions and frames of reference during problem sensing and definition.

A number of researchers have examined the nature and influence of core cognitive structures in some detail by focusing on organizational beliefs about strategic issues (Dutton et al., 1989), organizational identities (Albert and Whetten, 1985; Dutton and Dukerich, 1991), and strategic reference points (Fiegenbaum et al., 1996). With respect to strategic issues, Dutton et al. argued that organizational members must 'sort the wheat from the chaff' by isolating the key conditions and

concerns that impact the functioning of their organization. These researchers studied the types of issue beliefs held consensually by employees of two departments in a public agency in New York City. Dutton et al. observed that issue beliefs tended to cluster into three categories: external issues, internal issues, and issues involving the interaction of external environment and internal organizational processes. External issues encompassed such topics as rivalry and competition, technology, international trade, and social changes. Internal issues focused on funding, staffing, morale, and culture. Interactive issues focused on infrastructure, image, and the agency's mission and role. On the basis of these content categories, Dutton et al. concluded that issue beliefs vary along a number of dimensions such as abstractness, locus, controllability, immediacy, and impactfulness, and that these dimensions significantly influenced the time and attention given to an issue by the organization.

Organizational 'identity' is a second type of organizational cognitive structure that has been implicated in the strategy process. According to Albert and Whetten, 'Organizations define who they are by creating or invoking classification schemes and locating themselves within them' (1985: 267). An organization's identity is a belief structure that summarizes what members view as the organization's central, enduring, and distinctive characteristics. Albert and Whetten suggest that these characteristics can be quite varied and include organizational ideologies, management philosophy, culture, ritual, and strategic predispositions toward risk, rivalry, and cooperation. Rather than being a completely deterministic cognitive structure that represents a singular identity over time, Albert and Whetten imply that an organization's identity is really a pool of cognitive representations that can be selected from according to the identity demands of a situation. In their words, 'there is no one best statement of identity, but rather, multiple equally valid statements relative to different audiences for different purposes. From our point of view, the formulation of a statement of identity is more a political-strategic act than an intentional construction of a scientific taxonomy' (1985: 268).

Dutton and Dukerich (1991) examined how the collective identity of the New York Port Authority influenced the organization's response to the issue of homelessness in New York City. Dutton and Dukerich's interview protocol elicited identity statements that suggested that employees viewed the Port Authority as professional, ethical, scandal free, altruistic, and high quality. Employees also believed that the organization was a 'can do' organization in which loyal employees and a family atmosphere promoted superior service to local citizens. Dutton and Dukerich then went on to trace how this situated identity influenced the course of the Authority's response to the homeless population over a period of several years. They observed that the Port Authority's identity induced employees to view the homeless issue as a threat that elicited negative emotions because the presence of homeless individuals in bus terminals and other facilities was inconsistent with their view of the organization as professional, ethical, and action-oriented. When the problem of homelessness proved intractable, the Authority responded in its typically action-oriented way to a problem, but the resulting adaptation was constrained by the organization's identity as an ethical entity. Rather than simply banishing the homeless from its facilities and turning them out onto the streets, the Authority subsidized 'drop in' facilities that gave temporary shelter to those in need. This course of action attracted favorable publicity, and eventually positioned the Authority as a leader in the handling of the homeless population in the region.

Dutton and Dukerich's analysis of the Port Authority's response to homelessness reveals that embedded in identity beliefs are implicit assumptions about 'who we are' in relation to other organizations in the environment and in relation to the Authority's own perceived characteristics across time. Port Authority employees, for example, defined their organization as a transportation rather than a social service agency, a definition that delimited the scope of their response to the homeless problem by inducing the agency to subsidize drop-in centers that were managed by other organizations rather than managing such centers themselves. These implicit categorizations defined the relevant domain for the organization's activities and established a plausible set of external 'strategic reference points' that provided useful and informative interorganizational comparisons.

According to Fiegenbaum et al. (1996), a strategic reference point is a performance target that is embedded in a reference matrix defined by the three dimensions of internal capabilities, external conditions, and time. An organization's identity is centrally involved in creating particular reference points because any answer to the question, 'Who are we?' necessarily dimensionalizes that organization's reference matrix within a space of beliefs about internal (organizational capabilities), external (peer organizations), and temporal (future threats and opportunities) variables. Fiegenbaum et al. (1996) suggest that organizations with consensual and multidimensional reference points will consistently outperform organizations with contested and simple referents that myopically emphasize only selective aspects of internal and external targets.

All of the above work conceptualizes organizations as interpretation systems in which retention mechanisms store collective strategic beliefs about firms and their environments. This conceptualization highlights the fact that strategy is not simply a top management task. Instead, an organization's strategy reflects, and is constrained by, member ideologies, identities, beliefs about threats and opportunities, and key internal and external referents that guide problem formulation, the process of strategizing, and the choice of performance targets. This interpretive conceptualization of the strategy process has its roots in a wholistic view of strategy as an emergent activity with both bottom up and top down components, a process in which organizational actors collectively create and enact a strategic space.

And yet, an organization is not a strategically isolated entity. It is one element in a broader population of organizations, each of which is using the others as a reference point for their own strategizing and sensemaking activities. This industry-level sensemaking must be incorporated into any discussion of the cognitive bases of strategy. It is yet another level of cognitive analysis that must be explored and articulated, and a level to which we now turn.

INDUSTRY COGNITIVE COMMUNITIES AND THE STRATEGY PROCESS

An examination of collective beliefs in industry contexts should be anchored in a micro theory of market relationships and market making. Because most cognitive researchers take an actor-centered perspective on population-level beliefs, a useful micro theory would be one that assumes that industries are social constructions that emerge from the interplay of cognition and action over time (Table 8.4). In this regard, White (1981, 1992) suggests that producer markets are networks of actors who are bound together in equivocal transactions that are stabilized by shared assumptions and frames-of-reference. Market networks can be further subdivided on the basis of two identity constructs – a 'producer' community and a 'buyer' community. An industry network evolves around activities and artifacts that are traded across these two communities. Activities and artifacts are sets of informational cues that attach to interpretations that become commonly accepted and taken for granted. Over time, as social interactions occur within and between producer and buyer communities, an explicit population language evolves to capture aspects of what is being traded, the terms of trade, and the competitive regime controlling strategic choices among the actors involved. These nomenclatures, and their associated cognitive structures, are what we call 'industry belief systems'.

Industry belief systems are created and shared among firms by means of stories. Stories are important sensemaking tools within social systems (Weick, 1995; White, 1992). Through conversations among and between buyers, producers, and other industry actors (journalists, stock analysts, etc.), stories externalize internal cognitive representations and put them into play as public interpretations of industry events, conditions, and accepted practices that can be either accepted or contested. Once they become publicly available, such interpretations are grist for institutionalizing processes in which they are internalized by industry firms and incorporated into their

existing operating routines and strategies. As DiMaggio and Powell (1991) noted, the institutionalization of cognitive models is aided by any number of social processes such as rote imitation of other organizations, the coercive influence of powerful central authorities and legal environments, and expertise that has become codified and diffused through formalized professions. Regardless of the institutionalizing mechanisms involved, however, the result is that industry communities are characterized by a set of shared beliefs that consistently shape the strategies and actions of member firms. Research suggests that industry belief systems are comprised of at least three constituent belief types.

The first type consists of beliefs about the boundaries of markets and competitive interactions. As White (1981) suggested, a market is a small number social construction enacted when firms observe each other's actions and define unique product positions vis-à-vis each other. The key sensemaking task is to collectively establish a 'frame of comparability' (Leifer, 1985) that defines some producers to be members of the market while excluding others. Frames of comparability are often evident in statements of identity such as 'We're a knitwear producer' (Porac et al., 1995) or 'We're in the grocery business' (Hodgkinson and Johnson, 1994). Given that any single producer 'defines its role in terms of the similarities and differences it has with respect to other producers' (White and Eccles, 1987: 984), boundary beliefs emerge to stabilize markets by locking in inter-firm comparisons to create a reproducible competitive order.

That such beliefs do, in fact, emerge within industry communities has been well established in a number of empirical studies (see Hodgkinson, 1997 for a complete review). One well known example of this research is Reger and Huff's (1993) investigation of 'cognitive strategic groups' within the Chicago banking community. The notion of strategic group emerged in the management literature to recognize that industries tend to be stratified into multiple sets of firms whose members pursue similar business strategies. Slanting their study in a cognitive direction, Reger and Huff (1993) mapped the similarities and differences among 18 Chicago banks as perceived by key strategists in the industry. Through structured interviews, Reger and Huff asked 23 executives from six of these

Table 8.4 *Cognitive communities level of analysis cognitive models*

	Causes	Description	Consequences
Papers	White (1981, 1992)	Porac et al. (1995)	Phillips (1994)
	DiMaggio and Powell (1991)	Porac et al. (1989)	Benjamin and Podolny (1999)
	Fombrun and Shanley (1990)	Phillips (1994)	Porac et al. (1989)
		Abrahamson and Fairchild (1999)	
		Fombrun and Shanley (1990)	
Key concepts/ findings	Market identities	Boundary beliefs	Industry cultures found in wine, museum, grocery and knitwear contexts
	Institutionalizing processes	Industry recipes	
		Reputational structures	Predicted rivalry and cognitive network influences on outcomes

banks to compare each of the 18 banks with each other and to specify the strategic dimensions along which the banks were similar or different. The results suggest that bank executives parse the local banking industry into three separable groups of firms: large money center banks concentrating on wholesale and commercial activities in a national or global market, regional mid-market banks that focus on local small businesses and consumers, and a miscellaneous group that includes banks of different kinds that are hard to categorize.

Reger and Huff's results support the claim that boundary beliefs emerge within industries to segment firms into market networks. More direct evidence for this market structuring role comes from Porac et al.'s (1995) study of Scottish knitwear producers. Porac et al. asked knitwear executives to rate their firms on a number of relevant product and organizational dimensions. Respondents were also asked to check off from an exhaustive list of industry members those knitwear firms that they considered competitors and whom they regularly monitored. Porac et al. then clustered the firms on the basis of their attributes and uncovered six distinct clusters of attributes that suggested six different product markets exist in the industry. These six markets are associated with distinct 'rivalry networks' in the sense that producers embedded within a given market tend to view each other as rivals and pay little attention to the firms in the other product groups. Firms rarely cite more than five to nine competitors, and these competitors are almost always firms within their own product category. Porac et al. concluded that the rivalry networks they observed in the industry seem to be stable

cognitive orderings that structure competition in the industry. These networks derive from a collective 'industry model' (Porac et al., 1995) that is partially shared with others in the same industry community. The knitwear model channels the attention of actors toward firms that are embedded within the same product space such that rivalry networks are denser within understood market boundaries than they are across boundaries.

The second component of industry belief systems is what Spender (1989) called 'industry recipes'. By channeling the attentional focus of organizations toward comparable peers, consensual boundary beliefs create the conditions for the development of industry specific logics for action vis-à-vis competitors, suppliers, customers, the capital markets, and regulatory agencies. The notion of recipe reflects the fact that such beliefs constitute rule systems for reasoning through strategic problems and justifying organizational action across a community of firms. Research suggests that these industry-level rule systems exist at different levels of depth and articulation. For example, some researchers have viewed industries as cultural milieus and have studied the stable and fundamental assumptions that shape the worldview of industry members. A good example of this type of research is Phillips' (1994) study of wineries and art museums. Through unstructured ethnographic interviews with a variety of employees from firms within each industry, Phillips assessed industry differences in assumptions about the relationship between the industry and the environment, the origins of truth, the nature of time and space, the nature of innate human qualities, the purpose of work, and work relationships. Her results suggest that employees in the museum industry orient towards an evangelical educational mission with respect to their constituents, emphasize formal education rather than experience as a basis for expertise, and desire collaborative and egalitarian work relationships. Wineries, on the other hand, identify more with a geographical region, consider experience more important than formal education, and prefer work relationships to be organized hierarchically along distinct chains of command.

While Phillips chose to study industry variation in deep seated conceptions of time, space, professional identifications, and work relationships, others have explored middle range beliefs about the cause–effect relationships influencing business outcomes (Porac et al., 1989; Spender, 1989). Porac et al. (1989), for example, studied the small subset of Scottish knitwear producers that manufacture very expensive cashmere garments for sale at exclusive retail shops around the world. These firms are bound together by a very stable collective identity as purveyors of 'classically elegant' knitwear. Porac et al. found evidence for a consensual business model that emphasizes production expertise and manufacturing flexibility over high fashion design. This model locks these firms into producing certain types of garments which are then sold to particular kinds of high-end retail shops that cater to wealthy consumers preferring classic clothing designs. Porac et al. suggest that this industry recipe is self-reinforcing and taken for granted, and is contested only by outsiders who come into the industry with different business logics and beliefs about knitwear production, design, and marketing.

Both Phillips (1994) and Porac et al. (1989) studied the relatively enduring components of industry recipes that create bedrock justifications for organizational action over time. Abrahamson (1991, 1996, 1997; Abrahamson and Fairchild, 1999) has shown, however, that certain elements of industry beliefs are in constant flux, and that transient logics come and go according to the fads and fashions of the time. Abrahamson and Fairchild (1999), for example, studied the rise and decline of the quality circle logic during the period from 1974 to 1995. These researchers argued that managerial fads are generated through market stories passed along by consultants, the popular press, and academic journals. Using counts of articles written about quality circles as their dependent variable, Abrahamson and Fairchild

traced the pattern of quality circle discourse over time. Their results suggest that after a quiet period of gestation during the late 1970s, the quality circle logic exploded into the consciousness of American management in the early 1980s. After peaking in 1983, however, discussions about quality circles entered a decade-long decline until, by 1995, the frequency of topical stories had returned to the levels evident in the 1970s. Abrahamson and Fairchild provide evidence that this popularity curve in quality circle discourse reflects the transient acceptance and subsequent rejection of the logic over time.

The third component of industry belief systems consists of the reputation orderings that develop from the social coding and interpretation of interorganizational differences in performance over time. Stable and consensual industry boundaries and taken-for-granted strategic recipes together create the conditions for measuring and evaluating the performance of firms within an industry. These evaluations take place at different levels and encompass different metrics. At the level of face-to-face interactions, informal assessments of product quality permeate most industries, and industry insiders usually have quite detailed status rankings for judging one organization's outputs against another's. In the Scottish knitwear industry, for example, Porac et al. (1995) reported that managers have finely calibrated mental models for comparing the products of their firms. What appear to be identical garments to a novice are in fact easily identified by managers as having been manufactured by two different firms in the industry, each with their own technical proclivities and competencies. Similarly, Benjamin and Podolny (1999) noted the subtleties of California wine appellations as quality markers among producers and wine connoisseurs. These informal technical metrics are consistent with White's (1981) claim that producers in a market eventually structure themselves into role positions that reflect an implied quality ordering. This ordering, and the attentional interlocks that support it, are the defining features of a producer's market from an interpretivist's perspective.

Insider quality assessments, however, are only weak signals to outsiders such as customers, financial investors, and government regulators who are often not privy to the specialized technical nomenclatures of an industry. As Fombrun (1996) notes, the informational needs of these outsiders have provided the impetus for a multibillion dollar information infrastructure that amplifies and refracts weak quality signals for broader public consumption. Rating agencies, consumer testing laboratories, enthusiast magazines, securities analysts, and news agencies all play a role in this refraction process. These evaluators provide alternative assessments of firm quality using metrics constructed for their own purposes. To the extent that these metrics attract publicity and widespread public appeal, however, firms within an industry must recognize the reality of the resulting reputational order and respond accordingly.

Research on reputation and status orderings within industries has been steadily accumulating (see Fombrun, 1996 for a review) as organizational scholars explore both their causes and consequences. A good example of research examining the former is Fombrun and Shanley (1990). Each year *Fortune* magazine solicits ratings of corporate quality from outside directors, executives, and securities analysts familiar with different industries. These ratings are then summarized by ranking companies in different business sectors. Using data from *Fortune*'s 1985 rankings, as well as company information obtained from the COMPUSTAT database, Fombrun and Shanley sought to account for reputational differences among the 119 firms in their sample. Their results suggest that firms with better public reputations are more profitable, have lower market risk indicators, spend more on advertising, and are larger in size than less reputable firms. Fombrun and Shanley concluded that both economic (profitability, market risk) and non-economic (visibility) factors are involved in shaping a firm's perceived status among informed observers.

A study of California wine producers by Benjamin and Podolny (1999) is a good example of research examining the consequences of an industry's reputational order. Benjamin and Podolny reason that a firm's reputation in an industry is more than an epiphenomenon generated through public appraisals, that it has implications for the opportunities available to the firm and, in particular, for the prices that the firm can charge for its products. They distinguish between the quality of a firm's wines, as indexed by the judgments of wine experts, and a firm's status, which they suggest is a function of a wine's appellation linking it to a particular growing region in the state. Quality, status, and price data for a 10-year period were collected from various guides to California wines and from the US government. After controlling for a number of non-reputational variables such as the age and size of the producing winery and the cost of the varietal grapes in the bottle, Benjamin and Podolny found that wines of higher perceived quality and status garner higher prices in the marketplace. They conclude that a winery's position in the reputational hierarchy of the industry influences the amount of attention given to its wines and the general regard that consumers and wine experts have for these products. Because they command more attention in the marketplace, and their wines are more highly prized, highly reputable wineries are able to command a higher price for their outputs.

Boundary beliefs, industry recipes, and reputational orderings together represent the cognitive foundation of industry communities. In a very real sense, they are the cognitive cement that binds firms into identifiable populations with unique logics of action and status orderings that reflect the relative skill of member firms in enacting these logics. As such, they form a macro context for the strategic actions of individual firms that is both enabling and constraining. Industry beliefs are enabling because they are a pool of ideas and routines from which individual firms can draw in building their idiosyncratic resource positions within the community. No firm starts as a blank slate since cognitive models of successful action are available to copy, refine, and reformulate in creative ways. But industry beliefs are also constraining since they create expectations and norms about the appropriate ways of conducting business. These expectations are very much the price of admission into an industry community, and firms must be prepared to align their strategies in ways that conform to such expectations or risk being perceived as illegitimate by industry stakeholders. It is this enabling and constraining dialectic that produces what Porac et al. (1989) label the 'competitive cusp' – the thin edge between being different enough from the core tendencies in an industry to capture better than average returns and being similar enough to other industry members to be perceived as a legitimate actor within the relevant market space. As Deephouse (1999) notes, at the level of individual firms, the cognitive macro context of an industry necessitates a strategic 'balance' between differentiation and isomorphism that is quite simple to conceptualize but quite difficult to implement profitably in practice.

CONCLUSIONS AND FUTURE RESEARCH DIRECTIONS

Although cognitive theories of organizing have been fundamental to management and organizational studies at least since the work of March and Simon (1958), it has only been in the last 15 years that serious efforts have been made to systematize and understand the intersection of cognition and business strategy. The literature exploring this topic has literally exploded within the past decade, and although cognitive strategy researchers are continuously refining and altering what they study, the volume of work in this general area shows no signs of abating. In this chapter, we have reviewed key research findings that explore the intersection of cognition and strategy at four different levels of analysis: individual manager, top management team, organization, and industry population. We will use this last section of our chapter to reflect briefly on the summary characteristics of the work that we have reviewed and also to anticipate what the near-term future might hold for additional research in this area.

Cognitive strategy research broadly concerns the strategy formulation and implementation process that unfolds as organizations adapt to ever changing environmental conditions. At the same time, however, not all research on strategizing is 'cognitive' in nature. The research that we have reviewed above is distinct from other behavioural analyses of the strategy process in three ways. First, and perhaps most importantly, it is characterized by a clear emphasis on dimensionalizing and mapping the cognitive structures that give meaning to strategic environments. Concepts such as 'schemas', 'frames', 'categories', 'cognitive maps', 'belief systems', and 'mental models' have proliferated in the cognitive strategy literature as researchers have sought to incorporate insights from general cognitive science into their explorations of the strategizing process. While the proliferation of terms used to describe the content of strategic knowledge is sometimes confusing, this variety should not obscure the fact that tremendous strides have been made during the past decade to articulate the intangible and hard to measure contents of the strategic mind. These efforts have produced cognitive mapping techniques and research findings that are both theoretically rich and practically useful.

Second, while the terms used to describe strategic knowledge structures are quite varied, a key concept that binds all such terms together is 'strategic interpretation'. Interpretation is the act of carving out meaning from ambiguous cues and is the very core of the sensemaking process (Weick, 1995). It is a fundamental assumption of all strategic cognition research that knowledge structures provide a set of lens for strategists to make sense of their firms' strategic predispositions, competitive position, and internal capabilities. These lens are essentially cognitive filters that admit certain bits of information into the strategizing process while excluding others. It is the recognition and measurement of this filtering role of strategic knowledge that is truly a unique and important contribution of cognitive strategy research.

Third, cognitive strategy research has clearly evolved around what we view as a homogeneity–heterogeneity dialectic. The core issue in this dialectic has been the degree to which strategic knowledge structures are consensual across actors in and between organizations. On the one hand, it has been assumed by many cognitive researchers that strategic knowledge is social in nature and provides collective interpretive frameworks that bind individuals together into top management teams, organizations, and industries. On the other hand, empirical measurements of strategic knowledge structures often find significant disagreement among actors in how they interpret the business contexts in which they operate. To make matters even more complicated, it is clear that extreme homogeneity and extreme heterogeneity both have positive and negative consequences for top management teams, organizations, and industries, and research has yet to uncover the precise tradeoffs involved.

Although these three characteristics have distinguished cognitive from non-cognitive strategy research in the past, we anticipate that the research literature will evolve in slightly different directions in the future. First, we anticipate that there will be a shift in emphasis from the static mapping of strategic knowledge structures in a given business context to understanding the dynamic evolution of such structures over time and in multiple contexts. Cognitive change is substantially more difficult to conceptualize and measure. The progress made in developing cognitive mapping techniques over the past decade will be put to good use in more dynamic ways in the future.

A second, and related, trajectory for future research will be a movement away from studying single cognitive constructs (categorizations, identities, recipes, etc.) at a given point in time toward exploring the interactions of different cognitive structures over multiple points in time. In the case of industry belief systems, for example, researchers will be less interested in mapping and understanding the nature of boundary beliefs alone, and will be more interested in understanding how strong boundary beliefs create the conditions for the development of status orderings among firms defined within those boundaries. In other words, researchers will begin to actively search for the situated interactions of multiple types of knowledge that endow the strategizing process with much of its complexity.

REFERENCES

Abrahamson, E. (1991) 'Managerial fads and fashions: diffusion and rejection of innovations', *Academy of Management Review*, 16: 586–612.

Abrahamson, E. (1996) 'Management fashion', *Academy of Management Review*, 21: 254–85.

Abrahamson, E. (1997) 'The emergence and prevalence of employee management rhetorics: the effects of long waves, labor unions, and turnover, 1875 to 1992', *Academy of Management Journal*, 40: 491–533.

Abrahamson, E. and Fairchild, G. (1999) 'Management fashion: lifecycles, triggers, and collective learning processes', *Administrative Science Quarterly*, 44: 708–40.

Abrahamson, E. and Fombron, C. (1994) 'Macro-cultures: determinants and consequences', *Academy of Management Review*, 19: 728–53.

Agle, B. R. and Sonnenfeld, J. A. (1994) 'Charismatic chief executive officers: are they more effective? An empirical test of charismatic leadership theory', *Academy of Management Best Papers and Proceedings*, 2–6.

Albert, S. and Whetten, D. A. (1985) 'Organizational identity', in L. L. Cummings and B. M. Staw (eds), *Research in Organizational Behavior*, Vol. 7. Greenwich, CT: JAI Press. pp. 263–95.

Axelrod, R. M. (ed.) (1976) *The Structure of Decision: Cognitive Maps of Political Elites*. Princeton, NJ: Princeton University Press.

Bantel, K. A. and Jackson, S. E. (1989) 'Top management and innovations in banking: does the composition of the top team make a difference?', *Strategic Management Journal*, 10: 107–24.

Barnes, J. H. (1984) 'Cognitive biases and their impact on strategic planning', *Strategic Management Journal*, 5: 129–37.

Barr, P. S., Stimpert, J. L. and Huff, A. S. (1992) 'Cognitive change, strategic action and organisational renewal', *Strategic Management Journal*, 13: 15–36.

Benjamin, B. A. and Podolny, J. M. (1999) 'Status, quality, and social order in the California wine industry', *Administrative Science Quarterly*, 44: 563–89.

Bougon, M., Weick, K. and Binkhorst, D. (1977) 'Cognition in organizations: an analysis of the Utrecht Jazz Orchestra', *Administrative Science Quarterly*, 22: 606–39.

Burt, R. S. (1980) 'Cooptive corporate actor networks: a reconsideration of interlocking directorates involving American manufacturing', *Administrative Science Quarterly*, 25: 557–82.

Calori, R., Johnson, G. and Sarnin, P. (1994a) 'CEOs' cognitive maps and the scope of the organization', *Strategic Management Journal*, 15: 437–57.

Calori, R., Lubatkin, M. and Very, P. (1994b) 'Control mechanisms in cross-border acquisitions: an international comparison', *Organization Studies*, 15: 361–79.

Daft, R. L. and Weick, K. E. (1984) 'Toward a model of organizations as interpretation systems', *Academy of Management Review*, 9: 284–95.

Dearborn, D. C. and Simon, H. A. (1958) 'Selective perception: a note on the departmental identification of executives', *Sociometry*, June: 140–8.

Deephouse, D. L. (1999) 'To be different, or to be the same? It's a question (and theory) of strategic balance', *Strategic Management Journal*, 20: 147–66.

Dess, G. G. and Keats, B. W. (1987) 'Environmental assessment and organisational performance? An exploratory field study', *Academy of Management Proceedings*, 21–25.

Di Maggio, P. and Powell, W. W. (1983) 'The iron cage revisited: institutional isomorphism and collective rationality in organisational fields', *American Sociological Review*, 48: 147–60.

Di Maggio, P. and Powell, W. W. (1985) 'The structure of corporate ownership: causes and consequences', *Journal of Political Economy*, 3: 1155–77.

Di Maggio, P. and Powell, W. W. (1991) 'The iron cage revisited: institutional isomorphism and collective rationality in organizational fields', in W. W. Powell and P. Di Maggio (eds), *The New Institutionalism in Organizational Analysis*. Chicago: University of Chicago Press. pp. 63–82.

Dill, W. R. (1958) 'Environment as an influence on managerial activity', *Administrative Science Quarterly*, 2: 409–43.

Dill, W. R. (1962) 'The impact of environment on organizational development', in S. Mailik and E. H. Van Ness (eds), *Concepts and Issues in Administrative Behavior*. Englewood Cliffs, NJ: Prentice-Hall. pp. 94–109.

Dutton, J. E. and Dukerich, J. M. (1991) 'Keeping an eye on the mirror: the role of image and identity in organisational adaptation', *Academy of Management Journal*, 34: 517–54.

Dutton, J. E. and Duncan, R. B. (1987) 'The creation of momentum for change through the process of strategic issue diagnosis', *Strategic Management Journal*, 8: 279–85.

Dutton, J. E. and Jackson, S. (1987) 'Categorising strategic issues: links to organizational action', *Academy of Management Review*, 12: 76–90.

Dutton, J. E., Walton, E. J. and Abrahamson, E. (1989) 'Important dimensions of strategic issues: separating the wheat from the chaff', *Journal of Management Studies*, 26: 379–96.

Eden, C. (1988) 'Cognitive mapping', *European Journal of Operational Research*, 36: 1–13.

Eden, C., Ackerman, F. and Cropper, S. (1992) 'The analysis of cause maps', *Journal of Management Studies*, 29: 309–24.

Fahey, L. and Naranayan, V. K. (1989) 'Linking changes in revealed causal maps and environmental change: an empirical study', *Journal of Management Studies*, 26: 361–78.

Fiegenbaum, A., Hart, S. and Schendel, D. E. (1996) 'Strategic reference point theory', *Strategic Management Journal*, 17: 219–35.

Finkelstein, S. (1992) 'Power in top management teams: dimensions, measurement and validation', *Academy of Management Journal*, 35: 505–38.

Finkelstein, S. and Hambrick, D. C. (1990) 'Top management team tenure and organisational outcomes: the moderating role of managerial discretion', *Administrative Science Quarterly*, 35: 484–503.

Finkelstein, S. and Hambrick, D. C. (1996) *Strategic Leadership: Top Executives and their Effects on Organisations*. St. Paul, MN: West Publishing.

Fiol, C. M. (1989) 'A semiotic analysis of corporate language: organizational boundaries and joint venturing', *Administrative Science Quarterly*, 34: 277–303.

Fiol (1993) 'Consensus, diversity and learning in organizations', *Organization Science*, 5: 403–20.

Fombrun, C. J. (1992) *Turning Points: Creating Strategic Change in Corporations*. New York: McGraw-Hill.

Fombrun, C. J. (1994) *Leading Corporate Change*. New York: McGraw-Hill.

Fombrun, C. J. (1994) 'Taking on strategy, 1-2-3', in J. A. C. Baum and J. V. Singh (eds), *Evolutionary Dynamics of Organizations*. New York: Oxford University Press. pp. 199–204.

Fombrun, C. J. (1996) *'Reputation: Realizing Value from the Corporate Image*. Boston, MA: Harvard Business School Press.

Fombrun, C. and Shanley, M. (1990) 'What's in a name? Reputation building and corporate strategy', *Academy of Management Journal*, 33: 233–58.

Ginsberg, A. (1989) 'Construing the business portfolio: a cognitive model of diversification', *Journal of Management Studies*, 26: 417–38.

Ginsberg, A. and Venkatraman, N. (1992) 'Investing in new information technology: the role of competitive posture and issue diagnosis', *Strategic Management Journal*, 13: 37–53.

Gripsrud, G. and Gronhaug, K. (1985) 'Structure and strategy in grocery retailing: a sociometric approach', *Journal of Industrial Economics*, 33: 339–47.

Gupta, A. K. and Govindarajan, V. (1984) 'Business unit strategy, managerial characteristics and business unit effectiveness at strategy implementation', *Academy of Management Journal*, 27: 25–41.

Hambrick, D. C. (1989) 'Putting top managers back into the strategy picture', *Strategic Management Journal*, 10: 5–15.

Hambrick, D. C. and d'Aveni, R. A. (1992) 'Top team deterioration as part of the downward spiral of large corporate bankruptcies', *Management Science*, 38: 1445–66.

Hambrick, D. C. and Mason, P. (1984) 'Upper echelons: the organisation as a reflection of its top managers', *Academy of Management Review*, 9: 193–206.

Hill, R. C. and Levenhagen, M. (1995) 'Metaphors and mental models: sensing and sense-giving in innovative and entrepreneurial activities', *Journal of Management*, 21: 1057–74.

Hodgkinson, G. P. (1997) 'The cognitive analysis of competitive structures: a review and critique', *Human Relations*, 50: 625–54.

Hodgkinson, G. P. and Johnson, G. (1994) 'Exploring the mental models of competitive strategists: the case for a processual approach', *Journal of Management Studies*, 31: 525–51.

Hogarth, R. M. (1980) *Decision and Choice*. Chichester and New York: John Wiley.

Huff, A. S. (1982) 'Industry influences and strategy reformulation', *Strategic Management Journal*, 3: 119–31.

Huff, A. S. (ed.) (1990) *Mapping Strategic Thought*. Chichester and New York: John Wiley.

Hunt, M. M. (1982) *The Universe Within: A New Science Explores the Human Mind*. New York: Simon and Schuster.

Jackson, S. E. (1992) 'Consequence of group composition for the interpersonal dynamics of strategic issue processing', *Advances in Strategic Management*, 8: 345–82.

Kahneman, D., Slovic, P. and Tversky, A. (eds) (1982) *Judgement Under Uncertainty: Heuristics and Biases*. Cambridge: Cambridge University Press.

Keats, B. W. and Hitt, M. A. (1988) 'A causal model of linkages among environmental dimensions, macro-organisational characteristics and performance', *Academy of Management Journal*, 31: 570–98.

Kelly, G. A. (1956) *The Psychology of Personal Constructs*. Vols. I and II. New York: W. W. Norton.

Kets de Vries, M. and Miller, D. (1984) 'Neurotic style and organisational pathology', *Strategic Management Journal*, 5: 35–55.

Kiesler, S. and Sproull, L. (1982) 'Managerial responses to changing environments: perspectives in problem-sensing from social cognition', *Administrative Science Quarterly*, 27: 548–70.

Leifer, E. M. (1985) 'Markets as mechanisms: using a role structure', *Social Forces*, 64: 442–72.

Lorsch, J. W. (1989) *Pawns or Potentates: The Reality of America's Boards*. Boston: Harvard Business School.

Lyles, M. A. and Schwenk, C. R. (1992) 'Top management strategy and organisational knowledge structures', *Journal of Management Studies*, 29: 155–74.

March, J. G. and Simon, H. A. (1958) *Organisations*. New York: John Wiley.

Mason, R. O. and Mitroff, I. I. (1984) *Challenging Strategic Planning Assumptions*. New York: John Wiley.

Meyer, A. D. (1982) 'How ideologies supplant formal structures and shape responses to environments', *Journal of Management Studies*, 19: 45–61.

Miller, G. A. (1956) 'The magic number seven plus or minus two: some limits on our capacity for processing information', *Psychological Review*, 64: 81–97.

Mintzberg, H. (1976) 'Planning on the left side and managing on the right', *Harvard Business Review*, July: 49–58.

Mintzberg, H. (1979) *The Structuring of Organisations*. Englewood Cliffs, NJ: Prentice-Hall.

Mintzberg, H. (1983) *Power In and Around Organisations*. Englewood Cliffs, NJ: Prentice-Hall.

Moore, P. G. and Thomas, H. (1975) 'Measuring uncertainty', *Omega*.

Pettigrew, A. M. (1973) *The Politics of Organisational Decision-Making*. London: Tavistock.

Pettigrew, A. M. (1985) *The Awakening Giant*. Oxford: Blackwell.

Pettigrew, A. M. (1992) 'On studying managerial elites', *Strategic Management Journal*, 13: 163–82.

Phillips, M. E. (1994) 'Industry mindsets: exploring the cultures of two macro-organisational settings', *Organisation Science*, 5: 384–402.

Porac, J. F. and Thomas, H. (1990) 'Taxonomic mental models in competitor definition', *Academy of Management Review*, 15: 224–40.

Porac, J. F., Thomas, H. and Baden-Fuller, C. (1989) 'Competitive groups as cognitive communities: the case of the Scottish knitwear industry', *Journal of Management Studies*, 26: 397–416.

Porac, J. F., Thomas, H., Wilson, F., Paton, D. and Konfer, A. (1995) 'Rivalry and the industry model of Scottish knitwear producers', *Administrative Science Quarterly*, 40: 203–27.

Prahalad, C. K. and Bettis, R. A. (1986) 'The dominant logic: a new linkage between diversity and performance', *Strategic Management Journal*, 7: 485–501.

Reed, S. K. (1982) *Cognition: Theory and Applications*. Monterey, CA: Brooks/Cole.

Reger, R. K. (1988) 'Competitive positioning in the Chicago banking market: mapping the mind of the strategist', Unpublished doctoral dissertation, University of Illinois at Urbana-Champaign.

Reger, R. K. and Huff, A. S. (1993) 'Strategic groups: a cognitive perspective', *Strategic Management Journal*, 14: 103–24.

Schneider, S. C. (1989) 'Strategy formulation: the impact of national culture', *Organization Studies*, 10: 149–68.

Schwenk, C. R. (1984) 'Cognitive simplification processes in strategic decision-making', *Strategic Management Journal*, 5: 111–28.

Schwenk, C. R. (1985) 'Management illusions and biases: their impact on strategic planning', *Long Range Planning*, 18(5): 74–80.

Schwenk, C. R. and Thomas, H. (1983) 'Formulating the mess: the role of decision aids in problem formulation', *Omega*, 11: 239–52.

Simon, H. A. (1955) 'A behavioural model of rational choice', *Quarterly Journal of Economics*, 69: 99–118.

Simon, H. A. (1956a) 'Dynamic programming under uncertainty with a quadratic criterion function', *Econometrica*, 24: 74–81.

Simon, H. A. (1956b) 'Rational choice and the structure of the environment', *Psychological Review*, 63: 129–38.

Simon, H. A. (1956c) 'A comparison of game theory and learning theory', *Psychometrika*, 21: 267–72.

Simon, H. A. (1957) *Models of Man*. New York: Wiley.

Sims, H. P. and Gioia, D. A. (eds) (1986) *The Thinking Organization: Dynamics of Organisational Social Cognition*. San Francisco: Jossey-Bass.

Spender, J. C. (1989) *Industry Recipes: An Inquiry into the Nature and Sources of Managerial Judgment*. Cambridge, MA: Basil Blackwell.

Starbuck, W. H. and Milliken, F. J. (1988) 'Challenger: fine-tuning the odds until something breaks', *Journal of Management Studies*, 25: 319–40.

Stubbart, C. I. (1989) 'Managerial cognition: a missing link in strategic management research', *Journal of Management Studies*, 26: 323–47.

Tversky, A. and Kahneman, D. (1974) 'Judgement under uncertainty, heuristics and biases', *Science*, 198: 1124–31.

Walsh, J. P. (1995) 'Managerial and organisational cognition: notes from a trip down memory lane', *Organisation Science*, 6: 280–321.

Walsh, J. P. and Ungson, G. R. (1991) 'Organisational memory', *Academy of Management Review*, 16: 57–91.

Weick, K. E. (1979) 'Cognitive processes in organisations', *Research in Organisational Behavior*, 41–74.

Weick, K. E. (1983) 'Managerial thought in the context of action', in S. Srivastana (ed.), *The Executive Mind*. San Francisco, CA: Jossey-Bass.

Weick, K. E. (1995) *Sense-Making in Organisations*. Thousand Oaks, CA: Sage Publications.

Weick, K. E. and Bougon, M. G. (1986) 'Organisations as cognitive maps: charting ways to success and failure', in H. P. Sims and D. Gioia (eds), *The Thinking Organisation*. San Francisco, CA: Jossey-Bass. pp. 102–35.

Westphal, J. D. and Zajac, E. J. (1994) 'Substance and symbolism in CEO's long-term incentive plans', *Administrative Science Quarterly*, 39: 367–91.

White, H. C. (1981) 'Where do markets come from?', *American Journal of Sociology*, 87: 517–47.

White, H. C. (1992) *Identity and Control: A Structural Theory of Social Action*. Princeton, NJ: Princeton University Press.

White, H. C. and Eccles, R. (1987) 'Producers' markets', in *The New Palgrave: A Dictionary of Economics*. London: Macmillan. pp. 984–6.

Wiersema, M. and Bantel, K. A. (1992) 'Top management team turnover as an adoption mechanism: the role of the environment', *Strategic Management Journal*, 14: 485–504.

Zahra, S. A. and Chapple, S. S. (1993) 'Blind spots in competitive analysis', *Academy of Management Executive*, 7: 7–28.

9

Strategy Process: Forming, Implementing and Changing Strategies

BALAJI S. CHAKRAVARTHY
and RODERICK E. WHITE

Strategy process research attempts to address the very difficult question of how strategies are formed, implemented and changed. Embedded in this work is the assumption that managers aspire to, and firms realize, something that can be called a strategy. What constitutes an effective strategy is addressed in the work of 'strategy content' researchers (reported elsewhere in this book). Content research describes attractive destinations, but without explaining how to get there. The getting there, the journey, is the task of strategy process researchers. Unfortunately, in their preoccupation with the journey, process researchers too often lose track of the destination, the strategy outcome. Thus despite the voluminous writings on strategy process (see Chakravarthy and Doz, 1992; Huff and Reger, 1987; Lechner and Müller-Stewens, 1999; Papadakis and Barwise, 1997; and Pettigrew, 1992 for extensive reviews), relatively little is known about how processes actually affect strategy. Unfortunately, the work in the strategy process area has been more about process and less about strategy. As Maritan and Schendel note, 'there has been surprisingly little work that has explicitly examined the link between the processes by which strategic decisions are made and their influence on strategy' (1997: 259).

Understanding the link between strategy process and outcome is important. Without it, process research is of little value to managers. As Pettigrew observes, 'the irreducible purpose of a processual analysis remains to account for and explain the what, why and how of links between context, processes and outcomes' (1997: 340). Without the link to outcomes process research is 'pragmatically endangered'.

In part, this disconnect is due to the complexity of the strategy process. Mintzberg and Lampel (1999), in a recent survey, suggest that there are at least ten different schools of thought on strategy process. We have collapsed their ten schools into four perspectives: rational, political, evolutionary, and administrative. All of these perspectives have been used to shed light on the strategy process. The process is variously seen as rational, intentional and goal-directed, as well as intuitive, political, emergent, and non-teleological. Different empirical studies find support for these seemingly disparate views of the process. Like the proverbial blind men describing different parts of an elephant, each perspective provides a different description of the beast unconnected with the others (Mintzberg et al., 1998). Lacking is a unifying theory that can reconcile and connect these multiple perspectives.

As Pettigrew (1992: 9) notes, holistic theorizing in strategy process research is 'barely an ambition and rarely an accomplishment'.

A related issue is that most theorizing and empirical studies on strategy process have focused on discrete decisions, like major investment decisions, which are easily identifiable and appear to be of strategic import. However, such a 'decision' is only one step in a long sequence of decisions and actions that culminates in a strategy. It may be a formal and visible step but it is neither the first nor the last, and may not even be the most significant. So while such decisions and how they are made are worthy of study they do not capture the entire strategy process. At most, a decision is a commitment by an individual or a group to action. In order to understand the strategy process more fully, research must focus not only upon a single decision but also on the patterns of decisions and *actions* that accumulate over time into a strategy.

Strategy process can span long periods of time and traverse multiple levels, bridging the cognitive processes of individual decision makers, the social psychological and/or political processes within groups of individuals, the organizational rules and routines that guide and constrain the decisions and actions of organizational members, and ecological considerations that affect the survival and success of firms. Typically, the process is studied only at one of these levels, depending on the disciplinary bias of the researcher, and that too at a cross-section in time. Rarely are these studies contextually and historically situated. Meaningful process research requires rich linkages through time and across levels.

In summary, while there is a vast and growing body of research on strategy process, it suffers variously from one or more of the following limitations: lack of explicit links to strategy outcomes; focus on discrete decisions rather than on patterns of decisions and actions that accumulate into a strategy over time; failure to view the process from multiple levels (and perspectives); and lack of insights on how the process can be managed better to produce the desired strategy outcomes. Addressing these limitations requires the application of a more holistic approach to strategy process research. Figure 9.1 sketches our view of the process. We will use it in this chapter to provide a selective review of the vast literature on the subject, and also to define an agenda for future research on strategy process.

The framework provided in Figure 9.1 is a composite of four distinct relationships. The first (the lower part of Figure 9.1) has to do with a firm's strategy and how, together with its business context, strategy determines a firm's performance. Investigating this relationship is normally the domain of strategy content researchers. However, as we will argue in this chapter, this is a relationship that should be of interest to process researchers as well. The next relationship, captured by the mid section of Figure 9.1, is between decisions, actions and strategy. Decisions and actions are often viewed as the core elements of the strategy making and implementation process, though their relative importance to a firm's strategy is a matter of some debate. The third relationship captured by the framework (the upper part of Figure 9.1) is between the organizational context of a firm and how it shapes the premises for both decisions and actions within it. Time is an important dimension for all elements in Figure 9.1. Firm performance, strategy, decisions, actions, business and organizational contexts, all change over time and influence each other dynamically. The final component of the framework captures this dynamic interaction.

Changes to the organizational context of a firm are normally the concern of organizational change scholars (reported elsewhere in this book). However, as Figure 9.1 illustrates, these changes have a direct influence on the decision and action premises that guide a firm's strategy process. Strategy process scholars must understand this dynamic better. Similarly, they must go beyond the traditional concern of strategy content researchers with the exploitation of a firm's business context through innovative strategies and also focus on how the business context itself can be changed. Strategy process influences the strategy dynamic of the firm, defined here as the overall predisposition of the firm, whether it is to improve, consolidate or change its strategy position. Understanding this dynamic requires the strategy process researcher to have a good grasp of the work of strategy content researchers. While the core elements of strategy process may be in the patterns of decisions and actions that are witnessed in a firm, these have to be understood with reference to changes in its organizational context and tied closely to its strategy dynamic.

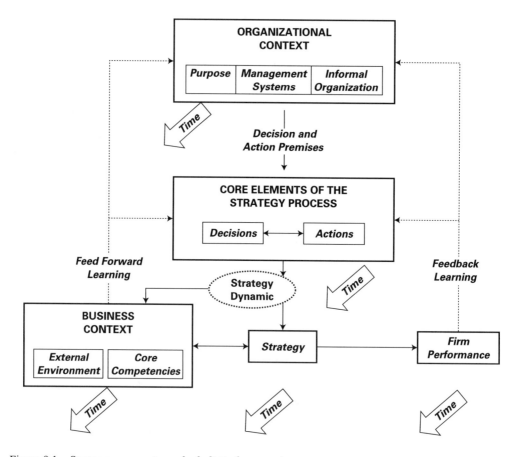

Figure 9.1   *Strategy process: toward a holistic framework*

As Figure 9.1 illustrates, strategy is realized through both emergent actions as well as planned actions that implement prior decisions. In turn, these decisions and actions are continuously revised based on feedback and feed forward learning. Strategy formation and implementation are closely intertwined. There is but one process for both. Similarly, we do not see it particularly useful to distinguish between steady state processes and processes of change. Strategy process should be concerned with improving, consolidating and changing a firm's strategy position. The task ahead of us is to develop a holistic understanding of a process that bridges the artificial divide between strategy formation and implementation, and steady state and change. It is not one that is amenable to theoretical or empirical reductionism.

The chapter is structured into five sections. The first four sections correspond to each of the four components of Figure 9.1. The first section discusses our concept of strategy dynamic and why it is relevant to process research. The next section examines the core elements of the process, using three different perspectives: rational, political, and emerging/evolutionary. In the third section, we examine how a firm's organizational context can be used to shape its decision and action premises. In the next section, we address the challenge of taking a more holistic view of the process, acknowledging its span over multiple periods and levels. We conclude by proposing an agenda for future research on strategy process.

STRATEGY DYNAMIC

Process researchers have not generally included a strategy outcome in their studies.

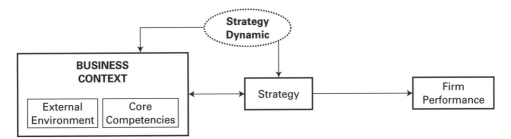

Figure 9.2 *Business context, strategy and performance*

When they do associate process characteristics with an organizational outcome, it is often financial performance. As the large body of content research (reported elsewhere in this book) shows, the financial performance of a firm is influenced not only by its strategy, but also by its business context (Figure 9.2). The business context of a firm includes both its external and internal environments. The former is defined by the economic, social, competitive and sectoral forces that it confronts (Pettigrew, 1992), and the latter by its core competencies (Hamel and Prahalad, 1994). Both the external (Porter, 1980) and internal (Barney, 1991) environments of the firm have an influence on its financial performance. Strategy defines how effective the firm has been in leveraging its business context. Its impact on performance cannot be seen in isolation from the firm's business context. The double-headed arrow linking business context and strategy in Figure 9.2 conveys this relationship.

Strategy content research has distinguished between three levels of strategy – business, multi-business, and multi-national – and offers a typology for each. The dimensions used to create these typologies reflect the key tensions inherent in any strategy. For example, at the level of business strategy, Porter (1980, 1985, 1996) suggests the two most salient dimensions are relative price/cost position and non-price buyer value delivered (or differentiation). At the level of multi-business or corporate strategy, there is tension between scale and scope – between vertical and horizontal integration (Chandler, 1990).

Scholars of international business have offered national responsiveness and global integration as the two key dimensions along which multi domestic, international, global and transnational strategies may be distinguished

(Prahalad and Doz, 1987; Bartlett and Ghoshal, 1989). Figure 9.3 presents a two-dimensional strategy space (S_1 and S_2). It can be employed with business, corporate, or multi-national strategies. The curved solid line represents a sort of strategy frontier, where those firms with the current best practice are positioned (Porter, 1996).

Even though most strategy typologies have limited the strategy space only to two dimensions, any number of dimensions are theoretically possible (S_1, S_2, ... S_n). In addition, the strategy frontier shown is hypothetical. Although there is considerable debate, researchers of business strategy, for example, have argued that only cost leadership and differentiation are feasible. 'Stuck-in-the middle' hybrid strategies are not. However, scholars of international management have conceptualized a feasible hybrid of global integration and national responsiveness, the transnational strategy. Our purpose here is not to argue for, or against, a continuous frontier or to determine the number of dimensions that define the strategy space, but rather to graphically represent the findings of the 'strategy content' researchers and build an agenda for strategy process research from such a representation.

Using the framework shown in Figure 9.3 we can think of four types of strategy dynamics or outcomes over time: improving/imitating, migrating, consolidating and innovating. It is important to note here that an effective strategy must not only seek to exploit the firm's external opportunities and internal competencies creatively, but it must also endeavor to stengthen its business context by exploring for new opportunities and renewing its competencies. Unfortunately, this latter aspect has not been the focus of strategy content researchers until recently. The arrows linking strategy

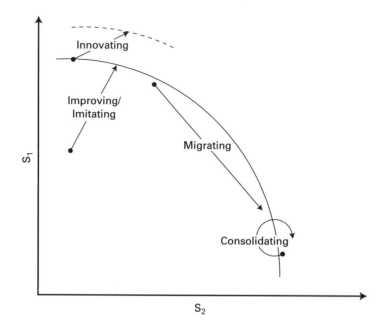

Figure 9.3   *Strategy dynamic*

dynamic with both business context and strategy in Figure 9.2 seek to convey this two-part agenda for strategy process research.

By its very nature, strategy process is dynamic. It is about becoming, becoming something else. The process must help bring about change. However, strategy process is also about being. Even maintaining a steady state requires a process. An active vocabulary is required to describe these processes. Mary Parker Follett (1924) was one of the first management scholars to stress the importance of active language to describe the processes of organizing. Karl Weick is a contemporary theorist who emphasizes the importance of 'ing' words: thinking, behaving, sense making, interacting, integrating, etc. However, Weick and Follett are the exceptions. Webb and Pettigrew (1999) complain about the largely static character of the language of strategy. The more dynamic vocabulary, con-solidat*ing*, improv*ing*/imitat*ing*, migrat*ing*, and innovat*ing*, which is proposed here, follows in the footsteps of Follett and Weick.

If a firm is not on the strategy frontier, improving/imitating advances the firm's strategic position toward the strategy frontier. Other firms on the strategy frontier, or those closer to it, provide the firm seeking improvement ready benchmarks to follow. Having reached the strategy frontier, a firm may start consolidating and maintaining this position by monitoring its competitors and making incremental improvements (Hammer and Champy, 1993), or it may seek to innovate. Innovating goes beyond established best practices and advances the strategy frontier (dashed line in Figure 9.3). Lastly, migrating involves a change in a firm's position along the existing frontier; for example from differentiation to low cost. While this is a significant change, it differs from innovating. A firm migrating from one generic strategy to another has exemplars. The position it seeks is not new. Other firms, elsewhere along the strategy frontier, have already achieved this strategy and provide benchmarks. An innovator does not have this luxury. Nevertheless, both innovating and migrating are more risky dynamics than improving, imitating or consolidating. These two dynamics place the current success of the firm at risk, in their search for greener pastures. Firms opting for innovation and migration not only seek a different market opportunity, they are also willing to redo their competence base.

Different types of process may be required to drive the four strategy dynamics described in Figure 9.3. For example, migrating from a differentiation to a cost leader business strategy or changing from a local responsive to a globally integrated multinational strategy may both require rebalancing the power structure in the organization (Prahalad, 1975). On the other hand, consolidating a successful business or corporate strategy may be more of a rational process. The typology of strategy dynamics offered in Figure 9.3 provides an approach for integrating process research on business, corporate and international strategies – as well as research on steady state (consolidating) and change (improving/imitating, migrating, innovating). The process should be similar for the same type of dynamic even across different levels of strategy.

Contrast this with the tendency to use generic strategies as outcomes in strategy process research. There is no reason to believe that the process required to deliver an *innovative* differentiation strategy should be any different from that required to deliver an *innovative* cost-leadership strategy. It is innovation that distinguishes the process and not the underlying generic strategy. Certainly, the cast of characters involved in decision making and action taking will vary with the generic strategy pursued. For example, product developers and marketers may be more important to differentiation and procurement experts and operations managers may be more relevant to a cost-leadership strategy. But the process they follow will be guided more by the strategy dynamic that is being pursued and not the generic strategy under consideration or the level (business, corporate or international) at which it is pursued.

Research exploring the relationships between a strategy dynamic and the underlying process is rare, the work of Miles and Snow (1978) being one of the few exceptions. These two researchers developed a typology of strategy dynamics: prospector, analyzer, defender and reactor, and aligned their four types with underlying organizational processes. Though their typology never gained wide acceptance amongst strategy content researchers, their pioneering effort still serves as an exemplar for the type of research that is needed to link process with a strategy dynamic.

THE CORE PROCESS ELEMENTS: DECISIONS AND ACTIONS

At its core, the strategy process involves decisions and actions, though not necessarily in that sequence. Three of the four major perspectives on strategy process research deal with decisions/actions.

Decision Making: A Rational Perspective

Rational decision making, both by individuals and within organizations, is a cornerstone of much of the thinking about strategy process: 'All behavior involves conscious or unconscious selection of particular actions out of all those, which are physically possible to the actor and to those persons over whom he exercise influence and authority' (Simon, 1976: 3).

Many process scholars agree with Simon. For them strategy process is essentially a decision making process, involving the rational application of knowledge to a choice problem. A rational process of decision making considers four questions: What are the alternatives?, What are the consequences of each alternative?, How desirable are the consequences?, and What rules or criteria should be employed to choose among the alternatives? (Simon, 1976: 91; March, 1994: 2). However, the individual trying to solve an unstructured problem (like most strategy problems are) does not know and cannot identify through search all of the possible alternative solutions. The consequences attached to the known alternatives are often ambiguous, and the decision-maker cannot specify a complete utility ordering for all possible sets of consequences even if these consequences are known. As Simon (1976: 79) concludes, for unstructured problems, 'it is impossible for the behavior of a single, isolated individual to reach any high degree of rationality'. Rather, individuals are more accurately described as 'boundedly-rational' (Cyert and March, 1963).

A boundedly-rational individual does not engage in a comprehensive search but only in a local search (guided by an organization's decision premises) and does not aspire to optimize, but rather more realistically to satisfy (Simon, 1945, 1976; March and Simon, 1958; Cyert and March, 1963). As March and Simon note: 'Most human decision making, whether individual or organizational, is concerned with the discovery and selection of satisfactory alternatives, only in exceptional cases is it

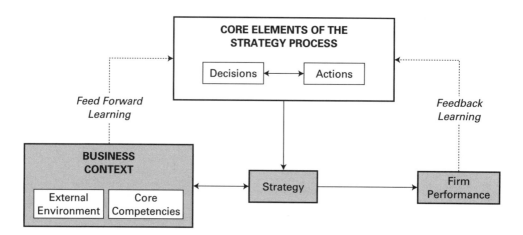

Figure 9.4   *Core elements of the strategy process*

concerned with the discovery and selection of optimal alternatives' (1958: 141).

Empirical studies on decision making using a rational, or boundedly-rational, perspective have been reviewed by Eisenhardt and Zbaracki (1992), and Rajagopalan et al. (1993). Most of the studies examined focused on linking process characteristics with process outcomes. Eisenhardt (1989) found that the comprehensiveness and extent of analysis influenced decision speed and effectiveness positively. Langley (1990) showed that formal analysis in strategic decisions helps convergence towards action. The available evidence suggests that procedural rationality leads to superior decisions in certain contexts. Other empirical studies have sought to understand the link between decision process characteristics and economic outcomes. These studies have been inconclusive.

Group decision making techniques for surfacing and resolving differences in fact and logic have been explored in laboratory studies. Dialectical inquiry (DI) or devil's advocacy (DA) have been employed to expand the set of alternatives considered and challenge factual and logic assumptions. As Rajagopalan et al. (1993) observed, these studies do provide some evidence that cognitive conflict in the decision process leads to improved decision quality. However, these studies typically assume that members of the decision making-group share the same goals and preferences. In large, complex organizations, differences in goals and preferences are commonplace.

Cyert and March (1963) have attempted to provide a comprehensive behavioral theory of the firm (BTF), using their boundedly-rational perspective. They recognize that individual members of an organization can have different goals and hence goal conflict is unavoidable in any organization. These conflicts can only be quasi-resolved. The emphasis is on local (sub-unit) rationality, an acceptable (satisfying) organizational solution, and a sequential attention to goals. The organization avoids uncertainty by using decision rules that emphasize reaction to short-run environmental feedback and by arranging a negotiated environment that controls uncertainty. Search within the firm is problem-oriented. A problem is recognized when the organization either fails to satisfy one or more of its goals or when such a failure can be anticipated in the immediate future. Furthermore, the search is simple-minded, deferring complex solutions, and biased by the training, experiences and goals of organizational members. However, the organization can learn, by changing its goals, shifting its attention, and revising its procedure for search, as a function of its experiences (feedback learning).

Many scholars have built on the ideas of Simon, March and Cyert and made important contributions to understanding the core elements of the strategy process, covering: decision making (Cohen et al., 1972; Eisenhardt, 1989; March and Shapira, 1987; Singh, 1986), organizational action taking (Thompson, 1967), organizational learning (Argote et al., 1990;

Cohen and Levinthal, 1990; Levitt and March, 1988), and organizational adaptation (Huff et al., 1992; Lant and Mezias, 1992). However, by anchoring their research in the rational perspective, these studies offer only a limited understanding of the process.

The BTF has been criticized on several counts. First, it is firmly rooted in a model of *individual* decision making. Even if this model provides a good description of individual choice, it is not clear that it can be extrapolated to the group and organizational levels. As Pettigrew (1985: 20) notes, by projecting individual processes of choice into statements about organizational processes of decision making 'there is a liberal bias to reconstructing the organization from the perspective of the individual, and not enough on demonstrating how the organization structures the perspectives and interests of the individual'.

Second, procedural rationality (Dean and Sharfman, 1993a) may not always be descriptive of how individuals take action. There is no obvious place for emotion in a (boundedly) rational process. Rational decision making theorists, at least at the level of the individual, commit what Damasio (1994) calls the 'Descartes error'. They assume that individuals separate their thinking self from their feeling self, their rationality from their emotion. Damasio's work on brain function and physiology suggests that this separation is neither possible, nor desirable. Emotion, or passion, may play an important role in generating novel actions (Hurst et al., 1989); actions that depart from the accepted norm and result in innovative outcomes.

Third, boundedly-rational models assume that decision makers have an established dominant logic that guides the generation of alternatives and the assessment of consequences. In part, this logic is what bounds the search process and the alternatives considered. The result is a locally satisfactory solution. Yet, the potential always exists for a better result. By abandoning optimality and settling for (local) satisfying, boundedly-rational models have difficulty explaining how innovative entrepreneurial strategies come about; how organizations discover and learn new logics. Most strategy situations present many opportunities for the exercise of intuition and the generation of novel actions. Indeed, Mintzberg and Lampel (1999) offer intuition

as the driver of entrepreneurial decisions and actions. Yet, intuitive insights or vision are by their very nature difficult to incorporate into a boundedly-rational process. As Bower and Doz note: 'Cyert and March focus on short-to-medium-term decisions in response to immediate problems. Longer-term change is achieved by organizational learning, i.e. adaptation of goals, attention rules and search rules. Combined with uncertainty avoidance, problematic search, and quasi-resolution of conflict, the process of adaptive learning lends to reactive behavior, not to the foresight and overall design implicit in a manager's vision of the future of his company' (1979: 155).

Foresight and vision, not just rationality, are important drivers of a firm's strategy. Besides feedback learning, feed forward learning (foresights about a firm's external environment) influences decisions and actions within a firm, and through them its strategy. The dotted lines in Figure 9.4 represent these learning loops.

Finally, some scholars contend that strategic decisions need not be precursors to all organizational actions (Mintzberg and Waters, 1990). If decisions are commitments to act, then the commitment that precedes can sometimes be vague, confusing or non-existent. Moreover, strategies are seldom made at one point or place. No single 'decision' leads to a strategy; rather it is the result of a stream of actions. Actions always leave a trail, whereas decisions may not always be revealed. Therefore, Mintzberg and Waters (1990: 5) argue that it makes more sense 'to study streams of actions, and then go back and investigate the role of decisions, *if any*, in determining these actions'. Butler (1990) concedes that studying discrete decisions has its limitations. Strategies do represent a stream of decisions made by multiple levels of decision-makers, over time. In addition, it is conceivable that some decisions are reflexive and some actions are initiated without a prior collective commitment or decision. Nevertheless, Butler argues that these stipulations do not negate the role of decision making and rationality in the strategy process. We conclude that both organizational actions that lead to strategy outcomes and the decisions that drive many of these actions should be considered as core elements of the strategy process. However, actions are a larger set than decisions, since many actions are not the result of decisions. Therefore, the strategy process cannot be fully understood just by studying the decision making process.

Resolving Goal Conflicts:
The Political Perspective

Power and politics generally carry negative connotations, and yet they are a vital perspective on the strategy process. The definition of what constitutes political behavior and a political process is broad. Most include 'behaviors associated with the use of power or influence' (Gandz and Murray, 1980: 237). Some researchers restrict their definition to the use of power to resolve important policy issues or resource allocation decisions (Wildavsky, 1964; March, 1962); others cast their net more widely and define any exercise of power or influence as political (Hickson et al., 1986). A few go even further and require that the exercise of power must be consciously self-serving to be deemed political (Mayes and Allen, 1977; Gandz and Murray, 1980).

Consciously self-serving behaviors and associated processes, such as the withholding or distortion of information, covert actions, agenda control, undue attention focused within the organization (coalition building) and incomplete enumeration of options (Cyert and March, 1963; Pettigrew, 1973; Nutt, 1993; Dean and Sharfman, 1993b, 1996), are often seen to be dysfunctional and undermine organizational effectiveness (Eisenhardt and Bourgeois, 1988). Gandz and Murray (1980: 246) reported 'respondents see politics as deviations from techno-economic rationality' and clearly disapproved of self-serving and self-advancing behavior. However, there are several possible reasons for this finding. First, large sample studies typically examine a wide range of decisions. A political process may not have been appropriate for all of these decision contexts. More importantly, these studies typically define political behaviors as self-interested. They do not distinguish between the self-interested use of power and power used in the broader interests of the organization. This shortcoming is critical. To find that balkanized organizations, with every group or individual out for its own self-interest, are ineffective is hardly surprising. While power may be used in this way, it need not be (Greenleaf, 1973).

Individuals or groups within an organization may genuinely disagree. This disagreement need not be grounded in a narrow calculus of each actor's self-interest. Allison's (1971) description of the Cuban missile crisis reported significant disagreement and conflict between the different actors. Each group came to the process with its own knowledge, experiences and biases. However, there is little evidence that they engaged in narrowly self-interested behaviors.

Moreover, as Barnard (1938) has observed, the self-interest of the organization is in a state of continual definition; seeking the common ground amongst the key contributors. A similar, but slightly less benign, view is that organizations are composed of a constantly shifting set of actors each seeking to have their interests defined as part of the organization's purpose (Burns, 1961; Butler, 1971). An organization does not have interests independent of the actors who make up the cooperative system. The organization's interests, such as they exist, represent the current common ground amongst the self-interests of the different actors affiliated with the organization. Actors naturally assert that their (self) interests and proposed actions are in tune with the future success requirements of the organization. The validity of their assertions is difficult to ascertain since the future is uncertain and equivocal. In situations like these where there is an absence of shared goals, a process that attempts to clarify and align the competing interests is very much needed (March and Simon, 1958). This is in essence a political process, with the final decision being swayed by the preferences of the group with the most power.

Choices made, or actions initiated, through the exercise of power are not necessarily bad for the organization. Such a choice may be better for the organization than no choice at all. Inaction is not necessarily the best course of action. In the face of uncertainty or ambiguity, choices based upon power and political processes may be the only feasible way to achieve change and adaptation (Daft, 1983; Pfeffer, 1981).

Action-Taking: The Emergent/
Evolutionary Perspective

The orderly decision process implied by procedural rationality is not always (some would contend, not often) observed in practice. The garbage can model proposed by Cohen et al. (1972) recognized that organizational action can result from a process more akin to organized anarchy where 'decision making occurs in a stochastic meeting of choices looking for problems, problems looking for choices, solutions looking for problems to answer, and decision-makers looking for something to decide' (Eisenhardt and Zbaracki, 1992: 27). In sharp contrast with the rational perspective, the evolutionary perspective views the strategy process as more emergent and non-teleological. However, within this perspective there are differences among scholars on the degree of randomness in the process.

At one extreme, Cohen et al. (1972) have suggested that organizational action could result from a purely emergent almost random process, a metaphorical organizational 'garbage can'. Organizational actions are not the result of decisions *per se*, but rather caused by a random intermingling of problems, people, issues, decisions, opportunities, ideas and solutions. For individuals as well as organizations, commitment does not have to precede action and 'whatever commitment does precede action can be vague and confusing' (Langley et al., 1995: 266). The original 'garbage can' formulation did not employ the evolutionary process of variation, selection, and retention. It incorporated variation but said little about the processes of selection and retention. The model cannot, therefore, account for stable persistent pattern of actions. It cannot explain strategy. However, subsequent field research shows that administrative, social and cognitive factors may serve as retention mechanisms that limit the randomness of this emergent process (Pinfield, 1986; Magjuka, 1988; Levitt and Nass, 1989).

According to Campbell, in order for a stable pattern of actions to emerge the process does not have to be teleological, it can be teleonomic (1991: 167). An evolutionary process can achieve regularity and a dynamic stability without prior knowledge of means–ends relationships and even without being goal-directed. Weick (1979) describes such a process. He applies an evolutionary process model to how individuals and groups make sense of their world – their process of organizing. Individuals interact and through the process of enactment–selection–retention make

sense out of a stream of experiences. Weick prefers the term enactment to variation because it 'captures the more active role that we presume organizational members play in creating the environments that then impose on them' (1979: 130). Selection selects meanings. It involves sense making (Weick, 1995) – the imposition of cognitive structures upon enacted events in an attempt to reduce their equivocality. Retention entails the storage of the products of successful sense making.

In a Weickian organization decision making becomes decidedly retrospective. As he explains, '... it is crucial to remember that decision making in the organizing model means selecting some interpretation of the world and some set of extrapolations from that interpretation and then using these summaries as constraints on subsequent acting' (1979: 175). Consequently Weick (1979) and Mintzberg (1994) share a similar view of strategic planning. As Weick observes: 'Organizations persistently spend time formulating strategy, an activity that literally makes little sense given the arguments advanced here. Organizations formulate strategy after they implement it, not before. Having implemented something – anything – people can then look back over it and conclude that what they have implemented is a strategy' (1979: 188).

In this view, the planning process can serve an important purpose. However, it is not to create strategy; but to retrospectively reduce equivocality, to discern a pattern in past action and explain it as a strategy. This explanation (with extrapolation) is then used to guide future actions.

For Weick, organizing is about producing stable interpretations of equivocal displays. Organizations embed these interpretations in their actions and their routines, and are reluctant to discredit them, resulting in inertia and an inability to adapt and change. The work of Nelson and Winter (1982) is consistent with and complementary to Weick, even though they were apparently unaware of his work. Nelson and Winter also employed an evolutionary model in which stable firm level routines feature prominently. As they explain:

> In our evolutionary theory, these routines play the role that genes play in biological evolutionary theory. They are a persistent feature of the organism and determine its possible

behavior; they are heritable in the sense that tomorrow's organisms generated from today's (for example, by building a new plant) have many of the same characteristics, and they are selectable in the sense that certain routines may do better than others, and, if so, their relative importance in the population is augmented over time. (1982: 14)

Evolutionary theory assumes that an established firm can replicate itself by replicating its routines. It implies that established routines can be applied on a larger scale, although not without costs. As the example in the quotation suggests, a firm with one successful plant could start a second similar plant relatively easily. By this logic the routines of other successful firms can also be imitated but perhaps at greater cost and/or with less accuracy. In the extreme, Nelson and Winter recognize that an imitator working with very little information about the routines of the source must largely solve the problem independently. Such a firm would merit the title of innovator except that 'the knowledge that a problem *has* a solution does provide an incentive for persistence in efforts that might otherwise be abandoned' (1982: 124).

Routines are by definition stable and resistant to change. But Nelson and Winter did suggest several sources for innovation (mutation). Puzzles or anomalies arising in relation to operation of established routines were identified as one possible source. Making sense of these anomalies may lead to a change in, or recombination of, routines. They also suggest that innovation may itself be routinized by the heuristics employed by top management. Periodic strategic challenges and changes to organizational structure initiated by top management can disrupt established routines and allow for change. Some of the change may result in positive innovation. Evolution can at least be facilitated, if not managed.

Evolutionary processes can also be guided by a broad organizational purpose. Quinn's (1980) work on 'logical incrementalism' recognized the practical impossibility within large organizations, with their many interlinked systems, of bringing together all the elements of a strategic decision at 'any precise moment'. Instead of seeing this as a problem, Quinn sees in this misalignment the source of new initiatives – opportunities that can spark a new strategy. He observed that 'top executives typically deal with the logic of each strategy subsystem largely on its own merits' and sequentially, not simultaneously.

While logical incrementalism is not a political process *per se*, political differences can be accommodated. Quinn noted, 'Strategic decisions do not come solely from power–political interplays. Nor do they lend themselves to aggregation in a single massive decision matrix' (1980: 51). They emerge from the process. Quinn goes on to note: 'Consequently, many successful executives initially set only broad goals and policies that can accommodate a variety of specific proposals from below yet give a sense of guidance to the proposers' (1980: 52).

Senior management frames and communicates the broad goals or intent. How to achieve this intent is not known, and it evolves incrementally over time. Ideas are proposed. Some are selected, others are not. Some sort of selection and retention mechanisms are necessary for regularities to emerge from an evolutionary process. Quinn suggests that this comes primarily from the firm's strategic intent. In addition, the administrative context of the firm may help guide, if not control, the evolutionary process.

MANAGING DECISION AND ACTION PREMISES

Strategy is the pattern that emerges over time from the decisions and actions taken by the members of an organization. For a pattern to form these decisions and actions cannot be purely random, they are influenced by the organizational context of a firm. The administrative perspective on strategy process focuses on how the organizational context of a firm shapes its decision and action premises. The rich field studies in this tradition provide credible descriptions of the action–decision dynamic in a strategy process and attempts by managers to influence it.

The Action–Decision Dynamic: An Integrated Perspective

In his pioneering study of the resource allocation process in diversified firms, Bower (1970) provides a rich description of decisions and action taking in a firm – the two core elements of the strategy process, and the dynamic inter-actions between the two. Even though he went into his fieldwork with the rational perspective in mind, Bower was not blinded by it. Contrary to his initial expectations, he found that in the resource allocation process, autonomous actions of individual managers often preceded formal decision. The process itself consisted of three distinct phases – defini-tion, impetus and approval – and spanned three levels of managers – functional managers, their divisional bosses and corporate manage-ment. Bower's narratives on the resource allo-cation process in diversified firms are rich and 'believable' (Bruner, 1986). At the risk of missing the nuances in Bower's rich narra-tives, we offer the following summary description of the resource allocation process as observed by him.

Bower noted that a resource allocation deci-sion often started as a discrepancy – a level of discomfort with the way things were versus how the functional manager would have liked them to be. 'Discrepancy' included a range of organizational problems like shortage of capa-city in the manufacturing plant, a technical invention in search of a commercial home, or a product seeking a market. A discrepancy arose not only because of an organizational problem, but also due to the passion that an individual had for a pet solution. Instead of a problem driven decision search, individual actions can also be solution driven (Cohen et al., 1972). In the 'definition' phase, actions of functional managers preceded the decision by the divisional manager. During this phase, functional managers sought to sell their felt 'discrepancy' to their divisional superiors. The divisional manager in turn tried to match the proposed investment with the priorities of top management. Of the many discrepancies that were brought to the divisional manager's notice, only a select few were chosen for fur-ther careful analysis. This analysis sought to provide 'definition' to the proposed investment, at times taking liberties with the numbers used in order to make the proposal fit the invest-ment criteria of the firm. The divisional manager's decision was at times intuitive and not based on a prior formal analysis. However, a formal analysis was always done later to support the decision that was made.

Once the divisional manager was satisfied with the definition of an investment proposal, he/she sought to position it in the most favor-able light given the priorities of top manage-ment and other competing requests for resource allocation. The proposal was prop-erly 'packaged' and communicated, giving it the necessary impetus towards approval by top management. This more subtle impetus process was less rational, and more political. When the divisional manager handled the impetus process well, approval by top man-agement was a mere formality.

Numerous follow-on studies have emplo-yed Bower's model to other strategic deci-sions, including: divestment (Gilmour, 1973), foreign investment (Aharoni, 1966), and glob-alization (Prahalad, 1975). These and other studies have confirmed the need to comple-ment the rational perspective on strategy process with the social/political and evolution-ary perspectives. Decisions and actions need not follow an orderly precedence. What may appear to be a decision made by top manage-ment may have had its origins in a process that was in part intuitive, social and political. Rational analysis may be done retrospectively to give proper authenticity and meaning to a firm's actions (as the evolutionary perspective would suggest), and not precede them (as the rational perspective would dictate).

Burgelman (1983, 1996) elaborated the action–decision dynamic in the Bower model in two important respects. The first was to pro-vide a more detailed account of the interactions between functional, middle and top managers of a firm as a strategic decision acquired defi-nition and built up impetus. The second was to show that even the three phases of acquir-ing definition, building impetus and giving approval, that Bower suggested, were by no means sequential or orderly. In the case of strategy exit, for example, the approval and impetus phases may actually precede the defi-nition phase. Top management, and not the functional managers, may be the instigator of this decision. The strategy process is thus bottom-up, top-down, and even middle-up-down (Nonaka, 1988). It is often iterative, in part due to the political and evolutionary imperatives of the process but also because of continuous learning.

While decisions may not always be deli-berate, articulate or consensual, they do manifest organizational cognition. Moreover, organizational cognition is not static and can be enhanced through learning (Walsh and Ungson, 1991). This learning can come both during the implementation of decisions and from the ensuing outcomes, as well as from actions that may be initiated without a prior decision (Starbuck, 1983). The latter type of learning has been called action-learning (Morgan and Ramirez, 1983). In addition, members of an organization can also learn vicariously by observing the consequences of the decisions and actions of others. Also, as noted earlier, learning can be driven by foresight. Learning is an important complement to decision making and action taking (see Figure 9.4). However, since other chapters in this book focus exclusively on cognition and learning, we will not dwell on these in this chapter.

Managing Premises

The above discussion would suggest that all levels of managers in a firm, from functional managers to top management, are engaged in the strategy process. They make decisions and take actions, which through interaction and iteration lead to the shaping and realization of a strategy. We now turn to the question: how can this decision–action dynamic be managed?

According to Simon (1945) there are two kinds of premises that top management can establish to guide decisions in an organization: value premises and factual premises. Value premises establish the goals for the organization, with each step down in the hierarchy implementing 'the goals set forth in the step immediately above' (Simon, 1976: 5). Factual premises specify the alternatives that may be considered in pursuit of the prescribed goals: 'Given a complete set of value and factual premises, there is only one decision which is consistent with rationality' (Simon, 1976: 223). This extreme prescription would not apply to any of today's large organizations, given their great diversity. If it ever was, top management is certainly not the 'one big brain' today, making all of the firm's decisions.

Nevertheless, Simon (1945) is right in pointing out the important role that purpose plays in shaping behaviors within an organization. The extent of discretion available to organizational members is determined by the number and importance of the premises that are specified (and unspecified). A guiding philosophy or strategic intent is not aimed at severely constraining discretion, but rather at helping bound discretion within the firm. Organizational purpose is, therefore, an important lever that top management can use for managing the strategy process. Bower (1970) suggested that the structural context of a firm – its organization and associated systems of information, measurement, reward and punishment – also plays an important role in shaping the decision and action premises of managers. Burgelman (1983) introduced the notion of a 'strategic context' – the process through which the current corporate strategy is extended to accommodate the new business activities resulting from bottom up initiatives that fall outside the scope of the current strategy. The strategic and structural contexts of the firm together must allow for both the exploitation of existing business domains as well as the exploration of new ones (March, 1991). Finally, Barnard (1938) emphasized the role of the informal organization in influencing organizational behavior.

We use the broader term organizational context here instead of structural and strategic contexts, and include within it the purpose of the organization, its management systems and informal organization (Figure 9.5). Each of these helps shape the decision and action premises of an organization. Senior executives in a firm are not only decision-makers and actors in the strategy process, they are also the architects and managers of the organizational context that shapes these decisions and actions.

Setting Purpose

Intentionality or goal directedness has been at the heart of most research about strategy process. As Lewin and Volberda (1999) note: 'Intentionality is rooted in social-psychological theories of human behavior and purposeful action. It underlies theories of rationality in economics, strategic management and decision sciences. It has been the foundation of management practice and the raison d'être for the thriving enterprise of teaching and research in schools of business.' Intentionality requires managers to anticipate what the external environment will favor in the future. It is a

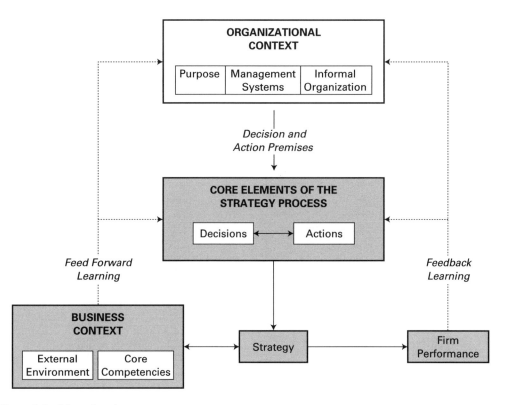

Figure 9.5 *Managing the strategy process*

tremendous challenge for a firm to have internal selection processes that accurately reflect external selection pressures. While accuracy may be hard to come by, intentionality cannot be abandoned all together. By setting purpose, top management influences the way in which the firm's managers see opportunities (and threats) in its environment, leverage and renew its competencies, and overcome its cultural inertia. As Quinn (1980) reminds us, goal directedness can play a central role in bringing stability to even an evolutionary process. It is useful, however, to distinguish between goals of different specificity.

Collins and Porras (1994) have demonstrated the importance of an enduring guiding philosophy for nurturing a firm's long-term success. They define guiding philosophy as a system of fundamental motivating assumptions, principles, values and tenets – the purpose of an organization and its core beliefs and values. Purpose defines the broad arena in which the firm seeks to contribute to society, whereas its core beliefs and values define how

it will go about achieving its purpose. Simons (1994) describes how defining the boundary system for an organization can help identify the opportunity space that its members can search in and specify the risks within it that are to be avoided.

However, it is not enough to bound the opportunity space within which bottom-up strategies can emerge, top management should also provide an inspirational strategic intent (Hamel and Prahalad, 1989) to vigorously stimulate the emergence of innovative strategies within this space. Strategic intent provides a tangible image, a mission which clearly focuses the efforts of the organization and a vivid description through which the mission is made more alive and engaging. Both an enduring guiding philosophy and its continuous interpretation through new and changing strategic intents are needed to guide strategy making within the firm. As Barnard noted: 'Most continuous organizations require repeated adoption of new purposes. This is concealed from everyday recognition by the practice of generalizing a complex series of specific purposes under one term, stated to be "the purpose" of this organization' (1968: 91).

Purpose can vary in its generality. When the desired strategy outcome is innovation or migration, purpose must allow for a lot of discretion. The strategy process will be bottom-up in nature. In addition, purpose has to be more general, because it will be harder for top management to sense the external selection pressures accurately in such a context. On the other hand, when the firm seeks improvement, imitation or consolidation, purpose can be more specific. The external selection pressures are better understood. The strategy process can also be top down. Understanding how the setting of purpose can influence the decision and action premises guiding a firm's strategy process is an important area that needs further research.

Architecting Management Systems

The study of management systems began gaining momentum in the 1960s when many large firms started diversifying, and resorted to a divisional structure for managing this diversity (Chandler, 1962). The use of a divisional structure meant more delegation in strategy making. Formal planning was employed to coordinate and control the strategies of the firm's divisions and their business units (Ansoff, 1965). The early writings on formal planning saw the process as rational (Ackoff, 1970; Steiner, 1979) and drew heavily on the work of Simon (1945). The driver of the process was top management. It set the goals for the organization and established the premises for other decision makers in the organization. However, given its own cognitive limits, top management had to rely on corporate staff for making and implementing strategic decisions. Strategic decision making was thus abdicated to staff executives in many companies and the resulting bureaucratization of the planning and control process has been criticized by many (Gluck et al., 1982; Mintzberg, 1994; Peters and Waterman, 1982).

The real problem with strategic planners in the 1970s was their mistaken belief that strategy is made top-down. But the remedy for this problem is not the abject surrender of the strategy process to random bottom-up initiatives. Each of these random trials requires resources and places the firm at risk. Goal incongruence and information asymmetry between top management and front line managers are endemic to diversified firms. More recent research on strategic planning and control systems (Chakravarthy and Lorange, 1991; Lorange, 1980; Simons, 1994) has sought to understand how a firm's administrative systems can address this agency problem. Their emphasis has been on tailoring these systems to suit the action and decision premises that top management desires in the firm's strategy process, rather than on designing systems to make or implement decisions. This is a nuance that has been missed by Mintzberg (1994) in his critique of strategic planning systems. These newer studies on management systems suggest that the degree of interactions and iterations in a firm's planning system and its orientation to control have an important role in determining whether the strategies its managers pursue will *explore* new strategy frontiers and seek new competencies or *exploit* existing markets and competencies (March, 1991).

Interactions in planning refer to the levels of managers who are involved in developing the firm's strategic plan. As observed by Bower (1970) and Burgelman (1983), strategy is shaped by functional managers, given impetus by divisional managers and finally approved by top management. The greater this interaction, the richer are the strategic alternatives which are considered. High interaction is crucial for exploration (Vancil and Lorange, 1977). Another consideration is the degree of iteration in the planning process. Lorange (1980) describes three distinct phases in a typical strategic planning process – agenda setting, strategic programming and budgeting. Abstract reflections of top management when cycled through these three phases result in concrete budgets for business units and functions within the firm. When the three phases are followed in a rigid sequential fashion, the intent is frozen when strategic programs begin to be developed. In turn, the programs are nonnegotiable once budgets are decided. There is no iteration in the planning process. In contrast, when each phase is seen more as a guide to the next without rigidly constraining it, the planning process is more iterative. For exploration, the planning process must encourage the continuous questioning of the relevance of approved strategic programs and the appropriateness of accepted goals. Frequent iteration is less important for exploitation.

A second important aspect of a firm's strategic and structural context is its control system (Simons, 1994; Vancil and Lorange, 1977). Vancil and Lorange make a simple distinction between capital and expense budgets that are needed to maintain the momentum of a business from those required to implement strategic programs for future growth and profitability. The former is referred to as the operating budget and the latter as the strategic budget. Failure to make this distinction can tempt managers to talk exploration but not invest in it. By separating the two, a business manager is not unfairly punished for taking a long view. His/her performance can also be measured more justly, on output delivered against the operating budget and on effort expended against the strategic budget. In business contexts that seek exploration, the control focus should be on the strategic budget and in the case of businesses that seek exploitation the control focus should be on the operating budget.

Other studies have focused on the important role that human resource management systems and incentive systems can play in support of the strategy process (Beer et al., 1987; Chakravarthy and Zajac, 1984; Fombrun et al., 1984; Gupta, 1986; Gupta and Govindarajan, 1984; Lawler, 1971; Pinchott III, 1985; Zaleznik, 1977). Chakravarthy and Lorange (1991) have provided a framework to design the planning, control, incentives and human resource management systems of a firm to suit the strategy outcome desired by top management. They suggest that management systems that encourage *exploration* are more conducive to strategy innovation and migration, whereas systems that support *exploitation* are better suited to strategies that seek improvement, imitation or consolidation.

Studies using the administrative perspective tend to have the most appeal for managers. The rich field studies in this tradition, like those by Bower (1970) and Burgelman (1983, 1996), provide convincing descriptions of the strategy process and useful insights on how it may be managed. However, these studies are hard to replicate and the frameworks offered difficult to validate. On the other hand, the more rigorous empirical studies on management systems tend to be very narrow in scope and are often inconclusive (Chakravarthy, 1987). Moreover, both field and survey research on management systems typically focus on one management system at a time without considering the combined effects of all systems. Quinn's (1980) work suggests misalignment between systems could provide the spark for a new strategy. On the other hand, Lorange (1980) has argued that alignment between the systems is essential for effectively exploiting the business context of a firm. The role of misalignment and alignment of a firm's management systems and their impact on *exploration* versus *exploitation* needs to be better understood.

Informal Organization

Barnard recognized the important complementary support that informal organization provides to a firm's management systems. He suggested that the leadership skills that are pertinent to it are: '"feeling," "judgement," "sense," "proportion," "balance," "appropriateness." It is a matter of art rather than science, and is aesthetic rather than logical' (1938: 235). The logical aspects of managing a firm's context – architecting its management systems – have to be balanced by the more aesthetic aspects of leadership (Doz and Prahalad, 1988).

The essence of leadership is to set the agenda for the organization and create the network to achieve it (Kotter, 1982). The agenda setting process requires top management to take the strategic intent of the firm, which can at times appear distant and abstract to its members, and break it down into more bite-sized challenges. Moreover, the emotion and passion that leaders impart to these challenges will decide whether members of the organization will accept them as their personal goals. The networking aspects of leadership have to do primarily with mobilizing support and cooperation to help individuals discharge their responsibilities.

Ghoshal and Bartlett (1994) define support as an attribute of an organization's context that induces its members to share and lend assistance to others. Mechanisms that allow them to access the resources available to others, and the personal orientation of superiors that gives priority to providing guidance and help over exercising authority, contribute to the establishment of support. The three key bottlenecks to sharing in an organization are poor predisposition, lack of opportunity, and low motivation (Chakravarthy et al., 1999). Whereas formal incentive plans can partially address the motivation problem, successful sharing requires an informal organization that is clan like in its predisposition to share, intense in its informal networking and high on trust.

Cooperation comes from a fair process. It is the role of top management to ensure that the strategy process is seen as fair. Dissenting voices must be heard and all concerns must be dealt with openly. This does not mean that members will always have their way, but when they don't they will be provided an explanation. Procedural justice theorists (Lind and Tyler, 1988) have argued that fair procedures serve two purposes. First, over the long run, fair procedures should help protect the interests of organizational members. Hence, perceptions of procedural justice can lead to freer sharing within the firm. The second function of fair procedures is symbolic, to signal to individuals that they are valued and respected members of the organization. In this regard, fair procedures would most likely promote harmony between organizational members and the development of other positive affective reactions. The overall consequence of fair procedures in organizations is the building of trust between members of an organization (Jones and George, 1998).

Senge (1990) and others have clearly articulated the importance of empowerment and cooperation of organizational members in order to create a supportive climate for learning. Empowered individuals are more likely to enhance their personal mastery and experiment with new mental models. But for such risk-taking behavior to occur, members of the organization must not feel vulnerable to either sanctions by superiors or abandonment by peers and subordinates. The ability of top management to provide coaching help and constructive feedback is important for nurturing risk-taking behaviors in the organization. In situations of organizational change, employees distrustful of management may regard management initiatives as subtle attempts to exploit employees. Trust is especially important when the desired strategy outcome is innovation or migration, each calling for risky decisions and

actions (Chakravarthy and Gargiulo, 1998). Top management must create a passion for the proposed change, mobilize the needed support and sharing, and nurture organizational trust. The informal organization is an important lever for making radical changes in a firm. Its role in strategy migration and innovation needs to be better understood.

TOWARD A MORE HOLISTIC VIEW OF THE PROCESS

Strategy process is a multi-level process, spanning more that just the levels of an organization's hierarchy. Cognition occurs within individuals, individuals interact with other members of their work group, work groups function within organizational structures and routines, organizations compete within industries and industries rise and fall within the broader political economy. What occurs at one level affects and is affected by what occurs at the other levels. Often this deeply embedded nature of the strategy process is not taken into account. The few researchers who attempt to deal with the levels challenge usually do so by considering 'context'. They isolate the level of the process they wish to study and consider anything beyond that level the context for the process being studied. We are equally guilty in this chapter of such a gross simplification. We isolated the core elements of the process from two of its 'contexts', business and organizational (see Figure 9.1).

However, context itself is the result of a process. For example, the organizational context that we described is, in large part, the distillation of the lessons learned from the past. The purpose, management systems and informal organization of a firm are influenced by the outcomes from the very actions and decisions that they seek to influence. Similarly, a firm's business context both influences its decisions and actions and is in turn influenced by their outcomes. Superior performance can influence the dynamics of a firm's environment in its favor and also enhance its core competencies. Figure 9.1 attempts to capture these mutual influences through double headed arrows and learning loops (shown by dotted lines). Context, if considered at all in strategy process research, is usually treated as stable and static, independent of the process being studied. We need a theory that will take more of a systems view of the process and accommodate dynamic interactions between context, process and outcomes.

This theory in its complete form does not exist as yet. However, it is possible to specify the requirements for such a theory. It must incorporate multi-level, longitudinal processes. The processes that occur at the individual level (cognition, for example) must be linked with processes at the group level (sense making), with processes at the organizational level (generation of routines), and with ecological processes at the level of the environment. Theories already exist at all of these levels, but these are not easily transferable between levels. For example, Simon's (1945) attempt – and the subsequent work by Cyert and March (1963) – to make organizational processes compatible with boundedly-rational decision-makers does not fit easily with others who view organizational processes as bundles of routines subject to ecological pressures (Nelson and Winter, 1982; Hannan and Freeman, 1989). The lack of a multi-level integrative theory is a major impediment to research on strategy process.

Developing such a theory will be not be an easy task. In the past, process theorists have been like individual musicians: violinists, trumpeters, woodwinds – each playing their own tune. The music they played can be appealing when heard independently. However, if you put them together in the same room playing at the same time, you have an unpleasant cacophony. To achieve a pleasing integrative result, the concerned musicians must share a common musical score. Any integrative multi-level theory must span disciplines as diverse as cognitive psychology and population ecology.

The broad outlines of such a macro-theory can be glimpsed in the work of Donald Campbell (Baum and McKelvey, 1999). Campbell and those who have followed in his tradition explore the evolutionary processes of variation–selection–retention across levels and over time. The use of evolutionary theory to explain internal organizational processes is at an early stage of development (Barnett and Burgelman, 1996; Baum and McKelvey, 1999). At the level of the firm emergent/evolutionary organizational processes are difficult to conceptualize and perhaps even more difficult to research. A large part of this difficulty is due to the nested and inter-related nature of these processes. A process of variation–selection–retention occurs at the individual cognitive level (Neisser, 1976), the group/social level (Weick, 1979, 1995), the organizational level (Nelson and Winter, 1982) and has been extended to the population of firms (Hannan and Freeman, 1989). Importantly, what occurs at one level affects the other levels. The process at one level creates the context for the next level. As Barnett and Burgelman recognize selection processes at one level are affected by selection at the next higher level. They note: 'A central proposition of this line of work is that external selection and internal selection, together, determine the fates of organizations. Those that continue to survive have an internal selection environment that reflects the relevant selection pressures in the external environment and produces externally viable new strategic variations that are internally selected and retained' (1996: 7).

However, internal selection processes have levels as well. The organizational level selection processes can only work with the behaviors that individuals and groups put forward. This is the essence of organizing. Moreover, there are processes of variation and selection working at these levels also.

Arguably, a multi-level evolutionary perspective has the potential to provide the metatheory that could unify much of strategy process research. The specifics of this macrotheory, formulated in a way that will help guide strategy process researchers and ultimately aid practitioners, remains to be developed. The challenge is significant but the benefits would be substantial. It is clearly too important to be left to evolutionary theorists alone.

A NEW RESEARCH AGENDA

Members of an organization, both individually and collectively, make decisions that affect its strategy outcomes. These decisions are not just rational (or boundedly-rational), but also driven by intuition and emotion. Research on strategy process has for the most part ignored the role of intuition and emotion in strategy making and implementation. This is an important new area for research.

Organizational actions should normally flow from its decisions. However, the actions of individuals and groups can be reflexive, evoking a 'routine' that is known to address the problem at hand. Even though such action is not preceded by a decision, some may argue that the 'routine', which drives it, is in essence a prepackaged decision. However, action can also be initiated without a decision, influenced more by organizational politics or the broader evolutionary forces to which the firm is subjected. Thus, strategy can be both intended and emergent. It results from action taking that may or may not be preceded by decision making. While there have been numerous studies that highlight the emergent nature of strategy, there have been very few studies that focus on the organizational politics that is associated with the strategy process. This needs to be redressed.

The organizational context influences both decisions and actions within the firm. By managing the firm's organizational context, top management can steer it to the desired strategy dynamic. It is important to view the outcome of strategy process dynamically – improving/imitating, consolidating, migrating or innovating the firm's strategy position, and not in terms of generic strategies or financial performance. This offers the best hope for cumulating research on strategy process, whether it is done at the level of buisness, corporate or international strategies. Strategy process research must be tied explicitly to both the organizational context of the firm and its strategy dynamic. Without this link its relevance to managers will remain questionable.

Furthermore, the research on strategy process is typically pursued from a single perspective – rational, political, evolutionary or administrative. Each provides a partial understanding of a complex process. Each perspective has its dogmatists, but luckily some dissenters as well. The best hope for an integrated theory lies in these dissenters, researchers who have a strong grounding in one of the four perspectives but are looking to others for stimulation. They are more likely to see the merits in a rival perspective and start forging a better integrated perspective.

Much of the current research on strategy process seems to be caught on a treadmill – doing more or less the same thing over and over again. It can be characterized in two ways. There is the work that begins with a strong theoretical perspective. This type of work usually takes a deductive reductionist approach and examines that theory in a 'controlled' experimental or quasi-experimental circumstance. Much of the empirical work on decision making falls into this category, and has been criticized for ignoring history and context (Pettigrew, 1990). In the other category there are the gestaltists who generally take a historical, multi-level approach, providing thick descriptions of the process, some aspects of its context, and the resulting strategy outcomes. While this work overcomes the shortcomings of the reductionist approach it has been criticized for being atheoretical. Patterns are described, and taxonomies developed, but there is no strong general theory resulting from this research. Thus the strengths of one category of research appear to be the weaknesses of the other.

These shortcomings are well understood. However, business as usual, continuing with these two types of research is unlikely to enhance our understanding of the strategy process. The reductionists typically use a single perspective on the process, whereas the gestaltists are more eclectical. It is hard for the two to share data, the former digs deep but in a very narrow area and the latter has a broader scope but not the depth. What is lacking is an integrative theory. Its development can be speeded up if we pursue two related empirical approaches, sequenced in their order of difficulty.

Cumulating Research Findings

Metaphors involving flow-waves (Mintzberg and Lampel, 1999) and rivers (Pettigrew, 1990) have been productively employed to describe the strategy process. This type of metaphor can be used to understand both the limitations of much of the strategy process research and how it can be remedied. Let us take the metaphor that strategy process is like a river. Many researchers take a sample of water from that river, or a number of samples, in order to get a statistically valid result. These samples describe something about the river – water quality, clarity, temperature, etc. However, they say little about its dynamic quality, the flow of the river 'where it has been and where it is destined'; how the surrounding terrain affects, and is affected by, the river; the impact of exogenous factors like rainfall or drought. This metaphor helps to understand why dynamic aspects of a larger active process cannot be fully explored with static samples from that process. Process, contexts and outcomes all change with time (see Figure 9.1). However, the river can be described comprehensively and consistently in terms of its chemistry, physics, hydrology, geography, meteorology, etc. For starters, it would be useful to define this metaphoric river for strategy process. Figure 9.1 is such an attempt.

Clearly, the proposed framework needs to be debated and modified. But assuming that Figure 9.1 represents such a shared understanding, we can start specifying what counts as strategy process research. In order to qualify, a study must deal explicitly with one of the strategy dynamics suggested here. Studies on decision making and action taking that do not relate to a strategy dynamic are just that, studies about decisions and actions and not about the strategy process. Further we suggested four strategy dynamics: improving/imitating, consolidating, migrating and innovating. Documenting the action–decision dynamic associated with each of these outcomes, the contextual factors associated with that dynamic, and its performance consequences are all separate studies that can be done in the current reductionist tradition. By focusing on discrete parts of the framework proposed in Figure 9.1, these studies have a better chance of accumulating their findings and complementing each other than they do currently.

Tracking Dynamic Interactions

While reductionist studies may be unavoidable given the 'publish or perish' culture within which many researchers operate today, the real progress in our understanding of strategy process will come from multi-disciplinary teams engaged in a longitudinal program of research. The research team should track all of the elements in Figure 9.1 at multiple levels, over time, by using all four of the major perspectives presented in this chapter. Programs of this kind are currently under way in both Europe and North America.

The real difficulty for gestaltists is to identify *ex ante* a decision or action as belonging to

a strategy stream. The ability to link outcomes with precursor actions and decisions is essential to strategy process research. Given the current state of the art, researchers should perhaps identify interesting strategy dynamics and work backwards to study across levels the precursor conditions and the processes that stimulated, guided, channeled, directed and limited subsequent actions and decisions. While single case studies done in this way are of interest, an even more powerful design includes comparative cases (Pettigrew and Whipp, 1991). Miles and Snow (1978) took essentially this retrospective comparative approach.

The retrospective methodology suggested above is like having a movie of the strategy process and running it in reverse. However, a movie does not capture everything that happens to all the characters in the movie. A movie has a perspective, a point of view. The perspective helps focus the movie and defines its audience, who it has relevance for. Clearly, choice of perspective depends upon the interests of the researcher. However, we would suggest that multiple perspectives be applied in strategy process research. If the research involves the collaborative efforts of a multi-disciplinary team willing to try and unify their differing perspectives then the likelihood of developing a common theory is enhanced.

Real time studies of strategy process are more difficult. It is unlikely that a firm engaged in a new strategy would allow a team of researchers to observe its evolution from multiple vantage points. Its mangers may perceive this as too intrusive. However, assuming that such a special access can be obtained, the research team has the added luxury of studying why a certain action–decision dynamic fails to result in a successful strategy or how top management resets the action and decision premises in an organization to redirect the process toward a successful outcome. We need to learn more about failed processes in order to be able to offer useful prescriptions to managers.

While there is a vast and growing literature on strategy process, it is often disconnected from strategy outcomes. It also tends to view the process rather parochially from a single perspective. The rational perspective is appropriate to individual level decision making but has been extended unconvincingly to organizational level decision making. The political perspective could be very useful in addressing goal conflicts and in managing change, but it is not popular among strategy process researchers. The evolutionary perspective handles dynamic interactions, but does not easily accommodate managerial intervention in the process. The administrative perspective is manager friendly, but it needs to validate its frameworks. Addressing these limitations requires more holistic thinking about the strategy process. In this chapter, we have tried to synthesize the current knowledge about various parts of this framework. To make real progress, strategy process needs an integrating theory. To build one, the field urgently needs a few ambitious multidisciplinary research programs. In the meanwhile, the deluge of reductionist papers that currently inundate the field are likely to end up as isolated puddles, not as part of the river that every one is waiting for.

ACKNOWLEDGEMENTS

The authors wish to thank Charles Baden-Fuller, Yves Doz, Peter Gomez, Anil Gupta, Peter Lorange, Leif Melin, Howard Thomas, Georg Von Krogh, and our doctoral students for their helpful critique and creative suggestions in developing this chapter. We are especially indebted to Andrew Pettigrew for his excellent guidance. While so many have helped, we are solely responsible for any shortcomings in this chapter.

REFERENCES

Ackoff, R. (1970) *A Concept of Corporate Planning*. New York: Wiley-Interscience.

Aharoni, Y. (1966) *The Foreign Investment Decision Process*. Boston: Division of Research, Harvard Business School.

Allison, G. T. (1971) *Essence of Decision*. Boston, Massachusetts: Little, Brown.

Ansoff, H. I. (1965) *Corporate Strategy: Business Policy for Growth and Expansion*. New York: McGraw Hill.

Argote, L., Beckman, S. L. and Epple, D. (1990) 'The persistence and transfer of learning in industrial settings', *Management Science*, 36: 140–54.

Barnard, C. I. (1938, reprinted 1968) *The Functions of the Executive*. Cambridge, Massachusetts: Harvard University Press.

Barnett, W. P. and Burgelman, R. A. (eds) (1996) 'Evolutionary perspectives on strategy', *Strategic Management Journal*, 17: special issue.

Barney, J. B. (1991) 'Firm resources and sustained competitive advantage', *Journal of Management*, 17: 99–120.

Bartlett, C. and Ghoshal, S. (1989) *Beyond Global Management: Transnational Solution*. Boston, MA: Harvard Business School Press.

Baum, J. and McKelvey, B. (eds) (1999) *Variations in Organization Science: In Honor of Donald T. Campbell*. Thousand Oaks, CA: Sage Publications.

Beer, M., Spector, B., Lawrence, P. R., Quinn Mills, D. and Walton, R. E. (1987) *Managing Human Assets*. New York: Free Press.

Bower, J. L. (1970 and 1986) *Managing the Resource Allocation Process*. Boston, MA: Harvard Business School Press.

Bower, J. L. and Doz, Y. (1979) 'Strategy formulation: a social and political process', in D. Schendel and C. Hofer (eds), *Strategic Management: A New View of Business Policy and Planning*. Boston: Little, Brown.

Bruner, J. (1986) *Actual Minds, Possible Worlds*. Cambridge, Mass: Harvard University Press.

Burgelman, R. A. (1983) 'A process model of corporate venturing in the diversified major firm', *Administrative Science Quarterly*, 28: 223–4.

Burgelman, R. A. (1996) 'A process model of strategic business? Exit: implications for an evolutionary perspective on strategy', *Strategic Management Journal*, 17: 193–214.

Burns, T. (1961) 'Micropolitics: mechanisms of institutional change', *Administrative Science Quarterly*, 6: 257–81.

Butler, E. A. (1971) 'Corporate politics – monster or friend?', *Generation*, 3: 54–8.

Butler, R. (1990) 'Studying deciding: an exchange of views', *Organization Studies*, 11–16.

Campbell, D. (1991) 'Autopietic evolutionary epistemology and internal selection', *Journal of Social and Biological Structures*, 14(2): 166–73.

Chakravarthy, B. S. (1987) 'On tailoring a strategic planning system to its context: some empirical evidence', *Strategic Management Journal*, 8: 517–34.

Chakravarthy, B. S. and Doz, Y. (1992) 'Strategy process research: focusing on corporate self-renewal', *Strategic Management Journal*, 13, Special Issue: 5–14.

Chakravarthy, B. S. and Gargiulo, M. (1998) 'Maintaining leadership legitimacy in the transition to new organizational firms', *Journal of Management Studies*, 35(4): 437–56.

Chakravarthy, B. S. and Lorange, P. (1991) *Managing the Strategy Process*. Englewood Cliffs, NJ: Prentice-Hall.

Chakravarthy, B. S., Zaheer, A. and Zaheer, S. (1999) 'Knowledge sharing in organizations: a field study', Working Paper, Strategic Management Research Center, University of Minnesota.

Chakravarthy, B. S. and Zajac, E. (1984) 'Tailoring incentive systems to a strategic context', *Planning Review*, 12, November: 30–5.

Chandler, A. D. (1962) *Strategy and Structure*. Cambridge, MA: MIT Press.

Chandler, A. D. (1990) *Scale and Scope: The Dynamics of Industrial Capitalism*. Cambridge, MA: Belknap Press.

Cohen, M. D., March, J. G. and Olsen, J. P. (1972) 'A garbage can model of organizational choice', *Administrative Science Quarterly*, 17(1): 1–25.

Cohen, W. M. and Levinthal, D. A. (1990) 'Absorptive capacity: a new prescriptive on learning and innovation', *Administrative Science Quarterly*, 35: 128–52.

Collins, J. C. and Porras, J. I. (1994) *Built to Last: Successful Habits of Visionary Companies*. New York: Harper Business.

Cyert, R. M. and March, J. G. (1963) *A Behavioral Theory of the Firm*. Englewood Cliffs, New Jersey: Prentice-Hall.

Daft, R. L. (1983) *Organization Theory and Design*. St. Paul: West Publishing.

Damasio, A. R. (1994) *Descartes' Error: Emotion, Reason, and the Human Brain*. New York: G. P. Putnam.

Dean, J. W. and Sharfman, M. P. (1993a) 'Procedural rationality in the strategic decision making process', *Journal of Management Studies*, 30(4): 607–30.

Dean, J. W. and Sharfman, M. P. (1993b) 'The relationship between procedural rationality and political behavior in strategic decision making', *Decision Sciences*, 24(6): 1069–83.

Dean, J. W. and Sharfman, M. P. (1996) 'Does decision process matter? A study of strategic decision making effectiveness', *Academy of Management Journal*, 39(2): 368–96.

Doz, Y. and Prahalad, C. K. (1988) 'Quality of management: an emerging source of global competitive advantage', in N. Hood and J. E. Vahlne (eds), *Strategies in Global Competition*. London: Croom Helm. pp. 345–69.

Eisenhardt, K. M. (1989) 'Making fast strategic decisions in high velocity environments', *Academy of Management Journal*, 32: 543–76.

Eisenhardt, K. M. and Bourgeois, L. J. (1988) 'Politics of strategic decision making in high velocity environments: toward a midrange theory', *Academy of Management Journal*, 31(4): 737–70.

Eisenhardt, K. M. and Zbaracki, M. J. (1992) 'Strategic decision making', *Strategic Management Journal*, 13: 17–37.

Follett, M. P. (1924) *Creative Experience*. New York: Longsmans Green.

Fombrun, C. J., Tichy, N. M. and De Vanna, M. A. (1984) *Strategic Human Resources Management*. New York: John Wiley.

Gandz, J. and Murray, V. (1980) 'The experience of workplace politics', *Academy of Management Journal*, 23: 237–51.

Ghoshal, S. and Bartlett, C. A. (1994) 'Linking organizational context and managerial action: the dimensions of quality of management', *Strategic Management Journal*, Summer Special Issue.

Gilmour, S. C. (1973) 'The divestment decision process', unpublished doctoral dissertation, Harvard Business School, Boston, MA.

Gluck, F. W., Kaufman, S. P. and Walleck, A. S. (1982) 'The four phases of strategic management', *The Journal of Business Strategy*, 2(3): 9–21.

Gupta, A. K. (1986) 'Matching managers to strategies: point and counterpoint', *Human Resource Management*, 25, Summer: 215–34.

Gupta, A. K. and Govindarajan, V. (1984) 'Business unit strategy, managerial characteristics, and business unit effectiveness at strategy implementation', *Academy of Management Journal*, 27: 25–41.

Greenleaf, R. (1973) *Servant as Leader*. Cambridge, MA: Center for Applied Studies.

Hamel, G. and Prahalad, C. K. (1989) 'Strategic intent', *Harvard Business Review*, 67(3): 63–76.

Hamel, G. and Prahalad, C. K. (1994) *Competing for the Future*. Boston: Harvard Business School.

Hammer, M. and Champy, J. (1993) *Reengineering the Corporation*. New York: Harper Business.

Hannan, M. T. and Freeman, J. (1989) *Organizational Ecology*. Cambridge, MA: Harvard University Press.

Hickson, D. J., Butler, R. J., Cray, D., Mallory, G. R. and Wilson, D. C. (1986) *Top Decisions: Strategic Decision Making in Organizations*. San Francisco: Jossey-Bass.

Huff, A. S. and Reger, R. K. (1987) 'A review of strategy process research', *Journal of Management*, 13(2): 211–36.

Huff, J. O., Huff, A. S. and Thomas, H. (1992) 'Strategic renewal and the interaction of cumulative stress and inertia', *Strategic Management Journal*, 13, Summer Issue: 55–76.

Hurst, D. K., Rush, J. C. and White, R. E. (1989) 'Top management teams and organizational renewal', *Strategic Management Journal*, 10: 87–105.

Jones, G. R. and George, J. M. (1998) 'The experience and evolution of trust: implications for cooperation and teamwork', *Academy of Management Review*, 23(3): 531–46.

Kotter, J. P. (1982) *The General Managers*. New York: Free Press.

Langley, A. (1990) 'Patterns in the use of formal analysis in strategic decisions', *Organization Studies*, 11: 17–45.

Langley, A., Mintzberg, H., Pitcher, P., Posada, E. and Saint-Macary, J. (1995) 'Opening up decision making: the view from the black stool', *Organization Science*, 6(3): 260–79.

Lant, T. K. and Mezias, S. J. (1992) 'An organizational learning model of convergence and reorientation', *Organization Science*, 3(1): 47–71.

Lawler, E. E. (1971) *Pay and Organizational Effectiveness: A Psychological View*. New York: McGraw-Hill.

Lechner, C. and Müller-Stewens, G. (1999) 'Strategy process research: what do we know? What should we know?', Working Paper No. 33, Institute of Management, University of St. Gallen.

Levitt, B. and March, J. G. (1988) 'Organizational learning', *Annual Review of Sociology*, 14: 319–40.

Levitt, B. and Nass, C. (1989) 'The lid on the garbage can: institutional constraints on decision making in the terminal core of college-text publishers', *Administrative Science Quarterly*, 34: 190–207.

Lewin, A. Y. and Volberda, H. W. (1999) 'Prolegomena on coevolution: a framework for research on strategy and new organizational forms', Working paper, Duke University, Fuqua School of Business.

Lind, E. A. and Tyler, T. R. (1988) *The Social Psychology of Procedural Justice*. New York: Plenum.

Lorange, P. (1980) *Corporate Planning: An Executive Viewpoint*. Englewood Cliffs, NJ: Prentice-Hall.

Magjuka, R. (1988) 'Garbage can theory of decision making: a review', *Sociology of Organizations*, 6: 225–59.

March, J. G. (1962) 'The business firm as a political coalition', *Journal of Politics*, 24: 662–78.

March, J. G. (1991) 'Exploration and exploitation in organizational learning', *Organization Science*, 2: 71–87.

March, J. G. (1994) *A Primer on Decision Making: How Decisions Happen*. New York: Free Press.

March, J. G. and Shapira, Z. (1987) 'Managerial perceptions on risk and risk taking', *Management Science*, 33(11): 1404–18.

March, J. G. and Simon, H. A. (1958) *Organizations*. New York: John Wiley.

Maritan, C. A. and Schendel, D. E. (1997) 'Strategy and decision processes: what is the linkage?', in V. Papadakis and P. Barwise (eds), *Strategic Decisions*. London: Kluwer Academic Publishers. pp. 259–65.

Mayes, B. T. and Allen, R. W. (1977) 'Toward a definition of organizational politics', *Academy of Management Review*, 2: 672–7.

Miles, R. E. and Snow, C. C. (1978) *Organizational Strategy, Structure and Process*. New York: McGraw-Hill.

Mintzberg, H. (1994) *The Rise and Fall of Strategic Planning*. New York: Free Press.

Mintzberg, H., Ahlstrand, B. and Lampel, J. (1998) *Strategy Safari: A Guided Tour through the Wilds of Strategic Management*. New York: Free Press.

Mintzberg, H. and Lampel, J. (1999) 'Reflecting on the strategy process', *Sloan Management Review*, Spring: 21–30.

Mintzberg, H. and Waters, J. (1990) 'Does decision get in the way?', *Organization Studies*, 11: 1–5.

Morgan, G. and Ramirez, R. (1983) 'Action learning: a holographic metaphor for guiding social change', *Human Relations*, 37(1): 1–28.

Neisser, U. (1976) *Cognition and Reality*. San Francisco: W. H. Freeman.

Nelson, R. R. and Winter, S. G. (1982) *An Evolutionary Theory of Economic Change*. Boston, MA: The Belknap Press.

Nonaka, I. (1988) 'Toward middle-up-down management: accelerating information creation', *Sloan Management Review*, Spring: 9–18.

Nutt, P. (1993) 'The formulation processes and tactics used in organizational decision making', *Organization Science*, 4: 226–35.

Papadakis, V. and Barwise, P. (1997) 'What can we tell managers about strategic decisions?' in V. Papadakis and P. Barwise (eds), *Strategic Decisions: Context, Process and Outcomes*. London: Kluwer Academic Publishers.

Peters, T. J. and Waterman, R. H. (1982) *In Search of Excellence*. New York: Harper & Row.

Pettigrew, A. M. (1973) *The Politics of Organizational Decision Making*. London: Tavistock.

Pettigrew, A. M. (1985) *The Awakening Giant: Continuity and Change in Imperial Chemical Industries*. London: Basil Blackwell.

Pettigrew, A. M. (1990) 'Longitudinal field research on change: theory and practice', *Organization Science*, 1(3): 267–92.

Pettigrew, A. M. (1992) 'The character and significance of strategy process research', *Strategic Management Journal*, 3, Special Issue: 5–16.

Pettigrew, A. M. (1997) 'What is a processual analysis?' *Scandinavian Journal of Management*, 13: 337–48.

Pettigrew, A. M. and Whipp, R. (1991) *Managing Change for Competitive Success*. Oxford: Basil Blackwell.

Pfeffer, J. (1981) *Power in Organizations*. Marshfield, MA: Pitman Publishing.

Pinchott III, G. (1985) *Intrapreneuring*. New York: Harper & Row.

Pinfield, L. T. (1986) 'A field evaluation of perspectives on organizational decision making', *Administrative Science Quarterly*, 31: 365–88.

Porter, M. E. (1980) *Competitive Strategy*. New York: Free Press.

Porter, M. E. (1985) *Competitive Advantage: Creating and Sustaining Superior Performance*. New York: Free Press.

Porter, M. E. (1996) 'What is strategy?', *Harvard Business Review*, November–December, 61–78.

Prahalad, C. K. (1975) 'The strategic process in a multinational corporation'. Unpublished doctoral dissertation, Harvard Business School, Boston, MA.

Prahalad, C. K. and Doz, Y. (1987) *The Multinational Mission*. New York: Free Press.

Quinn, J. B. (1980) *Strategies for Change: Logical Incrementalism*. Homewood, IL: Irwin.

Rajagopalan, N., Rasheed, A. M. A. and Dutta, D. K. (1993) 'Strategic decision processes: an integrative framework and future direction', in P. Lorange, B. S. Chakravarthy, J. Roos and A. Van de Ven (eds), *Implementing Strategy Processes*. London: Basil Blackwell.

Senge, P. (1990) *The Fifth Discipline*. New York: Doubleday Currency.

Simon, H. A. (1945 and 1976) *Administrative Behavior: A Study of Decision Making Processes in Administrative Organization*. New York: Free Press.

Simons, R. (1994) *Levers of Control*. Boston: Harvard Business School Press.

Singh, J. V. (1986) 'Performance, slack and risk taking in strategic decisions', *Academy of Management Journal*, 29: 562–85.

Starbuck, W. H. (1983) 'Organizations as action generators', *American Sociological Review*, 48: 91–102.

Steiner, G. A. (1979) *Strategic Planning: What Every Manager Must Know*. New York: The Free Press.

Thompson, J. D. (1967) *Organizations in Action*. New York: McGraw-Hill Book Company.

Vancil, R. F. and Lorange, P. (eds) (1977) *Strategic Planning Systems*. Englewood Cliffs, NJ: Prentice-Hall.

Walsh, J. P. and Ungson, G. R. (1991) 'Organizational memory', *Academy of Management Review*, 16: 57–91.

Webb, D. and Pettigrew, A. M. (1999) 'The temporal development of strategy: patterns in the UK insurance industry', *Organization Science*, 10(5): 601–21.

Weick, K. E. (1979) *The Social Psychology of Organizing*. New York: Random House.

Weick, K. E. (1995) *Sensemaking in Organizations*. Thousand Oaks: Sage Publications.

Wildavsky, A. (1964) *The Politics of the Budgeting Process*. New York: Little, Brown.

Zaleznik, A. (1977) 'Managers and leaders: are they different?', *Harvard Business Review*, 55, May–June: 67–78.

10

Strategic Change Processes

RAGHU GARUD and ANDREW H. VAN DE VEN

Strategy process research is at a crossroads. We are bombarded by an ever-increasing number of strategy concepts and frameworks. Some of these concepts and frameworks are normative whereas others are descriptive. Some are anchored at the individual level of analysis whereas others recognize the collective and distributed nature of strategy and strategizing. It is easy to get lost in this complexity.

The proliferation of strategy concepts and frameworks is perhaps a reflection of key changes that are occurring in our environment. First, the pace at which products, technologies, organizations, industries, and economies are changing is increasing. In some cases, change has become so rapid that a new term has been coined – internet time. Second, interdependencies between economic and social agents are becoming increasingly complex. In many instances, boundaries between once distinct entities are blurring to such an extent that it is difficult to discern where one entity begins and another takes over (Davis and Meyer, 1998; Garud et al., 1998a).

Historically, strategy process has been viewed as a logic used to explain a causal relationship in a variance theory, or a category of concepts dealing with the actions of leaders or organizations (Van de Ven, 1992). These perspectives were sufficient for examining change as a discrete shift from one stable state to another. However, the increasing pace of change and complexity of operation leads us to recognize change as an ongoing dynamic journey, not a discrete event shifting from one unfrozen state to another frozen state (Van de Ven et al., 1999).

Under these conditions, it is more productive to view change as nested sequences of events that unfold over time in the development of individuals, organizations, and industries. In these settings, we are challenged to examine how different mutually dependent groups co-evolve in their efforts. No longer is it appropriate to view organizational change as produced solely by full-blown strategic plans in response to industry life cycle dynamics or as adaptations and partisan mutual adjustments amongst conflicting entities within an evolutionary process (Chakravarthy and Doz, 1992). Instead, organizational change is more appropriately characterized as a 'duality' (Giddens, 1979) wherein organizations are shaped by a continual flow of events that they, in turn, help to shape (Garud and Karnøe, 2001).

Our objective is to explicate this notion of organizational change as duality. To do so, we begin with a review of four basic process theories of change. Van de Ven and Poole (1995) point out that each theory has an implicit 'motor' driving change. An explication of these motors provides a way to systematically explore strategic change processes. In doing so, we can generalize insights between settings driven by similar motors. Moreover, scholars

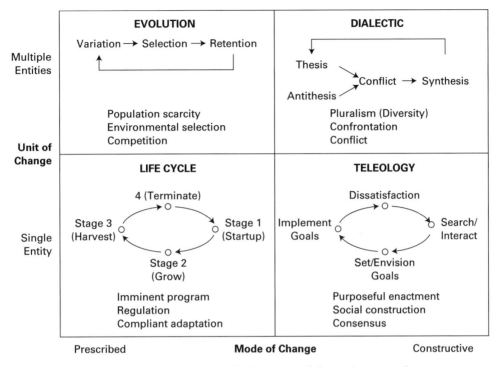

Figure 10.1   *Process theories of organizational development and change (arrows on lines represent likely sequences among events, not causation between events)*
From Van de Ven, A.H. and Poole, M.S. (1995) 'Explaining development and change in organizations', Academy of Management Review, *20(3): 510–40.*

and practitioners can generate additional insights by combining motors to explore more complex processes. Illustrative of such complex processes are non-linear dynamics[1] that are representative of strategic change in contemporary environments; processes that we explore in the conclusion of this chapter.

CHANGE THEORIES

Most organizational scholars would agree that change is a difference in form, quality, or state over time in an entity. The entity may be a strategy, an individual's job, a work group, a strategic business unit, the overall organization, or an industry. Change in any entity manifests itself in differences on a set of dimensions across time.

Much of the literature on organizational change focuses on the nature of these differences, what produced them, and the consequences. The literature offers several useful distinctions about change: planned or unplanned, incremental or radical, evolutionary or revolutionary, emergent or realized, induced or autonomous, recurrent or unprecedented, and more (cf. Burgelman, 1983; Mintzberg and Waters, 1985; Pettigrew, 1985; Tushman and Anderson, 1986). As is apparent from even this short list of distinctions, explaining how and why organizations change has been a central and enduring quest of management scholars and in other social science disciplines (see reviews in Sztompka, 1993; Van de Ven and Poole, 1995).

Van de Ven and Poole (1995) propose a typology of this literature by categorizing change processes along two dimensions: *mode of change* and *unit of change. Mode of change* distinguishes between change sequences that are constructed and emergent in contrast to change sequences that are prescribed *a priori* by either deterministic or probabilistic laws. *Unit of change* distinguishes between change processes that involve the development of a single organizational entity in contrast to processes that involve interactions between two or more entities.

By cross-classifying these two dimensions, Van de Ven and Poole identify four ideal theories that are often used to explain how and why organizational changes unfold – life cycle, teleology, dialectics, and evolution (Figure 10.1). We review these four theories here, for they represent fundamentally different bases for strategic change. Each theory focuses on a different set of change generating mechanisms and causal cycles to explain the processes that unfold.

Teleological Theory

Van de Ven and Poole (1995) describe a teleological theory as based on the assumption that change is guided by a goal or desired end-state. It assumes that the organization is populated by purposeful and adaptive individuals. By themselves, or in interaction with others, they construct an envisioned end-state, take action to reach it, and monitor their progress. This approach underlies many organizational theories of change, including functionalism, decision making, adaptive learning, and most models of strategic choice and goal setting.

Teleological theory views development as a cycle of goal formulation, implementation, evaluation, and modification of goals based on what was learned or intended. The theory can operate in a single individual or among a group of cooperating individuals or organizations who are sufficiently like-minded to act as a single collective entity. Since the individual or cooperating group have the freedom to set whatever goals they like, teleological theory inherently accommodates creativity; there are no necessary constraints or forms that mandate reproduction of the current entity or state.

Teleology does not presume a necessary sequence of events or specify which trajectory development will follow. However, it does imply a standard by which development can be judged – development is that which moves the entity toward its final state. There is no prefigured rule, logically necessary direction or set sequence of stages in a teleological process. Instead, theories based on teleology focus on the prerequisites for attaining the goal or

end-state: the functions that must be fulfilled, the accomplishments that must be achieved, or the components that must be built or obtained for the end-state to be realized. These prerequisites can be used to assess when an entity is developing; it is growing more complex, it is growing more integrated, or it is filling out a necessary set of functions. This assessment can be made because teleological theories posit an envisioned end-state or design for an entity and it is possible to observe movement toward the end-state *vis-à-vis* this standard.

While teleology stresses the purposiveness of the individual as the generating force for change, it also recognizes limits on action. The organization's environment and its resources of knowledge, time, money, etc. constrain what it can accomplish. Some of these constraints are embodied in the prerequisites, which are to some extent defined by institutions and other actors in the entity's environment. Individuals do not override natural laws or environmental constraints but make use of them in accomplishing their purposes.

Life Cycle Theory

Van de Ven and Poole (1995) observe that many management scholars have adopted the metaphor of organic growth as a heuristic device to explain changes in an organizational entity from its initiation to its termination. Witness, for example, often-used references to the life cycle of organizations, products, and ventures, as well as stages in the development of individual careers, groups, and organizations: startup births, adolescent growth, maturity, and decline or death.

Life cycle theory assumes that change is immanent; that is, the developing entity has within it an underlying form, logic, program, or code that regulates the process of change and moves the entity from a given point of departure toward a subsequent end that is already prefigured in the present state. What lies latent, rudimentary, or homogeneous in the embryo or primitive state becomes progressively more realized, mature, and differentiated. External environmental events and processes can influence how the immanent form expresses itself, but they are always mediated by the immanent logic, rules, or programs that govern development.

The typical progression of events in a life cycle model is a unitary sequence (it follows a single sequence of stages or phases), which is cumulative (characteristics acquired in earlier stages are retained in later stages) and conjunctive (the stages are related such that they derive from a common underlying process). This is because the trajectory to the final end-state is prefigured and requires a specific historical sequence of events. Each of these events contributes a certain piece to the final product, and they must occur in a certain order, because each piece sets the stage for the next. Each stage of development can be seen as a necessary precursor of succeeding stages.

Life cycle theories of organizations often explain development in terms of institutional rules or programs that require developmental activities to progress in a prescribed sequence. For example, a US legislative bill enacting state educational reform cannot be passed until it has been drafted and gone through the necessary House and Senate committees. Other life cycle theories rely on logical or natural properties of organizations. For example, Rogers' (1983) theory posits five stages of innovation – need recognition, research on the problem, development of an idea into useful form, commercialization, and diffusion and adoption. The order among these stages is necessitated both by logic and by the natural order of Western business practices.

Dialectical Theory

A third family, dialectical theories, is rooted in the assumption that the organization exists in a pluralistic world of colliding events, forces, or contradictory values that compete with each other for domination and control. These oppositions may be internal to an organization because it may have several conflicting goals or interest groups competing for priority. Oppositions may also arise external to the organization as it pursues directions that collide with those of others (see Burawoy and Skocpol, 1982).

Dialectical process theories explain stability and change by reference to the relative balance of power between opposing entities. Stability is produced through struggles and accommodations that maintain the status quo between oppositions. Change occurs when these opposing values, forces, or events gain sufficient power to confront and engage the status quo. The relative power of an opposing paradigm or antithesis may mobilize to a sufficient degree to challenge the current thesis or state of affairs and set the stage for producing a synthesis. More precisely, the status quo subscribing to a thesis (A) may be challenged by an opposing entity with an antithesis (Not-A), and the resolution of the conflict produces a synthesis (which is Not Not-A). Over time, this synthesis can become the new thesis as the dialectical process recycles and continues. By its very nature, the synthesis is something created new that is discontinuous with thesis and antithesis.

Creative syntheses to dialectical conflicts are not assured. Sometimes an opposition group mobilizes sufficient power to simply overthrow and replace the status quo, just as many organizational regimes persist by maintaining sufficient power to suppress and prevent the mobilization of opposition groups. In the bargaining and conflict resolution literature, the desired creative synthesis is one that represents a win–win solution, while either the maintenance of the status quo or its replacement with an antithesis are often treated as win–lose outcomes of a conflict engagement. In terms of organizational change, maintenance of the status quo represents stability, while its replacement with either the antithesis or the synthesis represents a change, for the better or worse.

Evolutionary Theory

Van de Ven and Poole (1995) restrict 'evolution' to cumulative and probabilistic changes in populations of organizational entities. As in biological evolution, change proceeds through a continuous cycle of variation, selection, and retention (Hannan and Freeman, 1989). Variations, the creation of novel forms, are often viewed to emerge by random chance; they just happen. Selection occurs principally through competition among forms, and the environment selects those forms that are best suited to the resource base of an environmental niche. Retention involves the forces (including inertia and persistence) that perpetuate and maintain certain organizational forms. Retention serves to counteract the self-reinforcing loop between variation and selection (Aldrich, 1979). Thus, evolutionary theory explains changes as recurrent, cumulative, and probabilistic progression of variation, selection, and retention processes.

Alternative theories of social evolution distinguish how traits can be inherited, whether change proceeds incrementally or radically, and whether the unit of analysis focuses on populations or species. A Darwinian perspective argues that traits can be inherited only through inter-generational processes, whereas a Lamarkian argues that traits can be acquired within a generation through learning and imitation. A Lamarkian view appears more appropriate than strict Darwinism applications of social evolution theory to organization and management (March, 1997). As McKelvey (1982) discusses, few solutions have been developed to operationally identify an organizational generation and an intergenerational transmission vehicle.[2]

Social Darwinian theorists emphasize a continuous and gradual process of evolution. In *The Origin of Species*, Darwin (1936) wrote, 'as natural selection acts solely by accumulating slight, successive, favorable variations, it can produce no great or sudden modifications; it can act only by short and slow steps'. Other evolutionists posit a saltational theory of evolution, such as punctuated equilibrium (Gould, 1989), which Tushman and Romanelli (1985) introduced to the management literature. Whether an evolutionary change proceeds at gradual versus saltational rates is an empirical matter, for the rate of change does not fundamentally alter the theory of evolution – at least as it has been adopted thus far by organization and management scholars.

rules exist to regulate the process. *Teleological* theory explains change processes within an entity or among a cooperating set of entities when a desired end-state is socially constructed and consensus emerges on the means and resources to reach the desired end-state. *Dialectical* theory explains change processes when aggressor entities are sufficiently powerful and choose to engage opposition entities through direct confrontation, bargaining, or partisan mutual adjustment. *Evolutionary* theory explains change processes within and between a population of entities as they compete for similar scarce resources in an environmental niche.

These theories are a useful way of thinking about strategic change. In this chapter, we use these theories to understand how change is 'driven' by underlying motors or generative mechanisms. These motors, as we have described earlier, are inferred from a systematic analysis of the sequence of events underlying the development of phenomena. Such an assessment reveals a set of motors that determine the scope and nature of strategic change.

In our use of strategic change one can see how we both build upon and depart from common uses of the term in the strategic management field. For instance, strategic change has been commonly used to denote 'key' organizational changes. Complementing this view is the use of strategic change as being purposive and goal oriented. Strategic change has also been used to denote changes undertaken to align an organization with its environment. The perspective that we have adopted suggests that one applies the theory that best fits the specific conditions to explain change processes.

Summary

Life cycle, teleology, dialectics, and evolutionary theories provide four useful ways to think about and study strategic change in organizations. The relevance of the four theories varies depending upon the conditions surrounding organizational change. Specifically, Van de Ven and Poole (1995) posit that the four theories explain processes of organizational change under the following conditions. *Life cycle* theory explains change processes within an entity when natural, logical, or institutional

IMPLICATIONS FOR STRATEGIC CHANGE

Each theory has important implications for strategic change in organizations. For instance, the notion of teleology has been central to the field of strategy as it offers a way of building theories that celebrate human agency (Child, 1972). In such theories, strategic choice is a key motor driving change with humans possessing an ability to plan and the power to shape economic, social and technological systems. Human agency becomes progressively circumscribed as we begin introducing other change motors. For instance, strategic initiatives may need to be conditioned by life cycle dynamics. Or, change processes could be circumscribed and shaped by a multitude of conflicting social forces that deny planners an ability to unambiguously navigate a stream of unfolding events. Or, change can unfold within an even larger evolutionary process of variation, selection and retention.

Strategic change processes are fundamentally different within each of these theories. Change driven by teleology is planned and deliberate, based on an assessment of the possibilities involved. Change driven by life cycle dynamics represent transitions from one stage to another as an organization progresses along a prescribed sequence and adapts to forces. With dialectical theories, change as adaptation gives way to political processes of partisan conflicts and mutual adjustments among opposing parties. Finally, evolutionary theory examines processes of variation, selection, and retention of alternative organizational forms as generated by competition for scarce resources among competition for processes, adaptation and adoption occur as organizations cycle between periods of exploration and exploitation within an overall punctuated equilibrium process.

We delve deeper into these motors in the rest of this section (Table 10.1). Our objective is to provide readers with a way of thinking about strategic change based on the kinds of motors that one might encounter in different settings. In doing so, we also offer readers with an illustrative survey of the literature on strategic change.

Strategic Issues Associated with Teleology

Of the four change theories, teleology has been the most frequently used theory by strategy scholars and practitioners. This is not surprising as the field of strategic management is presupposed on the assumption that humans are purposeful with a capacity to make strategic choices. Indeed, these approaches underlie most models of strategic choice and goal setting. These models include what Mintzberg and his colleagues label as the positioning,

design and planning schools of thought (Mintzberg et al., 1998). It also includes Allison's (1971) Model I that ascribes rationality to purposeful actors pursuing goals and objectives as they attempt to make consistent value maximizing choices within specified constraints. Indeed, these assumptions have been used by many game theorists in the field of strategy to model strategic behaviors (Schelling, 1960; Camerer, 1991; Postrel, 1991; Saloner, 1991).

Common to rational models of choice is a synoptic view of strategic decision making. In such a perspective thinking is separated from doing as decision makers apply a rational calculus to make optimal choices. However, because decision makers have limited information processing capabilities, most rational choice models accept Simon's (1957) perspective of bounded rationality.

The adaptive learning school is an important extension of this basic teleological model (March and Simon, 1958; March and Shapira, 1987; Levinthal and March, 1981; Lant and Mezias, 1992; Mezias, 1988). Changes in organizations are viewed as movements towards a desired purpose, goal, function, or aspiration. The ability of an organization to meet the aspirations of top managers has an impact on their risk preferences and, consequently, on how the firm might behave in the short run. In the long run, organizational decision makers may adjust their aspiration levels based on the organization's long run performance capabilities.

Those employing strategy theories around teleology often describe the genesis of novelty as being serendipitous (Garud and Karnøe, 2001). Variations from existing plans and standards of measurement are 'mistakes' that only by chance become successful. This is the benign side of such theories. A more pernicious side is evident when an application of these theories results in the active resistance to any deviations from existing standards (Garud and Rappa, 1994; Christensen, 1997). In doing so, practitioners may stamp out the very sources of novelty.

Perspectives on organizational change based on teleology possess many strengths. Most important is that they provide a way of thinking of change as being purposeful, one based on a rational calculation of contexts and contingencies. However, the emphasis on rationality

Table 10.1   *Overview of strategic organizational change*

Process model	Motor	Definition	Strategic organizational change issues
Teleological	Purposeful enactment and social construction.	Is based on the assumption that change proceeds toward a goal or end state. It assumes that the organization is populated by purposeful and adaptive individuals. By themselves or in interaction with others they construct an envisioned end state, take action to reach it, and monitor their progress.	Ex-ante attempts to weigh pros and cons and manage trade-offs employing a rational calculus; Strategic choices dictated by an understanding of interdependencies and end-state outcomes as in game theory.
Life cycle	Compliant adaptation to rules and routines programmed into or outside of the system.	Assumes that change is immanent; that is, the developing entity has within it an underlying form, logic, program, or code that regulates the process of change and moves the entity from a given point of departure toward a subsequent end that is already prefigured in the present state.	Context monitoring and matching; Managing transitions and inflexion points.
Dialectical	Confrontation and conflict among pluralistic entities.	Is rooted in the assumption that the organization exists in a pluralistic world of colliding events, forces, or contradictory values that compete with each other for domination and control. These oppositions may be internal to an organization because it may have several conflicting goals or interest groups competing for priority. Oppositions may also arise external to the organization as it pursues directions that collide with those of others.	Change as negotiated settlement, strategy as representation and governance, resolution of paradoxes and tensions with the articulation of higher order constructs and super-ordinate goals.
Evolutionary	Resource scarcity, competition, and environmental selection.	Change proceeds through a continuous cycle of variation, selection, and retention. Variations, the creation of novel forms, are often viewed to emerge by blind or random chance; they just happen. Selection occurs principally through the competition among forms, and the environment selects those forms that optimize or are best suited to the resource base of an environmental niche. Retention involves the forces (including inertia and persistence) that perpetuate and maintain certain organizational forms.	Trial and error adaptation and adoption processes.

(Contd.)

Table 10.1 *(Contd.)*

Process model	Motor	Definition	Strategic organizational change issues
Complex non-linear	Divergent–convergent cycles of resource infusions and self organizing criticality.	Non-linearity implies that there are feedback loops which vary in strength (loose or tight coupling) and direction (positive or negative) over time between opposing forces or demands. Such non-linear dynamic models are often path dependent or sensitive to initial conditions. This means that small initial differences or fluctuations in trajectories of variables may grow into large differences over time, and as they move far from equilibrium they bifurcate into numerous possible pathways resembling a complex decision tree in a chaotic fractal structure.	Strategy as path creation, bricolage and duality.

places a heavy burden on strategists to have a comprehensive view of the many contingencies that they may encounter in the future (Simon, 1957). They may also assume that interdependent actors will subscribe to the same set of goals and react to the same set of stimuli and information – see Zajac and Bazerman (1991) for situations with games between interdependent parties with competitive blind-spots. Social construction (Berger and Luckmann, 1967; Latour, 1987; Law, 1992; Callon, 1986) and enactment (Weick, 1979) theories relax these assumptions and adopt an interactionist perspective in which organizational purposes and meanings emerge from shared reflections among decision makers.

Strategic Change Issues Associated with Life Cycle Dynamics

The genesis of life cycle dynamics in the strategy literature may be traced to early work in technology studies. Two counter-forces shape the development and diffusion of technological systems. One is a 'law of progress' (Adams, 1931) that points to an exponential growth in the development of a technological system after a relatively slower start. A second force is the 'law of limits' that represents the physical limits one invariably confronts with the performance of a technological system. Together, these two forces combine to prescribe an 'S' shaped curve in the development and diffusion of a technological system (Foster, 1986).

Life cycle dynamics implicit in the 'S' shaped curve were productively employed in other disciplines as well. In the marketing literature, for instance, these dynamics are manifest in product life cycle issues (Kotler, 1994; Mahajan et al., 1990). In the economics literature, life cycle dynamics are apparent in the works of economists such as Vernon (1966). In the organizational field, life cycle dynamics can be found in conceptualizations of organizations progressing from one crisis to another as it grew in scale and scope (Greiner, 1972). They are also implicit in the contagion models that have been employed in diffusion studies and the creation of bandwagons in the development of fads and fashions (Abrahamson, 1991; Rogers, 1983). Clearly this is not an inclusive but an indicative list of those who have contributed to this way of thinking. However, as is apparent from even this short survey, life cycles unfold at various levels.

Several issues confront practitioners associated with processes exhibiting life cycle dynamics. First, there is a need to determine the stage in the life cycle of the organizational entity that is undergoing change. Monitoring internal and external contexts is an approach that has been advocated for this purpose. Although monitoring might appear to be a routine task, cognitive biases may create many difficulties in accomplishing this task (Kahneman et al., 1982; Kiesler and Sproull, 1982; Dutton and Jackson, 1987). Despite these difficulties, some tell-tale signs that have been employed to determine what stage an industry might be in its development are product price, the level of commoditization, the number of new entrants and exits.

In addition to correctly recognizing the stage of development of the entity being examined, another managerial challenge is determining the appropriate mode of operation in each stage of a life cycle. For instance, Utterback (1994) suggests that strategy implies competition based on functionalities during a 'fluid' stage of technology development whereas it implies competition based on reliability, quality and price during a 'specific' stage of development. Similar considerations have led others to suggest that a firm should be organized to 'explore' during early growth stages and organized to 'exploit' during later stages (March, 1991).

The most difficult challenge in managing processes driven by life cycle dynamics is to make transitions in between stages. Transitions are difficult as they imply changing one set of competencies well suited for one stage of operation to a different set of competencies required for a different stage of operation. Indeed, appropriate forms of behavior at one stage of operation may be the very forces that prevent organizations from transiting to the next stage. In other words, transitions become difficult as competencies at one point become traps (Levitt and March, 1988; Leonard-Barton, 1992).

While life cycle models are seductively simple to understand, they are easy for managers to misread. For instance, in the development of cochlear implants (a bio-medical prosthetic device), proponents of the single-channel device that gained early FDA approvals concluded to their peril that industry dynamics had switched to a growth and maturity stage (Garud and Van de Ven, 1992). This belief turned out to be misplaced when other firms continued developing their cochlear implants under the assumption that the industry was still at an introductory stage.

In a similar vein, Henderson (1997) illustrates how beliefs about the limits of a technology

based on its internal structure can be misleading. Using the development of optical photolithography as an example, Henderson shows how the 'natural' or 'physical' limits of the technology were relaxed by unanticipated progress on three fronts: significant changes in the needs and capabilities of users, advances in the performance of component technologies (lenses), and unexpected development in the performance of complementary technologies. These observations lead Henderson to caution against using a life cycle model to predict the limits of a technology. Such predictions must be tempered by a recognition that many other factors (beyond the immediate grasp of those forecasting) may play a role in extending the life of a technology.

Life cycle dynamics are at play in a key field that drives change in contemporary times – semiconductors. For about three decades, Moore's law described progress that has been made with semiconductor chips – a doubling of the number of chips that might fit into a silicon chip every 18 months. Announcements by scientists at Intel suggest that the silicon substrate may be reaching its limit (Markoff, 1999). In Grove's terminology, these limits may represent the onset of a strategic inflexion point with the potential to create a '10X change' (Grove, 1996). As this limit is reached, semiconductor firms will have to decide whether to continue with silicon chips, shift to a new architecture or to a new substrate. To ensure that Intel makes appropriate decision as it encounters this and other such inflexion points, Grove and his colleagues have put in place 'dialectical processes' that shape decision making at Intel. We explore issues associated with dialectical processes as they pertain to strategic change in the next sub-section.

Strategic Change Issues Associated with Dialectical Tension

Since Barnard (1938), organization and management theorists have largely accepted the premise that cooperation and consensus among organizational members are prerequisites for achieving organizational goals. This 'consensus orientation' views conflict between organizational constituents and disagreement about organizational direction as counterproductive activities that divert organizational resources from the coordinated and efficient attainment of commonly accepted goals. Proponents of a consensus orientation cite empirical research demonstrating that organizational performance is facilitated by executive consensus on means (Bourgeois, 1980), consensus regarding both means and ends (Dess, 1987), and that cognitive diversity inhibits comprehensive and thorough long-range planning (Miller et al., 1998).

An alternative perspective suggests that unity and consensus among organizational members is only effective in stable environments and for unambiguous or routine organizational tasks (Nehmeth and Staw, 1989; Jehn, 1995). According to this alternative perspective, disagreement about goals and direction may be a critical organizational dynamic leading to innovation, change, and renewal (Coser, 1957). Organizations that squelch disagreements and foster consensus become rigid and myopic, unable to adapt to changing circumstances or respond to competitive threats. In the words of Dahrendorf (1959: 170), a consensus orientation can answer the question 'What holds organizations together?' but only an orientation that includes conflict and disagreement can answer the question 'What drives organizations on?'.

Dialectical change processes are becoming increasingly relevant as organizations become complex and pluralistic. Dialectical processes are generated as actors with different bases of power and from different cultures interact with one another to influence organizational directions and compete with one another for scarce organizational resources. In a multi-cultural context, a change effort may produce counter reactions that affect the balance of power and associated social structures. Consequently, change itself spawns dialectical reactions in its wake.

Dialectical tensions between people with different values and preferences automatically increase as an organization opens up to change and pluralism. Opening up a firm to multiple constituencies raises a fundamental question – 'In whose interest should a firm be run?' Pursuing such a question takes us to a stakeholder view of the firm (Cyert and March, 1963; Freeman, 1984; Dunbar and Ahlstrom, 1995; Garud and Shapira, 1997; see the *AMJ* issue on stakeholders, social responsibility and performance edited by Harrison and Freeman, 1999).

In such a view, a firm consists of multiple constituencies, each with different interests and values. Organizational actors act in their self-interest, and in doing so, may be in opposition to one another (Pfeffer and Salancik, 1978). An organized entity, then, is not necessarily a unitary actor with an unified purpose. Instead, it consists of many actors with different value systems and preferences who act in their best self-interests.

From this perspective, a firm is a forum for facilitating processes that generate superordinate goals from the meaningful representation of different stakeholders. However, such a synthesis is not always assured. Sometimes one group may gather sufficient power to suppress and prevent the mobilization of opposition groups. Those in authority and power can address conflict in two ways. First, they can use the 'hierarchy' to address conflicts at one level through command and control exercised at a higher level. Or, they can use 'time' to address conflicts through the sequential attention to goals (March and Simon, 1958).

A different set of issues surface as one considers the oppositions that firms encounter as they pursue courses of actions that collide with those pursued by other firms (Van de Ven and Garud, 1993a, b; Garud and Rappa, 1994). For instance, the directions that any firm may pursue along a technological trajectory may be in opposition to those pursued by rivals. Each technological trajectory trades off one dimension of merit for another, thereby generating multiple and conflicting cues.

The presence of multiple and conflicting cues generates ambiguity (Daft and Lengel, 1986). In the presence of resources such ambiguity generates 'action persistence' (Brunsson, 1982; Garud and Van de Ven, 1992; Starbuck, 1983). Researchers developing cochlear implants encountered these conditions in the 1980s (Garud and Van de Ven, 1992). Their response was to close themselves from feedback. Metaphorically it was akin to saying 'damn the torpedoes, full steam ahead'. Indeed, where future states may be enacted in a self-fulfilling manner, such action persistence may be appropriate.

However, as was the case with cochlear implants, these dynamics can result in an escalation of commitment (Staw, 1976). To avoid this eventuality, proactive firms may institute checks and balance to reduce the possibilities of needless escalation of commitments. For instance, Intel has put into place internal mechanisms to engage in critical inquiry (Argyris et al., 1985). Not only do they have mechanisms in place to discuss contrarian inputs from their employees, but their CEO also engages in 'discrediting' (Weick, 1979) by being 'paranoid' (Grove, 1996).

A broader principle implicit in Intel's practices is that ambiguous, uncertain, and changing situations require a more pluralistic leadership structure that encourages the requisite variety of perspectives needed for learning by discovery (Hedberg et al., 1976; Van de Ven and Grazman, 1997; Van de Ven et al., 1999). The value of conflict and disagreement in organizations is based on the assumption that the consideration of multiple perspectives is a critical requirement for effective decision making. Organizations and groups that foster multiple points of view are less likely to overlook critical competitive contingencies that affect their ability to accomplish goals and are more likely to anticipate the need for changes in organizational strategy and structure (Bantel and Jackson, 1989; Lant et al., 1992; Wiersema and Bantel, 1992). They are also more likely to develop creative 'syntheses' (Bartunek, 1993) and less likely to suffer from problems like groupthink (Janis, 1972).

In this regard, Van de Ven et al. (1999) offer insights on the virtues of fostering pluralistic leadership processes. They suggest that the roles of sponsors and champions be countered by a critics' role. It is through the dynamic interplay between these different leadership roles that strategy is forged over time.

However, internal diversity is difficult to maintain. Depending upon the nature of diversity and how it is managed, 'vicious' cycles may emerge (Raghuram and Garud, 1995). Perhaps this is why organizations with executive teams that value contradictory perspectives and keep them in balance are seldom observed. However, studies of these exemplary outliers provide some useful clues. First, Levinthal (1997) discusses structural mechanisms for maintaining diversity within the firm by establishing multiple sources of resources and bases of legitimate authority that promote multiple communities of practice or learning groups (Brown and Duguid, 1991). Second, Bartunek (1993) points out that achieving balanced internal diversity requires strong

institutional leadership to tolerate the ambiguity of holding multiple perspectives, to be able to truly balance the power between managers with different perspectives, and to enable their interaction toward a creative outcome.

Strategic Issues Associated with Evolutionary Processes

At first blush, evolutionary theories challenge the applicability of teleology as a driver of strategic organizational change. Perhaps this is because evolutionary theories are indifferent or 'blind' to the source of variations. As Campbell (1969) discussed, blind variations may reflect purposeful creative acts of individuals, or a mutation of a life cycle process, or a dialectical synthesis from conflict and confrontation between opposing groups. Traces of evolutionary thinking are commonly embedded in emerging perspectives on strategy (see for example the *SMJ* special issue edited by Barnett and Burgelman, 1996).

Indeed, the applicability of evolutionary theories to strategic organizational change can be seen at various levels of analyses. For instance, at a very macro level, technological change can be conceptualized as proceeding through cycles of variation, selection and retention (Tushman and Anderson, 1986). Blind variations are the genesis of novelty, punctuating existing equilibrium that defines status quo. An era of ferment presages the emergence of a selection environment that is manifest in the form of a dominant design (Utterback and Abernathy, 1975). After the emergence of a dominant design, technological change takes on an incremental character as retained competencies and practices are fine honed. The cycle repeats itself as new variations disturb the equilibrium established by old technologies.

Another application of evolutionary theory can be found in the structure–conduct–performance (SCP) perspective as proposed by industrial organization economists such as Bain (1959) and Mason (1957). The SCP perspective attempts to explain inter-industry differences by examining industry structures that, in evolutionary terms, determines its carrying capacities. Specifically, industry structure influences firms' conduct which in turn dictates firms' performance (Porter, 1980).

Random variation, as manifest in technological innovations, often emanates from the 'outside' (Kamien and Schwartz, 1975). Selection environments (the industry structure) are exogenous. And, firms are powerless to abandon their retained competencies, thereby making it difficult for them to change their membership from their strategic groups.

A different application of evolutionary theory can be found in the resource-based view of the firm (Barney, 1986; Conner, 1991; Dierickx and Cool, 1989; Penrose, 1959; Rumelt, 1984; Wernerfelt, 1984; Garud and Nayyar, 1994). Over time, a firm accumulates resources, capabilities and organizational routines for developing new capabilities (Nelson and Winter, 1982; Teece et al., 1997). These core competencies develop in a path dependent manner, thereby making them somewhat unique (David, 1985; Arthur, 1988).

Such uniqueness is a cushion for firms against imitability. However, because of this very uniqueness, a firm's competence may become mismatched with the environment within which it operates (Dunbar et al., 1998). Consequently, firms attempt to shape and co-opt their environments to gain legitimacy (Hirsch, 1975; Hamel and Prahalad, 1994; Porac and Rosa, 1996a; Baum and Oliver, 1991; Rao, 1994; Aldrich and Fiol, 1994; Van de Ven and Garud, 1993a). Others may embed themselves in a constellation of relationships (Granovetter, 1985; Uzzi, 1996; Gulati, 1998). Successful firms gain a competitive advantage. Others may try to adapt themselves to their broader realities, and if successful, are able to overcome competency traps and core rigidities (Levitt and March, 1988; Leonard-Barton, 1992).

At the organization level of analysis the firm itself can be viewed as a selection environment (Bower, 1970; Burgelman, 1983). A firm's administrative context powerfully shapes resource allocation. Innovation within firms occurs through processes that are autonomous and emergent even as they are shaped through processes that are strategically induced by top management (Burgelman, 1983; Mintzberg, 1978; Noda and Bower, 1996).

Applications of evolutionary theory at different levels of analysis often produce different stories of strategic change. Organizational learning provides a good example. Learning is seldom invoked to explain evolution at a

population level. Whole species of firms may appear and disappear depending upon contextual changes that are oftentimes exogenous to firms' choices. Strategy implies stumbling onto a situation of competitive advantage and then protecting the resource niche. Firms protect their niches by actively managing the forces (from rivals, suppliers and buyers, substitutes and new entrants) that might dissipate their profits (Porter, 1980). However, other scholars entertain the possibility of inter-generational learning. Individuals and firms do not passively react to the environments that they confront. Instead, they are capable of adapting to their environments as they learn across different generations of technologies and products (Udayagiri and Schuler, 1999; Garud and Kumaraswamy, 1996).

A Lamarkian view of evolution admits to learning processes within generations. Innovation can be a systematic learning process as firms employ dynamic capabilities (Teece et al., 1997). Moreover, firms attempt to shape emerging structures to complement their competencies (Porac and Rosa, 1996a; Garud et al., 1997). In addition, firms may possess 'meta-capabilities' that provide them with an ability to change the genetic code driving innovation (Garud, 1999).

DYNAMIC INTERACTIONS BETWEEN CHANGE PROCESS THEORIES

Most processes of strategic change that have been systematically observed in field studies are far more complicated than any one of the four process theories that we have discussed so far. Van de Ven and Poole (1995) say this is so for two reasons. First, strategic change extends over space and time in any specific case. Spatial dispersion means that different influences may be acting simultaneously on different parts of the organization, each imparting its own particular momentum to the developmental process. In some cases more than one change motor may influence development and change. Development and change also take time to occur. As time passes, there is opportunity for different motors to come into play, especially given the dispersion of influences. For these reasons, resulting processes are multi-layered and complex.

The complexity of contemporary phenomena is well illustrated by a study of innovation in the development of a biomedical technology, the cochlear implant (Garud and Van de Ven, 1992; Van de Ven and Garud, 1993b). This innovation was shaped by change processes occurring on numerous fronts. A teleological process seemed to explain the course of development of the implant in the firm's R&D lab. The action of top managers in purposefully selecting and funding the program was also consistent with a teleological model. However, the decision premises and timing of managerial interventions moved at a different pace than the pace of efforts of the development team. At a certain point in its development, the product had to achieve FDA approval, which required a sequence of proposals, clinical trials, and regulatory reviews and approvals. This prescribed sequence, which embodied a life cycle motor, came into play later than the teleological motors, but it was so important that the other two spheres of change had to rearrange their efforts to meet its requirements. A fourth influence operated at the larger field of researchers and clinicians concerned with hearing health. The firm's pioneering implant design was initially supported by the field, but evidence mounted which led most researchers and clinicians to switch allegiance to a competing firm's design. The complex interplay of these different motors, which operated in different times and places, created a complicated developmental sequence that was difficult to understand until these diverse influences were sorted out.

A second reason for the complexity of specific strategic change theories is the inherent incompleteness of any single motor. Each theory has one or more components whose values are determined exogenously to the model. For example, in the evolutionary model, variations are assumed to arise randomly, but the process that gives rise to variation remains unspecified. In the dialectical model, the origin of the antithesis is obscure, as is the source of dissatisfaction in the teleological model, and the processes which trigger startup and termination in the life cycle model.

In this regard, generative mechanisms from one theory can be used to account for exogenous components of another. For instance, the selection process in the evolutionary model can be used to account for termination in the life cycle. So also, the implementation step in the teleological cycle can trigger the startup event in the life cycle and the antithesis in the dialectic. The synthesis in the dialectic could be the source of variation in the evolutionary cycle. There are many other possible interrelations. In short, events from one model can be used to remedy the incompleteness of another model of change.

It is for these reasons that Van de Ven and Poole (1995) suggested that most specific theories of organizational development and change are actually composites of two or more ideal type motors. Observed change and development processes in organizations are often more complex than any one of these theories suggest because conditions may exist to trigger an interplay between several change motors and produce interdependent cycles of change. While each of these types has its own internal logic, complexity and the potential for theoretical confusion arise from the interplay among different motors. In the remainder of this chapter we focus attention on the complex non-linear dynamics that may be produced by interplays between the theories of change.

Complex Non-Linear Dynamics

A dynamic model is one where the variables (here the operation of different change processes) at a given time are a function (at least in part) of the same processes at an earlier time (Koput, 1992). Complex dynamics are generated because of non-linear positive or negative feedback. Non-linearity implies that the response is not directly proportional to the feedback stimulus. Van de Ven and Poole (1995) point out that temporal shifts in the relative balance between positive and negative feedback loops in the operation of different change motors can push an organization to flow towards a fixed-point equilibrium, oscillate in a periodic sequence between opposites, bifurcate far from equilibrium and spontaneously create new structures, or behave in a random fashion.

Fixed-Point Equilibrium

Organizational stability occurs when a negative feedback loop exists between the operation of prescribed (outcomes determined or governed by probabilistic laws) and constructive (outcomes 'enacted' as change unfolds) motors of change. For example, the institutional routines or the established goals of the organization are sufficient to keep the creation of new programs or conflicts between alternative programs within limits so that the organization does not fly apart from too much novelty, and thereby produce incremental adaptations flowing toward a stable equilibrium.

Oscillation in a Periodic Sequence

Organizational cycles, fads, or pendulum swings occur when the relative influence of positive and negative feedback loops between change motors alternate in a periodic pattern and push the organization to oscillate somewhat farther from its stable equilibrium orbit. Such recurrent cycles are exemplified in some models of vicious circles in organizations (Masuch, 1985), group entrainment processes (McGrath and Kelly, 1986), and creative destruction (Schumpeter, 1942).

Bifurcation Far from Equilibrium

Organizational transformations and spontaneous novel structures can be produced when strong imbalances occur between constructive and prescribed change motors, which may push the organization out of its equilibrium orbit and produce bifurcations (Prigogine and Stengers, 1984) or catastrophes (Zeeman, 1976) leading to chaotic patterns of organizational change.

Random Behavior

The behavior of change motors in a developing organization may be so complicated and indeterminate to render deterministic modeling infeasible – the best one can do is to stochastically model the behavior as a random process. Stochastic models based on the theory of random processes allow us to make better predictions than we could make with no model at all (Eubank and Farmer, 1990: 76).

As this discussion suggests, a major emerging direction for scholarship on strategic change is studying non-linear dynamical systems models of organizational change and development (see the *Organization Science* issue on complexity edited by Anderson et al., 1999 and the journal on *Emergence* edited by Michael Lissac). When we move from a world

that is linear to one that is non-linear, we need a different way of describing processes associated with strategic change. Paraphrasing Pettigrew (1992), we need a way of explaining phenomena in a manner that: acknowledges the embeddedness of actions, explores temporal interconnections between processes, provides a role in explanation for context and action, is holistic rather than linear, and links process analysis to the location and explanation of outcomes. We direct our attention to these facets of an emerging paradigm.

IMPLICATIONS OF NON-LINEAR DYNAMICS FOR STRATEGIC CHANGE

Contemporary phenomena are driven by dynamics that arise from rich connections between economic and social agents. Partly induced by the introduction of new information technologies, these rich connections are blurring the boundaries between once distinct spheres of activities across technological, organizational and cultural domains. Elements that may once have functioned independently of one another are now becoming coupled. With such coupling, changes in one entity can trigger changes in others in a domino fashion. Indeed, because of interactive complexity (Perrow, 1984), the system begins exhibiting complex non-linear dynamics. As a result, the system becomes prone to processes that can generate vicious or virtuous circles (Masuch, 1985). Continual change is a key part of this new landscape. To keep up with change, any actor, in an interactively complex landscape, has to draw upon others' capabilities, thereby establishing links with them. And, in the very process of doing so, these inter-linked actors foster greater change. The reciprocal relationship between change and interdependence is a key facet of network fields such as computer hardware and software (see, for instance, Garud and Kumaraswamy, 1993; Garud et al., 1998a).

Change and interdependence point to another facet of contemporary phenomena – the value of belonging to a network with members who subscribe to a common architecture. Belonging to a common network gives rise to positive externality effects. Specifically, as the size of the network increases, so do the benefits to members because of knowledge spillover or module substitution effects (Garud and Kumaraswamy, 1995; Katz and Shapiro, 1985; Farrell and Saloner, 1986). Indeed, these benefits increase at an increasing rate, a path-dependent dynamic that has been labeled as representing increasing returns (Arthur, 1988).

Phenomena with increasing returns are path dependent and sensitive to initial conditions (Arthur, 1988). This means that small initial differences or fluctuations in trajectories of variables may grow into large differences over time, and as they move far from equilibrium they bifurcate into numerous possible pathways resembling a complex decision tree in a chaotic fractal structure. In a chaotic state the pathways that are taken in the branching cannot be predicted; they represent spontaneously-created new structures that emerge in a seemingly random order (Ginsberg et al., 1996). However, such chaotic processes have a hidden order which typically consists of a relatively simple nonlinear system of dynamic relationships between only a few variables (Eubank and Farmer, 1990: 75). Underlying the indeterminate and seemingly random processes of strategic change processes often observed in organizations there may be such a relatively simple system of nonlinear dynamic relationships between a few of the motors of change examined here.

How might one navigate a flow of events that exhibit complex nonlinear dynamics? An answer lies in appreciating the dualities associated with interactively-complex systems. Duality alludes to the mutual dependence of agency and structure wherein structure is both medium and outcome of practices (Giddens, 1979). Any action produces a ripple effect on interdependent actors – the 'structure'.[3] This ripple effect, in turn, shapes actions. Stated differently, any activity occurs and unfolds within an overall landscape that represents the residuals of prior actions. In other words, actions are embedded in the structures that they generate.[4]

One way to think about the nature of embedding is to appreciate the 'dimensionality' space within which action unfolds (Dooley and Van de Ven, 1999). Dimensionality space represents the degrees of freedom that are available for strategic choice. To the extent that the dimensionality space for strategic choice is small (phenomena are 'over embedded') there are few degrees of freedom to

maneuver. In contrast, to the extent that the dimensionality space is large (phenomena are 'under embedded'), there are larger degrees of freedom to maneuver.

The nature of embedding of actions in structures has a bearing on the type of dynamics that may unfold (Garud and Jain, 1996). For instance, if actions are unconstrained by existing structures, random (or path independent) behavior is likely to unfold. Random behavior is likely to unfold as the residues from the past have little influence on present outcomes. There are many techniques to foster such 'disembedded' processes. One technique is to engage in re-engineering, a technique that advocates beginning afresh by obliterating the past (Hammer and Champy, 1993). Another technique is to embrace an outsider's perspective. And, often associated with these techniques is an infusion of resources to sponsor initiatives that have the potential to breakthrough existing structures.

A different set of path-dependent dynamics ensue when actions are totally constrained by the structures that they generate. Rather than possibilities of the future, sediments of the past shape action. Such systems are governed by 'periodic attractors' wherein any perturbation sets in motion a counter reaction that brings the system back into equilibrium. It is not uncommon to find such systems in situations that demand reliability and standardization. Such systems are typically governed by institutionalized rules and routines accumulated over time. Indeed, many firms that adopted mass production systems are examples of such 'over embedded' systems designed to celebrate the past.

Thus, we suggest that the nature of embedding is a strategic variable. The extent to which a system is designed to exhibit one or the other dynamics is partly dependent upon how the organizational system is designed. In this context, strategic organizational variables that can be manipulated are the level of resources deployed for exploration, the number and kinds of rules that are in play, the flexibility in the interpretation of rules, rules for changing the rules, and the like. Such processes have been observed in studies of semi-conductor architectures (Garud and Kumaraswamy, 1995) and browser architecture (Garud et al., 1998a).

If the nature of embedding is a strategic variable, is it possible to design systems that are neither over embedded nor disembedded but, instead, lie somewhere in between? If we can accomplish such 'just' embedding, then it may be possible to generate dynamics that are neither random nor determined (Garud and Jain, 1996; Baum and Silverman, 2001). Instead, they may be characterized by path creation processes that harness continuity and change at the same time.

Organizational systems designed to spawn actions that are neither constrained nor unconstrained by the structures that they generate are poised at the 'edge of chaos' (Stacey, 1995; Cheng and Van de Ven, 1996; Polley, 1997; Brown and Eisenhardt, 1998). The extent to which resources are allocated to a set of activities and the number and type of rules that shape them are strategic variables that can be manipulated to shape the dynamics that are set in motion. In addition, the type of coupling between activities is another strategic variable (Weick, 1979). 'Loose' coupling between activities sponsors co-evolutionary dynamics where there are slippages in time and space between actions in one arena of activities and actions in another.

Systems characterized by such embedding are driven by 'strange attractors' and exhibit chaotic behavior. The nature of these processes are such that the structuration landscape bifurcates as agents make choices. Any action builds upon the past and yet departs from it. Indeed, any action opens up several associated possibilities almost in the form of a complex decision tree.[5] Within such a tree, any path can be traced to an earlier path but cannot be predetermined by it. That is, it may be possible to trace existing choices to earlier choices, but it may not be possible to predict future choices based on present choices. This is because future states are based on possibilities that have yet to be realized based on choices yet to be exercised. More importantly, these future possibilities are enacted at any point in time in a self-fulfilling manner as resources are deployed to undertake an initiative. In other words it is possible to trace a 'pattern' but not predict the exact 'path' (Dooley and Van de Ven, 1999).

These dynamics have important implications for strategic organizational change. New landscapes emerge in the very act of 'trying' something. This structurating facet of action rationality (Brunsson, 1982; Pettigrew, 1992;

Polley and Van de Ven, 1995) places a premium on trying something rather than endlessly analyzing a situation for an optimal course of action. Such an action rationality allows one to probe the system even as it is being created. Feedback that is generated from such a probe becomes the basis for making appropriate changes as new possibilities open up.

These processes are illustrated in several studies including a study of the development of VCRs (Rosenbloom and Cusumano, 1987), a comparative study of wind turbine development in the US and in Denmark (Garud et al., 1999), the emergence of brightness enhancement films at 3M (Garud, 1999), the emergence of browsers (Garud et al., 1998a), and the emergence of 'new media' initiatives in Silicon Alley (Garud and Lant, 1999).

Action rationality, however, can lead to an escalation of commitment to a failing course of action. Consequently, a key question is 'How large should these action steps be?'. One answer is to keep action steps as small as possible to avoid an escalation of commitment yet large enough to gain meaningful feedback. Such a process embraces a 'real options' approach to the navigation of complex dynamic flow of events (Kumaraswamy, 1996; Garud et al., 1998b). Options value is realized because investments in any step generates an outcome that serves as a basis for deciding in real time whether or not to continue, modify or abandon a course of action. In this way, a practitioner navigates a flow of events by generating a set of compound options that represents a sequence of steps that evolves through the choices made by practitioners at each stage of a complex journey.

The creation of a landscape even as agents probe their embedding structures represents a process of 'path creation' (Garud and Karnøe, 2001; Karnøe and Garud, 2000). Those who attempt to create new paths are embedded in existing structures even as they attempt to embed out of these structures. Mindful of these processes, those attempting to create paths take steps that are able to mobilize rather than alienate interdependent actors. Moreover, such steps are taken consistent with the time and resources required to complete each step.

It is here one can begin seeing how the four motors (teleology, life cycle, dialectics and evolutionary) apply, albeit in different ways. For instance, teleology, in this context, is 'muted' agency as agents attempting to create paths come to realize that they are enabled and constrained by the structures that they are embedded in. Indeed, actions and structures co-evolve, thereby creating a duality. The embeddedness of any strategic initiative is underscored by the responses that are evoked with any initiative; the trick being to take appropriate steps that mobilize rather than alienate interdependent constituencies. Indeed, managing the thin line between initiatives that can mobilize as compared to those that can alienate is a critical factor in determining whether practitioners harness increasing returns associated with growth or fall prey to the diminishing returns associated with maturity and decline. In other words, life cycle issues are manifest in the ways in which practitioners shape emerging structures and actions so as to benefit from increasing rather than diminishing returns.

Implicit in action rationality and the process of path creation is strategy as bricolage (Garud and Karnøe, 2001). Bricolage is a French word with two meanings. One meaning is of a process connoting resourcefulness and adaptiveness. A second meaning is of a final product created with materials at hand. Such a dual meaning is similar in intent to dual meanings associated with words such as 'building', 'construction' and 'work', designating both a process and its finished product (Dewey, 1934). As Dewey explains, for these words 'Without the meaning of the verb that of the noun remains blank' (Dewey, 1934: 51).

It is as both noun and verb that we introduce strategy as bricolage. Bricolage embodies loose coupling between actions and structure (Giddens, 1979), wherein actors probe their worlds even as they create them through a process of negotiation with others. It is this structuration quality that we want to capture with our use of the term bricolage where strategic organizational change represents a duality. In this conceptualization, actors navigate a flow of events by being mindful of when to persist and when to desist, when to credit and when to discredit, when it might be possible to make changes to boundary conditions – all the while cognizant of the fact that they are placing bets, the outcomes to which can be only described in probabilistic terms. When we allow for practical experimentation coupled with thoughtful modifications, a process of

bricolage, we allow for the evolution of a system in an emergent way.[6]

Such a process of bricolage is similar to processes observed by other scholars. For instance, recognizing the challenges of navigating through complexity, scholars have offered notions such as the 'science of muddling through' (Lindblom, 1959) or 'logical incrementalism' (Quinn, 1978). Mintzberg et al. (1976) are additional process proponents who recognize the importance of bricolage for dealing with emergent strategies. In a similar vein, Burgelman's (e.g. 1983) work offers considerable insights on autonomous approaches in contradistinction to the notion of induced approaches. More recently, Brown and Eisenhardt (1998) offer observations on how product development efforts can unfold in an emergent fashion within minimal structures across product generations.

RESEARCH AGENDA

We encourage scholars to study strategic change processes as an understanding of how organizations change lies at the very core of our discipline. Van de Ven and Huber (1990) note that study of strategic change tends to focus on two kinds of questions: What are the antecedents or consequences of strategic changes? How does a strategic change process emerge, develop, grow or terminate over time?

Although the vast majority of research to date has focused on the first question, we encourage much greater research attention to the second question. The 'how' question is concerned with describing and explaining the temporal sequence of events that unfold as a strategic organizational change occurs. Process studies are fundamental to gaining an appreciation of dynamic organizational life, and to developing and testing theories of organizational adaptation, change, innovation, and redesign.

The change topics that might be included in this research agenda are limitless, and can vary greatly in scope, complexity, and novelty. For example, to stay in business, most organizations follow routines to reproduce a wide variety of recurring changes, such as adapting to economic cycles, periodic revisions in products and services, and ongoing instances of personnel turnover and executive succession. These commonplace changes within organizations are typically programmed by pre-established rules or institutional routines and can be analyzed and explained using a life cycle theory of change. At the industry or population level, competitive or environmental shifts in resources typically govern the rates of reproduction (and resulting size and number) of various forms of organizations. Evolutionary theory is useful for explaining these population-level changes as the probabilistic workings of variation, selection, and retention processes.

Occasionally, organizations also experience unprecedented changes for which no established routines or procedures exist. They include many planned (as well as unplanned) changes in organizational creation, innovation, turnaround, reengineering, cultural transformation, merger, divestiture, and many other issues the organization may not have experienced. These kinds of novel changes can be usefully analyzed and explained with a teleological theory if they are triggered by a reframing or frame-breaking strategy of powerful people in control of the organization. Alternatively, a dialectical theory might better explain the novel change process when conflicts and confrontations between opposing groups occur to produce a synthesis out of the ashes of the conflict engagements.

The processes through which these novel changes unfold are far more complex and unpredictable than routine changes because the former require developing and implementing new change routines, while the latter entail implementing tried-and-tested routines. Novel changes entail the creation of originals, whereas routine changes involve the reproduction of copies. Novel changes are strategic innovations, whereas routine changes are business as usual.

Having said this, it is important to recognize a caveat. Existing theories of strategic organizational change are explanatory, but not predictive. Statistically, we should expect most incremental, convergent, and continuous changes to be explained by either life cycle or evolutionary theories, and most radical, divergent, and discontinuous changes to be explained by teleological or dialectical theories. But these actuarial relationships may not be causal.

For example, the infrequent statistical occurrence of a discontinuous and radical mutation may be caused by a glitch in the operation of a life cycle model of change. So also, the scale-up of a teleological process to create a planned strategic reorientation for a company may fizzle, resulting only in incremental change.

Studies of more complex strategic organizational changes are often more challenging to explain because several generative mechanisms may be driving the underlying dynamics of the specific change being investigated. An appreciation of these complexities is useful for identifying the scope of the research, including issues such as the research question, the levels and units of analysis, the granularity of the data that must be gathered and the time frame within which data must be gathered.

For example, consider a large scale project that we have tracked over a decade – the development of cochlear implants. Our early preliminary discussions with those associated with cochlear implants revealed that this was a field where the Food and Drug Administration (FDA) played a key role in the strategic success and failure of products and firms. At that time, the FDA 'life cycle' motor involving Investigational Device Exemption (IDE), clinical trials, and 'Pre Market Approval' (PMA) could take seven years or more. Recognizing this fact, 3M Corporation set aside a 10-year time frame for its cochlear implant program.

To be sure, there were intermediary mileposts indicative of the sub-processes and motors unfolding within the larger 'unitary' FDA driven sequence. For instance, one could see teleological driven change as 3M practitioners allocated resources to develop single-channel devices based on their judgments as to what would benefit profoundly deaf the most. Or, one could see dialectical change processes as opposing approaches to the development of cochlear implants informed and shaped emerging regulatory mechanisms. Or, one could see evolutionary processes at play as institutional and technical environments co-evolved.

We studied all these processes in our 10-year longitudinal research program with cochlear implants. We started our study in the early 1980s when 3M was initiating its cochlear implant program and when the cochlear implant industry was just starting to emerge. We concluded our longitudinal study in 1989 when a dominant design emerged at a 'consensus development conference' organized by NIH/FDA and when 3M decided to withdraw from cochlear implants. Along the way, the specific sub-processes that we observed (within the overall FDA logic) guided the type of questions we pursued, the level of granularity of data that we gathered and the approaches to the analysis of the data that we adopted.

This heuristic of developing a research agenda based on an unfolding understanding of the main and sub-drivers of a phenomena is a useful strategy for research in any setting. In the rest of this section, we will offer additional thoughts on the kinds of research questions, data collection approaches, analytical schemes and interpretive mechanisms that are appropriate. They are discussed in greater depth by Poole et al. (2000).

Research Questions

Because of its strong teleological underpinnings, strategic management scholars tend to gravitate towards studies that seek answers to our first type of question about the antecedents and consequences of strategic changes. Answers to this kind of question invariably drives us to take a variance approach (Mohr, 1982). Variance studies are concerned with establishing necessary and sufficient causation between dependent and independent variables. Such an approach to knowledge creation is valuable in contexts that are stable and where the boundaries of the phenomenon under consideration are clear. However, such an approach is less useful for examining process questions about the order and sequence of events that unfold in a change process being studied.

A process perspective is implicit in a 'how' question, such as 'How does a strategic change process emerge, develop, grow or terminate over time?'. Process theories explicate the confluence of forces that are individually necessary but only collectively sufficient for the occurrence of an outcome (Pettigrew, 1987; Tsoukas, 1989; Van de Ven and Poole, 1995; Drazin and Sandelands, 1992). Process theories offer a story of how these events occur – what are the necessary conditions, and how do they co-occur and interact in a probabilistic manner to yield the manifest phenomena

that we now observe? The basis of explanation is probabilistic combinations of precursors and focal units in such a way as to yield the outcome (Poole et al., 2000).

Nature of Generalizations

The bases of generalization in most process theories is not from a sample to a population but from a case to a theory (cf. Garud and Rappa, 1994). The way this is accomplished is not by teasing out efficient causation between variables, but, instead, by teasing out the deeper generative mechanisms that account for observed patterns in the events. And, these drivers can only be explicated if we have recorded events over time. That is, rather than look at co-variations between observable variables *at a point in time*, this approach attempts to look at the deeper drivers that account for the co-variations of variables *over a point in time*.

The 'degrees of freedom' required to make generalizations from an in-depth process study is different from those required to generalize from a large sample variance study. Specifically, as Campbell suggests:

> In a case study done by an alert social scientist who has thorough local acquaintance, the theory he uses to explain the focal difference also generates predictions or expectations on dozens of other aspects of the culture, and he does not retain the theory unless most of these are also confirmed. In some sense, he has tested the theory with degrees of freedom coming from the multiple implications on any one theory. The process is a kind of pattern-matching in which there are many aspects of the pattern demanded by theory that are available for matching with his observations on the local setting. (Campbell, 1975: 181–2)

Data Collection

Gaining access to longitudinal data is a key requirement for conducting process research. Equally important is to study 'phenomenon-in-the-making'. That is, researchers must be able to consider possible states *as they unfold* from the point of view of the actors involved at that point in time. Under these circumstances, potential successes and failures have to be studied symmetrically (Bijker et al., 1987).

Ideally, this task would require data gathering on a real time basis. This can be time consuming and a difficult task to accomplish. A viable alternative would be to track events on a 'seemingly' real time basis based on archival data. That is, researchers would have to put themselves at the time of the event without knowledge of the end-states that emerged.

These deliberations lead to another methodological facet – event neutrality (Garud, 1999). An event that occurs at any point in time has to be understood from a larger perspective spanning time and interpretive systems. For instance, the value of an event may differ over time, across levels of an organizational hierarchy and across the interpretive frames of different firms. It is for these reasons that what may appear to be a neutral event to a key stakeholder at one point in time may set in motion a sequence of events that shapes the evolution of phenomena in the future (Arthur, 1988; David, 1985).

Event neutrality has several implications for data collection. Besides gathering data over time, it is key to gather data from multiple sources and from multiple levels of analyses. Such a strategy allows the researcher an opportunity to track both continuity and change. Specifically, tracking events over time offers an opportunity to perceive and record change as a departure from existing forms and functions. Tracking change from multiple perspectives offers an opportunity to view who perceives change when. And tracking change at multiple levels offers an opportunity to see how change at one level of analysis unfolds with continuity at a different level of analysis.

Data Analysis

In preparation for a more detailed analysis of the data (as discussed by Poole et al., 2000), there are several basic steps one might take. A first step is to generate a chronology of events within and across constructs of the interest. A simple eyeballing of this chronology might reveal patterns that provide a clue as to the types of drivers at play. To supplement this effort, one might generate plots of events across constructs of interest. These plots can provide a visual representation of rates and directions of change of events within and across constructs.

These analyses serve as groundwork for a more detailed analysis of the data. Three strategies cover the many variations of more detailed data analysis. The first is to begin forming connections between concepts and identifying the complex feedback connections between them. Eventually, these cause maps can be displayed as a graphic and presented in the form of a narrative (Garud and Van de Ven, 1989; Van de Ven and Garud, 1993b).

In contrast to this qualitative process research approach, the variance theory approach begins identifying relationships between variables appropriately lagged in time by employing structural equations and other similar statistical tools (Garud and Van de Ven, 1992). More recently, Poole et al. (2000) describe how it is possible to identify the 'attractors' that might underlie the events by applying advances in non-linear dynamics to management research (see also Baum and Silverman, 2001).

A third strategy is to run computer simulations that might reveal the evolution of phenomena that exhibit complex non-linear dynamics. For running meaningful simulations, one has to have a sense of the range of values that simulation parameters can take. Data that has been gathered can serve as a good starting point for establishing the range. Mezias and Eisner (1997) have employed such a strategy to show that the interaction between levels of competition and imitability in the context of complex population dynamics can produce surprising patterns of innovation and refinement of technology.

CONCLUSION

It is easy to get lost in theories on strategic organization change processes unless we possess a systematic way of understanding this ever growing literature. We adopted Van de Ven and Poole's (1995) typology to make sense of this literature and to compare change processes in terms of the generative motors that derive from four theoretical perspectives – teleology, life cycle dynamics, dialectical processes and evolutionary processes. Each theory has different implications for strategic change. For instance, strategic change associated with teleology occurs in response to preset plans and goals. Strategic change associated with life cycle dynamics occurs in response to changes in the stages in the life cycle of an entity that occurs because of an inherent life cycle logic. Strategic change associated with dialectic processes occurs through mutual partisan adjustment of pluralistic entities. And strategic change in response to evolutionary processes occurs in response to firms' attempts to endogenize variation, selection and retention processes.

As organizations open themselves to a multitude of stimuli, change processes will become more complex than any of these four pure forms can suggest. Under these conditions, it is important for us to have a way of thinking about strategic change that matches the complex environments that we have to navigate. We would indeed be conducting a procrustean transformation if we were to use a uni-dimensional motor as the basis for the articulation of strategic change when the phenomena itself asks for a more sophisticated analysis involving the interplay of more than one motor.

In this regard, we showed how the interactions between motors can generate complex non-linear dynamics. These dynamics challenge us to think about strategic change in ways that are different from those we may encounter in traditional settings. Specifically, we must conceptualize strategic change as a fluid emerging process that is closer to a process of bricolage than it is to brilliance. We suggest that this represents a new view of strategic organizational change as duality. Understanding strategic organizational change as duality represents a central and productive challenge for strategy and management scholars.

ACKNOWLEDGEMENTS

We thank Andrew Pettigrew, Sanjay Jain, Arun Kumaraswamy, Daniel Beunza and Roger Dunbar, Scott Poole, and Bala Chakravarthy for their inputs.

NOTES

1 These complex dynamics are created because of non-linear feedback. Feedback can be negative or positive. Non-linearity implies that a response is not directly proportional to the feedback stimulus. Non-linear feedback produces complex dynamics in organizational systems.

2 Recent work on intra- and inter-generational learning holds the promise for developing such solutions (Garud and Kumaraswamy, 1996; Garud and Nayyar, 1994; Udayagiri and Schuler, 1999; Wade-Benzoni, 1999).

3 We use the term structure synonymously with context. Strategic choice by one actor manifests itself as context when viewed from the perspective of another interdependent agent. Another way of looking at this is to recognize the existence of reciprocal interactions between a group of variables wherein one variable affects, and is in turn affected by, another variable (Maruyama, 1963).

4 This structuration process is illustrated in several studies including emergence of wind turbines in Denmark (Garud and Karnøe, 2001), the emergence of cochlear implants (Van de Ven and Garud, 1993a; Garud and Rappa, 1994), the co-evolution of CT Scanners and radiology departments (Barley, 1986), the co-evolution of organizational forms and technologies (Orlikowski, 1992).

5 This process is illustrated by dynamics of change associated with the microreplication technology platform as described in '3M innovation: a process of mindful replication' (Garud, 1999).

6 These processes are explicated in greater detail in a paper that explores path creation and path dependence in the emergence of wind turbines (Karnøe and Garud, 2000).

REFERENCES

Abrahamson, E. (1991) 'Managerial fads and fashions: diffusion and rejection of innovations', *Academy of Management Review*, 16: 586–612.

Adams, H. (1931) *The Education of Henry Adams*. New York: The Modern Library.

Aldrich, H. (1979) *Organizations and Environments*. Englewood Cliffs, NJ: Prentice Hall.

Aldrich, H. E. and Fiol, C. M. (1994) 'Fools rush in? The institutional context of industry creation', *Academy of Management Review*, 19(4): 645–70.

Allison, G. T. (1971) *Essence of Decision: Explaining the Cuban Missile Crisis*. Boston: Little, Brown and Co.

Anderson, P., Meyer, A., Eisenhardt, K., Carley, K. and Pettigrew, A. (1999) 'Introduction to the special issue: application of complexity theory to organization science', *Organization Science*, 10: 233–6.

Argyris, C., Putnam, R. and Smith, D. M. (1985) *Action Science*. San Francisco: Jossey-Bass.

Arthur, B. (1988) 'Self-reinforcing mechanisms in economics', in P. Anderson et al. (eds), *The Economy as an Evolving Complex System*. Reading, Mass: Addison-Wesley.

Bain, J. S. (1959) *Industrial Organization*. New York: Wiley.

Barnard, C. (1938) *The Functions of the Executive*. Cambridge, MA: Harvard University Press.

Bantel, K. A. and Jackson, S. E. (1989) 'Top management and innovations in banking: does the composition of the top team make a difference?', *Strategic Management Journal*, 10: 107–24.

Barley, S. (1986) 'Technology as an occasion for structuring: evidence from observations of CT scanners and the social order of radiology departments', *Administrative Science Quarterly*, 31: 78–108.

Barnett, W. P. and Burgelman, R. A. (1996) 'Evolutionary perspectives on strategy', *Strategic Management Journal*, 17: 5–20.

Barney, J. B. (1986) 'Strategic factor markets: expectations, luck and business strategy', *Management Science*, 33: 1231–41.

Bartunek, J. M. (1993) 'Multiple cognitions and conflicts associated with second order organizational change', in J. K. Muringham (ed.), *Social Psychology in Organizations*. Englewood Cliffs, NJ: Prentice Hall. pp. 343–437.

Baum, J. A. C. and Oliver, C. (1991) 'Institutional linkages and organizational mortality', *Administrative Science Quarterly*, 36: 187–218.

Baum, J. A. C. and Silverman, B. (2001) 'Complexity, attractors, and path dependence and creation in technological evolution', in R. Garud and P. Karone (eds), *Path Dependence and Creation*. Mahwah, NJ: Lawrence Earlbaum Associates.

Berger, P. and Luckmann, T. (1967) *The Social Construction of Reality: A Treatise in the Sociology of Knowledge*. London: Penguin.

Bijker, W. E., Hughes, T. P. and Pinch, T. J. (1987) *The Social Construction of Technological Systems*. Cambridge, MA: MIT Press.

Bourgeois, L. J. (1980) 'Strategy and environment: a conceptual integration', *Academy of Management Review*, 5: 25–39.

Bower, J. L. (1970) *Managing the Resource Allocation Process*. Boston, MA: Harvard University Press.

Brown, J. S. and Duguid, P. (1991) 'Organizational learning and communities of practice: toward a unified view of working, learning and innovation', *Organizaton Science*, 2: 40–57.

Brown, S. L. and Eisenhardt, K. M. (1998) *Competing on the Edge: Strategy as Structured Chaos*. Boston, MA: Harvard Business School Press.

Brunsson, N. (1982) 'The irrationality of action and action rationality: decisions, ideologies, and organizational actions', *Journal of Management Studies*, 19: 29–34.

Burawoy, M. and Skocpol, T. (1982) *Marxist Inquiries: Studies of Labor, Class, and States*. Chicago: University of Chicago Press.

Burgelman, R. A. (1983) 'A process model of internal corporate venturing in a diversified major firm', *Administrative Science Quarterly*, 28: 223–4.

Callon, M. (1986) 'The sociology of an actor-network: the case of the electric vehicle', in M. Callon, J. Law and A. Rip (eds), *Mapping the Dynamics of Science and Technology: Sociology of Science in the Real World*. London: Macmillan.

Camerer, C. (1991) 'Does strategy research need game theory?', *Strategic Management Journal*, 12: 137–52.

Campbell, D. (1969) 'Variation and selective retention in socio-cultural evolution', *General Systems*, 16: 69–85.

Campbell, D. T. (1975) ' "Degrees of freedom" and the case study', *Comparative Political Studies*, 8: 178–93.

Chakravarthy, B. S. and Doz, Y. (1992) 'Strategy process research: focusing on corporate self-renewal', *Strategic Management Journal*, 13: 5–14.

Cheng, Y. and Van de Ven, A. (1996) 'Learning the innovation journey: order out of chaos?', *Organization Science*, 7(6): 593–614.

Child, J. (1972) 'Organizational structure, environment and performance: the role of strategic choice', *Sociology*, 6: 1–22.

Christensen, C. M. (1997) *The Innovator's Dilemma: When New Technologies Cause Great Firms to Fail*. Boston, MA: Harvard Business School Press.

Conner, K. R. (1991) 'A historical comparison of resource-based theory and five schools of thought within industrial organization economics: do we have a new theory of the firm?', *Journal of Management*, 17: 121–54.

Coser, L. (1957) *The Functions of Social Conflict*. New York: Free Press.

Cyert, R. and March, J. G. (1963) *A Behavioral Theory of the Firm*. Englewood Cliffs, NJ: Prentice Hall.

Daft, R. L. and Lengel, R. H. (1986) 'Organizational information requirements, media richness and structural design', *Management Science*, 32: 554–71.

Dahrendorf, R. (1959) *Class and Class Conflict in Industrial Society*. Stanford, CA: Stanford University Press.

Darwin, C. (1936) *The Origin of Species*. New York: Modern Library.

David, P. (1985) 'Clio and the economics of QWERTY', *Economic History*, 75: 227–332.

Davis, S. and Meyer, C. (1998) *Blur: The Speed of Change in the Connected Economy*. Reading, MA: Addison-Wesley.

Dess, G. G. (1987) 'Consensus on strategy formulation and organizational performance: competitors in a fragmented industry', *Strategic Management Journal*, 8: 259–77.

Dewey, J. (1934) *Art as Experience*. New York: Minton, Balch. p. 51.

Dierickx, I. and Cool, K. (1989) 'Asset stock accumulation and sustainability of competitive advantage', *Management Science*, 35: 1504–11.

Dooley, K. J. and Van de Ven, A. H. (1999) 'Explaining complex organizational dynamics', *Organization Science*, 10: 358–72.

Drazin, R. and Sandelands, L. (1992) 'Autogenesis: a perspective on the process of organizing', *Organization Science*, 3: 230–49.

Dunbar, R. and Ahlstrom, D. (1995) 'Seeking the institutional balance of power: avoiding the power of a balanced view', *Academy of Management Review*, 20: 171–92.

Dunbar, R., Garud, R. and Kotha, S. (1998) *Substance and Style: The Case of Steinway and Sons.* NYU Working Paper.

Dutton, J. E. and Jackson, S. E. (1987) 'Categorizing strategic issues: links to organizational action', *Academy of Management Review*, 12: 76–90.

Eubank, S. and Farmer, D. (1990) 'An introduction to chaos and randomness', in E. Jen (ed.), *1989 Lectures in Complex Systems: SFI Studies in the Sciences of Complexity*, Volume II. Reading, MA: Addison-Wesley. pp. 75–190.

Farrell, J. and Saloner, G. (1986) 'Installed base and compatibility: innovation, product preannouncements and predation', *American Economic Review*, 76: 940–55.

Foster, R. J. (1986) *Innovation: The Attacker's Advantage.* New York: Summit Books.

Freeman, R. E. (1984) *Strategic Management: A Stakeholder Approach.* Boston: Pitman.

Garud, R. (1999) 'Suggestions for developing long term relationships with organizations to study change', presented at the NSF IOC Panel at the Annual Academy of Management Meetings, Chicago.

Garud, R. and Jain, S. (1996) 'Technology embeddedness', in J. Baum and J. Dutton (eds), *Advances in Strategic Management*, Vol. 13. Greenwich, CT: JAI Press. pp. 389–408.

Garud, R., Jain, S. and Phelps, C. (1998a) 'Technological linkages & transience in network fields: New competitive realities', in J. Baum (ed.), *Advances in Strategic Management*, Vol. 14. Greenwich, CT: JAI Press. pp. 205–37.

Garud, R. and Karnøe, P. (2001) 'Path creation as a process of mindful deviation', in R. Garud and P. Karone (eds), *Path Dependence and Creation.* Mahwah, NJ: Lawrence Earlbaum Associates.

Garud, R., Karnøe, P. and Garcia, E. A. (1999) 'The emergence of technological fields', in M. R. Lissack and H. P. Gunz (eds), *Managing the Complex.* New York: Quorum Books.

Garud, R. and Kumaraswamy, A. (1993) 'Changing competitive dynamics in network industries: an exploration of Sun Microsystems' open systems strategy', *Strategic Management Journal*, 14: 351–69.

Garud, R. and Kumaraswamy, A. (1995) 'Technological and organizational designs to achieve economies of substitution', *Strategic Management Journal*, 16: 93–110.

Garud, R. and Kumaraswamy, A. (1996) 'Technological designs for retention and reuse', *International Journal of Technology Management*, 11: 883–91.

Garud, R., Kumaraswamy, A. and Nayyar, P. (1998b) 'Real options or fool's gold: perspective makes the difference', *Academy of Management Review*, 3: 212–4.

Garud, R. and Lant, T. (1999) 'Navigating Silicon Alley: kaleidoscopic experiences', NYU Working Paper.

Garud, R. and Nayyar, P. (1994) 'Transformative capacity: continual structuring by inter-temporal technology transfer', *Strategic Management Journal*, 15: 365–85.

Garud, R., Nayyar, P. and Shapira, Z. (1997) 'Beating the odds: towards a theory of technological innovation', in R. Garud, P. Nayyar and Z. Shapira (eds), *Technological Innovation: Oversights and Foresights.* Cambridge, UK: Cambridge University Press. pp. 20–40.

Garud, R. and Rappa, M. (1994) 'A socio-cognitive model of technology evolution', *Organization Science*, 5: 344–62.

Garud, R. and Shapira, Z. (1997) 'Aligning the residuals: risk, returns and responsibility', in Z. Shapira (ed.), *Organizational Decision Making.* Cambridge, UK: Cambridge University Press. pp. 238–56.

Garud, R. and Van de Ven, A. H. (1989) 'Technological innovation and industry emergence: the case of cochlear implants', in A. H. Van de Ven, H. L. Angle and M. S. Poole (eds), *Research on the Management of Innovation: The Minnesota Studies.* New York: Harper and Row. pp. 489–535.

Garud, R. and Van de Ven, A. H. (1992) 'An empirical evaluation of the internal corporate venturing process', *Strategic Management Journal*, 13: 93–109.

Giddens, A. (1979) *Central Problems in Social Theory.* Los Angeles: University of California Press.

Ginsberg, A., Larsen, E. and Lomi, A. (1996) 'Generating strategy from individual behavior: a dynamic model of structural embeddedness', in J. Baum and J. Dutton (eds), *Advances in Strategic Management*, Vol. 13. Greenwich, CT: JAI Press. pp. 121–47.

Gould, S. J. (1989) 'Punctuated equilibrium in fact and theory', *Journal of Social and Biological Structures*, 12: 117–36.

Granovetter, M. (1985) 'Economic action and social structure: the problem of embeddedness', *American Journal of Sociology*, 91: 481–510.

Greiner, L. (1972) 'Evolution and revolution as organizations grow', *Harvard Business Review*, July–August: 165–74.

Grove, A. S. (1996) *Only the Paranoid Survive.* New York: Doubleday.

Gulati, R. (1998) 'Alliances and networks', *Strategic Management Journal*, 19: 293–317.

Hamel, G. and Prahalad, C. K. (1994) *Competing for the Future.* Boston: Harvard Business School Press.

Hammer, M. and Champy, J. (1993) *Reengineering the Corporation.* New York: Harper Business.

Hannan, M. T. and Freeman, F. (1989) *Organizational Ecology.* Cambridge, MA: Harvard University Press.

Harrison, J. S. and Freeman, R. E. (1999) 'Stakeholders, social responsibility and performance: empirical evidence and theoretical perspectives', *Academy of Management Journal*, 42: 479–87.

Hedberg, B. L. T., Nystrom, P. C. and Starbuck, W. (1976) 'Camping on seesaws: prescriptions for a self-designing organization', *Administrative Science Quarterly*, 21: 41–65.

Henderson, R. M. (1997) 'On the dynamics of forecasting in technological complex environments: the unexpected long old age of optical lithography', in R. Garud,

P. Nayyar and Z. Shapira (eds), *Technological Innovation: Oversights and Foresights*. Cambridge, UK: Cambridge University Press. pp. 147–66.

Hirsch, P. M. (1975) 'Organizational effectiveness and the institutional environment', *Administrative Science Quarterly*, 20: 327–44.

Janis, I. (1972) *Victims of Groupthink*. Boston: Houghton Mifflin.

Jehn, K. A. (1995) 'A multimethod examination of the benefits and detriments of intragroup conflict', *Administrative Science Quarterly*, 40: 256–82.

Kahneman, D., Slovic, P. and Tversky, A. (eds) (1982) *Judgment Under Uncertainty, Heuristics and Biases*. New York: Cambridge University Press.

Kamien, M. I. and Schwartz, N. L. (1975) 'Market structure and innovation: a survey', *Journal of Economic Literature*, 1–37.

Karnøe, P. and Garud, R. (2000) 'Path creation and dependence in the Danish wind turbine field', in J. Porac and M. Ventresca (eds), *The Social Construction of Industries and Markets*. Oxford: Pergamon Press.

Katz, M. L. and Shapiro, C. (1985) 'Network externalities, competition, and compatibility', *The American Economic Review*, 75: 424–40.

Kiesler, S. and Sproull, L. (1982) 'Managing responses to changing environments: perspectives on problem sensing from social cognition', *Administrative Science Quarterly*, 27: 548–70.

Koput, K. (1992) 'Dynamics of innovative idea generation in organizations: randomness and chaos in the development of a new medical device', Berkeley, CA, University of California School of Business, Unpublished Ph.D. dissertation.

Kotler, P. (1994) *Marketing Management: Analysis, Planning, Implementation and Control*. Englewood Cliffs, NJ: Prentice Hall.

Kumaraswamy, A. (1996) 'A real options perspective of firms' R&D investments', Unpublished doctoral dissertation, New York University.

Lant, T. and Mezias, S. (1992) 'An organizational learning model of convergence and reorientation', *Organization Science*, 3: 47–71.

Lant, T., Milliken, F. J. and Batra, B. (1992) 'An organizational learning model of convergence and reorientation in strategic persistence and reorientation: an empirical exploration', *Strategic Management Journal*, 13: 585–608.

Latour, B. (1987) *Science in Action: How to Follow Engineers and Scientists through Society*. Cambridge, Mass: Harvard University Press.

Law, J. (1992) 'Notes on the theory of the actor-network: ordering, strategy, and heterogeneity', *Systems Practice*, 5(4).

Leonard-Barton, D. (1992) 'Core capabilities and core rigidities: a paradox in managing new product development', *Strategic Management Journal*, 13: 111–26.

Levinthal, D. (1997) 'Adaptation on rugged landscapes', *Management Sciences*, 43, July.

Levinthal, D. and March, J. G. (1981) 'A model of adaptive organizational search', *Journal of Economic Behavior and Organization*, 2: 307–33.

Levitt, B. and March, J. G. (1988) 'Organizational learning', *Annual Review of Sociology*, 14: 319–40.

Lindblom, C. E. (1959) 'The science of "muddling through"', *Public Administration Review*, 19: 79–88.

Mahajan, V., Muller, E. and Bass, F. M. (1990) 'New product diffusion models in marketing: a review and directions for research', *Journal of Marketing*, 54: 1–26.

March, J. G. (1991) 'Exploration and exploitation in organizational learning', *Organization Science*, 2: 71–87.

March, J. G. (1997) 'Foreword', in R. Garud, P. Nayyar and Z. Shapira (eds), *Technological Innovation: Oversights and Foresights*. Cambridge, UK: Cambridge University Press.

March, J. G. and Shapira, Z. (1987) 'Managerial perspectives on risk and risk taking', *Management Science*, 33, November.

March, J. G. and Simon, H. A. (1958) *Organizations*. New York: Wiley.

Markoff, J. (1999) 'Chip progress forecast to hit a big barrier: scientists seeing limits to miniaturization', *The New York Times*, Saturday, October 9, pp A1.

Maruyama, M. (1963) 'The second cybernetics: deviation-amplifying mutual causal processes', *American Scientist*, 51: 164–79.

Mason, C. S. (1957) *Economic Concentration and the Monopoly Problem*. Cambridge, MA: Harvard University Press.

Masuch, M. (1985) 'Vicious cycles in organizations', *Administrative Science Quarterly*, 30: 14–33.

McGrath, J. E. and Kelly, J. R. (1986) *Time and Human Interaction: Toward a Social Psychology of Time*. New York: Guilford Press.

McKelvey, B. (1982) *Organizational Systematics: Taxonomy, Evolution, Classification*. Berkeley, CA: University of California Press.

Mezias, S. J. (1988) 'Aspiration level effects: an empirical investigation', *Journal of Economic Behavior and Organizations*, 10: 389–400.

Mezias, S. and Eisner, A. (1997) 'Competition, imitation, and innovation: an organization learning approach', in A. Huff and J. Walsh (eds), *Advances in Strategic Management*, Vol. 14. Greenwich, CT: JAI Press. pp. 261–94.

Miller, C. C., Burke, L. M. and Glick, W. H. (1998) 'Cognitive diversity among upper-echelon executives: implications for strategic decision processes', *Strategic Management Journal*, 19: 39–58.

Mintzberg, H. (1978) 'Patterns in strategy formation', *Management Science*, 24: 934–48.

Mintzberg, H., Ahlstrand, B. and Lampel, J. (1998) *Strategy Safari: A Guided Tour Through the Wilds of Strategic Management*. New York: The Free Press.

Mintzberg, H., Raisinghani, O. and Theoret A. (1976) 'The structure of unstructured decision processes', *Administrative Science Quarterly*, 21: 246–75.

Mintzberg, H. and Waters, J. A. (1985) 'Of strategies, deliberate and emergent', *Strategic Management Journal*, 6: 257–72.

Mohr, L. B. (1982) *Explaining Organizational Behavior: The Limits and Possibilities of Theory and Research.* San Francisco, CA: Jossey-Bass.

Nelson, R. and Winter, S. G. (1982) *An Evolutionary Theory of Economic Change.* Cambridge, MA: Harvard University Press.

Nehmeth, C. J. and Staw, B. (1989) 'The tradeoffs of social control in groups and organizations', *Advances in Experimental Social Psychology*, 22: 175–210.

Noda, T. and Bower, J. L. (1996) 'Strategy making as iterated resource allocation', *Strategic Management Journal*, 17: 159–92.

Orlikowski, W. J. (1992) 'The duality of technology: rethinking the concept of technology in organizations', *Organization Science*, 3: 398–427.

Penrose, E. T. (1959) *The Theory of the Growth of the Firm.* New York: John Wiley.

Perrow, C. (1984) *Normal Accidents: Living with High-Risk Technologies.* New York: Basic Books.

Pettigrew, A. M. (1985) *The Awakening Giant: Continuity and Change in ICI.* Oxford: Basil Blackwell.

Pettigrew, A. M. (ed.) (1987) *The Management of Strategic Change.* Oxford: Basil Blackwell.

Pettigrew, A. M. (1992) 'Character and significance of strategic process research', *Strategic Management Journal*, 13: 5–16.

Pfeffer, J. and Salancik, G. (1978) *The External Control of Organizations: A Resource Dependence Perspective.* New York: Harper and Row.

Polley, D. (1997) 'Chaos as metaphor and science: applications and risks', *Organization Science*, 8(5): 445–57.

Polley, D. and Van de Ven, A. H. (1995) 'Learning by discovery during innovation development', *International Journal of Technology Management*, 11: 871–82.

Poole, M. S., Van de Ven, A. H., Dooley, K. J. and Holmes, M. (2000) *Studying Processes of Organizational Change and Development: Theory and Methods.* New York: Oxford University Press.

Porac, J. F. and Rosa, J. A. (1996a) 'In praise of managerial narrow-mindedness', *Journal of Management Inquiry*, 5: 35–42.

Porac, J. F. and Rosa, J. A. (1996b) 'Rivalry, industry models and the cognitive embeddedness of the comparable firm', in J. Baum and J. Dutton (eds), *Advances in Strategic Management.* Greenwich, CT: JAI Press. pp. 363–88.

Porter, M. (1980) *Competitive Strategy.* New York: Free Press.

Postrel, S. (1991) 'Burning your britches behind you: can policy scholars bank on game theory?', *Strategic Management Journal*, 153–5.

Prigogine, I. and Stengers, S. (1984) *Order Out of Chaos.* New York: Heinemann.

Quinn, J. B. (1978) 'Strategic change: logical incrementalism', *Sloan Management Review*, 20: 7–21.

Raghuram, S. and Garud, R. (1995) 'Vicious and virtuous facets of work-force diversity', in M. N. Ruderman, M. W. Hughes-James and S. E. Jackson (eds), *Selected Research on Work Team Diversity.* Washington DC: APA. pp. 155–78.

Rao, H. (1994) 'The social construction of reputation: certification contests, legitimation and the survival of organizations in the American automobile industry, 1895–1912', *Strategic Management Journal*, 15: 12–29.

Rogers, E. (1983) *Diffusion of Innovations*, third edition. New York: Free Press.

Rosenbloom, R. S. and Cusumano, M. A. (1987) 'Technological pioneering and competitive advantage: the birth of the VCR industry', *California Management Review*, 29(4): 3–22.

Rumelt, R. P. (1984) 'Toward a strategic theory of the firm', in R. B. Lamb (ed.), *Competitive Strategic Management.* Englewood Cliffs, NJ: Prentice Hall. pp. 557–70.

Saloner, G. (1991) 'Modeling, game theory and strategic management', *Strategic Management Journal*, 12: 119–36.

Schelling, T. (1960) *The Strategy of Conflict.* Cambridge, MA: Harvard University Press.

Schumpeter, J. A. (1942) *Capitalism, Socialism, and Democracy.* New York: Harper & Row.

Simon, H. A. (1957) *Administrative Behavior.* New York: Macmillan.

Stacey, R. (1995) *Strategic Management and Organizational Dynamics.* London: Pitman Publishing.

Starbuck, W. (1983) 'Organizations as action generators', *American Sociological Review*, 48: 91–102.

Staw, B. M. (1976) 'Knee-deep in the big muddy: a study of escalating commitment to a chosen course of action', *Organizational Behavior and Human Performance*, 16: 27–44.

Sztompka, P. (1993) *The Sociology of Social Change.* London: Blackwell.

Teece, D. J., Pisano, G. and Sheun, A. (1997) 'Dynamic capabilites and strategic management', *Strategic Management Journal*, 18: 509–33.

Tsoukas, H. (1989). 'The validity of idiographic research explanations', *Academy of Management Review*, 14: 551–61.

Tushman, M. L. and Anderson, P. (1986) 'Technological discontinuities and organizational environments', *Administrative Science Quarterly*, 31: 439–65.

Tushman, M. L. and Romanelli, E. (1985) 'Organizational evolution: a metamorphosis model of convergence and reorientation', in B. Staw and L. Cummings (eds), *Research in Organizational Behavior.* Greenwich, CT: JAI Press. pp. 171–222.

Udayagiri, N. D. and Schuler, D. A. (1999) 'Cross-product spillovers in the semiconductor industry: implications for strategic trade policy', *The International Trade Journal*, XIII: 249–71.

Utterback, J. M. (1994) *Mastering the Dynamics of Innovation.* Boston, MA: Harvard University Press.

Utterback, J. M. and Abernathy, W. J. (1975) 'A dynamic model of process and product innovation', *Omega*, 3: 639–56.

Uzzi, B. (1996) 'The sources and consequences of embeddedness for the economic performance of organizations', *American Sociology Review*, 61: 674–98.

Van de Ven, A. H. (1992) 'Suggestions for studying strategy process: a research note', *Strategic Management Journal*, 13: 169–88.

Van de Ven, A. H. and Garud, R. (1993a) 'The co-evolution of technical and institutional events in the development of an innovation', in J. Baum and J. Singh (eds), *Evolutionary Dynamics of Organizations*. New York: Oxford University Press. pp. 425–43.

Van de Ven, A. H. and Garud, R. (1993b) 'Innovation and industry development: the case of cochlear implants', in R. Burgelman and R. Rosenbloom (eds), *Research on Technological Innovation and Management Policy*. Vol. 6. Greenwich, CT: JAI Press. pp. 1–46.

Van de Ven, A. H. and Grazman, D. (1997) 'Technological innovation, learning and leadership', in R. Garud, P. Nayyar and Z. Shapira (eds), *Technological Innovation: Oversights and Foresights*. Cambridge, UK: Cambridge University Press. pp. 345–54.

Van de Ven, A. H. and Huber, G. P. (1990) 'Longitudinal field research methods for studying processes of organizational change', *Organization Science*, 1: 213–19.

Van de Ven, A. H., Polley, D., Garud, R. and Venkatraman, S. (1999) *The Innovation Journey*. Oxford: Oxford University Press.

Van de Ven, A. H. and Poole, M. S. (1995) 'Explaining development and change in organizations', *Academy of Management Review*, 20: 510–40.

Vernon, R. (1966) 'International investment and international trade in the product cycle', *Quarterly Journal of Economics*, 80: 190–207.

Wade-Benzoni, K. A. (1999) 'Thinking about the future', *American Behavioral Scientist*, 42: 1393–405.

Weick, K. E. (1979) *The Social Psychology of Organizing*, second edition. Reading, MA: Addison-Wesley.

Wernerfelt, B. (1984) 'A resource-based view of the firm', *Strategic Management Journal*, 5: 171–80.

Wiersema, M. F. and Bantel, K. A. (1992) 'Top management team demography and corproate strategic change', *Academy of Management Journal*, 35: 91–121.

Zajac, E. J. and Bazerman, M. (1991) 'Blind spots in industry and competitive analysis: implications of inter-firm (mis)perceptions for strategic decisions', *Academy of Management Review*, 16: 37–56.

Zeeman, E. C. (1976) 'Catastrophe theory', *Scientific American*, 234, April: 65–83.

11

Top Management, Company Directors and Corporate Control

GERALD F. DAVIS and MICHAEL USEEM

Theory and research on the relations among top managers, company directors, investors, and external contenders for corporate control – broadly, the field of *corporate governance* – experienced a remarkable flowering during the 1990s. Early work addressed the central puzzle raised by the widespread separation of ownership and control among large American corporations, namely, why would any sensible person – much less thousands or millions of them – invest their savings in businesses run by unaccountable professional managers? As Berle and Means (1932) framed the problem, those who ran such 'managerialist' corporations would pursue 'prestige, power, or the gratification of professional zeal' (1932: 122) in lieu of maximizing profits. Weak shareholders could do little to stop them. Yet generations of individuals and financial institutions continued to invest in these firms. Why?

Answering this question led to the creation of a new theory of the firm that portrayed the public corporation as a 'nexus of contracts'. In the contractarian model, the managers of the corporation were disciplined in their pursuit of shareholder value by a phalanx of mechanisms, from the way they were compensated, to the composition of the board of directors, to the external 'market for corporate control'. Taken together, these mechanisms worked to vouchsafe shareholder interests even when

ownership was widely dispersed. Research in this tradition flourished in the 1980s, as takeovers of under-performing firms became common and restive institutional investors made their influence known. Studies focused on assessing the effectiveness of devices such as having boards numerically dominated by outsiders, tying compensation to share price, or ensuring susceptibility to outside takeover (Walsh and Seward, 1990, provide a review). Following the dictates of financial economics, 'effectiveness' was commonly measured via stock market reactions to various actions by top management and/or the board. The results of these studies provided proof of which actions and structures promoted shareholder value, and which promoted 'managerial entrenchment' of the sort feared by Berle and Means.

Corporate governance research during the 1990s expanded from a narrow focus on large corporations to a broader concern with issues of political economy. The transition of state socialist societies to market economies, and the spread of financial markets to emerging economies around the globe, infused the puzzle of managerialism with enormous policy relevance. What mechanisms could be put in place to inspire the confidence of investors in businesses housed in distant and often unfamiliar cultures? The place of financial markets in the project of globalization, as a means to channel investment funds from wealthy nations to emerging markets with limited local capital, assured that corporate governance would be a topic of intense interest for years to come.

The decade of the 1990s saw three developments that moved the governance literature beyond the simple assessment of mechanisms in US firms. The first development was the examination of the governance structure of the firm – the set of devices that evolve within the organization to guide managerial decision-making – as an *ensemble*. Rather than regarding any particular aspect of the firm's structure as essential, researchers began to study them as complements or substitutes. Compensation strongly tied to share price may act as a substitute for a vigilant board, for instance, while a vigilant board is not sufficient to make up for a poorly integrated top management team. Governance structures, in short, were configurations of interdependent elements (Beatty and Zajac, 1994; Anderson et al., 1998).

The second development was the growth of comparative and historical governance research, which highlighted the idiosyncrasy of the American system. American-style corporate governance, aimed at 'solving' the problems created by the separation of ownership and control, is only one of several possible governance systems and reflected a path-dependent developmental trajectory. A range of alternatives is consistent with economic vibrancy, and the American system is not the crown of creation (Roe, 1994). Indeed, even among wealthy economies with well-developed corporate sectors, corporations with separated ownership and control were quite rare as late as the mid-1990s (La Porta et al., 1999). Moreover, empirical findings on the dynamics of the American system often held only for specific times; for instance, the takeover market of the 1980s, when hostile 'bust-ups' were common, was much different from takeovers of the 1990s, when friendly deals were the norm (Davis and Robbins, 1999). The nexus of contracts approach seemed increasingly like a theory of US corporate governance in the 1980s rather than a general theory of the firm.

The third development was the articulation of a reflexive stance on the theory of governance. While agency theory can be viewed as an empirical theory of the corporation, it can equally be considered a prescriptive theory, that is, not an explanation of what *is* but a vision of what *could* or *should* be. Its influence on public policy debates during the 1980s is evident in documents of the time (Davis and Stout, 1992) and in the subsequent spread of the rhetoric of shareholder value. But it is important to recognize that corporate managers are quite skillful in their use of this rhetoric (Useem, 1996). Declarations of share buy-backs are met with share price spikes, whether or not they are subsequently implemented (Zajac and Westphal, 2001). The announcement of a new compensation plan is met by more positive reactions from the stock market when described as means of aligning management with shareholder interests than when the identical plan is described as a human resources tool; naturally, managers gravitate toward the sanctioned rhetoric (Westphal and Zajac, 1998). And even earnest attempts to meet the demands of shareholders for transparency and accountability, as prescribed by the agency theory of governance, often have unintended consequences. Firms that improve the quality of their disclosure attract more transient institutional investors, which in turn *increases* the volatility of their share prices – exactly the opposite of what was anticipated (Bushee and Noe, 1999). In short, the dominance of the American system described by the agency theory of governance may take the form more of rhetoric than reality, a point worth bearing in mind in the ongoing debates about the convergence of national systems of corporate governance.

If the prototypical research question in the corporate governance literature of the 1980s was 'Is it better for shareholders for a corporation's board to have more "outside" directors?', the characteristic question of the early 21st century is 'What ensemble of institutions best situates a nation for economic growth in a global, post-industrial, information-based economy?'. Put another way, the vital questions going forward are not about why some stalks of corn in a field grow taller than others, but about the characteristics of soil and farming techniques that make corn in some fields grow taller than in others. Thus, research has come to span levels of analysis from within the organization to the nation-state and beyond. Behind this development is a recognition that

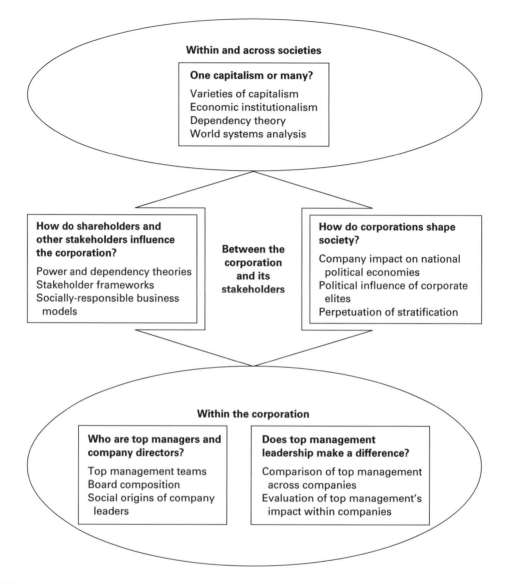

Figure 11.1 *Research on top management, company directors and corporate control*

what works for a particular firm is highly contingent on its institutional surround, that the institutional surround in a particular nation reflects its history and level of economic development, and that 'what works' for a national economy depends in turn on its place in the larger world system. Firms and economies, in short, are embedded in larger social and institutional structures that critically condition their structures and performance (Polanyi, 1957; Granovetter, 1985; Bebchuk and Roe, 1999).

We would like to be able to report that the earlier questions have now been answered

definitively. Much prior research relied on archival data several steps removed from the phenomenon (for example, crudely classifying directors as 'insiders' or 'outsiders' depending on whether they were current employees of the firm). Crude data led, unsurprisingly, to crude results (see Pettigrew, 1992 for a critique). Progress has certainly been made in moving beyond simple dichotomies of directors as inside or outside. Pettigrew and McNulty (1995, 1998a, b), for instance, have done much to unpack the processes and power dynamics of the boardroom through gathering extensive qualitative data from directors on 'critical incidents'. But an 'embedded' perspective makes clear that there is unlikely to be a generalized answer to questions of corporate governance.

Moreover, global financial integration has spurred major changes in corporate governance regimes around the world, for better or worse. Policy in this area is guided to a great degree by research and theory, making it both a vibrant intellectual domain and a consequential one. Law and economics scholars become Federal judges and treasury secretaries, well-known economists serve at the World Bank and IMF, and corporate directors take short courses at business schools to learn their trade. Corporate governance is an area where, at all levels of analysis, good research can have an impact.

Figure 11.1 maps out the terrain and locates research on top management, company directors, and corporate control in the larger academic discourse. Our aim in this chapter is to assay developments in this area at the beginning of the 21st century and outline promising areas for future research. We must, of necessity, be highly selective: research on top management and corporate governance spans multiple disciplines, from accounting and finance, to management and strategy, to sociology and political science. As research has proliferated, so have reviews (see, for instance, Blair, 1995; Shleifer and Vishny, 1997; Zingales, 1998). Even definitions of the object of study vary widely: Shleifer and Vishny state that 'Corporate governance deals with the ways in which suppliers of finance to corporations assure themselves of getting a return on their investment' (1997: 737), while Blair (1995: 3) argues that corporate governance implicates 'the whole set of legal, cultural, and institutional arrangements that determine what publicly traded corporations can do, who controls them, how that control is exercised, and how the risks and returns from the activities they undertake are allocated'. We take the broadest definition, and as such implicate a wide range of disciplines.

As our embedded framing would suggest, we review research across levels of analysis. We start by outlining and critiquing the contractarian model of corporate governance, which has dominated the academic discourse in law and economics as well as the policy debates around economic development. *Within the firm*, we then ask, who are top managers and corporate directors, and does their leadership make a difference? These questions connect to studies in diverse disciplines, including the sociology of elites, strategy research on top management teams, the study of organizational demography, and research across fields on leadership. Relevant chapters elsewhere in this handbook include Thomas and Porac's chapter on 'Managing cognition and strategy'; Chakravarthy and White's 'Strategy process'; and McGrath's 'Entrepreneurship, small firms and wealth creation'. *Between the firm and its stakeholders*, we ask, how do shareholders and stakeholders influence the corporation, and how do corporations in turn shape society? These questions link to stakeholder models of the corporation, research on power and dependence in organization theory, studies of business and society, socially responsible business, the study of political economy, power elites, and inequality. Whetten, Rands and Godfrey's chapter 'What are the responsibilities of business to society', elsewhere in this handbook, reviews additional relevant work. Finally, *at the level of the nation-state*, we ask, is there evidence of convergence in management practice and corporate governance around the world? The question of societal convergence or divergence has been an animating question in economics – particularly in the work of institutionalists such as Douglass North – in the political science literature on 'varieties of capitalism', in sociological theories of modernization, dependency, and world systems, and in the popular literature on globalization. Interested readers are encouraged to read Kogut's chapter in this handbook on 'International management and strategy'.

ONE CAPITALISM OR MANY?

Around the world, large corporations are the most visible institutions of modern capitalism. A few thousand corporations produce the bulk of the world's economic output and employ a significant part of the world's labor force. What forces determine who wields corporate power and how it is used? The answer is best framed in terms of institutions – 'the humanly devised constraints that structure political, economic and social interaction' (North, 1991: 97).

A nation's system of corporate governance can be seen as an institutional matrix (North, 1990) that structures the relations among owners, boards, and top managers, and determines the goals pursued by the corporation. The nature of this institutional matrix is one of the principal determinants of the economic vitality of a society. By hypothesis, getting the institutions of corporate governance right means ensuring that those who run corporations make decisions that lead to superior national economic performance. This means making sure that top managers and their supervisory board are appropriately responsive to signals from the product markets and the capital markets (Gordon, 1997). Thus, corporate governance can be seen as the institutional matrix that links market signals to the decisions of corporate managers.

According to Douglass North (1990: 6), 'The central puzzle of human history is to account for the widely divergent paths of historical change. How have societies diverged? What accounts for their widely disparate [economic] performance characteristics?' Accepted theory in economics predicts that through trade, national economies would converge in institutions and thus performance, as inferior institutions were weeded out and politicians in weaker economies adopted the policies of stronger ones. Yet economies are immensely diverse in their institutional structures and performance, leading to an enormous gap between rich and poor nations (see Firebaugh, 1999 for a recent assessment). Two questions arise from this observation. First, given that large corporations are disproportionately responsible for the economic wellbeing of a society, is there a best model of corporate governance? That is, is there an institutional matrix that reliably encourages corporate managers to make choices leading to economic growth for a society? Second, can an institutional matrix be emulated? The structures of particular organizations may be copied with more or less fidelity, but the institutions of corporate governance, such as a system of corporate and securities law, operate largely at a national level and thus entail politi- cal choices. Is it possible for a nation to move from one system of corporate governance to another?

The first question – what is the right model? – is deceptively simple. It should be a straightforward matter to rank economies by their economic vitality, select the top performer, and abstract the crucial elements of its institutional matrix. The experience of the 1990s suggested to many commentators that the American model of investor capitalism was the obvious winner (see Soros's [1998] critical account and Friedman's [1999] affirmative account of free market triumphalism). The American economy experienced the longest expansion in its history, generating millions of new jobs, countless new business starts, and a long stock market boom. This contrasted sharply with its rich-country rivals, particularly Japan, as well as with the emerging markets that entered deep slumps in the late 1990s. Moreover, the American model appeared especially amenable to a world of borderless capital, in which geography was of little concern in the process of matching investment flows to business opportunities. In principle, even a nation with little indigenous savings could achieve prosperity by adopting a system of American-style investor capitalism and opening itself to foreign investment. In the words of Treasury secretary Larry Summers, 'Financial markets don't just oil the wheels of economic growth – they *are* the wheels' (*Wall Street Journal*, 8 December 1997).

The institutional matrix that makes up the American system of corporate governance is codified in the contractarian approach to the firm, also known as agency theory. Agency theory was developed primarily within financial economics to describe the various mechanisms that 'solve' the agency problems created by the separation of ownership and control, by ensuring managerial devotion to increasing the company's share price:

> Managers' wealth is tied to share price through numerous devices, including outright ownership, stock options, and compensation keyed to stock performance that align executive and shareholder interests. Because share price does not necessarily reflect detailed inside information about how well the firm is being managed, firms have adopted other devices to monitor managers, including shareholder-elected boards of directors that ratify important decisions (Fama and Jensen, 1983), concentrated and thus powerful ownership blocks for firms whose performance is difficult to monitor (Demsetz and Lehn, 1985), efficient managerial

labor markets that ensure that managers are paid over the long run according to their contribution (Fama, 1980), and high debt that compels managers to meet regular payment hurdles and optimal returns to capital markets (Jensen, 1986). If all these mechanisms fail and bad management drives the firm's share price down far enough, superior managers will acquire control of the firm, fire incumbent managers, and run the firm better themselves; they are rewarded for their trouble by their personal gain from the recovery of firm value, while shareholders are compensated by the premium paid. Thus, capital markets ensure that the structure of the nexus of contracts that survives is the one that minimizes agency costs and maximizes shareholder wealth. Managers who sought to sell company shares that, say, made it too difficult for shareholders to remove them if they did a poor job or paid themselves too much would find few buyers. Thus, managers have built-in incentives to propose organizational structures that limit their own discretion. (Davis and Thompson, 1994: 144–5)

Each element of the theory – from management compensation and board composition to the structure of ownership and dynamics of takeovers – has received extensive research attention as it applies to large US corporations, particularly during the 1980s (see virtually any issue of the *Journal of Financial Economics* published during this period). If a cross-national adoption of American corporate governance institutions proved desirable, agency theory provides the blueprint: in the words of one recent review, 'the Anglo-American governance system, born of the contractarian paradigm, is the most flexible and effective system available. Indeed, notwithstanding its idiosyncratic historical origins and its limitations, it is clearly emerging as the world's standard' (Bradley et al., 1999: 14).

But questions of institutional transfer are premature. Those with long memories recall that at the beginning of the 1990s, it was the Japanese and German systems that served as the world's models, and pundits advocated a system of bank-centered relationship capitalism to cure the social disruption caused by America's myopic shareholder orientation. The virtues of 'Toyotaism' and the remarkable success of East Asian economies emulating Japanese business organization led the business

press to herald the emergence of American-style keiretsu. 'Unfettered Anglo-Saxon capitalism is finding it difficult to cope with the present' and thus American corporations should be encouraged to form keiretsu-like groups, which 'insulate management from short-term stock-market pressures without creating incompetent managers' (Thurow, 1992: 19, 281). In short, the most productive economies got that way because their systems of corporate governance, sometimes called communitarian or relationship capitalism, muffled the signals from impatient financial markets and encouraged cooperation among firms and their suppliers – exactly the opposite of the American system of investor capitalism.

Determining the best system of governance – investor capitalism, 'crony capitalism', or something else – thus turns out to be far from trivial. Indeed, choosing which measure of performance to use and which time period to focus on yields rather divergent results – while the US economy expanded continuously from 1992 through 1998, expanding the time horizon to a full decade creates a rather different picture. From 1989 to 1998, both Germany and Japan experienced substantially higher productivity growth than the US, Germany displayed a higher per capita growth in GDP, and Japan recorded lower average unemployment (*The Economist*, 10 April 1999). Locating the effective ingredient in a national economy's institutional matrix may be a hopeless endeavor and the safest course may be to call it a draw among the three major contenders (cf. Roe, 1994).

Even the pleasing simplicity of an abstract 'governance model' may imply more coherence than is warranted. The American system is often referred to as the Anglo-American system because key elements are held to be common between the US and the United Kingdom. Yet even these two are rather divergent on several dimensions, which suggests strong limits on the extent to which institutions can be adopted across cultures. In the UK, for instance, the positions of chairman of the board and the chief executive officer are held by different persons on more than four out of five boards among the largest 500 firms; the shared understanding is that 'the CEO runs the company and the Chair runs the board' (Pettigrew and McNulty, 1995). In contrast, three quarters of *Fortune* 500 firms in 1999 were led by CEOs who also held the chair's job, and seasoned directors are virtually unanimous in viewing the forced separation of the two jobs as undesirable because of the ambiguity it creates about 'who's in charge' (Neiva, 1996). On another contrasting front, 22% of the typical *Fortune* 1000 firm's directors are 'insiders' (executives of the firm), while the comparable figure in the UK is roughly 50%. These facts are attributed to cultural differences in the boardrooms of the two nations, and neither nation shows much sign of budging in the other direction (Davis, 1998). Thus, even between the two named practitioners of Anglo-American corporate governance, there are sharp divergences on such basic matters as the organization and composition of the board. There are also, notably, sharp differences in economic performance, favoring the US. Adopting Anglo-American governance practices is evidently not sufficient to ensure superior economic performance for an economy, even supposing one could determine what these practices were.

These cultural differences notwithstanding, the attractions are undeniable in emulating American corporate governance for firms seeking outside investment. The number of non-US firms listed on the New York Stock Exchange increased from 96 in 1990 to 379 in 1998, while the value of US equity investment abroad increased more than six-fold during the same period (Useem, 1998; New York Stock Exchange, 1999; Federal Reserve System, 1999). Effectively borderless financial markets are perhaps the strongest force in encouraging the adoption of American corporate governance and its valorization of 'transparency' and 'accountability'. But while a particular *firm* may come to adopt an American model of governance – just as many manufacturers sought to adopt the Toyota model of production in the 1980s and 1990s – a system of governance, as an institutional matrix embedded in a particular culture, is far less prone to such wholesale change (cf. Coffee, 1998). Species may adapt, but it is far more difficult for an entire ecosystem to do so.

WHO ARE TOP MANAGERS AND COMPANY DIRECTORS?

Though market capitalism can epitomize impersonality – and some company headquarters seem as remote as Kafka's castle – they are nonetheless intensely personal at the top. A handful of individuals make the defining decisions, whether to launch a new product, enter a promising region, or resist a tender offer. It is they who set the rules and fix the procedures that come to constitute the impersonal bureaucracy.

Top management is the catchphrase for those who work at the apex, and companies often define their 'top' as no more than the seven or eight most senior officers. Their color photos adorn the annual report's early pages. They speak for the company to inquisitive journalists and skeptical analysts. They are *the* 'they' when employees grumble about nasty work or shareholders gripe of shortchanged expectations.

To much of the world beyond the company walls and capital markets, however, top management is personified almost solely by the chief executive. Readers of the American business press know that Jack Welch 'runs' General Electric, Michael Eisner rules Walt Disney Company, and Warren Buffett *is* Berkshire Hathaway. Attentive Japanese recognize that Fujio Cho drives Toyota and Germans that Jurgen Schrempp steers DaimlerChrysler. It is enough to know the commanding general, it seems, to anticipate the strategy of attack. The upper apex of top management is what really counts.

Academic researchers had long been drawn to the same pinnacle of the pyramid, partly on the conceptual premise that the chief executive is the manager who matters, and partly on the pragmatic ground that little is publicly known about anybody except the CEO. We have thus benefited from a long accumulation of work on their family histories, educational pedigrees, and political identities, and we know as a result that their origins are diverse, credentials splendid, and instincts Republican. More contemporarily, we have learned much about their tangled relations with directors and investors as well. To know the CEO's personal rise and board ties is to anticipate much of the firm's strategic intent and performance promise. They are also a good predictor of the CEO's own fortunes – an elite MBA degree accelerates movement to the top, a prestigious background attracts outside directorships, and a handpicked board enhances pay and perquisites (Belliveau et al., 1996; Useem and Karabel, 1986).

The conceptual and pragmatic underpinnings for shining the light solely on the CEO, however, have eroded in recent years, as companies redefined their operations and researchers reconceived their methods. A central thrust of company restructuring during the past two decades has been to transform the chief executive's office into the office of the executive. At many companies, CEOs have fashioned teams among their top officers that meet frequently and resolve jointly, their vertical control giving way to lateral leadership. Henry Schacht served as chief executive of Lucent Technologies from 1995 to 1997, and upon taking office, he devoted his first six months to building a shared strategy and culture among his top 14 officers. Unless his top managers were all working from the same script, he believed, the spin-off from AT&T would not succeed. He certainly would not be capable of making it succeed on his own.

Observers and consultants during the 1990s consequently came to extol the pragmatic virtues of 'top management teams'. If well formed, executive teams could assure prosperity; if poorly led, they could spell disaster. Predictably, stock analysts and professional investors frequently came to appraise not only the capabilities of the chief but also the lieutenants before they recommend a stock or buy shares (Hambrick et al., 1998; Katzenbach, 1997; Katzenbach and Smith, 1992).

Similarly, academic researchers expanded their field of view from the chief executive to the entire upper echelon. They applied fresh strategies, ranging from personal interviews to direct observation and internet surveys, to acquire data on top managers other than the chief executive who now matter far more to company performance and stock analysts – if still not to the editors of *Who's Who*. A host of studies have subsequently confirmed what many executives already appreciated – a better predictor of a company's performance than the chief executive's capability is the quality of the team that now runs the show. To pinnacle analysis has been added top team appraisal (Finkelstein and Hambrick, 1996; Useem, 1995).

In conducting such studies, researchers have also discovered that the devil is in the detail, with a top team's composition and culture affecting company actions and results in ways that do not neatly fit into tidy frameworks. Some research results are straight-forward. A study of 54 US multinational corporations, for example, found when top managers brought more foreign experience to the executive suite, their companies moved more production offshore and booked more sales abroad.

But other inquiries yielded more complex results, as seen in a study of 32 US airline companies in the wake of industry deregulation in 1979. The researchers focused on competitive moves such as price-cutting, advertising campaigns, and fresh routes. They assessed the extent to which the companies' top executives varied in their educational backgrounds (engineering, economics, business, law), functional specialization (finance, marketing, operations), and years with the company, and they discovered that the airlines with top management teams diverse in these areas were more likely to take competitive actions but slower to make their moves. Overall, they found that companies with greater diversity at the top built greater market share and generated greater operating profits (Sambharya, 1996; Hambrick et al., 1996).

Yet even this widening of research attention beyond the chief executive has not broadened enough. Many companies have expanded the concept of top management to include one, two, or even three hundred senior managers whose decisions have significant bearing on firm performance. Prior to its merger with Travelers in 1998, for instance, Citibank had designated the bank's senior-most 300 executives as its 'corporate leverage population', and its 300 most vital jobs as its 'corporate leverage positions'. For Citibank, its future lay in the hands of 300 managers, not 3. Or consider how top management is defined at ARAMARK Corporation, a $6.5-billion managed-services firm with 150,000 employees worldwide. Its chief executive, Joseph Neubauer, formed an Executive Leadership Council in the 1990s comprising the top 150 executives in the company, including business unit presidents, staff vice presidents, top general managers, and corporate department heads. The Council charts company strategy and exchanges best practices, and it is, in the words of Neubauer, the firm's 'leadership team'. Its members are 'free to make their own decisions', says the CEO, but also 'as leaders', they're 'all accountable' for company results.

Top management, then, has expanded in the minds of company managers and, to a lesser extent, academic researchers, from the boss to the boss's team to the boss's court. Presiding over them are the directors, those elected representatives who in law must serve as fiduciaries of the investor electorate but in fact have virtually no contact with their electoral base. Their working contact is almost entirely confined to the top management team, and in the nexus of that relationship – the 'commanding heights' of the market economy – are fashioned the strategies and decisions that drive the company's future and determine the country's prosperity (Yergin and Stanislaw, 1998).

If companies make semiconductors and concrete much the same way the world around, they organize their directors in almost as many ways as their national economies. Boards of large publicly-traded companies in the US range in size from 4 to 35 directors (at least among the *Fortune* 1000), averaging 11 members. Boards average 12 directors in Italy, 11 in France, and 9 in the UK, with standard deviations of 3 to 4 directors. But cross-national comparability in size is about as far as it goes. American boards tend to include only two or three insiders, while Japanese boards rarely include even two outsiders. German and Dutch governance is built around a two-tier governance structure, employees holding half of the upper tier seats. British and Swiss governance is designed around a single-tier, management-dominated structure. Some systems give formal voice to labor, others none – German law requires that labor representatives serve on the board, while French law places labor observers in the boardroom. American law mandates nothing, but some boards have added a labor leader on their own (Charkham, 1994; Charkham and Simpson, 1999; Chew, 1997; Conyon and Peck, 1998; Franks, 1997; Hunter, 1998).

Such variety in national practices may well diminish for two reasons. First, as equity markets internationalize, with companies seeking capital from all corners of the globe, investors predictably prefer relatively consistent director models that they believe will optimize shareholder value and performance transparency. Their mental models of what's right may not indeed be right, but that is beside the point. Consider the preference expressed by some institutional investors in the US for a board chair who is not a sitting executive, believing that separation improves monitoring. Under pressure from investors in the wake of a $6 billion

loss in 1992, for instance, General Motors did split the roles, installing an outside chairman – John G. Smale, retired chief executive of Procter & Gamble – to breathe down the neck of new chief executive Jack Smith. Whatever the separatist penchant and however well it may have served General Motors, research reveals that such a division creates no advantage for company performance. But for some investors, persuasive preconceptions still prevail over research facts, and they press for common practices around the world (Baliga et al., 1996).

Another example can be seen in US investor preference for non-executive directors, believing the board's capacity for vigorous monitoring of top management to be a direct function of its independence from top management. The California Public Employees' Retirement System advocates that 'a substantial majority of the board consists of directors who are independent'. The Council of Institutional Investors avows that 'at least two-thirds of a corporation's directors should be independent'. TIAA-CREF prefers that 'the board should be composed of a substantial majority of independent directors'. Yet recent studies yield ambiguous support for the premise. Yes, independent directors often behave in more shareholder-friendly ways, but they also may be less likely to dismiss under-performing executives and less prone to render useful strategic guidance (California Public Employees' Retirement System, 1999; Council of Institutional Investors, 1999; Millstein and MacAvoy, 1998; TIAA-CREF, 1999; Ocasio, 1994; Westphal, 1999; Bhagat and Black, 1999).

The diversity in directorship practices is likely to diminish, however, for a second, more factual reason. Certain practices do engender better performance, regardless of the setting, and as companies increasingly compete worldwide for customers and investors, they are likely to adopt what indeed does prove best. A case in point here is the number of directors on the board. Research on team success suggests that bigger is not better when boards exceed 15 or 20 members. When the number of directors climbs far above middle range, the engagement of each diminishes, and so too does their capacity to work in unison. Study of the boards of 450 large US industrial firms in 1984–91 reveals that, net of company size, manufacturing sector, and inside ownership, companies with smaller boards displayed: stronger incentives for their chief executive, greater likelihood of dismissing an under-performing CEO, and larger market share and superior financial performance. In a parallel study, the same is found to prevail among large companies in Denmark, France, Italy, Netherlands, and the UK (Yermack, 1996; Conyon and Peck, 1998).

It is not surprising, then, to see companies worldwide migrating toward smaller boards in a search of improved performance. In their 1999 report to the stockholders, Sony's chief executive Norio Ohga and co-CEO Nobuyuki Idei wrote that they had launched a new 'corporate reorganization' to 'maximize shareholder value'. A central feature of their reorganization is to improve their directors' 'monitoring ability', and, to that end, Sony reduced its roster of 35 directors to just 9. Japan Airlines moved in parallel fashion. The company had reported losses during three of its past five years, and its largest investor, Eitaro Itoyama (holding 3.4% of its shares), had announced a campaign to oust top management to 'save JAL'. To improve its directors' effectiveness and, hopefully, company performance, the airline shrank its board from 28 directors to 15 and required that they stand for election yearly rather than bi-annually (Institutional Shareholder Services, 1999; Sony, 1999).

Directors in principle protect owner interests, direct company strategy, and select top management. In practice, they had concentrated more on strategy and selection and less on owner interests. But the rising power of investors has made for greater director focus on creating value and less coziness with top management. American and British directors, following the 'Anglo-Saxon' model, are already more focused on value than most. But directors in other economies can be expected to slowly gravitate toward the mantra of shareholder supremacy as well.

How Do Shareholders and Other Stakeholders Influence the Corporation?

The Uncommon Problem of the Separation of Ownership and Control

Imagine that the owners of a public corporation had a simple goal: to maximize the value of their investment at minimum risk. The most straightforward measure of the achievement of this goal is growth in the price of the firm's shares, and effective managers are those that successfully endeavor to maximize share price. Governance systems vary widely in the means by which owners can influence managers – owners might have a direct say in corporate strategy and in selecting members of the top management team, they might delegate these functions to a board but ensure that compensation and other incentives are aligned with share price maximization, or they might rely on mechanisms such as takeovers to ensure managerial devotion to share price. Corporations where management was not held accountable for achieving the corporation's goals would attract little outside support: as Gilson (1996: 333) puts it, 'any successful [governance] system must have the means to replace poorly performing managers'. This is the essence of the 'agency problem' identified by Berle and Means (1932) in managerialist corporations with dispersed ownership.

The problem of managerialism, however, turns out to be of surprisingly little relevance outside the US and the UK. In virtually every other economy, even the largest businesses are typically owned by controlling shareholders. A study of the largest 20 corporations in 27 of the world's richest economies found that 'controlling shareholders – usually the State or families – are present in most large companies' (La Porta et al., 1999: 473), while another survey found that 'a large majority of listed companies from Continental European countries have a dominating outside shareholder or investment group' (Goergen and Renneboog, 1998: 2). While minority shareholders may have little direct influence on the management of such firms, controlling shareholders presumably act to ensure the pursuit of shareholder value since it is their own. Outside the wealthiest tier of nations, stock markets are of relatively less significance, and thus managerialist corporations are unimportant. The influences of owners on managers are direct and unproblematic.

The general idiosyncrasy of the American system received surprisingly little attention from corporate governance scholars before the publication of Mark Roe's book *Strong Managers, Weak Owners* in 1994. Prior to this, 'the corporate governance systems of other nations were largely ignored because the American system was thought to represent the evolutionary pinnacle of corporate governance. Other systems, with different institutional characteristics, were either further behind the Darwinian path, or at evolutionary dead-ends; neither laggards nor Neanderthals compelled significant academic attention' (Gilson, 1996: 331).

In the late 1990s, however, a flourishing research interest focused on documenting and explaining the diversity of systems of governance. New systems of corporate and securities laws were installed in transitional East European economies to facilitate the process of privatization (with varied success – see Spicer and Kogut, 1999), and enthusiasm for financial markets as a tool for development in emerging markets created a practical need for understanding of cross-national variation in institutional structure (see the World Bank's corporate governance agenda at www.worldbank.org/html/fpd/privatesector/cg/index.htm). Nations vary in the extent of legal protection for shareholders and the quality of enforcement, and the strength of legal protection for shareholders is positively related to the degree of ownership dispersion. In other words, managerialist corporations are most common in countries with strong investor protections, while concentrated ownership is most common when investor protection is weak (La Porta et al., 1998). Stock markets are larger, and there are more public corporations per person, when investor protections are stronger (La Porta et al., 1997).

The single biggest factor distinguishing nations with strong legal protections for investors, and thus large capital markets and more dispersed ownership, was the origin of the legal system. Countries whose commercial law derived from a common law tradition, which includes most English-speaking countries as well as former British colonies, have stronger shareholder protections than countries with civil or 'code' law (La Porta and Lopez-de-Silanes, 1998). Absent strong legal protections against the types of self-aggrandizing managers contemplated by Berle and Means sensible people would avoid investing in companies with dispersed ownership because they would fear the loss of their investment. Concentrated ownership allows control of management without relying on uncertain legal enforcement.

The pole for market-centered (as opposed to relationship-based) capitalism is clearly the United States. In contrast to corporations throughout the rest of the world, large American corporations have relatively dispersed ownership. Roughly three-fourths of the 100 largest US corporations lack even a single ownership block of 10% or more. Of the 25 largest companies in 1999, the largest single shareholder averaged only 4% of the holdings, while the comparable percentages are 11 in Japan, 18 in Germany, and 19 in France (Brancato, 1999).

The dispersion of ownership in the US effectively rules out the direct control available in firms where a single family or bank owns most of the shares. Dispersed shareholders therefore delegate control to a board of directors that they elect to act as their agents in choosing and supervising the top management team. Control by minority shareholders generally extends only as far as buying and selling shares, and voting for directors and other matters on the annual proxy. Minority shareholders almost never have a say in the selection of top managers, or even in who ends up on the board. Indeed, by some accounts inattention is the only sensible course of action for dispersed shareholders ('rational ignorance'), as the cost of being well informed about the governance of the firm is not outweighed by the marginal benefit of improved corporate performance that might result from informed voting or activism (Fama, 1980). But while in other contexts this collective action problem would result in management unaccountable to shareholders, investors in US corporations can rest easy because of the well-developed set of institutions that have arisen to ensure share price maximization without their active participation (see Easterbrook and Fischel, 1991).

Takeovers

The most essential mechanism for enforcing attention to share price is the takeover market or 'market for corporate control'. By hypothesis, a poorly-run corporation will suffer a low stock market valuation, which creates an opportunity for outsiders with better management skills to buy the firm at a premium from shareholders, oust the top management team, and rehabilitate the firm themselves, thus increasing its value (Manne, 1965). This provides an economic safety net for shareholders and an opportunity for outsiders who detect undervalued firms. Moreover, it provides a mechanism to discipline top managers that fail to serve shareholder interests, as they generally end up unemployed following a takeover. In the contractarian model, the market for corporate control is the visible hand of Darwinian selection, weeding out badly run firms and protecting shareholders from bad management. Internal control mechanisms may fail, as boards are compromised by 'cronyism', and thus the hostile takeover – as an objective, market-based mechanism – is an essential weapon in the armory of the contractarian system (Jensen, 1993). US public policy in the 1980s made it considerably easier for outsiders to mount hostile takeover bids, and the result was a massive wave of takeovers in which nearly one-third of the largest publicly-traded manufacturers faced takeover bids (Davis and Stout, 1992).

Reams have been written about the US takeover wave of the 1980s (see Blair, 1993) but the high points are easily summarized. The typical target had a low stock market valuation relative to its accounting or book value, as one would predict based on the contractarian model (Manne, 1965; Marris, 1964), and the source of this low valuation was often excessive diversification by conglomerate firms (Davis et al., 1994). Conglomerates were typically purchased with the intention of busting them up into more focused components, which were sold to buyers in related industries (Bhagat et al., 1990), while non-targets restructured to achieve industrial focus and avoid unwanted takeover (Davis et al., 1994). In the US, takeovers are regulated both at the federal and state level, and by the early 1990s most states had passed legislation to make takeovers attempted without the consent of the target's board of directors extremely difficult. Thus, hostile takeovers virtually disappeared in the US after 1989.

Two results of the 1980s hostile takeover wave stand out. The first is that the manufacturing sector overall ended the decade much more focused than when it began, and the trend toward within-firm focus continued unabated through the mid-1990s (Davis and Robbins, 1999). With a few notable exceptions, such as General Electric, the industrial conglomerate would appear to be a thing of the past in the US, in spite of its prevalence

elsewhere in the world. The second result is a decisive shift in the rhetoric of management toward 'shareholder value' – to the virtual exclusion of other conceptions of corporate purpose. This is realized in efforts at managing investor relations (Useem, 1996), in the kind of spin that management puts on practices such as compensation plans (Westphal and Zajac, 1998), and in more tangible actions such as acquisition and divestiture strategies. US manufacturers in the 1990s eschewed diversification in favor of 'strategic' (horizontal) mergers and acquisitions, resulting in behemoths in oil, defense, autos, and other sectors that would have been unthinkable in previous decades. Notably, this shift toward a monomaniacal focus on shareholder value occurred in spite of the fact that – in stark contrast to the 1980s – hostile takeovers had virtually disappeared in the 1990s, and takeover targets were no longer 'underperforming' firms but rather those that were strategically attractive to acquirers (Davis and Robbins, 1999). Evidently, the hostile takeover is less essential to investor capitalism than had previously been thought.

Shareholder Activism

Hostile takeovers are a rather blunt instrument for transferring corporate control, and the message they send is not especially fine-grained. But short of takeover, the channels of shareholder influence are surprisingly limited in the US (see Davis and Thompson, 1994). The formal means of shareholder voice is through proxy voting at the annual meeting. Shareholders vote on who serves on the board of directors, which accounting firm audits the firm's books, whether to approve certain types of executive compensation plans, and other significant matters such as mergers, changes in the corporate charter, or changes in the state of incorporation. Almost without exception, these votes consist of approving (or not) proposals put forth by the current board of directors – competing director candidates, or competing proposals, are extremely rare. The primary means of direct shareholder voice is through shareholder proposals. Any shareholder owning a non-trivial stake in the corporation can submit a proposal relevant to the corporation's business to be included in the proxy statement and voted on by shareholders.

But the board may exclude proposals relating to the 'ordinary business' of the corporation, a term of art defined fairly broadly by the Securities and Exchange Commission, the regulatory body responsible for governing the proxy process.

The most famous and controversial case of the 1990s involved Cracker Barrel Old Country Stores, Inc., a restaurant chain headquartered in Tennessee. In 1991, the corporation announced a policy that it would not employ individuals 'whose sexual preferences fail to demonstrate normal heterosexual values' and fired more than a dozen gay employees. Subsequent public protests led the company to rescind the policy, but it did not explicitly include gays in its anti-discrimination policy, and gays continued to be fired. An institutional investor, the New York City Employees' Retirement System (NYCERS), submitted a proxy proposal in 1991 calling for Cracker Barrel to add explicit prohibitions against employment discrimination based on sexual preference to its employment policy statement. Cracker Barrel sought to exclude the proposal under the ordinary business exception, which had previously been considered to cover employment matters, and in October 1992 the SEC issued a 'no-action letter' (indicating that it would not take action against Cracker Barrel for excluding the proposal from its proxy materials). The SEC's position prevailed in court in 1994, and thus all employment-based matters were put beyond the scope of shareholder voice. The business case for NYCERS' position seemed clear: employment discrimination may subject the corporation to protests, tarnished reputation, lost business, and class action lawsuits, to the detriment of shareholder value; yet the SEC held even such highly consequential employment matters to be ordinary business by definition (McCann, 1998). In May 1998, the SEC eventually reversed its position on Cracker Barrel to allow 'employment-related proposals that raise sufficiently significant social policy issues' (cited in Ayotte, 1999). In October of that year, after a year-long battle, NYCERS' proposal appeared on Cracker Barrel's proxy statement, receiving 5.5 million votes (shares) in favor and 26.5 million votes against.

What is perhaps surprising is that even if NYCERS' proposal had won a solid majority,

it would have had no binding force on Cracker Barrel's board. Shareholder proposals are advisory ('precatory') only and cannot be used to compel management or the board to take any specific actions (see Davis and Thompson, 1994, for a discussion of the limits of shareholder voice). In other words, once they have delegated authority to the board of directors, dispersed shareholders have almost no legal standing to intervene further on matters of strategy and management. Why, then, do activist shareholders bother? In the US, the most prominent corporate governance activists are public pension funds run by political appointees, and thus some skeptics see their motivation as political rather than economic, and their qualifications as wanting (Useem et al., 1993). One seasoned director said of activist pension fund officials, 'These guys are not part of the business community. They're politicians' (Neiva, 1996). In its 1994 proxy statement, Cracker Barrel management said of NYCERS: 'Your management is convinced that the proponents of Proposal 3 are attempting to circumvent the legislative process by using corporate proxies as a forum to promote a "social policy" concerning gay and lesbian sexual preferences, thereby forcing your Company to do what Congress has declined to force companies to do. Your management is also convinced that the proponents of this proposal are more interested in gay and lesbian concerns as a social issue than in any economic effect these concerns may have on your Company.'

Yet research suggests that activist pension funds are motivated by financial concerns, not politics. Funds that pursue a buy-and-hold indexing strategy (which benefit from a general rise in the value of their portfolios) tend to field generic proposals for the purpose of promoting shareholder-oriented governance generally, while actively-managed funds (which can realize shorter-term trading gains) tend to focus on firm-specific governance proposals, consistent with the argument that the economically appropriate style of activism varies with the fund's investment style (Del Guercio and Hawkins, 1999). Proposals sponsored by pension funds (as opposed to individuals or religious groups) get higher favorable votes on average, occasionally achieving a majority vote (Gillan and Starks, 1998). And while there is little evidence that shareholder activism has an immediate positive impact on the share price of target firms, targeted firms do respond with significantly more governance changes than non-targets (Del Guercio and Hawkins, 1999). Thus, one survey of the literature on shareholder activism concludes that activism has had modest effects on governance structures but negligible impact on earnings and share price (Karpoff, 1998). It is possible that activism has a more diffuse impact by raising the visibility of directors who had previously toiled in anonymity; as one director put it, 'If you kill one wildebeest, then all the other wildebeests will start running a little faster' (Neiva, 1996). Perhaps activism serves to raise the general awareness of shareholder value and shareholder-oriented governance practices. It is hard not to conclude, however, that this would be pushing through an open door.

Financial Analysts

If takeovers are too blunt an instrument and shareholder activism too diffuse, then financial analysts may serve as a more intermediate form of influence on behalf of shareholders. Analysts investigate companies in order to render judgments on their prospects (to be realized in future earnings) and thus to estimate their appropriate valuation. Analysts are often allowed privileged access to corporate executives and facilities and are in a position to give strategic and governance advice directly to senior managers, something rarely afforded to the firm's own shareholders (Useem, 1996). In principle, the rewards go to the most accurate analysts, giving them incentives to act as corporate watchdogs. In practice, however, analysts are rarely dispassionate observers: those that work for firms doing business with a corporation they follow give systematically more positive evaluations than those that work for other firms, and analysts are discouraged from giving negative evaluations of potential clients of their employer (Hayward and Boeker, 1998). As *New York Times* financial writer Gretchen Morgenstern put it, 'What analysts are selling increasingly today is not the ability to plumb a company's business and uncover investment gems or scams but rather the ability to make investors buy the stocks they follow' (*New York Times*,

July 18, 1999). 'Sell' recommendations are therefore almost non-existent. Moreover, on average analysts are not especially accurate: according to Malkiel (1996: 169), 'Security analysts have enormous difficulty in performing their basic function of forecasting earnings prospects for the companies they follow.... Financial forecasting appears to be a science that makes astrology respectable.' In short, while analysts may be seen as a means to promote shareholder interests, this function frequently goes unrealized.

Although takeovers, shareholder activism, and financial analysts are fixtures on the American corporate landscape, and are uniquely suited to managerialist corporate governance, in the 1990s they spread beyond the borders of the US and the UK. In continental Europe, 1999 was a watershed year for hostile takeovers. In the first three months of the year, 13 hostile bids were unveiled, compared to 55 in the prior nine years, and the value of the proposed deals was far greater than the value of all prior hostile deals in the history of Europe (*Economist*, 17 April 1999). In Italy, Olivetti made a successful bid for the far larger Telecom Italia, the former Italian state telephone company and the sixth-largest telecom organization in the world. In France, Banque Nationale de Paris (BNP) simultaneously bid for banking rivals Societe Generale and Paribas, while oil giant TotalFina bid for Elf Aquitaine. Remarkably, Paribas, which was advising Total on its bid, had executives on the boards of both Total and Elf; Societe Generale's chair was on the board of Total, BNP's chair was on the board of Elf; Elf's chair was on the board of BNP, while Total's chair was a BNP director. Even the dense ties of the French financial elite were not sufficient to withstand the economic attractions of these deals. Due to much more stringent legal restrictions, it remains to be seen whether hostile takeovers will catch on outside Europe.

Shareholder activism, on the other hand, has achieved a global reach, partly through the actions of American institutional investors and partly through indigenous governance activists. The California Public Employees' Retirement System (CalPERS), a pension fund for government employees in California, promulgated corporate governance standards for Britain, France, Germany and Japan, and formed an alliance with Hermes (the pension fund manager for British Post Office and British

Telecom staff) to increase their mutual heft in issues of international corporate governance (CalPERS document can be found at www.calpers-governance.org/principles/international/). Given the vast growth of US institutional investment in equities outside the US, American-style investor activism is poised to go global. Already, investor pressures are credited with forcing the ousters of Cie. De Suez's chair in 1995 and Olivetti's chair in 1996 (Useem, 1998). In South Korea, Jang Ha Sung formed the People's Solidarity for Participatory Democracy to press for corporate governance reform, and while he met with little success prior to the Asian financial crisis of 1997, he has subsequently become 'the darling of the international crowd' and has formed successful alliances with foreign institutional investors to press for governance changes (*Economist*, 27 March 1999). In France, Colette Neuville formed the Association for the Defense of Minority Shareholders to push for corporate governance reform and to strengthen investor protections in takeovers (*Business Week*, 18 September 1995). Both non-local and indigenous investors can draw on the principles and tactics of shareholder activism in the US. Given the relatively weak minority shareholder protections outside common law countries, however, it is likely that any such activism will have modest impact at best (La Porta et al., 1998).

Do Top Managers Really Make a Difference?

If shareholders are increasingly insistent that board directors require top managers to deliver steadily rising returns on their investments, investor activism is premised on a critical assumption that top managers can make the difference. While the premise may seem intuitively obvious to those inhabiting this world, it is far from self-evident to those who study it. Observers diverge from the assumption of influential executives in two opposing directions, one viewing top managers as all-powerful, others seeing them as all but powerless. Jay Lorsch had examined company boards with both views in mind, and his book title well captures the bi-polar thinking about the clout of company executives as well: *Pawns or Potentates* (1989).

Gaetano Mosca, Vilfredo Pareto, and kindred 'elite' theorists early articulated the all-powerful view, but C. Wright Mills captured it best in his classic work, *The Power Elite* (1956). Company executives, in his acid account, had joined with government officials and military commanders in an unholy alliance that observers, including US president Dwight D. Eisenhower, would later dub the 'military–industrial complex'. Seen from this parapet, top management and their allies exercise commanding control over the company and the country. In E. Digby Baltzell's critique, *The Protestant Establishment* (1987), and G. William Domhoff's rendering, *Who Rules America* (1967), they have even come to constitute a self-conscious class, favoring descent over deed. Others discern comparable customs in British business and elsewhere (Bottomore, 1993; Scott, 1990, 1997). To the extent that top management is indeed all-powerful, shareholders and directors possess a silver bullet for righting whatever has gone wrong: install new management.

For the community of management scholars, Jeffrey Pfeffer (1978, 1981) well articulated the opposite, all-power*less* view with the contention that market and organizational constraints so tied top management's hands that it was much the captive, not a maker, of its own history. Production technologies and competitive frays in this view are far more determining of company results than the faceless executives who sit in their suites. Structures matter, personalities don't. It counts little who serves in top management, and, by extension, on the board. Managers and directors are controlling and caste-conscious in Mills' and Domhoff's critique, while they are both powerless and classless in Pfeffer's hands. If top management is quite as powerless as the latter imagery suggest, investors seeking new management are surely wasting their time.

Though probably less often than university deans, company executives do complain of a seeming helplessness at times. Yet almost anybody in personal contact with top managers reports just the opposite. Direct witnesses typically describe instead a commanding presence of their top management, an organizational dominance. It is the senior executives who shape the vision and mobilize the ranks, and it is they who make the difference between success and failure (Tichy, 1997;

Charan and Tichy, 1998). Also consistent with the concept of the prevailing executive is evidence from the flourishing executive search industry, where companies pay hundreds of headhunting firms millions of dollars to find the right men and women for the executive suite. They are engaged, in the phrasing of a widely circulated assessment by McKinsey & Co. (1998), in a 'war for talent'. It would hardly be deemed warfare or worth millions if senior managers made so little difference when they arrived in office.

Investors themselves think otherwise as well. When companies announce executive succession, money managers and stock analysts are quick to place a price on the head of the newly arrived, and, depending on the personality, billions can be added to or subtracted from the company's capitalization. On the addition side, consider the appointment of Christopher Steffen as the new chief financial officer of Eastman Kodak in 1993. Steffen had been hired to help turn around a company whose earnings and stock price had been languishing. He was characterized as the 'white-knight chief financial officer who could save stodgy Eastman Kodak'. Investors applauded his hiring. The company's stockprice soared in the days that followed, adding more than $3 billion to the company's value. In an immediate clash with chief executive Kay Whitmore, however, Steffen resigned just 90 days later. Investors dumped Kodak shares with vigor, driving the company's value down the next day by $1.7 billion, further affirming his worth in the eyes of discerning investors. It would seem that just a single individual with the right talent could augment a company's value by billions in days (Useem, 1996).

On the subtraction side, consider the selection of John Walter as the new chief operating officer and CEO-apparent of AT&T in 1996. In the five trading days that followed, in a period when little else was transpiring in the market, AT&T's value dropped by $6 billion. One business writer had hailed Christopher Steffen as the 'three-billion-dollar man'. John Walter might comparably be dubbed the 'six-billion-dollar disappointment' (Rigdon, 1993).

The importance that investors and directors attribute to top management for growing their fortunes can also be seen in the ultimate punishment for failure to do so: dismissal. Whether in the US, Japan, or Germany, the likelihood of a CEO's exit is increased by as much as half in the wake of a stock free fall. And investors are often the engines behind the turnover. Studies of Japanese companies stunned by a sharp reversal of fortune, for example, reveal that those whose top ten shareholders control a major fraction of the firm's stock dismiss the president and even bring in new directors more often than others (Kaplan, 1994a, b, 1997; Kang and Shivdasani, 1997).

To obtain a metric for the longer-term value that a chief executive brings to a company, we turn to several studies that have examined company results several years after a chief executive has left office, not just several days. The successor brings a distinctive blend of talents to the office, and if those talents make a difference, the firm's performance should be different as well. Net of confounding factors such as the company's sector and economy's momentum, investigators find that company performance does vary with executive personality. Yet compared to the firm's structure and identity, the chief executive's contribution can seem modest. After all, if Bill Gates retired as chief executive at Microsoft or Jack Welch at General Electric, the companies are such product juggernauts that their successors are sure to look good for some years to come. But in absolute terms, the studies report, performance can rise or fall by as much as 10 to 15% over several years after the CEO's departure depending upon the specific successor. To put that in perspective, think of a new manager of a professional baseball team that had won 80 games and lost 80 games during the past season. If the new manager's limited talents lead the team to win 15% fewer games next season, the team's win–loss record would drop from .500 to .425, and the coach will become the heel. If instead the new manager's excellent talents would yield 15% more wins, the team's record rises to .575, and coach will be the hero (Lieberson and O'Connor, 1972; Thomas, 1988).

As strong as they are, these results may still underestimate the difference that top management makes now compared to the past. In a study of 48 large manufacturing firms among the *Fortune* 500, the researchers asked two immediate subordinates of the chief executives the extent to which their boss, the CEO: was a visionary showed strong confidence in self and others, communicated high performance expectations and standards, personally exemplified the firm's vision, values, and standards, and demonstrated personal sacrifice, determination, persistence, and courage. The investigators also assessed the extent to which the firms faced environments that were dynamic, risky, and uncertain. Taking into account a company's size, sector, and other factors, they found that these executive capabilities made a significant difference in the firm's net profit margins among companies that faced highly uncertain environments. When the firms were not so challenged, however, the chief executive's qualities had far less of an impact on performance (Waldman et al., 1999).

Top management matters more, it seems, when it is less clear what path the company should pursue. Given the intensification of global competition and technological change in many markets, leadership is thus likely to make more of a difference in the future than it has in the past. We remember wartime prime ministers and presidents better than peacetime leaders, and the same is likely to be true for company executives. Thus, it not surprising that directors are observed to replace failing executives more quickly now than in years past (Ocasio, 1994). Similarly, directors are observed to more generously reward successful executives than in the past. For each additional $1,000 added to a company's value in 1980, directors on average provided their chief executive an extra $2.51. By 1990, the difference in their payments had risen to $3.64, and by 1994 to $5.29. Put differently, in 1980 the boards of companies ranked at the 90th percentile in performance gave their CEOs $1.4 million more than did boards whose firms ranked at the 10th percentile (in 1994 dollars). But by 1990, the boards had expanded that gap to $5.3 million, and by 1994 to $9.2 million (Hall and Liebman, 1998).

The specific leadership or teamwork capabilities that do account for the varying performance among top managers is beyond the scope of this chapter. But broadly speaking, leadership within the company is a critical component. Unless the troops are mobilized and their mission understood, they are unlikely to deliver the value top management wants. But so too is leadership out and up, building confidence and understanding among the money managers and stock analysts who can

turn against a poorly appreciated or understood company as quixotically as they did against the Asian nations when Thailand devalued its currency in July 1997.

Skillful top management work with professional investors is thus becoming more of a virtue since money managers and stock analysts have become less tolerant of languishing results and are better able to demand stellar performance. Moreover, globally minded investors are now comparing opportunities worldwide, and top managements and their performance are judged less against their domestic neighbors and more against the best anywhere. To assure investor favor and assuage doubt, companies and directors are therefore increasingly likely to stress executive ability to deliver the strategy story to the stock analysts and, ultimately, share value to the money managers. Research confirms that when chief executives present their strategies to groups of stock analysts, institutional interest and stockholding does indeed rise (Byrd et al., 1993). While some top managements will be tempted to create defenses against shareholder pressures, more are likely to be drawn to affirmative measures, including improved disclosure of information and stronger governing boards (Useem, 1998).

HOW DO CORPORATIONS SHAPE SOCIETY?

At stake in discussions of corporate governance and top management are questions of corporate power and accountability, and ultimately of the welfare of society. Corporations are *legal fictions*, created by systems of law to serve social ends for consumers, workers, and investors. Systems of corporate governance are, in essence, genres – styles of thinking about the corporation, its purposes, to whom it is accountable. There is a long-standing antinomy between the social entity model of the corporation and the property or contractarian conception (Allen, 1992). The entity conception, central to organization theory, sees corporations as 'containing' members, for whom the corporations provide various goods (for example, income security, social identity) as part of a social contract. In the most expansive version of this view, corporations directly shape almost every aspect of society. According to Perrow (1991), 'the appearance of large organizations in the United States makes organizations the key phenomenon of our time, and thus politics, social class, economics, technology, religion, the family, and even social psychology take on the character of dependent variables.... [O]rganizations are the key to society because *large organizations have absorbed society.*' The social entity conception of the corporation is associated with communitarian or relationship-based capitalism, in which law and custom accord the corporation obligations beyond shareholder wealth maximization (Thurow, 1992; Bradley et al., 1999; Blair and Stout, 1999).

In contrast, the contractarian model takes the notion of the corporation as a legal fiction to its logical extreme: it is nothing more than a nexus of contracts among freely contracting individuals, with no further 'entitivity'. This yields a substantially more circumscribed view of how the corporation shapes society, namely, through its impact on economic growth. Although the contractarian model denies the existence of the corporation as a social entity with obligations to any constituencies other than shareholders, the most sophisticated theoretical rationale for the contractarian model is framed in terms of social welfare. In stylized form, it runs as follows. Firms maximize social welfare by maximizing profits. The pursuit of profit leads firms to offer goods or services that the public will voluntarily pay for (thus benefiting consumers), and creating those products provides employment (thus benefiting workers). A firm's share price is the best measure of its sustainable profitability into the future, according to the well-documented efficient market hypothesis (according to Jensen [1988] 'no proposition in any of the sciences is better documented' than the efficient market hypothesis). Thus, as a measure of corporate performance, share price is ideal, and devices that encourage corporate managers to maximize share price thereby achieve a trifecta of benefiting consumers, workers, and shareholders simultaneously. These benefits may be unintentionally undermined when firms pursue other ends in addition to shareholder value (as advocated in the social entity conception), because serving two (or more) masters may lead in effect to serving none (Friedman, 1970). As 'residual claimants',

shareholders are the appropriate constituency for the corporation to serve because maximizing their interests automatically serves the interests of the corporation's other constituencies. Shareholders have the best incentives to monitor and, if necessary, replace management that goes astray. As Gilson (1981) memorably put it, 'if the statute did not provide for shareholders, we would have to invent them'.

Note that this case does not rest on anything sacred or mystical about shareholders and their property rights. Compare the apologia provided by Al Dunlap, former CEO of Sunbeam famous for his expansive approach to layoffs: 'The shareholders own the company. They are my number-one constituency, because they take all the risk. If the company goes bust, they lose their life's savings. I can't give them their money back.' Of course, actual ownership patterns are quite different from this 'widows and orphans' portrayal: most large US firms are owned primarily by highly diversified institutional investors, and individuals who focus their investments in one particular firm are typically employees of that firm, whose interests are more complex. In the sophisticated version of contractarianism, shareholders are as much a legal fiction as the corporation itself. It just happens that they are, by hypothesis, part of a social welfare-maximizing genre of corporate governance. As Allen (1992) puts it, this conception of the corporation 'is not premised on the conclusion that shareholders do "own" the corporation in any ultimate sense, only on the view that it can be better for all of us if we act as if they do'.

As a corporate genre, the contractarian approach is as distinctive to the US as Faulkner and Hemingway. The emphasis on voluntarism and individual liberty, and the suspicion of viewing the corporation as a social entity with obligations to constituencies other than shareholders, are recurrent themes in American law and economics (Allen, 1992; Bradley et al., 1999). According to Roe (1994), these individualist themes coupled with a populist mistrust of concentrated economic and political power to produce the managerialist corporation as we know it. Roe's (1994) study told a path-dependent tale of the American system in which the obvious 'solution' to the problem of managerialism – concentrated ownership in the hands of financial intermediaries – was repeatedly prevented by legislation driven by fears of concentrated economic power. At each point when corporate control threatened to become concentrated in a few hands, populist political pressures prevented such centralization. Thus, American corporate governance evolved like an ecosystem in an idiosyncratic climate, getting by as best it could, given its constraints. Along the way a number of means to ensure corporate attentiveness to share price evolved, including most notably the takeover mechanism. In many cases, these were second-best solutions that arose because the first-best was ruled out; the end product is the institutional equivalent of a Rube Goldberg invention: it ain't pretty, but it gets the job done – in this instance a riveting on shareholder value.

The histories of present-day institutions lend themselves to alternative interpretations, even within a general evolutionary framework. In contrast to Roe, Coffee (1999) argues from the recent evidence that the managerialist corporations characteristic of the American system are the product of legal success. Rather than seeing political pressures as *preventing* concentrated ownership, he sees strong legal protections as *allowing* managerialism and all the benefits of a system of arms' length investment without the intervention of powerful intermediaries. Along similar lines, Modigliani and Perotti (1998) portray arms' length financing (via securities markets) and network-based relationship capitalism as functional alternatives – if reliable legal enforcement is available, then a managerialist system centered on financial markets is possible. In contrast, the absence of reliable legal enforcement prompts the formation of 'noncontractual enforcement mechanisms' – often realized in bank-centered networks. In other words, it is relationship-based systems that are the poor cousins of the more arms' length system, and not the other way around.

The value of having a dominant corporate owner with direct control over management, as opposed to dispersed (and presumably powerless) shareholders that delegate authority to a board, has been an object of faith since Berle and Means wrote their famous book. But research in the 1990s, echoing the populist sentiments described by Roe (1994), has instead emphasized the social and economic costs of concentrated economic power. After the East Asian financial crisis of the late

1990s, systems of relationship capitalism, in which dominant owners (banks or families) are tied together into social networks, came to be called 'crony capitalism', reflecting the changing evaluations of personalistic vs arms' length business ties. Dominant shareholders may encourage profit maximizing, but they may instead use the corporation to pursue their own ends, which need not contribute to general economic welfare. Managers in family-controlled firms are difficult for outside shareholders to oust, no matter how bad their performance, and the impact can extend to dozens of firms through control pyramids (Morck et al., 1998). While the ventures of well-connected cronies may be lavishly funded, promising business ideas generated by those outside the network are denied access to capital and die on the vine. 'The opacity and collusive practices that sustain a relationship-based system entrench incumbents at the expense of potential new entrants', rendering the economic system resistant to reform (Rajan and Zingales, 1998: 14). Moreover, economies characterized by concentrated wealth in the hands of 'old money' families grow more slowly than economies without such families, again suggesting a political entrenchment that limits economic adaptability (Morck et al., 1998).

Recent research in financial economics thus suggests that social welfare is enhanced by a strong independent state and undermined by concentrated inherited wealth and power. The implications are ironic. Whereas Berle and Means feared that dispersed ownership would create a class of managers with control over large corporations but little accountability to shareholders, the late 20th century assessment suggests that *concentrated* ownership leads to cronyism, political favoritism, and weak economic growth. The irony runs deep. 'Managerialist' firms in the US pursue shareholder value with little regard for other stakeholders, while firms with concentrated ownership elsewhere in the world cannot help but attend to other stakeholders. Yet the explicit ignoring of other stakeholders may ultimately yield more favorable benefits for them.

The tradeoffs in social welfare of treating the corporation as a social entity vs as a nexus-of-contracts are thus quite subtle. The difficulty of displacing managers that are unsatisfactory to investors is seen as a critical failing of relationship capitalism because it renders firms too lethargic in the face of change (see Gordon, 1997). Without the prospect of outside takeover or other mechanisms that focus decision making on shareholder value, corporations are too slow to exit low-growth industries by closing plants and laying off employees (Jensen, 1993). When Krupp-Hoesch Group made a hostile takeover bid for steel rival Thyssen in March 1997, Thyssen workers fearful of the inevitable job losses mounted a demonstration at Krupp headquarters, pelting Krupp's CEO with eggs and tomatoes. Krupp was convinced by local political leaders to suspend the bid and enter into friendly negotiations. As the two firms sought to hammer out a joint venture agreement, 25,000 workers massed at Deutsche Bank headquarters in Frankfurt to protest the bank's role in the takeover – Deutsche Bank was helping to finance Krupp's bid, but it also had a representative on the Thyssen board – and the final, friendly agreement resulted in considerably fewer lost jobs at Thyssen. One person's 'industrial lethargy' is another person's job security.

In the US, by contrast, layoffs are so common as to arouse little comment, and it is difficult to imagine mass protests in response to takeovers. (The US Department of Labor estimates that 40% of the American labor force changes jobs in any given year.) It is hard to imagine mass protests against dispersed shareholders, and public debate over the social obligations of the corporation has virtually disappeared. Indeed, those corporations that try to serve the ends of stakeholders other than shareholders find it difficult to do so. In the 1919 case of *Dodge vs Ford Motor Co.*, the Michigan Supreme Court laid down a foundational view of the purpose of the corporation in a contractarian world:

> There should be no confusion of the duties which Mr. Ford conceives that he and the stockholders owe to the general public and the duties that he and his co-directors owe to protecting minority shareholders [i.e., the Dodge brothers]. A business corporation is organized and carried on primarily for the profit of the stockholders. The powers of the directors are to be employed for that end. The discretion of directors is to be exercised in the choice of means to attain that end, and does not extend

to a change in the end itself, to the reduction of profits, or to the nondistribution of profits among stockholders in order to devote them to other purposes.

Indeed, as we have seen from our discussion of the Cracker Barrel case, the board of an American corporation would not necessarily be required to attend to other constituencies even if their own shareholders wanted it! (Blair and Stout [1999: 251] make a compelling case that the discretion of the board of directors over the use of corporate resources is 'virtually absolute' under American corporate law, and this discretion can be used to implement something like a social entity model. They recognize, however, that custom among law and economics scholars – if not the law itself – treats the shareholders as the sole owners and legitimate 'stakeholders' of the corporation, and this notion has achieved the status of doxology among American corporate managers in the 1990s [Davis and Robbins, 1999].)

The beneficial effects of the shareholder-oriented corporation on society thus rest on the stylized argument at the beginning of this section – that corporations serve consumers, workers, and shareholders best when they focus exclusively on maximizing share price.

IS A WORLDWIDE MODEL FOR TOP MANAGEMENT AND CORPORATE GOVERNANCE EMERGING?

We have described corporate governance as an institutional matrix that structures the relations among owners, boards, and top managers and determines the goals pursued by the corporation. The corporation is a legal fiction, and different systems of governance represent different genres, with relationship capitalism (in which the corporation is treated as a social entity) and investor capitalism (in which the corporation is a nexus-of-contracts) as the two major distinct sub-types. Can both types survive, or will global trade and investment flows prompt a Darwinian struggle in which one system drives out the other, leading to global convergence?

The question of societal convergence – is it possible, likely, or desirable? – has been mulled over by sociologists (Guillen, 2000) and economists (North, 1990) for decades. It is fair to say that the majority opinion, if not the consensus, is that convergence has not occurred in the past and is unlikely to occur in the future. But the institutions of corporate governance, and the means of organizing top management, are considerably more circumscribed in scope. While the flow of trade across national borders may not induce convergence (North, 1990), the flow of global capital dwarfs that of trade and can have far more important impacts for corporate organization. The economic benefits of opening an economy to international investment, particularly through financial markets, are great, at least in theory – it can increase the availability and reduce the cost of capital for both new and established businesses, thereby boosting economic growth overall. But these benefits of financial markets require corporate governance practices that reassure arms' length investors that they will get a return. The US in particular is seen as having evolved a well-articulated system of institutions for ensuring that shareholders can make arms' length investments in corporations with a reasonable degree of confidence that management will do its job as well as possible. Given the manifest benefits of the contractarian model, some commentators see movement toward this system as 'inexorable.... The nature of this movement is unarguably in the Anglo-American direction rather than the other way around' (Bradley et al., 1999: 76). Others see a global spread of American-style management as extremely unlikely, and the purported benefits as ephemeral (Guillen, 2000). In short, there is no sign of convergence in the scholarly literature on convergence.

Before answering the question, it is worth asking it well. Those examining convergence often focus on very different units of analysis. At the *national* level, impediments to convergence on American-style corporate governance institutions are imposing. Common law, which is an inheritance of many former British colonies and relatively few other nations, is especially shareholder-friendly, civil law, which characterizes most nations in the world, is not (La Porta et al., 1998). The quality of legal enforcement also varies widely by nation. Entrenched and politically powerful economic interests are unlikely to abandon the basis of their economic dominance easily

(Morck et al., 1998). Moreover, relationship capitalism centered around powerful financial institutions has clear advantages over financial market-based ones in facilitating rapid economic development; a well-trained government bureaucracy guiding investment flows through affiliated banks can create an infrastructure of basic industry quite rapidly (Evans, 1995). Thus, the most sophisticated accounts of the link between national systems of corporate governance and economic vitality do not assume that there is one best way, but that the best system is contingent on a nation's level of economic development. In an exemplary work of this sort, Carlin and Mayer (1998) find that 'there is a positive relation in the less developed countries between activity in bank financed industries and the bank orientation of the countries and a negative relation between concentration of ownership and activity in high skill and external financed industries. In more developed countries, the relations are precisely reversed.' Thus, forcing an American system of governance on less-developed nations could be disastrous. On the other hand, it suggests that nations that have moved from 'emerging' to 'developed' may benefit by effecting a shift from relationship capitalism to investor capitalism, however unlikely this may be in practice (Rajan and Zingales, 1998).

The picture shifts when one considers not nations but firms. For the largest global corporations with the greatest need for capital, such as those listing on the New York Stock Exchange, movement toward the American style appears almost inevitable, just as adoption of the Toyota system of manufacturing seemed inevitable for the largest manufacturers (see Useem, 1998). In his thoughtful discussion of the convergence debate, Coffee (1998) argues that formal convergence is unlikely but 'functional convergence' is plausible. His argument runs as follows. Firms with higher stock market valuations have advantages in acquiring other firms around the globe and thus are more likely to survive global industry consolidations. As large global corporations seek the benefits of higher market valuations by listing on American stock exchanges, they thereby become subject to US legal standards. This moots the issues raised by La Porta et al. (1998): firms, in effect, choose their legal regime, and nations need not seek to become 'more American' for their indigenous firms to gain the benefits of American-style governance. The outcome of this process could be a world in which the largest global corporations 'look American' while nations retain their distinct national institutions of governance for smaller domestic firms.

In short, the most plausible scenario is for a global standard of governance to emerge for the largest global corporations, while national variation persists both in institutions of governance and in the practices of small- and medium-sized domestic corporations. The impediments for nations to move substantially toward the American system are almost certainly too large to be readily overcome, even if such a transition were desirable: many national distinctions will inevitably persist.

The Road Ahead

Top company managers have always drawn academic and applied interest, if for no other reason than they can seem larger than life at those pivotal moments when a company's ownership and its executive careers hang in balance. The loss of control of RJR Nabisco by chief executive F. Ross Johnson to leverage-buyout king Henry Kravis in 1987 provided ample material for a best-selling book and subsequent film (Burroughs and Helyar, 1991). The two CEOs – Gerald M. Levin and Stephen M. Case – who merged America Online and Time Warner in 2000 drew enormous media interest. Corporate directors have attracted less attention, partly because they avoid the limelight but also because few outsiders believed directors brought much to the table, vanquished as they were by Berle and Means' managerial revolution. For understanding company strategy, production technologies, and market dynamics, neither senior executives nor company directors could be viewed as fertile ground for theory building.

With the rise of professional investors and their subjugation of national boundaries, however, those who occupy the executive suite and those who put them there are drawing far more research and policy attention, and justifiably so. In a bygone era when markets were more steady and predictable, when airline and telephone executives confidently knew what to expect next year, the identity of top management mattered little. When shareholders were far smaller and decidedly quieter, when airline and telephone directors comfortably enjoyed inconsequential board meetings, the composition of the governing body mattered little either. During the past decade, however, all of this has changed in the US and the UK, with other economies close behind. As shareholders have sought to reclaim authority over what they owned, they have brought top management and company directors back in. Company strategy and financial results can no longer be understood without understanding the capabilities and organization of those most responsible for delivering them.

Research investigators have risen to the occasion. A solid flow of studies has sought to discern and dissect the dynamic relations that now characterize the world of investors, directors, and managers. The market is no longer viewed as so impersonal, the company no longer so isolated. Economic and financial decisions are embedded in a complex network of working relations among money managers, stock analysts, company directors, senior executives, and state regulators. Given the right combination of features, that lattice can yield high investment returns and robust national growth. Given the wrong amalgam, it can lead instead to self-dealing, frozen form, and economic stagnation.

The road ahead will thus depend on how well researchers understand what governance arrangements and leadership styles work well both within national settings and across cultural divides, and on the extent that top managers, company directors, and active investors learn and apply what is best. Five key areas deserve concerted research attention if we are to know what works and what does not, and which theories are useful and which are not:

Boards and directors: What does the decision process inside the boardroom look like? What are the sources of power and influence of inside and outside directors? How are the decision process and director influence contingent on the 'institutional matrix' in which a board is embedded? (Example: Pettigrew and McNulty, 1998a, b.)

Comparative governance: What really accounts for the astonishing and remarkably persistent diversity in the national systems of corporate governance? How do national institutions, cultures, and social structures shape and constrain the evolution of corporate governance systems? (Examples: Kogut and Walker, 1999; Bebchuk and Roe, 1999.)

Financial globalization: If the surge of cross-border investing is a major driver of corporate change, what can we expect of financial flows and their regulation in the years ahead? How is the evolving organization of investors and companies likely to affect the internationalization of capital flows? What aspects of corporate governance will affect the attractiveness of a national economy for international investors? How are actions by the International Monetary Fund and World Bank likely to affect national systems of corporate governance? (Examples: Evans, 1995; Mizruchi, 2000.)

Inequality in a 'globalized' world: How do systems of corporate governance affect distributions of wealth within and among nations? What is the likelihood that social movements for change may mobilize in the face of – or to resist – globalization? Does the globalization of finance lead to a leveling up or a leveling down of national standards for labor relations, environmental protection, and income inequality? (Example: Firebaugh, 1999.)

Business and Political Leadership: To what extent is a shared leadership style emerging among top company managers and government officials around the world? Are such institutions as the World Economic Forum creating a global network among those who govern the major commercial and political institutions in the leading economies? As worldwide relations among business and political elites do emerge, are they undermining traditional relations among elites within economies? (Examples: Davis and Mizruchi, 1999; Khanna and Palepu, 2000.)

The research is unlikely to reveal worldwide best practices in corporate governance, but it is likely to yield a host of better measures that, when deftly combined, adapted to legal context, and sensitive to cultural nuance, should produce what executives, directors, and stockholders all want. The academic and policy debate will wisely focus not on whether the opening of capital markets and ascendance of global companies will flatten alternative forms, but rather on what forms of organization and leadership are best suited for success in local or regional operations in an era when equity investing and company competitors can move in and out of markets with the click of mouse.

REFERENCES

Allen, W. T. (1992) 'Our schizophrenic conception of the business corporation', *Cardozo Law Review*, 14: 261–81.

Anderson, R. C., Bates, T. W., Bizjak, J. M. and Lemmon, M. L. (1998) 'Corporate governance and firm diversification', Unpublished, Washington and Lee University.

Ayotte, C. L. (1999) 'Comment: reevaluating the shareholder proposal rule in the wake of Cracker Barrel and the era of institutional investors', *Catholic University Law Review*, 48: 511–56.

Baliga, B. R., Moyer, R. C. and Rao, R. S. (1996) 'CEO duality and firm performance: what's the fuss?', *Strategic Management Journal*, 17: 41.

Baltzell, E. D. (1987) *The Protestant Establishment: Aristocracy and Caste in America*. New Haven: Yale University Press.

Beatty, R. P. and Zajac, E. J. (1994) 'Managerial incentives, monitoring, and risk bearing: a study of executive compensation, ownership, and board structure in initial public offerings', *Administrative Science Quarterly*, 39: 313–35.

Bebchuk, L. A. and Roe, M. J. (1999) 'A theory of path dependence in corporate ownership and governance', *Stanford Law Review*, 52: 127–70.

Belliveau, M. A., O'Reilly III, C. A. and Wade, J. B. (1996) 'Social capital at the top: effects of social similarity and status on CEO compensation', *Academy of Management Journal*, 39: 1568–93.

Berle, A. Jr. and Means, G. C. (1932) *The Modern Corporation and Private Property*. New York: Macmillan.

Bhagat, S. and Black, B. (1999) 'The uncertain relationship between board composition and firm performance', *Business Lawyer*, 54: 921–63.

Bhagat, S., Shleifer, A. and Vishny, R. W. (1990) 'Hostile takeovers in the 1980s: the return to corporate specialization', in M. N. Baily and C. Winston (eds), *Brookings Papers on Economic Activity: Microeconomics 1990*. Washington, DC: Brookings Institution. pp. 1–84.

Blair, M. M. (ed.) (1993) *The Deal Decade: What Takeovers and Leveraged Buyouts Mean for Corporate Governance*. Washington: Brookings Institution.

Blair, M. M. (1995) *Ownership and Control: Re-Thinking Corporate Governance for the Twenty-First Century*. Washington: Brookings Institution.

Blair, M. M. and Stout, L. A. (1999) 'A team production theory of corporate law', *Virginia Law Review*, 85: 247–328.

Bottomore, T. (1993) *Elites and Society*, 3rd edition. London: Routledge.

Bradley, M., Schipani, C., Sundaram, A. K. and Walsh, J. P. (1999a) 'Corporate governance in a comparative setting: the United States, Germany, and Japan', Durham, NC: Duke University.

Bradley, M., Schipani, C. A., Sundaram, A. K. and Walsh, J. P. (1999b) 'The purposes and accountability of the corporation in contemporary society: corporate governance at a crossroads', *Law and Contemporary Problems*, 62(3): 9–86.

Brancato, C. (1999) *International Patterns of Institutional Investment*. New York: Conference Board.

Burroughs, B. and Helyar, J. (1991) *Barbarians at the Gate: The Fall of RJR Nabisco*. New York: HarperCollins.

Bushee, B. J. and Noe, C. F. (1999) 'Unintended consequences of attracting institutional investors with improved disclosure', Unpublished, Harvard Business School.

Byrd, J. F., Johnson, M. F. and Johnson, M. S. (1993) 'Investor relations and the cost of capital', Ann Arbor, Mich: University of Michigan, School of Business Administration.

California Public Employees' Retirement System (1999) US Corporate Governance Principles, at http://www.calpers-governance.org/principles/domestic/us/page04.asp

Carlin, W. and Mayer, C. (1998) 'Finance, investment, and growth', Unpublished, University College, London.

Charan, R. and Tichy, N. M. (1998) *Every Business Is a Growth Business*. New York: Times Books/Random House.

Charkham, J. (1994) *Keeping Good Company: A Study of Corporate Governance in Five Countries*. New York: Oxford University Press.

Charkham, J. and Simpson, A. (1999) *Fair Shares: The Future of Shareholder Power and Responsibility*. New York: Oxford University Press.

Chew, D. H. (ed.) (1997) *Studies in International Corporate Finance and Governance Systems: A Comparison of the US, Japan, and Europe*. New York: Oxford University Press.

Coffee, J. C. Jr. (1998) 'The future as history: the prospects for global convergence in corporate governance and its implications', Columbia University Center for Law and Economic Studies Working Paper # 144.

Coffee, J. C. Jr. (1999) 'The future as history: the prospects for global convergence in corporate governance and its implications', *Northwestern University Law Review*, 93: 641–707.

Conyon, M. J. and Peck, S. I. (1998) 'Board size and corporate performance: evidence from European companies', *European Journal of Finance*, 4: 291–304.

Council of Institutional Investors (1999) Core Policies, at http://www.ciicentral.com/ciicentral/core_policies.htm

Davis, G. F. (1998) 'Corporate boards in times of turbulent change', in D. C. Hambrick, D. A. Nadler and M. L. Tushman (eds), *Navigating Change: How CEOs, Top Teams, and Boards Steer Transformation*. Boston: Harvard Business School. pp. 278–87.

Davis, G F., Diekmann, K. A. and Tinsley, C. H. (1994) 'The decline and fall of the conglomerate firm in the 1980s: the de-institutionalization of an organizational form', *American Sociological Review*, 59: 47–70.

Davis, G. F. and Mizruchi, M. S. (1999) 'The money center cannot hold: commercial banks in the US system of corporate governance', *Administrative Science Quarterly*, 44: 215–39.

Davis, G. F. and Robbins, G. E. (1999) 'The fate of the conglomerate firm in the United States', in W. W. Powell and D. L. Jones (eds), *Bending the Bars of the Iron Cage: Institutional Dynamics and Processes*. Chicago: University of Chicago Press.

Davis, G. F. and Stout, S. K. (1992) 'Organization theory and the market for corporate control: a dynamic analysis of the characteristics of large takeover targets, 1980–1990', *Administrative Science Quarterly*, 37: 605–33.

Davis, G. F. and Thompson, T. A. (1994) 'A social movement perspective on corporate control', *Administrative Science Quarterly*, 39: 141–73.

Del Guercio, D. and Hawkins, J. (1999) 'The motivation and impact of pension fund activism', *Journal of Financial Economics*, 52: 293–340.

Demsetz, H. and Lehn, K. (1985) 'The structure of corporate ownership: causes and consequences', *Journal of Political Economy*, 93: 1155–77.

Domhoff, G. W. (1967) *Who Rules America*. Englewood Cliffs, NJ: Prentice-Hall.

Easterbrook, F. H. and Fischel, D. R. (1991) *The Economic Structure of Corporate Law*. Cambridge, MA: Harvard University Press.

Evans, P. (1995) *Embedded Autonomy: States and Industrial Transformation*. Princeton, NJ: Princeton University Press.

Fama, E. (1980) 'Agency problems and the theory of the firm', *Journal of Political Economy*, 88: 288–307.

Fama, E. and Jensen, M. C. (1983) 'Separation of ownership and control', *Journal of Law and Economics*, 26: 301–25.

Federal Reserve System, Board of Governors (1999) *Flow of Funds Accounts of the United States*. Washington, DC: Federal Reserve System.

Finkelstein, S. and Hambrick, D. C (1996) *Strategic Leadership: Top Executives and Their Effects on Organizations*. Minneapolis–St. Paul: West Publishing Company.

Firebaugh, G. (1999) 'Empirics of world income inequality', *American Journal of Sociology*, 104: 1597–630.

Franks, J. (1997) 'Corporate ownership and control in the UK, Germany, and France', *Journal of Applied Corporate Finance*, 9: 30–45.

Friedman, M. (1970) 'The social responsibility of business is to increase its profits', *New York Times Magazine*, September 13.

Friedman, T. L. (1999) *The Lexus and the Olive Tree: Understanding Globalization*. New York: Farrar, Strauss, Giroux.

Gillan, S. L. and Starks, L. T. (1998) 'Corporate governance proposals and shareholder activism: the role of institutional investors', Unpublished, Securities and Exchange Commission Office of Economic Analysis.

Gillan, S. L. and Starkes, L. T. (1999) 'Corporate governance proposals and shareholder activism: the role of institutional investors', *Journal of Financial Economics*, 47: 275–505.

Gilson, R. C. (1981) 'A structural approach to corporations: the case against defensive tactics in tender offers', *Stanford Law Review*, 33: 819–91.

Gilson, R. C. (1996) 'Corporate governance and economic efficiency: when do institutions matter?', *Washington University Law Quarterly*, 74: 327–45.

Goergen, M. and Renneboog, L. (1998) 'Strong managers and passive institutional investors in the UK', Unpublished, University of Reading.

Gordon, J. N. (1997) 'The shaping force of corporate law in the new economic order', *University of Richmond Law Review*, 31: 1473–99.

Granovetter, M. (1985) 'Economic action and social structure: the problem of embeddedness', *American Journal of Sociology*, 91: 481–510.

Guillen, M. (1999) 'Corporate governance and globalization: three arguments against convergence', Unpublished, Wharton School, University of Pennsylvania.

Guillen, M. F. (2000) 'Corporate governance and globalization: is there convergence across countries?', *Advances to International Comparative Management*, 13: 171–206.

Hall, B. J. and Liebman, J. B. (1998) 'Are CEOs really paid like bureaucrats?', *Quarterly Journal of Economics*, 113: 653–91.

Hambrick, D. C., Cho, T. S. and Chen, M-J. (1996) 'The influence of top management team heterogeneity on firms' competitive moves', *Administrative Science Quarterly*, 41: 659–84.

Hambrick, D. C., Nadler, D. A. and Tushman, M. L. (eds) (1998) *Navigating Change: How CEOs, Top Teams, and Boards Steer Transformation*. Boston: Harvard Business School Press.

Hayward, M. L. A. and Boeker, W. (1998) 'Power and conflicts of interest in professional firms: evidence from investment banking', *Administrative Science Quarterly*, 43: 1–22.

Hunter, L. W. (1998) 'Can strategic participation be institutionalized? Union representation on American corporate boards', *Industrial and Labor Relations Review*, 51: 557–78.

Institutional Shareholder Services (1999) *The ISS Friday Report*, August 6: 5–6.

Jensen, M. C. (1986) 'Agency costs of free cash flow, corporate finance and takeovers', *American Economic Review (Papers & Proceedings)*, 76: 323–9.

Jensen, M. C. (1988) 'Takeovers: their causes and consequences', *Journal of Economic Perspectives*, 2: 21–48.

Jensen, M. C. (1993) 'The modern industrial revolution, exit, and the failure of internal control systems', *Journal of Finance*, 48: 831–80.

Kang, J-K. and Shivdasani, A. (1997) 'Corporate restructuring during performance declines in Japan', *Journal of Financial Economics*, 46: 29–65.

Kaplan, S. N. (1994a) 'Top executives, turnover, and firm performance in Germany', *Journal of Law, Economics and Organization*, 10: 142–59.

Kaplan, S. N. (1994b) 'Top executive rewards and firm performance: a comparison of Japan and the US', *Journal of Political Economy*, 102: 510–46.

Kaplan, S. N. (1997) 'Corporate governance and corporate performance: a comparison of Germany, Japan, and the US', *Journal of Applied Corporate Finance*, 9: 86–93.

Karpoff, J. M. (1998) 'The impact of shareholder activism on target companies: a survey of empirical findings', Unpublished, University of Washington.

Katzenbach, J. R. (1997) *Teams at the Top: Unleashing the Potential of Both Teams and Individual Leaders*. Boston: Harvard Business School Press.

Katzenbach, J. R. and Smith, D. K. (1992) *The Wisdom of Teams: Creating the High-Performance Organization*. Boston: Harvard Business School Press.

Khanna, T. and Palepu, K. (2000) 'The future of business groups in emerging markets: long-run evidence from Chile', *Academy of Management Journal*, 43: 268–85.

Kogut, B. and Walker, G. (1999) 'The small world of firm ownership in Germany: social capital and structural holes in large firm acquisitions – 1993–1997', Unpublished, Wharton School, University of Pennsylvania.

La Porta, R. and Lopez-de-Silanes, F. (1998) 'Capital markets and legal institutions', Unpublished, Harvard University.

La Porta, R., Lopez-de-Silanes, F. and Shleifer, A. (1999) 'Corporate ownership around the world', *Journal of Finance*, 54: 471–517.

La Porta, R., Lopez-de-Silanes, F., Shleifer, A. and Vishny, R. W. (1997) 'Legal determinants of external finance', *Journal of Finance*, 52: 1131–50.

La Porta, R., Lopez-de-Silanes, F., Shleifer, A. and Vishny, R. W. (1998) 'Law and finance', *Journal of Political Economy*, 106: 1113–55.

Lieberson, S. and O'Connor, J. F. (1972) 'Leadership and organizational performance: a study of large corporations', *American Sociological Review*, 37: 117–30.

Lorsch, J. W. (1989) *Pawns or Potentates: The Reality of America's Corporate Boards*. Boston: Harvard Business School Press.

Malkiel, B. G. (1996) *A Random Walk down Wall Street*. New York: W. W. Norton.

Manne, H. G. (1965) 'Mergers and the market for corporate control', *Journal of Political Economy*, 73: 110–20.

Marris, R. (1964) *The Economic Theory of 'Managerial' Capitalism*. New York: Free Press.

McCann, M. (1998) 'Shareholder proposal rule: Cracker Barrel in light of Texaco', *Boston College Law Review*, 39: 965–94.

McKinsey War for Talent Team (1998) *Winning the War for Talent*. New York: McKinsey & Co.

Mills, C. W. (1956) *The Power Elite*. New York: Oxford University Press.

Millstein, I. M. and MacAvoy, P. W. (1998) 'The active board of directors and performance of the large publicly traded corporation', *Columbia Law Review*, 98: 1283.

Mizruchi, M. S. (2000) 'The globalization of American finance: sources and consequences of foreign activity among large US commercial banks', Unpublished, Department of Sociology, University of Michigan.

Modigliani, F. and Perotti, E. (1998) 'Security versus bank finance: the importance of a proper enforcement of legal rules', Unpublished, MIT Sloan School of Management.

Morck, R. K., Stangeland, D. A. and Yeung, B. (1998) 'Inherited wealth, corporate control, and economic growth', National Bureau of Economic Research, Working Paper # 6814.

Neiva, E. M. (1996) 'The current state of American corporate governance', Columbia University Law School, Institutional Investor Project.

New York Stock Exchange (1999) *Fact Book for the Year 1998*. New York: New York Stock Exchange.

North, D. C. (1990) *Institutions, Institutional Change and Economic Performance*. Cambridge, UK: Cambridge University Press.

North, D. C. (1991) 'Institutions', *Journal of Economic Perspectives*, 5: 97–112.

Ocasio, W. (1994) 'Political dynamics and the circulation of power: CEO succession in US industrial corporations, 1960–1990', *Administrative Science Quarterly*, 39: 285–312.

Perrow, C. (1991) 'A society of organizations', *Theory and Society*, 20: 725–62.

Pettigrew, A. (1992) 'On studying managerial elites', *Strategic Management Journal*, 13: 163–82.

Pettigrew, A. and McNulty, T. (1995) 'Power and influence in and around the boardroom', *Human Relations*, 48: 845–73.

Pettigrew, A. and McNulty, T. (1998a) 'Control and creativity in the boardroom', in D. C. Hambrick, D. A. Nadler and M. L. Tushman (eds), *Navigating Change: How CEOs, Top Teams and Boards Steer Transformation*. Boston: Harvard Business School. pp. 226–55.

Pettigrew, A. and McNulty, T. (1998b) 'Sources and uses of power in the boardroom', *European Journal of Work and Organizational Psychology*, 7: 197–214.

Pfeffer, J. (1978) 'The ambiguity of leadership', in M. W. McCall, Jr. and M. M. Lombardo (eds), *Leadership: Where Else Can We Go?* Durham, NC: Duke University Press.

Pfeffer, J. (1981) 'Management as symbolic action: the creation and maintenance of organizational paradigms', in L. L. Cummings and B. M. Staw (eds), *Research in Organizational Behavior*, Vol. 3. Greenwich, CT: JAI Press.

Polanyi, K. (1957) 'The economy as instituted process', in K. Polanyi, C. M. Arensberg and H. W. Pearson (eds), *Trade and Market in the Early Empires: Economies in History and Theory*. Glencoe, IL: Free Press.

Rajan, R. G. and Zingales, L. (1998) 'Which capitalism? Lessons from the East Asian crisis', *Journal of Applied Corporate Finance*, 11(3): 40–8.

Rigdon, J. E. (1993) 'The new finance chief at Kodak has a style quite unlike his boss's', *Wall Street Journal*, April 28, A1, A13.

Roe, M. J. (1994) *Strong Managers, Weak Owners: The Political Roots of American Corporate Finance*. Princeton, NJ: Princeton University Press.

Sambharya, R. B. (1996) 'Foreign experience of top management teams and international diversification strategies of US multinational corporations', *Strategic Management Journal*, 17: 739–46.

Scott, J. (ed.) (1990) *The Sociology of Elites*. Hants, UK: Edward Elgar Publishing Ltd.

Scott, J. (1997) *Corporate Business and Capitalist Classes*. New York: Oxford University Press.

Shleifer, A. and Vishny, R. W. (1997) 'A survey of corporate governance', *Journal of Finance*, 52: 737–83.

Sony Corporation (1999) Annual Report 1999, at http://www.world.sony.com/IR/AnnualReport99/index. html

Soros, G. (1998) *The Crisis of Global Capitalism: Open Society Endangered*. New York: Public Affairs.

Spicer, A. and Kogut, B. (1999) 'Institutional technology and the chains of trust: capital markets and privatization in Russia and the Czech Republic', Unpublished, University of California at Riverside.

Thomas, A. B. (1988) 'Does leadership make a difference to organizational performance?', *Administrative Science Quarterly*, 33: 388–400.

Thurow, L. (1992) *Head to Head: The Coming Economic Battle among Japan, Europe, and America*. New York: William Morrow.

TIAA-CREF (1999) TIAA-CREF Policy Statement on Corporate Governance, at http://www.tiaa-cref.org/site-line/index.shtml

Tichy, N. M. (1997) *The Leadership Engine: How Winning Companies Build Leaders at Every Level*. New York: Harper Business.

Useem, M. (1995) 'Reaching corporate executives', in R. Hertz and J. B. Imber (eds), *Studying Elites Using Qualitative Methods*. Newbury Park, CA: Sage Publications.

Useem, M. (1996) *Investor Capitalism: How Money Managers Are Changing the Face of Corporate America*. New York: Basic Books/HarperCollins.

Useem, M. (1998) 'Corporate leadership in a globalizing equity market', *Academy of Management Executive*, 12: 43–59.

Useem, M., Bowman, E. H., Irvine, C. and Myatt, J. (1993) 'US investors look at corporate governance in the 1990s', *European Management Journal*, 11: 175–89.

Useem, M. and Karabel, J. (1986) 'Pathways to top corporate management', *American Sociological Review*, 51: 184–200.

Waldman, D. A., Ramirez, G., House, R. J. and Puranam, P. (1999) 'Does leadership matter? CEO leadership attributes and profitability under conditions of perceived environmental uncertainty', Phoenix: Arizona State University.

Walsh, J. P. and Seward, J. K. (1990) 'On the efficiency of internal and external corporate control mechanisms', *Academy of Management Review*, 15: 421–58.

Westphal, J. D. (1999) 'Collaboration in the boardroom: behavioral and performance consequences of CEO–board social ties', *Academy of Management Journal*, 42: 7–24.

Westphal, J. D. and Zajac, E. J. (1998) 'The symbolic management of stockholders: corporate governance reforms and shareholder reactions', *Administrative Science Quarterly*, 43: 127–53.

Yergin, D. and Stanislaw, J. (1998) *The Commanding Heights: The Battle Between Government and the Marketplace That Is Remaking the Modern World*. New York: Simon & Schuster.

Yermack, D. (1996) 'Higher market valuation of companies with a small board of directors', *Journal of Financial Economics*, 40: 185–211.

Zajac, E. J. and Westphal, J. D. (2001) 'Do markets learn? Institutional vs market learning perspectives on the consequences of stock repurchase programs', Working Paper, Northwestern University.

Zingales, L. (1998) 'Corporate governance', in P. Newman (ed), *The New Palgrave Dictionary of Economics and the Law*. New York: Macmillan.

Part Three
CHANGING CONTEXTS

12

International Management and Strategy

BRUCE KOGUT

The field of international strategy concerns the study of international activities of firms and their interactions with foreign governments, competitors, and employees. It seeks to address not only the question of why do firms go overseas, but also how they do it. The globalization of markets, and rapid changes in economic and political systems, has forced a re-thinking of the meaning of location, of competitive advantage, and of the transmission of knowledge among countries. Because of the dominance of the multinational corporation in trade and in world production, international business focuses on the manager's challenge to coordinate and organize people – despite large variations in their national origins and culture – within the boundaries of a single firm that spans borders.

The international business literature has strong roots in international economics that has influenced the discussion of corporate strategy and organizational structure. By 1980, this tradition culminated in the eclectic theory of the multinational corporation that is widely accepted today. This theory in many regards is a more complete statement of why firms exist than the partial theories found in strategy. It is a statement, in current parlance, that emphasizes the capabilities of the firm as subject to transaction costs and location constraints. However, this theory has also undergone an important re-interpretation over the past two

decades that has stressed more importantly the view of the multinational corporation as a repository of knowledge that has evolved in specific national settings.

The international business literature shares many similarities with the strategy theories that emphasize the industry as well as the resource-based theory of the firm. The former is not surprising, as both strategy and international business took inspiration from the work of Joe Bain (1956) in the 1950s and 1960s on the industrial economics that determine firm profitability. Moreover, much like industry analysis was shaped by Richard Caves and his student Michael Porter, Caves (1971) had an important influence on shaping the methodological approaches to understanding foreign direct investment. However, the capabilities, or knowledge, approach in international business has more distinctive roots than those found in strategy. Because of the importance of technology transfer in international markets, capabilities in the international literature started from asking why it is hard to transfer technology and knowledge across the borders of countries. From this perspective grew the view that an alternative definition of foreign direct investment was the transfer of organizational capabilities, and organizing principles, across borders and within the boundaries of the firm.

International management and strategy is a field that evolves along with the domain of its inquiry. Given the tremendous changes in the geo-political frontiers of East and West, current studies are far more sensitive to the institutional context of enterprises. It is understood much better now that the capabilities of firms are strongly influenced by national systems and institutions. At the same time that there is a growing appreciation of national context, there is also an awareness that the diminution in transport and communication costs, and the rise of the internet economy, poses fundamental changes in thinking about location and place. These empirical concerns feed back into theoretical understanding. These new phenomena do not so much contradict previous theory as enrich it.

WHY INVEST IN ANOTHER COUNTRY?

It is helpful to start with the basics. Multinational corporations have long been the primary players in particular industries, for example, consumer products (from toothpaste to electronics), transportation, and chemicals. Choose an industry such as washing machine detergent, and look at the names of the firms that compete in Mexico, France, Japan, Poland, and Saudi Arabia – Proctor and Gamble, Hertel, Kao, Colgate, Unilever. This is a long-standing oligopoly, an industry of a few players who compete and produce in a recognized world market and whose business strategies are dictated as much by what their rivals are doing as by what their customers need. Yet, while all multinationals tend to be part of an oligopoly, not all oligopolistic firms become multinationals or even invest abroad. Why?

The conventional answer had been that foreign investment occurs because money flows to countries that promise higher rates of return. The empirical evidence shows that companies expand their operations elsewhere even when the returns are not that attractive. Moreover this pattern is widespread enough that it cannot be discounted as the result of the mistakes made by overeager managers playing with shareholders' money.

In fact, the rise of multinational corporations, meaning companies that own and exert

centralized control over companies in several other countries, was the puzzle that the first generation of scholars in international business sought to solve. Prior to the publication of an MIT doctoral dissertation by Stephen Hymer in 1960, most economists and policy makers indeed thought that differences in the rates of return to capital among countries explained why money moves across borders. It had been hundreds of years since British and Dutch firms began contracting production to local businesses in Asia and elsewhere. American firms such as Singer and Westinghouse built large factories in England prior to 1900. Despite so much history and experience, the naive theory was that direct investment and portfolio investment were the same thing – both were investments seeking higher rates of return on invested capital.

Hymer simply asked why any firm would invest physical capital in a country (exposed as it is to commercial and political risk) when they could invest financial capital in small amounts across many firms and countries. To want to invest and own physical capital in a foreign country, a firm must believe that it has some additional advantage that outweighs the added costs of operating at a distance in an unknown business environment. Moreover, it must also believe that this advantage can only be exploited through the ownership and control over foreign operations. Otherwise a company could rely on exports to tap foreign markets without incurring the troubles of investing abroad. Hymer eliminated the country as an important factor in understanding direct investment. Now the focus would be on industries and firms themselves.

Since Hymer, there has been fairly universal agreement that the distinctive characteristic of direct investment is the intent to *control*. As a consequence, governments define foreign direct investment (FDI) as the controlling ownership of assets by foreign private individuals or firms. In the United States, only purchases of at least 10% of a firm's equity can be considered a direct investment; in other countries, this critical threshold percentage may be set at a different level. Thus, foreign direct investment is quite distinct from foreign *portfolio* investment, which usually implies the ownership of non-controlling equities in companies whose shares are traded in a foreign stock market.

WHY ARE SOME BUSINESSES MORE INTERNATIONAL THAN OTHERS?

Recognizing that multinational corporations tend to populate industries in which only a few firms dominate sales (oligopolistic enterprises), Hymer basically set out a necessary condition for direct investment and multinational corporations – namely, these firms should own some hard-to-replicate proprietary advantage (brand label, technology, efficiency due to size) that enables them to dominate in home markets and, later, foreign markets. Ironically, this tendency to domination that Hymer first came to identify as the outcome of the multinational corporation's advantage is also the quality that is the target of popular political and economic attack – an attack that Hymer later came to join.

These basic ideas were more fully developed by MIT's Charles Kindleberger (1969) and Harvard's Richard Caves and their students. Caves, in particular, constructed a methodological template that came to dominate empirical studies on foreign direct investment (1971). This template consists of finding a measure of direct investment as the dependent variable and then regressing this measure on explanatory proxies for barriers to entry that characterize industries. In this sense, the early work on direct investment set the stage for the latter development in strategy on industry analysis. The oligopolistic theory of direct investment still failed, however, to capture the differences among firms and industries. Why is Boeing, which clearly enjoys important competitive advantages and competes in an oligopoly, still largely a domestic producer that operates internationally through exports? In contrast, why is it that so early in history companies manufacturing tires or sewing machines felt the need to establish similar operations in other countries?

In the decades after Hymer's contribution, there emerged an integrated view that John Dunning, a professor at the University of Reading in England, dubbed the eclectic theory of foreign direct investment (1977, 1980). Dunning employed the acronym of OLI to summarize the theory's three elements: *ownership, location, and internalization.* Ownership is simply the Hymer idea that a firm has to own some unique advantage in order to offset the added costs of competing overseas. Location seems obvious enough: a firm will locate its activities either to gain access to cheap labor, capital, materials and other inputs, or to sell close to its customers and avoid transportation and tariff costs. In the parlance of economics, the sourcing decision is an act of 'vertical' investment – the sales decision represents a 'horizontal' investment.

ENTRY MODE AND ALLIANCES

A tremendous amount of intellectual labor has been invested in the third element – *internalization.* Scholars, such as Peter Buckley and Mark Casson (1976), Alan Rugman (1981) and Jean Francois Hennart (1982), sought to explain why a firm would choose to exploit its advantage internationally through ownership – as opposed to through a joint venture, license, franchise, or a simple export sales agreement. This line of thought bears strong affinities to transaction cost economics of Oliver Williamson, with an important exception. Williamson's (1975) theory of transaction costs was motivated by the desire to explain why vertical integration, even if it entailed some monopoly power, could nevertheless be efficiency improving. The international business literature did not assume that internalization leads to a globally efficient outcome. In fact, Buckley and Casson were explicit in noting that firms sometimes internalize to correct for market imperfections that nevertheless might lead to unusual monopoly powers.

Internalization theory has been most useful to explain the *entry* mode decision, for example, joint ventures, licensing, acquisition. In practice, these different modes of entry into overseas markets are not mutually exclusive. A firm commonly decides to establish a joint venture (share the equity ownership in a foreign operation with another partner) and also allow others to 'rent' its technology by granting them a license to use it. This license sells the right to use the technology against various kinds of payments, usually fees and royalties.

An earlier literature, started by Stopford and Wells (1972), had analyzed the choice of entry modes as determined by the strategy of the firm. They related entry choices also to the organizational structure of the firm. The internationalization hypothesis, suggested by Aharoni (1966) but proposed by Johanson and Vahlne (1978), states that a firm would move from exports, to joint ventures, to fully owned operations as it became more experienced. Subsequent work by Davidson (1980) and Wilson (1980) further developed the idea that entry is influenced by the degree of international experience held by the firm. Caves and Mehra (1986) were the first to confirm the internationalization hypothesis by a discrete choice model. Again, a Caves model served as a canonical template for future studies on entry. Kogut and Singh (1988) used a multinomial model to confirm the effect of experience and cultural distance – for which they built a construct using the data of Hofstede (1980) – on entry choice. Among others, Barkema et al. (1996) confirmed their results.

The internalization literature adopted the discrete model choice, but re-interpretated many of the earlier variables used in entry and direct investment studies as measures of transaction costs. Gatignon and Anderson's (1988) careful study, also using binary and multinomial choice models, showed that research and development, advertising and other measures of asset specificity pushed a firm toward full ownership over its foreign affiliates. They found, however, that these variables did not predict well the degree of equity ownership. In general, studies have been far less successful in explaining the degree of ownership than the mode of entry. The Gatignon and Anderson study served to frame subsequent internalization studies on entry, such as Hennart and Park (1993) and Henisz (2000).

The focus on entry mode has been an almost obsessive feature of the international management field, because it offers such a stunning insight into the problems of governance choice. There has been a growing movement toward the study, more generally, of global alliances and networks. The importance of networks was already suggested by Burenstam-Linder in his comments on how trade arises from relationships within the home market. The Uppsala School, in particular, developed a series of extensive studies on the use of networks for expansion into foreign markets and the problems of power and coordination in these networks (see, for example, Johanson and Mattsson, 1989; Forsgren and Johanson, 1992).

Though not aware of the Uppsala tradition, Jarillo (1988) was one of the first to merge the studies of alliances and networks in international markets. Walker (1987), however, was the first to show rigorously how the extant network methodologies developed in sociology could be used to show important theoretical patterns in joint venture activity. Similar to Walker, Nohria and Garcia-Pont (1991) used block analysis to show how the international auto industry broke into strategic constellations. Gomes-Casseres (1996) proposed that global networks could be classified into different types, with important implications for strategic interactions. This line of work could be much more developed, if not for the difficulties in collecting alliance data across borders. The database of Hagerdoorn has, for this reason, been instrumental in advancing research in international alliances (Hagerdoorn, 1993 and Oxley, 1997 are representative examples). Dunning (1997) has subsequently dubbed international markets as characterized by alliance capitalism. But, as alliance formation appears to vary by industry and by country, this claim represents more a forecast at this time.

THE ADVANTAGE OF MULTINATIONALITY

While for most of the 1970s and 1980s, the eclectic theory (or OLI) provided a useful perspective, the growing globalization of markets is increasingly undermining its conceptual value. The earlier theories of direct investment sought to explain direct investment as if a firm was investing in a foreign country for the first time. But already by the 1980s, there existed hundreds of multinational corporations with extensive holdings around the globe. Increasingly, managers of such corporations understood that the global nature of their operations provided an important advantage. Kogut (1983) proposed that direct investment, when seen as a sequential process, is also influenced by the advantage accrued by operating as a multinational corporation.

One of the most important, and controversial, sources of advantage for a multinational corporation is its ability to *arbitrage* internationally, which means profiting from the differences in costs and prices across borders.

These activities deeply trouble governments and workers. A multinational corporation very often buys and sells across borders within its own network. Ford produces parts in many places in the world, and then ships these parts for final assembly. For some countries, it is estimated that this 'intra-firm' trade is responsible for 30–50% of their international trade in manufactured products.

Given such internal trade, it makes sense not just to produce in countries where the costs are lower, but also to realize profits where the tax rates are lower. This is where arbitrage becomes important. By changing the price at which a transaction between two units of the same company located in different countries is accounted for, companies like Ford can realize a profit either in the country where a car part is made and sold to another subsidiary (by charging a high price), or in the country where the final car is assembled and sold (by buying the part at a low price). In principle, the subsidiary does not care if the price is high or low; its parent company will know how well the subsidiary did without being misled by a transfer price whose only purpose is to lower the total *global* taxes paid by the corporation.

Since multinational corporations tend to be large and visible, they are closely monitored by tax authorities, and therefore are careful to remain within tax laws. But other kinds of arbitrage that defy effective government intervention are also possible and provide huge profit opportunities to multinational corporations. It is astounding, for example, the extent to which exchange rates move. A few years ago, the dollar was worth 70 yen, or 1.4 Deutschmarks. A short period after, the dollar was at more than 140 yen, and 1.9 DM, appreciations of about 100% and 35%. This shift means that if productivity and inflation are about the same in these countries, it is now twice as expensive to produce in the United States as in Japan, and 40% more in the United States than in Germany. To exporters from the United States, these are tough times. And the subsequent sharp drops in the exchange rates of Asian currencies only adds further competitive pressure. But American multinationals also own facilities in Asia and Europe (and, of course, in other countries too). Some of the production done in the United States can be moved to these locations. This shifting is arbitrage in response to exchange rates.

In this and other senses, the contemporary multinational corporation is best viewed as a global network of subsidiaries. Thanks to advances in communication, transportation, and managerial science, managers enjoy an unprecedented degree of flexibility in moving production around, transferring know-how and knowledge from one place to the next, and reacting to threats and opportunities. In short, the national diversity of its global operations has become a source of advantage. The simple hypothesis to explain this advantage is that firms learn better how to run multinational operations over time, and this learning makes subsequent investments easier. But learning how to operate a multinational corporation better does not constitute itself a competitive advantage. However, the idea of the firm as an arbitrageur suggests that multinationality creates the opportunity to exploit the flexibility in its international operations. In other words, multinationality provides a firm with embedded options to respond to profit opportunities.

The theory of the multinational advantage as derived from embedded options was proposed by Kogut (1983, 1985) and formalized in Kogut and Kulatilaka (1995). Caves (1989) also noted that investments in a country set up subsequent investments. In this sense, it is useful to distinguish between 'within-country' and 'across-country' options (Kogut and Kulatilaka, 1995). An across-country option represents the value of multinationality that is recognized by arbitraging borders, such as by shifting production, exploiting tax regimes, or transferring innovations from one country to the next. A within-country option is the value of establishing a platform (brand label recognition, for example) that sets up later investments.

The evidence for the importance of multinational options is suggested by many studies. Rangan's (1998) careful study of production shifting showed that multinationals' exporting patterns are sensitive to exchange rate fluctuations. Kogut and Chang (1996) showed that foreign entry in the United States responds to exchange rate movements conditional on previous entries, as predicted by a within-country option. The evidence, however, for the benefits of multinationality are mixed. Doukas and Travols (1988) found that returns to acquiring firms increased for acquisitions that added subsidiaries in countries where they had no previous presence. Morck and Yeung (1991) found little evidence for such an effect. The results of Geringer et al. (1989) and Kim et al. (1989) were mixed, with some indication that performance increased with multinationality. Tsetsekos and Gombola (1992) find general evidence that investors recognize the option value to open and close plant operations.

Studies on multinational advantages confront the confound between the transfer of intangible assets and multinationality. Mitchell et al. (2001) invert this logic to argue and to find evidence for a subtle effect. They examined the temporal causality between international expansion and investment in intangible assets. In cross-sectional studies, previous research had shown that international presence was associated with the possession of intangible assets (often proxied by R&D and advertising intensity). However, this research did not address the temporal sequence of international expansion and investment in intangibles. Did firms invest in intangibles before expanding internationally, did firms expand internationally and then invest in intangibles, or did both occur simultaneously? Examining a sample of US manufacturers over a decade and employing a Granger causality test, *they found that international expansion preceded investment in intangibles, but not vice versa.* This finding is consistent with the interpretation that firms expand overseas to apply their current intangible skills, and that the expanded scope of the firm allowed it to increase its investment in intangibles. Moreover, they found that performance improvements stemmed from the investment in intangibles, not international expansion *per se*. These results suggested that international expansion plays a role in improving firm performance through the increased incentive of firms to invest in intangibles and, in turn, investment in intangibles benefits firm performance.

If direct investment establishes a platform for future expansion, it also kills the option to wait for a more propitious time to enter a market. Shaver et al. (1997) explored the mechanisms that would lead to advantages in delaying foreign investment. They argued that a benefit of delaying investment was that later entrants could benefit from the earlier entrants' experiences. Firms without any experience in the foreign market would lack the knowledge to effectively take advantage of information from previous entrants. Firms

with existing operations in the industry within the target country could draw on their own experiences and had little use for the experiences of previous entrants. The results from the empirical analyses were consistent with these arguments.

MULTINATIONAL CORPORATIONS AND THEIR MANAGEMENT

The international strategy literature has often been interpreted as the search for better management practices. It has been unfortunate that there has been a failure to link aggressively the reasoning why certain organizational practices are better to the studies that analyze international strategy directly. This divorce is all the more odd because the seminal work of John Stopford and Lou Wells (1972) explicitly investigated the relationship between organizational choices and the investment in strategic assets, such as R&D. They found, for example, that technology-intensive firms tend to have product divisions and to enter countries by control over their subsidiaries. Over all, they found a passage from a functional organization, to a divisional structure, with some experimentation with matrix dual command.

The findings of Stopford and Wells matched roughly the typology of Howard Perlmutter (1965) regarding three types of firms – ethnocentric, polycentric, and geocentric. Whereas the ethnocentric firm tended to be functionally organized or organized by an international division, the polycentric firm was organized by areas and the geocentric firm by global product divisions. Unlike Stopford and Wells, however, Perlmutter emphasized the human resource dimension to understanding a firm's cognitive orientation toward world markets.

The influence of the Harvard studies on the relationship between form, such as divisionalization, and strategy, such as diversification, is apparent. (See, for example, Chandler, 1962; and the theses organized under Bruce Scott's direction, Channon [1973], and Dyas and Thanheiser [1976].) Yet, at the same time, the influence of Raymond Vernon (1971) is also clear in the dual focus of understanding the strategic basis for organizational choices, as well as in the collection of careful data for the verification of hypotheses. The important contribution of Vernon's group at Harvard was not only theoretical, but also to organize historical observations on 180 American multinationals, and eventually on multinationals from other countries (see Curhan et al., 1977, for the first effort). These data became the basis for many subsequent theses that became books or articles, such as Davidson (1980), Gomes-Casseres (1989), Hladik (1985) and Delacroix (1993). It is a pity that the success of this program of research did not inspire others.

The emphasis on an empirical and historical understanding of firm evolution that bridges strategy and structure is also reflected in a study by Lawrence Franko (1976) on European multinationals. Franko found that many European multinational corporations did not disband their holding structure for the organization of their activities. European multinationals were organized much more by a mother–daughter structure involving a reliance on the transfer of managers than on strict accounting rules. Franko's findings were confirmed for Swedish multinationals by Hedlund (1981) and more broadly for other European multinational corporations. Later work on Japanese corporations also found a pattern different than that observed for American companies (Kono, 1984; Suzuki, 1991).

These European findings lead to a belief that Europe was lagging the US. It was later recognized, however, that European structures provided a favorable entry point into structures that were responsive both locally and globally. Influenced by Lawrence and Lorsch's (1969) distinction between integration and differentiation, Doz et al. (1981) analyzed the challenge facing multinationals in addressing local markets (differentiation) while organizing (integration) globally. Bartlett and Ghoshal (1990) proposed a simple matrix by which products could be mapped into a two-dimensional space representing the pressure to conform to local markets (because of government intervention or national tastes and standards) and the pressure to integrate activities globally (because of scale economies or low transportation costs). These dimensions captured easily the Stopford and Wells distinction between area- and product-organized firms. Area organization tended to reflect relatively stronger pressures for national differentiation, whereas product divisions reflected the dominance of pressures to integrate globally. Thus, this matrix captured the dimensions of competitive environments and organizational structure as one snapshot.

This line of analysis identified that multinational corporations in some industries face unusual demands in the need to respond both to national conditions and to integrate globally. The telecommunication industry is often cited as an example, where government agencies are buyers but research outlays require access to a global market. The early studies on matrix organizations indicated that this form was especially unstable (Davidson, 1976) and underperformed more simple structures (Davidson and Haspeslagh, 1982).

Research in the 1980s culminated in a better understanding of organizational resolutions to this problem. The European weakness in adopting American structures suddenly became heralded as offering greater flexibility in responding to these dual national and global pressures. Prahalad and Doz (1987) discussed the importance of lead country structures, in which certain subsidiaries played a vital role in global strategies. Bartlett and Ghoshal (1989) proposed the transnational corporation as relying on an internal network that provides the flexibility to manage the dual pressures. Hedlund (1986) developed the concept of the 'heterarchy' in which a firm no longer had a single headquarters responsible for world activities, but rather subsidiaries might take on global responsibilities; firms were multi-head in their organization. European firms, such as Asea Brown Boveri, became prototypes for this new organization.

Hedlund developed this idea further with Dag Rolander in proposing that the multinational corporation is a meta-institution (Hedlund and Rolander, 1990). By this, they meant that the multinational created its own capabilities through actively engaging in exploratory search as well as exploiting current markets and assets. This emphasis on the proactive capabilities and innovative search of the multinational corporation distinguished international research from its counterparts in management, in which the focus at that time was on industry competition and organizational inertia. This tradition of seeing firms as proactive players is reflected in more recent work, such as Birkinshaw's (1997) study of subsidiaries seeing entrepreneurial and global roles.

Unlike, however, the earlier studies by Vernon and his colleagues, this line of work has lacked broad empirical studies that provide an adequate survey of changes across a large sample of firms. (One might add the competition around terminological contribution, and the payoff to managerial applications to these contributions, perhaps dampened the incentive to develop academic research programs around these ideas.) The approach of Bartlett and Ghoshal on the 'transnational' corporation led to a number of studies that attempted to validate the concept and to test for performance results (see Birkinshaw et al., 1995, for an excellent representative work). In one of the few in-depth empirical studies, Malnight (1996) analyzed the internal operations of multinational corporations over time at a detailed micro-level of analysis. His results suggest that there were important variations in the timing, sequence, and objective of organizations' adjustments across individual functions over time. International coordination evolves at different paces for different functions. He, thus, was able to explain the structural rhythms of international growth and cross-border management.

The more novel contribution was to emphasize the importance of the internal network to provide the flexible response to local and global pressures. The pathbreaking article by Ghoshal and Nohria (1990) introduced network methods into the international literature. This approach understood that, if the proposition that the multinational corporation is a network, then it should develop managerial systems that support the coordination across borders. With the exception of Hansen's work discussed below, there has been relatively little work in this area.

It is not surprising that the study of the organization of the multinational corporation has been deeply intertwined with strategy. Because global markets and coordination are complex, a good strategy is to develop good management. However, the emphasis on good management had often the unfortunate consequence of suggesting that global advantages are simply the result of better managed firms. In other words, there has often been a disconnect between the organizational line of research and the studies described above on the sources of multinational advantage or motives for entry (the Stopford and Wells study remains one of the few that does both). It is very well possible that clearer progress could have been made if

the concern was less over typologies of firms and more directed to understanding the links between organizational structures and strategic advantage. It is still poorly understood how network structures support cross-border flexibility, how information technologies or incentives signal the timing of exercise of embedded options, or how firms organizationally manage currency fluctuations (see, however, Sharp, 1994, and Lessard and Zaheer, 1996).

STRATEGY AND LOCATION

It is not surprising that the literature in international strategy has been deeply concerned with location as a factor in understanding firm behavior. Strategy as rivalry *per se* has been surprisingly of secondary importance in international studies. There are a number of reasons for this. First, strategic positioning across borders present a complex array of multi-market interactions that defy an easy assessment. Second, templates of research were developed for the problem areas of understanding foreign entry and multinational coordination. These templates were not clearly developed for understanding rivalry. Lastly, strategic rivalry became at one time increasingly the province of economics and yet also required often detailed knowledge of a single industry in many national markets.

Vernon's (1976, 1979) product life cycle established a set of ideas that have often served as a theoretical entry into understanding international rivalry. His central idea is that firms start in their home markets carefully attentive to local conditions of supply and demand. Innovations consequently reflect the home market. High labor costs lead to labor saving processes; high incomes lead to a demand for product innovations. Though Vernon did not initially recognize the historical dimension to his argument, this theory very much described the emergence of American multinationals in the post-war period. Later work by Davidson (1980) showed that Europeans tended to innovate around the saving of relatively expensive materials and energy resources. In other words, innovation is influenced by home market conditions. The strategic element in Vernon's thinking was then to argue that as innovations diffuse in the home market, competition eventually pushes firms to export and then later to invest in foreign markets. Thus, home market competition drives the international expansion of firms. Or as Staffan Burenstam-Linder (1961) wrote in his theory of intra-industry trade, foreign trade is simply the extension of the local market to foreign locations. This thesis was re-iterated again in Porter's (1990) study of the country foundations to competition.

This theme of domestic rivalry was developed further by Vernon's student Frederick Knickerbocker (1973) in his historical study of the expansion of US multinationals. Knickerbocker collected data on the concentration ratios of major US industries, very much in the industrial economics tradition of Bain, Caves, and others. He showed that foreign investment decisions by large companies tended to bunch together – that is, tire firms invested at the same time in one country – particularly for industries with high levels of concentration. This bunching was more prominent for industries with high 8-firm measures of sales concentration. Knickerbocker argued that this finding implied that unstable oligopolies tended especially toward follow-the-leader behavior in their timing of foreign investments. Graham (1978) argued that, eventually, foreign competitors retaliate through cross-hauling investments in the home market of their competitors. Choi et al. (1986) used a gravity model to investigate the interpenetration by banks from 14 major financial centers into each other's home centers. The paper finds evidence consistent with exchange of threat behavior and mutual non-aggression pacts. Brander and Krugman (1983) later formalized this idea without knowledge of the previous tradition. This line of work left begging the question of who invests first. Mascarenhas (1992) showed that the first investment tended to be done by the firm who was at a competitive disadvantage in the home market. Thus, it was Ford who invested overseas; General Motors followed. Yu and Ito (1988) showed that this pattern tended to hold for Japan too, in which dominated firms such as Sony or Honda invested first overseas in their markets. More recently, Miotti and Sachwald (2001) found a similar pattern for Korea.

Given the common roots in the industrial economics tradition of Bain, the Caves tradition

also reflects the assumption of the importance of home market rivalry. The Caves template identifies variables to describe rivalry in the home market as an explanation of 'pushing' investment into other countries. The early studies by Horst, including his remarkable analysis of the food industry (1974), explored the heterogeneity of firms to understand why some firms invested overseas and others did not. His work, informed by simple yet incisive formal models, emphasized the importance of size and scale as a factor in explaining firm heterogeneity. He also found that foreign investment often was a response to tariffs, a result that has been reconfirmed many times in subsequent work (Kogut and Chang, 1991). Solvell (1987) further developed the Caves–Horst tradition through extensive case studies of international industries.

The development of new economic models of trade by Helpman (1981), Krugman (1991), Ethier (1986) and others stylized the ideas of Burenstam-Linder and Vernon in more formal models. With a few exceptions, the models generally worked with simple consumer utility functions (hence are not in the spirit of Burenstam-Linder's contribution) but rather focused on the combination of scale and location economics. Some of the models suggested a role for a strategic commercial policy. It is fairly widely recognized that such policies are rarely warranted by actual industrial conditions.

An alternative line of modeling, though not specifically international, is Sutton's work on why industries differ in their degrees of concentration (1991). Though his work is largely unexplored in the international area, his models address directly why industry leaders may only be national or regional. In this regard, one of the most important contributions is the study by Baden-Fuller and Stopford (1991) that first demonstrates the persisting higher profits to national players in the white goods industry and second shows how marketing and flexible manufacturing strategies can offset global economies in production.

LOCATION AND TECHNOLOGY PULL

John Cantwell's (1989) important contribution was to re-orient dramatically the emphasis away from the push of home rivalry toward the 'pulling' effect of certain regions on direct investment. Through an analysis of patenting over a long period of time, Cantwell established that countries tend to focus in areas of 'comparative technological advantage'. Germany, for example, has maintained a comparative lead in chemical innovation over the course of the last century. Once having established this 'path dependent nature' of investment, Cantwell then showed that foreign investment tended to flow to the locations where a country has a technological advantage. In other words, he added a very important dimension to previous studies, namely, that direct investment flows not only to low cost locations, but also to innovative centers. Suddenly, the puzzle established by such studies as Swedenborg (1979) that foreign direct investment and high labor costs of the host nation are correlated became resolved. The Silicon Valley has high labor costs and high levels of foreign direct investment because firms come to *learn* and to *exploit* local knowledge.

The importance of foreign market conditions had been neglected in earlier work, with the important and major exception of the large literature in business history on foreign expansion of firms (see, for example, Wilkins, 1974, and Chandler, 1962). Very few studies followed through on Graham's observation on the importance of understanding retaliation in the foreign market. Some studies even used American industry data for foreign countries, even though Bain (1966) had shown early on that industry conditions were correlated but varied dramatically across countries. Yamawaki (1988) was the first to make the effort to collect data systematically in both the home and foreign market. In his study on Japanese exporting to the US, he observed that brand labels and high levels of concentration deterred Japanese exports.

Kogut and Chang (1991) utilized Yamawaki's approach to analyze Cantwell's contention of the pull effect of certain regions. They transformed measures of Japanese and US R&D to separate out Japanese direct investment pulled to the US for technology sourcing from the pushing of this investment by rivalry. They found that Japanese investments in joint ventures appeared to be sensitive to the pull of American comparative technological advantage in certain industries.

This approach has subsequently been utilized by Miotti and Sachwald (2001) in the context of European and Korean investments.

The pull of regions on foreign investment is of critical importance to understanding the evolution of capabilities on a world basis. As tariffs fall, international competition becomes increasingly influenced by non-tangibles, including the institutional and economic advantages associated with particular countries. Krugman (1989) sought to explain this effect on the basis of scale and dynamic cost advantages, while discounting technological advantages. Porter (1990) suggested a broad framework that stressed home market rivalry, much in the Vernon and Burenstam-Linder tradition, that drove the acquisition of local competence.

Whereas Krugman was indifferent, if not hostile to technological factors (that do not leave a 'paper trace' and hence could not be observed, he claimed), Porter's approach did not seek a micro-analytic understanding of location advantages. More recent work has sought to investigate the paper trace of local advantages at a micro level. Some of this work consists of intense studies of local industry networks, such as the Italian industrial districts (Giannetti et al., 1991), that point to the importance of regional networks. More recent work has built upon Jaffe et al. (1993) on patenting to show that technology accumulates in particular locations. Almeida and Kogut (1999) showed that this aggregate pattern is, at least for semiconductors, a reflection of the extraordinary performance of certain regions, such as the Silicon Valley. Almeida (1996) also showed that foreign semiconductor firms located in the US draw upon this local knowledge.

EVOLUTIONARY STUDIES

The internalization literature was open to the criticism that its proxies for asset specificity could also be used as measures of firm capabilities. Capability-based theories challenged the internalization theory that entry choice, and hence direct investment, is determined by transactional hazards due to market inefficiencies. A capability refers to the organizational and technological competence of a firm in achieving higher rates of productivity or innovation. Such a capability, in turn, reflects underlying principles of organization as well as location advantages.

In many respects, this view point places ownership and location advantages as jointly sufficient explanations for the multinational corporation. Casson (1985) had argued earlier that multinational organizations can exist in the absence of ownership and internalization advantages when there was a gain to arbitraging across borders, such as through tax avoidance. The capability approach logically implies that internalization is not a necessary factor for the explanation for the multinational corporation, though it can be causally important for some kinds of transactions.

The international emphasis on capabilities, and knowledge, arose out of the work on technology transfer and the many historical and empirical studies on the operations of multinational corporations in foreign markets. It was Caves (1971) who first clearly argued that multinational corporations have an advantage in transferring assets across borders because they were quasi-public goods inside the corporation. Their marginal costs of transfer were not zero, as expected of a public good, but lower than their sale or transfer through the market. Similarly, many studies in technology transfer found that foreign countries and firms did not have the absorptive capacity, to use the term common in this literature, to adopt new technologies. The classic studies by Johnson on the transfer of aircraft manufacturing to Japan, or by Linsu Kim (1997) on the absorption of technology by Korea, pointed to organizational and institutional factors that influenced the cost of transfer.

Caves did not, however, explain his reasoning for the claim that marginal costs should be lower inside the multinational corporation. Teece (1977) had shown that technology transfer across borders entailed considerable costs that varied across projects. This study raised the important question of what constitutes a 'public good'. Kogut and Zander (1993) argued and tested the argument that these costs varied because technology transfer was essentially the transfer of knowledge that was often tacit and poorly understood. They argued that, because replication is the *sine qua non* of an evolutionary theory of the firm, the critical test is whether the governance and entry mode choice is influenced by the difficulty

of replication or conventional measures of market hazards. Based on the work of Rogers (1983) and Winter (1987), they built scales to proxy for tacitness and showed that the choice between licensing and ownership was explained by these scales. They concluded that the difficulty of transferring tacit knowledge outside the boundaries of the firm determined the entry mode choice. To them, direct investment is the transfer of hard-to-codify organizational knowledge that a firm acquires as it evolves from its home market overseas. Consequently, direct investment has to be seen, as suggested by the earlier work of Burenstam-Linder and Vernon, as the outcome of an evolutionary process by which the growth of a firm in its home market spills across national boundaries. In this sense, the evolutionary and knowledge theories of the firm provided complementary perspectives on the internationalization of the firm.

It is clear that the terms of 'ownership', 'internalization', and even 'location' do not capture this global role of the multinational corporation. Recent efforts to look at the multinational corporation start with a redefinition of what is meant by ownership. In this new work, a multinational corporation does not simply own an advantage. Rather, a firm is viewed as a repository of valuable knowledge that can be exploited either through new products or through the dissemination of existing products to new locations. This knowledge consists not just of what employees know, but also of the way in which people, machines, and technology are organized and directed. This approach leads to a redefinition of foreign direct investment to encompass the spread of a firm's organizational knowledge across national borders. Direct investment very often consists of technology transfer, but this technology should be broadly understood to include organizational and management skills. Toyota's investments in America surely consisted of real estate and capital equipment. But its knowledge of how to organize workers and suppliers in a new system for fabricating cars is a crucial element that cannot be overlooked.

This approach has the advantage of integrating the many important historical studies on the development of different national and regional patterns in the evolution of multinational corporations (see, for example, the above discussion on differences in patterns in organizational structures among European and American firms). Given the emphasis on understanding the long-term evolution of firm capabilities in specific national settings, historical studies of the rise of banking (Jones, 1993), or multinational corporations (Wilkins, 1974, 1988), or national patterns in competition (Kogut, 1987; Chandler, 1990) provide critical insight into the interaction of location and ownership factors.

Another implication of the evolutionary approach is to pose questions regarding the demography of foreign firms and the factors that influence their growth and survival. Statistically, Delacroix (1993) inaugurated this approach by submitting the Harvard multinational data collected by Vernon and his students to hazard modeling. He found broad evidence for demographic effects on survival of entries. Li (1995) introduced this approach more directly into the international literature through his study of the survival of foreign entrants into the US. About the same time, Mitchell et al. (1993) made a major return to the concerns of Vernon and Burenstam-Linder by asking how international expansion influences the survival of firms in their home market. They explored how changing international presence affected firm survival and market share in industries where firms with international operations did not have performance advantages. They found that international expansion was necessary for firm survival in industries where international operations became associated with performance advantages over time. Moreover, only firms with existing international operations or large market share were able to expand successfully.

Zaheer (1995) returned to a central claim of Hymer that foreign firms start at a disadvantage in a host country. She insightfully renamed this hypothesis the liability of foreignness borrowing from ideas in organizational ecology. The popular claim is that firms, as they gather experience, are less susceptible to such liabilities. She is able to test this idea that opens a window on a much larger issue.

Because of these efforts to understand the dynamics of foreign expansion, the international management literature is systematically incorporating more recent theories of foreign direct investment. The focus is no longer on the one-time entry into a country, or simple analyses of multinational corporations by a few dimensions. We are now forced to understand the evolution of multinational corporations as systems, with subsidiaries competing *without* a liability of foreignness in national markets.

An important consideration is then to rephrase the earlier literature on technology transfer as a hierarchical transfer of knowledge from one country to another. In this new phrasing, technology, or more broadly, knowledge transfer, is a permanent feature of the operation of a multinational corporation. Kogut (1987), Gupta and Govindarajan (1991), and Bartlett and Ghoshal (1990) stressed the importance, and difficulty, of the replication of knowledge for the understanding of the advantage and limitations of multinational corporations. Szulanski (1996) epitomizes the new approach to the study of technology transfer by analyzing the impediments of the transfer of best practices from the perspective of both the sender and receiver. Yet, while these studies break new ground, they are, from another angle, incremental studies to the long line of research on the problems of foreign countries to absorb technologies.

Of the many subsequent studies on knowledge transfer, the article by Hansen (1999) is unique in combining ideas on tacitness with a network analysis of the structure of community in a multinational corporation. He thus merged the efforts of Ghoshal and Nohria (1990) on networks with the empirical measurement of tacitness of Kogut and Zander (1993). His finding that tacit knowledge and structure interact to shape the communication in the firm is the first systematic study of knowledge management that is sensitive to organizational structure. In other words, he moved the level of analysis from the microanalysis of the determinants of transfer to the larger organizational context.

CURRENT RESEARCH STUDIES AND FUTURE RESEARCH DIRECTIONS

The field of international management presents a research record in which many debates are now settled. The evolution of the multinational corporation, and the capabilities of different structures, is well studied and documented. The factors that determine entry have been thoroughly investigated, with the understanding that transaction (or internalization) costs and knowledge as capabilities both matter to the choice of mode. Historical studies have made, and continue to make, a critical contribution to the research on the evolution of firms, and their interaction with national settings, over time.

Much of the radically different work currently is addressing more the institutional influence on firms in their national and international settings. It is still a wide open area to understand the country and regional basis of competition. Kogut (1991) proposed the paradox that sustained differences in the performance of countries suggests that better management practices flow more easily among firms within a country than across geographical borders. Clearly, institutional and political factors matter, then, to the 'permeability' of borders. One of the most exciting developments has been the work on why business practices might differ. Westney's (1987) work on the transfer of management practices to Meiji Japan inaugurated research on why and how practices are 'emulated' by particular countries, but not by all countries. Kogut and Parkinson (1993) argue that diffusion will be influenced by the existing social and political situation in a country. Djelic (1998) stressed the normative reception of foreign practices into a country.

One of the most exciting debates in the international area concerns the viability of multiple organizational forms. Whittington et al. (1999) argue from evidence on developed countries that holding companies are dying out due to the preference for more focused divisional strategies. Yet, Khanna and Palepu (1999) argue and find that business groups in developing countries are efficient in these contexts. This debate is far from resolved, and has major implications for understanding corporate policies in industrial and emerging economies. For example, Spicer (1998) argues that western policies in eastern Europe and Russia stressed a single solution rather than designing measures appropriate to the institutional contexts of these countries. In a different vein, Gittelman (2000) investigates how national institutional contexts influence innovation by examining biotechnology patents in France and the United States. She shows that firms in both countries

performed similarly, with the difference being that the United States simply had proportionally more start-up companies.

The proposition of Williamson (1991) is to understand governance choice on the basis of the effect of institutions, or their absence, on transaction costs. He labels this effect as a 'shift' parameter, suggesting that institutions shift the costs of transacting up or down. Others have offered more nuanced, and yet also more complicated, proposals regarding national systems. Thus Aoki (1990) and Soskice (1990) propose that national systems are tightly coupled and complementary institutions. These proposals of national systems confront the problem of diffusion that suggests a greater resiliency than can be explained by tight complements. Yet, at the same time, their approach rightfully frames the contention of Khanna and Palepu, as discussed above, that a variety of forms can be viable depending on national circumstances. That institutions can influence the growth of their economies and national differences can remain persistent despite global financial markets is shown at length by Garrett (1998).

The increasing concern with institutional effects is apparent also in the revived interest in political risk. Earlier work established that political risk has a domino effect, with the decision of one country to nationalize spreading to other countries (Kobrin, 1985). However, the earlier work on the effect of political factors on direct investment largely stalled due to a lack of empirical measures of risk, if not of adequate theorizing concerning the causes of instability. Recent work shows a shift from simple models of political risk to more sophisticated attempts to understand why certain countries are more risky. Henisz (2000) offers, for example, an analysis of direct investment flows that are influenced by a unique measure of the political stability inside countries.

Sometimes, powerful insights are achieved by simple recognitions. Shaver's (1998) study in many ways offers the conventional test of what determines entry and entry success. However, Shaver observed that entry success was simply not based on governance choice and context, but was also contingent on the wisdom of the initial decision to enter the market. His conclusion was that it was necessary to control for the endogenous strategy choice (the first decision to enter) when looking at performance.

However, once he corrected for endogenous
strategy choice, there was no performance difference between new plants and acquisitions.
The corrected estimation led to substantially
different conclusions regarding strategy performance and showed the importance of considering endogenous strategy choice when
empirically estimating performance outcomes
and guiding managerial action. Though
methodological, this contribution is theoretically very important. It says to researchers in
both strategy and international management
that performance is an outcome of capability,
be it the decision to first invest in a foreign
market or to enter a new product market, or to
build a plant. Shaver put forth, in other words,
an econometrically correct way to sort out
capability and governance effects.

Perhaps the most exciting area, though, is
the research done on the impact of new technologies on the work and strategies of multinational corporations. Sri Zaheer has initiated
this work through her studies on international
currency trading and the possibility to compete on global time (forthcoming). With such
exceptions as Peter Hagström's (1992) fine
study of the 'wired' multinational corporation,
there is little research on how multinationals
are increasingly deploying information technologies. This is an exciting area of work that
challenges the meaning of place and poses far
reaching questions about the value of local and
virtual communities. The field of international
management has shown that theory evolves
along with the phenomena under study. The
rise of the virtual office will, no doubt, create
a broad tension for better theorizing on the role
of international institutions and norms, and
their interaction with the broad strategies of
multinational corporations to exploit these
technologies to their advantage.

Thus, current work in international management and strategy poses a far more sophisticated
insight into the underlying dimensions of
international competition than possible 20 years
ago. Location is no longer simply cheap
factors, but institutional context. Transportation
costs is no longer the cost of expedition but the
difficulty in coordinating and innovating at a
distance. We understand more about the micro-
basis of what location means, while we are also
more knowledgeable of institutional factors in
enterprise, capabilities and behavior.

REFERENCES

Aharoni, Y., (1966) *The Foreign Investment Decision Process.* Boston: Div. Of Research, Graduate School of Business Administration, Harvard University.
Almeida, P. (1996) 'Knowledge sourcing by foreign multinationals: patent citation analysis in the US semi-conductor industry', *Strategic Management Journal,* 17: 155–65.
Almeida, P. and Kogut, B. (1999) 'Localization of knowl-edge and the mobility of engineers in regional net-works', *Management Science,* 45: 905–17.
Aoki, M. (1990) 'Toward an economic model of the Japanese firm', *Journal of Economic Literature,* 28: 1–27.
Baden-Fuller, C. and Stopford, J. (1991) 'Globalization frustrated: the case of white goods', *Strategic Management Journal,* 12: 493–507.
Bain, J. S. (1956) *Barriers to New Competition: Their Character and Consequences in Manufacturing Industries.* Cambridge: Harvard University Press.
Bain, J. S. (1966) *International Differences in Industrial Structure: Eight Nations in the 1950s.* New Haven, CT: Yale University Press.
Barkema, H. G., Bell, J. H. and Pennings, J. M. (1996) 'Foreign entry, cultural barriers, and learning', *Strategic Management Journal,* 17: 151–66.
Bartlett, C. A. and Ghoshal, S. (1989) *Managing Across Borders: The Transnational Solution.* Boston: Harvard Business School.
Bartlett, C. A. and Ghoshal, S. (1990) 'Managing innova-tion in the transnational corporation', in C. Bartlett, Y. Doz and G. Hedlund (eds), *Managing the Global Firm.* London and New York: Routledge. pp. 215–55.
Birkinshaw, J. M. (1997) 'Entrepreneurship in multi-national corporations: the characteristics of subsidiary initiatives', *Strategic Management Journal,* 18: 207–29.
Birkinshaw, J., Morrison, A. and Hulland, J. (1995) 'Structural and competitive determinants of a global integration strategy', *Strategic Management Journal,* 16: 637–55.
Brander, J. S. and Krugman, P. R. (1983) 'A "reciprocal dumping" model of international trade', *Journal of International Economics,* 15: 3113–21.
Buckley, P. and Casson, M. (1976) *The Future of the Multinational Enterprise.* London: Macmillan.
Burenstam-Linder, S. H. (1961) *An Essay on Trade and Transformation.* Uppsala: Almquist & Wiksells.
Cantwell, J. (1989) *Technological Innovation and Multinational Corporations.* Oxford: Blackwell.
Casson, M. (1985) 'Transaction costs and the theory of the multinational enterprise', in P. Buckley and M. Casson (eds), *The Economic Theory of the Multinational Enterprise.* London: Macmillan. pp. 20–38.
Caves, R. E. (1971) 'International corporations: the industrial economics of foreign investment', *Economica,* 38: 1–27.

Caves, R. (1974) 'Causes of direct investment: foreign firms' shares in Canadian and United Kingdom manufacturing industries', *Review of Economic Statistics*, 56: 79–93.

Caves, R. (1989) 'Exchange rate movements and foreign direct investment in the United States', in D. B. Audretsch and M. P. Claudon (eds), *The Internationalization of U.S. Markets*. New York: New York University Press. pp. 199–228.

Caves, R. and Mehra, S. (1986) 'Entry of foreign multinationals into U.S. manufacturing industries', in M. Porter (ed.), *Competition in Global Industries*. Boston: Harvard Business School Press.

Chandler, A. D. (1962) *Strategy and Structure: Chapters in the History of the Industrial Enterprise*. Cambridge, MA: MIT Press.

Chandler, A. D. (1990) *Scale and Scope: The Dynamics of Industrial Capitalism*. Cambridge, MA: Belknap Press of Harvard University.

Channon, D. F. (1973) *The Strategy and Structure of British Enterprises*. Boston: Div. Of Research, Graduate School of Business, Harvard University.

Choi, S-R., Tschoegl, A. E. and Yu, C-M. (1986) 'Banks and the world's major financial centers, 1970–1980', in R. Roberts (ed.), *International Financial Centres: Concepts, Development and Dynamics*. Aldershot, UK: Elgar. pp. 498–514.

Curhan, J. P., Davidson, W. H. and Suri, R. (1977) *Tracing the Multinationals: A Sourcebook on U.S.-Based Enterprises*. Cambridge, MA: Ballinger.

Davidson, W. (1980) 'The location of foreign direct investment activity: country characteristics and experience effects', *Journal of International Business Studies*, 11: 22.

Davidson, W. H. (1976) 'Patterns of factor-saving innovation in the industrialized world', *Journal of Industrial Economics*, 32: 253–64.

Davidson, W. H. and Haspeslagh, P. (1982) 'Shaping a global product organisation', *Harvard Business Review*, 60: 125–32.

Delacroix, J. (1993) 'The European subsidiaries of American multinationals: an exercise in ecological analysis', in S. Ghoshal and E. Westney (eds), *Organizational Theory and the Multinational Enterprise*. New York: Macmillan. pp. 105–31.

Djelic, M-L. (1998) *Exporting the American Model: The Postwar Transformation of European Business*. Oxford: Oxford University Press.

Doukas, J. and Travols, N. G. (1988) 'The effect of corporate multinationalism on shareholders' wealth: evidence from international acquisitions', *Journal of Finance*, 43: 1161–75.

Doz, Y. L., Bartlett, C. A. and Prahalad, C. K. (1981) 'Global competitive pressures and host country demands: managing tensions in MNCs', *California Management Review*, 23: 63–74.

Dunning, J. (1977) 'Trade, location of economic activity and the MNE: a search for an eclectic approach', in B. Ohlin, P-O. Hesselborn and P. M. Wijkman (eds), *The International Allocation of Economic Activity: Proceedings of a Nobel Symposium Held at Stockholm*. London: Macmillan. pp. 395–418.

Dunning, J. H. (1980) 'Towards an eclectic theory of international production: some empirical tests', *Journal of International Business Studies*, 11: 9–31.

Dunning, J. (1997) *Alliance Capitalism and Global Business*. London: Routledge.

Dyas, G. P. and Thanheiser, H. T. (1976) *The Emerging European Enterprises: Stratgey and Structure in French and German Industry*. London: Macmillan.

Ethier, W. J. (1986) 'The multinational firm', *Quarterly Journal of Economics*, 101: 805–33.

Forsgren, M. and Johanson, J. (1992) *Managing Networks in International Business*. Philadelphia: Gordon & Breach.

Franko, L. (1976) *The European Multinationals: A Renewed Challenge to American and British Big Business*. Stamford, CT: Greylock.

Garrett, G. (1998) *Partisan Politics in the Global Economy*. New York: Cambridge University Press.

Gatignon, H. and Anderson, E. (1988) 'The multinational corporation's degree of control over foreign subsidiaries: an empirical test of a transaction cost explanation', *Journal of Law, Economics and Organizations*, 4: 305–36.

Geringer, J. M., Beamish, P. W. and da Costa, R. C. (1989) 'Diversification strategy and internationalization: implications for MNE performance', *Strategic Management Journal*, 10: 109–19.

Ghoshal, S. and Nohria, N. (1990) 'Internal differentiation within multinational corporations', *Strategic Management Journal*, 10: 323–38.

Giannetti, R., Fredrico, G., Toninelli, P. A. and Bezza, B. (1991) 'Size and strategy of Italian industrial enterprises: empirical evidence and some conjectures', conference paper, History of Enterprise, Milan, ASSI Foundation.

Gittelman, M. (2000) 'Scientists and networks: a comparative study of cooperation in the French and American biotechnology industry', Ph.D. thesis, Wharton School, University of Pennsylvania.

Gomes-Casseres, B. (1989) 'Ownership structures of foreign subsidiaries: theory and evidence', *Journal of Economic Behavior and Organization*, 11: 1–25.

Gomes-Casseres, B. (1996) *The Alliance Revolution: The New Shape of Business Rivalry*. Cambridge, MA: Harvard University Press.

Graham, E. M. (1978) 'Transatlantic investment by multinational firms: a rivalistic phenomenon?', *Journal of Post-Keynesian Economics*, 1: 82–99.

Gupta, A. K. and Govindarajan, V. (1991) 'Knowledge flows and the structure of control within multinational corporations', *Academy of Management Review*, 16: 778–92.

Hagerdoorn, J. (1993) 'Understanding the rationale of strategic technology partnering: interorganizational modes of cooperation and sectoral differences', *Strategic Management Journal*, 14: 371–86.

Hagström, P. (1992) 'Inside the "wired" MNC', in C. Antonelli (ed.), *Economics of Information Networks*. Amsterdam: North Holland. pp. 325–45.

Hansen, M. T. (1999) 'The search–transfer problem: the role of weak ties in sharing knowledge across organization subunits', *Administrative Science Quarterly*, 44: 82–111.

Hedlund, G. (1981) 'Autonomy of subsidiaries and formulation of headquarters–subsidiary relationships in Swedish MNCs', in L. Otterback (ed.), *The Management of Headquarters–Subsidiary Relationships in Multinational Corporations*. Aldershot: Gower.

Hedlund, G. (1986) 'The hypermodern MNC: a heterarchy?', *Human Resource Management*, 25: 9–36.

Hedlund, G. and Rolander, D. (1990) 'Action in heterarchies – new approaches to managing the MNC', in C. Bartlett, Y. Doz and G. Hedlund (eds), *Managing the Global Firm*. New York: Routledge. pp. 15–46.

Helpman, E. (1981) 'International trade in the presence of product differentiation, economics of scale, and monopolistic competition: a Chamberlin–Heckscher–Ohlin approach', *Journal of International Economics*, 11: 305–40.

Henisz, W. (2000) 'The institutional environment for multinational investment', Reginald H. Jones Center Working Paper Series: WP2000–01, Philadelphia: The Wharton School.

Hennart, J. F. (1982) *A Theory of Multinational Enterprise*. Ann Arbor: University of Michigan Press.

Hennart, J. F. and Park, Y. R. (1993) 'Greenfield vs. acquisition: the strategy of Japanese investors in the United States', *Management Science*, 39: 1054–68.

Hladik, K. J. (1985) *International Joint Ventures: An Economic Analysis of U.S. Foreign Business Partnerships*. Lexington, MA: Lexington Books.

Hofstede, G. (1980) *Culture's Consequences: International Differences in Work Related Values*. Beverly Hills: Sage Publications.

Horst, T. (1974) *At Home Abroad: A Study of the Domestic and Foreign Operations of the American Food-Processing Industry*. Cambridge, MA: Ballinger.

Hymer, S. (1960) 'The international operations of national firms: a study of direct foreign investment', PhD dissertation. Cambridge: MIT Press.

Jaffe, A. B., Trajtenberg, M. and Henderson, R. (1993) 'Geographic localization of knowledge spillovers as evidenced by patent citations', *Quarterly Journal of Economics*, 108: 577–98.

Jarillo, J. C. (1988) 'On strategic networks', *Strategic Management Journal*, 9: 31–41.

Johanson, J. and Mattsson, L. G. (1989) 'The internationalization in industrial systems: a network approach', in N. Hood and J. E. Vahlne (eds), *Strategies in Global Competition*. New York: Wiley.

Johanson, J. and Vahlne, J-E. (1978) 'A model for the decision making process affecting pattern and pace of the internationalization of the firm', in M. Ghertman and J. Leontiades (eds), *European Research in International Business*. Amsterdam: North Holland. pp. 9–27.

Jones, G. (1993) *British Multinational Banking, 1830–1990*. New York: Oxford University Press.

Khanna, T. and Palepu, K. (1999) 'Policy shocks, market intermediaries, and corporate strategy: the evolution of business groups in Chile and India', *Journal of Economics & Management Strategy*, 8: 271–310.

Kim, L. (1997) *Imitation to Innovation: The Dynamics of Korea's Technological Learning*. Boston: Harvard Business School Press.

Kim, W. C., Hwang, P. and Burgers, W. P. (1989) 'Global diversification strategy and corporate profit performance', *Strategic Management Journal*, 10: 45–57.

Kindleberger, C. (1969) *American Business Abroad: Six Lectures on Direct Investment*. New Haven: Yale University Press.

Knickerbocker, F. (1973) *Oligopolistic Reaction and Multinational Enterprise*. Boston: Div. Of Research, Graduate School of Business Administration, Harvard University.

Kobrin, S. (1985) 'Diffusion as an explanation of oil nationalization: or the domino effect rides again', *Journal of Conflict Resolution*, 29: 3–32.

Kogut, B. (1983) 'Foreign direct investment as a sequential process', in C. P. Kindleberger and D. Audretsch (eds), *The Multinational Corporation in the 1980s*. Cambridge: MIT Press.

Kogut, B. (1985) 'Designing global strategies: comparative and competitive value-added chains', *Sloan Management Review*, 26: 15–28.

Kogut, B. (1987) 'Country patterns in international competition: appropriability and oligopolistic agreement', in N. Hood and J. E. Vahlne (eds), *Strategies in Global Competition*. New York: Wiley.

Kogut, B. (1991) 'Country capabilities and the permeability of borders', *Strategic Management Journal*, 12: 33–47.

Kogut, B. and Chang, S-J. (1991) 'Technological capabilities and Japanese foreign direct investment in the United States', *Review of Economics and Statistics*, 73: 401–13.

Kogut, B. and Chang, S-J. (1996) 'Platform investments and volatile exchange rates: direct investment in the US by Japanese electronic companies', *Review of Economics and Statistics*, 78: 221–31.

Kogut, B. and Kulatilaka, N. (1995) 'Operating flexibility, global manufacturing, and the option value of a multinational network', *Management Science*, 40: 123–39.

Kogut, B. and Parkinson, D. (1993) 'The diffusion of American organizing principles to Europe', in B. Kogut (ed.), *Country Competitiveness: Technology and the Organizing of Work*. Oxford: Oxford University Press.

Kogut, B. and Singh, H. (1988) 'The effect of national culture on the choice of entry mode', *Journal of International Business Studies*, 19: 411–32.

Kogut, B. and Zander, U. (1993) 'Knowledge of the firm and the evolutionary theory of the multinational enterprise', *Journal of International Business Studies*, 24: 625–45.

Kono, T. (1984) *Strategy and Structure of Japanese Enterprises*. London: Macmillan.

Krugman, P. (1989) 'Industrial organization and international trade', in R. Schmalensee and R. D. Willig (eds), *Handbook of Industrial Organization*, vol. 2. Amsterdam: North Holland. pp. 1179–223.

Krugman, P. (1991) *Geography and Trade.* Cambridge, MA: MIT Press.

Lawrence, P. R. and Lorsch, J. W. (1969) *Developing Organizations: Diagnosis and Action.* Reading, MA: Addison-Wesley Pub. Co.

Lessard, D. and Zaheer, S. (1996) 'Breaking the silos: distributed knowledge and strategic responses to volatile exchange rates', *Strategic Management Journal,* 17: 513–33.

Li, J. T. (1995) 'Foreign entry and survival: effects of strategic choices on performance in international markets', *Strategic Management Journal,* 16: 333–51.

Malnight, T. W. (1996) 'The transition from decentralized to network-based MNC structures: an evolutionary perspective', *Journal of International Business Studies,* 27: 43–65.

Mascarenhas, B. (1992) 'Order of entry and performance in international markets', *Strategic Management Journal,* 13: 499–510.

Miotti, L. and Sachwald, F. (2001) 'Korean multinational strategies and international learning', in F. Sachwald (ed.), *National Champions Going Multinational: The Case of Korea.* Paris: Harwood Academic Press.

Mitchell, W., Morck, R., Shaver, M. and Yeung, B. (2001) 'Causality between international expansion and investment in intangibles, with implications for financial performance and firm survival', in J-F. Hennart (ed.), *Global Competition and Market Entry Strategies.* Amsterdam: North Holland.

Mitchell, W., Shaver, J. M. and Yeung, B. (1993) 'Performance following changes of international presence in domestic and transition industries', *Journal of International Business Studies,* 24: 647–69.

Morck, R. and Yeung, B. (1991) 'Why investors value multinationality', *Journal of Business,* 64: 165–87.

Nohria, N. and Garcia-Pont, C. (1991) 'Global strategic linkages and industry structure', *Strategic Management Journal,* 12: 105–24.

Oxley, J. E. (1997) 'Appropriability hazards and governance in strategic alliances: a transaction cost approach', *Journal of Law, Economics and Organization,* 13: 387–409.

Perlmutter, H. (1965) *Towards a Theory and Practice of Social Architecture: The Building of Indispensable Institutions.* London: Tavistock Publications.

Porter, M. E. (1990) *The Competitive Advantage of Nations.* New York: Free Press.

Prahalad, C. K. and Doz, Y. L. (1987) *The Multinational Mission: Balancing Local Demands and Global Vision.* New York: Free Press.

Rangan, S. (1998) 'Do multinationals operate flexibly? Theory and evidence', *Journal of International Business Studies,* 29: 217–37.

Rogers, E. (1983) *The Diffusion of Innovations,* 3rd edition. New York: Free Press.

Rugman, A. M. (1981) *Inside the Multinationals: The Economics of Internal Markets.* London: Croom Helm.

Sharp, D. J. (1994) 'The effectiveness of routine-based decision processes: the case of international pricing', *Journal of Socio-Economics,* 23: 131–47.

Shaver, J. M. (1998) 'Accounting for endogeneity when assessing strategy performance: does entry mode choice affect FDI survival?', *Management Science,* 44: 571–85.

Shaver, J. M., Mitchell, W. and Yeung, B. (1997) 'The effect of own-firm and other-firm experience on foreign direct investment survival in the United States', *Strategic Management Journal,* 18: 811–24.

Solvell, O. (1987) *Entry Barriers and Foreign Penetration – Emerging Patterns of International Competition in Two Electrical Engineering Industries.* Stockholm: IIB, Published Doctoral Dissertation.

Soskice, D. (1990) 'Wage determination: the changing role of institutions in advanced industrialized countries', *Oxford Review of Economic Policy,* 6: 36–61.

Spicer, A. (1998) 'Institutions and the social construction of organizational form: the development of Russian mutual fund organizations, 1992–1997', Philadelphia: The Wharton School, University of Pennsylvania, Ph.D. Dissertation.

Stopford, J. M. and Wells, L. T. Jr. (1972) *Managing the Multinational Enterprise: Organization of the Firm and Ownership of Subsidiaries.* New York: Basic Books.

Sutton, J. (1991) *Sunk Costs and Market Structure: Price Competition, Advertising, and the Evolution of Concentration.* Cambridge, MA: MIT Press.

Suzuki, Y. (1991) *Japanese Management Structures, 1920–80.* New York: St. Martin's Press.

Swedenborg, B. (1979) *The Multinational Operations of Swedish Firms: An Analysis of Determinants and Effects.* Stockholm: Industrial Institute for Economic and Social Research.

Szulanski, G. (1996) 'Exploring internal stickiness: impediments to the transfer of best practices within the firm', *Strategic Management Journal,* 17: 27–44.

Teece, D. J. (1977) 'Technology transfer by multinational firms: the resource cost of transferring technological knowhow', *Economics Journal,* 87: 242–61.

Tsetsekos, G. P. and Gombola, M. J. (1992) 'Foreign and domestic divestments: evidence on valuation effects of plant closings', *Journal of International Business Studies,* 23: 203–23.

Vernon, R. (1971) *Sovereignty at Bay: The Multinational Spread of U.S. Enterprises.* London: Basic Books.

Vernon, R. (1976) 'International investment and international trade in the product cycle', *Quarterly Journal of Economics,* 80: 190–207.

Vernon, R. (1979) 'The product cycle in the new international environment', *The Oxford Bulletin of Economics and Statistics,* 41: 255–67.

Walker, G. (1987) 'Network analysis for interfirm cooperative relationships', in F. Contractor and P. Lorange (eds), *Cooperative Strategies in Multinational Business.* Lexington, MA: D. C. Heath.

Westney, D. E. (1987) *Imitation and Innovation: The Transfer of Western Organizational Patterns to Meiji Japan.* Cambridge: Harvard University Press.

Whittington, R., Mayer, M. and Curto, F. (1999) 'Chandlerism in post-war Europe: strategic and structural change in France, Germany and the UK, 1950–1993', *Industrial & Corporate Change*, 8: 519–50.

Wilkins, M. (1974) *The Maturing of Multinational Enterprise: American Business Abroad from 1914 to 1970*. Boston: Harvard University Press.

Wilkins, M. (1988) 'The free-standing company, 1870–1914: an important type of British foreign direct investment', *Economic History Review*, 2nd Series, 41: 259–82.

Williamson, O. (1975) *Markets and Hierarchies, Analysis and Antitrust Implications: A Study in the Economics of Internal Organization*. New York: Free Press.

Williamson, O. E. (1991) 'Comparative economic organization: the analysis of discrete structural alternatives', *Administrative Science Quarterly*, 36: 269–96.

Wilson, B. D. (1980) 'The propensity of multinational companies to expand through acquisitions', *Journal of International Business Studies*, 11: 59–65.

Winter, S. (1987) 'Knowledge and competence as strategic assets', in D. Teece (ed.), *The Competitive Challenge – Strategies for Industrial Innovation and Renewal*. Cambridge: Ballinger.

Yamawaki, H. (1988) 'Import share under international oligopoly with differentiated products: Japanese imports in US manufacturing', *Review of Economics and Statistics*, 70: 569–79.

Yu, C-M. J. and Ito, K. (1988) 'Oligopolistic reaction and foreign direct investment: the case of the US tire and textile industries', *Journal of International Business Studies*, 19: 449–60.

Zaheer, S. (1995) 'Overcoming the liability of foreignness', *Academy of Management Journal*, 38: 341–63.

Zaheer, S. (2001) 'Time-zone economies and managerial work in a global world', in P. C. Earley and H. Singh (eds), *Innovations in International and Cross-Cultural Management*. Thousand Oaks, CA: Sage.

13

Quasi Strategy: Strategic Management in the Contemporary Public Sector

EWAN FERLIE

This chapter analyses decision making within contemporary public sector organizations through a strategic management perspective. It argues that the analysis of public sector organizations should be taken more seriously within the strategic management literature. Three major themes are developed throughout the chapter. The first theme draws on increasing evidence of widespread and profound restructuring occurring within many current public sectors. This macro level change process is sometimes referred to as the rise of the 'New Public Management' (NPM) and is apparent in many countries, although some (mainly Anglo Saxon) jurisdictions have moved faster. The NPM should be seen as a broad restructuring, rather than the superficial managerial fad or fashion (Abrahamson, 1991) often encountered within managerial practice.

The second theme draws on the debate between generic and sectorally specific models of management. The question is: to what extent can generic models of strategic management be validly applied to current public sector organizations? A framework is outlined using a public management perspective which analyses the extent of similarity between the private sector and the contemporary public sector in respect of the senior managerial tasks undertaken. An important consequence of the NPM has been to make public sector

management less distinctive by moving managerial tasks 'downgroup' (Dunleavy and Hood, 1994). Given partial convergence, so generic management techniques (including those of strategic management) are increasingly valid within the current public sector, as long as continuing inter-sectoral differences are recognized.

The chapter then reviews various approaches to strategic management and explores how applicable they might be within contemporary public sector settings. It is concluded that a group of these models is potentially helpful, although some customization to the sector may still be required. The criticism of the strategic management wave that it is no more than a discursive claim to power by a new public sector elite is considered but not accepted. This forms the basis for a proposed research agenda in order to take what is still an emerging field forward. The view is taken that current public sector organizations can be seen as engaging in *quasi strategy* making in which customized versions of some strategic management models used in the private sector are valid and helpful. Certain conditions are specified under which the process of convergence with private sector styles of strategic management would accelerate further.

A wide definition of strategy which goes beyond the rational planning models historically

Table 13.1   *General government total outlays as % of nominal GDP*

	1981	1990	1997
USA	31.7	32.8	32.0
Japan	32.8	31.3	35.2
Germany	48.7	45.1	47.7
France	48.6	49.8	54.1
UK	44.2	40.7	39.7
Spain	34.9	42.0	42.2
Sweden	62.6	59.1	62.3
OECD total	37.6	38.4	39.1

Source: OECD (1998), Annexe Table 28.

dominant within the public sector – which are surprisingly resilient in practice – is used and various models are reviewed. The tone adopted here is descriptive rather than prescriptive and pluralist rather than proclaiming 'one best way' of strategy. 'Strategy' has been defined (Johnson and Scholes, 1993) in relation to the overall direction and scope of the organization, as expressed over the long term. Strategic decision making is distinctive when compared to operational management, characterized by higher levels of ambiguity, greater complexity and few decision rules. Strategic management has also been defined as the achievement of a fit across different activities so that a coherent positioning is achieved (Porter, 1996). There are many models of strategy on offer which succeed each other with bewildering rapidity. Emergent or processual models of strategy have been well reviewed by Mintzberg et al. (1998) and the systemic or 'embedded' model of strategy by Whittington (1993). A research overview suggested that strategic decision making can be seen as both political and boundedly rational in nature (Eisenhardt and Zbaracki, 1992). So we need to be open to many different definitions and models of strategy. However, the questions addressed here are somewhat more limited than these global analyses of the whole field of strategic management. First, what are the models of strategy apparent within the public sector? Secondly, to what extent do they 'fit' with the managerial tasks undertaken?

Within such jurisdictions as the USA and the UK, recent work indicates increased use of strategic management models and language within current public sector organizations (Bryson, 1988; Nutt and Backoff, 1992; Moore, 1995; Ferlie et al., 1996; Greer and

Hoggett, 1997; Thorne, 1999; Joyce, 1999) and also non profit organizations (Ostler, 1995). At first sight, this is a curious development. Within the private sector, strategic management activity may result in firm repositioning, enhanced market share, greater profitability and perhaps the elimination of rival firms. As these outcomes are not apparent within the public sector (due to the lack of markets, prices or private property rights), why should public sector organizations adopt techniques of strategic management? Why has there been this turn to the models and language of strategy? This chapter will argue that this shift reflects the changed nature of senior managerial tasks within a profoundly restructured public sector.

THE RISE AND CONSEQUENCES OF THE NEW PUBLIC MANAGEMENT

Large Continuing Public Sectors

Current public sectors remain of considerable scope and scale and continue to present important managerial and organizational challenges. Recent data on the proportion of gross domestic product (GDP) accounted for by government revenues suggest that substantial government expenditure levels continue, even in such neo liberal jurisdictions of the USA and the UK as shown in Table 13.1.

The USA continues to display one of the smallest public sectors internationally. This is one explanation of the relatively marginal position of the public sector within the strategic management literature, as much management research is American based and assumes a large private sector. The UK is interesting as a 'midway' jurisdiction where overall public expenditure is projected to remain at about the 40% of GDP level in the near future. France and Germany have displayed greater resistance to the lowering of public expenditure levels. Spain is an interesting case of a country where the public sector grew sharply in the 1980s, associated with a period of socialist government. Sweden, as always, remains an extreme case of the social democratic model, although the upward drift of public expenditure there has recently been contained.

The Organisation for Economic Cooperation and Development (OECD) uses a wide definition of public expenditure which includes transfer payments such as publicly financed pensions. Some might argue that such expenditures should be excluded from any definition of the 'real' public sector, although the continuing role of the public sector in the provision of pensions and income support is noteworthy. In many jurisdictions (including the USA), it has proved difficult to cut back on such entitlement programmes and replace them by private insurance based forms of provision. These limits to privately based income support may continue, given the growth of self-employment and short-term contract based forms of employment. By 1995, social spending accounted for about 25% of OECD GDP, requiring increased taxation levels (including on low income earners). The public sector also continues to provide core human services which have proved difficult to privatize or even contain at previous expenditure levels (such as the example of Medicare in the USA).

Pressure to Lower Taxation Levels

There is a strong link between changes in the wider political economy and the scope and shape of the public sector. A political drive to lower tax rates and increase incentives has been evident internationally from the early 1980s and key indicators of taxation levels have been falling, in such jurisdictions as Sweden and France as in the UK and the USA. There are few signs that this trend to lower income tax rates will be reversed as it is electorally popular, particularly with key groups of aspirant middle income earners that make up the new dominant electoral coalition. There is a technical debate about whether the overall burden of taxation has in fact reduced, as there has also been a tendency for indirect or 'hidden' taxes to rise. Nevertheless, there has been a switch from a presumption of continuing governmental expansion – and a willingness to accept higher taxation levels – to a new political agenda dominated by the search for value and effectiveness. This combination of buoyant demand and a decreased willingness to tax and spend represents a powerful combination of forces which have impacted on the organization and management of the public sector.

Some International Experiences

OECD surveys on individual countries are illuminating. For example, the American report (OECD, 1997) draws attention to the continuing failure to agree a bipartisan reform of the major entitlement programmes which are driving up public expenditure levels and potentially leading to fiscal deficits, given the strong continuing political demand for tax cuts. The report for Germany (OECD, 1998a) stresses the need to reduce marginal tax rates, control social spending and increase public sector efficiency through optimizing incentive structures and deregulation. The 'Leaner State' ('Schlanker Staat') programme includes pilot projects for contracting out, outsourcing and a growth of private finance. The report on Sweden (OECD, 1998b) notes an increased political emphasis on ensuring expenditure control, but further expenditure reduction was still seen by OECD as needed. Local government was starting to outsource, but levels of transfer payments were still high so that pension reform was a further priority. Their analysis of the French case (OECD, 1999) noted an increase in privatization and public sector restructuring, with the selling off of public enterprises, a downsizing of public sector staffs and an opening up of capital flows within the public sector.

The Rise of the New Public Management and its Consequences

These OECD reports suggest that substantial change is occurring in a number of current public sectors. But how does the academic literature describe and analyse these mega shifts? Some have detected the rise of the new public management (Hood, 1991, 1995; Dunleavy and Hood, 1994) as a successor to the old public administration template. This movement has been apparent for some 20 years and on an international basis, although with more impact in some jurisdictions (notably the UK, Australia and New Zealand triad of 'high impact' cases) than others. Texts on the rise of the NPM now offer analyses of the USA (Pollitt, 1990; Barzelay, 1992), UK (Pollitt, 1990; Ferlie et al., 1996), Canada (Aucoin, 1995), New Zealand (Boston et al., 1996), Australia (Campbell and Halligan, 1992; Zifcak, 1994) and Brazil

Table 13.2 *From public administration to new public management*

Dimension	Public administration	New public management
Focus of attention	Policy advice; constitutional and judicial tasks	Operational and strategic management; value for money
Organizational form	Vertically integrated organizations; strong lines of upwards accountability	Disaggregation into purchasers and providers; management through contract; greater managerial autonomy
Performance pressures	Low; poor IT base	High; advanced IT base
User focus	Inward facing; producer led	More outward facing; greater user orientation
Managerial roles	Modest; facilitative; 'administrators'	Expanded; directive; also professional/managerial hybrids
Change orientation	Low; many routines and operating procedures	High; past as a negative role model

(Bresser Pereira, 1998), suggesting that this is a movement of some breadth and depth.

Lynn (1998) argues that the NPM movement will fade, as political and issue succession takes its toll and that it is no more than the usual managerial fad (Abrahamson, 1991). The argument here, by contrast, is that the NPM represents a deeply rooted shift towards both a more managed and also 'market like' orientation (and there may indeed be tensions between these two principles) within continuing public sectors. As a result, there is convergence with private sector models of organization and management in some specific ways.

This descriptive analysis is advanced as a characterization of the new organizational order apparent in the contemporary public sector: it is not intended to be normative or prescriptive in tone. Some have criticized the NPM model for eroding traditional notions of due process, equity and probity which were seen as important advantages of the public administration model (du Gay, 1993). It typically places less emphasis on democratic accountability than traditional public sector modes of organization, being driven instead by strong notions of performance and efficiency. Key dimensions in the transition between the two models are summarized in Table 13.2.

Greater Focus on Operational and Strategic Management Rather than Policy Advice, Constitutional or Judicial Tasks

Within the restructured public sector, the dominant focus of interest and attention moves

from 'policy' to 'management'. The earlier public administrative template stressed the distinctive and indeed unique role of the State as lawgiver, governor and monopolist of legitimate force. While the constitutional, judicial and policy advisory roles associated with this model (the drafting and passing of new laws, the system of judicial scrutiny, provision of advice to ministers) represent the old core of the public sector, they have long been dwarfed by the mass service delivery tasks performed by large scale welfare bureaux. Such tasks may have been larger scale, but they were also historically less prestigious or politically visible. With the rise of the NPM, political attention shifted to more effective management of bureaux which account for the bulk of public sector expenditure (such as social security programmes) where better value can be sought.

Disaggregation of Public Organizations and Greater Managerial Autonomy

The public administration model produced vertically integrated organizations with strong upward lines of accountability. The NPM separates out responsibility for purchasing public services from providing them, so previously integrated organizations have been decoupled in order to increase pressure for performance and break up excessive collusion. On the providing side, greater managerial freedoms in the fields of budgeting, capital and human resources have been devolved to new operating units distinct from a policy making core. These agencies still operate under a framework set by the centre and enforced through a contract, but have more internal freedoms (at least rhetorically). Within the UK, a good example would be the new devolved agencies within the civil service (such as the Benefits Agency, which delivers a vast welfare programme as a 'hands off' agency).

These organizations typically display better developed managerial capacity and possess (within the agreed framework) greater autonomy, choice and flexibility. There is a debate about how much discretion has in reality been delegated, but it may be significant in some cases. Such shifts open up the possibility of some strategic choice and repositioning. Organizational diversity within the public sector may be increasing (Ferlie et al., 1996) rather than decreasing, as a wider range of organizational forms and management approaches is acceptable.

From Plans to Quasi Markets

The public administration model used the hierarchy and the plan as key vehicles for resource allocation. The NPM facilitates the growth of quasi markets in some settings. Public services may still be financed through public money but increasingly provided by a wider range of providers than the old public sector monopolists. Providers may include new entrants from the private sector, not for profit organizations or newly independent management buy outs. Barriers to entry are high in some areas (such as clinical health care) but lower in others (such as cleaning services). A number of peripheral functions have been externalized, contracted out or subjected to market testing, in order to stimulate performance and ensure value for money.

While there is not day to day competition *in* markets, there is periodic competition *for* markets (Baumol et al., 1982), such as in the auction of TV or media franchises, the provision of hotel services in health care or even intense competition between university research groups for publicly supported research and development (R and D) contracts. The letting and reletting of contracts represent key decision points, where the dynamics of the quasi market become clear. The quasi market has stimulated the growth of quasi firms, where the search for competitive advantage is no

longer an entirely inappropriate concept. Purchasers, too, wish to shape quasi markets, perhaps through market development and fostering possible new entrants.

Increased Pressure for Performance

The transition to the NPM is associated with a demand for public sector performance and productivity. Within the managerial sphere, there is greater use of efficiency targets, market testing, performance indicators and expanding audit systems (Power, 1997). There is increased interest in assessing performance, developing performance management systems and indeed in how to create high performance public sector organizations (Moore, 1995). Far more sophisticated information technology (IT) systems have led to the rapid development of performance indicator data systems and the comparative benchmarking of performance, in the public as in the private sector. Where market forces remain weak, public sector managers face individual performance targets set by their Boards on which their careers will depend. There is a greater willingness to expose low performing public sector providers and credible threats to replace them with new private providers (in the UK case, even in such 'core' areas as education and prison services).

From Producers to Users

Public sector organizations have historically been seen as highly inward facing, dominated by strong producer groups and insulated from the expression of client preferences. The new quasi markets within the public services have led to the introduction of novel mechanisms (decentralized budgets, micro purchasing, lessening of restrictions on client choice) designed to increase user voice. There has been a growth of 'customer care' initiatives designed to combat traditional producer dominance, associated with a new rhetoric of choice and quality.

For example, various quality oriented change programmes (such as total quality management and business process reengineering) are apparent within the public sector. The newly privatized utilities (such as British Airways) have been taken as a role model by the continuing public sector as they have often made sustained efforts to build a strong customer focus. Providing a consistently high quality service is increasingly a major objective for public sector organizations, as well as ensuring cost efficiency (Scally and Donaldson, 1998).

From Administrators to Managers

These developments have had implications for individual careers as well as for corporate organizational forms, with a shift from the old public administrators to the new public managers. Within the public administration model, often the real power lay in the hands of senior professional staff (for example, clinicians) with administrators taking on a modest, facilitative, role. The new public managers often enact an expanded and more directive role in their local settings. There is a growth of more active senior managerial roles with the hiring of chief executive officers (CEOs) (often brought in from outside) to act as change managers on higher salaries but also on short term contracts. The newly created non executive director roles (rather than the old 'member' model associated with the public administration model) on boards of public sector organizations provide another expanded focus for senior level leadership (Ferlie et al., 1996). More recently, senior professional managerial hybrid roles have been created (Montgomery, 1990; Fitzgerald, 1994; Thorne, 1997), in an attempt to tie together the historically different worlds of public sector managers and public sector professionals.

Many models of strategic management (for example, the strategic planning model) often presuppose the existence of a senior corporate management or board level team to drive the strategic process. Directors are here encouraged to take a corporate view and not remain within their particular functions or departments. In many public service organizations, such a corporate approach has not emerged until recently but policy changes have strengthened such senior management roles.

From Maintenance Management to the Management of Change

The emphasis on due process and insulation from external forces characteristic of the old public administration model led to the reproduction of decision making routines and standard operating procedures. Steady state management has been replaced by an emphasis on the management of change as the old public sector is taken as a negative role model – as something to escape from, rather than to perpetuate. There is interest in the management of strategic change (Pettigrew et al., 1992) within the public sector and even talk of radical 'organizational transformation' to quite new styles of management (Osborne and Gaebler, 1992). The earlier presumption of a dominant bureaucratic style with an emphasis on steady state management has been superseded by a post bureaucratic or an entrepreneurial style of management (Barzelay, 1992). This leads to a new interest in transition management and the management of change, including strategic as well as operational change.

This analysis concludes that the transition to the NPM has shifted the managerial tasks undertaken by public sector managers 'down-group' so that there has been partial convergence with private sector management tasks. Specifically, there is a greater focus on generic management tasks such as strategic management, quality management and the management of change. This shift is supported by the new architecture of the public sector – quasi markets have developed as resource allocation vehicles, new organizational forms now allow for greater managerial autonomy, and public sector boards have been empowered to engage in strategic management.

A PUBLIC MANAGEMENT PERSPECTIVE
ON STRATEGIC MANAGEMENT
WITHIN THE PUBLIC SECTOR

There is, of course, a general debate around the extent to which managerial roles and tasks in the private and public sectors should rightfully be seen as alike or as different – the greater the difference, the less useful the exporting of generic or indeed specifically private sector based models of strategic management into the public sector. Three different positions can be identified.

The first *public administration* perspective stresses the continuing importance of inter-sectoral differences including in relation to strategic management tasks (Smith and Perry, 1985; Allison, 1993). Legal or political science based perspectives (rather than more managerial forms of analysis) typically emphasize the special character of the State as an organization. The State is not like a private firm: its unique tasks include the establishment of the rule of law and of good governance, and it enjoys a monopoly of the use of legitimate force. The State operates on the basis of public rather than private property rights and is not concerned with profit maximization. Due process, public legitimacy and equity of treatment between cases are important objectives in service delivery which are not achieved within a purely business driven and profit maximizing approach. This is because the legitimacy needs of the democratic State imply that there is a strong concern for fair means as well as successful outcomes. Overall direction is here rightfully set by politicians who operate through an electoral mandate and are accountable to the legislature and periodically to the electorate for their performance. There are mandates from legislation to which public agencies have to respond and they cannot withdraw services from client groups on the grounds that there is no market.

By contrast, a second *general management* perspective emphasizes the similarity in key management tasks between sectors. General management involves the performance of similar tasks across all large organizations, such as leadership, team building, making best use of financial and human resources, ensuring satisfied customers and formulating long-term direction. An implication is that public sector organizations have underperformed because these general management disciplines and skills have been absent. However, primary management research does not in general support the argument that general management concepts and models can be applied irrespective of the organizational context even within the private sector (Hales, 1986) and a unified management science remains as distant as ever (Whitley, 1989).

A third model is developed within the *public management orientation* (Gunn, 1989). Within this framework, there are typically attempts to adapt generic management ideas generated within private sector contexts (such as quality management and organizational learning) to still distinctive public service settings. The generic management ideas are potentially useful, but also require adaptation. The flow of learning is two-way in nature (from the public sector to the private sector) rather than the uni-directional flow to the public sector often assumed. For example, Stewart and Clarke (1987) developed a public services orientation model which borrows from the generic literature such concepts as strong organizational culture, quality assurance and consumer responsiveness, but applies them in a distinctive public sector context where users are seen as citizens as well as customers.

The argument within the public management perspective that there are both similarities and differences between the sectors is too general and bland. The model needs to specify in more much detail the nature of these similarities and differences in terms of the managerial tasks performed. For example, Gunn (1989) argues that tasks become more similar across the sectors the higher one goes in the managerial hierarchy – strategic management tasks are hence more similar than operational management tasks.

When analysed as an organizational form, public sector organizations are situated within the same very broad historical and cultural milieu as private sector firms. Within Anglo American case examples, the post-war welfare state bureaucracy can be seen as a public sector analogue of the Fordist corporation; the successor form of the NPM 'quasi firm' is the analogue of a more decentralized and knowledge-based small or medium enterprise. While some public sector organizations (policy analytic departments such as Foreign Ministries or Treasuries; the judicial and legislative departments that should handle cases equitably and with due process) are highly distinctive, most public sector organizations deliver mass human services where generic management concepts are more applicable. Electors increasingly judge these organizations in their role as users, 'customers' or taxpayers as well as citizens. The key test is: can these agencies deliver high quality, cost effective, services when they are needed by users/electors?

While public sector organizations should not be seen as a radically different organizational form, they do lie on the extreme end of many organizational dimensions. In particular, they are often characterized by a distinct combination of: weak and ambiguous goals; multiple stakeholders; high degrees of professionalization and politicization; very large organizational size; weak markets; and few private property rights. While some of these dimensions may also apply to private sector firms, nevertheless this cluster of traits is distinctive when taken as a whole. These traits are not fixed, and may be reshaped over time, so increasing or decreasing intersectoral compatability. The rise of the NPM has changed the managerial tasks performed within current public sector organizations and aligned them with more generic models of management.

STRATEGIC MANAGEMENT APPLIED TO THE CONTEMPORARY PUBLIC SECTOR

Within the public management perspective, much of the strategic management literature can be usefully applied to contemporary public sector settings, where due regard is paid to the continuing inter-sectoral differences. This section reviews some of the key generic approaches to strategic management and considers their application within contemporary public sector settings.

Corporate Planning

The earliest model of strategic management grew out from its roots within the corporate planning movement. This model emerged in the 1950s and 1960s and is rational analytic in nature, set within a command and control model of the large organization. Chandler (1962: 13) famously defined strategy as 'the determination of basic long term goals and objectives of an enterprise and the adoption of courses of action and the allocation of resources necessary for those goals'. The corporate plan drove the flow of resources across the organization, based on the collection of data, and the use of option appraisal and other formal analytic techniques. Strategy was made by the board, after taking account of specialist advice from corporate planning staffs, and then transmitted downwards by line management. Grant (1998: 15–18) sees the early corporate planning movement as a tool for supplying direction – or at least a degree of coordination – to the internal resource allocation processes of the large and complex firms increasingly dominant within the mid 20th century American economy.

The assumption of a large, relatively stable, top down directed organization that needed a formal framework to guide the allocation of internal resources (especially capital resources) applied perhaps to a greater extent to public sector organizations, given their insulation from market forces, their presumption of incremental growth and the key role of scarce public sector capital as a lever for development. Rigorous investment appraisal of many competing internal bids could assure maximum value for money for the taxpayer, at least rhetorically.

It is not then surprising that these corporate planning approaches quickly diffused into the public sector. As a UK example, long range plans emerged in the early 1960s in hospital and university sectors and continued to be extremely dominant until the mid 1970s. They were seen as devices for managing growth, particularly major capital investment decisions. They were highly formalistic in orientation, often extremely detailed in nature and prepared by a new cadre of public sector corporate planners. Similar techniques – such as the corporate management approach (Hinings and Greenwood, 1988), zero based budgeting, and programme review – rolled out as management tools into the public sector as a second generation of analytic techniques in the early 1970s. Certain subsectors, for example defence with its large purchasing and project management decisions, found these techniques especially attractive. Influential planning based texts such as Bryson (1988) reflect this strategic planning model as applied to the public sector.

However, these long range planning techniques were badly adapted to the increasingly turbulent and discontinuous environment of the late 1970s. [As Mintzberg et al. (1998) argue, the failure of strategic planning is the failure of formalization. This failure is if anything more acute in politicized public sector settings.] Two successive 'oil shocks' in 1974 and 1979 led to reduced growth rates, and a novel combination of high unemployment and high inflation ('stagflation'), which sabotaged the presumption of incremental public sector growth and made long run financial projections meaningless. The shift to monetarism and tight cash limits within the public sector placed a premium on securing cost reduction at an operational level rather than planning for growth at a strategic level.

At the political level, the old consensus of the 1960s broke down with the growth of socialist Left and then New Right alternatives to the social democratic mixed economy and Welfare State. Radically different models were on offer for the organization and management of the public sector which were not amenable to technocratic control. The Left model promised rapid expenditure growth (but also possibly high inflation), but combined with both the unionization and democratization of professionalized service settings. In fact the 1980s were to usher in a period of radical right regimes, at least in an Anglo American context. Within the New Right analysis, the large public sectors characteristic of the social democratic state were a problem rather than a solution. The core aim was to downsize the State, reduce levels of taxation and expand the role of markets and prices (rather than planning based styles of resource allocation) through privatization and public sector restructuring. There was also increasing evidence of massive implementation deficits within the public sector as the centre might proclaim targets for rapid service change, but the localities could not deliver them. Such problems escalated with the higher level of governmental ambition and intervention apparent from the mid 1960s onwards, as for example within the American Great Society programmes (where implementation failure was seen as early as Pressman and Wildavsky, 1973). In the mid 1970s, many of the UK corporate plans collapsed under pressure from economic failure and political polarization.

In its adoption of corporate planning – and its experience of its limitations – the public sector mirrored rather than contradicted that of the private sector. Within the private sector, however, this led to the development of alternative approaches which could handle discontinuity (such as scenario planning). The public sector, by contrast, has failed to learn and has often recycled corporate planning techniques which have been shown to be badly flawed (Green, 1998).

Industrial Organizational Economics and the Search for Competitive Advantage

Within the private sector, the increased turbulence of the late 1970s and strong market mindedness of the 1980s led to a search for flexible forms of strategic management, with an increased stress on competition as the central characteristic of the business environment and on competitive advantage as the primary goal of strategy (Grant, 1998: 17). A second set of ideas flowed into the strategy field from industrial organizational economics, with a focus on competitiveness, profitability and the analysis of market structures. This perspective was useful in guiding the search for profitable industry sectors for investment, and then for profitable niches within a sector. It could be used to explore critical factors associated with higher levels of success by a firm within markets and guide strategic action which might improve performance (Grant, 1998: 109).

These ideas are developed in the highly influential work of Michael Porter (1980), whose five forces of competition model offers a framework for analysing the intensity of competition within an industry and the associated level of profitability: the level of competition from substitutes; a credible threat of market entry so that a market is contestable (Baumol et al., 1982); the extent of competition from established rivals; and the relative bargaining power of suppliers and buyers. Key success factors for profitability could be specified through this analysis. The framework could also be used for lower level segmentation analysis, enabling firms to identify which market segments they want to remain in or should expand into. Firms which have adopted similar strategies can be classified into 'strategic groups' for purposes of analysis and competitor analysis undertaken to profile each firm active in the market place and identify comparative weaknesses and strengths. From this emerges the concept of 'competitive advantage' where a firm outperforms its rivals on key performance criteria, usually profitability. An important question is whether such advantage can be quickly eroded through imitation or innovation by rivals. The idea of first mover advantage implies that a market leader may be able to develop certain assets (patents, reputation, possession of scarce human or physical capital) which are difficult to seize. Firms develop a range of different strategies, such as competing on cost leadership or on high quality, while firms 'stuck in the middle' between these positions are vulnerable (Porter, 1980). The nature of competitive advantage may also vary by market, as there may be very different patterns evident in new and mature markets.

How applicable is this Porterian model of strategic management to the current public sector? With its strong focus on markets, profitability and competitiveness, such models are difficult to apply literally, as prices, markets and profits all remain underdeveloped within the public sector. Where public sector quasi markets are developing, however, a similar analysis of market structure, market power and barriers to entry and exit may be helpful. Despite high barriers to market entry and exit and massive sunk costs, there is some evidence of the evolution of contestable markets within some public services, at least on the provider side. There is a process of market development, with the emergence of social businesses which seek to 'invade' other territory.

A good UK example would be the private and non profit education providers who are now bidding to run public sector schools where local public sector management has been deemed by central government to have failed (such externalization has if anything increased since the 1997 change of government with the central government determined to remove failed public sector monopolists). Such bidders have to calculate the investments needed to make a credible bid, the criteria and competences on which the contract will be awarded and the likelihood of their capturing the contract.

These Porterian models do not imply neo classical markets or perfect competition as sustained competitive advantage may be easier in imperfect or 'sticky' markets in which oligopolies can assume dominance and extract profits. Porterian concepts can certainly be adapted to analyse quasi markets as in Challis et al.'s (1994) typology of different UK public sector quasi markets. Market power varies according to the degree of concentration within both the purchaser and provider sides. The greater the degree of concentration, the greater the degree of market power. In regulatory terms, the optimal balance between contracts and regulatory institutions as control strategies will depend on the degree of provider and (especially) purchaser concentration. Porterian models and concepts may prove especially useful for public sector regulators and purchasers, guiding them in their market development tasks.

The 'competitive advantage' model has also proved fruitful in stimulating the development of analogous models such as that of 'collaborative advantage' (Kanter, 1994; Huxham, 1996), which develop, but also build on, early Porterian insights and apply them to alternative organizational settings.

The Resource Based View of the Firm

If 'strategy' springs from the match between a firm's capabilities and external opportunities, then an internal analysis of the resources and capabilities of the firm is as important as the more common assessment of the external environment. There has within the last decade been a significant growth of interest in the resources and competences of the firm as a prime basis for strategy (Barney, 1991; Mahoney and Pandian, 1992).

Increasing market volatility, accelerating rates of technological change and unpredictable changes in customer behaviour place a greater premium on core internal capabilities as flexibility, innovation and rapid response rates which enable the firm to cope with many different scenarios. The firm is a bundle of capabilities which provides the basis for its underlying competitive position and hence profitability. In order to forge a viable strategy, this perspective implies that the firm needs a deep understanding of its own resources and actual (and potential future) capabilities (Grant, 1998). The strategy selected should therefore reflect a firm's principal resources and capabilities, including a consideration of both tangible resources (financial and physical) and intangible resources (technology stock, reputation and human capital base). This perspective leads on to related concepts of organizational capability or core competence (Hamel and Pralahad, 1990) to describe those functions that the firm can perform well in relation to its competitors. The focus is on underlying generic capability rather than the ability to develop a particular product or service.

Resource-based models can be applied to public sector organizations, as their profile of intangible assets is surely closely correlated with their performance in such important managerial tasks highlighted by the NPM template as the management of strategic change. For example, Pettigrew and Whipp (1991) inductively derived a model of generic factors associated with the comparative success of UK private sector firms within a matched pair design of higher and lower performers. This template was then applied and adapted to the UK health care sector by Pettigrew et al. (1992). The ability to manage strategic change was a key performance dimension within the health care sector and varied markedly by locale depending on the configuration of local factors. A modified set of predictors was derived inductively on the basis of comparative case study material to explain these outcomes within health care organizations. These factors included the presence of an effective local leadership team and a supportive managerial subculture to energize change. The result was that some localities appeared to be far more effective at the management of strategic change than others.

Internal roles and relationships may be another organizational 'intangible' which explains organizational performance. Goold et al. (1994) use the concept of 'parenting advantage' to model the relationship between a corporate core and its subsidiaries. They identify three different parenting styles (strategic planning, strategic control, and financial control). They consider how these different styles can add value and in what sorts of businesses they are suitable and unsuitable. While this literature emerged within the context of complex multi national corporations, it is useful in large public sector organizations trying to add value by delayering and downsizing their corporate staffs.

Process Models of Strategy Formulation and Implementation

In the 1970s, implementation 'deficits' emerged as the limitations of a purely rational and planning based approach to strategy within large and complex organizations became apparent (Mintzberg et al., 1998). This critique was developed early on and sharply in public sector organizations by such authors as Pressman and Wildavsky (1973) and Alford (1975). A concern for the implementation *process* is a noticeable feature of much academic work on strategic management in the public sector.

'Weaker' models of the implementation deficit stress more effective approaches to top down change, where more sophisticated change management interventions (e.g. organizational development techniques) could be used to ensure that wider groups of participants 'owned' the top level strategy. 'Stronger' models stress the essentially negotiative and interactive nature of strategy generation as well as its implementation (indeed, the two stages cannot be usefully separated out and remain in iterative dialogue). Strategy should not be seen as explicit or 'intended' by the top management team but is of a more 'emergent' and diffuse nature (Mintzberg and Waters, 1998). Within an emergent strategy, the key patterning is seen in terms of consistency in a stream of actions across the organization. Mintzberg (1989) argued that strategy making is much more a craft like activity than an exercise in rational analysis. It may involve a much larger number of decision makers within an organization than solely senior management. It may involve creativity and intuition as well as reason so that there may be a need for a 'Big Idea' to provide strategic vision, energy and commitment across the organization.

In the 1980s, specific management techniques emerged which sought to operationalize this theoretical perspective, such as the use of mission statements or attempts to supply a broad organizational vision at the front end of a strategic change process (although it is unclear whether a credible vision can be manufactured to order). These Mintzbergian frameworks also permit a wider typology of strategies, such as 'umbrella' strategies in which leaders set broad guidelines but within which local actors have much discretion (Mintzberg and Waters, 1998).

Pettigrew's work (1973, 1985) developed these processual perspectives, seeing strategy formulation and implementation as shaped by a political bargaining process within the firm. There were both political and cognitive limits to the exercise of rational choice. The nature of the strategy process was shaped by the local organizational context which could best be revealed through the use of intensive, comparative and longitudinal case study techniques. This marked a methodological break away from the use of survey or scale based techniques associated with earlier schools, such as contingency theory. Other authors highlighted the importance of cognitive frameworks (Weick, 1978; Argyris and Schon, 1978; Johnson, 1987) in mediating the receipt and interpretation of external information by managers.

Such process-based models of strategy have analytic resonance in many public sector settings which often display: a high degree of politicization and of political behaviour; multiple stakeholders that engage in bargaining behaviour to form dominant coalitions; vague and multiple objectives that are reinterpreted at local level; the lack of strong market pressures that can drive change; and the limited power of the top echelons to impose direction. These processual models of strategy have been usefully applied within empirical studies of particular settings. For example, Pettigrew et al.'s (1992) analysis of strategic change processes within UK health care supported Mintzberg's contention that a shared broad vision was a more effective lever for change than a detailed blueprint.

The critique of processual models by Grant (1998: 22) argues that they overconcentrate on the role of vision and intuition, and hence provide no basis for informed choice. At worst (he argues), they can stray into 'New Age' form of organizational mysticism. In their defence, these concepts have been developed through empirical data, often of a case study based form. Implementation difficulties continue to be reported in the case of ambitious corporate change programmes so that the managerial experience which fuels interest in processual models of strategy is not likely to fade away. It appears that processual models have proved influential in theory but not in public sector practice. Recent empirical studies continue (Green, 1998; Cherry, 1999) to demonstrate the dominance of formalistic

planning models within the public sector, with the exception of the use of mission statements which appears to have widely diffused.

Strategy Making within Professionalized Organizations and Garbage Can Models

The nature of the strategic process may vary with the sector or organizational type under consideration (Mintzberg, 1998; Miller, 1998). Specifically, the professionalized organization is distinctive both in its basic form and in the way it makes strategy (Mintzberg, 1989). With the privatization of its industrial functions and its buoyant human service core, the contemporary public sector is now highly professionalized. Within it are located many established or aspirant professional groupings (including medicine as an ideal typical profession, but also university professors, teachers, nursing and social workers), fractions of other elite professions such as lawyers and some newer professional groups (such as accountants and management consultants) that have come into the public sector with the growth of the NPM.

Within professionalized organizations, professional dominance theory (Freidson, 1970) states that real power lies not with managers but with a college of senior professionals. Of course, professional dominance is not confined to the public sector and it may be seen in partner based organizations within the private sector as in law, accountancy or management consultancy. For example, Hinings et al.'s (1991) analysis of the capacity of senior partners within accountancy firms to block unwanted top down change indicates similar conditions. However, the public sector may display professional dominance to a more extensive degree, given the large number of professional workers located within it.

There may therefore be special dynamics of strategy making within public sector professionalized bureaucracies, such as universities and hospitals (Mintzberg, 1989). They are 'honeycomb' organizations in which small self-contained cells emerge and differentiate themselves in a relatively unplanned manner. While these conditions are resistant to standard planning based techniques, decision making is not highly random but is patterned by intense cultural socialization, norm bound behaviour, elaborated professional ideologies which stress autonomy, institutions of self regulation and a powerful college of senior professionals. Such professionals have low loyalty to their employing organization but high loyalty to an external 'invisible college' of professional colleagues located elsewhere.

At its most extreme this leads to the view that settings such as hospitals and universities may be seen as 'organized anarchies' where serendipitous forms of decision making (the 'garbage can' model) predominate (Cohen et al., 1972). The degree of purposeful behaviour is low and there is little patterning of decision making. Participants dip in and out of decision making processes, often selling pet solutions to invented 'problems'. Empirical support for this model in the private sector is relatively modest (Eisenhardt and Zbaracki, 1992), but it is possible that the model could fit highly professionalized public sector settings.

So how does strategic management and change ever take place within such organizations? One motor is deprofessionalization whereby previously dominant professional groups lose power and autonomy, in the face of tighter legislative constraints or sharper market forces. Such deprofessionalization may be occurring to American medicine, leading to the evolution of new decision making systems (Greer, 1984) which complement the traditional professionally-based system. Strategic management decisions with major investment implications (for example, an expensive new piece of equipment) here rest with an empowered senior managerial cadre or boards of trustees rather than segments of professionals. A second motor is that a new group of professional managerial hybrids (Montgomery, 1990; FitzGerald, 1994; Thorne, 1997) emerges that links the clinical and the managerial worlds. Such clinical managers undergo a secondary socialization into management after their primary training as clinicians and are comfortable with the use of management concepts, including models of strategic management. A third scenario is that purely professional leadership groups act strategically in the face of a frank crisis and threat to remove the autonomy of professionals (as in the case of UK medicine), leading to an acceleration of internally sponsored reform proposals and new modes of self regulation. These changes are strategic in scale as they

cross the traditional boundaries thrown up by a large number of distinct professional segments, but they are designed to preserve the autonomy of the profession as a whole against managerial incursions.

Many of the received analyses of strategy making within professionalized organizations date from the 1970s. Some more recent accounts suggest a sharpening of the strategic management capacity of some public sector professionalized bureaucracies as the degree of patterning in effect increases and the managerial 'grip' on these organizations tightens. Clark (1998) describes an emergent subtype of 'entrepreneurial' universities, characterized by a strong corporate core as well as the traditional departmentally based periphery.

A Critique: Strategic Management as Novel Discourse

A number of writers now agree that the language of strategy has recently diffused widely within current public sector organizations (Nutt and Backoff, 1992; Moore, 1995; Ferlie et al., 1996; Joyce, 1999; Thorne, 1999). The chapter takes a relatively benign view of this trend, arguing that many of the key models of strategic management can be usefully adapted to reflect the senior managerial tasks now undertaken within current public sector organizations. Others take a more critical view, in line with broadly based radical analyses of the growth of strategic management within the private sector (Knights and Morgan, 1991). Managerial innovations such as new techniques of strategic management are a subjective instrument of ideological dominance rather than an objective reflection of managerial tasks.

Using perspectives derived from critical theory, Laughlin (1991) and Broadbent et al. (1991) see NPM style reforms as an alien discourse and a form of cultural colonization by a hegemonic private sector. However, they predict that public sector professionals will retain control over their front line work practices and that these ideas will have only a peripheral impact. NPM ideas should be seen more as an expression of a dominant managerial ideology than a set of useful models and techniques.

Thorne (1999) highlights the growth of strategic management talk within the current public sector, characterizing it as a newly dominant discourse. It is a constitutive part of a major power shift (Knights and Morgan, 1991) whereby new public sector elites such as general managers and non executive directors increase their power still further by creating a private language (thus colonizing new discursive spaces) which makes a claim to overall organizational control. Professionals who have moved into management have also been drawn into the new discourse and this serves to cement their new alliance with general managerial elites.

But how constitutive is the language of strategy or does it rather reflect prior restructuring driven by the world of policy? The radical critique can itself be criticized for overestimating the role of management ideas within the rise of the NPM. Public sector restructuring was initially highly policy and practice led, provoked by fundamental changes in the political economy, and driven through by senior policy advisers who often had been practical businessmen. Only much later did the NPM as a concept emerge within the domain of management theory, more as an inductive description of what was happening within the field. Within the UK case, for example, large scale managerializing developments within the domain of policy and practice were evident from the early 1980s (Griffiths, 1983), yet the first academic text describing them in terms of the NPM did not appear until Hood (1991) and a bibliographic search indicates that the academic debate did not take off until the mid 1990s (Dawson and Dargie, 1999). Management theory has lagged behind changes in policy and practice, rather than led them.

'QUASI STRATEGY' WITHIN THE CURRENT PUBLIC SECTOR – A FUTURE RESEARCH AGENDA

So the greater use of strategic management models within current public sector settings reflects a convergence with private sector forms of organization and modes of management. Some inter-sectoral differences remain (such as the greater level of political control, the absence of fully developed markets or prices, mandated forms of provision, the importance of due

process as well as outputs), but these are diminishing as hybrid forms of organization (such as public/private alliances) become more common. Within this perspective, the devolution of decision making to local managers contains a genuine element and should not be seen purely as rhetoric. As a result, the scope for strategic managerial choice and behaviour has increased. The presence of the language and techniques of strategic management within the public sector does not therefore represent an ideological artefact, but reflects background shifts to the organization of work.

Just as we have seen the growth of 'quasi markets' within many public sectors, so we are now seeing the growth of 'quasi strategy' with the distinctive modification of generic strategic management models and tools within public sector organizations. This field is in a highly emergent state – and old models no longer apply – so that new streams of research and enquiry are now badly needed. One way of encouraging the creation of such a research agenda is to advance a set of high level propositions which might guide future debate.

Proposition 1: There is Substantial Convergence between the Managerial Activities Undertaken by Current Public Sector Agencies and those Typical of Private Sector Organizations

Inter sectoral convergence is not merely cosmetic in nature but a trend of some breadth and depth. In essence, the public sector is moving towards more business like models of organization and management. The concept of 'quasi strategy' applies only where there are conditions which support this transition of a public sector agency to firm like status. Argumentation and research are needed to define these parameters theoretically and to estimate their prevalence empirically. Critics may well argue that this perspective assumes that major change is occurring when in fact it is not. Candidate processes which might trigger such convergence include:

1 developing and powerful quasi markets; market based processes of resource allocation replacing plans; public sector organizations positioning themselves in relation to these developed quasi markets; market entrance and exit occurs; these quasi market forces are not damped down politically;

2   shifts in property rights (growing flows of
    private finance) and governance regimes;
    creation of public/private hybrids; emer-
    gence of long-term contracts enforceable
    in the courts regulating such hybrids; these
    contracts reduce the scope for political or
    governmental influence;
3   a 'hands off' judicial or regulatory system
    so that demands for due process, audit and
    review are contained to those levels preva-
    lent in the private sector; a move to 'light
    touch' forms of regulation;
4   a managerial presence and cadre across
    public service organizations which prevent
    the old 'garbage can' processes from
    reemerging, perhaps implying the loss of
    power by previously dominant public
    sector professional groupings and their
    incorporation within the organization; the
    presence of a strategic management knowl-
    edge base and capacity;
5   a strong corporate identity and culture so
    that a strategy is enacted in behaviour
    across the whole organization; a reduction
    in the multiple objectives and large range
    of autonomous stakeholders characteristic
    of the old public sector.

   These (or other) convergence conditions can
be traced to assess the degree to which inter-
sectoral convergence is occurring. Where there
are signs of movement on all or most dimensions, then there might well be a rapid growth
of strategic management activity and capacity.

Proposition 2: Decision Makers within the Public Sector Have Enhanced Discretion to Manage Strategically

A second condition for the emergence of quasi
strategic behaviour is a real and sustained
devolution of authority from politicians and
civil servants to local managers. Such devolution should include a strategic as well as an
operational dimension, where local managers
enjoy the freedom to reposition public service
agencies as a whole. The decentralization of
managerial authority is often proclaimed in
current public sector reform efforts, but sceptics argue that politicians will never give away
real control and that top down accountability
regimes will remain dominant.

   So there is a need to discover whether
processes of devolution are real or merely

rhetorical, and whether they extend to the
strategic domain. Tracing the career of
strategic issues would be one approach to
investigating this problem. Another method
would be to examine the governance structures
which mediate between local managers and
politicians, and how these may be changing.
For example, are the local boards which govern public sector agencies accorded enhanced
strategic roles? Who is on these boards and
how are they appointed? Where there is an
increased flow of private finance into public
sector settings, what happens to property rights
and accountability regimes? How are the contracts governing these public/private transactions written and how are they to be enforced,
in the event of dispute?

Proposition 3: There are New Models of Strategic Management Which Can Usefully be Applied and Developed within Current Public Sector Organizations

This chapter has confirmed – but within the
context of the public sector – that there is not
just one strategic management literature but
many (Mintzberg et al., 1998). Table 13.3
offers a framework for assessing various strategic management models within private sector,
NPM and traditional public administration settings respectively. As might be expected, the
NPM literature represents a hybrid field
between perspectives traditionally associated
with the private sector and those which have
emerged within the old public administration
settings. It is here argued that the four models
in the middle of the spectrum show most
promise and need more development work
within current public sector settings: industrial
economics; resource based model of the firm;
process models of strategy; and implementation and strategy making within professionalized organizations. The task of theoretical
renewal is a considerable one if the public
sector is shifting in the manner suggested by
this chapter and work has as yet only just started.

   On one end of the spectrum presented in
Table 13.3, highly rationalistic models (such
as corporate planning) have been heavily critiqued, yet survive in practice. The key question here is why so much management
research has had such little impact on managerial practice. On the other end of the spectrum,
very loosely coupled models (such as 'garbage

Table 13.3   *A framework for assessing strategy models on a cross sectoral basis*

Model	Private sector literature	NPM literature	Public administration literature
Corporate planning	Criticized – much survives but not dominant	Much criticized but dominant in practice	Much criticized but dominant in practice
Industrial economics	Increasingly influential from the 1980s	Emerging with quasi markets	Absent
Resource based model	Increasingly influential from the 1990s	Emerging with 'core competences'	Absent
Process models of strategy making and implementation	Apparent from the 1970s – but not dominant	Very strong	Very strong from the 1970s
Professionalized organizations	Present but not dominant	Strong – but now more assertive management	Strong – often invented here!
Garbage can models	Weak – little empirical support	Weak – little empirical support	Strong – often invented here!
Critical management	Theory leads to practice; minority undercurrent – rejected by the 'mainstream'	Practice leads to theory; minority undercurrent – rejected by the 'mainstream'	Absent

can' theories) no longer fit the more managed nature of NPM organizations.

The middle grouping of theories outlined in Table 13.3 is then of especial interest. Accessing these theories, it will be particularly interesting to explore such themes as: What is the nature of strategic decision making and competitive forces within quasi markets? What are the core competences or internal resources of a public sector agency? How is strategy made and enacted within a public sector setting? Does the presence of public sector professionals continue to shape the process of strategy making or is there a move to a more corporate form?

Proposition 4: Public Sector Professionals Will be Increasingly Incorporated within the Organization

The behaviour and indeed power base of the many public sector professions should be seen as a major theme in its own right. With the privatization of old economic functions and a buoyant human service core, current public sectors are highly professionalized organizations. This includes the presence of elite professions (medicine, law, accounting), mass professions (nursing, teaching, social work) and indeed the new professions (IT, marketing, management

consultancy). It is clear that strategic change and management within highly professionalized settings poses particular issues and challenges (Brock et al., 1999).

Traditionally the elite professions (such as medicine) have been accorded a high level of autonomy in working practices so that they have not been incorporated fully within public sector organizations which instead resemble a professionalized bureaucracy. Such disaggregation could be seen at its most extreme in large scale and complex organizations with many professions and professional segments (such as a hospital) which typically communicate poorly and engage in turf disputes. In addition, professional and managerial arenas here remained largely separated so that strategic management was highly problematic. The result is that incremental change may be pervasive at a micro level, but that strategic change across the organization remains highly underdeveloped.

The development of a strong strategic management capacity implies major reductions in these traditional behaviours and power bases. There are various processes which might lead to this outcome. One would be a frank process of deprofessionalization, either through the growth of sharper market forces or through the actions at a policy level of an increasingly hostile State. A second would be the growth of professional managerial hybrids (professionals who also undertake part-time managerial roles) which adopt the managerial agenda and take it to their professional colleagues. The knowledge base of these hybrids would look very different from a purely professional knowledge base, and would include much more education in management. The question here is whether these hybrids can attract a critical mass of support amongst rank and file professionals or whether they will remain an isolated outpost. A third might be the use of integrative tools (such as business process reengineering or a integrated client focus) which stimulate organizational-wide rather than segment-specific thinking. A fourth might be a reduction of top down performance pressures on public sector managers so that they are better able to look sideways to professional colleagues in their own agenda formation.

The progressive alignment of professional and managerial perspectives and agendas is then fundamental to the growth of strategic management capacity within the public sector and without such alignment, effective strategic management is unlikely. This theme clearly requires empirical tracking.

Proposition 5: Within Current Public Sectors, There Will be Continuing Variation between Settings and Jurisdictions

The convergence conditions outlined in proposition 1 may well vary between one agency and another (even within the same jurisdiction) and also between jurisdictions. Comparative work is needed to capture these tendencies and patterns. Even within the same jurisdiction, strategic management capacity may be easier to develop in those public sector settings which exhibit receptive conditions (that is, they are politically low profile, have a contained and focussed task, and do not contain strong professional groups).

Comparative work between jurisdictions is also needed as the experience of even neighbouring countries may sharply differ. The underlying principles lying behind public sector reform in the Netherlands, for example, appear to be radically different from the Anglo American model and to be based much more on participation and local networking (Kickert et al., 1997) rather than the NPM.

Within the more subjective realm of managerial thought, the diffusion of strategic management models and ideas within public sectors may also vary sharply. Is the use of these models, culturally specific to Anglo American cultures, linked to the presence of strong business schools and MBA programmes which have educated a new generation of public sector managers? Is there a similar use of strategic management models within other public sectors which are culturally distinct? Are these models 'home grown' or are they imported from Anglo American business schools?

Proposition 6: This New Field Requires the Use of a Mix of Exploratory Research Methods

This whole field is new and dynamic, so that many of the old models of decision making within the public sector no longer work. The field is also contested and controversial, as critics may well dispute the scale and significance of new forms of strategic behaviour within the public sector. A vigorous debate in theory is to be expected and welcomed. Institutionalists, for instance, would argue that the adoption of a language of strategic management is no more than a superficial badge of modernism, designed to increase the legitimacy of public service agencies in the eyes of market orientated governments. Political scientists may argue that the characteristic institutional architecture of the public sector has shifted much more modestly than management scholars assume. While such theoretical controversies are valuable and welcome, there are currently major empirical gaps in our knowledge of how current public sector organizations make strategy. The implication is that the field also requires an ambitious programme of primary empirical research, as opposed to secondary reviews of existing research.

The methods indicated are common to any emergent field within management studies which is trying to build a coherent knowledge base. Different research groups will prefer different methods, and at this stage methodological pluralism is indicated in order to get a range of different approaches up and running.

Ethnographies could be usefully employed initially to provide a richer picture of contemporary organizations and also to generate further propositions. 'High change' settings could be identified and studied as extreme cases where these processes can be seen with most clarity. Descriptive surveys across populations of public sector organizations would complement this qualitative work and provide basic statistical data on indicators of structure. Such work should proceed over time so as to generate a longitudinal data set. Comparative case studies are badly needed to identify patterns, and some of them should be of a considerable scale and sophistication (perhaps including international comparative studies). Texts such as annual reports could be subjected to contents analysis, perhaps to identify the key words and phrases which are recurrently used. Key documents such as contracts could also be collected and analysed, perhaps from a socio legal perspective.

Proposition 7: There is a Need for Two-Way Learning

In the 1980s and 1990s, much of the strategy literature was uni-directional and flowed from the private sector to the public sector. Sometimes the degree of adaptation required to the public sector context was underestimated. This is surprising as Eisenhardt and Zbaracki (1992) make the point that much of the early strategy literature (such as 'garbage can' theory) was developed in the non profit sector, and that there was if anything a need to bring in firms and markets further into the picture and to reduce the dependence on not for profit settings. Some classic implementation studies were also conducted in public sector settings (Pressman and Wildavsky, 1973; Alford, 1975), precisely because implementation processes were so complex and interesting. By the 1990s, the pendulum had swung sharply the other way and public sector settings have virtually disappeared from much of the new strategy literature. The public sector was seen as an alien setting where the ideas of strategic management could not apply.

By contrast, it is here argued that current public sector settings offer rich research sites for contemporary themes within the more general strategy literature, for example, such themes as the operation of relational markets,

the management of embedded social networks, the management of expert workers, and the barriers to the implementation of strategy within complex organizations. The organization and management of the public sector has changed to a greater extent than is realized by many strategic management scholars. Such organizations undertake societally strategic roles, are often research friendly and keen to use the results of research to improve their own managerial practice. The research and learning process should thus be much more two-way in nature: the current public sector may well be the increasing recipient of strategic management models and techniques but it also has much to give the discipline of strategy.

REFERENCES

Abrahamson, E. (1991) 'Managerial fads and fashions', *Academy of Management Review*, 16(3): 586–612.
Alford, R. (1975) *Health Care Politics*. London: University of Chicago Press.
Allison, G. T. (1993) 'Public and private management – are they fundamentally alike in all unimportant respects?', in J. L. Perry and K. L. Kraemer (eds), *Public Management – Public and Private Perspectives*. CA: Mayfield Publishing.
Argyris, C. and Schon, D. (1978) *Organisational Learning*. Reading, MA: Addison Wesley.
Aucoin, P. (1995) *The New Public Management: Canada in Comparative Perspective*. Montreal: IPPR.
Barney, J. B. (1991) 'Firm resources and sustained competitive advantage', *Journal of Management*, 17: 99–120.
Barzelay, M. (1992) *Breaking Through Bureaucracy*. Berkeley: University of California Press.
Baumol, W. J., Panzar, J. C. and Willig, R. D. (1982) *Contestable Markets and the Theory of Industry Structure*. New York: Harcourt Brace Jovanovich.
Boston, J., Martin, J., Pallot, J. and Walsh, P. (1996) *Public Management: The New Zealand Model*. Auckland: Oxford University Press.
Bresser Pereira, L. C. (1998) *Reforma do Estado para a Cuidandania*. ENAP, Editora 34, Brazil: Sao Paolo.
Broadbent, J., Laughlin, R. and Read, S. (1991) 'Recent financial and administrative changes to the NHS: a critical theory analysis', *Critical Perspectives on Accounting*, 2: 1–29.
Brock, D., Powell, M. and Hinings, C. R. (1999) *Restructuring the Professional Organisation*. London: Routledge.
Bryson, J. M. (1988) *Strategic Planning for Public and Non Profit Organisations*. San Francisco: Jossey Bass.

Campbell, C. and Halligan, J. (1992) *Political Leadership in an Age of Constraint*. Pittsburgh: University of Pittsburgh Press.

Challis, L., Day, P., Klein, R. and Scrivens, E. (1994) 'Managing quasi markets – institutions of regulation', in W. Bartlett et al. (eds), *Quasi Markets in the Welfare State*. University of Bristol: School of Advanced Urban Studies.

Chandler, A. D. (1962) *Strategy and Structure*. Cambridge, MA: MIT Press.

Cherry, J. (1999) 'Strategic planning in Ministry of Defence agencies', MBA Project, London: Imperial College Management School.

Clark, B. (1998) *Entrepreneurial Universities: Pathways to Organisational Transformation*. Oxford: Pergamon.

Cohen, M. D., March, J. G. and Olsen, J. P. (1972) 'A garbage can model of organisational choice', *Administrative Science Quarterly*, 17: 1–25.

Dawson, S. and Dargie, C. (1999) 'New public management – an assessment and evaluation with special reference to UK health', *Public Management*, 1(4): 459–82.

du Gay, P. (1993) 'Entrepreneurial management in the public sector', *Work, Employment and Society*, 7(4): 643–8.

Dunleavy, P. and Hood, C. (1994) 'From old public administration to new public management', *Public Money and Management*, 14, July/Sept: 9–16.

Eisenhardt, K. M. and Zbaracki, M. J. (1992) 'Strategic decision making', *Strategic Management Journal*, 13, Special Issue: 79–98.

Ferlie, E., Ashburner, L., Fitzgerald, L. and Pettigrew, A. (1996) *The New Public Management in Action*. Oxford: Oxford University Press.

FitzGerald, L. (1994) 'Moving clinicians into management', *Journal of Management in Medicine*, 8(6): 32–44.

Freidson, E. (1970) *Professional Dominance – The Social Structure of Medical Care*. New York: Atherton Press.

Goold, M., Campbell, A. and Alexander, M. (1994) *Corporate Level Strategy*. New York: John Wiley.

Grant, R. M. (1998) *Contemporary Strategy Analysis*. 3rd edn. Oxford: Basil Blackwell.

Green, S. (1998) 'Strategic management initiatives in the civil service: a cross cultural comparison', *International Journal of Public Sector Management*, 11(7): 536–52.

Greer, A. (1984) 'Medical technology and professional dominance theory', *Social Science and Medicine*, 18: 809–17.

Greer, A. and Hoggett, P. (1997) *Patterns of Accountability Within Local Non Elected Bodies*. New York: Joseph Rowntree Foundation.

Griffiths, R. (1983) *Report of NHS Management Enquiry*. London: Department of Health.

Gunn, L. (1989) 'Public management: a third approach', *Public Money and Management*, 8: 21–5.

Hales, C. (1986) 'What do managers do? A critical review of the evidence', *Journal of Management Studies*, 23(1): 88–113.

Hamel, G. and Pralahad, C. K. (1990) 'The core competences of the corporation', *Harvard Business Review*, May/June: 79–91.

Hinings, C. R. and Greenwood, R. (1988) *The Dynamics of Strategic Change*. Oxford: Basil Blackwell.

Hinings, C. R., Brown, J. and Greenwood, R. (1991) 'Change in autonomous professional organisations', *Journal of Management Studies*, 28(4): 375–93.

Hood, C. (1991) 'A new public management for all seasons?', *Public Administration*, 69(1): 3–19.

Hood, C. (1995) 'The new public management in the 1980s – variations on a theme', *Accounting, Organisation and Society*, 20(2/3): 93–110.

Huxham, C. (ed.) (1996) *Creating Collaborative Advantage*. London: Sage.

Johnson, G. (1987) *Strategic Change and the Management Process*. Oxford: Basil Blackwell.

Johnson, G. and Scholes, K. (1993) *Exploring Corporate Strategy*. London: Prentice Hall.

Joyce, P. (1999) *Strategic Management for the Public Services*. Buckingham: Open University Press.

Kanter, R. M. (1994) 'Collaborative advantage: the art of alliances', *Harvard Business Review*, July/Aug: 96–108.

Kickert, W., Klijn, E. and Koppenjan, J. (eds) (1997) *Managing Complex Networks*. London: Sage.

Knights, D. and Morgan, G. (1991) 'Corporate strategy, organisations and subjectivity: a critique', *Organisation Studies*, 12(2): 251–73.

Laughlin, R. (1991) 'Can the information system for the NHS internal market work?', *Public Money and Management*, 11: 37–41.

Lynn, L. (1998) 'The new public management – how to turn a theme into a legacy', *Public Administration Review*, 58(3): 231–7.

Mahoney, J. and Pandian, R. (1992) 'The resource based view within the conversation of strategic management', *Strategic Management Journal*, 13: 363–80.

Miller, D. (1998) 'Configurations of strategy and structure: towards a synthesis', in S. Segal-Horn (ed.), *The Strategy Reader*. Oxford: Basil Blackwell.

Mintzberg, H. (1989) 'Crafting strategy', in *Mintzberg on Management*. London: Collier Macmillan.

Mintzberg, H. (1998) 'The structuring of organisations', in S. Segal-Horn (ed.), *The Strategy Reader*. Oxford: Basil Blackwell.

Mintzberg, H. and Waters, J. A. (1998) 'Of strategies, deliberate and emergent', in S. Segal-Horn (ed.), *The Strategy Reader*. Oxford: Basil Blackwell.

Mintzberg, H., Ahlstrand, B. and Lampel, J. (1998) *The Strategy Safari*. London: Prentice Hall.

Montgomery, K. (1990) 'A prospective look at the specialty of medical management', *Work and Occupations*, 17(2): 178–98.

Moore, M. (1995) *Creating Public Value – Strategic Management in Government*. Cambridge, MA: Harvard University Press.

Nutt, P. and Backoff, R. W. (1992) *Strategic Management of Public and Third Sector Organisations*. San Francisco: Jossey Bass.

OECD (1997) *Economic Survey – The United States of America*. Paris: OECD.

OECD (1998a) *Economic Survey – Germany*. Paris: OECD.

OECD (1998b) *Economic Survey – Sweden*. Paris: OECD.

OECD (1999) *Economic Survey – France*. Paris: OECD.

Osborne, D. and Gaebler, T. (1992) *Reinventing Government: How the Entrepreneurial Spirit is Transforming the Public Sector*. Reading, MA: Addison-Wesley.

Ostler, K. (1995) *Strategic Management for Non Profit Organisations*. New York: Oxford University Press.

Pettigrew, A. M. (1973) *The Politics of Organisational Decision Making*. London: Tavistock.

Pettigrew, A. M. (1985) *The Awakening Giant: Continuity and Change in ICI*. Oxford: Basil Blackwell.

Pettigrew, A. and Whipp, R. (1991) *Managing Change for Competitive Success*. Oxford: Basil Blackwell.

Pettigrew, A., Ferlie, E. and McKee, L. (1992) *Shaping Strategic Change*. London: Sage.

Pollitt, C. (1990) *The New Managerialism and the Public Services: The Anglo American Experience*. Oxford: Basil Blackwell.

Porter, M. (1980) *Competitive Strategy*. New York: Free Press.

Porter, M. (1996) 'What is strategy?', *Harvard Business Review*, 74: 61–78.

Power, M. (1997) *The Audit Society: Rituals of Verification*. Oxford: Oxford University Press.

Pressman, J. and Wildavsky, A. (1973) *Implementation*. Berkeley: University of California Press.

Scally, G. and Donaldson, L. (1998) 'Clinical governance and the drive for quality improvement in the new NHS in England', *British Medical Journal*, 317: 61–5.

Smith, R. P. and Perry, J. L. (1985) 'Strategic management in public and private organisations: implications of distinctive contexts and constraints', *Academy of Management Review*, 10(2): 276–86.

Stewart, J. and Clarke, M. (1987) 'The public services orientation: issues and dilemmas', *Public Administration*, 65(2): 161–78.

Stewart, J. and Walsh, K. (1992) 'Change in the management of public services', *Public Administration*, 70: 499–518.

Thorne, M. (1997) 'Being a clinical director: first among equals or just a go between?', *Health Services Management Research*, 10(4): 205–16.

Thorne, M. (1999) 'What is the use of strategy?' Paper for the Third International Research Symposium on Public Management, University of Aston, Bristol: Bristol Business School.

Weick, K. (1978) *The Social Psychology of Organising*. Reading, MA: Addison Wesley.

Whittington, R. (1993) *What is Strategy and Does it Matter?* London: Routledge.

Whitley, R. (1989) 'On the nature of managerial tasks – their distinguishing characteristics and organisation', *Journal of Management Studies*, 26(3): 209–40.

Zifcak, S. (1994) *New Managerialism: Administrative Reform in Whitehall and Canberra*. Buckingham: Open University Press.

14

Entrepreneurship, Small Firms and Wealth Creation: A Framework Using Real Options Reasoning

Ultimately, strategy and entrepreneurship researches share a common interest in economic performance. Both streams are commensurately concerned with economic change, particularly change brought about by Schumpeter's (1942) 'waves of creative destruction'. My objective in this chapter is to show how an entrepreneurial research agenda has much that is of interest for strategic management research (McGrath and MacMillan, 2000), and show how real options reasoning can help provoke interesting questions and new research directions for both streams.

DEFINITIONAL AND METHODOLOGICAL QUAGMIRES

There is no consensus whatsoever on a precise definition for what entrepreneurship is, or on the distinction between entrepreneurship and the founding and management of a small or medium sized enterprise (SME) (Cunningham and Lischeron, 1991). Definitions often center on new organizations and their founder(s), on the premise that new firms drive economic change and therefore productivity increases and new wealth.[1] Unhappily, research relevant to

economic change and wealth creation is often not labeled 'entrepreneurship research', and research that is so labeled is often marginalized by its indiscriminate focus on new, small, firms, without any particular significance for economic change. This has led to fragmented research and only piecemeal understanding of the relationship between startup firms and wealth creation. The reality is that new companies that eventually transform economies are a tiny sub-group of all startups (Aldrich, 1999).

Most small firms remain that way. Harrison (1994) for instance finds that only 735 out of 245,000 firms (0.3%) accounted for 75% of the jobs created by all new firms identified by Dun and Bradstreet. Brander et al. (1998), in an exhaustive Canadian study, found that only 0.2% of startups employed more than 100 employees within 10 years.[2] Dennis (1997) found that less than half of the millions of startups in his study (47.5%) have a separate business telephone number; and three out of four employed only the founder. Only 11% of all entrants employed someone other than the owner and were located outside the home. Each year, only about 30,000 firms receive funding beyond that available through 'friends, family and fools' sources (Ason, 1999). An even smaller number – perhaps 250 to 500 firms – go as far as an initial public offering. Few of these go on to effect economic transformations.

In short, the high-growth firm that creates substantial wealth is unusual, located at the extreme right tail of a highly skewed firm size distribution. The wealth creation effects of entrepreneurship thus occur under conditions of high uncertainty in which large numbers of businesses are started, most don't grow, and a very few contribute a disproportionate societal upside. Conventional social science methodologies that examine means and central tendencies are not, as a consequence, appropriate (MacMillan and Katz, 1992).

Given this pattern, I propose that real options reasoning, which has been applied to important problems in strategy, also offers a powerful metaphor for analyzing the entrepreneurial process (see for instance Mitchell and Hamilton, 1988; Kogut, 1991; McGrath, 1996, 1999). Startups are analogous to options (Dixit and Pindyck, 1994). They are investments in real assets that preserve the right to make a decision at some point in the future. Should conditions not prove favorable, resources can be withdrawn and redeployed elsewhere, at a loss only of the amount of the sunk cost invested in the business at the time.

Characterizing startups as real options is consistent with observed aspects of the entrepreneurial process. Options increase in value when uncertainty increases, because the potential downside loss remains constant, while the upside performance distribution increases. Similarly, under uncertainty (Knight, 1921) new businesses can be highly valued. Consider internet stocks during their boom period. The huge potential upside of the area attracted investment, even though many of the firms in the arena faced a high hazard of failing, and many, in retrospect, did fail. No matter – as with financial options, failures (in the sense of options that are terminated or allowed to expire) are not only acceptable, but expected (McGrath, 1999). Just as not all options are worth exercising, not all businesses are worth pursuing over the long run. Finally, just as with financial options, returns to investments in startups are asymmetric, in that very few startups generate large returns.

In this chapter, I will explore how options reasoning may be systematically applied to a range of entrepreneurial problems, and discuss

the resulting issues for further research in entrepreneurship and strategy.

AN ORGANIZING FRAMEWORK FOR ENTREPRENEURIAL PROCESSES

Start-Ups and Creative Destruction

Venkataraman (1997) encourages scholars to focus on economic change as the distinctive core process of entrepreneurship. Because options investments proceed sequentially, we can build on this idea to specify four processes through which entrepreneurial activity leads to economic change, which I use as a means of organizing a discussion of the diverse relevant literature.

The first process involves identifying opportunities to take out options. Building on Hayek's (1945) insight that knowledge is asymmetrically distributed among individuals in a society, Kirzner (1997) has called the identification of opportunities a process of 'discovery' by 'alert' entrepreneurs. Unlike search in behavioral learning theory, opportunity identification does not occur in response to a problem in achieving goals. Rather, it is a process of what Bowman and Hurry (1993) termed 'recognition' of the value of shadow options. The natural culmination of the opportunity recognition process is investment in an option, which I will consider here to be investment in a new business (either an independent start-up or a corporate venture, consistent with Gartner, 1988).

Having recognized an opportunity and invested to create an option, the next process involves reduction of uncertainty, in order to determine whether further investment to exercise the option is warranted. During this process, new businesses are usefully characterized as experiments (Starr and MacMillan, 1990). Uncertainty can either be reduced as time passes and more information becomes available, or by an actor making investments, to create additional information or to strategically amplify the value of the entrepreneurial option (McGrath, 1997).

Uncertainty reduction figures prominently in research exploring patterns of founding and growth among new firms. Fichman and Levinthal (1991), for instance, found that

Table 14.1 *Real options reasoning and entrepreneurial processes*

Core processes → Level of analysis	Identification of an option: Alertness	Formation of a new business: Uncertainty reduction	Growth, development and profit: Exercise	Business closure: Termination
Individual	1. Factors influencing individual recognition of opportunity	2. Factors influencing individual perception of and reduction of uncertainty	3. Factors influencing individual profit from exercising an entrepreneurial option	4. Factors that influence individual choices to terminate or close a business
Network	5. How network ties influence the opportunity recognition process	6. How network ties influence uncertainty reduction for a new venture	7. How do network ties influence the flow of profits to investment in entrepreneurial ventures?	8. Network ties and the closure of or exit from a venture
Organizational	9. How do members of organizations recognize opportunities?	10. Factors influencing the organizational commitment to a new venture, after uncertainty is reduced	11. How organizations capture rents from investments in ventures	12. How do organizations allow exit from less productive businesses?
Regional	13. Local policies that facilitate the new business formation process within a region	14. Regional policies that encourage growth and investment after uncertainty is reduced	15. Issues having to do with regional distribution of entrepreneurial proceeds	16. Resource redirection and adjustment cost absorption at a local level
Institutional	17. Institutional payoff regimes	18. Institutional factors that help or hinder entrepreneurial growth	19. Issues having to do with institutional distribution of entrepreneurial proceeds	20. Resource redirection and adjustment cost absorption at an institutional level

new firms experienced a 'honeymoon' after founding. During this period, initial resource endowments are consumed to validate (or not) initial expectations. After the initial honeymoon period, new ventures experience a liability of adolescence manifest in high hazard of failure.

If the option continues to appear to have value through the uncertainty reduction process, it can be exercised. Exercising an entrepreneurial option implies making the follow-on investments necessary to extract profit streams from it. This might imply rapid growth. Alternatively, value can be extracted through other means, such as sale of the fledgling business to a more established one, equivalent to trading or selling the option.

The fourth process involves the termination of businesses that were launched, but which are no longer viable. Although this process is often ignored when entrepreneurship is being

investigated, it is core to the Schumpeterian idea of creative destruction in economic change (see Lichtenberg, 1998). An outcome of the closure process is the creation of slack, or unallocated, resources, which can be redirected.

The processes of entrepreneurial change involve actors at different levels of analysis. Just as the general manager is the primary actor upon which strategic management research focuses, the individual business founder is central to entrepreneurship research. Enormous energy has been expended on studies of entrepreneurial individuals, unfortunately with inconclusive results (Gartner, 1988).[3] Recently, researchers have shifted their attention away from understanding who acts to create economic change toward understanding the *behavior* of such actors (Aldrich and Zimmer, 1986; Birley, 1985; Burt, 1992). Accompanying this shift has been an increased attention in the literature away from a preoccupation with the individual level, to a broader concern with networks, with entrepreneurial organizations (or organizations that would like to become entrepreneurial), to regions and to institutions. Unlike strategic management research, entrepreneurship research at these different levels often attempts to derive policy implications, on the premise that entrepreneurial change can be, if not directed, then channeled, in socially productive ways (see Baumol, 1993).

I use the four processes of real options reasoning operating at five different levels of analysis to flesh out an organizing framework, presented in Table 14.1. The rows categorize behaviors depending upon whether they relate to the individual, network, organizational, regional or institutional level.

INDIVIDUAL LEVEL OF ANALYSIS

1. Factors Influencing Individual Recognition of Opportunity

Processes in this cell involve those factors that influence individuals to identify that an opportunity exists. In a world of perfect information, where everyone would know everything known to others, there would be little for an entrepreneur to do, an objection often leveled at economic characterizations of entrepreneurship (Baumol, 1993). Hayek (1945) took issue with the perfect information hypothesis, arguing that in a competitive market economy, knowledge is unevenly dispersed. Kirzner (1973, 1979) built upon this idea to argue that 'alert' entrepreneurs engage in non-random discovery. Discovery, he claimed, lies 'midway between that of the deliberately produced information in standard search theory and that of sheer windfall gain generated by pure chance' (1997: 72). Whether opportunity recognition is a purely random process, or whether it is amenable to systematic study and theory building, continues to be the subject of debate. Some authors argue that entrepreneurs are of a type. Hence, McGrath and MacMillan (1992) found that even across different cultures, entrepreneurs tended to share certain beliefs (such as a greater belief in the efficacy of individual effort) to a greater extent than did a contrast sample of non-entrepreneurs.

Other researchers have pointed to the breathtaking array of ways entrepreneurs find

opportunity (Vesper, 1990) and have concluded that the factors that determine which will be identified and acted upon must lie in the cognitive processes of entrepreneurs (Baron, 1998; Palich and Bagby, 1995). Unfortunately, as Shaver and Scott (1991) observe, much cognitively-oriented entrepreneurship research is conceptually or methodologically flawed. They observe (1991: 39) that it has been 'discarded, debunked, or at the very least, found to have been measured ineffectively'.

An exception to the largely disappointing body of work on entrepreneurial traits is work that jointly considers the entrepreneur's characteristics and the context. Shane (2000), for instance, found in a field study that prior experience strongly influenced entrepreneurs' perception of opportunity. Amit et al. (1995) found evidence that low opportunity cost and lack of other alternatives are associated with the urge to start.

The new economy may allow us to test premises involving opportunity recognition more easily than has previously been possible. For instance, there is some evidence that creativity and divergent thinking can be purposefully enhanced by exposure to variety (see Woodman et al., 1993 for a review). When virtual environments make exposure to variety inexpensive and broadly available, we might expect to see many more people identify interesting ideas for starting a business.

The implications of the new economy for individual learning and coping capacity, however, are not clear. We may find that rather than fuelling an entrepreneurial explosion, at some point our information saturated society will face an entirely new limitation on entrepreneurial capacity – the ability to sort through the vast array of inputs and to synthesize them into meaningful wholes. The role which cognitive limits play in the entrepreneurs' ability to synthesize, the double-edged sword of relentless variety generation and the effects of information being readily and cheaply disseminated are all worthwhile subjects for future research.

Another emerging issue relevant to the opportunity recognition process involves an increasingly visible group of 'habitual' entrepreneurs (MacMillan, 1986; Wright et al., 1999). They view their primary job as starting businesses that can then be sold to other organizations. A fascinating example is Idealab, a company that incubates and guides internet startups such as eToys, Free PC and GoTo.com. Similar incubating organizations spawned dozens of startups in the late 1990s, and have created critical connections between founders, venture capitalists and other investors (Armstrong and Grover, 1999). Rather than being represented as unusual or unique events, the economic role of entrepreneurs is increasingly regarded as business-as-usual, and taken for granted as legitimate. In short, at least in the United States, we are beginning to see evidence of the institutionalization of entrepreneurship.

The problem is that when entrepreneurial activity becomes business-as-usual, actors can easily fall victim to the same problems of myopia and competence entrapment that bedevil more established organizations. Previous experience is not always an asset. Starr and Bygrave (1992) document liabilities of previous entrepreneurial experience, including inhibited recognition of problems, unwillingness to take in disconfirming information, a tendency to stop making new network ties and a tendency to operate later ventures less parsimoniously than earlier ones.

This suggests an intriguing area of overlap with conventional strategy, namely, problems in the purposive pursuit of novel business ideas, whether as startups or corporate ventures. Clearly, understanding those factors, psychological and otherwise, that lead to the pursuit of opportunity continues to be a compelling issue for the entrepreneurial research agenda.

2. Factors Influencing Individual Perception of and Reduction of Uncertainty

Traditionally, entrepreneurial uncertainty reduction was characterized in terms of individual boldness or courage. Founders were assumed to be risk-takers, who engage in activities that more rational (or cautious) individuals would not – in other words, they don't reduce uncertainty, they simply take action notwithstanding. This characterization of entrepreneurs as risk-takers has had little empirical support (Brockhaus, 1980). Some recent studies, however, suggest that

business founders do differ systematically from non-founders in their approach to managing uncertainty.

Corman et al. (1988), for instance, found that two-thirds of the entrepreneurs in their sample of high technology venture founders did not perceive themselves to be doing anything risky, because they felt they understood the technological and market requirements needed to succeed. Busenitz and Barney (1997) and Busenitz (1999) found further evidence suggesting that cognitive factors may make entrepreneurs comfortable with investing under uncertainty. Founders were more likely to generalize from small samples and to exhibit overconfidence than were a matched sample of managers working in large firms. An interesting implication is that from the perspective of the larger society, such cognitive errors may have great utility. Were they to be stamped out and a more realistic assessment of probabilities to occur, many founders might never try to pursue an entrepreneurial option.

Of course, it is also possible to make downside risk less painful when the downside is minimized, a logical application of option thinking to the new venture. One way of doing this is to make investments with extreme parsimony, minimizing sunk costs and commitments to fixed capital expenditures (Hambrick and MacMillan, 1984; MacMillan, 1985). The recent wave of internet startups illustrates the point: since it is possible to set up shop at no cost other than opportunity costs to the founder, the downside to potential founders (at least in a full-employment economy) is limited. Such low downside risk is commonly associated with entrepreneurial environments – witness the famous Silicon Valley phrase, 'fail fast, fail cheap, move on' (Saxenian, 1994).

Interestingly, we have not made much progress on resolving the questions raised by Knight (1921), who long ago argued that a distinguishing characteristic of the entrepreneurial process is uncertainty, in which neither outcomes nor their probability can be predicted. Scholars are still divided roughly into two camps. One concludes that business founders ignore the potential for downside loss. The other suggests that founders instead engage in systematic forms of uncertainty reduction or downside risk avoidance. The debate remains unresolved.

3. Factors Influencing Individual Profit from Exercising an Entrepreneurial Option

A taken-for-granted assumption, at least in most of the United States-based research on entrepreneurship, is that entrepreneurs are highly motivated by the pursuit of profit. Given the widespread consensus on this point, it is surprising that little systematic research has examined why some routes to profit are preferred to others. Many vehicles exist. A founder can be compensated for services rendered, can sell rights to company equity (through an IPO, acquisition by or merger with another firm or to investors), can be offered stock options, or can be paid some form of franchise, royalty or licensing fee. The choices are often mutually exclusive. Given that the decision to grow, invest, or sell a business directs the disposition of knowledge and assets, scholars interested in economic change through entrepreneurship need to be more concerned with better understanding the considerations that influence the choice.

An entrepreneurs' preferred strategy may be influenced by fads such as 'hot markets' (Abrahamson, 1996; Ibbotson and Jaffe, 1975) and by institutional factors that make certain exercise routes more or less easy to pursue. In Japan, for instance, financial markets have not yet embraced the IPO, and other routes are often blocked. Such restrictions are often blamed for creating an environment hostile to entrepreneurship (Birley, 1997). Among the issues are that establishing a value for an unproven venture is difficult, leaving the profit to be captured the subject of negotiation.

Negotiating increases the potential for opportunism and rent-seeking. Interpersonal and psychological processes can then have enormous influence over the realized price of a business. The temptation on the part of founders to artificially seek to achieve high valuations can be enormous, leaving investors vulnerable to the 'winners' curse'. This refers to the phenomenon that when bidding for an asset of unknown worth, the winning bid will tend to exceed the value of the asset (Thaler, 1992; Samuelson and Bazerman, 1985). From a societal perspective, this matters because funds that could otherwise be invested productively instead may flow to those who make the most compelling sales pitch.

Conventionally (Vesper, 1990) people started a business to grow it and run it. This is no longer the dominant model among entrepreneurs. In some instances, founders now sometimes simply demonstrate the feasibility of the business proposition, then sell out. Thus, rather than having a long-term interest in the business, a founder might view it as a transient engagement. A policy question this raises is whether large firms are actually co-opting entrepreneurial enterprises rather than engaging in competition with them. If new businesses are critical for the productivity-enhancing change they provoke, what happens to productivity if entrepreneurs prefer to sell out rather than challenging incumbents' dominance?

4. Factors that Influence Individual Choices to Terminate or Close a Business

The activities in this cell have to do with option expiration, specifically, the factors that lead individuals to shut down businesses. Despite recognition of the learning benefits of intelligent failures (Sitkin, 1992), our theory for the most part continues to operate with a profound anti-failure bias (McGrath, 1999). In this, the entrepreneurship literature is consistent with other bodies of thought in organization studies.

In the ecological literature, for instance, exit is normally equated with firm-level 'death' (see Baum, 1996 for a review), and is considered to be the product of external selection forces, most commonly resource starvation. In the strategy literature, similarly, exits have typically been equated with the failure of a business, and have been considered negative outcomes (Suarez and Utterback, 1995). If, however, exit can be thought of as a strategic choice, many of the theoretical assumptions that underlie our ideas about business failure may simply be wrong. Gimeno et al. (1997), for instance, found that exit decisions were based upon individuals' alternative opportunities, regardless of whether their businesses were performing well or not. It is high time that assumptions regarding failure and selection were more precisely examined.

An aspect that has received very little attention is how entrepreneurs themselves define failure, and how this influences behavior such as persistence in the face of adversity. This would be a nice opportunity for psychological research to inform work in entrepreneurship. Attribution theory, for instance, focuses on how people's interpretation of outcomes influences their propensity to persist with a course of action. Several highly regarded studies have found linkages between individuals' attributions and their later behavior, finding that some attributions systematically generate a 'helpless' state, while others stimulate greater effort (Heider, 1958; Weiner and Kukla, 1970; Dweck and Leggett, 1988; Wortman and Brehm, 1975).

Cardon and McGrath (2001) extended these ideas to entrepreneurship. Results from a sample of pre-start entrepreneurs suggested that there is considerable variance in their predisposition to interpret negative events. If psychological variables affect the decision to persist, as it seems likely that they do, then characterizations of entrepreneurial failure as a Darwinist 'selection out' process misses a crucial explanatory construct. Similarly, characterizing those who persist as strategically astute may not reflect the whole picture either. It might be useful to apply insights from the escalation of commitment literature to this set of issues. For instance, Staw and Ross (1987) suggest ways in which the temptation to persist with a doomed effort can be addressed.

Relative to the considerable amount of work that has been done on the startup and growth processes of firms, individual actions relevant to business termination is relatively understudied and poorly understood. Given real options reasoning, failures may simply be a reasonable and expected part of the process, not an outcome to be avoided.

NETWORK LEVEL OF ANALYSIS

By the network level of analysis, I mean to touch upon phenomena that cannot be explained absent reference to ties between individuals and organizations.

5. How Network Ties Influence the Opportunity Recognition Process

Burt (1992) and many others (Castells, 1996; Granovetter, 1985) have suggested that the ties

between actors are as important for understanding the entrepreneurial process as the actors are themselves. An ongoing unresolved issue concerns whether weak or dense ties facilitate the recognition of an opportunity.

Some researchers have made strong arguments that weak ties facilitate opportunity identification (Granovetter, 1973). Looselycoupled relationships permit variance in perspective for each party, while greater distance between parties in terms of their knowledge bases improves the chances that novel ideas can move from actor to actor. Burt (1992) proposes that entrepreneurs spot opportunities by making connections across 'structural holes', meaning creating a tie between networks that are otherwise not connected. This suggests that weak ties and greater distance from others in one's network facilitate opportunity recognition.

The dilemma is that connections across networks can yield information that is of little value to a prospective entrepreneur because it is not relevant to a particular commercial problem-solving context. The work of von Hippel (1988) illustrates why weak ties can be a poor vehicle to opportunity recognition. He found that the source of innovative ideas come from dense ties, namely, from future customers. Because both customers and manufacturers shared a common base of information, mutual recognition of the benefits of a proposed solution can emerge quickly.

Dense, not weak, ties are similarly important in industries in which the work of recognizing opportunity is divided between large and small firms, and in which collective invention (Allen, 1983) represents a core process for technological advance. An example is the commercialization of biotechnology in the pharmaceutical industry. Today, much of the opportunity recognition is being done by entrepreneurial firms. Small firms are able to attract and reward stellar talent, while larger firms have the financial and marketing resources to successfully bring new drugs to market. The emergence of this division of entrepreneurial labor has been accompanied by increasing density of ties and better developed linkages between the networks of the small firms, the large firms, and their backers (Stuart et al., 1999).

Another, relatively unexplored, arena in which dense ties matter to the creation and recognition of opportunity concerns firms that compete in a network against networks of other firms. The most familiar form of this is when a network supporting a common standard faces off against an opposing group supporting a different standard. To the extent that the network makes opportunities more visible to all members, each member benefits from the adoption of the standard and improves the ability of the collective to recognize opportunities (Tushman and Rosenkopf, 1992). This again represents a situation in which dense, not weak, ties facilitate opportunity recognition.

Open questions for understanding opportunity recognition within and across networks thus involve when and with what consequences dense versus weak ties are useful, and at what stage in the evolution of a technology or market.

6. How Network Ties Influence Uncertainty Reduction for a New Venture

Arrow long ago observed that a fundamental problem for entrepreneurs is that resource commitments to a venture must be made by suppliers, customers, supporters and investors under uncertainty, because performance information will only be available in the future (Arrow, 1974). A taken-for-granted assumption is that social network ties are beneficial – allowing uncertainty to be reduced more quickly and at lower cost than could be accomplished by more arms-length transactions.

Research does suggest that network-based exchanges can provide entrepreneurs with critical information and resources. Social capital, or at least human capital in the form of previous experience (see Chandler and Hanks, 1998), can substitute for other kinds of capital in the startup process. Entrepreneurs might, for instance, use their social capital to create trusting relationships (Larson, 1992; McGee et al., 1995; Starr and MacMillan, 1990), which in turn allow them to address liabilities of newness and smallness through affiliations with well-established or prestigious network members (Stinchcombe, 1965).

Despite this general enthusiasm for the benefits of network affiliation, recent evidence suggests that whether social ties are beneficial or not may be a function of the level of uncertainty facing an entrepreneur. Venkataraman

and Van de Ven's research (1993) implies that it makes sense to leverage social capital *only* in the early stages of a new venture. As the venture progresses, parties base their decisions on economic criteria, and social capital has less impact. Ironically, the very network relationships that help to reduce uncertainty fade in importance with increasing certainty.

Uncertainty can further create confusion and mistrust as easily as positive social interchange. Potential stakeholders in a new business have few alternatives but to rely on the founding team for information, creating information asymmetry. Among the hazards are adverse selection, in which transaction partners are persuaded to commit resources to ventures which they would have avoided if they had accurate information, and moral hazard, in which entrepreneurs work out the best deal for themselves without regard to investor interests (see Amit et al., 1998). Information asymmetry creates incentives for misrepresentation (Cable and Shane, 1997).

A further open question with respect to the advantages of entrepreneurial networks has to do with tighter coupling created by investment connections. Venture capitalists often create relationships between the firms in their portfolios, for instance. Bygrave and Timmons (1992) reported that the top 61 venture capitalist firms out of a total of 464 represented 57% of the pool of venture capital in 1992. As a group, these top 61 had implemented 22% of all possible pairs of co-investment ties, with a much higher reported co-investment tie density as geographic density increased and business uncertainty increased.

Although it may seem like common sense for venture capitalists to form networks in which participants can share experience and information, there may be poorly understood dark sides to this activity. For one thing, while co-investing may reduce uncertainty, it potentially increases coordination and transaction costs, provides the incentive for selfish behavior and increases the likelihood of what Sahlman and Stevenson (1985) have termed 'capital market myopia'. This is the tendency for investors in capital markets to ignore the collective implications of their individual investment decisions. Investing together can create the illusion of greater certainty by reducing diversity of perspective.

Bringing portfolio firms together and sharing ideas and people between them induces tighter coupling within the portfolio. An unintended side effect is to create a situation in which single decisions affect multiple ventures in the portfolio. Real options reasoning predicts that this will decrease option value, because making a decision for one business affects others (Bowman and Hurry, 1993). Similarly, endorsements made by high-profile investors may direct the investment behavior of other investors, again increasing coupling between investments.

To attend to the nuances of entrepreneurial networks, scholars are going to have to go beyond identifying the presence of network ties to probing how ties are constructed and what sort of information flows between them at various stages in a venture. Electronic commerce may offer new vehicles to efficiently examine such processes. Networks based on electronic interchange, for instance, may be analytically tractable in that electronic communications act as visible tracers for interchanges that in traditional exchange are hard to track.

7. How Do Network Ties Influence the Flow of Profits to Investment in Entrepreneurial Ventures?

For profits to occur, an entrepreneurial venture must succeed in the creation of a transaction set (Venkataraman and Van de Ven, 1993). The transaction set refers to businesses' exchange partners (customers, suppliers, co-producers and so forth). One glaring gap in the literature concerns the implications of differences in the composition and behavior of transaction sets. As with the literature in strategy on strategic alliances, while we know a great deal about the conditions under which alliances between organizations are formed and broken, the 'so what' question has for the most part not been addressed (Gulati, 1998).

Although I have not found any empirical research to this effect, it stands to reason that major differences in realized outcomes relative to what network members expected might strain the mechanisms through which collective activity is governed, and that such disparities are more likely in high-variance entrepreneurial contexts. Even agreements that begin as cooperative may collapse in the event of unexpected upside results (in which partners might feel cheated of profits) or downside results (in which partners might feel resentful of losses).

A basic question has to do with how any rents emerging from investment in a venture are distributed between partners. We know little about how deals are cut under uncertainty and volatility. For businesses in general, Dyer and Singh (1998) advocate governance of exchange relationships to ensure equitable distribution of 'relational rents'. They concluded that self-enforcing mechanisms relying on social controls are more effective than those that rely on third party enforcement and formal controls. Most entrepreneurial firms, however, are disadvantaged in terms of power, legitimacy and resource depth. If equity is sought, this can be a difficult problem to navigate.

Outright acquisition of a smaller firm by a larger one is therefore an attractive way of using ties to profit. For the acquiring firm, however, the same dilemmas of internal opposition and resource allocation are as likely for an acquisition as for a new venture in-house. Loss of the small firm's talent may lead to an empty victory (Jemison and Sitkin, 1986; Buono and Bowditch, 1989). Leaving the small firm as is, however, leaves the option unexercised.

An intermediate solution is to exercise through network ties rather than through ownership. Such arrangements have been observed to spring up in economic clusters, often within industrial districts (Lorenzoni and Ornati, 1988; Lipparini and Maurizio, 1994; Lorenzoni and Lipparini, 1999). Specialist firms sustain high levels of innovation, while achieving scale through network ties with other firms. Districts begin when technicians or designers spin-off new firms from an established incubator organization. Their previous involvement with the parent firm gives them access to knowledge and resources, that they in turn can use to exercise their options.

When rents are shared, there is always the danger of self-serving rent-seeking among partners. Lorenzoni and Ornati (1988) find that one of the reasons firms within their 'constellations' do well is that they adhere to a joint set of rules regarding competitive rules of engagement. Absent such rules, enormous difficulty can arise for the small firm. They may, for instance, overreach and find themselves unable to handle large volumes of orders, consequently finding themselves in a cash flow catastrophe (Schilit, 1994). Large players can then easily take over the vulnerable target. Information asymmetry can put the small firm at a disadvantage, because large players can use their more comprehensive understanding of the market to negotiate advantageous terms. Bigger players can also, of course, renege on their deals with much less concern regarding the reaction of the SME.

Large players may also be tempted to manipulate small ones. Firms operating in multiple markets are known to seek stable sphere-of-influence arrangements relative to other large multiple point players (Bernheim and Whinston, 1990). They may thus be tempted to use the small firm instrumentally to divert their opponent's resources in a manner that suits them, a process that McGrath et al. (1998) call 'resource diversion'. Absent information about the motivations and behavior of their partners, small firms may be vulnerable to machinations in a game in which they don't know the rules. In short, an open question for researchers is who really benefits when options are exercised through network arrangements.

Critics (Harrison, 1994) have argued that the way work is divided between large firms and small ones simply allows large firms to parcel out the least profitable parts of their businesses, while retaining control of the profitable core. As network arrangements become more prevalent, researchers would do well to better understand issues of who benefits under what conditions, and what the consequences are.

Recent massive cash flows into the venture capital industry make the governance question particularly relevant. Although at first blush, one would think that greater capital availability would increase resources available to entrepreneurial firms, the effect has been the opposite. Investor pressure has increased expectations for venture capitalists to deliver results. Counter-intuitively, this appears to have increased the minimum deal size and made small ventures less attractive. Since, as Ruhnka et al. (1992) report, 40% of all venture capital investments fail to provide a satisfactory return, this pressure is only likely to increase further.

Whether increased performance pressure will shift the governance mechanisms utilized by venture capitalists from the self-reinforcing and informal part of the spectrum toward the third-party reinforcing and formal part, and with what consequences, is a crucial question. It is particularly pressing, given recent evidence that venture capitalists themselves are not explicitly aware of how they make decisions. In an experiment using a psychological technique called 'policy capturing', Zacharakis and Meyer (1998) found evidence that venture capitalists do not consciously understand the intuitive decision-making processes they actually use. The implication is that if venture capitalists shift their behavior toward more formal approaches due to pressure from investors, they may not be able to anticipate adverse effects on their decisions.

8. Network Ties and the Closure of or Exit from a Venture

Just as understanding the transaction set is vital to the exercise of an option, it can also help us better understand the end of a business. A strong assumption in the population ecology literature is that loss of a network is a powerful selection force. Despite this assertion, research examining how network collapse leads to organizational collapse is sparse.

We do know that bad news, in the form of hostile environmental jolts, can cause some network members to leave the transaction set (Venkataraman, 1989). The resulting instability consumes important resources as lost ties are replaced. This places enormous strain on the small organization. Retaining members in the transaction set is also more difficult after a hostile jolt, because it sends a negative signal to them. The relationships are more complex, however, than one might at first imagine.

Venkataraman and Van de Ven (1993) find that although hostile environmental jolts influence parties to an existing transaction set to leave, they appear to have no effect on the propensity of new parties to join in. They speculate that this may be because decisions to enter are based on such factors as social capital, while exit decisions are based more on economic criteria.

Part of the problem is that network effects can amplify downsides as much as they do upsides. Losing a network partner, for instance, has been empirically linked to the failure of the remaining partner, unless the relationship is replaced quickly (Singh and Mitchell, 1996). This suggests that business dissolution may operate with self-reinforcing negative cycles as devastating to the survival of a network as the creation of a new network depends on self-reinforcing positive cycles. The question this raises is whether, and what, mechanisms exist to transform a network. Even fabled Silicon Valley hit a very difficult period in the late 1970s as its leading firms began to operate as hugely asset-intensive manufacturers. They 'abandoned the networks' as Saxenian observed (1994: 84–95).

A special case of breakdown in the transaction set can be observed in situations in which venture capitalists dismiss members of a new venture team that they have previously funded (Fiet et al., 1997). This is interesting, but not because a change in leadership of the small business is unusual. Rosenstein for instance (1988) found that nearly 40% of even well-performing firms had replaced their CEOs, while 74% of firms seen as underperforming had done so. Instead, dismissal is interesting because disruptions in the transaction set are likely to have an extremely negative effect on small firms. Therefore financial backers must have concluded that the damage to be done by forcing a disruption is less than the damage that would be done by retaining an entrepreneurial team member.

The question of how transaction sets break down is thus vital, yet poorly understood. We don't know, for instance, whether different processes are involved in the choice to join or leave a network. We also don't know if and when the collapse of a transaction set is useful because it frees members to form new transaction partnerships. My encouragement here is for researchers interested in the impact of networks on the entrepreneurial process to pay as much attention to the expiration of options and the closure of businesses as they have to problems of business creation and network formation.

Organizational Level of Analysis

9. How Do Members of Organizations Recognize Opportunities?

This cell refers to the process of identifying new options within an organization – what

Bowman and Hurry (1993) term 'recognition'. As Ashby long ago observed, high-variety environments require equally high internal variety if an entity is to summon an adaptive response. The greater the environmental uncertainty, the greater the number of options an organization must sustain if requisite variety is to be maintained (Ashby, 1956). Increasing the variety of an organization's repertoire by pursuing new directions helps avoid dangerous 'simplicity' (Miller, 1993).

Thus, processes associated with the generation of organizational variety have been extensively studied, although mostly within the context of the large, established organization (for a good overview, see Block and MacMillan, 1993). A major conclusion from this literature is that to prevail over time, organizations must be capable of continually looking for opportunities and extending the reach of existing knowledge (March, 1991; Teece et al., 1994). They must also be capable of storing and recalling the knowledge they have previously created in order to deploy it if future situations warrant it, equivalent to exercising the option to postpone until conditions are favorable (Garud and Nayyar, 1994). Conditions that facilitate the recognition of option value include the introduction of newcomers, positive surprises (beyond base rate expectations) and the juxtaposition of people with differing points of view within the organization (Kogut, 1991; March, 1991).

The absence of good ideas is seldom the critical problem for SMEs (see Venkataraman et al., 1992). It is far more difficult to decide which of the ideas bubbling around the organization deserve scarce time and attention on the managerial agenda. As Van de Ven (1986) observed, managing ideas into 'good currency' is one of the central problems of the entrepreneurial process. It is interesting, therefore, that far more attention seems to have been lavished on the generation of ideas, and far less on the mechanisms through which some become regarded as important.

For managers of resource-constrained SMEs, this represents a critical gap. Sustaining requisite variety presents a substantial challenge when one has little slack. A wrong choice can easily lead to organizational-level disaster. Indeed, Brown and Eisenhardt (1998) found that one of the characteristics distinguishing successful from unsuccessful SMEs in the pursuit of new ideas is that the successful ones have a process for determining which ideas receive priority and which do not. Given substantial uncertainty, an area about which relatively little is known is how this process works. This discussion suggests two areas in which research has been more or less silent: what factors lead to some options receiving attention and enthusiasm while others are recognized but not pursued? and what is the carrying capacity of small organizations for options, given uncertainty and resource constraints?

10. The Uncertainty Reduction Aspect of New Ventures in Organizations

The uncertainty reduction process for new ventures within an established organization is usually conflict-ridden, because allocating resources to reduce uncertainty in a new idea implies denying resources both to other new ideas and to established organizational operations (see Bower, 1970; Brown and Eisenhardt, 1995; Block and MacMillan, 1993; Dougherty, 1992; MacMillan, 1983). SME managers can find themselves whipsawed by the simultaneous desire to keep options open until uncertainty is reduced and the imperative to make irreversible investments to capitalize on opportunities (Dixit and Pindyck, 1994; Ghemawat, 1991). A relevant finding from strategic management research is that the tools of rational management can lead to risk-avoidance that depresses variance and therefore option value (see March and Shapira, 1987). So, too, net present value calculations and decision-making can hinder needed investments in uncertainty reduction (McGrath, 1997).

One emerging mechanism for resolving the tension between the desire to allocate resources to sure bets and the necessity to make a commitment to new ventures is to use contingent resources until uncertainty has been sufficiently reduced that the outcome is predictable. Contingent resources are taken on only as they are needed, and retained only as long as they add value. The big questions are whether the flexibility gains from contingent relations come at the expense of a strong competitive position, and whether it is fair to the providers of the contingent resource (Harrison, 1994).

Research evidence suggests that the deployment of contingent resources is on the increase (Schilling and Steensma, 2001). Contingent labor, for instance, is increasingly legitimate in the eyes of a workforce that has become accustomed to lack of job security (Matusik and Hill, 1998). Other practices, such as outsourcing, decouple the possession of assets from the productive use to which those assets are devoted. The concept is for each firm to specialize in its own area, then use market mechanisms to find best-in-class resources to handle the rest of the required functions.

The appeal of contingent resources under uncertainty is seductive. Making no long-term investment reduces the cost of exercising options and can allow an SME to enter arenas that would not be feasible if permanent resources had to be deployed. Using contingent resources can also enhance speed. The dilemma is that the capabilities developed by using contingent resources may be ephemeral. Workers can leave and give competitors vital information. Subcontractors can sell to others, and even become competitors. And key knowledge may walk out the door. In other words, absent some way of controlling the value created from contingent relationships, the SME may find that it has wasted considerable resources on reducing uncertainty without a commensurate capability to exercise the resulting option.

The utilization and economic consequences of contingent resource deployment to reduce uncertainty is an extremely fertile area for further research.

11. How Organizations Capture Rents from Investments in Ventures

The concerns of this cell have to do with capturing profits from a new business. An issue that has emerged recently goes to the heart of real options reasoning, and this concerns timing of exercise, by which I mean making those follow-on investments required to release profits from a venture.

Influencing the timing of exercise is one of the ways in which managers can influence option value – for instance, by postponing, or speeding up, the program. As velocity in competitive markets increases, control over timing is more important than ever. For instance, as prices and costs become more transparent in an e-business environment, the time to identify the appropriate price and to adjust it has shrunk. Buyers know more, and mistakes in pricing are hard to correct. Traditional practices such as offering special deals to the first customers, or to utilize capacity once fixed costs are covered, are now potentially deadly, because buyers can find out what the best available price is worldwide, and insist on getting this price. One implication is that there is an advantage to moving as much activity as possible as early as possible, before buyers, suppliers and transaction partners catch on.

For the most part, we can expect big players to benefit from advances in the speed and flexibility of pricing. Consider internet auctions, in which prices can be adjusted rapidly based on market demand. Large firms targeting a market can easily use the information revealed by online pricing behavior to price aggressively below cost, until the small players are driven out of the market. This would be an interesting arena in which to test conventional ideas of pricing and signaling – for instance, small and short-term price moves may have far greater and swifter impacts when they happen in internet time than when they require communication via conventional media.

The news is not all bad for small firms, however. Short product life cycles may give them some real advantages. For one thing, they are apt to have less invested in specific assets and competences than larger firms, making change easier. It also can give small firms bargaining power. Large firms are likely to be eager to utilize the capacities of more agile smaller firms to capture short windows of opportunity, creating the chance for the small firm to profit in strategic factor markets.

Increased speed and shortening life cycles will also change traditional views of how competitors react to a product launch or other exercise move (see Chen, 1996). The traditional perspective that competitors are located in a similar industry space and produce offerings that are close substitutes for one another (Porter, 1980) may poorly account for dynamics that can have a huge impact on option value. Evans and Wurster (1997), for instance, point out that for newspapers, the most dangerous competition does not come from other newspapers, or even other news sources. The most deadly competitive battle they face has to do with losing classified ads as a source of revenue.

Timing dynamics may affect the SME in other ways. The software industry is an example. When significant irreversible costs are incurred to develop a product, but subsequent costs are close to zero, the ideal market share is 100% (Arthur, 1994). SMEs are likely to not only have trouble raising initial capital, but are also chronically short of cash to support their customer service costs. They are thus unlikely to price aggressively enough to capture a dominant position. This serves to create a price umbrella for competitors, and may well induce the entry of large-scale imitators.

Further, even fairly mundane SMEs are no longer competing in purely local markets. If SME managers must price to reflect local costs (such as high social welfare costs), the SME can be at a systemic disadvantage relative to firms that can avoid such costs. To my knowledge, this issue is sufficiently new that little attention has been paid to it in scholarly terms.

In short, some of the dynamics of the new economy will tend to favor smaller firms in exercising their options. When competitive advantages come not from scale, scope and entry barriers but from speed and secrecy, smaller players can compete quite effectively. Understanding the consequences for performance of both large and small firms are important and useful research areas.

12. How Do Organizations Allow Exit from Less Productive Businesses?

An options perspective only makes economic sense if those options not in the money expire. Although this is easy to say, empirically, organizations are observed to have a very difficult time abandoning businesses with a constrained future to redirect their efforts toward brighter prospects. Our understanding of this process is primitive, and is of vital concern not only to SME research but to mainstream strategy as well.

Venkataraman and Van de Ven (1993) suggest that one common way exit occurs is through an accumulation of negative jolts. A single jolt is usually survivable. A succession of them leads to the dissolution of the transaction set and the loss of resources to re-assemble it again. What is thus often described in retrospect as a decision at a single point in time (for instance, 'the decision to close the plant...') is often the end result of cumulative jolts. These leave the organization without the resources to compete further.

Burgelman's (1996) work on strategic business exit is consistent. He found that the process of exiting the dynamic random access memory (DRAM) business at Intel was not the consequence of a decisive choice by senior management. Rather, a series of local capacity and resource allocation decisions gradually shifted resources away from DRAM production and toward other lines of business. Ironically, even though senior managers were voicing continued commitment to the business, decisions being made at an operational level undermined it. Managing the release of resources by shutting down businesses within a hierarchy is very difficult, and scholars have few bright ideas to offer on how to do this better.

Christensen (1997) and Tushman and Anderson (1986) observe that rational managers tend to those markets, products and customers that provide current resource inflows (see Pfeffer and Salancik's 1978 concept of 'resource dependence'). When threatened, managers frantically shore up performance with existing technology (Cooper and Smith, 1992). Hence, empirical evidence suggests that exiting a business often does not happen by choice, yet making this a more conscious and well-managed process is clearly important in uncertain contexts.

Some new ideas relevant to a better approach have to do with revisiting the structure of incentives prompting managers to preserve the status quo. One financial innovation is the issue of tracking stocks. These are stocks in a business that represents a part (often a rapidly growing part) of the corporate parent. The difference in value between higher growth tracking stocks and the parents' stock can provide a powerful incentive to innovate in remaining businesses, and to shut down those that are chronic underperformers.

A second idea that might be useful is to use increased information transparency to extract maximum value from assets. If a high-quality global market for used equipment and people's skills emerges, the stickiness and sunk cost aspects of exit might to some extent be mitigated. This would be particularly useful

for SMEs, as they often lack the resources to transfer people elsewhere or upgrade older equipment and remain stuck with underperforming assets.

Another intriguing development is technology that allows assets to be reconfigured. In software, innovations such as object-oriented programming make it easier to modify complex systems from pre-programmed modules. In manufacturing, modularity is being advanced as a way in which variety can be sustained and reconfiguration made more easy without an explosion of costs (Baldwin and Clark, 1997; Langlois and Robertson, 1992; Sanchez and Mahoney, 1996). Such new technologies have the long run potential for eliminating, or at least reducing, costs such as overheads and other fixed costs and also to reduce the sunk cost burden that might inhibit business exit. In general, exit decisions as a matter of purposive choice need to be better understood, both for large firms and for SMEs.

Regional Level of Analysis

13. Local Policies that Facilitate the New Business Formation Process within a Region

In the economic development literature, the desirability of entrepreneurship is for the most part taken for granted, on the assumption that it is associated with wealth creation. Indeed, regional development officials sometimes give the impression that if only more entrepreneurial ideas could be identified, their economic woes would be over.

An underlying assumption of this enthusiasm is that idea generation is locally embedded in particular geographically centered places in which the SME is part of a relatively durable social structure. Research universities, high tech investment (such as Department of Defense contracting), and venture capital investment have all conventionally been characterized as adding value primarily within a geographic area (for a good overview, see Bygrave and Timmons, 1992: 227–61; see also Nelson, 1993).

Some research has tested the locality assumption. Von Hippel, for instance, found that informal ties between engineers in the same geographic area led to 'informal know-how trading' (1987). Saxenian (1994) argued that informal ties between Silicon Valley firms led to greater innovation. Inventions (measured in terms of patent counts) tend to cluster geographically (Jaffe et al., 1993). Local spillovers, however, have positive and negative strategic implications for the SME.

In conventional spillover theory in strategy, firms are motivated to try to prevent knowledge leakage, because they are not compensated for the costs of creating the knowledge. Spillovers reduce incentives to invest in R&D, starving an economy of good ideas (Spence, 1984). The network economy calls this conclusion into question (McGrath and McGrath, 1999). Spillovers may instead be essential to recognizing the potential value of options, particularly under conditions of increasing returns and network externalities (Shapiro and Varian, 1998; Appleyard, 1996).

Some (Daft and Lengel, 1986) have argued that some kinds of information simply cannot transfer without physical proximity and interpersonal contact, suggesting that regions will remain a vital unit of analysis for recognition of option value. Others (Boisot, 1995) hold that the new technologies are making it possible to transfer information from place to place in unprecedented new ways, de-emphasizing location to some extent. The outcome will have highly significant implications for the efforts of policymakers in regions to support new ideas, and represents a fertile field for scholarly inquiry.

14. Regional Policies that Encourage Growth and Investment after Uncertainty is Reduced

How should local policy encourage the growth of new businesses? This simple question has long puzzled both researchers and policymakers. Despite a lack of conclusive evidence on the effectiveness of such efforts, all manner of public resources have been poured into new business development efforts. They range from the creation of science parks, incubators, tax-advantaged enterprise zones, research centers and other subsidized resources, to the provision of services such as the consulting services offered by university-based small business development corporations (SBDCs). Notwithstanding a lack of conclusive evidence,

regions compete with each other to offer incentives such as tax savings, grants and relaxed compliance with regulations.

The whole notion of directing entrepreneurial growth through the manipulation of public resources may be flawed if it turns out that the most important development outcomes are driven by factors over which government policy has little effect (Thompson and Smith, 1991). Indeed, sometimes government policies can do more harm than good. Porter (1998) commented on the negative effects of policy efforts. Restrictions on industrial location and subsidies to invest in distressed areas, for example, can disperse companies artificially, inhibiting the formation of productive clusters. Protecting local companies from competition leads to excessive vertical integration and blunted pressure for innovation. Buffering startups for too long can create a false sense of security, leaving them unprepared to face competition when the subsidies end.

Romo and Schwartz (1995) find that non-economic factors tie small firms to regions, even if economic ones suggest that they might be better off moving, because they are dependent on 'core establishments' that themselves resist moving until competitive pressures threaten to undermine their viability. A socially embedded explanation for firm location suggests a limited impact for policy variables in influencing firms' location choices (see also Harrison, 1992).

One factor making conclusive research findings difficult is that the process through which public investment reduces uncertainty for the SME unfolds over a long period of time. Bygrave and Timmons (1992: 259) cite the example of the Research Triangle in North Carolina. The government funded a high tech research park in 1960. After nearly three decades of cumulative investment, the area finally saw the emergence of a 'self-sustaining high-tech metropolis' by the 1990s. A second factor making the evaluation of public policies difficult is that the evidence used by entrepreneurs to suggest whether or not further investment is warranted are often not visible, under governmental control, or easy to coordinate. Quality of life issues, family and friendship networks, proximity to key suppliers and customers, dual-career concerns, school quality and so forth all have an enormous influence on entrepreneurial location choices, but are hard to manipulate.

The conclusion emerging from the literature is that although government policymaking can help new businesses to form, helping them grow is a complex and counterintuitive process. Among the things we need to understand better are how and in what ways local governments can enhance the option value of a business and reduce the cost of trying and failing, in a way that does not create dysfunctional long-term incentives.

15. Issues Having to Do with Regional Distribution of Entrepreneurial Proceeds

When it comes to sharing the spoils of an entrepreneurial effort, the interests of regional policymakers within a region are often at odds with those of entrepreneurs. What matters to those making choices for a region is whether the exercise of the entrepreneurial option translates into wellbeing for the greater community (Cornwall, 1998). Many have argued that community wealth is essential for the operation of a just society – the best-known advocate of this position is probably Etzioni (1993, 1996). This focuses attention on a fascinating set of assumptions regarding the nature of entrepreneurship's contribution to community wealth.

Many successful entrepreneurs are famous for their penchant for philanthropy (Steinberg, 1999). Many others make no contribution whatsoever, save a negative contribution (Coleman, 1997; Zapalska, 1997; Ivy, 1997; Nafukho, 1998). This calls into question the pervasive belief in the economic development literature that supporting growing businesses will help community development.

Take Silicon Valley as an archetype. Many (for instance, Simon, 1992) reject the disloyalty and transience of ties in Silicon Valley as an appropriate model for generating community wealth. They argue that the best firms seek small towns or villages in order to create and protect a self-reliant, loyal operation far from the temptations of communities with more employers and from cities. Further, some have criticized the Valley for its social schism – on the one hand, highly paid technical workers and business founders and on the other, low-status assembly and

technical workers who are paid poorly and have no access to the upside gains of the major firms.

A major methodological flaw in research on regional effects of SME activity is that little systematic investigation has been done that compares regions enjoying wealth creation with those which are not. If we were to try to answer the question, 'how does starting small businesses benefit the region?' we would need to include both region types. As things stand, we are back to the perennial problem of sampling on the dependent variable – this time, on the emergence of a 'successful' regional economy (for example, Dorfman, 1983).

In addition, a factor that many of the 'small business as the seed for communities' perspectives seem to overlook is that small businesses are typically resource constrained. Even if their founders are enthusiastic, such community-building activities as allowing flexible schedules to permit employees to engage in community activities, allowing family and parental leaves, giving to local civic and charitable organizations, and other forms of community support are difficult for the small business to afford.

In many parts of the world personal or family needs overwhelm any opportunity for the entrepreneur to extract profits which could be used to contribute to the larger community. Diomande (1990) for instance finds that in Africa, the proceeds from a business success are often rapidly appropriated by needy relatives, depriving the enterprise of the ability to accumulate critical resources and grow.

In short, as scholars, we need to progress beyond the blanket assumption that new firms contribute to social wealth. Doing so could build a useful research agenda with the promise of integrating topics of interest both to students of entrepreneurship and public policy.

16. Resource Redirection and Adjustment Cost Absorption at a Local Level

Changes that render the businesses located in a region obsolete present policymakers with a terrible dilemma. On the one hand, introducing artificial supports to help preserve established businesses is likely to be counterproductive in the long run, because these businesses will become less and less competitive. On the other, the collapse of the regional economy in the name of free markets and Schumpeterian competition is apt to precipitate a voters' revolt. One can speculate why there has been rather little work done on this problem. Perhaps it is because shutting businesses down is generally not regarded as economically useful, although establishing and growing businesses are seen as positive.

Regional policymakers are stuck with finding solutions to the problem of assets and people corporations can no longer use. The troubles show up as boarded-up brownfield sites that produce no tax revenue and as faces in local unemployment and assistance offices. Markets for obsolete resources are highly imperfect. Even if people do have marketable skills, and that old brownfield site near the railroad might be great for a startup distribution company, it is hard for potential acquirers to get information about the resource and hard to price it. This can make efforts at restructuring counterproductive (Anand and Singh, 1997).

Part of the solution may simply be to change the practices through which entrepreneurs exercise their options, diverting to some extent the rents they can earn. Some states, for instance, New Jersey, are putting greater value on public resources by placing strict limitations on the rights of firms to create isolated greenfield facilities, while providing subsidies that make it more financially attractive to redevelop older areas. This suggests three research implications.

First, if exercising the entrepreneurial option is going to involve the destruction and devaluation of once-valuable resources (such as open space), the costs of this need to be borne by someone. Better understanding of how costs are, and should be, allocated might help us to develop creative alternatives. Second, there may be the opportunity for entrepreneurship and economic development researchers to intersect with the interests of urban planning and public policy researchers. Finally, if processes of decline and change could be couched as part of the entrepreneurial process, rather than as the unpleasant end of the development road, perhaps more researchers would be willing to try to understand them.

INSTITUTIONAL LEVEL OF ANALYSIS

17. Institutional Payoff Regimes

Institutional forces fundamentally shape the direction in which inventive capacity in an economy is directed (and indeed on how the other levels of analysis are constructed). Differences in what Baumol (1993) terms the 'payoff structure' have a powerful influence on motivation to think up new ideas, on what ideas are perceived as legitimate, and on how freely information and ideas are shared (Boisot and Child, 1988). Here, I will limit my use of the term 'institutional' to focus on effects stemming from high-level structures influencing monetary policy, property rights, labor laws, regulations, tax rates, social welfare provisions, educational policy and so on.

One easily forgotten point is that historically, the production of new ideas has not always been honored. Technological improvements are not always desirable. Citing Finley (1965: 32) Baumol offers the following illustration: 'There is a story, repeated by a number of Roman writers, that a man – characteristically unnamed – invented unbreakable glass and demonstrated it to Tiberius in anticipation of a great reward. The emperor asked the inventor whether anyone shared his secret, and was assured that there was no one else; whereupon his head was promptly removed, lest, said Tiberius, gold be reduced to the value of mud.' The Emperor's reaction suggests that public policies can profoundly influence the recognition of opportunity. The nature of the policy/ entrepreneurship connection, however, continues to be controversial.

For instance, in Korea, small firms often find themselves the victims of aggressive imitation and direct competition from the huge conglomerate chaebol groups that dominate the economy. As a consequence, many would-be entrepreneurs view the effort as futile because anti-competitive redress against the larger firms has not been routinely practiced. In Japan, poorly developed financial infrastructure means that small business founders find financing by co-signing one another's loans. While this works just fine when their businesses succeed, let one of them fail, and all of them become involved. In a famous recent incident, three Japanese businessmen committed suicide together in a Tokyo hotel, unable to see any way to escape the shame and loss of their failed collaboration.

There are also disincentives to individual initiative that a generous government can unintentionally promote. Indeed, there is some evidence that high tax rates, generous unemployment allowances and various combinations of the two depress the rate of new business formation – for instance, in Scandinavian countries. Ironically, such environments create an incentive for the able and ambitious to leave, while simultaneously creating an incentive for the less able to remain.

As the debate continues, evidence is beginning to accumulate that employees in industries labeled as the information based, entrepreneurial 'New Economy' are enjoying more growth in compensation than employees in non-information based professions (Mandel, 1999a, b). Such dramatic imbalances in prospects and rewards might prove politically destabilizing, as those who are left out resort to institutional action to correct perceived inequalities. Johnson and Loveman (1995: 235) for instance report on how people who suffered as state-owned enterprises were sold reacted: 'In almost every country in Eastern Europe and the former Soviet Union there has been a political swing back to the left. People become dissatisfied and disillusioned…'

Institutional forces also influence which options will be regarded as legitimate. Dunbar and Ahlstrom (1995) offer a fascinating analysis of how institutional negotiations regarding appropriateness of treatment created a $6 billion for-profit kidney dialysis industry, despite ample evidence that less costly in-home dialysis was an acceptable alternative. They attribute this result to a combination of factors: the inability of advocates for in-home dialysis to persuade relatively ignorant 'outsiders' (as in members of Congress and regulatory agencies) of the efficacy of the procedure; and the presence of a large and growing for-profit corporation intent on financial gain from the widespread commercialization of dialysis techniques. They conclude that in such cases, the public good may be poorly served.

Although the debate between traditional and endogenous growth theorists has drawn attention to the link between technological improvement, entrepreneurship, and growth, understanding how policy influences outcomes is still at an early stage (Romer, 1990; Grossman and Helpman, 1991; Aghion and Howitt, 1992).

18. Institutional Factors that Help or Hinder Entrepreneurial Growth

A key question here concerns the effects of institutional rules on the availability of factor inputs to new and small businesses, and government intervention to support new businesses. As with regional policies, the connection between government action and business outcomes is not clear.

The most important way in which the government can be of use to entrepreneurs, many argue, is to provide the resources they need to determine whether a business is worth pursuing, and to invest in growth. Immigration policies fall squarely into the midst of a huge debate on this point. In the United States, cries of labor and skills shortages on the part of small business owners have prompted some to press for relaxation of immigration restrictions for people with unique skills. At the same time, other officials argue that importing such skilled people will eliminate opportunities for native citizens, arguing for more restrictive rules.

From the perspective of net exporters of talent, changes in immigration policy in desirable destinations such as the United States can dramatically affect their supply of skilled individuals, and by implication, of individuals knowledgeable enough to be able to reduce uncertainty. Having expended funds on education, one can excuse policymakers for feeling frustrated if the most capable and ambitious of the people they educate bring their skills elsewhere. Net out-migration of such skilled people represents a huge cost to the country that has educated them, not only in immediate terms but in terms of creating or enhancing the entrepreneurial infrastructure.

Government support of startups seems to operate on the presumption that they are competitively neutral. In fact, what can happen is that unintentionally, government support intensifies competition in the sectors in which new businesses compete, having the counter-intuitive consequence of making their failure more likely by putting pressure on a limited number of transaction partners.

An unglamorous issue that does not figure prominently in our theory or literature is how at a day to day operating level governments help or hinder the pursuit of opportunity by entrepreneurs. An interesting study by Kuratko et al. (1999) suggests that policymakers should give this some thought. They report some startling statistics on the impact of government on new businesses, citing some United States evidence: 'The Code of Federal Regulations has 65,000 pages of new and modified regulations each year; there are fifty-two federal agencies employing more than 122,000 workers to administer 5,000 regulations; the federal regulatory budget for these agencies is $13 billion; and the total annual cost of federal regulations fell from $443 billion in 1977 to $369 billion by 1986, but recent increases in government activity has brought that figure back to over $400 billion' (1999: 82). The costs of compliance clearly put SMEs at a disadvantage relative to larger competitors, since they can ill-afford the people to monitor, track and comply with governmental requirements. This is an area ripe for innovative thinking and solid research.

19. Issues Having to Do with Institutional Distribution of Entrepreneurial Proceeds

Abundant evidence suggests that if appropriate institutional norms and controls are not in place, entrepreneurial effort can just as easily produce self-serving rent seeking at best, and criminality and violence at worst (Volkov, 1999), despite widespread assumptions that more wealth is better (for instance, Arzeni, 1997).

What then shapes how the proceeds to entrepreneurship are distributed? Hamer (1998) finds that social forces play a vital role in answering this question. Historically, he suggests, entrepreneurs have used their investments in symbolic capital to improve their economic capital by seeing 'the potential for wealth beyond the logic of the market' (1998: 147). In a fascinating critique of philanthropic behavior, he shows how entrepreneurial proceeds were spent to create a number of social and factor-input advantages by the philanthropists John P. Crozer, John D. Rockefeller, Andrew Mellon, John Wanamaker, John P. Morgan, and Andrew Carnegie. Hamer ends his discussion with some cautionary observations

regarding the underlying moral basis for entrepreneurship in the late 20th century. He suggests that we may be contemplating a situation in which 'short and long-term values have become one, in support of greed' and that social contributions today have to do with 'gaining prestige, self-promotion and identity building' rather than with making more substantive contributions (1998: 148).

Indeed, many of today's entrepreneurs seem to sport a latter day version of 'Social Darwinism'. The term originated in the late 19th and early 20th centuries and referred to the belief that those who accumulated vast wealth did so because they were naturally more fit or gifted than those who did not (Hall, 1982). By analogy, if wealth is created through hard work, persistence and risk-taking, those who are less successful are simply less deserving – indeed, by supporting them, one is only supporting the less 'fit' elements in a society and depressing its capability over the long run. Dated as this idea may seem, it has considerable purchase, even today. For instance, as Barna (1999) reports, the United Way, a major philanthropic organization, finds that donations from the many individuals who have grown wealthy from the emergence of Silicon Valley firms are extremely low relative to wealthy individuals elsewhere.

One recent development from the riches generated by the new economy is that SMEs are finding that they can attract talent that would otherwise only have been accessible to large firms. The lure of internet riches is one factor. Another, more subtle, factor is that with the collapse of the traditional employment contract, a job with a large employer is not perceived as secure. Since large firms do control considerable social resources, whether it benefits an economy to have its brightest people dedicated to the entrepreneurial sector is an open question (although the taken for granted assumption is yes, of course).

This is particularly pressing because most small businesses are not great places to work. Those few firms with the potential to go to IPO or grow rapidly can offer rich incentives to join (Judge and Burrows, 1999). Most, however, are not in this position. A reporter for *Business Week*, citing Bureau of Labor Statistics, found that not only do larger firms systematically pay better than small ones, even controlling for type of job, but that this gap has been widening throughout the 1990s. In 1993, white-collar workers earned 33% more than similar employees in small firms. This gap increased to 39% in 1995, reaching 47% by 1999 (Mandel, 1999). Among the issues the relative unattractiveness of working for an SME raises at a policy level is the control of an economy's slack resources. It may be all very well to enthuse about high growth entrepreneurial firms, but empirically, they don't on average appear to be very attractive employers.

Not only that, but government programs ostensibly designed to help them have gotten extremely mixed reviews. In the US, Kuratko et al. (1999) report that 'the vast majority of owners have never attempted to take advantage of these programs' while Moini (1998) reported general ignorance of programs intended to support export-oriented SMEs. Masten et al. (1995) found similar ignorance of programs intended to foster technology transfer as a form of SME assistance. Bygrave and Timmons (1992) somewhat cynically observe that most entrepreneurial activity doesn't benefit at all from those government programs intended to support it.

Different societies have different institutions governing the disposition of entrepreneurial profits, but there is little consensus on the connection between these institutions and social wealth. At the moment, the dominant view in the literature is largely drawn from conceptions of appropriateness embedded in the American system. Premises in this system – for instance, that wealth and property belongs to individuals rather than collectives or groups, that property and environment not explicitly protected by law or contract is available for profit-making use by entrepreneurs, and that the interests of shareholders far outweigh those of other stakeholders – are regularly questioned by those from other theoretical and cultural traditions (for instance, Johnson and Loveman, 1995). Globalization promises to make such issues fascinating for future research work.

20. Resource Redirection and Adjustment Cost Absorption at an Institutional Level

This final cell has to do with institutional influences on the demise of businesses. The process of redirecting a society's resources to more productive uses often reflects the intersection of uncertainty reduction and option exercise for smaller firms, and the exit choices of larger ones.

Although it is romantic to think of a small firm winning over a large one, for the most part large incumbents don't really suffer until the new entrant has attained efficient scale (Audretsch, 1995). This suggests the need to refine the David and Goliath metaphor of creative destruction. Real options reasoning suggests that it might be more prudent for scholars and policy makers to focus on the processes that allow a very few small firms to not only survive, but grow (Brander et al., 1998).

Changes in political regime is one factor that leads to wholesale business closure. With the end of communism, for instance, massive numbers of state-owned enterprises have been closed (Blanchard et al., 1993; McMillan and Naughton, 1992). Even successful economic transformations have their problems. The failure, on a mass scale, of formerly successful businesses creates enormous social adjustment costs. Jobs are lost, skills are made obsolete, and communities are disrupted. Luttwak (1999) offers a searing portrait of the consequences of failing to control capitalism's excesses – people living with a permanent sense of insecurity, broken homes when people's jobs are lost, an entire population of nomadic individuals with little interest in where they live or who they interact with, and decimated neighborhoods.

It would be helpful for scholars to focus on research that might offer some guidance, or at least some conceptual alternatives. For instance, if supporting new startups is unlikely to yield a buffer against economic dislocation, perhaps making investments to support companies that have demonstrated they have the capacity to grow would be better. There may be ways to humanize the pain of economic transitions without creating unproductive side effects. This becomes an urgent issue for policymakers in developing economies, such as that of South Africa, where unemployment is running at a stunning 30% or more. Even the most ardent advocates of a free market system there are unsure of whether a frustrated electorate will give policymakers enough time for economic forces to sort the situation out.

What little we do know about these issues has mostly to do with what doesn't work.

We know that many status-quo preserving interventions only exacerbate the problem of economic shift over the long run. For instance, throwing up protective trade barriers often means that the entire domestic base industry is vulnerable to invasion from superior technology from afar. The United States, for instance, banned the manufacture or sale of encryption technology for use in mobile telephones and other devices. The result is that the cutting edge of encryption technology is being pursued by firms that can market products that would result, not one of which is based in the United States. National protection of many industries, such as automobile manufacture and energy production, left incumbent firms without the incentive to innovate, protected from the forces of Schumpeterian change. The premise that stability and security can lead to dangerous ossification at the institutional level was developed in some depth by Olson (1982). He argues that societies experiencing long periods of political stability are likely to find their economic vitality sapped by the self-serving behavior of powerful special interests.

Throwing one's domestic markets completely open to foreign competition, however, raises the specter of large, capable firms from overseas swooping in and not only destroying domestic organizations but competing so effectively that they remove the incentive for home-grown entrepreneurial activity. This suggests another point at which researchers interested in entrepreneurship and economic change could be helpful at an institutional level. What kinds of policies create an appropriate balance of comfort and competition to ensure a healthy national economy while making sure that valuable resources are not trapped in obsolete businesses?

CONCLUSION

I have used real options reasoning to frame a selective overview of emerging issues relevant to strategy and entrepreneurship in the small firm. I hope to have demonstrated that the options lens offers a parsimonious way to raise issues and frame problems, because it is particularly suited to the highly uncertain, performance skewed world of the SME. As I bring the discussion to a close, let me suggest ways in which a real options perspective may add value.

The continuing debate over definitions of entrepreneurship (much like the ongoing debate about the definition of strategy), although intellectually stimulating, has interfered with our ability to undertake consistent, cumulative work that can be understood by all interested readers. Without insisting on paradigmatic unity, surely we as scholars can clearly define our level of analysis, presumed core processes, and explicit or implicit dependent variables when we undertake entrepreneurship research. Here, I have built upon a growing stream of research in strategy to suggest that option recognition, uncertainty reduction, exercise and exit are useful metaphors for entrepreneurial activities. I have further used this framework to show how the consistent application of a perspective like real options reasoning can highlight places in which existing research could stand further development.

I am struck by the similarity and relevance of work that has often been characterized as work in 'strategic management' to the problems that have often been characterized as problems of entrepreneurship or innovation. If we accept the premise that even large, established firms will be subject to the forces of Schumpeterian reconfiguration, I believe that the distinction between theories relevant to the two areas of inquiry will become further blurred. What may remain is what Venkataraman (1997) has defined as the core distinction between entrepreneurship research and other areas of management inquiry – the intersection of the drive for private gain and social wealth.

If strategy and entrepreneurship are merging, as I believe they are, this suggests some important implications for both fields. Strategy's central question concerns the influence of management action on firm performance. As the uncertainty that has always been a core issue for entrepreneurship research becomes a dominant feature of the world of all general managers, the predictive power of formerly useful frameworks and relations between constructs in strategy will fade.

We have already seen this, as historically well-defined relationships in strategy become less clearly relevant, such as the ability of market share to predict future profitability. Share and size, once prized as a key to profitability, are often seen now as a dangerous burden (MacMillan, 1985). Top management team demographics are seen as less effective in explaining attitudes and decisionmaking (Markoczy, 1997). Prediction, planning and control are giving way to ideas such as enactment, adaptation and discovery. The most valuable managerial skills may involve making sense of complexity, absorbing uncertainty and aligning interests, skills that are vital in an entrepreneurial world. In this way, the two fields share a set of common concerns with strategic intent under conditions of uncertainty and the social consequences of entrepreneurial action.

I have attempted in this chapter to suggest ways in which real options reasoning changes the way we consider entrepreneurial phenomena, and by extension, the world of strategy as well. If one looks at the world through an options lens, taken for granted assumptions are called into question. Discovery becomes a manageable process. Uncertainty can create value. Failure may simply be a necessary price paid to obtain information that isn't available any other way. Endings become as important to understand as beginnings. As the business world hurtles into this next millennium, we are thus blessed with a rich set of fascinating research issues to pursue.

ACKNOWLEDGEMENTS

I appreciate funding from the Eugene Marion Kauffman Foundation, DuPont Corporate New Business Development and the Sonera Corporation. Raffi Amit, Max Boisot and Ian MacMillan provided helpful comments and suggestions, as did the editorial team of this volume.

NOTES

1 This may in part be an artifact of the circumstance that much of what we consider to represent the literature on entrepreneurship is based on research done in the United States. As Mowery and Rosenberg (1993: 29) observe, new firms in the US have played a significant role in the commercialization of new technologies; a role which the new, small firm does not necessarily play in the innovation systems of other countries.

2 Although the actual number of new business entries remains the subject of considerable debate, Dennis (1997) finds that one half to one million annually, in the United States, is the 'popular range'. The Small Business Administration, he reports, found about 807,000 new firms and 944,000 new and successor firms that were formed in 1994. His own research, done for the National Federation of Independent Businesses, finds a staggeringly greater number of entries, namely 4.5 million, primarily by uncovering new businesses that other surveys and methods had overlooked.

3 A recurring topic of interest is whether certain characteristics, or traits, distinguish business founders from other people. A rich literature has addressed such topics as personality, motivation, demographic background, aspirations, gender and cultural beliefs (for instance, McClelland, 1961; Hornaday and Aboud, 1971). For the most part, empirical work has failed to support the hypothesis that entrepreneurs are systematically different from other people.

REFERENCES

Abrahamson, E. (1996) 'Management fashion', *Academy of Management Review*, 21: 254–85.
Aghion, P. and Howitt, P. (1992) 'A model of growth through creative destruction', *Econometrica*, 60: 323–51.
Aldrich, H. (1999) *Organizations Evolving*. Newbury Park, CA: Sage Publications.
Aldrich, H. and Zimmer, C. (1986) 'Entrepreneurship through social networks', in D. L. Sexton and R. W. Smilor (eds), *The Art and Science of Entrepreneurship*. Cambridge, MA: Ballinger Publishing. pp. 2–23.
Allen, R. C. (1983) 'Collective invention', *Journal of Economic Behavior and Organization*, 4: 1–24.
Amit, R., Brander, J. and Zott, C. (1998) 'Why do venture capital firms exist? Theory and Canadian evidence', *Journal of Business Venturing*, 13: 441–66.
Amit, R., Muller, E. and Cockburn, I. (1995) 'Opportunity costs and entrepreneurial activity', *Journal of Business Venturing*, 10: 95–106.
Anand, J. and Singh, H. (1997) 'Asset redeployment, acquisitions and corporate strategy in declining industries', *Strategic Management Journal*, 18: 99–118.
Appleyard, M. (1996) 'How does knowledge flow? Interfirm patterns in the semiconductor industry', *Strategic Management Journal*, 17: 137–54.
Armstrong, L. and Grover, R. (1999) 'Where net startups go to be born', *Business Week*, September 13, 1999: 46–8.
Arrow, K. J. (1974) *Limits of Organizations*. New York: W. W. Norton & Co.
Arthur, W. B. (1994) *Increasing Returns and Path Dependence in the Economy*. Ann Arbor: University of Michigan Press.
Arzeni, S. (1997) 'Entrepreneurship and job creation', *The OECD Observer*, December, 1997–January, 1998: 18–20.

Ashby, W. R. (1956) *An Introduction to Cybernetics.* London: Chapman and Hall.

Ason, J. (1999) 'Business angels and investment in entrepreneurial companies', Speech before the New Jersey Entrepreneurial Network, The Forrestal Hotel, Princeton, NJ, March 3, 1999.

Audretsch, D. B. (1995) *Innovation and Industry Evolution.* London: MIT Press.

Baldwin, C. and Clark, K. B. (1997) 'Managing in an age of modularity', *Harvard Business Review*, September–October.

Barna, M. (1999) 'The mythical land of type A techies: One insider dispels all the illusions of the famed Silicon Valley', *San Francisco Chronicle*, September 5, 1999: 3/Z3.

Baron, R. A. (1998) 'Cognitive mechanisms in entrepreneurship; why and when entrepreneurs think differently than other people', *Journal of Business Venturing*, 13: 275–94.

Baum, J. A. C. (1996) 'Organizational ecology', in S. R. Clegg, C. Hardy and W. R. Nord (eds), *Handbook of Organization Studies.* Thousand Oaks, CA: Sage Publications. pp. 77–114.

Baumol, W. J. (1993a) *Entrepreneurship, Management and the Structure of Payoffs.* Cambridge, MA: MIT Press.

Baumol, W. J. (1993b) 'Formal entrepreneurship theory in economics: existence and bounds', *Journal of Business Venturing*, 8: 197–210.

Bernheim, B. D. and Whinston, M. D. (1990) 'Multimarket contact and collusive behavior', *Rand Journal of Economics*, 21: 1–26.

Birley, S. (1985) 'The role of networks in the entrepreneurial process', *Journal of Business Venturing*, 1: 107–17.

Birley, S. (1997) 'Entrepreneurship in the UK', Presentation to the Waseda University Entrepreneurial Research Unit 1997 International Symposium, October 23–24, 1997, Tokyo, Japan.

Blanchard, O., Boycko, M., Dabrowki, M., Dornbush, R., Layard, R. and Schleifer, A. (1993) *Post Communist Reform: Pain and Progress.* Cambridge, MA: MIT Press.

Block, Z. and MacMillan, I. C. (1993) *Corporate Venturing: Creating New Business Within the Firm.* Cambridge, MA: Harvard Business School Press.

Boisot, M. (1995) *Information Space: A Framework for Learning in Organizations, Institutions and Culture.* New York: Routledge.

Boisot, M. and Child, J. (1988) 'The iron law of fiefs: bureaucratic failure and the problem of governance in the Chinese economic reforms', *Administrative Science Quarterly*, 33: 507–27.

Bower, J. L. (1970) *Managing the Resource Allocation Process.* Boston, MA: Harvard Business School Press.

Bowman, E. H. and Hurry, D. (1993) 'Strategy through the option lens: an integrated view of resource investments and the incremental-choice process', *Academy of Management Review*, 18: 760–82.

Brander, J., Hendricks, K., Amit, R. and Whistler, D. (1998) 'The engine of growth hypothesis: on the relationship between firm size and employment growth', Working paper, University of British Columbia.

Brockhaus, R. H. (1980) 'Risk taking propensity of entrepreneurs', *Academy of Management Journal*, 23: 509–20.

Brown, S. and Eisenhardt, K. M. (1995) 'Product development: past research, present findings and future directions', *Academy of Management Journal*, 20: 343–78.

Brown, S. and Eisenhardt, K. (1998) *Competing on the Edge.* Boston: Harvard Business School Press.

Buono, A. F. and Bowditch, J. L. (1989) *The Human Side of Mergers and Acquisitions.* San Francisco: Jossey Bass.

Burgelman, R. (1996) 'A process model of strategic business exit: implications for an evolutionary perspective on strategy', *Strategic Management Journal*, 17: 193–214.

Burt, R. S. (1992) *Structural Holes: The Social Structure of Competition.* Cambridge, MA: Harvard University Press.

Busenitz, L. (1999) 'Entrepreneurial risk and strategic decision making: it's a matter of perspective', *The Journal of Applied Behavioral Science*, 35: 325–40.

Busenitz, L. W. and Barney, J. B. (1997) 'Differences between entrepreneurs and managers in large organizations: biases and heuristics in strategic decision making', *Journal of Business Venturing*, 12: 9–30.

Bygrave, W. and Timmons, J. (1992) *Venture Capital at the Crossroads.* Boston: Harvard Business School Press.

Cable, D. M. and Shane, S. (1997) 'A prisoners' dilemma approach to entrepreneur–venture capitalist relationships', *Academy of Management Review*, 22: 142–76.

Cardon, M. and McGrath, R. G. (2001) 'When the going gets tough – toward a psychology of entrepreneurial failure and re-motivation', *Frontiers in Entrepreneurship Research*, Babson College.

Castells, M. (1996) *The Rise of the Network Society.* Malden, MA: Blackwell Publishers.

Chandler, G. N. and Hanks, S. H. (1998) 'An examination of the substitutability of founders' human and financial capital in emerging business ventures', *Journal of Business Venturing*, 13: 353–69.

Chen, M-J. (1996) 'Competitor analysis and interfirm rivalry: toward a theoretical integration', *Academy of Management Review*, 21: 100–34.

Christensen, C. (1997) *'The Innovator's Dilemma: When New Technologies Cause Great Firms to Fail.* Boston: Harvard Business School Press.

Coleman, S. (1997) 'Crime in Russia: implications for the development of training programs for Russian entrepreneurs', *Journal of Small Business Management*, 35: 73–7.

Cooper, A. C. and Smith, C. G. (1992) 'How established firms respond to threatening technologies', *Academy of Management Executive*, 6: 55–70.

Corman, J., Perles, B. and Vancini, P. (1988) 'Motivational factors influencing high-technology entrepreneurship', *Journal of Small Business Management*, 26: 36–42.

Cornwall, J. R. (1998) 'The entrepreneur as a building block for community', *Journal of Developmental Entrepreneurship*, 3: 141–8.

Cunningham, J. B. and Lischeron, J. (1991) 'Defining entrepreneurship', *Journal of Small Business Management*, 29: 45–61.

Daft, R. L. and Lengel, R. H. (1986) 'Organizational information requirements, media richness and structural design', *Management Science*, 32: 554–71.

Dennis, W. J. (1997) 'More than you think: an inclusive estimate of business entries', *Journal of Business Venturing*, 12: 175–96.

Diomande, M. (1990) 'Business creation with minimal resources: some lessons from the African experience', Working paper, Sol C. Sinder Entrepreneurial Center, University of Pennsylvania, April 27.

Dixit, A. and Pindyck, R. (1994) *Investment Under Uncertainty*. Princeton, NJ: Princeton University Press.

Dorfman, N. S. (1983) 'Route 128: the development of a regional high technology economy', *Research Policy*, 12: 299–316.

Dougherty, D. (1992) 'Interpretive barriers to successful product innovation in large firms', *Organization Science*, 3: 179–202.

Dunbar, R. L. M. and Ahlstrom, D. (1995) 'Seeking the institutional balance of power: avoiding the power of a balanced view', *Academy of Management Review*, 20: 171–92.

Dweck, C. S. and Leggett, E. L. (1988) 'A social-cognitive approach to motivation and personality', *Psychological Review*, 95: 256–73.

Dyer, J. H. and Singh, H. (1998) 'The relational view: cooperative strategy and sources of interorganizational competitive advantage', *Academy of Management Review*, 23: 660–79.

Etzioni, A. (1993) *The Spirit of Community: The Reinvention of American Society*. New York: Simon and Schuster.

Etzioni, A. (1996) 'The responsive community: a communitarian perspective', *American Sociological Review*, 61: 1–11.

Evans, P. B. and Wurster, T. S. (1997) 'Strategy and the new economics of information', *Harvard Business Review*, September–October: 71–82.

Fichman, M. and Levinthal, D. A. (1991) 'Honeymoons and the liability of adolescence: a new perspective on duration dependence in social organizational relationships', *Academy of Management Review*, 16: 442–68.

Fiet, J. O., Busenitz, L. W., Moesel, D. D. and Barney, J. B. (1997) 'Complementary theoretical perspectives on the dismissal of new venture team members', *Journal of Business Venturing*, 12: 347–66.

Finley, M. I. (1965) 'Technical innovation and progress in the ancient world', *Economic History Review*, 18: 29–45.

Gartner, W. B. (1988) 'Who is an entrepreneur? is the wrong question', *American Journal of Small Business*, 12: 11–32.

Garud, R. and Nayyar, P. R. (1994) 'Transformative capacity: continual structuring by intertemporal technology transfer', *Strategic Management Journal*, 15: 365–85.

Ghemawat, P. (1991) *Commitment: The Dynamic of Strategy*. New York: The Free Press.

Gimeno, J., Folta, T. B., Cooper, A. C. and Woo, C. Y. (1997) 'Survival of the fittest? Entrepreneurial human capital and the persistence of underperforming firms', *Administrative Science Quarterly*, 42: 750–83.

Granovetter, M. S. (1973) 'The strength of weak ties', *American Journal of Sociology*, 78: 1360–80.

Granovetter, M. (1985) 'Economic action and social structure: the problem of embeddedness', *American Journal of Sociology*, 91: 481–510.

Grossman, G. M. and Helpman, E. (1991) *Innovation and Growth in the Global Economy*. Cambridge, MA: MIT Press.

Gulati, R. (1998) 'Alliances and networks', *Strategic Management Journal*, 19: 293–317.

Hall, P. (1982) *The Organization of American Culture, 1700–1900*. New York: New York University Press.

Hambrick, D. and MacMillan, I. C. (1984) 'Asset parsimony – managing assets to manage profits', *Sloan Management Review*, Winter: 67–74.

Hamer, J. H. (1998) 'Money and the moral order in late nineteenth and early twentieth-century American capitalism', *Anthropological Quarterly*, 71: 138–50.

Harrison, B. (1992) 'Industrial districts: old wine in new bottles?', *Regional Studies*, 26: 469–83.

Harrison, B. (1994) 'The myth of the small firm as the predominant job creators', *Economic Development Quarterly*, 8: 3–18.

Hayek, F. (1945) 'The use of knowledge in society', *American Economic Review*, 35: 519–30.

Heider, F. (1958) *The Psychology of Interpersonal Relations*. New York: Wiley.

Herbert, R. F. and Link, A. N. (1988) *The Entrepreneur.* New York: Praeger.

Hornaday, J. A. and Aboud, J. (1971) 'Characteristics of successful entrepreneurs', *Personnel Psychology*, 24: 141–53.

Ibbotson, R. G. and Jaffee, J. J. (1975) '"Hot Issue" Markets', *Journal of Finance*, 30: 1027–42.

Ivy, R. L. (1997) 'Entrepreneurial strategies and problems in post-communist Europe: a survey of SME's in Slovakia', *Journal of Small Business Management*, 35: 93–7.

Jaffe, A. B., Trajtenberg, M. and Henderson, R. (1993) 'Geographic localization of knowledge spillovers as evidenced by patent citations', *Quarterly Journal of Economics*, 108: 577–98.

Jemison, D. B. and Sitkin, S. B. (1986) 'Acquisitions: the process can be a problem', *Harvard Business Review*, 64: 107–16.

Johnson, S. and Loveman, G. (1995) *Starting Over in Eastern Europe: Entrepreneurship and Economic Renewal*. Boston: Harvard Business School Press.

Judge, P. C. and Burrows, P. (1999) 'Suddenly the suits are jumping ship: but what do corporate vets bring to the Net?', *Business Week*, September 27, 1999: 46–7.

Kirzner, I. (1973) *Competition and Entrepreneurship*. Chicago, IL: University of Chicago Press.

Kirzner, I. (1979) *Perception, Opportunity and Entrepreneurship*. Chicago, IL: University of Chicago Press.

Kirzner, I. (1997) 'Entrepreneurial discovery and the competitive market process: an Austrian approach', *Journal of Economic Literature*, 35: 60–85.

Knight, F. H. (1921) *Risk, Uncertainty and Profit*. 1971 Midway reprint. Chicago: University of Chicago Press.

Kogut, B. (1991) 'Joint ventures and the option to expand and acquire', *Management Science*, 37(1): 19–33.

Kuratko, D. F., Hornsby, J. S. and Naffziger, D. W. (1999) 'The adverse impact of public policy on microenterprises: an exploratory study of owners' perceptions', *Journal of Developmental Entrepreneurship*, 4: 81–93.

Langlois, R. N. and Robertson, P. L. (1992) 'Networks and innovation in a modular system: lessons from the microcomputer and stereo component industries', *Research Policy*, 1–17.

Larson, A. (1992) 'Network dyads in entrepreneurial settings: a study of governance of exchange relationships', *Administrative Science Quarterly*, 37: 76–104.

Lichtenberg, F. (1998) 'Pharmaceutical innovation as a process of creative destruction', Working paper, Columbia University and the National Bureau of Economic Research, February, 1998.

Lipparini, A. and Maurizio, S. (1994) 'The glue and the pieces: entrepreneurship and innovation in small-firm networks', *Journal of Business Venturing*, 9: 125–40.

Lorenzoni, G. and Lipparini, A. (1999) 'The leveraging of interfirm relationships as a distinctive organizational capability: a longitudinal study', *Strategic Management Journal*, 20: 317–38.

Lorenzoni, G. and Ornati, O. (1988) 'Constellations of firms and new ventures', *Journal of Business Venturing*, 3: 41–57.

Luttwak, E. (1999) *Turbo-Capitalism: Winners and Losers in the Global Economy*. New York: Harper-Collins.

MacMillan, I. C. (1983) 'The politics of new venture management', *Harvard Business Review*, 62: 8–13.

MacMillan, I. C. (1985) 'How business strategists can use guerrilla warfare tactics', *Journal of Business Strategy*, 1: 63–6.

MacMillan, I. C. (1986) 'To really learn about entrepreneurship, let's study habitual entrepreneurs', *Journal of Business Venturing*, 1: 241–3.

MacMillan, I. C. and Katz, J. A. (1992) 'Idiosyncratic milieus of entrepreneurial research: the need for comprehensive theories', *Journal of Business Venturing*, 7: 1–8.

Mandel, M. (1999a) 'Big players offer better pay: for workers, company size matters', *Business Week*, August 30, 1999: 30.

Mandel, M. (1999b) 'The prosperity gap', *Business Week*, September 27, 1999: 90–102.

March, J. G. (1991) 'Exploration and exploitation in organizational learning', *Organization Science*, 2: 71–87.

March, J. G. and Shapira, Z. (1987) 'Managerial perspectives on risk and risk taking', *Management Science*, 33: 1404–18.

Markoczy, L. (1997) 'Measuring beliefs: accept no substitutes', *Academy of Management Journal*, 40: 1228–42.

Masten, J., Hartmann, G. B. and Safari, A. (1995) 'Small business strategic planning and technology transfer: the use of publicly supported technology assistance agencies', *Journal of Small Business Management*, 33(3): 26–37.

Matusik, S. F. and Hill, C. W. L. (1998) 'The utilization of contingent work, knowledge creation and competitive advantage', *Academy of Management Review*, 23: 680–97.

McClelland, D. C. (1961) *The Achieving Society*. Princeton, NJ: Princeton University Press.

McGee, J. E., Dowling, M. J. and Megginson, W. L. (1995) 'Cooperative strategy and new venture performance: the role of business strategy and management experience', *Strategic Management Journal*, 16: 565–80.

McGrath, B. and McGrath, R. G. (1999) 'Competitive advantage from knowledge spillovers: implications of the network economy', Paper presented at the Strategic Management Society Meetings, Berlin, October 2–6, 1999.

McGrath, R. G. (1996) 'Options and the entrepreneur: towards a strategic theory of entrepreneurial wealth creation', Best Papers Proceedings Academy of Management Annual Meetings, Cincinnati, Ohio, August, 1996, 101–5.

McGrath, R. G. (1997) 'A real options logic for initiating technology positioning investments', *Academy of Management Review*, 22: 974–96.

McGrath, R. G. (1999) 'Falling forward: real options reasoning and entrepreneurial failure', *Academy of Management Review*, 24: 13–30.

McGrath, R. G. and MacMillan, I. C. (1992) 'More like each other than anyone else? A cross-cultural study of entrepreneurial perceptions', *Journal of Business Venturing*, 7: 419–29.

McGrath, R. G. and MacMillan, I. C. (2000) *The Entrepreneurial Mindset: Strategies for Continuously Creating Opportunity in an Age of Uncertainty*. Boston, MA: Harvard Business School Press.

McGrath, R. G., Chen, M-J. and MacMillan, I. C. (1998) 'Multimarket maneuvering in uncertain spheres of influence: resource diversion strategies', *Academy of Management Review*, 23: 724–40.

McMillan, J. and Naughton, B. (1992) 'How to reform a planned economy: lessons from China', *Oxford Review of Economic Policy*, 8: 130–43.

Miller, D. (1993) 'The architecture of simplicity', *Academy of Management Review*, 18: 116–38.

Mitchell, G. R. and Hamilton, W. F. (1988) 'Managing R&D as a strategic option', *Research Technology Management*, 27 (May/June): 15–22.

Moini, A. H. (1998) 'Small firms exporting: How effective are government export assistance programs?', *Journal of Small Business Management*, 36: 1–15.

Mowery, D. C. and Rosenberg, N. (1993) 'The US national innovation system', in R. R. Nelson (ed.), *National Innovation Systems: A Comparative Analysis*. New York: Oxford University Press. pp. 29–75.

Nafukho, F. M. (1998) 'Entrepreneurial skills development programs for unemployed youth in Africa: a second look', *Journal of Small Business Management*, 36: 100–3.

Nelson, R. R. (ed.) (1993) *National Innovation Systems: A Comparative Analysis*. New York: Oxford University Press.

Olson, M. (1982) *The Rise and Decline of Nations: Economic Growth, Stagflation, and Social Rigidities*. New Haven: Yale University Press.

Palich, L. E. and Bagby, D. R. (1995) 'Using cognitive theory to explain entrepreneurial risk-taking: challenging conventional wisdom', *Journal of Business Venturing*, 10: 425–38.

Pfeffer, J. and Salancik, G. (1978) *The External Control of Organizations: A Resource Dependence Perspective*. New York: Harper & Row.

Porter, M. E. (1980) *Competitive Strategy*. New York: Free Press.

Porter, M. (1998) 'Clusters and the new economics of competition', *Harvard Business Review*, 76: 77–90.

Romer, P. M. (1990) 'Endogenous technological change', *Journal of Political Economy*, 998: S71–S102.

Romo, F. P. and Schwartz, M. (1995) 'The structural embeddedness of business decisions to migrate', *American Sociological Review*, 60: 874–907.

Rosenstein, J. (1988) 'The board and strategy: venture capital and high technology', *Journal of Business Venturing*, 3: 159–70.

Ruhnka, J. C., Feldman, H. D. and Dean, T. J. (1992) 'The "living dead" phenomena in venture capital investments', *Journal of Business Venturing*, 7: 137–55.

Sahlman, W. A. and Stevenson, H. (1985) 'Capital market myopia', *Journal of Business Venturing*, 1: 7–30.

Samuelson, W. F. and Bazerman, M. H. (1985) 'The winner's curse in bilateral negotiations', *Research in Experimental Economics*, 3: 105–37.

Sanchez, R. and Mahoney, J. T. (1996) 'Modularity, flexibility, and knowledge management in product and organizational design', *Strategic Management Journal*, 17: 63–76.

Saxenian, A. (1994) *Regional Advantage: Culture and Competition in Silicon Valley and Route 128*. Cambridge, MA: Harvard Business School Press.

Schilit, W. (1994) *Rising Stars and Fast Fades: Successes and Failures of Fast-Growth Companies*. New York: Macmillan.

Schilling, M. and Steensma, H. K. (2001) 'Industry determinants of the adoption of modular forms: an empirical test', *Academy of Management Journal*.

Schumpeter, J. A. (1942) *Capitalism, Socialism and Democracy*. New York: McGraw-Hill.

Shane, S. (2000) 'Prior knowledge and the discovery of entrepreneurial opportunities', *Organization Science*, 11: 448–69.

Shapiro, C. and Varian, H. R. (1998) *Information Rules: A Strategic Guide to the Network Economy*. Boston, MA: Harvard Business School Press.

Shaver, K. G. and Scott, L. R. (1991) 'Person, process, choice: the psychology of new venture creation', *Entrepreneurship, Theory and Practice*, Winter: 23–42.

Simon, H. (1992) 'Lessons from Germany's midsized giants', *Harvard Business Review*, 70: 115–23.

Singh, K. and Mitchell, W. (1996) 'Precarious collaboration: business survival after partners shut down or form new partnerships', *Strategic Managment Journal*, 17: 99–115.

Sitkin, S. B. (1992) 'Learning through failure: the strategy of small losses', in B. M. Staw and L. L. Cummings (eds), *Research in Organizational Behavior*, 14. Greenwich, CT: JAI Press. pp. 231–66.

Spence, M. A. (1984) 'Cost reduction, competition and industry performance', *Econometrica*, 52: 101–21.

Starr, J. and Bygrave, W. D. (1992) 'The second time around: assets and liabilities of prior start-up experience', in S. Birley, I. C. MacMillan and S. Subramony (eds), *International Perspectives on Entrepreneurship Research*. Amsterdam: Elsevier. pp. 340–63.

Starr, J. A. and MacMillan, I. C. (1990) 'Resource cooptation and social contracting: resource acquisition strategies for new ventures', *Strategic Management Journal*, 11: 79–92.

Staw, B. M. and Ross, J. (1987) 'Knowing when to pull the plug', *Harvard Business Review*, March–April: 68–74.

Steinberg, J. (1999) 'Nation's wealthy, seeing a void, take steps to aid public schools', *The New York Times*, Thursday, September 23, 1999: 1, 25.

Stinchcombe, A. L. (1965) 'Organizations and social structure', in J. G. March (ed.), *Handbook of Organizations*. Chicago: Rand McNally.

Stuart, T. Hoang, H. and Hybels, R. C. (1999) 'Interorganizational endorsements and the performance of entrepreneurial ventures', *Administrative Science Quarterly*, 44: 315–49.

Suarez, F. F. and Utterback, J. M. (1995) 'Dominant designs and the survival of firms', *Strategic Management Journal*, 16: 415–30.

Teece, D., Rumelt, R., Dosi, G. and Winter, S. (1994) 'Understanding corporate coherence: theory and evidence', *Journal of Economic Behavior and Organization*, 23: 1–30.

Thaler, R. (1992) *The Winner's Curse: Paradoxes and Anolomies of Economic Life*. Ithaca, NY: Cornell University Press.

Thompson, J. K. and Smith, H. L. (1991) 'Social responsibility and small business: suggestions for research', *Journal of Small Business Management*, 29: 30–9.

Tushman, M. and Anderson, P. (1986) 'Technological discontinuities and organizational environments', *Administrative Science Quarterly*, 31: 439–65.

Tushman, M. L. and Rosenkopf, L. (1992) 'Organizational determinants of technological change: toward a sociology of technological evolution', *Research in Organizational Behavior*, 14: 311–47.

Van de Ven, A. H. (1976) 'On the nature, formation and maintenance of relations among organizations', *Academy of Management Review*, 1: 24–36.

Van de Ven, A. H. (1986) 'Central problems in the management of innovation', *Management Science*, 32: 590–607.

Venkataraman, S. (1989) 'Problems of small venture start up survival and growth: a transaction set approach', Ph.D. dissertation, University of Minnesota.

Venkataraman, S. (1997) 'The distinctive domain of entrepreneurship research', in J. Katz and R. Brockhaus (eds), *Advances in Entrepreneurship, Firm Emergence, and Growth*. Greenwich, CT: JAI Press. pp. 119–38.

Venkataraman, S. and Van de Ven, A. H. (1993) 'Hostile environmental jolts, transaction set, and new business', *Journal of Business Venturing*, 13: 231–55.

Venkataraman, S., MacMillan, I. C. and McGrath, R. G. (1992) 'Progress in research on corporate venturing', in Sexton and Kasarda (eds), *State of the Art in Entrepreneurship Research*. Boston, MA: PWS Publishing Co. pp. 487–517.

Vesper, K. H. (1990) *New Venture Strategies*. Englewood Cliffs, NJ: Prentice-Hall.

Volkov, V. (1999) 'Violent entrepreneurship in post-communist Russia', *Europe–Asia Studies*, 51: 741–54.

von Hippel, E. (1986) 'Lead users: a source of novel product concepts', *Management Science*, 32: 791–805.

von Hippel, E. (1987) 'Cooperation between rivals: informal know-how trading', *Research Policy*, 16: 291–302.

von Hippel, E. (1988) *The Sources of Innovation*. New York: Oxford University Press.

Weiner, B. and Kukla, A. (1970) 'An attributional analysis of achievement motivation', *Journal of Personality and Social Psychology*, 15: 1–20.

Weiner, B., Russell, D. and Lerman, D. (1978) 'Affective consequences of causal ascriptions', in J. H. Harvey, W. Ickes and R. F. Kidd (eds), *New Directions in Attribution Research*. Hillsdale, NJ: Lawrence Erlbaum Associates. pp 59–90.

Woodman, R. W., Sawyer, J. E. and Griffin, R. W. (1993) 'Toward a theory of organizational creativity', *Academy of Management Review*, 18: 293–321.

Wortman, C. B. and Brehm, J. W. (1975) 'Responses to uncontrollable outcomes: an integration of reactance theory and the learned helplessness model', in L. Berkowitz (ed.), *Advances in Experimental Social Psychology (Vol. 8)*. New York: Academic Press.

Wright, M., Westhead, P. and Sohl, J. (1999) 'Editor's introduction: habitual entrepreneurs and angel investors', *Entrepreneurship, Theory and Practice*, 22: 5–21.

Zacharakis, A. L. and Meyer, G. D. (1998) 'A lack of insight: do venture capitalists really understand their own decision process?', *Journal of Business Venturing*, 13: 57–76.

Zapalska, A. (1997) 'Profiles of Polish entrepreneurship', *Journal of Small Business Management*, 35: 111–17.

15

The Strategy and Management of International Institutions

WINFRIED RUIGROK

International institutions such as the European Union (EU), the International Monetary Fund (IMF) and the World Trade Organization (WTO) have acquired a crucial role in the international political and economic arena. International institutions provide 'the rules that govern elements of world politics and the organizations that help implement those rules' (Keohane, 1998: 82). International institutions are a relatively recent phenomenon. Most of them date back to the post-war era, and some only to the 1990s. Demand for international institutions has grown steadily over the 1980s and 1990s, as a result of which many international institutions have been founded or upgraded (cf. Abbott and Snidal, 1998). At the basis of this development is the globalization of firms and markets, which eroded the effectiveness of states and of institutions whose role had been defined largely in a national context (Braithwaite and Drahos, 2000).

As international institutions have become more important, expectations have risen regarding the content, speed, and effectiveness of international institutions' policies. However, a big obstacle is that international institutions are very difficult to manage. An international institution usually does not have a strong CEO who can define its direction, nor one dominant nation that can fully impose its will upon other nations. Instead, international institutions tend to face highly diverse demands that somehow need to be accommodated. A case in point are the variety of demands that member states had of how the IMF should handle the Asia crisis, or how the North Atlantic Treaty Organization (NATO) should handle the Balkan crisis. Additionally, international institutions often need to conquer their position in the face of dissent by powerful nations or domestic institutions, as in the case of the European Central Bank and its management of the Euro currency.

For these and other reasons, there has been widespread frustration about the way that many international institutions are being operated. International institutions are being criticized for the policies that they pursue, for the limited effectiveness of implementing these policies, for the lack of transparency and accountability, and for the costs of maintaining their bureaucracies.

Over the 1980s and 1990s, institutions have become a popular area of research in management, economics, political science and sociology, though scholars in these four disciplines often define the concept of 'institution' in somewhat different terms. *International* institutions have been studied primarily by political scientists and international relations scholars. Much of this research has focused on the policy *content* of international institutions, and on the international or epistemological *context* in which international institutions operate (Braithwaite and Drahos, 2000). Management scholars have so far paid much less attention to international institutions. In view of the ongoing rise of international institutions and the concurrent critique on their effectiveness, this chapter argues in favor of building a research agenda on the strategy and management of international institutions. Such research should especially address the *processes* taking place in international organizations, with an eye on identifying ways to raise the effectiveness of international institutions.

The first part of this chapter traces the evolution of international institutions. The second part reviews the broad literature on domestic and international institutions produced in the area of political science and international relations, as well as in fields such as sociology, economics, and international law, and in the area of management itself. The third part then discusses how notions and approaches from the strategy and management field could help modify the research agenda in studying the effectiveness of international institutions.

THE RISE OF INTERNATIONAL INSTITUTIONS

The rise of international organizations is often dated at 1919, when the League of Nations was established (Archer, 1983: 3). Before this year, however, specialized international institutions were founded, such as the International Telecommunications Union (ITU), which was established in 1865 and became a UN agency in 1947. According to some, '(i)n the longer sweep of years the ITU has been the most important organization of states' (Braithwaite and Drahos, 2000: 347), due to its ability to shape global regulation on a technical rather than a political basis. The ITU works through technical committees in which interested large firms have often played a key role. Other early specialized organizations striving for the global dispersion of technical standards included the International Electrotechnical Commission (IEC), created in 1906, and the International Federation of the National Standardizing Associations (ISA), set up in 1926, both predecessors

of the International Standards Organization (ISO), founded in 1947.

However, the League of Nations represented the first *universal* international organization of which all independent nations in the world could voluntarily become a member. The League of Nations created an umbrella for already existing conventions and specialized organizations which also included the International Court of Justice (situated in The Hague, the Netherlands). Before 1919, several factors had hindered the rise of universal international organizations.[1] First, international relations in the 19th century were dominated by considerations of state formation and national sovereignty. In 1860, for instance, the United States (US) were yet to experience the Civil War, whereas Italy and Germany were yet to complete their process of state-formation, unifying formerly independent states. Second, 19th century transport and communication techniques precluded international organizations with complex decision-making processes and continuous consultation with the home front. Third, companies did not have the structures and processes in place to manage extended international operations. As a result, the scope of international business before 1880 was still limited (Jones, 1996).

The League of Nations collapsed in 1939, and World War II marked the end of European economic dominance as well as the beginning of US supremacy in the world. By 1944, the US government had developed a vision to include the entire world into one liberal economic order (Van der Pijl, 1992). The main focus of this multilateral vision was the United Nations (UN) family of international organizations, consisting of the UN itself (set up in 1945) and the 1944 Bretton Woods system of the IMF and the World Bank (International Bank for Reconstruction and Development). The US also played a crucial role in rebuilding Europe, using international organizations such as the Organization for European Economic Cooperation (OEEC, 1948), which was to coordinate the spending of the Marshall funds provided by the US. The OEEC would subsequently transform into the Organization for Economic Cooperation and Development (1961). Other post-war organizations that were established included the General Agreement on Tariffs and Trade (GATT) (1947), the European Payments

Union (1950) and the European Economic Community (1957).

The leading role of the US in creating these international institutions was never undisputed. The US emphasized multilateralism and non-discrimination rather than national sovereignty. Even Keynes 'wavered between this and a belief that Britain and the other European countries would only be able to pursue policies of full employment and reconstruct their wartorn economies if they could maintain strict controls on trade and capital flows' (MacBean and Snowden, 1981: 2). In the end, however, many in continental Europe felt that 'industrial countries ... were too advanced, specialized and interdependent to consider genuine, lasting improvements in economic welfare after the war without re-establishing some sort of a new economic order' (Panić, 1995: 38). Also, it was felt that governments had to play a leading role in this process, in view of the market limitations that had come to the fore in the 1930s.

After their establishment, many international organizations rapidly gained importance. By 1992, there were 15,000 International Governmental Organizations (IGOs) and International Non-Governmental Organizations (INGOs). This total did not include multinational corporations and Business International Non-Governmental Organizations (abbreviated as BINGOs) (Waters, 1995: 113).

Many international relations scholars distinguish between international organizations and international institutions. Young sees the distinction between institutions and organizations as follows: 'organizations are material entities possessing offices, personnel, budgets, equipment and, more often than not, legal personality. Put another way, organizations are actors in social practices. Institutions are frameworks affecting the behavior of actors by defining social practices and spelling out codes of conduct appropriate to them. But they are not actors in their own rights' (1996a: x). Thus international institutions can be analyzed both as organizations (with their own rules and organizing principles) and as institutions (affecting their environment).

As international institutions can only act on the basis of the authority delegated to them by nation states, international institutions have been facing huge and highly diverse expectations on the way they should affect their environment. If and when international institutions could not meet these expectations, they have been criticized for their lack of effectiveness (Feldstein, 1998; Joyner, 1999) (Table 15.1). The UN has been blamed of peacekeeping failures in countries such as Somalia and Bosnia, and the IMF has been criticized for failing to react properly to the Russian and Asian economic crises. These and other institutions have also been criticized for the costs of operating their expensive bureaucratic organizations. The US long withheld financial contributions due to the UN to enforce it to reduce costs and to shift their priorities, and even retreated from agencies that it considered to be ideologically biased such as the United Nations Educational, Scientific, and Cultural Organization (UNESCO) and the United Nations Industrial Development Organization (UNIDO).

Yet despite the costs and difficulties of running international institutions, their significance has only increased over the 1990s: the European Community evolved into the EU, and the GATT was upgraded to the WTO. While some international institutions have a global scope, others deliberately do not. In the case of the EU, an international institution emerged with substantial *regional* powers: the European Commission and the European Court of Justice can enforce member states' governments into compliance on a range of pre-defined issues. Since 1995, more than 67 Regional Integration Agreements (RIAs) have been notified at the WTO, representing 60% of all RIAs in the world (Dent, 1997; Ethier, 1998; OECD, 1996). Accepted under WTO rules (article XXIV), trade-regulating RIAs may act as a countervailing force against the WTO *global* institution as much as they represent attempts to strengthen regional integration. The WTO adopted a pragmatic and case-by-case approach to RIAs, acknowledging that RIAs may in fact serve as an added guarantee for the survival of multilateral institutions (Ethier, 1998).

Table 15.2 presents a categorization of some important state-based international institutions. This table shows that in many areas, there is more than one international institution trying to make its mark. This 'diversity' goes about with frequent differences of opinion between states as to the appropriate international institution to discuss certain issues. The less developed

Table 15.1 *A selection of important international institutions (2000)*

Institution	Established	Members	Purpose(s)	Managerial issues and critique
United Nations	1945	188 member states	To promote and protect democracy and human rights; to save children from starvation and disease; to provide relief assistance to refugees and disaster victims; to counter global crime, drugs and disease; and to assist countries devastated by war and the long-term threat of land-mines	Fiercely criticized for its ineffective peacekeeping and enforcement mechanisms, and for its inefficient bureaucracy
International Monetary Fund	1946	182 member states	To promote international monetary cooperation, exchange stability, and orderly exchange arrangements; to foster economic growth and high levels of employment; and to provide temporary financial assistance to countries under adequate safeguards to help ease balance of payments adjustment	IMF decision-making depends on capital supplied, leading to over-representation of Western points of view (US + EU = 48.3% of voting rights), exerting isomorphism to other economies. IMF handling of the Russia and Asia crises has been severely criticized, even by its sister organization, the World Bank, on the grounds that IMF policies are postulated on Western economic structures and solutions
World Trade Organization	1995 (1947)	135 member states (30 more have applied)	To ensure that international trade flows as smoothly, predictably and freely as possible	WTO relies on member states' willingness for further trade liberalization; only limited sanctions to enforce compliance
European Union	1993 (1957)	15: Austria, Belgium, Denmark, England, Finland, France, Germany, Greece, Ireland, Italy, Luxembourg, the Netherlands, Portugal, Spain, Sweden	To promote economic and social progress which is balanced and sustainable, to assert the European identity on the international scene and to introduce a European citizenship for the nationals of the Member States	'Enlargement' with Central and Eastern European countries could imply 'overstretch'; lack of transparency and democratic control of European decision-making structures; scandals on spending EU funds; almost 50% of EU budget is on agriculture, sustaining agricultural excess production
North American Free Trade Agreement	1994 (1985)	US, Canada and Mexico	To promote trade and investments through North America	Follow-up to 1985 US–Canada Free Trade Agreement; many non-tariff barriers remain

(Contd.)

Table 15.1 (Contd.)

Institution	Established	Members	Purpose(s)	Managerial issues and critique
Organization of Petroleum Exporting Countries	1960	11: Algeria, Libya, Nigeria, Indonesia, Iran, Iraq, Kuwait, Qatar, Saudi Arabia, United Arab Emirates, Venezuela	To promote stability and prosperity of the international petroleum market	Decision-making by consensus, incomplete membership and lack of enforcement mechanisms often hindered OPEC in reducing output to raise prices
North Atlantic Treaty Organization	1949	19 member states	To establish a collective defense for the preservation of peace and security in the North Atlantic area	Set up as US-dominated military alliances against former Soviet Union; after 1989 vehicle in persuading Central and Eastern European countries to adopt market economy principles
Asia Pacific Economic Cooperation forum	1989	21 member economies	To promote open trade and economic cooperation among member economies around the Pacific Rim	Has so far been unsuccessful in defining independent role due to highly diverse membership
International Olympic Movement	1894	International sports federations and National Olympic Committees	To organize summer Games of the Olypiad and Winter Olympics every four years	International Olympic Committee has max. 115 members, elected for 8 years; strong rule by president Samaranch; several corruption scandals on allocating organizing city

Note: Years in brackets refer to establishment of legal predecessor organizations.
Source: International institutions' websites; *FT*, 20 February 2000; Preston and Windsor (1997).

Table 15.2 *Categories of international institutions and influential actors*

Areas → Key actors	Trade and competition	Finance	Labor	Environment	Contract and property rights	Telecommunications	Nuclear safety
Leading institutions – organizations of states	OECD, GATT/WTO, EU	IMF, World Bank, OECD, Bank for International Settlements, EU, G-7	ILO	OECD, EU, World Bank, International Maritime Organization	WTO, EU, World Intellectual Property Organization	ITU, OECD, World Bank, WTO	International Atomic Energy Agency, EURATOM, OECD
Dominant states[1]	US, UK (EU)	US, UK, Germany (EU)	US, France, Germany	US, Germany, Sweden, Norway, Netherlands	US	US, UK	US, France, UK, Russia
International Business Organizations	International Chamber of Commerce (ICC)	ICC	International Organization of Employers	Union of Industrial and Employers' Federations in Europe (UNICE), Business Council for Sustainable Development	Intellectual Property Committee, International Intellectual Property Alliance, UNICE, Keidanren	International Telecommunications User Group, Society for Worldwide Interbank Funds Transfer, ICC	World Association of Nuclear Operators
International NGOs	Consumers International, International Confederation of Free Trade Union (ICFTU), Third World Network	International Accounting Standards Committee	ICFTU	ISO, Greenpeace, International Union for the Conservation of Nature, World Rainforest Network	International Law Assn, International Assn. for the Protection of Intellectual Property	ISO, International Electrochemical Commission	Greenpeace

[1] Though not a state, the EU as a 'rival' institution often plays a similar role as states in defining other institutions' agendas.

Source: Largely based on Braithwaite and Drahos, 2000: 476–7.

countries, for example, often seek to involve UNCTAD in World trade negotiations since less developed countries play a much stronger role in UNCTAD. As the example of the RIAs suggests, co-existing institutions may sometimes be *rival* institutions since they offer alternative fora for international negotiations or conflict resolution. Table 15.2 suggests that such rivalry may also be found in the interaction between different *types* of international institutions – between state-based and industry-based institutions or international NGOs.

While especially governments of smaller and open economies have often sought to strengthen the role of international institutions in providing international transparency and in departing from *ad hoc* rules, the 1980s and 1990s also marked the rise of large companies seeking a stronger (or a different) role for international institutions. For instance, large European technology companies between 1983 and 1985 campaigned at a European level for further economic integration, in a bid to create a level playing field with US and Japanese competitors who enjoyed large and integrated home markets. The European Roundtable of Industrialists (ERT), established in 1983, was a major support to the European Commissioner Davignon to formulate the 'Europe 1992' project (Van Tulder and Junne, 1988: 215). Companies may also seek to reform existing global regimes. A case in point are the European mobile phone producers, which in the year 2000, based on their edge in mobile phone technology, challenged the role of the ITU. Since the ITU became a UN agency in 1947, it has been heavily dominated by US interests (Braithwaite and Drahos, 2000: 347).

Notwithstanding the effectiveness issue, and the problem of overlapping or rival mandates of international institutions, recent work offers an explanation why international institutions have gradually come to adopt a more significant role in the world economy. Kaul et al. suggest that certain international institutions provide 'global public goods' (1998: 3), that is, goods whose benefits are non-rivalrous in consumption (consumption by one does not rival consumption by another, such as clean air, peace, or stable exchange rates) and non-excludable (benefiting all people, countries and generations). Examples of such institutions are the UN and the IMF. Other international institutions provide international public goods only for the members of the club (hence called 'club goods'), such as the G7 (group of seven industrialized countries), the EU, or NATO. Phrased in economic terms, international institutions, once established, shape actors' expectations and provide more reliable information, helping states to move toward the Pareto frontier. Thus, studying international institutions is of great relevance to international business.

APPROACHES IN STUDYING INTERNATIONAL INSTITUTIONS

According to Webster (2000), the word 'institution' refers both to the process of establishing an institution, and to its outcome. The outcome can be 'a significant practice, relationship or organization in a society or culture', or 'an established organization or corporation, especially of a public character'.

Institutions have been studied in many social sciences, such as political science, sociology, economics, management, geography and law. In each of these disciplines, institutional theory has developed specific concepts, approaches and 'star authors' appearing in the bibliographies of other institutional research carried out in these disciplines. In many disciplines, institutional theory has made a considerable impact, though usually it has not become the mainstream approach. Below, the insights and advances of institutional theory in political science, sociology, economics and management will be evaluated.[2]

Institutions in Political Science/ International Relations

The area of international relations (IR) is often seen as a subset of political science, therefore these are treated here under the same heading (for a different view, however, see Milner, 1998: 762ff.). To most political scientists and IR scholars, states are the central unit of analysis. States are taken to be sovereign entities, possessing the freedom to decide to cooperate with other states or not (an example of the latter would be North Korea). Thus international cooperation can only emerge on the basis of bargaining between governments. Inevitably, this produces a level of analysis problem (Singer, 1961): should one start the analysis at the state or at the international level, and how to link these two levels? Since it is not self-evident to many IR scholars that states will cooperate with other states in the first place, a central question to be answered is why and how 'governance without government' (Rosenau and Czempiel, 1992) emerges and functions. The most tangible form in which governance without government manifests itself is in the international institutions (other forms include informal, non-institutionalized mechanisms, which are accepted by the majority or the most powerful of those it affects [cf. Rosenau and Czempiel, 1992: 4]). IR is the only area discussed here that explicitly studies *international* institutions.

Initial work on international institutions had a distinct basis in International Law. After World War II, research on international institutions focused on formal organizations, such as the UN, and IR scholars found an outlet in the academic journal *International Organization*. Over the 1970s, attention shifted to the role hegemonic states (such as Great Britain in the 19th and the US in the 20th century) played in maintaining a stable and open world (Kindleberger, 1973). So-called 'realist' authors argued that since states were rationalistic and self-interested actors, the relative decline of the US economic and political dominance over the 1960s and 1970s would eventually undermine world stability and trade. In response, some scholars arose who argued that international *regimes* (such as the International Energy Agency or the IMF) could substitute for the hegemonic power after hegemony had lapsed (Keohane, 1984). Krasner defined international regimes as 'implicit or explicit norms, rules, and decision-making procedures around which actors' expectations converge in a given area of international relations' (1983). In the subsequent flood of literature on international regimes, two broad approaches emerged. Referring to transaction cost economics (see below), the *rationalistic* approach argued that 'institutions reduce uncertainty and alter transaction costs' (Keohane, 1988: 386). Adopting a sociological perspective, the *reflective* approach criticized the former approach for its lack of endogenous dynamic, and emphasized that institutions themselves are the product of prior existing institutions.

Several authors have sought to address the issue of international institutions' effectiveness. Young argued in favor of a symmetry of power within the international institution. He suggests that 'the more symmetrical the distribution of power, the harder it is to establish institutional arrangements initially but the more effective they are once formed' (1994: 15; Young, 1992). Woods suggested that international institutions' effectiveness depends on three often overlapping principles: participation, accountability, and fairness (1999).

The IR literature on international institutions produced some important findings. Firstly, many scholars found that state interests are not given, but 'depend in part how people define their identities' (Keohane, 1998: 90), pointing at the importance of ideas, norms and information at institutions' constituent partners. This suggests that crafty domestic or international institutions' leaders may be able to re-arrange perceptions and expectations. Secondly, Putnam (1988) emphasized the importance of two-level bargaining games (both at the home front and at the international institution), showing how asymmetrical information and actors' beliefs help shape outcomes. Two-level games assume that domestic leaders typically seek to manipulate domestic and international politics simultaneously (Moravcsik, 1993: 15). Analyses conducted at the level of international institutions will fail to capture this important dimension, which also determines whether international institutions are perceived as 'effective'. Thirdly, international institutions' effectiveness depends on such variables as perceived common interests, the distribution of power among actors (an even distribution may thwart effectiveness), the extent to which members share values, and the state of members' domestic politics (Keohane, 1998).

The political science literature on international institutions is characterized by a strong focus on content and on the influence wielded by member states on concrete issues. Surprisingly, in view of the criticism of international institutions' effectiveness, detailed and longitudinal studies of decision-making processes within international institutions do not appear to dominate the field.

Institutions in Sociology

The sociological analysis of institutions goes back to Robert Merton (1948). Early work adopted a functionalist perspective, analyzing the formal structures of organizations and understanding institutionalization as the 'formalized procedures that perpetuate organizing principles of social life' (Blau, 1964: 273). Initially, the focus was on organizations as isolated entities (Blau, 1970). In the second half of the 1960s, sociologists began to relate organizations to their environments (Lawrence and Lorsch, 1967), eventually guiding Pfeffer and Salancik to analyze organizations as somewhat static and reactive structures seeking to manage their external 'resource dependency' (1978). Much of the work produced afterwards focuses either on organizations' internal structures and processes of institutionalization (Giddens, 1984), or regarded organizations primarily as 'embedded' actors in external institutions (Granovetter, 1985).

In their seminal work *The Social Construction of Reality* (1967), Berger and Luckmann presented institutions and the process of institutionalization as important objects of sociological analysis. They defined an institution as 'a reciprocal typification of habitualized action by types of actors' (1967: 54). In this definition, reciprocal typification refers to the emergence of shared meanings among constituent actors, and habitualized action refers to the patterns of problem solving that these actors develop in response to external stimuli. One decade later, Meyer and Rowan (1977) launched the term 'institutionalized organizations', referring to organizations' formal structures *and* to their socially shared meanings and symbolic interactions and artifacts. Based on the work by Berger and Luckmann (1967) and Meyer and Rowan (1977), most sociologists today regard institutions as socially constructed and enacted in discourse (that is, the object of ongoing debates). Anthony Giddens (1984) explained why institutions may nevertheless have stable structures. In his view, actors within a given context have a 'practical consciousness' to '"go on" within the routines of social life' (1984: 4). Actors' knowledge of the implicit and explicit 'rules' effectively *structure* and reproduce social practices. Thus, Giddens interpreted institutionalization as a 'structuration' process. Inevitably, however, a

level-of-analysis problem emerged, and two broad approaches emerged: the so-called *methodological individualism* takes calculating individuals as the starting point of analysis (Coleman, 1990) whereas the *methodological holism* rather focuses on institutions than on the individuals constituting these institutions (cf. Tolbert and Zucker, 1997: 170ff).

Reviewing the sociological literature on institutions, Tolbert and Zucker (1997: 175ff) suggested a set of three sequential processes of institutionalization: habitualization, which refers to the generation and formalization of formal arrangements, representing the pre-institutionalization stage; objectification, which refers to the rise of some degree of social consensus on the value of a structure and to its adoption, effectively diffusing the structure; and sedimentation, by which they mean the virtually complete spread of structures across the relevant group of actors and its perpetuation over a lengthy period of time. Tolbert and Zucker suggest that these three processes help to explain variability in levels of institutionalization, and it would make sense to refer to them when studying the emergence and functioning of international institutions. However, these three processes fail to take into account institutions' environments, which in the case of international institutions play a dominant role.

In Keohane's (1988) words, the sociological approach to institutions is the reflective one. The work by sociologists on institutions has greatly influenced other social sciences, especially the management sciences. Unfortunately, the sociological literature may be relatively complicated and operationalizing sociological concepts in the management sciences is not always easy.

Institutions in Economics

Institutions have also been the object of study of economists. *Institutional* economics does not take the individual but rather the institutions created by individuals as the focal point of analysis and studies 'the emergence, development and functions of the institutions that are part of the economic system' (Hodgson, 1993a: xi). Institutional economists think of firms and other economic actors as institutions. Economic institutions have been defined as 'systems of enforced norms, routines, conventions and traditions in which individual economic activity is embedded' (Groenewegen et al., 1995: 6). Institutional economists emphasize that 'institutions and routines, other than acting simply as rigidities and constraints, enable decisions and action by providing more-or-less reliable information regarding the likely actions of others' (Hodgson, 1993a: xvii). Just as sociologists do, many institutional economists argue that institutions are 'being founded or constituted in or by human interactions and exchanges' (Sjöstrand, 1995: 21). Providing an 'infrastructure that facilitates or hinders human co-ordination and the allocation of resources', institutions effectively are 'public goods, relevant to and shared by many, and they are in principle characterized by non-excludability' (Sjöstrand, 1995: 21).

As in the management sciences (see below), an 'old' and a 'new' institutional economics have been distinguished (Hodgson, 1993b; Vanberg, 1989). The old institutionalist school provided a dominant paradigm in the US over the 1920s and 1930s, and included such illustrious names as Thorstein Veblen, John Commons and Wesley Clair Mitchell. The major difference between the two lies in the fact that the old institutionalism 'developed, theoretically and methodologically, in *opposition* to the neo-classical tradition in economics, while the new institutionalism emerges from *within* this tradition' (Vanberg, 1989: 335, original italics). Veblen critiqued the neoclassical notions of the 'rational economic man' and of economic equilibrium, paving the way for Herbert Simon's idea of 'bounded rationality' and pointing at the importance of understanding *evolution* rather than static equilibria (Hodgson, 1993b: 14ff). As early as 1919, Veblen defined institutions as 'settled habits of thought common to men' (Hodgson, 1993a: xii). Interestingly, early writings on social structures were already influenced by the biological metaphor of evolution, such as the natural selection of institutions.

The 'new' institutional economics emerged from the mid-1970s onwards. Much of this resulted from work 'within or close to mainstream economics' (Hodgson, 1993b: 1), which may be illustrated by the Nobel prizes that have been awarded to institutional authors such as James Buchanan, Ronald Coase, Douglas North and Herbert Simon. New institutional economists share with neo-classical economists the assumption of the 'abstract individual', meaning that the individual is taken as a calculating *Homo economicus* whose demands and preferences do not need to be explained. Although also referred to as methodological individualism, it is a different type than the one discussed under the heading of sociology. New institutional economists focus on the institution as a whole rather than on its constituent actors, and seek to explain institutions' structural evolution in objective terms, rather than to explain the origins of this evolution.

Oliver Williamson is one of the best-known neo-institutional economists, attempting to develop a theory of the firm by explaining the rise of capitalist institutions such as the multidivisional and vertically integrated firm (1975, 1985). Williamson focused on transactions between economic actors (hence the name transaction costs economics) and considered Herbert Simon's bounded rationality and opportunism as crucial motives in the creation of economic institutions. Other scholars explored the development of trust, and the role of power (Groenewegen et al., 1995).

Institutions in Management

Institutional theory in management scholars has drawn heavily from the work by sociologists and, to a lesser extent, institutional economists. As a result, it is frequently difficult to classify an institutional theorist unambiguously as a sociologist or a management scholar. Just as in the case of economics, management scholars have distinguished between an old and new institutionalism (Powell and DiMaggio, 1991: 13). However, in terms of content, the old and the new institutionalism bear perhaps more resemblance to developments we have seen in sociology. The old institutionalism focused on conflicting values, power issues and symbolism (mission statements) at the level of the individual organization (Selznick, 1957). The new institutionalism combines elements of Meyer and Rowan (1977), Pfeffer and Salancik (1978) and Giddens (1984), in that it analyzes the development of habits, routines and legitimacy *in response to an organization's embeddedness*. An important difference with new institutional economists is that new institutional management scholars do not necessarily see institutions (or their constituents) as rational economic actors. A central notion of the new institutionalism in management is that of isomorphism: the phenomenon that organizations become increasingly similar due to (external) institutional pressures, norms and expectations (DiMaggio and Powell, 1983).

In essence, the distinction between the old and the new institutionalism may be seen as another manifestation of the level of analysis problem that we encountered above. Whereas the old institutionalism had its strengths in the internal analysis of institutions, the new institutionalism explains how environments provide organizations with similar experiences and expectations, which leads to similar patterns of interpretation and thus helps to account for the stability of organizational arrangements and the similarity of firms' strategic behavior. Work in the second half of the 1990s has sought to integrate the old and the new institutionalism. Royston Greenwood and Bob Hinings suggested that indeed 'when theorists research the *interaction* of organizational actors with institutionalized contexts (…) they will find new directions. It is at the intersection of two forces that explanations of change and stability can be found' (1996: 1048) (see also Lawrence, 1999). This is exactly what Putnam's two-level game (1988) has sought to provide in the area of political science and international relations.

THE EFFECTIVENESS OF INTERNATIONAL
INSTITUTIONS

As the above section shows, there is 'very little consensus on the definition of key concepts, measures or methods within this theoretic tradition' (Tolbert and Zucker, 1997: 169). This lack of consensus hampers the development of a cross-disciplinary approach to studying international institutions. One sees an overwhelming divergence in the conceptual bases, the approaches and the foci of analysis. The political science literature focuses especially on *policy content*, the (international) *context* in which these policies emerge, and the *concepts* underlying domestic and international institutions. The institutional literature originating from economics, sociology and management rather address the *effect* of institutions. Contributions from these disciplines tend to emphasize the effects in theoretical terms, however, and refer to domestic institutions. There is a real gap in identifying and documenting the effects of *international* institutions.

In none of the four disciplines does the issue of the *effectiveness* of international institutions appear to figure highly on the research agenda. This may seem surprising to a management audience used to an ongoing stream of research aimed at helping organizations to raise their efficiency and effectiveness. Much of the research in the political sciences and sociology has been theory-driven and aimed at the development of specific theories and concepts, rather than inspired by practical problems or empirical phenomena. The economics literature does not address the effectiveness of international institutions, much in the same way as the firm itself has remained a black box to many economists.

The primary reason for the lack of empirical research into the effectiveness of international institutions has probably been the focus on institutions as 'social practices and … codes of conduct' (Young, 1996a) affecting actors' behavior, rather than on the organizations that help to realize these practices and codes of conduct. This has shifted attention away from empirical research and away from issues such as implementation and effectiveness. Additional reasons of the limited research into the effectiveness of international institutions are that the number of international institutions are still quite limited and that the number of people working in international institutions are many times smaller than those working at firms or government organizations. Therefore, demand for practical research into the effectiveness of international institutions has also been weaker than for research into firm effectiveness and efficiency.

Finally, it has also been less obvious in the case of international institutions as compared with other organizations that research into international institutions' effectiveness actually matters that much. A major variable moderating the effectiveness of international institutions has been the international context which permitted or enabled international institutions to be more effective. For instance, the European Commission itself did not decide to establish the European Union or a common currency – it was confronted with political considerations and decisions taken by important member states. Likewise, NATO's decision to expand to countries of the former 'East Bloc' was not made at its Brussels headquarters, but in Washington, London and Paris.

This indicates that research into the effectiveness of international institutions should not just take into account the actual policies pursued and the circumstances under which decisions were taken and had to be implemented. In studying the effectiveness of international institutions, it may help to distinguish between the policy or strategy *content*, *process* and *context* (Pettigrew, 1985). The policy or strategy content refers to the institution's explicit or implicit policy, plans, goals or strategy. The policy or strategy process refers to the development and formulation of the institution's policy or strategy, and to the implementation and internal monitoring of the policy or strategy content agreed upon. Finally, the policy or strategy context refers to the national and international circumstances under which policies and strategies are being adopted and implemented, and to the role of stakeholders seeking to influence these policies and strategies. The content, process, and context dimensions all matter in studying the effectiveness of international institutions, and different disciplines have their own strengths in addressing these aspects. Yet it is in examining policy and strategy processes that the management field may contribute most clearly to raising the effectiveness of international institutions.

Process Research into the Effectiveness of International Institutions

The UN Secretary General arguably faces a management challenge more formidable than the CEO of a *Fortune* 100 company. The UN CEO is facing a dispersed, heterogeneous and unpredictable group of owners, without any majority shareholder. This CEO can never look at immediate or more distant competitors to inform the organization's own decision-making. The organization employs a highly diverse workforce, yet it cannot offer any incentive schemes to set some common goals and motivate its employees. Possibilities to insert a common identity are further limited by the fact that there is no majority nationality, not one set of values shared by a majority of its employees, nor even one language spoken by its workforce – partly because the organizations usually had to adopt several official corporate languages. This CEO cannot refer to any existing markets in order to argue for internal changes. And perhaps most importantly, the organization can never be sure whether this CEO has done a good job, since there are few transparent performance indicators to help distinguish good from average or poor performance.

The methodologies and concepts developed for studying firms and other organizations will often require some kind of adjustment when studying international institutions. In his chapter on 'Strategic management in the contemporary public sector', elsewhere in this volume, Ewan Ferlie argues that generic management notions may be useful for studying the public sector, yet that some adaptation will often be required (Ferlie, 2001). It is crucial to appreciate the heterogeneous and at times quickly changing international context in which international institutions need to act, which seriously affects their ability to plan in advance, and which forces them to build up and maintain considerable organizational slack to be prepared for a sudden change of course. Likewise, concepts used in the strategy content literature may not always be applicable: it is often impossible to indicate what products or services international institutions generate, and ownership structures are such that states as owners cannot easily discard stock in an international institution which they consider badly run.

In selecting their methodologies, management researchers will also have to make certain adaptations when studying international institutions. Researchers will be hard put to generate large data sets consisting of individual international institutions in order to identify certain patterns or causal relationships. Organizational performance measures, such as various types of return rates or cost measures, cannot be applied to international institutions to check their performance relative to peer or rival institutions. Despite these disclaims, numerous issues tackled in the management literature could be applied to studying international institutions. Process research in international institutions could focus on a single issue or on a number of the below issues.

A first set of research questions could focus on the nature of leadership in international institutions. Leadership has been defined as 'an instrument of goal achievement' (Bass, 1990: 15–16) and as 'an interaction between two or more members of a group that often involved a structuring or restructuring of the situation and the perceptions and expectations of the members... Leadership occurs when one group member modifies the motivation or competencies of others in the group. Any member of the group can exhibit some amount of leadership' (Bass, 1990: 19–20).

Following this definition, research could focus on the ways in which individual or successive figureheads at international institutions have sought to motivate their organizations' people, to utilize existing or instill new competencies into the organization, and to create 'winning formulas' for important internal stakeholders. There do not appear to be many systematic studies of the role of leaders in international institutions and their ability to sway perceptions of their institutions' bureaucrats, member states, multinational corporations, NGOs and of the people at large. There are, of course, abundant conspiracy analyses available (for one anecdotal example on Maurice Strong, the former Deputy Secretary-General of the UN and head of the UN Environmental Program, see Lawson, 1996/7). Yet what did Jacques Delors do to the European Commission that made him a more successful leader than his predecessor or successor – if indeed he was. In addition, research could assess whether leaders at international institutions attempted to distribute leadership through their organizations, and with what results. Can one distinguish between leadership styles in different international institutions?

A second set of research questions could target the nature of decision-making in international institutions. March and Simon (1958) have pointed out that decision-makers are typically facing a much larger number of stimuli than they could possibly process and comprehend, and moreover that these stimuli are vague, ambivalent or even contradictory. Consequently, decision-makers are constantly facing a so-called 'weak situation' (Mischel, 1968) which is not clear enough to dictate an apparent course of action. In such circumstances, as Finkelstein and Hambrick explain, 'the decision maker's personal frame of reference, not the objective characteristics of the situation, becomes the basis for action' (1996: 20).

If corporate executives and managers are often facing a 'weak situation', the same must hold for decision-makers in international institutions. Top ranking officials at international institutions invariably must engage into a balancing act, keeping one eye on the institutions' mandate and another eye on important member states' views, knowing that important member states may well change their views if circumstances change. Research could track decision-making within an international institution on important strategic decisions, for instance to impose sanctions or to send a military intervention power to an outcast country, and identify the extent to which organization-specific, managerial characteristics or environmental factors explain the eventual outcome.

A third area of research could be the impact that decision-makers have, or are believed to have, on international institutions' 'performance'. A fruitful avenue here could be to apply agency theory, by regarding top ranking officials at international institutions as delegates appointed by nation states in order to maximize the institutions' value and/or performance (Berle and Means, 1932; Jensen and Meckling, 1976). Essentially, the situation of a separation of capital owners and managers, and the ensuing dilemma of aligning the former and the latter interests, is not altogether dissimilar from the problem that member states are facing when delegating authority to an international institution likely to be subject to its own dynamism and producing policies that may well deviate from its actual mandate.

Based on agency theory, a large body of research has examined the relationship between board or more generally senior management characteristics and such outcome variables as innovation, inter-organizational relationships, strategic choices or performance levels, using a range of methodologies and empirical data. At an aggregate level, the results of this research demonstrate little consistency, which leads Dalton et al. (1998) to suggest research should examine more specific categories (such as board committees) or features in order to capture the subtleties of these relationships. However, Finkelstein and Hambrick

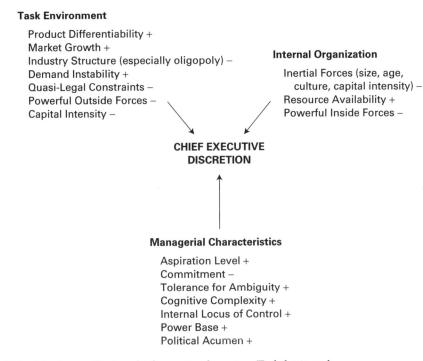

Task Environment

Product Differentiability +
Market Growth +
Industry Structure (especially oligopoly) –
Demand Instability +
Quasi-Legal Constraints –
Powerful Outside Forces –
Capital Intensity –

Internal Organization

Inertial Forces (size, age,
  culture, capital intensity) –
Resource Availability +
Powerful Inside Forces –

**CHIEF EXECUTIVE
DISCRETION**

Managerial Characteristics

Aspiration Level +
Commitment –
Tolerance for Ambiguity +
Cognitive Complexity +
Internal Locus of Control +
Power Base +
Political Acumen +

Figure 15.1   *The forces affecting chief executive discretion (Finkelstein and
Hambrick, 1996: 27)*

showed that managerial effects on corporate performance differ substantially across industries (1996: 27–8). *Mutatis mutandis*, researchers could measure the effects that 'top management teams' or 'upper echelons' at different international institutions have on their institutions' performance. Figure 15.1 presents some specific determinants of managerial discretion, many of which could also play a role at international institutions.

A final area of process research at international institutions could focus on change processes and the role of organizational culture. The concept of organizational culture came up over the late 1970s (Pettigrew, 1979) and although it has proven rather difficult to define and operationalize (cf. Getschmann, 1992), many authors agree that organizational culture refers to a set of values, norms and patterns which are shared by people in an organization and which direct people into specific patterns of performance-enhancing or problem-solving. Research could seek to establish patterns in international institutions' organizational culture, and identify whether certain organizational culture characteristics have proven to facilitate

important change processes, or indeed with perceived or actual superior performance.

The Content and Context Dimensions of International Institutions

Since international institutions owe their role and legitimacy to the delegation of authority by nation states, any process research of international institutions should always be accompanied by research on content and context dimensions. Such research has traditionally been the realm of political science and international relations. However, management research has produced some notions and approaches that may also be applied to studying content and context issues. For instance, when new international institutions are being established, or when existing institutions have partly overlapping domains (such as the WTO and the UNCTAD), newcomer or weak rival institutions should consider how to position and/or differentiate themselves. In this way, UNCTAD partly redefined itself by publishing its annual review of the world's most transna-tional corporations (UNCTAD, 1999).

An important area for future research on international institutions could be the notion of 'rival institutions', for example, between the WTO and UCTAD, between RIAs and the WTO or the ISO, or between the EU and NATO (in the case of strengthening the EU's foreign policy profile). Rival institutions offer rival platforms, are usually controlled by dif-ferent countries, are made up of different constituencies, and offer modes of conflict resolution.

Since pressures for higher effectiveness rarely originate and crystallize spontaneously from the inside, analyses of the effectiveness of international institutions would best adopt a multi-level approach (Putnam, 1988). This implies first conducting an outside analysis of the institutions' major stakeholders (both state and non-state actors), their strategic intents and potential involvement in rival insti-tutions, and the extent to which their agendas match. Research on the World Bank suggests that such outside forces, including NGOs, can influence and sway international institutions' policies in important respects (Biekart, 1999). Research could also seek to identify the ways institutions manage their contexts or stake-holders, whether nation states, multinational corporations or NGOs. As Braithwaite and Drahos conclude in their impressive study of dozens of international institutions, effective institutions nudge multinational corporations, 'to surpass the commitments of the states in which they operate' (2000: 295), leading a gradual and virtual cycle from norms to rules to actual enforcement. The same authors conclude that large companies frequently controlled international institutions' agendas, just as in many instances, 'NGOs are the key to invigo-rating global good governance' (2000: 36).

Finally, research on the context of inter-national institutions could benefit from research carried out by evolutionary ecologists, who argue that all organizations are characterized by *relative inertia*, due to the unpredictability of the environment, information constraints, the political nature of the internal decision-making process and the uncoupling of inten-tions and organizational outcomes (Hannan and Freeman, 1977: 133–5). Thus, organiza-tional ecology argues that organizations are often less able to respond properly to radical changes in the environment, and that therefore the environment selects organizations. Organi-zational ecology may help to explain the fate of an institution such as the Western European Union (WEU), that was established in the 1950s to develop a European 'pillar' in NATO yet that gradually developed to little more than a sleeping secretariat. However, should inter-national circumstances call for a more inde-pendent European defense organization member states could easily decide to restore the WEU.

CONCLUSIONS

Despite widespread disillusionment with their achievements and the way they are being run, international institutions have come to adopt a role of increasing importance in the interna-tional arena. The globalization of technolo-gies, capital markets, and corporations as the main carrier of Western capitalist values con-stitute a combined force compelling the fur-ther development of international institutions, helping to overcome the at times deep frustra-tions at governments, companies and the public at large about the ineffectiveness of international institutions.

International institutions are a relatively recent phenomenon. Apart from the EU there are few international institutions that have any jurisdiction of their own. The two-level game within international institutions as well as between institutions and their member states often makes it difficult for international insti-tutions to be effective in the first place.

Research by institutional authors has focused more on domestic than on interna-tional institutions, and more on institutions as frameworks guiding the actions of member states than on the material organizations administering the institutions. As a result, institutional effectiveness has hardly been identified as a theme. Management researchers, and the management literature, may help to shift research attention away from the rela-tively abstract and theoretical approaches that have dominated the study of institutions and that postulated rather than examined institu-tional effects, towards concrete and empirical research that may help to expose sources of international institutions' effectiveness.

The number of issues that have been dealt with in the management field and that may be applied to studying the effectiveness of international institutions is huge. Indeed, many of the topics dealt with in the other chapters of this volume could aid the researcher of international institutions. While suggesting that various notions and approaches developed in the management field may be applied successfully to the study of international institutions, this chapter in fact argues in favor of combining content, process and context research – for interdisciplinary research into the effectiveness question. By their very nature international institutions owe their existence to the delegation of authority by nation states who for the time being remain the ultimate actors on an international scale. Political scientists offer invaluable insights here that no management researcher should ignore.

ACKNOWLEDGEMENTS

I thank Andrew Pettigrew, Rob van Tulder and Geoffrey Underhill for their useful comments on an earlier draft.

NOTES

1 Some informal platforms did temporarily emerge, such as the 'Concert of Europe', which developed out of the Vienna Congress of 1815, and which represented an attempt by the victors of the Napoleonic Wars to coordinate international policy in Europe (Cameron, 1997: 388). Indeed, the League of Nations fitted into this tradition, since it was established by the victors of World War I – even if the US did not join the League of Nations which its president Woodrow Wilson himself had proposed.

2 The scope of the discussion below is limited in its ability to discuss all important streams within these four disciplines, and biased in its selection of disciplines and approaches that appear particularly interesting to a management audience.

REFERENCES

Abbott, K. W. and Snidal, D. (1998) 'Why states act through formal international organizations', *Journal of Conflict Resolution*, 42(1): 3–42.

Archer, C. (1983) *International Organizations*. London: Allen & Unwin.

Bass, B. (1990) *Bass and Stogdil's Handbook of Leadership*. New York: Free Press.

Berger, P. and Luckmann, T. (1967) *The Social Construction of Reality*. New York: Anchor Books.

Berle, A. and Means, G. (1932) *The Modern Corporation and Private Property*. New York: Macmillan.

Biekart, K. (1999) *The Politics of Civil Society Building: European Private Aid Agencies and Democratic Transitions in Central America*. Utrecht: International Books.

Blau, P. (1964) *Exchange and Power in Social Life*. New York: John Wiley.

Blau, P. (1970) 'A formal theory of differentiation in organizations', *American Sociological Review*, 35: 201–18.

Braithwaite, J. and Drahos, P. (2000) *Global Business Regulation*. Cambridge: Cambridge University Press.

Cameron, R. (1997) *A Concise Economic History of the World: From Paleolithic Times to the Present*. New York and Oxford: Oxford University Press.

Coleman, J. (1990) *Foundations of Social Theory*. Cambridge, MA: Harvard University Press.

Dalton, D. R., Daily, C. M., Ellstrand, A. E. and Johnson, J. L. (1998) 'Meta-analytic reviews of board composition, leadership structure, and financial performance', *Strategic Management Journal*, 19(3): 269–90.

Dent, C. (1997) *The New European Economy*. London: Routledge.

DiMaggio, P. J. and Powell, W. W. (1983) 'The iron cage revisited: institutional isomorphism and collective rationality in organizational fields', *American Sociological Review*, 48: 147–60.

Doz, Y. (1997) 'The evolution of cooperation in strategic alliances: initial conditions or learning processes?', *Strategic Management Journal*, 17: 55–83.

Ethier, W. (1998) 'Regionalism in a multilateral world', *Journal of Political Economy*, 106(6): 1214–45.

Feldstein, M. (1998) 'Refocussing the IMF', *Foreign Affairs*, 77(2): 20–33.

Ferlie, E. (2001) 'Strategic management in the contemporary public sector', in A. Pettigrew, H. Thomas and R. Whittington (eds), *Handbook of Strategy and Management*. London/Thousand Oaks: Sage. pp. 281–300.

Finkelstein, S. and Hambrick, D. C. (1996) *Strategic Leadership: Top Executives and their Effects on Organizations*. Minneapolis/St. Paul: West Publishing Company.

Getschmann, D. (1992) '"Unternehmenskultur": Bemerkungen zum Handelswert eines Begriffes', *Zeitschrift Führung und Organisation*, 5: 299–303.

Giddens, A. (1984) *The Constitution of Society*. Cambridge: Polity Press.

Granovetter, M. (1985) 'Economic action and social structure: the problem of embeddedness', *American Journal of Sociology*, 91: 481–510.

Greenwood, B. and Hinings, C. R. (1996) 'Understanding radical organizational change: bringing together the old and the new institutionalism', *Academy of Management Review*, 21(4): 1022–54.

Groenewegen, J., Pitelis, C. and Sjöstrand S. E. (1995) *On Economic Institutions: Theory and Applications.* Aldershot: Edward Elgar.

Hambrick, D. C. and Abrahamson, E. (1995) 'Assessing the amount of managerial discretion in different industries: a multimethod approach', *Academy of Management Journal*, 38: 1427–41.

Hannan, M. and Freeman, J. (1977) 'The population ecology of organizations', *American Journal of Sociology*, 82: 929–64.

Hodgson, G. (1993a) *The Economics of Institutions.* Aldershot: Edward Elgar.

Hodgson, G. (1993b) 'Institutional economics: surveying the "old" and the "new"', *Metroeconomica*, 44(1): 1–28.

Jensen, M. and Meckling, W. (1976) 'Theory of the firm: managerial behavior, agency costs and ownership structure', *Journal of Financial Economics*, 4(10): 305–60.

Jones, G. (1996) *The Evolution of International Business.* London and New York: Routledge.

Joyner, C. C. (1999) 'The United Nations and democracy', *Global Governance*, 5(3): 333–67.

Kaul, I., Grunberg, I. and Stern, M. A. (1998) 'Defining global public goods', in I. Kaul, I. Grunberg and M. A. Stern (eds), *Global Public Goods*. Oxford: Oxford University Press. pp. 2–19.

Keohane, R. O. (1984) *After Hegemony: Cooperation and Discord in the World Political Economy.* Princeton: Princeton University Press.

Keohane, R. O. (1988) 'International institutions: two approaches', *International Studies Quarterly*, 32(4): 379–96.

Keohane, R. O. (1998) 'International institutions: can interdependence work?', *Foreign Policy*, Spring: 82–96.

Kindleberger (1973) *The World in Depression, 1929–1939.* Berkeley: University of California Press.

Krasner, S. D. (ed.) (1983) *International Regimes.* Ithaca/London: Cornell University Press.

Lawrence, P. R. and Lorsch, J. W. (1967) *Organization and Environment.* Boston: Graduate School of Business Administration, Harvard University.

Lawrence, T. B. (1999) 'Institutional strategy', *Journal of Management*, 25(2): 161–88.

Lawson, R. L. (1996/1997) 'Plots, plans, and partnerships: global governance and US mining', *Executive Speeches*, 11(3): 7–13.

Lyles, M. (1996) 'New ventures in Hungary: the impact of US partners', *Management International Review*, 36(4): 335–70.

MacBean, A. I. and Snowden, P. N. (1981) *International Institutions in Trade and Finance.* London: Allen & Unwin.

March, J. G. and Simon, H. A. (1958) *Organizations.* New York: Wiley.

Merton, R. (1948) *Social Theory and Social Structure.* Glencoe, IL: Free Press.

Meyer, J. W. and Rowan, B. (1977) 'Institutionalized organizations: formal structures as myth and ceremony', *American Journal of Sociology*, 83: 340–66.

Milner, H. (1989) *Resisting Protectionism: Global Industries and the Politics of International Trade.* Princeton: Princeton University Press.

Milner, H. (1998) 'Rationalizing politics: the emerging synthesis of international, American, and comparative politics', *International Organization*, 52(4): 759–86.

Mischel, W. (1968) *Personality and Assessment.* New York: John Wiley.

Moravcsik, A. (1993) 'Introduction: integrating domestic and international theories of international bargaining', in P. B. Evans, H. K. Jacobson and R. D. Putnam (eds), *Double-Edged Diplomacy: International Bargaining and Domestic Politics.* Berkeley: University of California Press. pp. 3–42.

OECD (1996) *Regionalism and Its Place in the Multilateral Trading System.* Paris: Organisation for Economic Co-operation and Development.

Panić, M. (1995) 'The Bretton Woods system: concept and practice', in J. Michie and J. G. Smith (eds), *Managing the Global Economy.* Oxford and New York: Oxford University Press. pp. 37–54.

Pettigrew, A. M. (1979) 'On studying organizational cultures', *Administrative Science Quarterly*, 24: 570–81.

Pettigrew, A. M. (1985) *The Awakening Giant.* Oxford: Blackwell.

Pfeffer, J. and Salancik, G. (1978) *External Control of Organizations.* New York: Harper & Row.

Powell, W. W. and DiMaggio, P. J. (eds) (1991) *The New Institutionalism in Organizational Analysis.* Chicago: University of Chicago Press.

Preston, L. E. and Windsor, D. (1997) *The Rules of the Game in the Global Economy: Policy Regimes for International Business.* Boston and Dordrecht: Kluwer Academic Publ.

Putnam, R. D. (1988) 'Diplomacy and domestic politics: the logic of two-level games', *International Organization*, 42(3): 427–60.

Richards, J. E. (1999) 'Toward a positive theory of international institutions: regulating international aviation markets', *International Organization*, 53(1): 1–37.

Rosenau, J. N. and Czempiel, E. O. (eds) (1992) *Governance Without Government: Order and Change in World Politics.* Cambridge: Cambridge University Press.

Ruigrok, W. and Van Tulder, R. (1995) *The Logic of International Restructuring.* London and New York: Routledge.

Ruigrok, W., Pettigrew, A., Peck, S. and Whittington, R. (1999) 'Corporate restructuring and new forms of organising: evidence from Europe', *Management International Review*, 19(2): 41–64.

Scott, W. R. and Meyer, J. W. (eds) (1994) *Institutional Environments and Organizations.* London and Thousand Oaks: Sage.

Selznick, P. (1957) *Leadership in Administration.* New York: Harper & Row.

Singer, J. D. (1961) 'The level of analysis problem in international relations', *World Politics*, 14: 77–92.

Sjöstrand, S. E. (1995) 'Towards a theory of institutional change', in Groenewegen, J., Pitelis, C. and Sjöstrand S. E. (eds) *On Economic Institutions: Theory and Applications*. Aldershot: Edward Elgar, 19–44.

Tolbert, P. S. and Zucker, L. G. (1997) 'The institutionalization of institutional theory', in S. R. Clegg and C. Hardy (eds), *Studying Organizations: Theory and Method*. London and Thousand Oaks: Sage.

UNCTAD (1999) *World Investment Report 1999*. Geneva: United Nations Conference on Trade and Development.

Vanberg, V. (1989) 'Carl Menger's evolutionary and John R. Common's collective action approach to institutions: a comparison', *Review of Political Economy*, 1(3): 334–60.

Van der Pijl, K. (1992) *Wereldorde en Machtspolitiek: Visies op de Internationale Betrekkingen van Dante tot Fukuyama*. Amsterdam: Het Spinhuis.

Van Tulder, R. and Junne, G. (1988) *European Multinationals and Core Technologies*. Chichester and London: Wiley.

Waters, M. (1995) *Globalization*. London and New York: Routledge.

Webster (2000) http://www.m-w.com/cgi-bin/dictionary March 8, 2000.

Williamson, O. E. (1975) *Markets and Hierarchies Analysis and Antitrust Implications*. New York: MacGraw-Hill.

Williamson, O. E. (1985) *The Economic Institutions of Capitalism*. New York: Free Press.

Woods, N. (1999) 'Good governance in international organizations', *Global Governance*, 5(1): 39–61.

Young, O. R. (1992) 'The effectiveness of international institutions: hard cases and critical variables', in J. N. Rosenau and E. O. Czempiel (eds), *Governance Without Government: Order and Change in World Politics*. Cambridge: Cambridge University Press.

Young, O. R. (1994) *International Governance: Protecting the Environment in a Stateless Society*. Ithaca: Cornell University Press.

Young, O. R. (ed.) (1996a) *The International Political Economy and International Institutions, Volume I*. Cheltenham (UK): Edward Elgar.

Young, O. R. (ed.) (1996b) *The International Political Economy and International Institutions, Volume II*. Cheltenham (UK): Edward Elgar.

16

Technology in Corporate Strategy: Change, Continuity and the Information Revolution

KEITH PAVITT and
W. EDWARD STEINMUELLER

The accumulation and application of engineering knowledge (technology) in order to improve and change products and services, and how they are produced and delivered (technical change), have been central features of all recorded civilizations. Since the industrial revolution, the process has become increasingly deliberate, specialized, continuous, endogenous to firms' activities, and applicable across a wider range of sectors and functions.[1] The industrial revolution also initiated the dialogue between scientific knowledge (systematic observation and experimentation aimed at the discovery of general principles) and technology.

These characteristics have been noted by the major social observers of the past 200 years, and analysed by several generations of historians.[2] But they have been incorporated in management theory and in the recipes provided by management consultants only in the past 20 years. These come barely in time to provide some of the ideas needed for coping with the competitive, organizational and strategic consequences of the explosion of opportunities in information and communication technologies (ICTs). ICTs promise to accelerate the accumulation of knowledge by augmenting the effectiveness of processes of discovery, and to

hasten application by facilitating new patterns of firm organization and divisions of labour between firms. However, the potential of ICTs can only be assessed in the context of the longer historical development of technical change as a continuous rather than an episodic process, and as a pervasive rather than isolated feature of business activity.

The relatively young field of strategic management itself, like many of the 'modern' disciplines concerned with human behaviour, has only recently recognized the central importance of scientific and technological knowledge in corporate competitiveness. This recognition is overdue as rethinking the ends and means of modern organizations should lead directly to a consideration of the role of science and technology. Among the first scholars to receive widespread attention for doing so are Prahalad and Hamel (1990) who have argued that corporate organizational practices, methods of evaluation and strategy formulation should reflect not only the products and services that they make, but the underlying bodies of knowledge – the corporate core competencies – on which present and future products and services are based. Research by business historians serves to remind us that leading firms in the chemical and electrical industries were already practising at the beginning of the 20th century what Prahalad and Hamel preached at its end.

To take one not insignificant example, Hounshell and Smith (1988) have shown that, by the 1920s, Du Pont in the USA had already established a dual structure in R&D, with some laboratories linked to established product divisions, and a central laboratory performing more fundamental research in scientific fields of common interest; the latter's research in polymers eventually led to the discovery of nylon and world corporate leadership in synthetic fibres. Similarly, Plumpe (1995) has shown that, in the 1920s, IG Farben in Germany had already established numerous 'Technical Committees' at the corporate level, in order to exploit emerging technological opportunities. These enabled the firm to diversify progressively over the next 15 years out of dyestuffs into plastics, pharmaceuticals, and other related chemical products. However, later experience at Du Pont (Hounshell and Smith, 1988) showed that such knowledge-based diversification was neither automatic nor easy. In the 1960s, new ventures in Du Pont were generally unsuccessful because they were too closely linked to the well-established fibres division – yesterday's core competencies had become today's core rigidities.

In addition to the contributions of historians, those involved in what have come to be called 'innovation studies'[3] have considerably broadened and deepened our empirical understanding of the nature, sources and consequences of technological change since the industrial revolution. It is against these empirical findings that the contributions of the various disciplines to our understanding of corporate innovative activities will be assessed. We present the evidence on technology in the corporation in four sections. Section two deals with the nature and implications of increasing specialization in innovative activities; section three with the growing complexity of innovation and its implications for uncertainty, learning and organization; section four with how technology shapes competitive dynamics amongst firms; and section five with the impact of the rapid improvements in the ICTs. We finish by proposing some future directions of research.

We shall comment in passing on the implications of our evidence for theory. Our approach will mirror what we say in section three below about the contributions of scientific theory to technological practice – no one social science theory can encompass all the complexities of the innovation process, but they can each offer valuable insights. Beforehand, what can we say in general about the contributions of various theoretical approaches to our understanding of technology, strategy and the information society?

Since the industrial revolution, contemporary observers have been well aware of the importance of the systematic application of technological knowledge in the rapid growth of material welfare. Adam Smith, Alexis de Tocqueville and Karl Marx between them identified many of the key interactions between technology and corporate behaviour that we shall explore below. In particular: increasing specialization in the production both of goods and of the knowledge on which they are based; increasing variety and complexity in the sources of technical change, with machine-building and what we would now call research and development (R&D) of particular importance; and the importance of competitive pressures and the profit motive in firms' decisions to improve and change their products and production methods.

However, whilst recognizing the importance of technical change, mainstream economic theories in the 20th century have assumed that its generation is exogenous. One reason is the theoretical convenience of assuming that firms have perfect knowledge of production possibilities, since this makes the origin of technological knowledge irrelevant to the analysis of the dynamics of competition between firms, and of management behaviour and choice. In addition, there are profound difficulties in assessing the value of technical activities and inventions before they are commodified and exchanged in markets, typically by embodying them in products. From a management perspective, this is a totally unsatisfactory state of affairs, since economic theory is unable to distinguish effectively between firms, except through glib generalities about comparative efficiency of the firm's production function. However, it has also given free rein to scholars of management to explain issues that 'really matter', including the processes of leadership, control and organization. Viewing technology as exogenous has allowed both scholars of business management and micro-economics to avoid the gritty particularities of technology.

Scholars of management can also provide a re-examination of the mainstream tradition in ways that illuminate the role of technology. In particular, Porter (1980, 1983) has turned industrial economics on its head and defined the purpose of corporate strategy as the mini-mization of the competitive threats that the corporation faces. This has led to improved understanding of the role of technological change in corporate marketing positioning, and to a useful taxonomy of different forms of technology strategy that underpin corporate strategy. The weakness of the approach is one to be expected, given its idealization of the management process, namely, the neglect of factors internal to the firm that constrain cor-porate choice and behaviour – in particular, competencies, power struggles, and the mis-alignments between technological and other organizational practices.

There have, of course, been other exceptions to the prevailing mainstream trend. Schumpeter and many other economists believed that the historical development of the means of pro-duction is central to an understanding of issues such as business cycles, the aggregate rate of growth and sectoral composition of individual economies, and the interactions between strat-egy and structure in specific industries. Nelson and Winter (1982) have built on these founda-tions to develop an evolutionary theory of eco-nomic change that (amongst other things) explains intersectoral differences in industrial structure by differences in the range of techno-logical opportunities that firms face, and their ability to appropriate the benefits flowing from their exploitation. They have also devel-oped corporate decision rules that explicitly encompass uncertainty, tacit knowledge and firm-specific organizational practices ('rou-tines'). However, the concept of 'routines' – and especially those related to innovation and change – has remained abstract. Based on our review, we identify at the end of section three the key routines (corporate organizational prac-tices) that must be matched with the nature and sources of technological opportunities.

More recently, Teece and Pisano (1994) and others have given greater operational content to notions of competencies that are both firm-specific – and therefore a basis of competitive advantage – and dynamic and changing through continuous renewal. In particular, they identify three dimensions of such compe-tencies – market positioning, technological paths, and organizational processes. Whilst useful as a tool for describing and analysing the past, this approach has limited ability to prescribe the future. This is because successful positioning, paths and processes are not pre-ordained. They become clear after experimen-tation, trial and error, and therefore cannot in practice be cleanly separated from perfor-mance. We may therefore caricature failed corporate competencies, and glorify those of a successful rival, even though they encompass tacit knowledge and dynamic learning, and are not either properly identified or repro-ducible. Given these limitations, the dynamic-capabilities approach explains and predicts best when building on relatively slow-moving trajectories.

More generally, models and theories grow-ing out of economics are weak in coping with the internal organizational dimensions of tech-nological change that – we shall argue – are of increasing importance. The 40-year-old dis-tinction by Burns and Stalker (1961) between a mechanistic management system adapted to stable conditions, and an organic one adapted to change and uncertainty, has been amply confirmed by subsequent empirical studies but not yet incorporated in formal models of cor-porate co-ordination. With distinguished exceptions of Woodward (1965) and Chandler (1977, 1990), there has been very little recent analysis of how particular forms of technical change co-evolve with specific dimensions of corporate organizational practice. As a consequence, the analytical base for making confident predictions about the future organi-zational implications of ICTs is a flimsy one. Table 16.1 summarizes briefly the main fields contributing to our understanding of the role of technology in corporate strategy.

SPECIALIZATION: DISCIPLINARY, FUNCTIONAL, INSTITUTIONAL

Adam Smith's identification of the benefits of specialization in the production of knowledge

Table 16.1   *Key contributions on technology and corporate strategy*

Field	Some key authors	Main contributions
Classical economics	A. Smith, K. Marx	Description and explanation of nature, sources and impact of technological change in long-term historical processes
Contemporary observers	A. de Tocqueville, B. Franklin, S. Smiles	
Economic history	A. Toynbee, D. Landes, L. Mumford, S. Kuznets	
Business history	A. Chandler, D. Hounshell	Setting the empirical agenda of phenomena to be explained, and offering some explanations
Innovation studies	C. Freeman, N. Rosenberg, D. Mowery, R. Rothwell, E. von Hippel	
Management theory	M. Porter	Analysing the importance of market positioning in corporate innovative activities
Evolutionary economics	J. Schumpeter, R. Nelson and S. Winter, G. Dosi, S. Metcalfe	Up-dating the research agenda of classical economics
Organizational studies	T. Burns and G. Stalker, J. Woodward	Analysing the interactions between technology and organization
Dynamic competencies	D. Teece and G. Pisano	A theory of the firm encompassing incentives, competencies and organizational routines

has been amply confirmed by experience. Professional education, the establishment of laboratories, and improvements in techniques of measurement and experimentation have progressively increased the efficiency of discovery, invention and innovation. Increasingly difficult problems have been tackled and solved (de Solla Price, 1984; Mowery and Rosenberg, 1989; Rosenberg, 1974).[4] Three complementary forms of specialization have developed in parallel – disciplinary, functional and institutional.

Disciplinary Specialization

In addition to increasing specialization and discovery in the established scientific disciplines, new disciplines emerged in the early years of the 20th century to encompass the accumulation of specialized knowledge about specific features or elements of technology. Specialization has led to the emergence of the engineering disciplines as distinct from the disciplines of physical science: hence chemical engineering rather than applied chemistry and electrical engineering as distinct from applied physics (Rosenberg and Nelson, 1994). These new disciplines have become useful over a growing range of applications, so that products incorporate a growing number of technologies: compare the 18th century loom with today's equivalent, with its fluid flow, electrical, electronic and software elements improving the efficiency of its mechanical functions. In other words, products are becoming increasingly 'multi-technology', and so are the firms that produce them (Granstrand et al., 1997). Each specific body of technical knowledge consequently cannot be associated uniquely with a single, specific class of product. Products and related technologies co-evolve within firms, but their dynamics are different. For example, Gambardella and Torrisi (1998) have recently argued that a number of the successful electronics firms over the past 10 years have been those that have simultaneously broadened their technological focus and narrowed their product focus. In other cases, firms have used their range of technological skills to create or enter new product markets (Granstrand, 1982; Granstrand and Oskarsson, 1994; Granstrand and Sjølander, 1990). Technological change has also opened up opportunities for customization and differentiation of products, and for the integration of complex system innovations, such as mechatronics (Kodama, 1991). Similarly, production organization and product reconfiguration and redesign to increase efficiency in production have required the development and deployment of specialized engineering competencies.

Despite the increasing organization and professionalization of technological activities, the rate and direction of innovation has not become smooth and predictable. Fields of technological knowledge and their exploitation have developed at different times and in different directions. For reasons well explained by Mowery and Rosenberg (1979), the differences in timing of the emergence of new opportunities for innovation have not simply been the result of changing market demands.[5] More important in the long-term scheme of things have been radical but uneven improvements in the knowledge base underlying technological change.

For example, the latent demands for more powerful machines to alleviate physical burdens, and for better medicines to cure diseases, are both of long standing. The former were satisfied before the latter, in part because the knowledge of mechanics and metallurgy could be obtained with craft skills and through trial and error. Knowledge of the origins of disease in the human body, by contrast, depended upon specialized knowledge in chemistry and biology, coupled with sophisticated measurement instruments. It is still true today that the state of the knowledge base continues to influence powerfully the locus of technological opportunities and the shape of corporate technological strategies. In particular, our capacity to store, transmit and manipulate information continues to increase by orders of magnitude every few years, thereby influencing the corporate strategies of virtually all firms in one way or another. At the same time – and despite threats of global warming and environmental degradation and of major corporate investments in related R&D – our capacity to store energy still depends essentially on a technology developed in the

18th century (Volta's battery), and remains two orders of magnitude less efficient than naturally-occurring petroleum.

According to Freeman et al. (1982; Freeman, 1984), periodic waves of productive improvement and new business opportunities have emerged after big jumps in the performance–cost ratio of key technological inputs into the economy. Each of these jumps has been closely tied to rapid improvements in specific bodies of technological knowledge: mechanics and metallurgy (textiles, coal, railways, machinery, automobiles), chemistry (petroleum, synthetic materials), physics (electricity, communications).[6] These major changes may be described as the emergence of a new technological paradigm (Dosi, 1982). A new technological paradigm encompasses the growth of new fields of engineering knowledge (see Rosenberg and Nelson, 1994), new sectors of development and application of technology, new forms of organization and management, and new means of appropriating economic returns from knowledge (for example, new forms of intellectual property rights or industrial secrecy).

New technological paradigms are associated with the emergence of large dynamic firms that have been successful in exploiting the new opportunities. The largest R&D spenders today are in companies that grew with the emergence of the mechanical (and automobile), chemical and electrical–electronic paradigms.[7] The fastest growing R&D spenders today are those closely associated with ICTs and software technology. Although these firms master an increasing range of technologies, their fields of relative technological strength are closely linked to their product markets, and both change relatively slowly over time. At the same time, such changes can be the beginnings of a new paradigm. Griset (1995) describes how the electronic (communications) paradigm emerged alongside the electrical (power) paradigm in the period between the two world wars. A similar pattern can be seen in the 1960s and 1970s with the emergence of software alongside micro-electronics and computing (Steinmueller, 1996).

Major waves of innovation have also helped shape the characteristics of business firms and the tasks of management. Chandler (1977) has shown that the rise in the USA at the end of the nineteenth century of the large, multi-unit firm, and of the coordinating function of professional middle managers, depended critically on the development of the railroads, coal, the telegraph and continuous flow production. Similarly, the later development of the multidivisional firm in part reflected the major opportunities for product diversification in the chemical industry opened up by breakthroughs in synthetic organic chemistry.

But change has not only been of a revolutionary nature. Whilst old firms and products have disappeared and new ones emerged, the development of the underlying bodies of technological knowledge has been complementary rather than destructive. Thus, knowledge of ICT is an essential input into the design and production of the contemporary automobile, but certainly has not displaced the central importance of mechanical engineering and metallurgy. Similarly, successful innovations depend not only on the spectacularly new, but also on the steady improvement of what is already established and working. The continuous and incremental accumulation of knowledge and practice in such fields as production organization, quality control, process instrumentation, materials and (now) applications software has been just as important to the growth of modern economies as to the strategic success of individual firms (Mowery and Rosenberg, 1989).

Functional Specialization

In addition to the benefits of the cognitive division of labour into more specialized fields, the functional division of labour within business firms has augmented the rate of technical change. Functional specialization has led to the organizational specialization of the corporate R&D laboratories and similar groups devoted full-time to inventive and innovative activities (Mowery, 1995; Hounshell and Smith, 1988; Cusumano, 1991; and Gomory, 1989). These organizational units provided an effective method for combining and coordinating increasingly specialized knowledge. They also provided a functional role for knowledge generation activities within the firm, enabling the professionalization of the functions of knowledge generation and application, and supporting the construction of laboratories with improved and specialized

instrumentation. This organizational specialization of the industrial research laboratory enabled firms to monitor and benefit more systematically and effectively from advances in specialized academic disciplines. In the 20th century, Bell Laboratories has been an archetype:

> Perhaps the outstanding characteristic of [the Bell Laboratories], the one that sets it apart a little from others, is its conduct of research and development by a group method of attack…the result is the necessity of a high degree of specialization. So in all of these technical departments we have specialists…who are trained and skilled in their particular branches of science and engineering. Their activities are so co-ordinated by means of this organization, that their best brains can be brought to bear upon any specific problem…When a problem is put up to the Labs for solution, it is divided into its elements and each element is assigned to that group of specialists who know the most about that particular field but they all cooperate and make their contribution to the solution of the problem as a whole. (Craft, 1925: 43–4, as reproduced in Noble, 1977: 119)

The organizational specialization of the industrial research laboratory created a growing body of experience in the development and testing of laboratory concepts and prototypes and the translation of these into commercialized products. Firms adopting the industrial laboratory have engaged in systematic experimentation with a wider range of products and processes than had previously been possible through incremental improvements constrained by established products and production lines. In fields rich in technological opportunity, firms have in consequence become multi-product as well as multi-technology.

Institutional Specialization

Corporate R&D laboratories have come to depend increasingly on a supply of scientists and engineers aware of the latest research results and trained in the latest research techniques. Even with continuous expansion in the scope of in-house research activities, the extent of external cognitive specialization and knowledge generation continuously threatens to outrun the ability of companies to monitor and acquire useful technological knowledge. The maintenance of corporate dynamism in technological change requires the reproduction and renewal of research personnel, as well as the continuous infusion of new ideas and opportunities.[8] Industrial research has therefore become increasingly dependent upon higher education to deliver suitably prepared researchers, and upon the complex mixture of public and private knowledge creating institutions (including universities) to deliver variety and novelty for commercial exploitation. The dynamics of capitalist competition, through invention and innovation, created (and continues to create) demands for institutional specialization and the creation of sustainable 'systems' of knowledge transfer (see David et al., 1992; Klevorick et al., 1995; Hicks and Katz, 1997; Martin and Salter, 1996).

Individual entrepreneurs and philanthropists have therefore been progressively displaced by the privately funded laboratories of business firms and the publicly funded laboratories of universities, as the main sources of invention, innovation and of the underlying skills and knowledge needed to make them. Increasing disciplinary and functional specialization has had subtle yet major implications for the management of innovation and for the role of technology in corporate strategy.

Implications for Management Practice

First, the increasingly specialized and professionalized production of knowledge has gone hand-in-hand with the proliferation of knowledge-based networks that cross corporate boundaries, and permit exchanges of knowledge both inside and outside market transactions. This is most prevalent in exchanges between the corporate and university sectors (see, for example, Galambos and Sewell, 1995; Graham, 1986) but also happens amongst corporate practitioners (see von Hippel, 1987). However, corporate participation in such networks is not costless. The entrance fee is the cost of the skills and competencies necessary to contribute to network exchanges. These costs can be considerable. Many large firms based in the chemicals and electronics industries publish hundreds of papers yearly in order to signal their research

interests to the academic research community (Hicks, 1995).

There appear to be significant differences between industries in the types of knowledge that are valued by networks of innovating firms. In electronics, for example, a broad common base of knowledge allows widespread anticipation of how new developments may be put into practice. Publication is often aimed at establishing links with others about the most productive means of implementing new technological capabilities, rather than signalling the uniqueness of particular corporate capabilities. In the chemical industry, by contrast, publication often serves as a signal of capabilities and knowledge that are highly differentiated, and that provide a clear foundation for collaboration or licensing of technologies.

Second, and contrary to many predictions, the growth of specialized knowledge has not been accompanied by the dominance in innovative activities of firms specialized in providing such knowledge. In spite of a wide range of markets for technology in the form of contract research organizations, biotechnology firms, plant designers and providers of applications software, most firms perform in-house most of the R&D and related activities that they fund (Mowery, 1983, 1995). Various explanations have been suggested, based for example on transaction costs, complementary assets and other factors (Lamoreaux and Raff, 1995; Teece, 1986). But perhaps the most plausible explanation is that the benefits of an increasing specialization in knowledge production emerge only after co-ordination and integration of the component parts. In-house technical competence is necessary both for the effective assimilation of external knowledge that is increasingly specialized and varied, and for its effective technical integration into specific artefacts and its organizational integration with production and marketing. The current fashion for, and increase in, 'outsourcing' of R&D activities does not contradict this conclusion (see section four).

This leads to the third major implication of technology for corporate strategy. Successful innovation depends upon corporate capacities to coordinate and to integrate many strands of specialized knowledge in order to improve or change the provision of goods and services. Given high uncertainty and much tacit knowledge, this requires close physical and organizational proximity – especially in the phase of developing and launching major innovations. A series of empirical studies have arrived at the same, robust conclusion: the capacity to innovate depends on effective horizontal communications and learning between the R&D function, on the one hand, and the production and marketing functions, on the other (Cooper, 1986; Maidique and Zirger, 1985; Rothwell et al., 1974). These organizational skills are themselves partly tacit and difficult to imitate. As the sociologists of science have stressed, scientific and technological capabilities are socially embedded, and therefore cannot be readily transferred because each social grouping requires a process of working out the specific forms of power, negotiation, decision, delegation and monitoring functions (Callon, 1993). The capacity to innovate has therefore become an important strategic asset for the corporation.

Finally, different technologies and their related products require different organizational practices for their successful development. For example, direct links with the results of published academic research are essential for firms competing through innovation in the pharmaceutical industry. They are less important for innovating firms in the automobile industry, where the interface between R&D and manufacturing is much more critical. In addition, the required practices evolve over time: pharmaceutical firms now have to monitor publication in biology much more closely than in the past, given the promise of molecular biology. This lack of homogeneity makes it impossible to offer simple recipes and procedures for successful innovation that will ensure success in all circumstances and at all times. As we shall see in the next section, the increasing complexities of the innovation process lead to the same conclusion.

COMPLEXITY, UNCERTAINTY AND LEARNING

The requirements for the effective management of technology and innovation have become ever more varied and stringent during the past 200 years. In the early stages, leading corporations mobilized technological knowledge, in order to cut costs and increase quality of established products through the introduction of mechanical innovations and analytical instruments into manufacturing processes (Mowery and Rosenberg, 1989). Management progressively learned that the science-based technological opportunities then emerging in the chemical and electrical industries were applicable over a range of existing and new product markets, and therefore opened up opportunities for what is now called 'related' product diversification (Hounshell and Smith, 1988; Reich, 1985; Rumelt, 1974). As a consequence, we have seen increasing demands on corporate technology management along all three of the following dimensions: the range of fields of knowledge – and related products, components and systems – to master, combine and exploit; the variety of possible market applications to identify, assess and exploit; and the need to match technological opportunities with market needs through appropriate organizational structures and practices.

These trends have meant that, in spite of the increases in scientific understanding and in corporate R&D activities, the uncertainties surrounding innovative activities have not been reduced, learning from experience (including failure) remains essential, and finding the appropriate organizational designs and practices are more important than ever.

Uncertainty

In spite of increasing scientific understanding and the growth of R&D activities as a central feature of corporate 'routines', innovative activities are still highly uncertain. Business firms remain incapable of predicting accurately the technical and commercial outcomes of their own (and others') innovative activities. On average, research scientists and engineers tend to be over-optimistic about the costs, benefits and time periods of their proposed projects, but the variance of the ratio of ex post outcomes to ex ante estimates in any specific corporate portfolio of projects tends to be large (Freeman, 1982; Mansfield, 1995). As a consequence, high proportions of corporate R&D and corporate patenting activity are associated with commercially failed projects (Griliches, 1990).

In addition, business firms (and others) are incapable of defining fully the possible futures that might come into existence as a consequence of innovations, especially radical ones. Examples of inaccurate predictions about what turned out later to be spectacularly successful technologies and innovations are legion. Rosenberg (1994) has pointed out that, in the 19th century, the Western Union turned down Bell's patent for the telephone, which it perceived as an inferior product to the telegraph. In the early 20th century, the pioneers of radio communication conceived it as a system of point-to-point communications, particularly between naval vessels; it was only much later that the much larger market for mass radio communications was recognized. And after World War II, the owner of IBM foresaw a world market for computers in single figures. For the more recent period between the 1960s and the 1980s, Schnaars and Berenson (1986) concluded that only about half the major new product families announced in the USA turned out to be commercially successful.

This uncertain world, where corporate managers and others have a poor record – not only in assigning probabilities to future outcomes, but also in identifying the full range of such outcomes – is a necessary consequence of the complexity of the processes through which knowledge, artefacts, producers and users are linked. It is commonplace to acknowledge our inability to predict potential users' reactions to the radically new (for example, which combination(s) of telephone, television, computing and the internet will succeed commercially in the next 10 years?). It is equally true that theory is an insufficient guide to practice even in the technical development of many physical artefacts, since interactions amongst components and subsystems cannot always be predicted, and because they involve many bodies of technological knowledge, none of which individually gives a full picture of potential behaviour. For example, physicists saw the potential benefits of fast breeder nuclear reactors in terms of favourable fuel requirements, whilst (less influential) process engineers pointed to the nasty, dirty and potentially dangerous processes and materials involved (Keck, 1981). This is why business firms are constrained to spend most of their technical resources, not on scientific research, but on the development and testing of often full-scale prototypes and pilot plant. As we shall see in section five, one of the greatest potential and

pervasive benefits of the development of the ICTs will be the increasing use of virtual prototypes and pilot plant to complement real ones.

The theoretical and practical implications of these conclusions are far-reaching and can only be touched upon in a chapter of this length. In economics, they suggest that models and techniques based on risk cannot automatically be applied to innovations, since the range of possible futures is not known, let alone susceptible to realistic attributions of *a priori* probabilities.[9] In strategic management, they suggest that formal and rational models of technology and innovation strategy are likely to be based on mistaken assumptions, especially in fields with rapid technological change. Under such circumstances, incremental 'muddling through' (Lindblom, 1959) and 'emergent strategy' (Mintzberg, 1987) models are likely to offer greater insights.

In practice, they suggest that top-down corporate visions can be a poor guide to innovation strategies. In the academic and business literatures, the failures of such visions are easily forgotten[10] and the successes oversimplified. For example, as told by Prahalad and Hamel (1990), the story of Canon's successful diversifications from optics and precision mechanics into electronics technology, and from cameras into photocopying and computer peripheral products, do not touch on Canon's failed diversifications into recording products and electronic calculators (Sandoz, 1997).

Learning

However, from another perspective, such failures are inevitable and a rich source of information and experience to guide future corporate action. Investments in R&D and innovation are not once-for-all commitments in a perfectly known and understood world, but part of a process of learning and improvement, with continuous feedback between hypotheses (or predictions, or hunches, or design configurations, etc.) and experiments (or experience, or events, or prototype and pilot plant testing, etc.). Hence – among other things – the expression, coined by Maidique and Zirger (1985), of 'learning by failing' in product innovation. According to one eminent engineering practitioner:

...we construct and operate...systems based on prior experiences, and we innovate in them by open loop feedback. That is, we look at the system and ask ourselves 'How can we do it better?' We then make some change, and see if our expectation of 'better' is fulfilled.... This cyclic, open loop feedback process has also been called 'learning-by-doing', 'learning by using', 'trial and error', and even 'muddling through'. Development processes can be quite rational or largely intuitive, but by whatever name, and however rational or intuitive, it is an important research process...providing means of improving systems which lie beyond our ability to operate or innovate via analysis or computation. (Kline, 1995: 63)

Detailed studies of early developments in electronic switching in Ericsson (Granstrand and Sjølander, 1990) and in opto-electronics in Japanese companies (Miyazaki, 1995) suggest that successful processes of corporate learning about a potentially promising new technological field begin with 'bottom up' initiatives that take a long time. They involve trial and error accompanied by progressive concentration on specific fields of application, and require the fusing of old competencies with acquired knowledge of new fields, with a consequent broadening of the range of technological competencies mastered within the firm.

Similarly, the introduction and spread of new production technologies take a long time. Devine (1983) has shown that the full potential for production improvement, opened up by the replacement of steam and water power sources in factories by electricity, was only slowly recognized and realized. More recently, the same has been true for factory automation (Bessant and Hayward, 1988). In addition, the same long process of learning takes place between producers and users in the development of radically new consumer goods, as is shown in the development of both the video-cassette recorder and the personal computer (Ferguson and Morris, 1993; Rosenbloom and Cusumano, 1987).

Two points of analytical importance emerge from research on these learning processes. First, successful innovation often requires effective learning (effective feedback between hypotheses and experience) across functional boundaries – an empirically robust conclusion emerging from numerous studies of product

development (Cooper, 1986; Rothwell et al., 1974), and from business histories (Graham, 1986, on RCA; Reich, 1985, on ATT and GE). Such cross-functional learning has not yet, however, been adequately represented in models of corporate learning (see, for example, Aoki, 1986).

Second, activities that are often represented in mainstream economics as potential substitutes become complements, when considered in the context of dynamic learning. Consider the debate about the balance between radical innovations, incremental innovations and failed innovations. According to the mainstream view, we now know about all possible future states and their probabilities, so good decision-makers will decide the mix between radical and incremental innovations by comparing the marginal products and probabilities of success of each possible innovation. According to the learning model we have described above, good decision-makers will recognize that the three types of innovation are serially inter-related. In particular, a successful radical innovation may well be preceded by some failures and learnt lessons, and will almost certainly be followed by a series of incremental improvements in cost, quality and embodied features. The degree of emphasis placed on radical compared to incremental innovations will reflect *a priori* corporate judgements about the extent of future technological and market opportunities, and the capacities of the corporation to exploit them. Needless to say, these judgements will be continually revised in the light of experience.

A similar contrast can be made in decisions about the balance between in-house R&D activities and what have come to be called 'strategic alliances' involving the purchase, sale and exchange of technological knowledge, and which have grown massively over the past 20 years (Hagedoorn, 1992). The mainstream view is that such alliances reflect a more general trend towards the outsourcing, with a view to increasing efficiency, reducing R&D costs and concentrating on 'core competencies' (see Whittington, 1991). The dynamic learning view is that the main purpose of such alliances is to help assimilate new knowledge rather than to outsource it (Granstrand et al., 1997). Most of the strategic alliances are in three fields – biotechnology, ICT and materials – where a growing number of large firms themselves have been acquiring new competencies, as well as increasing their own R&D expenditures, rather than reducing them. Strategic alliances and in-house R&D are complementary activities, rather than substitutes. As Cohen and Levinthal (1987) have pointed out, corporate R&D has two faces, promoting both innovation and imitation.

Organizational Routines

Over time, business firms have learned to evaluate and master new bodies of technological knowledge, mainly through the medium of the R&D laboratory, which has become a powerful means of insuring against future technological surprises (Mowery, 1983). Firms competing against each other in specific product markets have remarkably similar profiles of technological competence.[11] Compared to the past, fewer contemporary firms in advanced countries appear to fail purely because of lack of technological competence.[12] The main causes can be found in the difficulties of matching technological and market opportunities with organizational routines and practices. Successful matching requires skills in the transformation of the knowledge base into working artefacts, together with further skills necessary for their production and sale. In a world of specialized knowledge and functions, these skills are largely organizational, often informal and embedded, and difficult to codify and replicate. Business histories and contemporary studies point to two sets of reasons why these skills of organizational practice are difficult to acquire and implement – the weight of conventional management practices, and the organizational implications of disruptive technological changes.

First, there is the inevitable tension between conventional methods of corporate monitoring and control, and the practice of R&D and related innovative activities. The former involves plans, thorough ex ante evaluations, and the monitoring of performance against plans through vertical hierarchies. The latter involves uncertainties, (often interesting) divergences from plans, and important horizontal rather than vertical linkages. This tension leads to specific pathologies (and continuing debates) observable in a wide range of firms in different historical periods.

In all cases, the 'right' answer is hard to find, since it depends on difficult to define trade-offs between established activities and new opportunities, which vary amongst technologies, firms and time periods. Practices therefore tend to oscillate in the light of recent corporate experience and management fashion, and are often focussed on the following three activities.

The Monitoring and Control of Corporate R&D Workers

Tension continues between R&D workers and their managers about how closely the work of the former should be monitored and controlled. The result is the frequent practice of what is called 'bootlegging', namely, bottom-up, non-programmed R&D activity without official authority. As Augsdorfer (1996) and Pearson (1997) have shown, the extent of bootlegging is often exaggerated, as are the supposed freedoms proffered on R&D workers by supposedly enlightened firms. Bootlegging is nonetheless necessary in any organization hoping to combine strategy with creativity.

The Evaluation of Corporate R&D Programs

The burgeoning of research in ICI, in theory universally approved of, was in practice watched, in some quarters, with narrowly critical eyes, for to the tidy commercial mind it had grave disadvantages. First, everything about it – the genesis of ideas, the method of carrying them out, above all the results – were irritatingly unpredictable and not susceptible to methodical planning according to well-known rules of procedure. Secondly, it was freely admitted to be very expensive, but nobody, least of all the scientists themselves, had devised a method for calculating the return – if any – on the heavy investment that was demanded. (Reader, 1975: 84–5)

The above tensions, observed in the late 1920s, can still be seen in many companies today, with debate and controversy between the R&D function and the rest of the organization about how R&D programs and projects should be evaluated. Rigorous quantitative methods to the liking of conventional managers can give a spurious sense of scientific accuracy to what are often no more than inspired guesses. They can also give research scientists and engineers the opportunities to manipulate their less numerate bosses (Thomas, 1970). And there is no evidence that accurate ex ante estimates of costs and markets are positively associated with ultimate commercial success.

After reviewing more than 100 R&D selection methods, European corporate practitioners have recently argued that formal evaluation methods are most useful as a means of mobilizing and integrating expert opinion, rather than as a substitute for such expertise (EIRMA, 1995). And each must be tailored to the nature and purpose of the R&D being considered. Mitchell and Hamilton (1988) have proposed three categories of R&D, each requiring different treatment – knowledge building, strategic positioning and business investment.

The Organizational Location of R&D

A related and long-standing cause of continuing debate is how corporate R&D should be organized.[13] In particular, what should be the balance between the R&D paid for and performed in the established product divisions, and the more speculative central – or 'corporate' – R&D aimed at monitoring new technological opportunities and threats emerging from outside these divisions? Over the past 20 years, spectacular failures of certain corporate central laboratories[14] have combined with increased financial pressures to curb more speculative R&D, but precisely at the time of the emergence of pervasive new opportunities in ICTs, biotechnology and materials. Writing in the mid-1980s, Graham concluded: 'Whether or not corporate R&D organizations continue to generate long-term research in-house, the ability to translate research performed elsewhere into usable technology for a specific firm will almost certainly remain a responsibility internal to the firm. For this purpose, if corporate R&D did not exist in some form, sooner or later it would have to be invented' (1986: 100).

The second set of organizational skills that corporations find difficult to acquire are those needed to cope with (often major new) technologies that disrupt their established markets, knowledge sources, and organizational

practices. In his recent book, Christensen (1997) shows how successful and well organized firms fail to recognize and deal in time with the development of radically new markets for their technologies, when these are distant from their established areas of strength. The slow reaction of mainframe computer companies to the emergence of the personal computer is a case in point. Similarly, some pharmaceutical firms have had difficulty in integrating skills and knowledge from molecular biology to complement their established knowledge in organic chemistry.[15] Radical technical change can also require radical changes in corporate methods of monitoring and control. For example, the development and commercialization of the personal computer, with low development costs, fast development times, and large-scale production and sales, required more decentralized and flexible systems of monitoring and control than those prevailing in companies specialized in making large mainframe computers.

The difficulties of making major shifts in large corporations from one market, from one knowledge source and from one method of monitoring and control, to another is not simply one of skills and learning. It is also profoundly political. In the world of specialized and professionalized competencies that prevail in contemporary corporate activities, such shifts inevitably result in changes in the relative power, status and influence of different professional and functional groups. Professional and functional interests and loyalties will therefore inevitably influence perceptions of – and attitudes towards – potential radical changes. Carlson (1995) and Sutton (1995) show the importance of such factors in the early development of the US electrical industry. Today, we may surmise that some research chemists will be tempted to see the triumphant molecular biologists as a threat rather than an opportunity, and to downplay their potential importance,[16] salesmen used to selling large mainframe computers will not fancy selling PCs, and the managers running today's corporate monitoring and control systems will often reflect yesterday's successes rather than tomorrow's opportunities.

Intelligent arguments will therefore readily (and often sincerely) be found to explain why the proposed changes will be unnecessary, unsuccessful or just plain wrong. Under such circumstances, corporate 'core competencies' can become corporate 'core rigidities' (Loasby, 1983; Leonard-Barton, 1995). But this generally becomes apparent only in the light of subsequent corporate performance, and is very difficult to recognize at the time. Such a powerful mixture of cognitive blinkers and political interests in resisting change was recognized a long time ago:

> It must be considered that there is nothing more difficult to carry out, nor more doubtful of success, nor more dangerous to handle, than to initiate a new order of things. For the reformer has enemies in all those who profit from the old order of things, and only lukewarm defenders in all those who would profit by the new order, this lukewarmness arising partly from fear of their adversaries ... and partly from the incredulity of mankind, who do not truly believe in anything new until they have had actual experience of it. Thus it arises that on every opportunity for attacking the reformer, his opponents do so with the zeal of partisans, the others only defend him half-heartedly ... (Machiavelli, 1950: 21–2)

Implications for Management Practice: Innovative Routines

This growing body of empirical research enables us to identify some of the key organizational features associated with successful and unsuccessful innovating firms, and therefore to give greater practical and operational substance to the notion of the 'routines' that govern innovative activities. These features centre on the matching of the characteristics of technology with organizational practices: external linkages with potential customers and with the important sources of knowledge and skills; internal linkages in the key functional interfaces for experimentation and learning; degree of centralization of resource allocation and monitoring consonant with the costs of technological and market experimentation; criteria for resource allocation consonant with levels of technological and market opportunity; and alignment of professional groups with power and control with fields of future opportunity.

As we concluded above, key organizational practices will vary across firms and sectors. They will also vary over time, particularly

with the advent of radically new technologies. As a general rule, the greater the number of the above organizational routines that require radical change, the greater the likelihood that established firms will have difficulties exploiting a radically new technology.

However, given the uncertainties of innovative activities, the proper routines cannot easily be identified before the event, and – even when they are – applying them cannot guarantee success. From society's point of view, dynamic competition amongst firms is therefore essential, and can be seen as a means both of increasing the incentive to innovate, and of ensuring that a range of 'innovation experiments' take place, some of which turn out to be successful (Nelson, 1990). How firms cope with dynamic competition will be explored in the next section.

TECHNOLOGY AND THE DYNAMICS OF COMPETITION

In *Capitalism, Socialism and Democracy* (1942), Schumpeter (1962) asked one of the most fundamental questions that can be asked about the interaction between technology and management: 'Is it possible to make routine the innovation process and, thereby, to institutionalize change?' We have seen in the previous section of this chapter that support for the inputs to technological development has been 'routinized' in large firms in corporate R&D laboratories and related activities, but that the technical and commercial outputs remain highly uncertain and non-routine. He also approached the same issue from another perspective when he proposed that major technological change brought with it a process of 'creative destruction' which would dislodge incumbent firms and favour entrants. We shall show in this section that, whilst such creative destruction can be observed in some sectors, it is absent from others. The reasons are varied, as are its sources when it happens.

Creative Destruction or Creative Accumulation?

Large firms best institutionalize the process of innovation when integrated development on a large scale is necessary for competitive entry. This is the case in the industries that have historically been amongst the largest investors in R&D, including the pharmaceutical, aircraft and aircraft engine, and chemical industries. In these industries, the development of new products is often intimately connected with the development of new processes and the total scale of activity is sufficiently high to be intimidating to new entrants. Although major technological advances during the second half of this century have challenged each of these industries, most of the incumbent players have maintained their market leadership.[17] It is not obvious that scale in R&D alone explains the persistence of incumbents in these markets. The reasons, however, differ across industries. In pharmaceuticals, the costs of clinical testing arguably favour incumbents (Comanor, 1986; Grabowski, 1968). In aircraft and aircraft engines, long established and complex patterns of supplier relationships perform a similar function (Bonaccorsi and Giuri, 1999; Mowery, 1987; Prencipe, 1997). In chemicals, the scale of pilot plant prototyping and development processes favour companies with established positions.

In other industries of similar scale and technological sophistication, such as consumer electronics, automobiles and steel making, incumbent positions were either overturned or seriously challenged by rivals innovating either in products or production methods. One of the most attractive explanations is that, in situations in which the incumbent does not confront adequate competition, it fails to develop strategies for technological development and diversification that provide a defence against the entry of determined rivals. However, it is always easier to see in retrospect that an industrial leader had become insulated from processes of change after that insularity is challenged by successful entry. It is rarely clear before the event how much development and diversification of technological competencies is enough to hold the forces of 'creative destruction' at bay. Some caution is therefore in order in accepting prescriptions that exhort firms to develop and diversify their technological competencies.

Whilst most corporate R&D investment occurs in industries where large firms dominate, they are not the only sources of persistent innovative activities. In the machine-building

sector, small and specialized innovating firms are predominant, and their importance is often neglected.[18] And since World War II, new technology based firms (NTBF) have supplemented, and in some cases complemented, the intensification of R&D activities of large firms. NTBFs may be found in virtually all of the industrial classifications, but are particularly prominent in industry segments that have experienced fundamental shifts in technological paradigm following World War II. These include the telecommunication, computer, office machinery, new material, medical device and scientific instrument, software and biotechnology industries. NTBFs are also conspicuous in other industries where, although new technologies have emerged, they co-exist with well-established paradigms. Thus, we may speak of NTBF 'segments' in chemicals and pharmaceuticals (based upon recombinant DNA and other fundamental advances in biochemistry), and in machine tool and producer goods (robotics and the diversity of process control instrumentation based upon microelectronics). While almost all NTBFs begin their life as specialized producers, some have grown to rival the scale of large incumbent companies, particularly in the areas where fundamental shifts in technological paradigms have occurred.

Much of the discussion of NTBFs has either explicitly or implicitly addressed the role of these firms as agents of 'creative destruction' in displacing incumbent firms and technologies. There are a handful of industries in which NTBFs have had this role: for example, semiconductors vs valves in electronic components, electronic vs mechanical in calculators and cash register machines, and epoxy resin and cyanoacrylate vs glue in adhesives. However, in a number of other industries, the 'creative destroyers' have been larger and older firms whose strategies of technological diversification open up the opportunities to displace similar or older firms: for example, laser vs impact computer printers, fibre optics vs microwave transmission in telecommunications, and cold (photographic) vs hot 'type' in printing. In this second case, the firms may have had their origins as NTBFs: for example, Hewlett-Packard began as an instrument producer, with its first product, an audio-frequency generator, and its first major success in the oscilloscope market.

To sum up, the model in which 'creative destruction' is accomplished by the simultaneous substitution of new technologies and actors for old has been validated in certain industries. However, it overstates the technological inflexibility and static qualities of incumbents and it reinforces the overly simplistic view that technological change is simply about the creation of substitute products and processes. Instead, and until relatively recently, Schumpeter's model of institutionalized technological change within the confines of the large enterprise opportunities seemed to be a more consistent and reliable account of the sources of technology and innovation. The operations and competitive interactions of large incumbent firms were central to the development and diffusion of new technology. Companies like IBM, Alcoa, General Electric, ICC, Siemens, Philips, NEC, Toyota and Mitsubishi were conducting research on such a broad scale, or implementing organizational innovation with such effectiveness, that a gap was opening between them and potential competitors. More recently, however, each of these companies has faltered. They have not been replaced, but some of those that have prospered over the past two decades have adopted new models for using knowledge to produce competitive advantage. These new models have not directly followed the narrowly framed model of new and superior technology substituting for older and inferior technology. Instead, the process has also involved the restructuring of organizations and markets.

The Perils of Size and Specialization

Whilst large-scale research and development laboratories have demonstrated their capacity to coordinate the production and absorption of knowledge, the capacities of the large organization to experiment simultaneously with a wide variety of innovative opportunities is limited. The reasons for this have already been touched upon above.

First, the large-scale organization faces the daunting task of reproducing the successes responsible for its size. Thus, even though the central research laboratory may provide numerous options for the development of new products and markets, the delays in building these markets to substantial size will often appear unattractive relative to the incremental extension of established products and markets. In short, large organizations most often choose to proceed through the innovation process in large and lumpy bites at what they already know.

Second, even though central corporate research laboratories have proven their capacity to illuminate likely paths forward in technological development, their capacity to coordinate and mobilize new ideas as viable commercial innovations is limited. In part, this is a direct consequence of the functional specialization that has produced them. Their function is more often identified with the process of invention and demonstration of concept than with commercialization or manufacturing process. Indeed, as noted earlier, the difficulties of coordination between central research laboratories and manufacturing and marketing operations are often the reef upon which otherwise excellent new ideas founder.

Third, while numerous academics have abandoned the 'linear model' of innovation in which the creation of new scientific and technical knowledge is progressively refined and developed to become a product innovation, this model continues to influence the organization and incentives of many corporate research efforts. Many companies have been reluctant to implement management practices for the 'chain linked' model (Kline and Rosenberg, 1986), with its feedback loops from customers and downstream development processes or parallel development ladders (Gomory, 1989), and its requirements for concurrent development of multiple generations of product technology. Moreover, the recognition of the problems of the 'linear model' can lead to dysfunctional changes, such as when central research laboratories are made to fund their operations mainly through subventions of the established manufacturing or product marketing departments of the organization.

Thus, although large organizations have been able to institutionalize the process of knowledge creation, their capacity to exploit this knowledge in commercial application is often hindered by the difficulties of demonstrating that a project will have a measurable impact on the corporate balance sheet, of coordinating the specialized competencies of R&D and manufacturing, of harnessing 'feedback' processes from customers, downstream development processes, and of organizing parallel development cycles. These difficult issues are all consequences of the uncertainties about the rate and the direction of technological change. They raise fundamental doubts about the ability of single organizations to coordinate the commercialization of new technologies, especially radically improving ones.

Technology-Based Clusters

The principal alternative to routines of innovation within the large organization is the generation of variety through the development of independent or quasi-independent firms that specialize in the risk taking associated with new product and market development. Complete or partial independence provides powerful incentives to the individuals involved as investors and managers in these companies. It also provides a rapid means of discontinuing lines of development that prove inferior to competitive alternatives, and often provides large companies with the opportunity to acquire successful technologies at a relatively early stage in their development.

In recent years, the development of firms that are specialized in technological risk taking has been associated with 'technological clusters' such as those found in the biotechnology industry (Kenney, 1986), and 'regional high technology centres' such as Silicon Valley or Route 128 in the USA (Saxenian, 1994). Although this model of technological development is very popular with policy makers looking for regional development initiatives (Whittington, 1985), it has been criticized as very difficult to implement, and as problematic as a means to generate large and stable firms (Hobday, 1994).

Three features characterize innovative clusters and regions. The first is a mobile labour force that moves between organizations, thereby cross-fertilizing the 'pool' of knowledge associated with a particular industry and allowing the rapid construction of specialized supplier companies. The second is the availability of a technology that offers substantial opportunities for testing a variety of different approaches to products, markets and organizational practices. Third, innovative clusters and regions are often characterized by the availability of 'venture capital', although the precise forms of financing practice differ substantially in different countries. In the USA, the most important characteristic is its role in coordinating the assembly and monitoring of the management team of the risk-taking enterprise. In other, usually less successful contexts, the terms venture and risk capital are synonymous and a more passive investor role is often adopted.

Over time, large companies have come to recognize that a successful innovative cluster or region provides large companies with the sort of variety generation mechanism that is difficult for them to construct internally. The fluid movement of personnel, simultaneous experimentation with competing implementations, and direct link between risk and reward are difficult things for the large organization to do. For these reasons, fields of high technological opportunity like biotechnology have seen the growth of strategic alliances between established large firms and small entrants, with the former promoting experimentation in the latter and sometimes assimilating those with successful outcomes (Pisano, 1990; Zucker and Darby, 1997).

Networked Structures and the New Competition

The innovative cluster or region is one method for externalizing a part of the functional specialization of the large enterprise which is particularly well adapted to radically changing technologies. A second method – better suited to more stable technologies – entails the replacement of internally coordinated and hierarchical management structures with incentive structures based upon franchise and affiliation. We shall limit our focus to the technological issues involved in such activities.

It is useful to recall that economics views the existence of the firm as a means of reducing the transaction costs that would be involved in more dis-integrated structures of economic organization. One implication is that organizational or technological innovations that reduce transaction costs improve the prospects for their 'outsourcing' or externalization from the company. Progressive and incremental improvements in a wide range of manufacturing inputs and services employed in the manufacturing and distribution of products have improved companies' abilities to outsource components and services. In many cases, outsourcing involves the international transfer of specific manufacturing operations to countries where wage rates are lower, providing a cost-based advantage. This approach has, however, become problematic as companies tighten their manufacturing operations with regard to time, to delivery and quality assurance. The consequent tensions have been an unusually forceful impetus to technological transfer.

Rather than losing the advantages of lower-wage production or the value of export potential, companies in the industrialized and industrializing world have cooperated in the international harmonization and standardization of manufacturing methods and quality assurance. The same process has been responsible for high levels of direct foreign investment in those economies that have demonstrated their capacity and interest in continuous improvement of manufacturing method and of the skill base of the population. This new competition is one in which the large organization retains core competencies, particularly in the areas of integration and coordination, while pursuing a continuing search of its own business and manufacturing processes for activities that could be more effectively performed by external suppliers. The discipline for the internal operations that remain is strengthened as the result of this process.

The development of outsourcing and globalization are symptoms of the maturity of many industries in the current technological paradigm. Thus, while the development of key components of modern transportation or communication equipment remains the domain of the large company, many of the components required to construct these 'system' products have become standardized commodity-like items, for which there is no particular advantage in self-sourcing. Similar developments have occurred in other consumer durables and even in many categories of producer goods. However, the optimism of managers with regard to the 'non-essentiality' of particular components or capabilities is often misplaced. Outsourcing activities can proceed too rapidly or too dramatically, resulting in the loss of capabilities that become costly to rebuild once their absence is noted. In particular, activities of

the large firm that involve extensive systemic integration, or the coordination of rapidly involving components, are inappropriate candidates for outsourcing activities (Prencipe, 1997). Nonetheless, as an aggregate process, and taking account that outsourcing from time to time imposes heavy costs, the collective effect of outsourcing has been to improve competitive discipline and performance.

Implications for Management Practice

Large organizations persist, despite setbacks arising from the challenges of new technology based firms, alternative means of organization for innovative risk-taking and the development of outsourcing as a source of competitive advantage. Understanding the reasons for this persistence is particularly important for management practice and is one of the most fertile fields for research. Over the last 20 years, each of the challenges to the role of the large organization has been accompanied by the claim that the large organization's role was to be supplanted by an alternative organizational model with a superior means for achieving commercial success. Each of these alternative models has been adapted and employed by large firms to their advantage, although often only after making substantial investments in organizational and technological change. The large organizations that have survived these transformations are more resilient and adaptable organizations as a result of these changes. There are several specific lessons to be learned from this experience.

First, organizations that are outward looking in their perspective are generally able to identify and incorporate important technological changes before rivals grow large enough to constitute a major competitive threat. Ignoring external developments generally does not doom a company, but delay in recognizing change and beginning to respond to it enormously increases the cost of responding when it does become necessary.

Second, the development of external networks of knowledge generation and supplier competence are a particularly rich source of long-term competitive advantage to those companies that learn to use such networks effectively. Perhaps the most difficult management problem that the large organization faces is in distinguishing where it has advantages in systemic integration and coordination. For the manager accustomed to internal procurement and development, the advantages of systemic integration and coordination are likely to appear to be pervasive. In many cases, however, this is an expensive illusion waiting to be exposed by rivals, who either take a harder look at their internal capacities or are forced to make their way in the world without such capabilities. The capacity to outsource capabilities is particularly important in industries where technological change in components has slowed and may be amenable to standardization.

Third, the management of external networks is a function in which large companies can and should take an active role. Active involvement with innovative and supplier networks provides an important source of learning for the company that can be used to cross-fertilize its own competencies and to enable it to recognize the most innovative and effective players in external networks.

Fourth, large companies play a particularly important role in fostering the improvement and development of their suppliers and customers. Much of the strategic partnership and other alliance building activity of recent years reflects the need for the coordination of technological development in supply chains, and for building an in-house competence to do this. Engaging in cooperation, while preserving advantage, requires a clear differentiation between proprietary and 'industry standard' sets of knowledge and competency.

These developments define the broad framework within which we can assess Schumpeter's belief in the ability of large companies to routinize the innovative process. Specifically, can they create and maintain the competence and vision needed to coordinate the more complex structures following these developments? In the light of the evidence presented above, the answer to this question is uncertain, and makes Schumpeter's original formulation particularly ironic:

To act with confidence beyond the range of familiar beacons...requires aptitudes that are present in only a small fraction of the population and that define the entrepreneurial type as well as the entrepreneurial function. This function does not essentially consist in either

inventing anything or otherwise creating the condition which the enterprise exploits. It consists in getting things done.

This social function is already losing importance and is bound to lose it at an accelerating rate in the future even if the economic process itself of which entrepreneurship was the prime mover went on unabated. For, on the one hand, it is much easier now than it has been in the past to do things that lie outside familiar routine – innovation itself is being reduced to routine.

Technological progress is increasingly becoming the business of teams of trained specialists who turn out what is required and make it work in predictable ways. The romance of earlier commercial adventure is rapidly wearing away, because so many more things can be strictly calculated that had of old to be visualized in a flash of genius. (Schumpeter, 1962: 132)

We have seen that having an innovative vision and bringing it into existence is not the same as the full institutionalization of new knowledge creation and the achievement of predictable results. The romance of the entrepreneurial adventure has failed to be extinguished during the 20th century. Instead, we must reject the view that the large organization can effectively 'internalize' innovation and vertical supply through rational planning. As a result, the large organization has had to resurrect its role as entrepreneur, in creating and maintaining a vision (sometimes in competition with 'creative destroyers') in order to survive and prosper. It would seem that Machiavelli had the clearer perception of the persistent features of human nature.

WHICH REVOLUTIONS FROM ICTs?

Existing theories relating technology to firm behaviour embed the important assumption that, whilst technological constraints and opportunities may change over time, the cognitive processes of decision-makers, as well as the means to implement their decisions, are similar from one time to another. Technological change, including the advance of ICTs, therefore remains largely extrinsic to the decision processes of management. Technology is what management acts upon; management is not acted upon by technology. The governing constraints on the formulation and implementation of strategy are therefore human capabilities and limitations (for example, Nelson and Winter's 'routines'). This section questions whether this assumption is likely to remain true in the face of the continuous development of ICTs, with regard to both the generation of innovation, and the implementation of strategy.[19]

Incremental Revolutions

We shall argue that progress in the ICTs is opening up opportunities for technical changes that are revolutionary, in the sense that the rates of related new product and process development and improvement are much higher than the normal, and that they are having major impacts on knowledge-creation and managerial decision processes themselves.[20] However, the revolution is an incremental one, in that learning and improvement grow directly out of past experience and accumulated competencies, even when these are associated with technical, commercial and organizational failure rather than success. We do not conclude from this – as Tushman and Anderson (1986) might do – that innovations are competence-enhancing and will reinforce incumbents at the expense of new entrants. As we saw in sections three and four, revolutionary technical changes often require organizational changes which incumbent firms find particularly difficult to make (Pavitt, 1998).

ICTs are advancing on a trajectory that is extraordinary when compared to almost any prior technology. The rate of advance in processing power, storage and transmission capacity, and artefact complexity of microelectronic technologies are driving forward so rapidly that our abilities to recognize and exploit useful applications are the principal constraint on realizing their potential. The unique qualities of this extraordinary rate of technological advance suggest such profound and far-reaching effects that Perez (1983) coined a new term, 'techno-economic paradigm', to encompass them. Key features of this new techno-economic paradigm are the ubiquity of ICTs as a general-purpose technology employed throughout the economy, and the extent of the adjustments required for fully exploiting the

technology. Perez (1983) and later Freeman and Perez (1984) were particularly concerned with whether capitalist economies would successfully negotiate the transitions and adjustments implied by the continuing expansion of this paradigm. Although substantial caution remains in order, a crisis has yet to emerge from the processes of adjustment.

Impact in Services: Transactions and Logistics

ICTs are having a major impact upon processes of knowledge generation, distribution and use in the industrialized world. Focussing on the process of knowledge use, many important changes have occurred in the service industries where information collection and processing are essential prerequisites to the definition and delivery of services. Considerable attention has been devoted to the investment and retail banking industry (including finance and real estate), since it has sustained the highest rate of investment in ICTs. These have facilitated major and sometimes controversial innovations in investment banking including security-packaging innovations such as derivatives and the extension of international security trading markets. In retail banking, the development of automatic teller machines, online and telephone banking, and the vast extension of credit card payment systems has only been possible due to the existence of ICTs (Barras, 1990).

It is a mistake, however, to take these developments as the paradigm for the future role of ICTs in technological change. As important as ICTs have been in banking and financial services, their influence is seriously constrained by regulatory structures and industry traditions, as well as by the profound difficulties of developing new market models for many financial services. Financial services demonstrate the importance of ICTs in facilitating transactions, only one of their potentialities and, in many ways, the least revolutionary. Nonetheless, important strategic developments in these industries are often based on the extension and elaboration of ICT networks, and on their role in augmenting the decision-making capabilities of individuals.

If we consider ICTs in retailing and distribution, a richer and somewhat more complete picture of their potentialities begins to emerge. Retailing and distribution services involve a complex mixture of financial transactions and the purchase, storage and transport of goods. A vast quantity of information is generated in managing the flow of goods through distribution and retail channels, and the evolution in the use of ICTs has been a gradual and somewhat piecemeal process, just as in manufacturing automation (Bessant and Hayward, 1988). As in banking, the partial automation of transactions has allowed the restructuring of activities, and savings in some of the traditional processing functions. This, in turn, has created opportunities for larger companies to adopt the strategy of price reduction and quality improvements that support their further expansion, often at the expense of smaller and less sophisticated rivals.

The realization of the potential advantages of ICTs for retailing is, however, constrained by the technical problems of fully utilizing the flow of information generated in their operations. Although ICT-based point of sale and shipping and receiving systems in principle allow the instantaneous assessment of inventories, and the development of sophisticated predictive models of purchasing behaviour and logistical management, there is considerable unevenness in the development and utilization of these systems.[21] One reason is that fully integrated information systems are rare. While the use of ICTs is nearly ubiquitous, there are still many businesses in which ICTs are principally utilized on a 'stand-alone' basis and the extent of inter-firm integration in distribution and retailing is therefore uneven. This state of affairs is temporary. Large retailers are among the most aggressive investors in system integration and in methods for coordinating supplier networks, such as EDI and the more recent applications of internet technologies to create intranet and extranet networks. The latter developments offer substantial advantages in solving the coordination problems in complex supplier networks, such as those encountered in retailing.

A second reason is that the development of the capabilities to utilize such systems fully requires complementary investments in advertising and other proven means of retaining or expanding market share. Increased investment in ICT-related capabilities alone makes little sense if the initial advantages that they provide have not been exploited through complementary and expensive advertising and promotional programmes. A third reason is that the development of integrated inventory management and sales prediction models is difficult and demanding. Although there are many generalized solutions to abstract problems such as the 'travelling salesperson', the adaptation of these abstractions to the real world requires the elaboration of special software.

A significant issue in these and other developments in ICTs is that, while the cost–performance characteristics of microelectronics are plummeting down a uniquely rapid trajectory, the costs of software are falling less rapidly.[22] Correspondingly, the costs of training and of skills development that are necessary for many software and information system applications are relatively constant. The costs of implemented information systems consequently fall at a much slower rate than the price performance of microelectronics. The level of investment continues to increase in the applications identified above, but at a moderate pace, which is one of the reasons that the change in techno-economic paradigm has not yet provoked an adjustment crisis.

The examples from the service industry therefore suggest that ICTs are not disrupting nor soon will disrupt patterns of incremental change in the service industries. In the context of services, ICTs appear to offer a manageable pattern of technological innovation and upgrading, with equipment and software systems developed by suppliers being integrated and improved by growing technological competencies in user firms. Although we have confined our attention to some of the larger service industries, it is possible to see similar processes at work in other service industries such as health care, passenger transportation and shipping.

Impact in Manufacturing: Virtual Prototypes and Pilot Plant

The use of ICTs in manufacturing involves a further set of characteristics that may, on balance, offer greater potential for revolutionary change than the service industry examples that we have considered. This is because manufacturing industries offer a much broader range of opportunities to employ scientific and technological knowledge than has so far been revealed in the service industries. Manufacturing shares many of the transactional and logistical issues of finance and distribution, and therefore the opportunities to apply ICT improvements to these business processes. What distinguishes manufacturing from other economic activities is the range of opportunities for employing knowledge in process and product improvements and innovations. As we have already observed, there is great diversity and unevenness in the extent to which scientific and technical knowledge has been generated and applied across the manufacturing industries.[23] We have also indicated that the process of technological change in these industries is generally incremental and continuous.

To what extent are ICTs disrupting these historical patterns at present, or likely to do so in the near future? The answer to this question hinges upon an evaluation of the technological potential of ICTs. If, on the one hand, the traditional process of incremental knowledge generation, drawing upon a broad infrastructure of scientific and technological knowledge, continues to predominate, the impacts of ICTs will be confined to the improvements they offer in accessing external knowledge and helping to distribute knowledge throughout the organization. These opportunities are, of themselves, major in scope and substance, as the literature on knowledge management has emphasized in recent years. If, on the other hand, ICTs can be more effectively employed to generate the knowledge necessary for incremental improvement or innovation, they will have a much more revolutionary influence on established patterns of technical change. Weether this can happen depends on the potential of virtual modelling and simulation as a means to facilitate the knowledge creation process. These techniques for augmenting human creativity and analytical capability, or even generating 'independent' results, is where ICTs might have their greatest impact.

It is important to recall that computers were created as general-purpose scientific instruments and that they have steadily progressed in filling this role. Major families of scientific and technical problems have been solved only through the use of computer technique. Information technology-based instrumentation has come to characterize both the experimental laboratory and a considerable share of theoretical

investigation. There are still many physical and biological systems for which computer modelling and simulation techniques have yet to offer a convincing alternative to other investigative methods. At the same time, however, one way to characterize the progress in computer application is that it, too, is incremental, building upon systems with fewer variables and less complexity toward systems with more variables and complexity. As computational power increases and costs fall, computerized techniques are deployed across a wider range of scientific and technological investigations.

As is well known, there is frequently a major gap between laboratory and factory practice. In the science-based industries, deliberate efforts to scale up laboratory practice (and thereby preserve many of the controls and much of the knowledge gained in the laboratory) are systematically pursued. Factories are fundamentally different than laboratories but these differences are themselves often subject to scientific and technical investigation, measurement and experimentation. In other industries, the precise science and technology of production processes are less well understood. Considerable effort may be devoted to scientific and technical investigations of particular issues involving quality control or the alleviation of major bottlenecks. But key processes and methods have not been investigated, with the knowledge needed for production residing in the tacit experience of individuals and the transfer of this knowledge from generation to generation.

There are, however, significant prospects for change in this state of affairs from two directions. First, the continuing expansion in computational power and modelling capability employed in the science-based industries is creating a growing collection of techniques and capabilities for modelling processes that are increasingly complex and similar to the real world problems of the factory. Second, the continuing decline in the cost–performance characteristics of all forms of instrumentation by which real world processes can be measured, modelled, simulated and ultimately controlled makes these techniques accessible to a widening range of users. Like the process of computerizing scientific and technical investigation, this process of 'informatizing' the factory proceeds at an uneven pace and, even in the science-based industries that have proceeded the furthest with such techniques, there remain many processes which are only to be understood as art, craft, or tacit knowledge. Our concern is not with whether it will be possible, ultimately, to specify fully a given factory through a virtual model or simulation. Instead the relevant question is: 'Has there been enough progress in this direction to guide the search for process improvements and innovations, or to better design and hasten the manufacturing of product innovations?'

The answer to this question is a qualified 'yes'. In many industries, the product design process is informed by models of the manufacturing process so that the manufacturing characteristics of specific designs may be simulated in virtual models of the factory process (Nightingale, 1997). These models are incomplete, subject to verification and tuning in practice, and sometimes totally inappropriate. They are nonetheless having an important impact on the practice of engineering design in many industries (integrated circuits, electronics more generally, computer printers, telecommunication switches, aircraft bodies and avionics, athletic shoes and other athletic equipment, pleasure boats, tyres, sub-systems of the automobile including suspension and power transmission systems). In other industries, there is no comprehensive model, but there have been important advances in the connection of the design to the manufacturing process (cutting cloth for apparel, rapid prototyping for plastic injection moulding, simulation of food processing operations).

Implications for Management Practice: ICTs in Strategy and Learning

To the extent that the potentials of ICTs are realized, corporate strategy and management are likely to become far more interdependent with the evolution of these applications of ICTs. More specifically, the processes of cognition and learning are likely to become far more interactive with extensions in the use of ICTs within companies. This suggests that the process of making strategy will increasingly be bounded and shaped by systemic considerations related to the effective integration of technologies with supplier and customer networks. The abilities to conceive and implement

strategy will increasingly depend upon the availability of detailed information from these networks and, more importantly, the ability to process this information in ways that lead to coherent and timely decision-making. Strategy must therefore embrace not only what can be done with the information at hand, but what might be possible through the elaboration and extension of the existing systems for gathering and processing information. As we have seen above, strategy in the modern corporation already has many systemic features. ICTs will extend and link many of the existing interdependencies, as well as creating new ones.

As we observed in the case of the service industries, a primary constraint on the use of ICTs is the extent of integration of information processing functions throughout the chain of business processes comprising the operation of the firm. Achieving this integration within the firm and between the firm and its suppliers and, in some cases, customers are processes that advance unevenly. The process of achieving integration will require important strategic decisions that in turn will shape future strategic options. For example, it is possible for a retailer to achieve a high degree of integration with a particular supplier that opens up a wider range of strategic options for the retailer than a more generic and loosely coupled integration. Achieving the tighter integration is likely to require co-investment – what Teece (1986) calls co-specialized assets – between the supplier and the retailer and to constrain that supplier's strategic options for supplying other retailers. Information system integration thereby becomes a kind of virtual vertical integration in which the traditional problems of bilateral monopoly may transform into actual vertical integration. It does not follow, however, that vertical integration between suppliers and retailers is the most efficient solution for either party.

Similarly, in manufacturing we observed that a principal constraint on more use of ICTs was the extent to which virtual modelling and simulation could accurately represent products and production processes. There is, however, unlikely to be a single solution to the problems of virtual modelling and simulation. Differences will arise from the diversity in existing production methods. They will also arise from conditions of complexity and uncertainty that will result in differences in opinions amongst modellers about the features that are most important to model. This new modelling capability, like the established patterns of incremental and continuous improvement, is therefore likely to generate diversity in performance and in response to new opportunities. Firms pursuing an ICT intensive strategy to improvement and innovation are likely to choose from amongst a variety of strategies. Some will build models that are very flexible but less precise, requiring more time-consuming and expensive trials and shakedowns. Others will build systems that are very precise but rather inflexible, delivering incrementally improvements to products at a faster rate, but unable to accommodate larger shifts in market demand or opportunity. Still others might over-determine their virtual models and simulations, allowing a combination of tight and loose specifications to be chosen as the occasion demands.

As the constraints on virtual modelling and simulation and the integration of information systems loosen with the progress in ICTs and continued investments in capabilities and software, new forms of vertical and horizontal integration as well as spin-off and dis-integration are likely. The questions raised by Schumpeter will once again come to the fore, now as central components not only of corporate strategy but also of the research agenda of scholars of strategic management. Will the larger incumbent enterprises prove to be more effective in developing these models as a means to institutionalize the process of innovation? Will smaller firms be able to develop specialized competencies in information systems that will prove more effective either technologically or in combination with a smaller, more highly motivated human workforce than it is possible to attract to the larger enterprise?

CONCLUSIONS

Consistent with what we said at the start of this chapter, we do not believe that there is any one best way to improve our understanding of the links between technology and corporate strategy. Empirical studies, corporate practitioners and events will continue to generate things to be explained. Scholars will hopefully be responsive to practical concerns, without claiming to provide instant and easy solutions

to complex problems. It would also be a help if scholars could communicate with each other across disciplinary fields – more specifically, if organization specialists would read what economists say about the influences on innovation of factors external to the firm, and economists would read what organization specialists say about factors internal to the firm.

But exactly the same paragraph could probably be written about most aspects of strategic management. For the specific objective of improving our understanding of technology in corporate strategy, we can identify three characteristics of corporate innovative activities that we expect to continue in future – the production and distribution of scientific and technological knowledge will continue to be increasingly specialized, and to flow through professional as well as corporate networks; the application of ICTs will certainly maintain – and probably accelerate – the dual trends identified since the industrial revolution: increasing fundamental understanding (through cheaper experiments and simulations) and increasing complexity (involving more bodies of knowledge, and more systemic linkages through the cheap communications and applications software); innovative large firms will persist, but not fully control the process of innovation. On this basis, we identify three major research challenges.

Knowledge Networks

Two factors are beginning to change how knowledge networks operate. First, the increasing global reach of business firms is changing what used to be the mainly national basis for links between knowledge generation and application. Second, advances in ICTs are changing the content of such networks, reducing the costs of scientific and technological experimentation, and changing the means of communication. Together with the traditional means of case studies, recent advances in bibliometrics – involving analysis of authorship and citation patterns in published scientific papers and patents, and themselves facilitated by advances in ICTs – will be an increasingly powerful means of describing and understanding how these science and engineering networks operate and are changing, and their implications for corporate strategy.

The Co-evolution of Technology and Organization

There is no uniformity or inevitability in the nature of successful or unsuccessful corporate practice in coping with technology. This is highly contingent upon the technologies and markets in which the firm is engaged. It is not a technologically deterministic position to argue that corporations know better how to make continuous and radical changes in technologies than to make continuous and radical changes in accompanying organizational practices. However, some corporations are capable of learning, from their own and others' experience and mistakes, how to match changing technologies with products, markets, and methods of production and delivery. This is why it is premature to predict the demise of the large corporation and the universal advent of the virtual firm. It is also why we are clearly not on the path suggested by Schumpeter, where change is safely institutionalized within the boundaries of the large enterprise. At the end of section three, we propose some key organizational practices that have to be dovetailed with the particularities of specific technologies. They are mostly about linkages amongst specialized professional skills and corporate functions, and the matching of decision criteria and monitoring systems to the range of technological opportunities and the scale of activities required to exploit them. One aim of future research should therefore be to develop a robust taxonomy that classifies and matches the nature of technologies (their source, rates and directions of change, costs of experimentation) with the products, markets and organizational practices associated with their successful exploitation.

Impacts of the ICTs

ICTs can be considered an area where such a taxonomy will be particularly timely. For example, we have seen in our discussion in section five that advances in the ICTs offer the potential for integrating a number of previously separate functions – transactions, distribution, product development, manufacturing – and thereby creating more complex systems, involving an ever greater number of sub-systems and components. At the same time,

the costs of experimentation in particular sub-systems are declining with the increasing use of simulations. What implications do these apparently conflicting trends have for product development and corporate strategy?

ACKNOWLEDGEMENTS

We are indebted to Richard Whittington and Joe Tidd for their constructive and helpful comments on earlier drafts of this chapter.

NOTES

1 Kuznets (1957) argued that the essence of modern economic growth was precisely the deliberate application of scientific and technical knowledge to the industrial (and other) production processes.

2 Comparing the social observations of A. de Tocqueville (1980), B. Franklin (1987) and A. Smith (1937) is a persistently fruitful exercise for understanding the early perception of these developments. Notable historical works include A. Toynbee (1956), J. D. Bernal (1939), A. P. Usher (1954), P. Mantoux (1961), D. Landes (1969), and L. Mumford (1964) while A. Chandler (1977, 1990) offers a similar breadth of vision in business history.

3 Broadly speaking, innovation studies are concerned with improving empirical and theoretical understanding of the nature, sources and societal impact of technical change. They touch upon a number of disciplines, in particular, economics and economic history, industrial sociology and the sociology of science, business management, and political science. They have also built increasingly on advances in bibliometrics. Their contributions include: the empirical confirmation of the significant influence of national technological investments on national economic performance; helping lay the empirical foundations for the evolutionary theory of economic change; identifying key management factors distinguishing successful from unsuccessful innovations; criticizing heavy government funding of big technologies; advancing the debate on the relative importance of the knowledge base and societal factors in influencing the rate and direction of technical change. The research findings emerging from innovation studies are the basis of the textbook on managing innovation by Tidd et al. (1997).

4 For recent research on increasing specialization in invention in the 19th century, see Lamoreaux and Sokoloff (1999a).

5 Although patterns of specialization in demand in specific regions do influence the evolution of local technological capabilities (Fagerberg, 1995; Rosenberg, 1976).

6 A similar concept of a 'technical system' had been developed earlier by B. Gille (1978).

7 Aerospace is a special case, having been technologically force-fed, especially since World War Two, by Government R&D subsidies and procurement linked to military requirements.

8 We consider here only the main institutions directly involved in the creation and application of knowledge. Other specialized institutions concerned with (for example) finance and intellectual property clearly influence the incentive to produce and diffuse knowledge, but will not be considered. For systematic exploration of their influence, see von Tunzelmann (1995).

9 This point is made strongly by analysts in the evolutionary economic tradition; see Saviotti and Metcalfe (1991).

10 Because the failed managers disappear from view, or the corporation does not like talking about failure, or because failures do not make such good stories or case studies.

11 As measured by the distribution of their US patenting amongst technological fields; see Patel and Pavitt (1997).

12 In Tushman and Anderson's influential paper (1986), the most plausible cases of competence-destroying innovations are those at the beginning of the twentieth century; see Pavitt (1987).

13 See Dornseifer (1995) for a fascinating comparison of the organization of R&D in IG Farben and in Dupont between the world wars.

14 In particular, the failure of Xerox to exploit the major inventions underlying the personal computer that it made in its PARC laboratory (Uttal, 1983).

15 This has particularly been the case for German and Swiss firms, whose considerable strengths are based on organic chemistry. Martin (1998) has suggested that the greater success of British and US pharmaceutical companies in assimilating advances in molecular biology may in part reflect their stronger competencies in traditional biology, reflecting their origins in food processing activities.

16 One of Adam Smith's less well recognized achievements in *The Wealth of Nations* was to have described the then emerging disciplines in science (then called philosophy) as 'tribes'.

17 Some of the most significant changes have occurred in the chemicals industry where the leadership of companies (mainly from Germany) with their origins in the dyestuff branch of the industry is now shared with the relatively newer companies (mainly from the USA) that emerged from petroleum refining.

18 More than a third of all US patenting is in fields of mechanical technology; see Patel and Pavitt (1994).

19 As we have pointed out in section two, Chandler is very aware of the historical effects of changes in technology on changes in management tasks and corporate strategies. He does not, however, analyse the effects of technological change on processes of knowledge generation.

20 We shall not discuss here one of the sector-specific consequences of advances in the ICTs, namely, the growing importance of 'information goods'; see Shapiro and Varian (1999).

21 In addition, in many industrialized countries, it is possible that significant market power of large retailers may blunt incentives to fully develop or employ these systems; see section four above.

22 There is little basis for concluding, as some have, that the costs of software production are increasing. It is, however, probably the case that total investment in software is increasing. The uncertainty arises because a major share of software cost is not recorded separately in national income and product accounts. Individuals that are employed within companies to produce software, as well as many of the software production costs of information system suppliers, are not separately recorded. Software that is sold in 'packaged' form is recorded and it appears likely that the costs of this software are declining as the development costs are spread over larger numbers of users. The problem with making conclusive statements about packaged software costs is that there is no reasonable method for indexing quality change.

23 The same may be said for the manufacturing and related industries such as construction where physical production processes and complex production scheduling are part of the production process.

REFERENCES

Aoki, M. (1986) 'Horizontal vs vertical information structure of the firm', *American Economic Review*, 76: 971–83.

Augsdorfer, P. (1996) *Forbidden Fruit: An Analysis of Bootlegging, Uncertainty, and Learning in Corporate R & D*. Aldershot: Avebury.

Barras, R. (1990) 'Interactive innovation in financial and business services: the vanguard of the service revolution', *Research Policy*, 19: 215–37.

Bernal, J. D. (1939) *The Social Function of Science*. London: Routledge & Kegan Paul (reprinted by MIT Press, 1967).

Bessant, J. and Hayward, B. (1988) 'Islands, archipeligoes and continents: progress on the road to computer-integrated manufacturing', *Research Policy*, 17: 349–62.

Bonaccorsi, A. and Giuri, P. (1999) 'Network structure and industrial dynamics: the long term evolution of the aircraft-engine industry', Draft Paper, Sant'Anna School of Advanced Studies, Pisa, Italy.

Burns, T. and Stalker, G. (1961) *The Management of Innovation*. London: Tavistock (republished in 1994 by Oxford University Press).

Callon, M. (1993) 'Variety and irreversibility in networks of technique conception and adoption', in D. Foray and C. Freeman (eds), *Technology and the Wealth of Nations*. London: Pinter. pp. 232–68.

Carlson, W. B. (1995) 'The coordination of business organization and technological innovation within the firm: a case study of the Thomson-Houston Electric Company in the 1980s', in N. Lamoreaux and G. Raff (eds), *Coordination and Information: Historical Perspectives on* the *Organization of Enterprise*. Chicago: University of Chicago Press. pp. 55–99.

Caron, F., Erker, P. and Fischer, W. (eds) (1995) *Innovation in the European Economy between the Wars*. Berlin: de Gruyter.

Chandler, A. (1977) *The Visible Hand. The Managerial Revolution in American Business*. Cambridge, MA: Belknap.

Chandler, A. (1990) *Scale and Scope: The Dynamics of Industrial Capitalism*. Cambridge, MA: Belknap.

Christensen, C. (1997) *The Innovator's Dilemma*. Boston: Harvard University Press.

Cohen, W. and Levinthal, D. (1987) 'Innovation and learning: the two faces of R&D', *Economic Journal*, 99: 569–96.

Comanor, W. S. (1986) 'The political economy of the pharmaceutical industry', *Journal of Economic Literature*, 24: 1178–217.

Cooper, R. (1986) *Winning at New Products*. Reading, MA: Addison-Wesley.

Craft, E. B. (1925) *Bell Educational Conference, 1925*. New York: Bell System.

Cusumano, M. (1991) *Japan's Software Factories: A Challenge to US Management*. New York: Oxford University Press.

David, P. A., Mowery, D. and Steinmueller, W. E. (1992) 'Analysing the economic payoffs from basic research', *Economics, Innovation, and New Technology*, 2: 73–90.

de Solla Price, D. (1984) 'The science/technology relationship, the craft of experimental science, and policy for the improvement of high technology innovation', *Research Policy*, 13(1): 3–20.

de Tocqueville, A. (1840) *Democracy in America*. English language version 1980. New York: Vintage Books.

Devine, W. (1983) 'From shafts to wires: historical perspectives on electrification', *Journal of Economic History*, 43: 347–72.

Dornseifer, B. (1995) 'Strategy, technological capability, and innovation: German enterprises in comparative perspective', in F. Caron, P. Erker and W. Fischer (eds), *Innovations in the European Economy between the Wars*. Berlin: de Gruyter. pp. 197–226.

Dosi, G. (1982) 'Technological paradigms and technological trajectories: a suggested interpretation of the determinants and directions of technical change', *Research Policy*, 11: 147–62.

European Industrial Research Management Association (EIRMA) (1995) *Evaluation of R & D Projects*. Paris: EIRMA.

Fagerberg, J. (1995) 'User–producer interaction, learning and comparative advantage', *Cambridge Journal of Economics*, 19: 243–56.

Ferguson, C. and Morris, C. (1993) *Computer Wars: How the West Can Win in a Post-IBM World*. New York: Random House.

Franklin, B. (1987) *Writings*. New York: Library of America.

Freeman, C. (1982) *The Economics of Industrial Innovation*. London: Frances Pinter.

Freeman, C. (1984) 'Prometheus unbound', *Futures*, 16: 494–507.

Freeman, C. and Perez, C. (1984) 'Long waves and new technology', *Nordisk Tidsskrift for Politisk Economi*, 17: 5–14.

Freeman, C., Clark, J. and Soete, L. (1982) *Unemployment and Technical Innovation: A Study of Long Waves and Economic Development*. London: Frances Pinter.

Galambos, L. and Sewell, J. (1995) *Networks of Innovation*. New York: Cambridge University Press.

Gambardella, A. and Torrisi, S. (1998) 'Does technological convergence imply convergence in markets? Evidence from the electronics industry', *Research Policy*, 27: 445–63.

Gille, B. (1978) *Histoire des Techniques*. Paris: Gallimard.

Gomory, R. E. (1989) 'From the "ladder of science" to the product development cycle', *Harvard Business Review*, 67(6): 99–105.

Grabowski, H. G. (1968) 'The determinants of industrial research and development: a study of the chemical, drug and petroleum industries', *Journal of Political Economy*, 76, March/April: 292–306.

Graham, M. (1986) *RCA and the Video-Disc: The Business of Research*. Cambridge: Cambridge University Press.

Granstrand, O. (1982) *Technology, Management and Markets*. London: Frances Pinter.

Granstrand, O. and Oskarsson, C. (1994) 'Technology diversification in "multi-tech" corporations', *IEEE Transactions on Engineering Management*, 41: 355–64.

Granstrand, O. and Sjölander, S. (1990) 'Managing innovation in multi-technology corporations', *Research Policy*, 19: 35–60.

Granstrand, O., Patel, P. and Pavitt, K. (1997) 'Multi-technology corporations: why they have "distributed" rather than "distinctive core" competencies', *California Management Review*, 39(4): 8–25.

Griliches, Z. (1990) 'Patent statistics as economic indicators', *Journal of Economic Literature*, 28: 1661–707.

Griset, P. (1995) 'Innovation and radio industry in Europe during the interwar period', in F. Caron, P. Erker and W. Fischer (eds), *Innovations in the European Economy between the Wars*. Berlin: de Gruyter. pp. 37–63.

Hagedoorn, J. (1992) 'Trends and patterns in strategic technology partnering since the early seventies', *Review of Industrial Organisation*, 11: 601–16.

Hicks, D. (1995) 'Published papers, tacit competencies and corporate management of the public/private character of knowledge', *Industrial and Corporate Change*, 4: 401–24.

Hicks, D. and Katz, S. (1997) *The Changing Shape of British Industrial Research*. STEEP Special Report No. 6. Brighton: Science Policy Research Unit, University of Sussex.

Hobday, M. (1994) 'Innovation in semiconductor technology: the limits of the Silicon Valley network model', in

M. Dodgson and R. Rothwell (eds), *The Handbook of Industrial Innovation*. Aldershot: Edward Elgar. pp. 154–68.

Hounshell, D. and Smith, J. (1988) *Science and Corporate Strategy*. Cambridge: Cambridge University Press.

Keck, O. (1981) *Policy-making in a Nuclear Program: The Case of the West German Fast Breeder Reactor*. Lexington, MA: D. C. Heath and Co.

Kenney, M. (1986) *Bio-Technology: The University–Industry Complex*. New Haven, Conn: Yale University Press.

Klevorick, A. K., Levin, R., Nelson, R. and Winter, S. (1995) 'On the sources and significance of inter-industry differences in technological opportunities', *Research Policy*, 24: 185–205.

Kline, S. (1995) *Conceptual Foundations for Multi-disciplinary Thinking*. Stanford: Stanford University Press.

Kline, S. and Rosenberg, N. (1986) 'An overview of the process of innovation', in R. Landau and N. Rosenberg (eds), *The Positive Sum Strategy: Harnessing Technology for Economic Growth*. Washington DC: National Academy Press. pp. 275–305.

Kodama, F. (1991) *Analyzing Japanese High Technologies: The Techno-Paradigm Shift*. London: Pinter.

Kuznets, S. (1957) *Modern Economic Growth: Rate, Structure and Spread*. New Haven, Conn: Yale University Press.

Lamoreaux, N. and Raff, G. (eds) (1995) *Co-ordination and Information: Historical Perspectives on the Organization of Enterprise*. Chicago: University of Chicago Press.

Lamoreaux, N. and Sokoloff, K. (1999a) 'Inventive activity and the market for technology in the United States, 1840–1920', Working Paper 7107. Cambridge, MA: National Bureau of Economic Research, Inc.

Lamoreaux, N. and Sokoloff, K. (1999b) 'Inventors, firms and the market for technology in the late nineteenth and early twentieth centuries', in N. Lamoreaux, D. Raff and P. Temin (eds), *Learning by Doing: In Markets, Firms and Countries*. Chicago: University of Chicago Press. pp 19–60.

Landes, D. (1969) *The Unbound Prometheus*. Cambridge: Cambridge University Press.

Leonard-Barton, D. (1995) *Wellsprings of Knowledge*. Boston: Harvard Business School Press.

Lindblom, C. (1959) 'The science of "muddling through"', *Public Administration Review*, 19: 79–88.

Loasby, B. (1983) 'Knowledge, learning and enterprise', in J. Wiseman (ed.), *Beyond Positive Economics*. London: Macmillan. pp. 104–21.

Machiavelli, N. (1950 edition) *The Prince*. New York: Modern Library College Editions.

Maidique, M. and Zirger, B. (1985) 'The new product learning cycle', *Research Policy*, 14(6): 299–313.

Mansfield, E. (1995) *Innovation, Technology and the Economy*. Aldershot: Edward Elgar.

Mantoux, P. (1961) *The Industrial Revolution in the Eighteenth Century: An Outline of the Beginnings of the Modern Factory System in England*. New York: Harper and Row.

Martin, B. and Salter, A. (1996) *The Relationship between Publicly-Funded Science and Economic Performance*. Report to HM Treasury. Brighton: SPRU, University of Sussex.

Martin, P. (1998) 'From eugenics to therapeutics: science and the social shaping of gene therapy', Unpublished DPhil thesis, Brighton: SPRU, University of Sussex.

Mintzberg, H. (1987) 'Crafting strategy', *Harvard Business Review*, 87(4), July–August: 66–75.

Mitchell, G. and Hamilton, W. (1988) 'Managing R & D as a strategic option', *Research Technology Management*, 31: 15–22.

Miyazaki, K. (1995) *Building Competences in the Firm: Lessons from Japanese and European Optoelectronics*. Basingstoke: Macmillan.

Mowery, D. C. (1983) 'The relationship between intrafirm and contractual forms of industrial research in American manufacturing 1900–1940', *Explorations in Economic History*, 20: 351–74.

Mowery, D. (1987) *Alliance Politics and Economics: Multinational Joint Ventures in Commercial Aircraft*. Cambridge, MA: Ballinger.

Mowery, D. (1995) 'The boundaries of the US firm in R & D', in N. Lamoreaux and D. Raff (eds), *Co-ordination and Information. Historical Perspectives on the Organization of Enterprise*. Chicago: University of Chicago Press. pp. 147–82.

Mowery, D. and Rosenberg, N. (1979) 'The influence of market demand upon innovation: a critical review of some recent empirical studies', *Research Policy*, 8: 102–53.

Mowery, D. and Rosenberg, N. (1989) *Technology and the Pursuit of Economic Growth*. Cambridge: Cambridge University Press.

Mumford, L. (1964) *The Myth of the Machine: The Pentagon of Power*. New York: Harcourt Brace Jovanovich.

Nelson, R. (1990) 'Capitalism as an engine of progress', *Research Policy*, 19(3): 193–214.

Nelson, R. and Winter, S. (1982) *An Evolutionary Theory of Economic Change*. Cambridge, MA: Belknap.

Nightingale, P. (1997) 'Knowledge and technical change: computer simulations and the changing innovation process', DPhil. thesis, Brighton: SPRU, University of Sussex.

Noble, D. (1977) *America by Design: Science, Technology and the Rise of Corporate Capitalism*. New York: Alfred A. Knopf.

Patel, P. and Pavitt, K. (1994) 'The continuing, widespread (and neglected) importance of improvements in mechanical technologies', *Research Policy*, 23: 533–45.

Patel, P. and Pavitt, K. (1997) 'The technological competencies of the world's largest firms: complex, path-dependent, but not much variety', *Research Policy*, 26: 141–56.

Pavitt, K. (1987) 'Commentary on Chapter 3', in A. M. Pettigrew (ed.), *The Management of Strategic Change*. Oxford: Blackwell. pp. 123–7.

Pavitt, K. (1998) 'Technologies, products and organisation in the innovating firm: what Adam Smith tells us and Joseph Schumpeter doesn't', *Industrial and Corporate Change*, 7: 433–52.

Pearson, A. (1997) 'Innovation management – is there still a role for "bootlegging"?', *International Journal of Innovation Management*, 1: 191–200.

Perez, C. (1983) 'Structural change and the assimilation of new technologies in the economic and social system', *Futures*, 15: 357–75.

Pisano, G. (1990) 'The R & D boundaries of the firm: an empirical analysis', *Administrative Science Quarterly*, 35: 153–76.

Plumpe, G. (1995) 'Innovation and the structure of the IG Farben', in F. Caron, P. Erker and W. Fischer (eds), *Innovations in the European Economy between the Wars*. Berlin: de Gruyter. pp. 163–74.

Porter, M. (1980) *Competitive Strategy*. New York: Free Press.

Porter, M. E. (1983) 'The technological dimension of competitive strategy', in R. S. Rosenbloom (ed.), *Research on Technological Innovation, Management and Policy*, Vol. 1. London: JAI Press. pp. 1–33.

Prahalad, C. K. and Hamel, G. (1990) 'The core competencies of the corporation', *Harvard Business Review*, 90(3), May–June: 79–91.

Prencipe, A. (1997) 'Technological competencies and product's evolutionary dynamics: a case study from the aero-engine industry', *Research Policy*, 25: 1261–76.

Reader, W. (1975) *Imperial Chemical Industries: A History. Vol II, The First Quarter Century*. London: Oxford University Press.

Reich, L. (1985) *The Making of American Industrial Research: Science and Business at GE and Bell, 1876–1926*. Cambridge: Cambridge University Press.

Rosenberg, N. (1974) 'Science, invention and economic growth', *Economic Journal*, 84: 333.

Rosenberg, N. (1976) 'Technological innovation and natural resources: the niggardliness of nature reconsidered', in N. Rosenberg (ed.), *Perspectives on Technology*. Cambridge: Cambridge University Press. pp. 229–48.

Rosenberg, N. (1994) *Exploring the Black Box: Technology, Economics and History*. Cambridge: Cambridge University Press.

Rosenberg, N. and Nelson, R. (1994) 'American universities and technical advance in industry', *Research Policy*, 23: 323–48.

Rosenbloom, R. and Cusumano, M. (1987) 'Technological pioneering and competitive advantage: the birth of the VCR industry', *California Management Review*, 29: 51–76.

Rothwell, R., Freeman, C., Horsley, A., Jervis, V., Robertson, A. and Townsend, J. (1974) 'SAPPHO updated – project SAPPHO phase II', *Research Policy*, 3: 258–91.

Rumelt, R. (1974) *Strategy, Structure and Economic Performance*. Boston: Graduate School of Business Administration, Harvard University.

Sandoz, P. (1997) *Canon*. London: Penguin.

Saviotti, P. and Metcalfe, J. (1991) *Evolutionary Theory and Economic and Technological Change: Present Status and Future Prospects*. Reading: Harwood Academic Publishers.

Saxenian, A. (1994) *Regional Advantage: Culture and Competition in Silicon Valley and Route 128*. Cambridge, MA: Harvard University Press.

Schnaars, S. and Berenson, C. (1986) 'Growth market forecasting revisited: a look back at a look forward', *California Management Review*, XXVIII: 71–88.

Schumpeter, J. (1962) *Capitalism, Socialism and Democracy*, Third Edition. New York: Harper Torchbooks Edition (originally published, 1942, by Harper and Brothers).

Shapiro, C. and Varian, H. (1999) *Information Rules: A Strategic Guide to the Network Economy*. Boston: Harvard Business School Press.

Smith, A. (1937) *An Inquiry into the Nature and Causes of the Wealth of Nations*. New York: Modern Library Edition.

Steinmueller, W. E. (1996) 'The US software industry: an analysis and interpretive history', in D. Mowery (ed.), *The International Computer Software Industry: A Comparative Study of Industry Evolution and Structure*. Oxford: Oxford University Press. pp. 15–52.

Sutton, J. (1995) 'Comment', in N. Lamoreaux and D. Raff (eds), *Co-ordination and Information. Historical Perspectives on the Organization of Enterprise*. Chicago: University of Chicago Press. pp. 94–9.

Teece, D. (1986) 'Profiting from technological innovation: implications for integration, collaboration, licensing and public policy', *Research Policy*, 15: 285–305.

Teece, D. and Pisano, G. (1994) 'The dynamic capabilities of firms: an introduction', *Industrial and Corporate Change*, 3: 537–56.

Thomas, H. (1970) 'Econometric and decisions analysis: studies in R & D in the electronics industry', DPhil. thesis, Edinburgh: University of Edinburgh.

Tidd, J., Bessant, J. and Pavitt, K. (1997) *Managing Innovation: Integrating Technological, Market and Organisational Change*. Chichester: Wiley.

Toynbee, A. (1956) *The Industrial Revolution*. Boston: The Beacon Press (originally published 1884).

Tushman, M. and Anderson, P. (1986) 'Technological discontinuities and organisational environments', *Administrative Science Quarterly*, 31: 439–65.

Usher, A. P. (1954) *A History of Mechanical Inventions* (Revised Edition). Cambridge, MA: Harvard University Press (published in facsimile by Dover Publications, Inc., New York, 1988).

Uttal, B. (1983) 'The lab that ran away from Xerox', *Fortune*, September 5, 97–102.

Von Hippel, E. (1987) 'Co-operation between rivals: informal know-how trading', *Research Policy*, 16(6): 291–302.

von Tunzelmann, G. N. (1995) *Technology and Industrial Progress: The Foundations of Economic Growth*. Aldershot: Edward Elgar.

Whittington, D. (ed.) (1985) *High Hopes for High Tech: Microelectronics Policy in North Carolina*. Chapel Hill: University of North Carolina Press.

Whittington, R. (1991) 'Changing control strategies in industrial R & D', *R & D Management*, 21: 43–53.

Woodward, J. (1965) *Industrial Organisation: Theory and Practice*. Oxford: Oxford University Press.

Zucker, L. and Darby, M. (1997) 'Present at the biotechnological revolution: transformation of technological identity for a large incumbent pharmaceutical firm', *Research Policy*, 26: 429–46.

17

What Are the Responsibilities of Business to Society?

DAVID A. WHETTEN, GORDON RANDS
and PAUL GODFREY

Some readers might be wondering: Why include a chapter on business ethics and social responsibility in a handbook on strategy and management? Our short answer is that we see many benefits from greater integration between business and society scholarship and more mainstream approaches to the study of strategy and management. Following are three supporting arguments, each associated with a major section of our chapter.

First, organizational science scholarship, broadly defined, can benefit from a better understanding of the history of thought regarding the troubling matter of business responsibilities. We offer two brief examples.

Although debates regarding the control and accountability of organizations have receded into the background of organizational scholarship, generally, this subject continues to energize much of the scholarship on business and society relations. When these scholars scan the business landscape they 'see' social activists and special interest groups expending tremendous energy changing business practices that impact society in ways they see as adverse. Whether one agrees with the activists' intentions or not, they are undeniably exerting increasingly greater pressure on, and in many cases control over, the strategies and actions of firms. Achieving a better understanding of these

powerful, organization-bending social forces is at the heart of business and society scholarship.

Given that the term used to characterize this area of focus, 'business and society', denotes the study of relationships, it should not be surprising that scholarship in this area has specialized in the subject of external relations management. Business strategy scholars interested in this subject can learn a great deal about the categorical arguments used to justify the claims regarding what constitutes a firm's legitimate responsibilities. In particular, scholars who tend to focus on the instrumental aspects of external relations involving suppliers, channels of distribution, unions, etc., can gain a better understanding of the full range of relationships firms must manage, including those external claims made on firm resources that are represented as 'moral obligations'. In addition, the recent theoretical work pertaining to stakeholder relations has the advantage of being more bi-directional in orientation than the dominant inside-out models of customer relations, supplier relations, etc., that populate the broader organizations literature.

The first section of our chapter details the history of scholarship on business and society relations, showing how the number and variety of claims regarding corporate social responsibility have increased through the years, and how the scholarship on stakeholder relations has

Table 17.1 *Business and society terminology*

Term	Definition
Attitudes	Situation-specific beliefs
Behavioral intentions	Planned actions
Behaviors	Actions
Corporate social performance	Actual behavior regarding social issues (may be used to refer either to responses, outcomes and impacts of responses, or the entire set of inputs, throughputs, and outputs resulting in social impacts of corporate behavior); a stakeholder's assessment of the degree of acceptability of a company's social responses
Corporate social responses	Actions taken by a company that are intended to or actually do impact a social issue
Corporate social responsibility	Societal expectations of corporate behavior; a behavior that is alleged by a stakeholder to be expected by society or morally required and is therefore justifiably demanded of a business
Corporate social responsiveness	Processes of responding to social demands
Descriptive ethics	Description of the actions engaged in and how these compare to societal moral expectations
Duties	An action which is obligatory in order to protect the right of another
Ethical, moral	Behavior consistent with principles that define what is good or bad
Ethics	The study of moral obligations and behavior; a set of principles or rules that judges or guides decisions made or actions taken by individuals or groups
Justice	Fairness in treatment; various forms exist including distributive (allocation of benefits and burdens associated with some action), compensatory (providing recompense for harm suffered), retributive (imposing punishment for wrong behavior), and procedural (establishment of/adherence to/consequences of following administrative rules)
Morality	Questions of fundamental right/wrong action (good/bad as opposed to correct/incorrect)
Negative rights	Those rights which a person will enjoy unless interfered with (the duty is one of 'negative action', i.e., non-interference in the other party's enjoyment of the right), e.g., life and liberty. The creation of harm frequently involves interfering with negative rights, and negative rights have primary importance in ethics
Normative ethics	Articulation/prescription of desirable behavior or a desirable principle on which to make moral decisions
Positive rights	Those rights which a person can sometimes enjoy only if others take action to see that it is provided (the duty is one of 'positive action', i.e., provision of the entitlement), e.g., food for the starving, shelter for the homeless. The production of social good frequently involves the provision of positive rights, and positive rights have secondary importance in ethics
Rights	Things to which an individual is entitled either by virtue of citizenship or humanity
Utilitarianism	The philosophical theory which states that the morally best action is that which produces the greatest net benefits for society as a whole
Values	Fundamental preferences for outcomes or modes of existence, which are used as a guide for making decisions

emerged as a prominent framework for understanding the process by which external claims are presented, investigated, and negotiated.

Second, the obligatory dimension of the myriad and often conflicting litmus tests of social responsibility facing contemporary firms raises some vexing conceptual challenges that should appeal to organizational theorists interested in the general subject of organizational dilemmas and paradoxes.

Business and society scholars have identified four generic responsibilities of business. These encompass a wide spectrum of 'duties', including creating wealth, obeying laws and regulations, avoiding harm, and ameliorating social ills. Firms attempting to discharge these responsibilities confront a multitude of dilemmas, arising both within and between the four responsibility categories. The conceptual and practical conundrums associated with this

THE RESPONSIBILITIES OF BUSINESS

classification of corporate social responsibilities are the focus of the second section of our chapter.

Finally, the business and society literature contains numerous intriguing leads for new areas of investigation in related areas of management scholarship. Whereas the purpose of the first section is to expose readers with a general interest in organizations to the business and society literature, the purpose of this final section is to suggest opportunities for boundary-spanning collaboration on topics hitherto unstudied. Hence, the final section of our chapter has a distinct forward-looking orientation, inviting readers to consider a variety of research ideas stimulated by our reading of the business and society literature. Given our space limitations, we have opted to introduce a wide variety of topics rather than exploring a handful in detail. This is consistent with our overall objective of inviting the broadest possible range of readers to become more familiar with this literature and to add their theoretical and methodological perspectives to the contemporary discussions in this field regarding some of the most practically challenging and intellectually interesting issues facing tomorrow's business executives.

Before proceeding, we are concerned that because many readers will be new to the business–society literature (within which we include the business ethics literature), some of the terminology may be unfamiliar. Accordingly, in Table 17.1 we present a summary list of major terms – including brief definitions – used in this literature.

HISTORICAL OVERVIEW OF BUSINESS AND SOCIETY SCHOLARSHIP

Significant concerns about the role of business in the larger American society first arose at the end of the 19th century, with the rise of large corporations and the 'robber barons'. Theodore Roosevelt and other progressive politicians of the 1900s and 1910s responded to these concerns by creating the first modern wave of government regulation to curb abuses, such as the meat packing industry's scandalous practices, which were the subject of muckraker Upton Sinclair's *The Jungle*. The earliest 'management scholar' to address this

issue was scientific management pioneer Henry Gantt, who in 1919 advocated that companies should serve society (Wren, 1979). Four years later, English businessman Oliver Sheldon included this argument in his 'philosophy of management'. More specifically, Sheldon suggested that every manager needed to adopt three principles:

(1) 'that the policies, conditions, and methods of industry shall conduce to communal well-being'; (2) that 'management shall endeavor to interpret the highest moral sanction of the community as a whole' in applying social justice to industrial practice; and (3) that 'management … take the initiative … in raising the general ethical standard and conception of social justice'. (Wren, 1979: 207)

The incorporation of social concerns in management education came after the Second World War. Dean Donald David of the Harvard Graduate School of Business Administration suggested in a *Harvard Business Review* article (1949) that business involvement in community and public affairs must be a quality promoted by business education. From 1952 to 1958 a series of articles on the subject of business and society appeared in *HBR*. According to Paul (1987: 8), 'the basic theme of much of this work is the necessity for the individual to integrate personal values and managerial action. On a more general level, the idea was presented that social responsibility should be a guiding principle for corporations.' This period also saw the publication of Howard Bowen's (1953) *The Social Responsibilities of the Businessman*, and a suggestion by participants in a 1955 AACSB meeting of deans that business schools offer courses in business–society relations and social responsibility.

This section of our chapter picks up the story in the 1960s and continues to the present by briefly reviewing five major themes in the business–society literature.[1] As shown in Table 17.2, our discussion of these five themes highlights topics that are particularly relevant for the study of strategic management. We will first present an overview of the five themes, and then examine each, particularly the first, in more detail. Our added measure of attention to the first theme reflects its foundational nature.

Table 17.2 *Themes in the study of business and society relations*

Lines of inquiry	1960s	1970s	1980s	1990s
Organizing principles				
Business ethics	Meaning of business ethics (different than ethics of individuals in business?)	Descriptive ethics – articulation of ethical issues	Review and application of major ethical theories (rights, justice, utilitarianism) to social and ethical issues	Review and application of additional ethical theories (esp. virtue ethics, social contract theory, ethic of care); ethical theory – organizational theory relationships
Corp. social responsibility	Existence of social responsibilities; articulation of different responsibilities	Why social responsibilities exist; categories of CSR; principle of public responsibility	Social performance – financial performance relationship	Principles of social responsibility; refinement of measures of social performance; exemplary practices of 'socially responsible businesses'
Ideology/attitudes/values	Change in individuals' ethical values over time	Social and ethical values of managers; comparison to those of business critics; manager's opinions re CSR arguments	Social/ethical values/attitudes of business students; models of individual ethical decision making; organizational influences on ethical decision making in organizations	Comparative ethical values (nationality, race, gender); empirical studies of moral reasoning and decision making; moral intensity of issues
Organizational processes				
Corp. social performance	Desirability and appropriate beneficiaries of philanthropy; social movements	Understanding social issues – scanning the environment/ link to strategic planning; social auditing proposed; growth of public affairs and community relations functions; social responsiveness; advocacy advertising	Crisis management; public affairs management; issues management; cause-related marketing, strategic philanthropy; corporate governance; industry self-regulation; CEO leadership; models of CSP	Managing employee voluntarism; environmental audits/reports; environmental affairs function; corporate ethics codes; creating ethical cultures; issue-specific control systems: diversity management, whistle blower protection, ethics hot-lines, sexual harassment policies, etc.

(Contd.)

Table 17.2 (Contd.)

Lines of inquiry	1960s	1970s	1980s	1990s
Stakeholder management			Stakeholder concept, analysis and management	Stakeholder partnerships; prioritizing stakeholders; determinants of stakeholder tactics
Social issues				
Minorities	Hiring	Purchasing from minority owned businesses	Advancement	Diversity, anti-AA
Women		Hiring	Advancement, work and family pressures, comparable worth, child care	Sexual harassment, elderly dependent care
Community	Poverty, riots	Urban renewal	Education, homelessness, drug education, community impacts of closings/takeovers	Education, hiring welfare recipients
International	Corporate political intervention in other countries	Bribery	Disinvestment from South Africa, plant safety, marketing practices	Human rights of workers, local community benefits, global operating standards
Consumers	Consumer rights, planned obsolescence, auto safety	Product safety, deceptive advertising claims	Product quality, advertising to children	Liability regarding inherently harmful products, over-consumption, sex in advertising; internet marketing and privacy/security
Employees	Labor law violations, wage increases	Wages, quality of work life, layoffs, workplace safety, free speech, employee assistance programs	Plant closings, wage and benefit cuts, AIDS, privacy, whistle-blower protection, age and disability discrimination, nonsmoker's rights, employee wellness, employee crime	Downsizing, e-mail privacy, too much overtime, work-life balance, CEO/worker pay ratio, religion/spirituality and work, disability access, domestic partner benefits, smoker's rights, workplace violence

(Contd.)

Table 17.2 (Contd.)

Lines of inquiry	1960s	1970s	1980s	1990s
Environment		Air, water, noise pollution; energy conservation; endangered species	Toxic waste, solid waste, acid rain, ozone depletion, environmental racism	Global warming, recycling, recycled content, pollution prevention, disclosure, biodiversity, sprawl, sustainable development
Stockholders			Greenmail, golden parachutes	CEO compensation
Business–government relations				
Government action	Determinants and legitimacy of corporate political activities	Federal chartering of corporations; social regulatory policies; regulation's impact on business	Economic deregulation; social deregulation attempts; privatization of govt. services; pro-business govt. activity; corporate PACs; regulatory compliance	International trade policies; comparative public policy; international regulation
Business political activity	Implications for business of governmental response to social unrest	Political contributions/ scandals; corporate crime		Political action in other countries; corporate political strategy and competitive advantage

Business and Society Themes

The first theme, *organizing principles*, examines the basis for claims that corporations should act on social and ethical issues. In a sense, authors addressing this theme are answering the 'why' question of business and society relations – Why should firms be good corporate citizens? Within this broad theme are three major streams of scholarship: business ethics, corporate social responsibility (CSR), and ideology/values/attitudes. Each of these streams claims kinship to different disciplines: business ethics is based in philosophy, ideology/ values/attitudes is based in psychology and sociology, and CSR is based in sociology and management. The three streams are inter-related. Individuals have values, attitudes and ideologies that influence, and are the product of, the issues they pay attention to and the decisions they make. These beliefs shape, and are influenced by, their views regarding what corporations should do. Individuals articulate these values in terms of claims that businesses have certain social responsibilities – often framed as ethical responsibilities or moral obligations. To make these claims obligatory, actors weave in the scholarship and thinking of major moral systems or philosophies, as well as legal and economic reasoning.

The second theme, *organizational processes*, focuses on firms' responses to claims that they 'ought' to act in certain ways. Literature on this subject focuses on the 'how' question that has been central to the business and society field – How do firms manage their interactions with the external environment? The major streams of scholarship within this area are corporate social performance, corporate social responsiveness, issues management, crisis management, stakeholder management, and corporate governance. These streams have their roots in business strategy and policy, organizational behavior, organizational theory, psychology, sociology and political science. Corporate social performance (CSP) has become the dominant stream within this category, but stakeholder management has rapidly grown in prominence.

The third theme, *social issues*, examines the specific concerns expressed by various stakeholders. Scholarship on this theme addresses the 'what' component of business and society relations – What are the specific claims made

on the business enterprise by agents of social change? Research in this area involves description of social problems, and of the corporate activities that give rise to or contribute to the exacerbation of these problems. This stream of research tends to be descriptive and issue specific. Unlike the literature in the principles category it tends to focus on the specific impacts of the harm and the mechanisms by which it occurs, rather than making a philosophical or strategic case for why companies should respond to the issue. Unlike the literature in the processes category, it tends to describe practices of companies that are framed in issue specific terms rather than in relational or functional terms. In addition, when corporate practices are described, the focus is on how they increase or lessen the harm done, rather than on their intended effects, in terms of the development of the issue or the company's relationships with the concerned stakeholders. As noted above, unlike the business–government relations literature, the stakeholders involved have no direct, legitimate coercive power over the corporation. It is important to point out that fewer business and society scholars currently emphasize this theme in their writings than did in the past – much of the literature in this area now stems from sociology, political science, and journalism, including the general, business, and social advocacy press. Although it is an important source perspective in this field, it is seldom the focus of actual scholarship.

The fourth theme, *business–government relations*, focuses on activities directed at business by government (such as regulation and trade policies), and on activities directed at government by business (such as lobbying and PAC contributions). To the extent that government is just another stakeholder group, it should be managed by a process like public affairs (under theme 2). To the extent that government is concerned about specific issues scholarship on this topic spills over into theme 3. However, government is such a powerful stakeholder – different in degree (size and power vis-à-vis other stakeholders) and kind (it can enforce its demands through laws and regulations) – that we place it in its own category. For this reason, this theme can be viewed as a specific focus on a unique 'who' in business and society relations. Scholars in this area commonly study both governmental and business actions, making separation of these interactions awkward. These scholars frequently have different training than those who study the interactions of business with other social stakeholders. The root disciplines of business–government relations scholars tend to be political science, economics and law.

Theme 1: Organizing Principles – 'Why'

The pioneers in the business–society field came from many disciplines, but most notably from economics, political science, law, and business policy. In part because of their professional background, as well as the nature of public discourse, the search for principles to guide business in its relationship with society was framed primarily in terms of corporate social responsibility (CSR), rather than ethics or values – although these latter topics have been of great significance. Because of CSR's prominence, we will focus primarily on spend most of our effort detailing this concept. Readers interested in an extensive discussion of the evolution of the CSR concept are advised to see Carroll (1999).

Corporate Social Responsibility

The early advocates for CSR (Bowen, 1953; Davis, 1967; Votaw and Sethi, 1969) advanced many pragmatic arguments on behalf of CSR. These included the ideas that CSR activities: would help limit increases in government regulation; would develop a socially and economically stronger society more conducive to business success; would improve corporate reputation among existing and potential customers; would help attract and retain high quality employees; and had the potential to turn social problems into business opportunities. Arguments that business had a moral obligation to help society were also advanced, but were not generally articulated in as much detail.

This growing acceptance in the late 1950s and the 1960s of the concept of social responsibility within both business and business education elicited a vigorous attack on the concept, led by conservative economist Milton Friedman. Friedman's (1962, 1970) criticisms

of the concept will be explored in some detail in the third section of this chapter. Put simply, Friedman argued that the proper social responsibility of business is to focus on wealth creation, and to leave other social institutions to solve social problems. Other critics charged that giving business the power to address issues traditionally reserved for government and charitable organizations would be damaging to the concept of a pluralistic society (Levitt, 1958).

This challenge to the CSR concept resulted in attempts in the 1970s to build a stronger, more logically grounded and articulated case for the adoption of CSR. Preston and Post (1975) looked for a principle to decide what issues a company was obliged to respond to. They articulated the 'principle of public responsibility', which argues that a business should deal with the social issues that are impacted by the normal operating activities of the company. This principle suggests, for example, that an automobile manufacturer has the responsibility to address issues such as auto safety, vehicular air pollution, and the impacts of its manufacturing plant activities on the local community, while it has no responsibility to become engaged in activities such as philanthropic support for the arts. Sethi (1975) suggested that corporate social responsibility (or performance) had three logically distinct elements: social obligation (responsibility to obey the law), social responsibility (congruence with prevailing societal norms, values and expectations), and social responsiveness (development of policies, programs and capabilities that would minimize adverse consequences of societal demands). These three elements were considered by Sethi (1975) to be proscriptive, prescriptive, and anticipative, respectively.

Building on this conceptual work, Carroll (1979) suggested another approach to establishing principles of social responsibility. He attempted to defuse the economic responsibility vs social responsibility argument by acknowledging that economic profitability is a fundamental social responsibility of business. Carroll articulated three other categories of responsibility: legal, ethical and discretionary. He argued that these four categories could serve as principles for managers deciding how to meet their social responsibility regarding a specific issue. The economic responsibility of the firm is to take those actions regarding the issue that helped the firm make money. The legal responsibility of the business on the issue is to obey whatever laws existed regarding the issue. The precise nature of the ethical and discretionary responsibilities is more vague, in part because Carroll offered differing explanations of them in different writings (Carroll, 1979, 1991). Ethical responsibilities consist either in doing what society expects on the issue or in doing whatever is necessary to avoid causing harm. Discretionary responsibilities (or philanthropic responsibilities, as they were later referred to) consist of taking actions not expected of the firm by society, or actions which bring about social benefits. The differences in Carroll's earlier, more pragmatic, formulation of these responsibilities and his later, more theoretically based, formulation reflects growth in the influence of ethics on the CSR concept, which we discuss shortly.

In the 1980s and 1990s, much of the CSR research focused on the relationship between corporate social performance and financial performance. This attention reflected both the increased empirical orientation of the field, as well as the desire to empirically test (or for many, to provide support for) the claim that good corporate citizens would be good economic performers. Over 50 such studies have been done, and several reviews and meta-analyses of this literature have been conducted (Ullmann, 1985; Griffin and Mahon, 1997; Preston and O'Bannon, 1997; Roman et al., 1999; Wood and Jones, 1995; Frooman, 1997). The empirical results are mixed. In general, the studies suggest a somewhat positive association between CSR and financial performance, although the causal nature of the relationship is unclear. At the very least, relatively little support exists for the view that CSP and economic performance are negatively related. However, many of these studies are methodologically weak and the robustness of their findings is thus in doubt. For example, Wood and Jones (1995) attribute some of the ambiguity in these results to a mismatching of independent and dependent variables and the lack of available data on theoretically relevant intervening variables.

Scholars have increasingly attempted to refine measures of social performance. Single issue, single measure studies have been supplanted by measures which use multiple indicators, most notably the Kinder, Lydenberg, Domini & Co. (KLD) index. This index of social performance currently measures performance on 10 different social issue areas (community, diversity, employees, product, environment, non-US operations, nuclear power, military contracting, alcohol/tobacco/gambling, and 'other') for all of the S&P 500, and is available on a longitudinal basis. Several studies of the KLD database have concluded that, despite some weaknesses, it is a far more accurate and reliable measure of social performance than its predecessors (Sharfman, 1993; Starik, 1993; Waddock and Graves, 1997b).

In the 1990s, attention also turned back to articulating theoretically sound and practical principles for CSR. Wood (1991) drew from previous CSR research to suggest three fundamental principles. At the institutional level, the legitimacy of business as an institution depends upon proper use, rather than abuse, of its power. At the organizational level, the business should minimize harmful impacts stemming from its normal operating activities. At the individual level, managers should utilize whatever individual discretion they may have to benefit society. These principles, Wood argued, provide logically defensible guidelines which managers can use to determine what issues they should respond to and in what ways.

Many CSR scholars in the 1990s have called attention to and described the exemplary practices of so-called 'socially responsible businesses' (SRBs) (Altman and Post, 1995). These organizations, generally relatively young small to midsize companies, publicly state their commitment to CSR, particularly to engage in activities which can be regarded as falling in Carroll's (1979) discretionary category. The Body Shop, Ben & Jerry's, Odwalla, Tom's of Maine, Patagonia, South Shore Bank of Chicago, and Hanna Andersson are among the companies whose exemplary commitment to CSR have been widely recognized. However, critics argue that when one considers the full range of corporate activity, few companies deserve the SRB label (see Entine, 1994 for an application of this argument to the Body Shop).

Ethics

The sub-field of business ethics has benefited from an increasing presence of business faculty with a rich training in ethics. In the 1950s and 1960s scholars wondered whether business ethics was anything more than individual ethics applied in a business setting. Guiding ethical principles were often religiously based (Johnson, 1957). As CSR focused on organizational actions regarding externally generated social demands, ethics to some degree focused on individual actions within the company. Such topics include falsification of expense reports and other records, dishonesty, theft and extortion, etc. To some degree this distinction between social and ethical issues continues, particularly as this subject is treated in textbooks. But recognition that ethical considerations apply to external social issues grew, and in the 1970s many studies identified and catalogued the ethical questions involved in a wide variety of personal and organizational issues. These works were often used in conjunction with the pedagogical question: What should be done in this situation in order to be ethical?

As ethicists began to write and teach in the business–society area, the tools of normative ethical analysis entered the discussion. During the 1980s, the ethical theories of utilitarianism, rights, and justice (Cavanagh et al., 1981) were applied to business situations. Philosophers and non-philosophers alike began to apply these theories to organizational and individual behaviors, as well as to social problems, to determine if an ethical responsibility exists in conjunction with a particular issue, and, if so, what is the nature of the organization's or individual's obligations. While the application of ethical analysis fostered a more rigorous analysis of social responsibility claims, these theories did not end the debate about business ethics. While rights theory is preferred by most business ethicists, there is hardly a general consensus on this matter. Recognizing that different ethical principles often yield conflicting implications for action, a common recommendation is that potential decisions be analyzed using each of the major theories (Velasquez et al., 1983). If a course of action is adjudged ethical by all of the theories, it can be confidently engaged in. However, if no course of action passes all theoretical screens, the decision-maker must choose among those options that pass one or two screens, or continue to search for additional options. While this is a reasonable guideline for academic analysis, its limitations for management practice should be fairly obvious – few managers have the time, understanding, or energy to perform this type of detailed comparative analysis.

In the 1990s, additional ethical theories entered the field and attracted substantial interest: chief among these are social contracts theory (Donaldson and Dunfee, 1994), virtue ethics (Solomon, 1992), and the ethics of care or feminist ethics (Liedtka, 1996). Virtue ethics represents a qualified return to the 1960s treatments of business ethics as individual ethics, but with a firmer philosophical grounding. Recent scholarship also asks a new question: do ethical business practices lead to competitive advantages? (Hosmer, 1994; Quinn and Jones, 1995.)

Ideology, Attitudes and Values

This component focuses on the beliefs that individuals hold which shape their decisions and behaviors. As such it is based in psychology, sociology, and social psychology. In the 1960s a key question in this area, stemming from such ethical fiascos as the electrical price fixing scandals of the 1950s, was whether individual managers' ethical values were in decline (Baumhart, 1961). In the 1970s attention to the role of values in decision making led to a number of studies about the values of executives (Ostlund, 1977), employees (Collins and Ganotis, 1973) and social activists (Sturdivant, 1977). The focus on executives' attitudes continued in the 1980s with studies examining whether executives' attitudes toward types of social responsibilities might be related to company social performance (Aupperle et al., 1985). In the 1980s and 1990s a number of studies examined the social and ethical values and attitudes of business students (see Glenn, 1992, for a review of these studies) in an attempt to determine whether ethics education had an impact on ethical values and attitudes. Another area of increased attention in the 1990s was comparative studies of ethical values and decision making in companies and societies around the world (Al-Kazemi and Zajac, 1999; Batten et al., 1997; Nakano, 1997).

Scholars interested in empirically investigating ethics and values looked to studies such as those of Rokeach (1973), England (1967), and Hofstede (1980) for insight and instrumentation (Frederick and Weber, 1987). But these psychologically and managerially based values instruments were not found to be especially helpful, and in the 1980s and 1990s a major shift in this literature occurred. Scholars moved away from descriptive studies of values and attitudes presumed to be important in decision making and towards psychological theories of ethical reasoning – including conceptual models of individual ethical decision making in organizations. Kohlberg's (1981) theory of moral reasoning has been widely used in studies of managers' and business students' moral reasoning (Weber, 1990; Elm and Nichols, 1993). Trevino (1986) developed a model of ethical decision making incorporating aspects of both the individual and the organization. Victor and Cullen (1988) investigated the ethical climate of organizations, and how this affected individuals' ethical decision making. Jones' (1991) model calls particular attention to the moral intensity of the issue that is the focus of an ethical decision. This scholarship attempts to move values and attitudes research away from social responsibility and brings it into closer alignment with ethics. It also offers the potential to offer descriptive evidence and prescriptive suggestions for actually *managing* ethical and social behavior and performance within the firm. It is to this subject that we now turn as we examine the organizational processes theme.

Theme 2: Organizational Processes – 'How'

The CSR literature of the 1950s, 1960s, and 1970s focused on establishing the case for the existence of corporate social responsibility. However, other than Bowen's (1953) proposal that companies conduct a social audit, the literature had little to say about how corporations should be managed in order to fulfill these responsibilities. In 1971 the first article focusing on managing for social responsibility appeared in a business journal, suggesting the creation of committees of senior officers and of departments of social affairs (Mazis and Green, 1971). By 1976 at least 39 other articles focusing on social issue management process topics had appeared, which were collected in two volumes (Carroll, 1977; Sethi,

1974). From these works, especially those of Ackerman (1973) and Paluszek (1973), it became apparent that many companies had been grappling with how to effectively manage corporate social responsibility issues during the 1960s. Ackerman (1973) suggested that a three-stage process was typically associated with effective corporate social performance: social obligations were recognized and policies developed; staff specialists were hired and substantial learning about the problem occurred; and line managers assumed responsibility for social policy implementation, usually accompanied by changes in resource allocations and rewards.

This trend suggested a shift in the field from identifying a general set of corporate social responsibilities to describing processes whereby firms could become more socially responsive to the social issues in their task environment. For example, research during this period focused on topics like identifying and forecasting social issues (Wilson, 1974), creating social responsibility officials (Eilbirt and Parket, 1973), issues management (Chase, 1977), social reporting (Butcher, 1973), changes in organizational structures and systems (Steiner, 1975), reforming corporate governance through changing board composition (Blumberg, 1974), and a revival of the call for social auditing (Bauer, 1973). This trend was also reflected in actual corporate practice, as reflected in the proliferation of public affairs departments responsible for public relations, community relations, corporate philanthropy, issues management, crisis management, advocacy advertising, and governmental relations and lobbying (Post et al., 1983). By the end of the decade Frederick (1978, 1995) suggested that corporate social responsiveness (CSR2) had replaced social responsibility (CSR1) as the key topic in business–society scholarship.

Carroll (1979) brought these two facets of CSR (social responsibility and social responsiveness) together in a model of corporate social performance (CSP). He proposed that effective performance in this arena required managers to: reflect on the issues their companies face, identify types of social responsibilities these issues invite, and select the mode of responsiveness (reactive, defensive, accommodative, proactive) they will pursue. This model motivated CSP research for the next two decades (Miles, 1987; Mitnick, 1993; Rands, 1991; Strand, 1983; Swanson, 1995, 1999; Wartick and Cochran, 1985; Wood, 1991). The models developed by Strand, Rands, and Mitnick differ from the others in that they frame the CSP process in systems theory terms of inputs (demands for CSR), throughputs (responsiveness processes), and outputs (actions which affect social issues). While not firmly grounded in a systems framework, Wood (1991) is the most well known CSP model and has become a widely used reference tool on this topic. CSP now serves for many as an overarching framework for the business–society field.

CSP models are lacking in two areas, however. First, the models fail to adequately specify relationships between key constructs. This failure impedes the development of testable hypotheses that would further advance scholarship regarding relationships between and among issues, stakeholders, principles, processes, and outcomes. Second, the models fail to effectively integrate normative perspectives into their descriptive focus (Swanson, 1999). Possible outcomes of this lack of normative–descriptive integration include: reinforcing the notion that business and ethics are distinct and incompatible domains – the 'separation thesis' – (Wicks, 1996); reducing the value of CSP models to practicing managers; and inhibiting the development of a coherent theory of business and society (Swanson, 1999).

Stakeholder theory (Freeman, 1984) emerged in the 1980s not as a theory, but rather as a useful concept for communicating the need to manage relationships with persons and organizations concerned with social issues, not just those concerned with economic issues identified by strategy scholars such as Porter (1980). In the 1990s, however, the stakeholder concept moved toward a more complete theory, and became a leading competitor to the CSP framework for theoretical dominance. Numerous scholars have elaborated stakeholder theory by developing models for identifying and prioritizing stakeholders (Mitchell et al., 1997) and applying network theory to stakeholder theory (Rowley, 1997). Managing relationships with stakeholders is increas-ingly being viewed as a more robust means of conceptualizing or studying companies' actions in the social realm than is

managing issues (Clarkson, 1995). Some scholars (Waddock and Graves, 1997a) have suggested that the quality of relationships with a broad set of primary (economic) and secondary (social) stakeholders may in fact be synonymous with the quality of management generally. Hence, several scholars (Clarkson, 1995; Waddock and Graves, 1997a; Wood and Jones, 1995) have suggested that stakeholder theory provides *the* basis for adequately understanding and assessing CSP.

Given the increasing emphasis on stakeholder relations, it is important to draw attention to the literature on stakeholder tactics. Scholarship in this area has focused on the influence strategies employed by various stakeholder groups to shape corporate practice (Frooman, 1999). As such, it complements the firm-centric, inside-out orientation of stakeholder theory. The combination provides the conceptual foundation for a bi-directional study of stakeholder relations. Consistent with this broadened view of stakeholders, Wood and Jones (1995) note that stakeholders play three fundamental roles regarding CSP: they are the source of CSP expectations, they are affected by company actions, and they evaluate how well companies meet CSP expectations. In addition, they are frequently considered by managers during the process of developing and implementing social responses. Thus, in systems terms, stakeholders are critical providers of inputs, explicit and implicit factors in throughput processes, primary recipients of outputs, and predominant sources of feedback.

Just as the number of social issues facing business has increased, so have the number of tactics available to and utilized by stakeholder activists, as indicated in Table 17.3. In part, this is an outcome of the conservative revolution (and to a lesser extent the GOP control of the US Congress throughout much of the 1990s). Lobbying for new laws and regulations was unproductive in that political climate, so stakeholders had to devise new ways that were more congruent with the prevailing ideology. Within the business and society field, although the breadth of tactics has been noted, little research has focused on in depth investigation of specific tactics, or on the implications of the choice of tactics for subsequent corporate response. There are signs that this deficiency is beginning to be addressed.

Table 17.3 *Examples of stakeholder tactics by decade*

1960s	1970s	1980s	1990s
Protests/demonstrations	Federal chartering proposals	Issue specific codes of conduct	Corporate practices-oriented partnerships
Lobbying for laws/regulations	CSR-based boycotts	Social investing and consuming	CSR awards
Proxy resolutions	Suing government agencies	Encouraging whistle-blowing	Multi-stakeholder negotiations
Unionization/strikes	PACs/endorsements by other social activists	Lobbying against social deregulation	Independent certification of products for CSR practices targeting retailers
Labor PACs/endorsements	Labor-management partnerships	Cause-related event partnerships	'Monkey-wrenching'
		Community issue partnerships	Lobbying against corporate subsidies
		Ballot initiatives	Internet-based activism
		Calls for product labeling based on CSR activities	
		Worker ownership	

For example, Frooman (1999) uses resource dependence theory to examine the conditions under which stakeholders are likely to select four different types of influence strategies.

In conclusion, as corporate practice related to CSP has evolved, research on organizational processes has both expanded and improved. New corporate practices/research topics include strategic philanthropy, cause-related marketing, industry self-regulation, CSP-related executive leadership behaviors, creation of ethical cultures, management of new corporate functions (such as environmental affairs departments), creation of ethics codes, partnerships with social activist stakeholders, corporate social and environmental auditing and reporting, corporate governance, and various issue specific control systems and mechanisms. Research on these topics generally follows the pattern of documenting current practice, then explaining variance in these practices, including their effectiveness as tools for managing the social environment.

Theme 3: Social Issues – 'What'

Whereas stakeholder relations focuses on the dynamics of relationships between firms and their stakeholders, scholarship on social issues has focused on the content, or purpose, of these relationships. An external group's concern about a social issue is often the generative force that propels them to declare a stake, or interest, in a firm's capacities and competencies. As Table 17.2 indicates, new social issues emerged during each of the past four decades. Since most of these remain with us, the number of social issues with which business must deal is very large. The anti-regulatory mood of the 1980s did little to slow this pattern, and may have even increased the expectation that corporations would voluntarily address social issues since little new regulation emerged during that period. The likelihood of new issues continuing to emerge is great, and several that have emerged during the 1990s are likely to grow in importance. Among these are environmental issues (such as sustainable consumption and industrial ecology); work and family issues (such as support for nursing mothers and those caring for elderly parents); national sovereignty implications of

trade treaties such as NAFTA, WTO, and the proposed Multilateral Agreement on Investments (MAI); sexual orientation issues (such as domestic partner benefits and nondiscrimination on the basis of sexual orientation); workplace violence and its relationship to free speech and privacy rights; international social justice issues (for example, workers' rights in sweat shops, the impact on minorities of corporate practices allowed by majority-controlled governments); and the significance of religion and spirituality in the workplace.

Through four decades, business–society scholars have documented and analyzed these various issues, increasingly in the context of building or testing theories. The emergence of a stronger theoretical perspective and more sophisticated analytical tools, combined with an ever-growing list of challenging issues, bodes well for the future of scholarship in this area.

Theme 4: Business–Government Relations – 'A Unique Who'

Because government differs in kind from other stakeholders, business–government relations has been treated as a special case, or form, of stakeholder relations in the business and society field. The business–government literature has focused on three basic topics: the actions of government to affect business, companies' nonpolitical responses to government activity, and the political involvement of business.

In the 1960s and 1970s social regulation increased and the implications of this trend for business generated a fair amount of descriptive attention, as well as theoretical attention (Mitnick, 1980). Business–society researchers also examined existing control efforts by government and generated proposals that government adopt new means of controlling business behavior. Schwartz (1974) proposed that the federal government charter corporations and use the attendant power to more strictly require socially beneficial corporate action. A more recent example is an examination of the growing movement to reduce or eliminate the federal government's subsidies of corporations (Stevens et al., 1995). In the 1990s, however, an analysis of the business–society relationship from the perspective of both partners has been relatively uncommon. Business and society researchers focus primarily on the description or analysis of corporate political activity aimed at *effecting* such government actions (Christensen, 1995), leaving to political scientists and/or the popular press the task of examining government's actions and reactions. This has the unfortunate result of leaving some potentially significant government experiments, such as the substitution of market-based incentives (pollution taxes, tradable emission permits) for traditional command and control regulations, relatively unstudied by business and society scholars.

The major decision firms face regarding nonpolitical responses to government activity is whether or not to comply with a government regulation. Research on this topic has tended to fall under the topics of corporate crime or illegal corporate behavior (Baucus and Near, 1991; Clinard and Yeager, 1980) and its flip side, regulatory compliance. The illegal corporate behavior literature has studied both the antecedents and consequences of illegal behavior. The smaller literature studying compliance has primarily focused on the question of what induces firms to comply with laws and regulations. Variables studied have included factors such as environmental munificence and dynamism, firm size, industry, and past behavior (Baucus and Near, 1991). Baron (1995) has recently reoriented these discussions by suggesting that firms tend to integrate their market and non-market activities. This suggestion makes the separability of political and product-market strategies problematic, and if correct, would seem to require strategy scholars to pay close attention to business–government relations.

The study of the means by which and conditions under which corporations attempt to influence government was pioneered by Epstein (1969), who identified 25 questions regarding business–government relations. Recent reviews of the corporate political activity literature include those by Getz (1997), Mahon and McGowan (1996), Shaffer (1995) and Vogel (1996). Getz (1997) describes the scope of corporate political activity (CPA) research using the journalistic questions of why, where, when, who and how. *Why* firms participate in CPA has been, she suggests, the most commonly

studied question, and is the one most likely to examine the nature and implications of government activities. *Where* (local, state or federal governments; legislative, executive or regulatory agency; etc.) CPA takes place has received little separate attention apart from its relationship to why CPA occurs. *When* CPA takes place also has been studied primarily in the context of why firms engage in political activity. The question of which firms (*who*) engage in CPA has also been studied extensively, and researchers have found that a large number of firm and industry characteristics are related to political involvement. Finally, the question of *how* firms engage in political activity has also received a great deal of research attention.

Getz (1997) has noted the opportunistic rather than systematic nature of this research, in that it has focused on political tactics and political issues that have been in the public eye. For example, in the 1970s researchers focused on tactics like direct company lobbying activities and direct political contributions, and on political issues, such as environmental, consumer, and safety. In the 1980s the focus was on grassroots lobbying, trade associations, and political action committees, as well as on issues like economic deregulation and government protection from foreign imports. Research on political tactics during the 1990s has continued to examine the use of PACs, as well as the formation of political coalitions containing firms from several industries. In terms of research on political issues in the 1990s, corporate political involvement in trade issues has received attention (Rehbein and Schuler, 1997; Schuler, 1996), as well as the development of international regulatory regimes, such as the Montreal protocol to limit ozone depletion (Getz, 1993). Also receiving increased attention have been political strategies of multinational corporations in different countries and under different political regimes (Boddewyn and Brewer, 1994; Hillman and Keim, 1995). Looking to the future, Oberman (1993) and Hillman and Hitt (1999) have developed typologies of political tactics predicting which tactics will most likely be used in what contexts and in support of what political strategies. These offer the potential for increasing the rigor of research on this topic.

In conclusion, our objective in this brief overview of the business and society literature has been to expose management and strategy scholars to the key themes and intellectual trends within this subfield of organizational studies. We will now narrow our focus and concentrate on the core question that has both energized and confounded scholarship on this topic for decades: just what are business' responsibilities to society?

WHAT ARE BUSINESS' RESPONSIBILITIES TO SOCIETY?

Having reviewed the evolution of thinking on business and society relations, we now narrow our focus. Within the context of the four major themes described in the preceding section, this question is primarily a matter of principle. That is, answers reflect competing paradigmatic arguments regarding whether (and if so, then *why*) businesses should attend to expectations originating outside the realm of business.

We organize our discussion using the four types of business responsibilities proposed by Carroll (1979). Carroll postulated that, 'The social responsibility of business encompasses the economic, legal, ethical, and discretionary expectations that society has of organizations at a given point in time' (1979: 500). As shown in Table 17.4, we have broadened two of his categories to reflect a more contemporary 'institutional' perspective and to make the categories more consistent. It is important for our purposes to underscore Carroll's conclusion that what constitutes a social responsibility of business is a decision made by society, not by business.

As noted in the previous section, Carroll's model of social responsibility has exhibited a remarkable degree of resilience, although it has its critics. One of the most common criticisms is that the model assumes that economic responsibilities are most fundamental, followed by legal, ethical and discretionary responsibilities (Kang and Wood, 1995; Swanson, 1999). Kang and Wood (1995) offer an alternative view, in which they turn the hierarchy upside down, before re-conceiving it in different terms, in which moral responsibilities are framed as most important, followed by social responsibilities, economic responsibilities, and benevolence. Ferrell et al. (2000) meanwhile retain Carroll's

categories but prioritize their order as legal, ethical, economic, philanthropic (discretionary).[2]

In one way or another this simple hierarchical framework continues to give form and shape to contemporary discussions of business' responsibility to society. We will briefly review the contemporary arguments supporting each claim regarding what constitutes these responsibilities and highlight the fundamental conceptual issue, framed here as a dilemma, at the core of each perspective.

Our purpose in invoking this particular analytical frame is to encourage management and strategy scholars to more closely examine a variety of vexing conceptual challenges that while they are particularly prominent and troublesome in the business and society literature lurk beneath the surface of most contemporary scholarly accounts of managerial and organizational actions.

Legal Responsibility: Obey Laws and Regulations

Legal regulations are considered to be society's 'safety net' for regulating business activity. Given the widespread evidence that market forces and moral persuasion are not sufficient to curb the harmful externalities resulting from business leaders' myopic focus on short-term earnings, governmental regulations and laws have been historically seen as a necessary buffer between business and society. However, as we mentioned earlier, a reduction in the rate of growth of business regulation is one of the enduring legacies of the conservative political revolution. Therefore, very little attention has been paid to this position in the 'what is business' responsibility' debate since that era. However, there is some evidence that this trend line may be reaching a deflection point. We'll briefly mention three examples of fairly recent proposals to experiment with new forms of business regulations: market incentives, federal chartering of corporations, and international regulations.

Many proponents of stronger controls on pollution have advocated various forms of market-based incentives in preference to traditional 'command-and-control' regulation (Stavins and Whitehead, 1992). Examples of market incentives include pollution charges, tradeable permit systems, deposit refunds and

Table 17.4 *A comparison of business' responsibilities to society*

Type of responsibility	Common description	Focus of imperative	Claim on business	Conceptual dilemma
Legal responsibility: obey laws and regulations	'Doing what is required'	Legal requirements	Obligatory	Market efficiency versus regulation effectiveness
Economic responsibility: maximize shareholder wealth	'Doing well'	Owners' rights	Obligatory	Accuracy versus generality of the 'rules of the game'
Moral responsibility: discharge moral duties	'Doing what is expected' ('not doing harm')	Moral obligations	Obligatory	Conflicting moral standards and expectations
Social responsibility: go beyond obligatory responsibilities	'Doing what is desired/ doing good'	Citizenship responsibilities	Discretionary	Instrumental justification for 'doing good'

user fees. The nature of these mechanisms, under which companies incur greater financial costs for greater amounts of pollution, encourages companies to engage in innovation in order to reduce costs. In contrast, traditional regulations, by specifying exactly what actions are to be taken to limit pollution, can actually discourage innovation. In addition, market incentive mechanisms encourage firms to continue reducing pollution even after the level of pollution that is permitted by regulations is attained. Various applications of this approach are being experimented with in both the US and Europe, including elements of the 1990 Clean Air Act and the recently formulated global warming treaty. An example of an application outside of the environmental arena is the proposal to bestow favorable tax treatment on corporations that voluntarily engage in socially responsible practices, such as limiting CEO/worker pay ratios to a certain level (Kuttner, 1996).

The federal chartering of businesses has been advocated by those who believe that government needs greater leverage over the actions of business (Mokhiber, 1998). If all firms were federally chartered, then government could revoke a company's charter (and thus its right to exist) if it engaged in a pattern of egregious behavior. While states currently have this power, the economic benefits they derive from issuing charters or from being the home of a large corporation discourages them from using this power. Advocates of this form of regulation argue that government simply can't levy big enough fines to deter businesses from engaging in a class of reprehensible offenses that generate significant financial gains. They believe that nothing short of the threat of losing the right to operate as a business will be sufficient to prevent these social disasters.

Recently, there has been an increase in the demands for international business regulation (Post et al., 1996). Advocates argue that even if the world's major trading nations agree on a common set of ethical standards and business regulations, given that contracts are generally awarded to the lowest bidder and that pollution knows no boundaries, the only guarantee that harmful business activities occurring in any given country aren't allowed to affect members of societies half way around the globe is to create a minimal set of international business regulations. Notable examples

are the Montreal Protocol adopted in 1987 to eliminate certain ozone-depleting chemicals, and the 1998 Kyoto global warming treaty. A major impediment to the use of international regulations is that no acknowledged enforcement body exists, so the implementation and enforcement of these regulations is dependent upon action by individual countries.

The legal responsibility position wrestles with a core management dilemma, familiar to strategy scholars, namely the tradeoff between effectiveness and efficiency. The critique of the traditional form of government regulation is that it is inefficient for business, government, and society. Because they permit greater flexibility and require less oversight, market incentives are championed as a more efficient form of regulation. However, numerous concerns have been raised regarding the effectiveness of market-based forms of regulation. For example, some environmentalists oppose this approach because it doesn't carry the same degree of moral sanction. They are concerned that the underlying objective of protecting the environment will be overshadowed by debates over pricing mechanisms, etc. They view the prospect of an extremely wealthy firm being willing to pay a severe financial penalty for producing high levels of pollution as an untenable proposition. They also point out that in order for the market form of deterrence to work, prices have to be right. Given that pricing is inherently a trial-and-error process, they worry that if the initial prices are too low to produce the expected results, government officials will lack the political will to raise the fees.

Business and government leaders have expressed related concerns about the unknown aspects of this new approach. For example, although business leaders complain about the current form of regulation, they know how the current system works and they have learned how to operate successfully within this set of parameters. Therefore, although they, in general, prefer market solutions over government solutions, many business leaders are uncomfortable with the uncertainty inherent in switching to an entirely new form of regulation. The same type of ambivalence can be observed among government officials. On the one hand, they see merit in off-loading an extremely unpleasant, unpopular, and onerous oversight responsibility. But, they too are uncertain about the implications of trading a known set of goals, responsibilities, competencies, etc., for a new approach whose potential to regulate is unproven and whose implications for regulators are unknown.

Economic Responsibility: Maximize Shareholder Wealth

This is the traditional view of business responsibility, commonly attributed to Milton Friedman's classic *New York Times Magazine* article, 'The social responsibility of business is to make profits' (1970). Advocates of this position argue that the ultimate decision criteria in business affairs is the interests of the owners – the shareholders. Their agents (senior managers) are expected to maximize profits, within the 'rules of the game'. From this perspective, the firm has but one stakeholder – stockholders – and they have but one interest – financial gain. Therefore, if managers engage in 'socially responsible actions' that reduce the return to shareholders they are in effect levying a tax on the company's assets. Furthermore, by appointing themselves as de facto policy makers they subvert the rightful control of the market place. As such, 'doing good' is always at the expense of 'doing well', and, therefore, it is not only bad for business it is also bad for society. Why? Because, shareholder advocates claim (using utilitarian logic) that the 'greatest good for the greatest number' results from business doing what business does best – creating wealth that through lawful and appropriate means like wages and taxes enables other social institutions (families, governments, and churches) to do what they do best – attending to the charitable needs of society.

In summary, the Friedmanesque view of business and society relations can be reduced to two statements: The responsibility of business is to make money, and management should stay focused on this goal, as long as they are playing by the rules. If a corporation engages in socially beneficial practices that add value to the firm that is simply good economics. (As such, these practices should not be heralded as evidence of socially-enlightened management.)

This view of business and society relations has been criticized on several fronts (Wartick and Cochran, 1985; Sethi, 1999; Baumol, 1991). We have chosen to synthesize many of these critiques into two broad dilemmas facing advocates of the 'maximize shareholder wealth' position. These dilemmas are linked to the corresponding summary statement in the preceding paragraph.

First, the tradeoff between accuracy and generality. Weick (1979) observed that theoretical propositions can be classified as simple, general, or accurate. In addition, he argued that because it is logically impossible for a statement to be simple, general, and accurate, these attributes are, as a set, incommensurable. Applying this logic to Friedman's 'rules of the game', critics have argued that although this general and simple statement is adequate as a boundary condition for the maximize shareholder wealth proposition, its lack of accuracy makes it unacceptable as a practical guide for discharging moral responsibilities.

Initially, Friedman proposed that the rules of the game included laws and ethical standards. However, in his later writings he argued in favor of restricting legal encumbrances on business (Friedman and Friedman, 1980), which places the bulk of the responsibility for restraining the excesses of business on unspecified ethical standards and moral principles. Advocates of the moral responsibility position have insisted that matters this important shouldn't be passed off this casually – morality is too important to be summarily dismissed with a forward definition. Although they don't fault Friedman for not providing a definitive set of ethical rules, they fear that his simple and general treatment of the subject marginalizes the role of ethics in the minds of practitioners. The expressed need for adding greater specificity and clarity to the 'rules of the game' is reflected in the search for the Holy Grail of business ethics – a definitive moral credo for business. As we will discuss in more detail shortly, although this quest has not yet accomplished its avowed objective, the crusaders involved in this effort are both numerous and zealous.

Second, the tradeoff between core and comprehensive. It is clear that Friedman was focusing on the core objective of business – to generate wealth. However, when wealth generation is proposed as a comprehensive statement of business practice, critics consider this an impoverished view of business' role in society. They argue that placing all other organizational intentions and effects secondary to the wealth-creation imperative of business increases the risk that devotees of Friedman's philosophy will intentionally or unintentionally precipitate social calamities because of what they have been trained 'not to see' in terms of their firm's web of embedded interdependence.[3]

To better inform discussions about this broader set of issues, it is useful to note that these two broad critiques of the economic responsibility position have served as the defining issues for the moral responsibility and social responsibility positions, respectively. In the next section we will summarize the efforts by the advocates of the moral responsibility position to remove the vagueness from Friedman's notion of the 'rules of the game'. Then, in the following section on social responsibility, we will examine the position that responsible businesses, like citizens, should do more than the bare minimum to advance the goals of the larger society.

Moral Responsibility: Discharge Moral Duties

This position challenges the presumption of privilege underlying the shareholder wealth position. Rather than granting economic activity an exemption from basic ethical obligations, this perspective characterizes business and markets (like all other forms of human activity) as social artifacts, consisting of socially constructed and sustained 'practices' (Wicks, 1996; Freeman and Gilbert, 1988). By stressing the commonality between business activity and other forms of human endeavor, advocates bring economic activity under the jurisdiction of fundamental moral principles and responsibilities. Given that no social institution can legitimately claim that their contribution to society is uniquely exempted from the moral codes required to sustain the common good, then all institution-specific goals, rules, or requirements must be subordinated to common moral law. This is an essential requirement for sustainable social action.

There have been several attempts to codify the moral 'rules of the road' that under-gird all business activity. For example, DeGeorge (1990), following the lead of Velasquez et al. (1983), proposed a 'normative code' that encompasses three principles – rights, justice,

and utility. Quinn and Jones' (1995) moral rule book is less expansive: avoiding harm to others, respecting the autonomy of others, avoiding lying, and honoring agreements. In an ambitious statement of the 'universal moral minimum' that should regulate all business activity in any national or cultural setting, Donaldson (1989) proposes a list of 10 fundamental international individual rights, including such things as freedom of physical movement, nondiscriminatory treatment, subsistence, and freedom of speech.

An encyclical letter from Pope John Paul II, 'Centesimus Annus', represents one of the most comprehensive and articulate efforts to establish a moral code for business activity. Following is an excerpt from this 114 page document, written by one of the foremost moral authorities of our time.

> The Church acknowledges the legitimate *role of profit* as an indication that a business is functioning well. When a firm makes a profit, this means productive factors have been properly employed and corresponding human needs have been duly satisfied. But profitability is not the only indicator of a firm's condition. It is possible for the financial accounts to be in order, and yet for the people – who make up the firm's most valuable asset – to be humiliated and their dignity offended. Besides being morally inadmissible, this will eventually have negative repercussions on the firm's economic efficiency. In fact, the purpose of a business firm is not simply to make a profit, but is to be found in its existence as a *community of persons* who in various ways are endeavouring to satisfy their basic needs, and who form a particular group at the service of the whole society. Profit is a regulator of the life of a business, but it is not the only one; *other human and moral factors* must also be considered which, in the long term, are at least equally important for the life of a business. (1991: 68–9) (italics in the original text)

The dilemmas associated with the moral responsibility position that we feel have the greatest relevance for organizational scholars are rooted in the social nature of moral codes, including their creation, their enactment, and their enforcement. Several organizational scholars have examined the social context conducive to on-the-job moral behavior, including the effects of ethics statements, ethics committees, in-house ethics advisors, ethics audits, ethics training programs, and so forth (Smith and Carroll, 1984; Trevino, 1986; Weber, 1993). The most commonly examined source of organizational influence on moral behavior is organizational culture, or climate (Victor and Cullen, 1988; Toffler, 1986; Trevino, 1990). Summarizing these studies, Frederick finds, 'Ethics is essentially an experiential phenomenon, so that finding ways to affect one's working experience is more likely to have moral impact than exhortations to adopt abstract philosophic principles, laudable as they may be' (1995: 242).

In reading this literature, one is left wondering, 'Given what we know about "effective" organizational practices, is there anything unique about their "moral" counterparts?' For example, referring to the preceding quote from Frederick, wouldn't we expect to hear basically the same sentiments from an expert on improving productivity, or quality, or customer satisfaction?

If we assume that our 'best practice' management processes are agnostic – what is being implemented, and for what purpose, does not significantly affect how it should be implemented – then the primary obstacle inhibiting the widespread adoption of the moral responsibility position is lack of interest. If, on the other hand, we conclude that organizational practices legitimated by the moral imperative are inherently and fundamentally different from practices legitimated by the effectiveness imperative, then not only may 'effective managers' be unskilled as 'moral managers', but in addition the blurring of this distinction (in discourse and in practice) will likely exacerbate this 'folly of ignorance'.

These alternatives highlight a core dilemma in the business and society field – the tradeoff between feasibility of moral practice and distinctiveness of moral practice. Their common peril, reflected in the respective extreme positions, is straightforward: If moral management practices are characterized as just another form of organizational best practices, then their adoption is facilitated by the assurance of familiarity, but justifications used to support these practices must yield their 'moral high ground'. On the other hand, if moral practices are treated as wholly separate from, even antithetical to, standard business practice, then the

moral voice is likely to be marginalized as unknown, impractical and, therefore, irrelevant.

Although the dilemma involving moral and effective organizational practices has not received much attention in the business and society literature, it is related to a conundrum that has been the focus of considerable debate: the apparent 'contradiction-by-definition' relationship between a firm's economic and moral duties. A standard technique for resolving dilemmas and paradoxes is to invoke a frame-changing moderator, such as time intervals, or levels of analysis. The later has figured prominently in the efforts of business and society scholars to develop an 'integrated' view of business' moral and economic duties. For example, Wood (1991) argues that different levels of analysis, or organization, incur different forms of social responsibility, and furthermore, she believes there is a natural order to these nested requirements. The observation that businesses have 'nested' responsibilities to society echoes Freeman and Gilbert's (1988) argument that all organizations sanctioned by a society must support the underlying normative rules that make social intercourse possible. More specifically, they propose that it is only after a business has satisfied its common obligations as a member of society (to support and sustain foundational moral/ethical principles) that it should focus on its institution-specific responsibilities (to generate wealth) (see Quinn and Jones, 1995, for an excellent summary of this general argument).

Another dilemma that figures prominently in this literature involves compliance with codes of ethics. It is widely recognized that many, if not most, unethical decisions in business are the result of conflicting obligations and priorities, rather than manifestations of morally defective decision makers (Frederick, 1995). Work in this area has examined inter-role conflicts (Wicks, 1996) as well as inter-group conflicts (Wood, 1991). Individuals sucked into the vortex of incompatible moral force fields often feel like they are 'damned if they do and damned if they don't'. These conflicting force fields can take the form of incompatible codes of conduct governing the home office of a multinational corporation and a field operation in a different country. They can also manifest themselves as conflicting norms regarding social intercourse, in general, versus codes of conduct pertaining to a specific type of business transaction.

Various strategies have been proposed for resolving the potentially paralyzing tension associated with seemingly incompatible ethical requirements. Invoking the levels of analysis moderator to reconcile seemingly contradictory moral and economic duties, Donaldson and Dunfee (1994) propose an 'integrative social contracts theory', that specifies two requirements for an ethical contract. First, it must conform to the universal 'hypernorms' that apply to all contracts among economic participants. Second, it must be consistent with the local, or 'micro', ethical specifications within an economic community (an industry, an organization, a market). Using different levels of analysis fulcrum for logical leverage, Wicks (1996) argues that there has been an excessive emphasis on creating a shared moral organizational culture at the expense of helping individuals better understand how their personal moral sensibilities should be used as guidelines for determining what constitutes a moral business practice. In brief, he argues that personal moral codes should take precedence over organizational codes of conduct, because the latter are too easily corrupted by other organizational responsibilities.

Social Responsibility: Go Beyond Fulfilling Basic Obligations to Society

There are numerous forms of the social (discretionary) responsibility position, but they all acknowledge the need for firms to go beyond simply meeting their economic, moral, and legal responsibilities. While some tend to advantage one set of obligatory responsibilities over others (Ferrell et al., 2000; Kang and Wood, 1995), all accept the inherent legitimacy of all obligatory claims on the enterprise of business. However, advocates of the social responsibility position generally hold that for a business to only do the bare minimum is no more responsible than it is for a citizen to only do what is minimally required.

The difference between negative and positive rights in philosophy is pivotal to the distinction between obligatory and discretionary business responsibilities (Swanson, 1995; Velasquez, 1992). Negative rights are those rights that a person will enjoy unless interfered with. Therefore, the resulting moral duty

involves 'negative action' – non-interference in the enjoyment of a right. The common terminology for violating this duty is 'doing harm'. In contrast, positive rights are those rights that a person can enjoy only if they are provided by someone else. The common terminology for enabling someone to enjoy positive rights is 'doing good'. If a business does not provide an entitlement, it is creating harm. If it does not provide a privilege (benefit) then it is not, by definition, creating harm, but it also isn't doing good. As reflected in the medical creed, 'First do no harm', moral philosophy places greater importance on avoiding harm than on doing good. Hence, the distinction between business' obligatory (moral) responsibility to avoid harm, and its discretionary (social) responsibility to do good.

As noted in our historical overview, the term philanthropy was used by Carroll (1991) in his later description of discretionary social responsibilities. However, over time the discretionary aspect of business' responsibility to do more than avoid causing harm has proven problematic for those who see the need for our most powerful and resourceful organizations to address pressing social issues like improving literacy, caring for the homeless, and protecting the environment. They bridle at the implication that corporate support for foundational social goods is classified as philanthropy, which is equated with support for the local arts council or symphony guild.

The passionate commitment shared by many business and society scholars to increase the 'clout' of the social responsibility claims on the business enterprise highlights a vexing dilemma in this literature. On the one hand, it is unacceptable to relegate important social responsibilities to the status of discretionary. But, on the other hand, efforts to enhance the authority of these claims by aligning them with business' obligatory moral, legal, or economic duties tends to yield illogical or unverifiable arguments. Space does not permit a detailed analysis of the logical and empirical problems resulting from the practice of invoking the authority of each of the three categories of obligatory duties. Therefore, we will focus on the overarching fallacy of using instrumental arguments to justify moral positions.

Given the avowed purpose of the social responsibility advocates to influence business practice, it is not surprising to find many of their espoused positions buttressed by instrumental justifications. For example, Hosmer (1994) argues that ethical firm behavior fosters trust among stakeholders, which in turn generates commitment, which is manifest as increased organizational support.[4] An alternative form of this argument makes the case for the instrumental benefits of trust within the contest of principle–agent relations and social contract management (Freeman and Evan, 1990; Hill and Jones, 1992; Jones, 1995). In rebuttal, critics argue that despite their natural appeal, instrumental justifications for moral behavior are both logically and empirically suspect (Donaldson and Preston, 1995; Quinn and Jones, 1995; Wicks, 1996; Freeman and Gilbert, 1988).

Logically, the instrumental argument isn't supported by either the economic or moral responsibility positions. To say that one should 'do good' in order to 'do well' violates a fundamental tenant of moral reasoning: moral principles require no external validation and that moral practice should be intrinsically valued. Furthermore, as noted by Friedman (1962), it is neither necessary nor appropriate to characterize business activities that create economic value for the firm as moral or ethical – it's just good economics, period.

Empirically, the research on the relationship between corporate social performance and financial performance has so far yielded ambiguous results (Wood and Jones, 1995). As we described in our historical overview, it is far from an established fact that socially responsible firms have a competitive advantage over social slackers. Irrespective of what the numbers suggest about this relationship, some authors have expressed concern about the practice of using empirical evidence to support a moral argument. For example, Donaldson and Preston (1995) express concerns about succumbing to the 'naturalistic fallacy' (Moore, 1959) – moving from description to evaluation, from 'what is' to 'what should be', without careful attention being paid to the underlying explanation and analysis. In addition, they point out a practical concern regarding the use of 'descriptive justification'. If businesses adopt socially responsible practices because they believe doing good will enhance their financial performance, but their experience doesn't support their expectations, then managers feel justified in abandoning their commitment to socially responsible business practices.

Before closing this discussion of social responsibility, we wish to draw attention to an emerging effort to finesse the use of instrumental arguments to justify moral behavior. Recently, several scholars (Litz, 1996; Waddock and Graves, 1997a) and practitioners (Long and Arnold, 1995; Svendsen, 1998) have argued that internal and external stakeholders are so essential to the effectiveness of a company that partnering and collaborating with stakeholders are essential strategic activities. Furthermore, they posit that the ability to do so effectively is a strategic asset – a source of competitive advantage. This perspective asserts that *collaborating with*, rather than the *management of*, stakeholders requires a positive, rather than a defensive or manipulative, orientation toward stakeholders (Svendsen, 1998). Empirical evidence is used by supporters of this position to suggest that the quality of stakeholder relations may be synonymous with the quality of management (Waddock and Graves, 1997a).

To provide a sampler of the specifics, many of these partnerships have focused on environmental issues, such as the McDonald's–Environmental Defense Fund collaboration. A key element of collaboration has been increased communication and trust between the parties. Disclosure and transparency are the key watch words in companies attempting to build collaborative relationships with stakeholders, frequently expressed through the issuance of environmental reports, as championed by the Coalition for Environmentally Responsible Economies (CERES). The increased attention to sustainable development has broadened the focus on environmental concerns to include collaboration on issues of social justice or equity, and is reflected in the 'triple bottom line' (economics, environment, equity), that is increasingly being used by companies, particularly in Europe, and addressed in their 'sustainability' reports (Elkington and Stibbard, 1997).

Now we turn to the crucial, supporting arguments. As noted earlier, collaborative relationships with stakeholders can be justified on the basis of a purely instrumental view of business relations (Donaldson and Preston, 1995), and, if profit-enhancing, would be considered by

Friedman (1970) to be perfectly appropriate and justifiable, simply on economic grounds. But the emerging argument that firm performance will improve as a result of consistent attention to, and concern for, the satisfaction of all stakeholders (not just primary/economic stakeholders) is similar to, but not the same as, the 'do well *as a result of* fulfilling non-obligatory social responsibilities' argument discussed above. It is actually more consistent with the moral responsibility perspective, with the 'duty claim' being provided by the ethic of care perspective (Liedtka, 1996). Although this stakeholder-collaboration approach to social responsibility obviously does not preclude the adoption of these practices on the basis of their perceived instrumental benefits to the firm, it does not rely on, nor tout, an instrumental justification. Said another way, although proponents do not ignore the potential instrumental benefits of these practices, they characterize them as neither necessary nor sufficient conditions for organizations discharging their universal moral obligation to be prudent and judicious stewards.

In summary, this section has focused on the core question in the business and society literature: What are the responsibilities of business to society? We have briefly reviewed contemporary thought on the four leading 'answers' – legal, economic, moral, and social responsibilities. In addition, as summarized in Table 17.4, we have examined various dilemmas associated with each position. These dilemmas reflect in various ways and through various forms a distinctive, and some would argue unique, feature of the business and society literature – it treats as problematic what too often the encompassing discipline takes for granted. Authors in this area debate the utility of the prevailing economic model of business – worrying as much about what it leaves unstated as about what it explicitly claims. They also worry about what happens when the business model 'works too well', for example, when firms successfully create market niches with high barriers to entry, or when they convince employees that their personal values and interests are identical to (or, at least compatible with) the company's goals and practices. Their distrust of the enlightened self-interest, self-policing, view of ethical business practice has also led them to examine the competing claims of alternative 'institutional' approaches to the social control

of business, for example, the effectiveness of government regulation versus the efficiency of economic markets (Scott, 1995).

We have chosen to highlight the theme of dilemmas in this section for two reasons. First, they serve as prominent intellectual topographical reference points for constructing a 'map' of the business and society literature. This is a field of study that has chosen to establish its base camp astride a maze of intellectual fault lines. Second, our immersion in this literature has sensitized us to the relative paucity of concern being expressed about these critical matters within the broader intellectual context of organizational science. The proposition that the practice of organizational science, broadly defined, can benefit from a better understanding of the contemporary study of business and society relations will be more fully developed in our next section.

FUTURE DIRECTIONS FOR RESEARCH AND STUDY

The previous sections of this chapter provide a general overview of the CSR literature – its history and the current state of thinking. Because this is a handbook for scholars of strategy and management, we have chosen to focus our final section on promising research leads implied by business and society scholarship, that represent promising opportunities for collaboration with scholars in other fields of organizational science. We believe this call for boundary-spanning collaboration is timely given the increased interest in business and society relations within contemporary businesses and societies. Anticipating greater emphasis on socially responsible business practices, we present opportunities for research that consider the strategic and managerial challenges facing firms that are committed to discharging their social responsibilities (commonly referred to as socially responsible businesses – SRBs). One way of conceptualizing our research agenda for studying SRBs is that it brings business and society scholars and their more mainstream counterparts together to examine what Weick (1979) refers to as an 'extreme case' within the general business population. Following his lead, we believe that studying outlier organizations often produces more insights than focusing on more typical organizations. Throughout this section we'll draw attention to the significant reasons why we believe SRBs represent a particularly promising venue for research and theory development on business management and strategy.

Effective and/or Moral Practices

Earlier, we drew attention to the lack of research on the relationship between effective organizational practices and moral organizational practices. If managers want to foster a moral culture should they basically follow the known recipes for producing other forms of strong organizational culture? Asked a different way, are there any significant differences between the 'best bets' for increasing work performance, that are standard fare in any introductory management course, and the list of 'how tos' for improving ethical performance? Or, as one of the authors regularly asks his MBA students, 'Is there a difference between being an ethical manager in an effective organization, and an effective manager in an ethical organization?'

Because they speak directly to the assumption of uniqueness that pervades the business and society literature, it is remarkable that questions this fundamental to a field's claim of a unique domain have not been examined more fully. Studies of socially responsible firms comparable to our numerous studies of effective organizations (Collins and Porras, 1994) would provide a context for addressing the core question: Are SRBs a type of effective organization, or does the addition of the moral imperative fundamentally change their basic constitution? The answer to this question is equally important to business management and strategy scholars because it would identify the extent to which, and in what ways, SRBs require modifications of our standard, mainstream organizing models and principles.[5]

Before leaving this topic, we want to draw attention to an intriguing variation. Although the theory development literature emphasizes the importance of using variables, rather than values of a variable (for example, height, rather than tall or short) (Whetten, 1989), many of our theories in organizational science do not cover the full range of the core variables, or constructs. (When was the last time you heard a scholarly presentation on poor leadership, weak cultures, lousy strategies, or ineffective organizations?) One of the benefits of studying SRBs as an organizational population is the abundance of information about socially 'irresponsible' organizations. This brings us to the proposed variation on our questions regarding the organizational cultures of SRBs: Do socially irresponsible firms – those that are regularly cited (given citations for violating government regulations and cited in the press for their irresponsible actions) for ignoring their social responsibilities – have equally strong cultures? Self-interest taken to the extreme requires that organizational actors be willing to violate legal and other regulatory statutes. To do so may require an extremely strong set of enabling norms, values, and artifacts. The alternative proposition is that socially irresponsible firms have weak cultures. Because these organizations appear to value everything very little, their employees are left on their own to sort out the messiness of an organizational milieu awash in self-interest.

Reputation, Image and Identity

Questions regarding the unique constitution of SRBs are closely linked to the emerging interest in the theoretical distinctions between reputation, image and identity, as well as their respective implications for management practice (Whetten and Godfrey, 1998; Fombrun, 1996). Given the skepticism expressed by some (Entine, 1994) regarding the level of commitment exhibited in companies professing to support SRB principles and practices, this area represents a richly-textured context for sorting out conceptual conundrums, like the following.

How does one distinguish between SRB practices that are intended to burnish a firm's image, by enhancing its reputation, and those that emanate from an organization's identity? How can we determine if a firm's SRB claims are truly foundational (constitutional)? Would we expect to observe different SRB practices in firms whose SRB claims appear to be motivated by reputation-enhancement versus identity-articulation?

The study of SRBs also provides a fairly unique opportunity to examine what Albert and Whetten (1985) call hybrid identity organizations. First and foremost, one wonders: To what extent do SRB firms represent true hybrid identity organizations, in the sense that their dual commitment to 'doing good' and 'doing well' constitutes the core of their organizational identity? If so, then: What is the etiology of these firms? Is it necessary for their unique constitution to be established by the founders at the time of founding? Or: How likely is it that a hybrid identity can be propagated in mature organizations by means of 'ideology grafts'? And finally: Can we isolate a unique organizational hybrid identity management competence in these firms?

Sources of Competitive Advantage

Scholars in both the academic literature (Hart, 1995, 1997) and the popular press (Dalla Costa, 1998) postulate a positive relationship between an ethical orientation and competitive advantage. For example, firms that are committed to environmental sustainability often gain cost advantages over rivals, because by avoiding pollution (or other environmental degradation) there is less waste in the economic operations of the firm. Conversely, firms with strong ethical claims (such as the Body Shop) may generate and sustain a clear position of valuable differentiation from competitors. This differentiation may result in a very loyal customer base, that is willing, among other things, to pay significantly higher prices for the firm's products.

Sidestepping for now the debate over using instrumental arguments to justify moral action, we commend SRBs as an apt setting for examining some of the core arguments regarding competitive advantage in the strategy literature. Specifically, does an ethical orientation, or a stated commitment to socially responsible business practices, constitute a unique, valuable, non-substitutable, and difficult to imitate source of competitive advantage? (Barney, 1991; Peteraf, 1993.) Godfrey and Hill (1995) have noted that much of the research on the resource-based view of strategy is hampered by the unobservability of resources. The commitment to being an SRB seems to overcome this problem: firms make public commitments to being

socially responsible, and external stakeholders increasingly have access to metrics for evaluating firm performance, relative to their claims.

Considering this question within organizations in 'basic' industries, like mining, would provide a nice counterpart to the heavy focus in the popular press on SRBs from the consumer products industry. One wonders, for example, do mining firms that practice 'beyond compliance' environmental reclamation gain competitive advantages over rivals, as suggested by Porter and van der Linde (1995), or do they simply incur more costs? Because of the commodity-like nature of these industries, it would appear that ecological sustainability is unlikely to provide any noticeable differentiation in the firm's product offering. These industries have particular relevance for the business and society field, because of the severity, and permanence, of potential damage that could be done. Ironically, we might find that those industries where society has the greatest stake in ethical behavior are the least likely to be influenced by an appeal to enlightened self interest.

There is another way in which the study of firm-specific competitive assets could be expanded and enhanced through collaboration with business and society scholars. The bulk of the research on competitive advantage has focused on market-oriented competencies (Hosmer, 1994). It is self evident that firms also gain competitive advantages through the regulatory process, either by tempering the impact of regulations governing their operations, or by encouraging stronger regulation of their competitors. This suggests that some firms, particularly large firms in highly visible and socially sensitive industries (bulk chemicals, mining and extraction, agriculture), would develop competencies related to business–government relations. This type of indirect effort to increase a firm's competitive advantage might take the form of influencing the processes pertaining to the granting of licenses, patents, and other forms of government approval to conduct business.

Collaborative Strategies

One of the most natural connections that can be made between strategy and management, and business and society scholarship involves the study of stakeholder relations. In reading the discussions of interorganizational collaboration in these fields one gets the sense of two tunnels being drilled from opposite ends of the mountain. On the one side the effort is being framed as effective stakeholder relations (Waddock and Graves, 1997a), while on the other side it is characterized as effective business strategy (Dyer and Singh, 1998). Common to both is the assumption that competitive advantages accrue to firms that successfully implement and manage interorganizational alliances. Business and society scholars bring to this joint scholarly venture a strong sense of purpose. Many of the social problems facing our world, from environmental degradation to poverty to drug use, will require interorganizational, and even intersectoral, cooperation and collaboration. Strategy scholars bring complementary assets, including an in depth understanding of how effective alliances are created and managed. Together they might examine questions like: Assuming that SRB managers are very responsive to stakeholder claims, are the resulting stakeholder networks different in kind from those typically studied by strategy scholars – both in terms of membership and relationship?

Given that most social problems can't be solved by the private sector alone, the study of interorganizational relations within the context of SRBs necessarily expands the set of collaborating organizations to include government agencies (Feyerherm, 1993, 1994; Feyerherm and Milliman, 1995; Starik and Rands, 1995). Studying interorganizational collaboration within this setting will allow strategy scholars to assess the boundary conditions of their current models of alliances and joint ventures. Specifically, this enterprise would seek to understand how well existing models of joint ventures and other forms of inter-firm collaboration apply to different kinds of partnerships (between businesses and government agencies) and to different types of activities (reducing poverty versus developing a new technology).

The Pathological Relationship between Strategy and Society

Our earlier comment about socially irresponsible firms foreshadowed this broader, more theoretical, and clearly more controversial observation. The field of business strategy emerged into the limelight via the writing of Michael Porter (1980, 1985), who advocated turning many of the propositions of welfare economics on their ear. For example, welfare economists hold that barriers to entry in an industry impede competition, encourage monopolistic behavior, and lead to a net loss in welfare over the economy as a whole. Porter, however, advocates that firms erect barriers to entry in order to enhance their own monopolistic position – irrespective of the welfare effects on the economy as a whole. Current work in strategy focuses on gaining competitive advantage at the level of individual firms. Consequently, concern that firms or industries as a whole may gain competitive advantages at the expense of the welfare of the encompassing society is seldom expressed. Korten (1996) and others writing in a more popular vein have impaled much of economics (and by implication strategy) in their attacks on the emerging global capitalist order. In response, we suggest that business and society and strategy scholars need to develop a carefully reasoned and non-incendiary articulation of the conditions under which the pursuit of individual firm competitive advantage leads to negative outcomes for the social order as a whole.

Such an endeavor might foster a long overdue critical examination of the economic models underpinning much of the thinking on this subject. For example, while much of game theory supports the notion that unethical strategies will not lead to competitive success (Axelrod, 1984; Hill, 1990), there is no prescription that encourages firms to go beyond obligatory moral, legal, and economic responsibilities. In fact, according to game theory logic SRBs may be at a disadvantage in many trades (as games) because their ethical commitment signals a strategy that can be exploited by firms unencumbered by these commitments. While the literature on organizational trust (Barney and Hansen, 1994; Wicks et al., 1999) argues that trust creates advantages in trades, the progress of this literature has been halting to date. More importantly, these arguments are disadvantaged by a lack of empirical support – data comparable to the years of accumulated results that buttress the game theory view of business transactions.

Before leaving this topic, we need to note an interesting counterpoint to the notion of a pathological relationship between strategy and society. Ironically, it is reflected in the evolution in strategic thinking exhibited by Michael Porter. While the work referenced above arguably contains pathological elements, Porter's more recent work relies heavily on notions of social capital and socially beneficial inputs and outputs to the strategy process. For example, in his work on inner city revitalization (Porter, 1995), he argues that the exercise of sound strategic thinking and the principles of competitive advantage work to improve the condition of America's inner cities. Even more to our point, his 1998 addition to the strategy literature (Porter, 1998) holds that when social and intellectual capital is concentrated into geographic clusters, businesses flourish (with concomitant gains for the communities composing the cluster).

Social Issues and Environmental Niches

A review of Table 17.2 indicates that the burning social issues facing business have evolved and expanded over time. Because of the existence of sympathetic stakeholder and special interest groups, social issues may create munificent niches for organizations. For example, firms deemed to have family-friendly HR practices have received a windfall in favorable publicity during the past decade. Given how key the concept of niche is to the study of business strategy (Porter, 1980), business and society scholars can inform their understanding of the emergence of social issues by viewing this process through the analytical lens of niche formation. Relevant research questions in this vein include: How do social issue niches form, and how long do they last? How do organizations identify and evaluate the consequences of new niches? Do new issues-based niches encourage new organizational forms?

There is another way in which the concept of niche suggests a promising opportunity for discipline-spanning collaboration. The bulk of research in strategy and management aims to be content free. This is consistent with the broad scientific objective of providing generalizable theories and models of business behavior and performance. While organizational theories typically emerge from observations of a specific organizational context, the focus of the theorist is to move beyond the limitations of any given context and formulate general propositions. For example, Porter (1980) advocates the adoption of generic strategies of low cost or differentiation. In similar fashion, the literature on managing legitimacy (Suchman, 1995) provides researchers and managers with a menu of possible strategies seemingly without regard to the contextual factors that may make certain alternatives less efficacious than others. Thus, scholars live comfortably in a world of offering prescriptions for action devoid of diagnosis of the contextual richness of the situation.

Because much of the business and society interface is still defined in terms of issues and practices, rather than general theoretical propositions, research on how firms deal with social issues tends to emphasize the contextual features of firm activities rather than automatically abstracting from specific observations to general formulations. The application of known techniques for grounded theory development (Eisenhart, 1989) can significantly extend the reach of the business and society 'bottom-up' understanding of the moderating effects of contextual conditions on strategizing. On the other side of the theoretical breach, the business strategy, 'top-down' view needs to be calibrated using various social contexts to test the utility of their general models. Granovetter (1985) shows how this type of contextual analysis changes the prescriptions of strategy paradigms. He argues that the rich cultural context of Japanese society voids certain prescriptions of transaction costs economics about the structuring of firm boundaries.

Social Institutions, Population Dynamics, and Socially Responsible Businesses

Some of the most promising and critical opportunities for scholarly collaboration involve the application of institutional theory and population ecology to the study of SRBs. Following are a few illustrative examples. Activity by critical stakeholders represents an attempt to modify the organization, or at least some of its actions. Applying the lens of institutional theory (Scott, 1995) to this subject highlights promising new lines of inquiry. Given the growth and diversity of stakeholder tactics, outlined in Table 17.3, we need a better understanding of how new forms of stakeholder activity (bad publicity, consumer boycott, letter writing campaigns to board members) become legitimated. In particular, it would be interesting to compare the institutionalization processes of stakeholder tactics that seek to punish firms with those that reward firms. The 'socially responsible investment' mutual fund business provides an ideal context for this type of comparison, because some funds use screens to 'select out' offensive firms, whereas other funds 'select in' acceptable firms (Lavelle and Whetten, 1997).

Examining the development of the 'institution' of socially responsible business practices represents another important opportunity for collaborative scholarship. One straightforward, framing question is: How has the institutionalization of this form of business been aided by various enabling factors? Candidates for investigation would include: the formation of professional associations devoted to providing expertise on this topic (for example, Businesses for Social Responsibility), the articulation and endorsement of SRB principles by industry leaders (the CERES Principles, the Caux Roundtable), the emergence of specialized trade publications (*The Green Money Journal*), the development of formal criteria for rating the social performance of firms (Council on Economic Priorities, the Domini 400 Social Index), the organization of academic professional associations (International Association for Business and Society, European Business Ethics Network), the development of specialized roles in firms, along with accompanying professional associations (Business Ethics Officers, Public Affairs Directors), support service firms providing social consulting assistance in conducting social performance audits and ethics training (Institute of Social and Ethical Accountability, Praxis Consulting Group), the legitimating endorsements of a Papal Encyclical and a White House Conference, the attention focusing impact of bad publicity (Exxon, Shell) or good publicity (the Corporate Conscience Awards of the Council on Economic Priorities, the Business Enterprise Trust Awards).

This type of institutional theory analysis needs to be augmented by population ecology studies of the (collective) growth of the socially responsible business organizational form (Hannan and Freeman, 1989), and the SRB practices diffusion process (Oliver, 1997). The business and society field would benefit from a more systematic, theory-guided, understanding of the environmental dynamics that encourage (or discourage) the success of SRBs. An incentive for population ecologists to examine this population of organizations is the availability of rich data on the genesis of both the new form and the niche (Stinchcombe, 1965). In addition, this setting provides an opportunity to test the limits of our prevailing maxims regarding population dynamics. How does the presence of SRBs in a population of businesses impact their joint evolution? Do SRBs and non-SRBs tap into different resource bases? Do they have different bases of competition? How well do our existing theories of organizational forms (specialists, generalists) predict the competitive profile of SRBs?

Strategic Human Resource Management

To this point we have argued that SRBs warrant study because they appear to represent atypical organizations, in some way or another. Continuing that theme, we conclude our discussion of future opportunities for collaborative research on SRBs by drawing attention to their implications for our understanding of human resource management practices. The literature on human resource management (HRM) continues to widen its scope to contemplate the importance of human resources in the overall strategy of the firm (Barney, 1998). Applying this 'strategic human resources' frame of reference to our discussion of SRBs, we wonder: If a firm's business strategy includes a strong commitment to socially responsible business practices, how does this affect the HRM practices of the firm? For example, assuming for the moment that the leadership of SRBs requires a different (or at least modified) skill set, how must a firm's management development and career mapping functions change? Also, how should compensation programs be altered to encourage and reward both ethical behavior and ethical learning?

One particularly intriguing area of inquiry involves the viability of management fast-track programs in firms committed to a strong moral code of conduct. While much of the business of a business can be learned during a fast-track rotation, ethical learning is of a different ilk. In particular, ethical learning may be subject to strong time compression diseconomies (Dierickx and Cool, 1989). Because ethical challenges are ambiguous and fraught with peril, management fast-trackers may passively ignore or actively avoid contact with the ethical issues surrounding the organizational units they visit. Further, the nature of fast-track programs means that managers will often have moved on before the ethical consequences of their decisions become clear. In this light, there appears much to investigate about how SRBs can develop managers with both a diverse and complex understanding of the business and a keen awareness of the ethical choices and dilemmas involved in running the business.

Another set of fascinating questions pertaining to the strategic HRM practices of SRBs involves the topic of executive succession. Anecdotal evidence suggests that many SRBs are founded with a specific social agenda in mind. This makes the task of finding a suitable successor to the founder particularly difficult. For example, Ben and Jerry's had several well-publicized miscues in their repeated efforts to select a suitable new CEO – resulting from the difficulty of finding leaders capable of both growing and greening the business. Given the critical nature of executive succession for both firm strategy and survival, strategic HR scholars interested in this topic might consider questions like the following in a study of SRBs. What is the impact of these 'additional' selection criteria on the succession process? Does it simply mean that SRB successors must be selected from within a restricted pool of candidates? Or does it mean that the selection process itself is fundamentally changed? For example, how would a head-hunter firm go about the task of assessing (let alone certifying) the character of prospective CEO candidates?

CONCLUSION

The relationship of business to the larger social enterprise is not a neutral one. The actions taken by business firms in pursuit of competitive advantages and profits impact the society in which that business operates, for good or for ill. Similarly, society is no longer a passive actor in relationship to business. Stakeholder and special interest groups are increasingly well organized, and becoming more vocal and encompassing in the demands they make on businesses. As a consequence, management scholars and practitioners are becoming increasingly aware of the agenda-shaping impact of these powerful voices.

To encourage broader participation in scholarly conversations about business and society relations, we first examined the evolution of the scholarship on this broad topic. It is apparent from this overview that the interdependence between business and society is extremely complex, and the opportunity for different theoretical and methodological perspectives informing the analysis of this interdependence is extremely rich. Debates within this literature regarding the control and accountability of businesses and the components of effective external relations management need to inform related conversations scattered throughout the discipline.

The narrower focus of the second section was directed at the nature of the claims made by society on business. In addition to examining contemporary scholarship on the topics of economic, moral, legal, and social responsibilities, we also explored several dilemmas associated with each of the four perspectives. One of our purposes in highlighting the tensions within and between Carroll's categories is to encourage organizational scholars to examine their assumptions about the justifications for organizational action. In particular, the challenges facing scholars who attempt to blend instrumental and moral justifications was highlighted.

The theme of bridging the substantive questions pertaining to business' responsibilities to society and the expertise and interests of the broader community of organizational scholars was amplified in the 'implications' section. Here we highlighted examples of promising, discipline-spanning, collaborative research and theory development opportunities, placing particular emphasis on the 'macro' topics of interest to our readers.

It is our perception that stakeholders are becoming increasingly bold in making claims on businesses' resources, in the name of reducing harm or doing good. Given the number and severity of the social issues clogging the political agendas in all contemporary societies, we can expect to see increasing pressure on the largest, most powerful, and most resourceful organizations to become active, integral contributors to their resolution. In addition, it is apparent that many firms believe that representing themselves as a socially responsible 'corporate citizen' is good for business. Whether this pattern of increasing social involvement is stimulated by the push of threat or the pull of opportunity, it appears that business firms are broadening their list of salient decision criteria beyond the narrow considerations suggested by Friedman.

One implication of these trends is that organizational scholars must become more conversant with the issues and challenges associated with the social responsibilities of business. We believe that the resulting boundary-spanning conversations will both broaden and enrich scholarship within the field of business and society relations and highlight opportunities for research and theory development in allied management fields on vexing issues facing managers striving to discharge their firm's social responsibilities. These organizational matters are far too important to society and to business to be compartmentalized within our discipline – bounded by the domain statement of a single, small, marginal field of scholarship. This 'very important stuff' warrants the attention of all organizational scholars.

ACKNOWLEDGEMENTS

The authors wish to thank Brad Agle, Dan Greening, Jamie Hendry, Andrew Pettigrew, Doug Schuler, Sandra Waddock, Steve Wartick, Jim Weber, and Donna Wood for their many helpful suggestions on this chapter.

NOTES

1 Although many different typologies of the major streams of business and society scholarship have been developed, we will draw primarily from one suggested by Gerde and Wokutch (1998) in their review of 636 Social Issues in Management (SIM) division papers and abstracts published in the *Academy of Management Proceedings*.

Their typology in turn roughly corresponds with the categories of the corporate social performance model proposed by Wood (1991). It is also influenced by the categories Collins (1996) used to group 497 papers presented at the first six annual meetings of the International Association for Business and Society (IABS) and published in the *IABS Annual Proceedings*. Unlike the typologies of Gerde and Wokutch, and of Collins, we do not consider research methodology or teaching issues in the field. Neither is our discussion based on an empirical review of a coherent set of papers. Rather it is an attempt to present a brief overview of some of the major themes that have developed in this field over the past four decades.

2 The order of our discussion of Carroll's categories is different from his original model. This choice was guided solely by our present expository preferences and should not be interpreted as a general comment on the 'proper' order of his categories.

3 Before leaving the subject of what people have been trained not to see, we would like to insert a reflexive observation. Across the length and breadth of organizational science there is a general lack of concern regarding the inconsistency between the 'behavioral assumptions' underlying the prevailing models of motivation, leadership, organizational change, etc., and the 'business assumptions' dictating acceptable practice within the vast majority of organizations for which our organizing models are intended (see Hosmer, 1994, for a business and society version of this critique). In contrast to the pitched battles between notable scholars regarding the merits of adopting one unifying paradigm of 'organizing business' (Pfeffer, 1993; McKinley, 1995), it is curious that the field as a whole accepts without concern the dominant economic paradigm of 'doing business'. Given this general condition, it is worth noting to our readers that there is an active discourse among business and society scholars regarding the merits of accepting the net present value model of business management as an unassailable assumption, or as merely one point of view (Freeman and Gilbert, 1988; Gilbert, 1992).

4 Organizational behavior scholars will recognize this as an incarnation of the 'satisfied workers produce more' instrumental argument conundrum that played itself out in the motivation literature some time ago. Briefly, not only did subsequent research determine that the simple correlation between worker satisfaction and job performance is extremely modest (this is one of the most moderated relationships in our literature), it also demonstrated that the 'arrow' goes the opposite direction (if productive workers are rewarded commensurate with their performance then they will be satisfied).

5 Given our objective of fostering greater collaboration between business and society scholars and business management and strategy scholars, and given the absence of disconfirming information, the remainder of this section is predicated upon the assumption of uniqueness. However, we have drawn attention to the need to test this assumption here at the beginning of this 'implications' section to emphasis its foundational significance.

REFERENCES

Ackerman, R. (1973) 'How companies respond to social demands', *Harvard Business Review*, 51(4): 88–98.

Albert, S. and Whetten, D. A. (1985) 'Organizational identity', in L. L. Cummings and B. M. Staw (eds), *Research in Organizational Behavior*. Greenwich, CT: JAI Press. pp. 263–95.

Al-Kazemi, A. A. and Zajac, G. (1999) 'Ethics sensitivity and awareness within organizations in Kuwait: an empirical exploration of espoused theory and theory-in-use', *Journal of Business Ethics*, 20(4): 353–61.

Altman, B. W. and Post, J. E. (1995) 'Achieving corporate social rectitude? The results of an empirical survey of BSR (Business for Social Responsibility) companies', in D. Nigh and D. Collins (eds), *Proceedings of the Seventh Annual Meeting of the International Association for Business and Society*. pp. 314–19.

Aupperle, K. E., Carroll, A. B. and Hatfield, J. D. (1985) 'An empirical examination of the relationship between corporate social responsibility and profitability', *Academy of Management Journal*, 28(2): 446–63.

Axelrod, R. (1984) *The Evolution of Cooperation*. New York: Basic Books.

Barney, J. B. (1991) 'Firm resources and sustained competitive advantage', *Journal of Management*, 17: 99–120.

Barney, J. B. (1998) 'On becoming a strategic partner: the role of human resources in gaining competitive advantage', *Human Resource Management*, 37: 31–46.

Barney, J. B. and Hansen, M. H. (1994) 'Trustworthiness as a source of competitive advantage', *Strategic Management Journal*, 15 (special issue): 175–90.

Baron, D. P. (1995) 'Integrated strategy: market and non-market components', *California Management Review*, 37(2): 47–65.

Batten, J., Hettihewa, S. and Mellor, R. (1997) 'The ethical management practices of Australian firms', *Journal of Business Ethics*, 16(12/13): 1261–71.

Baucus, M. S. and Near, J. P. (1991) 'Can illegal corporate behavior be predicted? An event history analysis', *Academy of Management Journal*, 34(1): 9–36.

Bauer, R. A. (1973) 'The corporate social audit: getting on the learning curve', *California Management Review*, 16(1): 5–10.

Baumhart, R. (1961) 'How ethical are businessmen?', *Harvard Business Review*, July–August: 156–66.

Baumol, W. J. (1991) *Perfect Markets and Easy Virtue: Business Ethics and the Invisible Hand*. New York: Blackwell.

Blumberg, P. I. (1974) 'Reflections on proposals for corporate reform through change in the composition of the board of directors: "special interest" or "public" directors', in S. P. Sethi (ed.), *The Unstable Ground: Corporate Social Policy in a Dynamic Society*. Los Angeles: Melville Publishing. pp. 112–34.

Boddewyn, J. J. and Brewer, T. L. (1994) 'International business political behavior: new theoretical directions', *Academy of Management Review*, 19(1): 119–43.

Bowen, R. H. (1953) *The Social Responsibilities of the Businessman*. New York: Harper & Row.

Butcher, B. (1973) 'Anatomy of a social performance report', *Business and Society Review*, Autumn.

Carroll, A. B. (ed.) (1977) *Managing Corporate Social Responsibility*. Boston: Little, Brown.

Carroll, A. B. (1979) 'A three-dimensional model of corporate performance', *Academy of Management Review*, 4(4): 497–505.

Carroll, A. B. (1991) 'The pyramid of corporate social responsibility: toward the moral management of organizational stakeholders', *Business Horizons*, July–August: 39–48.

Carroll, A. B. (1999) 'Corporate social responsibility', *Business and Society*, 38(3): 268–95.

Cavanagh, G. F., Moberg, D. J. and Velasquez, M. (1981) 'The ethics of organizational politics', *Academy of Management Review*, 6(3): 363–74.

Chase, W. H. (1977) 'Public issue management: the new science', *Public Relations Journal*, 33(10): 25–6.

Christensen, S. L. (1995) 'The new federalism: implications for corporate political activity', in D. Nigh and D. Collins (eds), *Proceedings of the Seventh Annual Meeting of the International Association for Business and Society*. pp. 195–9.

Clarkson, M. B. E. (1995) 'A stakeholder framework for analyzing and evaluating corporate social performance', *Academy of Management Review*, 20(1): 92–117.

Clinard, M. B. and Yeager, P. C. (1980) *Corporate Crime*. New York: Free Press.

Collins, D. (1996) 'An annotated bibliography of the 1990–1995 IABS Annual Proceedings', *Business & Society*, 35(3): 240–63.

Collins, J. C. and Porras, J. I. (1994) *Built to Last*. New York, NY: HarperCollins.

Collins, J. W. and Ganotis, C. G. (1973) 'Is social responsibility sabotaged by the rank and file?', *Business and Society Review/Innovation*, Fall(7): 82–8.

Dalla Costa, J. (1998) *The Ethical Imperative: Why Moral Leadership is Good Business*. Reading, MA: Perseus Books.

David, D. K. (1949) 'Business responsibilities in an uncertain world', *Harvard Business Review*, 27(1): 1–8.

Davis, K. (1967) 'Understanding the social responsibility puzzle', *Business Horizons*, 10(1): 45–50.

DeGeorge, R. (1990) *Business Ethics* (third edition). New York: Macmillan.

Dierickx, I. and Cool, K. (1989) 'Asset stock accumulation and sustainability of competitive advantage', *Management Science*, 35: 1504–11.

Donaldson, T. (1989) *The Ethics of International Business*. New York: Oxford University Press.

Donaldson, T. and Dunfee, T. W. (1994) 'Toward a unified conception of business ethics: integrative social contracts theory', *Academy of Management Review*, 19(2): 252–84.

Donaldson, T. and Preston, L. E. (1995) 'The stakeholder theory of the corporation: concepts, evidence, and implications', *Academy of Management Review*, 20: 65–91.

Dyer, J. H. and Singh, H. (1998) 'The relational view: cooperative strategy and sources of interorganizational competitive advantage', *Academy of Management Review*, 23: 660–79.

Eilbirt, H. and Parket, I. R. (1973) 'The corporate responsibility officer: a new position on the organization chart', *Business Horizons*, 16(1): 45–54.

Eisenhart, K. M. (1989) 'Building theories from case study research', *Academy of Management Review*, 14: 532–50.

Elkington, J. and Stibbard, H. (1997) 'Socially challenged', *Tomorrow*, 7(2): 54–9.

Elm, D. R. and Nichols, M. L. (1993) 'An investigation of the moral reasoning of managers', *Journal of Business Ethics*, 12(11): 817–34.

England, G. W. (1967) 'Personal value systems of American managers', *Academy of Management Journal*, 10(1): 107–17.

Entine, J. (1994) 'Shattered image', *Business Ethics*, 8(5): 23–8.

Epstein, E. A. (1969) *The Corporation in American Politics*. Englewood Cliffs, NJ: Prentice-Hall.

Ferrell, O. C., Fraedrich, J. and Ferrell, L. (2000) *Business Ethics: Ethical Decision Making and Cases* (fourth edition). Boston: Houghton Mifflin.

Feyerherm, A. E. (1993) 'Regulation through collaboration: a longitudinal study of two interorganizational rule-making groups', in J. Pasquero and D. Collins (eds), *Proceedings of the Fourth Annual Meeting of the International Association for Business and Society*. pp. 524–9.

Feyerherm, A. E. (1994) 'The influence of dialogue on multiple stakeholders in interorganizational, collaborative networks', in S. Wartick and D. Collins (eds), *Proceedings of the Fifth Annual Meeting of the International Association for Business and Society*. pp. 517–22.

Feyerherm, A. E. and Milliman, J. F. (1995) 'Community advisory (CAPs) and corporate environmental management: a model and research agenda', in D. Nigh and D. Collins (eds), *Proceedings of the Sixth Annual Meeting of the International Association for Business and Society*. pp. 508–13.

Fombrun, C. (1996) *Reputation: Realizing Value from Corporate Image*. Boston, MA: Harvard Business School Press.

Frederick, W. C. (1978) 'From CSR1 to CSR2: the maturing of business-and-society thought', Pittsburgh: University of Pittsburgh working paper No. 279. *Business & Society*, 33(2): 150–64.

Frederick, W. C. (1995) *Values, Nature and Culture in the American Corporation*. New York: Oxford University Press.

Frederick, W. C. and Weber, J. (1987) 'The values of corporate managers and their critics: an empirical description and normative implications', in W. C. Frederick (ed.), *Research in Corporate Social Performance and Policy*. Greenwich, CT: JAI Press. pp. 131–52.

Freeman, R. E. (1984) *Strategic Management: A Stakeholder Approach*. Marshfield, MA. Pitman.

Freeman, R. E. and Evan, W. M. (1990) 'Corporate governance: a stakeholder interpretation', *Journal of Behavioral Economics*, 19(4): 337–59.

Freeman, R. E. and Gilbert, D. (1988) *Corporate Strategy and the Search for Ethics*. Englewood Cliffs, NJ: Prentice-Hall.

Friedman, M. (1962) *Capitalism and Freedom*. Chicago: University of Chicago Press.

Friedman, M. (1970) 'The social responsibility of business is to increase profit', *New York Times Magazine*, September 13, 33.

Friedman, M. and Friedman, R. (1980) *Free to Choose*. New York: Harcourt Brace.

Frooman, J. S. (1997) 'Socially irresponsible and illegal behavior and shareholder wealth: a meta-analysis of event studies', *Business & Society*, 36(3): 221–49.

Frooman, J. S. (1999) 'Stakeholder influence strategies', *Academy of Management Review*, 24(2): 191–205.

Gerde, V. W. and Wokutch, R. E. (1998) '25 years and still going strong: a content analysis of the first 25 years of the Social Issues in Management Division proceedings', *Business & Society*, 37(4): 414–46.

Getz, K. A. (1993) 'Corporate political tactics in a principal-agent context: an investigation in ozone protection policy', in J. E. Post (ed.), *Research in Corporate Social Performance and Policy*. Greenwich, CT: JAI Press. pp. 19–55.

Getz, K. A. (1997) 'Research in corporate political action: integration and assessment', *Business & Society*, 36(1): 32–72.

Gilbert, D. R. Jr. (1992) *The Twilight of Corporate Strategy*. New York: Oxford University Press.

Glenn, J. R. Jr. (1992) 'Can a business and society course affect the ethical judgment of future managers?', *Journal of Business Ethics*, 11: 217–23.

Godfrey, P. C. and Hill, C. W. L. (1995) 'The problem of unobservables in strategic management research', *Strategic Management Journal*, 16: 519–34.

Granovetter, M. (1985) 'Economic action and social structure: the problem of embeddedness', *American Journal of Sociology*, 91(3): 481–510.

Griffin, J. J. and Mahon, J. F. (1997) 'The corporate social performance and corporate financial performance debate: twenty-five years of incomparable research', *Business & Society*, 36(1): 5–31.

Hannan, M. T. and Freeman, J. (1989) *Organizational Ecology*. Cambridge, MA: Harvard University Press.

Hart, S. L. (1995) 'A natural resource-based view of the firm', *Academy of Management Review*, 20: 986–1014.

Hart, S. L. (1997) 'Beyond greening: strategies for a sustainable world', *Harvard Business Review*, January–February: 66–77.

Hill, C. W. L. (1990) 'Cooperation, opportunism, and the invisible hand: implications for transaction cost theory', *Academy of Management Review*, 15: 500–13.

Hill, C. W. L. and Jones, T. M. (1992) 'Stakeholder-agency theory', *Journal of Management Studies*, 29: 131–54.

Hillman, A. and Hitt, M. A. (1999) 'Corporate political strategy formulation: a model of approach, participation, and strategy decisions', *Academy of Management Review*, 24(4): 825–42.

Hillman, A. and Keim, G. (1995) 'International variation in the business–government interface: institutional and organizational considerations', *Academy of Management Review*, 20(1): 193–214.

Hofstede, G. (1980) *Cultures's Consequences: International Differences in Work-Related Values*. Beverly Hills, CA: Sage.

Hosmer, L. T. (1994) 'Strategic planning as if ethics mattered', *Strategic Management Journal*, 15: 17–34.

Johnson, H. L. (1957) 'Can the businessman apply Christianity?', *Harvard Business Review*, 35: 68–76.

Jones, T. M. (1991) 'Ethical decision making by individuals in organizations: an issue-contingent model', *Academy of Management Review*, 16(2): 366–95.

Jones, T. M. (1995) 'Instrumental stakeholder theory: a synthesis of ethics and economics', *Academy of Management Review*, 20: 404–37.

Kang, Y. C. and Wood, D. J. (1995) 'Before-profit social responsibility: turning the economic paradigm upside down', in D. Nigh and D. Collins (eds), *Proceedings of the Sixth Annual Meeting of the International Association for Business and Society*. pp. 408–18.

Kohlberg, L. (1981) *The Philosophy of Moral Development*. San Francisco: Harper & Row.

Korten, D. C. (1996) *When Corporations Rule the World*. West Hartford, CN: Kumarian Press.

Kuttner, R. (1996) 'Rewarding corporations that really invest in America', *Business Week*, February 26: 22.

Lavelle, J. and Whetten, D. A. (1997) 'The evolution of CRS and the relationship between doing well and doing good: a social investment analysis', paper presented at the Academy of Management Conference, Boston.

Levitt, T. (1958) 'The dangers of social responsibility', *Harvard Business Review*, 36: 41–50.

Liedtka, J. M. (1996) 'Feminist morality and competitive reality: a role for an ethic of care?', *Business Ethics Quarterly*, 6(2): 179–200.

Litz, R. A. (1996) 'A resource based view of the socially responsible firm: stakeholder interdependence, ethical awareness and issue responsiveness as strategic assets', *Journal of Business Ethics*, 15: 1355–63.

Long, F. J. and Arnold, M. B. (1995) *The Power of Environmental Partnerships*. Fort Worth, TX: Dryden Press.

Mahon, J. F. and McGowan, R. A. (1996) *Industry as a Player in the Political and Social Arena: Defining the Competitive Environment*. Westport, CT: Quorum Books.

Mazis, M. and Green, R. (1971) 'Implementing social responsibility', *MSU Business Topics*, Winter: 68–76.

McKinley, W. (1995) 'Towards a reconciliation of the theory-pluralism in strategic management – incommensurability and the constructivist approach of the Erlangen school', *Advances in Strategic Management*, 12A: 249–60.

Miles, R. H. (1987) *Managing the Corporate Social Environment: A Grounded Theory*. Englewood Cliffs, NJ: Prentice-Hall.

Mitchell, R. K., Agle, B. R. and Wood, D. J. (1997) 'Toward a theory of stakeholder identification and salience: defining the principle of who and what really counts', *Academy of Management Review*, 22: 853–86.

Mitnick, B. M. (1980) *The Political Economy of Regulation: Creating, Designing, and Removing Regulatory Forms*. New York: Columbia University Press.

Mitnick, B. M. (1993) 'Organizing research in corporate social performance: the CSP system as core paradigm', in J. Pasquero and D. Collins (eds), *Proceedings of the Fourth Annual Meeting of the International Association for Business and Society*. pp. 2–15.

Mokhiber, R. (1998) 'Death penalty for corporations comes of age', *Business Ethics*, 12(6): 7–8.

Moore, G. E. (1959) *Principia Ethica*. Cambridge, England: Cambridge University Press.

Nakano, C. (1997) 'A survey study on Japanese managers' views of business ethics', *Journal of Business Ethics*, 16(16): 1737–51.

Oberman, W. D. (1993) 'Strategy and tactic choice in an institutional resource context', in B. M. Mitnick (ed.), *Corporate Political Agency: The Construction of Competition in Public Affairs*. Newbury Park, CA: Sage.

Oliver, C. (1997) 'Sustainable competitive advantage: combining institutional and resource-based perspectives', *Strategic Management Journal*, 18: 697–714.

Ostlund, L. E. (1977) 'Attitudes of managers toward corporate social responsibility', *California Management Review*, 19(4): 35–49.

Paluszek, J. L. (1973) 'How three companies organize for social responsibility', *Business and Society Review/Innovation*, Summer (6): 16–20.

Paul, K. (ed.) (1987) *Business Environment and Business Ethics: The Social, Moral, and Political Dimensions of Management*. Cambridge, MA: Ballinger.

Peteraf, M. (1993) 'The cornerstones of competitive advantage', *Strategic Management Journal*, 14: 179–92.

Pfeffer, J. (1993) 'Barriers to the advance of organizational science: paradigm development as a dependent variable', *Academy of Management Review*, 18: 599–620.

Porter, M. E. (1980) *Competitive Strategy*. New York: Free Press.

Porter, M. E. (1985) *Competitive Advantage*. New York: Free Press.

Porter, M. E. (1995) 'The competitive advantage of the inner city', *Harvard Business Review*, May–June: 55–71.

Porter, M. E. (1998) 'Clusters and the new economics of competition', *Harvard Business Review*, November–December: 77–92.

Porter, M. E. and van der Linde, C. (1995) 'Green and competitive: ending the stalemate', *Harvard Business Review*, 73(5): 120–34.

Post, J. E., Frederick, W. C., Lawrence, A. T. and Weber, J. (1996) *Business and Society: Corporate Strategy, Public Policy, Ethics* (eighth edition). New York: McGraw-Hill.

Post, J. E., Murray, E. A. Jr., Dickie, R. B. and Mahon, J. F. (1983) 'Managing public affairs: the public affairs function', *California Management Review*, 26(1): 135–50.

Preston, L. E. and O'Bannon, D. P. (1997) 'The corporate social–financial performance relationship: a typology and analysis', *Business & Society*, 36(4): 419–29.

Preston, L. E. and Post, J. E. (1975) *Private Management and Public Policy*. Englewood Cliffs, NJ: Prentice-Hall.

Quinn, D. P. and Jones, T. M. (1995) 'An agent morality view of business policy', *Academy of Management Review*, 20: 22.

Rands, G. P. (1991) 'The corporate social performance model, revisited', in *Proceedings of the Second Annual Meeting of the International Association for Business and Society*. pp. 64–77.

Rehbein, K. and Schuler, D. (1997) 'An exploratory analysis of how manufacturing industries influenced the Uruguay round of GATT', in *Proceedings of the Eighth Annual Meeting of the International Association for Business and Society*. pp. 169–76.

Rokeach, M. (1973) *The Nature of Human Values*. New York: Free Press.

Roman, R. M., Hayibor, S. and Agle, B. R. (1999) 'The relationship between social and financial performance: repainting a portrait', *Business & Society*, 38(1): 109–25.

Rowley, T. J. (1997) 'Moving beyond dyadic ties: a network theory of stakeholder influences', *Academy of Management Review*, 22(4): 887–910.

Schuler, D. A. (1996) 'Corporate political strategy and foreign competition: the case of the steel industry', *Academy of Management Journal*, 39(3): 720–37.

Schwartz, D. E. (1974) 'The federal chartering of corporations: a modest proposal', in S. P. Sethi (ed.), *The Unstable Ground: Corporate Social Policy in a Dynamic Society*. Los Angeles: Melville Publishing. pp. 152–67.

Scott, W. R. (1995) *Institutions and Organizations*. Thousand Oaks, CA: Sage Publications.

Sethi, S. P. (ed.) (1974) *The Unstable Ground: Corporate Social Policy in a Dynamic Society*. Los Angeles: Melville Publishing.

Sethi, S. P. (1975) 'Dimensions of corporate social responsibility', *California Management Review*, 17(3): 58–64.

Sethi, S. P. (1999) 'Imperfect markets: business ethics as an easy virtue', *Journal of Business Ethics*, 13: 803–17.

Shaffer, B. (1995) 'Firm-level responses to government regulation: theoretical and research approaches', *Journal of Management*, 21(3): 495–514.

Sharfman, M. (1993) 'A construct validity study of the KLD social performance ratings data', in J. Pasquero and D. Collins (eds), *Proceedings of the Fourth Annual Meeting of the International Association for Business and Society*. pp. 551–6.

Smith, H. R. and Carroll, A. B. (1984) 'Organizational ethics: a stacked deck', *Journal of Business Ethics*, 3: 95–100.

Solomon, R. (1992) *Ethics and Excellence*. New York: Oxford University Press.

Starik, M. (1993) 'Using and improving the KLD data base for research and teaching', in J. Pasquero and D. Collins (eds), *Proceedings of the Fourth Annual Meeting of the International Association for Business and Society*. pp. 563–6.

Starik, M. and Rands, G. P. (1995) 'Weaving an integrated web: multilevel and multisystem perspectives of ecologically sustainable organizations', *Academy of Management Review*, 20(4): 908–35.

Stavins, R. N. and Whitehead, B. W. (1992) 'Dealing with pollution', *Environment*, 34(7): 7–11, 29–42.

Steiner, G. (1975) 'Institutionalizing corporate social decisions', *Business Horizons*, December: 12–18.

Stevens, J. M., Rands, G. P. and Cochran, P. L. (1995) 'Corporate welfare: a new issue for business?', in D. Nigh and D. Collins (eds), *Proceedings of the Sixth Annual Meeting of the International Association for Business and Society*. pp. 295–300.

Stinchcombe, A. L. (1965) 'Social structure and organizations', in J. G. March (ed.), *Handbook of Organizations*. Chicago, IL: Rand McNally. pp. 142–93.

Strand, R. (1983) 'A systems paradigm of organizational adaptations to the social environment', *Academy of Management Review*, 8(1): 90–6.

Sturdivant, F. D. (1977) 'Executives and activists: test of stakeholder management', *California Management Review*, 22(1): 53–9.

Suchman, M. E. (1995) 'Managing legitimacy: strategic and institutional approaches', *Academy of Management Review*, 20(3): 571–610.

Svendsen, A. (1998) *The Stakeholder Strategy: Profiting from Collaborative Business Relationships*. San Francisco: Berrett-Koehler.

Swanson, D. L. (1995) 'Addressing a theoretical problem by reorienting the corporate social performance model', *Academy of Management Review*, 20(1): 43–64.

Swanson, D. L. (1999) 'Toward an integrative theory for business and society: a research strategy for corporate social performance', *Academy of Management Review*, 24(3): 506–21.

Toffler, B. L. (1986) *Tough Choices: Managers Talk Ethics*. New York: Wiley.

Trevino, L. K. (1986) 'Ethical decision making in organizations: a person-situation interactionist model', *Academy of Management Review*, 11: 614.

Trevino, L. K. (1990) 'A cultural perspective on changing and developing organizational ethics', *Research in Organizational Development*, 4: 195–230.

Ullmann, A. A. (1985) 'Data in search of a theory: a critical examination of the relationships among social performance, social disclosure, and economic performance of U.S. firms', *Academy of Management Review*, 10(3): 540–57.

Velasquez, M. (1992) *Business Ethics: Concepts and Cases* (third edition). Englewood Cliffs, NJ: Prentice-Hall.

Velasquez, M., Cavanagh, G. F. and Moberg, D. (1983) 'Organizational statesmanship and dirty politics', *Organizational Dynamics*, Autumn: 65–80.

Victor, B. and Cullen, J. B. (1988) 'The organizational bases of ethical work climates', *Administrative Science Quarterly*, 33: 101–25.

Vogel, D. J. (1996) 'The study of business and politics', *California Management Review*, 38(3): 146–65.

Votaw, D. and Sethi, S. P. (1969) 'Do we need a new corporate response to a changing social environment?', Parts I and II, *California Management Review*, 12(1): 3–16, 17–31.

Waddock, S. A. and Graves, S. B. (1997a) 'Quality of management and quality of stakeholder relations: are they synonymous?', *Business & Society*, 36: 250–79.

Waddock, S. A. and Graves, S. B. (1997b) 'The corporate social performance–financial performance link', *Strategic Management Journal*, 18: 303–19.

Wartick, S. L. and Cochran, P. L. (1985) 'The evolution of the corporate social performance model', *Academy of Management Review*, 10: 758–69.

Weber, J. (1990) 'Managers' moral reasoning: assessing their responses to three moral dilemmas', *Human Relations*, 43(7): 687–702.

Weber, J. (1993) 'Institutionalizing ethics into business organizations', *Business Ethics Quarterly*, 3: 419–36.

Weick, K. E. (1979) *The Social Psychology of Organizing* (second edition). Reading, MA: Addison-Wesley.

Whetten, D. A. (1989) 'What constitutes a theoretical contribution?', *Academy of Management Review*, 14(4): 490–5.

Whetten, D. A. and Godfrey, P. C. (1998) *Identity in Organizations: Building Theory Through Conversations.* Thousand Oaks, CA: Sage Publications.

Wicks, A. C. (1996) 'Overcoming the separation thesis: the need for a reconsideration of business and society research', *Business & Society*, 35(1): 89–118.

Wicks, A. C., Berman, S. L. and Jones, T. M. (1999) 'The structure of optimal trust: moral and strategic implications', *Academy of Management Review*, 24: 99–116.

Wilson, I. H. (1974) 'Reforming the strategic planning process: integration of social responsibility and business needs', in S. P. Sethi (ed.), *The Unstable Ground: Corporate Social Policy in a Dynamic Society.* Los Angeles: Melville Publishing. pp. 245–55.

Wood, D. J. (1991) 'Corporate social performance revisited', *Academy of Management Review*, 16: 691–718.

Wood, D. J. and Jones, R. E. (1995) 'Stakeholder mismatching: a theoretical problem in empirical research on corporate social performance', *International Journal of Organizational Analysis*, 3(3): 229–67.

Wren, D. A. (1979) *The Evolution of Management Thought* (second edition). New York: Wiley.

Part Four

LOOKING FORWARD

18

The Conduct of Strategy Research

HARIDIMOS TSOUKAS and CHRISTIAN KNUDSEN

More than in any other field in management studies, the study of corporate strategy is the study of reason in action. What course of action a firm chooses to follow over time, with what effects; how such choices are made and put into action; and how continuity and novelty are interwoven in corporate behaviour, are some of the most important questions studied in strategic management (SM). As Mintzberg et al. (1998: 299) have aptly remarked, what distinguishes strategic management (SM) from other fields in management is 'its very focus on *strategic choice*: how to find it and where to find it, or else how to create it when it can't be found, and then how to exploit it' (emphasis added).

Focussing on strategic choice raises all sorts of interesting questions: What is choice and how is it explained best? To what extent can it be said that human choices are an expression of free will rather than a deterministic reflection of circumstances? How is thinking related to action? How are choices made at one point in time related to choices made at earlier points in time, and to what extent do they foreclose choices to be made at later points in time? Are there certain strategic choices that are systematically connected to creating competitive advantage? Do such choices already exist waiting to be discovered, or are they uniquely created? How are both corporate coherence and corporate renewal achieved over time?

Grappling with these questions, SM has been predominantly preoccupied with studying choice in different types of situations and finding optimal solutions that may be prescribed for these situations. In fact, much of the literature in SM that has its origin in economics (such as the 'positioning school' and 'modern game theory') starts from such a clear rational choice foundation. However, much of this literature seems to be limited to decision making situations that are relatively stable and repetitive, involving no surprises and few uncertainties (no changes). The development of the rational choice approach in economics has shown that there are strict limitations as to how complex a problem may be if it should have an optimal solution (March, 1994; Simon, 1983).

More recently, several SM scholars have been arguing for a better theoretical understanding of the change processes that are fundamentally transforming firms and industries in the contemporary global economy. However, attempting to conceptualize change processes, some researchers have tended to build models that reduce the element of human agency to a minimum, relying on selection forces rather than on human intentionality to design viable organizations and strategies. Within this stream of research, the process rather than the content of strategy is emphasized, and 'emergent' rather than 'planned' strategies are highlighted (Nelson and Winter, 1982).

The field of SM seems to be confronted with a dilemma: strategy thinkers have either drawn on theories that account for strategic choices but no changes, or they have drawn on theories that account for changes but no strategic choices. However, the crucial question is: how can strategy thinkers model change processes involving genuine uncertainties and non-repetitive situations *and*, at the same time, model individuals and organizations as being able to make strategic choices? Like in other fields, the existence of such a dilemma may motivate a thorough investigation of the philosophical foundations of SM. It is often by making more explicit the ontological, epistemological and praxeological presuppositions of existing perspectives that we identify the reasons for the existence of a dilemma. Identifying the limiting constraints and presuppositions may also give us some idea of how to build a framework that would allow us to simultaneously model 'strategic choices' and 'change processes'. That is, a theory of how individuals and/or organizations make 'strategic choices' by gradually building their 'opportunity sets' in fast changing and partly unpredictable 'environments'.

Motivated by presumably similar concerns, Porter (1991) argued that SM has been in need of a 'dynamic theory of strategy'. Coming from an orthodox industrial economics perspective that has traditionally put its emphasis almost exclusively on 'choice' rather than 'change', Porter interestingly formulated the following four desiderata which a 'dynamic theory of strategy' would need to fulfil. First, such a theory should simultaneously deal with the firm and its environment. Second, it should allow for endogenous change. Third, it should make room for creative action. And fourth, such a theory should acknowledge the roles of historical accident and chance.

Porter's first desideratum refers to the tendency in strategy research to focus exclusively either on the firm (as in the resource-based approach) or on its environment (as in the positioning approach). Porter's (1980) first contribution to strategy took its point of departure in the structure–conduct–performance (SCP) paradigm, with its black box view of the firm. As a consequence, his theory presupposes that competitive advantage may be explained by the firm's ability to exploit the opportunities and threats in its industry, rather

than by the building of its strengths and the minimization of its weaknesses (as in the resource-based view). One suggestion for overcoming the one-sidedness of each theory would be to synthesize the positioning school and the resource-based school. However, such a solution neglects that one theory takes a rather static and short-term view of industries while the other assumes a much more long term and dynamic view.

Porter's second desideratum is that a 'dynamic theory of strategy' should allow for *endogenous change*. Most economic approaches to SM build on the neo-classical paradigm that assumes that preferences and technology are exogenous variables. In this paradigm, changes would be explained by assuming certain shifts in these exogenous variables. However, since the process of obtaining competitive advantage has often been associated with processes of endogenous changes in the technology and knowledge structure of the firm, relying only on exogenous changes would be highly unsatisfactory from the point of view of a dynamic theory of strategy.

The third desideratum is that a dynamic theory of strategy should make room for *creative action*. This desideratum derives from the fact that several of the major approaches to SM have viewed human behaviour and strategies as 'situationally determined' or 'externally enforced', rather than intentionally chosen or constructed. As we will argue later in this article, desiderata 2 and 3 are interrelated. If the 'strategizing subject' is viewed as an evolving and creative actor that co-constructs, through a historical process, his or her own 'set of opportunities', we have not only fulfilled the third but also the second desideratum (by having modelled an endogenous process of an expanding set of opportunities). Desiderata 2 and 3 imply, therefore, a view of the 'strategizing subject' as an evolving historical entity.

Finally, according to Porter's fourth desideratum, a 'dynamic theory of strategy' must acknowledge the *historicity* of strategy development. An important implication of this desideratum is that strategy researchers should abandon the classic view of scientific method and explanation founded on the covering law (or deductive-nomological) model. As will be argued later in the chapter, a 'dynamic theory of strategy' is unlikely to be developed if SM researchers persist in merely recording 'social regularities' or discovering allegedly 'invariant laws' by which firms' strategic behaviour may be explained and predicted. Rather, a dynamic theory of strategy should aim to outline the processes or generative mechanisms that produce specific empirical events (Hedstrom and Swedberg, 1998). A 'process approach' should replace the standard 'variance approach' (Mohr, 1982: Ch. 2).

Despite the enormous significance of the preceding issues for SM, one is surprised by the paucity of systematic reflection on them. True, there have been notable attempts to explicate some of the philosophical issues involved (see Calori, 1998; Scherer and Dowling, 1995; Singer, 1994), focussing especially on questions of epistemology and theory development (Camerer, 1985; Mahoney, 1993; Thomas and Pruett, 1993; Schendel and Hoffer, 1979; Spender, 1993). However, the bulk of research has been in the tradition of 'normal science' (Kuhn, 1970): the meaning of key notions such as 'choice' and 'rational action' has been taken as given (that is to say, unproblematically borrowed from positivist approaches to the social sciences and neoclassical economics) with the view of generating knowledge of relevant empirical regularities (Ansoff, 1987, 1991). As sociologists of science would probably tell us, this may have been a necessary feature of the process of maturation of a relatively young field (as SM undoubtedly is – see Rumelt et al., 1994), whereby the meaning of fundamental concepts is established, albeit provisionally, to enable the accumulation of empirical findings. It was to be expected that a field anxious to legitimate itself would most likely adopt the language and method of 'science' (as SM did) rather than let itself be permeated by a speculative, self-questioning spirit (Toulmin, 1990; Mirowski, 1989; Cohen, 1994). As we will see later, and as some SM researchers have already pointed out (Mintzberg et al., 1998: 37–8), the type of knowledge claims made in SM is crucially shaped by the audiences they are addressed to. If to be seen as relevant and useful meant that one needed to be 'scientific', it was to be expected that the knowledge produced would exhibit certain analogous features. Nothing surprising, at least to those remotely familiar with the history and the sociology of sciences.

Be that as it may, it will be enlightening to critically examine the key assumptions that have characterized the conduct of research in SM. Such meta-theoretical reflection will elucidate the manner in which certain key notions have been used in SM and will contribute to outlining alternative sets of assumptions that may guide research in the future. Our goal is to enable researchers to see more clearly what is implicitly involved in adopting particular theoretical perspectives and, by so doing, to better appreciate what is at stake when different conceptualizations of strategy are suggested (Tsoukas, 1994).

The chapter consists of two parts. In the first we undertake an epistemological exploration of the theoretical foundations of strategy research, which mostly lay in economic models. The purpose of that section is to assess the different modes of explanation that have been adopted in strategy research and tease out their implications. This analysis is followed, in the second part, by an outline of a meta-theoretical framework that enables us to see where different perspectives in SM stand with regard to the following two questions: how is thinking related to action? and who sets strategy? Our thesis will be that SM has been dominated by one particular mode of explanation (the covering law model) and one particular view of how thinking is related to action (representationalism), both of which have their problems. We argue that strategy research will become more relevant, encompassing, and subtle if it moves closer towards a process-oriented view of the firm and lets itself open to a constructivist view of strategy making.

ECONOMIC MODELS AND STRATEGY RESEARCH: TWO CONCEPTIONS OF EXPLANATION

The core argument of this and the following sections is that there seem to be at least two very different sets of ideas concerning what a good explanation is and, therefore, how to build theories within the field of SM. By identifying these differences we think that it is also possible to identify at least two sets of very different ontological and epistemological presuppositions that separate two major research streams in SM.

The dominant tradition in SM argues that the goal of strategic management is to find statistical associations between important variables in order to identify regularities, causal statements and even laws in firms' behaviour. This tradition builds on what some organization researchers have called the 'variance approach' (Mohr, 1982) and philosophers of science refer to as the 'deductive-nomological model' or the 'covering law model' of explanation (Bohman, 1991; Rosenberg, 1988; Camerer, 1985). According to this model, a social regularity or law takes the form 'If conditions C1, C2, C3,....Cn then always E'. The conditions used to explain are called the *explanans* and the phenomenon E to be explained is called the *explanandum*. A covering-law explanation consists in explaining an instance of E by demonstrating the presence of C1, C2, C3,....Cn. Furthermore, the covering-law model postulates that explanations have the same logical structure as predictions (the *symmetry thesis*). If we are able to predict an empirical phenomenon, we have simultaneously explained it, and vice versa. And if we are able to identify a regularity, we may make use of it to control or intervene in the social world.

It is this view of what constitutes an explanation or a 'good theory' that researchers subscribing to a 'process approach' (Mohr, 1982; Pettigrew, 1990, 1992, 1997) or a 'mechanism approach' (Elster, 1983; Hedstrom and Swedberg, 1998) criticize. Let's assume now that some strategy researchers have observed a systematic relationship between two variables, for instance, between market share and profitability. Such a correlation does not constitute an explanation, because it could be a 'spurious relationship', should it be caused by a third variable. From the perspective of the 'process/mechanism approach', we have not established a social regularity, say between I and O, before a mechanism/process M, describing how O is produced by I has been specified. Giving an explanation is therefore closely associated with the possibility of showing *how* I and O are linked to each other – how the cause I produces the effect O through a mechanism M. By specifying a mechanism and thereby providing the details of a causal story we will reduce the risk of spurious explanations. The problem with the covering-law model is, according to Elster (1983), that it is

too coarse-grain. It allows too wide a gap between causes and effects. Such a gap may exist if there is too long a time lag between the cause and the effect, or if we provide a too aggregated description by using a macro-variable instead of a micro-variable. For the process researcher, the goal is to close such gaps and to 'open up the black box and show the nuts and bolts, the cogs and wheels of the internal machinery' (Elster, 1983: 24–5). While the 'covering-law' approach is very outcome-oriented, the 'mechanism' approach focuses on the process that produces an outcome.

Equilibrium Models as 'Outcome' Explanations

Having formulated the main difference between the 'covering-law model' and the 'mechanism' approach, we will try now to show how these two basic approaches to explanation pervade the different research traditions within the field of SM.

Historically, the 'covering-law model' has been by far the most influential in SM, since both equilibrium models (used by industrial economics, including the SCP paradigm, the positioning school and part of modern game theory) and structural functionalist models (early business policy models, contingency theory, transaction cost economics, nexus-of-contract theory) build on it.

Let us start by studying the structure of equilibrium models and the closely related comparative-static method in economics. Drawing on Machlup (1955) we can show how the covering law model lies at the very foundation of equilibrium models and the comparative-static type of analysis that is so common in economics. For Machlup (1955), an economic theory may be viewed as a 'machine' that consists of fixed and variable parts (see right side of Figure 18.1). Let us take the case of the neo-classical theory of the firm. The fixed part of the theory is the 'assumed type of action' or the profit-maximizing hypothesis. The variable part consists of assumptions about which type of situation a firm is confronted with (type of economy, type of market structure, etc.) and what information the firm has access to when taking decisions.

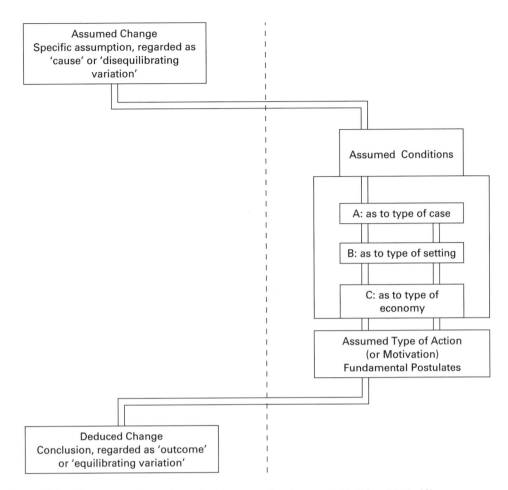

Figure 18.1   *The comparative-static method in economics. Source: F. Machlup (1955: 13)*

It is from such a machine model of fixed and variable assumptions that we may derive comparative static theorems, that tell us what happens when an exogenous variable is changed – when we have a 'disequilibrium variation'. Assuming that the system studied is a stable equilibrium system, we will then be able to get an 'equilibrium variation' that tells us what happens to an endogenous variable. The predictions/explanations of the 'machine' consist of conditional statements of the type: 'If the exogenous variable Y is increased under the conditions X1, X2, X3,...Xn, then the endogenous variable Z will decrease.'

This description of the comparative static method can tell us something about what equilibrium theorists presuppose about the reality or the empirical systems they study. By looking more closely to these models, we may reveal what ontological assumptions they make about reality. To make these assumptions more explicit, we may ask the following question: Why have economists (and especially equilibrium theorists) not been interested in studying social systems without equilibria, systems with several equilibria, and systems with unstable equilibria?

An answer to this question was given by Samuelson (1947: 5) in his famous book *The Foundation of Economic Analysis*: 'Positions of unstable equilibrium, even if they exist, are transient, non-persistent states, and hence on the crudest probability calculation would be observed less frequently than stable states. How many times has the reader seen an egg standing upon its ends?' A necessary condition for obtaining empirical knowledge (identifying empirical regularities) about a social system is that the system demonstrates a relatively high degree of stability or it is relatively invariant. According to Samuelson's *correspondence principle*, a necessary condition for deducing what he somewhat misleadingly calls 'operationally meaningful' (falsifiable) comparative static theorems about a system is that the system has a stable equilibrium. It is only within such a stable system that a change in an exogenous variable, by introducing a 'disequilibrium variation', will lead to a new equilibrium position (or an 'equilibrium variation') which may be compared to the original equilibrium position. The main argument is therefore that it will be impossible to obtain any knowledge (comparative static theorems) about systems that are not stable systems; i.e. systems that after a 'disequilibrium variation' do not return to a new equilibrium position. As a consequence, economists have restricted themselves to the study of systems with stable equilibria and reproductive processes, thereby avoiding the study of irreversible and cumulative change processes (cf. Boudon, 1981).

The underlying worldview that economists have taken as an exemplar for setting up equilibrium models is Newtonian mechanics (cf. Mirowski, 1989). If we want to obtain knowledge (empirical regularities or causal statements) about a mechanical system, it needs to fulfil, according to Bhaskar (1978), two criteria of closure. First, it should be possible to isolate the system from its environment so that it is not influenced by external variables. This is the criterion of *external closure* (or *isolationism*) (cf. Lawson, 1997). However, even if we are able to isolate the system from external influences, we may still not be able to derive social regularities or laws from it. The reason for this is that most systems have a certain internal structure or complexity, which implies that a system will not necessarily behave in the same way when exposed to the same external conditions. A complete closure of a system will therefore imply, according to Bhaskar (1978) and Lawson (1997), that the system must also meet the criterion of *internal closure* (or *atomism*). According to this criterion, not only the environment but also the internal structure of a system must remain constant over time, in order for us to be able to derive laws or regularities describing a system's behaviour. The condition of internal closure implies a preference for a purely atomistic type

of analysis, as well as for a unit of analysis that is not allowed to change endogenously but responds identically to identical environmental changes (Gharajedaghi and Ackoff, 1984).

In the standard microeconomic paradigm, we find the criterion of internal closure expressed in the methodological rule of 'De Gustibus non est Disputandum' (cf. Stigler and Becker, 1977). This rule prescribes that the behavior of consumers and firms should be explained by considering their preferences and production functions as constant and that changes in behavior has to be explained by changes in their situational constraints. This rule implies that consumers and firms are viewed as the 'atoms' or the basic units of analysis, whose behavioral dispositions are invariant over time, since the possibility of behavioral changes due to endogenous changes in preferences and production functions has been ruled out by definition. For instance, had we assumed that 'learning-by-doing', 'learning-by-using' or other endogenous changes in knowledge have been taking place inside the firm, then the criterion of internal closure would not have been fulfilled and we would have been unable to discover social regularities.

It was exactly this feature of the standard microeconomic theory of the firm that got Latsis (1976) to describe it as a research program: in his words: 'Viewing economic actions as highly constrained reactions has provided a research program for the neoclassical theory of the behaviour of the firm. That is, the approach to the explanation of the decisions and actions of sellers in all the diversity of market structures is handled in a unified way, in accordance with certain principles and certain problem solving rules' (1976: 17). The most important of these rules was, according to Latsis (1976), that the behavior of the firm should be seen as determined by its external situational constraints. As a consequence, Latsis (1972) uses the term *situational determinism* to describe this program. He argues that the goal of this program is to reduce the number of alternatives by putting more and more external constraints on the firm, until a 'single exit' solution emerged as the maximizing outcome.

The fulfillment of the criteria of 'external' and 'internal closure' has several implications for how the firm has been conceptualized within the standard microeconomic research program, as well as for how this program has been used within SM. First, since the primary intellectual task of the microeconomic research program has been to explain the formation of prices within different market structures or industries rather than to account for the behavior of the single firm, they have used a 'black box' or at least a 'grey box' view of the firm. And precisely because microeconomists, including many modern game theorists, see the industry as their primary level of analysis, all explanatory factors are located in the environment of the firm rather than inside the firm and its organization. Strategy theorists that build on this tradition (such as Porter, 1980) retain a similar 'black box' view and identify strategy with the positioning of the firm in an industry. Strategy is therefore mainly concerned with the opportunities and threats of the market rather than related to the internal strengths and weaknesses of the firm.

Second, in accordance with the criterion of internal closure, the firm is viewed as an unchanging atom that displays identical behavior in identical situations. In accordance with the research program of situational determinism, the firm is viewed as an entity that has no history and can only change behavior due to changes in exogenous situational variables, rather than due to endogenous change processes. This may be substantiated by looking at how orthodox microeconomists have conceptualized changes in knowledge over time as related to production possibilities. In accordance with the 'production function' view, firms are conceptualized as having access to a set of different production techniques that can be matched with different relative factor prices in order to produce a certain product in the most efficient way. All these production techniques are assumed to be common knowledge among the firms in an industry – all firms are assumed to have access to exactly the same 'cookbook' of production techniques (cf. Nelson, 1991). According to the criterion of internal closure of the model, only exogenous changes in the knowledge of the firm are allowed. In the world of standard microeconomic theory, firms cannot be seen as building competitive advantages through firm-specific knowledge accumulation processes, since firms are analyzed from a cross-sectional rather than a longitudinal perspective.

Third, the criterion of internal closure in microeconomic models does not only imply that firms in an industry are viewed as entities without a history. Firms in the same industry are also viewed as identical in the sense that they are assumed to face the same demand curve and to have identical cost curves. Often industries are studied from the point of view of a 'representative firm' or firms have been assumed to be homogenous within an industry. This has been very unfortunate for the field of SM, since it made it impossible for the microeconomic paradigm to answer the fundamental question: why do firms differ?

Structural Functionalist Models as 'Outcome' Explanations

The structural functionalist model (SF model) that has dominated both organizational sociology and organizational economics has both similarities and differences with the standard equilibrium model. Like equilibrium models, SF models are based on the covering law model of explanation. Both types of models are also studying social phenomena from an 'outcome' rather than a 'process' perspective. However, SF models differ from standard equilibrium models by studying a much broader variety of systems. Structural functionalists argue that more enduring social structures, such as institutions, organizational structures, norms, social conventions, etc, are solutions to repeated problems of social interaction (cf. Ullmann-Margalit, 1977). In order to understand the specific functions that an institution, norm, organizational structure or convention may have, we need to reconstruct the social problem of interaction that it solves.

For instance, we explain the right hand rule in traffic as an efficient solution to an underlying coordination game with at least two players that have two strategies: right-hand driving (R) and left-hand driving (L), and the four outcomes: (R, L), (R, R), (L, R) and (L, L). In this case, structural functionalists start by studying a system with two Nash equilibrium-solutions ((R, R) and (L, L)) and analyze the institution as the selection of, or convergence towards, one of these two equivalent Nash-equilibria. The underlying assumption in the structural functionalist explanations is that the most 'efficient' instituation would emerge as the solution to the problem of social interaction, either through a reinforcing learning process or through a selection process.

In SF models the existence of a firm and the structure of its organization are the main phenomena to account for (its explanandum). In transaction cost economics, the existence of the firm has been explained as an institutional solution to a market failure problem that economizes on transaction costs. In the nexus-of-contracts theory the capitalist firm has been assumed to emerge as a solution to a team production problem that helps to solve a metering problem. In the case of agency theory, the firm has been assumed to emerge as a solution to the separation between ownership and control by minimizing agency costs. And finally, in the case of contingency theory, a firm's organizational structure has been considered as being adaptive to its environment to make it as efficient as possible. Compared to orthodox equilibrium theorists, structural functionalists take their point of departure in systems without any equilibria, systems with several equilibria, as well as systems with different types of coordination failures, such as market failures, organization failures, etc. The goal of the analysis has been to account for the institutional framework that emerges as a solution to this problem, arguing that it is the most efficient solution by either minimizing or at least economizing on some type of costs (agency costs, transaction costs, adaptation costs, metering costs, etc.).

While equilibrium models have had their foundation in Newtonian mechanics, structural functionalist models have taken their point of departure in the Darwinian theory of natural selection. Organizations and firms are studied as if they were organisms in need of fitness with their environment. In fact, many of the early contributions in SM (at that time called business policy) build on a SF model. Among the most important works are Chandler's (1990) *Strategy and Structure*, Ansoff's (1965) *Corporate Strategy* and Learned et al.'s (1965) *Business Policy*.

While an orthodox equilibrium model tries to explain and predict what happens within a stable system by comparing two states of equilibrium before and after a change in exogenous variables, an SF model tries to explain the existence of the different institutional structures that are taken as given in the orthodox

equilibrium model. The comparative static type of analysis, that is used in an orthodox equilibrium model to explain *empirical events* within an existing institutional structure, is replaced, in the SF model, with a comparative institutional model used for explaining the existence of different *structural arrangements* as a response to different situational circumstances (cf. Simon, 1978).

Process Explanations in Strategy Research

Although equilibrium theorists and structural functionalist theorists have different explananda, they are both using the covering law model of explanation. Both camps share the common feature of studying social phenomena from an 'outcome' rather than a 'process' perspective. This implies that social systems are studied when they are in a stationary state and when there is no further tendency for changes in terms of new learning or new knowledge. The regularities studied within such systems are of a 'synchronous' rather than of a 'diachronous' nature. Though most 'outcome' oriented models only study the end state of social processes, they often have an *ad hoc* story of how the 'outcome' may have been produced tacked onto a more formal model. In most equilibrium models, a so-called 'adjustment' story is often tacked onto the formal equilibrium analysis in order to legitimate why it is relevant to study a specific equilibrium outcome and how the equilibrium came about. In a similar way, many structural functionalists try to legitimate the study of an efficient institutional arrangement by arguing that it has been produced by a 'natural selection' process or through a reinforcement learning process.

However, as Hayek (1948) stated some time ago, most equilibrium models do not provide us with an explanation as to *how* the equilibrium state has been produced in the first place: 'The statement that, if people know everything, they are in equilibrium is true simply because that is how we define equilibrium. The assumption of a perfect market in that sense is just another way of saying that equilibrium exists, but does not get us any nearer an explanation of when and how such a state will come about. It is clear that if we want to make the assertion that under certain conditions people will approach the state *we must explain by what process they will acquire the necessary knowledge*' (1948: 46, our emphasis). In a similar fashion, SF researchers have studied the efficient outcomes of social processes without demonstrating what process or mechanism may in fact have produced such a state. In most cases, structural functionalists just assume that an adjustment process has been operative without demonstrating that empirically.

The choice between an 'outcome perspective' and a 'process perspective' is a choice between two very different ontologies: a closed-world ontology and an open-world ontology. Following the 'outcome perspective', one sees the world as closed (as having a finite set of states), which implies that economic agents can never be surprised. Following the 'process perspective' one views the world as open-ended, allowing fundamentally new and unexpected events to happen (cf. Popper, 1988; Rorty, 1991: 93–7). But what implications do these two different onto-epistemological views have with regard to the way we model firms and, consequently, to the way we understand the concept of strategy? We may address this question by first finding out in what ways the 'process approach' diverges from the 'outcome approach' as exemplified by the standard microeconomic theory or the research program of situational determinism.

As it was earlier argued, according to the 'outcome approach', it will be possible to obtain knowledge (social regularities) about a social system only if it fulfills the criterion of internal closure. This criterion implies that firms should be conceptualized as entities without a history, identically responding to identical situations. It was in opposition to the criterion of internal closure that the behavioral theory of the firm emerged. According to Simon, both the internal structure of the firm and its historical evolution were important factors in understanding its behavior: 'Responses to environmental events,' notes Simon (1979: 509), 'can no longer be predicted simply by analyzing the "requirements of the situation", but depend on the specific decision processes that the firm employs […] If in the face of identical environmental conditions, different decision mechanisms can produce different firm behaviors, this sensitivity of outcomes to processes can have important

consequences for analysis at the level of the markets and the economy.' According to this 'multiple-exit' heuristic of the behavioral research program, one should never assume that goals, technology and preferences are exogenous, but must instead be accounted for within an endogenous process perspective (cf. Latsis, 1976).

The most important implication of abandoning the criterion of internal closure is that it enables us to model organizations as *historical* entities. In the behavioral theory of Cyert and March (1963), the firm is characterized as an adaptive institution whose short term behavior is determined by its 'standard operating procedures'. The latter are viewed as the memory of the organization, since they contain solutions to standard problems the firm confronted in the past. The firm's knowledge of how to solve repeated problems is embodied in its behavioral rules. The key for understanding the short term behavior of a firm consists in the analysis of its procedural rules. The conception of strategy following from the behavioral theory of Cyert and March (1963) has been described as 'logical incrementalism' (Quinn, 1980). In the behavioral theory, the firm is often viewed as a 'political coalition' between different interest groups that the strategist must constantly try to find a truce for (Lindblom, 1968). However, from a classical strategy perspective, logical incrementalism is thought to lead to a 'purposeless' or even an 'anti-strategic' view of the firm (Andrews, 1980).

It was Nelson and Winter's (1982) *An Evolutionary Theory of Economic Change* that extended Cyert and March's short-term behavioral analysis of the firm, into a long-term analysis of how firms within an industry adapt to new environments, through a process of search for new and more profitable routines. In the evolutionary theory of Nelson and Winter, the firm has been conceptualized as an historical entity more consistently than in the short-term analysis of Cyert and March (1963). By viewing the firm as a bundle of routines into which knowledge is stored, the productive knowledge of the firm is seen to be the result of an endogenous and historical learning process. In opposition to the criterion of internal closure in orthodox equilibrium and SF models, evolutionary economists find it necessary to uncover the cumulative process leading to the firm's current ways of doing things.

By viewing the firm as a historical entity that has emerged through a cumulative causal process, the evolutionary theory not only clashes with orthodox equilibrium theories, but also with SF models, such as Williamson's transaction cost economics. As Winter argues: 'In the evolutionary view – perhaps in contrast to the transaction cost view – the size of a large firm at a particular time is not to be understood as the solution to some organizational problems. General Motors' […] position at the top [of the *Fortune* 500] reflects [alternatively] the cumulative effect of a long string of happenings stretching back into the past […] A position atop the league standing is not a great play. It does not exclude the possibility that there were several not-so-great plays' (1988: 178).

Indirectly, this is a critique of the assumption of internal closure and of the ahistoric view of the firm adopted by SF models. Transaction cost theory decomposes the firm into a series of interdependent transactions, arguing that the firm organizes transactions in a way that economizes on transaction costs. Since the firm consists of complex networks of interdependent transactions, it is the totality of the transactions, and not the individual transaction, that is subject to the 'market test' of efficiency. In such a bundle of transactions, it is very likely that some will be inefficient. From the perspective of the evolutionary theory of Nelson and Winter, a firm should rather be viewed from a *holistic* perspective, since it is assumed to emerge from a cumulative causal process. According to the 'process approach' favored by Winter, the selection mechanism will always have to mold already existing structures rather than create them *de novo*. Therefore, changes will consist of incremental adaptations to a complex and interdependent system and the selection mechanism will, according to Winter, 'produce progress, but […] not […] an "answer" to any well-specified question or list of questions about how activities should be organized', as in SF models of Williamson's transaction cost economics (1988: 177).

The process approach questions the rather simplistic view of causality that is often assumed by the outcome approach. Well known examples that are relevant to SM can be found both within equilibrium models and within SF models. The best known example within equilibrium models is the structure–conduct–performance paradigm that assumes a one-way causal relationship from the market structure to the performance variable. According to the so-called market concentration doctrine in the SCP paradigm, the higher the concentration of an industry, the higher the profitability in that industry. However, as argued by Demsetz (1973), the causal relationship between concentration and profitability may be a spurious relationship, since the causal relationship may just as well go the other way – from profitability to market structure. According to Demsetz, it is even more likely that a higher concentration is caused by the fact that more efficient/profitable firms outcompete less efficient firms, thereby increasing the concentration of the industry.

Similarly, a simplistic view of causality can be seen in the SF model of the strategy–structure–performance paradigm. It was Chandler's (1990) *Strategy and Structure* that first established this paradigm. According to contingency theorists such as Donaldson (1995: Ch. 2), Chandler's major thesis was that the introduction of the M-form in four major American corporations was due to a prior diversification strategy and could be reconstructed as 'structure follows strategy'. Corporations such as General Motors, Sears, Dupont, etc. had all introduced the M-form, the argument goes, in order to solve 'control loss' and other 'inefficiency' problems that had been caused by an earlier diversification strategy. Later empirical studies within the strategy–structure–performance paradigm viewed 'strategy' as the independent variable and 'structure' as the dependent variable. However, such an interpretation may be too simplistic.

From a process perspective, the simple one-way causal relationship assumed in the strategy–structure–performance paradigm needs to be replaced with a more complex cumulative causal model that, over time, allows causality to go both ways. Though the emergence of the M-form may be explained by a strategy of diversification, an explanation of the persistence and later diffusion of the M-form may be built on the opposite causal relationship. When first introduced, the main advantage of the M-form over the U-form was the superior ability of the M-form to 'digest' acquisitions. In the M-form, an acquired firm needs just to be assigned the status of profit center to become part of the new firm. In the U-form the integration of a new firm is much more difficult, since all the new assets need to be integrated with the old assets. However, after the introduction of the M-form, the diversification strategy may be reinforced by the M-form structure. In this case, 'strategy follows structure' rather than the reverse.

As Chandler himself remarks in a new introduction to his *Strategy and Structure*: 'structure had as much impact on strategy as strategy had on structure. But because the changes in strategy came chronologically before those of structure, and perhaps also because an editor at The MIT Press talked me into changing the title from *Structure and Strategy* to *Strategy and Structure*, the book appears to concentrate on how strategy defines structure rather than on how structure affects strategy. My goal from the start was to study the complex interconnections in a modern industrial enterprise between structure and strategy, and an ever changing external environment' (1990, no pagination). In fact, Chandler (1992) has recently opposed the atomistic and ahistorical perspective of firms that characterizes SF models, in favor of a more holistic and historical perspective that is characteristic of process models.

A process approach has been claimed to be at the core of game theoretical approaches to strategy and is worth considering here the modelling of strategic rational agents in modern game theory. The shift from the SCP-paradigm (Scherer, 1970) to game theory (Tirole, 1988) has been described as a shift from 'old' industrial organization to 'new' industrial organization (cf. Ghemawat, 1997). Compared with the SCP-paradigm, the introduction of game theory presents several advantages. First, while the SCP-paradigm took the industry structure as an independent and given variable, industry structure has been endogenized in much of modern game theory. Second, compared with the rather static framework of the SCP-paradigm, the introduction of extensive games has given game theorists a language for modelling intertemporal or dynamic competitive interactions. Third, compared with the SCP-paradigm, game theory has been able not only to accommodate situations with imperfect information but also to handle the much more difficult situations with asymmetric information.

However, like much of the SCP-paradigm, game theory has mostly been applied to the study of competitive interactions at the industry level and has, therefore, to a large degree, adopted the 'black box view' of the firm from orthodox microeconomics and the SCP-paradigm (Saloner, 1991). This seems to be due more to tradition than to methodological limitations of game theory itself. With the diffusion of extensive games, an increasing number of game theorists has abandoned the view of the firm as an *ahistoric* entity and has either modelled the firm as an entity that builds its reputation over time (cf. Kreps, 1990) or as an entity that makes different types of precommitments in order to constrain its future behavior (cf. Ghemawat, 1991, 1997; Besanko et al., 1996: Ch. 9). However, it seems to us that even if game theory has made major progress in terms of modelling strategic rational agents in an intertemporal perspective, there are still some deep-seated methodological and ontological problems to be solved in this research program.

The solution to intertemporal games is found through *backward induction* (Selten, 1975). This method advises us to unravel the game backwards by solving the very last subgame first. After we have solved the last subgame, we may then move on to the next-to-last subgame. Since we know the outcome of the last subgame, it will then be possible to determine what is a rational choice in this subgame. Continuing in this way we will be able to unravel the whole game finding a rational strategy for the whole game.

Besides being haunted by a number of logical paradoxes (cf. Binmore, 1990; Bicchieri, 1993; Knudsen, 1993), the backward induction method in extensive games raises some important ontological questions. By using this method, game theorists seem to have broken down an inter-temporal game, in which time plays an important role, into a set of separate static games in which time (and therefore process) is no longer an essential variable. Indeed, it seems to be a general principle not only in game theory, but more generally within economics, that what constitutes a rational choice is never allowed to depend on what happened earlier. In economics, the status quo has no special advantage over its alternatives. In defining rational behavior, only future states matter. This implies that we overlook, by defintion, the path-dependency of our decisions, since each new decision is assumed to be taken *de novo*. All decisions are therefore fully reversible and there are no historical constraints. McClelland (1993) argues that strategic players in extensive games make use of what he calls a *principle of separability*, which is the foundation of Selten's (1975) subgame perfect equilibrium:

> It is separability that drives the form that backward reasoning, or 'folding backward,' takes in the analysis of sequential choice games. Separability implies that in evaluating any coordination plan, what that plan calls upon a given agent to choose, at any given point, must be consistent with what that agent would choose, were she to make a *de novo* choice at that point. This is what licenses proceeding from the evaluation of the last segment of that plan, *taken in isolation from the rest of the plan*, successively backward, to the evaluation of the whole plan. (McClelland, 1993: 192–3)

It is by using the principle of separability as a foundation for defining rational behavior in extensive games that it becomes impossible to model the decision-maker as being able to coordinate his or her decisions over time and, therefore, as an adequate behavioral foundation for a truly process approach.

Moreover, game theory treats all firms (players) in an industry as fundamentally uniform. For example, when defining what constitutes rational behavior, the principle of symmetry is assumed to hold, implying that a player has to ascribe the same form of rationality to his opponent that he applies to himself (maximizing expected utility). However, by applying the principle of symmetry, game theorists ignore information about the *identity* of opponents that real world actors typically will use to make 'rational' decisions. As Schelling (1960) remarks: 'If a man knocks at the door and says that he will stab himself on the porch unless given 10 dollars, he is more likely to get the 10 dollars if his eyes are bloodshot.' To signal what type of an agent one is (one's identity) is therefore of great importance to the outcome of the social processes studied by game theorists. This implies that the conception of the firm as an invariant entity in game theory needs to be replaced by a conception of the firm in which firm-specific *history*

is important for understanding differences in firms' behavior within the same industry.

It is this emphasis on the historicity of the firm that has been the hallmark of Penrose's (1959) work. While Nelson and Winter (1982) have primarily been interested in developing an evolutionary theory of industries and firms, Penrose (1959) was more focussed on building a theory of the individual firm and its growth process. She based her theory on what she described as an 'unfolding perspective' (Penrose, 1955) and used the gradual unfolding of an organism as an analogy for studying the growth of the firm. Penrose's focus was especially directed towards understanding how resources, capabilities and knowledge are gradually created through an irreversible and cumulative causal process. New knowledge is gradually built into the formal and informal structure of the organization, thereby becoming a significant factor for the direction of future knowledge accumulation, where more complex knowledge structures are created on the basis of already existing structures. As opposed to both the research program of situational determinism (orthodox microeconomics) and Porter's strategy framework, Penrose emphasized the internal over the external limits to growth (cf. Knudsen, 1996).

THEORIES OF ACTION IN STRATEGY RESEARCH: A META-THEORETICAL FRAMEWORK

Most researchers agree that the chief purpose of corporate strategy is the creation of sustainable competitive advantage. They also seem to agree that such an advantage is created through a continuous effort on the part of managers to align their organization's strengths with the opportunities and limitations present in their environment. There is near unanimity that whatever else strategy may be thought to be, it certainly is *consistent corporate action over time*. Strategic behaviour, in other words, is a systematic attempt to shape the future in a coherent way (Araujo and Easton, 1996).

There are two crucial issues in seeking to understand strategic behaviour. First, how does organizational consistency develop? To a large extent (although not exclusively) this is a question concerning the role of human intentionality in setting up patterns of corporate actions. Put differently, how is thinking related to acting? Secondly, who is responsible for the development of strategy? Who sets it? As soon as these questions are raised, differences between the several perspectives in SM start cropping up. For example, there are those who believe that, more than anything else, strategy is systematic thinking by a single person (or, at most, a few individuals), using relevant concepts and analytical techniques in order to decide on an appropriate course of action, which will be implemented in the future. At the other end, there are those for whom strategy making is primarily a social process of continuous experimentation, the outcome of which is the formation of a distinct (as well as unique) pattern of action over time. What is worth noting is that behind a seemingly common understanding of strategy as corporate consistency over time, there are significant differences over the way thought is related to action, generating contrasting interpretations of strategy (Tsoukas, 1994). Ultimately, as we hope to show in this chapter, these differences are the result of competing theories of action implicit in the different perspectives.

Strategic management is a very diverse field. It is commonly acknowledged that the diversity of SM is, by and large, the result of, on the one hand, the different disciplines which take corporate strategy as their object of study, ranging from economics to sociology and psychology and, on the other hand, the multiple audiences addressed by strategy researchers (Gopinath and Hoffman, 1995; Shrivastava, 1987). To cope with an ever-increasing theoretical pluralism, there have been several attempts to bring some taxonomic order to the field by grouping research findings into distinct schools of thought (Bowman, 1995; Gilbert et al., 1988; Mintzberg, 1990a; Mintzberg et al., 1998; Scherer and Dowling, 1995; Zan, 1990). Such an attempt is inherently fraught with conceptual difficulties, given the contrasting disciplinary allegiances of competing perspectives. However, after nearly 40 years of research in SM, we have seen enough to be able to make meaningful comparisons.

The 10 schools of thought identified by Mintzberg (Mintzberg, 1990a; Mintzberg et al., 1998) serve as a useful guide to an already large SM literature. Mintzberg's scheme is comprehensive enough to cover most developments in the field and will be used throughout this chapter as a point of reference. The ten schools of thought are the following: the design school (strategy formation as a process of conception); the planning school (strategy formation as a formal process of analysis); the positioning school (strategy formation as an analytical process of positioning the firm in its industry); the entrepreneurial school (strategy formation as a process of envisioning new possibilities and taking advantage of opportunities); the cognitive school (strategy formation as a mental process); the learning school (strategy formation as a social learning process); the power school (strategy formation as a process of negotiation); the cultural school (strategy formation as a process for building collective uniqueness); the environmental school (strategy formation as a reactive process); and the configuration school (strategy formation as a process of quantum-like transformation) (Mintzberg et al., 1998: 5–6).

There are several ways these perspectives may be classified. For example, Mintzberg et al. (1998) group them in two categories. The first three schools are avowedly *prescriptive*: their proponents do not attempt to describe or explain how strategies form, but, rather, they seek to prescribe how strategies should be formulated. The reverse is the case with all the other perspectives. Another way of grouping them would be to distinguish between those schools concerned with the *content* of strategy (the positioning school) vis-à-vis those concerned with either prescribing the *process* of strategy formulation (the design school, the planning school, and the entrepreneurial school), or *explaining the process of strategy formation* (the learning school, the power school, and the cultural school).

Despite what the authors of several leading textbooks in SM have argued (Johnson and Scholes, 1997; Mintzberg et al., 1998), the environmental and the configuration schools are not really concerned with describing, explaining or prescribing *strategy* – at least not if we take human agency to be a necessary feature of strategy – and, therefore, we will not include them in our discussion in the rest of this chapter. There are good reasons for doing this. To the extent that strategy involves making choices, it cannot be said that the environmental school is in any way concerned with strategy since, on the environmental view, corporate actors do not choose but they are chosen (selected by the environment). One may certainly discern, *ex post facto*, failed strategies or strategies selected by the environment, but this hardly constitutes an argument concerning corporate strategy *per se*. As said earlier, strategy implies coherent action over time, and any theoretical framework which does not engage with (or assume) it cannot properly be said to be about strategy *per se*. It may well be about the evolution of corporate behaviour but, in order to qualify as an account of strategy, it needs to make provisions for human agency unfolding in time.

Similarly, the configuration school seeks to explain organizational change, drawing on the model of paradigmatic change. Within such a model, particular types of strategy are shown to match particular types of structure and particular types of context. How, however, strategies form or should form are not issues with which the configuration school is preoccupied. A particular strategy is simply seen to occupy a place within a particular configuration. Why this should be the case and how it came to be the case are not dealt with. In fact, when it comes to the nitty gritty of strategy, the proponents of the configuration school offer extremely general advice to practitioners (of the type 'everything matters' – see Mintzberg et al., 1998: 305–6) to the point where such advice, because it nearly leaves nothing out, risks being vacuous. This is not to belittle the contribution of the configuration school, only to point out that it is not a theory of strategy but a theory of corporate change.

Representationalism vs. Enactivism in Strategy Research

As mentioned earlier, there are two key questions, the answers to which will help us distinguish the different theories of action underlying perspectives on strategy. First, *how is thinking related to acting*? By and large, there have been two answers to this question. First, thinking is a basically representational activity, according to which the mind represents the world 'outside' as well as depicts ends desired 'within' the individual (Rorty, 1980, 1991; Taylor, 1993). Action is following

the rules dictated by such representations. In its strong version, which is the one most often found in SM, the representationalist approach consists, more precisely, of the following principles: the world has certain pre-given features; there is a cognitive system which represents those features; and the cognitive system acts on the basis of those representations (Varela et al., 1991: 135). It is assumed that, ontologically, the world is pregiven and that, epistemologically, its features can be specified prior to any cognitive activity. Moreover, as Varela et al. (1991: 147) remark, a representationalist approach tacitly assumes that 'the world can be divided into regions of discrete elements and tasks. Cognition consists in problem solving, which must, if it is to be successful, respect the elements, properties, and relations within these pregiven regions.'

According to this view, largely Cartesian in origin, human experience is made up of atoms of subjective sensation. Knowledge of the world is built by assembling those atomic sensations to make up a picture of the world (Reed, 1996: 24; Rorty, 1991). Cognition consists of two stages: first the gathering of sensations, and then the drawing of inferences (thinking) on the basis of those sensations. In other words, first we experience, then we think. However, according to Descartes (1968), the two steps are not equally trustworthy. Sensory experience, gathered through the bodily mechanisms, is not dependable. Our senses may deceive us: we may mistake (as we often do) one thing for another and, therefore, we cannot possibly base our judgements on such shaky foundations. In Descartes' (1968: 103) graphic language, 'there is some deceiver both very powerful and very cunning, who constantly uses all his wiles to deceive me'. For true knowledge of the world to be obtained, sensory experience needs to be purified through the rigorous scrutiny of reason. Hence, for Descartes, only pure thought can ever be completely reliable. The second step in the process of cognition (that of inference) is more trustworthy than the first (that of sensory experience). The evil demon lurking to deceive the individual can eventually be defeated. 'Let him deceive me as much as he likes,' says Descartes (1968: 103), 'he can never cause me to be nothing, so long as I think I am something.' In other words, I may mistake that robot for a person, my rival's silence for cowardice, my competitor's new product for a short-lived project, but I cannot deceive myself that I am thinking – hence *cogito, ergo sum* (I think, therefore I am).

Because thinking is more reliable than sensing, we should base our actions on a set of distinct and clear ideas, which we know to be true and, therefore, we trust. This has been the mainstream theory of knowledge in the 20th century: 'knowledge involves taking one's subjective states and trying to test whether they fit current or upcoming realities' (Reed, 1996: 58; see also MacIntyre, 1985; Rorty, 1991; Taylor, 1985). For example, a firm wants to enter a new market. What, on this view, should it do? For a start, it should identify what are the formally known (that is, scientifically validated) ways of entering new markets and establishing competitive advantage, and then connect this generic knowledge with the knowledge of the particular market the firm is interested in (see Ansoff, 1991). Actors, on this view, are deductive reasoners: from an abstract set of generically valid premises and from a particular set of current observations, they deduce conclusions which they proceed to implement (Devlin, 1997). Another way of putting it is to say that actors are propositional thinkers: they follow explicit rules of the type 'If X, then Y, in conditions Z' (Tsoukas, 1998a).

Thus, to sum up, the representational approach is characterized by the following principles. Ontologically, it assumes a pregiven world. Epistemologically, it is based on the belief that only pure thinking can yield reliable knowledge by allowing a deductive approach. And praxeologically, it adheres to instrumental action: actors follow explicit rules or apply explicit precepts, in order to achieve their goals. Action is driven by reliable prior knowledge.

The second answer to the question of how thinking is related to action is the *enactive* approach. According to this, knowing is action. In Varela et al.'s (1991: 149) words, 'knowledge is the result of an ongoing interpretation that emerges from our capacities of understanding. These capacities are rooted in the structures of our biological embodiment but are lived and experienced within a domain of consensual action and cultural history. They enable us to make sense of our world.' On this view, rather than the mind passively reflecting

a pregiven world, the mind actively engages with the world and, by so doing, it helps shape the world. Meaning is enacted (constructed) – it is brought forward from a taken-for-granted background of understanding (Winograd and Flores, 1987: 36–7; Taylor, 1993: 47; Varela et al., 1991: 49). It is when we lack a common background that misunderstandings arise, in which case we are forced to articulate the background, and explain it to ourselves and to others (Winograd and Flores, 1987: 36–7).

The world causes us to form beliefs but does not dictate the content of our beliefs (Rorty, 1991). Objects 'out there' are the loci of causal powers providing the stimuli for manifold uses of language. But the moment we ask for *facts* about an object we are asking how it should be described in a particular language, and that language is not – it cannot be – neutral: its vocabulary is necessarily loaded with meaning. Notions, for example, such as 'trust', 'work' or 'authority' do not mirror an independent reality, but are inextricably bounded with having certain *experiences* (concerning trust, work, authority, etc.), which involves seeing that certain *descriptions* apply. Particular languages mark particular qualitative distinctions concerning what *is* work, trust, etc. and how actors ought to respond to them. The language, therefore, actors use to describe their goals, beliefs and desires defines also the meaning these terms have for them (Taylor, 1985: 71; Tsoukas, 1998b).

Moreover, as well as goals, beliefs and desires being language-dependent, so are social practices and institutions: they incorporate particular background distinctions (distinctions of worth). Without such distinctions a particular practice would not be what it is. What, for example, a firm is (its particular competencies, the way it combines resources) incorporates a particular self-understanding as to what matters and what does not. Knowledge, therefore, is action in the sense that when statements about the world are made, these are not merely denotative but connotative: utterances do not merely describe the world but, by interpreting it, they help create it (Austin, 1962; Moch and Huff, 1983; Winograd and Flores, 1987; Tsoukas, 1998b). Seeing a particular market as saturated, a competitor as threatening, or a product as fulfilling a particular need, a firm is helping to create those objects and properties it describes by undertaking appropriate action (Soros, 1987). Thinking *is* doing.

If social institutions and practices are what they are by virtue of the particular sets of background distinctions they incorporate, where do those distinctions derive their meaning from? As Wittgenstein (1958) insightfully observed, the meaning of our signs and symbols comes from the use we put them to. Social practices and meanings are mutually constituted. Without a particular practice, a set of meanings would be unintelligible. And without a set of meanings, a practice could not exist. Actors learn to follow certain rules by being socialized into the meanings constituting a particular practice. An actor's understanding, therefore, does not reside in his/her head but in the *practices* in which he/she participates. In other words, understanding is implicit in the social activity in which the individual participates.

This Heideggerian and Wittgensteinian insight is perhaps the single most important difference between representationalism and enactivism: the social activity, rather than the cognizing subject, is the ultimate foundation of intelligibility (Heidegger, 1962; Wittgenstein, 1958). For example, a quartermaster does not need to form explicit representations of his sensing instruments. His ability to act comes from his familiarity with *navigating* a ship, not by his representation of the navigation instruments in his mind (Hutchins, 1993). The world for him is, to use Heidegger's (1962) expression, 'ready-to-hand'. Activity is much more fundamental than representational knowledge. Doing comes before thinking.

Knowing may be understood as action in an additional sense. As Polanyi (1975) observed, in order to make sense of our experience we necessarily rely on some parts of it subsidiarily in order to attend to our main objective focally. We comprehend something as a whole (focally) by tacitly integrating certain particulars, which are known by the actor subsidiarily. Polanyi's (1975: 36) classic example is the man probing a cavity with his stick. The focus of his attention is at the far end of the stick while attending subsidiarily to the feeling of holding the stick in his hand. This is an important point for it underscores the personal-cum-constructed character of knowledge – something which Polanyi (1962) was so keen to point out. All knowledge, for Polanyi,

involves personal participation (action): the individual *acts* to integrate the particulars of which he/she is subsidiarily aware in order to *know* something focally. Knowing is action.

To sum up thus far, the enactive approach consists of the following three principles. Ontologically, it assumes that actors are beings-in-the-world and, thus, takes social activity as the fundamental building block of the social world. Epistemologically, it highlights the personal-cum-constructed character of human knowledge. And praxeologically, it conceives of action as experimentation, or, to put it differently, thinking and acting are seen as being perpetually engaged in a dialogue (Schon, 1983).

The second question is about who sets strategy. This is an important question since, in focussing our attention on who is involved in the formation of strategy, it enables us to see how different perspectives in SM have conceptualized organizational agency. Three answers can be found in the literature. First, the strategy is set by the strategist(s) who, typically, is the CEO or, at any rate, a few designated individuals in the organization. The important thing to note is that the formation of strategy is a largely *individual* responsibility. Secondly, the strategy is set by the planning system. By this is meant an administrative system of data collection and analysis which, on a routine basis, is charged with formulating the strategy of the organization. Like an expert system, a planning system is supposed to tap into formal knowledge concerning the organization and its environment in a systematic manner, in order to suggest particular courses of action. It is a machine-like version of human cognition: the planning system stands to the strategist as artificial intelligence stands to natural intelligence (Devlin, 1997; Hageuland, 1985). It is recognized that the formulation of strategy is a complex task involving specialist knowledge, which entails the formal setting up of a planning system to cope with such complexity. And thirdly, strategy formation is a fundamentally social process: it occurs in a social context in which there are relations of influence and power as well as social bonds among those involved. In this case, strategy is no longer seen as an individual accomplishment but as a collective endeavour.

Putting these two questions together (How is thinking related to action? Who sets strategy?)

Table 18.1   *Theories of action in strategy research: a meta-theoretical framework*

		How is thinking related to action?	
		Representationalism	Enactivism
Who sets strategy?	Individual	Design School Game-theoretical approach Cognitive School	Entrepreneurial School Constructionist approach
	Planning System	Planning School Positioning School	Scenario-based planning
	Social Process		Culture School Learning School Power School

we obtain Table 18.1, in which the different perspectives on strategy are laid out.

The design school, the cognitive school and game theoretical approaches – which Mintzberg et al. (1998) include in the positioning school – are shown to share the same individualist assumptions with regard to who sets the strategy, and a representationalist approach. Likewise, the planning and positioning schools remain within a representationalist approach while substituting a formal system for analysing and deciding strategy for the individual strategist(s). Here, whatever else strategy may be, it is above all else a systematic analysis of relevant information. Strategy, therefore, as an outcome of such a process, is seen as the commitment of substantial resources in a particular direction over the long term. Driven by already available information, strategy appears as the rational inference to be drawn from a mass of data, rather than as the creative synthesis; it is a measured continuation of past and present trends, not the bold step into the unknown future.

The entrepreneurial school, by privileging the decisive role of the entrepreneur in shaping strategy, is committed to an avowedly individualist conception of strategy formation while, at the same time, showing a much more experimental orientation to action. The entrepreneur does not so much analyse the environment as playfully interacts with it. The world outside the firm is an occasion for creative action not for detached calculation. Scenario-based planning shares also the same enactive approach with the entrepreneurial school while, at the same time, privileging the planning system for constructing scenarios for the

future. It combines the open-endedness towards the world that is characteristic of the enactive approach with an emphasis on a systemic understanding of organizational agency – ultimately it is the system for making scenarios that produces strategies.

The constructionist view – which Mintzberg et al. (1998) include in the cognitive school – is possibly the best illustration of the enactivist approach. It is based on individualist assumptions, since it is the individual strategist who interprets his/her environment and acts on the basis of those interpretations. As Smircich and Stubbart (1985: 726) nicely put it: 'The world is essentially an ambiguous field of experience. There are no threats or opportunities out there in the environment, just material and symbolic records of action. But a strategist – determined to find meaning – makes relationships by bringing connections and patterns to action.'

Finally, the cultural, the power, and the learning schools are paradigmatic cases of both strategy-making-as-a-social-process and the enactive approach. Strategy making is seen taking place within a social context, and this has led researchers to explore the contextual influences on strategy – typically those of power, social learning and culture. Here action is accorded a significant place in explaining strategy. Actors are not detached thinkers making their plans within a social vacuum; rather, they are beings-in-the-world, partaking in social activities, having locally situated knowledge, being connected to networks of influence and power, and mobilizing their political and cultural resources in order to get things done.

Strategy research has opened up over time from a representationalist-cum-individualist approach to include an enactive-cum-social process approach. This has been a reflection of the growing awareness that strategy is a much more complex affair than its formulation by a single decision-maker, or the outcome of detached rational planning. Instead, it has been increasingly realized that the formation of strategy is a primarily social process whose outcome should ideally be a novel one; that the future is not out there to be discovered but is rather invented; that strategy is not plucked out of the tree of some already available strategies but is painstakingly developed to suit a firm's unique profile and circumstances. Such a widening of the agenda of strategy research, a view of which is very engagingly provided by Mintzberg et al. (1998), has also been reflected in the epistemology used: process explanations have increasingly become as prominent as conventional variance-model explanations (Mohr, 1982). Methodologically, case studies and historical analyses have been especially popular in an attempt to capture the contextual dynamics of strategy formation (Mintzberg and Waters, 1982, 1985; Pettigrew, 1985, 1992, 1997; Malerba et al., 1999).

The Missing Element in Strategy Research: A Theory of Creative Action

Although strategy formation as an object of study has been complexified, and such complexity has been reflected in the methodology used in relevant empirical studies, this has not been followed by an equally sophisticated attempt to reconceive the relation between strategy research and business policy advice. In other words, when it comes to praxeology – how should knowledge about strategy be used? – representationalism prevails: there is a difficulty in translating those more contextually sensitive research findings into business policy advice. This is amply illustrated in SM textbooks.

Johnson and Scholes' (1997) best-selling textbook is a good case in point. The authors offer the reader a comprehensive view of SM, including those perspectives that are more explanatory and descriptive in orientation (the power school, the cultural school, etc.). Acknowledging also the influence of context on strategy formation, they encourage managers

to take into account the important issues of politics and culture when designing strategies. However, the bulk of the textbook is taken by the positioning and planning schools. When it comes to offering the reader the necessary conceptual tools with which they may think strategically, the authors tend to resort to industry analysis, generic strategies, and planning techniques. This is also manifested in the way even politics and culture are tackled. They are reduced to quasi-measurable concepts, not substantially different from those used for industry analysis. The representationalist approach is evident throughout the text – it is clearly manifested in the multitude of tables, checklists, and graphs. The organization and its environment are objects that need to be mapped by an independent cognizing subject (that is, the managerial elite) and, on the basis of such mapping, the strategy needs to be formulated.

Even when authors such as Johnson and Scholes are sensitive enough (as they clearly are) to appreciate the difference between strategy formation and strategy formulation, their analysis pays lip service to the former and places emphasis, instead, on the latter. What they seem to be saying is something like this: 'We know that realized strategies are always different from those intended, but in aiming to offer managers advice about how to design their strategies, we need to give them those tools that will enable them to do so.' However, by doing so, they find it difficult to adopt any other but a representationalist position. Consequently, any references to the *unique* features of a firm's dynamic context tend to be downgraded, insofar as such references cannot be expressed but in a (necessarily generic) propositional language. Additionally, *creative action* is downgraded too, since strategic choice is seen to be the outcome of an overtly analytical process that seeks to force the organization to choose from the already existing menu of generic strategies.

The same difficulty is also evident in Mintzberg et al.'s (1998) account of the learning school. Since the essence of the learning school, according to the authors, is the emergence of strategy through experimentation, Mintzberg et al. are also keen to point out that continuous experimentation is not an end in itself, but needs to be balanced with a sense of direction. The key is, note the authors, 'to know what to change when. And that means balancing change with continuity' (Mintzberg et al., 1998: 227). This is indeed the case, but how can one know 'what to change when'? How can one know 'when to cut off initiatives that venture beyond the [strategic] umbrella as opposed to when to enlarge the umbrella to recognize their benefits'? Such questions, to which Mintzberg et al. provide no answer, are especially pertinent, given that Mintzberg et al. criticize certain perspectives (such as the cultural school) for failing 'to let managers know when and how to go about challenging [successful strategies]' (1998: 282) in order to develop their own.

The difficulty Mintzberg et al. (1998) and Johnson and Scholes (1997) have with providing contextually sensitive business policy advice stems from the lack of a theory of creative action (Joas, 1996). Johnson and Scholes (and most authors of SM textbooks) are trapped within a representationalist theory of action, thus being unable to incorporate contextual uniqueness and creative choice into their generic policy advice, while Mintzberg et al., although explicitly espousing novelty as a constitutive feature of strategic action, have not developed it into a coherent theory of creative action.

A good illustration of the difficulties of a representationalist theory of action to conceive of human action as anything else but instrumental application of propositions is Goold's (1992) reply to Mintzberg (1990b), regarding the latter's account of a BCG (1975) report – especially the report's handling of the development of Honda's strategy to enter the American motorcycle market. Goold (1992: 169), a co-author of the report, points out that the report never attempted to answer historical questions such as 'how did this situation arise?' but managerial questions such as 'what should we do?'. As Goold (1992: 169–70) remarks, 'its purpose was to discern what lay behind and accounted for Honda's success, in a way that would help others to think through what strategies would be likely to work. [...] [The report tried] to discern patterns in Honda's strategic decisions and actions, and to use these patterns in identifying what works well and badly.'

How did the report achieve this? By mobilizing an array of concepts borrowed from the positioning school, especially pointing out

Honda's dedication to low cost aided by its large-scale domestic production. 'The basic philosophy of the Japanese manufacturers,' says the report, 'is that high volumes per model provide the potential for high productivity as a result of using capital intensive and highly automated techniques. Their marketing strategies are, therefore, directed towards developing these high model volumes, hence the careful attention that we have observed them giving to growth and market share' (BCG, 1975: 59).

Notice the rationalizing language of the BCG report. Honda's success in the American motorcycle market is explained by making use of concepts from the positioning school. But this is exactly where the problem lies. What the report says does make sense, but it does so by giving an *ex post facto* rationalizing account of events. Looking *back* at Honda's success, the BCG report reconstructs it in its own image, so to speak. It shows us the structure of an already built system, but tells us very little about *how* that system came to be built in the first place; it is silent on precisely those *action* questions which are most important for practitioners: how did it occur to Honda to follow the strategy it did? How did it happen? How did they do it, at that particular time and place? Why this strategy and not something else?

BCG's explanation of the Honda success leaves *action* out of the picture: we see nothing in the account provided by BCG, about Honda managers' *reasons* for doing what they did; no statement describing their *beliefs* and *desires* that led them to undertake the actions they did. BCG's account is a paradigmatic case in SM of what philosophers call 'extensional descriptions': any true description of behaviour will remain true whenever we substitute equivalent descriptions into it (Rosenberg, 1988: 48). Indeed, one can easily imagine countless other managers in BCG's account being substituted for Honda's particular managers, without changing the content of the account provided. That those particular Honda managers, at that particular point in time, at that particular place, held those particular beliefs and desires, which led them to undertake that particular stream of actions, are of no consequence to BCG's explanation. Yet our common experience tells us, and philosophical analysis shows, that explaining human action without reference to non-substitutable beliefs and desires is profoundly flawed (Rosenberg, 1988; Bohman, 1991).

Goold dismisses *action* questions as irrelevant for managers and that is why he describes, misleadingly, the learning school as advocating 'random experiments' (Goold, 1992: 170). History is irrelevant, he is, in effect, saying; strategic action needs to be based on strong foundations consisting of 'extensional models' (Rosenberg, 1988) derived from past experiences. For Goold (and for several others), to answer the managerial question 'what should we do now?' implies that a generic model should be built from *past* experiences, and this model should then be used by others in the *future*. Strategic action is seen as being propositional in structure: if in a situation like Honda's, then do something similar to what Honda did. Or if you want to do what Honda did, try to create conditions similar to those of Honda's. On this view, managers should look for those (Cartesian) 'clear and distinct ideas' on the basis of which they may reliably base their actions. Successful action is derived from reliable, codified knowledge, not from an experimental orientation towards the world. The strategist should not let himself/herself be surprised by the world; instead, the world should fit into the strategist's categories – the latter have logical priority over the former. Taken to its logical extreme, such a position encourages imitation, not creativity – do what others did, or what is typically done, slightly adapted, perhaps, to your circumstances. Needless to say that such a mode of thinking cannot accommodate Porter's (1991) desiderata for a dynamic theory of strategy.

CONCLUSIONS

Searching for a dynamic theory of strategy has been something like searching for the Holy Grail in SM. It has increasingly been recognized that for a firm to create and sustain a competitive advantage it must position itself uniquely in its industry and develop its internal capabilities in such a way as to make it very difficult for its competitors to imitate it. Moreover, a firm must do these things continuously. To put it simply, the current orthodoxy

in SM underlines the uniqueness of the firm, the novelty of its choices, and the time-dependent nature of its development (Hamel and Prahalad, 1994; Kay, 1995; Porter, 1991; Markides, 1999). All this may sound obvious to practitioners but not necessarily to theorists!

As we hope we have shown in this chapter, the economic models that have provided the bedrock for most of the research on business strategy have been unable to adequately account for endogenous change, for process and time, and for creative action. Insofar as the neo-classical firm has had any theoretical reason to exist at all, it has been thought to be an entity possessing no internal complexity and without a history, since changes in its productive knowledge are attributed entirely to exogenous shifts in its production function. Focussing predominantly on explaining outcomes, economic models have tended to view the firm from 'outside': firms strive to optimally respond to environmental conditions or to organizational problems rather than creatively engage with them in real time (cf. Rumelt et al., 1991).

As the Honda illustration mentioned earlier shows, on this view, strategy exists as a theoretically validated set of prescriptions waiting to be discovered by particular firms. There is a set of generic strategies that has been deduced and validated from the study of firms' aggregate strategic behaviour in the past, which serves as a menu for a particular firm to choose from. Such a deductive mode of explanation has been linked with a closed-world ontology and an instrumental praxeology. Even when economic actors behave in new and unexpected ways, as for example in the case of Honda, the dominant tendency has been to explain their novel strategic choices in terms of the existing vocabulary of strategy theories (to be precise, in terms of the vocabulary of the positioning school). Novel outcomes are accounted for by extensional descriptions containing substitutable actors who apply timeless, generic, subject-free formulae.

As well as strategy research being largely dominated by a preference for outcome explanations, it has tended to cluster around a theory of action that privileges representationalism and individualism. Strategy has been conceptualized as the exercise of (mostly) individual cognition followed by implementation (Huff, 1990). From that perspective, the purpose of strategy research has predominantly been the supply of managers with increasingly sophisticated formal models capturing essential features of firms and their environments. Knowledge of such models has been thought to be propositional in structure and thus instrumentally applicable by practitioners.

In this chapter we critiqued that view (which is best represented by the planning and cognitive schools) and argued that formal strategy models cannot offer contextually sensitive and time-sensitive advice, nor can they formally suggest novel ways of acting. Their analyses are heavily skewed towards past behaviours while they incorporate the premise that a firm needs to choose its strategy from a currently available menu of ideal-type strategies. Strategy, on that view, is discovered; it is not invented; it is more an inferential rather than a creative process.

The field of SM (and much of management studies, for that matter) has suffered from what Bergson (1946) and James (1909/1996) called 'intellectualism'. Intellectualism is the reduction of human experience into a conceptual order. Why is this a problem? It is a problem for the reason that, as James (1909/1996) notes, 'an immediate experience, as yet unnamed or classed, is a mere *that* that we undergo, a thing that asks, *"What* am I". When we name and class it, we say for the first time what it is, and all these whats are abstract names or concepts' (emphasis in the original). Using concepts is an efficient way of handling experience, for once we have classed the various parts of experience in concepts, we can treat them by the law of the class they belong to. However, the real problem intellectualism presents consists in the fact that when we start identifying experience with concepts, we tend to treat the latter as a substitute for the former and, thus, 'deny the very properties with which the things sensibly present themselves' (James, 1909/1996: 218–19). To put it simply, reality is much more complex and rich than our concepts and theories allow for.

Social scientific understanding aims at a level of generality which glosses over particularities, imperfections, uniqueness. Yet it is taking advantage of those particularities and imperfections that gives a company an edge over its competitors (Nelson, 1991; Spender, 1996). For these features of reality to be made sense of, the faculty of perceiving needs to be given higher priority over the faculty of conceiving. Whereas concepts class our experiences and thus obliterate differences, in perception we are attentive to qualitative differences. Action is always situational and it takes place in time. Practitioners necessarily act *in concreto*, no matter how much they have been informed *in abstracto* about certain regularities (Schon, 1983; Tsoukas, 1996, 1998a).

Remember the language of the BCG (1975) report? Honda's success in America was thought to be due to their emphasis on high volume, which led them to pursue market share, which was linked with high productivity, and so on. This is a prime example of intellectualism. The situated action of those particular Honda managers is described via a timeless, generic proposition that has been validated through the study of aggregates of firms in the past. Details, personalities, interpretations, timing, context – all these particularities do not seem to matter. They are mere appearances that can be glossed over in search of the essential forces that move companies – the Four Principles, the Seven Dilemmas, the Key Drivers. What is, however, missing from such intellectualist accounts is something which practitioners intuitively understand: uniqueness; an answer to the question 'why them and not others?'. Countless companies tried to enter foreign markets, but having codified such experiences would not necessarily have given the Honda managers concrete advice as to what to do when contemplating penetrating the American market. What made the difference was how *they read* the situation; their perceptiveness in seeing connections (Strawson, 1992: Ch. 2); their sense of unease; their boldness in undertaking action in the face of uncertainty about the consequences of their action. Such an understanding is not nomological, and such action is not propositional (Berlin, 1996: 15–39).

In order to explain distinctiveness and singularity, and incorporate time and creative action in their theoretical accounts, strategy researchers need to engage in ethnographic and historical modes of research. They need to adopt process explanations, if they wish to do justice to potential novelty, to human agency, and to the situatedness of strategy making. In process explanations, it is possible to show the links between thought and action as they unfold in time, and to focus on the historicity of the social context (the cultural and political dynamics) surrounding strategy making. It is also possible to avoid the dilemma choice vs change that was mentioned in the introduction, since, in process explanations, change is all there is, and change cannot be comprehended without human agency (strategic choice).

There is a respectable tradition of qualitative research in strategy that is close to process explanations, but it has tended to be relatively atheoretical. As well as thick descriptions of strategy making, we also need theories of creative action in organizations. How new actions emerge and how they cohere to constitute a pattern (Mintzberg and Waters, 1985); how re-description through the metaphorical use of language occurs (Rorty, 1991) and how new descriptions are legitimated in particular contexts (Burgelman, 1988); and how key actors' historically formed webs of beliefs influence strategic choice (Pettigrew, 1985; Woiceshyn, 1997), are important issues such theories ought to address. Process explanations, however, lack the generality of outcome explanations. It will not be possible to offer practitioners propositional advice, transcending context and time. If actors are not substitutable and their actions are not interchangeable, business policy advice will not be possible to be algorithmic – it can at best draw attention to things that matter. But what process accounts lose in scope they gain in depth: by re-entering the world of practitioners hermeneutically, process accounts may connect with the concrete experiences of practitioners, thus inviting them to reflect on their circumstances in novel ways (Tsoukas, 1998a: 56–7; Weick, 1990: 7). The utility of process accounts lies not so much in the standard reactions they evoke but in their mode of use: they offer practitioners the chance to reflect on, and make links with, others' experiences thus leading to potentially new forms of action. To paraphrase Weick (1990: 7), good strategy theorizing, like good strategies, invites practitioners to 'rewrite' their experiences in order to construct new strategies. From a process-cum-enactivist perspective, just like thought and action are reflectively connected, so are strategy theorizing and strategy making.

REFERENCES

Andrews, K. R. (1980) *The Concept of Corporate Strategy*. Homewood, Ill: Richard D. Irwin Inc.

Ansoff, I. H. (1965) *Corporate Strategy*. London: Penguin Books.
Ansoff, I. H. (1987) 'The emerging paradigm of strategic behavior', *Strategic Management Journal*, 8: 501–15.
Ansoff, I. H. (1991) 'Critique of Henry Mintzberg's "The design school: reconsidering the basic premises of strategic management"', *Strategic Management Journal*, 12: 449–61.
Araujo, L. and Easton, G. (1996) 'Strategy: where is the pattern?', *Organization*, 3: 361–83.
Austin, J. L. (1962) *How to Do Things with Words*. Cambridge, MA: Harvard University Press.
Bergson, H. (1946) *The Creative Mind*. New York: Citadel Press.
Berlin, I. (1996) *The Sense of Reality*. London: Pimlico. pp. 1–39.
Besanko, D., Dranove, D. and Shansley, M. (1996) *Economics of Strategy*. New York: John Wiley.
Bhaskar, R. (1978) *A Realist Theory of Science*. Hassocks, England: The Harvester Press.
Bicchieri, C. (1993) *Rationality and Coordination*. Cambridge: Cambridge University Press.
Binmore, K. (1990) *Essays on the Foundations of Game Theory*. Oxford: Blackwell.
Bohman, J. (1991) *New Philosophy of Social Science*. Cambridge: Polity Press.
Boston Consulting Group, Inc. (BCG) (1975) *Strategy Alternatives for the British Motorcycle Industry*. London: Her Majesty's Stationery Office.
Boudon, R. (1981) *The Logic of Social Action*. London: Routledge & Kegan Paul.
Bowman, E. H. (1995) 'Strategic history: through different mirrors', *Advances in Strategic Management*, 11A: 25–45.
Burgelman, R. A. (1988) 'Strategy making as a social learning process: the case of internal corporate venturing', *Interfaces*, 18: 74–85.
Calori, R. (1998) '*Essai*: philosophizing on strategic management models', *Organization Studies*, 19: 281–306.
Camerer, C. (1985) 'Redirecting strategy research in business policy and strategy', *Strategic Management Journal*, 6: 1–15.
Chandler, A. (1990) *Strategy and Structure*. First edition, 1962. Cambridge, Mass: MIT Press.
Chandler, A. (1992) 'Organizational capabilities and the economic history of the industrial enterprise', *Journal of Economic Perspectives*, 6: 79–100.
Cohen, B. (1994) 'Newton and the social sciences, with special reference to economics, or, the case of the missing paradigm', in P. Mirowski (ed.), *Natural Images in Economic Thought*. Cambridge: Cambridge University Press. pp. 55–90.
Cyert, R. M. and March, J. G. (1963) *A Behavioral Theory of the Firm*. Englewood Cliffs, NJ: Prentice Hall.
Demsetz, H. (1973) 'Industry structure, market rivalry, and public policy', *Journal of Law and Economics*, 16: 1–9.
Descartes, R. (1968) *Discourse on Method and the Meditations*. London: Penguin.
Devlin, K. (1997) *Goodbye, Descartes*. New York: Wiley.

Donaldson, L. (1995) *American Anti-Management Theories of Organizations*. Cambridge: Cambridge University Press.

Elster, J. (1983) *Explaining Technical Change*. Cambridge: Cambridge University Press.

Gharajedaghi, J. and Ackoff, R. (1984) 'Mechanisms, organisms, and social systems', *Strategic Management Journal*, 5: 289–300.

Ghemawat, P. (1991) *Commitment: The Dynamic of Strategy*. New York: Free Press.

Ghemawat, G. (1997) *Games Businesses Play*. Cambridge, Mass: The MIT Press.

Gilbert, D. R. Jr, Hartman, E., Mauriel, J. J. and Freeman, R. E. (1988) *A Logic for Strategy*. New York: Ballinger.

Goold, M. (1992) 'Design, learning and planning: a further observation on the design school debate', *Strategic Management Journal*, 13: 169–70.

Gopinath, C. and Hoffman, R. (1995) 'The relevance of strategy research: practitioner and academic viewpoints', *Journal of Management Studies*, 32: 575–94.

Hagueland, J. (1985) *Artificial Intelligence*. Cambridge, MA: The MIT Press.

Hamel, G. and Prahalad, C. K. (1994) *Competing for the Future*. Boston, MA: Harvard Business School Press.

Hayek, F. (1948) 'Economics and knowledge', in F. Hayek, *Individualism and Economic Order*. London: Routledge.

Hedstrom, P. and Swedberg, R. (1998) *Social Mechanisms*. Cambridge: Cambridge University Press.

Heidegger, M. (1962) *Being and Time*. New York: Harper & Row.

Huff, A. S. (ed.) (1990) *Mapping Strategic Thought*. Chichester: Wiley.

Hutchins, E. (1993) 'Learning to navigate', in S. Chaiklin and J. Lave (eds), *Understanding Practice*. Cambridge: Cambridge University Press. pp. 35–63.

James, W. (1909/1996) *A Pluralistic Universe*. Lincoln: University of Nebraska Press.

Joas, H. (1996) *The Creativity of Action*. Translated by J. Gaines and P. Keast. Cambridge: Polity Press.

Johnson, G. and Scholes, K. (1997) *Exploring Corporate Strategy*, fourth edition. London: Prentice Hall.

Kay, J. (1995) *Foundations of Corporate Success*. Oxford: Oxford University Press.

Knudsen, C. (1993) 'Equilibrium, perfect rationality and the problem of self-reference in economics', in U. Mäki, B. Gustafsson and C. Knudsen (eds), *Rationality, Institutions and Economic Methodology*. London: Routledge.

Knudsen, C. (1996) 'The competence perspective: a historical review', in N. J. Foss and C. Knudsen (eds), *Towards a Competence Theory of the Firm*. London: Routledge. pp. 13–37.

Kreps, D. M. (1990) 'Corporate culture and economic theory', in J. E. Alt and K. Shepsle (eds), *Perspectives on Positive Political Economy*. Cambridge: Cambridge University Press.

Kuhn, T. (1970) *The Structure of Scientific Revolutions*. Chicago: University of Chicago Press.

Latsis, S. (1972) 'Situational determinism in economics', *British Journal for the Philosophy of Science*, 23: 207–45.

Latsis, S. (1976) 'A research programme in economics', in S. Latsis (ed.), *Method and Appraisal in Economics*. Cambridge: Cambridge University Press. pp. 1–42.

Lawson, T. (1997) *Economics and Reality*. London: Routledge.

Learned, E. P., Christensen, C. R., Andrews, K. R. and Gush, W. D. (1965) *Business Policy*. Homewood, IL: Richard D. Irwin.

Lindblom, C. E. (1968) *The Policy Making Process*. Englewood Cliffs, NJ: Prentice-Hall.

Machlup, F. (1955) 'The problem of verification in economics', *Southern Economic Journal*, 21: 1–21.

MacIntyre, A. (1985) *After Virtue*. London: Duckworth, Second Edition.

Mahoney, J. (1993) 'Strategic management and determinism: sustaining the conversation', *Journal of Management Studies*, 30: 173–91.

Malerba, F., Nelson, R., Orsenigo, L. and Winter, S. (1999) '"History-friendly" models of industry evolution: the computer industry', *Industrial and Corporate Change*, 8: 3–40.

March, J. G. (1994) *A Primer on Decision Making*. New York: The Free Press.

Markides, C. C. (1999) 'A dynamic view of strategy', *Sloan Management Review*, 40: 55–64.

McClelland, E. F. (1993) 'Rationality, constitutions, and the ethics of rules', *Constitutional Political Economy*, 4: 173–210.

Mintzberg, H. (1990a) 'Strategy formation: schools of thought', in J. W. Fredrickson (ed.), *Perspectives on Strategic Management*. New York: Harper Business. pp. 105–236.

Mintzberg, H. (1990b) 'The design school: reconsidering the basic premises of strategic management', *Strategic Management Journal*, 11: 171–95.

Mintzberg, H. and Waters, J. A. (1982) 'Tracking strategy in an entrepreneurial firm', *Academy of Management Journal*, 25: 465–99.

Mintzberg, H. and Waters, J. A. (1985) 'Of strategies, deliberate and emergent', *Strategic Management Journal*, 6: 257–72.

Mintzberg, H., Ahlstrand, B. and Lampel, J. (1998) *Strategy Safari*. London: Prentice-Hall.

Mirowski, P. (1989) *More Heat than Light: Economics as Social Physics, Physics as Nature's Economics*. Cambridge: Cambridge University Press.

Moch, M. and Huff, A. S. (1983) 'Power enactment through language and ritual', *Journal of Business Research*, 11: 293–316.

Mohr, L. (1982) *Explaining Organizational Behavior*. San Francisco: Jossey-Bass Publishers.

Nelson, R. (1991) 'Why firms differ, and how does it matter?', *Strategic Management Journal*, 12: 61–74.

Nelson, R. and Winter, S. (1982) *An Evolutionary Theory of Economic Change*. Cambridge, MA: The Belknap Press of Harvard University Press.

Penrose, E. T. (1955) 'Limits to the growth and size of firms', *American Economic Review, Papers and Proceedings*, 45: 531–43.

Penrose, E. T. (1959) *The Theory of the Growth of the Firm*. Oxford: Oxford University Press.

Pettigrew, A. M. (1985) *The Awakening Giant*. Oxford: Blackwell.

Pettigrew, A. M. (1990) 'Longitudinal field research on change: theory and practice', *Organization Science*, 1: 267–92.

Pettigrew, A. M. (1992) 'The character and significance of strategy process research', *Strategic Management Journal*, 13: 5–16.

Pettigrew, A. M. (1997) 'What is a processual analysis?', *Scandinavian Journal of Management*, 13: 337–48.

Polanyi, M. (1962) *Personal Knowledge: Towards a Post-Critical Philosophy*. Chicago: University of Chicago Press.

Polanyi, M. (1975) 'Personal knowledge', in M. Polanyi and H. Prosch, *Meaning*. Chicago: University of Chicago Press.

Popper, K. (1988) *The Open Universe*. London: Hutchinson.

Porter, M. E. (1980) *Competitive Strategy*. New York: The Free Press.

Porter, M. E. (1991) 'Towards a dynamic theory of strategy', *Strategic Management Journal*, 12: 95–117.

Quinn, J. B. (1980) *Strategies for Change*. Homewood, IL: Irwin.

Reed, E. S. (1996) *The Necessity of Experience*. New Haven: Yale University Press.

Rorty, R. (1980) *Philosophy and the Mirror of Nature*. Oxford: Blackwell.

Rorty, R. (1991) *Objectivity, Relativism and Truth*. Cambridge: Cambridge University Press.

Rosenberg, A. (1988) *Philosophy of Social Science*. Oxford: Clarendon Press.

Rumelt, R. P., Schendel, D. and Teece, D. J. (1991) 'Strategic management and economics', *Strategic Management Journal*, 12: 5–29.

Rumelt, R. P., Schendel, D. E. and Teece, D. J. (1994) 'Fundamental issues in strategy', in R. P. Rumelt, D. E. Schendel and D. J. Teece (eds), *Fundamental Issues in Strategy*. Boston, MA: Harvard Business School Press. pp. 9–47.

Saloner, G. (1991) 'Modelling, game theory, and strategic management', *Strategic Management Journal*, 12: 5–29.

Samuelson, P. (1947) *The Foundations of Economic Analysis*. Cambridge: Harvard University Press.

Schelling, T. (1960) *The Strategy of Conflict*. Cambridge: Harvard University Press.

Schendel, D. E. and Hofer, C. (1979) 'Theory building and theory testing in strategic management', in D. E. Schendel and C. Hofer (eds), *Strategic Management*. Boston, MA: Little, Brown and Co. pp. 382–94.

Scherer, F. M. (1970) *Industrial Market Structure and Economic Performance*. Chicago: Rand-McNally.

Scherer, A. G. and Dowling, M. J. (1995) 'Towards a reconciliation of the theory-pluralism in strategic management – incommensurability and the constructivist approach of the Erlangen school', *Advances in Strategic Management*, 12A: 195–247.

Schon, D. (1983) *The Reflective Practitioner*. London: Avebury.

Schwenk, C. R. and Dalton, D. R. (1991) 'The changing shape of strategic management research', *Advances in Strategic Management*, 7: 277–300.

Selten, R. (1975) 'Reexamination of the perfectness concept for equilibrium points in extensive games', *International Journal of Game Theory*, 4: 25–35.

Selten, R. (1990) 'Bounded rationality', *Journal of Institutional and Theoretical Economics*, 146: 649–58.

Shrivastava, P. (1987) 'Rigor and practical usefulness of research in strategic management', *Strategic Management Journal*, 8: 77–92.

Simon, H. (1978) 'Rationality as process and as product of thought', *American Economic Review, Papers and Proceedings*, May: 1–16.

Simon, H. (1979) 'Rational decision making in business organizations', *American Economic Review*, 69: 493–513.

Simon, H. (1983) *Reason in Human Affairs*. Stanford: Stanford University Press.

Singer, A. E. (1994) 'Strategy as moral philosophy', *Strategic Management Journal*, 15: 191–213.

Smircich, L. and Stubbart, C. (1985) 'Strategic management in an enacted world', *Academy of Management Review*, 10: 724–36.

Soros, G. (1987) *The Alchemy of Finance*, second edition. New York: Wiley.

Spender, J-C. (1993) 'Some frontier activities around strategy theorizing', *Journal of Management Studies*, 30: 11–30.

Spender, J-C. (1996) 'Organizational knowledge, learning and memory: three concepts in search of a theory', *Journal of Organizational Change Management*, 9: 63–78.

Stigler, G. J. and Becker, G. (1977) 'De gustibus non est disputandum', *American Economic Review*, 67: 76–90.

Strawson, P. F. (1992) *Analysis and Metaphysics*. London: Oxford University Press.

Taylor, C. (1985) *Philosophy and the Human Sciences*, Vol. 2. Cambridge: Cambridge University Press.

Taylor, C. (1993) 'To follow a rule...', in C. Calhoun, E. LiPuma and M. Postone (eds), *Bourdieu: Critical Perspectives*. Cambridge: Polity Press. pp. 45–59.

Thomas, H. and Pruett, M. (1993) 'Editorial: perspectives on theory building in strategic management', *Journal of Management Studies*, 30: 3–10.

Tirole, J. (1988) *The Theory of Industrial Organization*. Cambridge, MA: The MIT Press.

Toulmin, S. (1990) *Cosmopolis*. Chicago: The University of Chicago Press.

Tsoukas, H. (1994) 'Refining common sense: types of knowledge in management studies', *Journal of Management Studies*, 31: 761–80.

Tsoukas, H. (1996) 'The firm as a distributed knowledge system: a constructionist approach', *Strategic Management Journal*, 17 (Winter Special Issue): 11–25.

Tsoukas, H. (1998a) 'Forms of knowledge and forms of life in organized contexts', in R. Chia (ed.), *In the Realm of Organization*. London: Routledge. pp. 43–66.

Tsoukas, H. (1998b) 'The word and the world: a critique of representationalism in management research', *International Journal of Public Administration*, 21: 781–817.

Ullmann-Margalitt, E. (1977) *The Emergence of Norms*. Oxford: Clarendon Press.

Varela, F. J., Thompson, E. and Rosch, E. (1991) *The Embodied Mind*. Cambridge, MA: The MIT Press.

Weick, K. (1990) 'Introduction: cartographic myths in organizations', in A. S. Huff (ed.), *Mapping Strategic Thought*. Chichester: Wiley. pp. 1–10.

Winograd, T. and Flores, F. (1987) *Understanding Computers and Cognition*. Reading, MA: Addison-Wesley.

Winter, S. (1988) 'On Coase, competence and corporation', *Journal of Law, Economics and Organizations*, 4: 163–80.

Wittgenstein, L. (1958) *Philosophical Investigations*. Oxford: Blackwell.

Woiceshyn, J. (1997) 'The role of management in the adoption of technology: a longitudinal investigation', *Technology Studies*, 4: 62–99.

Zan, L. (1990) 'Looking for theories in strategy studies', *Scandinavian Journal of Management*, 6: 89–108.

19

Business History and Strategy

DAVID J. JEREMY

For long one of the Cinderellas of the MBA curriculum, 'longitudinal', 'temporal', alias historical, perspectives on organizational strategy are now seen as increasingly useful. This is hardly surprising: the present is after all the product of the past. However, over the past two or three decades the old axiom has been given new relevance and explanation by several outstanding historical contributions to concepts of strategic management. Alfred D. Chandler, Jr. has demonstrated the evolutionary and historical nature of strategic change. Douglass C. North has stressed the role of institutions in shaping both organizational environments and organizations themselves. Their work has been highly influential and widely recognized, with Chandler receiving a Pulitzer and North a Nobel prize.

Chandler and North have built their generalized theoretical insights on a foundation of empirical research. A lot of this has been done by historians of business over the past half century. Chandler and North represent the peaks of business history research. Yet most of this work is unknown to and unused by management theorists. The purpose of this chapter is to explore the relationship between business history and the study of strategy; briefly to describe the development of business history as an intellectual discipline; to outline what business history has contributed to an understanding of management strategy; and to introduce the techniques of the business historian. Finally, the chapter

offers some items for a future research agenda.

In contrast to economic history, which deals with the history of economic activity at the level of an economy (national or international) or an industry, business history is concerned with the history of firms (singly or collectively), their members (entrepreneurs, managers, or employees, singly or collectively), and relationships between firms or their members and the larger contexts of economy and society. Business history draws upon several disciplines, including history (Lee, 1990b), economics (Lee, 1990a), and management (Hendry, 1992). However, the dominant discipline is history.

Strategic management, as the essays in this volume emphasize, is concerned with explaining and predicting 'how firms achieve and sustain competitive advantage' (Teece et al., 1997: 509). In essence it entails 'the determination of the basic long-term goals and objectives of an enterprise, and the adoption of courses of action and the allocation of resources necessary for carrying out these goals' (Chandler, 1962: 13).

THE RELATIONSHIP BETWEEN BUSINESS HISTORY AND THE STUDY OF STRATEGY

If two of the central elements of strategic management are sustaining competitive advantage and engaging with long-term horizons, how do historical dimensions mesh with strategic ones? The first element in strategic management, sustaining competitive advantage, would be enriched, if it does not demand historical inputs. Competitive advantage theory has centred on three or four frameworks since 1980 (Teece et al., 1997). Porter (1980, 1985, 1990), whose paradigm was dominant for a decade, related the company to its environment. At the industry level, five forces threatened or advantaged the firm: entry barriers, rivalry between industry incumbents, substitute products or services, the bargaining power of suppliers, and the bargaining power of buyers. At an international level, four forces were sources of national competitive advantage: factor conditions; firm strategy, structure, and rivalry; demand conditions; and clusters of related industries (the 'diamond'). In addition government policies, culture, and chance might, much less predictably, play a part. None of these forces acts outside time frames. The present is always to some extent the product of the past. Business historians, aware of the usefulness of Porter's categories, have begun exploring past-to-present strategies using his framework (Singleton, 1997).

Another competitive advantage framework was the strategic conflict approach, using game theory. However, more widely accepted has been the resource-based view of the firm, going back to Penrose (1959). While industrial organization theorists like Porter explain competitive advantage in terms of market positioning, the resource-based theorists point to 'internally generated competencies' (Scarbrough, 1998: 220). The firm is seen as a bundle of 'firm-specific capabilities and assets' (Teece et al., 1997: 510). Resources are firm-specific assets difficult or impossible to imitate (such as trade secrets). Competencies or capabilities are firm-specific assets spread across individuals or groups enabling them to perform distinctive activities. Teece et al. (1997: 510) argue that the competitive advantage of a firm lies with organizational processes 'shaped by its (specific) asset position, and the paths available to it'. Most pertinent for the business historian, by managerial and organizational processes they mean the firm's 'routines, or patterns of current practice and learning. By position [they] refer to its current specific endowments of technology, intellectual property, complementary assets, customer base, and its external relations with suppliers and complementors. By paths [they] refer to the strategic alternatives available to the firm, and presence or absence of increasing returns and attendant path dependencies' (Teece et al., 1997: 518).

A pillar in Teece et al.'s model of 'dynamic capabilities framework' is the concept of path dependencies. 'Where a firm can go is a function of its current position and the paths ahead. Its current position is often shaped by the path it has traveled' (1997: 522). Earlier investments and routines shape the firm's current endowment. Their concept is predicated on the assumption that the firm's opportunities for learning are 'local' (close to previous activities), because learning is a matter of trial and error. Spreading too widely beyond previous activities threatens the ability to learn clearly what brings success (increasing returns to scale or to adoption of new techniques) or failure (the reverse). Path dependency reaches into the future because of its implications for technological opportunities. A firm engaging in R&D is likely to find that its prior research activities will constrain what opportunities its management may perceive or justify for future investment (Teece et al., 1997: 524).

A resource-based view of the firm pays much attention to the role of the past. As Teece et al. emphasize, 'history matters' (1997: 522). However, as yet, business historians have produced no major studies intensively utilizing this resources and capabilities framework. Since Teece et al. proposed their model, attention to the resource and capabilities framework has increased among theorists of strategic management. History is now well recognized as one tool for exploring firm origins, failure, and growth paths (Helfat, 2000).

The second element in strategic management is long-termism into the future. In contrast, business history is about long-termism into the past. Presumably there are linkages between the two. Potential meeting points are suggested by the themes which preoccupy the business historian, as much as any other kind of historian: change, continuity, constraint, and context. Change over time is the historian's core perspective. Contrasts between past and present allow change to be tracked, measured, assessed. Business growth and performance, indicators of the effectiveness of strategic choices, cannot be evaluated without the use of past evidence. In learning from past experience, drop-outs, failures, dead-ends are as instructive as success. Countering change, invariably there are continuities. Ritual, symbol, myth, and story have pointed the mortar of family, class, social structure, and network, by which social stability in the face of change is preserved.

The greatest of all continuities, of course, is human nature. While this might undergo evolutionary change over aeons of time, within recorded history there is little or no evidence to show that in their collective or individual behaviours 21st century people are essentially different from the peoples of ancient Greece or Rome, of Meiji Japan, or of the Progressive Era of the American Republic. Cultural differences of course exist but essential 'humanness' persists. Constraints in the organization have come from groups or single individuals threatened by change beyond their control – a managerial elite threatened by corporate change following a merger, or the dynamic entrepreneur threatened by advancing age, for example. Outside the organization constraints have been imposed by contexts – political or market or technological changes, for example. Last, historians are interested in contexts and circumstances. Organizational behaviour, of individuals or groups, always occurs in a wider setting – within the firm, the industry, the national economy, the global economy, the local community, the region, the nation, the international alliance. As much as change and continuity, constraints and contexts are rooted in the past and reach into the present.

From their side, strategists are rediscovering the significance of the historical (Barnett and Burgelman, 1996). As already seen, the pace and path of strategic change emerges from predecessor organizational experience, even when a new organization is formed. The process of strategy selection is affected by previous rates and paths of organizational change – strategy is 'path-dependent'. Again, past examples show that there is no single route for achieving the strategic goals of an organization. Awareness of past trajectories is therefore important. In learning from the past, failures are as important as successes. Within the organization a process (processes) of strategy selection occurs. Choice, amendment, and rejection of strategies is pursued via an interactive consideration of strategic goals and tactical means. Decision-making quality rests upon a reliable knowledge of organizational resources, many of which have been accumulated over time. People resources, in contrast to capital, have all manner of cultural 'baggage'. Without taking this into account (as Japanese firms do with their intensely consultative *ringi* system), top-down, long-term decision-making becomes time-consuming and problematic to implement.

Bridging the perspectives of the business historian (historian) to those of the strategist meets one potentially serious problem: their respective presuppositions about time. Strategic concepts of time have been summarized and classified by Mosakowski and Earley (2000). Historians' views of the past and how it should be understood have been debated and reviewed for centuries (see Marwick, 1970; Bebbington, 1979). Both historians and strategists, for the most part, agree that the *nature of time* is real (rather than epiphenomenal). On the *experience of time*, while most strategists have viewed it as objective, historians would usually see it as both objective and subjective, pinning their narratives around objective events (like an individual's birth or death) but readily taking subjective perspectives, offered by, say, an actor's diaries, at other points.

On the *flow of time* (novel, cyclical, punctuated – repetitive events punctuated by novel ones), strategists can be found for all views. Western historians, following Christian tradition, see time as linear (novel in the long run) but meanwhile characterized by cycles (life, dynastic, seasonal; trade, for example). In contrast, the Asian view of history, deriving from Buddhism, is based on cosmic cycles within which the other cycles move. The *structure of time* (the fourth dimension according to Mosakowski and Earley) may be discrete (equal units of time), continuous (with events being regarded as more significant than units of time), or epochal (units of time being regarded as unequal). Again, strategists have used each of these and the same can be said for historians. Last, there is the *referent anchor in time*: 'whether time perceptions are anchored with a referent point in the past, present, or future' (Mosakowski and Earley, 2000: 800). Strategists espousing a resource-based view of strategy emphasize past and future, rather than the present. Historians tend to think along a past-and-present axis. This last dimension of time is the one at which the widest divergence occurs between historians and strategists. Strategists want to predict the future using the past. Historians want to understand the past using the present.

This points to a second difficulty: the predictive power of the past. On this historians have divided (Bebbington, 1979: 140–60). Positivists hold that there are regularities to be traced in human behaviour. The historian's task is then to conduct empirical investigations to establish general laws. For this the appropriate methods are those of the social sciences. In contrast, the idealists (following Ranke and the German historians of the 19th century) consider the historical method unique. Human beings are unique and distinctive because they have ideas. Particularity, not generalization, is the concern of an historian. The historian's method is therefore distinctive from that of the social scientist. Many business historians would claim sympathy with both schools of historiography. In studying organizations or groups of individuals they would turn to the methods of the social sciences. In addition, and certainly with single individual profiles, they would resort to the position and approach of the idealists.

While the positivist approach seems most useful for the strategists, it should be noted that, following Popper (1957), few today would accept the idea that the past is determined, in the sense that movements and events happened inevitably. If the past is not determined, how can the future be predicted? The answer, presumably, is that choices made in the past limit possible outcomes in the present; into the future, choices made in the present limit possible outcomes five, ten, or whatever years ahead.

Mosakowski and Earley (2000: 806) note that research on decision-making often avoids individual decision-makers and simply anthropomorphizes the firm. An historical idealist approach would avoid that pitfall. However, there is still the problem of linking individual managers to firm-level strategies. This involves either finding explicit evidence for cause and effect, with specific strategies and outcomes traceable to particular managers, or it requires finding links between different levels of analysis (the individual and the firm in this case). Mosakowski and Earley (2000), and earlier

Pettigrew (1990, 1997), suggest that attention to perceptions of time may be one such link. For example, the manager may 'focus on long-term planning around hypothesized past critical events in an effort to predict and plan for the punctuated change' (Mosakowski and Earley, 2000: 806).

The skills and techniques of the historian thus offer two complementary approaches to management strategists seeking to track the past. One brings in the armoury of social science methods, assuming that past behaviour (in firm, economy, or society) presents regularities that may be detected, analysed, explained, related to the present. A second approach recognizes that the past (on top of the imperfect evidence it offers) is shaped by much that is beyond social science analysis: the nooks and crannies of an individual powerful personality; the unpredictable power of passion or ideology; the surprising strength and direction of personal relationships; unexpected surges of human creativity; events; chance – to name some elusive elements.

A HISTORY OF BUSINESS HISTORY

The history of business since the advent of the modern corporation in the second half of the 19th century has been spearheaded by American historians. Initially business history was the province of mythmakers (Diamond, 1955) or muckrakers (Lloyd, 1894; Tarbell, 1904; Josephson, 1934). However, the conventions of German-inspired historical scholarship were applied to corporate history at Harvard Business School two decades after its foundation. In 1927 the appointment of Norman S. B. Gras as the first Isidor Straus Professor of Business History and a year later of Henrietta M. Larson as Associate Professor of Business History marked the beginning of a new era for the subject.

By 1950 the group recruited by Gras and Larson had published 16 titles in the series 'Harvard Studies in Business History'. One and two volumes each in length, nearly all were single-company histories, of firms such as Macy's, Barings, Hancock, Whitin, and Saco-Lowell. Each was based on its firm's records (often deposited in the Harvard Business School Library, headed by the economic historian

Arthur H. Cole) (Copeland, 1958). All were written by academic economic or business historians writing with maximum independence of judgment. Equally importantly for the professionalization of the subject, the *Business History Review*, the first scholarly journal of the discipline, was established in 1926 and Larson published her pioneering annotated bibliography, *Guide to Business History*, in 1948.

The study of the history of business in the UK began before the First World War with accounts of 18th century firms, using their records as a way of exploring the Industrial Revolution. Until the 1950s the modern history of the individual company was left to companies themselves. The results were invariably unsatisfactory. Authors were trusted retired directors or hack journalists, rather than independent professional historians. Corporate success was emphasized, company weaknesses or failures conveniently ignored. The storyline was in tedious chronological sequence, displaying little broad historical understanding or concern for theory.

The American lead was followed in the UK in 1954 when the first two volumes of *The History of Unilever: A Study in Economic Growth and Social Change* by Charles Wilson, Fellow of Jesus College, Cambridge, appeared. A third volume was published in 1968. Other commissioned studies of single companies began to appear.

In the USA the attention of business historians was shifting from the individual business company to generic themes. First to attract a great deal of research effort was entrepreneurship. At Harvard Business School a Research Center in Entrepreneurial History flourished for a decade, from 1948 until 1958. Arthur H. Cole was its 'leading spirit' but its inspiration came from the ideas of Joseph A. Schumpeter, former Austrian Minister of Finance, who was an economics professor at Harvard from 1932 until his death in 1950. Fritz Redlich, Thomas C. Cochran, Leland H. Jenks, William Miller, Irene D. Neu, Douglass North, Hugh G. J. Aitken, David S. Landes, and Alfred D. Chandler Jr. were all associated with the Center. These and others produced studies as wide-ranging as collective biographies of American business elites, biographies of individual business figures, accounts of the 'business mind in action' and of business leaders in their community settings (Miller, 1952).

After the Research Center in Entrepreneurial History dissolved in 1958, and with it hopes of establishing an entrepreneurial paradigm for business history, the initiative was taken by Alfred D. Chandler Jr. Almost single-handed, he shifted the focus of business historians from entrepreneurs to organizations. He did so by moving from entrepreneurs to managers, and from the milieu of heroic capitalists (or robber barons, depending on your viewpoint) to the administrative core of the corporate managerial revolution. His three volumes, *Strategy and Structure* (1962), *The Visible Hand* (1977), and *Scale and Scope* (1990), began respectively with case studies of a clutch of American firms, advanced to larger American samples, and then encompassed international comparisons. Research on strategy and structure, using the Chandler model, was extended to Europe by a team led by Bruce Scott at Harvard Business School (Whittington and Mayer, 2000: 12).

A major departure in the UK came in 1979–80 with the foundation of the Business History Unit (BHU) at the London School of Economics & Political Science. Jointly sponsored by the LSE and the Imperial College of Science & Technology, its mainsprings were Theo Barker, Leslie Hannah (first Director of the BHU), and W. J. Reader (*LSE Calendar*, 1979–80: 88) on the academic side; and Sir Alastair Pilkington (of the glassmaking firm) on the business side. Funding came from private business and national research bodies. Over 80 firms and charities contributed £250,000, while research foundations gave just over £200,000 (*BHU Annual Reports*, 1979, 1979–80).

The BHU was formed specifically to undertake research into business history that would span many single companies. In other words, this new initiative would regard single company histories as building blocks. Supplementing these with archival research, BHU staff would investigate large themes across a multitude of businesses. The staff recruited in the first year reflected this policy. Leslie Hannah worked on nationalized industries, completing his study of the electricity supply industry. Geoffrey Jones launched his studies of UK multinational activity. David Jeremy began studying entrepreneurs by editing the *Dictionary of Business Biography* (6 vols, 1984–86), which *inter alia* aimed to extend the ground-breaking collective biography of business leaders by Charlotte Erickson (1959).

Jonathan Liebenau was appointed to develop the BHU's work on the business history of technology. Besides Bill Reader, the first visiting scholars were Howard Gospel and Shin'ichi Yonekawa of Hitotsubashi University (funded by the Japan Foundation) (*BHU Annual Reports*, 1979, 1979–80).[1]

The BHU at the LSE was not the only centre in the UK for business history in the 1980s and 1990s. Sydney Checkland and Anthony Slaven established at Glasgow University a Centre for Business History in Scotland, secured by a private benefaction of £1 million. The development of business in Scotland was their focus, the first fruits being the *Dictionary of Scottish Business Biography* (2 vols, 1986–90). Michael Moss in the Glasgow University Archives continued Peter Payne's pioneering work of collecting the business records of Scottish firms. Also at Glasgow, Rick Trainor studied business elites and developed computing techniques while Charles Munn worked on the history of Scottish banking.

In the last two decades of the 20th century business historians in the UK became distinctly more professionalized. Partly under pressure from the UK government's four-yearly Research Assessment Exercise, journals, societies, and conferences multiplied. The spread of the subject out from the USA and the UK is suggested by the appearance of other national journals, such as the *Japanese Yearbook on Business History* (1984–) or the *German Yearbook on Business History* (1988–). The *Proceedings of the Fuji Conference* (1976–) series is not a journal but the very useful papers and discussions of an international conference annually convened. In addition, the Association of Business Historians, an international group, was launched in 1990. A few years later a European Business History Association followed. Both sponsored annual conferences.

What Has Business History Contributed to Thinking about Strategy?

That Organizational Change is Evolutionary and Can be Managed

This is the essence of Alfred D. Chandler's findings. By arduous empirical research in corporate archives published in numerous articles and three major volumes, he forged the most persuasive analysis yet of the historical development of business strategy. After the Research Center in Entrepreneurial History at the Harvard Business School dissolved in 1958, he became 'a founder of the organizational school of American historians' (John, 1997: 171). Chandler perceived an historical pattern to the emergence of the bureaucratic firm and its managerial hierarchies. Technical change in the 19th century (particularly factory production and the railway) widened markets, created mass demand, and drove the transition from craft to mass production. First movers (entrepreneurs in the UK and the USA, bank-guided managements in Germany) made three-pronged investments in manufacturing, marketing, and management initially in order to gain economies of scale.

By the early 20th century three broad developments were clear. In the USA and in Germany corporate managerial hierarchies ran the largest firms. In the UK family-run firms remained dominant. Secondly, although first movers, by making their three-pronged investments, raised barriers to entry against challengers, nevertheless challengers appeared. Sometimes the challengers invoked government aid. Sometimes they exploited shifts in resource markets. Sometimes they took advantage of new technologies. Changes in fashion offered challengers fresh opportunities. Elsewhere challengers found niches. Thirdly, as the volume of activities rose, large firms reduced their costs by removing more and more transactions from outside suppliers, assigning them to units of their own. This achieved economies of scale, scope, and transactions. Administrative coordination (by hierarchies of managers within one firm) replaced market coordination (by arrays of firms comprising the market).

Chandler explored the American experience, first in four case studies (Du Pont; General Motors; Standard Oil; Sears, Roebuck) in *Strategy and Structure* (1962) and then in 200 or so largest enterprises in the USA (benchmarked at 1917) in *The Visible Hand* (1977). He found that an early corporate strategy was horizontal integration, taking over rivals in the same industry. Such a strategy reinforced reorganization along functional lines. To achieve further economies in production and to increase market share, American firms possessing new technology in the 1870s and 1880s pursued strategies of vertical integration, effected by the use of holding company structures. Diversification strategies in the early 20th century, again driven by new technologies and changing markets, led after 1918 to the multi-divisional structure (the M-form).

In his third magnum opus, *Scale and Scope* (1990), Chandler drew international comparisons between the competitive managerial capitalism of the USA, the personal capitalism of the UK, and the cooperative managerial capitalism of Germany. Concentrating his attention on the 200 largest enterprises in each of the three nations between the 1880s and the 1940s, he argued that the core dynamic was organizational capabilities ('physical facilities and human skills') nurtured by managerial hierarchies. Britain, Chandler maintained, has been the least effective in developing a form of managerial capitalism, as many features of UK business apparently testified. The UK had relatively fewer large firms able to achieve economies of scale, scope, and transactions. British entrepreneurs failed to make (or to make large enough) the critical triple investment in manufacturing, marketing, and management in the capital-intensive industries of the Second Industrial Revolution (metals, machinery, industrial chemicals, and oil). They invested too little and too slowly in distribution. They recruited smaller managerial hierarchies. They were slow to adopt the M-form. In many firms the founder's family dominated management, either by recruiting a few salaried managers or by forming federations of small family-managed firms. The consequences of this pattern, alleged Chandler, were detrimental. Firms were starved of investment. Instead of exploiting their own resources to maintain output and prices, UK firms looked outside themselves to sources of market power like patents, advertising, and collusion. Foreign competitors entered and won UK markets relatively easily. Among the UK's large firms growth rates were much lower than those of American enterprises.

Chandler's model greatly influenced the definition of strategy and the components of strategy, such as the relationship between strategy and structure, work on multinationals, and studies of organizational analysis (Hendry, 1992). More than that, Chandler's model of the development of the American corporation (the great shift to diversification strategies and M-form structure) has been found in the USA after 1940 (Rumelt, 1974) and in British, French, and German firms 1970–93 (Whittington and Mayer, 2000).

Fundamental to any long-term historical estimates of firm structure, strategy, and performance has been the construction of databases providing capital and labour measures of the sizes of the largest 50, 100 or whatever firms in the various national economies at benchmark dates. Estimates of the largest United States firms by capital measure have been made by Kaplan (1954) and by Chandler (1969, 1984) but these do not go beyond 1960. For UK firms there are estimates by capital measure by Payne (1967) and Hannah (1983). Conspicuous by their absence are lists of largest US firms ranked by employment measure, though Wardley (1999) has a tentative list for the pre-1914 decade. These have been compiled for the UK by Shaw (1983), Johnman (1986), Jeremy (1991a), and Wardley (1999). They have been extended to French and German firms (Cassis, 1997). Refinements are possible, such as suggested by Jeremy and Farnie (2001). One result of the availability of these new data is that we can plot the survival rates of largest firms. Among the world's largest firms in 1912, 19% survived until 1995, suggesting that global dominance required particular powers of survival, minimally the ability to adjust speedily to markets radically differing with place and changing in time (Hannah, 1999).

That There is No Single Path for Organizational Development

The assumption that managerial capitalism is optimally achieved by following the American path is confounded by the case of Japan (Fruin, 1992, 1998). The Chandler thesis, predicated on competitive forms of capitalism, does not fit the experience of Japan, the second largest economy of the late 20th century. Between the 1880s and the 1930s the zaibatsu (a group of diversified businesses owned exclusively by a single family or extended family) built up multi-sector businesses spanning all industries except cotton and railways. The Mitsubishi zaibatsu even adopted a divisional structure in 1908 (Morikawa, 1992: 112–13). After 1945, when the old zaibatsu were broken up under the Allied Occupation, Japanese business has been characterized by competitive strategies and cooperative structures (Fruin, 1992).

Three structures have been identified by Fruin: firms which act strategically, focal factories, and networks. Firms may be enterprise groups, the heirs of the zaibatsu, controlling a core of major subsidiaries from all sectors (Mitsui, Mitsubishi, Sumitomo), or they may be the heads of vertical chains in a single industry (Toyota in motor vehicle manufacturing). Focal factories, emergent between the wars, developed multi-function capabilities exploiting economies of scope in a variety of ways. They appeared widely across Japan in the post-war period. Networks linked big business with small business and core firms with subcontractors. Toyota, for example, in 20 years developed three tiers of suppliers totalling 47,000 firms. While strategies between dominant firms are based on competition, a great deal of cooperation is admissible in the furtherance of those strategies (Hirschmeier and Yui, 1981; Morikawa, 1992; Fruin, 1992; Yuzawa, 1994; Wada, 1991). Variation on networks, the N-form (Hedlund, 1994 – quoted Whittington and Mayer, 2000: 80), not the divisional structure, characterized Japanese business development.

A variation on the theme of different paths for organizational strategies has been pursued by Scranton. Not a different country, but a different sector of the economy, revealed that small firms (initially in the textile industries of 19th century Philadelphia) followed very different strategies and structures from those of big US businesses. Small and medium enterprises in 19th century USA survived and flourished by pursuing strategies of flexibility, specialization, and niche marketing (Scranton, 1983, 1989, 1997).

Strategy in a regional context has gained new significance from Porter's (1990) attention to clustering. Again business historians have responded. Tweedale (1995) has examined the roles of entrepreneurship, strategy, and technology in the rise and decline of Sheffield's steel industry. Manchester business historians have collaborated with their Osaka counterparts in tracing the different 100-year paths taken by firms that started in similar textile-dominated regions at the end of the 19th century (Farnie et al., 2000).

That Organizations are Shaped by and Shape their Institutional Environment

This is the message of Douglass North (1990) who outlines the likely mechanisms by which institutions shape and are shaped by organizations. Institutions (or rules) range from customs and values (informal institutions) to constitutions and laws (formal). Deciphering the rules, especially the informal ones, is costly for individuals and organizations engaging in economic transactions. Transaction costs arise from seeking to discover the value of the attributes of a good or service offered in a market, and then enforcing the contract under which the exchange is made. In complex societies transactions are impersonal, involving many intermediaries (such as a sale between a computer manufacturer and a private purchaser, or an employment contract between the corporation and one of its middle managers). Enforcement is then passed to a third party, an agent (lawyers, police, managers).

Immediately this raises the principal–agent problem (adverse selection of the agent; moral hazard when the agent acts outside his principal's orbit of control). When organizations and their entrepreneurs seek change, therefore, they encounter transaction costs (on top of transformation costs).[2] Lowering those costs will involve exploiting or adjusting the institutional constraints – that is, tapping informal rules for opportunities to change motivation (of agents, or customers), or else marginally changing the rules (say, to legalize or prohibit a transaction opportunity). More frequently, organizations are locked-in to their previous patterns of behaviour (path-dependence). By defining institutions as all rules by which a society reduces uncertainty and by suggesting that non-economic behaviour (for example, religious or political belief) has a price in any society, with a trade-off relationship between preference and price (high price implying low willingness to stick to beliefs), North expands the earlier model of the institutional economists, confined to firms and markets (Jones, 1997;

North, 1990), to encompass all manner of social behaviour.

North's theoretical synthesis has yet to be tested by business historians. However, parts of the new institutional economists' theory (for North has built on institutional economics as well as empirical history) have been explored by business historians. Lazonick (1986) used the case of the Lancashire cotton industry to argue that institutional rigidities lay at the root of Britain's relative industrial decline (as measured by economic growth rates, relative to the USA, France, Germany). A prime illustration of these rigidities, Lazonick believed, was the persistence of the family firm. Family-run and controlled business, he argued, prevented the reorganization of British industry along American lines. The result was 'a prolonged technological backwardness and industrial decline' (Lazonick, 1986: 45). If the institutionalists' theoretical models are still under debate (Jones, 1997; Casson, 1997a), business historians are certainly taking up the challenge to test them (Westall, 1997; Casson and Rose, 1997; Sunderland, 1999; Rose, 2000).

Like the sponge in the ocean, organizations absorb and float in a sea of social institutions. What is clear is that informal institutions can either promote or retard economic behaviour. For example, the rules by which families function in differing societies have been critical in admitting or denying economic development. Family business, as the Chinese in South-East Asia have demonstrated (Redding, 1990; Weidenbaum and Hughes, 1996), can be highly successful businesses (Church, 1993; Rose, 1995). On the other hand the routinized stranglehold of the extended family on business in most African states has choked their economic path (Kindleberger, 1965; Nafziger, 1969). Using a transaction cost approach, Pollak (1985) suggested a variety of interesting bargains negotiable between family and economic governance structures.

The presence of family networks in the managements of big business, which Chandler regarded as a major handicap, was not a phenomenon peculiar to Britain or to big business. In the USA big business has to some degree remained in the hands of the descendants of founding families, such as the Du Ponts (Chandler's own ancestors), Mellons, Rockefellers, and many more (Lundberg, 1969;

Burch, 1972; Rubinstein, 1981). Intermarriage and nominee shareholdings make it difficult to measure the extent of kin networks. Other industrial states also present the same family business phenomenon, particularly France and Germany (Cassis, 1997; Whittington and Mayer, 2000) and pre-1940s Japan (Morikawa, 1992).

Another important aspect of the business environment that historians on both sides of the Atlantic have studied has been relationships between business and government. In the USA, where the state was seeking new ways to curb national monopolies, aspects of the long experience of competition and regulation have been examined. Particularly good are Temin and Galambos (1988) on the struggles leading to the 1981 break-up of American Telephone & Telegraph, a regulated monopoly, into competitive units. In the UK the experience of nationalization has been tracked through several industries, such as coal (Ashworth, 1986), electricity (Hannah, 1979, 1982), and railways (Gourvish, 1986). Privatization is currently in the business historians' sights.

From an entirely different direction, the collective mind and values of business leaders have long been the subject of historians' interest, more in the USA (Cochran, 1953, 1985; Kirkland, 1956; Krooss, 1970; Thimm, 1976) than in the UK (Boswell and Peters, 1997; Jeremy, 1988, 1990, 1998b, 1998c).

That Organizational Strategies Need to be Complemented by Subsidiary Strategies

A model in which firms have just three organizational strategies (horizontal integration, vertical integration, diversification) overlooks the possibility of other organizational strategies, such as locational strategies (local, regional, national, multinational) (Dunning, 1993; Jones, 1996). It also ignores the possibilities for other kinds of strategy to be deployed in other corporate functions, for example, technological strategies (Pavitt, 1980; Porter, 1985; Hounshell and Smith, 1988; Campbell-Kelly, 1989; Jeremy, 1994b), labour strategies (Gospel, 1992), financial strategies (Ingham, 1984; Capie and Collins, 1992), and culture-shaping strategies (Kanter, 1983; Hofstede, 1994; Hampden-Turner and Trompenaars, 1993).

Two of these are illustrative. A great deal of research effort has been directed on multinationals, increasingly relevant in view of the dominance of global companies. Most notable are Mira Wilkins on American multinationals abroad (Wilkins, 1970, 1974) and on foreign multinationals in the USA (Wilkins, 1989); Geoffrey Jones on UK multinationals (Jones, 1986, 1993, 1996; Bostock and Jones, 1994); and various European historians (Jones and Schroter, 1993) on multinationals originating in their own countries. Their work has improved estimates of the direction and scope of multinational activity and has shown that it was pursued much sooner (well before 1914) than earlier thought. It has exposed the variable quality of management overseas and also the paradox, since the 1940s, of British managerial failure at home and success abroad. Individual company studies (Ferrier, 1982; Bamberg, 1994, 2000; Corley, 1983, 1988) of course change the magnification from panoramic survey to close-up when individual entrepreneurs and executives come into view.

Second, in the 1980s and 1990s some business historians moved towards the interests of labour historians and looked at aspects of corporate cultures (Brown and Rose, 1993; Godley and Westall, 1996). Particularly interesting was Jacoby's (1986) investigation of employee attitude testing at Sears, Roebuck & Co., 1938–60. This, the broadest and most enduring corporate attitude survey to date, was designed to forestall unionism but had the side-effect of improving personnel relations by alerting managements to employee responses to company policies and practices. Significantly, it gave senior managements a control device in relation to local managements.

Church's (1996) attempt to deconstruct the managerial culture of the British motor industry left post-modernists dissatisfied because he neglected to engage with the theory and techniques of uncovering meaning (Rowlinson and Procter, 1999). Lloyd-Jones et al. (1999) have utilized Alvesson's post-modern categories of culture in pursuing the important linkage between culture and strategy, but the methodology is not sustained, for example, by a content analysis of evidence emanating from the boardroom. Griffiths' (1996) study of corporate communication in four UK firms since the 1930s attempts this approach.

That Technical Change, though Exogenous to a Degree, has Displayed Patterns that Offer Indicators to Management Strategists

Technical change, according to Thomas P. Hughes, hinges on systems and salients. His systems 'contain messy, complex, problem-solving components. They are both socially-constructed and society-shaping' (Hughes, 1987: 51). Systems include physical plant, organizations, books. People (inventors, engineers, managers, financiers, workers) are also part of these systems. They have inputs and outputs. They solve problems, invent, innovate, transfer technology, have style and momentum. Technical change, according to Hughes, comes when a component in a technical system is developed beyond other components (for example, when the power of an aircraft engine vastly exceeds the performance limits of, say, wings or fuselage) and catch-up in the lagging components is undertaken. Reverse salients emerge when the development of one component is left behind. Hughes's generalizations arose from work on the electricity supply industry of the USA, Britain, and Germany that emphasized that technology has social and economic contexts (Hughes, 1983).

Work by Smith (1977), Hounshell (1984), Hoke (1990) and Cooper (1991) has explored with much insight the processes of invention and innovation in 19th century America – particularly the rise of the interchangeability principle in manufacturing technology and the emergence of the professional inventor. Comparably perceptive studies on invention in the UK, centring on the 18th century, have been made by Dutton (1984) and MacLeod (1988).

Technology transfer has been studied by Rosenberg (1982), Jeremy (1981, 1991c, 1992, 1998b), Bruland (1989, 1991), Harris (1998), and Taylor (1994) among others. Rosenberg has emphasized the incremental and gradual nature of technical change. Harris underscored the role of tacit knowledge, the ubiquity of attitudes of secretiveness among possessors of new technology, and their rivals' incessant resort to industrial espionage. Bruland, like Jeremy, discovered the critical roles of human carriers of new technology. Jeremy, influenced by sociological models of the communication of innovations, proposed a stage analysis model for the process of transfer and, perhaps more usefully, a framework for analysing technology transfer.

The management of R&D in the 20th century has been massively illuminated by Hounshell and Smith's (1988) analytical history of R&D at Du Pont. This shows in detail the choices faced by managers, how they came to realize that science was a central pillar in corporate strategy, and how they adjusted the organization of their R&D laboratories over time. Wider and internationally comparative surveys have been made by Mowery (1986), Edgerton and Horrocks (1994), and Edgerton (1996). Campbell-Kelly's (1989) business and technical history of ICL, Britain's leading computer firm, traces the persistence of a firm in the new technology sector. However, taken over by Fujitsu soon after he wrote, it did not fulfil its historian's optimistic prognosis.

That Management Strategies Need to Take into Consideration an Ethical Dimension if their Governance Structures are to Secure Social Legitimacy

Sidney Pollard, a doyen of British economic historians and close observer of modern German developments, noted of *Scale and Scope*, 'Possibly the gravest weakness is the aseptic economic purity with which industrial history is presented here. In Chandler's world no one ever bribes an American judge or an Asiatic prime minister, no one sets armed police or private armies on strikers, no one manipulates the stock exchange. This purity may possibly be justifiable in econometric studies where the numbers of variables have to be reduced to a minimum; in an empirical study, especially of giant and multinational firms, one would have expected rather more realism' (Pollard, 1990).

Both the imperatives of historical truth (see below) and of present realities demand that the awkward, unpleasant, dark side of corporate capitalism be revealed in order to understand not just why economic failure occurred but why social injustice was fostered and tolerated. Paths from the past sometimes need to be remade or abandoned.

In this respect the environmental concerns of the late 20th century have most recently caught the business historians' attention (Darby, 1997). Nature, medicine, business, government, unions, and the intersections of some or all of these, are the themes. Of course, big business is reluctant to open its archives on some episodes or policies of the past. However, the greater openness of American government and courts has enabled European business historians to follow their American counterparts. British scholars working on the boundaries between business, medicine, science, culture, and ethics have secured ample funding from the Wellcome Trust. The first-fruits of this funding (and the discovery judgements of American courts) is Tweedale's (2000) study of Turner & Newall, the asbestos multinational. His volume brings into sharp focus corporate irresponsibility, regulatory failure, union negligence, and professional ambivalence in the medical community. Behind attitudes, of course, are values differing with culture (Engelbourg, 1980; Cochran, 1985; Jeremy, 1988, 1990, 1998b, 1998c; Rose, 2000).

Summary

In sum all this effort generated a prolific output, much recorded in the profession's international directory (Jeremy, 1994a). In aggregate, in its directions and methods, this research produced what amounted to 'new business history'. This may be characterized as utilizing company archives and commissioned company histories to address cross-company issues informed by management theory, assisted by the tools of current information technology (Coleman, 1992; Jeremy, 1994b). Much of it has been disseminated to wider audiences though textbooks, like Hannah (1983), Kirby and Rose (1994), Wilson (1995), and Jeremy (1998a). In addition, the St James's *Company Histories* series, now running to 29 volumes, has provided summary histories of individual companies in the capitalist world.

In no way do these subjective remarks do justice to the research achievement of business historians in the second half of the 20th century. For example, nothing has been said about management education and the debate unleashed by Robert Locke's (1984, 1989, 1996) assault on the universal efficacy of the American MBA model (Gourvish and Tiratsoo, 1996; Amdam, 1996; Engwall and Zamagni, 1998). The research achievement of business historians requires an analysis of the journal articles and monographs produced in the period, in order to uncover not only research achievements but also the biases of the journals accepting articles for publication – a scrutiny similar to that performed for historians of technology by Staudenmaier (1985).

BUSINESS HISTORY TECHNIQUES

The Approach of the Historian

In the first place it should be emphasized that business history is about history – about what actually happened in the past. It is not primarily an exercise in defending or assaulting currently-fashionable management theories. Of course a large component of the historian's technique is interpretation and to this he may well bring the theoretical insights of the social sciences. However, the historian's first task is to establish the facts of the matter. Facts based on reliable evidence are required initially because they keep the historian close to the realities of the past; because they will provide accurate chronology, and thus will open the way to the perception of logical cause-and-effect relationships; and because rudimentary and elaborated facts will save the historian from clothing his history with fantasy, rather than with imagination. J. W. Reader, in preparing his superlative history of ICI, was keenly aware of this responsibility:

> great corporations are bound to be the subject of public concern and controversy. Controversy ought to be founded on fact, and on historical fact not least, for otherwise all manner of mythology, folklore, and prejudice will gain currency and respectability. Anything, it seems to me, that helps to dispel these mental mists – or at any rate helps to remove the excuse for being misled by them – must be a contribution worth making to the understanding of industrial society, and that is what gives a history of ICI, on the present scale, something more than merely an antiquarian interest. (Reader, 1970: xi)

Yet, second, the historian can never be satisfied with Mr Gradgrind's 'Facts alone are wanted in life' recipe (Dickens, 1854). Reality is too complex for that. Individuals and society, unceasingly changing over time, defy exhaustive definition and exact prediction. 'Facts' are viewed and understood by their participants from numerous and differing angles. The historian has to do justice to these participatory divergencies. In making sense of a welter of details, stories, and evidence about the past he/she must also try to perceive wider trends and patterns. Interpretation becomes necessary.

This starts with a close examination of the documentary evidence (Boyd, 1950). The records of the past are not equally reliable. There are rules of evidence to be observed similar to those of the law court. The first is that primary or eyewitness evidence is the best. Historical truth is the truth of the eyewitness record, as the 19th century German historian Leopold von Ranke laid down. The physical, textual, and contextual characteristics of documents have to be evaluated and kept in view. The likely perspectives and motives of author and recipient need to be borne in mind. Interpretation continues with the aid of secondary sources, those written by people at a distance in time or place from the historical moment under consideration. Last, the social sciences, philosophy, theology even, of the historian's own day can be used, perhaps to frame a preliminary hypothesis to be tested as the historical evidence is reviewed. Thus an initial question or interest engendered in the historian's present can be tested against the realities of the historical past (Evans, 1997).

In struggling to reach their interpretations historians find themselves torn between three contending claims to be heard: the views, contexts, and horizons of the historical actors, the people of the past; the broad concerns of the society in which the historian functions and to whom he seeks to relay meaningful perspectives of the past; and the historian's own personality and particular ideological and psychological biases. The most common conflict is between history which is focused on reconstructions of the past and history which is used simply to buttress a current ideology or theory. The former can lapse into antiquarianism, the latter into propaganda.

Third, in reaching interpretations that draw upon past voices, present concerns, and personal preferences, most historians would argue that their first allegiance is to voices past. That is, the historian's primary interpretative task is to understand the contexts of the past, the social, political, economic horizons, which bounded and shaped the choices of predecessor communities, organizations, leaders; to understand as closely as possible the choices that were made or rejected; and the consequences of the courses followed. This is important because the historian will sooner or later have to make assessments and judgments about the people and societies of the past and the decisions they took. Unless the historian is careful to judge them by the circumstances and knowledge that bounded them in their own time, unfair appraisals will result. Instead of the richness of a painting the historian will produce a poor caricature.

These are large issues. A major challenge for practitioners of business history is to research and write about business developments in ways that satisfy these three concerns.

Historical Methods for Investigating Strategy

If business history allows us to compare the past with the present, to explore how the past has evolved into the present, and to test current theory against past reality, how can strategy be investigated from historical sources? Some of the more frequently used methods would include the following, which are summarized in Table 19.1.

Narrative History

Since time immemorial, stories have been the staple medium of the historian. Despite the modern, and econometric, tendency to reduce managerial problems to statistical solutions, language, being so much more subtle than number, ensures that human experience in all its particularity, variety, and richness is best captured in story: narrative, anecdote, retold myth. If by narrative is meant a chronologically-told story, scarcely any historians use the form. Their narratives move between time and place as suits their overall analysis of a topic. Their aim is to preserve a sense of chronology whilst bringing in the actors and events of the unfolding historical situation they are trying to reconstruct. Rather, for the business historian, narrative history means drawing heavily upon description in writing about the past.

For strategists, narrative has recently taken on post-modern meanings. It is all about how the historical narrative of the current managerial storyline has been or might be manipulated to shape strategic outcomes (Barry and Elmes, 1997; Pentland, 1999). Such techniques might be valuable for probing corporate myths. Apart from analyses of myth, very different are business historians' narratives. These are predicated on the view that the past has a reality independent of the historian and that therefore there is historical truth (the truth of the evidence closest to past moments) waiting to be uncovered. Among business historians, masters of the narrative form include Reader (1970, 1975), Davenport-Hines (1984), and Kynaston (1994, 1995, 1999).

Analysis

While necessary, narrative is not sufficient for an historian seeking explanation for past patterns of behaviour. Analysis, or breaking down an event, issue, personality, company's past development, or whatever, is essential. Historical analysis will always encounter at least three tensions:

1 The historian's old conflict between the chronological and the topical is the first. While it is essential to establish and re-check chronology (so that a later effect cannot be identified as an earlier cause, since real time moves in one direction only), chronology must not be regarded as an iron framework. After coherent time periods are selected, a mixture of narrative and reflective discussion, or deconstruction, can be deployed within the various themes or topics comprising the units of analysis.

2 The tension between the qualitative (invariably described and discussed in language) and the quantitative (optimally presented and explored mathematically) frequently appears. Of course, appropriate tools of statistical analysis can be brought to bear within a narrative framework. Rarely will the statistical alone suffice in conducting any historical study of human activity.

Table 19.1 *Historical methods for investigating strategy*

Type	Definition	Advantages	Disadvantages
Narrative	Descriptive writing about the past	Brings the past into focus with vividness and dramatic movement	Can be excessively constricted by the 'iron cage' of chronology
Analysis	Breaking down past events, issues, careers etc. into components in the search for explanation and insight	Offers many angles on the historical topic being considered	Encounters tensions between chronology and theme; the qualitative and the quantitative; the inductive and the deductive use of evidence
Company history	History of a single company, usually commissioned by the board of directors	Company records and employees are fully accessible to the historian	The historian's treatment of the company might be biased in its favour. If the board of directors did not like what they got from the historian they might suppress the history
Case study	Academic analysis of a particular company and one or more of its corporate decisions	Clarifies managerial analysis of corporate decision-making	Runs risk of neglecting the company's historical contexts
Biography	Profile of a single business person, whose career is usually examined chronologically	Allows individual personality and behaviour to be held under the lens of highest magnification of detail	Excessively focused on the individual, to the neglect of other figures and circumstances
Collective biography	An objectively-chosen group of individuals with some kind of shared experience are treated as a whole and their collective characteristics are analysed	Exposes changes over time in the social origins and social mobility of a group of individuals	Difficult to relate collective careers to collective performance, unless there is also an examination of processess, for example, in the functioning of the group's networks
Oral history	Recording the evidence of participants in historical events	Offers primary evidence	Open to the distortions of memory
'Instrumental' history	The analysis of the history of a particular episode or facet of corporate behaviour to illuminate that matter	Focuses the investigator's mind on a single corporate issue, rather than the total life of the organization	Possible to understate the impact of influences extraneous to the issue under consideration
Post-modern approaches	Viewing the past through the lens of language and meaning, relying heavily on the viewer's own subjective understanding of 'text'	Directs attention to meanings and the 'rich texture' of the historical evidence	Neglects almost all historical conventions, especially in its denial that the past has a verifiable existence independent of the living observer of the past

3   In drawing conclusions from the evidence, historians find themselves either tending towards inductively-reached conclusions (building up a description or theory from a multitude of empirical details) or towards deductively-reached ones (assuming that the general case applies to particular instances). The safest resolution to this tension lies in testing the general against the particular and vice-versa. By and large, as stated earlier, historians are interested in the particular, those things that make for difference and individuality. Hence the preferred research method is induction.

In addition, the business historian will find himself torn between the competing claims of the related disciplines which have been used to open up his subject: economics, sociology, psychology, management, for example. While narrative and analysis will be used by any kind of historian, investigations of past business behaviour, including strategic issues, have utilized more specific methods.

The Company History

As seen above, it was not until the commissioned company history, researched and written by academic business historians, first appeared from Harvard in the 1930s that reliable accounts of company developments were available. Until then company history was either muckraking or glorification. However, within the genus of the individual company history there are subspecies. Most authors begin with a boardroom viewpoint.

Like Bill Reader (1970, 1975), some see company history as essentially political history, interpersonal struggles for power. In the preface to his magisterial history of ICI he wrote:

> The backbone of my narrative is the intricate diplomacy of the international chemical industry – in this volume between 1870 and 1926 – and what I conceive myself to be writing is political history, dealing with the interplay of men and events, rather than economic or social history, concerned with the description and analysis of impersonal forces and conditions. This is because I hold that individuals, singly or in groups, can and do influence events (often in unintended ways, but still the influence is there) and that until some attempt has been made to establish who the principal characters were, what they were trying to do, and what they did – that is, until the political history has been written – it is idle, or at least very risky, to proceed to economic or social analysis, because you simply have not got the facts you need for making statistical, social, or ethical judgments. (Reader, 1970: xii)

Others like Donald Coleman (1969) follow the economic and social historian's perspective. Coleman, aware of a need to satisfy both the theoretical demands of the economist and the human focus of the historian, prefaced his three-volume history of Courtaulds with the view that he did not think both audiences could be satisfied. He therefore 'presented in statistical form' the quantifiable aspects of the company history but simultaneously gave 'a good deal of attention ... to the character and performance of leading figures of the firm; to the influence exercised by their attitudes of mind upon the company's reaction to external stimuli; and to the social context of their activities' (Coleman, 1969: I, x).

The problem with the commissioned company history is that there is always the suspicion of subverted historical judgment – that 'the author's elbow has been steered'. There is no easy way round this. The company must allow the historians to ask and explore awkward questions, and to publish the answers discovered. For their part, historians must perform their research and exercise their critical faculties to the full.

The Case Study

Developed at Harvard Business School, where the form was adopted in the teaching of commercial law at the foundation of HBS in 1908, case studies were formally used across all subjects from the 1920s. When business history became a separate course at HBS in 1930 the case study method was naturally used (Copeland, 1958).

Case study methods are usefully outlined in Eisenhardt (1989). However, the case method has its problems. Unless the company being studied monopolized its market, the individual case could not be assumed to have representativeness and hence any wider usefulness in theory building. Defenders of case study research have justified the method in terms of internal validity (alternative interpretations or arguments), construct validity (appropriate case evidence), replicability, and external validity. Numagami (1998) argues that only the first two are relevant unless there are invariant laws in the social sciences (which, he believes, there are not). Countering Eisenhardt's (1989) arguments that case studies can be used to build theory is Dyer and Wilkins' (1991) view that case studies have a richness of their own and what is needed are 'better stories'.

The Biography

While biography has been a traditional form of the historian's art, an adequate biography of a business figure calls for familiarity with the technicalities of business as well as abilities both to empathize with and to level critical appraisal at the subject. Two exemplars may be cited. Chandler and Salsbury's magisterial biography of Pierre S. Du Pont, pioneer of the multi-divisional corporation, is avowedly 'as much [business] history as biography ... a way to get inside an enterprise to see how its business was carried on and how and why basic decisions affecting its destiny were made' (Chandler and Salsbury, 1971: xix). Richard Davenport-Hines's biography of Dudley

Docker – a secretive but highly influential mergerer and corporatist intriguer – scans a wide array of unpublished and published evidence which vividly portrays personality, activity, and business-political contexts. Ostensibly only giant figures merit full-scale biography. Lesser individuals need to be representative in some way if the historian's resources are not to be squandered.

Collective Biography

Techniques for writing collective biography (prosopography) have been outlined by Stone (1971) and for collective business biography in particular by Jeremy (1991b). Pioneering studies of American business elites were Gregory and Neu (1952), Miller (1952), and Newcomer (1955). They inspired Erickson's (1959) study of UK leaders in the steel and hosiery industries between 1850 and 1950. In essence, the historian objectively chooses a group of actors in history (an elite or a mass) who in life have shared some common feature such as position or experience. By analysing their group characteristics (beginning with individuals' parentage, early years, schooling, training), it is possible to discover how the group's social origins may have changed over time, whether social mobility has increased or decreased, or (if two or more groups of actors are chosen) whether there were linkages of any significance between social groups.

The technique is especially appropriate for studying networks of directors and managers (Jeremy, 1990). The starting point is the assembly of outline biographies of each individual in the group. For business leaders in the USA these may be found in Ingham (1983); for those in England and Wales, in Jeremy and Shaw (1984–86); and for those in Scotland, in Slaven and Checkland (1986–90). Shorter biographies of British business leaders are in Jeremy and Tweedale (1994).

Britain's perceived industrial decline in the 1960s and 1970s and then the Thatcher revolution pulled British business historians back to entrepreneurs. Some of the new work built on the LSE and Glasgow dictionary projects of the 1980s. Empirically, networks have been explored in monographs on bankers at the beginning of the 20th century (Cassis, 1984, 1997), business leaders and church leaders in the first half of the 20th century (Jeremy, 1990),

and wealth-holding among the richest (Rubinstein, 1981). Slaven (1995) offered the first glimpse of his analysis of the careers of Scottish business leaders. Nicholas (1999), using *Dictionary of Business Biography* data, reached new conclusions about the distribution of fortunes between careers in industry and careers in commerce. This triggered a lively debate between himself (2000) and Rubinstein (2000).

The problem with collective biography is that it is difficult to relate collective biographies to collective performance. As Pettigrew (1992) observed, they do not sufficiently expose the processes by which linkages internal or external to the group take place. The anatomy of corporate elites like boardrooms or interlocking directorates needs to be complemented with studies of 'what flows across the links' (Stinchcombe, 1990 – cited Pettigrew, 1992). Casson (1997a, 1997b) argues that it is information that flows across networks, the economic motivation being to lower information costs. This has yet to be empirically demonstrated by the business historians.

Oral History

Oral history is as old as pre-literate society, as new as the portable tape recorder. Historians in the USA led when in 1948 they organized their Oral History Association, following on from earlier work by anthropologists and New Deal writers' projects. The invention of the cheap and portable tape recorder led to the spread of the technique in the 1950s and 1960s but in the UK it was not until the 1980s that a National Sound Archive, part of the British Library, was established (Thompson, 1988: 68). Allan Nevins (1954) in his massive study of Henry Ford (Nevins and Hill, 1957, 1963) applied the technique to 'great men' in the 1940s and 1950s. In the UK the oral history of business figures is much more recent. Paul Thompson, one of the pioneers and a founder of the National Life Story Collection (formerly the NSA), and his collaborators moved into the business world with a project to record the memories of figures in the City of London's (mostly) financial markets. From over 120 recordings of memories sometimes going back half a century Courtney and Thompson (1996) assembled a fascinating and rich collection of excerpts arranged topically.

Accountants in much smaller samples have also yielded memory material (Mumford, 1991; Matthews, 2000). Single company histories now regularly utilize oral history material (Jones, 1995: 385–6). There are of course problems with using oral history data, primarily the distortions of memory. These are discussed fully in Thompson (1988).

'Instrumental' Business History

The analysis of corporate history to illuminate a particular corporate problem, what might be called 'instrumental' business history, is also relatively new. Again two or three exemplars may be cited. An early one was Boswell's (1983) study of the making of business policy in three steel companies between the wars. Given his time period, he was heavily reliant on historical sources. Very different, because it was much more of an 'insider job', was Pettigrew's (1985) investigation of how large organizations achieve adjustment to their changing economic and political environments.

In exploring managerial strategies in ICI, at the centre and in four of its divisions, Pettigrew paid attention to culture as much as to organization, using history as one of the ways of exposing company culture. His research technique, contextualism (proposed by the philosopher Stephen Pepper in 1942), or the contextualist analysis of process, *inter alia* relates 'vertical level' phenomena (individual–company–industry–economy, for example) to 'horizontal level' phenomena (other individuals, for example) (Pettigrew, 1990, 1997). The result is a framework which reminds the investigator to look for interchanges between agents and contexts which occur over time and are cumulative.

Different again was Gillespie's (1991) revisiting of Western Electric's famous Hawthorne experiments of the 1920s and 1930s. Gillespie's object was to discover how the research was conducted. Going through the evidence with a toothcomb, he reconstructed the various interpretations of the fatigue evidence made by company researchers, workers, academics, and supervisors. Equally importantly, he showed how personal, professional, and political interests shaped these interpretations; and by what personal and institutional processes one interpretation, that of Elton Mayo (whose use of research data was 'rather

cavalier' – Gillespie, 1991: 182–7), became the dominant one.

Brave in concept but much less successful as history is Mintzberg and Waters' (1982) attempt to plot the development of strategy in an entrepreneurial firm, Steinberg Inc. of Montreal, a diversified retail chain. Boardroom, management, and workforce actors are absent. No attempt is made to present and triangulate a variety of participants' experiences of emerging strategies under the constraints of past horizons. The complexities of changing business environments are heavily generalized. In short, the authors are so focused on the concept of strategy that they miss the chance of 'getting inside the skin of the past'. For some historical studies an article-length treatment is too short.

Post-Modern Approaches

Post-modernism is an 'umbrella term for various discussions concerning "language, culture, the subject, rationality, and writing"' (Alvesson, 1995: 1048 – cited in Rowlinson and Procter, 1999). In arranging the hierarchy of competing 'voices', the idealist historian pays closest attention to past voices; the positivist, to present sociological voices; the postmodernist, to his own inner perspectives and pre-suppositions. This is a caricature, but it indicates where emphases lie in the rival approaches to historical evidence. A postmodern approach is predicated on the assumption that in-depth, qualitative case studies result from 'a relationship between the researcher, the research community, and the actors in the organization being studied' (Rowlinson and Procter, 1999). For post-modernists, objectivity is problematic, impossible even. Following Geertz, organizational symbolists move to the position that at any point in time 'the real history of the organization is what its members imagine it to be' (Geertz, 1980: 136 – quoted in Rowlinson and Procter, 1999).

While post-modernism has valuably brought language and meaning into the historian's kit-bag of analytical tools, it is otherwise alien to the position taken by the majority of historians (Evans, 1997). While post-modernists claim that time is meaningless, historians assume that real time is unidirectional and its chronology must be respected. While post-modernists say there are no facts in history, historians assume that 'A historical fact is something that happened in history and can be verified as such through the traces history has left behind' (Evans, 1997: 76). Where post-modernists say nothing exists outside language and that the meaning of documents changes every time they are read, historians assume that it is historical interpretation, not historical reality, that alters with each new reading. Where post-modernists reduce all past happenings to the level of present perceptions, historians assume that past realities were not all equally significant: that Hitler and Stalin and their tyrannies were genocidal monsters of a quite different order from some 19th century capitalist bosses and their oppressive workplaces. Where the post-modernist makes him or herself the master of historical experience (by confining all historical reality to their own 'discourses'), the historian approaches the past with humility. The truth is, business history, and most history, simply cannot be written by staring through a post-modern monocle.

AN AGENDA FOR FUTURE RESEARCH

Business historians (and historians generally) have usually been mindful of the overriding issues of their own day and have tried to respond by supplying historical perspectives. In the light of organizational and strategic management literature, a wide range of topics awaits the attentions of the business historian.

One of the challenges is to test Porter's positioning theory of competitive advantage against the evidence of corporate archives, actors and histories. Singleton's (1997) application of competitive advantage theory to the global textile industries is one example of what might be done.

A resource-based theory of strategic management is another theme demanding historical investigation. As Scarbrough (1998) has shown, the theory itself is not without problems. Not least is the difficulty in demonstrating how competencies relate to performance. In this context the focus is now on knowledge in the firm. How is it generated? Where is it located? How is it modified? How is it transmitted across intra- and inter-firm boundaries? How does it relate to performance? Concepts of path dependency and networking need to be examined in historical

cases. Changing sources of changing business values need to be explored afresh.

Looking for gaps in the achievements of business history, it appears to this author that some or all of the following additional strategy topics (listed in no special rank order) merit serious study by business historians (some have already begun to be addressed):

1 The behaviour of middle managements, as they admitted or resisted strategic change; work on the professionalization of managements has started (Brech, 1997; Matthews et al., 1998).
2 The culture and governance of boardrooms in relation to corporate strategies.
3 Changes in strategy formation in small and medium enterprise.
4 Ethical/non-ethical business strategies and their role in affecting market efficiency, following the work of Tweedale (2000).
5 Location and regional strategies in an international context, as attempted by Farnie et al. (2000).
6 Foreign, especially Japanese, multinationals in Europe; their impact on European management strategy.
7 The impact of new technology on business strategy, particularly the effects of the computer, the WorldWideWeb, and telecommunications revolution, comparing American, European, Japanese, and other Asian experiences.
8 British entrepreneurs after the Thatcher revolution; their career patterns and strategic performance.
9 Marketing strategy and consumer markets, from UK high streets to US shopping malls.
10 Personality in management strategy.
11 Strategy perceptions among ethnic businesses.
12 The role of women in strategic management.
13 Age and business strategies – the grey generations of the West, as markets and as a managerial resource; Hannah (1986) pointed in one direction, pension strategies.
14 Appropriate strategies for Third World Development.
15 Business strategies and their impacts on the natural environment.

For each of the above topics, the basic historical questions are, 'What has happened in the past?' and 'How have we got to the present?'

In terms of new methods, some of the attention paid to language and meaning by the post-modernists (heavily supplemented with traditional historical techniques) may prove fruitful in understanding path dependency. Similarly, business historians might be able to contribute to the econometric, counterfactual computer modelling of past decisions and outcomes, to plot the might-have-beens, or to see where some strategies led to dead-ends while others brought survival and expansion, or where the same strategy succeeded in one set of historical circumstances but failed in another.

Conclusion

History is more an art than a social science. It is most concerned with the intricacies of human nature, thought, and action, in the past. Its central skill is empathy, the ability to get inside another mind, another community, another situation. Its central methodology is familiarity with and assessment of sources. Immersion in the sources: finding better primary evidence; testing the reliability of the sources; triangulating source against source; placing one contemporary viewpoint against another; questioning the sources with the aid of current theory; buttressing the evidence with scholarly apparatus which allows statements and interpretations to be checked and verified; presenting the results in narrative and analysis. These seem to me to be the essential skills of the historian/business historian. Modern theory (sociological, economic, management, or whatever) will help the historian in framing the hypotheses he may wish to explore with the aid of the evidence of the past. Modern methodology may allow the historian to shortcut some of his otherwise wasted archival reading. But to get into the minds, decisions, events, circumstances, and unfolding developments of the past, there is no substitute for soaking in the sources.

History has value for management strategists because it illuminates such crucial issues as organizational capabilities, path dependency, and corporate culture. In fact every theme strategists may care to mention has an historical dimension. Furthermore, practitioners, as much as theorists, need to be mindful of history, as Sir Peter Parker, former chairman of British Rail and chairman of Mitsubishi UK, has underscored:

'The historical conditioning of individuals and their communities is the proper basis of an understanding of their present and future fears and hopes ... History is not what is over and done with, it runs alongside any of us who run anything, reminding us of what the individual can do, of what surprises the unforeseen predictably springs on us, of what a lot of cant clutters our way' (Parker, 1989: 46).

While the past offers patterns, and certainly patterns for management strategists, empirical historians invariably find that the past does not neatly fit the current theory they might espouse. The unexpected happens. Events break in. Illness and death intervene. Chance meetings make connections. Private personal crises affect judgment. Disastrous courses are followed. Surprising success emerges. Such awkwardnesses of the past remind theorists and practitioners that human behaviour, individual or collective, is never wholly subject to regular and predictable patterns. For those trying to understand the past, these inconveniences induce the humility that will avoid the old historical conceit of believing that the past only has relevance if it can be related to a superior present (Butterfield, 1931). The past has its own horizons and they need to be discovered and understood.

Appendix: Sources for Business History

Bibliographies

The two most useful are the following: Francis Goodall, Terry Gourvish and Steven Tolliday (eds), *International Bibliography of Business History* (1997); Francis Goodall, *A Bibliography of British Business Histories* (1987).

Academic Journals

Economic history journals: *Economic History Review* (1950–); *Journal of Economic History* (1972–). Business history journals: *Business History Review* (1926–); *Business History* (1958–); *Business and Economic History* (1971–99), superseded by *Enterprise and Society* (2000–). Specialist business history journals: *Accounting Business and Financial History* (1990–); *Business Archives* (1934–); *Financial History Review* (1994–); *German*

Yearbook on Business History; *Japanese Yearbook on Business History* (1984–); *Journal of Industrial History* (1999–); *Journal of Transport History* (1953–); *Service Industries Journal* (1980–); *Technology and Culture* (1959–); *Textile History* (1971).

Archives

Baker Library, Harvard Business School, Boston, MA, USA; Hagley Library, Wilmington, DE, USA; The (UK) National Register of Archives at the Royal Commission on Historical Manuscripts, London; The Business Archives Council, London.

ACKNOWLEDGEMENT

I am grateful to the editors for their comments on this chapter, and especially to Richard Whittington who provided strategic management materials and challenging comments on the first draft; also to the Leverhulme Trust for their research report.

NOTES

1 By the mid-1980s numerous other business historians were associated with the BHU. Among them were Christine Shaw, Margaret Ackrill, Sir Arthur Knight, Richard Davenport-Hines, Edgar Jones, Shirley Keeble, Frances Bostock, Geoffrey Tweedale, Mari Williams, Youssef Cassis, Francis Goodall, Stephen Nicholas, Nuala Zahadieh, John Hendry, Stefanie Diaper, Judy Slinn, Jean-Jacques Van Helten, and, from Japan, Takeshi Yuzawa and Kazuo Wada, among others. Over the course of its seventh year, 1984–85, the BHU employed 34 staff, full or part-time, including five secretaries (*BHU Annual Report*, 1984–85).

2 Total production costs = costs of land, labour and capital required in transformation (converting the physical attributes of a good) and transaction (defining, protecting, enforcing property rights to goods) (North, 1990: 28).

REFERENCES

Amdam, R. P. (ed.) (1996) *Management Education and Competitiveness: Europe, Japan and the United States*. London: Routledge.

Ashworth, W. (1986) *The History of the British Coal Industry*, Volume 5 *1946–1982: The Nationalized Industry*. Oxford: Clarendon Press.

Bamberg, J. H. (1994) *The History of the British Petroleum Company*, Vol. 2 *The Anglo-Iranian Years, 1928–1954*. Cambridge: Cambridge University Press.

Bamberg, J. H. (2000) *The History of the British Petroleum Company*, Vol. 3 *British Petroleum and Global Oil, 1950–1975: The Challenge of Nationalism*. Cambridge: Cambridge University Press.

Barnett, W. P. and Burgelman, R. A. (1996) 'Evolutionary perspectives on strategy', *Strategic Management Journal*, 17: 5–19.

Barry, D. and Elmes, M. (1997) 'Strategy retold: toward a narrative view of strategic discourse', *Academy of Management Review*, 22: 429–52.

Bebbington, D. (1979) *Patterns in History*. Leicester: Inter-Varsity Press.

Bostock, F. and Jones, G. G. (1994) 'Foreign multinationals in British manufacturing, 1850–1962', *Business History*, 36: 89–126.

Boswell, J. S. (1983) *Business Policies in the Making: Three Steel Companies Compared*. London: George Allen & Unwin.

Boswell, J. S. and Peters, J. (1997) *Capitalism in Contention: Business Leaders and Political Economy in Modern Britain*. Cambridge: Cambridge University Press.

Boyd, J. P. (ed.) (1950) *The Papers of Thomas Jefferson*, Vol. 1. Princeton, NJ: Princeton University Press.

Brech, E. (1997) *A History of Management*, Vol. 1 *The Concept and Gestation of Britain's Central Management Institute, 1902–76*. Corby: Institute of Management.

Brown, J. and Rose, M. B. (eds) (1993) *Entrepreneurship, Networks and Modern Business*. Manchester: Manchester University Press.

Bruland, K. (1989) *British Technology and European Industrialisation: The Norwegian Textile Industry in the Mid-Nineteenth Century*. Cambridge: Cambridge University Press.

Bruland, K. (ed.) (1991) *Technology Transfer and Scandinavian Industrialization*. New York: Berg.

Burch, P. J. (1972) *The Managerial Revolution Reassessed: Family Control in America's Large Corporations*. Lexington, MA: D. C. Heath.

Butterfield, H. (1931) *The Whig Interpretation of History*. London: G. Bell & Sons.

Campbell-Kelly, M. (1989) *ICL: A Business and Technical History*. Oxford: Oxford University Press.

Capie, F. and Collins, M. (1992) *Have the Banks Failed British Industry?* London: Institute of Economic Affairs.

Cassis, Y. (1984) *City Bankers, 1890–1914*. Cambridge: Cambridge University Press.

Cassis, Y. (1997) *Big Business: The European Experience in the Twentieth Century*. Oxford: Oxford University Press.

Casson, M. C. (1997a) 'Institutional economics and business history: a way forward?', *Business History*, 39(4): 151–71.

Casson, M. C. (1997b) *Information and Organization: A New Perspective on the Theory of the Firm*. Oxford: Clarendon Press.

Casson, M. C. and Rose, M. (1997) 'Institutions and the evolution of modern business: introduction', *Business History*, 39(4): 1–8.

Chandler, A. D. Jr. (1962) *Strategy and Structure: Chapters in the History of the American Industrial Enterprise*. Cambridge, MA: MIT Press.

Chandler, A. D. Jr. (1969) 'The structure of American industry in the twentieth century: a historical overview', *Business History Review*, 43: 255–98.

Chandler, A. D. Jr. (1977) *The Visible Hand: The Managerial Revolution in American Business*. Cambridge, MA: Harvard University Press.

Chandler, A. D. Jr. (1984) 'The emergence of managerial capitalism', *Business History Review*, 58: 473–503.

Chandler, A. D. Jr. (1990) *Scale and Scope: The Dynamics of Industrial Capitalism*. Cambridge, MA: Harvard University Press.

Chandler, A. D. Jr. and Salsbury, S. (1971) *Pierre S. Du Pont and the Making of the Modern Corporation*. New York: Harper & Row.

Church, R. (1993) 'The family firm in industrial capitalism: international perspectives on hypotheses and history', *Business History*, 35(4): 17–43.

Church, R. (1996) 'Deconstructing Nuffield: the evolution of managerial culture in the British motor industry', *Economic History Review*, 49(3): 561–83.

Cochran, T. C. (1953) *American Railroad Leaders, 1845–1890: The Business Mind in Action*. Cambridge, MA: Harvard University Press.

Cochran, T. C. (1985) *Challenges to American Values: Society, Business and Religion*. New York: Oxford University Press.

Coleman, D. C. (1969) *Courtaulds, An Economic and Social History*, Vol. 1 *The Nineteenth Century: Silk and Crape*. Oxford: Clarendon Press.

Coleman, D. C. (1992) 'New business history for old?', *The Historical Journal*, 35: 239–44.

Cooper, C. C. (1991) *Shaping Invention: Thomas Blanchard's Machinery and Patent Management in Nineteenth Century America*. New York: Columbia University Press.

Copeland, M. T. (1958) *And Mark an Era: The Story of the Harvard Business School*. Boston: Little, Brown & Co.

Corley, T. A. B. (1983) *A History of the Burmah Oil Company, 1886–1924*. London: Heinemann.

Corley, T. A. B. (1988) *A History of the Burmah Oil Company, 1924–1966*. London: Heinemann.

Courtney, C. and Thompson, P. (1996) *City Lives: The Changing Voices of British Finance*. London: Methuen.

Darby, J. (1997) 'The environmental crisis and the origins of Japanese manufacturing in Europe', *Business History*, 39(2): 94–114.

Davenport-Hines, R. P. T. (1984) *Dudley Docker: The Life and Times of a Trade Warrior*. Cambridge: Cambridge University Press.

Diamond, S. (1955) *The Reputation of American Businessmen*. Cambridge, MA: Harvard University Press.

Dickens, C. (1854) *Hard Times*.

Dunning, J. H. (1993) *The Globalization of Business: The Challenge of the 1990s*. London: Routledge.

Dutton, H. I. (1984) *The Patent System and Inventive Activity During the Industrial Revolution*. Manchester: Manchester University Press.

Dyer, W. G. and Wilkins, A. L. (1991) 'Better stories, not better constructs, to generate better theory: a rejoinder to Eisenhardt', *Academy of Management Review*, 16(3): 613–19.

Edgerton, D. E. H. (1996) *Science, Technology and the British Industrial 'Decline', 1870–1970*. Cambridge: Cambridge University Press.

Edgerton, D. E. H. and Horrocks, S. M. (1994) 'British industrial research and development before 1945', *Economic History Review*, 47(2): 213–38.

Eisenhardt, K. M. (1989) 'Building theories from case study research', *Academy of Management Review*, 14(4): 532–50.

Engelbourg, S. (1980) *Power and Morality: American Business Ethics, 1840–1914*. Westport, CT: Greenwood Press.

Engwall, L. and Zamagni, V. (eds) (1998) *Management Education in Historical Perspective*. Manchester: Manchester University Press.

Erickson, C. (1959) *British Industrialists: Steel and Hosiery, 1850–1950*. Cambridge: Cambridge University Press.

Evans, R. J. (1997) *In Defence of History*. London: Granta Books.

Farnie, D. A., Nakaoka, T., Jeremy, D. J., Wilson, J. F. and Abe, T. (2000) *Region and Strategy in Britain and Japan: Business in Lancashire and Kansai, 1890–1990*. London: Routledge.

Ferrier, R. W. (1982) *The History of the British Petroleum Company*, Vol. 1 *The Developing Years, 1901–1932*. Cambridge: Cambridge University Press.

Fruin, W. M. (1992) *The Japanese Enterprise System: Competitive Strategies and Co-operative Structures*. Oxford: Clarendon Press.

Fruin, W. M. (1998) 'To compare or not to compare: two books that look at capitalist systems across centuries, countries and industries', *Business History Review*, 72(1): 123–36.

Gillespie, R. (1991) *Manufacturing Knowledge: A History of the Hawthorne Experiments*. Cambridge: Cambridge University Press.

Godley, A. and Westall, O. M. (eds) (1996) *Business History and Business Culture*. Manchester: Manchester University Press.

Gospel, H. F. (1992) *Markets, Firms, and Management of Labour in Modern Britain*. Cambridge: Cambridge University Press.

Gourvish, T. R. (1986) *British Railways, 1948–73: A Business History*. Cambridge: Cambridge University Press.

Gourvish, T. R. and Tiratsoo, N. (eds) (1996) *Missionaries and Managers: American Influences on European Management Education, 1945–60*. Manchester: Manchester University Press.

Gregory, F. W. and Neu, I. D. (1952) 'The American industrial elite in the 1870s: their social origins', in

W. Miller (ed.), *Men in Business*. Cambridge, MA: Harvard University Press.

Griffiths, J. R. (1996) 'A comparative analysis of company magazines and company cultures in four firms, 1930–1990', PhD thesis, Business School, Manchester Metropolitan University.

Hampden-Turner, C. and Trompenaars, F. (1993) *The Seven Cultures of Capitalism*. London: Piatkus.

Hannah, L. (1979) *Electricity before Nationalisation: A Study of the Development of the Electricity Supply Industry in Britain to 1948*. London: Macmillan.

Hannah, L. (1982) *Engineers, Managers and Politicians: The First Fifteen Years of Nationalised Electricity Supply in Britain*. London: Macmillan.

Hannah, L. (1983) *The Rise of the Corporate Economy*. London: Methuen.

Hannah, L. (1986) *Inventing Retirement: The Development of Occupational Pensions in Britain*. Cambridge: Cambridge University Press.

Hannah, L. (1999) 'Marshall's "trees" and the global "forest": were "giant redwoods" different?', in N. R. Lamoreaux, D. M. G. Raff and P. Temin (eds), *Learning by Doing in Markets, Firms, and Countries*. Chicago: University of Chicago Press.

Harris, J. R. (1998) *Industrial Espionage and Technology Transfer: Britain and France in the Eighteenth Century*. Aldershot: Ashgate.

Helfat, C. E. (2000) 'Guest editor's introduction to the special issue: the evolution of firm capabilities', *Strategic Management Journal*, 21: 955–9.

Hendry, J. (1992) 'Business strategy and business history: a framework for development', *Advances in Strategic Management*, 8: 207–25.

Hirschmeier, J. and Yui, T. (1981) *The Development of Japanese Business, 1600–1980*. London: George Allen & Unwin.

Hofstede, G. (1994) *Cultures and Organizations: Software of the Mind*. London: HarperCollins.

Hoke, D. R. (1990) *Ingenious Yankees: The Rise of the American System of Manufactures in the Private Sector*. New York: Columbia University Press.

Hounshell, D. A. (1984) *From the American System to Mass Production, 1800–1932: The Development of Manufacturing Technology in the United States*. Baltimore: The Johns Hopkins Press.

Hounshell, D. A. and Smith, J. K. (1988) *Science and Corporate Strategy: Du Pont R&D, 1902–1980*. Cambridge: Cambridge University Press.

Hughes, T. P. (1983) *Networks of Power: Electrification in Western Society*. Baltimore: Johns Hopkins University Press.

Hughes, T. P. (1987) 'The evolution of large technological systems', in W. E. Bijker, T. P. Hughes and T. Pinch (eds), *The Social Construction of Technological Systems: New Directions in the Sociology and History of Technology*. Cambridge, MA: MIT Press.

Ingham, G. (1984) *Capitalism Divided? The City and Industry in British Social Development*. London: Macmillan.

Ingham, J. N. (1983) *Biographical Dictionary of American Business Leaders*, 4 vols. Westport, CT: Greenwood Press.

Jacoby, S. M. (1986) 'Employee attitude testing at Sears, Roebuck and Company, 1938–1960', *Business History Review*, 60(4): 602–32.

Jeremy, D. J. (1981) *Transatlantic Industrial Revolution: The Diffusion of Textile Technologies between Britain and America, 1790–1830s*. Cambridge, MA: MIT Press.

Jeremy, D. J. (ed.) (1988) *Business and Religion in Modern Britain*. Aldershot: Gower.

Jeremy, D. J. (1990) *Capitalists and Christians: Business Leaders and the Churches in Britain, 1900–1960*. Oxford: Clarendon Press.

Jeremy, D. J. (1991a) 'The hundred largest employers in the United Kingdom in manufacturing and non-manufacturing industries in 1907, 1935 and 1955', *Business History*, 31(1): 93–114.

Jeremy, D. J. (1991b) 'The prosopography of business leaders: possibilities, resources and problems', *Proceedings of the Annual Conference (1990) of the Business Archives Council*, 35–61.

Jeremy, D. J. (ed.) (1991c) *International Technology Transfer: Europe, Japan and the USA, 1700–1914*. Aldershot: Edward Elgar.

Jeremy, D. J. (ed.) (1992) *The Transfer of International Technology: Europe, Japan and the USA in the Twentieth Century*. Aldershot: Edward Elgar.

Jeremy, D. J. (ed.) (1994a) *An International Directory of Business Historians*. Aldershot: Edward Elgar.

Jeremy, D. J. (ed.) (1994b) *Technology Transfer and Business Enterprise*. Aldershot: Edward Elgar.

Jeremy, D. J. (1994c) 'New business history?', *The Historical Journal*, 37(3): 717–28.

Jeremy, D. J. (1998a) *A Business History of Britain, 1900–1990s*. Oxford: Oxford University Press.

Jeremy, D. J. (1998b) *Artisans, Entrepreneurs and Machines: Essays on the Early Anglo-American Textile Industries, 1770–1840s*. Aldershot: Ashgate.

Jeremy, D. J. (ed.) (1998c) *Religion, Business and Wealth in Modern Britain*. London: Routledge.

Jeremy, D. J. and Farnie, D. A. (2001) 'The ranking of firms, the counting of employees, and the classification of data: a cautionary note', *Business History*, 43(3): 105–18.

Jeremy, D. J. and Shaw, C. (eds) (1984–86) *Dictionary of Business Biography*, 6 vols. London: Butterworths.

Jeremy, D. J. and Tweedale, G. (1994) *Dictionary of Twentieth Century British Business Leaders*. London: Bowker Saur.

John, R. R. (1997) 'Elaborations, revisions, dissents: Alfred D. Chandler, Jr's *The Visible Hand* after twenty years', *Business History Review*, 71(2): 151–200.

Johnman, L. (1986) 'The large manufacturing companies of 1935', *Business History*, 28(2): 226–45.

Jones, E. (1995) *True and Fair: A History of Price Waterhouse*. London: Hamish Hamilton.

Jones, G. (1986) *British Multinationals' Origins, Management and Performance*. Aldershot: Gower.

Jones, G. (1993) *British Multinational Banking, 1830–1990.* Oxford: Clarendon Press.

Jones, G. (1996) *The Evolution of International Business: An Introduction.* London: Routledge.

Jones, G. and Schroter, H. G. (eds) (1993) *The Rise of Multinationals in Continental Europe.* Aldershot: Edward Elgar.

Jones, S. R. H. (1997) 'Transaction costs and the theory of the firm: the scope and limitations of the new institutional approach', *Business History,* 39(4): 9–25.

Josephson, M. (1934) *The Robber Barons.* New York: Harcourt, Brace & Co.

Kanter, R. M. (1983) *The Change Masters: Corporate Entrepreneurs at Work.* London: Unwin.

Kaplan, A. D. H. (1954) *Big Enterprise in a Competitive System.* Washington DC: The Brookings Institution.

Kirkland, E. C. (1956) *Dream and Thought in the Business Community, 1860–1900.* Ithaca, NY: Cornell University Press.

Kindleberger, C. P. (1965) *Economic Development.* New York: McGraw-Hill Book Co.

Kirby, M. W. and Rose, M. B. (eds) (1994) *Business Enterprise in Modern Britain from the Eighteenth to the Twentieth Century.* London: Routledge.

Krooss, H. E. (1970) *Executive Opinion: What Business Leaders Said and Thought on Economic Issues, 1920s–1960s.* Garden City, NY: Doubleday.

Kynaston, D. (1994) *The City of London,* Vol. 1 *A World of Its Own 1815–1890.* London: Pimlico.

Kynaston, D. (1995) *The City of London,* Vol. 2 *The Golden Years, 1890–1914.* London: Pimlico.

Kynaston, D. (1999) *The City of London,* Vol. 3 *Illusions of Gold, 1914–1945.* London: Chatto & Windus.

Larson, H. M. (1948) *Guide to Business History.* Cambridge, MA: Harvard University Press.

Lazonick, W. (1986) 'The cotton industry', in B. Elbaum and W. Lazonick (eds), *The Decline of the British Economy.* Oxford: Clarendon Press.

Lee, C. H. (1990a) 'Corporate behavior in theory and history: I, the evolution of theory', *Business History,* 32(1): 17–31.

Lee, C. H. (1990b) 'Corporate behavior in theory and history: II, the historian's perspective', *Business History,* 32(2): 163–79.

Lloyd, H. D. (1894) *Wealth against Commonwealth.* New York: Harper & Bros.

Lloyd-Jones, R., Lewis, M. J., and Eason, M. (1999) 'Culture as metaphor: company and business strategy at Raleigh Industries, c. 1945–60', *Business History,* 41(3): 93–133.

Locke, R. R. (1984) *The End of the Practical Man: Entrepreneurship and Higher Education in Germany, France and Great Britain, 1880–1940.* Greenwich, CT: JAI Press.

Locke, R. R. (1989) *Management and Higher Education since 1940: The Influence of America and Japan on West Germany, Great Britain, and France.* Cambridge: Cambridge University Press.

Locke, R. R. (1996) *The Collapse of the American Management Mystique.* Oxford: Oxford University Press.

Lundberg, F. (1969) *The Rich and the Super Rich: A Study in the Power of Money Today.* London: Nelson.

MacLeod, C. (1988) *Inventing the Industrial Revolution: The English Patent System, 1660–1800.* Cambridge: Cambridge University Press.

Marwick, A. (1970) *The Nature of History.* London: Macmillan.

Matthews, D. (2000) 'Oral history, accounting history and an interview with Sir John Grenside', *Accounting, Business and Financial History,* 10(1): 57–83.

Matthews, D., Anderson, M. and Edwards, J. R. (1998) *The Priesthood of Industry: The Rise of the Professional Accountant in British Management.* Oxford: Oxford University Press.

Miller, W. (1952) *Men in Business: Essays on the Historical Role of the Entrepreneur.* New York: Harper & Row.

Mintzberg, H. and Waters, J. A. (1982) 'Tracking strategy in an entrepreneurial firm', *Academy of Management Journal,* 25(3): 465–99.

Morikawa, H. (1992) *Zaibatsu: The Rise and Fall of Family Enterprise Groups in Japan.* Tokyo: University of Tokyo Press.

Mosakowski, E. and Earley, P. C. (2000) 'A selective review of time assumptions in strategy research', *Academy of Management Review,* 25(4): 796–812.

Mowery, D. C. (1986) 'Industrial research, 1900–1950', in B. Elbaum and W. Lazonick (eds), *The Decline of the British Economy.* Oxford: Clarendon Press.

Mumford, M. J. (1991) 'Chartered accountants as business managers: an oral history perspective', *Accounting, Business and Financial History,* 1(2): 123–40.

Nafziger, E. W. (1969) 'The effect of the Nigerian extended family on entrepreneurial activity', *Economic Development and Cultural Change,* 18(1): 25–33.

Nevins, A. (1954) *Ford: The Times, the Man, the Company.* New York: Scribner.

Nevins, A. and Hill, F. E. (1957) *Ford: Expansion and Challenge, 1915–1933.* New York: Scribner.

Nevins, A. and Hill, F. E. (1963) *Ford: Decline and Rebirth, 1933–1962.* New York: Scribner.

Newcomer, M. (1955) *The Big Business Executive: The Factors that Made Him.* New York: Columbia University Press.

Nicholas, T. (1999) 'Wealth making in nineteenth and early twentieth-century Britain: industry v. commerce and finance', *Business History,* 41(1): 16–36.

Nicholas, T. (2000) 'Wealth making in the nineteenth and early twentieth century: the Rubinstein hypothesis revisited', *Business History,* 42(2): 155–68.

North, D. C. (1990) *Institutions, Institutional Change and Economic Performance.* Cambridge: Cambridge University Press.

Numagami, T. (1998) 'The infeasibility of invariant laws in management studies: a reflective dialogue in defense of case studies', *Organization Science,* 9(1): 2–15.

Parker, P. Sir (1989) *For Starters: The Business of Life*. London: Jonathan Cape.

Pavitt, K. (ed.) (1980) *Technical Innovation and British Economic Performance*. London: Macmillan.

Payne, P. L. (1967) 'The emergence of the large scale company in Great Britain, 1870–1914', *Economic History Review*, 30(3): 519–42.

Penrose, E. T. (1959) *The Theory of the Growth of the Firm*. Oxford: Basil Blackwell.

Pentland, B. T. (1999) 'Building process theory with narrative: from description to explanation', *Academy of Management Review*, 24(4): 711–24.

Pettigrew, A. M. (1985) *The Awakening Giant: Continuity and Change in ICI*. Oxford: Blackwell.

Pettigrew, A. M. (1990) 'Longitudinal field research on change: theory and practice', *Organization Science*, 1(3): 267–92.

Pettigrew, A. M. (1992) 'On studying managerial elites', *Strategic Management Journal*, 13 (Winter Special Issue): 163–82.

Pettigrew, A. M. (1997) 'What is processual analysis?', *Scandinavian Journal of Management*, 13(4): 337–48.

Pollak, R. A. (1985) 'A transaction cost approach to families and households', *Journal of Economic Literature*, 23: 581–608.

Pollard, S. (1990) 'The world according to Mammon', *The Times Higher Education Supplement*, 27 April.

Popper, K. (1957) *The Poverty of Historicism*. London: Routledge & Kegan Paul.

Porter, M. E. (1980) *Competitive Strategy: Techniques for Analyzing Industries and Competitors*. New York: The Free Press.

Porter, M. E. (1985) *Competitive Advantage: Creating and Sustaining Superior Performance*. New York: The Free Press.

Porter, M. E. (1990) *The Competitive Advantage of Nations*. London: Macmillan.

Reader, W. J. (1970) *Imperial Chemical Industries*, Volume 1 *The Forerunners, 1870–1926*. Oxford: Oxford University Press.

Reader, W. J. (1975) *Imperial Chemical Industries*, Volume 2 *The First Quarter Century, 1926–1952*. Oxford: Oxford University Press.

Redding, S. G. (1990) *The Spirit of Chinese Capitalism*. Berlin: De Gruyter.

Rose, M. B. (ed.) (1995) *Family Business*. Aldershot: Edward Elgar.

Rose, M. B. (2000) *Firms, Networks and Business Values: The British and American Cotton Industries since 1750*. Cambridge: Cambridge University Press.

Rosenberg, N. (1982) *Inside the Black Box: Technology and Economics*. Cambridge: Cambridge University Press.

Rowlinson, M. and Procter, S. (1999) 'Organizational culture and business history', *Organization Studies*, 20(3): 369–96.

Rubinstein, W. D. (1981) *Men of Property: The Very Wealthy in Britain since the Industrial Revolution*. London: Croom Helm.

Rubinstein, W. D. (2000) 'Wealth making in the nineteenth and early twentieth centuries: a response', *Business History*, 42(2): 141–54.

Rumelt, R. P. (1974) *Strategy, Structure and Economic Performance*. Cambridge, MA: Harvard University Press.

Scarbrough, H. (1998) 'Path(ological) dependency? Core competencies from an organizational perspective', *British Journal of Management*, 9: 219–32.

Scranton, P. (1983) *Proprietary Capitalism: The Textile Manufacture at Philadelphia, 1800–1885*. Cambridge: Cambridge University Press.

Scranton, P. (1989) *Figured Tapestry: Production, Markets, and Power in Philadelphia Textiles, 1885–1941*. Cambridge: Cambridge University Press.

Scranton, P. (1997) *Endless Novelty: Specialty Production and American Industrialization, 1865–1925*. Princeton, NJ: Princeton University Press.

Shaw, C. (1983) 'The large manufacturing employers of 1907', *Business History*, 25(1): 42–60.

Singleton, J. (1997) *The World Textile Industry*. London: Routledge.

Slaven, A. (1995) 'Entrepreneurs and business success and business failure in Scotland', in D. H. Aldcroft and A. Slaven (eds), *Enterprise and Management: Essays in Honour of Peter L. Payne*. Aldershot: Scolar Press.

Slaven, A. and Checkland, S. (eds) (1986–90) *Dictionary of Scottish Business Biography*, 2 vols. Aberdeen: Aberdeen University Press.

Smith, M. R. (1977) *Harpers Ferry Armory and the New Technology: The Challenge of Change*. Ithaca, NY: Cornell University Press.

Staudenmaier, J. M. (1985) *Technology's Storytellers: Reweaving the Human Fabric*. Cambridge, MA: MIT Press.

Stone, L. (1971) 'Prosopography', *Daedalus*, 100: 46–79.

Sunderland, D. (1999) '"Objectionable parasites": the Crown Agents and the purchase of Crown Colony government stores, 1880–1914', *Business History*, 41(4): 21–47.

Supple, B. (ed.) (1977) *Essays in British Business History*. Oxford: Oxford University Press.

Tarbell, I. M. (1904) *The History of the Standard Oil Company*, 2 vols. New York: Macmillan.

Taylor, G. D. (1994) 'Negotiating technology transfers within multinational enterprises: perspectives from Canadian history', *Business History*, 36(1): 127–58.

Teece, D. J., Pisano, G. and Shuen, A. (1997) 'Dynamic capabilities and strategic management', *Strategic Management Journal*, 18(7): 509–33.

Temin, P. and Galambos, L. (1988) *The Fall of the Bell System: A Study in Prices and Profits*. Cambridge: Cambridge University Press.

Thimm, A. L. (1976) *Business Ideologies in the Reform-Progressive Era, 1880–1914*. University, AL: University of Alabama Press.

Thompson, P. (1988) *The Voice of the Past: Oral History*, second edition. Oxford: Oxford University Press.

Tweedale, G. (1995) *Steel City: Entrepreneurship, Strategy & Technology in Sheffield, 1743–1993.* Oxford: Clarendon Press.

Tweedale, G. (2000) *From Magic Mineral to Killer Dust: Turner and Newall and the Asbestos Hazard.* Oxford: Oxford University Press.

Wada, K. (1991) 'The development of tiered inter-firm relationships in the automobile industry: a case study of Toyota Motor Corporation', *Japanese Yearbook on Business History,* 23–47.

Wardley, P. (1999) 'The emergence of big business: the largest corporate employers of labor in the United Kingdom, Germany and the United States c. 1907', *Business History,* 41(4): 88–116.

Weidenbaum, M. and Hughes, S. (1996) *The Bamboo Network: How Expatriate Chinese Entrepreneurs Are Creating a New Economic Superpower in Asia.* New York: Free Press.

Westall, O. M. (1997) 'Invisible, visible, and "direct" hands: an institutional interpretation of organizational structure and change in British general insurance', *Business History,* 39(4): 44–66.

Whittington, R. and Mayer, M. (2000) *The European Corporation: Strategy, Structure, and Social Science.* Oxford: Oxford University Press.

Wilkins, M. (1970) *The Emergence of Multinational Enterprise.* Cambridge, MA: Harvard University Press.

Wilkins, M. (1974) *The Maturing of Multinational Enterprise.* Cambridge, MA: Harvard University Press.

Wilkins, M. (1989) *The History of Foreign Investment in the United States to 1914.* Cambridge, MA: Harvard University Press.

Wilson, C. (1954) *The History of Unilever: A Study in Economic Growth and Social Change,* 2 vols. London: Cassell & Co.

Wilson, J. F. (1995) *British Business History, 1720–1994.* Manchester: Manchester University Press.

Yuzawa, T. (ed.) (1994) *Japanese Business Success: The Evolution of a Strategy.* London: Routledge.

20

Theorizing the Future of Strategy: Questions for Shaping Strategy Research in the Knowledge Economy

N. VENKATRAMAN and MOHAN SUBRAMANIAM

Much is being said today about how our economy is being transformed into a knowledge-based economy. There is a growing belief that intangible knowledge-based assets are replacing tangible physical assets as the primary impetus behind competitive advantage. Performance differentials seem to be explained more by intellectual, rather than physical, resources. Scholars and practitioners alike now appear to think that the traditional rules of competition may be increasingly losing relevance in this new economy, and there is a pressing need for organizations to find and embrace 'new' rules to survive and prosper.

What are these 'new' rules? How do they challenge our traditional ideas of strategy that we hold dear in our research and teaching? Do they change our traditional wisdom about strategy? What directions should future research in strategy take? In this chapter, we provide a framework to discuss these issues. We believe that strategy as a field of inquiry is at a crossroads today as it was in the late 1970s at the time of the Pittsburgh conference that led to Schendel and Hofer (1979). We need to look at the key issues facing corporations today and develop a proactive approach so that the theory of strategy continues to guide and shape leading-edge practice.

We present our ideas in this chapter in two sections. In the first section, we discuss how our current understanding of strategy has evolved over time. We capture this evolution in our thinking about strategy over three eras: first, wherein strategy was viewed as a *portfolio of businesses*, second, as a *portfolio of capabilities*, and third, as it is now surfacing in the current knowledge based economy, as a *portfolio of relationships*. Each of these eras represents how organizations have rallied around a particular concept of strategy with an associated set of norms for creating competitive advantage. Also, underlying each of these norms are distinct paradigms: *economies of scale* for the first era, *economies of scope* for the second era, and finally, *economies of expertise* for the third and current era (see Table 20.1).

In discussing the evolution of strategy over these eras, we synthesize and put forward our *cumulative* state of the art understanding of strategy. We emphasize *cumulative*, as we believe that the emerging new concepts are not replacements, but supplements of old concepts. Economies of scale and scope, for example, are undoubtedly necessary for companies to compete even in the new knowledge-based economy. The difference, however, is in

Table 20.1   *The evolution of strategy from a theorizing perspective*

	Era 1	Era 2	Era 3
Description	Portfolio of businesses	Portfolio of capabilities	Portfolio of relationships
Key drivers of competitive advantage	Economies of scale	Economies of scale and scope	Economies of scale, scope and expertise
Key resources	Physical assets	Organizing skills for managing relatedness across businesses	Position in the network of expertise
Unit of analysis	Business unit	Corporation	Network of internal and external relationships
Key concept	Leverage industry imperfections	Leverage intangible resources	Leverage intellectual capital
Key questions	What products? What markets?	What capabilities?	What streams of expertise?
Dominant view	Positioning	Inimitability of processes and routines	Network centrality

their significance. From being key drivers of distinctive competitive advantage in earlier eras, scale and scope have now become parity factors. That is, while the benefits of scale and scope are necessary for companies to continue competing, they are no longer sufficient to create distinctive advantage. New concepts, such as the economies of expertise that we are proposing in this chapter, are emerging as providers of vital supplements to the benefits of scale and scope, for companies to break parity and surge ahead of their rivals.

In presenting this cumulative understanding of strategy we also set the stage to question the validity of the emerging concepts in light of what we observe to be the needs and characteristics of the knowledge-based economy. And, in doing so, we attempt to forge new directions for future research on strategy. We proceed to do so in the second section by raising four questions that represent the key conundrums and challenges for theorizing the future of strategy in the knowledge economy. Our discussion around each of these questions provides avenues for future studies to unravel, further develop and validate the 'new' rules to effectively compete in the knowledge economy.

EVOLUTION IN OUR CONCEPTUALIZATION
OF STRATEGY

Table 20.1 represents our view of how the concept of strategy has evolved over the years

in terms of three eras. These are stylized so that we are able to highlight the key themes and perspectives on theorizing about strategy. They are also meant to provide a foundation for us to develop a set of questions that epitomize our new challenges.

Era 1: Strategy as a Portfolio of Businesses (circa 1970s)

We begin with the first era wherein the concept of strategy could be described as a portfolio of businesses (Aaker and Day, 1986; Harrigan, 1981; Hofer and Schendel, 1978; Woo and Cooper, 1981). Note the focus on 'business', as this was the domain in which strategy was largely conceptualized. Even for multi-business corporations, the strategic thinking was at the level of each of its individual businesses. Competitive strategy was at the business unit level (Galbraith and Schendel, 1983; Govindarajan, 1989; Huff, 1982; Karnani, 1982; Porter, 1980) and industrial organization economics played a significant role in shaping our thinking about strategy and competitive advantage (see Bain, 1956; Mason, 1939; Porter, 1981, for a historical perspective). Business performance was explained by factors of industry structure and the conduct of firms within the industry (Scherer and Ross, 1990; Gale, 1972). Corporate performance was believed to be an aggregate of performances across the individual business (Kurt and Montgomery, 1981;

Rumelt, 1974). This era can be classified through the lens of strategy as a *portfolio of businesses*.

In this view, early thoughts of competitive business strategy largely revolved around gaining advantage through *economies of scale*. Concepts of learning and experience curves (Hall and Howell, 1985; Henderson, 1979; Lieberman, 1987) dominated strategic thinking, as firms fought to dominate businesses through gaining market share (Buzzell et al., 1975). And this experience curve logic bridged the link between an individual business unit and the corporation as a portfolio of businesses through the generation and utilization of cash as a key strategic resource. Balancing the generation and use of cash led to constructs like the BCG portfolio matrix and its variants. The BCG matrix highlighted the need for every business in a company's portfolio to focus on relative market share in high growth industries – businesses that did not achieve dominance were expected to be divested. Academic research echoed these views with several studies based on the PIMS database reinforcing the strategic significance of market share (Buzzell and Wiersema, 1981; Ramanujam and Venkatraman, 1984; Wensley, 1982).

Porter's (1980) influential work further refined and legitimized this thinking by anchoring it within the concepts of industrial organization economics (Caves, 1980). Industry boundaries defined businesses for the purpose of strategic analysis. And, industries were evaluated based on their attractiveness – a function of the imperfections in their structural characteristics (for example, degree of concentration, barriers to entry/exit, rivalry). From a strategist's perspective perfect markets were unattractive, as these markets did not provide above normal profits, or rents. Imperfect markets in contrast were the strategist's ideal, as these markets enabled firms to earn monopoly rents. The concept of strategy thus evolved into finding ways by which firms could *leverage imperfections* in industry structures, so as to gain monopoly power. Exploiting learning curves and striving for market share represented some of the means by which firms could create imperfections in the structure of the industry and leverage monopoly power (Amit, 1986).

Companies competed with *physical assets* as their key resources, because they were primary means to create imperfections within the industry. For example, investments in physical assets and associated fixed costs raised barriers to entry, and investments in physical capacities were means to signal the potential for protracted price wars and hence deterred rivalry (Dixit, 1980; Salop, 1979; Wernerfelt and Karnani, 1987). Moreover by increasing the intensity of physical assets firms could further take advantage of their economies of scale. The specific means by which a firm leveraged market imperfections were captured in its *positioning*. A strong position implied that the firm was leveraging market imperfections very well; a weak position in contrast implied that the firm was not leveraging market imperfections very well. Business units were found to cluster around specific positions in an industry to form strategic groups (Cool and Dierickx, 1993; Hatten and Hatten, 1987; McGee and Thomas, 1986) – and these positions determined their competitiveness (Caves and Ghemawat, 1992; Porter, 1980). Positioning thus became the dominant view of strategy.

Although IO economics largely influenced this view, research in organization theory provided complementary ideas in the form of analyzing environmental characteristics and matching organizations' structures with these characteristics. For example, environmental certainty (Thompson, 1967; Lawrence and Lorsch, 1967) or environmental munificence (Pfeffer and Salancik, 1978) were concepts similar to that of industry attractiveness as proposed by industrial organization economics. Our objective in this chapter is not to be exhaustive, but to develop the logic behind a dominant view of strategy that could be characterized by a portfolio of businesses. A list of representative studies of this era is presented in Table 20.2.

Era 2: Strategy as a Portfolio of Capabilities (circa mid-1980s)

While industrial organization theory gave the field of strategy much-needed conceptual rigor, two shortcomings of theorizing strategy from this perspective soon became apparent. First was the absence of a persuasive logic for managing multiple businesses. Viewing strategy for a multi-business corporation as a mere

Table 20.2   *Representative studies for era 1 (strategy as a portfolio of businesses)*

Key concepts	Representative studies
Market share, learning curves, and scale related advantages	Buzzell et al., 1975; Henderson, 1979; Lieberman, 1987; Prescott et al., 1986.
Significance of physical assets for rivalry deterrence	Dixit, 1980; Salop, 1979; Wernerfelt and Karnani, 1987.
Positioning businesses for competitive advantage, strategic groups	Hatten and Hatten, 1987; McGee and Thomas, 1986; Porter, 1980.
Fundamentals of industrial organization theory as applied to corporate strategy	Caves, 1980; Porter, 1981.
Industry as a unit of analysis for business strategy	Harrigan, 1981; Porter, 1980; Woo and Cooper, 1981.
Broader environmental analysis for strategy/ Matching business unit strategy to fit environmental conditions	Abell, 1980; Andrews, 1971; Ansoff, 1965; Hofer and Schendel, 1978; Lawrence and Lorsch, 1967; Pfeffer and Salancik, 1978.

aggregation of strategies in individual businesses was clearly not adequate. Rumelt's (1974) ambitious attempt to develop a scheme to understand the different logics of diversification was an important contribution that pioneered a different line of inquiry. Research in the area of corporate diversification provided compelling evidence that unrelated diversification – or managing unrelated businesses – was rarely successful (Bettis, 1981; Montgomerry, 1979; Palepu, 1985; Varadarajan and Ramanujam, 1987). These findings highlighted the fact that even if a firm crafted out strong positions in multiple businesses, it need not be successful at the aggregate level (Rumelt, 1982). Clearly, some synergies across businesses had to be leveraged for effectively managing a multi-business corporation (Prahalad and Bettis, 1986). The concept of strategy based on 'positioning' did not adequately address cross-business synergies, and hence the value-added of a corporation.

Second, industrial organization theory was largely about industry structure. As a result, theorizing strategy from this viewpoint leads to a highly 'industry focused' view of strategy. The emphasis on market imperfections made strategic analysis focus more on *what* objectives to achieve, as opposed to *how* to achieve those objectives. There was thus a pressing need for a framework that enabled a systematic analysis of internal workings of a company (to answer the 'how to' question), and more importantly, for a theory to explain how organizations could effectively compete both within and across industries.

A stream of research described as the *resource-based theory* of the firm evolved to address these shortcomings. As opposed to focusing on market imperfections through product-market positions, this research stream focused on how organizations conducted its activities – or, on an organization's processes and routines. The logic was that if organizational processes and routines were valuable and difficult for rivals to imitate, firms could create and sustain competitive advantage (Barney, 1991; Conner, 1991; Peteraf, 1993). Note that this framework does not limit its frame of reference to any particular industry, but does consider competitors in its analytical lens by underscoring the inimitability of processes and routines as a necessary condition for competitive advantage.

The significance of this framework was that it allowed a strategist to systematically analyze and understand the internal processes and routines by which an organization competed in the market place (Collis, 1994; Robins and Wiersema, 1995). For embedded within these processes and routines were an organization's distinctive capabilities that determined how effectively they could compete either within or across businesses and industries (Hitt and Ireland, 1985; Nelson, 1991). The theory of strategy thus evolved from a portfolio of businesses to a *portfolio of capabilities*.

Prahalad and Hamel's (1990) influential work on core competencies underscored the key differences between these two perspectives of strategy (portfolio of businesses and portfolio of capabilities). They argued that firms that restricted their strategic analysis to single industries, and limited their attention to how they were positioned in their focal industry alone, often failed to anticipate the potential for new competitors to transform the structure of their industry and to seriously undermine prevailing product-market positions. They made their case through examples of several such new competitors (Honda, Canon, Sharp and so on), who were different from conventional competitors in several ways.

One, they came in with strengths absorbed from different industries. For example, Canon entered the photocopier business to challenge Xerox by leveraging their strengths in optics and imaging garnered from their camera business. Two, prevailing product-market positions in the focal industry did not pose significant barriers to them as they could leverage their strengths gained from other industries to create new (and more effective) product-market positions. Again, Canon bypassed the entry barriers Xerox had erected for its large copiers sold to big corporations by choosing to compete with small copiers for copy-service franchisers (such as Copy Cop). Three, they could generate a stream of products that were difficult to foresee and plan counter-attacks for, as they were not necessarily based upon the conventional wisdom accumulated in the focal industry. Xerox for example could not anticipate Canon's entry into their industry with small copiers and for years could not retaliate with equivalent products because their business model was designed only to reinforce their existing product-market position (Henderson and Clark, 1990).

The core logic that competitors such as Canon competed with was rooted in developing a portfolio of capabilities. These capabilities were embedded in their internal processes and routines that cut across several organizational functions and levels. These processes and routines constituted activities that systematically absorbed learning from different businesses, shared and integrated this learning across the organization, and then leveraged this shared learning through a stream of new products (Galunic and Rodan, 1998; Teece and Pisano, 1997). For example, Honda's focus was not so much in its product-market positioning in any single industry but on reinforcing its capabilities in 'power-trains' and leveraging them to generate a stream of new products cutting across different businesses such as lawn-mowers, motor-cycles, outboard boats and automobiles (Prahalad and Hamel, 1990). The competitive advantage for

this company did not stem from any specific product-market position in any single industry, but from they way it organized its activities – or its processes and routines – that enabled it to execute cross-functional learning across multiple businesses and effectively harness it in its new products.

This new lens modified the focus of competitive strategy from that of creating industry imperfections through product-market positioning to understanding how to develop and leverage organizational capabilities. Consequently, the key drivers of competitive advantage shifted from economies of scale to *economies of scope*. Economies of scope were about leveraging *organizational relatedness* (Grant, 1988; Farjoun, 1998). That is, competitive advantage was no longer merely a function of how well an organization could leverage imperfections in any one specific industry, but a consequence of how learning across industries could be transferred, shared and effectively deployed in any of several businesses (Markides, 1994). Over and above physical assets in any one business, the *organizing skills* that enabled companies to achieve the transfer and deployment of learning across industries through their processes and routines became vital for competitive advantage. In addition to creating impregnable product-market positions in any specific industry for deterring rivalry, the *inimitability* of processes and routines – that enabled organizations to leverage learning across industries in ways their rivals could not – became critical to create and sustain competitive advantage (Galunic and Rodan, 1998). These processes and routines and related organizing skills constituted the *intangible assets* of organizations that critically supplemented the benefits of physical assets for competitive advantage (Hall, 1992; Itami, 1987).

Even though this line of thinking was conceptually elegant and supported by anecdotes and case studies, empirical tests of key propositions are limited. Some of the key problems include the measurement of processes and routines that typically span across different organizational levels, and the development of valid metrics for the causal ambiguity or inimitability of these routines. Some critics have also called this view tautological, because of arguments such as: a resource has to be valuable for competitive advantage. We, however, believe

Table 20.3 *Representative studies for era 2 (strategy as a portfolio of capabilities)*

Key concepts	Representative studies
Fundamentals of the resource-based theory of the firm	Amit and Schoemaker, 1993; Barney, 1991; Conner, 1991; Peteraf, 1993.
Core competence of the corporation, organizing skills	Collis, 1994; Hitt and Ireland, 1985; Prahalad and Hamel, 1990; Robins and Wiersema, 1995.
Leveraging relatedness across businesses	Chatterjee and Wernerfelt, 1991; Galunic and Rodan, 1998; Farjoun, 1998; Markides, 1994; Prahalad and Bettis, 1986.
Leveraging intangible resources	Itami, 1987; Subramaniam and Venkatraman, 2001; Zander and Kogut, 1995.

that this perspective is equally valid today and is attractive for researchers to develop further points of view and hypotheses that are tested with data from companies. We present a representative, but not exhaustive, list of studies that represent this view in Table 20.3.

Era 3: Strategy as a Portfolio of Relationships (circa mid-1990s)

While the concept of strategy evolved from product-market positioning in individual businesses or industries to processes and routines for managing multiple businesses and leveraging relatedness across them, one important premise remained unchanged. This premise was that the key drivers of competitive advantage were internal to the organization. Strategic success was based on the strength of the organization's own ability to craft a strong position in its market, or, its own superior processes and routines giving it the necessary capabilities to out compete its rivals.

Over the last few years, however, corporations have not limited their strategies to those based on capabilities that they fully own through ownership. The evolving view is that firms now need to generate a wider range of capabilities that are difficult to generate internally, and can be developed only through a *portfolio of relationships*. In this view, companies complement their internal capabilities with a wide array of relationships with external entities (Baum et al., 2000). These may include standard outsourcing but more importantly involve co-creation of capabilities with partners using complex governance structures and processes (Quinn, 1992; Lewis, 1994, 2000; Stork and Hill, 2000).

The notion of relationships in strategic thinking is by no means new. An impressive stream of research based on transaction cost economics (for example, Coase, 1937; Williamson, 1975) has long recognized that firms do not conduct all activities concerning their businesses internally. Instead they create relationships with other firms and invite them to share their business value creation process. More specifically, these studies suggest that firms may elect to let external suppliers – through market-based contracting or even longer-term contracting – provide a value adding business service, despite the firm possessing the necessary expertise to execute that process.

The evolving view of strategy as a portfolio of relationships however is different from this traditional viewpoint. From this new perspective, firms create relationships not because they choose to outsource a business process (based on transaction cost criteria) despite having the requisite expertise to conduct it internally. Relationships are formed because the firm does not possess the requisite expertise for that business process. The demand for new skills and know-how far outstrips the capacities of firms to develop them on their own. Put differently, most organizations have limitations in terms of the band-with of capabilities they can develop, and hence necessarily have to look for external sources for meeting environmental demands. Moreover, as these environmental demands change, organizations also have to re-configure the nature of complementary capabilities that they need and are relevant under the changing circumstances. In such an environment, organizations that do not develop the right set of relationships for dynamic value creation and rely only on their internal strengths to reinforce prevailing product-market positions, or consolidate a particular set of processes and routines, are very likely to be out-maneuvered by more nimble organizations.

Table 20.4   *The distinctive roles of relationships in the industrial era versus expertise era*

	'Who'	'Why'	'How'	'When'
Traditional	Upstream suppliers and downstream distributors in the different boundary-spanning functional domains	Reduction in transaction costs	Standard contracts based on clear delineation of decision rights and defined performance metrics	Dependent on operational conditions
Emergent	Those in possession of critical expertise that support current strategies as well as possible trajectories of strategic evolution	In addition to reducing transaction costs, firms need to have mechanisms to identify, nurture and exploit a broader range of expertise necessary for strategic adaptation	A portfolio of relationships that balance differential types of expertise and intellectual properties; this might involve equity investments, joint R&D, licensing and joint ventures – often without ex-ante specification of performance metrics	Dynamic shifts in the business landscape brought about by the broader evolution to a knowledge economy; the implications are competitors now jockey across traditional industry boundaries

Table 20.4 further describes the key differences in the concept of relationships from the traditional industrial economy perspective and the emergent perspectives.

Although outsourcing of non-core capabilities could still be studied from the standard lens of organizational economics and the constructs of the second era, what's needed now is a way to understand how a corporation acquires capabilities through relationships – where these capabilities are core drivers of value delivery to customers. This view has become popular with themes like virtual organizations and strategic sourcing for capabilities. The key premise being that in the knowledge economy, no one firm can have all the required capabilities inside the corporate boundaries. Knowledge resources cannot be appropriated like physical, tangible resources. As corporate boundaries get blurred with companies entering into cross-licensing, co-sourcing as well as joint R&D and joint venturing for leveraging knowledge resources, we need to take a different perspective to look at strategy. We believe that this emergent perspective takes the form of *economies of expertise*. This view provides a new logic for strategy, and supplements the concepts of economies of scale and scope that shaped our thinking in the previous eras.

What are economies of expertise? They are advantages that come from leveraging knowledge flows in a complex network of relationships. They require a different set of strengths, both in terms of understanding where the potential sources of knowledge reside and the ability to absorb and deploy external knowledge in their businesses. The strategic focus thus shifts from strengthening internal processes and routines for leveraging internal capabilities to building mechanisms that enable identifying, sharing, and absorbing knowledge in a broader network of organizations (Kogut, 2000).

It is important to highlight that this is not just about the recent euphoria about knowledge management systems and processes for managing knowledge and expertise inside the firm (Davenport, 1997; Nonaka, 1994; Stewart, 1997). Instead it is about conceptualizing how a company develops superior strategy by understanding the knowledge flows in a complex network of relationships. Let's look at the network of relationships within Kleiner Perkin's keiretsu of expertise to highlight the salient concepts of this era. We see that the strategy of individual firms, which can be represented as nodes in the network, is incomplete if we look at them only in terms of their scale and scope. The reason is that they benefit by accessing and leveraging the expertise of complementary entities that are tied together through financial capital, cross-technology licensing as well as important interlocking directorates. In addition, these companies have a rich and complex array of relationships that is independent of Kleiner Perkin's own business activities (and consequently, its scale and scope). They develop multiple avenues to access and leverage expertise to succeed in this fast-changing marketplace.

It should be noted however that this concept of strategy is still evolving. It has to be refined, grounded in organizational data and validated through systematic tests. We believe that this era is rich in opportunities for rethinking the important role of strategy. However, more work needs to be done to formalize this thinking and transform it into a framework that can not only steer academic research but also guide the decision-making processes of practitioners. So, in the section below, we discuss a set of questions that mold and refine our thinking on strategy in this era.

THEORIZING STRATEGY IN THE EXPERTISE ERA

What are the implications of this shift in our conception of strategy? Do they simply provide a new context to apply traditional strategy theories? Or do they compel us to rethink how we theorize about strategy? There have been many discussions about the new business landscape. Some focus on the internet as if technology is the driving force. Others focus on knowledge and expertise. We believe that the internet as a technological force is a subset of the larger shift to the economy based on knowledge and expertise. This is not a forum to lay out the broader shifts underway. Instead, we focus on a set of four questions, which over time will allow us to better understand the role of strategy as a portfolio of relationships where the relationships are formed for accessing and leveraging expertise that drives value creation.

Question 1: How Do We Conceptualize Economies of Expertise?

By now the theoretical and practical implications of economies of scale and scope are very well understood. Our challenge is to develop

ways to delineate how economies of expertise differ from these well-understood concepts. One way to begin doing so is to contrast how each of these phenomena has to be leveraged for obtaining their benefits.

The benefits of economies of scale come from leveraging the depth of physical assets. That is, greater capacities, or larger investments in plant and machinery, lead to more scale based advantages (Porter, 1980). Similarly, the benefits of economies of scope come from leveraging organizational relatedness. That is, the more organizations derive common knowledge from their businesses and utilize them across these businesses, the greater their benefits of scope (Chatterjee and Wernerfelt, 1991; Prahalad and Hamel, 1990). In contrast, the benefits of economies of expertise come from a firm's *centrality in the knowledge network*.

Centrality within a network matters because of preferential access through understanding the likely trajectories of knowledge. These relationships could be through linkages with leading laboratories for developing pilot ideas and prototypes. These are different from passive, tangential relationships in the limited domain of high-technology areas in the industrial age and are emerging as central to acquire and leverage expertise in a faster knowledge life cycle. For example, venture capitalists are centrally connected to the creation of new knowledge today as they have preferential access to expertise through the rights that they have received as part of their initial investments. And these venture capitalists are not limiting their domain of influence over start-ups but are increasingly applying it to established companies. Cisco has relied on its interlinkages with Sequoia Capital for being the nucleus in the evolution of the internet network over the last decade. It has made several acquisitions of critical technologies through the investments that Sequoia Capital placed with different technology start-ups. Similarly, Microsoft and Intel have used a significant part of their venture funds as investments in a wide domain of expertise. They use these funds to probe, test and stimulate how the technology might evolve in this fast-changing era. Unlike in the era of portfolio of businesses and portfolio of capabilities, the role of corporate ventures and investments now has emerged as an important mechanism to create network centrality and consequently increase economies of expertise.

While expertise has long been considered a critical resource for strategy, the new challenge today is to conceptualize how economies of expertise are being leveraged through relationships. Earlier strategy frameworks have helped us understand how firms create and leverage expertise within their organizational boundaries (Grant, 1996; Leonard-Barton, 1995). However, the new challenge for us is to theorize how firms create and leverage expertise from a broader network of relationships. In this domain we believe the notion of network centrality offers a promising area for theorizing.

It is important to note that economies of expertise through centrality in the network of relationships need not be treated as independent of economies of scale and scope. In fact economies of expertise are likely to be enhanced through economies of scale and scope. Firms having a strong position because of their scale, or unique capabilities because of their scope of businesses, become attractive partners for others to form relationships with them. The greater these advantages, the more likely they would occupy an important position in the network (see Gulati et al., 2000 for a discussion on these issues). It may be premature to come up with operational indicators for this concept. However, viewing relationships through network analyses may be promising to develop new metrics of networks that capture the different dimensions of acquiring and leveraging expertise.

If we are on the threshold of a new logic of strategy and value creation through expertise, then we need a set of constructs that reflect expertise as a driver of advantage. Economies of expertise is a meta-concept that is worthy of some serious attention by researchers so that we go beyond anecdotal evidence or untested assertions.

Question 2: Do We Need a New Unit of Analysis for Theorizing about Strategy?

The evolution of theorizing about strategy over the three eras allows us to highlight a shift in the unit of analysis. The typical unit of analysis in strategy has been the business unit for era 1 and has been the corporation for era 2. This is because competitive advantage has been largely a function of how activities within a business unit or a corporation are managed.

The shift to an expertise era brings with it some important challenges about selecting the unit of analysis. The 'entity' which determines the competitiveness of a firm is amorphous – a function of a shifting myriad of networks and relationships as we observed earlier with companies such as Cisco, Intel and Microsoft. Interestingly, this is not limited to these companies as more companies can be seen as a portfolio of relationships to assemble and use complementary capabilities. If that is the case, how do we determine our unit of analysis for strategy?

Let us, for a moment, revisit how we have framed strategy questions neatly into the four 'levels of analyses' – individual, group, organization and inter-organization as they roughly correspond to the levels in organization theory. To the extent that our research is discipline-driven, these levels proved useful for researchers to embrace and build on theoretical arguments from the referent disciplines like psychology, sociology and economics.

The inter-organizational level of analysis was always the most bothersome since the relevant theoretical underpinnings were considered to be weaker than the 'cleaner' levels inside the organization. But now, in an era of dynamic cooperation and competition (Brandenberger and Nalebluff, 1998), we do not have the luxury of only studying easy-to-track entities. An increasing number of studies are now dealing with networks of activities. Moore (1996) in his provocatively titled book *The Death of Competition* highlights the evolution of eco-systems. We may be tempted to accept the ideas of eco-systems and alliance clusters and value networks as useful ways to describe emergent phenomena. But, how do we define them in a parsimonious way? What are the different building blocks or fundamental principles that shape these networks? We are compelled to think about strategy as a network-centric concept and treat it as such. So, how do we best conceptualize a business entity that is embedded within an organizational system but is intricately connected to knowledge networks outside? What unit of analysis can we develop and use?

Question 3: Does Economies of Expertise Lead to Differential Performance?

If the above two questions are addressed systematically, we may have better clarity around the meta-concept of economies of expertise and we may have derived dimensions of this concept at different levels. Now, we can begin to assess the relationships between this concept and important criterion variables like competitive advantage and performance.

Strategy as a field has always been called upon to explain performance through strategic actions – whether they relate to business unit strategy or corporate strategy. That requirement has not changed now. If we have to make progress in understanding the notions of strategy in the knowledge era, we need to ask the question: Can we explain the success of today's business leaders with the concepts of scale and scope or can this success be better explained by concepts rooted in expertise? In other words, what's the additional explanatory power of the concepts that differentially reflect knowledge and expertise?

If expertise is to become a central anchor, we need theories and models that demonstrate the unique and salient role in the creation and capture of value in the marketplace. Researchers seeking to understand the drivers of markct capitalization are calling for better measures of understanding knowledge-based advantages (see for instance: Baruch Lev's research program at NYU). Practitioners in companies like Skandia, Xerox and BP are experimenting with different ways of assessing how their approaches to managing knowledge drive their bottom line. There have been many attempts at developing ways to manage knowledge – both reflecting a western culture and an Asian (Japanese) culture. Anecdotally, we know the importance of knowledge and expertise. But, what's missing is a systematic link between the concept of economies of expertise and performance.

We can develop a simple stylized functional form to tease out the relationships that could make an important contribution:

$$\text{Performance} = f\,(\text{scale, scope}) \qquad (1)$$
$$\text{Performance} = f\,(\text{scale, scope, expertise}) \qquad (2)$$

The functional forms of the above equations may be intuitive but the empirical tests are not straightforward and call for simultaneous and path-dependent formulations. The complicating factor is that expertise may indeed be a common cause of scale and scope based effects. For instance, knowledge may enhance an organization's ability to manage scale and scope (by deploying managerial expertise across divisions and across relationships).

Consider GE for example. This company offers a unique setting that we can use to derive working propositions to support the above model and develop a design to test it more systematically across multiple companies. Clearly, GE has significant economies of scale in the individual businesses – attesting to scale effects. Jack Welch as the CEO has always strived for the individual business units to be dominant players in their respective markets. In addition, it's well known that GE has scope effects as a portfolio across the business units. This is particularly true in recent years as the internet and e-business has allowed consolidation of activities across different business units and coordinate purchases and sales.

Moreover, GE is a setting that provides insights for economies of expertise. The Corporate Learning Center has spearheaded the sharing of best practices across the different business units in areas such as globalization, services, six-sigma quality processes and the internet/e-business. In addition, GE is in the midst of developing and extending its learning activities to tap into and learn from its extended network of alliances and partnerships. So, how do we tease out the differential effects of scale, scope and expertise in driving GE's performance? By studying a leading-edge company such as GE, we can develop insights that can be used to study other large corporations that are in the midst of maximizing their performance across these three sets of drivers – scale, scope and expertise. We may even derive a different categorization of the effects than the traditional tri-partite classification that we have used thus far.

Question 4: Do We Need New Organizing Principles?

The fourth question focuses on organizing principles for the expertise era. Our traditional principles of organizing have revolved around efficiency. Right from Frederick Taylor to the more recent information processing views of Galbraith, we have been preoccupied in designing work-units that limit uncertainty, or, what the organization considers the realm of the unknown.

Today's economy however thrives by leveraging uncertainty. Successful organizations do not choose environments that limit uncertainty but strive for increased uncertainty. Competitive advantage may no longer be a function of a 'fit' between uncertainty and information processing capacity as we have traditionally understood – but a function of an organization's ability to continually navigate its way into realms of the unknown and concurrently develop requisite new expertise. Newer organizing principles like self-organizing teams, with dynamic capabilities based on increasing absorptive capacities, may replace the more conventional structures designed to process information efficiently.

What has not changed is the view that organization design needs to be still aligned with the strategic requirements in order to maximize performance. That basic treatise offered by Chandler in 1962 is still valid – although we may have adapted and revised our concept of strategy (from firm-specific to network-centric) and structure (to include alliances and relationships as well as multiple forms of contracts).

At least two strands of ideas are worthy of exploration in terms of conceptualizing organization governance in this era. One is a view that an organization is not merely a nexus of contracts but is a generator of future options. This calls for a greater degree of interdisciplinary thinking, where strategy as a field needs more integration with recent developments in corporate finance – especially real options (Merton, 1998; Jensen, 2000; Amram and Kulatilaka, 1999). A firm exists to create future options and this potential drives its value. Executing current strategies consequently becomes a necessary but not sufficient condition for success. Accordingly, we have to understand not just what a company does in the short term but what it does to generate options so that it is best positioned for the uncertain and fast-changing future through its investments in relationships.

The second strand is about employment contracts for expertise. Human resource policies have become central to organizational design and governance issues. The relationship between strategy and human resource was at best a tangential and peripheral theme in the industrial age. Now, strategic capabilities are through knowledge, which is embodied in people. And we may now find a direct and significant link between the talent pool of the employees and firm performance. The next evolution of strategic human resource management may prove to offer useful insights. This calls for understanding who takes the risks and who gets the rewards in the knowledge economy. Microsoft went public not to raise financial capital for its operating cash-flow but to monetize the value of knowledge and expertise of its workers and to provide an external perspective on how their expertise creates value (Stewart, 1997). In the knowledge economy, the organization is a network of expertise with positively reinforcing and escalating network effects (feeding off each other).

Alfred P. Sloan struggled with the design of organizations in era 1 with General Motors. Reginald Jones and Jack Welch struggled with the organization design and governance issues within GE in era 2 to manage degrees of relatedness (scope). We are yet to anoint a leader who may be seen as the architect of the organizational design for the new expertise era.

We are still in the experimental stages with different organizational forms to understand how they function as mechanisms for expertise leverage. Quinn's starburst model of organization has the potential to scan and cover a broader span of expertise. Inverted pyramids are organizational designs that allow those closer to the operations to bring their expertise to solve customer requirements and thereby create a competitive advantage through knowledge in action.

Companies are in the midst of trying out many other forms. Organization design then is one of facilitating the acquisition and use of expertise across boundaries including the portfolio of relationships. What we need is a typology of organizational governance that is particularly suited to the idea of generating future options through expertise and recognizing closer alignment between expertise and employment contracts. Then, we can assess how the specific organizational design type supports and shapes the strategic requirements in the expertise era. The evolution can be seen as shifting from knowledge sharing across functions (era 1) to across businesses (era 2) to across companies (era 3). The first two are clear and well established. And, if we are to make progress in strategy, we need to think through a network-centric view of organizational design.

CONCLUSIONS: FUTURE CHALLENGES

The winners in the new economy appear to be rewarded in the market place not necessarily by their current earnings but by what their key stakeholders appear to think as promising strategies. How do we communicate strategic logic when the focus is on obtaining capabilities through relationships? How do we communicate strategies if the focus is on generating future options? Are generic strategies that proved comforting to understand the complexity of strategy in the 1980s still valid? If not, what constructs and logics should we use? What we have tried to do in this chapter is to develop a broad picture of the changing landscape. Admittedly, it's biased as seen through our lenses. But, they offer some interesting and important avenues to pursue. The four questions serve as a starting point in this journey.

Over the years, strategy scholars have incorporated the theoretical logic of industrial organization economics and the methodological rigor of social sciences and econometrics to address key strategic questions. In-depth case studies provided the phenomenological underpinnings to frame research questions and test them using data collected under fairly steady-state conditions. Now, we are at a crossroads: the strategy phenomenon is becoming network-centric – compelling us to look beyond traditional units of analyses of business units and corporations. Industries are blurring due to technological convergence of digitization and the internet – compelling us to broaden the competitive landscape beyond narrowly defined industry boundaries. The key resources that drive value creation are becoming knowledge and expertise – compelling us to rethink the drivers of competitive advantage. And since expertise is not limited to any given organization, we need to develop newer and more powerful lens of relationship expertise and positioning in the network of fast-changing expertise.

We also need to recognize a parallel shift. Strategy has been preoccupied with accounting performance and to some extent on financial market performance. What's a good indicator of success and performance in the knowledge economy? Should we track and order companies based on asset productivity metrics like ROA, ROI when most of the assets and investments (in employees and expertise) are not seen on the accounting statements? Event studies that proved attractive under relatively predictable conditions are not as attractive today. This is because 'clean events' are difficult to discern with so many potentially confounding actions that companies pursue today. How do we develop better linkages between a network-view of strategy and performance? The challenge for strategy researchers is clear but the path ahead is open for us to collectively recognize the limitations of current approaches to theorizing – not because they are wrong but because they have outlived their usefulness. As the business landscape shifts to knowledge-based competition, it will be counterproductive if we continue to take our well-tested and widely accepted approaches without adapting them and when necessary discarding some of them in favor of newer approaches.

What we have attempted to do in this chapter is to provide a starting point for this journey. It's our responsibility to reframe how we theorize if we are to be taken seriously by researchers in other branches of management as well as by practitioners.

REFERENCES

Aaker, D. A. and Day G. S. (1986) 'The perils of high growth markets', *Strategic Management Journal*, 7: 409–21.

Abell, D. F. (1980) *Defining the Business*. Englewood Cliffs, NJ: Prentice-Hall.

Amit, R. (1986) 'Cost leadership strategy and experience curves', *Strategic Management Journal*, 7(3): 281–93.

Amit, R. and Schoemaker, P. (1993) 'Strategic assets and organizational rents', *Strategic Management Journal*, 14: 33–46.

Amram, M. and Kulatilaka, N. (1999) *Real-Options*. Boston: HBS Press.

Andrews, K. J. (1971) *The Concept of Corporate Strategy*. Homewood, IL: Dow-Jones Irwin.

Ansoff, I. (1965) *Corporate Strategy*. New York: McGraw Hill.

Bain, J. S. (1956) *Barriers to New Competition.* Cambridge, MA: Harvard University Press.

Barney, J. B. (1991) 'Firm resources and sustained competitive advantage', *Journal of Management,* 17(1): 99–120.

Baum, J. A. C., Calabrese, T. and Silverman, B. S. (2000) 'Don't go it alone: alliance network composition and startups' performance in Canadian biotechnology', *Strategic Management Journal,* 21(3): 267–81.

Bettis, R. A. (1981) 'Performance differences in related and unrelated diversified firms', *Strategic Management Journal,* 24(4): 379–93.

Brandenberger, A. and Nalebuff, G. (1998) *Co-opetition.* Boston: Harvard Business School Press.

Buzzell, R. D., Gale, B. T. and Sultan, R. G. M. (1975) 'Market share – a key to profitability', *Harvard Business Review,* January–February: 97–106.

Buzzell, R. D. and Wiersema, F. D. (1981) 'Modeling changes in maket share: a cross-sectional analysis', *Strategic Management Journal,* Jan–March: 27–42.

Caves, R. E. (1980) 'Industrial organization, corporate strategy and structure', *Journal of Economic Literature,* 18: 64–92.

Caves, R. E. and Ghemawat, P. (1992) 'Identifying mobility barriers', *Strategic Management Journal,* 13(1): 1–13.

Chandler, A. D. (1962) *Strategy and Structure.* Cambridge, MA: MIT Press.

Chatterjee, S. and Wernerfelt, B. (1991) 'The link between resources and type of diversification: theory and evidence', *Strategic Management Journal,* 12(1): 33–49.

Coase, R. H. (1937) 'The nature of the firm', *Economica,* 4: 386–405.

Collis, D. J. (1994) 'Research note: how valuable are organizational capabilities?', *Strategic Management Journal,* 15 (Winter): 143–53.

Conner, K. (1991) 'A historical comparison of resource based theory and five schools of thought within industrial economics: do we have a new theory of the firm?', *Journal of Management,* 17(1): 121–54.

Cool, K. and Dierickx, I. (1993) 'Rivalry, strategic groups and firm profitability', *Strategic Management Journal,* 14(1): 47–60.

Davenport, T. H. (1997) *Working Knowledge: Managing What Your Organization Knows.* Boston: Harvard Business School Press.

Dixit, A. K. (1980) 'The role of investment in entry deterrence', *Economic Journal,* 90: 95–106.

Farjoun, M. (1998) 'The independent and joint effects of the skill and physical bases of relatedness in diversification', *Strategic Management Journal,* 19: 611–30.

Galbraith, C. and Schendel, D. (1983) 'An empirical analysis of strategy types', *Strategic Management Journal,* 4(2): 153–74.

Gale, C. (1972) 'Market share and rate of return', *Review of Economics and Statistics,* 54(4): 412–13.

Galunic, C. D. and Rodan, S. (1998) 'Resource recombinations in the firm: knowledge structures and the potential for Schumpeterian innovation', *Strategic Management Journal,* 19(12): 1193–209.

Govindarajan, V. (1989) 'Implementing competitive strategies at the business unit level', *Strategic Management Journal,* 10(3): 251–70.

Grant, R. M. (1988) 'On "dominant logic", relatedness and the link between diversity and performance', *Strategic Management Journal,* 9(6): 639–43.

Grant, R. M. (1996) 'Prospering in dynamically-competitive environments: organizational capability as knowledge integration', *Organization Science,* (7)4: 375–87.

Gulati, R., Nohria, N. and Zaheer, A. (2000) 'Strategic networks', *Strategic Management Journal,* 21(3): 203–15.

Hall, G. and Howell, S. (1985) 'The experience curve from the economist's perspective', *Strategic Management Journal,* 6(3): 197–203.

Hall, R. (1992) 'The strategic analysis of intangible resources', *Strategic Management Journal,* 13(2): 135–45.

Harrigan, K. R. (1981) 'Barriers to entry and competitive strategies', *Strategic Management Journal,* 2(4): 395–413.

Hatten, K. J. and Hatten, M. L. (1987) 'Strategic groups, asymmetrical mobility barriers and contestability', *Strategic Management Journal,* 8(4): 329–43.

Henderson, B. (1979) *Henderson on Corporate Strategy.* Cambridge, MA: ABT Books.

Henderson, R. and Clark, K. B. (1990) 'Architectural innovation: the reconfiguration of existing product technologies and the failure of established firms', *Administrative Science Quarterly,* (35)1: 9–30.

Hitt, M. A. and Ireland, R. D. (1985) 'Corporate distinctive competence, strategy, industry and performance', *Strategic Management Journal,* 6(3): 273–94.

Hofer, C. W. and Schendel, D. (1978) *Strategy Formulation: Analytical Concepts.* West Publishing Co.

Hofer, C. W. and Schendel, D. E. (1979) *Strategic Management: A New View of Business Policy and Planning.* Boston: Little, Brown and Company.

Huff, A. S. (1982) 'Industry influences on strategy reformulation', *Strategic Management Journal,* 3(2): 119–32.

Itami, H. (1987) *Mobilizing Invisible Assets.* Boston: Harvard University Press.

Jensen, M. (2000) *A Theory of the Firm: Governance, Residual Claims and Organizational Forms.* Boston: Harvard University Press.

Karnani, A. (1982) 'Equilibrium market share – a measure of competitive strength', *Strategic Management Journal,* 3(1): 43–52.

Kogut, B. (2000) 'The network as knowledge: generative rules and the emergence of structure', *Strategic Management Journal,* 21(3): 405–21.

Kurt, C. H. and Montgomerry, C. A. (1981) 'Corporate economic performance: diversification strategy versus market structure', *Strategic Management Journal,* 2(4): 327–44.

Lawrence, P. R. and Lorsch, J. W. (1967) *Organization and Environment.* Boston, MA: Harvard Business School Press.

Leonard-Barton, D. (1995) *Well-Springs of Knowledge: Building and Sustaining the Sources of Innovation.* Boston: Harvard Business School Press.

Lewis, J. (1994) *Partnership for Profit.* New York: Free Press.

Lewis, J. (2000) *Trusted Partners.* New York: Free Press.

Lieberman, M. (1987) 'The learning curve, diffusion, and competitive strategy', *Strategic Management Journal,* 8(5): 441–53.

Markides, C. C. (1994) 'Related diversification, core competences and corporate performance', *Strategic Management Journal,* 15: 149–66.

Mason, E. S. (1939) 'Price and production policies of large-scale enterprise', *American Economic Review,* March: 61–74.

McGee, J. and Thomas, H. (1986) 'Strategic groups: theory, research and taxonomy', *Strategic Management Journal,* 7(2): 141–61.

Merton, R. C. (1998) 'Applications of option-pricing theory: twenty-five years later', Les Prix Nobel 1997, Stockholm: Nobel Foundation; reprinted in *American Economic Review.*

Montgomerry, C. A. (1979) 'Diversification, market structure and firm performance: an extension of Rumelt's model', Unpublished doctoral dissertation: Purdue University.

Moore, J. F. (1996) *The Death of Competition.* New York: HarperCollins.

Nelson, R. (1991) 'Why do firms differ, and how does it matter?', *Strategic Management Journal,* 12 (Winter): 61–75.

Nonaka, I. (1994) 'A dynamic theory of organizational knowledge creation', *Organization Science,* 5(1): 14–37.

Palepu, F. (1985) 'Diversification strategy, profit performance and the entropy measure', *Strategic Management Journal,* 6(3): 217–39.

Peteraf, M. A. (1993) 'The corner-stones of competitive advantage: a resource-based view', *Strategic Management Journal,* 14: 179–91.

Pfeffer, J. and Salancik, G. (1978) *The External Control of Organizations: A Resource Dependence Perspective.* New York: Harper and Row.

Porter, M. E. (1980) *Competitive Strategy: Techniques for Analyzing Industries and Competitors.* New York: Free Press.

Porter, M. E. (1981) 'The contributions of industrial organization to strategic management', *Academy of Management Review,* 6: 609–20.

Prahalad, C. K. and Bettis, R. A. (1986) 'The dominant logic: a new linkage between diversity and performance', *Strategic Management Journal,* 7(6): 485–502.

Prahalad, C. K. and Hamel, G. (1990) 'The core competence of the corporation', *Harvard Business Review,* 68(3): 79–91.

Prescott, J. E., Kohli, A. K. and Venkatraman, N. (1986) 'The market share-profitability relationship: an empirical assessment of major assertions and contradictions', *Strategic Management Journal,* 7(4): 377–405.

Quinn, J. B. (1992) *Intelligent Enterprise: A Knowledge and Service Based Paradigm for Industry.* New York: Free Press.

Ramanujam, V. and Venkatraman, N. (1984) 'An inventory and critique of strategy research using the PIMS database', *Academy of Management Review,* 9(1): 138–52.

Robins, J. and Wiersema, M. (1995) 'A resource-based approach to the multibusiness firm: empirical analysis of portfolio interrelationships and corporate financial performance', *Strategic Management Journal,* 16(4): 277–300.

Rumelt, R. P. (1974) *Strategy, Structure and Economic Performance.* Cambridge, MA: Harvard University.

Rumelt, R. P. (1982) 'Diversification strategy and profitability', *Strategic Management Journal,* 3(4): 359–70.

Salop, S. C. (1979) 'Strategic entry deterrence', *American Economic Review,* 69: 335–8.

Schendel, D. E. and Hofer, C. W. (1979) *Strategic Management: A new view of Business Policy and Planning.* Boston: Little Brown and Company.

Scherer, F. M. and Ross, D. (1990) *Industrial Market Structure and Economic Performance.* Boston: Houghton Mifflin Company.

Stewart, T. A. (1997) *Intellectual Capital: The New Wealth of Organizations.* New York: Currency Doubleday.

Stork, J. and Hill, P. A. (2000) 'Knowledge diffusion through strategic communities', *Sloan Management Review,* Winter: 63–74.

Subramaniam, M. and Venkatraman, N. (2001) 'The determinants of transnational new product development capability: testing the influence of the transfer and deployment of tacit overseas knowledge', *Strategic Management Journal,* 22: 359–78.

Teece, D. and Pisano, G. (1997) 'Dynamic capabilities and strategic management', *Strategic Management Journal,* 18(7): 509–22.

Thompson, J. D. (1967) *Organizations in Action.* New York: McGraw Hill.

Varadarajan, P. and Ramanujam, V. (1987) 'Diversification and performance: a reexamination using a new two-dimensional conceptualization of diversity in firms', *Academy of Management Journal,* 30: 380–97.

Wensley, R. (1982) 'PIMS and BCG: new horizons or false dawn?', *Strategic Management Journal,* 3(2): 147–59.

Wernerfelt, B. and Karnani, A. (1987) 'Competitive strategy under uncertainty', *Strategic Management Journal,* 8(2): 187–95.

Williamson, O. E. (1975) *Markets and Hierarchies.* New York: Free Press.

Woo, C. Y. Y. and Cooper, A. C. (1981) 'Strategies of effective low share businesses', *Strategic Management Journal,* 2(3): 301–19.

Zander, U. and Kogut, B. (1995) 'Knowledge and the speed of transfer and imitation of organizational abilities: an empirical test', *Organization Science,* 6(1): 76–92.

21

Conclusion: Doing More in Strategy Research

RICHARD WHITTINGTON, ANDREW PETTIGREW
and HOWARD THOMAS

There is a wonderful impatience in the chapters of this Handbook. There is impatience with the boundaries of orthodox strategy research. Grant (Chapter 4) wants more than routine volumes of inconsistent and inconsequential empirical testing. Chakravarthy and White (Chapter 9) see too much 'business as usual'. At the same time, there is impatience to get on and do new kinds of strategy research. Both Garud and Van de Ven (Chapter 10) and Venkatraman and Subramaniam (Chapter 20) use the same phrase: strategy is at a 'crossroads'. Sure, one path pushes straight ahead, but there are also new turnings available, going beyond the beaten tracks. In this impatience we have a store of energy and enthusiasm that promises some exciting new directions for strategy research in the coming years.

This concluding chapter will not attempt a comprehensive review of prospects for strategy – that has been the collective endeavour of our contributors. What we shall do is pick out some common themes that arise from the more focused reviews of the earlier chapters. We shall be drawing together arguments that are made in many different ways, with respect to many different topics, but which seem to share a fundamentally similar orientation. Our discussion will not represent all the contributors to this Handbook – we do not have, and

would not wish for, uniformity. But we do detect a widespread sense of both frustration and opportunity to which we can add our own voice. If we wanted to summarize this sense, it is that strategy is at last pressing beyond the constraints of its origins in the modernist social sciences of the mid 20th century.

To say that strategy research is reaching beyond modernism is not to commit to the sometimes extravagant notions of post-modernism. Rather it is to accept a position that accepts the mature diversity that comes 'after modernism' (Clark, 2000; Whittington and Mayer, 2000). We are at a point when traditional modernist streams of research need be less exclusive in their definitions of appropriate science, and when challengers can relax their loud iconoclasm. The mainstream and its challengers can co-exist; both may need to reappraise their roles in the conversations that necessarily arise as they share a common territory.

What we take from many of the chapters here is exactly this readiness to construct a more pluralistic discipline (see Chapter 2 – Bowman et al.), in which new perspectives amplify rather than displace the old. After modernism, research in strategy will continue its search for general truths, but give greater weight to temporal and spatial context. Where methodological convenience imposes clear-cut distinctions and hard-and-fast boundaries, research will be more frank in recognizing the fuzzy and holistic realities that may lie beneath and more ready to approve alternative methodologies to bring them out. The power of abstraction and reduction can be admitted, so long as change, action and complexity are accepted alongside. By taking seriously this commitment to pluralism, strategy research after modernism has the opportunity to extend the scope of its scientific enquiry at the same time as enhancing its leverage on the messy, shifting world of practice.

This world of practice is both intellectually challenging and empirically utterly important. Strategy as a discipline is concerned with how actors place their bets on the future, investing and innovating in a manner that determines their own fates individually and collectively shapes the nature of the world we live in. As such, strategy addresses the direction of some of the largest and most enduring institutions ever built – great corporations such as General Electric, Mitsubishi and Shell whose origins date to the century before last and whose scope stretches to every corner of the earth. It also strives to make sense of the myriads of small, entrepreneurial companies, mostly fleeting but some makers of the innovations that will change life everywhere (see Chapter 14 – McGrath). Strategy now pervades even the large public and non-profit making institutions that remain so central to our lives both within and outside the strictly economic spheres (see Chapter 13 – Ferlie). In short, as students of strategy, we could hardly have a more important subject, or one whose breadth and dynamism could demand greater things of us intellectually.

Strategy researchers are fortunate too in having a head-start over our sister disciplines. For a long time, economics, sociology and psychology have left the field of strategy largely open, while yet furnishing us with many of the tools with which to plough it. We need all the analytical tools we can get if we are to grasp adequately the messy, shifting world of practice. At the same time, however, our head-start has protected us from the imperialism of adjacent disciplines and provided the breathing-space to bed down the foundations of what increasingly is and always should be a pluralistic discipline. We must remain open to whatever perspectives we

might need to understand one of the most central sets of issues in contemporary life.

Our argument here, therefore, is for more strategy research and for more ways of doing it. Our difference with the modernist tradition is not so much with what it has done as with what it has left out. This chapter continues in the next section, therefore, by reviewing what we conceive of as strategy's modernist heritage. This tradition has achieved a lot and has plenty more to do. But it has also tended to limit the kinds of issues that are chosen, the contexts that are explored and the methods that are drawn upon. The following section, therefore, will take up various opportunities that lie beyond modernism and that are proposed by many of the contributors to this volume. We shall highlight particularly the potential for research that is more contextually-sensitive and plural, that is wider-ranging in its disciplinary resources and that is more ready to deal with the imprecise and emergent. Finally, we conclude by proposing concrete measures for research training, international collaboration and engagement with practitioners that together would help take the strategy community forward with the kind of research agenda we develop here.

STRATEGY'S MODERNIST HERITAGE

As Bowman et al.'s historical review (Chapter 2) points out, the strategy discipline is just four decades old, emerging during the 1960s. The discipline has made significant advances in this period and incorporates an increasing breadth of strands. Yet strategy remains profoundly marked by its origins, especially in the work of Alfred Chandler and his followers. Rumelt et al. (1994: 16) write: 'The foundation of strategic management as a field may very well be traced to the 1962 publication of Chandler's *Strategy and Structure*.' Although Rumelt et al. (1994) find that Chandler's own work was insufficiently systematic and deductive, it was on this foundation that they describe the field as moving forwards to the 'positive science' that emerged in the 1970s. The deductive theorizing and empirical testing of Rumelt's (1974) *Strategy, Structure and Economic Performance* proved a model for much of the strategy research that was to follow.

It is worth pausing on the significance of both strategy's foundation in Chandler's pioneering work and the positive model of science which Rumelt and his colleagues espouse. The 1960s were what Toulmin (1990) identifies as the last years of modernism. Modernist social science had taken from the Enlightenment a faith in progress based upon reason. Scientific progress constructed a kind of knowledge expressed in universal laws. Knowledge was best advanced through the dedicated work of scientists in their disciplines. Truth would be determined through scientific testing. This testing required precision and reduction. Only then could science hand over to practice what its laboratories had produced. This stiff scientific detachment had been constructed to escape the arbitrary authorities of the pre-Enlightenment. More recently, it has been a stalwart bastion against the bloody ideologies of the early and mid 20th century. Modernism is suspicious of alternatives – understandably perhaps.

Chandler and his early successors in the strategy field were deeply imbued with this modernist notion of science. Gray (1998) has called the United States the last Enlightenment regime, and certainly during the immediate post-war decades, the American social sciences were confident in their modernism. Chandler's (1962) foundational *Strategy and Structure* appeared only four years after the Ford and Carnegie reports on management education had called for a more scientific and analytical approach to business research (Gordon and Howell, 1959; Pierson et al., 1959). While at Harvard in 1940s, Alfred Chandler had been taught by Talcott Parsons, the dominant sociologist of the day and author of an influential account of 'Evolutionary Universals' that had placed the United States at the pinnacle of world development (Parsons, 1964). Chandler's colleague at MIT, Walt Rostow (1960), was one of the most prominent exponents of this stage theory of modernization, in which the American model was proposed as the logical end-point of economic and political development.

Chandler's (1962) foundational work reflected these origins closely. His 'four chapters of enterprise' – from simple business to diversified multidivisional – expressed the same teleological sense of progress as the stage models of the modernization theorists. The diversified corporation called on general skills of management that had little respect for the demands of specific contexts and sectors. The multidivisional's rigid separation of strategy from operations embodied a confidence in hard distinctions and top-down rationality utterly characteristic of the modernist ideal. Chandler's (1977) faith in the United States as 'seedbed' for a world-wide managerial capitalism restated the old modernization thesis in the terms of the contemporary corporation.

Ideological threats have faded and American ascendancy diminished, yet still the old modernist spirit makes itself felt in strategy research today. The aspiration to construct a deductive, law-like science closer to the apparent model of the natural sciences remains (Camerer, 1985; Seth and Zinkhan, 1991). If the precise, invariant relationships that might be found within the carefully-controlled laboratory sciences are elusive, then we are urged to probe beyond surface noise to uncover 'the background laws' that determine tendencies and probabilities (McKelvey, 1997). But even this more sophisticated deductivism supports what Numagami (1998) calls the dominant 'theory-in-use', one that operates as if invariant laws remain to be discovered. In practice, research conduct '… is still implicitly dominated by research procedures that would be relevant only if the search for invariant laws were predominant in the social world' (Numagami, 1998: 3).

The deductive ambition holds a strong appeal, promising both scientific legitimacy within academe and substantial pay-offs in practice. The discovery of robust and general relationships between strategic actions and performance outcomes would rank alongside the scientific achievements of engineering, at the same time as offering practising managers reliable guidelines for business policy. But, as Lowendahl and Revang (1998) have recently remarked, this is an ambition founded on just one model of scholarship, one moreover that may be of diminishing relevance to the contemporary world. Some of the contributors to this Handbook see continuing potential in this model, but others chafe impatiently at its limits. As many of the chapters here indicate, there are some exciting opportunities beyond the boundaries we set in the early days of strategy research. It is these especially that this concluding chapter will explore.

OPPORTUNITIES AFTER MODERNISM

For Lowendahl and Revang (1998), postmodernism implies an end to the deductive ambition of constructing grand, universal theories. Our phrase 'after modernism' is more open. Modernism's legacy to the contemporary strategic management discipline has been the development of sophisticated statistical tools and large empirical databases. These have a continuing role in the discipline. However, the deductive tradition can now be more flexible in constituting its own role at the same time as more relaxed about the boundaries of what it conceives as proper science. There is no need anymore to reduce induction to the role of slightly apologetic under-labourer, handing over intriguing propositions for the real science of deductive theory-testing (Montgomery et al., 1989; Eisenhardt, 1989). Deduction may need to be more modest in its aspirations to building universal, timeless theories, but can also be more proud of its achievements in developing theory through its tireless quest for better 'fit' (Seth and Zinkhan, 1991). Both induction and deduction help us think better and anew as each gropes forward in a world whose empirical complexity and dynamism will for ever escape law-like closure.

We shall approach the changing roles of deductive and inductive thinking in the strategic management discipline 'after modernism' in five ways. First, we shall see how the two can work together in prompting more creative thinking about strategy. Next we shall explore their different but complementary roles in marking out and learning from the limits of a contextually plural world. We shall go on to argue for the importance of dynamic thinking in a world whose accelerating changes constantly undermine the careful piles of deductively accumulated evidence. We shall pursue the impact of contemporary change in its challenges to the neat distinctions required by deductivism and its invitation to think more beyond the boundaries of either single disciplines or discrete business entities. One crucial boundary supported by deductivism has been that between theory and practice. Our final argument, then, will concern the importance of conceiving theory and practice as a more tightly linked duality, in which progress in at least some kinds of scientific endeavour depends crucially on its intimate engagement with practice.

More Creativity

As we have suggested, the modernist instinct in strategic management research has been to cumulate evidence and construct laws. Prescription is based upon the general and the regular. As Garud and Van de Ven (Chapter 10) observe, the typical movement has been upwards, generalizing from samples to populations. The exceptional has been smoothed over. Part of our argument here, however, is that exceptions are disregarded resources for more creative thinking. The strategic management discipline should do more to seek out and actively confront the empirically irregular.

This Handbook's verdict on the traditional modernist endeavour is ambivalent. Kogut (Chapter 12) is positive about achievements in the field of international business. General theories concerning, for instance, the sequence and mode of entry into foreign markets seem to hold up well against empirical evidence. Likewise, the simple performance variable of international firm survival follows predicted patterns. Regarding the resource-based view that has been so influential for a decade or so, Cool et al. (Chapter 3) find promising statistical work in support, but admit that this is still limited and unsatisfactory (cf Thomas and Pollock, 1999; Priem and Butler, 2001). As to its more recent elaboration, Eisenhardt and Santos (Chapter 7) state that 'there is no cumulative demonstration of the power of the KBV (knowledge-based view) as a theory of strategy for any specific conception of performance'. In their view, the knowledge-based view is stimulating and useful, but does not yet qualify as a theory of organization. Venkatraman and Subramaniam (Chapter 20) find the alleged importance of knowledge and expertize to be 'largely an untested assertion'.

For new perspectives such as the resource and knowledge-based views, the absence of firm results may be allowable at this early stage. We need more deductive studies in these areas. They will benefit as concepts are more rigorously defined and more clearly operationalized (Thomas and Pollock, 1999). But the empirical record of more established areas of the discipline does not lead us to be confident that evidence will cumulate in quite the way that deductive researchers might hope.

Strategy falls often into a typically modernist predicament: the more studies there are in an area, and the greater the proliferation of methodologies, the more ambivalent are the findings (Lyotard, 1984). We can cite the heavy-weight ping-pong over the role of firm, corporate and industry effects (Rumelt, 1991; McGahan and Porter, 1997; Bowman and Helfat, 2001). This Handbook highlights the issues of diversification strategy and corporate structure, both of which have attracted large volumes of repeated testing against financial measures of performance since the 1970s, yet are still empirically unresolved. As Grant (Chapter 4) observes regarding product diversification: 'More than a hundred academic studies have failed to determine if diversification enhances profitability or whether related diversification outperforms unrelated diversification.' As for the advantages of the multidivisonal and similar forms of organization, Whittington (Chapter 6) reports that decades of empirical research have produced 'few convincing results'. Despite enormous efforts, law-like certainty still eludes us – in these areas at least.

Yet there is at least one gain even in these areas of deductive frustration. Empirical disappointments have pushed strategy researchers towards theoretical sophistication. As Grant (Chapter 4) indicates, in its tireless search for some kinds of regularity, the discipline has gradually abandoned the simple theories with which it started in favour of more complex and thoroughly-worked-through theories. On diversification, we distinguish more clearly now between types of strategy and likely relationships (Palich et al., 2000); on structure, we have moved steadily from one-size-fits-all theories, through contingency theory, towards theories of configurations and complementarity (Whittington et al., 1999). Where firm research results are elusive, therefore, the deductive tradition has at least created a resource of better theory.

Better theory, even uncorroborated, is no small achievement. For Tsoukas and Knudsen (Chapter 18), the deductive aspiration to create a set of general laws is misplaced. They suggest that a more productive way forward is to help strategy practitioners think better and

more creatively. The practitioner's arts rely only partly on the kinds of relationships that can be described in the deductive models of modernist science (see Chapter 6 – Whittington). One achievement of the deductive tradition is somewhat paradoxical, therefore. It is not so much the construction of law-like relationships, as the constant elaboration of more complex theory to deal with the empirical frustrations of an inherently unpredictable world. In developing theory, rather than delivering certainty, the deductive tradition furnishes practitioners with the complexity and even contradiction required for strategic reflection and creativity.

The deductive effort has a continuing role in strategic management, therefore, but it might do well to moderate its expectations of conclusive results at the same time as valuing more its achievements in theoretical development. The voguish pursuit of the novel, at the expense of painstaking replication, is often regretted by those in the deductive tradition (Montgomery et al., 1989; Hubbard et al., 1998; Schendel, 2000). But if the inconclusive work on diversification and the multidivisional turns out to be representative of the strategic management discipline more widely, then we should admit that replication is likely to have largely a cautionary role. So long as the deductive tradition is frank about its fragile empirical foundations, its main contribution to practical knowledge will be precisely in conceptual and theoretical innovation. It is in the accumulation of the novel and the complex, rather than cumulative confirmation of the old, that we should look for progress. We should not worry too much about the limited empirical support for the resource and knowledge-based views – so long as they are not allowed to congeal into orthodoxy.

The complement to this shifting focus in deductive work should be continued investment in inductive research. The role of induction has long been recognized for its potential to generate theoretical insight (Montgomery et al., 1989) and Garud and Van de Ven (Chapter 10) too join in underlining the potential of generalizing from singular cases to deeper theory. The benefits of inductively-generated theory do not depend upon the kind of statistical confirmation that the deductive position might expect, however. According to Jeremy (Chapter 19), the contribution of the inductive approach of the business historian is to develop empathy with decision-makers and sensitivity to the particularities of their situations. While hardly amenable to detached statistical testing, this inductive approach does produce both the ability to get deeply inside strategic dilemmas and the respect for uniqueness that are essential to strategic originality. Tsoukas and Knudsen (Chapter 18) argue that it is a hermeneutical and historical approach that is most likely to prompt practitioners to creative reflection on their opportunities and constraints. Again, therefore, the value of new theory, whether generated inductively or deductively, need not wait for general empirical confirmation, but can be exploited early for the innovativeness of the strategic thinking it prompts.

The argument so far, then, is that the deductive and inductive approaches can march in step. The deductive approach should not be less energetic in its empirical testing, for even if firm results elude it, its theoretical struggle to make sense of an intractable world will still push forward the frontiers of understanding. Here the deductive tradition should recast its objectives, taking them closer to those of induction. Induction, meanwhile, has more to do than mere under-labouring. The primary role of both deductive and inductive approaches is not in laying down laws, but helping practitioners think more creatively about the complex, shifting world in which they operate.

More Context

In their historical review of the strategic management discipline, Bowman et al. (Chapter 2) point to a propensity towards premature generalization. General statements are particularly challenged by the power of context. Context can be conceptualized in a number of ways, internal and external, temporal and sectoral (Pettigrew, 1985). Here we shall concentrate on one aspect of context that emerges as a particularly strong theme in this Handbook, that of national context. We shall touch on temporal context in the next section, but many of the questions raised by national context apply to contextual issues more broadly. With the spread of the strategic management research community around the world, national context is inescapably claiming more attention (Khanna and Rivkin, 2001).

As we indicated in the introduction (see Chapter 1 – Pettigrew et al.), the strategic management discipline was born in the USA and for a long time operated primarily as an American export industry. The discipline's very success is now taking it beyond these territorial roots. Time and time again, the chapters of this Handbook have reminded us of the complex findings that arise from the new more international research community. Generalizations are hard to sustain across borders. It will be our argument here, however, that these other contexts do not just pose constraints; they may also furnish opportunities for innovative thinking.

Whetten et al. (Chapter 17) and Ruigrok (Chapter 15) both underscore the deep embeddedness of firms within their institutional contexts. The specific institutional arrangements of different countries can substantially alter the local economics of strategy. As Grant (Chapter 4) and Markides (Chapter 5) both notice, conglomerate strategies condemned – rightly or wrongly – in advanced Western economies seem to have done surprisingly well in the developing economies of Asia and South America. Similarly, Whittington (Chapter 6) remarks on the equivocal performance advantages of the multidivisional outside the United States, and the persistence of alternative forms of organization such as the Chinese family network. McGrath (Chapter 14) outlines carefully the important implications that different national institutional regimes can have for entrepreneurship in a manner that could be extended to strategy more generally. As she shows, variations in institutional regimes are liable to alter local capacities to identify business options, actually to act on new business opportunities, then to grow and develop businesses and finally to terminate them.

The strategic management discipline needs to take the limits imposed by national context extremely seriously. Davis and Useem (Chapter 11) warn of a characteristically modernist tendency towards assuming unthinkingly that the American experience represents an inevitable pinnacle of development. The consequence is a too-easy transfer of American formulae into contexts where they are unwarranted. In their specific field, Davis and Useem warn that '... forcing an American system of governance on less-developed nations could be disastrous'. Similarly dangerous repercussions are to be expected in wider fields of strategy. It becomes incumbent upon strategy researchers to demarcate very carefully the territorial and institutional contexts in which they believe their propositions hold.

Jeremy (Chapter 19) argues that recognition of the distinctive national pathways of economic development comes naturally to the inductive approach favoured by business historians. Induction is likely to highlight the particular. But we should hang on to the possibility of some generalization. An important task for those engaged in deductive models of research, therefore, becomes one of seeking replication in different institutional contexts. In an institutionally plural world, we must expect the scope for scientific generalization to be limited. Nevertheless, there are valuable returns to demarcating these boundaries carefully: it would be as much an error to draw the bounds on generalization too tightly as to extend them too confidently (Whittington and Mayer, 2000).

This Handbook does provide grounds for some generalization across different contexts. Davis and Useem (Chapter 11) themselves note international convergence in certain corporate practices. Ferlie (Chapter 13) points to considerable successes in the transfer of management concepts between public and private sectors, while Ruigrok (Chapter 15) suggests a similar potential regarding international institutions. What this suggests is that we need to be sensitive to context, not paralysed. We should both develop our grounds for judging which knowledge is transferrable from one context to another, and understand better how this knowledge can most effectively be translated.

This sensitive translation from one context to another is potentially a significant source of value. As Kogut (Chapter 12) observes regarding the European origins of the transnational model, and Ferlie (Chapter 13) argues for the public sector innovations of recent decades, different contexts can be the source of important novelty and change. An important task for strategy research, therefore, is not so much to impose universality, but rather to hunt out valuable idiosyncrasies and then generalize them as far as contextual limitations will allow. In this way, strategy research need neither adopt an unwarranted universalism nor succumb to narrow particularism, but instead play-off the two extremes. Familiarity with different territorial contexts may provide a steady reservoir of local practices amenable, with appropriate adjustments, to translation into best practices more generally. The discipline will become richer as we seek out and integrate international diversity, rather than avoid it.

More Dynamism

Contexts not only differ internationally; they change over time. Change represents both a scientific challenge, jeopardizing knowledge accumulation, and a practical challenge, forcing upon managers repeated flux and uncertainty. The modernist tradition has been uncomfortable with dynamism. Chia (1995) characterizes modernist science as most typically dealing with states rather than the complex processes that lead to them. States are easier to model and more reassuring for audiences: 'properties such as unity, identity, permanence, structure and essences etc are privileged over dissonance, disparity, plurality, transience and change' (Chia, 1995: 582). Of course, the greater challenge for practitioners is precisely the dissonance and change that modernist social science avoids and masks.

Since its Chandlerian foundations in the problems of the large corporations of the early 20th century, the strategy discipline has particularly privileged the stable and established as against the new and entrepreneurial (Michael et al., 2000). Strategy has been more about controlling losses rather than creating value. The challenge now, for strategy practitioners and researchers alike, is how to bring more dynamism into a discipline that has traditionally been static and conservative (cf Pettigrew, 1990; Helfat, 2000; Mosakowski and Earley, 2000).

Temporal context presents a particular challenge for the cumulation of research results in the manner of traditional deduction. Thus Grant (Chapter 4) points to the instability over time of the value attributed to acquisition and conglomerate strategies, while Whittington (Chapter 6) notes the diminishing returns found to divisionalization. Venkatraman and Subramaniam (Chapter 20) even propose the possibility of radical 'new rules' for competing in the emerging knowledge economy. Generalization over time is likely to be a frustrating project.

The problem of temporal instability is not specific to strategy, of course. Giddens (1987) has described as a general predicament of the social sciences that its most striking findings are condemned to banalization or erosion as they become accommodated within everyday popular practice. There would be grounds for suspecting any longstanding correlation of strategic advantage and performance as spurious, for the very fact of its continuity would indicate that practitioners had insufficient confidence actually to act upon it. Tsoukas and Knudsen (Chapter 18) urge us to take seriously the creative capacity of practitioners to generate new strategies and supersede old (cf Mir and Watson, 2000). In their terms, good strategy is not lying out there to be discovered; it is continuously invented. We should expect, and welcome, contradictory empirical returns to strategies over time.

The call to take time seriously is not a simple one, however. This Handbook offers alternative approaches. Chakravarthy and White (Chapter 9) point to the proclivity of strategy content researchers to prescribe outcomes without understanding the change processes involved in reaching them. In this way, contingency theorists have concentrated on designs at the expense of the designing (see Chapter 6 – Whittington). Chakravarthy and White blame the prevailing static orientation of the language of strategic management. In place of the traditional static nouns, they offer an active vocabulary of 'consolidat*ing*, improv*ing*/ imitat*ing*, migrat*ing* and innovat*ing*' (their emphases). They argue that this perspective will provide a unifying language that will help reconnect strategy process research to research on strategy outcomes. There is a more radical view of change, however. Garud and Van de Ven (Chapter 10) warn against the traditional characterization of change within strategy research as merely transition from one state to another. In the contemporary environment, 'the increasing pace of change and complexity of organization lead us to recognize change as an ongoing dynamic journey, not a discrete event shifting from one unfrozen state to another frozen state'. In other words, there is hardly anything that does not, in some sense, involve change. It is not a matter of understanding the processes that lead to outcomes, but of recognizing that the outcomes are themselves implicated in continuous processes of change. To worry about the link between process and outcome is to risk perpetuating a false distinction. For Garud and Van de Ven, therefore, the language of nouns is not necessarily a lost cause. They propose the notion of strategy as 'bricolage'. The word has both a process connotation and a reference to a final product. They cite Dewey: 'without the meaning of the verb, that of the noun remains blank'. As Grant et al. (1988) observe of diversification, nouns can imply both state and process. Strategy research has assumed too much state, without attending to the processes that are a necessary part of its accomplishment.

This stronger appreciation of change and continuity has important implications for the practice of research. Above all, there is entailed a respect for history. History chronicles change, but also reveals pattern. According to Jeremy (Chapter 19) 'change, continuity, constraints and context' are the core themes of the business historian. Tsoukas and Knudsen (Chapter 18) likewise emphasize the 'historicity' of the firm in strategy, understanding it in a Penrosian sense as a gradually unfolding organism. In this kind of view, a firm's current state is not innocent with regard to either its specific past or its future. Identical strategic states may have different implications forwards according to different paths of arrival. Tsoukas and Knudsen conclude therefore strongly for modes of research that do not rely on surface similarities in terms of states, but ethnographic and historical approaches that uncover the significant processes by which states are achieved and reproduced. The past is one way forward in strategy research.

More 'Out of Bounds'

Prahalad and Hamel (1996) point to how the changing nature of the contemporary world requires increasing readiness to work 'out of bounds'. Modernist social science, on the other hand, has preferred clear boundaries. Empirically, its characteristic research methods rely upon the notion of ideally isolatable systems and discrete entities (Chia, 1995). In terms of research organization, it has privileged specialization within distinct disciplines, arranged in ordered hierarchy (Lyotard, 1984). If not before, certainly now we have to grapple with much more blurred empirical entities than those of modernist science. But after modernism we also have a greater capacity to reach across disciplines for the multiple methods and perspectives necessary to grasp this more complex reality. If the world has fewer neat boundaries, at least we can be less bounded in the tools we use to study it.

The deductive variance studies that have prevailed within strategic management so far rely, as Garud and Van de Ven (Chapter 10) suggest, upon both stable contexts and clear boundaries to phenomena. But neither stability nor boundaries can be taken for granted anymore. Even the fundamental concepts of industry, competitors and firms start to crumble. Here the cognitive tradition of research has been particularly important, revealing how industries and competitors are frequently perceived in different ways by different actors or groups of actors (see Chapter 8 – Porac and Thomas; Porac et al., 1995). It is not just a matter of whether they are right or wrong in their different perceptions. Even the most discrepant cognitive maps must be taken seriously, because they may be real in their effects. Beyond any empirical reality, strategy also deals with the inconsistent, semi-conscious and sometimes shifting cognitive maps of competitors, actual or imagined.

The boundary problem is becoming even starker with regard to the most basic unit of analysis, the firm. It is important for deductivists to be able to count firms, to trust that these firms are essentially the same from one period to another, and that performance outcomes can be traced back reliably to these stable essences. These conditions are confronted first of all by the challenge of national context. Widening international perspectives have already shown how the key units of resource control in many market economies may not be identical to legally constituted firms, but rest with opaque families or loosely-defined networks (Whitley, 1994). A firm is not always and everywhere a firm. These conditions for deductivism are also confronted by the contemporary transformation in the nature of business, the rise of what Castells (1996) has described as the 'network society' (cf Gulati et al., 2000).

Several chapters in this Handbook address the challenge presented by the shift from an economy of discrete business units to one that is increasingly enmeshed within webs of alliances, partnerships, supply chains and joint ventures. Grant (Chapter 4) raises the role of joint ventures and alliances as an alternative to full internalization for firms wishing to diversify. Pavitt and Steinmueller (Chapter 16) emphasize the growing importance of networks in strategy, especially with regard to technology. These kinds of networks complicate the link between performance and the firm. According to Pavitt and Steinmueller, it is the resources and knowledge that reside in the network as a whole, rather than the focal firm in particular, that determine the capacity for continuous innovation. Drawing out the implications for future management research, Venkatraman and Subramaniam (Chapter 20) suggest that the move towards a network society jeopardizes the firm as the traditional unit of analysis in strategic management research: 'in an era of dynamic co-operation and competition .... we do not have the luxury of studying only easy-to-track entities'. A strategic management discipline that confines itself to the stable and quantifiable risks engaging with an increasingly marginal portion of strategic activity. We shall have to be more patient with the fuzzy, more dependent on the qualitative.

There is an intriguing parallel between the increasingly networked character of economic activity and the organization of our own research endeavours. Pavitt and Steinmueller (Chapter 16) argue that the network society is forcing firms to become increasingly adept at integrating many different kinds of knowledge, even within narrower product ranges. Traditional technological boundaries do not demarcate the knowledge required for innovation any more. Something similar is true of strategy research as well. The integrative nature of the strategy problem has always entailed some inter-disciplinarity for strategic management as a field (Seth and Thomas, 1994), but now the calls are more urgent. Chakravarthy and White (Chapter 9) complain of the tradition of reductionist, single-lens studies in research on strategy processes. The result is 'puddles' of isolated studies, not going anywhere. They argue that progress in strategy process research requires the integration of many perspectives in large-scale longitudinal studies bringing together many disciplines and perspectives. For the puddles to meld into a river with some direction, the economics of outcome research needs to be joined with the more subtle sociology and psychology of process.

Davis and Useem (Chapter 11) make an equivalent plea for multidisciplinarity in urging the need to go beyond the abstract 'contractarian' approach to corporate governance of finance to a recognition of embeddedness that draws upon sociological and historical appreciations of context. Again, Whetten et al. (Chapter 17) suggest that research progress in addressing increasingly salient issues of social responsibility will require 'boundary-spanning' collaborations across disciplines. Openness to many disciplines is a strong theme running through this Handbook (see Chapter 1 – Pettigrew et al.). Dealing with an increasingly boundary-less world requires us to think beyond the bounds of our disciplines.

More Practical

A typical modernist boundary is between science and practice. In the early modernist struggle, the philosopher Pascal made his name by scorning the practical wisdom sought by the Jesuits in the case study: he wanted general principles (Toulmin, 1990). Something of this distinction lingers on in the deductive tradition within strategic management (Mir and Watson, 2000). Thus Montgomery et al. (1989) are quite comfortable with the notion of strategy research achieving a certain detachment from practice. There is no reason to insist that knowledge should always be closely tied to practice, but we must admit that the kind of science that cuts itself off is a rather lop-sided one. Bowman et al. (Chapter 2) quote the late Herbert Simon's strictures on academia for being more interested in 'what is' questions, and less concerned with the professional questions of 'how to'. It is part of our argument that, after modernism, we can construct a better science by reinforcing the link back to practice.

A detached science risks being left on the margins. Ferlie (Chapter 13) notes how strategy and management research has lagged behind policy and practice rather than changed it. We are too often the obituarists of past practices. Deductive concern for general relationships easily degenerates towards reproduction of the average. There is no competitive advantage there – in the world of entrepreneurial small firms, indeed, the average result is failure (Michael et al., 2000). Especially in a world of increasingly hectic change, practical science should concern itself more with the pioneering and the exceptional (cf Lowendahl and Revang, 1998; Daft and Lewin, 1993). The purpose is exploration, innovation and inspiration. Whetten et al. (Chapter 17) likewise advocate the study of 'extreme cases'. The extremes are both more likely to produce practical insight and make the kinds of intellectual demands only to be met by commitment to interdisciplinary research.

Thinking practically is not, however, just a matter of getting close to leading-edge practice. It also involves thinking about the practical requirements of ordinary performance. As Garud and Van de Ven (Chapter 10) insist, we must be concerned with the 'how' questions. Here the strategy literature is still too silent. Whittington (Chapter 6) observes that the literature on corporate structure is profuse with its advice on what organizational types to adopt, but says little about how these types should be implemented and maintained. Tsoukas and Knudsen (Chapter 18) point to the absence of effective praxeology – how should knowledge about strategy actually be used – in strategy research and textbooks. They argue that the answer lies in constructing theories of creative action in organizations, which again highlights the practical 'how': how new actions emerge, how they come to be described and legimated and how they relate to key actors' webs of belief. Such theories of creative action will not offer general rules for strategy, but rather help practitioners towards the kind of good strategy theorizing capable of generating novel forms of practical action. Tranfield and Starkey (1998) quote Kurt Lewin's famous remark that there is nothing more practical than a good theory.

Getting closer to practice need involve no loss of rigour, only an extended set of criteria. To be sure, the jagged complexities of the real world are hard to reconcile with the instinct towards regularity and predictability we inherit from modernism. But it is a peculiar sort of rigour that force-fits an intractable world into law-like regularities or which privileges the average at the expense of the exceptional. A greater sensitivity towards practical complexity prompts a more comprehensive notion of rigour.

Practical science faces 'double-hurdles' (Pettigrew, 1997). There are the standards of the scientific community – not necessarily those of deductive science, but the broader criteria of well-crafted studies, transparent methods and appropriate conclusions that we can properly expect of all kinds of empirical endeavour. Then there are the standards of the practitioner audience, expecting insight and advice that meet the demands of particular and changing circumstances. There is no necessary 'softness' here: practitioner audiences will require hard-headed connections to performance outcomes (Pettigrew, 2000). Jumping the two hurdles is a more rigorous challenge than just jumping one. Meeting the standards of both science and practice should be a legitimate source of scholarly satisfaction and cause for reward.

SOME RESEARCH POLICY IMPLICATIONS

The chapters of this Handbook are very diverse, in positions as well as topics. Here, though, we have tried to pick out some repeated themes, linking them where necessary to the wider literature of our discipline. We have not been comprehensive in our choice of themes and certainly we have stamped them with our particular mark. But we can hope that our readers will draw out from this chapter and the preceding ones a reasonably coherent and positive message about how the strategy discipline might progress.

The message amounts to this. The strategy discipline is now moving beyond its modernist origins to a new and more plural maturity, with some exciting opportunities ahead of it. The discipline will put increasing value on theoretical creativity and innovation. It will be more prepared to seek out the novel in unfamiliar contexts, and less eager to prescribe conformity for a diverse world. Rather than starting from the assumption of stability, the discipline will now take seriously issues of change and process, while yet respecting the sheer accomplishment of continuity. The changing nature of the world, moreover, is challenging traditional distinctions, whether

empirical or disciplinary. As the boundaries of the firm dissolve, so too should the traditional disciplinary borders and hierarchies of our field. All these changes will help us researchers to think better and anew about strategy. They should, moreover, reinforce our connections to practice.

This message has important repercussions for research policy in our discipline. We shall limit ourselves to three main thrusts that follow particularly from the argument so far. As modernist divisions relax, we must assert multi-disciplinarity right from the start of research training. With our growing appreciation of context, we should promote international collaborations. Less protectively detached from the world, we should be more ready to engage as researchers directly with practice. All three of these thrusts involve in some way the reaching across traditional boundaries.

Research Training

The strategic management discipline has long been sensitive to the need to develop the capability of communicating with, and even contributing to, adjacent disciplines (Montgomery et al., 1989). This Handbook's contributors repeatedly draw attention to the interdisciplinary nature of strategy problems. But the very success of the strategic management discipline in generating growing masses of research continually challenges this openness to outside disciplines as the task of mastering our own increases. We can easily overwhelm our students with just what our own discipline has produced in the last four decades.

Doctoral training programmes will need to make some hard choices. We would argue for Nelson-like selectivity of vision. Programmes may have to refuse to recognize some parts of the discipline in favour of cultivating a readiness from the beginning to look outside to other disciplines. Disciplinary gaps in knowledge can be filled later as needs be; the interdisciplinary habit of mind is harder to cultivate later in a career than earlier. Right from the start, students should be offered the opportunity to work with other social scientists on foundational course such as epistemology and research methods. More advanced courses might centre on the big issues to which not only we but other disciplines have a great deal to contribute – globalization, corporate governance, the future of the large-scale corporation, for example. Inviting teachers in from adjacent disciplines to debate these big issues will remind our students that our subject involves greater things than simple technique, at the same time as exposing them to a far wider range of problems and methods than most business schools can easily express. In an environment in which traditional disciplinary boundaries are blurring, new researchers will need to be prepared to work increasingly in interdisciplinary teams capable of tackling the fuzzy, awkward-shaped problems the world will keep throwing us (Pettigrew, 1997).

International Projects

Research will have to reach not just over disciplinary divides but also across national boundaries. This chapter has emphasized the importance of contexts – temporal and institutional. One implication is the need for more longitudinal and historical work (Pettigrew, 1990), but we shall underline here the opportunities for more international collaborative projects. What we draw from many of the chapters of this Handbook is that testing theories internationally, and teasing out the implications of apparent anomalies, can be a crucial source of innovation in the strategic management discipline. As Laurent and Pras (1999) argue for the adjacent discipline of marketing, an international dimension for doctoral training would be an important start. But we also need to build more international collaborative project teams amongst mature researchers. Teagarden et al. (1995) record that international research, collaboration and publication has been popularly regarded as career-limiting rather than career-enhancing. We must reverse this position. Cross-national research programmes should be routine, for no knowledge generated in one context can be trusted in another and – at the same time – the idiosyncratic practices of one nation may have practical implications for others. As we build these teams, too, we should guard against the simple export of assumptions and concepts from dominant nations to others (Easterby-Smith and Danusia, 1999). We are no longer in a world where strategy can be a US export

industry; intellectual trade is most beneficial when multilateral.

Collaborating with Practice

Several contributions here have singled out the limiting artificiality of the traditional distinction between theory and practice. These reflect a broader sense of change within business schools. It is now argued increasingly widely that we need to move beyond what has been characterized as Mode 1 research, in the modernist mould of scientific detachment, towards a more practically-engaged Mode 1.5 or Mode 2 research model (Tranfield and Starkey, 1998; Huff, 2000).

Again, there is a research training dimension. The United Kingdom especially has seen the rise of the Doctorate in Business Administration (Bourner et al., 2000). In distinction from the traditional PhD and in line with the Masters in Business Administration, this DBA is more focused on practical problems and typically recruits students with practical experience. New problems, new sensitivities and new experience are thus drawn into the research community. But also there is potential for more collaborative projects with practitioners, whether organized through consortia of firms or direct sponsorship by single corporations or consultancies (Pettigrew, 1997). More than simply welcoming the additional material resources, we should seize the intellectual insights generated through practitioners' more immediate confrontation with the leading edges and complexities of practice. Practitioners can be intellectual partners as well. The discipline has already seen successful collaborations with practice – witness the Harvard programme on the workings of the multidivisional (Vancil, 1978), Bartlett and Ghoshal's (1993) research on multinationals, Porter's (1990) government-sponsored work on national competitiveness and the recent INNFORM programme on innovative forms of organizing (Pettigrew and Fenton, 2000). Such projects can comfortably meet the double hurdles of academic rigour and practical relevance. We should look for more such collaborations in the future.

These calls for more interdisciplinarity, more internationalism and more collaboration with practice are just three kinds of proposal for a discipline that, in the coming decades, will doubtless be changing in as many ways as its subject matter. What we take from the contributions to this Handbook, however, is that the strategy discipline is ready to seize the challenges and opportunities of a fast-moving field. The chapters here speak of an energy and openness that will push strategy research forward in many directions. We are enthused by this. After all, as a discipline we have a great topic, understanding the evolution of the key institutions of our age – whether large corporations, hi-tech ventures, international networks or even not-for-profits. From the advances of the first four decades, and with an openness to other disciplinary perspectives, we have also a store of empirical data and a wealth of tools and concepts. The discipline has important things to do and a good base from which to go. We hope our readers will share our enthusiasm about doing more strategy research and finding more ways in which to do it.

REFERENCES

Bartlett, C. A. and Ghoshal, S. (1993) 'Beyond the M-form: towards a managerial theory of the firm', *Strategic Management Journal*, 14, Special Issue: 23–46.

Bourner, T., Bowden, R. and Laing, S. (2000) 'Professional doctorates: the development of researching professionals', in T. Bourner, T. Katz and D. Watson (eds), *New Directions in Professional Higher Education*. Buckingham: SRHE and Open University Press.

Bowman, E. H. and Helfat, C. E. (2001) 'Does corporate strategy matter?', *Strategic Management Journal*, 22: 1–24.

Camerer, C. (1985) 'Redirecting research in business policy and strategy', *Strategic Management Journal*, 6: 1–16.

Castells, M. (1996) *The Rise of the Network Society*. Oxford: Blackwell.

Chandler, A. D. (1962) *Strategy and Structure: Chapters in the History of the American Industrial Enterprise*. Cambridge, MA: The MIT Press.

Chandler, A. D. (1977) *The Visible Hand: The Managerial Revolution in American Business*. Cambridge, MA: Harvard University Press.

Chia, R. (1995) 'From modern to postmodern organizational analysis', *Organization Studies*, 16: 580–601.

Clark, P. (2000) *Organisations in Action: Competition between Contexts*. London: Routledge.

Daft, R. and Lewin, A. (1993) 'Where are the theories of the new organizational forms?', *Organization Science*, 4: 1–16.

Easterby-Smith, M. and Danusia, M. (1999) 'Cross-cultural collaborative research: toward reflexivity', *Academy of Management Journal*, 42: 78–86.

Eisenhardt, K. (1989) 'Building theories from case study research', *Academy of Management Review*, 14: 532–51.

Giddens, A. (1987) *Social Theory and Modern Sociology*. Cambridge: Polity.

Gordon, R. and Howell, J. (1959) *Higher Education for Business*. New York: Columbia University Press.

Grant, R. M., Jammine, A. P. and Thomas, H. (1988) 'Diversity and profitability among British manufacturing companies, 1972–1984', *Strategic Management Journal*, 9(4): 333–46.

Gray, J. (1998) *False Dawn: The Delusions of Global Capitalism*. London: Granta.

Gulati, R., Nohria, N. and Zaheer, A. (2000) 'Strategic networks', *Strategic Management Journal*, 21: 203–16.

Helfat, C. E. (2000) 'Guest editor's introduction to the special issue: the evolution of firm capabilities', *Strategic Management Journal*, 21: 955–60.

Hubbard, R., Vetter, D. E. and Little, E. L. (1998) 'Replication in strategic management: scientific testing for validity, generalization and usefulness', *Strategic Management Journal*, 19: 243–54.

Huff, A. S. (2000) 'Presidential address: changes in organizational knowledge production', *Academy of Management Review*, 25: 288–93.

Khanna, T. and Rivkin, J. W. (2001) 'Estimating the performance effects of business groups in emerging markets', *Strategic Management Journal*, 22: 45–74.

Laurent, G. and Pras, B. (1999) 'Research in marketing: some trends, some recommendations', in D. Brownlie, M. Saren, R. Wensley and R. Whittington (eds), *Rethinking Marketing: Towards Critical Marketing Accountings*. London: Sage.

Lowendahl, B. and Revang, O. (1998) 'Challenges to existing theory in a post industrial society', *Strategic Management Journal*, 19: 755–74.

Lyotard, J-F. (1984) *The Postmodern Condition: A Report on Knowledge*. Manchester: Manchester University Press.

McGahan, A. M. and Porter, M. E. (1997) 'How much does industry matter, really?', *Strategic Management Journal*, Summer Special Issue, 18: 15–30.

McKelvey, B. (1997) 'Quasi-natural organization science', *Organization Science*, 8: 352–80.

Michael, S., Storey, D. and Thomas, H. (2000) 'Reflections on the linkages between strategic management and entrepreneurship', paper presented to the Conference on Strategy and Entrepreneurship, Kansas City.

Mir, R. and Watson, A. (2000) 'Strategic management and the philosophy of science: the case for a constructivist methodology', *Strategic Management Journal*, 21: 941–53.

Montgomery, C. A., Wernerfelt, B. and Balakrishnan, S. (1989) 'Strategy content and the research process: a critique and commentary', *Strategic Management Journal*, 10: 189–97.

Mosakowski, E. and Earley, P. E. (2000) 'A selective review of time assumptions in strategy research', *Academy of Management Review*, 25: 796–812.

Numagami, T. (1998) 'The infeasibility of invariant laws in management studies: a reflective dialogue in defence of case studies', *Organization Science*, 9: 1–15.

Palich, L. E., Cardinal, L. B. and Miller, C. C. (2000) 'Curvilinearity in the diversification–performance linkage: an examination over three decades', *Strategic Management Journal*, 21: 155–74.

Parsons, T. (1964) 'Evolutionary universals in society', *American Sociological Review*, 29: 339–57.

Pettigrew, A. M. (1985) *The Awakening Giant*. Oxford: Blackwell.

Pettigrew, A. M. (1990) 'Longitudinal field research on change: theory and practice', *Organization Science*, 3: 267–92.

Pettigrew, A. M. (1997) 'The double hurdles for management research', in T. Clarke (ed.), *Advancement in Organizational Behaviour: Essays in Honour of Derek S. Pugh*. London: Dartmouth Press.

Pettigrew, A. M. (2000) 'Linking change processes to outcomes: a commentary on Ghoshal, Bartlett and Weick', in Beer and Nohria (eds), *Breaking the Code of Change*. Boston: Harvard Business School Press.

Pettigrew, A. M. and Fenton, E. (eds) (2000) *The Innovating Organization*. London: Sage.

Pierson, F. C. et al. (1959) *The Education of American Businessmen*. New York: McGraw Hill.

Porac, J., Thomas, H., Wilson, F., Paton, D. and Kanfer, A. (1995) 'Rivalry and the industry model of Scottish knitwear producers', *Administrative Science Quarterly*, 40: 203–27.

Porter, M. E. (1990) *The Competitive Advantage of Nations*. London: Macmillan.

Prahalad, C. K. and Hamel, G. (1996) 'Competing in the new economy: managing out of bounds', *Strategic Management Journal*, 17: 237–42.

Priem, R. L. and Butler, J. (2001) 'Is the resource-based "view" a useful perspective for strategic management research?', *Academy of Management Review*, 26: 22–40.

Rostow, W. W. (1960) *Stages of Economic Growth: A Non-Communist Manifesto*. Cambridge: Cambridge University Press.

Rumelt, R. P. (1974) *Strategy, Structure and Economic Performance*. Cambridge, MA: Harvard Business School Press.

Rumelt, R. P. (1991) 'How much does industry matter?', *Strategic Management Journal*, 12: 167–85.

Rumelt, R. P., Schendel, D. and Teece, D. (1994) 'Fundamental issues in strategy', in R. P. Rumelt, D. Schendel and D. Teece (eds), *Fundamental Issues in Strategy*. Boston: Harvard Business School Press.

Schendel, D. (2000) 'Fresh challenges for the future', in *Mastering Strategy*. London: Financial Times Pitman.

Seth, A. and Thomas, H. (1994) 'Theories of the firm: implications for strategy research', *Journal of Management Studies*, 31: 165–92.

Seth, A. and Zinkhan, G. M. (1991) 'Strategy and the research process: a comment', *Strategic Management Journal*, 12: 75–83.

Teagarden, M. B., von Glinow, A. M., Bowen, D. E. and Frayne, C. E. (1995) 'Toward a theory of comparative management research: an idiographic case study of the best international human resources management project', *Academy of Management Journal*, 38: 5.

Thomas, H. and Pollock, T. (1999) 'From I-O economics' SCP paradigm through strategic groups to the puzzle of competitive strategy', *British Journal of Management*, 10: 127–40.

Toulmin, S. (1990) *Cosmopolis: The Hidden Agenda of Modernity*. Chicago: University of Chicago Press.

Tranfield, D. and Starkey, K. (1998) 'The nature, social organization and promotion of management research: towards policy', *British Journal of Management*, 9: 341–53.

Vancil, R. E. (1978) *Decentralization: Managerial Ambiguity by Design*. Homewood, Ill: Dow Jones-Irwin.

Whitley, R. D. (1994) 'Dominant forms of economic organizations in market economies', *Organization Studies*, 15: 153–82.

Whittington, R. and Mayer, M. (2000) *The European Corporation: Strategy, Structure and Social Science*. Oxford: Oxford University Press.

Whittington, R., Pettigrew, A. M., Peck, S., Fenton, E. and Conyon, M. (1999) 'Change and complementarities in the new competitive landscape', *Organization Science*, 10: 583–600.

Author Index

Subject Index